CW00666201

THE HANDBOOK OF

EXPERIENTIAL LEARNING AND MANAGEMENT EDUCATION

THE HANDBOOK OF

EXPERIENTIAL LEARNING AND MANAGEMENT EDUCATION

Edited by

MICHAEL REYNOLDS

and

RUSS VINCE

OXFORD
UNIVERSITY PRESS

OXFORD
UNIVERSITY PRESS

Great Clarendon Street, Oxford OX2 6DP

Oxford University Press is a department of the University of Oxford.
It furthers the University's objective of excellence in research, scholarship,
and education by publishing worldwide in

Oxford New York

Auckland Cape Town Dar es Salaam Hong Kong Karachi
Kuala Lumpur Madrid Melbourne Mexico City Nairobi
New Delhi Shanghai Taipei Toronto

With offices in

Argentina Austria Brazil Chile Czech Republic France Greece
Guatemala Hungary Italy Japan Poland Portugal Singapore
South Korea Switzerland Thailand Turkey Ukraine Vietnam

Oxford is a registered trade mark of Oxford University Press
in the UK and in certain other countries

Published in the United States
by Oxford University Press Inc., New York

British Library Cataloguing in Publication Data
Data available

Library of Congress Cataloging in Publication Data
The handbook of experiential learning and management education/edited
by Michael Reynolds and Russ Vince.
p.   cm
Includes index.
ISBN 978–0–19–921763–2
1. Experiential learning–Handbooks, manuals, etc.   2. Management–Study and teaching–Handbooks,
manuals, etc.   3. Organizational learning–Handbooks, manuals, etc.   I. Reynolds, Michael, 1939–
II. Vince, Russ.
LB1027.3.H365 2007
650.071′1–dc22   2007025804

Typeset by SPI Publisher Services, Pondicherry, India
Printed in Great Britain
on acid-free paper by
Biddles Ltd., King's Lynn, Norfolk

ISBN 978–0–19–921763–2
1 3 5 7 9 10 8 6 4 2

Contents

PART III POLITICALLY GROUNDED EXPERIENTIAL LEARNING

PART IV EXPERIENTIAL LEARNING AND SYSTEMS PSYCHODYNAMICS

List of Contributors

Chris Argyris has received thirteen honorary doctorate degrees and is author of thirty-three books and monographs as well as numerous articles. Recognition of his lifetime contribution includes awards from the Academy of Management, American Psychological Association, American Society for Training and Development, and the *Financial Times*. His most recent books include *Flawed Advice* (2000) and *Reasons and Rationalizations* (2004), both Oxford University Press.

Joseph E. Champoux is a Regents' Professor of Management at the Robert O. Anderson Schools of Management of the University of New Mexico. His research activities focus on film as a teaching resource and enhancements for on-line courses. He has published articles in several scholarly journals, eleven book chapters, and thirty print or electronic books.

John Coopey, a visiting fellow in Management Learning at Lancaster, has created unusual links between organizational learning and power and politics. Currently John is attempting to theorize how pressures from campaigning groups within global civil society trigger processes of learning and institutional and structural change in the business organizations they target.

Nelarine Cornelius is Reader in Human Resource Management and Organizational Behaviour, Brunel Business School, where she is Director of the Centre for Research into Emotion Work (CREW) and Head of the Organizational Behaviour and Employment Relations Research group. Her research interests include workplace diversity and inequality, and emotion and work.

Liz Creese engaged with a Group Relations approach to experiential learning some eighteen years ago as an arts manager studying a Graduate Diploma in Organization Behaviour at Swinburne University of Technology. She has since continued the 'struggle' in both her research and teaching, face to face and on-line, at various Australian universities.

Gordon E. Dehler (Ph.D., University of Cincinnati) is on the management faculty at the College of Charleston. His scholarly interests centre on critical views of organizations and management, particularly in understanding the place of critical pedagogy in management education. His published work includes papers in *Management Learning, Academy of Management Journal*, and *Journal of Managerial Psychology*. He is an associate editor for the journal *Management Learning*.

Andrea D. Ellinger is an Associate Professor in the Department of Human Resource Education at the University of Illinois at Urbana-Champaign. She holds a Ph.D. in Adult Education from the University of Georgia with a functional concentration in Human Resource and Organization Development. Her research interests include informal learning in the workplace, organizational learning, and the concept of the learning organization.

Silvia Gherardi is Professor of Sociology of Work at the University of Trento, Italy, where she coordinates the Research Unit on Communication, Organizational Learning, and Aesthetics (RUCOLA), devoted to the exploration of different 'soft' aspects of knowing in organizations, with an emphasis for emotional, symbolic, and discursive aspects of organizational process.

Jeff Gold is Principal Lecturer at Leeds Business School. He has presented conference papers on a variety of topics relating to leadership, management, and organization learning. He is the co-author of *Management Development: Strategies for Action* (with Alan Mumford), published by the Chartered Institute of Personnel and Development in 2004.

Steve G. Green is a Professor of Management in the Department of Management at United States Air Force Academy. He is also the department's Director of Consulting. His research interests focus on cost analysis, government financial management, managerial and financial accounting, performance measurement, and education.

Kurt A. Heppard is an Associate Professor of Management in the Management Department at the United States Air Force Academy. He is also the department's Director for Accreditation. His current research and teaching interests include entrepreneurial strategies, performance measurement, and strategic innovation.

Anne Herbert completed her Ph.D. in Education in Australia. In recent years she has worked as Academic Director of Executive Education at Helsinki School of Economics. Among her current research interests are managing learning and education and the practices of academic work.

Robin Holt is currently a Roberts University Fellow at Leeds University Business School having received his Ph.D. from the London School of Economics. Robin works as a philosophy and management academic, primarily on research collaborations between universities and the private and public sectors. He has an enduring interest in investigating the use of philosophical perspectives in the business world.

Martin J. Hornyak, Associate Professor of Management, University of West Florida, teaches Strategic Management, Human Resource Management, and Principles of

Management. He completed his DBA in strategy/marketing from Cleveland State University. Dr Hornyak authored/co-authored several publications on strategic alliances, management education, and service learning.

Paula Hyde is Senior Lecturer in leadership and experiential learning at Manchester Business School, University of Manchester, England. Her teaching includes management of change, experiential learning, and personal leadership development. Her research interests are organizational dynamics and change, and organizational leadership. She is particularly concerned with psychodynamic approaches to understanding organizational life.

Tusse Sidenius Jensen has worked as a research assistant at the Department: Learning Lab Denmark, the Danish University of Education. She has been a member of the research group Neuroscience, Corporality, and Learning and has researched the impact of the surroundings and embodied learning. Her research field is 'embodied learning processes'.

Sandra Jones is the Associate Professor of Employment Relations at the University of the Royal Melbourne Institute of Technology. She supervises a number of doctoral candidates and in 2004 received a Research Supervision Award for her innovation in introducing a Doctoral Community of Practice to her supervisory practice.

Anna B. Kayes is Assistant Professor of Management in the School of Business at Villa Julie College. Her doctorate in Human and Organizational Learning is from the George Washington University. Her research focuses on power and trust dynamics and how people learn from experience. Her research has appeared in publications such as the *Journal of Management Education* and *Journal of Managerial Psychology.*

D. Christopher Kayes (Ph.D., Case Western Reserve) holds positions at George Washington University and the University of Hull. He is author of *Destructive Goal Pursuit: The Mt. Everest Disaster* (Palgrave-Macmillan). His article on experiential learning was nominated for the first best paper award by the journal *Academy of Management Learning and Education.*

Kirsi Korpiaho, M.Sc. (Econ.), is a researcher and doctoral student in organization studies at the Helsinki School of Economics. Kirsi is researching management education and students' learning. She is a founding member of the Management Education Research Initiative at HSE (www.hse.fi/meri).

Tracy Lamping is a Senior Lecturer in the Faculty of Business and Law at the University of Lincoln. She has designed and delivered a range of management education/development courses. Her particular interest is creating a sociological and psychological awareness of management development at undergraduate level.

Dale L. Murray is an Associate Professor in Industrial Design and is the coordinator of the Industrial Design programme in the College of Design Architecture, Art, and Planning at the University of Cincinnati. He holds a BS and a master's degree in Industrial Design and specializes in sustainable product design.

Dr Jean E. Neumann serves as Director of Studies and Core Faculty for the Tavistock Institute's Advanced Organizational Consultation programme. She has undertaken over 450 projects in the USA and Europe concerned, in some way, with 'good' organizational change. Jean's publications use practice to inform a more critical OD&C theory.

Enrico Maria Piras is a Ph.D. student in Information Systems and Organization at the University of Trento, Italy, and a junior member of RUCOLA (Research Unit on Communication, Organizational Learning, and Aesthetics). His research interests are Organizational Aesthetics, micro-practices of organizing, and research methodologies in organizational settings.

Barbara Poggio is researcher at the Department of Sociology and Social Research at the University of Trento, Italy, and member of the Research Unit on Communication, Organizational Learning, and Aesthetics (RUCOLA). Barbara is lecturer in Sociology of Organization. Her research interests and publications focus on gender practices in work and organizations and on narrative analysis.

Keijo Räsänen is Professor in Organization and Management at the Helsinki School of Economics. He is a founding member of the Management Education Research Initiative at HSE. The MERI group studies academic work and educational activities in the business school (www.hse.fi/meri). He is also researching and teaching practices of workplace development.

Peter Reason is Director of the Centre for Action Research in Professional Practice at the University of Bath, which has pioneered graduate education and research based on collaborative, experiential, and action-oriented forms of enquiry. His major concern is with the devastating and unsustainable impact of human activities on the biosphere, grounded in our failure to recognize the participatory nature of our relationship with the planet.

Michael Reynolds is Emeritus Professor of Management Learning at Lancaster University Management School. His research interests are in the development and application of experiential learning theory with particular interest in illuminating differences between tutor intentions and students' experiences. More recently he has developed these interests in studies of the application of critical perspectives to participative management pedagogies such as the 'learning community'.

Clare Rigg is Senior Lecturer at the Institute of Technology, Tralee, Ireland. She has worked with practitioners from all sectors, integrating action learning and action research to individual, organizational, and inter-agency development. She researches and writes on action learning, critical action learning, management learning and human resource development.

Dr Burkard Sievers is Professor of Organizational Development at Bergische Universität Wuppertal/Germany, where he teaches and writes on management and organization theory from a psychoanalytic perspective and an action research approach. He is President of the International Society for the Psychoanalytic Study of Organizations for the period 2005–7.

Stephen Smith is a member of Brunel Business School with research interests in methodology, emotional labour, applied theatre, and the 'infrastructure' of authority—all of which collide in his chapter. Steve is currently exploring the emotional labour of consensus building at the local level, the well-being of air transport workers, and the emotional labour of police work. He is a founder member of the 'Working with Emotions Network' and Centre for Research in Emotion Work and edits the *International Journal of Work Organisation and Emotion.*

Sari Stenfors is an Associate Director of Scandinavian Consortium for Organizational Research at Stanford University. Her academic interests, born out of fifteen years as an international business executive and consultant in the healthcare, advertising, and design industries, are strategy tools, experiential learning methods, and methods of business research. Sari is the CEO of Innovation Democracy, Inc., a global NGO.

Antonio Strati is Professor of Sociology of Organization and lectures at the Universities of Trento and Siena, Italy. He is a founder member of the Standing Conference on Organizational Symbolism (SCOS-EGOS), and of the Research Unit on Communication, Organizational Learning and Aesthetics (www.unitn.it/rucola). His research interests focus on aesthetics and organization.

Elaine Swan is a senior teaching fellow at Lancaster University Management School where she is director of the Health Foundations' Leaders for Change programme and adviser on a new leadership programme for older people run by the charity Help and Care. She is interested in the interface between therapeutic cultures and the workplace, and diversity in organizations.

Jane Thompson lectures at the University of Lincoln (Hull Campus) and is also a tutor for the Centre for Labour Market Studies, University of Leicester. Her main area of research is in the field of management learning. She is a member of the editorial board for the *Journal of Gender Studies.*

Richard Thorpe is Professor of Management Development at Leeds University Business School. His interests lie in the field of Management Learning and Organizational Development as well as research methodology more generally. Richard is currently Vice-Chair of the British Academy of Management and is a member of the Economic and Social Research Council Training and Development Board.

Bente Rugaard Thorsen is a Ph.D. student at the Doctoral School of Organizational Learning at the Danish University of Education. She is a member of the research programme Lifelong Competence Development and she is investigating how academics affect the organizational learning arena in retail banking.

Kiran Trehan is Professor of Management Learning/Human Resource Development and Head of Department at the University of Central England. Her fields of interest include critical approaches to human resource development, management learning, power, and emotions in organizational development. Kiran is an editorial board member of *Journal of European Industrial Training, Journal of Business Innovation,* and *Action Learning, Research and Practice.*

Russ Vince is Professor of Leadership and Change in the School of Management at the University of Bath. His research interests cover management and organizational learning, leadership, and change. Russ is Editor-in-Chief of the journal *Management Learning.*

Jane Rohde Voigt is a Ph.D. student at the Department: Learning Lab Denmark, the Danish University of Education. She is a member of the Doctoral School of Organizational Learning and the Research Programme Lifelong Competence Development. Her research field is social learning processes as a part of the clinical setting of nurse education within a hospital as an organization.

Tony Watson is Professor of Organizational Behaviour at Nottingham University Business School. His interests cover industrial sociology, organizations, managerial and entrepreneurial work, and ethnography. Current work, is on the relationship between the shaping of the 'whole lives' of managers and entrepreneurs and the shaping of the enterprises within which they work.

M. Ann Welsh (Ph.D., University of Missouri) is Professor of Management at the University of Cincinnati. Her research interests include political activity in organizations, new product development processes, and constructive deviance. Her published research includes papers in the *Academy of Management Review, Academy of Management Journal, Administrative Science Quarterly,* and *Management Learning,* as well as in various book chapters.

INTRODUCTION

EXPERIENTIAL LEARNING AND MANAGEMENT EDUCATION: KEY THEMES AND FUTURE DIRECTIONS

RUSS VINCE

MICHAEL REYNOLDS

EXPERIENTIAL learning is having a revival. We have been aware for some time of a new interest in the potential of experiential learning, particularly as a way of developing the practice of critical management education. In building this Handbook, we set out to illustrate some of the ways in which the social and political complexities of organizing can be raised and reflected on, both by managers and by management educators. In addition, we wanted to demonstrate the depth and creativity that experiential methods and approaches can bring to management learning.

As management teachers and researchers, experiential learning has long been an important, although by no means dominant, part of our educational approach. In general, management education in business and management schools is delivered through traditional, didactic approaches, sometimes with group work attached, and sometimes not. Where experiential methods have been used, they have attracted criticism for being unlikely to deliver the 'agreed' management curriculum and clear learning outcomes. Worse still, the approach has been seen as subverting the authority of the academic institution by legitimizing experience as a source of knowledge and understanding. So although experiential learning has been popular for decades, it has not made a significant impact in management and business schools. This Handbook is for scholars (like us) who would like to remedy this situation.

We have many colleagues in management education who are actively engaging with the various criticisms of experiential learning while introducing its methods into management and business schools at all levels. There are some exciting and challenging developments in both experiential methods and the ideas and theories which support them. Our starting point for this volume therefore was that this seemed to be a good time to bring together a selection of high-quality papers in order to reintroduce experiential learning and to remind management educators of its strengths and value. As the chapters in this volume illustrate, not only is the tradition of experiential learning and its considerable array of methods an emergent feature of contemporary management education, the theory and practice of experiential learning is being developed, applied, and evaluated at all levels of management education. Through these developments, there has been a significant shift in perspective from a predominantly personal development agenda to one in which experiential approaches are used to find ways of helping management students and managers understand and work with the complex social and political processes which characterize living and working in organizations. This Handbook represents this shift, providing twenty-five examples of experiential approaches to management education.

TOWARDS A CRITICAL PERSPECTIVE

It is no coincidence that this volume comes at a time when critical management education is gaining ground within the community of management teachers, and it was to the 'critical management studies' network that we first turned for contributions to this project. Over the years since the field was being given its foundations by such writers as Kurt Lewin, Donald Schön, Malcolm Knowles, and David Kolb—all of whose contributions are acknowledged in the chapters of this volume—experiential learning has attracted its share of critique. Questions have been raised, for example, about the ambiguities of tutor and student roles and relationships during experience-based programmes, and the appropriate degrees of power and control exercised by tutors—especially in the context of assessment. These questions were manifestations of more fundamental concerns that the experiential project was characterized by overly psychological interpretations of organizational behaviour and paid insufficient attention to the social, emotional, and political content of experience. Elaine Swan expresses this very well in this volume when she says that: 'experience isn't what it used to be.' In other words, we do not think that 'experience' provides 'neutral access to reality and selfhood', and this means at the very least that we should ask: what kind of 'microcosm' is being created through experiential methods, what versions of the social, and what versions of experience are being imagined in experiential methods?

These questions and the debates which pursued them have provided the platform through which the theory and practice of experiential learning has been developed recently. This is illustrated for example in the writing of Chris Kayes, who contributes the Conclusion to this volume. Chris has worked with critiques of experiential learning theory, reconciling the principles of a critical perspective with learning approaches which foreground experience—personal *and* organizational (Kayes 2002). In the same spirit, others (see, for example, Willmott 1994; Reynolds and Vince 2004) have argued the case for experiential learning as the basis for a critical pedagogy because it enables complex social and political processes to be observed and understood through both its content and its methodology.

While we believe that experiential learning has much to offer the future development of management education, we also take some pleasure in its limitations. We think that it is important to acknowledge the unreliability of experience as a concept because this encourages us to question assumptions about the nature of experience. For example, how can we know that our personal perception of experience is real? How are others accomplices in our perceptions and constructions of experience and how stable is experience as a concept related to learning? This last question is particularly important because we want to argue that the very value of experiential learning is in its unreliability and instability. It is an educational approach that mirrors the complexities and uncertainties of being in the role of manager; that can represent the contestation and change that takes place in organizations; and that reflects the ways in which organization is constructed and reconstructed within practice. The value of experiential learning is that it can discourage and disrupt our tendency to produce prescriptions for learning, our attempts to define 'best' practice, and it asks us to reflect again on the 'imagined stability' of organization (Vince 2002).

This Handbook presents a collection of new papers from leading international authors on experiential learning and management education. Its aim is to surface the developments and debates that currently characterize experiential learning in business and management schools, and to bring together a clear set of theory-based practices and recent developments within a range of settings. The chapters in the Handbook all discuss experiential events that have been designed to engage students in the complex emotional, social, political, and relational issues that underpin management education. These include: the emotional and/or aesthetic experience of managing and organizing; developing an understanding of power relations in organizations; the dynamics of organizational change; avoidance and/or human development in organizations; and an understanding of how control and/or compliance is mobilized in organizations. The richness and importance of experiential learning comes from the desire for management education to highlight the complexities involved in organization and organizing. Often, the reason for using experiential approaches is to generate lasting insights about management and organization thinking and practice.

EXAMPLES OF EXPERIENTIAL LEARNING

One way that we can explain what experiential learning means to us is by providing a couple of examples of how we use experiential learning in our own work with managers and management students.

Example 1: The 'Whole Group Task'

The 'whole group task' is designed to help managers to engage with the emotional and political dynamics that construct and often constrain organization. The exercise belongs to the 'group relations' tradition of experiential learning (French and Vince 1999). It is best done with groups of between twelve and twenty managers, in a room where the chairs can be arranged in a circle. The exercise runs for seventy-five minutes and then there is a short break before a thirty-minute plenary to debrief the event. At the start of the exercise, the tutor will say something like: 'This session is called the whole group task. It will finish at (give the group the finish time). The task is for the group to decide, and the management of the task is with the group. Your tutor will be commenting only on the process.' The first thing that happens, as soon as the tutor has finished making this initial statement, is some form of reaction to not having a clearly defined task. Some people express this through their silence; others, through attempts to take control (for example I'll write the ideas on the flip chart); through offering traditional or predictable solutions (for example let's vote on it); similarly, people decide that smaller groups would be easier or better; that a chairperson or leader would help to manage the group more effectively; that we should all go round and each say our idea for a task; that it is all a waste of time; that we should go for a walk; that that tutor is a...

The exercise raises a number of issues that are important to an understanding of behaviour in organizations. The person who jumps up to stand at the flip chart and write down the group members' ideas for a task is behaving in this way in order to alleviate her or his own anxieties as much as to help with the effective management of a group task. Similarly, splitting into smaller groups helps group members to dispel some of the uncomfortable feelings generated by such a task. Finding a task is, of course, not the main point of this exercise. The 'whole group event' is a method for exploring the complex interplay of emotions, relations, and politics as part of processes of organizing, as well as understanding the implications of organizational dynamics for leadership and change. The exercise can reveal how quickly (and often unconsciously) implicit rules and expectations are brought into groups; it shows how difficult it is to break free from 'the way we do things here'; and how readily individuals abandon their authority when faced with uncertainty.

Example 2: An Undergraduate Lecture on Management and Organizational Behaviour

This lecture was a response to a colleague who said that experiential learning was all very well with small groups of managers, but that it could not be used in a lecture room with 250 management undergraduates. The 'lecture' lasted for fifty minutes. When the students came into the lecture theatre they were each given one sheet of blank A4 paper. After they had settled down, they were given ten minutes to 'create something beautiful'. The students interpreted this task in many ways. For example, after a few minutes, paper aeroplanes started to float from parts of the lecture theatre. Some students sat with the sheet of paper in their hands, unclear what they were supposed to be doing. From the front the lecturer could see the students drawing, colouring with different pens, tearing shapes into the paper, folding it, screwing it into a ball, talking about other things, sending text messages, and making origami figures.

When the ten minutes were over, the ways students responded to the task could be used to illustrate some very common aspects of human behaviour in organizations. The behaviour that results from being asked to do a task, however well or ill defined it is, is likely to be varied. There will be, for example: predictable responses (paper aeroplanes); ambivalent responses (sending text messages); creative responses (elaborate colour pictures); and enquiring responses (talking with others to clarify or criticize the point of the task). There are many different interpretations possible of the things we are asked to do in organizations, as well as fantasies and expectations concerning what may be the 'right' and 'wrong' ways to do them. This exercise helps management students to understand that managing and being managed involve, for example, complicated relationships, varied interpretations, limited resources, and unclear commands. It also allows the lecturer to comment on the importance of collective reflection as one way of understanding the complexities and uncertainties of experience in organizations.

EXPERIENTIAL LEARNING: KEY THEMES

In both of the above examples there is a desire by the tutor to illustrate aspects of behaviour in organizations that can be *felt* as much as understood by those seeking to learn. Experiential learning is used to encourage students to become actively involved, and it is this activity that provides a means to generate 'here and now' examples in order to reflect on the emotional, relational, and political dynamics of managing and organizing. There are many more such examples represented and discussed in this Handbook and together, they present the reader with five main themes of experiential learning and management education. These are:

- Experiential learning is an approach that can reveal the 'underground organization'. The use of experiential learning implies a desire to examine emotional, unconscious, social, and political forces that shape learning, managing, and organizing.
- Experiential learning is a way of introducing concepts to students in depth, as well as representing complex work environments and allowing reflection on specific aspects of how and why we can and cannot learn.
- Experiential learning inevitably raises a tension that is inherent in both learning and organizing: that the 'radical potential' of experiential learning to challenge ways of thinking and ways of working cannot be separated from the 'political purpose' in educating managers to comply with organizational norms and expectations. In this volume, experiential learning is a method for generating critique. The value of critique is that it promotes a reflexive approach to both learning and organizing.
- Experiential learning is often a challenge to the educational institution in which it is situated.
- Experiential learning is an approach that encourages collective and critical reflection as well as individual learning.

We think that these themes provide an informal framework and an outline agenda for the future development of experiential learning. If we are trying to generate examples in order to reflect on the emotional, relational, and political dynamics of managing and organizing, then it is important to try to use a pedagogical approach that gets beneath the surface of organizing, which addresses conscious and unconscious dynamics, underlying power relationships, persistent expectations, and emotions. The chapters in this volume illustrate how experiential learning allows management educators to introduce such concepts to students in depth, and to represent work environments that encourage reflection on not only the possibilities for learning but also the restrictions and limitations on learning that are inevitably part of organization.

There are always tensions raised by the utilization of experiential methods in management education. At the same time as this approach might offer 'radical potential' (John Coopey, this volume) to challenge ways of thinking and working, it is important to start to question the 'political purpose' in educating managers in this way. This emphasizes the understanding of experiential learning we are seeking to support and develop in this Handbook, which can be called *experiential reflexivity* (Gherardi and Poggio, this volume). Experiential learning not only challenges what and how individuals and groups expect to learn, it often poses a challenge to the educational institution in which it is situated. Attempts to reflect on power relationships in the classroom are likely to connect to the broader institutional context within which such power relations are created and sustained.

In principle and in practice experiential learning challenges the assumption of learning as dissemination from expert to novice. Learning is seen as a collaborative process, one in which people critically examine the ideas they use to make sense of 'experience'. In the academy, teachers play a crucial part in providing the connections to research and theory which students use to elaborate and understand the complexities of their experience. But reflecting Paulo Freire's (1974) concept of pedagogy, this process of construction is co-authored rather than totally differentiated into students-with-experience and tutors-with-ideas to explain that experience. Our view about experiential learning is that it is not a solution but a way of reflecting within and on complexity. It is certainly not a simplistic or easy approach. As the chapters in this volume demonstrate, experiential learning is demanding theoretically, practically, and emotionally, because it mobilizes organizational politics and anxieties. However, this is exactly why it is important. In the tradition of Dewey, through an exploration of work and working relationships, experiential learning provides the basis of learning for living and working democratically.

THE CHAPTERS IN THIS VOLUME

All of the chapters describe an event and how this has been used within a process of management education and/or learning in organizations. They reveal the theories and intentions that inform the event, as well as explaining the thinking that underpins it, the reasons for using it, and the learning that it is designed to produce. Authors' thinking is linked to wider debates within and about experiential learning, to reflections on the experience of using the event, and to student responses and reactions to the experience. Authors are explicit about why the experiential event they are describing is important, and the themes in management and organization theory and behaviour that the event is designed to address.

The volume covers examples of experiential learning in undergraduate, postgraduate, doctoral, and post-experience management education. It provides the reader with new perspectives: on the importance of learning from experience; on the varieties of thinking behind the experiential approach; and how the approach has been used in management education to ensure interest, challenge, and in-depth learning.

Part I

We have called this part 'fundamental ideas and theoretical developments in experiential learning'. There are four chapters which between them demonstrate a considerable range of underlying ideas from applications of classic developments in experiential learning theories to applications which move into less familiar conceptual territory. In each case the authors illustrate how the theory is used in the education of managers and management students. The concept of double-loop learning is a well-established and fundamental theory in the lexicon of management education. In putting theory to work Chris Argyris (Chapter 1) describes an experience-based intervention designed to help managers understand the difficulties they have in generating a double-loop learning approach to solving organizational problems at work. This is an example of a classic contribution to theory developed as the means of helping managers to challenge and revise their assumptions. Through experience-based activities—including role-play—managers identify the defensive routines and mind-sets which all too often undermine their learning and effectiveness. In conveying the principles of double-loop learning, Chris Argyris draws a parallel between 'skilled unawareness' at an individual level and the 'underground organization' in which defensiveness has become culturally embedded. The aim of the intervention is that managers develop a theory-in-use which is supportive of a more creative, challenging organizational culture.

In Chapter 2, Jeff Gold, Robin Holt, and Richard Thorpe give their account of introducing activity theory as a perspective for experience-based learning for Master of Business Administration (MBA) students. The MBA students are encouraged to make sense of their experiences of organization—whether at work or on the MBA—as an activity system. The perspective they introduce emphasizes the importance of historical, contextual, and cultural influences as well as the ways in which experience is mediated by both 'sentient and non-sentient entities'. Gold, Holt, and Thorpe's intention is that through this approach MBA students should be able to understand better the nature of social realities from an experiential perspective and to develop the ability to engage with the complexities of business life in both a practical and critical manner.

Experiential learning makes possible the crossing of boundaries which subject disciplines protect. In Chapter 3, Ann Welsh, Gordon Dehler, and Dale Murray describe a course in which students studying different subjects (business, engineering, design, etc.) work in multidisciplinary teams on the design and development of various products. These action research projects bring together the principles of experience-based learning and critical pedagogy in that the student groups generate in the classroom the experience of working in multidisciplinary teams, learn to depend at least as much on their own ideas and experience as on input from the faculty, and analyse power relationships as they evolve within the programme. Ann Welsh and her colleagues emphasize the aesthetic nature of work experience as the basis of learning to form judgements, providing a balance to discursive knowledge.

Aesthetics is also the focus of Antonio Strati's chapter (Chapter 4) in which it becomes central to understanding the experience of organization. Through the application of a riddle and of a video as artistic performance—devices not often associated with academic pedagogy—students are encouraged to put value on their 'imaginings, tastes and intuitions' as the means of understanding organizational phenomena. Even 'the lecture' is used by Antonio Strati and a colleague to illustrate to students the dynamics of power and emotions within the classroom. Through this highly creative and challenging approach, experiential learning is a perspective through which organizations can be understood, rather than simply a particular form of pedagogic method.

Part II

The title of this part is 'the diversity of classroom experience'. The four chapters illustrate the richness in variety which characterizes experiential learning. There are considerable differences in the type and scope of the activities presented in this part which nevertheless share common ground in terms of the learning theories which support them.

Chapter 5 reminds us that the hard-and-fast distinction which is often made between 'experience' and other aspects of study is questionable. Reading, research-ing, or taking part in discussion is itself an experience which can confront be-haviour and beliefs. The problem with which Keijo Räsänen and Kirsi Korpiaho engage in this chapter is to develop a way of introducing experiential learning to management students who have no experience of work. These authors invite students to examine their ongoing experience of their own course as a 'practi-cal activity' employing a theoretical framework intended to be of later use when they become members of work organizations. This framework incorporates three perspectives: tactical, strategic, and moral. Keijo and Kirsi describe in detail the process of design, acknowledging the challenge of introducing such an approach to students who can regard academic work as out of touch with the 'real world' of management, even if they have no clear idea of what the 'real world' of management involves.

In Chapter 6 Ruth Colquhoun, Nelarine Cornelius, Meretta Elliot, Amar Mistry, and Stephen Smith present a detailed description of a simulation which develops Custody Sergeants' understanding of and capacity to deal with the arrival of a 'detained person' (DP) into their charge. In the tradition of the safe learning laboratory, the simulation recreates the complex interaction between police, members of the public, the physical arrangements of the police station, and the pervading presence of governmental regulations. Student actors are used to enact a series of detained persons arrested and brought to a police 'custody suite'. They develop their understanding of their part as DPs, based on brief police résumés describing actual 'circumstances of arrest'. Their drama tutor encourages them to create a 'back story' from which their role-play can be brought to life in a convincing fashion and with great realism. As well as enabling practice development in the student Custody Sergeants, practice development also takes place in the student actor. The design seen here dissolves the distinction between teaching, research, and practice development and, as the authors remind us, in representing in microcosm the relationship between police and the community, an important part of what is learned is the realization of civilized practice.

It can be argued that through the intermediary of technology, networked learning presents possibilities for tutors and students to work more democratically together. In Chapter 7, Joe Champoux discusses ways of introducing experiential learning into a networked environment. He describes on-line activities which have the aim of increasing students' involvement with course content, each other, and the tutor, enhancing not just subject learning but self-awareness—in the same way that experiential activities would contribute to students' experience in the face-to-face classroom. Joe draws on a number of learning theories—in particular experiential and constructivist—in support of this approach, which he illustrates with examples from individual and team-based activities—some of which use film—and through which students engage with concepts such as job design, decision making, and organizational culture.

In Chapter 8 the experiential component of the United States Air Force Academy programme described by Martin Hornyak, Steve Green, and Kurt Heppard is designed with the aim of equipping students with the knowledge and skills, technical, intellectual, and social, which they will need in their professional careers. In another example of crossing boundaries between disciplines, the learning experience in this case is a student team project, which involves the design and eventual launch of a satellite. This extraordinary and ambitious experiential project brings together both technical and non-technical aspects of the programme, including principles of engineering and management, by creating a student-centred environment in which students learn to identify and solve problems on their own as well as develop skills of communication and teamwork.

Part III

Part III of the Handbook addresses what we are calling 'politically grounded experiential learning'. In our view, experiential learning is always set within a political context. Sharing experience both generates politics and reflects the politicized nature of managing and organizing. In addition, addressing the politics and power relations mobilized within and by experiential learning encourages reflexive critique on the ways in which we position and interpret the meaning of 'experience' as well as the political function of experiential learning within organizations.

The chapter by Silvia Gherardi and Barbara Poggio (Chapter 9) is an exploration of the relational and emotional dynamics involved in leadership and situated practice. They consider the value of narrative knowledge in stimulating reflexive thought and they outline an approach to experiential learning based on the interaction between storytelling and listening. Their training approach is grounded in 'memory work' (the self as historical product, cultural product, relational practice) and designed to stimulate individual and group reworking of both leadership and the relationship between gender and leadership. The event they describe is a five-day workshop designed around 'core themes' of leadership (rationality, control, decision making, strategic thinking) each framed in relation to its opposite, what they call 'the suppressed term', reflecting an aspect of gendered experience and power relations that links to each of these themes. Participants within the workshop read and write stories of leadership, engaging with each other in dialogue for improvement or transformation. The chapter presents the reader with an example of 'experiential reflexivity', and the authors explain how 'the process of narrating leadership creates the context for experiencing leadership and reflecting on its practices'.

In Chapter 10, John Coopey discusses how 'theatre workshops' can be used to create the trust and the physical and emotional space for learning through 'playful experimentation'. He also highlights the broader political context within which this approach to experiential learning can be negotiated and performed, placing particular emphasis on its political function within organizational development. John argues that a specific value of theatre workshops is that they can be used to address the problem of potential harm that comes from trusting and being trusted within a political system. While such workshops can provide an 'aesthetic space' within which individuals might become visible and find voice, John also acknowledges that this is rarely achieved in practice and that theatre workshops can be created, consciously or unconsciously, to induce conformism and to rehearse emotional labour. They can become an exercise in learning how to behave in order 'to reflect the company's position'. John's chapter conveys a powerful message about the political dynamics of experiential learning, the inevitable tension present in experiential learning between its 'political purpose' and its 'radical potential'. His chapter also provides the reader with insights about the importance of understanding the paradoxical nature of experiential learning: that it contains both the hope of making change and the reinforcement of established power relations, expectations, and norms.

In Chapter 11, Peter Reason describes a 'wilderness experience', part of an exercise in education for ecology that occurs on the M.Sc. in Responsibility and Business Practice, a programme that has been running for the past ten years at the School of Management, the University of Bath. This M.Sc. programme is informed by strong values in relation to the global challenge of ecology and the issues of individual and social responsibility that arise from these values. The idea behind the wilderness experience is to take managers 'beyond the conscious, rational mind and into a literal and internal wilderness'. Experiential learning therefore provides the specific context of a 'profound challenge', a challenge faced both by individuals and by the global human community. Here, experiential learning is being used to explore a crisis of perception concerning the way we see ourselves in relation to the planet and as a way of developing forms of management education that might address these issues.

Elaine Swan provides the reader with a challenging and useful thought: that 'experience isn't what it used to be'. In other words, 'experience' does not provide us with neutral access to reality and selfhood. In Chapter 12, Elaine explores the meaning of the category of 'experience' in experiential learning. She positions experience as problematic and discusses how experiential learning is beset by its own contradictions. Elaine adds to the critique of experiential learning begun in John Coopey's chapter, acknowledging the tension in experiential learning, its connections both to social movements and to consumerism. She reminds us that 'experience' in all forms of experiential learning cannot and should not be taken for granted, and therefore of the need to interrogate what kind of microcosm is being created through experiential methods. Elaine's theme is: 'how social reality is being understood in experiential methods'. In particular, and through a discussion of a specific approach to race equality training, she examines what version of the social, and what versions of experience, are being imagined in experiential methods.

In Chapter 13, Anne Herbert and Sari Stenfors reflect on their use of action learning and problem-based learning within the institutional context of the Helsinki School of Economics (HSE). They explore the institutional tensions that can be generated by using experiential learning in a teacher-centred institution. We are sure that the Helsinki School of Economics is not the only institution that demonstrates a mismatch between the espoused mission to 'develop dynamic teaching programmes' and the actual practice of teaching and learning. They found that their attempt to change from traditional teaching methods to experiential methods was not easy, and that institutional forces make change challenging. They argue for a conscious comparison of experiential methods in order to develop the best possible fit between the experiential approach and the institutional context. The differences between experiential methods are seen to be important because different methods address different needs, demands, and constraints within the institution. They conclude that, while teachers have relative freedom to choose the teaching and learning methods they use, there is limited practical support for experiential learning methods.

Part IV

Part IV contains four chapters which are informed by a psychoanalytic perspective on experiential learning. There is a long tradition of experiential learning from a psychoanalytic perspective represented by the work of the Tavistock Institute, London, and many other organizations around the world. Within this tradition, experiential learning has been a preferred method because it provides opportunities to engage with unconscious dynamics, with the collective emotions of organizing and their implications for structure and action.

In Chapter 14, Burkard Sievers describes an action research project designed to examine feelings and emotions 'below the surface' of the university and of the experience of students and faculty within university settings. His experiential framework is the 'Social Photo-Matrix' (SPM), a method designed to 'allow access to the unconsciousness of the university' and to highlight what remains hidden or goes unnoticed. The method asks students to take digital photographs of the university. Students' images then provide access to a 'transitional space' between the inner world of the photographer and the outer one of the 'object'; the photographs capture both a picture of the university and a memory of experience. Burkard's analysis reveals that students predominantly see the university as a production line. His conclusion is that the university engages only in part of its task, the generation and transmission of technologically exploitable knowledge, while losing sight of the part of its task that might engage students in critical reflection. Such critical reflection may be of benefit to students and might also provide a way of rediscovering the role educational institutions have in activities that create new knowledge.

Jean Neumann (Chapter 15) discusses the ways in which experiential learning can be used in the education and development of organizational consultants. She describes the thinking and approach that she and colleagues have developed on the Advanced Organizational Consultation (AOC) programme run by the Tavistock Institute, London. Experiential learning is used to bring 'real life' consultancy work into the classroom and it serves as a basic strategy for teaching and learning about the dynamics of organizational analysis and intervention. Jean discusses 'five varieties' of experiential learning used in the programme. These are: curriculum and module design, experiential activities and reflection, consultancy experience and reflection, vicarious learning, and institutional reflexivity. She carefully outlines the experiences of learning and learners within these five varieties and thereby demonstrates the importance of actively working through the political and emotional dynamics of the institutional context. Jean then outlines 'patterns' for how each type of experiential learning contributes to the education of consultants. We find the category of 'institutional reflexivity' to be a particularly important description of the relationship between psychodynamic theory and experiential learning. Institutional reflexivity begins when the AOC programme begins, and the function of this variety of learning is to reveal 'regressive dynamics that excite political and psychological anxieties and conflicts' and 'substantially delay or block many strategically important changes and developments in organizations'.

In Chapter 16, Liz Creese provides the reader with a personal story about her own teaching and learning, an example of the experience in the role of teacher and how she was 'unable to learn in the very way I expected of my students'. Rethinking experience in the role of teacher is the theme of this chapter. In our minds, the chapter contrasts well with Jean Neumann's, providing an example of the emotional energy that can be given to resisting reflexivity. Anxieties about the learning experience initially undermined her ability to be effective in her role and then in sustaining and developing the design for learning. Liz uses her chapter to revisit the experience of 'not really knowing what experiential design we are teaching until we have been able to be critically reflexive about it'. There is much that is left open in this chapter and there is also a very clear sense of how difficult it can be to understand and accept that, as teachers, we can easily become accomplices in the failure to learn.

Paula Hyde (Chapter 17) discusses the use of 'live projects' in a Masters of Business Administration (MBA) programme and explores the challenges involved in attempting to integrate experiential approaches to management education in university settings: particularly how isolated experiential learning can be and that 'the possibility of accounting for what is learnt during an experiential event remains elusive'.

She contrasts three ways of thinking about the delivery of the MBA. First, the 'lecture-centred' MBA, which is taught and assessed by traditional means. This approach seeks to minimize uncertainty and to place opportunities for creativity with the teacher. The second way of thinking she calls the 'project-added' MBA, which builds on the lecture-centred approach by providing projects that allow for some personal and experiential learning. This approach increases the possibility for uncertainty, for unintended outcomes, and for creativity by the student in the completion of a project task. Paula's final approach is the 'experiential' MBA programme. This is not an easy approach to find or to create. However, the experiential approach has the capacity to contain anxiety in the face of uncertainty in order that students might move between 'not knowing', 'knowing', and 'established knowledge' as part of their experience of learning. Her conclusion is that, without opportunities for experiential learning, management education programmes will continue to produce students unprepared for the realities of organizational life.

Part V

Part V has three chapters that give examples of experiential learning with doctoral students. Experiential approaches to working with doctoral students might help them to understand the value of peer working and review; offer different models for doctoral supervision; and provide a method for qualitative data collection and analysis. In all three chapters there is an emphasis on collective reflection as a key element in the development of scholarly knowledge and practice.

In Chapter 18, Andrea Ellinger and her class of doctoral students present the reader with the work they did together to improve learning processes at the same time as reviewing the literature on the learning organization and writing a conference paper. Experiential learning was used as a way of reflecting on and developing the 'emerging scholar'. The approach was designed to help doctoral students become more immersed in the literature through a collaborative writing project. The idea was to experience scholarly writing through collaboration and reflection and through this to understand and develop skills and knowledge relating to scholarship and literature review. Andrea does not claim this as a new idea, but she does re-emphasize the importance of finding an appropriate and consistent learning process for understanding how to study organizational learning.

Sandra Jones (Chapter 19) focuses on a 'professional doctorate' and she addresses the question: 'what should an appropriate student–supervision relationship for practice-based research include?' Her chapter gives an example of an experiential research community of practice, designed 'to provide peer-supported knowledge sharing and discovery'. She explores how experiential learning can be used, outlines some principles for experiential designs with doctoral students, and she proposes a collective model for a 'more equal' supervisory–candidate relationship.

The final chapter in this section (Chapter 20) is by Tusse Jensen, Jane Voigt, Enrico Piras, and Bente Thorsen, who are all Ph.D. students who attended a research methodology workshop organized by the Doctoral School of Organizational Learning in Copenhagen. The chapter is the direct result of an experiential exercise run by one of the editors of this book (Russ Vince). The exercise was designed to help doctoral students understand how and why to use visual data collection methods within their research (see Vince 2007), and the particular value of this method in researching emotion in organizations. The exercise asked all the participants to produce images of their experience of being a Ph.D. student and then to use collective processes of data interpretation and analysis in order to build a short and contained study on the emotions involved in being a doctoral student. Workshop participants were invited to utilize the data generated to write a chapter for this Handbook, reflecting their understanding of this approach to research. Tusse, Jane, Enrico, and Bente took up this challenge.

Part VI

This part is called 'critically focused experiential learning'. We noted earlier in this introductory chapter the important debates as to both the 'critical' potential of experiential learning and, for some, its lack of criticality. Critical perspectives will be illustrated and applied throughout this volume but in this section we have presented four chapters which illustrate quite different expressions of this.

In Chapter 21, Anna Kayes describes an application of experiential learning which has the aim of helping management students to develop their understanding of the dynamics of power in organizations. Based on recent developments in Kolb's theory of experiential learning, Anna draws on 'conversational learning' as a means of surfacing different perspectives, contradictions, and possibilities for the interpretation of complex organizational processes as well as implications for action. Using the device of guided leadership narratives, groups of students are encouraged to reflect critically on their experiences of power and leadership so as to identify ways of deconstructing and transforming them. Anna illustrates how, in learning from experience in this way, students are encouraged to work with emotional and social processes and to engage with the inevitable complexity of organizational life.

In Chapter 22, Tony Watson introduces an approach though which undergraduate management students learn about aspects of organization through 'negotiated narrative'. He illustrates how students work with theory and research material from the literature and from lectures through reflection on their own experiences of being in organizations. In the examples in the chapter Tony shows how students are encouraged to make connections between their personal experience and case studies of people in employment through individual studies which provide the basis for classroom, student-led meetings in which ideas about management and organization are developed through discussion.

In Chapter 23, Jane Thompson and Tracy Lamping apply a critical perspective to both content and process in their work with HRM and business undergraduates. Their aim is to provide students with classroom activities which reflect the social and political behaviours they will encounter in organizations. In engaging with the uncertainties of the experiential activities designed for them, students encounter in the 'here and now' social issues including those of power, trust, responsibility, and gendering, connecting these with selected literature and developing the skills and insights which will support their development as reflexive practitioners.

Chapter 24 is also an account of critical pedagogy in practice. In this illustrated example by Kiran Trehan and Clare Rigg, educational practice is aimed at integrating the social and political into management education. The authors make clear the principles on which the course design is based, and as with the previous chapter, emphasize the ways experiential processes can be as much a source of learning as the curriculum. Trehan and Rigg show how, for example, action learning, student-led projects, and participative assessment, supported by psychodynamic theory, enable students to learn about social and organizational process through an understanding of their own experience of working with each other and with the staff of the programme.

Conclusion

We invited Chris Kayes to read all the chapters and to write a conclusion to the volume. He has called this 'Institutional Barriers to Experiential Learning Revisited'. Chris has sought to engage both with Kolb's theories of experiential and conversational learning, as well as critical perspectives on experiential learning. We thought that this meant that he was uniquely placed to reflect on the volume as a whole, and to provide a way of finishing the Handbook that connects back to and contrasts with our own Introduction. Chris focuses his Conclusion on institutional barriers to successful experiential learning and on the themes that emerge from his reading of the chapters in this Handbook.

He uses his reading of the chapters to 'take stock' of experiential learning in order to look at future directions for experiential learning theory and practice. He recognizes, amongst other things, that there is a strong connection between experience and narrative; that experiential learning shares something in common with critical theories; and that experiential learning is moving more toward social and group dynamics (from a concern with personal learning). Chris points to the bias inherent in the reading of experiential learning within the Handbook. He is right to surmise that, as editors, we have privileged 'a particular viewpoint', and that, looking outside of the examples here, there is likely to be a much wider selection of methods and approaches available (particularly 'of functionalist, quantitative, and outcome-driven experiential exercises'). His overall view is an optimistic one. He identifies the breadth, depth, and diversity of experiential learning, as well as the variety of settings in which it is being used and the wide range of content.

Our view of experiential learning is also optimistic. We have brought together what we consider to be a comprehensive range of high-quality examples of recent thinking about experiential learning. For us, this Handbook shows the richness of thought and action that experiential learning can bring to management education. It offers an overview of some new insights into this subject, and thereby provides a basis for increased interest in understanding how and why experiential learning is such an important component in the education of leaders and managers.

REFERENCES

Freire, P. (1974). *Pedagogy of the Oppressed*. Harmondsworth: Penguin.

French, R., and Vince, R. (1999). *Group Relations, Management and Organization*. Oxford: Oxford University Press.

Kayes, D. C. (2002). 'Experiential Learning and its Critics: Preserving the Role of Experience in Management Learning and Education', *Academy of Management Learning and Education*, 1/2: 137–49.

Reynolds, M., and Vince, R. (2004). 'Critical Management Education and Action-Based Learning: Synergies and Contradictions', *Academy of Management Learning and Education*, 3/4: 442–56.

Vince, R. (2002). 'The Politics of Imagined Stability: A Psychodynamic Understanding of Change at Hyder plc', *Human Relations*, 55/10: 1189–208.

—— (2007). 'Drawings and Images in Management Research', in R. Thorpe and R. Holt (eds.), *The Dictionary of Qualitative Management Research*. London: Sage.

Willmott, H. (1994). 'Management Education: Provocations to a Debate', *Management Learning*, 25/1: 105–36.

PART I

FUNDAMENTAL IDEAS AND THEORETICAL DEVELOPMENTS IN EXPERIENTIAL LEARNING

CHAPTER 1

DOUBLE-LOOP LEARNING IN A CLASSROOM SETTING

CHRIS ARGYRIS

IN this chapter I will focus on problems that require double-loop learning. For example, why do human beings appear to design and implement actions that are counterproductive to achieving their intentions? Why, even after they do see the counterproductivity of their actions, do they repeat them in the same and in other settings? Why is it that the context in which this occurs rewards and strengthens these actions even though they violate the norms of effective actions?

THE ORGANIZATION OF THE CHAPTER

I begin with some fundamental assumptions about how human beings strive to make sense of the context in which they are embedded. Next, I present some observations from cases written by participants in our session. Inferences are then made that begin to answer the questions raised at the outset. The concepts of single- and double-loop learning are introduced. A theory of action is presented that explains the problems described above.

Next, I turn to the Joe–Bill case used in the classroom seminar intended to focus on double-loop learning. I describe the dialogue and show how the participants are helped to become aware that they are not skilful at producing double-loop learning. After dealing with their bewilderment, I present an example by the faculty member of a double-loop learning solution for the Joe–Bill case. I conclude with some comments on the underground world in organizations.

SOME FUNDAMENTAL ASSUMPTIONS

Human beings strive to make sense of the context in which they are embedded. Three key activities required are to understand and explain what is going on, to design effective action, and to implement the design. Our task as educators and interventionists is to make sense of how they go about making sense.

I begin with several propositions that are relevant to the analysis. First, all actions that human beings produce they do so by using their mind/brain. Second, human beings hold theories of action that inform their action. Third, human beings hold espoused theories of action and theories that they use to act (theories-in-use). Fourth, in order to develop a valid diagnosis of sense-making process it is necessary to begin with their theory-in-use. Fifth, in order to do so, it is necessary to base the diagnosis upon actual behaviour. Sixth, from the fifth step, we can infer the reasoning human beings used to inform their actions.

THE DIAGNOSTIC METHODOLOGY: THE LEFT-HAND-RIGHT-HAND CASE

One method that has been used with, conservatively estimated, over 10,000 participants is a case method that is called the left-hand-right-hand case. Individuals are asked to write a case about a challenge that they are facing with individuals, groups, intergroups, or organizational behavioural systems. Next they are asked what they would do to begin to solve the problems (about a paragraph).

Finally, they are asked to divide several pages into left-hand and right-hand columns. In the right-hand column they are asked to describe the dialogue that occurred (or would occur if it has not happened). This data represents the actual behaviour as they recall it. In the left-hand column they are asked to describe any feelings and thoughts that they had (or would have) that they did not (or would not) communicate. The objective of this column is to ask the writer to make public what they kept secret.

Both columns exhibit certain patterns that are central to inferring the theory-in-use of the case writer. Examples of the left-hand column are:

1. Don't let the group upset you.
2. This is not going well. Wrap it up and wait for another chance.
3. He is clearly on the defensive.
4. He is playing hardball because he is afraid of losing power.
5. This guy is unbelievable.
6. You are nowhere near as good as you think you are.
7. I am losing her, so I have to go in for the kill.
8. Great, try patronizing me. That won't get you far. He cares about trust. Talk about trust.

These examples help us begin to develop insights into the sense-making processes used by human beings. They appear to focus on three behavioural strategies. They advocate their views, they evaluate their own and others' effectiveness. They make causal attributions about the others' intentions. They keep this information secret from the others. Indeed, they cover up the secrecy.

A second feature is to test the validity of these early sense-making activities. Unfortunately, their testing (that often is implicit) assumes that their evaluations and attributions are valid because they honestly believe this is the case. The reasoning they use to develop their views is based on their own sense-making process. Their logic is self-referential.

If you combine cover-up and biased testing, it is a recipe, as we shall see, for faulty and incomplete learning. When we ask the participants what leads them to believe that cover-up and biased testing are connected to effective action, they provide two interdependent answers.

First they could become vulnerable (for example 'Don't let these guys upset you', 'This is not going well'). If others knew this information they could take advantage of them. The second response is that if they made their left-hand column public, it would make the others defensive. They keep their left-hand columns secret out of caring and concern for the others.

We see a double bind. If they are to behave effectively, it is necessary to test the validity of the left-hand column. But if they do test they are likely to create defensiveness in others and themselves. We can begin to see how human beings act to create the condition described in our questions at the outset of the chapter.

Double binds are complex consequences to solve. They require a level of awareness that cover-ups do not permit. They also require independent testing that self-referential logic does not supply.

Double binds under these conditions produce further double binds. The individual must act as if they are not creating undiscussables. To do so, they must make the undiscussability of the undiscussable, undiscussable. To compound the problem

Left-hand column	Right-hand column
I am going to get attacked, straight out of the box.	I'm so happy to meet you and get to know you. I think we will have a great working relationship and can learn a lot from each other.
What a bunch of crap. I don't want to get drawn into this discussion.	I'd like you to know that I believe in open, direct communication.
Did he say our plan? He must have meant his plan. Doesn't he know I disagree with his decision?	No problem, it seems like we are at a crucial point.
Winning the Nobel Prize will not help the company. Perhaps it is time to expand the development stuff and downsize the research stuff.	I am sure that you all realize that we work in a for-profit industry and must be realistically oriented.

Fig. 1.1 'Skilful spinning': examples

they deny their causal responsibility by using skilful spinning (See Figure 1.1). The spinning blocks the learning required to check the effectiveness of the actions taken. The anti-learning processes are reinforced by the other recipients who infer that the individual is spinning. They too cover up and do not test their inferences. We now have a systematic, self-fuelling, self-reinforcing set of processes that are counterproductive to learning. These results hold regardless of colour, gender, education, wealth, culture, size, and type of organization (Argyris 1990, 1993, 2000, 2004; Argyris and Schön 1996).

The above again reminds us of the puzzle stated at the outset. Why do human beings choose to act in ways that are counterproductive? How do they come to learn to become skilful at acting skilfully incompetent (i.e. producing consequences that are counterproductive to their intentions)? How do they come to learn to live with these conditions by blaming others? How do they come to learn to believe that they are not responsible; indeed to believe that they are victims?

A THEORY OF ACTION

One explanation is generated by a theory called a theory of action. The same theory can be used to develop learning for human beings and for organizations. The theory hypothesizes that human beings produce action by activating designs for action that they have created and stored in their heads (mind/brain). Human beings also develop designs to assess the degree to which they are effective. This introduces the concept of learning defined as detecting and correcting error. There are two types of learning. Single-loop learning occurs when errors are corrected without changing the underlying programme. Double-loop learning occurs when an error

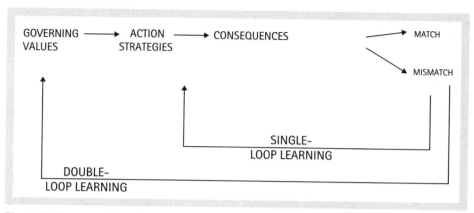

GOVERNING ⟶ ACTION ⟶ CONSEQUENCES   MATCH
VALUES   STRATEGIES

                                                     MISMATCH

                                    SINGLE-
                                    LOOP LEARNING

          DOUBLE-
          LOOP LEARNING

Fig. 1.2 Managerial and organizational learning

is corrected by first altering the underlying programme. For example, a thermostat is a single-loop learner. It is programmed to turn the heat up or down depending upon the temperature. A thermostat would be a double-loop learner if it questioned its existing programme that it should measure heat (Argyris 2004b).

The premiss of this approach is that all actions (behaviour with intentions) are produced as matches with the designs stored in our heads that we activate. These designs are developed by human beings as they strive to become skilful in whatever actions they intend.

If it is true that all actions are produced by activating designs for action stored in our heads, then actions that are counterproductive to our intentions must also be produced by activating appropriate designs stored in our heads. If this is true, the actions that are counterproductive must be consistent with the design that we have activated. If this is true, then even actions that are counterproductive are matches, and not mismatches. Counterproductive actions represent 'errors' that are designed, hence they are not errors.

How do we make sense of the puzzle? One way is to hypothesize that human beings are unaware of the errors that they are producing and the unawareness is skilful. But if unawareness is behaviour then it too must be designed. In what sense is unawareness skilful? One hypothesis is that the theories of action stored in our heads lead to actions that are counterproductive to our intentions and to being unaware that this is the case. We are programmed when dealing with double-loop problems to be skilfully incompetent and skilfully unaware. What kinds of programmes are we talking about?

Model I Theory-In-Use

There are two types of master programmes or theories of action. First, there are those that are espoused. Second, there are those that are used to produce the

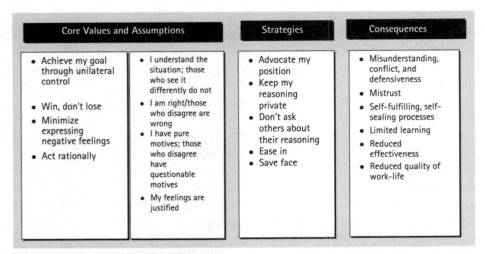

Core Values and Assumptions		Strategies	Consequences
• Achieve my goal through unilateral control • Win, don't lose • Minimize expressing negative feelings • Act rationally	• I understand the situation; those who see it differently do not • I am right/those who disagree are wrong • I have pure motives; those who disagree have questionable motives • My feelings are justified	• Advocate my position • Keep my reasoning private • Don't ask others about their reasoning • Ease in • Save face	• Misunderstanding, conflict, and defensiveness • Mistrust • Self-fulfilling, self-sealing processes • Limited learning • Reduced effectiveness • Reduced quality of work-life

Fig. 1.3 Model I: unilateral control

action (theories-in-use). We have identified a theory-in-use that we have labelled Model I.

Model I is said to be dominant because we have found it to be used regardless of gender, race, education, social status, wealth, age, and size of organization as well as culture (Argyris 1982, 1985, 1990, 1993, 2000, 2004; Argyris, Putnam, and Smith 1985; Argyris and Schön 1996).

The three most prevalent action strategies are, advocate ideas and positions, evaluate performance, and make attributions about causes of the actions of self and others. Action strategies are implemented in ways that are consistent with the governing values, which means enquiry into them is not encouraged nor is testing of claims, such as that the conclusions are self-seeking. Testing is based upon the use of self-referential logic. The logic used to generate a claim is the same logic used to test the claim (for example: trust me, my conclusion is valid because I know the organization, group, or individual). The consequences of Model I action strategies include misunderstanding and escalating error, self-fulfilling prophecies, and self-fuelling processes. These feed back to reinforce the governing values and the action strategies.

The use of Model I produces a defensive reasoning mind-set. Premisses and inferences are implicit and kept minimally transparent. The purpose of testing claims or conclusions is self-protective. A self-protective mind-set generates skills that produce consequences that are counterproductive to valid learning and systematic denial that this is the case. The incompetence and unawareness or denials are skilled. They have to be. Otherwise, they would not exist as theory-in-use designs in the human mind to produce the actions observed.

Model I theory-in-use and a defensive reasoning mind-set combine to produce organizational defensive routines. Organizational defensive routines are any actions or policies intended to protect individuals, groups, intergroups, or organizations as a whole from embarrassment or threat and do so in ways that prevent getting at the causes of the embarrassment or threat. Organizational defensive routines are anti-learning and overprotective. For example, organizations exhibit mixed messages. The theory-in-use to produce them is (1) state a message that is mixed, (2) act as if it is not mixed, (3) make 1 and 2 undiscussable, and (4) make the undiscussability undiscussable.

Defensive routines feed back to reinforce Model I, and the defensive reasoning mind-set. There is a tightly integrated relationship between individual theory-in-use and group, intergroup, and organizational factors. The result is an ultra-stable, self-fuelling, and self-sealing state. Under these conditions, it is difficult to call any factor (individual, group, intergroup, and organizational) the primary cause. They are highly interrelated. If so, then we may predict that if we give human beings a genuine opportunity to help others and themselves to create double-loop learning, they will fail to do so and be unaware of their failure, even if the conditions are ideal for double-loop learning. For example, thirty-eight CEOs came together in a seminar to learn more about effective leadership (Argyris 2000). They were asked to help 'Andy' who sought advice on how to overcome the blindness and incompetence that he admits he exhibits in the way he leads. Thus the CEOs were embedded in a context where Andy seeks help, where the credibility of the leadership of the CEOs is not in jeopardy, and where they do not come together with an organizational history and culture that contains organizational defensive routines. Moreover the context is not hierarchical and unilaterally controlling of their actions, and being without the pressures of everyday work life to act, the CEOs are not required to behave consistently with Model I, whether using defensive reasoning mind-sets or creating organizational defensive routines. Yet they produced these consequences. The same counterproductive consequences occur in the seminar to be described below.

The Joe–Bill Case

The first step is to help the participants to see the extent of their skilled incompetence and skilled unawareness. The methodology that we use has to be able to achieve this objective even though we can predict that the participants are going to be bewildered and baffled. They come to the seminar with the honest belief that they are not skilfully incompetent and unaware. The methodology should make it difficult to deny their personal causal responsibility for these two features. It should also help them to realize that if they are victims it is by their own design as well as the organizational norms and behavioural systems that they create in their organizations.

In this seminar, we used a two-prong methodology. The first was for them to complete a left-hand-right-hand case about a problem that they experienced in their setting that they wish to resolve. The second prong was to send them a one-page case of Joe and Bill written by Joe (the superior) about a sexual discrimination problem that Bill (the subordinate) was creating in their organization. The case was sent to the participants ahead of time. The participants were asked to help advise Joe on how to deal more effectively with Bill (Joe has stated in his case that the first session with Bill did not go well).

The session began with the faculty member (FM) asking the participants to become consultants to Joe. FM asked the participants to role-play their advice to Joe. FM said that he would role-play Joe receiving the advice. Finally, FM said that it was important for the dialogue to be stopped at any point in time when any participants believed that FM's role-playing of Joe's likely reactions was inaccurate or unfair.

Example of Advice Given to Joe by the Participants

Participant A: advises Joe to make sure that Bill understands the harassment policy.

Joe (as role-played by **FM**) 'I do not think that Bill will respond positively. As you read in the case Bill doesn't believe that he harasses anyone. Also he doesn't believe that the female co-workers believe that he has harassed them.'

Participant B: advises Joe to tell Bill that you have personally witnessed several of the incidents. 'Make it clear that you did not like what you saw. "Joe, you must find better ways to be specific without violating your promise not to identify the women"'.

FM: 'I agree with you. What would this behaviour look like? What do you advise me to say?'

B: 'I don't have the answer. I see problems but I am not sure how to get around it.'

Participant C: 'Joe, were you not offended with what you saw?'

FM: 'Absolutely'

C: 'Then use your feelings as a way into the problem.'

FM: 'What do you advise me to say? After all he says that I am making a mountain out of a molehill.'

C: 'So you feel he will reject your views?'

Participant D: 'Joe would it not be enough for you to tell B that you are personally offended with his behaviour?'

FM: 'I doubt it. He believes my discomfort is invalid because the women see him as being funny.'

Participant D: 'So why not explore with him the difference between his intentions to be funny and what is actually happening?'

FM: 'What do you advise me to say?'

D: 'You might say, "Bill you told a joke by the cooler. You thought it was funny"'

FM: 'Bill would say "correct" '

D: 'Ask him to share his experience honestly.'

FM: 'Again, I need advice as to what I would say to get him to be honest.'

FM: interrupts the dialogue. He notes that, so far, each of the advisers crafted advice with a sense of confidence that it would work. Joe's biggest problem is that he did not find the advice helpful. 'Do my interpretations make sense?'

D: 'yes.'

FM: 'Are you feeling a sense of failure?'

D: 'Just a tad' (group laughs)

FM: 'Please talk a bit about your feelings.

D: 'I feel stuck.'

FM: (role-playing Joe) 'I also feel stuck. I feel that you are highly motivated to help me. I believe that you are concerned about me. I conclude that I am faced with advisers who are concerned yet who are not helpful. I too feel stuck. It appears that we are creating a set of self-fuelling, self-sealing counterproductive processes.'

Reflections on the Experience

Reflecting on the dialogue we see that the advice given by the participants is consistent with Model I theory-in-use and defensive reasoning. For example:

1. Joe should act rationally. Tell Bill his actions are wrong and they are against company policy.
2. Joe should be in unilateral control. Joe should make it clear that if Bill does not change his actions Joe will not hesitate to punish him.
3. Joe should be cautious about being forthright. The advice crafted by the participants and given to Joe was consistent with easing in. If Bill did not respond favourably then Joe is advised to threaten Bill with punishment, including firing him.

The dialogue produced by the participants also illustrated the predicted consequences of Model I, namely, skilled incompetence, skilled unawareness, the use of self-referential logic to test claims.

Finally the FM helped the participants to realize that although they said they wanted to learn, although Joe pleaded for help, although they were in a classroom setting where their future was not at risk, they skilfully created a setting where as one of them said 'things are going nowhere' (consistent with the Andy case described above).

FM invited, at the outset, the participants to confront FM if they thought that FM, acting as Joe, was unfair. At the end of the dialogue FM asked again if anyone thought that FM role-played Joe irresponsibly. If so, would the individual please

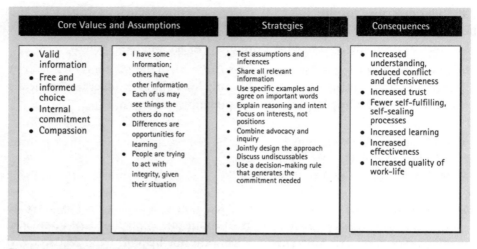

Core Values and Assumptions		Strategies	Consequences
• Valid information • Free and informed choice • Internal commitment • Compassion	• I have some information; others have other information • Each of us may see things the others do not • Differences are opportunities for learning • People are trying to act with integrity, given their situation	• Test assumptions and inferences • Share all relevant information • Use specific examples and agree on important words • Explain reasoning and intent • Focus on interests, not positions • Combine advocacy and inquiry • Jointly design the approach • Discuss undiscussables • Use a decision-making rule that generates the commitment needed	• Increased understanding, reduced conflict and defensiveness • Increased trust • Fewer self-fulfilling, self-sealing processes • Increased learning • Increased effectiveness • Increased quality of work-life

Fig. 1.4 Model II: joint control

say so and illustrate their claims by using Joe's behaviour as role-played by FM. No one volunteered an example. The participants expressed bewilderment because none of them expected that they or the members as a group would be responsible for creating the conditions for failure in double-loop learning. The next question is, how can the participants learn a new theory-in-use that will help them to reduce the stuckedness that they created? The first step is for them to learn a new theory-in-use called Model II.

Model II: Theory-In-Use

The governing values of Model II are valid knowledge, informed choice, and personal responsibility for one's actions. The action strategies are to advocate, to evaluate, to attribute in the service of the Model II governing values and productive reasoning. Productive reasoning emphasizes encouraging enquiry and robust testing of claims in the service of learning. The consequences are the reduction of self-fulfilling and self-sealing processes. These consequences feed back to reinforce Model II governing values and action strategies. This, in turn, produces organizational behavioural systems that encourage learning, especially double-loop learning.

An Example of Model II Strategy

The faculty member then said that he would like to present Model II strategy that Joe could use during his second session with Bill. The strategy is aimed at helping Bill become aware of his defensive mind-set that includes denial and blaming others, test his claims with the use of self-referential logic, and accept his share of personal responsibility.

FM first described his thinking in terms of a seven-point action strategy for the meeting.

1. I should begin the meeting by stating that some of the staff are upset about the comments and jokes that he (Bill) makes.
2. I should strive to do so in as constructive a manner as possible. By that I mean I will begin by describing the problem as I see it and then ask Bill for his reactions (confirms-disconfirms).
3. If Bill agrees then we can move to how he can begin to change and how I can help him to do so.
4. However, I doubt that this will be Bill's response. I hypothesize that he will continue to be defensive and self-protective.
5. My task will be to help him express as much of his defensive reactions as he wishes. The more he does, the more he is likely to produce directly observable data of his defensiveness. It is this kind of data that I can use to begin a constructive dialogue.
6. I will strive to react to Bill's responses by focusing on the impact they have on me. I will do my best not to use the staff's descriptions as evidence that Bill is a problem.
7. I will focus on what I might be doing wrong. I seek to learn. I seek to examine any behaviour, mine or his, which inhibits learning.

FM then role-played how he as Joe would implement the strategy.

Bill, let's review the bidding from the previous session.

1. I began by describing how upset the staff was over your unwanted behaviour. I asked for your reaction.
2. You responded, in effect:
   (*a*) Don't worry. My behaviour is always appropriate.
   (*b*) If they had a problem with me, they would tell me.
   (*c*) If this is a problem it means that no one has a sense of humour.
3. In effect your responses were I was wrong, they were wrong, and you were not wrong.
4. Let us first focus on me. I could be wrong. But it is difficult to learn about my possible errors from your responses.
5. Under these conditions, I want you to know that if your actions continue I will use my authority to 'order' changes or to implement other consequences. I do not prefer these actions. I prefer the actions that would help us both learn how to correct the situation in a way that the corrections persevere.

After the presentation FM asked the participants especially if they had doubts about the effectiveness of this strategy with Bill. Examples are:

1. What if Bill surfaces his fears that if he crafted a constructive response the women might get mad? Is there is a way to prevent their being held responsible for their defensiveness.
2. What if Bill tries and he too gets stuck? Are we not placing him in a vulnerable situation? Could the others take advantage of him?
3. What if Bill decided to mimic Joe? He would not have changed his theory-in-use yet he would act as if he did.

FM responded that their questions were valid. He asked that answering them be postponed until the end of the seminar when they would have had several days of practising Model II using their own left-hand-right-hand cases. He predicted that many of the questions would arise during these sessions

When they revisited these questions at the end of the week they found that they had learned:

1. The first step to prevent the defensiveness of others is to prevent one's own Model I actions and defences from informing their actions. If they become defensive then focus on how they can express these feelings. Begin by assessing the extent to which they unrealizingly acted in ways that helped to activate the defensiveness of others.
2. This also helps the others to see that you can be vulnerable without feeling weak. They may begin to observe how they might act to develop similar competence and confidence in the competence.
3. If Bill decided to mimic Joe, he would soon learn that he has not developed the skills to be able to go beyond Joe's crafting of actions. He will realize that Joe's advice may be fine for a first step but it is not adequate as the others continue their defensiveness. Mimicking may be helpful as a first step in practising (Argyris and Schön 1996). It is inadequate for helping develop new theory-in-use actions that do not evaporate under unexpected or expected hostile responses.

It is beyond the scope of this chapter to describe in detail the activities that the participants experienced while learning and internalizing Model II competencies. Examples are available (Argyris 1985, 1993, 2000, 2004a, 2004b; Argyris and Schön 1996).

CLOSING COMMENTS: THE UNDERGROUND WORLD IN ORGANIZATIONS

At the outset of this chapter, I asked why human beings design and implement actions that are counterproductive to achieving their intentions. Why do they keep repeating them? My response is that human beings appear to be programmed, through acculturation, to Model I theory-in-use and defensive mind-sets. When they design and create organizations, human beings inevitably create organizational systems that themselves have left-hand columns (underground world of organizational defensive routine). We do not seem to be the focus of the limitations because we focus on moving boxes around and redefining policies. These are important. But they are non-trivially limited in being implemented because of the Model I theories-in-use, organizational defensive routines, and defensive mind-sets.

The second strategy is to attempt to focus on these underground worlds by changing the culture. There are several problems with most of these efforts. They focus on espoused values and beliefs. They assume that the new values and beliefs can be imposed by charismatic leaders who champion these values. The trouble is that the fundamental process for such implementation leads to external commitment. Once the senior executive is gone, the touted accomplishments seem to disintegrate.

Recall that after the *Challenger* tragedy there was a special commission to make recommendations to prevent such a tragedy from happening again. The commission recommended a change in culture. NASA officials agreed. The implementation was top down. Several years later the *Columbia* tragedy occurred. Again the commission recommended changes in the culture. They were similar to the ones 'implemented' a few years before.

Recall ABB. This company was touted for several years as having produced a successful cultural change. The new culture emphasized openness, initiatives, trust, risk taking, and personal responsibility. A few years ago, the *Financial Times* interviewed the new CEO of ABB. He reported that the biggest challenge he faced was to create a new culture that emphasized openness, initiative, trust, risk taking, and personal responsibility. These were the same features the previous CEO had been acclaimed for creating (Argyris 2004a).

Recall 3M. 3M was a corporation acknowledged for several decades as a company that rewarded innovation. Last year, the new CEO told a *Wall Street Journal* reporter that his biggest challenge was to recreate a culture of innovation that had been lost. How do innovative cultures get lost? Why are these causes not foreseen (Argyris 2004a)?

One way to begin to explain all these puzzles is to realize that in all organizations there are managerial components that are above ground and underground. The above ground in organizations is managed by productive reasoning, transparency, and tough testing of performance. Truth (with a small 't') is a good idea.

The underground organization is dominated by defensive reasoning where the objective is to protect the players from embarrassment or threat. It rewards skilled denial and personal responsibility. Truth is a good idea, when it is not troublesome. If it is, massage it, spin it, and cover up.

The underground organization has several fascinating features. It develops even though it violates the current concepts of effective management. It survives even though there are no courses taught to executives on how to help it to survive. It flourishes by engaging the rules and regulations intended to smother it. It is a major cause for individuals using defensive mind-sets protected by organizational defensive routines that guarantee its survival.

These self-sealing processes are counterproductive to a productive reasoning mind-set. They make it difficult to produce trust, openness, transparency, and testing of ideas, all features that I suggest will be increasingly required for the future design of organizations and their management. Individual, group, intergroup, and organizational double-loop learning can help to meet these challenges.

References

Argyris, C. (1982). *Reasoning, Learning, and Action: Individual and Organizational.* San Francisco: Jossey-Bass.

—— (1985). *Strategy, Change and Defensive Routines.* New York: Harper Business.

—— (1990). *Overcoming Organizational Defenses.* Needham, Mass.: Allyn Bacon.

—— (1993). *Knowledge for Action: A Guide to Overcoming Barriers to Organizational Change.* San Francisco: Jossey-Bass.

—— (2000). *Flawed Advice and the Management Trap: How Managers Can Know When they're Getting Good Advice and When they're Not.* New York: Oxford University Press.

—— (2002). 'Double Loop Learning, Teaching, and Research', *Academy of Management Learning and Education*, 1/2: 206–19.

—— (2003a). 'A Life Full of Learning', *Organizational Studies*, 24/7: 1178–92.

—— (2003b). 'Actionable Knowledge', in H. Tsoukas and C. Knudsen (eds.), *Organizational Theory*. Oxford: Oxford University Press.

—— (2004a). *Reasons and Rationalizations: The Limits to Organizational Knowledge.* Oxford: Oxford University Press.

—— (2004b). 'Double-Loop Learning and Organizational Change: Facilitating Transformational Change', in J. J. Boonstra (ed.), *Dynamics of Organizational Change and Learning*. Chichester: John Wiley and Sons, Ltd.

—— Putnam, R., and Smith, D. (1985). *Action Science.* San Francisco: Jossey-Bass.

—— and Schön, D. (1996). *Organizational Learning II.* Reading, Mass.: Addison-Wesley.

....

CHAPTER 2

A GOOD PLACE FOR CHAT

ACTIVITY THEORY AND MBA EDUCATION

....

JEFF GOLD

ROBIN HOLT

RICHARD THORPE

INTRODUCTION

....

IN this chapter, we are going to argue that activity theory, specifically the approach offered by Cultural and Historical Activity Theory (CHAT) (Engeström 2000), has an instructive role on MBA programmes. We base our argument on the following grounds. First, as a theoretical model CHAT embodies rather than represses the multiplicity associated with business life; secondly, it offers users a mode of engaging with practical concerns; and, finally, it allows MBA students to reflexively engage with their educative and wider organizational experience. As such, it is, we argue, a theory that advocates aspect seeing above formal representation; practical knowledge above validity; and rigorous enquiry above imitation. In doing so its use on MBA programmes can go some way to addressing the concerns we have about orthodox thinking that informs the design and delivery of such programmes.

We connect these concerns to the criticisms that have surrounded the MBA degree in recent years. For example, Bennis and O'Toole (2005) have illustrated the extent to which MBAs and the professors who teach them are removed from business practices. Their claim, like those of Pfeffer and Fong (2002) and Mintzberg (1976, 2004) before, is that business schools, particularly represented in the MBA, have been too focused on 'scientific' research and analysis and less concerned with developing qualities and abilities that can accommodate the complexities of business life. The knowledge informing many textbook models and cases used in MBA teaching is of a condensed, formalized nature somewhat removed from the 'real' experience of managing. The problem occurs when students find that in re-applying these learning tools they have to struggle to make them 'fit' their experience; a struggle that in part is attributable to the intellectual abstraction and practical naivety of what they have been taught (Alvesson and Willmott 2003: 16–17).

Intellectual abstraction refers to how the data being used in models and cases is sifted from the experiences of managers and employees by means of surveys, or is replicated through experiments, in order to realize a coherent, generalized account of organizations and their management. The prevailing assumption is of an objectified world of passive resources that are bundled and managed by active managers using a rational, economizing calculus in order to secure economic rents. Unfortunately this clean and tidy representation does not embody fully the complexity and uncertainty of business life. Even in its own 'representative' terms, the static models and cases often fail to account for the choices and contradictions that ensue when resources from different organizations, or parts of organizations, are combined and recombined. More critically, the representations do little to convey how different organizational members view particular aspects of the organization differently, and how the resultant images can only ever present one of many possible perspectives (Sutton and Staw 1995). For example, within a model of good knowledge management one way of understanding patents as a 'knowledge resource' is to link their ownership to the revenue benefits accruing from exploitation. Yet even on this limited model and governing logic, questions arise as to what those benefits consist of and whether they would accrue to the shareholders, organizational stakeholders, or wider communities. Likewise, questions also arise as to whether rent-seeking behaviour is appropriate when the patent concerns human proteins, for example. And even if a human protein can be sensibly 'owned', are the associated rights and duties distinct from those associated with owning a piece of machinery or building? Here the simple logic of the knowledge management model equating the possession of a patent with the possession of an exploitable resource is not wrong, only inevitably incomplete. To understand patents as exploitable resources is one way of modelling them, but it is a partial selection of observable phenomena behind which lies a host of background assumptions. It is these assumptions that are rarely tested within MBA programmes (Ghoshal 2005).

Practical naivety refers to how models and cases often fail to convey how people grapple with the practical experience of doing management in which competence is as much an expression of tacit know-how as it is formal instruction. Business life is not simply the sum of bundles of resource ready to be marshalled into efficiency drives and value-adding initiatives for the good of a known and uncontested set of interests. Rather, it is people doing and using things for a whole host of reasons, utilizing a variety of practices each with potentially diverging theories of effectiveness and efficiency. From this more complex perspective, management is more a performance than the application of economic logic. Managers have to appreciate how they may need to create and work within 'an organizational landscape' consisting of people, things, and structures whose continued existence within the organization requires argument and justification (Shotter 1993). Here managers are not overseers, instructors, or conduits of enlightened vision, but practical authors who have to persuade others to enlist in the joint production of outcomes (Holman and Thorpe 2003: 7). The knowledge being taught on many MBAs fails to convey business life in such terms because it tends to shy away from appreciations of the ethnographic, personal, and rhetorical nature of these persuasive skills (Ghoshal 2005).

The final concern relating to the relevance of MBA teaching stems from a wider understanding of the practice of education itself, and is embodied in the question: 'To what extent should MBAs be seen vocationally as tools to improve and promote enterprise, and to what extent should they encourage an independent spirit?' Whilst these are no mutually exclusive concerns (namely, the importance of entrepreneurial spirit to wealth generation), there has been a tendency for business schools to critically consider academic credentials of rigour and pedagogy in the light of their practical relevance (as discussed above) rather than their contribution to intellectual autonomy. At present many MBAs embody such a skew. They teach students according to well-understood, academically established criteria to allow them to make contributions to established understandings about business and the economy. In doing so, students experience the weight of common-sense activity sustained by establishment *doxa* (unexamined opinion) without necessarily being exposed to doubt, challenge, and a sense of being engaged on an intellectual mission (Rorty 1999: 118).

It is in addressing these three concerns of abstractness, naivety, and teaching *doxa* that we see a significant role for approaches such as Cultural and Historical Activity Theory (CHAT) on MBA programmes. We will argue that CHAT encourages those who use it to adopt practical, mature, and critical attitudes to business life. The suggestion being that not all theory is bad theory. We go on to explain how this is so by discussing our use of CHAT in an experiential and learner problem approach to the teaching of two MBA modules. We will explain how the theory was introduced and discuss how it helped participants better understand the ideas they held about organizations and their roles within them. In conclusion we also note some problems with using the model.

CULTURAL–HISTORICAL ACTIVITY THEORY

Background

Cultural–Historical Activity Theory (CHAT) is not a theory that establishes valid propositions or predictions about the future, rather it provides people with a rigorous heuristic that allows them to configure and reconfigure the changing objects or goals of their activities. In this sense, it is a theory that establishes the importance of doubt rather than certainty. It draws on a number of strands. One is Marx's (1969) *Thesis on Feuerbach*, which provides a basic critique of the conception of social reality as an object 'of contemplation' rather than 'as sensuous human activity, practice' (p. 13). Another is the work of Vygotsky and other psychologists working in Soviet Russia in the 1920s and 1930s. CHAT aims to understand knowledge as the pragmatic product of open-ended, competent, social enquiry informed by historical and narrative traditions. As such, we argue that CHAT offers an effective model for MBA teaching; one that is both theoretical whilst at the same time being alive to the problems of intellectual abstraction, practical relevance, and *doxa*.

Understanding the composition of social reality in terms of activities rather than causally linked objects means the theories by which this reality is explained move from abstract representations to concrete considerations of practical use value. The truths about which we learn are not established by lawlike predictions but by understanding what assists people in realizing their goals in specific contexts. It is truth set within, and established by, the intentional relationships people have with objects and their causal links, rather than the objects themselves, that is of interest (Kaptelinin 2005). It is science that is concerned with understanding objects unadorned by human intention. Social science, argue exponents of activity theory, is different. It concerns itself with how we have built up relationships with one another, with other entities (sentient and non-sentient), with objects and symbols, and with our wider environments. Inspired by such a concern, academic models and cases must attest to the cultural and historical patterns (as well as deviations from these) by which people have gone about understanding their intentional relationships. In organization and management studies, this involves an active investigation of the informing values, the communities, the tools and symbols in use, and the procedural structures involved in activities such as the production of goods, the making of strategy, and so on, and how these are understood as being more or less useful in realizing collectively configured goals and outcomes. What is produced by this theory is insight into how the hurly-burly of everyday business life can be effectively captured with a sufficient degree of clarity and certainty that knowledge claims (not theoretical propositions) can be made of it.

Activity Theory and the Activity System Model

For activity theorists, to know something equates with the ability to use *things* in a meaningful and potentially innovative way. When used, *things* become tools. These tools include all those entities that mediate our experience, and in doing so are complicit with that experience. So as well as things like machines or tools we can also include symbols, aesthetic appearances, gestures, and, most pervasively of all, language itself. Mediation describes how tools impose limits on actions (where they have a material quality and become a prosthetic extension) and mental operations (where they are immaterial signs and become an extension of our thought, aspirations, etc.). These tools, then, engender meanings, patterns, and purposes that extend beyond the individual judgement of any single actor (Bedny, Seglin, and Meister 2000); they also carry with them the trace of previous uses. In so doing knowledge becomes less a representative statement about states of affairs and more a demonstration of practical skill, a know-how versed in learning from others how tools have been used in the past, and so how they might be used in the future. To know things is to know one's way about situations or problems, something that is achieved when the use of a tool conforms to, and resonates with, previous uses (Engeström 2000). Orthodoxy frames meaning, insofar as what we do and say carries itself not merely as an enactment of our self-understanding but also as a disclosure to others that we are someone of significance, an identity with plans and purposes that can be and wishes to be understood by others. Failure to conform to established standards within a context (to use language as others do, or to conform to certain manners or rituals) jeopardizes this disclosure. Yet this know-how is distinct from merely reiterating established opinions (*doxa*) about things. The use of tools remains potentially innovative because submission to established standards does not entail conformity to outcomes. Each use of a tool is unique; our personal 'style' and specific experiential focus breathes life into the meanings associated with it. Hence whilst we follow rules for using tools, we do not obey such rules. In following rather than obeying we have the capability to use tools in new situations and in novel ways—what counts as meaningful does so throughout its expression, its use, and not in its conforming to a template, or formula (Cavell 1969: 48–52).

In proposing that knowledge arises from competent, practical use, activity theorists are imbibing what Evald Ilyenkov called an 'epistemological responsibility'—an awareness of the socially configured scenes of significance through which we act. These scenes are normative, acting like a 'space of reasons' for doing things in certain ways; they filter our actions (Bakhurst 1997). The tiered benches and proscenium arrangement of a lecture theatre, for example, might elicit certain actions in both teacher and students. The teacher is invested with the role of 'vanishing point' in this scene of learning, not merely a material arrangement, but a normative one conveying a source of learned authority. The students are invested with the role of engagement, meaning they listen to, note, and, where appropriate, comment upon what they hear. This normative structure, defined by previous engagements (personal or vicarious) and tradition (collective), carries and sustains the meaning of the actions within the lecture theatre. Where such a proscenium arrangement is suggestive of an unwarranted and unhelpful distance between student and teacher the normative 'space of reasons' would be altered somewhat, perhaps eliciting exploratory interactions requiring less hierarchical room layouts and actions that were more conversational.

To understand these normative spaces in our social experiences, Engeström (2000, 2001) shifts the unit of analysis from the specific actions of individuals to what is called the activity system. This shift is particularly germane to understanding business life because the activity system uses a framework for representing and analysing organizational experience as a three-way interaction of subjects, objects of activity, and communities, each of which is mediated by rules (social norms), artefacts (technology/tools, symbols, language), and divisions of labour (organizational structures). To understand one aspect of business life is to understand it in relation to the other aspects set within one or multiple normative spaces. Understanding spaces as activity systems allows theorists to identify individual motives, structural conditions, localized norms, and available tools as things that exist in dynamic relations with one another rather than as entirely separate entities. Figure 2.1 shows Engeström's basic framework of an activity system.

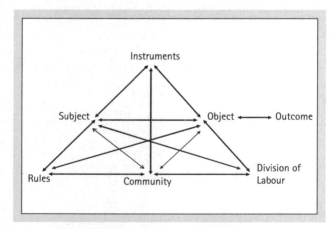

Fig. 2.1 A framework of an activity system

Source: Engeström (1999).

The MBA as an Activity System

Because activity, rather than action, is highlighted as the unit of analysis, it is only through situating actions and claims in previous experiences and traditions that they can be said to have sense and be acknowledged by others as legitimate. So, for example, the activity of studying for an MBA would provide the framework, logic, and impetus to actions such as: questioning; essay writing; grading; experiential learning; and so on. Outside of the activity these same actions and frames would 'hang' as meaningless or empty movements. Understood within the activity system these actions would be informed by a host of mediating influences: university premises, institutional repute, testimony from alumni, brochures, and so on. Defining this activity is an object, from which outcomes emerge. The object of studying for an MBA, for example, might be gaining a qualification and extending peer networks, gaining a symbolically powerful qualification, or alternatively learning how to better manage people; but it might also extend to internal goods associated with becoming more knowledgeable *per se*. As a subject within such an activity system, the student would develop know-how of the material arrangements and social/historical rules, purposes, and techniques by which MBAs are recognized and legitimized as things (qualifications) of significance. In doing so the student contributes to the collective understanding of the MBA as something that is both objective (understood by people as an object of intentional interest) and projective (it has outcomes that have a social use value linked to a repertoire of skills, norms, procedures and tools) (Miettinen and Virkkunen 2005; Engeström 2001). So there is an orthodoxy associated with the object of the MBA activity system; not anything counts as having an MBA, nor can an MBA be fully understood outside of the activity system itself. Yet the object is not fixed and there are a number of them. The object is characterized by what Miettinen (2001) calls 'horizons of possibility'. Studying for an MBA can be done in different ways, informed by different people and norms, and produce differing outcomes (in terms of expectation as well as results).

It is within such an open structure that we wish to understand how MBAs can evolve in response to their critics. Yet we also want to show that using this structure as an academic model is one way of realizing such an evolution. As a pedagogic tool we show how activity theory models allowed MBA students to better understand how theories and cases of organizational life provide knowledge claims that are informed by specific interests, aims, values, and communities. It also encouraged students to appreciate the fragmented and often contested views of the knowledge produced. As a practical tool we show how students were able to use it within their organizations to appreciate how procedures and aims were understood and the different perspectives taken on these understandings. It provided students with a model that they could use to critically orient themselves towards prevailing objects of concern within their organization. As a tool of personal development, we show how the model can lead students to question their own participation within any activity system, be it in this case educational or economic, and to understand the responsibility associated with knowledge claims made through such participation.

USING ACTIVITY THEORY

CHAT was incorporated into MBA programmes at both Leeds University and Leeds Metropolitan University. In total, thirty students were required to identify and analyse their 'own' organizations as an activity system for their study. For those studying part-time, the unit for study was straightforward and easily identified. For full-time students, 'own' organizations required further elaboration, even though the full-time students had work experience. This is because we were keen that all students could appreciate that working with CHAT should be achieved from a grounding of flux in actions and operations within an activity system and that to gain this understanding they needed to enter the activity system in a relevant and practical way (Engeström 1999). So full-time students were guided to consider the MBA programme itself as their 'own' organization and as an activity system and to examine it from the perspective of creating influence within such a system. All students therefore, both full- and part-time, could through their own actions engage with the system and this could in practice lead to new meanings and understandings among all who were part of the life of the activity system.

Completing a study using CHAT requires a multi-layered, multi-voiced approach where students can collect information on the different voices in a system as well as present their views as they participate in various tasks that contribute towards the realization of some defined objects and wider normative spaces. In addition students also need to be aware of the traditional patterns that exist and how they change over time. While no specified time period was allocated, it was clear to us that the time-bound nature of 'modules' and the additional constraints of assessment would limit the nature of the study that students could undertake. Our aim was to balance the time required for students to explore the working methods of CHAT with a realistic awareness that any study they conducted might well be only partial.

Our approach to assisting students in acquiring tools for their enquiries was to employ the metaphor of 'construction'. A Vygotskyian perspective informed the initial process adopted. Students in the role of problem solvers required guidance or what Wood, Bruner, and Ross (1976) refer to as 'scaffolding'. This scaffolding came from the teachers and was initially offered in quite a didactic way. However, through practice, there was an eventual transfer of direction to the inside. The 'building materials' adopted were as follows:

1. An explanation of the concept of mediation.
2. An understanding of the meaning and content of cultural and historical influence.
3. The role and nature of disturbance and contradiction.
4. The way different levels of operation, action, and activity influence and 'nest' within any activity.

We used these materials to build up Engeström's framework of an activity system as an amalgam of interrelated triangles. The triangles became the building blocks for the construction of understanding. The first of these is the 'triangle of production' in which an individual subject and a goal are understood as being mediated through cultural and historical tools. We used the example of a person lying on a beach wearing sunglasses on a sunny day, presented in the form of a reworking of Vygotsky's (1978) triangle.

This image (fig 2.2) was meant to connect directly to student experience and to quickly surface the cultural historical nature of human action. So, in relation to the diagram, humans in contrast to animals have goals which are cultural in origin: they set out to 'get a tan' rather than merely seek warmth in the sun. In order to achieve this goal, they make use of tools and this allowed us to introduce

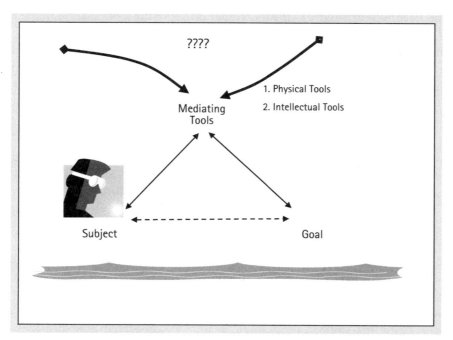

Fig. 2.2 The production triangle

the concept of mediation. The sunbather cannot achieve his or her goal directly but only through the use of physical tools such as trunks, sun cream, sunglasses, as well as psychological tools such as ideas about looking good, along with previous knowledge that exposure to the sun will provide a tan. The example was also useful in illustrating how tools also have a historical origin and cultural meaning. This introduces Engeström and Miettinen's (1999) contribution that 'objects, and the means by which we realize them, are complicit with historically and culturally framed resources that are common to society at large' (p. 8). We were also keen to illustrate that questions or 'hypotheses' can be introduced in order to explore the way certain tools work; for example: 'What exactly is the origin of sunbathing?', 'What are the perceived benefits of sun oils and whose interest is served by the sale of sun cream?', 'Is our understanding of the function of sun cream changing?', 'Will any old sunglasses do?'

These questions and others also highlight a further important exploration which relates to how tools act upon individuals through what Vygotsky (1978: 40) called 'reverse action', where a tool leads to behaviour 'that breaks from biological development and creates new forms of culturally-based psychological process'. So using the same example we were able to engage with students to consider the influence of tools such as designer as opposed to normal sunglasses, in the social construction of individuals, their identities and values and motivation. We were also able to consider how the influence of such tools, and fashion items more generally, can quickly become accepted as natural and normal rather than historical and cultural, in time becoming attributes of the individual as user of the tool rather than the tool itself (Pea 1993).

Finally, we considered the effect a change in tools might have. CHAT is centrally concerned with the dynamics of change and the tensions and learning that may be provoked. For example, students can consider the impact of new ideas about sunbathing and the connection with skin cancer; with sun cream being used protectively. This new orientation to a tool creates a disturbance to current ideas about lying on a beach, what to wear, where to go, etc. The ongoing tension and contradiction between tools, represented by a lightening arrow in the production triangle, can affect over time the motivation to sunbathe but also the goal, not to mention the sale of sun cream and sunglasses. Following this introduction, students were able to practise their use of the triangle to analyse actions in their organizations, with prompts to explore the cultural and historical features of mediation, posing questions as hypotheses for enquiry.

Following this session, the students met to share their findings, reporting their use of the 'production triangle' and clarifying their understanding of CHAT. We were then able to move towards the introduction of a collective activity system model, utilizing Leont'ev's (1981) three-level schema of operation, action, and activity. Using the sunbathing example again, we considered how locations for sunbathing such as beaches are often crowded with more than one sunbather, many of them wearing designer sunglasses but also obeying the rules of the beach and/or accepting the various roles that accompany life on the beach. In this way, students can recognize how sunbathing *actions* (lying down, spreading out towels, swimming to cool down) can be parsed into smaller physiological and cognitive *operations* associated with personal space, muscle movement, and memory, but also have to be situated in larger contexts of *activity*. There is a community of sunbathers, who occupy a space and who interrelate with others undertaking different activities, all of whom are governed by procedures and rules which guide behaviour. Further, we encouraged the students to reflect on how the individual or group achievement of goals only makes sense on the basis of social, cultural, and historical influences that provide the rationale for performing operations, taking action, and having objectives.

This move to the collective activity, as shown earlier in Figure 2.1, is made by breaking the framework into three more triangles, each showing the mediation of various contextual elements. Figure 2.3 shows this breakdown.

In each case the reader will see that the 'production triangle' remains but now students consider the cultural and historical mediation of rules, community, and division of labour respectively. We guided students to consider all aspects of mediation as they began to use the model to investigate activity systems of which they

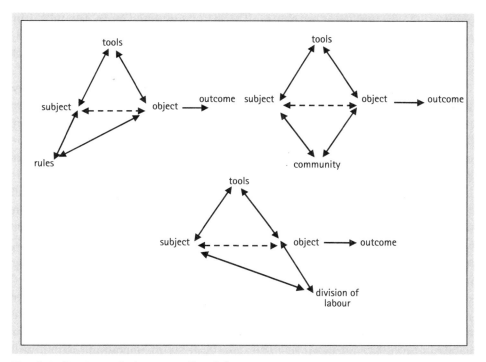

Fig. 2.3 Contextual elements of activity

Source: Adapted from Engeström (1999).

were a part. They were given two options upon which to focus their investigations; either the use of written human resource policies or to consider the relevance of Gronn's (2000) theory of distributed leadership for their own organizations (part-time) or for the MBA programme itself (full-time). Students were encouraged to pose questions for enquiry and explore tensions and contradictions, some of which may have been suppressed or 'patched over' to prevent difficulties or contradictions from surfacing.

THE STUDENT RESPONSE

The first observation to make was how quickly the students learnt to appreciate the mediating role of tools. To be able to recognize mediation is the anchor point here, as it is through acknowledgement of mediation that a better grasp can be gained of how people are complicit with their context and with those who work within and beyond it. For example, following the beach scenario, students investigating distributed leadership were asked to describe the practice of leadership. A number spoke of exerting influence (positive or negative) and others of the need to achieve specific goals by undertaking multiple tasks assisted by the use of certain tools (physical, intellectual, or imaginative). The actions undertaken by the would-be leader and the tools used were clearly seen by the students as being influenced by factors both cultural and historical. Some students went further and noted that leadership need not be influenced by people alone, nor need its influence be solely over people but a wider environment of which people are a part. A number even alluded to the potential for some leaders to share responsibility for exerting influence on others, as well as amongst themselves, so as to bring about a complementary effect of collective achievement. These observations, we believe, were fed from a general consensus amongst the students that purposeful actions were culturally and historically embedded through the established use of tools.

A second observation relates to the way an understanding of the mediating role of tools extends to an understanding to contextual elements such as rules, community, and the division of labour. Here the students began to deepen their awareness of the richness and depth of what exactly constitutes cultural and historical influences, and how these might be investigated using the conceptual structure of the activity system triangles. For example, one student studying human resource policies honed in on the issue of billing for time in their organization. Focusing on the role played by the mediating role of rules, they identified the way handbooks were laid out and how these formed rules about the completion of time sheets. These rules included procedures for how often time sheets should be handed in, how much time off in lieu could be accrued, and how much time 'debt' was allowed. When considering the mediating effects of community, the student began to understand how the staff team applied social pressure on individual members to concur with the orthodox system. Yet they were also able to reflect on how much cheating was allowed, reporting that 'if someone openly abuses the system—beyond social parameters—then the rules are brought into play more rigidly by that staff member being reminded of them'. This highlighted the effects of the division of labour and the role played by line managers responsible for checking and verifying time sheets by countersignature. The student observed that the fact that this official task rarely occurs—leaving finance assistants to query obvious errors—meant most abided by the rules because of community rather than official pressure. The student also identified how action by senior staff created room for manoeuvre through continual interpretation that 'bent the rules', allowing new rules or benchmarks to emerge. This dynamic appreciation of how rules shift is further appreciated in noting the influence of third parties, in this case external funders who, because of their own extensive audit procedures, put pressure on staff to allocate recorded time to specific projects rather than 'company' business. Here the student is identifying competing rule systems, contradictions whose consequence is to make a simple task more complex. These considerations were made in a presentation to us following the period of study in his own organization of the everyday strategic management of HRM. He concluded:

Notwithstanding the principle that many staff hold that they oughtn't be required to complete one [time sheet] since they are wholly employed on one project or that the time that they spend completing one is a waste since they could be doing 'actual work'; the payoff is that the system demands a TOIL be put in place. The activity system analysis helps a strategy manager to consider the whole cultural system of time recording and enables her to consider where changes can be introduced to encourage or incentivise different outcomes.

When identifying mediating influences, another student went even further in their use of the activity system model by investigating the practical use of an established academic model, namely 'communities of practice'. Their investigation highlighted a set of internally commissioned documents which outlined procedures the aim of which was to link business value, knowledge management, and structures to the concept 'communities of practice'. In this example, what the management team were attempting to create were communities of practice through the identification of particular roles and responsibilities.

Being a member of the central team, the student was able to investigate a specific community of practice very much like a participant observer (as opposed to a core member). During four sessions over two full days, they observed what took place and how the 'scaffold' for an activity system could be built up. Their analysis then provided an understanding of how the community of practice operated. They were able to summarize their observations so as to understand such things as: the use of rules, mediating artefacts, community, and so on. They then constructed an activity system model (Figure 2.4) which depicted the links and contradictions by which

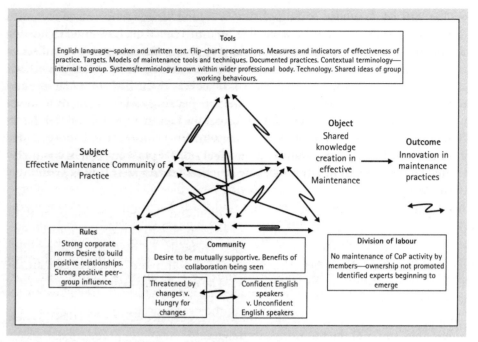

Fig. 2.4 The Community of Practice Activity System (CoPs)

the community of practice acted, made sense of its actions, and potentially challenged its actions through a critical awareness of its 'defining' objects of activity.

This analysis was useful in surfacing various tensions and contradictions within the activity system which were then explained in the following bullets:

- The existing maintenance practices were severely criticized following pressure to reduce production costs. As a result, practices benchmarked as excellent from plants in other regions were documented and presented to newly formed CoPs. These factors appeared to have a negative effect—especially among long-serving members who consequently exhibited defensive behaviours during discussions. Newly appointed managers, by contrast, were more positive.
- Diversity within the CoP highlighted different conventions in operation in the behaviour of groups. Ways of working were usually developed within the CoP and included in a 'charter'—the charter represented explicitly stated 'rules'. However, this particular CoP had not developed a charter. Nevertheless, strong corporate conventions along with an evident desire to form personal relationships had resulted in the development and use of strong conventions of its own.
- The principle of developing roles from members of the CoP, as set out in guiding documentation, had not been progressed. 'Thought-leaders' were emerging, but other roles were left to the facilitator. This appeared to discourage the ownership of 'systems/practices' as enablers to promote and maintain the CoP.

- The 'official' language of English was a second language for most members and this has the effect of limiting conversations but also accelerated the development of a 'contextualized' vocabulary implying the emergence of collective understanding. Another consequence was the reliance on 'alternative' methods of communication (tools) to spoken text such as the use of electronic presentations. Where this was recognized written materials were detailed; however where unrecognized, the impact on verbal exchanges was evident. Whilst all members raised questions, verbal exchanges during constructive discourse were dominated by more confident English-speakers. This to some extent was mediated by shared ideas in group working practices leading members to proactively include others.

Through mastering the concept of mediation and through the use of analytic tools the students on these programmes have been able to complete enquiries into practices embedded in their organizations. Through the method of storytelling they have identified characters, interpenetrated all within the context of continually changing themes, shifting causal influences. The enquiry formed an integral part of the module assessment.

When we asked students to reflect on their experience of using activity system models, they spoke of the following advantages:

- It allowed for an appreciation of the multiple 'sites' in which mutually influencing changes occur. One student remarked, for example: 'Far too often I have used the phrase: "Well that was the straw that broke the camel's back!" But what caused the camel to get overloaded in the 1st place? Well that depends on the experiences of the camel.'
- It allowed students to understand the inevitability of only ever understanding theories and frameworks as half-truths being used from different perspectives. For example, one student remarked on the theory itself: 'My perception of the value of Activity Theory might not be correct and then again, that is exactly the value of it!'
- A more instrumental view of the theory was the way it afforded a holistic vision, how individuals, structures, and cultures which occur in great complexity can be made sense of and brought into more harmonious alignment.
- It afforded an appreciation of the multi-voiced nature of social experiences characterized by disturbance. So that in relation to the above, the theory acknowledges that any alignment of interests and objectives is always only at very best an ongoing orchestrated engagement that will have an end or be superseded somehow.

However, we would also caution readers that in using the CHAT model there may still be a tendency to overly focus on individuals, objects, and tools and view them as isolate entities rather than as emerging, processual relations. This is perhaps something that is imposed by limits on the time students have to spend on the modules and would be rectified with a chance to develop a fuller study that allows them to be more critically reflective and pose critical questions about how they as managers act under which rubric, with what they identify, and for what ends. In addition the longitudinal and ethnographic requirements of the approach are demanding for students and often difficult to fit into an educative programme. Moreover, the identification of the contradictions in the cases does not then prompt interventionist action. These areas require further consideration and revision.

CONCLUSION

The specific focus of this chapter is an account of how we have attempted to introduce activity theory models to MBA students. But the chapter also opens up a number of debates surrounding management education in general and the curriculum of MBA programmes in particular. For many years now we have known (Davies and Easterby-Smith 1984) that much of the management knowledge used to tackle difficult problems at work occurs naturally, so that the more learning can be structured around activities at work and the more it promotes critical and reflective engagement, the more productive the experience. In this chapter we have illustrated an attempt at creating such a learning experience on MBA programmes. The designs adopted were to chosen explicitly to counter the already identified criticisms levelled at MBAs, namely their being too abstract, impractical, and too orthodox. The chapter shows how we developed the design to give the MBA programme participants the confidence and ability to work with theory. In so doing our objective was to provide them with working models and conceptual competences that would help them practically as managers to deal with complex and ambiguous information and yet also engage them as critical learners in their own right. This we achieved through introducing them to the concept of activity theory and providing them with a framework through which they could understand and relate the theory to a range of organizational experiences.

Activity theory enables students to reflect on the practical implications of their analysis and helps them to consider the next courses of action they might take. Further it helps them to understand that organizations are not static but dynamic and that current modes of operation have derived from cultural and historical factors and that these could themselves be further influenced by managerial action. It is from such awareness that students can then go on to consider themselves. The assignment, by asking participants for a collection of data about a particular object in their own activity system, focused attention on the participants' own motives, perceptions, values, and intentions. In so doing they became more conscious of the ideas they held, how they were formed, and how they might be changed, and potentially for a significant majority what next courses of action they would take as managers with the activity system to either change their behaviour, systems, or other mediating means.

By using activity theory we argue that the activity of management that is taught and critically investigated in MBAs might be viewed more like a design science (Van Aken 2004), much in the same way disciplines such as engineering or medicine are. If this were so, there might, in the ways we have illustrated, be a move away from simply understanding management towards an orientation that emphasizes and engages managers (students) in producing knowledge relevant to their own organizations linked to a commitment to make change and improvement (Gibbons et al. 1994), without thereby collapsing it into the unquestioning circulation of orthodoxy (*doxa*).

REFERENCES

Alvesson, M., and Willmott, H. (2003). *Studying Management Critically*. London: Sage.

Bakhurst, D. (1997). 'Meaning, Normativity and the Life of the Mind', *Language and Communication*, 17: 33–51.

Bedny, G., Seglin, M., and Meister, D. (2000). 'Activity Theory: History, Research and Application', *Theoretical Issues in Ergonomic Science*, 1: 168–206.

Bennis, W., and O'Toole, T. (2005). 'How Business Schools Lost their Way', *Harvard Business Review*, 83: 96–104.

Cavell, S. (1969). *Must We Mean What We Say?* New York: Charles Scribner.

Davies, J., and Easterby-Smith, M. (1984). 'Learning and Developing from Managerial Work Experiences', *Journal of Management Studies*, 21: 169–84.

Engeström, Y. (1999). 'Activity Theory and Individual And Social Transformation', in Y. Engeström, R. Miettinen, and R. Punamäki (eds.), *Perspectives on Activity Theory*. Cambridge: Cambridge University Press.

——(2000). 'Activity Theory and the Social Construction of Knowledge: A Story of Four Umpires', *Organization*, 7: 301–10.

——(2001). 'Expansive Learning at Work: Toward an Activity Theoretical Reconceptualisation', *Journal of Education and Work*, 14: 133–56.

——and Miettinen, R. (1999). 'Introduction', in Y. Engeström, R. Miettinen, and R. Punamäki (eds.), *Perspectives on Activity Theory*. Cambridge: Cambridge University Press.

Ghoshal, S. (2005). 'Bad Management Theories are Destroying Good Management Practices', *Academy of Management Learning and Education*, 4: 75–91.

Gibbons, M., Limoges, C., Nowotny, H., Schwartzman, S., Scott, P., and Trow, M. (1994). *The New Production of Knowledge*. London: Sage.

Gronn, P. (2000). 'Distributed Properties: A New Architecture for Leadership', *Educational Management and Administration*, 28/3: 317–38.

Holman, D., and Thorpe, R. (2003). *Management and Language*. London: Sage.

Kaptelinin, V. (2005). 'The Object of Activity: Making Sense of the Sense-Maker', *Mind, Culture and Activity*, 12: 4–18.

Leont'ev, A. N. (1981). *Problems of the Development of Mind*. Moscow: Progress.

Marx, K. (1969). *Marx/Engels Selected Works*, Vol. i. Moscow: Progress.

Miettinen, R. (2001). 'Artifact Mediation in Dewey and in Cultural-Historical Activity Theory', *Mind, Culture, and Activity*, 8: 297–308.

—— and Virkkunen, J. (2005). 'Epistemic Objects, Artefacts and Organizational Change', *Organization*, 12/3: 437–56.

Mintzberg, H. (1976). 'Planning on the Left Side, Managing on the Right', *Harvard Business Review*, 54: 49–58.

—— (2004). *Managers Not MBA's: A Hard Look at the Soft Practices of Managing and Management Development*. San Francisco: Berrett-Koehler Publishers.

Pea, R. D. (1993). 'Practices of Distributed Intelligence and Designs for Education', in G. Salomon (ed.), *Distributed Cognitions: Psychological and Educational Considerations*. Cambridge: Cambridge University Press.

Pfeffer, J., and Fong, C. T. (2002). 'The End of Business Schools? Less Success Than Meets the Eye', *Academy of Management Learning and Education*, 1: 78–95.

Rorty, R. (1999). 'Education as Socialization and as Individualization', in *Philosophy and Social Hope*. Harmondsworth: Penguin.

Shotter, J. (1993). *Conversational Realities: Constructing Life through Language*. London: Sage.

Sutton, R. I., and Staw, B. M. (1995). 'What Theory is Not', *Administrative Science Quarterly*, 40: 371–84.

Van Aken, J. T. (2004). 'Management Research Based on the Paradigm of the Design Sciences: The Quest for Field Tested and Grounded Technological Rules', *Journal of Management Studies*, 41: 219–45.

Vygotsky, L. S. (1978). *Mind in Society: The Development of Higher Psychological Processes*, eds. M. Cole, V. John-Steiner, S. Scribner, and E. Souberman. Cambridge, Mass.: Harvard University Press.

Wood, D., Bruner, J. S., and Ross, G. (1976). 'The Role of Tutoring in Problem Solving', *Journal of Child Psychology and Psychiatry*, 17: 89–100.

CHAPTER 3

....

LEARNING ABOUT AND THROUGH AESTHETIC EXPERIENCE

UNDERSTANDING THE POWER OF EXPERIENCE-BASED EDUCATION

....

M. ANN WELSH

GORDON E. DEHLER

DALE L. MURRAY

This course was a unique opportunity to participate in a project with a group of individuals with different backgrounds and who would hopefully give me a different perspective on how to approach a problem. The desire to understand how other disciplines work came from my experiences on co-op [where] I observed that the individuals running the show were people who could relate to professionals with differing backgrounds and direct their combined efforts. From this I concluded that if I wanted to effectively serve in a managerial position I need to refine this interpersonal skill.

(Donald, engineering student[1])

THIS chapter describes a transdisciplinary action research course created to help students understand the dynamics of innovation and change within an organizational setting. There are three distinct characteristics of the course context that contribute to its effectiveness: it is an aesthetic experience, emotionally intense, and politically real. Applying principles of critical pedagogy in this context produces a transformative learning experience for students where they not only learn about issues in product development but also become more effective learners.

Our chapter is organized as follows: first we present the learning objective and describe our pedagogical approach. Next we demonstrate how each of the three course characteristics identified above plays out in the students' experience. Then we discuss how this combination of attributes yields a distinctive learning experience.[2] Finally, we discuss why this experience is so valuable in helping students to develop a critical stance on both organizational action and their educational experience.

LEARNING OBJECTIVE: DESIGN A BRANDED EXPERIENCE

The course we describe introduces students to issues associated with the new product development process. In product design and development, the use of multidisciplinary creative teams that work concurrently throughout the development process is now widely accepted as the most effective practice. Since team-based multidisciplinary experiences are becoming the norm in professional product development situations, modelling those experiences in the classroom has great pedagogical value for students who plan to work in any aspect of new product development, including students in business, design (industrial, digital, graphic, fashion), engineering, science, and technology programmes. The course design is also intended to introduce students to a higher standard in product development: the formation of transdisciplinary creative teams capable of creating more significant innovations.

The course objective requires multidisciplinary student teams to create a branded experience for a corporate client. This entails 'designing a product system within a designed environment for a designated user group to create a significant, memorable, or poetic experience. The proposed solution should engage all of the senses and be socially responsible.' Examples of branded experiences developed in course iterations include:

1. Creating a customized brewing experience (for example, tea, coffee) for a range of venues including fine restaurants, drive-up kiosks, organizational workplaces, and private residences using a proprietary brewing technology developed by the corporate client. This course involved students from industrial design, digital design, and business.

2. Creating a branded experience for air travel for a legacy airline. Here students identified several underserved market segments and created travel experiences either consistent with the firm's existing brand equity or designed to build entirely new brands. This course involved teams of industrial design and business students.

3. Creating the concept for an alternative-fuel-powered vehicle targeted toward a global market fifteen years out for a major auto manufacturer. This course included students from industrial design, fashion product design, mechanical engineering, and business.

Students work in creative multidisciplinary teams using a concurrent product development model (for example, Cagan and Vogel 2002). Corporate partners act not only as the client but also as a co-learners and mentors to the students. Faculty members manage and monitor the interaction of the corporate representatives with the students to be sure the content of the course remains aligned with pedagogical goals.

PEDAGOGICAL FOUNDATION

Faculty members teaching the course use a critical pedagogical approach (Dehler, Welsh, and Lewis 2001). This involves creating classroom spaces which challenge students to question assumptions, analyse power relationships, critically reflect upon this embedded network of relationships with other students, and consider alternatives for the transformation of that network (Reynolds 1997). Application of critical pedagogy is relatively rare in each of the base disciplines. And indeed, adopting such an approach requires significant modifications in curriculum design and course content. Happily, because this course exists on the margins of our respective curricula, we have been able to develop a course that is entirely consistent with the aims of critical pedagogy. It has been our experience that success in the course is directly and strongly related to the extent to which faculty understand critical pedagogy and believe it to be valuable. The following sections describe the fundamental aspects of critical pedagogy.

Decentred Classroom

No one really knew what the faculty really wanted from us. (Jack, engineering student)

I consider myself a very good note taker, and when I walked into a class and there was little or no notes, it made me uncomfortable. I like for teachers to tell me what I need to know, not simply give me the keys to the car and say get there. (Mike, business student)

The designers were more experienced with these projects. It was difficult for the business students, who had never approached a design task such as the one laid out for us, to figure out how to manage the project. I must admit that even though I am accustomed to the 'fuzzy front end' I am also used to receiving more instruction from teachers and employers, so this was a challenge for me too. (Dave, industrial design student)

Adopting a critical pedagogy means creating a decentred classroom (Giroux 1997) with the instructor more of a collaborator, co-learner, and mentor than an authoritative figure dispensing factual information. While a departure in educational culture for business and engineering students and faculty, a decentred classroom is consistent with the established norms of the 'studio' approach to learning typically utilized by design educators, and is directly and emphatically related to our success in the course. Early on, design students exhibit greater comfort with the ambiguity and anxiety inherent in the course objectives. Their comfort level provides crucial reassurance for business and engineering students accustomed to highly structured courses and classrooms. The physical space of design studios—blank walls covered with tack boards, tables, and stools (but never enough stools for everyone!)—helps communicate to students from the start that 'this class is going to be different'.

This difference is further reinforced by the absence of a traditional syllabus with assigned readings, clear schedules, and benchmarks. Students receive a statement of the 'deliverable' expected by the client (for example, a branded experience for air travel), a set of background materials on the disciplines and industry involved, information on effective collaboration, and are introduced to their process consultant (the management faculty member). How the deliverable is to be developed (and what it should include) are decisions left to the teams. The absence of the pre-packaged road-map creates a higher than normal level of anxiety for students.

Multidisciplinary Approaches

I felt uncomfortable that I was taking a class that integrated so many different groups of people. I had not had the opportunity to work with students from different colleges, and to some extent, I had a fear that they would hate us as business students.

(Karen, finance student)

The most obvious obstacle was due to the diversity of majors participating in this collaborative. The first example of this to come to mind was a conversation between Bill [an industrial designer] and me. We were discussing the placement of fuel cell and hydrogen tanks, and how that would affect the outer proportions of the vehicle. Bill kept using terms like 'body-side' and 'demi' which I did not understand. I'm sure that I also used 'technical' terminology that was foreign to him. (Keith, engineering student)

Student anxiety is further exacerbated by the multidisciplinary approach. Not only are the 'classroom rules' suspended, students quickly learn that talking to each other is also going to be more difficult as a consequence of differences in behavioural norms, learning models, and language. In a multidisciplinary course, students are not expected to be proficient in any of the other disciplines. It is important to allow each discipline to participate equally and for students to excel in their area of expertise. Students develop an understanding of who has what skills, the answers they need, and how best to communicate with practitioners of those various disciplines. This is essential in learning to function effectively in creative teams and appreciating the skills and knowledge that the other disciplines bring to the problem. It takes some knowledge of other disciplines/functions to ask the right questions—those that allow expertise to flow into the decision process.

Over time, design students come to see that engineers or accountants are practising their craft rather than simply throwing unreasonable obstacles in the designer's way. Similarly, the manager-in-training begins to appreciate the intellectual quality of design and the integrity of the design process. This deeper understanding makes it more difficult to dismiss the designer as undisciplined or the manager as uncreative. Debate then is focused where it belongs, on the intrinsic merit of ideas and of the interests these ideas serve. The goal is to create a space where students start depending upon their own knowledge and experience as they try to gain more of each and begin to engage in critical self-reflection (Raab 1997). This is the essence of the multidisciplinary experience—creating a 'borderland' (Welsh and Murray 2003) where the expertise and interests of engineers, designers, and business students coexist and inform.

Power Relationships

I was surprised at the resistance to certain methods of approaching problems...As engineers...we were already pushing ourselves to think outside our 'three towered box'. I think the differences in priorities, and in problem-solving tactics, between colleges was a significant obstacle and took us much of the quarter to overcome.

(Keith, engineering student)

From an engineering standpoint...if it can't be done in two years don't bother because the technology will change; however, the design faculty swore on 15 years out...If reality is not to enter the picture, then engineering is not needed. You just do whatever sounds good in your head. I don't think this was engineering not wanting to come out of our box, it was designers not wanting to come out of never-never land. (Donald, engineering student)

An example of this was nuclear power. . . . A piece the size of a person's thumb could run the car for years . . . and never have to be refuelled. Current technology does not have a method to store the nuclear material on the car; however, we had fifteen years to design something to do this. A couple of group members in particular were strongly against nuclear . . . After a discussion, with strong negative feelings from some group members, the idea was put on the back burner as an option for the future, but not one we would pursue.

(Jack, engineering student)

Beyond exposing students to the cultural and intellectual differences, multidisciplinary learning experiences introduce students to the existence of disciplinary power as the interests and agendas of each discipline are represented and organized around a general conceptual scheme, core idea, or problem. Educational reality becomes problematic for students as they (at least momentarily) question the monolithic, conventional educational imaginary of their home discipline. The quotes above illustrate the tension characteristic of these collaborations.

Students come to understand the institutional and ideological authority expressed in those theories and how traditional faculty–student relationships reinforce this authority. Their typical experience has been faculty who, via their own power, alleviate the inherent tensions by making decisions on the 'students' behalf'. Once this is understood, it is a short step to understanding how managers, engineers, and designers are similarly positioned as a consequence of dominant theories about organizations. Instead of articulating the meaning in other people's theories, students theorize their *own* experience within the context of the discursive texts, ideological positions, and theories that are introduced as part of the course. From a critical perspective, by acquiring more skills in reappropriating knowledge, students acquire a greater capacity to act. As Stehr notes (1994: 259), setting specific pressures and interests (in our case the experience of design) heightens the learning potential of a critical discussion of discipline-based knowledge claims. Students become independent or, in the language of critical pedagogy, emancipated learners, ready to act.

Action Orientation

Some confusion came from the professors' leadership. They all had excellent advice, but often their advice conflicted . . . which forced us either to value one prof higher than another, or to side with the prof who would grade us . . . in the end we simply took it all in and made the decisions we felt were right. (Brant, marketing student)

The learning objective, to create a branded experience, provides students with the opportunity to act, as they are required to do relevant research, propose design solutions and marketing plans, refine and evaluate results. The deliverables of the course (the designed experience and a complementary business and manufacturing model) require them to demonstrate the efficacy and viability of their ideas in a specific situation. Creating a branded experience requires some combination of engineering, design, and marketing decisions to be made. The process of producing, articulating, defending, and advocating for their experience forces students to make choices and understand their implications.

Context Meets Process: Aesthetics, Emotion, and Power

Aesthetically Compelling

Creating a branded experience is like what graphic designer Edward Tufte (1997: 138) calls a 'visual confection', an assembly of many visual events brought together and juxtaposed on a flat piece of paper. Composed of a multiplicity of image events, confections 'illustrate an argument, present and enforce visual comparisons, combine the real and the imagined and tell us yet another story'. This is the essence of a branded experience. 'Confection makers cut, paste, construct and manage miniature theaters of information—a cognitive art that serves to illustrate an argument, make a point, explain a task, and show how something works, list possibilities, narrate a story' (p. 138). Creating a branded experience, like a visual confection, is an aesthetic experience.

Following Gagliardi (1996: 566), we use the term aesthetic to refer to 'all types of sense experience and not simply to experience what is socially described as beauty or defined as art'. Aesthetic experiences have long been viewed as valuable learning experiences. Dewey (1934) argued that all aesthetic experiences are by nature educational, because they invoke an active, reciprocal interaction instead of passive reaction. While Dewey was discussing the interaction between a work of art and its perceiver, the argument may easily be extended to educational experience as well. Langer (1942) held that aesthetic experience promotes a different way of knowing. He argued that while explicit knowledge is expressed through discursive forms, tacit knowledge can be represented through artistic, presentational, or symbolic forms. Csikszentmihalyi and Rochberg-Halton (1981) state that aesthetic experiences, whose inherent subjectivity leads them to be dismissed by social scientists as inessential, are in fact one of the essential ways in which we learn judgement. And as Nissley (2004) suggests, these ideas that different ways of knowing are suited to different forms of expression—and in particular, that tacit knowing and the development of judgement may best be expressed through art forms—challenge the dominant intellectual forms of knowledge. This is the distinctive contribution of aesthetic experience—it provides a needed balance to our traditional disciplinary emphasis on discursive, propositional knowledge.

As students from business or engineering initially watch, and eventually participate, with their design counterparts in creating the images necessary to depict an experience, they are simultaneously learning (or reinforcing lessons) about making effective judgements and supporting rationale. Tufte (1997) presents design strategies for presenting information, noting that the limits of visual confections (our branded experience) arise from thinness of content, flimsy logic, poverty of annotating text, and heavy-handed arrangements of structure (p. 141). We might say the same about any other form of composition. The value of the aesthetic experience is that students learn to *see* (*feel*, *hear*) whether a composition meets standards. Involvement in a design project thus trains the non-designer's eye. For example, images with subtle visual differences (for example, in colour) allow more differences to be presented in a clear and effective manner. Visual parallelism builds connections among images by position, orientation, overlap, synchronization, and/or similarities in content. Not simply a matter of design arrangements, however, it is the reciprocal interaction as the perceiving mind actively works to detect and make sense of the assorted visual elements that is the aesthetic experience. 'Embodying inherent links and connections, parallelism synchronizes multiple channels of information, draws analogies, enforces contrasts and comparisons' (Tufte 1997: 103). Thus, the criteria are the same but the lens through which they are viewed is significantly different. But it is a short distance between eye and the mind's eye. Excellence in the display of information requires clear thinking (Tufte 1997: 141).

When students have a direct and immediate aesthetic encounter, this experience adds dimensionality to their learning, as they can reflect appreciation of constructing images, i.e. presentational knowing, onto their experiences in writing position papers, i.e. propositional knowing (Heron and Reason 2001). This enables them to both build and debunk arguments more quickly and effectively. Further, it leads to practical knowing of how to construct the branded experience. When aesthetic encounter forms the basis for critical reflection, students are demonstrating the best of intentional learning (Dehler 1996), becoming more open-minded, risk taking, intellectually responsible, and emotionally committed to their work, making aesthetic experiential learning transformative (Weddington 2004).

Emotionally Intense

This was by far the most challenging thing I have done while in school. . . . I was stressed, nervous, anxious, unsure I knew what I was doing, challenged, excited, worried, happy, and all other emotions during this course however the feeling I had on Friday afternoon when we presented was by far the best feeling I have had academically. It was such an achievement and something I am very proud of. (Anita, marketing student)

The course has been a source of constant frustration and struggle. There were clear differences in expectations, commitment, and respect between the students and professors. This relationship obstacle was never fixed but it was overcome by the students grudgingly dealing with the issue. I hated this course and really see no value with the experience.

(Norm, finance student)

Dewey (1934) argued that an aesthetic experience is only possible if an emotional investment is made. He stated that emotion is the 'cementing force' connecting what is happening in the current experience with prior knowledge, experience, and sentiment, thus allowing a sense of continuity. The comments above capture the rollercoaster ride of emotions our students experience in the course as well as the variation in student response to the course.

Activating emotion is a necessary and important outcome of critical pedagogy. Decentred classrooms, multidisciplinary exchanges, problematizing issues and interests, taking action—because they alter traditional educational relationships (i.e. faculty–student, across disciplines)—promote anxiety in students. Learning and organizing are inherently emotional activities, yet for the most part proceed in an intentionally unemotional manner. Vince (1996) describes how anxiety can initiate cycles that either inhibit or promote learning. Traditional learning models reinforce student dependence upon the knowledge of others (for example, Freire 1972). Even the most accomplished graduates leave ill equipped to understand and use the emotions activated in either process. Experiential learning, by contrast, is directed toward helping students feel emotionally competent and in charge. Learning to work from and through emotions is a principal learning outcome of experience-based courses such as ours.

How much learning occurs, however, depends on the risk-taking propensity of students, whether they are willing to give themselves over to the experience (Weddington 2004). Our unhappy student Norm railed against what he perceived as the messy, inefficient, and unprofessional process. His proposed solution was to segregate students and tasks according to initial competence and hold faculty solely responsible for structuring activity—in other words, he wanted to turn this learning experience into one just like all the others. This behaviour is characteristic of students whose performance orientation outweighs their learning orientation (Dweck 1999). Individuals with a performance orientation seek validation; those with a learning orientation seek growth. This orientation influences an individual's response when encountering challenging tasks.

Relevant here is the tendency towards denial and avoidance in individuals with a strong performance orientation. Since negative feedback is perceived as a judgement of one's competency and self-worth, situations that present risk and uncertainty are to be avoided. In contrast, individuals with a strong learning orientation view novel, potentially risky situations as opportunities for additional self-development (Cron et al. 2005). Students with strong performance orientations are thus more likely to have anxiety followed by denial and avoid-ance, ending in 'willing ignorance', while those with a learning orientation find the struggle results in greater insight and a sense of personal authority (Vince 1996).

Politically Real

We had to negotiate with our marketing professor concerning the integration of the two classes. Originally, the thought was to integrate both ... but our marketing teacher strongly disagreed with the field study approach. (Karen, accounting student)

I hated the political pissing matches between professors and other external sources such as the university administration and CarCo. (Albert, industrial designer)

I learned that AirCo's culture is not very innovative at all. The AirCo executives that came in to speak with us did not appear to be very receptive of what people want in a flight. They kept telling us what they thought people wanted and what they thought needed to be done to fix it. If all their executives are like this, they will go bankrupt fast.

(Derrick, finance student)

The worst things about this course were: conflicting professor and industry expectations and resistance to come to a mutual understanding of student expectations; unwillingness from some professors to allow the expectations to be developed by the students as the scope of the project was more understood ... and to readjust the expectations and evaluate us on a more broad criteria than simply what we do in all our other classes. Since the curriculum expanded in some ways, I felt that the evaluation criteria should have expanded as well.

(Bill, industrial design student)

Another way in which our learning context is distinctive is in its illumination of power relationships within academia and the client firms. This occurs initially through the decentring of power within the classroom setting—grappling with dif-ferences in pedagogical approaches students wonder, 'Who is in charge here?' Over time, students begin to understand the intellectual 'contests' between disciplines, taking on the responsibility to work through them. Faculty disagreements about course process cause students to uncover normative and political processes of acad-emia. Situations become interpreted through a political lens, expanding the possible meanings of decisions. Through interactions with managers from the corporate clients, students begin to see corporate decisions as not necessarily reflecting the true 'merits' of a situation as much as the firm's cultural and political façade. Thus, students come to understand the political landscape (Welsh and Dehler 2004), the rituals and structures through which power identities are constituted within academia and client firms.

In our setting, learning about power involves using the inherent tension be-tween identifying with and negotiating over meaning. Students from each discipline begin the course with novel insights based on their experience. To accomplish their objectives, they have to learn to translate this knowledge to other disciplines. Through this process, ideas and interests are made explicit. Some are incorporated, others marginalized. Students come to appreciate influence processes—literally and figuratively! At the same time, as students achieve a more complicated understanding of the issue (i.e. necessitating a major infusion of funds, or cultural change) they can become assailed by feelings of powerlessness as the enormity of the problem becomes manifest. Thus their learning has greater depth; students come to see how the complexity of power relationships influences what happens during and because of their work.

How Learning Proceeds within Transdisciplinary Teams

There was not always a clear definition of the professors' roles in the course. The normal teacher–student relationship was challenged as both parties lacked clear direction and deliverables at most points in time. The absence of the traditional student–teacher relationship made me feel a bit more uncomfortable in the class. Eventually, instead of viewing the professors as knowledge boxes deciding your ultimate fate (grade), I began to see them as valuable resources and partners in the class. (Nina, marketing student)

Our first responsibilities were fairly easily defined. Team members researched a variety of facets of the project and reported their findings back to the group...we were a group of consultants working on a single project and acting fairly independently. As the quarter progressed, a time arrived where critical technical decisions had to be made in regard to the project. It was decided to present these questions to the group in such a format that everyone could contribute input to determine the most appropriate solution to be aligned with our thematic goal. This process opened the door for other issues to be brought up and discussed within the team. (Donald, engineering student)

The business kids surprised me last meeting when they asked how long they should set aside for story boarding. A lot of the other people thought that would be taken care of by the designers, but now it is hard to tell which students are which.

(Ally, industrial design student)

The outcome of learning in the borderland (Welsh and Murray 2003) is the creation of transdisciplinary teams. Geertz (1973: 33) characterized scientific advancement as the 'progressive complication of what once seemed a beautifully simple set of notions but now seems an unbearably simplistic one'. Viewing a project from a single lens is no longer satisfactory for our students. As they engage in course activities together, students learn that their underlying craft is similar, even if the targets are different. They also come to see how incomplete (and potentially misleading) either craft is when enacted in isolation.

Students also encounter three added layers of texture in this learning process, those of aesthetics, emotion, and power discussed earlier. Learning becomes more than a matter of making sense of interactions for instrumental ends, i.e. to solve the problem presented by the client or to learn how to navigate effectively among a firm's different subcultures. Sense making (Weick 1979) around what it means to 'be' a designer, engineer, marketer, or manager is also occurring. Mutual appreciation and interdependence lay the foundation for collaboration, now and in the future. Next, we describe how building a critical framework around an aesthetic experience provides the foundation for effective collaboration and transdisciplinarity.

According to Jantsch (1971), transdisciplinarity occurs when there is multi-level coordination within an entire system. In our teams, transdisciplinarity is expressed through transparency. When movement within and between disciplines becomes transparent despite still significant differences in expertise among team members, the barriers between disciplines are seen as permeable, rather than obstacles to be overcome. Students find that their own disciplinary expertise has been informed and expanded as a consequence of their involvement with new and different disciplines.

Because of the centrality of practice in the development of the transdisciplinary team's identity and the existence of significant coordinative requirements, learning within the teams can be analysed using the framework and processes of communities of practice (for example, Brown and Duguid 1991; Lave and Wenger 1991). When interacting, team members share understandings about what they do and what the doing means for them and for their speciality (discipline). Learning takes place in a participation framework, not in the individual mind (Orlikowski 2002), and is mediated by differences of perspective among the co-participants.

In the beginning, the team culture reflects the additive influence of each discipline. Students engage in different ways and at different levels of intensity as the task unfolds and their expertise is required. The changing locations and perspectives represent the learning trajectories of the participants. The shape of a transdisciplinary team emerges during its practice, rather than being assigned or created specifically. Members of each discipline are gradually socialized to the values and expertise of others, ultimately learning to function as a community.

Over time, team members take on the knowledge embedded in the community. The home discipline reproduces itself through the acculturation of newcomers yet is transformed as well (the necessary requirement for transdisciplinarity). This enables students to socially construct their own identity as a specialist practitioner as well as that of generalist team member and learn how to transition between these two roles. Thus membership in a transdisciplinary team enables students to enhance their specialist skills in practice and develop significant skills as learners. The combination of in-depth skill as a practitioner and the ability to continuously learn and unlearn in a social context is crucial to the student's professional development.

Learning within communities is collaborative, socially constructed, and proceeds through the development of narratives. Narratives (Bruner 1990) reflect the causal maps that community members develop in the course of their practice. As practitioners encounter new or unexpected events, they construct stories in which the new or unexpected make sense. Exchanging stories allows the community to uncover the implicit assumptions or interpretative structures with relevance to the situation. This interchange produces the friction of divergent or competing ideas necessary to spark experimentation and improvisation. At least initially, these new experiences create causal ambiguity and, in turn, encourage the participation of all team members as a means of constructing or elaborating narratives that reduce this ambiguity. From this process, new stories emerge that belong to the community and are modified by subsequent exposure to the new or unexpected.

Learning through narrative development is particularly suited to both our course objective (developing branded experience) and pedagogy. The narrative mode of thought is based on the goal of understanding and the construction of meaning, requiring an involved, self-relevant reflection on experience (Bruner 1990). Forming narratives to use in conveying the branded experience or forming narratives to understand how this new pedagogical experience operates—in each case we are asking for information to be organized in a story format. It suggests the possibility—indeed the likelihood—that there can be multiple interpretations of a particular experience. It does not necessarily seek to identify the best explanation because the idea of a correct interpretation has no meaning. Students want to know the 'correct answer'. All faculty struggle to prepare students for a world where definitive answers are all too rare. One of the most important contributions of learning the narrative mode of thought is that it provides students with a powerful tool to use in anxiety-provoking, ambiguous, novel, and challenging events in their future.

THINKING AND LEADING CRITICALLY

We conclude the chapter with a few remarks about why we continue to offer this course and recommend it to others. Our experience-based course is modelled on action research, intended to 'produce practical knowledge that is useful to people in the everyday conduct of their lives' (Reason and Bradbury 2001: 2). True to the roots of action research, real organizational problems serve as the starting point for students. But the approach extends beyond the pragmatic, problem-solving aspects of the pedagogy by guiding students into and through the less familiar terrain of aesthetics, emotion, and politics.

Action research, however, also requires students to question the motives for their proposed actions. According to McNiff, Lomax, and Whitehead (1996), action research requires praxis rather than just practice: 'Praxis is informed, committed action *that gives rise to knowledge rather than just successful action*' (p. 8, emphasis added). Learning takes precedence, but the linkage between learning and action is explicit. In this sense, action research is emancipatory in that it generates not only new practical knowledge, but the development of 'new abilities to create knowledge' (Reason and Bradbury 2001: 2). The overarching objective is the explicit connection of practice as it is currently being conducted (experience) with a more rigorous knowledge base (the curriculum). In other words, 'where the traditional teaching-centred approach privileges textbook learning for use later, i.e. *toward practice*, action research begins with practice and works the other way, i.e. *toward knowledge*' (Dehler 2006).

Knowledge is not something to be accessed; rather it is created (Dehler 1996). In an action research context, practice is transformed through the creation of knowledge (McNiff 1990). But our concern is with developing students' capacity to be critical. This requires reflexivity, i.e. turning the process back on itself through reflection (Reynolds 1998). By revealing heretofore unexplained, taken-for-granted assumptions, reflection serves as the primary mechanism for leveraging experience and translating knowledge into action. Through critical reflection, new insights are generated and their interpretation and understanding of the underlying problem reformulated. The candid student comments included in this chapter illustrate their recognition of how much of their prior training, and even their workplace context, is built upon a set of assumptions that fail to consider emotional, political, or cultural-symbolic perspectives. The culmination of critical reflection is emancipatory—developing the student as a change agent. Gregory (1994) suggests that adopting a critical attitude toward their own practice raises students above the ranks of technician. Engaging learners at a different level of experience, for example, critically reflective and freed from disciplinary constraints, leads to a transformation of perspectives—a two-way bond between theory and practice rather than theory-led practice (pp. 46–7).

Learning in the context of work has been proposed as a response to the 'changing articulation of the knowledge-based economy' (Rhodes and Garrick 2003: 447). The challenge for management educators and learners appears deceptively straightforward: 'How is it that competence is turned into performance?' (McNiff 1990: 54). This seemingly simple question presents a conundrum that defies simplistic solution and continues to perplex management educators. Our experience-based action research course provides a pedagogical mechanism for management educators to do this—by engaging students more directly into 'the messy real world of practice' (Griffiths 1990: 43).

First, it enriches students' learning by raising their level of 'complicatedness' (Dehler, Welsh, and Lewis 2001). Second, it expands the scope of potential learning. Students are often stumped and frustrated by the project, fearful about trusting their own competence absent someone checking their work or providing specific

task guidelines. For them, learning has been defined and experienced as performance related to propositional knowledge. This venture into experience-based
learning provides the opportunity to directly relate curricular learning to actual
workplace context, and to translate programmatic learning into workplace action.
Students experience the struggle of coping with turmoil, tension, and the social
embeddedness of real organizational problems, enhancing their competencies as a
result.

Third, it underscores the importance of integrating the 'critical theoretic' component of action research. Universities and business endeavour to foster closer link-
ages, yet Rhodes and Garrick (2003: 463) caution that it would not be 'completely
healthy to uncritically remove all aspects of the distance' between them. The risk
would be 'instrumental outcomes in which learning no longer requires critical
distance, dialogue, and critique—knowledge is only valued insofar as it produces
economically legitimated results' (p. 464).

Finally, a widely held supposition about innovation suggests that leadership
makes a difference in the nature and success of creative efforts. Mumford and
Licuanan (2004), after reviewing articles on this issue, suggest that leaders foster
innovation by facilitating the adoption of a creative identity by a team, effectively
managing the emotion relative to this identity, and competently utilizing influence
processes. As the final set of quotes from students indicates, successful execution
requires practice; our experience-based action research course is a crucial step in
this direction.

As we gained understanding of our respective fields, I believe we found it much easier to
respect, and contribute, to the other fields. (Keith, engineering student)

I would say that I did not 'get' what this course was about until our group met for the first
time out of class. This was when we finally decided what route we wanted to do for our
project. We had been brainstorming for a few weeks, and we all sat there and decided on
the . . . idea. It was then it hit me that we thought of this idea completely on our own, no
lecture or PowerPoint could have gotten us to where we were at this point. It was our little
'baby' if you will, and, at least for me, motivated me to work harder as we had spent so much
time and we were actually 'getting' somewhere. (Mike, business student)

I want to believe that my existence as a designer is more than just a product and that I can
change the way people live and feel by what we do. (Sharon, industrial designer)

NOTES

1. All student quotes were extracted from journals kept as part of the course requirements. Student names and corporate clients are disguised to maintain confidentiality.
2. This course is co-taught by the first and third authors.

REFERENCES

Brown, J. S., and Duguid, P. (1991). 'Organizational Learning and Communities of Practice: Toward a Unified View of Working Learning and Innovation', *Organization Science*, 2: 40–57.

Bruner, J. S. (1990). *Acts of Meaning*. Cambridge, Mass: Harvard University Press.

Cagan, J., and Vogel, C. M. (2002). *Creating Breakthrough Products*. Upper Saddle River, NJ: Prentice Hall.

Cron, W. L., Slocum, J. W., VandeWalle, D., and Fu, Q. (2005). 'The Role of Goal Orientation on Negative Emotions and Goal Setting when Initial Performance Falls Short of One's Performance Goal', *Human Performance*, 18: 55–80.

Csikszentmihalyi, M., and Rochberg-Halton, E. (1981). *The Meaning of Things: Domestic Symbols and the Self*. Cambridge: Cambridge University Press.

Dehler, G. E. (1996). 'Management Education as Intentional Learning: A Knowledge-Transforming Approach to Written Composition', *Journal of Management Education*, 20: 221–35.

—— (2006). 'Using Action Research to Connect Practice to Earning: A Course Project for Working Management Students', *Journal of Management Education*, 30/5: 636–69.

—— Welsh, M. A., and Lewis, M. W. (2001). 'Critical Pedagogy in the New Paradigm: Raising Complicated Understanding in Management Learning', *Management Learning*, 32: 493–511.

Dewey, J. (1934). *Art as Experience*. New York: Pedigree Books.

Dweck, C. S. (1999). *Self-Theories: Their Role in Motivation, Personality, and Development*. Philadelphia: Psychology Press.

Freire, P. (1972). *Pedagogy of the Oppressed*. Harmondsworth: Penguin.

Gagliardi, P. (1996). 'Exploring the Aesthetic Side of Organizational Life', in S. T. Clegg, C. Hardy, and W. R. Nord (eds.), *Handbook of Organization Studies*. London: Sage.

Geertz, C. (1973). *The Interpretation of Cultures*. New York: Basic Books.

Giroux, H. A. (1997). *Pedagogy and the Politics of Hope: Theory, Culture, and Schooling*. Boulder, Colo. Westview Press.

Gregory, M. (1994). 'Accrediting Work-Based Learning: Action Learning—a Model for Empowerment', *Journal of Management Development*, 13: 41–52.

Griffiths, M. (1990). 'Action Research: Grass Roots Practice or Management Tool?', in P. Lomax (ed.), *Managing Staff Development in Schools: An Action Research Approach*. Avon: Multilingual Matters Ltd.

Heron, J., and Reason, P. (2001). 'The Practice of Co-Operative Inquiry: Research "With" Rather Than "On" People', In P. Reason and H. Bradbury (eds.), *Handbook of Action Research: Participative Inquiry and Practice*. London: Sage.

Jantsch, E. (1971). 'Inter- and Transdisciplinary University: A Systems Approach to Education and Innovation', *Ekistics*, 32: 430–7.

Langer, S. (1942). *Philosophy in a New Key*. Cambridge, Mass. Harvard University Press.

Lave, J., and Wenger, E. (1991). *Situated Learning: Legitimate Peripheral Participation*. Cambridge: Cambridge University Press.

McNiff, J. (1990). 'Writing and the Creation of Educational Knowledge', in P. Lomax (ed.), *Managing Staff Development in Schools: An Action Research Approach*. Clevedon: Multilingual Matters.

——Lomax, P., and Whitehead, J. (1996). *You and your Action Research Project*. London: Routledge.

Mumford, M. D., and Licuanan, B. (2004). 'Leading for Innovation: Conclusions, Issues and Directions', *Leadership Quarterly*, 12: 163–71.

Nissley, N. (2004). 'The "Artful Creation" of Positive Anticipatory Imagery in Appreciative Inquiry: Understanding the "Art of" Appreciative Inquiry as Aesthetic Discourse', in D. L. Cooperrider and M. Avital (eds.), *Advances in Appreciative Inquiry*. Greenwich, Cana.: JAI Press.

Orlikowski, W. (2002). 'Knowing in Practice: Enacting a Collective Capability in Distributed Organizing', *Organization Science*, 13: 249–73.

Raab, N. (1997). 'Becoming an Expert in Not Knowing: Reframing Teacher as Consultant', *Management Learning*, 28: 161–75.

Reason, P., and Bradbury, H. (2001). 'Introduction: Inquiry and Participation in Search of a World Worthy of Human Aspiration', in P. Reason and H. Bradbury (eds.), *Handbook of Action Research*. London: Sage.

Reynolds, M. (1997). 'Towards a Critical Management Pedagogy', in J. Burgoyne and M. Reynolds (eds.), *Management Learning: Integrating Perspectives in Theory and Practice*. London: Sage.

——(1998). 'Reflection and Critical Reflection in Management Learning', *Management Learning*, 29: 183–200.

Rhodes, C., and Garrick, J. (2003). 'Project-Based Learning and the Limits of Corporate Knowledge', *Journal of Management Education*, 27: 447–71.

Stehr, N. (1994). *Knowledge Societies*. London: Sage.

Tufte, E. R. (1997). *Visual Explanations: Images and Quantities, Evidence and Narrative*. Cheshire, Conn.: Graphics Press.

Vince, R. (1996). 'Experiential Management Education as the Practice of Change', in R. French and C. Grey (eds.), *Rethinking Management Education*. London: Sage.

Weddington, H. S. (2004). 'Education as Aesthetic Experience: Interactions of Reciprocal Transformation', *Journal of Transformative Education*, 2: 120–37.

Weick, K. (1979). *The Social Psychology of Organizing* 2nd edn. Reading, Mass.: Addison-Wesley.

Welsh, M. A., and Dehler, G. E. (2004). 'P(l)aying Attention: Communities of Practice and Organized Reflection', in M. Reynolds and R. Vince (eds.), *Organizing Reflection*. Aldershot: Ashgate.

——and Murray, D. (2003). 'The Ecollaborative: Using Critical Pedagogy to Teach Sustainability', *Journal of Management Education*, 27: 220–35.

CHAPTER 4

AESTHETICS IN TEACHING ORGANIZATION STUDIES

ANTONIO STRATI

BRIEF INTRODUCTION

THE aim of the chapter is to illustrate how aesthetics activated experiential learning while I was teaching organizational subjects. The experiences recounted relate to undergraduate and master courses at an Italian university. The linking theme of the chapter is a module on organizational aesthetics which formed the final part of the Sociology of Organizations course on a specialist degree programme in Work, Organization, and Information Systems. This experience also enabled me to reflect on some ten years' experience of a 'riddle-based' process of learning. The second experience described is a performance (riddles have features characteristic of the performance as an artwork) that a student (and artist) on my course staged for her degree examination. The subject of the performance was Max Weber's ideal type of bureaucracy. I will focus on the use in teaching of the performance as a video artefact. The chapter will end with some 'inclusions' about the perceptual faculties and sensitive judgements involved in appreciating the performance, and/or the video of it, and then with reflection on academic teaching and the aesthetic understanding of organizational life.

OBSERVING THROUGH THE
LENS OF AESTHETICS

Last academic year I decided to devote a module of my Sociology of Organizations course to the aesthetic study of organizational life. My intention was to give students attending at the specialist degree programme on Work, Organization, and Information Systems an opportunity for the practical-factual learning of qualitative methods. My more specific purpose was to have the students experiment with their personal capacities to conduct qualitative empirical research on organizations.

Aesthetics lends itself well to this type of teaching because it induces students to activate their perceptual-sensory capacities and their aesthetic judgements in order to understand organizational phenomena, and to reflect upon those capacities and that judgement. When teaching the everyday practices of qualitative research, in fact, aesthetics immediately brings to light the constant dialogue between ordinary routine and personal configuration. It does so by inviting students to invest something of themselves in their research and to follow where their imaginings, tastes, and intuitions lead them.

But there is something else that aesthetics invites students to do: *pay very close attention to how they observe an organizational phenomenon in its setting*. The details of organizational action are extremely valuable for aesthetic understanding. Immersing oneself in those details, detaching oneself from them, and then letting oneself be absorbed by them, to evoke and relive them, finding representations for them: all this is involved in the 'aesthetic' study (i.e. analysis performed with all the senses and the sensibility) of organizations.

I therefore conceived the module as moving through the following phases:

(a) a review of the standard distinction between qualitative and quantitative analysis, preparing the students for aesthetic analysis of qualitative type by means of this theoretical introduction;

(b) a survey of the literature on the aesthetic dimension of organizational routine;

(c) an invitation to the students to conduct observations on some organizational setting, but as far as possible avoiding interviews with organizational personnel;

(d) classroom discussion of their field notes, and the formation of work groups;

(e) constructing a dialogue between their research and literature on the aesthetic approach; and

(f) monitoring and stimulating the learning process.

Hence an entire module of twenty-four hours was to be devoted to one single approach to organizational analysis—and indeed devoted to only that part of it involving observation and representing what has been observed. But the course as a whole amounted to seventy-two hours, and this final module was envisaged as a workshop on empirical studies or case studies drawn from the organizational literature. It was designed to follow on from the theoretical aspects examined in the two previous modules.

The problem, however, was that I could not foresee how things would turn out. I had devised the module without knowing the students, given that my course was scheduled for the first year of the specialist degree programme, the syllabuses for which were published in the spring term of the previous academic year. Yet with my syllabus the willingness of the students to participate actively was crucial. This participation I could not take for granted, however, because it required the students to 'risk' something of themselves. The texts studied could do little to protect them against this risk, because what I planned to activate was a largely experiential form of learning.

I also wanted to give a young researcher—particularly expert in the aesthetic study of organizations—an opportunity to conduct this learning experience together with me. I would thus introduce further plurality into the collective action. I told the researcher how I imagined the module, stressing its experiential nature, and asked him to draw up an outline programme. Just before the module began, we pooled our ideas and decided its structure. At that stage I had completed the first two modules of the course, and the students had acquired corporeality in my mind, and I in theirs, so that reciprocal trust had been established. A feature that had become apparent during the previous part of the course was that the roughly twenty students—the number varied, as did the composition of the class, because attendance was not compulsory—did not form an aggregate of individuals but a collective comprising diverse student subcultures besides that of the course as a whole. My assistant had also 'acquired corporeality' for some students—in part for institutional reasons (research and teaching) and in part for informal and personal ones.

At the first meeting with the students, I explained—alternating with my assistant—what we intended to do and what we intended to have them do. The students showed interest in our ideas, although I could see a certain amount of apprehension and uncertainty in their faces.

And so my lectures on the methodology of organizational empirical research began, followed by those of my assistant on the aesthetic approach. In the meantime, we had decided that the organizational setting investigated by the students would be the one most accessible to them: their faculty, the Facoltà di Sociologia. We asked the students, first, to write a brief note outlining their knowledge about the faculty. Then, we asked them to leave the classroom in the last half-hour of the lesson, conduct their observations for ten to fifteen minutes, return to the classroom and write their preliminary field notes, briefly tell the others where they had been, what they had seen, and what their first sensations had been. They would come to the next lesson with their field notes organized so that they could be read out and discussed by the class. They would also have studied an article—first Gagliardi (1996), then Strati (2000) and Martin (2002), and finally Barry (1996), one for each of the next four weeks—on the aesthetic approach, and they would have related it to their field notes.

The Aesthetic Experience of Power in Lecturing Practices

The first striking aesthetic experience came during a lecture by my assistant. He was describing certain features of the aesthetic approach. He was standing up and he had moved from behind the table at which we were sitting to face the students scattered around the benches in the classroom. I cannot remember exactly how, but he introduced a topic which aroused strong emotion in the room. He began to talk about his power, as well as my own, over the students; but this was a power deriving more from our teaching than from our hierarchical positions and institutional roles in the organization. Lecturing has intrinsic power, he explained, because it constructs knowledge artefacts which simultaneously establish teacher–pupil relations that—though subject to controvertible power dynamics—put me and him in a position of pre-eminence. But the students were not devoid of power, because the outcome of their learning depended on their active participation; and the reputation of our module, and to a certain extent his reputation as a teacher, depended on their assessment of the quality of our teaching—assessment made both informally and formally by the faculty questionnaire. As he was saying this, the assistant moved away from the table and towards the students. He then walked along the aisle between the left-hand block of desks and the wall, to the back of the room. There he turned and raised his arm to point at me. There was a further kind of power, he said: my power over him, or the fact that while he was teaching he felt that I was examining him. As he spoke he walked backwards without turning until, still facing the students, he passed the first row and moved into the centre of the space separating it from our desk, where I was sitting with his empty chair to my right. In other words, by moving and 'touching' the space of the classroom, he had placed himself physically between me and the students, albeit slightly to one side. His account was overtly offered to the students as a reflection on relational power within the organization tied to the construction of intangible artefacts like knowledge and learning: sentiment, openness, and corporeality of action in the organizational space that transformed the materiality itself of our organization. But it caused tension, irritation, and embarrassment in the room, which seemed no longer recognizable, now that it had lost the relaxed, sometimes playful, nature of its previous teacher–learner relations.

The students deemed me 'guilty' because I had power to evaluate the work of the young assistant. They understood what he felt, but they did so with the embarrassment of people suddenly involved in relational dynamics whose substance they do not know, and which they are unwilling to judge. But they knew me as well; they sympathized with the assistant but they sympathized with me too, perhaps realizing my surprise at what had happened from the expression on my face and my physical posture.

The students watched my reactions surreptitiously. As Simmel (1908) pointed out, sight is distinctive among the five senses of aesthetic-sensory perception in that it activates a relation of particular sociological interest. Unlike the other senses, hearing for example, it produces reciprocity: we look at others, and they look at us, in the same moment of time. I and the students looked at each other. We faced each other as my assistant moved from his initial lateral position to a central space between us. But numerous students avoided reciprocity of gaze. Although I was strongly aware of the embarrassment of the situation, I did not feel impelled to get rid of it. I just as strongly felt my duty not to leave the assistant alone in the complex of emotions that his speech on power had aroused. Hence, when the drama of the situation had subsided, though not entirely disappeared—when, that is, it was still heavily present in the room—I did my duty and spoke to the students. I stressed that the organizational event we had witnessed had been experienced 'aesthetically' and not just 'intellectually'.

My assistant's thoughts on power, I stressed, had been purged of neither emotion nor aesthetic feeling. Consequently, they had not been experienced as mental experience alone, but in the complexity, interferences, and con/fusion of experience that converts it from intellectual to bodily and material matter. My assistant's reflection on power in the organization had 'evidently' become an account of diverse dialogic experiences of power. It had brought out paradoxes and incongruities, powers and impotencies, conflicts and assonances. Power had been articulated, declined across several levels, echoed in the plurality and diversity of Italian academic practices, rather than being reduced to the more or less conflictual lecturer–student dynamic. We had been immersed in it with aesthetic-sensory feelings, with emotions, and also with aesthetic judgements based on various aesthetic categories, to wit: (a) 'the ugly'—the ugliness of the young teacher's situation, of relations among academic staff, or of power; (b) 'the tragic'—through sympathy with the young assistant's organizational heroism, the tragedy of his account of it; (c) and 'the comic'—what a good joke at the professor's expense!—in the human comedy that sets drama within lived experience. Power in organizations had become more than a theoretical notion; it now constituted aesthetic experience of lecturing practice performed—and manifest in its analytic and aesthetic complexity—in the lecture room. It did so for the following reasons:

(a) the participation by everyone, students and lecturers, had been intense, though not couched in speech, in that only my colleague and myself (now) had spoken;

(b) the interactions among us had been elicited by the words spoken, by their illocutionary force, by the emotion that they evinced, communicated, and passed from body to body through gesticulation, movement, gaze, silence, non-movement;

(c) the revelation of the power relations between professor, assistant, and students had occurred during theoretical analysis, which was suddenly transformed into aesthetic experience;

(d) the critical event caused by one organizational actor and experienced by all the others demonstrated that organizational experiences subject the same event to different and personal interpretations and to dynamics of organizational memory construction which intermingle corporeality, emotion, aesthetic judgement, and ratiocination;

(e) the event had given salience to the 'game' of organizational relations, in the twofold sense of playing and gambling, of pleasure and risk, of transparency and deception, of awareness and not knowing what will happen, of imagination and ignorance;

(f) the game had put aesthetics at the centre of organizational relations, while also showing that the reputation of every individual and collective actor and trust in others are not just 'known' but 'felt';

(g) involvement in the organizational event had provoked pleasure but also discomfort, thus further emphasizing that aesthetic experience is complex because it concerns the tragic, the ugly, or the grotesque, as well as the comical, the beautiful, or the elegant—as the aesthetic category of the sublime (the co-presence of profound pleasure and suffering) emblematically demonstrates.

At this point—I concluded—the students were ready to begin empirical analysis. We had already discussed both the empirical qualitative study of organizations and the main features of the aesthetic approach. We had completed the lectures with the riddle of the organizational artefact. Moreover, the students had also seen—during the first part of the course when Weber's bureaucracy was discussed—the 'Iron Cage Performance'. My reflections on the materiality and corporeality of power relations in organizational practices should, I said, further persuade them to rely on their capacities for aesthetic comprehension of organizational phenomena, to take personal responsibility for empirical research, to risk their reputations as students, to enjoy knowledge acquired in not exclusively analytical-rational manner. But what, then, of the riddle?

THE RIDDLE

I have used the riddle as a teaching device for the last ten years or so, although not on all my courses: sometimes I have been unable to use it; or sometimes, more simply, I have not wanted to do so because I have not felt that the situation was appropriate. But in the majority of cases, I have brought out this riddle in my courses on sociology of organizations. The students have been very different, both because they have been so by their very nature, and because they were attending different universities and faculties (I teach at the Faculty of Sociology, University of Trento, and at the Faculty of Letters, University of Siena).

Riddles are a somewhat bizarre teaching technique at university level. A riddle differs from a quiz in its 'serious irony', playfulness, and non-sense; and also because it is widespread in childhood game playing. Answering the riddle 'what was the colour of Napoleon's white horse' demonstrates, not knowledge of the correct answer, but an infantile ability to engage in play. Riddles are decidedly out of place at a university. Yet it is precisely this change of aesthetic-cognitive 'frame' which makes them enjoyable and rich with emotions that prompt reflexivity—as I have amply described elsewhere (Strati 1999).

Reflexivity in regard to what? The knowledge artefacts that populate the symbolic domain of Italian university-level teaching, we might say, paraphrasing the title of the collected volume edited by Pasquale Gagliardi (1990) on pathos and symbolism in artefacts. Hence, when I have deemed the didactic situation appropriate, I have introduced my riddle at the beginning, or during, or towards the end of a course, my purpose being:

(a) in the first case, to use the riddle to conduct joint reflection with my students on their knowledge of forms of organizational life at the beginning of the course. Later I have used the riddle to evoke an experience shared by myself and my students but which distinguishes us: a symbol, therefore, of ongoing styles of teaching and learning:

(b) in the other two cases, to conduct an 'experiential' test on student progress and my teaching input, as well as to support my lecturing style.

In all three cases, however, I have always introduced or recalled what in the literature is meant by 'organizational artefact'.

The ritual of the riddle differs according to the students, to the setting of the lesson, and to the moment. But the proposal of solving a riddle has always evoked surprise and pleasure: 'inner laughter' and the students' agreement to play as if they have become children again. Not all of them, though, because some have been loath to participate, and their grimaces and bodily movements protested that this was no way to conduct a serious lesson. In many cases these students translated it into a 'quiz' and tried to answer the quiz rather than experience the process engendered by the riddle. This situation is not always easy to handle, because the riddle loses its didactic value and its ability to have the students enjoy the game through their sensory faculties and aesthetic judgement. The situation has the awkwardness one feels when watching a comic film with someone who does not like that kind of comedy, or simply does not understand it; so that when you laugh you receive a stony gaze enquiring what it is that you find funny.

The riddle can be solved either individually or in small groups, according to the students' preference. I often ask them to pool their small change as a prize for the winning student or group. This process embedded within the larger one of the riddle always animates the students. Some of them collect the prize money, others count it. Some of them move around the room to form pairs or groups; others only do so to exchange quips and then go back to their seats. The atmosphere in the room changes: I hear giggling and laughter, names being called out, the noise of tables, chairs, and benches being moved. I see faces smiling and grinning, or bent over pieces of paper on which the names of group members are being written; bodies no longer still but in movement, leaning on desks, lounging across seats. I watch the negotiation and creation of a different organizational order distinguished by doing-in-movement, instead of doing-in-stillness. When the money has been collected and the name lists of pairs or groups have been placed on my table, the room is again different, the organizational order has again changed: before me are no longer students, but those particular students on their own, those students in couples, those in groups. They are scattered around the room if it is large, or bunched together if it is small. I now place the answer to the riddle on my table—after waving the envelope in the air to show that it is sealed—and press the button on the overhead projector to display the riddle.

Which organizational artefact in the broad sense:

1. is purchased more often than it is produced
2. extends beyond organizational boundaries
3. is simultaneously material and non-material
4. is individual and belongs to everybody
5. shows up anyone who does not have one
6. is constantly sought after
7. is a metaphor for the hierarchy of organizational levels
8. if flaunted may provoke criticism and invoke sanctions
9. if it shifts, may provoke hilarity
10. homogenizes positions downwards

?

The answers that I have collected over the years have always related to the lofty themes of university education; 'power', 'control', domination', 'money', 'professionalism', 'work', 'culture', 'emotion'. Only on two occasions have I received more mundane replies: 'toilet' and 'window'. These were given by a student and a group of three female students in Siena, on two different courses. When asked, in both cases they replied that they had come up with the answers by basing themselves on my 'unconventional' lecturing style.

Neither did the students on last year's course on organizational aesthetics depart from broad organizational themes like 'culture', 'gender', 'control', 'money', 'work', 'social position', 'fashion', 'power' (numerous answers), 'organization' itself. However, two answers were different from those offered on other occasions: 'marriage' and 'sex'. The former indicated organizational mergers; the latter meant sex both as a gender construct and as personal diversity among organizational actors and a dimension of interpersonal relations in the organization. However, although intrigued, I could not discuss these answers with the two female students who had proposed them because the class was anxiously awaiting the result of the riddle game, and the lesson was drawing to a close.

Also these students on the organizational aesthetics course were surprised by the answer to the riddle. Laughter, protests, and demands for explanation erupted as soon as a female student opened the envelope and incredulously read out the solution. Her incredulity was evident from the tone of her voice, which halted halfway through reading the short word written on the piece of paper. It then resumed, but too faintly to be heard by the other students because it was muffled by the girl's own laughter. However, the word flashed around the classroom, being repeated with different tones and emphases by the students. Now, as the girl student regained her composure and repeated out loud—with tears in her eyes—the answer to the riddle, the laughter of the other students was accompanied by bodies collapsing on the desks, gesticulations which emphasized the pleasure of the surprise, expressions of astonishment, signals of satisfaction with the ingenuity of the riddle, but also with its successful performance. The lecture room was once again changed by these bodily movements, facial expressions, shifts of gaze, the noise of voices and laughter. There was no longer a focus of interactions, but a plurality of loci of action which overlapped and merged. Then, as on previous occasions, attention returned to myself as I explained the answer to the riddle and showed why the students' solutions were wrong. But then, unlike on many other occasions, the students stopped arguing for their quasi-solutions and showed appreciation at the answer read out to them, which, with a minimalist touch, reduced grand abstract concepts to the banality of organizational routine and its corporeality. What was the right answer? It was an organizational artefact that all of them were using at that moment and which they constantly used in the organization. The artefact without which they would not feel accepted by the organization, nor feel they had a proper place in it, nor feel at ease in it, but which they did not 'see' because they took it for granted as if they were attached to it in their routine practice: the chair. In other words, the riddle had induced the students to:

(a) problematize their habitual learning practices, eschewing institutionally learned theories and relying instead on what they could see, touch, and feel—this being a phenomenon widespread in organizations, as documented by Zucker's (1977) ethnomethodological studies;

(b) conduct empirical analysis, because what matters when solving a riddle is the ability to grasp the meaning of the game and to play it; in other words, the ability to use one's intuition, imagination, and sensory perception to grasp the materiality of everyday organizational life in its details and nuances;

(c) to appreciate organizational aesthetics, because it had shown the ineludibility of sensible knowledge, the emotions, the aesthetic judgement, in short, the complexity of forms of action and knowledge in organizations; as well as demonstrating that many of these forms, though used in organizations as essential components of the experiential flow of quotidian routine—and therefore, as in the case of the chair, a crucial element in the personal experience of acting in organizations—are not grasped, studied, and understood but instead taken for granted and therefore paradoxically excluded.

The riddle has therefore been a teaching device in which the pleasure gained from participating, and the enthusiasm shown in doing so, the serious irony involved in collectively constructing the didactic event, the taste for constant change in the organizational setting, the pleasure of the game, and enjoyment of its humour, had been experiences acquired by participating corporeally in the flow of creating and recreating the organizational order, its 'spatial focuses', its rhythms, noises, and materiality. Some of these elements were also comprised in the students' experience of watching the video of the 'Iron Cage Performance'.

The 'Iron Cage Performance'

When during the first part of the course I discussed Weber's notion of bureaucracy, I did so by projecting a video of the 'Iron Cage Performance' (Gherardi and Strati 2003). This is an audio-visual artefact available on CD-ROM, cassette, or DVD which was produced on the occasion of the performance submitted by a student—and artist—Anna Scalfi as her project for the examinations in sociology of organization and sociology of work, and then as an essential part of her degree thesis. I have described this teaching experience in more detail in an essay on organizational artefacts (Strati 2005), where I dwell on the performance as an ephemeral organizational artefact difficult to explain to those who have not seen it/taken part in it. The topic is important in regard both to theoretical-methodological developments in the aesthetic study of organizational life and, more generally, to qualitative analysis of organizations. It is so because it centres on the issue of the knowledge and learning acquired experientially by a researcher and also, as stressed by Chris Steyaer and Daniel Hjorth (2002), on the issue of their representation and communication to different audiences. It was in these terms—representation of the organizational understanding acquired by the researcher—that I showed the 'Iron Cage' video to the students attending my organizational aesthetics course. Such representation was contextualized in the framework of empirical research, and therefore in a framework different from that of classroom discussion of Weber's ideal type of bureaucracy.

The video (which lasts about twenty minutes) has always aroused contrasting aesthetic and emotional reactions when I have shown it to students. Initially, there is pleasure that something artistic has been introduced into a lecture on a standard topic, and curiosity to see how that topic could be treated unconventionally. It is the diversity itself of the didactic experience which has in many respects aroused the students' interest and solicited use of their perceptual-sensory faculties and sensitive-aesthetic judgement. Although by now largely routine practices in university teaching, lowering a screen, switching on the computer and the projector (or video projector), turning off the lights, closing the window blinds, projecting images and sounds change the nature of the lecture room. They make it different in terms of both the physicality of the organizational context and the disposition of participants to activate their capacity for aesthetic understanding. The rituality of these practices changes the type of attention required, for it now focuses not on the goodness of the theories expounded but on the multiformity of the didactic experience in which the cognitive and analytical dimension is embedded in the *pathos* of sensible knowledge and the emotions connected with it.

Paradoxically, projection of the performance video benefits from the separation between art and science distinctive of university teaching in Italy and elsewhere. Videos and performances pertain to the world of art, which is institutionally kept distant from the seriousness of academic pedagogy, and with it student expectations of experiencing aesthetic sentiments and enjoying—or disliking—transgression of conventional teaching practices.

During the title sequence, the video shows a large cage consisting partly of rigid straight elements and partly of soft and sinuous ones, standing in the entrance lobby to the Faculty of Sociology. It is an installation by the artist Loris Cecchini which had previously been displayed at the Civic Gallery of Trento. The student had seen it and associated it with my treatment of Weber's bureaucracy. Prompted by a workshop on the organizational space of workplaces held during Gherardi's course, the student had decided to 'do something different' in the form of the 'Iron Cage' performance. This was based on extracts from Weber which were 'said'—not recited—by the female student and which alternated, as in counterpoint, with voices recorded at a supermarket, a railway station, and a dance school, and which recounted discursive practices in those workplaces. The video shows the student entering the installation and uttering Weber's words—taken from the Italian translation—on bureaucracy. From time to time she stops so that the voices from the everyday world of work can be heard. The students are usually very interested at the beginning. They strain to hear the oral exchanges on the workplaces, they are caught up by the alternation between the two vocal contexts evoked—Weber's text and discursive practice—and with the visual dialogue between the student's movements—only at the end does she emerge from the cage—and the rigid or sinuous parts of the installation. Later some of them grow tired, they begin to fidget, they create sensory distractions and emotional windows in their experience. They make small noises which give others an opportunity to relax the intensity of their emotional-aesthetic concentration on the video of the performance. When the video has ended and the lights have been switched back on, the air entering the opened windows accompanies the return of speech and bodily movement among the students. Their faces turn from the screen to their neighbours, and their gazes become communicative. Someone mutters a comment, and the students slowly abandon the aesthetic-emotional state in which their attention was focused on the screen. When I ask for their 'first impressions' and 'first sensations', there is always someone who answers 'anxiety'. And to illustrate this sensation, the final vocal counterpoint is usually cited (Strati 2005: 34):

Student: Already now, rational calculation is manifest at every stage. By it, the performance of each individual worker is mathematically measured, each man becomes a little cog in the machine and, aware of this, his one preoccupation is whether he can become a bigger cog. [...] it is horrible to think that the world could one day be filled with nothing but those little cogs, little men clinging to little jobs and striving towards bigger ones [...]. This passion for bureaucracy [...] is enough to drive one to despair.

Woman teacher at the dance school: Please take care with these movements because otherwise they become mechanical, and end themselves and they become...sort of sad. Please, let things start from within, from your soul, from your body, from your heart. And always filter, always, mind, heart, body. You.

The aesthetic experience of the performance has therefore generally evoked the aesthetic category of 'tragedy', with its heroes and innocent victims; and so it was with the students on the organizational aesthetics course. In this case, too, discussion of this sensation and the other feelings aroused centred on Weber's description of the functioning principles of bureaucracy. However, even when a performance is transformed into an enduring audio-visual artefact like the video, it is still an ephemeral experience that begins and ends with it. I have never backtracked the video to the Weber extracts to discuss them with the students, although I could have done so, given the audio-visual support technology: the performance, even if video projected, has always been absorbed and experienced in its totality. Also the sensations—of seduction or anguish, for example—have always been related to the totality of the didactic experience acquired with the projection of the video, and not apart from it, even when it has been highlighted by indicating some part of it—for example, the above-mentioned final vocal counterpoint. The intensity of the aesthetic experience of the performance-based didactic device has generally subdued rational discourse therefore. And it is to this aspect, though projected against the background of doing research, that I have directed the students' attention: representation of the results of their empirical analysis could draw on the evocative process of knowledge gathering and not rely solely on the analytical-rational one.

REPRESENTING AESTHETIC OBSERVATION

The co-presence of very different styles in the same account—the style which elicits the evocative process of knowledge gathering and the one inspired by richness of analytical detail—was much discussed by the students on the organizational aesthetics course, right from the first write-up of their field notes. Indeed, representation of their ethnographic study of the Faculty of Sociology—admittedly limited to observation alone, but using their capacities for aesthetic-sensory understanding—was perhaps the issue that provoked most debate in the classroom, and in relation to:

    (a) the perceptions of each sense, isolating it from the others and then re-merging it with them, as well as the sixth sense, which is better able than the others to intuit what to do and when;

    (b) the coexistence of several languages—those of images, sounds, and speech—and their aesthetic canons;

    (c) constant redefinition of their objects of enquiry, so that what was singled out at the beginning was gradually reconfigured until it assumed the form of a plastic, malleable, collectively constructed object.

The process of experiential learning was marked by cadences and stages so that progress enriched the experience, but also to ensure that enthusiasm did not wane and that the appeal of self-conducted research and collective debate did not diminish. After the first observation, when the students themselves selected the organizational and work practices to study, they were invited to explore the faculty further for aspects unknown to them. Finally, they were asked to focus their observations on only one of the various settings selected by them and considered.

This required a change of classroom, because the students' initial observations were overlapped by the considerations, discussions, and operational choices produced by their being grouped, on a voluntary basis, into small groups or pairs according to the setting or phenomenon selected. Moreover, some sort of dialogue began between what the students were observing and their required reading texts. To be stressed is that the core of the course was still the experience of conducting the observations and representing them, not the literature. The latter furnished further participants in the dialogue, besides the students and the lecturers with whom they regularly reflected and discussed, as well as the materials for the oral examination that followed discussion of a paper produced by the students.

At the end of the course, a comment by a student further highlighted the distinctive nature of the learning experience: it was different from other kinds of workshops; the good thing about this experience was that, instead of deepening research made by others, it was the students themselves who were the protagonists of the research.

INCLUSIONS

On rereading this chapter, and on reliving, once again with pleasure, both the contentment and the delicate tragicality of certain features of these didactic experiences, I have been struck by the fact that their *dominant tonality is the performance* of teaching and learning. This has its roots in the arts, rather than in organizational theories and managements studies, although these too have dealt with performances.

The performance has gained recognition and accreditation in the arts only recently, in the 1970s during the golden age of conceptual art (Goldberg 1988/2001). It is a form of expression which *mobilizes* understandings, intuitions, and ideas in *everyday life*—of organizations in our case—where *acting and knowing are intimately bound up with each other*: two features which, as we have seen, are crucial for aesthetics in the teaching of organization studies. But there is a third, and equally important, feature of artistic performance which resides in experiences of aesthetics-based experiential learning. Since its origins in Italian futurism, in fact, the central purpose of the performance has been to involve and to surprise the audience so that it reinterprets its conceptions of art and culture. It has enhanced, that is to say, the interaction between the humans and artefacts involved in the artistic process—as did the riddle, the 'Iron Cage Performance,' and the aesthetic field observation.

But a performance requires not only active participation in altering the focal points of the interaction among the students and between students and teachers, but also careful didactic supervision by the teachers, because it turns everyday routine into something exceptional. The image that best conveys the idea is that of 'learning in the face of mystery' (Gherardi 1999), which highlights both reliance on individual aesthetic capacities to activate processes of experiential learning, and the non-prescriptive nature of learning. As the papers by the students on the Sociology of Organizations course stressed, at the beginning you do not know what is going to happen, and this causes anxiety; it is only in the course of its 'doing' that aesthetics-based experiential learning allays fears and displays knowledge richness.

REFERENCES

Barry, D. (1996). 'Artful Inquiry: A Symbolic Constructivist Approach to Social Science Research', *Qualitative Inquiry*, 2/4: 411–38.

Gagliardi, P. (ed.) (1990). *Symbols and Artifacts: Views of the Corporate Landscape*. Berlin: de Gruyter.

—— (1996). 'Exploring the Aesthetic Side of Organizational Life', in S. R. Clegg, C. Hardy, and W. R. Nord (eds.), *Handbook of Organization Studies*. London: Sage.

Gherardi, S. (1999). 'Learning as Problem-Driven or Learning in the Face of Mystery?', *Organization Studies*, 20/1: 101–24.

—— and Strati, A. (eds.) (2003). *The Iron Cage: Dialogues from Max Weber about Loris Cecchini's Installation 'Density Spectrum Zone 1.0'* [DVD/VHS, 19′]. Performance by Anna Scalfi, 2 Apr. Trento: Faculty of Sociology.

Goldberg, R. (1988/2001). *Performance Art from Futurism to the Present*. London: Thames & Hudson.

Martin, P. Y. (2002). 'Sensations, Bodies, and the "Spirit of a Place": Aesthetics in Residential Organizations for the Elderly', *Human Relations*, 55/7: 861–85.

Simmel, G. (1908). *Soziologie. Untersuchungen über die Formen der Vergesellschaftung*. Berlin: Duncker & Humblot (partial Eng. trans. by K. H. Wolff, *The Sociology of Georg Simmel*. New York: Free Press of Glencoe, 1964).

Steyaer, C., and Hjorth, D. (2002). 'Thou Art a Scholar, Speak to it . . .': On Spaces of Speech: A Script', *Human Relations*, 55/7: 767–97.

Strati, A. (1999). *Organization and Aesthetics*. London: Sage.

—— (2000). 'The Aesthetic Approach in Organization Studies', in S. Linstead and H. Höpfl (eds.), *The Aesthetic of Organization*. London: Sage.

—— (2005). 'Organizational Artifacts and the Aesthetic Approach', in A. Rafaeli and M. Pratt (eds.), *Artifacts and Organizations*. Mahwah, NJ: Lawrence Erlbaum Associates Inc.

Zucker, L. G. (1977). 'The Role of Institutionalization in Cultural Persistence', *American Sociological Review*, 42/5: 726–43.

PART II

THE DIVERSITY OF CLASSROOM EXPERIENCE

CHAPTER 5

EXPERIENTIAL LEARNING WITHOUT WORK EXPERIENCE

REFLECTING ON STUDYING AS 'PRACTICAL ACTIVITY'

KEIJO RÄSÄNEN

KIRSI KORPIAHO

INTRODUCTION

WHEN business school students do not have previous experience in professional work, which is the case in many European master's programmes, the users of experiential methods meet a serious problem (cf. Reynolds and Vince 2004). What is the 'experience' that is supposed to be reflected on and learnt from? One answer to this question is that the students' lives are full of experiences, including the experiences of studying in the business school. However, the students are inclined to say that 'the real world' is outside the university and there is nothing worth reflecting on in their pre-real-work life. Even if teachers wanted to make studying experiences an object of reflection, their students might find this an unworthy effort. This chapter reports on a partially successful effort in solving this problem.

This story is an account of a course experience in the Helsinki School of Economics (HSE). We authors organized the course, called 'Professional Development' (in Finnish *Ammattitaidon kehittäminen*, hereafter PD) in January–March 2005. What was locally exceptional in this course was that the students actually did some work in examining their own studying practices, and found the exercise meaningful. Our previous attempts to accomplish similar events have more or less failed.

The key to this partial success was the conceptual ideas that guided the way in which we organized the learning process throughout the course. This was surprising to us teachers, because we had previously believed that the learning methods are the crucial and sufficient means in accomplishing learning from experience. In this case, the success cannot be wholly attributed to the working methods of cooperative and enquiry-based learning, although they were applied in the spirit of experiential learning.

Our account suggests that both teachers and students need also suitable conceptual resources for engaging in experiential learning (cf. Cunliffe 2004). In particular, when the relevant experiences concern student life, teachers need a suitable approach to, and understanding of, studying activities and experiences. We report here what our conceptual points of departure were and how we used them in creating a space for reflection. Practice-based understandings of studying as 'practical activity' seemed to work in this case, once we found a way to translate researchers' ideas into a form that was meaningful to the students.

THE EVENT IN CONTEXT

The PD course has had a crucial position in the curriculum of the subject organization and management.[1] The students, aiming at the master's degree in the norm time of four years, have chosen their major during the second year of studies, in December. Those who have chosen organization and management have had to first participate in the obligatory PD course. This course was launched in 2001 to serve as a key, introductory part of the discipline's programme.[2]

Since the first round, the purposes of the course have been many-sided and somewhat ambiguous. Teachers have agreed that it should work as an introduction to the discipline-specific studies and 'community', especially in regard to working methods, and also aid the students in planning their studies. The originators' idea was also that the course would serve students in approaching professional jobs and tasks, that is, the development of professional skills for further use after their studies. Several members of the staff believed that the concept of 'reflective practice' covered some of the skills needed, and they hoped that the course would teach the practices of reflection. In addition, quite a few teachers wanted to teach critical stances to managerial practice, although the staff never made an overall decision to educate the students into a 'critical management studies' approach. The ambiguity concerning the purposes has partly been due to the unit's diversity in terms of research and teaching interest, but it was also due to the originators' inability to design such a new and different course.

The PD course has been run by a varying combination of teachers. Keijo Räsänen[3] was one of the three teachers who planned and organized the first round in 2001. For him, the first round confirmed the need for this course, but the team did not really find a proper concept for it. The teachers did not doubt the learning methods used, because they had been involved in bringing in various new methods since the mid 1990s. After the first round, other teacher pairs developed the course, but they also did not quite come to a satisfactory idea of what the focus and content of the course should be. In the late 2004 Keijo Räsänen and Kirsi Korpiaho started to plan the 2005 course round, and they got a new idea.

The teachers of the PD course had been struggling with the basic problem of experiential learning methods with students who come to the business school directly from the high school. They do not have experience from 'professional' jobs, but value such experience highly. Consequently, they devalue academic studies as something 'theoretical' and out of touch with 'the real life'. Previous attempts to lead them into a reflective stance concerning their own experiences and studies have met attitudes of indifference or even resistance. The students ask: 'Why should we waste time in talking about our own studies and business-school experiences, when we want to learn tools that are needed in real work and valued by the employers?'

The question has been especially difficult for the teachers of organization and management, because the subject is not respected highly by the younger students as to its 'practicality' and value in terms of the managerial labour market (cf. Burke and Moore 2003). Most of the graduates from the subject have been happy with their choice, but newcomers raise serious questions of what they can actually learn and gain by choosing this particular field of study. The doubts are supported by the students' moral order in HSE, that is, the stories students circulate on what they consider 'good' and 'bad' in studying (Leppälä and Päiviö 2001; Päiviö 2005). In these accounts, keen interests in reflection, serious thinking, research, and theory are rather presented as vices than virtues. However, in certain majors like economics and management, students need to develop modifications to the general beliefs, making vices reminiscent of virtues. The PD course could, in principle, provide a good site for starting or advancing this slow process.

THINKING UNDERPINNING THE EVENT

The new concept for the course was based on research work in progress. The two teachers have been members of a researcher group called Management Education Research Initiative—MERI. The group had just been keenly interested in 'theories of practice' (see, for example, Nicolini, Gherardi, and Yanow 2003; Schatzki 2001; MacIntyre 1981; Räsänen et al. 2005), and Keijo and Kirsi came to the conclusion that they would apply this line of thinking to the PD course. That is, studies and studying would be treated from a practice-based approach.

The basic idea and approach can be summarized in the following way. (a) Students' activities at the university are understood as participation in 'study practices'. Instead of framing studying merely in terms of a learning rhetoric, this view presents studying first and foremost as practical activity, that is, concrete doings and everyday experiences. (b) Students' learning is approached in terms of 'situated learning' (Lave and Wenger 1991). This conception of learning is congruent with the basic view: learning means entry into and engagement in new, specific practices and relationships. (c) Professional development means entry into and participation in consequent sets of practices, ranging from study practice to subject-unit-specific 'academic practices' and business graduates' 'professional practices' in other workplaces. (d) In studies, one can learn to rehearse 'reflective practice', which will help in learning the professional practices when entering new workplaces and jobs later on.

Taken together, the propositions suggested a new way of framing what the PD course is about and how it serves the students'—and the teachers'—interests. It is important to notice that the teachers did not assume that the students are engaging in similar practices to the members of the local academic unit in organization and management. Quite the contrary, the teachers wanted to create a space where the students could think through and discuss if and how they want to become involved in what the academics do, that is, engage in practices that may be considered morally questionable or at least 'useless' by some other students. Hence the *distinction between studying practices and academic practices* (see Figure 5.1). This distinction signalled a point of reflection and choice for the students. Concretely, do they want to approach and trust the teachers and let them lead in the process of learning disciplinary practices?

As to the method of experiential learning, the distinctions between various sets of practices opened up the possibility to choose what is to be reflected on in the course. While only a few of the students at HSE have experience of professional practice typical of business graduates, they are all practitioners in 'doing their studies'. *Thus, the study practices are the only shared basis of experience and possible object for joint reflection.*

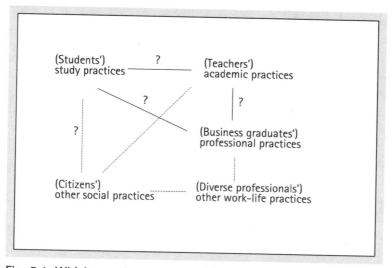

Fig. 5.1 Which practices are we talking about?
Source: Material of the PD course translated from Finnish.

There remained three difficult questions as to the use of this basic idea in organizing the course. First, how to translate the difficult 'theoretical' concept of practice entertained by the teachers and make it understandable and usable for the students. Secondly, how to teach them what the basic conceptual ideas of the course are, while the perspective is not familiar to them. Thirdly, how the teachers' frame of interpretation can be used in providing students with specific opportunities to study and reflect on their own experiences of studying.

On the basis of ongoing research on academic work and previous research in managerial work (see, for example, Räsänen et al. 2005; Räsänen 2005; Eriksson and Räsänen 1998; Räsänen, Meriläinen, and Lovio 1995), the teachers were able to present a particular version of the concept of practice. In this three-stance construct, any social and embodied 'practical activity' can be understood as dealing with the following three issues: how to do it, what to do, why do it and in this way?[4] These three stances towards an activity were named for the course as the 'tactical perspective' of how, the 'strategic perspective' of what, and the 'moral perspective' of why.[5]

In recent research texts, the teachers have used the term 'stance' rather than the term 'perspective' (in Finnish *näkökulma*), but they believed that the business students find it easier to use the latter term. For the same reason, they decided to label the second perspective 'strategic' instead of 'political'. As it would not serve the purpose of this story, the specific practice concept and the three stances cannot be opened up in detail here. It would require a discussion of the works by Michel de Certeau (on tactics), Pierre Bourdieu (on politics as proper positions), and Alasdair MacIntyre (on morals). In fact, the teachers did not take up the intellectual roots of the concept during the course either, and they had to invent another way to introduce what the term practice might mean. In HSE one cannot expect that students have read or will read social scientific literature, except for master's theses in a few cases.

Consequently, the course was organized according to the three perspectives to practical activity, which in this case was studying in the business school. The programme was planned to treat the following questions and in this particular order:

(a) Tactical perspective: *How can I perform my studies in organization and management? (That is, how can I pass courses—with satisfactory grade points?)*

(b) Strategic perspective: *What can I accomplish and achieve in my studies in HSE? (That is, what can I study in HSE?)*

(c) Moral perspective: *Why am I studying in HSE and in a certain way?*

The order was considered crucial. The teachers assumed that the students should be interested at least in the first question. They probably want to pass exams, and value the treatment of 'practical' how-questions. The second question may be more difficult. According to the teachers' previous experience, HSE students do not necessarily have clear plans for the studies as a whole, are bound by various practicalities preventing goal-focused action, and talk only about instrumental goals if any. As to the moral issues, the teachers were not at all sure if the students were willing and actually able to share their thoughts with the other students and the teachers. Anyway, trying it felt important. As a whole this order of proceeding seemed possible, realistic, and promising.

As to the problem of how to teach the basic ideas, the duo chose a rather traditional approach. In the beginning of the course they gave a lecture on the basic concepts: practice; situated learning; reflective practice. They also described how the concepts were to be used in the course. Moreover, they asked the students to read a text on each of the basic concepts (Brown and Duguid 1991; Tiuraniemi 1994; Atherton 2003) and search for 'resources' on the approach. The texts and resources were used in the consequent session as a basis for learning tasks, the purpose of which was to check that all the students had got a grasp of the starting points.

Brown and Duguid's article was chosen because it outlines in an accessible and attractive way the concept of community of practice, and thereby introduced a conception of practice to the students. Even if some of the students found this framework attractive, one dilemma remained: the students seemed to be attracted especially by the idea of community, while the teachers wanted to highlight and illuminate the relevance of practices and saw the term community as problematic (Eriksson et al. 1996; cf. Reynolds 2000). Especially when the focus is on relationships amongst the students or teachers, it is problematic to assume, or propagate, the existence of communities in a strict sense, but the teachers chose not bring up these complications as the point was in making practices worth their attention. And indeed, it turned out that the students found it at first difficult to understand what the teachers were after when they were speaking about practices. However, the next phases of the course made the perplexing starting points more understandable.

In treating the three main issues, one by one, the teachers used roughly the following script: first, they presented an orientation to the issue, saying what was at stake in this particular issue. Secondly, they provided the students with some 'resources' that can help in thinking about the issue, and asked them also to search for and collect their own resources for dealing with the issue. Thirdly, the issues were discussed in the sessions in terms of learning tasks based on preparatory work. And finally, the students wrote (individually): one personal text after each part of the course; a report on study skills (and their development); a study plan (with arguments for their choices); and an essay treating any issue considered personally relevant by a student.

The working methods were based on a combination of lecturing and reading tasks, cooperative learning, enquiry-based learning, and action learning. In this sense there was nothing new in the course in comparison to other courses arranged by the disciplinary unit during the last ten years. However, there was one minor deviation: in the PD course the teachers gave more emphasis on work done individually, i.e. privately, than in some other courses that are based strongly on collaborative work and on the assessment of accomplishments by groups. The assumption was that some of the issues are so difficult and even threatening that the students do not want to discuss them in groups composed of other, so far unfamiliar students. However, this did not solve the problem if they did not trust the teachers either.

LINKS TO DEBATES ABOUT EXPERIENTIAL LEARNING

While working methods of the course add nothing new to discussions about experiential learning, the specific conceptual solution may help in paying attention to some tricky issues in how to learn from experience in a business school.

The main point is that the idea of experiential learning can work only if it concerns what can be called 'authentic' experiences (cf. Tochon 2000; Edwards 2005: 7). The course concept was an answer to the tricky question of what to reflect on, when the young students do not have work experience in professional tasks. The solution is to draw on the fact that the students have experience of participating in the study practices. As practitioners of studies in higher education they share this common ground of experience, and these experiences are as authentic as any experiences can be.[6] They can also be different within a group of students.

The key problem with this idea is that students may not see the point in focusing on their everyday life as students. It has to be made somehow problematic and interesting for them, before they want to take part in the rather demanding exercises. The proposed solution was to start from the issues that the business school students usually consider relevant by necessity, namely being able to perform in a highly competitive and stressing context. If they feel that they learn something 'useful' in this stage of the course, they will probably be more interested in approaching the two other questions as well.

While reflection is considered an essential moment in experiential learning (Roberts 1996: 67), one can ask: where do the resources needed in reflection come from (cf. Guile 2003: 98)? Especially if the objective is to expand the resource base, how can it be done? During the course, the teachers both told about their ways of understanding studies as practical activity and guided the students in finding themselves new resources on the issues defined by the teachers. However, the success of the concept depends on the reception of the starting points: is the practice-based world-view acceptable, understandable, and interesting enough to the students?

In this case, the teachers relied on their previous experience of what might be possible with the students in HSE. While most students consider any interest in 'theory' morally dubious (Leppälä and Päiviö 2001), some students had already found the communities of practice approach interesting in their master's thesis projects. As a graduate said after finishing her thesis: 'Now I finally have a perspective of my own, from which I can communicate with the engineers in my workplace.' Although the approach questions some of the basic, taken for granted assumptions of a manager-centred world-view, it can be used to advance various interests. The two teachers thus tried to both provide the students with new, usable resources and let them make their own, individual choices as to the tactics, politics, and morals of studying. For instance, a study plan arguing well for specific instrumental or reputational goals could gain high points in assessment.

EXPERIENCES OF TUTORS AND STUDENTS

Overall the course was received positively, and it seemed to serve its now redefined purpose. However, the course cannot be considered a complete success, because there are better (elective) courses available in the subject's programme, at least according to the student feedback for this first round.

Thirty-four students participated in and passed the course. Students' experiences can be documented in two ways: (a) the kind of insights and conclusions they presented in the written reports—this tells something about the nature of their 'reflective' accomplishments during the course; (b) students' feedback asked for with two forms—the official feedback form of HSE and a form designed specifically for this event.

As to the teachers' experiences, we can speak for ourselves. For the two teachers the situation was very different in respect to previous experience in teaching tasks. The senior teacher had been teaching in HSE since 1979. He had been involved in a process of bringing in new learning methods, renewing several courses, establishing new ones, and revising the subject curriculum. For the junior teacher this was the first course for which she was fully responsible together with the senior teacher. Consequently, the experiences were different.

STUDENTS' 'EXPERIENCES'

The teachers have no direct access to the students' diverse experiences. However, it is possible to document what kind of thoughts they expressed in their written reports. In particular, we will give examples of what they presented as new ideas or conclusions from the exercises, and what we teachers found interesting in their reports.

In general, the written reports and essays contained richer and more fine-grained lines of thought than the oral conversations in the classroom. The texts were written individually, knowing that only the two teachers will read them, while in the sessions thoughts were shared with the other students, either in triads or in the whole group. The contents of the reports indicates that the course offered an opportunity to discuss and think about questions that are otherwise left unattended. They actually came to think of their own ways of engaging in the study practices. Here we can give only a few examples of insights and conclusions considered important by the students.

There were interesting differences in the students' ability and willingness to artic-ulate uncertainties and commitments across the three basic issues and perspectives: how, what, and why. Several students gained new ideas from the treatment of the *tactical* issue of how to study and perform in examinations. They became aware of the accessible resources concerning study skills, although there were significant differences in their efforts to search for the resources. They were able to list, and in some cases even frame, the skills needed in studying, as well as choose a skill that was personally critical and in need of development.

In the first assignment on 'how to study', the students chose to write about diverse skills, but the most favoured one was 'time management'. For example, one of the students noticed that the lack of time management is not really the problem but rather a symptom of something else:

Time management alone was too broad a definition to describe my real study problems. And as I ploughed through the 'study skills' pages in the Internet, I came across the term procrastination. This term appears in several Internet pages and there are even articles written about it. As I read more about this term and got more familiar with it, I realized that, although there surely are lots to improve in my time management skills, my real problem was procrastination. After this long process of getting acquainted with diverse study skills, I decided to choose time management and especially getting rid of procrastination as a focus of my deeper reflection.

However, the students presented very few ideas of how to go about improving a certain skill by themselves, possibly because their expectation has been that this is a task for the teachers. Another interesting point is that the students seemed to be hesitant in revealing to the teachers in detail what tactics they used in passing the courses. This interpretation is based on the fact that a different picture emerges in a study of the students' conversations in 'their own' media, namely the student union's internet forum (Korpiaho 2005).

The *strategic* issues were harder to reflect on. Planning studies is in itself a justified task and expectation in HSE, but there are a few major difficulties in this respect: the students say that any opportunities in the curricula are difficult to grasp, and many students talk only about instrumental, labour market-oriented goals. As the teachers brought in material that opened up the possibility that HE could also serve other than employment interests, several students recognized this view but explicitly argued for their 'practical' interests. This is why they are in the business school. However, there were a number of students who took the opportunity and expressed their feeling of being 'different' from the majority of HSE students.

In the second assignment on 'what to study', students wrote about their own study plans and presented arguments to support their choices. The essays were quite long and many of them very personal. Many of them reported on feelings of being different and trying to find one's own place within the students' circles. The following excerpt is from the essay where a student who feels herself deviant from the mainstream students reflects on her choices. This essay is especially fascinating because a reader can see that the author has revisited the paper and rewritten the end of it.

I have known from the beginning that I am not interested in mainstream business subjects, like accounting, finance or marketing. I knew that I have to find my motivation to perform obligatory courses elsewhere. In the beginning of my studies my goal was to perform these courses with satisfactory grades in order to study later on what I was really interested in. . . .

This year I applied for IDBM (international design business management)—programme. That feels almost too good to be true . . . .

I have learnt that in my lifetime I won't be able to please everyone around me; instead I go crazy and feel exhausted in trying to do so. This is why it is important to me, not for the sake of others, to justify and analyze my own choices. . . .

Now rereading this paper I realize that I really want to continue my studies after gradua-tion and apply for an MBA-programme in Milan, Italy. This MBA-programme feels already like my own thing. After getting this idea, studying, graduating and getting a job doesn't feel distressing anymore, since now I know that I have an opportunity to continue my studies—and additionally, I know where and when.

In another excerpt, the student reports on difficulties of being and maintaining a sense of 'self' in the relations with other business students.

During the time of major selection everybody seemed to think only about the money they could earn from different jobs. It took long for me to decide what to choose as my major: all the so called hard majors felt somehow false, that is if I had chosen one of those subjects, I would have deceived myself and other people involved in those subjects. The decision that I chose Organization and Management as my major was a concession to me, because I knew I wouldn't be happy working with numbers or curves. Until that moment, I had been convincing myself that I could work as accountant and that I could do brilliantly for example in Finance. Of course this was not the case....
Now I feel I have made a right choice. My goal is not a certain job, company or title. My goal is more like a state of mind, where I, and others, see and feel that I am 'the woman in the right place'. I want to do things in life that I enjoy and appreciate. For me, work is a big part of my identity.

In any case, the 'strategy' part of the course induced the students to think of and articulate their plans for several years ahead, which was the first time for many of them, as formal study plans had not been obligatory in HSE before the academic year 2005/6. Thinking and articulating what one can, and wants to, accomplish and achieve in the degree studies was something new to almost all of the students.
The *moral* stance was inspiring especially for some older students, in contrast to those who had entered the university immediately after high school. What seemed to focus attention and provide a point of reference for saying something about the vices and virtues of studying was a reading used in the course. Leppälä and Päiviö's (2001) report on the moral order in HSE evoked comments, as it has done in many other forums too. Some students want to defend the existing order, while some others are ashamed of, and want to distance themselves from, the instrumental values reproduced in students' conversations.
The following excerpt expresses an insight on how values—both personal and those of business education—are interwoven with the process of performing and developing certain study skills and with the participation in educational practices.

I realized that reading for exams is problem to me in many ways. First of all I have troubles in starting to read and concentrating on the text because I cannot make the anxiety and feeling of inadequacy, that hurry creates, go away. My reading also remains often [at a] superficial level because of the mismatch between my personal values and implicit values in required materials. I also fear that if I concentrate too much on studying, it becomes the most important thing in my life again.

Overall, the issue of why to study and in a certain way was not taken with a similar keen interest to the two other perspectives. One obvious reason for this fact may be that writing about the moral questions was not required as were the reports on

Table 5.1 Students' evaluation of the course

	1–2	3	4–5
Conceptual points of departure	1	3	22
Success in treating personal experiences	2	5	19
Improved understanding of studying	0	5	21
Impact on motivation	2	11	12
Implementation of the concept	1	4	21
Need for the course			
O and M	2	1	23
HSE	3	6	17

Questions (with numerical scales, 1–5):

1. The teachers chose to base the course on a conception of 'studying as practical activity' (practice). They said at the beginning of the course what they meant by practical activity, situated learning, and reflective practice. The course proceeded by treating studying from tactical, strategic, and moral perspectives.
   How good was this point of departure in your own experience? (Scale 1–5, from weak to excellent)
2. To what extent did the course succeed in treating things and issues that belong to your own world of experience? (From weak to excellent)
3. Did the course help you in understanding your studies in new ways? (From not at all to significantly)
4. Did the course influence your motivation to study? (From not at all to significantly)
5. How good was the implementation of the course concept? (From weak to excellent)
6. To what extent is there a need for this kind of a course? (From not all to strong)
   (a) In the programme of organization and management.
   (b) In HSE otherwise

Note: Numerical items in the form designed by the teachers of the course; n = 26.

skills and plans. It was an optional topic in the final essay. As one student said in the class: 'I can talk about morals for five minutes, but I don't want to write an essay on them.'

As to the 'feedback' collected in the end of the course, it seems that the course fulfilled the teachers' main hopes. Almost all of the students came to reflect on their studies as a form of practical activity. Answers to the questions posed in the form crafted by the teachers for this particular event show that there were only a small number of students who did not find the concept meaningful (see Table 5.1, reporting responses to four questions). Of the thirty-four students that participated in the course, twenty-six were present in the last session and filled in the form.

According to the numbers, twenty-two of the twenty-six students assessed the concept favourably. Only two of them did not feel that the course touched their lived experience and five others chose to mark the medium value for this question. Moreover, twenty-three of the students seemed to consider the course important rather than useless for studies in the major. This can be considered a success in respect to the teachers' goals, especially when the course was about something that goes against the moral order; that is, the course was focused on studying practices and on reflective activities (cf. Leppälä and Päiviö 2005).

Those who did not appreciate the course wrote, for instance:

The course was impractical, for example theory of practice?!!

The Tactic dimension was very distressing and unclear.

Those who found the course beneficial wrote, for example:

This course helped me to look for and to find direction to my studies—and to my future choices.

This clarified my own thinking about my studying practices and my goals.

Reflective practice has really been stored in my subconscious. I have noticed that nowadays I tend to reflect on my entire life constantly...It is good thing that we concentrated on studying issues, because they are not dealt with elsewhere.

Learning this kind of a reflective practice helped me to question and develop my thinking.

Personally, I want to thank you for giving this wonderful opportunity to stop and reflect upon some of the current and important issues of contemporary life.

However, the course was only a partial success, because (a) some of the participants did not find the course useful and meaningful, and (b) there are (smaller, elective, if not mandatory) courses in organization and management that receive higher points in the official feedback forms. Responses to the formal feedback form used in HSE gave the average points 5.83 (on the scale 1–7) to the question concerning the overall quality of the course. During the academic year 2004/5, the average for all courses in the subject was 5.6, and for all courses in HSE 5.4. There remains work to be done in improving the way the basic concept is used, but the concept itself seemed to be promising.

Tutors' Different Experiences

For the two tutors, the course was an important and meaningful experience. It was meaningful academic work, and an experience of collaboration—and also of joint risk taking that ended rather well. The teachers found it important that they could integrate their research work with the teaching task, and in a way that was also found sensible by the students. They were able to use an emerging conception of practice as a basis for organizing interaction with the students.

However, differences in starting points colour the interpretations. Räsänen et al. (2005) provide two different types of narrative of the teachers' experiences. On the one hand, the course can be presented as a further step in a series of innovative moves in improving local teaching and learning practices. The course added a new theoretical twist to these developments.

On the other hand, the course can be accounted for as a personal experience of working in academia. For the senior colleague, the course tested his motivation to continue a long-term struggle for teachers' autonomous development work, and under increasing pressure from enforced, top-down changes. Although the course was a fresh opportunity to realize his ideals of proper management education, he had to deal with his fatigue and frustration. For the junior colleague, teaching her first course, it was about entering a professionally crucial set of practices. For her, the themes of the course were not only related to her ongoing research project, but also to her situation (and learning) as a novice teacher. Teaching only a few years after her graduation, and as a doctoral student, she was acutely aware of being in the middle of two positions: a student and a teacher. Moreover, she had to pay most attention to the question of 'how' in carrying out the new teacher's role and, simultaneously, facilitate students' discussion on the 'how', 'what', and 'why' questions. Fortunately, the conceptual ideas of the course brought resources that helped her in meeting the challenges of reflexivity. As she wrote afterwards (Räsänen et al. 2005: 260): 'I lived the theory.'

CONCLUSION

The event storied here pays attention to a specific but important aspect of experiential learning in management education in the higher education context. When the students do not have extended experience from working life, teachers have to consider other sources of experience. One alternative is to focus on students' experiences of studying, and our account reports on an attempt at doing so. The PD course was based on the view that studying can and should be understood as an interesting form of practical activity among others. The art is in how to make their everyday life feel and look interesting and important enough to deserve reflective attention.

The key element in the solution was to apply a particular, three-perspective conception of practice (Räsänen et al. 2005; Räsänen 2005). Even if the construct of tactical, strategic, and moral stances in practical activity is still in a state of emergence, it guided the planning of the learning process well enough. The participants found the course meaningful and useful.

We suggest that theories of practice provide, in principle, a source of resources, when teachers want to create a motivating space for discussions on how, what, and why business school students learn—and want to learn. However, teachers need to find a way to build the theoretical ideas into their course design and into the learning tasks, that is, to practise what they preach.

Drawing on the practice-based approaches may also be an avenue for attempts to meet the ambitions of 'critical management education'. The course experience evokes two related conclusions in this respect. The first of these concerns the ways in which teachers lead students to approach such complicated and contested concepts as practice. The second concerns ways in which critically oriented teachers can contextualize power issues in various substantive topics.

The decisions to introduce practice-theoretic thinking through the 'community of practice' approach can be considered a matter of pragmatics, of sensitivity as to the local context. We teachers still think that this was a sensible move, because any practice ontology is hard to learn, especially for students who have already learnt to reproduce the theory/practice dualism with its political implications. While the 'communities of practice' stream of practice-based theorizing has recently divided researchers into two camps, one favouring a consulting-oriented rhetoric and the other one emphasizing power aspects (Wenger, McDermott, and Snyder 2002; cf. Contu and Willmott 2003; Vann and Bowker 2001), students who are familiar with the approach are one step nearer to making personal choices in this respect. Once they have questioned the taken for granted premiss that all the wisdom resides in managers' heads, they have stepped away from the 'managerial point of view': they have thought, for a moment at least, that managers are not the only knowers and knowledge is not necessarily in any heads. If the communities of practice vocabulary can aid in this move, why would we not use this particular version of practice thinking in teaching? The vocabulary is accessible just because of this possibility for multiple uses. Once the interest exists, learning can proceed towards more challenging forms of thinking, according to the choices of each individual student and her or his political drives.

Another conclusion in relation to critical management education concerns the applicability of the three-stance conception of practice in other courses and contexts. The course design, based on this conception, allowed for the treatment of tactical, political, and moral issues, and in a way that touched the students' everyday life and left the choices to the students themselves. This should be relevant for those who ask about the ethics of critical management studies and education (Wray-Bliss 2002; Fenwick 2005). Their concern stems from the fact that the advocates of critical management studies have been primarily concerned about political issues and explanations, especially power and social domination. When a part of these scholars have taken seriously the challenges of education and committed themselves to experiments with new pedagogical ideas and practices, they cannot but notice that teaching or any other practical activity is not only about politics (Roberts 1996; Cunliffe, Forray and Knights 2002).

The students, in particular, may experience that they have serious problems with various tactical or technical demands, as well as with various ethical issues that cannot be easily transformed into questions of politics. The same goes for the teachers, too. Therefore, the three-stance conception of practice could be taken as a device for the articulation of tactical, political, and moral concerns, and of complications between them. The advantage of this solution would then be in the possibility of explicitly dealing with the various stances in relation to each other. For instance, political issues could be related to an actor's skills in doing something specific and to her or his moral concerns or motives. Or, moral issues could be connected to political situations and tactical possibilities. The latter idea might in fact result in a specific way of teaching business ethics. And more generally, various substantive issues in management curricula might benefit from approaching them as 'practical activity' with its moral, political, and tactical issues. Why would this not be worth trying?

NOTES

Other members of the MERI researcher group at HSE have influenced this story in various, positive ways. Thank you to Hanna Päiviö, Hans Mäntylä, and Anne Herbert. We are also grateful to the students who participated in the course storied in this texts. A grant (no. 108645) from the Academy of Finland aided Keijo Räsänen's work in writing this piece.

1. Due to the Bologna process, the degree structures and programmes are currently changing. The new rules were followed for the first time during the academic year 2005/6.
2. The subject's curriculum was renewed gradually since 1999, as an autonomous and collective initiative by the unit's staff. The Bologna process, combined with other changes in HSE, destroyed some of the key accomplishments of this movement, and surely delayed many intended improvements. For instance, there is no space for the PD course in the new structure of two separate and shorter degrees (B.Sc. and M.Sc., 3+2 years), while in the old curriculum the students aiming at the master's degree had ahead three to four more years of studies after the PD course.
3. We refer also to ourselves, the authors of this text, in the third person in order to make clear whose experiences, thoughts, and deeds we are representing in each point. In accounting for collective efforts it is important not to assume consensus and shared interpretations, and the term 'we' may obscure differences.
4. The 'why question' is unavoidably twofold: it can concern either the goals or the means of an activity. The classical example of this is the reappearing debates on whether good intentions justify whatever (corrupt or violent) means. Procedural vs. outcomes-based conceptions of justice offer another example of discussions on the same theme. In the course, the teachers let the students focus on what they considered relevant without forcing attention on both sides of the issue.
5. For the sake of simplicity, the teachers only mentioned a fourth issue of 'who I am', that is, the issue of identity. They suggested that the answer to the 'who' question is accomplished by getting to know how to do, what to do, and why to do it in a certain way. They had in mind a 'doing identity' approach to the concept of identity. It was difficult enough to deal with the three questions, and the integration of the identity question to the course concept was left to further experiments.
6. This starting point does not preclude other sources of experience. Studying can be reflected in a way that appreciates what these young adults have gone through in

other spheres of life, and even their orientation towards the 'real', but so far unknown 'working life'.

REFERENCES

Atherton, J. S. (2003). 'Doceo: Competence, Proficiency and Beyond'. [On-line] UK. Available at: www.doceo.co.uk/background/expertise.htm.

Brown, J. S., and Duguid, P. (1991). 'Organizational Learning and Communities of Practice', *Organization Science*, 12/1: 40–57.

Burke, L. A., and Moore, J. E. (2003). 'A Perennial Dilemma in OB Education: Engaging the Traditional Student', *Academy of Management Learning and Education*, 2/1: 37–52.

Contu, A., and Willmott, H. (2003). 'Re-embedding Situatedness: The Importance of Power Relations in Learning Theory', *Organization Science*, 14/3: 283–96.

Cunliffe, A. (2004). 'On Becoming a Critically Reflexive Practitioner', *Journal of Management Education*, 28/4: 407–26.

—— Forray, J., and Knights, D. (2002). 'Considering Management Education: Insights from Critical Management Studies', *Journal of Management Education*, 26/5: 489–95.

Edwards, R. (2005). 'Learning in Context: Within and Across Domains'. Paper presented to ESRC Teaching and Learning Research Programme (TLRP) Thematic Seminar Series 'Contexts, Communities, Networks: Mobilising Learners' Resources and Relationships in Different Domains', Seminar One, Glasgow, 15–16 Feb. Retrieved 29 Nov. 2005 from: crll.gcal.ac.uk/docs/TLRP_ContextSeminars/TLRP_ContxtSem1_Edwards.doc.

Eriksson, P., and Räsänen, K. (1998). 'The Bitter and the Sweet: Evolving Constellations of Product Mix Management in a Confectionery Company', *European Journal of Marketing*, 32/3–4: 279–304.

—— Fowler, C., Whipp, R., and Räsänen, K. (1996). 'Business Communities in the European Confectionery Sector: A UK–Finland Comparison', *Scandinavian Journal of Management*, 12/4: 359–87.

Fenwick, T. (2005). 'Ethical Dilemmas of Critical Management Education: Within Classrooms and Beyond', *Management Learning*, 36/1: 31–48.

Guile, D. (2003). 'From "Credentialism" to the "Practice of Learning": Reconceptualising Learning for the Knowledge Economy', *Policy Futures in Education*, 1/1: 83–105.

Korpiaho, K. (2005). 'Students' Curriculum: What Do the Students Learn in the Business School?', in S. Gherardi and D. Nicolini (eds.), *The Passion for Learning and Knowing*. Trento: University of Trento e-books, vol. i. Available in e-form at: www4.soc.unitn.it:8080/dsrs/OLK6/content/e1220/Volume_1_ita.pdf.

Lave, J., and Wenger, E. (1991). *Situated Learning: Legitimate Peripheral Participation*. Cambridge: Cambridge University Press.

Leppälä, K., and Päiviö, H. (2001). *Kauppatieteiden opiskelijoiden moraalijärjestys: Narratiivinen tutkimus kolmen eri pääaineen opiskelusta Helsingin kauppa-korkeakoulussa*. Helsinki: Publications of the Helsinki School of Economics and Business Administration B-34.

MacIntyre, A. (1981). *After Virtue: A Study in Moral Theory*. Notre Dame, Ind.: University of Notre Dame Press.

Nicolini, D., Gherardi, S., and Yanow, D. (2003). 'Introduction: Towards a Practice-Based View of Knowing and Learning in Organizations', in D. Nicolini, S. Gherardi, and

D. Yanow (eds.), *Knowing in Organizations: A Practice-Based Approach*. Armonk, NY: M. E. Sharpe.

Päiviö, H. (2005). 'The Moral Order(s) of Studying at the Business School'. Paper presented to the 18th CHER Annual Conference 'Higher Education: The Cultural Dimension: Innovative Cultures, Norms and Values', University of Jyväskylä, 1–3 Sept. 2005.

Räsänen, K. (2005). 'Rehearsing Meaningful Academic Practice: Mission Impossible?' Paper presented to the symposium 'Universities as Worksites', 4th International Conference on Researching Work and Learning, Sydney, 11–14 Dec.

—— Meriläinen, S., and Lovio, R. (1995). 'Pioneering Descriptions of Corporate Greening: Notes and Doubts on the Emerging Discussion', *Business Strategy and the Environment*, 3/4: 9–16.

—— Korpiaho, K., Herbert, A., Mäntylä, H., and Päiviö, H. (2005). 'Emerging Academic Practice: Tempered Passions in the Renewal of Academic Work', in S. Gherardi and D. Nicolini (eds.), *The Passion for Learning and Knowing*. Trento: University of Trento e-books, vol. i. Available at: htttp://eprints.biblio.unitn.it/archive/00000828/.

Reynolds, M. (2000). 'Bright Lights and the Pastoral Idyll: Ideas of Community Underlying Management Education Methodologies', *Management Learning*, 31/1: 67–81.

—— and Vince, R. (2004). 'Critical Management Education and Action-Based Learning: Synergies and Contradictions', *Academy of Management Learning and Education*, 3/4: 442–56.

Roberts, J. (1996). 'Management Education and the Limits Technical Rationality: The Conditions and Consequences of Management Practice', in R. French and C. Grey (eds.), *Rethinking Management Education*. London: Sage.

Schatzki, T. (2001). 'Introduction: Practice Theory', in T. Schatzki, K. Knorr-Cetina, and E. von Savigny (eds.), *The Practice Turn in Contemporary Theory*. London: Routledge.

Tiuraniemi, J. (1994). 'Reflektiivisen ammattikäytännön käsitteestä'. Publications of the Centre for Extension Education, University of Turku. Available at: http://users.utu.fi/juhtiur/reflektio.htm.

Tochon, F. (2000). 'When Authentic Experiences Are "Enminded" into Disciplinary Genres: Crossing Biographic and Situated Knowledge', *Learning and Instruction*, 10/4: 331–59.

Vann, K., and Bowker, G. C. (2001). 'Instrumentalizing the Truth of Practice', *Social Epistemology*, 15/3: 247–62.

Wenger, E., McDermott, R., and Snyder, W. (2002). *Cultivating Communities of Practice: A Guide to Managing Knowledge*. Cambridge, Mass.: Harvard Business School Press.

Wray-Bliss, E. (2002). 'Abstract Ethics, Embodied Ethics: The Strange Marriage of Foucault and Positivism in Labour Process Theory', *Organization*, 9/1: 5–39.

CHAPTER 6

MAKING A DRAMA OUT OF A CRISIS? 'PERFORMATIVE LEARNING' IN THE POLICE SERVICE

RUTH COLQUHOUN

NELARINE CORNELIUS

MERETTA ELLIOT

AMAR MISTRY

STEPHEN SMITH

INTRODUCTION

POLICE station custody suites are subject to intense scrutiny, particularly through the UK Police and Criminal Evidence Act (PACE). Custody decisions are governed by myriad mandatory and discretionary regulations. Custody Sergeants must be conversant and comfortable with these regulations. They also need the nous to handle the emotions and the multiple dangers entailed by detention.

All sergeants must work as Custody Sergeants eventually. Although there is good training in the regulations and their interpretation, there is relatively little concerning the lively and complex interpersonal dynamics generated in custody, nor on their impact on decisions. Experience 'at the deep end' and informal knowledge sharing has been the main safeguard of good practice, which partly explains why few officers look forward to their stint as Custody Sergeants. Moreover specialization and accelerated promotion mean that many sergeants come to custody work with incomplete appreciation of the police process, full understanding of which is essential to wise decisions. When the cells are full, the combination of volume, complexity, and speed is intimidating. A 'Q-night' is preferred.[1]

Police cells present officers with a semi-scripted theatre in which they gauge their performance while under the gaze of many others. Get it wrong and the result can be catastrophic in terms of duty of care to detained persons and to justice. The way actors learn stagecraft has special practical relevance to officers. We will explain how 'performative learning' makes immediate sense in enabling Duty Sergeants to excel. This requires a learning laboratory including an imitation *custody suite* in which sergeants get a feel for how to *play* the role. We developed realistic simulations incorporating use of a front desk, four police cells, actual sergeants and arresting officers, with detained persons (DPs) played by actors—drama students who have researched and developed 'back stories' to inform their performances. These facilitate flowing enactment and convincing improvisation. Each 'circumstance of arrest' was devised by one of the authors: a sergeant with considerable custody experience.

The booking-ins were videoed for later analysis. One author undertook non-participant observation of three late shifts in real custody suites, partly to gauge the similarity between live 'booking-ins' (the initial registration of detained persons by the Custody Sergeant) and the simulations. No two booking-ins are ever identical; nevertheless 'life imitated art' closely. The simulations proved realistic in terms of the 'emotion work' performed by DPs and the 'emotional labour' enacted by Custody Sergeants. But reviews of the video coverage showed we had underestimated the impact of arresting officers in cooling down (or heating up) each turn of events. We argue that performative training develops practical appreciation of interactions between diverse DPs, Custody Sergeants, arresting officers, and the complex regulations governing custody. Indeed performative learning offers similar advantages to most front-line professions.

PERFORMATIVE LEARNING

Experiential learning involves use of the body as an investigative tool and as a repository for felt knowledge known-in-the-bones. Not all experiential learning involves *doing something to somebody, in the company of another*, or *someone doing something back* in a challenging way. Police 'do things to others' with cooperation and resistance; for example, colleagues learn to collaborate when containing a bar-room brawl between twenty angry men. Officers also *embody* the criminal justice system. Learning is also performative because they are on stage.

Jackall's observations of the NYPD (2000) highlight police work as high drama and confounding frustration. Knowledge gained in performing duties is, unsurprisingly, relayed through performances: storytelling, serious joking, and gallows humour (Fineman, Gabriel, and Sims 2005). Cunliffe advocates learning arenas which engage issues from the *learner's* perspective, in their language (2000, 2001). Fenwick (2003) addresses practice-based informal learning and embodiment; Green and Taber (1978) experimentation and experiential learning. Ibarra's research (1999) on identity work and professional selves, Fransella's on personal change through 'fixed-role therapy' (2003), and Kalekin-Fishman on socio-psychodynamic learning (2003) share similar assumptions. All treat experience in and beyond the classroom as a resource requiring courses designed to enable learners to incorporate new skills back into their practices outside the classroom. The test is 'Does this "ring true" and "feel right"?' Cunliffe urges *acting reflexively within circumstances*, rather than taking intellectual or behaviourist approaches to practice development:

[T]he learning process is...complex and non-linear, and encompasses informal ways of sense making that are often taken for granted. We therefore need to focus on singular events and conversations within which we construct practical accounts of our actions, identities and relationships with others, and which may guide our future action....process...should be open to reflexive critique, because in helping students create new readings of their experience, we can create possibilities for change in everyday interaction. (2001: 37)

This should enable students to identify what they did-not-know-they-knew: 'responsive and unselfconscious moments in which we respond to our embodied sense of what is happening...the tacit knowing/assumptions often deep within us.' (2001: 40). The facilitators involved in custody training were unaware of Cunliffe but adopted similar precepts.

PRACTICE DEVELOPMENT IN EMOTIONAL LABOUR

Though recent, the use of actors is quite common in police training with few evaluations of theatre techniques applied to practice development.

This is theatre because the officer is an actor; an *emotional labourer* (Hochschild 1983/2003). Emotional labour is 'the management of feeling to create a publicly observable facial and bodily display: emotional labour is sold for a wage and therefore has exchange value' (2003: 7). Police officers engage in varied and complex emotional labours, performed before many hostile audiences, scrutinized by CCTV, colleagues, and institutions beyond the police station, and challenged by DPs and by several constituencies.

Like acting, many branches of emotional labour invite performative learning. For example, Pam Smith's (1992) study of nursing and nurse training suggests to us similarities to (and differences from) police work, and we recommend inter-service dialogue. Like nursing the number of stakeholders with an interest in policing is high. Popular fiction, political, debate and newspaper headlines add faux familiarity with policing, and officers encounter these expectations in those arrested for the first time. DPs also: discovering 'the way it goes' as their own detention progresses.

The performance of a Custody Sergeant in relation to each DP here and now effects the judicial process ever after and many of these 'butterfly effect' outcomes are unforeseeable. The way Custody Sergeants interact with DPs, arresting officers, solicitors, official visitors, jailers, custody nurses, superintendents, and 'responsible adults' will be relayed far and wide, over time. Decent performance may be rewarded with greater compliance and consent when the DP is arrested next time, knowing the score. Good practice is infectious and other officers will incorporate it into their own work, with unknown future benefits, which could be large. 'Regular customers' will require less physical coercion; usually none, their anxiety lessened and easily contained by the sergeant.

Alternatively, events can escalate if the Custody Sergeant is insensitive to warning signs which most DPs 'give out' well before 'kicking off'. The next time *this* DP is in front of *this* Custody Sergeant—or another—the tipping point may come sooner; she or he may kick off quickly, be harder to contain, take longer to book in, and keep arresting officers off patrol for longer; poor use of police resources compromising public safety. The quality of information gathered might be lower, injury risk increased, periodic cell observations increased, confidence reduced in the DP's social circle; and death in custody more likely. Officers acknowledge that some constables manage to antagonize DPs. 'By the time they come in, blue lights flashing, we have got a *load* of work on our hands and it's a case of straight-into-the-holding-cell'.[2] Bad practice spreads too.

The DP, arresting officers, and Custody Sergeants interact, with Custody Sergeant as lead actor (or director) at the centre of transactions, using ingenuity to keep each episode within the plot indicated by the criminal justice system. The system calls for good-quality answers entered on a terminal, observation of accumulated contingent rules, and transparency. Finally, Custody Sergeants should uphold healthy and safe 'emotion regimes' (Hochschild 2001), which were palpable during field observations.[3] A robust approach to well-being was observed at all three police stations visited, modulated by individual differences between DPs.

EMOTIONAL LABOUR, EMOTION WORK

For realism, actors playing DP roles need compelling back stories from which informative feelings can be derived, such as anger or vulnerability caused by prior hardship, indignity, or injustice, imagined or actual. This ability to invest a role with the memory of a feeling is known as deep-acting, as distinct from expressions merely painted on ('surface acting').

Hochschild defined emotional labour as the paid work of inducing appropriate feelings in others, in the line of duty. This applies to the effect on clients by flight attendants, debt collectors, Custody Sergeants, and arresting officers alike. But what to call efforts between colleagues or by clients *towards* the emotional labourer? The police are paid to affect others but not especially each other. Hochschild applies the general term 'emotion work' to *any* effort to alter the mood of others (1983/2003) while emotional *labour* is the *paid*, or commercialized, subset of emotion work. Thus officers do emotional labour and DPs do emotion work. The police station is not meant to 'commercialize human feelings', except incidentally through lawyers' fees. Because the point is to uphold the law (not profit), policing has a sacred quality—despite dealing with the dark side of life. This suggests a higher moral benchmark than, say, commercial security work.

Fineman applies *emotion work* to cover all emotional efforts between work colleagues (Fineman 2000; Bannister 2003). Similarly Hochschild, when comparing the all-consuming warm American office with home, which has become colder, stressful, and shows 'care deficit' (Hochschild 1997). Police comradeship was obvious from field observations.

Distinctions apart, the most relevant poles in custody work are deep-acted conviction and surface-acted superficiality; sacred attainment of high standards and profane *losing it*. Custody Sergeants work on DPs' feelings to minimize messing about, provocation, fishing for sympathy, derailing, bargaining, delay, stealing of the initiative, usurping of authority, and to detect false calm which masks private turmoil, hidden ligatures, razor blades secreted inside the cheek. There are scores of risks. Experienced Custody Sergeants treat 'giving-out' as an invitation by the DP to have their mood recognized and to be taken off the path to kicking off. The possibility of losing it is always present, so Custody Sergeants must perceive all relevant goings-on around the custody suite *and* devote exceptional attention to the critical moment, through eyes-at-the-back-of-the-head and 'antennas'.

MAKING A DRAMA OUT OF A CRISIS

Project Preparation

We began with over eleven hours listening to police officers about what they do. Our key informant and co-author is an experienced sergeant. The theory of emotional labour was explained to enable her to judge its relevance. A performing arts tutor (an experienced actor) was introduced for her expertise in performance-making and especially problem-solving theatre (after Boal). We took to each other's approaches.

Our sergeant scripted several circumstances-of-arrest and preliminary characterizations of DPs. The tutor worked with actors on their back stories, refined through exchange visits and viewing coverage of real booking-ins which illustrated best and worst practice. The roles are fictionalized versions of persons known to the police. A male police officer added 'Victor', an especially dangerous DP arrested for GBH. One of the authors played 'middle-aged male arrested at the scene for criminal damage'. Each role entailed points of law, procedure, degrees of physical and mental illness, and duty of care issues.

Design

Credible representation of a custody suite, insider knowledge, learning and development expertise (practical and academic), and capable actors were needed. The scenarios had to be experienced as real. The convincing enactment of 'regular customers' by actors who had never seen inside a police station was especially creditable. Their back stories left no shortage of things-to-do-next.

Scenarios unfolded in about twenty-five minutes each and debriefings took thirty minutes. Actors debriefed *in role*, then as themselves. Debriefings were initiated by experienced sergeants. Comments were immediate, constructive, and lightened with humour—meeting Cunliffe's ideal of reflection 'within circumstances'. The researchers said little to avoid interrupting conversation between officers.[4]

Staging

The event is reproducible. It continues to run with other actors and is offered to another police authority. The mock-up contains a facsimile of four cells with standard (Victorian) doors, locks, inspection flaps, raised mattresses, and WC. There is a 'front desk' with raised floor giving the Custody Sergeant a height advantage over DPs;[5] a computer terminal built into the desk, booking-in forms, and statements of rights. CCTV is statutory and incidentally enables trainees to observe each booking-in, live, from another room, where debriefs were completed, immediately afterwards. Again typically, there is no natural light at the desk.

The set is unusual as it includes a sink and cells near to the desk. Normally cells would be off a corridor, away from the desk. There ought to be a back office behind the desk, containing CCTV monitors, VCRs (checked and logged by the jailer), a visual display summarizing circumstances of arrest, time of arrest (vital to obeying rules limiting how long DPs can be kept in custody), and details such as the frequency of periodic inspection of each DP's safety and well-being. This display assists the handover between shifts, when the suite is crowded with all (say) fifteen cells occupied by DPs with different circumstances of arrest, at different stages on their 'PACE clock'.[6] The back room would have phones, police radios, and notice boards extolling new practices and the availability of other agencies (drug referral, translation, mental health teams). Cartoons (ironic observations on police work), postcards, mugs, and tea bags domesticate this space. Field observations showed masses of deliberation, reflection, and advice happening here. Back offices allow Custody Sergeants to rebuke arresting officers discreetly and offer equally confidential praise. Mutual care and counselling is done, generally in an adult, comradely, and direct way; 'collective emotion work' certainly (Hochschild 1983/2003). Finally, the mock-up lacks the *smell* of real custody suites: sweaty-tar-the unwashed smell of fear, it was suggested.

While every custody suites varies, officers would recognize the mock-up as a plausible representation.

Participants

Each intake includes around eight sergeants new to custody suite work and about four with some experience. (The constabulary has about forty-five Custody Sergeants in post.) Two or three observers with considerable experience of custody were involved. One played the role of defence solicitor, another a CPS[7] agent, who presented particular types of challenge. We used between three and six actors, plus 'Victor' and one author as a 'criminal damage'. The arresting officers (usually two per DP) act as they would in practice, though it was agreed that no role would entail use of force. A research assistant provided video analysis.

Iterative Review

Given the dynamic complexity of booking in, they need immediate review while still fresh. This is collective, beginning with the actor, the Custody Sergeant, if necessary the arresting officers, and the trainers. This advice offered between colleagues deserves a separate paper. It addresses *split-second moments*, strategies—successful or otherwise—and suggested alternatives, with theories offered as to their probable outcomes.

Video reviews led to new questions. What is the Custody Sergeant doing *exactly*? What is the DP doing towards the arresting officers? How are they performing towards the others? Is this the *result* or the *cause* of the DP's behaviour? Ramping up or down? Is the Custody Sergeant being supported or dissipated by arresting officers? Are they wandering off-piste? Who's alert to what *now*? Why did they miss the signs that the DP was going to run down the corridor? Is it always the same episode we see each time? What feelings does this scene provoke? What scope for different understandings?

With Crabtree and Miller (1999), Borkan claims repetitive review is

invaluable as a qualitative, interpretive process that has the potential to be widely applicable, emotionally and intellectually stimulating, and highly productive. Immersion/crystallisation (I/C) consists of cycles whereby the analyst immerses him- or herself into and experiences the text, emerging after concerned reflection with intuitive crystallizations, until reportable interpretations are reached. . . . [Openness is a] critical tool. (1999: 180–1)

Observers should 'listen deeply'; engage; corroborate and consider alternatives; be patient and have a process orientation; be a mentor, tolerant of repetition.

Interestingly, officers tend towards consensus on the critical moments. They differ on what-could-have-been-done-about-it and between male and female officers' perception of risk (males perceive greater risk from close proximity to DPs). They are quick to cut-to-the-point—this is their pace, their professional *clockspeed*.

Professional theory is alive to these issues: identity work (Mirchandani 2003; Sveningsson and Alvesson 2003), physical attitude, embodiment and its influence on what is communicated and learned (Boal 2000; Boal and Jackson 1994, 2002; Laban 1963; Hodgson 2001), and learning through the role; similarly Kelly on 'fixed role therapy' as a means of 'reconstrual' and 'personal change' (1991) and Stanislawski's (1965) deep emotional reflection as a means of scoping embodied, emotion-informed performance.

After the Event

The videos from the first two sessions were replayed many times. The research assistant settled on:

- Narrative content,
- Non-verbal behaviour,
- Verbal behaviour,
- Emotional labour,
- Movement.

Narrative Content

We detected certain *prototypical* narratives which also fitted field observations:

- loud/agitated/on the edge/desperado/preparing to 'kick off'/obscene/'bring it on!'/roaring bear. (Officers choose from a wide repertoire of de-escalating measures. Place in cell if these fail to work, inspections every ten minutes, and resume booking in later.)
- too intoxicated or mentally distracted for any engagement. (Officers place in cell to await recovery; call for medical expertise if anxious about DP's well-being. Constant watch of cell.)
- bemused/bewildered/seeking orientation/struggling to comprehend, or feigning bewilderment. (Officers try explaining things in several different ways, searching for those that seem to 'catch' the DP's attention. Hold the DP's gaze.)
- lost soul/plaintive/disturbed/unsteady/had enough/agree-to-anything. (Officers try uphold the DP's rights in a meaningful way. Custody Sergeants may decide to place in cells while nursing assistance is called. But many other sympathetic strategies exist.)
- embarrassed/'I'm not really here'/'This is not really happening'. (Custody Sergeant tries to make 'reality dawn' while preserving DP's awareness of rights as 'reality hits', especially by quiet repetition of reminders that the DP can change their mind later about legal representation or having someone informed of their arrest.)
- rage-exhausted/compliant/pleading/quiet/in shock/retreating/apologetic/guilt. (As above; frequent observation.)
- negotiating/coy/messing/latching on to every opportunity/sustained mind games/preventing forward movement. (The Custody Sergeant uses all available mental stamina to stay ahead of whatever game is being played, anticipating each move if possible. Once a threshold is reached, may place in cell with little warning.)
- past caring/out-of-it/catatonic/trance-like/zonked/estranged. (Constant observation; custody nurse called.)
- needy/emanating neglect/lost child/whistling-in-the-dark. (Responsible adult called.)
- exceptional violent rage/DP biting own lips and cheeks/spitting blood and body tissue. (Rare. May call for as many as five officers for restraint.)

Non-Verbal Content

Movement, use of floor space, and gesture underlined narratives: repetitive gestures such as drumming on the desk, shifting weight from foot to foot, head swaying, and flapping the arms like appendages, also freezing. These evolved in relation to arresting officers' posture, eye contact, as the narrative unfolded. The importance of arresting officers was underestimated originally, but was apparent from reviewing the videos. DPs 'played off them', testing their reactions.

Verbal Content

Prototypes included:

- loud-aggressive
- voice with raised emotional content
- quiet voices, depleted emotional content
- voice launched from the stomach or hissed through teeth
- shouting to the gallery

… inviting containing attempts by officers.

We observed pace of voice for each individual; reactions if interrupted, turn-taking gaps (disallowed in the case of high-pitched, resistant, and affronted narratives), and withholding of acknowledgement of the other. More turn-taking gaps offered as the mood comes down.

Emotional Labour

Some officers' performances were

- knowing
- close tracking of every move
- restrained-powerful
- authoritative-but-not-authoritarian
- business-like
- kindly
- patient
- tolerant

These varied according to prototypes (above) to some degree, modified by individual mannerisms, customized case by case, moment by moment.

Movement Analysis

We noted position, posture, and elicited responses; who was talking to whom; the extent of eye contact. We looked at movements[8] and whether or not any individuals were 'near' or 'far' either spatially, or in demeanour. We noted how emotion work transmits bodily. We also marked positions at outset and at completion, pondering changes in distance. Participants relaxed visibly coming out of role (shoulders relaxed).

These subtleties were debated (in police day-language) during debriefing, particularly regarding *positioning* of both Custody Sergeant and DP at the desk and the conflicting needs for safety and rapport. The language of police work addressed issues precisely, consistent with Cunliffe's studies of what works well at management learning events (2000, 2001). Direct feedback from actors in and out of role (who come from the same age range as most detained persons) about how they felt at each stage gave an important reality check from outside the service. Academic observers could name the concepts which officers had picked up on. Naturally, officers prefer their terminology even where academic and lay concepts are similar.

By giving readers an over-our-shoulders description of a booking-in, followed by comments, they can judge the interpretations we are making:

> *Georgie* scenario with *police commentary* (25 minutes elapsed time). *Camera*: frontal view of Custody Sergeant and arresting officer, back of Custody Sergeant. Circumstances of Arrest: *Georgie* was detained by store personnel, claiming to have observed her leave an M & S store with £79 of smoked salmon without paying, then concealing it on another person. Full circumstances and back story omitted.

> A male arresting officer brings the detained person into the suite, guiding her lightly with his left palm on her upper back, indicating to her that she should 'Stand there', which places her about a metre from the Custody Desk. He stands aside, to her right, by a similar distance, having closed the door to the Custody Suite. The female Custody Sergeant's first act is to invite the DP to come forwards to the desk and a little to her right, so that she is now directly before her. Now the DP is nearer to the door than the arresting officer. [*Police comment: this arrangement shows that the officers do not anticipate threats from the DP. Inexperienced officers might be unaware that this is a judgement call that they should make in each case. Another example is when offensive weapons are taken from the DP and placed on the Custody Desk, within easy reach of the DP. This could result in injuries to the Custody Sergeant or arresting officer.*]

> Sergeant learns that her name is Georgie, age 21 and turns to the arresting officer for the 'circumstances of your arrest'. She asks Georgie, 'Will you let him speak?' She has been arrested for taking £79 worth of smoked salmon from a supermarket-far more than she could possibly need—without paying.

> Georgie does 'not remember any of that at all. I wouldn't do that at all . . . ' The Sergeant is struck by this and soon identifies that she is on an anti-depressant, the effects of which, according to the DP, can seem to cause lapses in awareness. [*Police comment: the need to notice this risk and the importance of recording it is part of the Custody Sergeant's role: the novice Sergeant did well to identify signs of a mental health problem very quickly—information that DPs may be reluctant to reveal. The Sergeant found this out without causing any embarrassment or distress to the DP. Good.*]

> Georgie reiterates that she is oblivious as to the circumstances of the arrest, complaining of feeling sick; beginning to shift her weight from one foot to the other. She places one

hand on top of the other on the Custody Desk and rests her chin on her hands, head rolling from side to side. In response to some questions, she lifts her head and looks up at the Custody Sergeant. She is of slight build and the Custody Sergeant towers above her.

'I don't feel very well.'

'A nurse will be called.'

The 'authorization of her detention' causes her some distress and there is rising anxiety in voice. It is a delicate moment. Though Georgie is not hostile, the flow of the booking-in is a little awry. [*Police comment: The DP is persisting with many side issues and there are key questions that must be answered for reasons of justice and to identify any other well-being issues. Although there is a need to avoid unsettling the DP unnecessarily, the right balance needs to be struck between drawing things out and keeping control.*]

Some routine questions re-establish the rhythm a little, though Georgie begins a side-conversation with the arresting officer, which the Sergeant 'pulls back'. Georgie offers another conversation on 'using computers' and 'how cold it is'. 'Have you been trained in computers?' 'I like your watch. Is it one of those under-water ones?' 'It wasn't this cold last time.' 'Have you repainted in here?' Coughing, she is offered water; but declines asking after the arresting officer's height to help her judge her own: 'Six foot.' ... 'Can I represent myself?' she asks. The Sergeant responds with a gentle 'smiling laugh' ... Georgie is quite talkative. It transpires that she has quit her university course in journalism. She says she is claustrophobic. A Police National Computer Check (PNC) indicates that she has tried to harm herself in the past. 'Did *you* go to university?' asks Georgie.

Having had her rights explained (slowly, the Sergeant checking for understanding) and given a form which gives them in writing, Georgie reaches out with her left hand to flick at the sheet of paper (placed on the desk) spinning it clockwise with the tips of her first and second fingers. Quickly losing interest in this, she rests her chin directly on the desk. Sometimes she reaches out with her left hand, as far as she can across the desk. Her continuing dance seems spontaneous and unaffected. The impression is child-like and charming, suggestive of dependency, helplessness; vulnerability, perhaps. Meanwhile the arresting officer preserves his distance, arms folded, but shadowing her smiles. He rests his own chin on his left hand, supporting his left elbow on his folded right hand. That is arresting officer and DP both rest chin in hands.

In response to questions about special needs, she says 'vegetarian'. .... 'Do you have any Jelly-babies?' she jokes.

'Can I not just go home?' ... 'I need to go home for my welfare.' ...

Georgie is gaining more and more 'air-time' tugging gently at 'who has the initiative?' 'I can't go in there!' Presented with the decision to place her in Cell 1 she suddenly makes a break and runs out and along the corridor. The officers laugh with mixture of shared surprise and bemusement. Brought back by the arresting officer, Georgie makes for the far wall of the Custody Suite as an alternative to going in the cell. 'I really can't. I Can-Not-Go-In-There.' She repeats this several times. This works for her. The Sergeant concedes that the custody nurse can assess her there, pending a decision.

[*Police comment: Georgie, has taken (or been given) some control. Welfare needs have been respected; but we are left with a DP in a semi-open area which could become busy with other 'customers' leading to a bit of a mess in the custody area, with Georgie, complicating the next booking in. The DP has managed to charm and divert the officers and takes her opportunity to escape. With a different DP the outcome could have been serious, with harm to the DP, the officers, or both, and a lot of disruption.*]

At the collective debrief, asked 'how was it?' the actor, *still in role*, said, 'You were OK...I suppose. Yes you were *alright*. You kept looking at me and yes, OK. It was fine, I suppose.'

Could the outcome have been different and by doing what?

Georgie in four categories (5 minute sample)

The arresting officer enters with Georgie, and he tells her where to stand. However the female Custody Sergeant tells her to move closer so she 'doesn't have to shout', suggesting a difference between the male and female officers and that she is not afraid of the DP and offers closeness.

Analysis of 5 minute video recording:

Non-verbal Language Georgie's body language shows that she is comfortable with the Custody Sergeant as she is leaning on the desk, getting closer to the female officer and further from the arresting officer. Georgie's hands are on the table, exploring its surface continuously. The DP and Custody Sergeant have full eye contact. The Custody Sergeant is kind and addresses Georgie's well-being. She is comforting, measured, and seems to acknowledge Georgie's distress.

Georgie takes up the invitation by making conversation with the Custody Sergeant on how to use computers, more typical of friendship than of custody. When the custody officer goes to the computer, Georgie stretches up so that she can look over and continue talking. She doesn't make any efforts to get closer to the male officer and this suggests that she is working at controlling the situation between the two officers.

The male officer seems defensive, arms semi-folded across the chest and positioned at arm's length from Georgie. He spends most of his time looking at her head. Georgie withholds eye contact with him. She seems indifferent to him. He looks a little distant but the Custody Sergeant's questions occupy him briefly. This is routine. Arms across his chest, authoritative, in control. But I feel that this is not what he feels. He looks a bit spare and must look the part despite the tedium, to preserve control. He sways when he is talking to the Custody Sergeant and looks at Georgie when she talks to the Custody Sergeant. He tends to look away when they directly talk to each other. He returns his arms from his side to across the chest, suggesting restlessness. He also occasionally rubs his ear, suggestive of him 'not wanting to hear any lies'.

Verbal exchanges The female Custody Sergeant is reassuring, she has a calm voice and gives Georgie time to talk. She listens. The Custody Sergeant doesn't talk over her as they work through the procedure. They seem close, and not just physically. Honorary Mother and Daughter? The female officer is 'between the toe and the heel' of the job as Hochschild might put it.

She questions Georgie, taking time to listen to the problem and establish whether Georgie's answers are credible. Trust is being built. A male Custody Sergeant could not be Mother and, even as Father, might be more blunt and less receptive. He might look straight past her and—given the circumstances of arrest-towards the more obvious fact of her guilt. Although the role of Custody Sergeant and arresting officer are scripted, there does seem to be another, male–female dynamic at work. Georgie is very quiet-spoken when talking to the female officer and she seems to curb her annoyance. Georgie knows the custody officer is looking after her because she's been asked if she wants an extra blanket for the cell. The arresting officer also speaks quietly, but the script allows him little to do in any case.

Emotional Labour   The Custody Sergeant is deep-acting and uses her experience to control Georgie while keeping her comfortable in unusual surroundings. Georgie sways throughout and is given spatial freedom. In placing her arm on her cheek she seems to be thinking about what has happened and the Custody Sergeant's calm approach invites truthful reflection. The arresting officer's acting shows looser attachment and neutrality. On a few occasions he checks his watch indicating he needs to be elsewhere. He is not very interested and only participates when instructed by the custody officer. This is expected of the arresting officer in this Constabulary.

Movement   Georgie talks to both officers. However, she forms a greater bond with the custody officer by eye contact, proximity, and conversation. They talk about other issues besides custody. When Georgie eventually talks to the arresting officers, she makes good eye contact and looks at him whenever it is relevant. The arresting officer offers Georgie less eye contact. Through a good relationship with Georgie and the arresting officer, the Custody Sergeant minimizes potential conflict in connection with asking the arresting officer what she stole. She answers some of his questions for him. The arresting officer is silent when Georgie asks him questions—again as would be expected.

Changes in the distance between Georgie and the male officer are shown to be large when the video is played 'fast-forward'. It shows that the male is always moving back in relation to her. In between, Georgie *hugs* and caresses the custody desk, to get closer to the female Custody Sergeant? This action suggests what a little trust and sympathy from an officer can bring to the relationship between Custody Sergeant and DP. Getting closer may elicit vital information. I also sense that the Custody Sergeant experiments with putting herself in Georgie's position to discover more.

At the start the distance between Georgie and the arresting officer is closer (15–46 cm) but at the end it is a social distance of 1.2 m–3.6 m. The distance between Georgie and the Custody Sergeant is close throughout, starting off social but straight away moving to intimate/confiding. This occurs as soon as the custody officer tells her to 'come closer' and it stays like that throughout the five-minute sample.

Conclusions

Hochschild drew attention to the special labour performed by service workers who stand in front of us. She noticed the emotional labour of the flight attendant and the possible estrangement caused by endless good cheer in the line of duty. What of police officers, required to switch between good cheer and coercion many times and return home to normal life? Flight attendants report difficulty switching off at the end of a shift and no doubt so do many police officers, especially after a busy custody shift.

Pam Smith (1992) addressed the emotional labour of nursing and of improved performance. By comparing clinical settings, Smith found connections between good emotional labour, reduced estrangement, and better patient care, noticing how different clinical leaders enabled or disabled good nursing. Some wards were happy, explained by senior clinicians; they enabled learning by novices, which worked its way through to improved patient recovery times.

We hinted at how *custody nous* is developed, embodied, and felt. Like Pam Smith, we are interested in how improvement is possible through learning and how a virtuous relationship can be created between *improved* emotional labour (especially improved quality) and *reduced* estrangement, avoiding burn-out. The lack of enthusiasm among sergeants contemplating custody work for the first time and the burn-out of nurses are related phenomena.

While *efficiency* and *estrangement* are not the same, there is usually some relationship between them in both services. Better emotional labour should mean less estrangement, not more; though the danger persists that improved labour means both more labour and more estrangement. We should only countenance improved emotional labour that brings gains for both provider (nurse, police officer) *and* client (patient, detained person). All parties have a stake in good technique. This type of two-way gain comes from good custody practice much as it does from good clinical practice, which nevertheless needs to be learned.

Cunliffe (2000, 2001) stresses 'singular events and conversations within which we construct practical accounts of our actions, identities and relationships with others'. We should 'respond to our embodied sense of what is happening … the tacit knowing/assumptions often deep within us'. We think this was happening. Custody training confirms that:

improvement = reduced estrangement + learning + client care.

Though police officers could say far more in their own words, *improvement, learning*, and *reduced estrangement* can be itemized:

1. Custody should uphold the physical, psychical, and emotional well-being of officer and client and meet public expectations for civility and justice. Custody training contributes in a significant way to these sacred aims. Officers, DPs, and visitors 'know it when they see it'.
2. Conversely poor practice leads to regrettable redirection of resources from public safety to custody control; this can foster righteous resentment.
3. The debriefings picked on immediate and wider consequence. How officers perform towards detainees is likely to be associated with how communities as

a whole, law abiding and law breaking, are viewed and policed. One provides an index for the other and good custody is a sign of good policing 'On Area'.

4. Custody is a marker of civility. To treat DPs as outlaws means unlicensed abuse by law officers and maximum estrangement (and disgrace) of all concerned. The world offers many dreadful examples and civilized practice should be exported.

5. Like senior nurses, the Custody Sergeant is also both emotional labourer and unit manager. In discussion officers stressed the need to be authoritative without being authoritarian—something which officers and nurses do not always achieve.

6. Practitioner involvement in the design and conduct of training events brings concreteness and relevance that would be impossible otherwise.

7. Actors know a great deal about performance know-how. Their nous is invaluable to other emotional labourers.

We think these items indicate reduced estrangement for providers and clients and practical means for achieving them, though the care of detained persons is not always pretty. Detainees who rage in custody are nevertheless vulnerable in many ways and we have been pleased to find that a language of care exists in police stations. Care is expressed in a more robust way by police officers compared with flight attendants, but it seems more *substantive*. And as we saw with Georgie's Custody Sergeant, who is not untypical, many officers express much the same care and concern as the good nurse.

NOTES

1. Officers are superstitious about saying 'Quiet night', preferring 'It's a Q. Night, Sarge.' Saying 'quiet night' tempts fate.

2. Ideally, low-threat DPs are brought straight to the desk. The DO will order an appropriate type of body search, at an appropriate point in the process (if this has not been done). However if the DP is difficult to restrain, they are taken straight from the patrol car to the holding cell, restrained, and searched there and then. Any available officers, the 'civilian' jailer, and, if necessary, the DO will cooperate in restraining the DP. There is the space to do this. The holding cell differs from other cells in that the front wall is replaced by bars along its full width (as in cells shown in 'Western' movies) so that everything can be seen from the outside. The holding cells we have seen are positioned immediately opposite the 'yard' entrance to the police station. This means that DPs can be taken directly through the back entrance and into the holding cell, without negotiating difficult corners or narrow corridors. While this does not usually present too much of a challenge, it is certainly not the preferred option for most officers! As for officers who provoke DPs, 'It's really the *last* thing I need.'

3. Hochschild first used the term 'emotion regime' during her public address at Brunel University on 4 Oct. 2001. She used it to identify what it was that the terrorists had

attempted to destroy just three weeks earlier on 11 Sept. 2001. We feel that this is a telling form of words which may be used also to describe any affective social order, for example the good or, for that matter, the bad atmosphere prevailing in a police station. Emotion regimes vary perceptibly from place to place and over time. Thus, in everyday language, people speak of a bar with a 'great atmosphere' or, say, of an intimidating 'no go area', where they are afraid to visit at night'. Feminist street campaigns to 'reclaim the night' may be described as acting to change the emotion regime. In our understanding, emotion regimes have a comparatively long half life, measured in years or decades. Short-term changes in mood (such as a crowd 'turning nasty' and there being 'ugly scenes') do not usually indicate a shift in the emotion regime as a whole. However, in very rare moments a change in emotion regime is indeed marked by a singular change of mood, such as accomplished by exceptional political oratory. The text version of Hochschild's public lecture at Brunel is found in *Soundings*, 20.

4. A mini seminar in 'emotional labour' was tried on the first custody course, but abandoned subsequently because, by common agreement, it 'did not feel right'.
5. Our confederate reported that this extra height can aggravate feelings of persecution in DPs with certain forms of mental illness.
6. PACE governs the maximum length of time of detention without charge.
7. Crown Prosecution Service.
8. The Fast-Forward/Play function makes the rhythm of position changes very clear.

REFERENCES

Bannister, D. (2003). 'The Logic of Passion', in F. Fransella (ed.), *International Handbook of Personal Construct Psychology*. London: Wiley.

Boal, A. (2000). *Theatre of the Oppressed*. London: Pluto Press.

——and Jackson, A. (1994). *The Rainbow of Desire: The Boal Method of Theatre and Therapy*. London: Routledge.

————(2002). Games *for Actors and Non Actors*. London: Routledge.

Borkan, J. (1999). 'Immersion/Crystalization', in B. F. Crabtree and W. L. Miller (eds.), *Doing Qualitative Research*. Thousand Oaks: Sage.

Crabtree, B. F. and Miller, W. L. (eds.) (1999). *Doing Qualitative Research. Thousand Oaks: Sage*.

Crabtree, B. F. and Miller, W. L. (1999). 'The Dance of Interpretation', in B. F. Crabtree and W. L. Miller (eds.), *Doing Qualitative Research*. Thousand Oaks: Sage.

Cunliffe, A. L. (2000). 'Reflexive Dialogical Practice in Management Learning', *Management Learning*, 33/1: 35–61.

——(2001). 'Managers as Practical Authors: Reconstructing our Understanding of Management Practice', *Journal of Management Studies*, 38: 351–71.

Fenwick, T. (2003). 'Reclaiming and Re-embodying Experiential Learning through Complexity Science', *Studies in the Education of Adults*, 35/2: 123–41.

Fineman, S. (ed.) (2000). *Emotion in Organizations*. London: Sage.

——Gabriel, Y., and Sims, S. (2005). *Organizing and Organizations*. London: Sage.

Fransella, F. (ed.) (2003). *International Handbook of Personal Construct Psychology*. London: Wiley.

Green, S. G., and Taber, T. D. (1978). 'Structuring Experiential Learning through Experimentation', *Academy of Management Review* (Oct.): 889–95.

Her Majesty's Inspectorate of Constabulary (2002). *Training Matters*. London: HMSO.

Hochschild, A. R. (1983/2003). *The Managed Heart: The Commercialisation of Human Feeling*. Berkeley and Los Angeles: University of California Press.

—— (1997). *The Time Bind: When Work Becomes Home and Home Becomes Work*. New York: Metropolitan Books/Henry Holt.

—— (2001). *Emotion Management in an Age of Global Terrorism*. Public lecture, 10 Oct., Brunel University; later published in *Soundings*, 20 (2002).

Hodgson, G. (2001). *Mastering Movement: The Life and Work of Rudolf Laban*. London: Methuen.

Ibarra, H. (1999). 'Provisional Selves: Experimenting with Image and Identity in Professional Adaption', *Administrative Science Quarterly*, 44/4: 764–91.

Jackall, R. (2000). 'A Detective's Lot: Contours of Morality and Emotion in Police Work', in S. Fineman (ed.), *Emotion in Organizations*. London: Sage.

Kalekin-Fishman, D. (2003). 'Social Relations in the Modern World', in F. Fransella (ed.), *International Handbook of Personal Construct Psychology*. London: Wiley.

Kelly, G. A. (1991). *The Psychology of Personal Constructs*. London: Routledge.

Laban, R. (1963). *Modern Educational Dance*. London: MacDonald & Evans.

Mirchandani, K. (2003). 'Challenging Racial Silences in the Studies of Emotion Work: Contributions from Anti-Racist Feminist Theory', *Organization Studies*, 24/5: 721–4.

Smith, P. (1992). *The Emotional Labour of Nursing*. Basingstoke: Macmillan.

Stanislawski, C. (1965). *An Actor Prepares*. New York: Theater Arts Books.

Sveningsson, S., and Alvesson. M. (2003). 'Managing Managerial Identities: Organizational Fragmentation, Discourse and Identity Struggles', *Human Relations*, 56/10: 1163–94.

CHAPTER 7

EXPERIENTIAL LEARNING IN THE ON-LINE ENVIRONMENT

ENHANCING ON-LINE TEACHING AND LEARNING

JOSEPH E. CHAMPOUX

PEDAGOGICAL and education research dating to John Dewey's (1916) foundation work has emphasized student interaction as a key part of an engaging student-centred learning environment. A focus on interaction has continued as a primary concern of contemporary on-line instructional researchers. They see it as a key way of reducing the emphasis on course content or the instructor (for example, Draves 2000; Kearsley 2000).

On-line teaching and learning often has a passive quality when instructors do not include course features that draw students into course content. A course design that features a collection of hyperlinked documents can lead to simple 'page turning'. Such designs do not increase student involvement with course material.

This chapter describes some on-line learning activities that can increase student involvement with course content, other students, and the instructor. Refinements in on-line course delivery and other technologies now allow more involvement and engagement of learners with on-line course material than ever before.

The chapter discusses ways of introducing experiential learning into the on-line environment. It presents some experiential exercises (eExercises) developed for on-line management and organizational behaviour courses. These exercises increase the focus on the learner and can help increase social interaction within an on-line course.

On-Line Management Education Issues

Four on-line management education issues guided the development of the eExercises described in this chapter. Each issue derives from Bloom's taxonomy of learning goals (Bloom 1956) and careful consideration of several learning theories discussed later. The four issues are:

- Learner involvement: increase learner involvement with course content and the instructor.
- Learner self-awareness: design course content that lets a learner become more aware of various aspects of self.
- Learner analytical skills: offer on-line course experiences that help a learner develop her or his analytical skills.
- Practical application of on-line course content: help on-line learners apply course content to practical situations.

A later section assesses each eExercise against this list of on-line management education issues.

Learning Theory and On-Line Experiential Learning[1]

Several learning theories offer some insights about experiential learning in the on-line environment.[2] These lines of research suggest different learning effects of on-line course content. The following summarizes some major learning theories and links them to teaching and learning in the on-line environment.

Behavioural learning theory views learning as happening because of a predictable and reliable link between a stimulus and a learner's response. A person learns from stimulus–response pairing. The connection between a stimulus and response strengthens the more it is practised. The need to link stimulus and response suggests the importance of the instructor's role in controlling the learning environment to align with an educational goal (Chance 1994; Skinner 1968; Thorndike 1932; Watson 1914).

Cognitive theory also views learning as happening in response to an environmental stimulus. It adds a person's internal mental processing system as a mediator between response and resultant learning. Internal mental states or schemata help a person organize, remember, and learn from environmental events. A person can learn across situations by framing new problems with familiar schemata (Bartlett 1932; Rumelhart and Norman 1981).

Humanistic theory views learning as involving the total person. It includes the person's uniqueness, individual potential, intrinsic motivation, and emotions. A person learns through all aspects of self, not only a reaction to the person's environment. An individual's feelings and views about experiences and behaviour are integral parts of learning. Humanistic theory sees behaviour resulting from human choice. Individuals have the freedom and responsibility to become what they can become (Bugental 1967; Patterson 1973; Rogers 1969).

Social learning theory uses the concepts and principles of operant learning, but assumes cognitive mediation of these associational processes. It adds a social context to learning, including social groups and the larger social order. This theory describes people as learning from observing other people within a social context. Much of human behaviour involves the interaction of people, with multiple stimuli bombarding the individual simultaneously. Social learning theory explains human learning based on the continuous reciprocal interaction between cognitive, behavioural, and environmental factors (Bandura 1977; Miller and Dollard 1941; Mischel 1973, 1979).

Constructivism or constructivist theory is an umbrella term for diverse views of learning. This perspective assumes learning is an active process of building not attaining knowledge. Learners construct knowledge as they try to make sense of their experiences. The most striking difference from previously described theories is the shift of focus from knowledge acquisition in a content domain to development of skills needed to navigate through the domain. Knowledge is not in the content but in the person's content domain activity. While the learning activity is embedded within the domain context, getting the content is peripheral not central to learning. This approach emphasizes the learning process not the products of learning (Brown, Collins, and Duguid 1989; Bruner 1961; Bruner, Oliver, and Greenfield 1966; Lave and Wenger 1991).

Experiential learning refers to a wide range of learning and teaching practices, policies, and ideologies. It is typically a multiple step process of reacting to experiences with observations and reflection (Brah and Hoy 1989; Jarvis 1987; Kolb 1984; Miller and Boud 1996; Weil and McGill 1989a, 1989b). A person reacts to and learns from experiences based on their cultural origin and a unique collection of beliefs, attitudes, and emotions—their unique personality. The experiential learner forms concepts and generalizations from the experience that he or she can test and use in new situations. The experience that forms the basis of experiential learning can happen as real life experiences (primary experience) or mediated (secondary experience) in a classroom setting by using exercises.

Each theory summarized above suggests that bringing an experiential exercise approach to on-line instruction can have potentially positive effects. Behavioural learning theory points to the reinforcement of concepts between print and on-line presentations and completing an appropriate eExercise. Cognitive theory strongly suggests that a well-designed eExercise can become a schema by which a person organizes and recalls otherwise abstract concepts. The holistic views of humanistic theory argue that a properly designed eExercise focused on the individual can tap more of the whole person, especially emotion. Using a team-based eExercise can create an on-line social context that supports learning contributions from the interaction of cognitive, behavioural, and environmental factors as argued by social learning theory.

The strongest theoretical support of teaching and learning functions of eExercises comes from constructivism and experiential learning theory. Constructivism implies that exercises are rich targets and activities from which a learner builds understanding and retention of theories and concepts. They represent an activity within a content domain from which a learner builds understanding. Experiential learning theory argues for using experience (eExercises) as the basis of learning. In the on-line environment, eExercises can become the secondary experience from which learners form concepts and generalizations that they take to new experiences. These two theoretical positions point strongly to enhancing the on-line learning experience with an integrated experiential learning approach.

An On-Line Experiential Learning Approach

An on-line experiential approach parallels what a student experiences in a face-to-face class. A major difference is the use of on-line technology as part of the experiential course design. The eExercises described later parallel the design and effect of experiential exercises in the face-to-face classroom.

The experiential exercises discussed in this chapter can give students an engaging and involving learning experience, reducing the passive character of on-line content. One can fully integrate these exercises into almost any on-line management or organizational behaviour course. They become a regular part of a student's on-line activity.

eExercises have two forms: (1) individual exercises for the single learner, and (2) virtual group exercises that teams complete in the on-line environment. The eExercises that focus on individuals ask individual students to assess themselves. Virtual group exercises ask virtual teams to complete the exercise. A unique feature of some exercises is their use of on-line film scenes as the exercise target. This mixture of experiential learning and different media helps enhance the on-line teaching and learning experience.

Experiential exercises can appear almost anywhere in an on-line course. Behavioural learning theory suggests placing the eExercise experience close to the presentation of concepts and theories to which it is related. Such presentations can have many forms: off-line text; on-line text; PowerPoint slides; and E-Lectures (voice-over PowerPoint slides).

Individuals or teams complete the body of the eExercise and identifying information on-line. A student or team enters identifying information at the bottom of the eExercise form. All exercises have the same format. They ask for the student's name, the student's e-mail address, and the instructor's e-mail address. When satisfied with the completion of the exercise, the student clicks the 'Submit Your Answers' button. The completed form passes through a forms processing program that summarizes the exercise contents and sends the summary to both the student and the instructor.

The results of the exercises become part of a course's discussion, either in a scheduled chatroom activity or with postings to a course's discussions area topics. An instructor can analyse the exercise results she or he receives and build those results into the discussion. These discussions are important parts of course design that increase student involvement and engagement with course content.

eExercises: On-Line Experiential Exercises

This section describes four eExercises drawn from a larger project that is developing exercises for many management and organizational behaviour topics. The larger project has exercises focused on workforce diversity, organizational socialization, power, political behaviour, motivation, and the like. The discussion below separately examines individual and virtual team exercises.

Each exercise closes with an identifying information section that includes the student's name, the course in which enrolled, the student's e-mail address, and the instructor's e-mail address. After clicking the 'Submit Your Answers' button, the forms processing program sends the processed form to the course instructor.

> **Table 7.1 Access and login information: chapter supporting website**
>
> URL: http://webct.unm.edu
> Click: LOGIN
> Login: guest_elol
> Password: guest_elol
> Click: Experiential Learning—On-Line
> Links to each eExercise appear on the Home Page.

Individual eExercises

Individual eExercises focus on the individual learner. Students complete the eExercise alone with no involvement of other course members while completing the exercise. This section presents two individual eExercises. One uses the student as the target; the other uses an on-line film scene as the target. Because of space limitations, the eExercises are not reproduced here. You may view and complete each exercise by going to the website that supports this chapter. Table 7.1 shows the access and login information.

Each eExercise description includes its purpose, typical ways in which to use the exercise, and some results you can expect when using the exercise. Expected results come from several sources, all based on the author's experiences with the exercise. Sources of typical results vary because each exercise is in a different development stage within the larger project. Some exercise results come from on-line course use; others come from face-to-face classroom use. The film-based eExercise results come from the instructor's manual that supports the noted film scene.

Your Conflict Orientations

The 'Your Conflict Orientations' eExercise lets a person assess the conflict orientations the person is likely to use in different situations. This exercise addresses the on-line management education issues of learner involvement and learner self-awareness described at the beginning of the chapter.

The exercise opens with an overview and instructions that orient the student to the exercise. This exercise defines the conflict orientations and presents the student with a set of rating scales to assess her or his conflict orientations. The exercise includes a text box where a student enters notes and makes some observations about her or his likely use of each orientation.

A course's design can require a discussion of each student's conflict orientation during a course's weekly scheduled chat activity. If a student does not attend the scheduled chat activity, a course can require the student to post observations

Table 7.2 eExercise: your conflict orientations

Champoux≫Let's take a look at your/our conflict orientations.
Student A≫different depending on who is involved
Champoux≫Around the room: Primary conflict orientation of each of you?
Student B≫mostly collaborative or compromise
Student A≫dominant with strangers but not with friends—collaborative with friends
Student C≫I am collaborative in most situations
Student E≫I am definitely a compromise-type, though collaborative efforts are always praised
Student A≫accommodative at work
Student D≫Cooperate.
Student F≫same as [Student B] ... don't like avoidance ... can be pressed into using dominance at times (usually defensive)
Student A≫definitely—but I think it's important to change orientation depending on who is on the other side of the conflict
Student D≫I agree. Avoidance, in my experience, is never the best approach.
Champoux≫Myself largely collaborative ... with a dusting of compromise and dominance.

Discussions Area Excerpts

Student X:
I consider myself to be dominant. I enjoy exploring issues and winning debates about the best way to deal with an issues. But, this has overlap with collaborative, since winning frequently requires meeting the needs of many different stakeholders and buiding consensus.

Student Y:
eExercise: This exercise made me consider how I do react when I am in a conflict. I have to fight my natural tendencies of avoidance and accommodation. This would really be hard for me to do if I was in a conflict with another person with a dominance orientation. I do not like dealing with people with strong dominance traits and would prefer to ignore the conflict or make it go away as quickly as possible. However, I realize that this accomplishes nothing. The conflict aftermath will leave room for latent conflict because none of my goals will have been met. This only means that I will have to deal with the same dominant person when the conflict resurfaces. It is better that I deal with the person the first time and focus on collaboration or compromise to solve the conflict. This is something that I am getting better with as I mature and gain more experience dealing with conflicts.

Chat activity and discussions area postings excerpts; chat activity excerpts.

on his or her eExercise results to a specific topic in the course's discussions area.

The upper part of Table 7.2 shows an excerpt of a chat activity discussion of the 'Your Conflict Orientations' eExercise for several students. I disguised students' names but show their observations as they appeared in the chatroom log. The lower part of Table 7.2 has excerpts from student postings to the discussions area. These are different students because they did not participate in the course's scheduled chat activity. The chat activity excerpts show interaction among participants; the discussion posting has no interaction. Both show the introspection produced by the exercise.

Diagnosing and Redesigning Jobs: Reality Bites *(1994)*

The diagnosing and redesigning jobs exercise is a film-based eExercise that uses a scene from the film *Reality Bites*. This scene comes from a film scene collection licensed for internet distribution in on-line courses (Champoux 2005).

Four Generation Xers meet life's realities after their college graduation. Life's realities play cruel tricks on them as they continue developing together. Lelaina Pierce (Winona Ryder) desperately seeks a job after her termination as a production assistant for a morning TV show. She has had three unsuccessful job interviews before the one shown in the 'Wienerdude' scene used for this eExercise. Just before this scene, Lelaina asked her mother (Susan Norfleet) for a loan. Lelaina's mother noted that times are hard and Lelaina should perhaps find a job at a fast food restaurant.

This exercise presents a student with an exercise overview and instructions for accessing the *Reality Bites* film scene. A student first views the film scene on-line. The on-line presentation of the scene includes a brief film description, scene description, scene context within the film, and a link to the film scene. This *Reality Bites* film scene is the exercise target, not the person. This exercise addresses the on-line management education issues of learner analytical skills and practical application of on-line course content described at the beginning of this chapter.

Separate sections of the exercise present various parts of the job characteristics theory of work motivation (Hackman and Oldham 1980). This theory is part of many management and organizational behaviour courses. The sections include the core job characteristics, moderator variables, critical psychological states (internal psychological reactions), and affective and behavioural responses. A 'Navigation Menu' lets a student conveniently move among the exercise's sections.

Students individually complete the form, using it to assess the job and work context they observe in the film scene. A course's design can include the discussion activities described for the previous eExercise.

Students should note in their exercise results several parts of the film scene analysis shown in Table 7.3. The core job characteristics of skill variety, task identity, and autonomy should appear low to most students. They will need to infer levels of these job characteristics from Wienerdude's (David Spade, uncredited) description of Lelaina Pierce's (Winona Ryder) potential job. They also can observe the other workers' behaviour to come to their conclusions. The work context has some negative factors such as closeness of workers, heat, and food odours. Students will vary in what they notice and emphasize. Work context can play a negative role as a moderator variable in the job characteristics theory of work motivation. Students also note low levels of most critical psychological states. As predicted by the theory, affective and behavioural outcomes also should appear low to most students. They also might note some observations from their experiences in a fast food restaurant.

Table 7.3 *Reality Bites.* Film scene analysis

Despite Wienerdude's fondness for his job and supervisory role, the job for which Lelaina applies
likely is low in most core job characteristics. The job has few skill requirements, little
wholeness, and does not appear important to almost anyone. This job likely has little
autonomy because of well-defined procedures for food preparation and customer interaction.
The work context has crowded working conditions, food particles scattered about, food odours,
and unenthusiastic coworkers. It likely is a hot work environment, especially in the summer.
Wienerdude's supervisory behaviour combines with crowded working conditions to produce a
potentially negative work context. If Wienerdude hires her, Lelaina should experience low
intrinsic motivation and general job satisfaction.

Source: J. E. Champoux, *Instructor's Manual* for *Our Feature Presentation: Organizational Behavior* (Mason,
Oh.: South-Western, a division of Thomson Learning, 2005), 38. Used with the permission of Thomson Learning.

Virtual Team eExercises

Teams of students complete the second group of eExercises. Team members interact
using on-line course technologies such as discussion areas and chatrooms. The
technologies described for the virtual team eExercises are common features of on-
line course delivery and management platforms.

Team members can interact by either of two methods. Asynchronous interaction
uses a private discussions area topic set for each team. Only team members can
access the topic. Synchronous interaction occurs in a scheduled chatroom activity
for team members. This communication method requires coordination among
teams and the instructor to assign the course's chatrooms.

Each team posts its results for the exercise to a public discussion topic for the exercise. The results of each team become part of the discussion during the scheduled
weekly chat activity or the alternative discussions area postings.

Alternative Social Processes for Decision Making

The 'Alternative Social Processes for Decision Making' eExercise presents two
decision-making scenarios to a team. Teams assess each scenario for the type of
decision process that best fits the scenario. Decision processes range from individually based processes to a group-based process that asks for consensus.

This exercise is based on the Vroom–Yetton (1973) model that commonly appears
in management and organizational behaviour courses. It is a normative decision-
making model that guides a person's choices from five alternative approaches to
decision making. The approaches are Autocratic (AI, AII), Consultative (CI, CII),
and Group Based (GII). The model uses a set of rules that protects a decision's

acceptance and quality. It picks the approach shown by the rules as best for the decision problem under consideration. This exercise addresses the on-line management education issues of learner involvement and learner self-awareness described at the beginning of this chapter.

Students who have completed this exercise usually pick all five approaches to decision making for 'Case I: Oil Pipeline'. Their reasons for choices vary highly. Those who pick AI or AII note that they have the information to decide. Students who pick the consultative approaches (CI and CII) note that they need more information to make a decision. Those who pick GII, the most time-consuming approach, say they want to build commitment to the decision to carry out the decision effectively.

'Case II: Data Collection' has about 90 per cent of a class choosing the GII social process. Discussion usually centres on the ambiguity of the situation, the need for more information, and the need for supervisory commitment described in the case's last sentence. Students often see the importance of this commitment to the decision to get effective implementation, a key part of the Vroom–Yetton decision model.

Organizational Culture Diagnosis: Backdraft *(1991)*

The film-based 'Organizational Culture Diagnosis' eExercise uses scenes from the film *Backdraft* as the exercise target. These scenes come from the collection of film scenes described earlier. Presentation of the *Backdraft* scenes proceeds as described for the *Reality Bites* scene. This exercise addresses the on-line management education issues of learner analytical skills and practical application of on-line course content described at the beginning of this chapter.

Two brothers follow their late father, a legendary Chicago firefighter, and join the department. Stephen 'Bull' McCaffrey (Kurt Russell) joins first and rises to the rank of lieutenant. Younger brother Brian (William Baldwin) joins later and becomes a member of Bull's Company 17. The scene appears early in *Backdraft* as part of 'The First Day' sequence. It shows Company 17 preparing to fight a garment factory fire.

The eExercise form's content follows common discussions about organizational culture and culture diagnosis found in management and organizational behaviour courses. Different exercise sections focus on an organizational culture's visible aspects such as physical characteristics and invisible aspects such as values. Students will typically have the required background from course content to assess the firefighter organizational culture shown in the *Backdraft* scenes. A 'Navigation Menu' allows convenient movement among the exercise's sections.

Virtual teams complete their organizational culture diagnosis of the *Backdraft* scenes. Team members interact with each other using the interaction methods described earlier. Each team posts its results to the exercise's public discussion topic.

Table 7.4 *Backdraft.* Film scene analysis

The scene shows many cultural artifacts of the Chicago Fire Department. Some are bold symbols such as the fire trucks, loud sirens, fast driving, the bright red fire hydrant, and the roaring fire. Others are equally important cultural symbols but less bold in presentation. For example, nicknames appear on the backs of the firefighter's jackets. Stephen McCaffrey's jacket says, 'Bull.'

In-use values guide much of the veteran firefighters' behaviour. No one told the firemen to smash the windows of the Mercedes Benz so they could get the fire hose to the fire hydrant. Brian quickly learns this value as he stares in disbelief. There is little time while fighting a fire to describe values (espoused values), although Stephen gives his brother some guidance about how to attach his equipment and stay beside him while fighting the fire.

Other aspects of a firefighter's culture appear in the scene. New firefighters ('probies') must accept their subordinate status during their first workdays, and take wanted or unwanted guidance from their more senior firemen.

Source: J. E. Champoux, *Instructor's Manual* for *Our Feature Presentation: Organizational Behavior* (Mason, Oh.: South-Western, a division of Thomson Learning, 2005), 42. Used with the permission of Thomson Learning.

The results of each team become part of the discussion during the scheduled weekly chat activity or the alternative discussions area postings.

Several parts of the film scene analysis in Table 7.4 should appear in submitted eExercises. The visible artefacts of a Chicago firefighter's organizational culture should appear in most submitted exercises. Uniforms, fire trucks, fast driving, status relationships, and language should get the attention of most students. Many students also will note in-use values from the behaviour shown in the scenes. For example, working together and properly attaching equipment appear at different places. Most students will not note any basic assumptions because they are hard for an outsider to see. One exception is breaking the window of the Mercedes Benz. The firefighter broke the window without hesitation, an example of a basic assumption.

Assessment of Each eExercise

This section assesses each eExercise discussed in this chapter against the on-line management education issues and learning theories described earlier. The discussion highlights the role of these exercises in on-line teaching and learning processes. Constructivism and experiential learning theory provide broad support for using the four types of eExercises in the on-line teaching and learning environment.

- *Individual eExercise: Your Conflict Orientations.* This exercise focuses on the on-line management education issues of learner involvement and self-awareness. Asking a student to assess her or his conflict orientations increases involvement with that course content. Self-awareness also likely increases because the student considers the conflict orientations and some likely occasions when she or he uses them. Behavioural, cognitive, and humanistic learning theories support the use of individually focused experiential exercises.

- *Individual Film-Based eExercise: Diagnosing and Redesigning Jobs.* Learner analytical skills and practical application of on-line course content are the on-line management education issues addressed by this exercise. The film scenes have some varying content that also can increase student involvement. Behavioural, cognitive, and humanistic learning theories support using this exercise.

- *Virtual Team eExercise: Decision Making: Individual versus Group Approaches.* This exercise helps with the on-line management education issues of learner involvement and self-awareness. The virtual team approach of this exercise receives strong support and guidance from social learning theory. Although virtual team members usually have no face-to-face contact, on-line chatrooms and discussion areas form a social context for student learning. Students still 'observe' the behaviour of other students, although they mediate their observations through on-line course technology.

- *Virtual Team eExercise: Organizational Culture Diagnosis.* This exercise addresses the on-line management education issues of learner analytical skills and practical application of on-line course content. Social learning theory lends its support to the virtual team design of this exercise as it did the previous exercise.

SOME NOTES ABOUT ON-LINE EXPERIENTIAL COURSE DESIGN

Bringing experiential learning to the on-line learning environment can help engage students with course content, other students, and the instructor. The eExercises introduced in this chapter emphasize a student-focused approach to on-line courses. Blending the exercises with on-line film scenes also brings multiple media and variety to on-line course design.

One also should address other aspects of on-line course design to ensure the desired effect of eExercises. Specifying the eExercise in that part of a course's assignments, and calling it out as a specific item in a discussion agenda, can help engage students with the exercise. Inserting a specific content element for the eExercise helps remind students of its presence and the need to complete the exercise during the required period. Each design element noted here can help increase student engagement with on-line course content.

NOTES

An earlier version of this chapter was presented at the Academy of Management meetings, 14 Aug. 2006. Atlanta, Georgia.

1. I thank Dr Kayleigh Carabajal, Executive Director, Organizational Learning, Central New Mexico Community College, for her invaluable help with this section of the chapter.
2. This discussion of learning theories drew from J. E. Champoux and K. Carabajal, 'Media, Cognition, and Learning: A Theoretical Basis for Using Film in Teaching', Albuquerque, N. Mex., the Robert O. Anderson Schools of Management, the University of New Mexico, 29 Sept. 2003, working paper.

REFERENCES

Bandura. A. (1977). *Social Learning Theory*. Englewood Cliffs, NJ: Prentice-Hall.

Bartlett, F. C. (1932). *Remembering: A Study in Experimental and Social Psychology*. Cambridge: Cambridge University Press.

Bloom, B. S. (1956). *Taxonomy of Educational Objectives: The Classification of Educational Goals*. New York: Longman.

Brah, A. and Hoy, J. (1989). 'Experiential Learning, a New Orthodoxy?', in S. Weil and I. McGill (eds.), *Making Sense of Experiential Learning*. Buckingham: Society for Research into Higher Education and the Open University Press.

Brown, J. S., Collins, A., and Duguid, P. (1989). 'Situated Cognition and the Culture of Learning', *Educational Researcher*, 18: 32–42.

Bruner, J. S. (1961). 'The Act of Discovery', *Harvard Educational Review*, 31: 21–32.

—— Oliver, R., and Greenfield, P. M. (1966). *Studies in Cognitive Growth*. New York: Wiley.

Bugental, J. F. T. (1967). *Challenges of Humanist Psychology*. New York: McGraw-Hill.

Champoux, J. E. (2005). *Our Feature Presentation: Organizational Behaviour*. Mason, Oh.: South-Western, a division of Thomson Learning.

Chance, P. (1994). *Learning and Behaviour*. Pacific Grove, Calif.: Brooks/Cole.

Dewey, J. (1916). *Democracy and Education: An Introduction to the Philosophy of Education*. New York: The Macmillan Company.

Draves, W. (2000). *Teaching Online*. River Falls, Wis.: LERN Books.

Hackman, J. R. and Oldham, G. (1980). *Work Redesign*. Reading, Mass.: Addison-Wesley.

Jarvis, P. (1987). *Adult Learning in the Social Context*. London: Croom Helm.

Kearsley, G. (2000). *Online Education: Learning and Teaching in Cyberspace*. Belmont, Calif.: Wadsworth Thomson Learning.

Kolb, D. A. (1984). *Experiential Learning: Experience as the Source of Learning and Development*. Englewood Cliffs, NJ: Prentice Hall.

Lave, J. and Wenger, E. (1991). *Situated Learning: Legitimate Peripheral Participation*. Cambridge: Cambridge University Press.

Miller, N. and Boud, D. (1996). 'Animating Learning from Experience', in D. Boud and N. Miller (eds.), *Working with Experience: Animating Learning*. London: Routledge.

—— and Dollard, J. (1941). *Social Learning and Imitation*. New Haven: Yale University Press.

Mischel W. (1973). 'Towards a Cognitive, Social Learning Reconception of Personality', *Psychological Review*, 80: 252–83.

Mischel W. (1979). 'On the Interface of Cognition and Personality', *American Psychologist*, 34: 740–54.

Patterson, C. H. (1973). *Humanist Education*. Englewood Cliffs, NJ: Prentice-Hall.

Rogers, C. R. (1969). *Freedom to Learn*, 3rd edn. Columbus, Oh.: Merrill/Macmillan.

Rumelhart, D. E. and Norman, D. A. (1981). 'Analogical Processes in Learning', in J. R. Anderson (ed.), *Cognitive Skills and their Acquisition*. Hillsdale, NJ: Erlbaum.

Skinner, B. F. (1968). *The Technology of Teaching*. Englewood Cliffs, NJ: Prentice Hall.

Thorndike, E. L. (1932). *The Fundamentals of Learning*. New York: Teachers College, Columbia University.

Vroom, V. H. and Yetton, P. (1973). *Leadership and Decision-Making*. Pittsburgh: University of Pittsburgh Press.

Watson, J. B. (1914). *Behaviour: An Introduction to Comparative Psychology*. New York: Holt, Rinehart & Winston.

Weil, S. and McGill, I. (1989a). 'A Framework for Making Sense of Experiential Learning', in S. Weil and I. McGill (eds.), *Making Sense of Experiential Learning*. Buckingham: Society for Research into Higher Education and the Open University Press.

—— —— (1989b). 'Continuing the Dialogue: New Possibilities for Experiential Learning', in S. Weil and I. McGill (eds.), *Making Sense of Experiential Learning*. Buckingham: Society for Research into Higher Education and the Open University Press.

CHAPTER 8

IMPLEMENTING EXPERIENTIAL LEARNING

IT'S NOT ROCKET SCIENCE

MARTIN J. HORNYAK

STEVE G. GREEN

KURT A. HEPPARD

INTRODUCTION

EXPERIENTIAL learning is a powerful pedagogical tool that recognizes that people learn best from their own experiences. This chapter presents a brief description of experiential learning, its relationship with the changing educational landscape, and insights into why the academic community is embracing it so actively. Experiential education in all of its contemporary forms, including active or participatory learning, self-directed learning, and service learning, to name a few, has been extensively studied and the many merits and shortcomings are well documented in education, business, and management literature (Henry 1989).

A virtual paradigm shift in educational theory is transitioning the focus of educators away from instruction and toward learning (Barr and Tagg 1995). Many feel that for this transformation to be successful, reform should be focused on the types of learning that give students the tools they need for a complex world. Experiential learning is an excellent example of a pedagogy that can answer this call for reform.

It is probably safe to state that teaching students to identify and take advantage of their own styles of learning, as well as recognize their weakness, would be beneficial in preparing them to address the complexities of the real world they will encounter (Berhman and Levin 1984; Luckmann 1996). After all, teachers will not be at their students'sides in the workplace after graduation.

Research supports the contention that more discovery-oriented and student-active teaching methods allow students to discover knowledge on their own (Nilson 1998) and the literature is replete with the avocation of this lifelong learning skill. There has been a groundswell of support for a mix of activities that teach independence and interdependence and interdisciplinary life skills that students will need, and which can be implemented across the curriculum (Association of American Colleges and Universities (AACandU) 2002). Experiential learning is an excellent example of the type of pedagogy that promises to address, in a meaningful and measurable way, the diverse expectations of students, faculty, and future employers by focusing on the learner and recognizing that with learning, one size does not fit all (Weigand 1995).

This chapter provides a brief description of experiential learning along with its relationship with broader changes in education. This is followed by a description of a course with exceptional experiential learning application. In many ways, this course is the quintessence of experiential learning. Not only does it simulate almost the exact engineering and procurement environment that many of the students will enter upon graduation, but it was developed in lock-step with institutional learning outcomes at its foundation while directly addressing assurance of learning issues.

EXPERIENTIAL LEARNING

The definition of experiential learning varies. Many are descriptive or compare it with traditional learning in that it combines direct experience with guided reflection and analysis and is student centred (Chapman, McPhee, and Proudman 1995). Additional definitions help link theory and practice while building upon established educational philosophies. Still other definitions are oriented toward education at institutions of higher learning, which will be the focus of this chapter.

It should be noted that there are other dimensions of experiential learning which address important educational considerations, but will not be the focus of this chapter. For example, there are many learning opportunities that take place beyond the 'school house' but are still an element of a formal curriculum. From co-ops and internships to international exchanges, many see these experiential learning opportunities as valuable complements to classroom activities. But some critics have viewed these as 'semester-long interviews' or 'on-the-job training' with future employers and post-graduation employment being the ultimate pay-off (Schofield and Caragata 1999). Also, from the business training industry, there are many different activity-based training approaches that incorporate experiential learning philosophies. These experiential learning activities have become increasingly diverse, high-profile, and occasionally controversial as they are applied in more settings by more mainstream organizations (Weaver 1999). This chapter will concentrate exclusively on experiential learning as it applies to classroom education.

EXPERIENTIAL LEARNING AND THE EVOLVING EDUCATIONAL LANDSCAPE

While experiential learning is arguably one of the most significant areas for current research and practice for adult education (Michelson 1996), there are also many that critically question and examine its implementation (Pickles 2005). Theoretical models have been developed to help frame experiential learning and explain why this particular pedagogy enhances the educational experience. Most models include the concepts of the actual experience, plus reflection upon that experience. They are usually described in some variation of a process or cycle that includes action, reflection, and application (Kolb 1984). The position of David Kolb, for example, is that while people are exposed to many life experiences, they do not 'learn' from all of them. Learning happens only when there is reflective thought and an internal processing of an experience by the learner in a way that links the experience to previous learning, and transforms the learner's previous understanding in some way (Fenwick 2001). In management education circles, Kolb's theory has been reported as 'extremely influential' and 'is rarely seen as problematic', while there are some critics that question, for example, the need to progress sequentially through the cycle (Beard and Wilson 2002).

In essence, experience alone, or what is often called 'learning by doing', is insufficient to be called experiential learning. While some argue that there must be a deliberate design and systematic implementation to maximize the educational experience of experiential learning, that is not to say there should be rigid rules with no flexibility. For example, while the learning environment may have been painstakingly designed, the actual classroom may even be 'teacher-less'.

Experiential learning, which is focused on capitalizing on experience to enhance learning, is in line with what some refer to as a new paradigm for higher education (Mailen 2000; Svinicki 1990). What was once the traditional dominant educational approach, commonly referred to as the 'instructional paradigm', has shifted to a 'learning paradigm' (Barr and Tagg 1995). The very purpose of the instruction paradigm is to offer courses, while the learning paradigm goal is not to merely transfer knowledge, but to create environments that allow students to discover and construct knowledge and to make discoveries and solve problems on their own (Barr and Tagg 1995). In an institution that has embraced the learning paradigm, the structure of courses, assessment, and the form of pedagogy all become negotiable. There is no one-size-fits-all best learning environment. But experiential learning is an excellent example of the type of pedagogy that promises to address, in a meaningful and measurable way, the diverse expectations of students, faculty, and future employers (Levine and Tompkins 1996).

The learning paradigm requires a constant search for new structures and methods that work better for student learning and success, and expects even these to be redesigned continually and to evolve over time (Barr and Tagg 1995). In addition, course content is very dynamic. What is 'known' twenty years from now will be very different from what is 'known' today (Haynie and Heppard 2005). This means students need to acquire not just knowledge as it currently exists, but also the skills and attitudes necessary to continue learning after they leave school. It is unlikely that they will be able to acquire these skills in a classroom in which they are 'told' everything they need to know.

Consequently, the role of a faculty member is evolving as well. In a learning-centred classroom, the educator is expected to provide a learning environment in which students learn by experience and by interacting with the instructor, as well as other students. In a classroom focused on learning, the students are not sitting passively; they are practising the skills they are learning, monitoring their own learning progress, and developing the adaptive capacities they will need to address the dynamic workplace that awaits them. They are what are referred to as 'intentional learners' who can adapt to new environments, integrate knowledge from different sources, and continue learning through their lives (AACandU 2002). These intentional learners are empowered through the mastery of intellectual and practical skills, informed by knowledge about forms of enquiry, and are responsible for their personal actions and civic values (AACandU 2002).

Educators have also focused attention on the benefits of teaching students to effectively work in teams or groups to satisfy employers' desire for students who can 'hit the corporate ground running' with cross-functional team experience (Chen, Donahue, and Klimoski 2004; Siegel and Sorenson 1999). Educators have embraced a wide range of experiential learning pedagogy attempting to make the classroom experience better reflect the real world as an effective member, or leader, of a team. As a result, instructional methods have shifted from traditional instruction-centred lecturing with a focus on individual effort as described earlier, to a variety of team-oriented experiential learning approaches (Johnson and Johnson 1974, 1989) including activities such as group projects (Michaelsen, Knight, and Fink 2002), student teams (Stein and Hurd 2000; Vik 2001), and cooperative learning (Ravenscroft and Buckless 1997).

While student learning has always been the central topic of higher education, there has also been a renewed emphasis on assessment, or what is currently referred to as 'assurance of learning', by national accreditation bodies such as the Association to Advance Collegiate Schools of Business (AACSB). Assurance of learning evaluates how well a school accomplishes the educational aims at the core of its activities and the learning process is separate from the demonstration that students achieve learning goals (Association to Advance Collegiate Schools of Business (AACSB) 2005). Institutions must use a well-documented, systematic process that assesses the impact of curricula on learning. Because of differences in missions, student populations, employer populations, and other circumstances, each programme's learning goals will differ (AACSB 2005). AACSB, for example, emphasizes that no single approach to assurance of learning is required and schools are encouraged to choose, create, and innovate learning measures that fit with the goals of the degree programmes, pedagogies in use, and the individual schools' circumstances (AACSB 2005). By any measure, experiential learning is an excellent pedagogy to facilitate achievement of educational outcomes.

In addition, as institutions search for justifications to modify or adapt their curricula to changes in education, and as they prioritize activities or realign resources, experiential learning appears to be very appealing in this regard as well. Experiential learning allows some objective means for ranking or prioritizing implementation decisions or budget allocations. This is in part because many institutions are embracing educational outcomes that are associated with a revised Bloom's taxonomy with respect to learning, teaching, and assessment (Anderson and Krathwohl 2001). These outcomes assure that students are learning what their stakeholders expect and need. Activities that do not directly and measurably support these outcomes may suffer in priority and resources allocation. Because of its promised positive impact on the student's ability to adapt in the workplace, experiential learning is enjoying this emphasis on assurance of learning.

INCREASED NEED FOR EXPERIENTIAL LEARNING

Based on Kolb, experiential learning may be more effective when it is integrated with educational objectives and classroom curriculum and activities, and contains opportunities for students to reflect on their experiences and grow intellectually (Kolb 1984). This chapter presents an example of how, through a capstone design course, a military service academy embraces experiential learning in much the same manner as the private sector and other universities have. However, a major difference is that this course has a final project that not only mimics the real world that many of the students are graduating into; it includes launching a small satellite and placing it into earth's orbit.

This senior capstone course at the United States Air Force Academy (USAFA) involves engineering systems design and programme management that almost identically replicates an engineering management environment. It allows students to experience and learn from designing, building, and finally launching a small (micro) satellite.

USAFA, like any other major university, has embraced many different forms of experiential learning including the service component. The widely practised form of experiential learning, service learning, is a method where reasoning, leadership, interpersonal skills, academic content, values, and citizenship are taught through real life community experiences (Katula and Threnhauser 1999). As the military's roles and missions are evolving and changing to new global responsibilities and citizenship, the Department of Defense (DOD), and particularly its service academies, must recognize the need to be able to prepare future officers with increasing agile skills sets.

For example, the Secretary of the Air Force has stated that one of the Air Force's core competencies is translating technology to war fighting (USAF Chief's Sight Picture 2003). The relationship between this core competency and translating technology to 'service' is closely related to war fighting. Developing an experiential learning pedagogy at a service academy helps groom future officers and leaders for new global and domestic requirements that will be expected of them. War fighting and service, such as humanitarian support missions, now draw upon the same human resource pool and officers must be prepared to respond to either diverse requirement.

Even before America embraced a new emphasis on homeland defence and the creation of the Department of Homeland Security (DHS), the DOD was experimenting with major initiatives associated with 'transformation' of the armed forces in a post-Cold War era (USAF Joint Vision 2020, 2000). With the fall of the Berlin Wall in 1991, Cold War posturing had ended and there was a renewed use of the military in peacekeeping, humanitarian actions, and contingency actions (Callander 1998).

The dynamics of an expeditionary military involved in direct combat in many different theatres, possibly simultaneously, has taken the need for experiential learning to the next level of sophistication. The old adage of 'train the way you fight', with its intuitive understanding of the ability to properly prepare military members for the battle they will encounter, has evolved to 'train while you fight', citing the need for continuation training and experiential learning to adapt to new environments (Haun 2005).

IMPLEMENTING EXPERIENTIAL LEARNING IN THE UNITED STATES AIR FORCE ACADEMY

The intent of this chapter is to extend the discussion of experiential learning and highlight this powerful methodology's application in USAFA's learning environment. Using USAFA's Small Satellite Program as a case study, its background, project histories, and experiential learning pedagogy are highlighted while showcasing one current project, the building of FalconSat 3. Finally, reasons for programme success are suggested with an emphasis on what aspects other institutions may be able to implement.

Given an apparent need for more experiential learning opportunities that meets the requirements of a modern DOD, it would stand to reason that this pedagogy would be embraced rigorously at all levels of the curriculum, particularly at a service academy like USAFA where its educational mission is to 'Inspire and educate cadets and faculty to serve our nation with integrity in peace and war' (United States Air Force Academy (USAFA) 2005d). This backdrop provides an excellent environment for experiential learning for many reasons including that USAFA can identify the specific functional and operational career fields that its students will enter upon graduation.

USAFA is an undergraduate institution located just north of Colorado Springs, Colorado. Since its first class graduated in 1959, approximately 38,000 graduates have entered the United States Air Force or other components of the DOD (Association of Graduates (AOG) 2004). Currently USAFA has just over 4,000 students (cadets), selectively recruited nationwide. Cadets are commissioned upon graduation as Air Force officers with the daunting, time-honoured challenge of national service. USAFA's Core Values, which mirror the Core Values of the entire Air Force, are 'Integrity First, Service Before Self, and Excellence in Everything We Do' (USAF Core Values 1997).

USAFA has been awarded all major institutional accreditations including North Central Association of Colleges and Schools and many discipline-specific accreditations such as ABET (Accreditation Board for Engineering and Technology) and AACSB (Association to Advance Collegiate Schools of Business) to name a few (USAFA 2005a). Also, USAFA has many examples of external validation of the quality of its education. In 2005, it was ranked as the twelfth 'best overall academic experience for undergraduates' and was ranked Number 1 in 'professors make themselves accessible' by *Princeton Review's* Best 361 Colleges (Frank, Meltzer, and Maier 2005).

Experiential learning has been specifically and deliberately incorporated in several courses at USAFA. Since the mid-1970s, a course entitled Engineering Systems Design (ENGR 410) served as a core curriculum capstone experience addressing a wide variety of community stakeholders in three basic categories: Community

Service, Assisting the Disabled, and USAFA Improvement (Hornyak, Green, and Ciccotello 2000). There currently is a course, Capstone for Operations Research (OR 420), that offers 'consulting' projects for actual public and private organizations in the greater Colorado Springs area, USAFA, and the Air Force at large. Also, recently two new interdisciplinary majors, Systems Engineering (SE) and Systems Engineering Management (SEM), have been initiated that also plan to have capstone courses that will heavily implement experiential learning (USAFA 2005e). But the senior level two-semester sequence course, Small Spacecraft Engineering I and II (ASTRO 436/437), is specifically focused on experiential learning. This course, referred to as the Small Satellite Program, serves as the case study for this chapter.

THE SMALL SATELLITE PROGRAM LEGACY

For decades USAFA has pursued the challenge of doing a better job of enhancing not only cognitive skills in the cadets but also their interpersonal, behavioural, and management skills. The Academy instituted its Small Satellite Program in 1993 to motivate cadets toward space by providing 'hands-on' satellite development and operational experience. This is a classic application of experiential learning.

Since 1965, USAFA has offered a major in astronautical engineering, one of the few accredited undergraduate astronautics programmes in the nation (USAFA 2005c). Cadets have developed and flown three student experiment packages on space shuttle missions. They have also been doing rocket propulsion research since 1990 (USAFA 2005c). Over the last decade, the Small Satellite Program has been administered and taught by the Department of Astronautics (DFAS). It was originally created as a dedicated systems analysis and decision-making process course for astronautics majors only. Since 1991, it has evolved into an interdisciplinary project-based course for students interested in synthesizing classroom learning from various disciplines to tackle 'real world' engineering design and programme management challenges. Furthermore, the Small Satellite Program incorporates additional capabilities taught in the Academy's four academic divisions (Engineering Sciences, Basic Sciences, Social Sciences, and Humanities) and has become a prototypical capstone experience replacing some of the previously required capstone courses (USAFA 2005c).

The actual 'products' of the Small Satellite Program are referred to as FalconSats. FalconSat modules enabled students to apply what they have learned in various technical and non-technical courses to find design solutions to problems. All of the FalconSat projects have an experiential learning orientation benefiting multiple facets of the Air Force, education, and space community at large. FalconSat teams are given minimal direction other than background on how technical systems are developed and produced within the Air Force systems acquisition process. In fact, this 'sink or swim' approach is identical to what students will experience as new officers designing, developing, and procuring major Air Force weapon systems.

However, one institutional stumbling block almost made the experience unachievable. Since a typical FalconSat project life cycle usually lasts more than one year from concept exploration to final production, it was necessary to constantly rotate student programme management teams due to graduation. To generate continuity and maximize the learning experience, the Small Satellite Program enrols interested third-year students (juniors) into the programme, giving them an opportunity to work with fourth-year students (seniors) and instructors over a two-year period. The course operates like any company under government contract, or a government agency charged with a specific programme development and management task. The project team selects a programme manager who is singularly responsible and accountable for successful task completion. Other team members perform functional duties such as finance, production, test, logistics, and documentation depending upon how the team decides to organize. This parallels very closely with how Air Force major weapon system programme offices are organized and operate. An integrated or 'systems' approach is stressed throughout the course.

With respect to assurance of learning, the groups are assessed, measured, and evaluated using specific acquisition milestones marked by graded briefings, demonstrations, and written reports. There are no examinations since milestone briefings are the vehicle for information transfer and assessment. As in the 'real world', a successfully completed project is a time-proven benchmark of excellence. The course emphasizes the economic and managerial aspects of the acquisition process, as well as technical performance. Unprecedented levels of student freedom are allowed in the course. Students determine the schedule, perform all planning, and accomplish all coordination within the milestone schedule.

Each FalconSat project receives funds and resources from customers and government organizations interested in the project's payload. Each project received an official ranking and a National Aeronautics and Space Administration (NASA) manifest number. Originally, FalconSat 2 was rank 21 out of thirty-four essential space payloads by the DOD Space Experiment and Review Board (SERB) and manifested to fly on Space Shuttle *Atlantis* (STS-114) on 16 January 2003 (Martin, Sellers, and Green 2002). The current satellite project, FalconSat 3, is another example of the students demonstrating the adaptive capacity that can be enhanced through experiential learning. FalconSat 3 underwent vibration testing in preparation for an anticipated launch from the Atlas V vehicle (USAFA 2005c).

From many perspectives, the Small Satellite Program is a benchmark for unique experiential learning projects nationwide. It clearly supports and develops the Air Force core competencies of 'translating technology to war fighting and service' as well as directly 'developing airmen', another core competency (USAF Chief's Sight Picture 2003). With worldwide organizational connections needing payload and launch assistance, FalconSat allows students to learn engineering, management, and acquisition processes through hands-on experience. Regardless of their future career speciality selection, students on the FalconSat team learn essential components of the Air Force systems project development and the acquisition process while assisting external stakeholders. From contracting officers to pilots, many will eventually hold positions designing and procuring major weapon systems, and the FalconSat programme prepares them through experiential learning.

WHY DOES THIS EXPERIENTIAL LEARNING PROGRAMME WORK?

There are distinct answers to the questions of why an experiential learning approach at this highly technical school is working so well, and what lessons other institutions can learn about developing their own experiential learning projects. The Small Satellite Program course philosophy and implementation have overcome barriers that might reduce the likelihood of successful implementation. First, faculty members from various departments within the Engineering Division, as well as the various departments from the Social Sciences Division, are invited, encouraged, and assigned as instructors/mentors for the projects. Participation is highly recognized, valued, and rewarded by the Dean and department heads. Besides the obvious appeal and 'status' of launching the final project into space, the course's overall significance to the core curriculum minimizes faculty and organizational resistance.

Second, the infrastructure for experiential activities is already in place. USAFA has an established machine and electrical shop with works areas and skilled professional personnel available for advice on design and construction. Most impressive, the Space Systems Research Center (SSRC) has been created and endowed with an impressive laboratory, fabrication site, permanent staff, and office area solely dedicated to the FalconSats and rocket research including a command centre and clean room (USAFA 2005c). Thus many of the 'infrastructure' concerns associated with viable experiential learning activities have been mitigated.

Third, major relevancy barriers are overcome by inexorably tying FalconSat to the Air Force's systems acquisition process in completing design projects. Courses such as ASTRO 436/437 require attention to technical details of systems design as well as the economics, management, and social aspects of the process. The processes used in this course are the identical major weapon system acquisition process students will experience upon graduation from the Academy if they enter the procurement, contracting, or various engineering career fields. Also the realism of managing group dynamics is apparent with teams involving students of a variety of academic majors many of which are non-technical in nature.

Lesson Learned: Linking Experiential Learning and Educational Outcomes

Perhaps the most impressive aspect of the Small Satellite Program's success is the linkage between experiential learning and USAFA Educational Outcomes and the development of Air Force core competencies. The lesson for institutions embracing experiential learning is to start with the educational outcomes you want to achieve. The direct links between the experiential learning pedagogy used in the Small Satellite Program and USAFA's Dean of the Faculty Educational Outcomes are evident. The Educational Outcomes were established to describe the desired intellectual capabilities of its graduates (USAFA 2005b).

- *Officers who possess a breadth of integrated, fundamental knowledge in basic sciences, engineering, the humanities, and social sciences, and depth of knowledge in an area of concentration of their choice.*

As complex as designing a satellite may sound, the students do not require knowledge above what they have achieved in their core classes. Even though some basic core skills have not been used or forgotten, they are re-emphasized in this capstone educational experience. Students should graduate recognizing where to get help, how to teach themselves again, and that people from every discipline can make meaningful project contributions.

- *Officers who are intellectually curious.*

When presented with a problem, or a seemingly unachievable obstacle, students are expected to apply appropriate models to assess the situation and solve the problem. When dealing with small satellites, there are no solutions manuals. Students are expected to address problems using intellectual curiosity as their compass and all their means available.

- *Officers who can communicate effectively.*

The students involved in the Small Satellite Program are not just communicating with peers and instructors. They must communicate ideas to external organizations and customers paying for the service. Students need to understand the immediate project needs/impact and be able to articulate and 'sell' what is being done for multiple clients and customers.

- *Officers who can frame and resolve ill-defined problems.*

By its very nature, the construction of a small satellite is an ill-defined problem. A 'Statement of Work' attempts to qualify and quantify what the user wants. As a team, they need to further clarify requirements and identify constraints in order to develop a solid understanding for application in design solution. The process may seem ambiguous but if time is taken to understand complexities, ask questions, understand the project requirements, and to develop a useful schedule, it can be done.

- *Officers who can work effectively with others.*

It would be difficult to construct a better opportunity uniting a team of people of different academic specialties to work toward a common goal. While this course offering is only one of many courses taken by cadets, the time, dedication, and tenacity required of individuals would be futile if not for the synergies of the team. Simply put, this is not a one-person job, so survival is predicated on teamwork, leadership, and followership.

- *Officers who are independent learners.*

One of the true course benefits is it challenges the students to teach themselves about their project. For the students, FalconSat offers situations and dilemma that they have never encountered. Answers to questions need to be discovered and independently applied to the solutions because there is literally no single source to rely upon.

- *Officers who can apply their knowledge and skills to the unique tasks of the military profession.*

Regardless of what assignment cadets receive upon graduation, there will always be some aspect of the systems engineering management process involved whether the job is in supply, acquisitions, maintenance, personnel, space operations, or flying. At some point, all Air Force members will be called on to head a major project team with all of its ambiguities (Bruno 1999).

These educational outcomes are crafted toward USAFA graduates becoming military officers. However, other institutions can develop or modify their own educational outcomes and integrate experiential learning opportunities to help accomplish those desired results.

Currently USAFA uses experiential learning in several courses as a vehicle to culminate its undergraduate education and meet its educational outcomes. The Small Satellite Program transitions students from a primarily academic environment to the challenges of 'practice' and the 'real world' they will face as Air Force project officers. By continuing to add new elements associated with the technologically dynamic space environment to its experiential learning pedagogy, the Small Satellite Program continues to succeed in developing excellent students, officers, and citizens. But of course, continuous improvement is also recognized as critically important.

How Can FalconSat Improve Its Experiential Learning?

Having a project actually launched into space has its own positive motivation and organizational inertia. But the reality of risks associated with such a task becomes apparent. In the beginning of each year, much excitement and enthusiasm is exhibited by the team as they meet to discuss the 'client and customers' needs and issues. However, this connection needs to be consistently reinforced as well as the tie to the educational outcomes. As the process moves into the design and fabrication stages, the team focus often fixates on production and meeting critical project milestones. The reality of the project's scope and significance becomes apparent, and, depending on the progress, may become disheartening. Also, many environmental factors, such as launch vehicle availability, intrude into the experiential learning classroom. There is a real and palpable chance of failure in this course. Instead of merely focusing on the deliverable, what may get lost is the sense of the value being added to the community, customers, or individuals through the team's work and effort, and instructors must keep students aware of this.

Also, students are required to make self-evaluations and peer evaluations to be included in the final grade. However, the evaluations rate individuals based on criteria important to the experiential learning's 'practical application'. Job performance, attitude, leadership, management of resources, and communication categories are self-assessed as well as peer rated. These performance categories are oriented toward project tasks, goals, and objectives. If USAFA desires to advance the impact of experiential learning, the students need more time to reflect, analyse, and openly discuss their experiences.

Final Thoughts

This presentation of experiential learning at USAFA suggests the planned and deliberate integration of classroom learning experiences and 'real world' projects can be a very important element in helping meet institutional educational outcomes. It also supports experiential learning arguments that this learning pedagogy is appropriate for a variety of disciplines (Sax and Astin 1997) including engineering and the military profession. Since the programme is directly related to developing Air Force core competencies in cadets, this example also demonstrates to educators how enhancing learning by integrating coursework with practical applications and stakeholder expectations can be achieved through experiential learning.

At the same time, this chapter illustrates the importance of the institutional commitment required for a successful experiential learning programme and the need of balancing any course's focus on both practical and educational aspects.

USAFA is committed to continue the investigation of innovative pedagogy with the ultimate goal of becoming the best educational institution possible (Born 2005). Experiential learning has helped provide real world projects for future Air Force leaders that have helped, and continue to help, accomplish this goal. We are hopeful that educators in other disciplines can find this example useful for their courses and that other educational institutions consider experiential learning as a part of a learner-centred curriculum. The design is replicable across disciplines and gives students the opportunity to experience projects that best imitate those that they will find in their future careers. While experiential learning is not rocket science, we have demonstrated that it certainly can be.

Note

The authors wish to thank Lt-Col. Timothy J. Lawrence, Ph.D., Director of the Space Systems Research Center, Department of Astronautics, United States Air Force Academy, for his invaluable assistance.

Opinions, conclusions, and recommendations expressed or implied within are solely those of the authors and do not necessarily represent the views of USAFA, USAF, the DOD, or any other government agency.

References

Anderson, L., and Krathwohl, D. (eds.) (2001). *A Taxonomy for Learning, Teaching and Assessing*. New York: Addison Wesley Longman.

Association to Advance Collegiate Schools of Business (AACSB) (2005). *Accreditation Standards: Assurance of Learning Standards*. Tampa, Fla.: AACSB International.

Association of American Colleges and Universities (AACandU) National Panel Report (2002). *Greater Expectations: A New Vision of Learning as the Nation Goes to College*. Washington: Association of American Colleges and Universities.

Association of Graduates (AOG) of the United States Air Force Academy (2004). *Register of Graduates of the United States Air Force Academy 2004 Edition*.

Barr, R., and Tagg, J. (1995). 'From Teaching to Learning: A New Paradigm for Undergraduate Education', *Change*, Nov.–Dec.: 21–7.

Beard, C., and Wilson, J. (2002). *The Power of Experiential Learning: A Handbook for Trainers and Educators*. London: Kogan Page.

Berhman, J., and Levin. R. (1984). 'Are Business Schools Doing their Jobs?', *Harvard Business Review*, 62/1: 140–7.

Born, D. (2005). 'On Being Learner-Focused: Are you on Board?', *USAFA Educator*, 13/3: 1.

Bruno, E. (1999). 'Engineering 410: An Experience for Life', *Warrior Update*, 13/4: 8–9.

Callander, B. (1998). 'Dissecting the Tempo Problem', *Air Force Magazine*, 81/4: 76–80.

Chapman, S., McPhee, P., and Proudman, B. (1995). 'What Is Experiential Education?', in K. Warren, M. Sakofs, and J. Hunt (eds.), *The Theory of Experimental Education*. Dubuque, Ia.: Kendall-Hunt Publishing Company.

Chen, G., Donahue, L., and Klimoski, R. (2004). 'Training Undergraduates to Work in Organizational Teams', *Academy of Management Learning and Education*, 3: 27–40.

Fenwick, T. J. (2001). 'Experiential Learning: A Theoretical Critique from Five Perspectives'. RIC Clearinghouse on Adult, Career, and Vocational Education, College of Education, Ohio State University, Information Series No. 385:11. Retrieved 19 Sept. 2005, from http://www.cete.org/acve/textonly/mp_fenwick_01.asp.

Frank, R., Meltzer, T., and Maier, C. (2005). *Best 361 Colleges 2006*. New York: The Princeton Review.

Haun, P. (2005). 'Train while you Fight', *Air and Space Power Journal*, 19/2: 37.

Haynie, M., and Heppard, K. (2005). 'From Content Delivery to Metacognitive Education: Using Inductive Pedagogies to Develop Cognitive Adaptability in Students', *USAFA Educator*, 13/3: 3.

Henry, J. (1989). 'Meaning and Practice in Experiential Learning', in S. Weil and I. McGill (eds.), *Making Sense of Experiential Learning*. Milton Keynes: SRHE and Open University Press.

Hornyak, M., Green, S., and Ciccotello, C. (2000). 'Putting Service into Service Learning: A Case Study at a Military Academy', *Academic Exchange Quarterly*, 4/4: 109–19.

Johnson, D., and Johnson, R. (1974). 'Instructional Goal Structure: Cooperative, Competitive or Individualistic', *Review of Educational Research*, 44: 213–40.

——— (1989). *Cooperation and Competition: Theory and Research*. Edina, Minn.: Interaction Books.

Katula, R., and Threnhauser, E. (1999). 'Experiential Education in the Undergraduate Curriculum', *Communication Education*, 48: 238–54.

Kolb, D. (1984). *Experiential Learning*. Englewood Cliffs, NJ: Prentice-Hall.

Levine, J., and Tompkins, D. (1996). 'Making Learning Communities', *AAHE Bulletin*, 48/10: 3–6.

Luckmann, C. (1996). 'Defining Experiential Education', *Journal of Experiential Education*, 19/1: 6–7.

Mailen, A. (2000). 'Towards the Essence of Adult Experimental Learning: A Reading of the Theories of Knowles, Kolb, Mezirow, Revans and Schon'. University of Jyvaskyla, Finland: So Phi Academic Press.Top of Form.

Martin, J., Sellers, J., and Green, S. (2002). 'Learn Space by Doing Space', *Program Manager*, 31/4, DAU 169: 2–6.

Michaelson, L., Knight, A., and Fink, L. (2002). *Team-Based Learning: A Transformative Use of Small Groups*. Westport, Conn.: Praeger Publishers.

Michelson, E. (1996). 'Usual Suspects: Experience, Reflection, and the (En)gendering of Knowledge', *International Journal of Lifelong Education*, 15/6, Nov.–Dec.: 438–54.

Nilson, L. (1998). *Teaching at its Best: A Research-Based Resource for College Instructors*. Bolton: Anker Publishing Company.

Pickles, T. (2005). Experiential learning articles and critiques of David Kolb's theory. Retrieved 18 Sept. 2005 from http://reviewing.co.uk/research/experiential.learning.htm.

Ravenscroft, S., and Buckless, F. (1997). 'Student Team Learning: Replication and Extension', *Accounting Education*, 2: 151–72.

Sax, L., and Astin, A. (1997). 'The Benefits of Service: Evidence from Undergraduates', *Educational Record*, Summer/Fall: 25–32.

Schofield, J., and Caragata, W. (1999). 'Learning on the Front Lines', *Maclean's*, 2485739 (15 Nov.), 12/46: 90.

Siegel, G., and Sorensen, J. (1999). *Counting More, Counting Less: Transformation in the Management Accounting Profession*. Montvale, NJ: Institute of Management Accountants.

Stein, R., and Hurd, S. (2000). *Using Student Teams in the Classroom: A Faculty Guide*. Bolton, Mass.: Anker Publishing.

Svinicki, M. (1990). 'Changing the Face of *your* Teaching?', in M. D. Svinicki (ed.), *The Changing Face of College Teaching*. San Francisco: Jossey-Bass.

United States Air Force Academy (USAFA) (2005a). *AACSB Accreditation*. Retrieved 19 Sept. 2005, from www.usafa.af.mil/superintendent/pa/factsheets/academic.htm.

—— (2005b). *Educational Outcomes*. Retrieved 19 Sept. 2005, from http://atlas.usafa.af.mil/df/df_ed_outcomes.cfm.

—— (2005c). *Fact Sheet: The Academy in the Space Age*. Retrieved 19 Sept. 2005, from http://www.usafa.af.mil/superintendent/pa/factsheets/space.htm.

—— (2005d). *Mission*. Retrieved 19 Sept. 2005, from http://atlas.usafa.af.mil/df/df_mission.cfm.

—— (2005e). *Systems Engineering/Systems Engineering Management (SE/SEM)*. Retrieved 19 Sept. 2005, from http://www.usafa.af.mil/df/dfsem/?catname=dean%20of%20faculty.

United States Air Force (USAF) Core Values (1997). USAF Pamphlet.

United States Air Force (USAF) Joint Vision 2020 (2000). USAF Pamphlet.

United States Air Force (USAF) Chief's Sight Picture (2003). USAF Pamphlet.

Vik, G. (2001). 'Doing More to Teach Teamwork than Telling Students to Sink or Swim', *Business Communication Quarterly*, 64: 112–19.

Weaver, M. (1999). 'Beyond the Ropes: Guidelines for Selecting Experiential Training', *Corporate University Review*, 10788638 (Jan.–Feb.), 7/1: 34.

Weigand, R. (1995). 'Experiential Learning: A Brief History', in C. Roland, R. Wagner, and R. Weigand (eds.), *Do it ... and Understand: The Bottom Line on Corporate Experiential Learning*. Dubuque, Ia.: Kendall/Hunt.

PART III

POLITICALLY GROUNDED EXPERIENTIAL LEARNING

CHAPTER 9

TALES OF ORDINARY LEADERSHIP

A FEMINIST APPROACH TO EXPERIENTIAL LEARNING

SILVIA GHERARDI

BARBARA POGGIO

INTRODUCTION

FEMINIST practice and theory have always conferred value on narrative knowledge produced through storytelling, mainly because of its ability to stimulate reflexive thought. In our contribution we intend to present and discuss a training methodology founded on memory work and designed to stimulate an individual and group reworking of the leadership dimension, and of the gender and leadership relationship.

We will describe a narrative workshop conducted with groups of women working in managerial positions and based on the perspective of workplace learning through experiential reflexivity. The training objective was to address the issue of leadership as situated practice. To this end, narrative stimuli were given to the participants in order to prompt more general reflection about male and female modes of power management (and about the connected practices of domination/exclusion). The purpose was to highlight the social and cultural factors that influence these differences, and to offer perspectives alternative to dominant patterns.

The narrative methodology proved to be a particularly effective tool: it gave the participants a chance to conduct retrospective analysis of their past work experiences (individual and organizational), and it generated—due to the interaction with other stories (those furnished in the training activity and those provided by other trainees)—different interpretative perspectives and new meaning configurations in order to face working life and organizational dynamics.

REFLECTION, REFLEXIVITY, AND NARRATIVE IN FEMINIST METHODOLOGY

The concepts of reflection and reflexivity have assumed great importance in the contemporary sociological literature, and especially in studies on workplace learning (Boud, Cressey, and Docherty 2006a).

Reflection concerns the rendering of personal experience amenable to awareness and analysis. It entails the actor's ability to engage in a process of introspection and to impose some sort of self-control on his or her intellectual operations. Its principal purpose is to conduct retrospection appraisal of individual action in order to improve future practice (Schön 1983, 1987). Michael Reynolds (1998: 183) makes a distinction between reflection and critical reflection. The crucial distinction of critical reflection is its confronting the tacit knowledge that underpins individuals' action and their taken-for-granted assumptions. Comparing the main processes of reflection from an individual and social relations perspective, Høyrup and Elkjaer (2006) see reflection as a collective capacity to question assumptions and therefore—from an organizational perspective—it can be understood as an organizing process that creates and sustain opportunities for organizational learning and change. For Vince (2002: 63) the questioning of assumptions is a practice that needs to be thought of as integral to organizing rather than the province of individuals.

Despite the diversity of the literature on reflection and learning at work, reflective practice is conceived as a means of examining and re-examining experience. The focus on re-examining experience is to notice tensions and contradictions in order not to take experience for granted. Uncertainties, discrepancies, and dissatisfactions are said to precipitate reflection and are central to any notion of reflection (Boud and Walker 1998; Boud, Cressey, and Docherty 2006b).

This conception leads to the development of a model for learning from experience that focuses on how reflection might be facilitated as a key element of learning.

Reflexivity, especially in the ethnomethodological meaning of the term (Garfinkel 1967), instead consists in the practices of accountability, observability, and referability of social action. It concerns the close interweaving among symbols, languages, and actions, and their connections with the context. It is the outcome of the separation or breakdown between subject and object and the need for 'accountability'—by which is meant making the world comprehensible to oneself and to the other members of a collectivity. To account for an event or an experience implies language use, narrative practices, storytelling. It is a relational practice, taking place in an interactional context, and it is mainly social and not simply cognitive and emotional.

Reflexivity is therefore a characteristic of all order-producing social activities. Moreover, 'the essential reflexivity of accounts' (Garfinkel 1967: 67) is used to create a sense of orderliness for action but reflexively creates that self-same context. While reflection looks back at the past in order to understand and to alter the future, reflexivity is anchored in present practice, in identification of the assumptions and priorities that shape our interpersonal relations. Introspection is not undertaken with a view to action, but is instead an integral part of it and is embedded in every interaction. Indeed, Rothman (1997) defines the reflexive process as 'interactive introspection'. When we refer to 'reflexive leadership' we wish to point out that the process of narrating leadership creates the context for experiencing leadership and reflecting on its practices.

Reflection and reflexivity perform a central role in the feminist debate, particularly with regard to so-called 'feminist methodology' (Bowles and Klein 1983; Harding 1987). Various writers have emphasized the need for reflexive approaches which enable individuals, and women in particular, to start from personal experience (Roberts 1981; Stanley and Wise 1983) and from self-awareness (Reinharz 1983; Held 1993) to question the traditional paradigms of 'objectivity' and 'detachment' that have supported the hegemony of maleness in the dominant models of science. The main means to foster reflexive thought is indubitably narrative, owing to its ability to enhance retrospective glance and memory work. What is meant by retrospective thought can be illustrated by referring to the story of the stork told by Karen Blixen in *Out of Africa* (1938).

The story runs as follows. A man lived in a small house near a pond. One night he was woken up by a loud noise. He ran out of his house and in the darkness headed towards the pond, repeatedly tripping, falling, and getting up again. Following the noise he found a leak in the pond wall, which he repaired and then went back to bed. When he looked out of the window the next morning, he saw that his footsteps had traced the outline of a stork on the ground. In this short story, retrospective glance is metaphorically represented by the man looking out of the window. His work of the night is finished, and it is only *a posteriori*, in the marks left on the ground, that he gives meaning to his movements, sees a pattern, and shapes his experience.

It is through recounting that the signs and traces of experience are pieced together and acquire complete meaning. The pattern of a life or an event emerges retrospectively when thought becomes reflexive, when it turns onto itself to compose a narrative, to give shape to what was indistinct.

Besides the backward introspection that induces reflexive thought to appropriate or reappropriate personal history, also of especial importance in feminist methodology is 'memory work'. In the 1980s a group of German women in Hamburg published a collected volume which reconstructed, on the basis of individual experiences, the social processes that construct female sexuality (Haug et al. 1987). The methodology of memory work was then transferred to other contexts, for instance the socialization of women to academic work, or the therapeutic treatment of women victims of abuse. Put briefly, the expression 'memory work' refers to the process by which the historical-cultural self is interwoven with practical/social relations. It looks at the self as a historical product, as an ongoing trajectory, as a cultural product (form of the discourse), and as a relational practice. It is based on the assumption that some change in the present can only be brought about if that past is subjected to 'dispassionate' analysis.

Narrating is a way to reappropriate experience, to're-member' in the sense of reconstructing a 'dismembered' body (Brady 1990), and to gain new awareness. Narrating makes it possible to construct a memory and to retrieve something that would otherwise be lost (Cavarero 1997). It is an opportunity for individuals to acquire renewed projectuality and a more sophisticated ability to interpret and make sense of the events that they encounter (Poggio 2004). In short, it is 'a practice of transformation, reflection, reconstruction, re-cognition and re-structuration of the self' (Gamelli 1995: 116).

LEADERSHIP AS A SITUATED AND GENDERED PRACTICE

Leadership has long been a topic of central concern for organizational studies. However, with the course of time attention has shifted from the role and function of the leader to the practice of leadership, from a personalized and functionalist view to one that emphasizes the relational and constructive dimension of leadership action and the process of the collective creation of meaning and consensus (Alvesson 1992; Piccardo 1998). Among the emergent features of this new view of leadership there are some that we believe to be particularly significant.

The first is the growing awareness that leadership is not so much a personality trait or a natural gift as a relational practice, something that 'one does' by relating to others (Manz and Sims 1991). Thus, a prescriptive approach intended principally to identify categories and models (the charismatic leader, the participative leader, the transactional leader, and so on) is replaced by an experiential one in which the focus is on experiences of leadership, the relational dynamics involved in leadership, its motivational and emotional features, and especially its relationship with power. The interweaving between leadership and power has been stressed by several authors (Kets de Vries 1993; Sievers 1996), but in this case the object of analysis is the subjective relationship with power and its implications for interpersonal relations.

The second emergent feature is connected to the 'situatedness' of leadership (Bruni, Gherardi, and Poggio 2005). Like every practice also leadership has a situated nature, in the sense that it cannot be conceived in absolute and general terms but must be contextualized in specific relational situations and systems. Situated leadership means that it is situated in a physical context, in the dynamics of interactions, in the language, and in the body.

Therefore, leadership is also gendered. It has been historically constructed as a male subtext by producing images of leadership which are difficult to relate to femaleness (Alvesson and Billing 1997) or by describing styles and models of female leadership which stand as alternatives to traditional leadership (Hegelsen 1990; Loden 1985). A frequent finding of these studies is that, whereas men are mainly characterized by a 'transactional' style of leadership (involving the exchange of results for rewards and command through control), women display distinct abilities in 'transformational' leadership: a management style which emphasizes relationality and seeks to foster positive interactions and trust relations with/among subordinates, to share power and information, and to encourage employees to subordinate their personal aims and interests to collective ends.

In short, these studies relate female leadership styles to a specific (natural or socialized) orientation of women towards communication, cooperation, affiliation, and attachment, and to a conception of power as control not over the group but by the group. Some authors explain this distinctive style of female leadership as resulting from the influence of primary socialization (Chodorow 1978), which develops women's affective and relational resources and a propensity to communicate with others, to listen to them, and to concern themselves with their needs. Accordingly, the argument runs, the activities that society has traditionally assigned to women (child raising, care for the physical and psychological well-being of family members, the settlement of conflicts) have developed a culture of responsibility and an ethic of care whereby women constantly endeavour to satisfy the needs of everyone.

A more critical interpretation (Kanter 1977; Beccalli 1991; David and Vicarelli 1994) suggests that, because women have not usually been able to wield formal authority in the organizations for which they work, they have been forced to develop other strategies to that end, most notably an ability (typical of those in positions of inferiority) to 'feel' and anticipate the reactions of others.

Moreover, analysis of the organizational literature on leadership shows that it is constructed to maintain and reinforce hegemonic masculinity. Images of male sexual functions and of patriarchal paternalism appear to be rooted in the way that the leader's action is described. One observes a seductive game, modulated in the masculine, which seduces those who identify with the stereotypes of maleness and virility (Calás and Smircich 1991).

A REFLEXIVE WORKSHOP ON LEADERSHIP

In recent years feminist critiques within organization studies (Gherardi 2003) have led to a redefinition of the concept of leadership and a redefinition of training practices. Approaches more oriented to relationality, empowerment, and reflexivity have appeared and therefore courses and methods designed to re-elaborate personal and professional experience, to create sense and consensus collectively, to develop creativity, and to foster autonomy and self-awareness. The aim is no longer to teach efficacious leadership styles or models, nor to define skills to be developed; rather, it is to stimulate individual and collective reflection, for example, through the sharing of leadership stories recounted by the trainees. A reflexive approach to leadership enables individuals, and women in particular, to start from personal experience and from self-awareness to question the traditional paradigms of 'objectivity' and 'detachment' that support the dominant models of knowing in organizations and producing knowledge on organizations.

Reflection and individual or group analysis of situations in which the participants have wielded authority in organizations furnish occasions for self-knowledge or even its redesign which involve not only the cognitive, cultural, and affective dimensions of the individuals concerned but also the strategic and structural ones of the organization. The assumption is that the group is a crucial learning resource because it enables different experiences to be shared and compared.

The importance of leadership learning workshops has been emphasized also outside the feminist approach by various authors, among them Senge (1991), and recent years have seen the growth of a large body of literature on the use of *self case studies* and narratives in learning workshops (Casula 2003; Griffith 1999; Piccardo 1998). During these workshops, accounts of work experiences written by the participants are discussed and analysed, and usually rewritten (Piccardo 1998). Or accounts are exchanged by the participants so as to foster a 'dialogic conversation' which generates multiple points of view, stimulates analysis and deconstruction of the assumptions of canonical stories, and encourages the creation of alternative plots, thereby fostering a learning process which is at once dialogic, divergent, emergent, and collaborative (Abma 2003).

We now describe a specific instance of a narrative workshop (Gherardi and Poggio 2006)[1] based on some of the assumptions just outlined, and the focus of which was the relationship between leadership and gender. Four editions of the workshop were organized, each of them attended by twelve women with managerial positions in the local administration of a north Italian town.

The course was designed around a number of themes representing the core of leadership in traditional textbooks: rationality, control, decision making, and strategic thinking. Each of them was framed in relation to its opposite (the suppressed term). On this basis, the workshop was divided into five day-long sessions entitled:

- *The retrospective gaze,* in which the temporal dimension in organizational life and in the individual working career seen as planning and anticipation was explored by contrasting it with the idea of looking backward and retrospective sense making. This session started with Karen Blixen's story of the stork.
- *Leadership in the feminine?* The interrogative form was proposed in order to explore the mainstream conception of leadership in contrast with its hypothetical translation 'in the feminine'. This session relied on a story by Italo Calvino.
- *Rationality and emotionality.* The two concepts were played one against the other starting with an excerpt from Daniel Pennac.
- *The myth of control.* Control and being in control is the founding myth of organization studies and it was contrasted with the image of flow and being in the flow of time and things. The image was based on a passage from Michel Tournier's *Friday or the Other Island* which describes the change of relationship between Robinson Crusoe and Friday after the explosion on the island and the end of its rational order.
- *Designing the future.* Strategy and decision making as anticipation of the future action was contrasted with a relational and contextual view of time, power, and future scenarios. The impetus was provided by Tolsto's description of the decision process of General Kutuzof about the Russian Army's retreat.

Each session required the participants to read and to write stories, according to the following schema:

- The facilitator read aloud 'the story of the day'; a literary passage intended to introduce the proposed theme in a imaginative way and in the context of mundane life.

- Following the narrative stimulus, each participant was invited to write a short story relating to her professional experience in the organization and which centred on the topic of the day.
- The stories were told, exchanged, and analysed in smaller groups. The group as a whole worked together in order to bring out shared and divergent views on the experience narrated, the plots used, the processes by which meaning had been reconstructed and attributed, and the underlying cultural models.
- Cutting across the various themes addressed provided the stimulus to reflect on a number of issues intrinsic to the topic of leadership: its relationship with power, recognition of its conflictual dimensions, and the importance of learning to recognize and understand the emotions connected with the exercise of authority in the participants' organizational contexts.

The key component of the workshop was reflexive learning, defined as 'a process which involves dialogue with others for improvement or transformation whilst recognizing the emotional, social and political context of the learner' (Brockbank, McGill, and Beech 2002: 75). Narrating leadership and analysing it collectively and in relation to organizational change is a way of constructing a more or less shared understanding of what leadership is and how it may be 'done' in a shared workplace. Storytelling provides not only the opportunity to discuss 'things that happened or could happen', but also the opportunity of performing one's identity as power holding in situated circumstances.

THE USE OF NARRATIVE METHODOLOGY: AN EXAMPLE

This section presents one day, and one theme, in our narrative workshop, in order to illustrate the process and reflect on managerial education. The subject of the day (the second in the course) was the relationship between gender and leadership.

The stimulus for reflection, narrative writing, and storytelling in groups was a story entitled 'Fanta-Ghiro' taken from Italo Calvino's *Italian Folktales*, of which a summary follows.

A king had three daughters but no sons. The king was of a sickly disposition. One day a Turkish king declared war against his land, but the king was too ill to take command of his army. So his three daughters offered to take his place. The father at first refused, because commanding an army was not women's work. But then, given the seriousness of the situation, he agreed to send his eldest daughter, but on the condition that she dressed and behaved like a man. He warned her that if she started talking about women's things, his trusted squire would bring her straight home. The daughter left for the war, but during the sea voyage she saw a gaily coloured fish and remarked that she wanted a ball gown in the same colours. So the squire took her straight back home. The same thing happened to the second daughter. During the voyage, when she saw the colourful sails of the fishing boats, she began talking about the fabrics she wanted to decorate her bed chamber. So the third daughter, Fanta-Ghiro, then set off to fight the war, even though she was still so small that her armour had to be padded before she could put it on. The sea voyage passed without incident, and the young princess went to parley with the enemy king. The king was intrigued by the 'iron general' and set traps to see whether he was not really a woman. He took Fanta-Ghiro into the armoury and then into the garden, asking question to catch her out. Fanta-Ghiro passed all the tests until the king invited her to go for a swim. This forced her to find an immediate excuse to return home. But she left behind a letter explaining who she really was. The king, by now in love, followed Fanta-Ghiro and asked her to marry him. Peace was made, of course, and when Fanta-Ghiro's father died he left his kingdom to his son-in-law.

This story was particular stimulating for the participants, owing to various features which emerged very clearly from both the narratives produced during the workshop and the group and plenary discussions. The first of these features concerned the symbolic order of gender apparent in the story, which the participants recognized as an organizational archetype (gender segregation) and a dilemma (adopt male or female behaviour?) that all of them had encountered to some extent in their professional lives.

Added to this was the fact that the plot of the story was substantially ambivalent. On the one hand, an unconventional figure of a woman was presented and valorized; but on the other, the end of the story depicted an absolutely canonical scenario in which the conventional order was restored through matrimony and inheritance by the male offspring, thereby complying with one of the essential principles of narrative: the restoration of the violated order (Bruner 1990).

The co-presence of these features was highly stimulating to the workshop participants. It elicited reactions ranging from admiration, through identification and frustration, to anger, and it generated numerous stories which developed aspects and nuances of the relationship between gender and leadership as experienced by the women. They recounted experiences of discrimination, episodes of revenge and affirmation, introspective analyses of their relationships with leadership and power, anecdotes about when they had to disguise themselves as men, or when they refused to do so.

There follows an example of one of the stories produced.

That morning Allegra climbed the stairs to her office thinking that yet another of those days was about to begin.

Another one of those difficult days in which tiredness due to work (positive) would be accompanied by the subtler, more insidious weariness (negative) that comes from fighting a losing battle.

Once again it was going to be the same old struggle, the one that since her promotion to a position of responsibility she had been fighting in a public organization still trapped in a formal, individualistic and—why not?—male mentality. Absorbed in her thoughts, as Allegra turned the corner she ran into Dr. Nero, her boss, who had always resented her promotion.

She tried to slip past him... too late! 'Allegra, good morning! I hope that today we can finally get that matter sorted out...'

'Right, that matter... for God's sake', thought Allegra.

The 'matter' concerned lessons on theory of organizations and old-style leadership which Nero based on his twenty-year experience of leadership declined in the masculine.

As if leadership can be taught! And then, what leadership? As if there's a universal model of it!

'Remember that personnel management requires an iron fist...!' Dr. Nero's voice boomed in the background as Allegra remembered the altercation between them the previous day: 'You give too much importance to others, to personal aspects. You want to understand everything and everyone... Set value on differences! What rubbish. And then let me say, all that baloney that you think is so important... creating a climate, building a team... it's nothing but a waste of time, it's just women's stuff...'.

The ringing of her mobile phone saved Allegra from her memories and from Dr. Nero. She rushed into her office slamming the door behind her.

For a moment she teetered towards the idea that Dr. Nero might be right, that there was no place for the emotions in work, no place for caring about others, for valuing differences... But then she shook her head, whispering 'But what sort of world would that be?' as she settled into her chair. 'No, I'm not the leader that Nero wants me to be, but what do I care? And then an iron fist would clash with my name!', she said to herself as she smiled and switched on her computer.

The story of Allegra is a mixture of invention and reality. However, when set within the training context and shared with the group, it immediately assumed a situated character and an explicit organizational significance, eliciting shared reflection on individual experiences of leadership and on the leadership models of the organizations to which the participants belonged. The story discloses a rejection of the symbolic order of gender dominant in the woman's organization and awareness that the female is constructed in organizations as the 'other' with respect to a maleness still hegemonic in concrete and discursive practices.

The emphasis on the diversity of leadership styles between men and women, and the reference to valuing differences, prompted the group to discuss the ambivalence inherent in its participants' organizational cultures. The discussion brought out a double-bind situation in which women filling leadership roles are required to behave like men but without abandoning their femaleness.

Finally the group's discussion of the story highlighted that leadership is tied to a person's relationship with power. This relationship is strongly gendered for social-cultural reasons: on the one hand there is the male view of power as power over others; on the other there is the female version of power as power for others, with the dichotomy being resolved by a view of power as with others, in a domain of relation, exchange, cooperation, and responsibility where gender has citizenship (Parker Follet 1924; Clegg 1989).

Concluding Remarks

In this chapter we have sought to demonstrate the importance of a narrative methodology in generating reflection and reflexivity with respect to working and organizational experience, and to leadership processes in particular. Our treatment has been based on feminist practice and theory, and the emphasis that these have placed on the centrality of reflexive thought and memory, as well as on the need to redefine the mainstream models of leadership aimed at maintaining and reinforcing hegemonic masculinity.

From this perspective, experiential learning is based on the interaction between two processes distinctive of narrative workshops: storytelling and listening. It is, in fact, above all in this interaction that individual indentities, as relational and performative processes, are produced and negotiated and that the meaning of experience is constructed. The collective processing of common experiences elicited in the workshops through the reciprocity of storytelling and listening stimulates the participants to reconsider their positioning in individual, professional, and organizational relations and to redefine the meaning of their experiences, generating transformative practices and processes.

By describing our reflexive workshops on leadership, therefore, we have sought to show how storytelling stimulates reflection and reflexivity, or retrospection and reflective learning from experience, on the one hand, and storytelling as a means to reflect on current practices and to create further contexts on the other.

This comes about in particular when the stimuli used consist of polysemic stories; that is, ones which stimulate different valid interpretations (Boje 1995) or which touch the deepest-lying emotions (Gabriel 2000), as in the case of the story of Fanta-Ghiro. The tale produced by Allegra in response to this stimulus, and its subsequent discussion by the group, furnishes a clear example of experiential learning where listening and storytelling interweave to produce occasions for reflecting upon and transforming leadership practices and power relations, not just at the individual level but within a process of sharing and exchanging.

In fact, the person's unique autobiographical narrative constitutes the occasion for collective experiential learning, since it represents the way that persons understand and act in their organization and how it can be done differently. Experiential learning has a developmental character since it builds agency among participants, confidence that they can act together in meaningful ways and develop their own organizational repertoire of practices for exerting power in future challenges.

NOTE

1. The reader who wishes to know more about the theoretical foundations of our methodology is referred to our 2006 article in which we explore storytelling within the framework of 'productive reflection at work'.

REFERENCES

Abma, T. A. (2003). 'Learning by Telling. Storytelling Workshop as an Organizational Learning Intervention', *Management Learning*, 342: 221–40.

Alvesson, M. (1992). 'Leadership as Social Integrative Action: A Study of a Computer Consultancy Company', *Organization Studies*, 13/2: 185–209.

——— and Billing, Y. (1997). *Understanding Gender and Organizations*. London: Sage.

Beccalli, B. (1991). 'Per una analisi di genere nella sociologia economica', in G. Bonazzi, C. Saraceno, and B. Beccalli (eds.), *Donne e uomini nella divisione del lavoro*. Milan: Angeli.

Blixen, K. (1937). *Den Afrikanske Farm*. Copenhagen: Gyldendal (Engl. trans. *Out of Africa*. London: Putnam, 1938).

Boje, D. (1995). 'Stories of Storytelling Organization: A Postmodern Analysis of Disney as "Tamara-Land" ', *Academy of Management Review*, 38/4: 997–1035.

Boud, D., Cressey, P., and Docherty, P. (eds.) (2006a). *Productive Reflection and Learning at Work*. London: Routledge.

——— ——— ——— (2006b). 'The Emergence of Productive Reflection', in D. Boud, P. Cressey, and P. Docherty (eds.), Productive Reflection and Learning at Work. London: Routledge.

Boud, D., and Walker, D. (1998). 'Promoting Reflection in Professional Courses: The Challenge of Context', *Studies in Higher Education*, 23/2: 191–206.

Bowles, G., and Klein, R. Duelli (eds.) (1983). *Theories of Women's Studies*. London: Routledge & Kegan Paul.

Brady, E. M. (1990). 'Redeemed from Time: Learning through Autobiography', *Adult Education Quarterly*, 41/1: 43–52.

Brockbank, A., McGill, I., and Beech, N. (2002). *Reflective Learning in Practice*. Aldershot: Gower.

Bruner, J. (1990). *Acts of Meaning*. Cambridge, Mass.: Harvard University Press.

Bruni, A., Gherardi, S., and Poggio, B. (2005). *Gender and Entrepreneurship: An Ethnographical Approach*. London: Routledge.

Calás, M. B., and Smircich, L. (1991). 'Voicing Seduction to Silence Leadership', *Organization Studies*, 12/24: 567–602.

Casula, C. (2003). *Giardinieri, principesse, porcospini: metafore per l'evoluzione personale e professionale*. Milan: Franco Angeli.

Cavarero, A. (1997). *Tu che mi guardi, tu che mi racconti*. Milan: Feltrinelli.

Chodorow, N. (1978). *The Reproduction of Mothering*. Berkeley and Los Angeles: University of California Press.

Clegg, S. (1989). *Frameworks of Power*. London: Sage.

David, P., and Vicarelli, G. (eds.) (1994). *Donne nelle professioni degli uomini*. Milan: Angeli.

Gabriel, Y. (2000). *Storytelling in Organizations: Facts, Fictions, Fantasies*. Oxford: Oxford University Press.

Gamelli, I. (1995). 'La conoscenza di sé e il pensiero introspettivo: la meditazione', in D. Demetrio (ed.), *Per una didattica dell'intelligenza: il metodo autobiografico nello sviluppo cognitivo*. Milan: Franco Angeli.

Garfinkel, H. (1967). *Studies in Ethnomethodology*. Englewood Cliffs, NJ: Prentice-Hall.

Gherardi, S. (2003). 'Feminist Theory and Organizational Theory: A Dialogue on New Bases', in H. Knudsen and H. Tsoukas (eds.), *The Oxford Handbook of Organizational Theory: Meta-theoretical Perspectives*. New York: Oxford University Press.

—— and Poggio, B. (2006). 'Feminist Challenges to Mainstream Leadership through Collective Reflection and Narrative', in D. Boud, P. Cressey, and P. Docherty (eds.), *Productive Reflection and Learning at Work*. London: Routledge.

Griffith, W. (1999). 'The Reflecting Team as an Alternate Case Teaching Model: A Narrative, Conversational Approach', *Management Learning*, 30/3: 343–61.

Harding, S. (1987). 'Is There a Feminist Method?', in S. Harding (ed.), *Feminism and Methodology*. Bloomington: Indiana University Press.

Haug, F., et al. (1987). *Female Sexualization: A Collective Work of Memory*. London: Verso.

Hegelsen, S. (1990). *The Female Advantage*. New York: Currency Doubleday.

Held, V. (1993). *Feminist Morality: Transforming Culture, Society and Politics*, Chicago: University of Chicago Press.

Høyrup, S., and Elkjaer, B. (2006). 'Reflection: Taking it beyond the Individual', in D. Boud, P. Cressey, and P. Docherty (eds.), *Productive Reflection and Learning at Work*. London: Routledge.

Kanter, R. M. (1977). *Men and Women of the Corporation*. New York: Basic Books.

Kets de Vries, M. F. R. (1993). *Leaders, Fools and Imposters*. San Francisco: Jossey-Bass.

Loden, M. (1985). *Feminine Leadership or How to Succeed in Business Without Being One of the Boys*. New York: Times Books.

Manz, C. C., and. Sims Jr., H. P. (1991). 'SuperLeadership: Beyond the Myth of Heroic Leadership', *Organizational Dynamics*, 19: 18–35.

Parker Follett, M. (1924). *Creative Experience*. New York: Peter Smith.

Piccardo, C. (1998). *Insegnare e apprendere la leadership*. Milan: Guerini.

Poggio, B. (2004). *Mi racconti una storia? il metodo narrativo nelle scienze sociali*. Rome: Carocci.

Reinharz, S. (1983). 'Experiental Analysis: A Contribution to Family Research', in G. Bowles and R. Duelli Klein (eds.), *Theories of Women's Studies*. London: Routledge & Kegan Paul.

Reynolds, M. (1998). 'Reflection and Critical Reflection in Management Learning', *Management Learning*, 29/2: 183–200.

Roberts, H. (ed.) (1981). *Doing Feminist Research*. London: Routledge & Kegan Paul.

Rothman, J. (1997). *Resolving Identity-Based Conflict: In Nations, Organizations and Communities*. San Francisco: Jossey-Bass.

Schön, D. A. (1983). *The Reflective Practitioner: How Professionals Think in Action*. New York: Basic Books.

—— (1987). *Educating the Reflective Practitioner*. San Francisco: Jossey-Bass.

Senge, P. M. (1991). 'The Leader New Work: Building Learning Organizations', *Sloan Management Review*, 3/1: 7–23.

Sievers, B. (1996). 'Greek Mythology as a Means of Organizational Analysis: The Battle at Larkfield', *Leadership and Organizational Development Journal*, 17/6: 32–40.

Stanley, L., and Wise, S. (1983). ' "Back into Personal" or: Our Attempt to Construct Feminist Research', in G. Bowles and R. Duelli Klein (eds.), *Theories of Women's Studies*. London: Routledge & Kegan Paul.

Tournier, M. (1967). *Vendredi ou limbes du Pacifique*. Paris: Gallimard (Eng. trans. *Friday or the Other Island*. London: Collins, 1969).

Vince, R. (2002). 'Organizing Reflection', *Management Learning*, 33/1: 63–78.

CHAPTER 10

....

THEATRE IN MANAGEMENT AND ORGANIZATION DEVELOPMENT

A CRITIQUE OF CURRENT TRENDS

....

JOHN COOPEY

THIS chapter presents a preliminary critique of the recent growth in the use of theatre in management education and training and organization development. It is preliminary in the sense that, because little empirical work seems to have been published on the use of theatre in this way, the review presented here draws mainly on journal and newspaper articles, claims made in theatre company brochures, and two case studies written up by the author.

In the first section of the chapter I try to explain the growth of business involvement in arts generally and in theatre in particular and discuss the services provided by theatre companies within the context of growing business influence on various aspects of UK society. Next, an attempt is made to explain how theatre workshops—depending on how radical is their purpose and form—can be used to create the trust and the physical and emotional space in which learning can be nurtured through playful experimentation with alternative ways of behaving and living.

The third section reviews some of the current applications of theatre in this mode. First, a conventional form, role-play, is examined, then I turn to consider examples of more creative workshops in the light of claims that they can prompt quite radical change in managers and organizations. Within this category are two specially prepared cases, one of theatre used within an in-company change programme and the other where it is part of an international programme of management education.

BUSINESS AND THEATRE

Several trends have contributed to the recent growth in the use of theatre in management education and training in the UK. First, there has been an ideological shift prompted by central government since the 1980s, continued by recent Labour governments. Increasingly, emphasis has been placed on the economic importance of the arts for the British economy. At the local level the targeting of the arts towards goals of economic development has been particularly marked (Gray 2000). There has also been some diminution of state funding which, when linked to increasing pressures on business organizations to show greater social responsibility, has tended to draw the arts and business sectors together. At the same time companies have been enhancing their capacity to deal with what they perceive as an ever more competitive and turbulent business environment, prompted in part by a growth in the number of consulting firms offering the arts as a way of responding to those challenges.

One important element in this changing context is an organization called 'Arts and Business' (A&B) established to broker the relationship between the two while changing the emphasis from sponsorship to contracts for the provision of arts-based services. A directory created by A&B lists over 160 arts organizations and individuals offering their services. Many are theatre companies delivering 'bespoke training packages' intended to 'influence behaviour ... accelerate change, improve communications and release creativity'.[1] At least fifty companies in the UK have been involved over recent years.

Hadfield (2000) records that eleven business and management schools were incorporating arts-based materials into their management programmes, including five that made use of theatre in various modes.

Regional arts organizations play their part in brokering arts–business connections, running 'taster' sessions where arts groups display their offerings to businessmen and managers. One of the actor/directors featured in this chapter demonstrated his company's workshop approach at such a session just as he and his partner were reappraising how the company might survive: how 'with integrity we could augment what we are earning...and find a better way of not going under'. The relevance of financial issues is shown by the admission that the two partners were 'really worried about...teaching people who were earning so much'. Ambivalence about working with business is also revealed in the remark that 'it is of interest [but] sometimes I'm frustrated if I commit myself to this and nearly give up a year of what we do...but you can't do everything'.

Conversely, non-business organizations where theatre has been used to nurture learning processes are feeling the pinch, in schools, prisons, and young offenders institutions. For example, the use of theatre in UK education took off in the early 1970s when various companies created drama as an educational tool. Campbell (1994), whose theatre company was involved in this work, argues that the 'idea of theatre as a universal language through which young people can be empowered to explore and express their own experience' became more controversial in a more politicized education system. For him, Margaret Thatcher's goal was to empower not individual pupils, but the business system comprising 'UK plc'. Hence, funding for experimental work in collaboration between actors and teachers was in short supply. It was only by adapting an existing form of radical theatre that his company was able to continue working effectively with school groups despite financial constraints.

The situation today is probably much worse for those involved in theatre in education given the more intense pressure on timetables exerted through governments' attachment to rational and examinable parts of the curriculum. Much of the impetus for this trend comes, again, from a need to serve the interests of British business in order to maintain its competitiveness. So the scope of business influence and power over aspects of cultural and political life has been extended into the arts and, in parallel, has increased within education.

As yet the situation does not approach closely that in the USA although the trends continue in the same direction. Over a long period, as noted by Bourdieu and Heeke (1995), these have led to such a growth of private patronage in the USA that it is used to 'justify the abdication of public authorities...with the extraordinary result that citizens still finance the arts and sciences through tax exemptions'. Meanwhile the act of business funding 'appears as an example of the disinterested generosity of the corporations [through] an extremely perverse mechanism which operates in such a way that we contribute to our own mystification' (p. 16). For the corporations this process is a form of 'symbolic bank account': the donations made serve to accumulate symbolic capital of recognition, assuring a 'positive image that...will bring indirect profits' (p. 18).

THEATRE AND LEARNING

The focus in this section is on the learning potential of theatre workshops; any reference to more traditional stage-based theatre is used by way of comparison. In a theatre workshop participants are both performers and audience, fluctuating between two roles: a *liminal* role, similar to that experienced by participants in rituals, placing them 'betwixt and between' more permanent social roles, able 'to accept that the events of the production are *both real and not real*', and a *ludic* role in which they 'participate in playing around with the norms, customs, regulations, laws which govern life in society'. Then, as the two roles are played more vigorously and openly, more progress can be made in constructing new understandings as a basis for action (Kershaw 1992: 24; author's emphasis).

Trust and Learning Space

Progress is difficult without trust which stems from people's shared concern about a common good. A person's trust grows with the confidence, based on experience of relating to others, that they will take care of something he or she values. Crucial therefore is the belief that no harm comes from trusting and being trusted.

However, whether someone is able to tolerate his or her vulnerability in the face of the other's use of discretion in safeguarding a valued object may well depend on the relative power of the two people. Hence, the surest foundation for trust is mutual love, where power is unlikely to be an issue for as long as the loving relationship lasts. Perhaps the next best basis for trust is equality of power as part of which each partner to the trusting relationship has free access to knowledge of the other's motives and reasons (Baier 1992: 374).

Creating theatre between people who participate voluntarily and on equal terms provides a 'learning space' where trust can flourish, enabling participants to act and interact such that the relationships they shape contain the potential for deep learning. Slowly, people offer more freely their representations of experiences and the emotions which memories evoke, especially fear. Learning happens as other actors draw on their own personal history in interpreting, elaborating, and creating new insights out of the others' offerings (Fulop and Rifkin 1997). In effect, the series of episodes of mutual self-disclosure serve as a vehicle for learning and for building up trust. The deeper the trust as each participant obtains freer access to the motives and reasons of the others, the deeper the learning.

The deepening of trust between members of a group is also a function of the success they achieve in fulfilling the task which confronts them: in a theatre workshop the performance itself. When all members of the group judge that they have been successful the shared experience of completing the task then tends to improve their relationships further. Opportunities given in the workshop for retrospective monitoring of what has happened, and for appraising the learning that has taken place, increase the strength of commitments and enhance relationships further. Hence, 'two distinguishable but strongly related levels of experience are interwoven: the socio-relational level concerning how the parties shape their mutual relationships, and the content-domain levels' concerning the task's meaning (Steyaert, Bouwen, and Van Looy 1996: 72).

This is how theatre creates an 'aesthetic space' in which participants can become visible and find their voice, allowing them to rediscover and revalue their experience, to overcome others' attempts to dismiss how they make sense of their lives, and to realize that technocrats and managers are not the sole sources of valid knowledge.

Conventional or Radical Workshops?

Now I consider how theatre workshops are used in practice and try to establish some broad criteria as to whether they might be considered as more or less radical in form and process and, therefore, more or less likely to foster radical learning on the part of workshop participants.

In professional playhouses workshops are used to develop actors' general skills and their approach to a specific play, and in exploring and shaping themes for a new play. Workshops have also been used for many years in education, personal therapy, and the rehabilitation of adult prisoners and young offenders. Clearly, given some of these uses, there may be quite radical purposes concerned with the promotion of personal change (for example Feldhendler 1994).

In stage-based theatre companies workshops help the ensemble prepare for a performance. The conventional workshop form involves reworking an existing text in order to put a contemporary gloss on it and to perform it well enough to ensure favourable reviews and high box-office receipts. Even so, the reworking process may well last many days and provide opportunities for some degree of learning on the part of the ensemble and its members.

More radical forms of workshop are found in the work of certain playwrights, directors, and companies of actors who develop both a text and the mode of its performance. For example, the highly acclaimed 'Theatre de Complicité' improvise a performance by working on some 'universal theme' during months of argument, rehearsal, and research. This allowed them in *Help! I'm Alive* to 'speak for the urban dumbos, deadbeats and dispossessed in a world where ugliness is endemic and dignity a luxury confined to the rich' (Ratcliffe 1995).

For the Brazilian theatre director Augusto Boal, this is insufficient: though the performances which emerge might 'create an opening for a critical consciousness' on the part of the audience, the power still rests with the character. So Boal uses his own form of workshop—called Theatre of the Oppressed or Forum Theatre—which he evolved during a programme to increase literacy in Peru. He placed theatre at the service of those on the programme so that, by using its language, they could take the protagonist role and express possible modes of living through which they could escape the meanings in which their oppression was grounded. In the process they moved beyond enquiry into a form of 'rehearsal theatre' for worlds that had to be created if people were to survive (Boal 1979).

Preliminary exercises are used to build trust and overcome participants' inhibitions as they devise one or more 'plots' from their own raw material based on real life modes of thought and behaviour which, though perceived generally as 'normal', they find oppressive. Each plot is then played out by some of the group, without interruption. The remainder are, in Boal's terms, 'spect-actors' who, in the unfolding of the drama on subsequent runs through, are encouraged to say 'stop' and take the part of one or more of the original 'actors' in order to change the course of the action. They strive to create 'a new vision of the world' in opposition to the original actors' attempts to maintain the original script.

Not surprisingly the difficulty and pain of this process can be such that participants may be driven to accept simple or comfortable answers (Jackson 1992). So workshops are 'led' not by a conventional 'director', or the 'facilitator' of training sessions, but by a 'Joker' whose role is to discourage the 'quick-fix'. A Joker serves 'as a "difficultator", undermining easy judgements, reinforcing our grasp of the complexity of a situation, but not letting that complexity get in the way of action or frighten us into submission or inactivity' (pp. xix–xx).

Workshops as used by Complicité and Boal provide a mirror image of the ideas of commentators such as Mangham and Overington (1987). Whereas the latter, using a dramaturgical metaphor, suggest how work in organizations is a form of theatre, Complicité and Boal demonstrate how theatre workshops can be used to change how life is lived, including organizational life. They too are aware that in every situation there are implicit texts on which we improvise our actions, texts that are 'often structured by the thoughts, words and actions of playwrights long dead' (Mangham and Overington 1987: 173). They also acknowledge that a successful interpretation of a text involves a mode of enactment that takes it well beyond that which is current, but their vision of the world that might be created is likely to be very different from those of the senior executives used as exemplars by Mangham and Overington, such as 'the Gambles, the Hewletts, Sloans, Geneens and Fords'. The approach taken by Complicité and Boal would produce a radically new reading of the texts which govern business life so as to take account of the interests of a multiplicity of stakeholders and the fragility of the ecosphere in the face of demands to yield up ever greater 'shareholder value'. When, in the final part of the chapter, I ask how radical are the interventions reviewed, this is the benchmark against which that question is posed.

In Fulop and Rifkin's (1997) terms such learning 'is potentially anti-foundational, anti-the system, and not easily orchestrated' (p. 58), a potential that is recognized by St George, Schwager, and Canavan (1999) in their 'consumer's guide [sic] to the use of drama in corporate training' in the USA. In this they warn companies that, 'inasmuch as drama has the potential to create poignant and highly successful learning opportunities, it may also have the capacity to manipulate, distort, and compromise training goals and participant integrity'. Hence, consistent with their concern with such goals as 'reducing the potential for litigation', they give this 'health warning': 'Those using drama-based training have an ethical imperative to ensure its appropriate application' (p. 79).

Alternatively, it could be argued that the current state of the world economy and environment requires training that is 'anti-foundational and anti-the system'. It would then be appropriate to use theatre workshops within a much more radical programme of training and development designed to encourage and help participants to imagine and experiment with creating 'a much more radical economic and business model of human development than that favoured in the 20th century', i.e. 'materials-intensive, driven by fossil fuels, based on mass consumption and mass disposal, and oriented primarily to economic growth—with insufficient regard for people's needs' (Worldwatch Institute, 2002: 4).[2] The new model might, as suggested by the New Renaissance Group, be more relevant to the achievement of 'a sustainable human future' implying a 'stable human population of diverse societies, living at peace with one another and within the Earth's carrying capacity . . . and a more rewarding quality of life for all human beings with benefits more evenly and fairly distributed'.[3]

A REVIEW OF SOME CURRENT APPLICATIONS

In this section I consider the use being made of theatre within business organizations mostly in the UK, including two cases studied in more detail for this review. The sources of information about other examples are journal or newspaper articles and brochures of theatre companies.

The critique which emerges from this review is based on a preliminary assessment of how conventional or radical are, first, the form and process of the actual workshops—assessed in a broad-brush way against the criteria discussed earlier— and the aims of those who design and manage the programmes of which the workshops are part.

Role-Play

One long-standing use of theatre in management training is role-play in helping, for example, to assess the role competence of candidates for jobs and of employees chosen to attend development centres, and to practise and explore strategies for playing work roles in various circumstances.

One of the biggest providers of role-play workshops in the UK is Role Call Limited: fifty actors on its books coach managers to enhance their capability in dealing with difficult situations such as breaking bad news to subordinates. The constrained form of theatre workshop employed is very unlikely to prompt any radical positive change either in the participants or their organizations. On the contrary it seems designed to induce greater conformism especially when the role acted out is a defensive one, as in dealing with redundancies.

Such a role can require a person to perform 'emotional labour', managing their feelings so as to 'sustain the outward countenance that produces the proper state of mind in others' (Hochschild 1983: 7). The interviewing of people to be made redundant, for example, requires the adoption of an 'emotional style' intended to ensure that they do not feel as upset as, in the circumstances, they are probably entitled to feel. In this encounter a manager may well experience feelings of empathy which the training helps to suppress, at least outwardly, in order to produce the desired effect on the other party. However, the recipient of bad news may have the sense of being dealt with well by both the manager and—via a process of transference—the company for whom that manager is 'fronting'

In behaving regularly in this way 'to reflect the company's position', the role incumbent may not find it easy to disengage other aspects of self and emotions. If repeated many times such behaviour can tend to estrange the person not only from their 'performance' in role but from their deeper sense of self. Such an experience may be quite disturbing for them whilst risking that those with whom they deal then become convinced of the manager's insincerity.

Workshops that Prompt Change and Creativity

A freer form of theatre workshop is used as part of change programmes as described by Arkin (1998), Caulkin (2000), and Hadfield (2000). They provide many examples including how members of a theatre ensemble coached managers in staging their own performance, how the use of the RSC's 'rehearsal room techniques of presentation, ensemble building and ideas generation' were borrowed 'as a powerful problem solving methodology', and how a theatre group helped to bring about a successful merger of two large companies by directing and coaching several hundred employees in a three-day workshop in which they mounted dance and theatre presentations, hence demonstrating the potential of the newly created company.

Certainly, such programmes may produce far-reaching outcomes, but without the opportunity for evaluation it is difficult to comment on their effects. On the other hand, it is perhaps illuminating to comment on claims that such programmes are intended to help companies to:

- cope with the speed of change;
- use the world of theatre as 'a paradigm for organisational structures and ways of working' relevant in the business world;
- achieve an 'injection of imagination and creativity' to increase companies' competitiveness;
- gear up for 'modern weightless economies' in which it will become possible 'to recombine resources in a way that redefines whole industries at a stroke' (*sic*);
- 'provide work that engages (employees') hearts and minds' now that old loyalties have been swept away in 'the earth-moving upheavals in employment relations' (Caulkin 2000; Coyle 1999; Handy 1997).

Despite the promise of radical change which this list might imply, several of the reasons suggested as to why organizations would choose to use theatre workshops for management development are quite traditional. What does seem different of late is that these needs have become much more pressing as a result of a spate of mergers, takeovers, downsizing, and managerial initiatives intended to undermine long-standing employment relations in order to introduce flexible working. In parallel, change programmes have been implemented, sometimes to help achieve these outcomes and, in others, to deal with their unexpected consequences. So managers and other employees have been subjected to a stream of 'fads' from 'Quality Circles' in the 1970s to 'Just-in-Time', 'TQM', and 'Search for Excellence' in the 1980s and programmes of 'Empowerment' and 'Business Process Re-engineering' most recently.

Turnbull (1999) comments on the effect of these interventions on middle managers who 'are required to manage the interface between the *authors* of the latest fads (the senior managers) and the *recipients* (the employees)'. Deeply involved in emotional labour, through a requirement to exercise emotional control while displaying the enthusiasm expected of them, they are in danger of 'entering into self-deception and inauthentic behaviour', a mode of behaviour that can begin to blur 'the boundaries between their own identities and those of the organization' (p. 3; original emphasis).

So it may take more than theatre—even alchemy—to undo pernicious effects of this period of corporate activity on the attitudes, beliefs, and sense of commitment of both managers and rank and file employees. Alchemy may certainly be needed in the creation of 'modern weightless economies'. If such a notion merits theatre at all, most fitting might be the modern 'theatre of the absurd' or, from the seventeenth century, Ben Jonson's play *The Alchemist*, in which a fake alchemist-cum-astrologer fleeces gullible characters fooled by his promises of bizarre ways to enrich themselves.

But there may be potential in some of the examples considered above to help participants to become more playful and self-questioning of behaviour and identity in ways that reinforce their personal values and other strengths and talents. In Hopfl's

(1994) terms, out of the unsettling experience of workshop activities participants may emerge with a nascent sense of self which promises to undermine the rhetoric on which organizational 'reality' is based and yet is more resistant to subjection and appropriation.

Also potentially radical at the organizational development level is the suggestion by both Arkin (1998) and Caulkin (2000) that managers can be coached by leading actor/directors to learn from the speed with which theatre companies use workshops to put on a new play. It is not clear, however, to what extent this facility to move quickly from rehearsal to performance can be transferred to other work organizations. Perhaps this is possible in some sectors such as communications where there are similarities between business firms and theatre companies in the sense that both are 'putting on a performance'. However, in numerous other sectors—such as nuclear energy, chemicals, pharmaceuticals, and insurance—where error in implementation can incur widespread damage to people and other elements of the natural environment, a lengthy period of planning, development, and testing is probably essential.

But when Caulkin (2000) refers to the use of theatre to enhance the creative potential of an existing group's member companies or to speed up the shaping of a creative culture in a company newly created from a merger of existing organizations, these events may yield somewhat more radical effects than could be achieved through traditional management development techniques.

Even so, a more elegant, much less costly prophylactic response to the latter issue may be to avoid mergers or acquisitions (M&As) in the first place. The great stream of M&As which have been a feature of global business in recent years have, time and time again, been shown to result in considerable disbenefits for many stakeholders, including shareholders (for example KPMG 1999; NEF 2002). Such outcomes merit not the application of 'doses of theatre' or any other form of panacea administered by boards of directors, but the imposition of constraints by stakeholders on boards themselves in order to prevent at least the worst of corporate excesses that lead to decisions to engage in takeovers and mergers (Girma, Thompson, and Wright 2002).

Two Case Studies

Finally, I describe and comment on two case studies in the UK which illustrate some of the potentially more radical uses it is claimed can be made of theatre workshops in management development. Information about these initiatives has been gleaned from various documents provided by their main sponsors and interviews with those sponsors, colleagues, and the actor/directors who were contracted to design and direct the workshops.

Case 1: International Executive Master's Programme

Here, a theatre workshop is part of an international executive master's programme run collaboratively by business schools in five countries including the UK. The programme's design is dictated by a desire to escape the fragmented functional focus of the traditional MBA and to concentrate on the processes and practice of managing. The learning mode emphasizes the contributions of an international group of mature executives from the five countries and the importance of drawing on and sharing the meanings each gives to managerial work.

A programme 'cycle' takes place over an eighteen-month period. At regular intervals during this time five two-week modules are spent in a classroom or similar environment, each devoted to a specific topic or 'mind-set'. Each collaborating school is responsible for designing and running one of the modules in that school's facilities. The cycle starts in the UK with a module linking general notions of managing with a *reflective* mind-set. The other modules are, in sequence: managing organizations with an *analytic* mind-set, managing context with a *worldly* mind-set, managing relationships with a *collaborative* mind-set, and managing change with an *action* mind-set.

The first part of the opening module is taken up with an introduction to the themes of the programme as a whole. After that, apart from the drama workshop—titled 'Players in a Game'—the remaining time is devoted to reflecting on self and identity, managing knowledge and self, the completion and review of a cultural audit, and a very brief introduction to issues concerning the natural environment.

In earlier cycles the drama session stretched over one and a half or two days but for the most recent, the cycle that started in 2002, this was restricted to one day. The session starts with simple physical warm-up exercises, in silence, so that participants can get to know the space and how to use it. Then they work in small groups on quite trivial tasks designed to build up trust even though an 'edge of competition' may be induced. All are encouraged to act as 'players in a game' and to express their pleasure through laughter which also helps relieve any stress invoked by the unfamiliar. They are 'kept at it', encouraged to 'go with the flow and suspend belief', given few opportunities to interpret and rationalize their experiences.

At this point the first piece of 'acting' is introduced in which small groups create for each other a mimed piece expressed through visual images. Following this they make up and tell stories often related to organizational life before moving on to 'produce the beginnings of theatre' when groups are given carte blanche to prepare quickly a piece for performance based on a story with a focus on leadership in organizational life. Rehearsal space is provided and a time limit set in which to try out their ideas. Finally, in turn, each group performs its piece to an audience, followed immediately by the director's initial comments. Once all have performed, a feedback session allows substantive issues to be commented on as a prelude to a discussion of what the performers have learned and how it might be useful in 'real life'.

Case 2: CompCo

Here, a theatre workshop was introduced as an element of an intervention made by a small consultancy firm specializing in facilitating executive and organizational change. One of their consultants was contracted to work with CompCo, a company created through the privatization and splitting up of a public utility. The board of CompCo had already worked with a major international consulting firm to develop a strategy designed to capitalize on opportunities to run part of the company as a fully competitive enterprise even though the bulk of its business is regulated. The role of the consultant in the case examined here was to help disseminate that strategy through the organization so that local policies and practices could be aligned with the company's overall goals.

This task is being addressed through individual and group work with the top cadre of executives below CompCo's board. The aim is to change the organization's orientation from one of public service to commercially based competitiveness. A central part of the intervention is a series of development programmes, each extending over a year and catering for a group of twenty-five executives. The programme is built around three 'core' modules in which conceptual and experiential approaches are linked. Participants are charged with carrying the learning process forward such that, by the end of the programme, they are expected to have produced their own personal development plan against which their performance and progress can be assessed.

In the first core module the emphasis is on leadership capabilities, the development of strategy, and its integration with operations. A major business simulation forms the second module concerned with market appreciation, benchmarking, and growing a new business. The final core element, of which the theatre workshop is part, is about 'shifting mind-sets', helping participants change from a set of public service values, beliefs, and practices to those appropriate to a more commercial, competitive environment.

The focus of this third element is both more personal and political in the context of a new set of stakeholders who are involved with the company. It affords opportunities for experimentation which takes participants out of their 'comfort zones' in order to help them build self-confidence, become less risk averse, and perform with more spontaneity in public.

Within this core element the form of the theatre workshop is very similar to that in the first case but with one difference which stems from the contrasting nature of the two groups. It seems that the in-company groups of executives are older, more inhibited, and more homogeneous than those on the international business school programme. So whereas the latter seem generally able and ready to perform a role behind their own faces, the in-company set is happier behind masks, using shadow puppets to create often powerful metaphors which tell their stories of leadership and life as it is lived on their shared home territory. To allow them to get to this point the workshop runs over a full three days.

Commentary

The form of workshop in the two cases is very similar in many respects to that used in other contexts including those run by Augusto Boal. However, the majority of those who attend his workshops are probably already amateur or professional actors, who may well intend to incorporate aspects of his Forum Theatre into their own work. Despite this, and the cost constraints most of them face, the programme runs over four days. This is consistent with the emphasis that ensembles such as Theatre de Complicité place on both the power of the radical learning process which is played out in workshops and, hence, on the time they are prepared to spend in workshops to capitalize on this.

However, in CompCo three days may well suffice to help executives realign their values, beliefs, and performance in support of the intervention's limited aims. There seems no intention of prompting any radical, thoroughgoing rethinking of personal and corporate values but merely to integrate into their business lives those values relevant to the sectors which their board of directors hope to penetrate.

What is more, the assumptions which frame the intervention seem very conventional in managerial terms: firmly top-down, aimed at helping 'the organization do things better' within the current business and market paradigm. The 'strategy work' completed prior to the phase in which the change consultant is involved enables him to design the intervention so as to turn key aspects of the emergent strategy 'into leadership capability'. As part of this process executives who participate are encouraged to consider how, once they have shifted their own mind-sets consistent with the strategy, they propose to go out and 'shift the organization' for which they are responsible.

In dramaturgical performance terms, this is similar to Mangham and Overington's (1987) view that, in business organizations,

much of the responsibility for the provision of a guiding interpretation . . . lies with senior managers often with the chief executive. Beyond all else, the leader . . . is the person to whom others look for the provision of a sub-text; once provided, the individual structures and processes which support it can be put in place by lesser mortals. (175–6)

But those lesser mortals, including middle managers up to the level of the board, may well experience the unsettling effects of the emotional labour they will have to perform to achieve these ends. In this they risk having to indulge in 'self-deception and inauthentic behaviour' of which Turnbull (1999) speaks, and experience the resultant threat to self-identity.

As for the business school programme, the use of theatre is consistent with the academic director's belief that the act of theatrical performance provides people with novel ways of relating to each other. This encourages them to engage with their experience in a non-analytical, more expressive mode, reflecting freely about things they may not have noticed from within their usual rationalist frame. It is hoped that this form of learning will be useful in the rest of the programme and when they are back at work.

However, given that only one day is devoted to theatre, it is difficult to believe that, of itself, it has more than a passing effect within the programme as a whole, even given that the executives enrolled on the programme are young, uninhibited, and heterogeneous relative to those in CompCo. The actor/director who runs the workshop believes from a professional standpoint that it would be better to devote more time to it and suggests that the programme director acknowledges this too, but is also concerned to do justice to all the other material 'they've got to pack into the time'.

A short workshop may still help to encourage the reflective mind-set of the first module. But it is surely insufficient as a way of preparing the group to slip easily into workshop mode—as theatre ensembles might do—when they work on the later externally focused themes with faculty who are not necessarily familiar with this approach. All in all it seems a missed opportunity in a very innovative programme.

So how do I explain the results of an informal poll among participants in the second cycle of whom all but one—who was unsure—agreed that the programme had been a 'life changing experience'? This response is credible only if we accept the two main promoters' argument that, apart from the tone they set and the venue and creative inputs they provide, 'the natural dynamics of a collection of bright, experienced and interested people from around the world takes over, and a remarkable learning experience results'.[4]

As for any radical effects on the sponsoring organizations, the promoters are disappointed that insufficient change has been induced *by virtue of what takes place during the program*. They are working on this issue.

But what sort of change do they have in mind? Is it akin to that favoured by those of London's West End theatre directors who use workshops so that they and their ensemble can rework an existing text in order to put a contemporary gloss on it and to perform it well enough to ensure favourable reviews and high box-office receipts? Or is it more like Theatre de Complicité's attempts to create and perform new radical texts from diverse sources that challenge and even trouble their audiences? Or, yet again, is it similar to the change which Schutzman (1994) managed to achieve using a Boal Forum workshop with middle-class Americans? Though expressing no sense of their own oppression they acknowledged that they belonged to a privileged group which oppressed members of other groups. Then, by sharing their feelings of impotence and complicity, workshop participants managed to create a 'map' to aid them in dealing with their 'non-prescriptive, unchosen, social positions within that oppressive territory' and with 'the cultural forces that so humiliated their wills and appropriated their differences' (p. 140).

In this latter sense, how does the programme help participants to produce their maps for dealing with oppression others might suffer at the hands of the companies they work for and for overcoming the cultural forces that may humiliate their own wills in such situations?.

Finally, do boards of directors of direct sponsoring companies really want radical change to be produced by their executives? Perhaps directors' views on this issue are better reflected in the reservations expressed by St George, Schwager, and Canavan (1999), noted earlier, about the potential risks they see in the use of drama in corporate training such that 'those using drama-based training have an ethical imperative to ensure its appropriate application' (p. 79). If one takes their position, the conventional theatre director's approach will probably suffice after all.

CONCLUSIONS

In the first part of the chapter it is suggested that growth in the use by UK-based companies of theatre in training and development programmes is best seen as part of a larger movement which has increased business influence over aspects of social, cultural, and political life in order to strengthen the competitiveness internationally of 'UK plc'.

Claims that such programmes can prompt change and creativity in participants and, through them, in the organizations they manage are designed to resolve problems which seem little different from those perceived as targets in the earlier history of initiatives designed to engineer management and organization development. Nowadays, there may be more urgency, created by changed perceptions of competitiveness and organizational failings. Ironically, though, some of these stem from ill-considered corporate strategies such as 'downsizing' and mergers and acquisitions. However, it is possible that some of the uses of theatre referred to in the literature may produce more creative and radical outcomes than is possible using traditional approaches.

As for the two specially prepared cases, they are examined for evidence that they fit this more radical scenario. In the CompCo case it is concluded that the inclusion of a theatre workshop in the programme of in-company executive training and development may have produced worthwhile outcomes for the organization. However, though some may also label those outcomes as 'radical', this seems to ring true only within the conservative framework of existing dominant economic and business paradigms. What is more, the use of workshops as part of change programmes may increase the pressures on the participants to perform emotional labour in ways that could have pernicious effects on their sense of self and the esteem that is associated with it.

As for the international business school programme, it is possible to infer from material produced by its main sponsors that their objectives are radical. These are probably realized in terms of the effects of the participants' experience within the programme on their own learning and, possibly, the transfer of this to their in-role behaviour back at work. However, even the promoters accept that it is doubtful how far this applies to the executives' potential to change their organizations.

The commentary suggests that, in any case, any such outcomes are likely to have been due only in small part, if at all, to the inclusion of a one-day theatre workshop. Much more important are other aspects of the very innovative design of the programme and the orientation and mix of participants. Even within the first reflective module the value of the workshop seems more as an 'ice-breaking' activity rather than one designed to fit participants to adopt easily a playful workshop mode of experimentation throughout the programme and back in the workplace.

Taking as a benchmark the practice of professional theatre companies, I conclude that, if workshops for managers are to help significantly in the process of producing more radical and lasting outcomes in both personal and organizational terms, two conditions are necessary. First, much more time and effort needs to be devoted to the use of workshops within training and development programmes. Second, if—as the promoters claim—those programmes can help participants to imagine how 'the world can be seen differently', perhaps the ideas introduced by faculty into a programme, and the way the theatre workshop is used in relation to those ideas, need to be responsive to the 'more radical economic and business model' proposed by the Worldwatch Institute (2002), directed to the 'sustainable human future' described by the New Renaissance Group.

NOTES

1. Quoted from Arts and Business website.
2. The Worldwatch Institute is a non-profit public policy research organization based in Washington, USA, dedicated to informing policy makers and the public about emerging global problems and trends and the complex links between the world economy and its environmental support systems. For each of the last nineteen years, including 2002, the Institute has published an assessment of the state of the world with special emphasis on the state of the environment, including human beings, and steps needed to protect it.
3. The New Renaissance Group, formed recently in the UK, is made up of a set of experienced people of established reputations drawn from a variety of fields. The quotation cited is from a statement that arose from a meeting of an International Multi-disciplinary Workshop organized by the NRG held at the Royal Society of Edinburgh, 4 to 6 July 2001.
4. From 'The Education of Practicing Managers', a paper posted on the programme website http://www.impm.org.

REFERENCES

Arkin, A. (1998). 'Treading the Boards', *People Management*, 13 Aug.

Baier, A. (1992). 'Trust and Antitrust', in J. Deigh (ed.), *Ethics and Personality: Essays in Moral Psychology*. Chicago: University of Chicago Press.

Boal, A. (1979). *Theatre of the Oppressed*. London: Pluto Press.

Bourdieu, P., and Heeke, H. (1995). *Free Exchange*. Cambridge: Polity Press.

Campbell, A. (1994). 'Re-inventing the Wheel: Breakout Theatre-in-Education', in M. Schutzman and J. Cohen-Cruz (eds.), *Playing Boal: Theatre, Therapy and Activism*. London: Routledge.

Caulkin, S. (2000). 'Performance!', *Management Today*, May: 62–7.

Coyle, D. (1999). *The Weightless World*. Oxford: Capstone Publishing.

Feldhendler, D. (1994). 'Augusto Boal and Jacob L. Moreno: Theatre and Therapy', in M. Schutzman and J. Cohen-Cruz (eds.), *Playing Boal: Theatre, Therapy and Activism*. London: Routledge.

Fulop, L., and Rifkin, W. D. (1997). 'Representing Fear in Learning in Organizations', *Management Learning*, 28/1: 45–63.

Girma, S., Thompson, S., and Wright, P. (2002). 'Merger Activity and Executive Pay'. Paper presented to the Annual Conference of the Royal Economic Society, Mar.

Gray, C. (2000). *The Politics of the Arts in Britain*. London: Macmillan Press.

Hadfield, C. (2000). *A Creative Education: How Creativity and the Arts Enhance MBA and Executive Development Programmes*. London: Arts and Business.

Handy, C. (1997) 'The Search for Meaning', *Leader to Leader*, 5 (Summer): 14–20.

Hochschild, A. (1983). *The Managed Heart*. Berkeley and Los Angeles: University of California Press.

Hopfl, H. (1994). 'Learning by Heart: The Rules of Rhetoric and the Poetics of Experience', *Management Learning*, 25/3: 463–74.

Jackson, A. (1992). 'Translator's Introduction', in A. Boal, *Games for Actors and Non-actors*. London: Routledge.

Kershaw, B. (1992). *The Politics of Performance: Radical Theatre as Cultural Intervention*. London: Routledge.

KPMG (1999). *Unlocking Shareholder Value: The Keys to Success: Mergers and Acquisitions*. London: KPMG, Global Research Report.

Mangham, I., and Overington, M. (1987). *Organizations as Theatre: A Social Psychology of Dramatic Appearances*. Chichester: John Wiley.

New Economics Foundation (NEF) (2002). *Five Brothers: The Rise and Nemesis of the Big Bean Counters*. London: NEF.

Ratcliffe, M. (1995). 'Collusion between Celebrants', in *Theatre de Complicité: The Three Lives of Lucy Cabrol*. London: Methuen.

St George, J., Schwager, S., and Canavan, F. (1999). 'A Guide to Drama-Based Training', *Employment Relations Today*, Winter: 73–81.

Schutzman. M. (1994). 'The Political Therapy of Augusto Boal', in M. Schutzman and J. Cohen-Cruz (eds.), *Playing Boal: Theatre, Therapy and Activism*. London: Routledge.

Spry, L. (1994). 'Structures of Power: Toward a Theatre of Liberation', in M. Schutzman and J. Cohen-Cruz (eds.), *Playing Boal: Theatre, Therapy and Activism*. London: Routledge.

Steyaert, C. R., Bouwen, R., and Van Looy, B. (1996). 'Conversational Construction of New Meaning Configurations in Organisational Innovation: A Generative Approach', *European Journal of Work and Occupational Psychology*, 5/1: 67–89.

Turnbull, S. (1999). 'Emotional Labour in Corporate Change Programmes: The Effects of Organizational Feeling Rules on Middle Managers', *Human Resource Development International*, 2/2: 125–46.

Worldwatch Institute (2002). *State of the World, 2002: Progress towards a Sustainable Society*. London: Earthscan Publications.

CHAPTER 11

....

WILDERNESS EXPERIENCE IN EDUCATION FOR ECOLOGY

....

PETER REASON

AT LEAST since the 1980s, and possibly long before that, humanity has been running an ecological deficit with the earth. The activities of humans are fast overwhelming the self-regulating capacity of the planet of which we are a part (see, for example, WWF 2004: 2–4). The Millennium Ecosystem Assessment (2005) reveals that approximately 60 per cent of the ecosystem services that support life on earth—such as fresh water, capture fisheries, air and water regulation, and the regulation of regional climate, natural hazards, and pests—are being degraded or used unsustainably and that this 'could grow significantly worse in the next 50 years'. The ecological footprint, a measure of humanity's use of renewable natural resources (Wackernagel et al. 1997), grew by 80 per cent between 1961 and 1999, to a level 20 per cent above the earth's biological capacity. The challenge of sustainability faces us now, not in some distant future. David King, Chief Scientific Adviser to the UK government, has described climate change as the greatest challenge facing the world in the twenty-first century (King 2004a, 2004b). James Lovelock has issued the grim warning that we are too late for 'sustainable development' and must make 'a well-planned sustainable retreat' (Lovelock 2006).

This chapter explores how wilderness experiences, as part of education for ecology, can be part of management education designed to address these issues. For the challenges we face are not simply economic and technical—although they have economic and technical dimensions. Rather the crisis is primarily one of mind and of how we perceive ourselves in relationship to the planet of which we are a part. As David Orr argues,

The crisis we face is first and foremost one of mind, perceptions, and values; hence, it is a challenge to those institutions presuming to shape minds, perceptions, and values. It is an educational challenge. More of the same kind of education can only make things worse.

(Orr 1994: 27)

The M.Sc. in Responsibility and Business Practice at the University of Bath seeks to address these educational challenges (see http://www.bath.ac.uk/carpp/msc.htm). It looks at the complex relationship between business decisions and their impact on local and world communities, economies, and environment, and helps participants develop management practices that are responsive to pressures for greater awareness in these areas. Many people would like to bridge the gaps between their beliefs and hopes as human beings, and the reality of their working lives. This course aims to equip participants with the skills, knowledge, and awareness to review their own practice and play an active part in moving organizations towards a more values-aware orientation.

Judi Marshall has described the educational design of this programme as 'matching form to content' (Marshall 2004). She argues that 'pedagogy matters...that we need to develop educational forms that are robustly congruent with the issues addressed' (2004: 197). Our pedagogy recognizes that there are no formulaic solutions to these issues; we invite participants to engage in active reflection and experimentation, and so become explorers and potentially pioneers in responsibility and business practice. Thus our educational model is both appreciative and question posing.

The programme is part-time and comprises eight intensive, five-day residential workshops over two years. Each workshop explores a content area in depth—the first two open the territory, looking at 'Globalization and the New Context of Business and New Economics'; the third workshop, the subject of the current chapter, explores the ecology of the planet of which business is a part; while the fourth brings participants back to the practices of 'Sustainable Corporate Management'; in the second year workshops develop these themes. We weave other, ongoing, strands of learning throughout the programme: systemic thinking, acting for change, power, gender, diversity, and leadership.

Our question-posing education practice is based on action research (Reason and Bradbury 2001). We invite participants to develop skills of reflective practice (Marshall 2001; Schön 1983; Torbert 2004), cooperative enquiry (Heron 1996), and large-scale change (Gustavsen 2001). For example, the programme is structured overall as cycles of action and reflection, with each workshop offering space for reflection in learning groups, and the periods between workshops as cycles of action. We bring into the classroom exercises which encourage reflective capabilities here and now—such as individual and group process reviews; and 'tools' to enhance off-line reflection such as the 'learning pathways grid' (Rudolph, Taylor, and Foldy 2001). The assessment process encourages learning through enquiry. Maybe most important and challenging is our attempt as staff to model a practice of enquiry moment to moment in all our engagements with students.

WILDERNESS EXPERIENCE

The staff team, when they originally designed it, were adamant that the programme, while clearly a business programme in a prestigious business school, should attend to questions of meaning, value, spirit, and in particular that students should be exposed to radical thinking about the nature of the planet earth as the originator of all human and non-human wealth. We wanted to explore deep ecology and Gaia theory and, as far as possible in the overcrowded British Isles, offer students a 'wilderness experience', an opportunity for a direct experience of the wildness of the natural world.

To this end we have teamed up with colleagues at Schumacher College in Devon,[1] and in particular with the resident ecologist Stephan Harding. Together we designed

---

Box 11.1 The Deep Ecology Platform

- All life has value in itself, independent of its usefulness to humans.
- Richness and diversity contribute to life's well-being and have value in themselves.
- Humans have no right to reduce this richness and diversity except to satisfy vital needs in a responsible way.
- The impact of humans in the world is excessive and rapidly getting worse.
- Human lifestyles and population are key elements of this impact.
- The diversity of life, including cultures, can flourish only with reduced human impact.
- Basic ideological, political, economic, and technological structures must therefore change.
- Those who accept the foregoing points have an obligation to participate in implementing the necessary changes and to do peacefully and democratically.

This version of the Deep Ecology Platform was formulated by those attending the Deep Ecology course at Schumacher College, May 1995 (Harding 2006: 241–2).

Box 11.2 Gaia

Gaia Theory proposes two radical departures from the conventional view [of life on earth]. The first proposal is that life profoundly affects the non-living environment, such as the composition of the atmosphere, which then feeds back to influence the entirety of the living world. The second property emerges out of this tight coupling between life and non-life. This 'emergent property' is the ability of Gaia, of the Earth System as a whole, to maintain key aspects of the global environment, such as global temperature, at levels favourable to life, despite shocks from both with and outside itself.

This sort of ability, which scientists call 'self-regulation' is exhibited by all living things.... So, according to this theory, Gaia is in some sense alive ...

Source: Adapted from Harding (2001: 17–19; see also 2006: ch. 3).

---

a week-long experience which includes lectures on deep ecology (Devall and Sessions 1985; Naess 1990) (see Box 11.1); Gaia theory (Harding 2006; Lovelock 1979, 2006) (see Box 11.2); and the state of the natural world, but where a lot of time is spent outside. We take participants on a night walk through woodland and spend an afternoon meditating by the River Dart. We summon the Council of All Beings, the ceremony developed by John Seed and Joanna Macy (Macy and Brown 1998; Seed et al. 1988) in which participants come to the council circle to speak as the many diverse beings of their concern for the state of the world. And we spend one whole day in a hike along the upper reaches of the River Dart, along what must be one of the last remaining stretches of wilderness in England. On this walk we leave the footpaths and scramble over rocks and under branches; we help each other through bogs and over torrential streams. And under Stephan's guidance we experiment with deep ecology exercises which shift our experience of the more than human world.

Through ten years of reflective practice conducting this workshop we have learned that education for ecology cannot be based solely on propositional knowing: it must be an experiential and aesthetic process. As Gregory Bateson argued in his essay 'Conscious Purpose vs Nature' (in Bateson 1972), the conscious rational human mind—what we in academia are proud to inculcate in our students-is itself antipathetic to natural ecological processes. He argues that the human mind, driven by rational conscious purpose, separates itself from the wider Mind embedded in the self-regulation of ecological systems. Consciousness as a 'short-cut device to enable you to get quickly at what you want' (1972: 443), when coupled with powerful technology, cuts through the balancing circuits of Mind and undermines the ecosystem's stability. Bateson wanted to find a way of accessing the lost sense of interconnectedness and intimate interdependency; and he calls this the recovery of 'grace', the sacred dimension of our being (for a fuller review of the implications of Bateson's ideas for ecological education, see Reason forthcoming 2007).

EXPERIENTIAL ENQUIRY

I have described the educational model of the M.Sc. programme as drawing on action research as a basis for learning, and throughout the programme there is an emphasis on enquiry processes and skills. The deep ecology workshop draws on the model of cooperative enquiry by inviting participants to engage in cycles of action and reflection in their exploration of the natural world. Cooperative enquiry is a form of collaborative action research-research *with* rather than *on* people—in which all participants contribute equally to the design of the enquiry and engage in the activities being researched (Heron 1996; Reason 2003). While, in traditional research, the roles of researcher and subject are mutually exclusive, cooperative enquiry is based on reciprocal initiative and control, so that all those involved work together as co-researchers and as co-subjects. It is argued that for a truly human science of persons, those involved in the enquiry process must engage as persons rather than as passive objects, contributing with awareness to both the ideas and the action that are part of the enquiry endeavour. It is important to emphasize that the workshop is not an example of a full practice of cooperative enquiry: the staff team retain a significant degree of (hopefully authentic and legitimate) hierarchical control of the design: we want to offer the cooperative enquiry model to participants and 'walk them through it'; and we want to offer activities which may open participants to a range of new experiences. However, within the overall design there is plenty of space for individual autonomy and collaboration among participants.

An important part of the cooperative enquiry that we want participants to understand and experiment with is the idea that our 'reality' is subjective-objective and involves an extended epistemology. As human persons we participate in and articulate our world in at least four interdependent ways: experiential, presentational, propositional, and practical. These four forms of knowing can be seen as aspects of human intelligence and ways through which we dance with the primal cosmos to co-create our reality.

Experiential knowing is through direct encounter, face-to-face meeting: feeling and imaging the presence of some person, place, process, or thing. It is knowing through participation and empathic resonance with what is there. As knower I am open to other and distinct from it. Experiential knowing is the foundation for the co-creative shaping of our world through mutual encounter, and thus articulates reality through inner resonance with what there is. It is the essential grounding of other forms of knowing.

Presentational knowing emerges from and is grounded on experiential knowing. It clothes our encounter with the world in the metaphors and analogies of aesthetic creation. Presentational knowing is profoundly embodied and draws on expressive forms of imagery, in movement and in visual, musical, vocal, and verbal art forms, and is the way in which we first give form to our experience.

Propositional knowing is knowing in conceptual terms; knowledge by description. It is knowing expressed in statements, theories, and formulae that come with the mastery of concepts and classes through language and number. Propositions themselves are carried by presentational forms—the sounds, or the visual shapes of the spoken or written word or number—and are ultimately grounded in our experiential articulation of a world.

Practical knowing is knowing how to do something, demonstrated in a skill or competence. It presupposes a conceptual grasp of principles and standards of practice, presentational elegance, and experiential grounding in the situation within which the action occurs. Practical knowing is based on and fulfils the three prior forms of knowing, brings them to fruition in our practice.

The process of cooperative enquiry draws on cycles of action and reflection which draw on the extended epistemology and thereby present the possibility of addressing Bateson's concerns. At each stage of the cycle a different way of knowing holds primacy. In Phase 1 a group of co-researchers come together to explore an agreed area of human activity. In this first phase they agree on the focus of their enquiry and the questions or propositions they wish to explore. They agree to undertake some action, some practice, which will contribute to this exploration, and agree to a set of procedures by which they will observe and record their own and each other's experience. Phase 1 is primarily in the mode of propositional knowing.

In the deep ecology workshop the focus of enquiry is established as part of the course content. The questions posed for the week are 'What is the experience of deep ecology?' and 'What activities and disciplines aid its development?' Within these broad questions individual participants are invited to develop their own specific questions as the week progresses. The enquiry is based propositionally in the ideas about deep ecology and Gaia theory offered by Stephan.

In Phase 2 the co-researchers now also become co-subjects: they engage in the actions agreed and observe and record the process and outcomes of their own and each other's experience. In particular, they are careful to notice the subtleties of experience, to hold lightly the propositional frame from which they started so that they are able to notice how practice does and does not conform to their original ideas. This phase involves primarily practical knowledge: knowing how (and how not) to engage in appropriate action, to bracket off the starting idea, and to exercise relevant discrimination.

Starting with the night walk the evening we arrive at Schumacher College, participants are invited into the range of activities outlined above. As faculty we have designed activities through which they can bracket their preconceptions and engage with the natural world in novel ways—to enter into relation with trees, to walk on the earth as a living being, to meditate with the River, to speak as a slug or as an oak tree ...

Phase 3 is in some ways the touchstone of the enquiry method. The co-subjects become fully immersed in and engaged with their experience. They may develop a degree of openness to what is going on so free of preconceptions that they see it in a new way. They may deepen into the experience so that superficial understandings are elaborated and developed. Or they may be led away from the original ideas and proposals into new fields, unpredicted action, and creative insights. Phase 3 involves mainly experiential knowing, although it will be richer if new experience is expressed, when recorded, in creative presentational form.

For many participants it is this experiential knowing that is the key to the workshop experience. For many, living for a week in community in an area of amazing natural beauty, having time just to sit by a river, and being given permission to open themselves to the voice of the more-than-human world is a great significance.

In Phase 4, after an agreed period engaged in Phases 2 and 3, the co-researchers reassemble to consider their original propositions and questions in the light of their experience. As a result they may modify, develop, or reframe them; or reject them and pose new questions. They may choose, for the next cycle of action, to focus on the same or on different aspects of the overall enquiry. The group may also choose to amend or develop its enquiry procedures—forms of action, ways of gathering data—in the light of experience. Phase 4 is primarily the stage of propositional knowing, although presentational forms of knowing will form an important bridge with the experiential and practical phases.

The course community is divided into small groups (who also work together each day on simply household tasks to maintain the ecology of the College) which meet at the end of each day to review and make their sense of the experiences. We invite participants to help each other articulate what has been important for them, to write reflectively, to draw or otherwise create visual images.

In a full enquiry the cycle will be repeated several times. Ideas and discoveries tentatively reached in early phases can be checked and developed; investigation of one aspect of the enquiry can be related to exploration of other parts; new skills can be acquired and monitored; experiential competencies are realized; the group itself becomes more cohesive and self-critical, more skilled in its work. Ideally the enquiry is finished when the initial questions are fully answered in practice, when there is a new congruence between the four kinds of knowing. It is of course rare for a group to complete an enquiry so fully.

The deep ecology workshop is designed with three cycles of enquiry: discussion of the philosophy of deep ecology followed by an afternoon in meditation with the River Dart;

an introduction to Gaia theory and the state of the world followed by the Council for All Beings; and the day-long eco-walk down the River Dart with mini-talks and exercises. Each of these cycles of followed by a review in small groups, and on the final morning we meet as a whole group. Each person is given 'post-it' stickers and asked to write three answers to each of the two questions of the enquiry: 'What is the experience of deep ecology? And 'How do you get there?' Participants take it in turn to present their answers to the group, and to place their stickers on a wall chart, with the aim of clustering them into meaningful groups.

This process of enquiry, based in experiential knowing, parallels and amplifies the learning cycle of deep ecology, which involves deep experience, deep questioning, and deep commitment.

Deep experience is 'often what gets a person started along a deep ecological path' (Harding 1997: 14); it often involves a spontaneous recognition of the interconnectedness of all things and thus the value of all things in their own right.

A key aspect of these experiences is the perception of gestalts, or networks of relationships. We see that there are no isolated objects, but that objects are nodes in a vast web of interconnections. When such deep experience occurs, we feel a strong sense of wide identification with what we are sensing. This identification involves a heightened sense of empathy and an expansion of our concern with non-human life. We realize how dependent we are on the well-being of nature for our own physical and psychological well-being. (Harding 1997: 16)

This sense of belonging to an intelligent universe revealed by deep experience often leads in the deep ecology framework to 'deep questioning'

which helps to elaborate a coherent framework for elucidating fundamental beliefs, and for translating these beliefs into decisions, lifestyle and action...By deep questioning, an individual is articulating a total view of life which can guide his or her lifestyle choices...In questioning society, one understands its underlying assumptions from an ecological point of view. (Harding 1997: 16)

Deep experience combined with deep questioning leads to deep commitment:

When an ecological world-view is well developed, people act from their whole personality, giving rise to tremendous energy and commitment. Such actions are peaceful and democratic and will lead towards ecological sustainability. Uncovering the ecological self gives rise to joy, which gives rise to involvement, which in turn leads to wider identification, and hence to greater commitment. This leads to 'extending care to humans and deepening care for non-humans'. (Harding 2001: 17)

By linking the process of cooperative enquiry to the perspective of deep ecology we hope to emphasize the importance of question posing in education. We are not offering deep ecology as a monolithic normative view to which all must conform. But we are saying, there is something really important in this view of a deeply interconnected world, please engage in an exploration of what this means for you in your life; use the enquiry process to make it your own.

WILDERNESS EXPERIENCE

Schumacher College is located on the edge of Dartmoor which, while by no means a pristine wilderness, contains pockets of land where the modern human imprint is minimal. One of these is a corridor along the River Dart in its higher reaches, where the river is swift flowing, tumbling over rocks and through narrow gorges as it falls off the moor. While we introduce participants to outside activities throughout the week, the 'ecohike' down the Dart on the fourth day is the major event. We take a coach up onto the moor, and walk downstream for about six hours. For most of the distance there are no paths: we scramble up and down, through boggy areas, over rocks, through oak woods; sometimes walking confidently on secure ground, while at other times cautiously on slippery rocks by the river's edge; sometimes walking alone, and at others helping each other up steep cliff climbs and over swollen streams where they join the main river. We have walked this route ten times now in many different weather conditions—on several occasions in pouring rain. I have found myself moved almost to tears as I watch group members look after each other, the stronger helping the less able over difficult patches—it is clear that as well as providing an education in ecology, the experience is emotionally bonding for the group.

We encourage participants to walk with open minds and hearts, to be aware of the world around them. We encourage them to walk with an attitude of deep ecology-that the world they are walking through is of intrinsic value; and of Gaia-that the world is in some sense a living being. We ask people to avoid everyday chatter as much as possible—for how can we hear what the trees might be saying if we don't listen to them? We invite them to try walking meditatively with a mantra on their lips—one of my favourites I learned from Joan Halifax, 'walking the green earth...Ah!' which is repeated in time with one's walking pace. From time to time on this walk we stop to hear from Stephan about ecological features—we can see directly the erosion of granite rocks by water and plants which is fundamental to the carbon cycle. At others we stop to invite participants to engage in 'deep ecology exercises'—simple activities which may radically shift perception.

Typically at our first stop, in a particularly wet and mossy glade overhung with ancient oaks growing improbably out of crevices in the granite, we invite participants to walk around in silence, touching the moss, rocks, and trees while exploring the sense that as they touch, these beings are touching them; and more broadly that as they see the world, the beings in the world are—in an entirely different way—'seeing' them. We are here drawing on anthropological evidence from hunter gathers (see Harding 2006: 48–9); and on David Abram's (1996) interpretation of Merleau-Ponty that we can touch because we ourselves are physical beings capable of being touched, so that touching is a transaction, 'certain ways the outside has of invading us and certain ways we have of meeting the invasion' (Merleau-Ponty 1962: 317).

Our second exercise is a variant of the 'blind walk' with the emphasis placed not on qualities of interpersonal trust but on the perception of the world with our primary sense of sight inhibited. Participants work in pairs to help each other experience the roughness of bark, the stickiness of mud, the delicacy of fungi, the coldness of rock—yet these qualities are experienced directly rather than described verbally. Later we may express them through poetic form such as haiku:

> Water drop on leaf
> a tear rolls down for times lost
> and new beginnings. (Ruth Townsley)

In the third formal exercise we invite participants to find a quiet spot and imaginatively identify with a part of the more than human world and how it partakes in the cycles of Gaia: *How a tree expires water, creating clouds which form rain which feeds the river which, amplified by the roots of the tree, erodes the granite releasing calcium which links with carbon to form calcium carbonate which sediments as chalk. . . .*

The last time we did this, I was sitting against a tree in a particularly lush and damp piece of woodland. I relaxed against the tree, experienced my body against the wood and the earth, and looked around me. As I quietened my thoughts, and looked at those beings I call trees, earth, stones, birds . . . and opened my imagination to include fungi, insects, bacteria . . . and then the various chemical substances, the elements and molecules . . . and then again the quantum reality of the particles that lie underneath even that . . . I realized everything I could see and imagine was in the process of becoming something else, that everything was participating in everything else. I realized quite suddenly that to see the world as separate things or beings was to have already abstracted from this ongoing process of being. And I think I understand what Whitehead and the Buddha might have meant.

(Reason 2002: 19)

We end the walk pretty exhausted, footsore, and 'full up' with experiences. However, participants usually have the energy for further reflection that evening. During the week we have introduced participants to creative ways of recording experience—freefall writing (Turner-Vesselago n.d.), poetry and haiku, drawing—and following the walk we encourage people to reflect together on their experience and to use these approaches to gather their reflections. We end the enquiry process with a round of sharing, usually centred about questions such as 'What is the experience of deep ecology?' and 'What activities and disciplines aid its development?'

WHAT IS THE EXPERIENCE OF
DEEP ECOLOGY?

Student Responses

This workshop is experience as both deeply moving and challenging. Looking directly at the state of the world through statistics and through the eyes of other Beings can be deeply disturbing. And the workshop can challenge deeply held views of those with a scientific education and those with strong religious commitments. On the whole, it opens new perspectives on the world we live in. The fourth M.Sc. group made a tape recording of their final enquiry cycle which formed the basis of a journal article (Maughan and Reason 2001). The following give some sense of the nature of the experience (the quotation marks indicate participants' actual words).

The experience of deep ecology started for most of us with a true appreciation, as if for the first time, of the simple beauty of the more-than-human world versus the human-made urban world many of us live in. This experience is one of profound joy expressed by one participant as 'post human exuberance, when you sit on a rock and feel happy, it's not like when you're happy because you've had a birthday present, it's a different, more profound sort of happiness'.

We found beauty in 'the wonder and magic of nature's complex cycles'. Through cycles of birth, death and re-use we became aware that 'everything is related in one way or another' and deep ecology provides us with an 'understanding of the intimate relationships which exist and which we have with nature as well'. Our 'connectedness to the rhythms of the natural world' is something which our urban lives allow us to forget and the experience of deep ecology places us back within our most fundamental context: 'we are nature'. One participant elaborated on this: 'I thought the core experience was to actually feel myself as part of the natural world. I don't think we normally actually feel that.'

We found our experience was particularly heightened by the exercises during our day long wilderness walk when we were invited to close our eyes, touch our surroundings and sense our surroundings touching and feeling us in reply. One participant spoke of 'the blur between me and the moss I was touching, it was difficult to know where I ended and the moss began. Then there was the exercise where we really probed our surroundings, I almost felt like asking permission of this other living entity, "May I?" and "Should I?" and "I've never done this before". I really experienced a wonderful balance between the blur and the sense of otherness, in our existence, our relationships with the living world, our very being.' This notion of otherness was also expressed in this way: 'Now I know the earth and everything on it has a heart and has feeling.' Throughout the week we felt welcomed by the more-than-human world and many of us shared this participant's feeling 'of coming home, of being accepted by the place like when I've had a really happy home, I've just walked in and been embraced...' (Maughan and Reason 2001: 21–2)

From the experiences of our students over many cycles of enquiry, we can summarize the experience of deep ecology as in Box 11.3.

Box 11.3 What is the experience of deep ecology?

- The experience of deep ecology is a feeling of joy and awe at the beauty of the more-than-human world
- It is an appreciation of the delicate balance between chaos and order
- It is the acknowledgement of the interconnectedness of all living beings, including ourselves, in the endless cycles of the planet
- This acknowledgement leads to the direct identification of ourselves with other living beings and a redefinition of our place, no longer dominating nature but one equal part of it
- It is a sense of the consciousness of other living beings and the reciprocal relationship between us
- The experience is both of the moment and of eternity
- The experience is that of a spiritual quest to reconnect with our true human nature and break down the artificial barriers we have erected
- It is the feeling of home-coming
- It is the celebration of the creator

Source: Maughan and Reason 2001: 21

So What?

The deep ecology workshop is for many a turning point on the programme. Our experience as staff is that participants join the programme with a strong value orientation toward making a difference but sometimes with a quite narrow view of 'responsibility and business practice' based, understandably, in their own career and experiences. For many, the first two workshops open their eyes to the extraordinary range of issues—economic, political, personal, and spiritual—that are presented when questions of justice and sustainability are placed at the centre of the curriculum; and the urgency of the ecological challenge. For many this is a daunting realization which modern humanist values do not prepare them for. In many ways the programme deeply challenges the assumptions and values of the modern capitalist world.

The experience of deep ecology can, we would argue, provide a new grounding in an earth-centred ethic. Not to say that as the result of a week's experience participants all become radical deep ecologists. But the experiences of the workshop do open the possibility of a different way of addressing what Thomas Berry (1999) calls the Great Work of our times—learning how to move from a devastating presence on the planet to a benign presence. How participants actualize this is highly individual, but the thread of the Schumacher College experience can be traced through their work on the rest of the course and into their final projects. I trace three examples.

Jane Brown worked as an equal opportunities adviser in the Fire Service. Her job, and her passion, is to open the service to women, people of colour, and other minorities, to promote equality. She writes of how she was moved and inspired by the ecology workshop and concludes that:

The claim that there is a deep interconnectivity at all levels of life...gives me a feeling of relief but also an increasing sense of responsibility. It lets me rest and releases me from taking on everything myself...It invites me to trust both the greater intelligence that is the universe and to myself as part of that universal intelligence. It also obliges me to take action and engage in...the 'real work' of becoming a whole person...My understanding of what 'equality' meant is fundamentally different...

Ian Nicholson is an engineer who has worked extensively in the construction and water industry. He recounts how the experience at Schumacher gave him a sense of unity with the natural world, 'because I was part of it and not different to it'. While these fundamental values are at the heart of his practice, he struggles with how to integrate this with the needs of his nascent environmental consultancy. It is tough going.

Christel Scholten works for a large international bank seeking a way toward sustainable banking. She writes of how the deep ecology perspective came to life for her on the ecology workshop in her experience of both the pain and the beauty of the planet. This informs her world-view that we can learn to live in harmony with nature, each of us unique yet part of one living system. She applies this to her practice as a 'tempered radical' (Meyerson and Scully 1995) in her bank, using her informal power to bring people together in different forms of dialogue to create a 'change community'.

The challenge of learning about deep ecology and Gaia theory offers a profound challenge to programme participants. For many, it changes their sense of who they are as humans in relation to the earth which penetrates and deeply challenges their practice as organizational members.

NOTE

1. Schumacher College is an international centre for ecological studies offering a range of educational opportunities including short courses and an M.Sc. in Holistic Science. http://www.gn.apc.org/schumachercollege/.

REFERENCES

Abram, D. (1996). *The Spell of the Sensuous: Perception and Language in a More than Human World*. New York: Pantheon.

Bateson, G. (1972). *Steps to an Ecology of Mind*. San Francisco: Chandler.

Berry, T. (1999). *The Great Work: Our Way into the Future*. New York: Bell Tower.

Devall, B., and Sessions, G. (1985). *Deep Ecology: Living as if Nature Mattered*. Salt Lake City: Gibbs M. Smith.

Gustavsen, B. (2001). 'Theory and Practice: The Mediating Discourse', in P. Reason and H. Bradbury (eds.), *Handbook of Action Research: Participative Inquiry and Practice*. London: Sage.

Harding, S. P. (1997). 'What is Deep Ecology'?, *Resurgence*, 185: 14–17.

—— (2001). 'Exploring Gaia', *Resurgence*, 204: 16–19.

—— (2006). *Animate Earth*. Totnes: Greenbooks.

Heron, J. (1996). *Co-operative Inquiry: Research into the Human Condition*. London: Sage.

King, D. (2004a). *Global Warming: The Science of Climate Change, the Imperatives for Action. Greenpeace Business Lecture*. Retrieved Dec. 2004, from http://www.ost.gov.uk/about_ost/csa.htm.

—— (2004b). 'Responding to Climate Change', *Science*, 303: 5655.

Lovelock, J. E. (1979). *Gaia: A New Look at Life on Earth*. London: Oxford University Press.

—— (2006). *The Revenge of Gaia*. London: Allen Lane.

Macy, J. R., and Brown, M. Y. (1998). *Coming Back to Life: Practices to Reconnect our Lives, our World*. Gabriola Island: New Society Publishers.

Marshall, J. (2001). 'Self-Reflective Inquiry Practices', in P. Reason and H. Bradbury (eds.), *Handbook of Action Research: Participative Inquiry and Practice*. London: Sage.

—— (2004). 'Matching Form to Content in Educating for Sustainability: The Masters (MSc) in Responsibility and Business Practice', in C. Galea (ed.), *Teaching Business Sustainability*. London: Greenleaf Publishing.

Maughan, E., and Reason, P. (2001). 'A Co-operative Inquiry into Deep Ecology', *ReVision*, 23/4: 18–24.

Merleau-Ponty, M. (1962). *Phenomenology of Perception*, trans. C. Smith. London: Routledge & Kegan Paul.

Meyerson, D. E., and Scully, M. A. (1995). 'Tempered Radicalism and the Politics of Ambivalence and Change', *Organization Science*, 6/5: 585–600.

Millennium Ecosystem Assessment (2005). *Experts Say that Attention to Ecosystem Services is Needed to Achieve Global Development Goals*. Retrieved Aug. 2005, from http://www.maweb.org/en/article.aspx?id=58.

Naess, A. (1990). *Ecology Community and Lifestyle: Outline of an Ecosophy*, trans. D. Rotherberg. Cambridge: Cambridge University Press.

Orr, D. W. (1994). *Earth in Mind*. Washington: Island Press.

Reason, P. (2002). 'Justice, Sustainability and Participation: Inaugural Professorial Lecture', *Concepts and Transformation*, 7/1: 7–29.

—— (2003). 'Doing Co-operative Inquiry', in J. Smith (ed.), *Qualitative Psychology: A Practical Guide to Methods*. London: Sage.

—— (2007). 'Education for Ecology: Science, Aesthetics, Spirit and Ceremony', *Management Learning*, 38/1: 27–44.

—— and Bradbury, H. (eds.) (2001). *Handbook of Action Research: Participative Inquiry and Practice*. London: Sage.

Rudolph, J. W., Taylor, S. S., and Foldy, E. G. (2001). 'Collaborative Off-line Reflection: A Way to Develop Skill in Action Science and Action Inquiry', in P. Reason and H. Bradbury (eds.), *Handbook of Action Research: Participative Inquiry and Practice*. London: Sage.

Schön, D. A. (1983). *The Reflective Practitioner*. New York: Basic Books.

Seed, J., Macy, J. R., Fleming, P., and Naess, A. (1988). *Thinking like a Mountain*. London: Heretic Books.

Torbert, W. R. (2004). *Action Inquiry: The Secret of Timely and Transforming Leadership*. San Francisco: Berrett-Koehler Publishers.

Turner-Vesselago, B. (n.d.). *Freefall: Writing without a Parachute*. Toronto: The Writing Space.

Wackernagel, M., Onisto, L., Linares, A. C., Falfán, I. S. L., García, J. M., Guerrero, A. I. S., et al. (1997). *Ecological Footprints of Nations: How Much Nature do They Use?—How Much Nature do They Have?* Retrieved July 2004, from http://www.ecouncil. ac.cr/rio/focus/report/english/footprint/.

WWF (2004). *Living Planet Report*. Retrieved Dec. 2004, from http://www.panda. org/downloads/general/lpr2004.pdf.

CHAPTER 12

BLUE-EYED GIRL? JANE ELLIOTT'S EXPERIENTIAL LEARNING AND ANTI-RACISM

ELAINE SWAN

INTRODUCTION

IT has become commonplace in many different academic disciplines to suggest that 'experience' is socially and culturally mediated. Thus, it is argued that our recalling of experience does not provide us with neutral access to 'raw' reality and to authentic selfhood. Given that experience isn't what it used to be, what does this mean for the category of experience in experiential learning, pedagogies? In this chapter I explore this question through an examination of race equality pedagogies. In particular, I discuss the 'equivalences' that are set up in one popular, but controversial form of race equality experiential learning, that of the 'Blue-eyed, brown-eyed' experiment of the North American primary school teacher, now consultant and public speaker, Jane Elliott, more of which later. In all forms of experiential learning method, assumptions are made about the relationship between the activity and reality. In this chapter, I ask what assumptions are made about the relationship between the experience created in the Blue-eyed, brown-eyed experiment and the realities of racism. Although there is a long history of anti-racist and equal opportunities education in the USA, and in the UK, there are relatively few examinations of these interventions within organizational and HRM studies. Perhaps this isn't surprising given that issues of race, racialization, and racism get very little coverage, as Stella Nkomo has consistently argued (1992; Nkomo and Cox 1999). But it is a major omission, particularly given the recent history of policy makers' intensified focus on multicultural and anti-racist training (Arora 2005; Bhavnani 2001; Penketh 2000).

EXPERIENTIAL LEARNING

In the various models of multicultural and anti-racist training, the use of experiential learning methods has been significant. Experiential learning, of course, is a 'diffuse concept' denoting a diverse range of practices, ideologies, and disciplines (Wildemeersch 1989; Fenwick 2003). It can refer to a whole range of practices from the political to the mainstream. For example, it is used by practices at the centre of different social movements—anti-colonial, feminist, or worker movements—whilst at the same time, albeit under different terms, it is being increasingly used in neo-liberal marketized, vocationalized, and consumerist approaches to education across the education sector (Brah and Hoy 1989; Usher, Bryant, and Johnston 1997). There are also different politics underpinning experiential learning from a bottom-up radical valuing of 'lived experience' as a challenge to top-down codified academic discipline knowledge, to a very different model: a more mainstream, neo-liberal technicist approach in which the consumer is sovereign. In general, the experience part of experiential learning therefore either refers to some model of lived experience or orientation in life, or to a present here-and-now sensing. In both, experience is taken to involve more than simply cognition and include emotions, bodily senses and sensations, and memories. Of course, as Tara Fenwick (2003) notes, there is a danger in all models that experience is idealized and romanticized, and that even in so-called radical models, only some types of experiences are seen as legitimate. Experience, particularly in its emotional and bodily representations, is sometimes presumed to be unmediated and unideological, as emotions and bodies are often thought to be more real, more natural, and more true than rationality or cognition.

As mentioned above, the category of experience has come under much critical scrutiny, particularly in feminist, post-structural and critical race studies (Scott 1992; Brah and Hoy 1989). The debates on humanism, universalism, essentialism, foundationalism, and epistemology in these studies have rendered the category of experience problematic in a number of ways leading to what Caroline Ramazanoglu and Janet Holland call 'the politics of the construction of experience' (1999: 387). In essence this politics suggests, as Ali Rattansi succinctly puts it, that 'experience . . . is *produced*, rather than simply *registered*' (1992: 33). Rattansi goes on to expand on this notion of the politics by arguing that the 'empiricism of . . . [the] notion of direct immediate experience . . . writes out the significance of the complex interpretive frameworks through which events, processes and facts are constructed' (Rattansi 1992: 33; Reynolds and Vince 2004). Experience cannot then be seen as raw material, a 'river of thoughts, perceptions and sensations into which we decide, occasionally, to dip our toes' (Brookfield 1995 cited at http://www.nl.edu/academics/cas/ace/facultypapers/StephenBrookfield_AdultLearning.cfm). It is culturally framed and shaped, and what we make of our experience depends on interpretative frames, discourses, and categories of analysis. And as Avtar Brah and Jane Hoy (1989) write, all experience is shaped by concrete social conditions, for example being black or white working class, and the significance and making sense of this experience is determined by how and by whom it is interpreted. In this view, this means that the pedagogical project is:

> to enable all students to develop analytical frameworks within which to examine and interrogate experience. In other words, the aim is to *critique* rather than *criticize* 'commonsense' understanding of experience. Depending on the context certain experiences may need to be valued while others may need to be challenged. (Brah and Hoy 1989: 72)

Experience in experiential learning cannot then be simply accessed or recalled as pure or special knowledge but must be understood as arising out of and produced within political relations.

This does not mean, however, throwing the proverbial baby out with the bathwater. As some recent feminist and post-structural writing indicates, there can be a rapprochement in relation to experience (Ramanzanoglu and Holland 1999). This does not mean a simple resurrection of experience as innocent or natural, but a recognition that lived and embodied experience cannot be simply condensed down to discourse and that the interpretative frameworks used to represent our experience themselves can contribute to a political agenda (Ramazanoglu and Holland 1999). Enabling us to make sense of our experience and its relation to power relations, this kind of politics of experience also allows us to find new concepts to make new sense of old experiences and to 'recognise that the experience of others can constantly disrupt our acceptance of what is the case' (ibid. 391).

Perhaps not recognizing some of these rapprochements, discussions of what experiential learning is and does has stalled somewhat in educational theory. Drawing upon a research study on 'diversity work' (Ahmed et al. 2006), in this chapter I want to pick up some of these themes to explore how social reality is being understood in experiential methods. In particular, I want to examine what version of the social, and what version of experience are being imagined in experiential methods for race equality. Using Michael Reynolds and Kiran Trehan's phrase (2001), what type of 'real world' is being conceptualized and how are complex processes of racialization and racism being seen as part of this 'real world'? What kinds of experiences, emotions, and ideas are imagined to produce anti-racism and social change?

Race Equality Training and Experiential Learning

Of course, experiential learning is not the main means of achieving social change. There are many ways in which black and minority ethnic women and men find ways to live with and against racisms. For some writers such as Alastair Bonnett (2000) these strategies and tactics can be understood as forms of anti-racist practice, but for others such as Paul Gilroy (1992) to call them anti-racist narrows down our understanding of their purpose and effects; for him, many of these activities are better understood as forms of emancipation. Thus, there have been innumerable formal and informal activities led by different parts of black communities: black mothers; black churches; black intelligentsia; grass roots black power groups; black trade unions and industrial action (Gilroy 1987, 1992). This chapter will not focus on these experiences but on more institutionalized forms of anti-racism in the form of training interventions. This is because in recent UK policy, training has been seen as one of the major problems in relation to institutional racism in public institutions and also one of its most promising solutions (Penketh 2000). Training as a field of power is important, involving a highly influential network of organizations, consultancies, agencies, policy makers, business schools, and authors, and is relatively under-researched and theorized (Swan 2004).

Writers who do discuss race equality training interventions in the UK suggest that there are three main clusters of practice which follow in chronological order: multicultural awareness training, anti-racist training, and diversity training (Bhavnani 2001; Arora 2005). In practice, these overlap and are more internally contradictory than the following overview will describe, but this simplification will give a sense of the differing theoretical, political, and pedagogical underpinnings around differing and contested notions of social reform, power, learning, and racism.

Multicultural Awareness Training

The first cluster of training practice that writers identify then is multicultural awareness in the 1980s. It can be found in school education but also in organizational training in schools, local authorities, social work practice, and universities (Penketh 2000). Related to discourses of relativism, cosmopolitanism, and anti-colonialism, and away from policies of assimilation and integration, according to Alastair Bonnett (2000), and spurred on by the Swann Report (1985), the main aim of multicultural education was to promote knowledge, recognition, and respect for different cultural traditions in the UK. Reproducing an idea that racism is the product of individual prejudice, and the result of ignorance or faulty knowledge of other cultures, the pedagogic approach was one of providing 'facts and empathy' (Rattansi 1992: 33). Cultures were understood as something which didn't 'melt' into the melting pot and therefore needed to be understood, experienced, and protected (Anthias and Yuval-Davis 1992).

Although there was much debate within education and local authorities, the predominant educational practices became focused on 'celebrating' cultural diversity. In her analysis of teaching training, Ramjit Arora refers to this as 'diversity of the festive kind' (2005: 22). This approach was largely based on experiential methods in schools and organizations which involved what Bonnett (2000) calls 'mini-ethnographies'. These involved children being involved in experiences that were imagined to represent 'other' cultures: the participation in eating 'different' foods, trying on 'different' dress, playing different music, watching different customs; the purpose of which was to enable white people to interact with people from different backgrounds, to learn from 'others', to see things from 'their' view, and to be 'at ease' with black and minority ethnic people (Bonnett 2000; Pederson, Walker, and Wise 2005). These experiential methods have been referred to, somewhat pejoratively, as the 3Cs (calypso, carnival, cricket) and the 3 Ss (saris, samosas, and steel bands) (Gaine 1995). The main learning technology was understood to be empathy, which was seen as the means through which prejudice could be reduced or eliminated by enabling white children to share in 'other cultures'.

CRITIQUES OF MULTICULTURALISM

The multicultural approach has been criticized by black and minority ethnic activities and a wide range of academics on a number of counts. I will focus on two of the main criticisms. The first major criticism is that the model of racism as the product of ignorance and prejudice is an impoverished account of the processes and relations of racism. It reduces cultural and structural analyses to individual psychological matters (Macdonald et al. 1989). Vikki Bell summarizes the tenor of this critique in her assessment of multicultural education as a pedagogy which was based on the erroneous assumption that all that would be required to be rid of racism was knowledge of other cultures. Such a stance ignored the fact that knowledge does not automatically result in respect, and that the politics of racism needs an analysis that does more than see racism as the result of ignorance. (2002: 510)

In terms of experiential learning, then, the relations between experiences in the classroom, subsequent actions, and social reform are not linear or guaranteed.

The second main criticism focuses on the assumptions about cultures that underpin much multicultural training and education. It assumes a narrow definition of multicultural, that cultures are static, that it is 'other ethnic' cultures that need exploring, not white cultures, and that white cultures are not already constituted through relations with black and minority ethnic people (Gilroy 1992). In spite of these weaknesses, Laura Penketh argues that it 'provided an important 'break from the violent and brutalising racism' (2000: 24).

MUNICIPAL ANTI-RACISM

The approach that emerged in the mid- to late 1980s, to some extent a reaction to the multicultural approach, was what Gilroy calls 'municipal anti-racism' (1992: 136). As a formalized and institutionalized set of practices, this form of anti-racism grew from the response to the UK governmental reviews on racism, including Lord Scarman's report (1981) in local authorities and schools, grass roots dissatisfaction with multiculturalism as an approach to racism, and the growth of 'the race relations industry' and the 'race professional' (Cohen 1992: 62). The focus on the 3Cs and the 3Ss was seen as superficial in their analyses of structures and relations of power, and processes of racism. As Chris Gaine writes, anti-racism as an approach is summarized in the slogans 'life chances not life styles' and 'we don't have culture riots' (1995: 42). Municipal anti-racism, funded by the government, developed into the setting up of race units, race experts, and practices such as positive action, ethnic monitoring, community engagement, contract compliance, and, of course, anti-racist training (Gilroy 1992).

RACE AWARENESS TRAINING

There were different forms of anti-racist training. Some were focused more on information exchange, so more facts than empathy in Rattansi parlance, comprising discussion on legislation, organization change, and equality policies

(Penketh 2000). But one approach called Race Awareness Training, also known as RAT, has become the stuff of infamy, generating a lot of 'heat and noise' (Brown and Lawton 1991). As Colin Brown and Jean Lawton write, RAT has 'generated more words than any single issue in the literature' (1991: 23). Drawing from the practice of an influential anti-racist trainer in North America called Judith Katz, who had developed a white awareness programme in 1978 and subsequently detailed it in her book *White Awareness: A Handbook for Anti-Racism Training*, the focus shifted from white people learning about other cultures to them learning about their own privilege, racism, and power (Anthias and Yuval-Davis 1992). This draws upon experiential learning as encounter group. Based on humanistic psychology and 'here and now' learning through technologies of confrontation and challenge which were aimed at getting white people to face up to how they had internalized racism (Lasch-Quinn 2002), it resembled the experiential method of encounter groups from the human potential movement. In this method, the expression of emotion— anger from black and minority ethnic participants and guilt from white people— was imagined as an authentic and purifying means of learning about the self and its effects on others. Racism was conceptualized as a disease of the white mind and soul that needed purging and eliminating through catharsis (Bonnett 2000). The training was seen therefore as an exorcizing and healing process through which challenge, confessions, witnessing, and revelation could banish irrational fears and raise white people's consciousness through involving white people emotionally as well as cognitively (Bonnett 2000). This is not to say that discussing emotions, including anger, doesn't have its place in race equality training but to question the pedagogies and frameworks that are used to make sense of these.

RAT was critiqued by left and right. It was seen by some black activists as a 'liberal sop to black demands' which led to 'white breast beating and learning the right rhetoric' (Gaine 1995: 128) and a 'perverse lust for guilt and the ritual cleansing of exposure' together with 'wallowing in white middle class guilt' (Brown and Lawton 1991: 26). For others, it was a highly moralistic, accusatory, and dangerous approach in which all white people were seen as 'baddies', a rotten barrel of apples not just a few rotten ones (Brown and Lawton 1991). In their account of their enquiry into the Burnage High School murder, Ian Macdonald et al. (1989) conclude that RAT as a form of race equality training was an unmitigated disaster, which caused white backlash, defensiveness, and guilt, and no real addressing of material inequalities.

With increasing government criticism and cutbacks in funding and growing media backlash, municipal anti-racism, and with it RAT, went into decline during the 1980s only to resurface in the form of diversity during the 1990s and 2000s. This was the time of a political climate of the 'loony left, race spies and green sheep' (Gaine 1995: 129) in which anti-racism and political correctness were, in the words of Gideon Ben-Tovim, ridiculed and exaggerated as 'authoritarian, illiberal, dogmatic or absurd' (1997: 209) and the discourse of tradition, moderation, and common sense was drawn upon by right-wing media and politicians to denounce what was seen as the extremism and excesses and professional obscuration of race professionals (Walker 2002). For some on the left, some of these criticisms were justified; thus for Gilroy (1992) municipal anti-racism was moralistic and dictatorial, applying what he calls a 'coat of paint theory of racism' in which racism is seen as an 'unwanted blemish' or 'unfortunate excrescence' which with the 'right ideological tools and political elbow grease, racism can be dealt with once and for all leaving the basic structures and relations of British economy and society unchanged' (1992: 52). Anti-racism in the form of corporate activity seemed to be coming to an end.

Diversity Training

In the 1990s and 2000s, anti-racism has been replaced, in name at least, by the concept of diversity, and anti-racist training with diversity training. The politics of this shift has been hotly debated, with some arguing that diversity is a dilution of anti-racism and equality, others arguing that it is a rejuvenation, and yet others suggesting that the concept of diversity can work in different ways, both radical and domesticated (see Ahmed et al. 2006 for more discussion). Derived more from the private sector and human resource models than legislation and policy, diversity is a concept that was first introduced to go 'beyond' what was seen by some as the narrow sectarianism of equal opportunities, and anti-racism. Referred to as a model 'beyond race and gender' by Thomas Cox, the leading influential 'academic-consultant' in North America on diversity in the 1990s, it was seen to broaden out the focus from collective differences such as race or gender to include all the ways in which individuals differ including, for example, personality and work style, thus offering 'less fractious analytical categories than race' (Mir, Mir, and Wong 2006). It seemed to offer a more celebratory narrative of the multicultural workplace (ibid.) which included white men and was therefore imagined to be more sustainable. As Pushkala Prasad and Albert J. Mills (1997) suggest this growing 'diversity industry' seemed to offer a more upbeat, happy new mood after anti-racism in the UK and affirmative action in the USA. This industry, which US diversity critic Frederick Lynch (2002) also refers to as the 'social policy machine', includes books, articles, lectures, workshops, videos, networking and conferences, consulting firms, board games, university courses, and training workshops (Prasad and Mills 1997; Lasch-Quinn 2002; Jack and Lorbiecki 2003). The latter, Elisabeth Lasch-Quinn suggests, is aimed at 'attitude change through workshopping' (2002: 166) and is the focus for the case study in this chapter.

Diversity training comes in many different forms, using different methods and eclectic content. In the UK in a recent survey, Taylor, Powell, and Wrench (1997) suggest that there are three main approaches, providing information, changing attitudes, changing behaviour, but that all have been influenced by the experiences or myths about the confrontational approach of RAT and therefore a more 'softly softly' pedagogical style is typical. Content can include aspects from multicultural-ism awareness, racism, legislation, sexism, homophobia, disability awareness, cross-cultural competencies, stereotyping, communication skills, and attitude awareness (Kossek, Lobel, and Brown 2006). There is also some variety in the length of training from short two-hour sessions to one-week workshops. Experiential meth-ods are still a core component in diversity training, although there is much less consistency of approach than in RAT.

Having given a brief, necessarily schematic overview of training interventions in promoting anti-racism, I now turn to a case study, which focuses on one particular approach to experiential approach to anti-racism used for over thirty years in North America, Australia, and the UK, to examine emotional pedagogies and their specificities in relation to anti-racism. What analogues are being presumed? What similarities seen to be created?

EXPERIENTIAL EYE

The case study examines the experiential approach used by Jane Elliott, a white North American diversity training consultant. Jane Elliott, however, is no ordinary diversity consultant. She has appeared on North American television shows such as the Oprah Winfrey, Donahue, and Johnny Carson television programmes, has won US awards, and is famous—some might say infamous—for an experiment called Blue-eyed, brown-eyed which she claims teaches people about discrimination. First used by Elliott in 1968 when she was a primary school teacher on her school class in Riceville, Iowa, after the assassination of the Reverend Dr Martin Luther King, this experiential learning method has been widely used as a tool for innumerable workshops over the past thirty years with public sector workers, educationalists, students, university workers in North America, Australia, and the UK. Thus, her work has straddled all three stages of race equality training described above: multi-culturalism, anti-racist, and diversity.

Called 'bold and ground breaking' by some and 'dangerous and unethical' by others, the experiment has been described by Elliott and commentators as teaching white people what racist discrimination feels like. In the original experiment based in her classroom, teacher Elliott divided her class into two groups on the basis of eye colour, blue-eyed and brown-eyed, and Elliott proceeded to set against the blue-eyed children and favour the brown-eyed children. The group of blue-eyed children was designated the 'inferior' group and wore a collar to denote that they were the 'oppressed' group; the brown-eyed children were the 'privileged' group, who witnessed, and joined in, the oppressive treatment of the blue-eyed children. After a couple of days, the roles were reversed. In her role as main oppressor Elliott criticizes and humiliates the blue-eyed children and praises and encourages the brown-eyed children, and eggs them on to also criticize the blue-eyed children. Very quickly the children treated as inferior appear dejected, sad, and distraught. Their academic work suffers. This is then understood to show how easily prejudiced behaviour can be initiated and how arbitrary it is. Subsequently, Elliott has repeated this experiential method with adults with whom she is even more confrontational.

Elliott's approach has received widespread publicity through TV documentaries and training videos, the latter used in much diversity training and teacher training. The initial experiment was documented in the ABC programme *The Eye of the Storm* (1970), and available as a video. Since then, many follow-up documentaries and replays of the exercise have taken place with college students and public sector workers in the USA, Australia, and the UK. At the age of 73, Elliott still runs a number of different workshops for public sector and private sector organizations. These include: 'The Anatomy of Prejudice', a three-hour presentation which introduces and discusses the *Eye of the Storm* video at a cost of $6,000; 'A Collar in my Pocket', a one-day workshop in which the Blue-eyed, brown-eyed experiment is run, discussed, and the video *Eye of the Storm* watched.

I first encountered her work when I attended one of her workshops based on 'The Anatomy of Prejudice' as part of a study on diversity training. In this case study, I draw upon my participation in the workshop, Elliott's videos, training manuals, and advertising. In relation to debates on experiential learning and anti-racist pedagogy, I want to examine what kind of real world is being produced by Elliott. What kinds of experiences are being created and how are they seen to be related to the real world? To start answering these questions, I shall describe and analyse a number of equivalences that are set up by Elliott between racism and the experiences produced through her pedagogical work.

WHOSE EYES?

Elliott's approach is akin to the type of experiential learning Susan Warner Weil and Ian McGill (1989) call 'personal growth' in which emotions are imagined to be the most important means and outcome for learning (Swan 2004). It is a recognizable approach in anti-racist training as Stella Dadzie notes (2000).

The most important equivalence claimed by Elliott and her supporters is between the social aggression experienced by the participants in the exercise and the lived experience of black and minority ethnic people. Hence, Elliott assumed that it is possible to recreate racism in such a way that the white participants can experience it and do so emotionally. For example, in the first video of the initial school experiment *Eye of the Storm*, Elliott is shown talking to the classroom of the white young schoolchildren and asking them: 'How do you think it would feel to be a Negro [*sic*] boy or girl? It would be hard to know, wouldn't it, unless we actually experienced discrimination ourselves?' Thus, for Elliott, the experiential activity of Blue-eyed brown-eyed reproduces the real lived experience of black and minority ethnic children. This is based on the assumption that black and minority ethnic experience is saturated by discrimination and can be reduced to matters of feeling. As Gilroy points out, this kind of approach reduces the 'rich complexity of black life by reducing it to nothing more than a response to racism' (1992: 60). This view, he argues, presents the black person as a victim whose identity and experience add up to nothing more than an answer to racism.

There are many examples of Elliott's take on the 'real world' produced in her experiential methods. One of the main websites that advertises her services suggests that her pedagogy enables the tables to be 'turned on white students so that they are forced to experience the racist treatment African American and other minority students have been receiving for years'. In some of her advertising, she suggests that the method enables participants on her workshop to live 'for one day as other people live for a lifetime'. In essence, she is claiming that the experiential approach she used enables dominant groups to 'get a taste' of discrimination (Burbules 2004: p. xxi). As with the mini-ethnographies of multicultural training, empathy is seen as a learning technology which produces white identification with black and minority ethnic groups. In contrast to multicultural mini-ethnographies in which sharing food or music is imagined to bring about empathy, in Jane Elliott's method a condensed feeling of discrimination, a sharing of suffering and pain not food and music, is seen to produce this learning technology of empathy. Through this empathy, then, it is imagined that white participants are offered a means of identification with black and minority ethnic people in which it is believed that they assume the place of the 'other' and replicate their thoughts and emotions. As a result they are imagined to have access to epistemic privilege into the experience of racism. This, in turn, privileges and reproduces the knowing and feeling white person.

This empathy is not simply an affective empathy but a 'cathartic empathy' which is believed to lead to self-transformation and social transformation (Woodward 2003). As Nicholas Burbules writes, her method of experiential learning is 'based on the idea that making people experience what it feels like to be discriminated against is a key step in transforming their attitudes about racism' (2004: p. xx). Pain and suffering are the emotional mechanisms which are seen to provide this step. In therapeutic cultures, and some related forms of experiential learning, pain is imagined to be a very special and effective means of learning because it is seen having an embodied clarity, unadulterated by the intellect.

It is Elliott's pedagogic style that brings about the empathy, pain, and suffering. Seen as a role, or performance, rather than authentic behaviour, Elliott's teaching style, in stark contrast to many race teachers who advocate reflective and dialogic styles, is confrontational, aggressive, and brash (Erickson 2004). Her approach is not what would be seen as progressive but rather is consciously oppressive, and is understood to be her simulating prejudice (Erickson 2004). Her unrelenting and unforgiving approach is seen to be part of the learning process, bringing with it a form of cathartic identification in which intense emotions of being on the receiving end of social aggression are seen to reproduce feelings of being subject to racism, and to act as a catalyst to exorcizing an individual's prejudices. This kind of intense masculine performance is counter to traditional feminized models of teaching and can also be read as a providing a shock to learners, potentially enhancing strong emotions in them. This kind of self-presentation and audience management cannot be an easy performance to muster, taking consider emotional labour on her part.

During all workshops she insults, badgers, belittles, and blames the blue-eyed participants. She began the workshop I attended, as she does in many of the workshops and videos, by declaring, 'I'm J. E. Elliott. I am your blue-eyed bitch for the day.' One of her recent videos is sold on the basis that she is 'mean and nasty' in it. The training manual accompanying some of her videos praises her use of sarcasm and humiliation as pedagogic techniques (Lasch-Quinn 2002). After a gruelling two-and-half-hour confrontation, participants are reduced to being angry, bewildered, tearful, and distraught, to which Elliott shows no sympathy. In fact, she silences belligerently any participant who tries to challenge her or tries to express their feelings. She reminds them that their suffering is nothing compared to that of black and minority ethnic people: 'If you have so much trouble accepting this kind of treatment for only a few hours, when you know it isn't even real, how do you think people of colour feel during a lifetime of treatment?' (Erickson 2004: 6).

Critical to this approach is a problematic notion of racism as something which is one-off, spectacular, and sadistic. In producing this conceptualization of racism, Elliott ignores other types of racism that are everyday, mundane, and repetitive (Essed 1991). Not underestimating the existence, harm, and inequality of the trauma model of racism, the latter type of banal racism is what many black and minority ethnic people have to live with. This type of one-off trauma racism also presumes a one-off shock solution in the manner of trauma/reparation narrative, which ignores the repetitiveness of racism and the need for ongoing recuperations (Berlant 2000).

Some of her academic supporters, Gregory Jay and Sandra Jones, argue that 'her manner is a far cry from the therapeutic, feel-good multiculturalism of many American workshops' (2005: 6). In light of what some might see as technologies of sadism, Jay argues that she 'wants her blue-eyed to really feel the pain of discrimination and inequality' (2005: 6). Somewhat more critically, Ingrid Erickson (2004) suggests that Elliott provides 'confrontation not education'. This leads on to the question of what Elliott is producing through these strategies of emotional surrogacy.

Central to these assumptions is the idea that emotions are a technology of self- and social transformation. This has been subject to considerable debate within educational studies, critical race studies, feminism, and cultural studies. In social science the main debate centres on the question of whether shared emotion, in particular, suffering, is the most productive foundation for collective politics (Berlant 2000). In relation to educational studies in management, therapeutic cultures such as personal development and humanistic psychology have been critiqued for naturalizing and over-psychologizing emotions, privileging them as the most truthful form of knowledge about the self and its place in the world (Vince 1996; Swan and Bailey 2004). In critical race studies, the focus for attention has been the effects of white people's emotions and their fantasies of affective identification with black and minority ethnic people as a form of pedagogy for race equality. I will discuss these in more detail in relation to Jane Elliott's work but first I want to outline the view of academics who support Elliot's emotional approach.

One such example is Justin Infinito (2003) who uses Elliott's technique in his own classroom. For him, Elliott's approach using empathy can bring about a 'deeper understanding of the indignity that comes with racist oppression' that then leads to participants coming 'to a level of caring about injustice so it can be eradicated from classroom and from the world' (Infinito 2003: 68). This works for Justin Infinito in a number of related ways: first, for him, sympathy with others is a higher order of knowledge than cognition; secondly, the experiential method of Blue-eyed provides a more direct and immediate route into an individual's emotions and reflections; thirdly, the group sharing the same experience enables communal, critical, and diverse reflection. In providing the opportunity for discussion in which different theoretical models are used to examine the 'politics of construction' around this experience, Infinito's pedagogy differs from Elliott's. The 'eye' at the centre of the storm for Elliott is the feeling of emotion, not the theorizing or discussing of those emotions. It is not clear which theoretical models Infinito uses, and as Brah and Hoy (1989) point out, therein lies the rub.

In both approaches, empathy is seen as a significant mechanism for white participants to get intimate with racism. As mentioned above this brings about a number of effects which have been problematized by some social and critical race theorists, which can help us understand some of the issues around Elliott's work. A key problem raised by critical race theorist Sara Ahmed (2005) in a discussion of the politics of good and bad feelings in relation to anti-racism is whose feelings become seen as important—those of white people, or those of black and minority ethnic people? One of the dangers for Ahmed of this is that in feeling bad on behalf of black and minority ethnic people, white people reduce black and minority ethnic people to being the object of their feelings. According to Ahmed this not only involves a fantasy that one can know how the other feels but also it can become a form of appropriation, in which 'the pain of others becomes ours' (2005: 74). In 'taking on' this feeling of pain, we can then start to feel good about our capacity for empathy, identification, and feelings of shame in relation to the other. As a result, white people can become absorbed in their own emotions rather than the material conditions affecting black and minority ethnic people (Ahmed 2005; Hytten and Warren 2003). As Audrey Thompson writes, 'the white pleasures of identification and empathy and redemption or guilt can lead to self-absorption' (2003: 17).

In a related discussion Sarit Srivastava (2005) argues that white women's attachment to feeling good about doing good to others can again lead to self-absorption. In this view, many white women, in particular white feminists, have an image of themselves as good, non-racist, kind, and caring. Emotions such as empathy as an anti-racist response uphold this self-image through the production of introspection and self-examination, a 'personalized antiracist ethic' of confession (2005: 31). Requiring techniques of purification or salvations by others, anti-racism becomes a white performance of anger and guilt at racism which is performative. These displays become proof of an individual's goodness as they prove themselves less ignorant and less racist and, hence, anti-racism in this form becomes a matter of an individual's moral self-development rather than organization change (2005: 44). According to Srivastava, with empathy, anti-racism becomes a character reference rather a form of political analysis. In her summary, Srivastava questions whether these forms of empathetic anti-racism, in which white people know better, feel better, and become better people, really mean that white people actually *do* any thing that is better.

These critiques relate to Elliott's work in a number of ways. First, it seems that it is white people's empathy and suffering that is the focus for the workshop and video. Although she silences any white participant who attempts to discuss her feelings, the narrative of the whole workshop is around whites feeling better. One of the ways that this operates is that Elliott is herself white. In fact, she is blue-eyed. In essence, she offers the white participants the therapeutic promise of progression. Presenting herself as a point of 'heroic identification' through embodying the good white person that they can become if they hang in there under the pressure (Woodward 2003), her aggression is seen as permissible because it will be transformative for the white participants. The intensity and unrelenting nature of her aggression is evidence of both her moral outrage and her crusading wish to purify them of racism and prejudice. Jay and Jones (2005) argue that Elliott does not work with a model of humanist empathy which results in complacency or congratulation, but I want to suggest that in presenting herself as enlightened, her performance is a congratulation of the white saved self, and her crusade to save other white selves. In contrast, the black and minority ethnic participants have no way out of the racism of which they are on the receiving end in life. Although there is room for them to express emotions of anger, frustration, and sadness during the workshop about the racism they encounter, the focus for the narrative is the fate of white people. There is no transformational narrative for the black and minority ethnic participants as theirs is not the main feature.

CONCLUSION

In summary, then, I have argued that experience in all forms of experiential learning cannot be taken for granted. This is particularly the case with emotional experiences which have been understood within some experiential philosophies and therapeutic cultures as the most raw, natural, internal, and therefore most authentic of experiences. I am not suggesting that this means that emotions are not important either to learning or politics. Using a case study of Jane Elliott's Blue-eyed, brown-eyed experiential method, I have examined some of the effects of using emotion, and, in particular, empathy and suffering, as technologies for race equality. One of the key questions for experiential pedagogy is what kind of microcosm is being created through experiential methods—what is the activity a miniature copy of? In drawing upon a representation of racism as simply about spectacular suffering, Elliott offers a reductionist model of racism. As many critical race theorists argue, racism is complex, fluid, plural, mundane, and dynamic: it cannot be reduced simply to matters of spectacularized suffering. Mobilizing the notion that empathy through white on white social aggression is the same as racism again trivializes the operation and experience of racism. Furthermore it is assumed that the emotions produced are to do with learning about racial discrimination not to do with any new humiliation that might be peculiar to the aggressive pedagogy and the experiential exercise itself (Lasch-Quinn 2002). I have argued then that instead of Blue-eyed, brown-eyed being a microcosm of racism, it stands more for the problems of empathy as a technology of white benevolence, salvation, and crusades. Finally I suggested that Blue-eyed, brown-eyed is actually about blue-eyed people, offering as it does a therapeutic narrative of catharsis and self-transformation for the blue-eyed in that it does not facilitate a real role reversal—where black and minority ethnic people have white power and privilege: indeed it cannot ever do this kind of work—but offers a therapeutic narrative of catharsis and self-transformation for the blue-eyed.

Of course teaching about anti-racism is complex and challenging. As critical race theorist Stuart Hall comments, it is full of 'pedagogic difficulties' because the subject is complex and therefore difficult to teach clearly (1981: 58). It is also emotionally charged and what he calls emotionally combustible (ibid.). Rattansi (1992) also draws our attention to the importance of the unconscious in understanding and education around racism. This suggests that an affective approach to teaching about race equality and anti-racism is important but we must be aware

of the complex politics of construction needed around how emotion is conceptualized and theorized in relation to experiential learning and anti-racism. In the
words of Hall again, 'racism is deeply resistant to attempts at amelioration, good
feeling, gentle reform and so on' (1981: 61). As Ahmed (2005) and Berlant (2000)
both point out, emotions, and empathy *per se* need not necessarily be apoliti-
cal, but neither should they be seen as a self-contained, self-explanatory form of
politics.

NOTE

Thanks to Sara Ahmed and Shona Hunter, the UCLAN MA in Promoting Equality class
2005–6 especially Andrew, Arun, James, and Jules, and also to Rosemary Crawley for
support and helpful comments on this work. Thanks to the editors for their insightful
comments and their patience. This chapter is based on research funded by the Centre for
Excellence in Leadership but does not necessarily reflect its views.

REFERENCES

Ahmed, Sara (2005). 'The Politics of Bad Feeling', *Australian Critical Race and Whiteness
Studies Association Journal*, 1: 72–85.
—— Hunter, Shona, Kilic, Sevgi, Swan, Elaine, and Turner, Lewis (2006). *Integrating Diver-
sity: Final Report*. London: Centre for Excellence in Leadership.
Anthias, Flora, and Yuval-Davis, Nira (1992). *Racialized Boundaries: Race, Nation, Gender,
Colour and Class and the Anti-Racist Struggle*. London: Routledge.
Arora, Ranjit (2005). *Race and Ethnicity in Education*. Aldershot: Ashgate.
Bell, Vikki (2002). 'Reflections on the "End of Antiracism" (P. Gilroy)', in Philomena Essed
and David Theo Goldberg (eds.), *Race Critical Theories*. Oxford: Blackwell.
Ben-Tovim, Gideon (1997). 'Why "Positive Action" is "Politically Correct"', in Tariq Mod-
ood and Pnina Werbner (eds.), *The Politics of Multiculturalism in the New Europe: Racism,
Identity and Community*. London: Zed Books.
Berlant, Lauren (2000). 'The Subject of True Feeling: Pain, Privacy, and Politics', in Jodi
Dean (ed.), *Cultural Studies and Political Theory*. New York: Cornell University Press.
Bhavnani, Reena (2001). *Rethinking Interventions in Racism*. Stoke-on-Trent: Trentham
Books.
Bonnett, Alastair (2000). *Anti-Racism*. London: Routledge.
Brah, Avtar, and Hoy, Jane (1989). 'Experiential Learning: A New Orthodoxy?', in Susan
Warner Weil and Ian McGil (eds.), *Making Sense of Experiential Learning: Diversity in
Theory and Practice*. Milton Keynes: Open University Press.
Brookfield, Stephen (1995). 'Adult Learning: An Overview', in Torsten Husen and
T. Neville Postlewaite (eds.), *International Encyclopedia of Education*. Oxford: Pergamon
Press.

Brown, Colin, and Lawton, Jean (1991). *Training for Equality: A Study of Race Relations and Equal Opportunities Training*. London: Policy Studies Institute.

Burbules, Nicholas C. (2004). 'Introduction', in Megan Boler (ed.), *Democratic Dialogue in Education: Troubling Speech, Disturbing Silence*. New York: Peter Lang.

Cohen, Philip (1992). ' "It's Racism What Dunnit": Hidden Narratives in Theories of Racism', in James Donald and Ali Rattansi (eds.), *'Race', Culture and Difference*. London: Sage.

Dadzie, Stella (2000). *Toolkit for Tackling Racism in Schools*. Stoke-on-Trent: Trentham.

Erickson, Ingrid M. (2004). 'Fighting Fire with Fire: Jane Elliott's Antiracist Pedagogy', in Megan Boler (ed.), *Democratic Dialogue in Education: Troubling Speech, Disturbing Silence*. New York: Peter Lang.

Essed, Philomena (1991). *Everyday Racism*. London: Sage.

Fenwick, Tara (2003). *Learning through Experience: Troubling Orthodoxies and Intersecting Questions*. New York: Krieger.

Gaine, Chris (1995). *Still No Problem Here*. Stoke-on-Trent: Trentham.

Gilroy, Paul (1987). *There Ain't No Black in the Union Jack*. London: Routledge.

—— (1992). 'The End of AntiRacism', in James Donald and Ali Rattansi (eds.), *'Race', Culture and Difference*. London: Sage.

Hall, Stuart (1981). 'Teaching Race', in Alan James and Robert Jeffcoate (eds.), *The School in the Multicultural Society*. London: Harper & Row.

Hytten, Kathy, and Warren, John (2003). 'Engaging Whiteness: How Racial Power Gets Reified in Education', *Qualitative Studies in Education*, 16/1: 65–89.

Infinito, Justen (2003). 'Jane Elliot Meets Foucault: The Formation of Ethical Identities in the Classroom', *Journal of Moral Education*, 32/1: 67–76.

Jack, Gavin, and Lorbiecki, Anna (2003). 'Asserting Possibilities of Resistance in the Cross-Cultural Teaching Machine: Re-viewing Videos of Others', in Anshuman Prasad (ed.), *Postcolonial Theory and Organizational Analysis: A Critical Engagement*. Basingstoke: Palgrave MacMillan.

Jay, Gregory, with Jones, Sandra (2005). 'Whiteness Studies and the Multicultural Literature Classroom', *Journal of the Society for the Study of the Multi-Ethnic Literature of the United States*, Spring.

Kossek, Ellen Ernst, Lobel, Sharon A., and Brown, Sharon (2006). 'Human Resources Strategies to Manage Workforce Diversity: Examining "The Business Case" ', in Alison M. Konrad, Pushkala Prasad, and Judith K. Pringle (eds.), *Handbook of Workplace Diversity*. London: Sage.

Lasch-Quinn, Elisabeth (2002). *Race Experts: How Racial Etiquette, Sensitivity Training, and New Age Therapy Hijacked the Civil Rights Movement*. Lanham, Md.: Rowman & Littlefield.

Lynch, Frederick (2002). *The Diversity Machine: The Drive to Change the 'White Male Workplace'*. New Brunswick, NJ: Transaction.

Macdonald, Ian, John, Gus, Khan, Lily, and Bhavnani, Reena (1989). *Murder in the Playground*. London: Longsight Press.

Mir, Raza, Mir, Ali, and Wong, Diana J. (2006). 'Diversity: The Cultural Logic of Global Capital', in Alison M. Konrad, Pushkala Prasad, and Judith K. Pringle (eds.), *Handbook of Workplace Diversity*. London: Sage.

Nkomo, Stella M. (1992). 'The Emperor Has No Clothes: Rewriting "Race" in Organizations', *Academy of Management Review*, 17/3: 487–513.

—— and Cox, Taylor (1999). 'Diverse Identities in Organizations', in Stewart Clegg, Cynthia Hardy, and Walter R. Nord (eds.), *Handbook of Organization Studies*. London: Sage.

Pederson, Anne, Walker, Ian, and Wise, Mike (2005). ' "Talk Does Not Cook Rice": Beyond Anti-racist Rhetoric to Strategies for Social Action', *Australian Psychologist*, 40/1: 20–31.

Penketh, Laura (2000). *Tackling Institutional Racism: Anti-racist Policies and Social Work Education and Training*. Bristol: Policy Press.

Prasad, Pushkala, and Mills, Albert J. (1997). 'From Showcase to Shadow: Understanding the Dilemmas of Managing Workplace Diversity', in Pushkala Prasad, Albert J. Mills, Michael Elmes, and Anshuman Prasad (eds.), *Managing the Organizational Melting Post: Dilemmas of Workplace Diversity*. Thousand Oaks, Calif.: Sage.

Ramazanoglu, Caroline, and Holland, Janet (1999). 'Tripping over Experience: Some Problems in Feminist Epistemology', *Discourse: Studies in the Cultural Politics of Education*, 20/3: 381–92.

Rattansi, Ali (1992). 'Changing the Subject? Racism, Culture and Education', in James Donald and Ali Rattansi (eds.), *'Race', Culture and Difference*. London: Sage.

Reynolds, Michael, and Trehan, Kiran (2001). 'Classroom as Real World: Propositions for a Pedagogy of Difference', *Gender and Education*, 13/4: 357–72.

—— and Vince, Russ (2004). 'Introduction', in Michael Reynolds and Russ Vince (eds.), *Organizing Reflection*. Aldershot: Ashgate.

Scarman, L. G. (1981). *The Brixton Disorders 10–12 April 1981: Report of an Inquiry*. London: HMSO.

Scott, Joan W. (1992). 'Experience', in Judith Butler and Joan W. Scott (eds.), *Feminists Theorise the Political*. New York: Routledge.

Srivastava, Sarit (2005). ' "You're Calling me a Racist?" The Moral and Emotional Regulation of Antiracism and Feminism', *Signs: Journal of Women in Culture and Society*, 31: 29–62.

Swan, Elaine (2004). 'Worked up Selves: Personal Development, Self-Transformation and Therapeutic Cultures', unpublished Ph.D. thesis, Lancaster University.

—— and Bailey, Andy (2004). 'Thinking with Feeling', in Michael Reynolds and Russ Vince (eds.), *Organizing Reflection*. Aldershot: Ashgate.

Swann Report (1985). *Education for All*. London: Department of Education and Science.

Taylor, Paul, Powell, Diana, and Wrench, John (1997). *The Evaluation of Anti-discrimination Training Activities in the United Kingdom*. International Migration Papers 21. Centre for Research in Ethnic Relations, University of Warwick.

Thompson, Audrey (2003). 'Tiffancy, Friend of People of Color: White Investments in Anti-racism', *International Journal of Qualitative Studies in Education*, 16/1: 7–29.

Usher, Robin, Bryant, Ian, and Johnston, Rennie (1997). *Adult Education and the Postmodern Challenge: Learning beyond the Limits*. London: Routledge.

Vince, Russ (1996). 'Experiential Management Education as the Practice of Change', in Robert French and Christopher Grey (eds.), *Rethinking Management Education*. London: Sage.

Walker, Hilary (2002). *A Genealogy of Equality: The Curriculum for Social Work Education and Training*. London: Woburn.

Weil, Susan Warner, and McGill, Ian (1989). 'A Framework for Making Sense of Experiential Learning', in Susan Warner Weil and Ian McGill (eds.), *Making Sense of Experiential Learning: Diversity in Theory and Practice*. Milton Keynes: Open University Press.

Wildemeersch, Danny (1989). 'The Principal Meaning of Dialogue for the Construction and Transformation of Reality', in Susan Warner Weil and Ian McGill (eds.), *Making Sense of Experiential Learning: Diversity in Theory and Practice*. Milton Keynes: Open University Press.

Woodward, Gary C. (2003). *The Idea of Identification*. Albany, NY: State University of New York Press.

CHAPTER 13

CHOOSING EXPERIENTIAL METHODS FOR MANAGEMENT EDUCATION

THE FIT OF ACTION LEARNING AND PROBLEM-BASED LEARNING

ANNE HERBERT

SARI STENFORS

INTRODUCTION

THE process of changing from traditional teaching methods to experiential methods is not easy. Institutional forces make change challenging, even when a university signals that it wants to change. We provide a framework for choosing an experiential learning method that takes into consideration institutional forces in the form of restricted resources. We argue for conscious comparison of methods for the best possible fit in a specific context.

As instructors in an established business university we reflect on our use of action learning (AL) and problem-based learning (PBL) that are not traditional nor widely used in our university. Our efforts are consistent with the university's publicly stated strategic intentions, yet the necessary institutional support for using experiential learning methods is not always readily available. This situation is typical for many instructors currently employed in ambitious business schools and universities.

The available management education literature does not address sufficiently the choice of learning methods. In practice, the choice of a method often is rendered secondary to considerations of content, and depends on institutional traditions and pressures, professional interests and abilities, fads and serendipitous circumstances. The choice between learning methods does not get the reflexive attention it deserves. But clarity about the details and distinctions of different teaching and learning methods allows clear descriptions of expectations for students and instructors and alignment of appropriate institutional support for teaching and learning. Understanding the distinctions also gives an opportunity to choose the methods that best answer the aspirations of the university and its curricula. Our case shows that the differences between experiential methods are important to acknowledge because different methods address different needs, and also that the demands and constraints of the teaching and learning context matter. The fit of a particular method in a specific course with the overall curricula, the goals of the teaching modules, the resources available to the instructors, and the individual learners' needs and readiness for a particular method, all play an important part in the choice to adopt new learning methods, and the effective implementation. In other words, choice in our study means selecting methods that match aspirations and available resources.

We suggest a framework of three questions for comparing learning methods before choosing:

1. How does the method help the learners orient to the course and the learning objectives?
2. What type of teaching and learning processes does the method encourage and support?
3. What type of material and non-material resources and support are needed for successful implementation of the method?

Answering these questions reveals opportunities and challenges that in turn allow us to examine the relative fit of the methods to the institutional context and the available resources offered by the business school, instructors, and learners.

First, we will provide a brief description of our university, Helsinki School of Economics (HSE). Then, we offer answers to our three questions above, based on AL and PBL as examples. The answers are initially drawn from literature and then from instructor and student comments on the experience of using these methods. The output is a description of differences between the AL and PBL in the business school context. Finally, we make recommendations about practical issues to be considered when choosing these particular methods and discuss the choice of learning methods in general.

THE INSTITUTIONAL CONTEXT

Helsinki School of Economics is an ambitious business university which 'seeks to develop dynamic teaching programmes that are competitive and comparable internationally...We train students for independent and interactive study and also in holistic *problem-based learning* ...' (HSE Strategies 2006; italics added).

Pedagogic methods vary throughout HSE and, until the publication of the strategy statement cited above, no preference for a specific teaching method had been stated. The traditions and disciplinary structure of the university best serve theory-focused teacher-centred methods, privilege individual learning concentrating on theory and reading books, and reward learners who compete to pass supervised written exams under time pressure (Leppälä and Päiviö 2001; Korpiaho 2005). Recently HSE has signalled that it intends the faculty to adopt more 'modern teaching methods' and increasingly 'involve students' in the teaching-learning process (HSE 2003). HSE has also invested in developing some on-line capacity for delivering course information, course material, and on-line discussion of course content. However, it has not provided any guidelines to faculty about exactly what constitutes desirable modern teaching methods or how appropriate teaching methods that involve students should be chosen and adopted.

Two recent external evaluations of the M.Sc. programme at HSE noted the apparent mismatch between the mission statement and the actual practice of teaching and learning at HSE. One of them specifically suggested, 'A more systematic use of internships, *action learning* ...would highly benefit the students' development, giving them the practical skills needed and the specific skills and knowledge appreciated by the recruiting companies' (Cavalle et al. 2003: 12; italics added). Both evaluation reports called for the development of theme-based study modules and teaching methods accenting teamwork and interpersonal skills, and curriculum design processes that would be more visibly and effectively responsive to corporate needs (Cavalle et al. 2003; Kettunen et al. 2003).

Based on our understandings of PBL and AL, elaborated below, and supported by the references cited above, we maintain that AL and PBL are in line with the published mission and strategies of HSE. Yet, in practice, these methods do not fit so readily at HSE because they require new kinds of teaching and learning competencies and different use of time and material resources. For example, AL and PBL learners and instructors need to collaborate rather than compete, student teams require space to work together at convenient hours, extensive library resources for reference, the critical information skills to use the resources, and responsive, cross-disciplinary learning support as specific needs emerge. Furthermore, the assessment and evaluation systems at HSE are designed more for assessing theoretical rather than practical knowledge, and tend to encourage competition between individual learners.

The current institutional arrangements at HSE most effectively support teacher-centred and lecture-based teaching methods. For example, all applicants for faculty positions are required to give a lecture as a means to assess their teaching. Also, instructors are implicitly discouraged from using time to experiment with new learning methods, as most of the instructors at HSE are primarily researchers whose accomplishments are measured by academic publication outputs. Being an instructor at HSE is often a secondary occupation because the tenure criteria, especially for higher-level positions, reward research not teaching. The recently introduced performance management system assesses both research performance and teaching, but has not provided any obvious increase in appreciation of teaching so far. At HSE, historically, individual instructors are the 'sole owners' of their individual course and its content. In many disciplinary areas, teaching is a personal and private matter, conducted behind closed doors. While there may be some discussion with peers of extraordinarily brilliant or difficult students, there is little public discussion of how to encourage learning. The standard course feedback form that students are invited to complete focuses on disciplinary content and the instructor as the 'transmitter' of content, and does not ask about group work, nor about other learning processes.

Despite the institutional barriers, we used AL and PBL methods to teach strategic management. A set of favourable circumstances made this possible. First, at HSE, there is no 'strategy department' and at each department the strategy courses are different. The subject of strategic management invites cross-disciplinary learning as it demands understanding of various functional areas. Secondly, individual instructors at HSE can decide the teaching methods they use. Generally, as long as the students do not complain too much about teaching, the instructors are left to concentrate on research work. The overall arrangement allows independence but little practical, material, or peer support for instructors who choose non-traditional methods. There is a small 'Centre for Innovative Education', providing technical support for eLearning and managing eLearning systems, and organizing briefings on broader teaching and learning issues when it can. In addition, HSE provides small grants for novel teaching efforts and sometimes hires instructors with skills in new teaching methods. We received some funds for a short introduction to PBL.

So, small changes are taking place, but institutional forces still hinder change (see, for example, DiMaggio and Powell 1991), for example continuing to align resources with traditional teaching methods, while offering a short course for teachers on PBL methods. Nonetheless, the changes can be advanced by individuals who create positive experiences with new methods (for example DiMaggio 1988; Garud, Jain, and Kumaraswamy 2002; Maguire, Hardy, and Lawrence 2004), so it is important to identify and throw light on learning methods that will lead to success.

COMPARING PBL AND AL METHODS

Our argument is based on our experiences with PBL and AL at HSE. There is little literature that specifically compares AL and PBL, but from articles on the individual methods and their use, we have made some comparisons.

The methods have different roots. PBL was largely conceived and developed in the academy, initially for training clinical practitioners and lawyers, and subsequently adopted for other professional courses (Savin-Baden 2000). AL was developed in workplaces with managers, first in the mining industry, then in other industries and for other levels of workers. Subsequently AL has also been adopted in business schools, but its domain remains largely work-based learning (Pedler 1997).

PBL and AL are both enquiry-based experiential methods that privilege practical knowledge, put the 'instructor' in a facilitating role, and emphasize learners' active role in taking responsibility for their own learning, most often working in teams. The students have to make choices about the contents and goals of their learning, and are forced by the demands of practice to reintegrate elements that are often separated in the disciplinary silos of management education. Both methods develop learners' capacity for new theory building through interaction around the learning problem. Academics sometimes debate the place of presentation of existing theories and ownership of the learning problem, yet both AL and PBL are generally described as valuable for management education curriculum. PBL and AL offer learners practice and support in business situations and in turn, employers gain well-prepared, or at least less naive, graduates.

The following discussion highlights the similarities and differences based on the three-question framework introduced at the beginning of this chapter.

Orientation to the Learning Objectives

Both AL and PBL achieve learning by engaging learners from the outset with the messy problems of working life that transcend academic disciplinary boundaries.

These complex learning problems present the learners, both as individuals and in groups, with challenges about their own resourcefulness, capacity to think creatively and critically, and their personal organization for finding, storing, and integrating information.

The choice of the problematic situation in PBL usually rests with the instructor or 'tutor'. The PBL literature discusses the choice of appropriate problems (for example Schmidt 1993), and the adequate design of problem situations (for example Stinson and Milter 1996) to ensure encounters with current theories deemed important in the academy. The learners are assumed to be inexperienced and unfamiliar with the complexity of the situations that are the focus of learning in PBL.

In AL, the participants are asked to bring problems to the learning process, to describe the problem with which they wish to work in the group, and to limit the problem so that learning outcomes will be achievable and discerniable (Marquardt 1999). The problem upon which learning is focused exists in the living world where the learners typically are employed, or otherwise actively trying to make an effect. Generally, AL learners are assumed to be the most expert people available regarding knowledge of their current context and the dimensions of their particular problems. Their role as a learner comes from the desire to act more effectively in their situation (Revans 1983, 1985; McGill and Beatty 2001). Thus, the discussion about the problematic situation in AL literature revolves around the suitability of the problems. Highly technical problems with little ambiguity are seen to be inappropriate (Revans 1983; Herbert 2002), and established theory is not typically in focus when choosing the problem.

Learning Process

In both AL and PBL the learners have to take an active role and responsibility for their own learning. They are expected to develop the ability to define their own learning needs and goals, and identify appropriate sources and relevant information to meet the goals. When most learners have been trained in an educational system where instructors have told them what needs to be learned, and with discipline-based textbooks to structure the content, the literature acknowledges that AL and PBL participants can find difficulty adapting to the responsibility and freedom (for example Duch, Groh, and Allen 2001; Raelin and Raelin 2006).

Learners in AL and PBL collaborate in small groups to share their perspectives, questions, and insights, with the intent to learn from one another about the presenting problem and possible solutions. Between group meetings, individuals are pursuing information or action that they have agreed with the group to pursue in order to achieve agreed goals with respect to the problem situation in focus. Learners encourage one another to delve more deeply, articulate more clearly, and justify claims more convincingly. Such group work provides space for the public expression of emotion that is not available in traditional lecture-based courses. Group work also provides space for interpersonal power dynamics among participants. Forming, storming, and norming in groups have to be anticipated and managed until the desired performance emerges.

Terms such as AL 'adviser' and PBL 'tutor' emphasize the facilitating role of the instructor. Instructors might provide input on certain skills such as listening, critical questioning, and problem analysis if required. A difference between the AL adviser and PBL tutor roles can be the degree of disciplinary expertise provided. The literature suggests that the PBL tutor is often a source of expert disciplinary input, where an AL adviser is more a process facilitator. Successful action learning depends on the participants having within themselves the experience, the knowledge, skills, and understanding necessary to engage in, and direct, their own learning. Revans (1983, 1985) even advocated that AL groups work without the 'interference' of any external adviser. Apart from the emphasis on theory in the orientation phase, PBL also offers a structured step-by-step process for group meetings (for example Wood 2003) which is not so common for AL.

Both AL and PBL stress the importance of ongoing iterative learning and assessment of learning at different points in time. The learning outcomes from AL and PBL are in some ways also less predictable than for some other methods. Often the assessment tasks concentrate on practical and functional abilities; however the PBL learners may also be tested for theoretical knowledge.

Evaluations of the effectiveness of PBL in use have focused more on the acquisition of disciplinary knowledge than evaluations of AL. Evaluations of AL more usually focus on the workplace effects and outcomes, and often comment on the balance of action and reflection in the learning process.

Resource and Support Requirements

In PBL, where problems are designed or chosen so that external multidisciplinary information will be required to address the problem, a team of teaching staff working together is preferable to ensure the breadth of information can be provided. This multidisciplinary teamwork is also an important difference between traditional case approach (for example Christensen and Hansen 1987) and PBL, although problem situations may be somewhat similar to traditional cases in management education. PBL goes well beyond the typical case by emphasizing the learners' acquisition of skills to seek and identify relevant information and to structure the situation to permit analysis. PBL manuals suggest ensuring the availability of the predictably required information and in addition training learners to seek, analyse, and use additional information from various sources (for example Duch, Groh, and Allen 2001). The learning materials are ideally tailored to the process, with resources and support to gain access to specialist knowledge and disciplinary theory. In many universities, institutional rearrangements are required to ensure support for instructor teams, recognition of the roles and work of instructors in PBL, training on information and critical literacy for learners, access to adequate learning resources, and arrangements for appropriate group work spaces (for example Duch, Groh, and Allen 2001; King forthcoming).

Compared with PBL, in AL the learners are expected to be more in charge of the learning problem and take greater responsibility. Effective AL requires management to sponsor action about the chosen problem (Marquardt 1999). The instructor's role is to facilitate the participants' learning from their action on the chosen problem, which includes limiting and framing the problem with regard to learning goals that can be linked to the curriculum. Instructors do not need to work in teams to achieve this focus, but instructors do often have to refer the participants to other scholars for assistance on particular cross-disciplinary issues. Like PBL, AL is more effective if there is institutional support for interdisciplinary work, literacy training, and provision of a wide variety of learning resources.

To briefly sum up this section comparing AL and PBL, we affirm that there are many similarities in these methods, and the main differences seem to be the assumptions about the amount of experience the learners bring with them, and the amount of prescription about the learning process for the participants.

INSTRUCTOR AND LEARNER RESPONSES TO PBL AND AL

PBL and AL strongly appeal to our professional and academic commitments to cross-disciplinary, enquiry-based, experiential learning for the living integration of management theories and practices. We wanted to encourage the development and use of lifelong learning skills, for example taking responsibility of own learning, team working, debating, constructively challenging one another, and reflecting. These skills are ones that employers seek, so we expected that motivating learners to practise and demonstrate the skills would be easy, and that the learners with working experience would quickly recognize their usefulness. What was not apparent from the literature was the effect of overall institutional constraints that in our case manifested as lack of support for experiential learning methods. These alignment problems were evident for example in how strongly the traditional ways of teaching conditioned the students' learning routines. We will elaborate on the effects more fully below.

The PBL was used in an elective course for M.Sc. and D.Sc. students. The course focuses on teaching management tools for strategy processes. The participants are a heterogeneous group, many with work experience, and at different stages of their studies in different disciplinary majors. The PBL participants have to attend meetings with the instructor each week and in addition are required to attend lectures, observe presentations, and produce short preliminary essays weekly on topics chosen by the instructors. Their schedule is structured around the weekly activities and requires outputs that lead to the main output of the course, the final essay.

The AL was used for a mandatory strategy project in the Executive MBA programme (EMBA). The participants are executives from a wide variety of educational backgrounds and business organizations. The project is a major element of the EMBA. There are three key deadlines and three compulsory workshop periods (eight days) with the adviser where project proposals, interim, and final reports are presented and discussed. Otherwise participants are responsible for organizing their own schedule of meetings, work, and production of required outputs.

We draw on the instructors' comments and the participants' post-course feedback to make sense of their experiential learning experiences at HSE in 2003. The data is:

1. Semi-structured feedback from all thirty AL participants and from twenty of the thirty-three PBL participants.
2. Twelve additional e-mail survey responses from the PBL participants.
3. Reflective discussions and interviews with other teachers using AL and PBL at HSE.

The course participants' and other instructors' identities have been protected by anonymity.

The course participants did not compare AL and PBL, but they compared, often implicitly, AL or PBL to the other methods they had experienced. We focus on our three guiding questions: first, on experiences of orientation to the learning objectives of the subject; secondly, on experiences of the learning process; and thirdly, we reflect on the resources and support available.

Orientation to the Learning Objectives

Both the PBL and AL participants reported uncertainty about defining the problem situation in the beginning, uncertainty about how to work with the instructor and other co-participants, and uncertainty about various aspects of the project and the processes:

At first the free-form way of working in PBL was a bit confusing and it felt like you couldn't get anything out of it.

One AL participant wrote:

The instructor's support was very good, even if we did not know how much we should ask and what better not. So we maybe did not ask enough, in order to avoid difficult situations.

Different assumptions about the learners' pre-existing expertise led to different approaches to theory and practice in PBL and AL. The PBL instructors did not anticipate that the participants would understand the complexities of the studied subject at the beginning of the course. The problem was introduced by a CEO describing everyday work issues. Course material included a number of theories and guest speakers from other companies discussing how these theories had been used by their companies. In contrast, at the AL course, the participants were seen as experts on the practical issues in their local situation, and were set to solve live practical problems in business. Each chose a practicable problem where they could extend their knowledge and skills while making a visible practical difference in a living business situation. The participants were expected to demonstrate stretching their understanding of the interdependency of management functions and market forces in an industry. They were also assumed to note and monitor the variety of possible ways to address and communicate key issues in a complex problem. The participants themselves had to arrange to consult people connected to the workplace sponsoring their learning project.

The different ways of setting the learning problems in AL and PBL have been reflected in the participants' comments. The AL participants' feedback expressed satisfaction and excitement regarding their ability to make decisions that affected the directions and outcomes of their chosen project. The AL course participants showed ownership of their learning problem, for example:

The assignment...was interesting and offers great opportunities in the near future. The scope of the project, taking a view of an entity in...business, was very interesting given my background, and relates to several other topics I am working with.

In contrast, the PBL participants showed frustration with the learning problem. Outlines of the problem were provided, but the participants themselves had to focus the problem. Some of the PBL participants were confused about the incomplete information about the case company and they longed for the extra background information and clearer learning objectives.

Defective information about the problem and its background caused a lot of confusion and wondering...

and

[We] didn't know the case company well enough to really solve problems. On the other hand, that was also good, because otherwise your free thinking would have been too bounded.

The confusion of the PBL participants may have partly been due to the participants' familiarity with solving cases in case method courses and relative lack of familiarity with enquiry-based learning methods.

The PBL instructors reflected on the participants' confusion and initial reluctance to engage with some feelings of inadequacy: not being able to manage and learn everything that the participants learned or would have needed to learn. They were anxious that so much time was used to orient to the subject. They commented on the need to limit learning objectives in order to adhere to HSE assessment procedures. For example, the final essays that concentrated on describing a solution to the course problem were instructed to cover certain theoretical parts to ensure that the course also met more traditional learning objectives. Overall, orienting the participants to the learning objectives was a major concern to the PBL instructors.

In contrast, the AL instructor reported no problems with the learning objectives and confidently assumed that the learners were experts in their fields and that the companies would assess the end product. The AL participants seemed to follow learning routines already used at their workplaces and the instructor reported paying attention to activating individual participants' learning processes by mainly helping to define the problem, aiding group work, brushing up research skills, and developing thinking. In sum, the AL instructor's main role was to facilitate the learning process.

Learning Process

In spite of the distinction identified above, the participants' comments on the role of the instructor were similar for both methods. The 'instructor' appeared as a facilitator, organizer, motivator, and an expert resource. The participants took responsibility for their own learning and understood that the instructor had a supportive role in this process. The learners' feedback showed a clear commitment to the learning process and the instructors talked about the importance of motivation as the key success factor with these learning methods.

Both the AL and PBL participants were clearly conscious that these methods integrate practice and theory. The AL participants' comments emphasized the excitement of putting theories into practice; whereas the PBL participants described reaching practice from a theory-oriented view:

The best parts of the course were the 'ah-ha!' experiences that occurred both during group-work and in situations where you could apply the given material . . . to the guest company.

Where the PBL participants' feedback talked about theories, the AL participants described actions. Particularly, in dealing with unclear issues the AL participants looked for practical ways to proceed with work, and PBL participants resorted to theoretical concepts and readings often provided for them to help finding the problem. This orientation showed also in the instructors' descriptions of the difficulties they experienced. When the PBL instructors worried about supplying theories and practice views that would help students accomplish learning objectives, the AL instructor talked about the challenge of being able to support the learners and their process so that the host company directly benefited from the project.

The collaborative aspect of both AL and PBL generated many comments. The instructors worried about learners' group work skills and best ways to facilitate them. Both participant groups acknowledged their dependence on collaborative work to succeed in individual learning.

The work in the [PBL] group depended on everyone's commitment and effort, so it was important that everyone did the preparatory work well and was ready to present it and to learn from others in the group and take others' perspectives into account.

The participants often commented on the importance of the work processes and the positive impact of individual differences. The challenges with teamwork seemed to be slightly different between the AL and PBL groups. AL participants indicated challenges in effectiveness of teamwork such as division of tasks, doing one's share, and managing difficult team members. The PBL participants commented on the challenges and difficulties of new ways of learning, and especially unfamiliarity with learning as a team, working collaboratively and reflectively in a group. For example, one PBL participant noted:

The worst experiences were in teamwork sessions, when it felt like the discussion or problem-solving did not proceed or that other people were thinking in completely different ways about the matter.

But the teamwork also helped some participants reflect. The AL participants often described reflecting on the situation in practice whereas in PBL the participants emphasized the reflection in the team.

Teamwork helped me develop my ideas further and increase perspectives based on ideas and thoughts made by other students.

In our context we saw that the PBL participants struggled with the group work more painfully and stressfully than the AL participants. This can be explained by the greater experience of the AL participants working in diverse groups, usually in their workplaces, that typically require collaborative working and learning.

The engaged, interactive collaborative learning in AL and PBL aroused emotions that were different from those in the lecture-based or book-exam courses. Both learning methods also provided space for expression. At HSE, emotions are usually kept private, separate from classes. Unprecedented public expression of frustration and stress during a course, in turn, stimulated emotions in the instructors who had to manage both themselves and the participants, at least to some extent. The repeated necessity to interact and work in groups meant that many participants of both AL and PBL courses learnt new interpersonal skills, and management of emotions in the group—skills needed well beyond university.

The instructors and the participants in the AL and PBL courses gave positive evaluations of the courses, acknowledging that the learning process enabled them to cross boundaries between different subjects, use different study methods from in other courses, appreciate diversity and diverse points of view, integrate different theories, increase critical, deep, and independent thinking, and practise lifelong learning skills. Also the companies reported high satisfaction with the outcomes of the courses. Both methods clearly contribute to HSE's stated aspirations to develop new practical knowledge and skills needed in the community.

Resources and Support

The HSE allowed the instructors the freedom to use AL and PBL methods, and the access to information technology provided support for communication on the content and the process of learning.

The university's business partnership programme did not readily provide teaching resources. The practical cooperation with business organizations for teaching purposes relied on the initiative and connections of the individual instructors and learners. The EMBA learners were able to provide this resource themselves, and identified the practical projects for action learning from their workplaces. The PBL instructors used their personal business networks to introduce speakers with living problems from Finnish businesses to the class.

The learners and the instructors of both courses would have benefited from support for handling feelings and emotions that emerged during the courses. PBL tutors and AL advisers do not need such well-honed lecturing skills, but must be able to handle enthusiasm and frustrations, mediate conflicts in groups, and be able to maintain their sense of professional and academic integrity even when they cannot answer all the students' questions. These sorts of skills can be developed, but are best sustained in a peer support group. Such peer support does not come easily in a business school where teaching is a private matter and secondary to research.

AL and PBL participants and instructors reported that the courses took more time than traditional courses at HSE, and a disproportionate amount of time without recognition. Although the courses were more labour intensive to administer and teach, the instructors were paid no extra, and in the financial accounts these courses look like any course taught with traditional methods. The expectation is for a course to require a student to work a set number of hours, and the course design and methods should be adjusted to the standard.

Despite both the courses being taught at HSE, they have somewhat different curricular settings. The M.Sc. and D.Sc. curricula provide a discipline-focused education teaching relevant theories to inform disciplinary practice and decision making. Being an optional course, the PBL instructors reported spending time marketing their course to students with different majors and making deals with different departments to accept the PBL course credits in their programmes. In contrast, strategic management is compulsory in the EMBA curriculum which is more practically oriented by design, without any option for a disciplinary major. An integrative method like AL that is very practical fits reasonably well with the overall intent of the EMBA general management curriculum.

Overall, the participants' and instructors' comments help us see that resources and support for AL and PBL come from the institutional context, and also from the instructor's personal knowledge, skills, and networks, and the learners' readiness. Whilst all were required for both methods, the balance was somewhat different. The PBL course relied very heavily on the instructors' resources, whereas the AL relied on the participants' commitment to the project and their team and the sponsor's interest in the project.

CHOOSING EXPERIENTIAL METHODS

Our case study has looked at the use of PBL and AL in a traditional business school that aspires to be more internationally competitive and involve students in modern teaching methods. We compared the use of PBL and AL because they were specifically mentioned in public documents referring to the desired improvements. We described how in our context, which we think is rather common, instructors have relative freedom to choose the teaching and learning methods they use, but limited practical support for experiential methods such as AL and PBL. The data generated was small scale and there were differences in the weighting and timing of the courses in the overall curriculum. The question of fit to topic areas is beyond the scope of this chapter, although it can be argued that the area of strategic management lends itself especially well to experiential methods. Additionally, we are well aware that the participants were given little choice about the use of these methods, and were not asked whether they prefer these methods to others. More case studies and more enquiries are needed, but this study contributes to establishing a discussion about the choice of experiential methods in management education.

Based on our case, we suggest key issues to consider when choosing an interactive, enquiry-based experiential and integrated method like AL or PBL at HSE or another comparable business school. Initially we began with a framework of three questions, respectively about the method orienting the learners to learning, the teaching and learning processes important in the method, and the material and non-material support required. Our approach could be used for comparing any learning methods. Based on our reflections and consideration of data from instructors and participants, we see that considerations regarding resources and support are of concrete practical importance. The main considerations that have emerged in this study are university support, instructors' resources, and learners' readiness.

Although experiential methods at first may look very similar, there are important differences. Table 13.1 points out the important considerations when choosing between AL and PBL. Note that Table 13.1 does not pay attention to considerations that are common to AL and PBL (for example access to a wide range of theoretical resources, information literacy skills to identify and critically assess appropriate resources, university recognition of the instructor's time to support the process, to name a few). The considerations in Table 13.1 become meaningful only after the university has indicated that collaborative enquiry-based experiential learning

Table 13.1 Differences in AL and PBL considerations

Considerations	Choose AL when	Choose PBL when
University support	Demonstration of practical outcomes is valued.	Learning of explicit theories and understanding of their practical use is important.
Instructor's resources	Practical experience, management consulting experience may help. Means to recognize unmanageable project proposals quickly. Ability to flexibly allocate his or her own time to support the learning process. Good process facilitation skills to encourage and guide the projects.	Means to find a relevant messy problem area and also organize introduction of it for the class. Ability to arrange input about relevant theories. Skills to control the learning objectives and to facilitate the learning process. Preparedness to face unpredictability and not being able to have all the answers. Willingness to cope with struggle and frustration.
Learner's readiness	Ability to bring live workplace problems to class. Practical experience and some theoretical knowledge. Social and management skills to handle a project with a business organization. Listening and feedback skills for constructively challenging group members about action and its effects.	Interested in new learning challenges, and taking responsibility for their own learning. Not easily deterred by struggle and frustration. Team working skills or time to develop them.

methods are consistent with its goals, and a decision has been made to compare the fit of AL with the fit of PBL.

When the final choice of the adoption of learning method is left to the instructor, the choice is best made consciously. Where the institutional context privileges theoretical knowledge in disciplinary silos and teacher-centred inputs, an instructor choosing between experiential methods must consider to what extent they will be working against the norms, and what that will require from themselves and the learners. Our study illustrates that much is expected from the instructor, yet points to the differences between methods that may help an instructor to choose a method that can succeed in meeting the educational purpose and not set oneself up for insurmountable challenges. The abilities to identify the available choices, to make and follow through with choices, take responsibility for one's choices, and face the consequences of those choices, are as fundamental to successful teaching practice as they are to management practice.

CONCLUSION

Choosing experiential methods, like AL and PBL, means facing the challenge of working with complex problems and in unfamiliar groups of co-learners, as indicated both in the literature and in our experience. Our comparisons developed our awareness of the demands of experiential methods; for example, the importance of institutional emphasis on achievement of learning objectives rather than time served in classes, the need for instructors to be willing to work across and beyond disciplinary silos, and the significance of learners' responsibility for their own learning. Thus, the university, the instructors, and the learners all contribute elements that are necessary for a method to succeed.

In business schools, traditions are difficult to change. Support for a change and understanding of its intended purpose are needed from the entire organization. Overall, AL and PBL methods work most effectively when designed with an overview of the whole curriculum in mind. Thus, explicit plans and decisions regarding the use of experiential methods should be made and implemented, and their effects evaluated. The participating teachers need to have development plans, training, and encouragement, otherwise they will feel overburdened. And not only the faculty, but also the learners and the business organizations should be involved in the process of making methodological choices explicit. There is a need to orient the students effectively to these different methods, to prepare, train, and support them to learn effectively in teams, and to identify and fulfil their individual learning needs. Responding to such needs sends waves through the entire organization of the degree programme.

NOTE

We gratefully acknowledge Mari Simola's help in data collection and early discussions for this chapter.

REFERENCES

Cavalle, C., de Leernyder, J. M., Verhaegen, P., and Nataf, J. G. (2003). 'Follow-up Review of the Helsinki School of Economics: An EQUIS Re-accreditation'. Helsinki: Edita Prima.

Christensen, C. R., and Hansen, A. J. (1987). *Teaching and the Case Method*. Boston: Harvard Business School.

DiMaggio, P. J. (1988). 'Interest and Agency in Institutional Theory', in L. B. Zucker (ed.), *Institutional Patterns and Organizations: Culture and Environment*. Cambridge, Mass.: Ballinger.

——and Powell, W. W. (1991). 'Introduction', in P. J. DiMaggio and W. W. Powell (eds.), *The New Institutionalism in Organizational Analysis*. Chicago: University of Chicago Press.

Duch, B. J., and Groh, S. E. (2001). 'Assessment Strategies in a Problem-Based Learning Course', in B. J. Duch, S. E. Groh, and E. D. Allen (eds.), *The Power of Problem-Based Learning*. Sterling, Va.: Stylus Publishing.

————and Allen, E. D. (eds.) (2001). *The Power of Problem-Based Learning*. Sterling, Va.: Stylus Publishing.

Garud, R., Jain, S., and Kumaraswamy, A. (2002). 'Institutional Entrepreneurship in the Sponsorship of Common Technological Standards: The Case of Sun Microsystems and Java', *Academy of Management Journal*, 45/1: 196–214.

Herbert, A. (2002). *Paradoxes of Action Learning*. Helsinki: HSE Print.

HSE (2003). EQUIS Self Assessment Report.

HSE Strategies (2006). Accessed on 14 May 2006 at http://www.hse.fi/EN/abouthse/introduction/mission.

Kettunen, P., Carlsson, C., Hukka, M., Hyppänen, T., Lyytinen, K., Mehtälä, M., Rissanen, R., Suviranta, L., and Mustonen, K. (2003). *Suomalaista kilpailukykyä liiketoimintaosaamisella. Kauppatieteiden ja liiketalouden korkeakoulutuksen arviointi* (Finnish Competitiveness through Business Knowledge. Assessment of University Level Business Education). Helsinki: Edita (in Finnish).

King, S. (forthcoming). 'The Emotional Dimension of Radical Educational Change'. Ph.D. dissertation, University of South Australia.

Korpiaho, K. (2005). 'Student's Curriculum: What Do the Students Learn in the Business School?', in S. Gherardi and D. Nicolini (eds.), *The Passion for Learning and Knowing*. Trento: University of Trento.

Leppälä, K., and Päiviö, H. (2001). 'Kauppatieteiden opiskelijoiden moraalijärjestys: Narratiivinen tutkimus kolmen eri pääaineen opiskelusta Helsingin kauppakorkeakoulussa' (Moral Order of Business and Economics Students: Narrative Research about Studying Three Different Majors at Helsinki School of Economics). Helsinki School of Economics Masters Thesis B-34 (in Finnish).

McGill, I., and Beatty, L. (2001). *Action Learning: A Guide for Professional Management and Educational Development*, 2nd edn. London: Kogan Page.

Maguire, S., Hardy, C., and Lawrence, T. B. (2004). 'Institutional Entrepreneurship in Emerging Fields: HIV/AIDS Treatment Advocacy in Canada', *Academy of Management Journal*, 47/5: 657–79.

Marquardt, M. (1999). *Action Learning in Action*. Palo Alto, Calif.: Davies-Black Publishing.

Pedler, M. (ed.) (1997). *Action Learning in Practice*, 3rd edn. Aldershot: Gower.

Raelin, J. A., and Raelin, J. D. (2006). 'Development Action Learning: Toward Collaborative Change', *Action Learning: Research and Practice*, 3/1: 45–67.

Revans, R. (1983). *The ABC of Action Learning*. Bromley: Cartwell-Bratt.

—— (1985). *Action Learning: Its Origins and Nature*. Aldershot: Gower.

Savin-Baden, M. (2000). *Problem-Based Learning in Higher Education: Untold Stories*. Buckingham: Society for Research into Higher Education and Open University Press.

Schmidt, H. G. (1993). 'Foundations of Problem-Based Learning: Some Explanatory Notes', *Medical Education*, 27: 422–32.

Stinson, J., and Milter, R. (1996). 'Problem-Based Learning in Business Education: Curriculum Design and Implementation Issues', in *New Directions in Teaching and Learning in Higher Education*. San Francisco: Jossey-Bass.

Wood, D. F. (2003). 'ABC of Learning and Teaching in Medicine: Problem-Based Learning', *British Medical Journal*, 326: 328–30.

PART IV

EXPERIENTIAL
LEARNING AND
SYSTEMS
PSYCHODYNAMICS

CHAPTER 14

PICTURES FROM BELOW THE SURFACE OF THE UNIVERSITY

THE SOCIAL PHOTO-MATRIX AS A METHOD FOR UNDERSTANDING ORGANIZATIONS IN DEPTH

BURKARD SIEVERS

A university should, I believe, provide an experience of living as well as an opportunity for learning.

(Sloman 1964: 51)

The university Business School is not a seat of learning and does not pretend to be. It is a factory run on Tayloristic principles of standardisation, measurement and control.

(Höpfl 2005: 65)

Thinking psychoanalytically means disturbing adjacent disciplines with a new method.

(Figlio 1996: 22)

INTRODUCTION

THE following is a first account and reflection on an experience with a 'Social Photo-Matrix' (SPM) as a method for experiential learning 'in the making'. I recently invited students from our department of economics and business administration at Bergische Universität Wuppertal in Germany to focus on the unconscious dynamics of the university by using photos. During this one-term event, students were asked to make their own photos of the university (with digital cameras) and to send them by e-mail to provide an 'archive' from which they would be selected and shown during a SPM. Since a majority of the fifteen students who attended this seminar had already taken previous ones, they were experienced with other approaches to experiential learning, for example Group Relations Conference, Organizational Role Analysis, and Social Dreaming.

Referring to my own lifelong experience with taking photos, I mentioned in the invitation that *making* pictures with a camera often allowed me to see 'things' with a different eye. Just as Magritte's picture *Ceci n'est pas une pipe* actually 'is' not a pipe—but 'just' a picture of a pipe—the students might have similar experiences that 'objects' in their pictures are not identical to 'objects in reality'. Like the experience of working with dreams in the context of Social Dreaming (Lawrence 1998, 1999a, 2003, 2005) and Bion's (1962/1967) notion of 'thoughts in search of a thinker', the work with photos might lead to the experience of 'photos in search of a photographer'.

From these first thoughts the following *working hypothesis* for this seminar was derived: the photos of the university taken by the participants would allow access to the 'unconsciousness of the university' to the extent that associating and amplifying the photos would allow the thinking of thoughts which had not been thought so far. The stated *aim* of the Social Photo-Matrix as an experiential learning method was to experience—through visualization (and subsequent associations, amplifications, and reflection)—the hidden meaning of what in an organization usually remains unseen and unnoticed.

In face of the almost endless amount of photos taken since the invention of photography and the innumerable photos one has seen (or even taken) during one's lifetime, one does soon recognize that what one is experiencing in a seemingly immediate individual experience of the world actually is mediated long since by schematism and clichés that are passed on by the mass media. Or, as Viola (2004: 265) put it, 'most of the pictures we encounter in everyday life are disposable articles'.

Stated differently, despite our often desperate longing to make photos and create pictures that are 'new' and an expression of our own creativity, more often than not our photos are actually 'replicas', in the sense that they capture something on film, paper, or chip that we already have seen in other photos taken either by others or ourselves. Such an insight may at first appear humiliating. It reaches a further, different meaning, however, if we bear in mind that, especially for fine arts, if not for art, science, and the humanities in general, progress 'does not mean anything else but increasing realization of the past' (Brock 2004: 323). The new in fine arts actually is a new view of the old and the familiar. In this sense, our photos of the university would certainly contribute to viewing and understanding what appeared to be familiar in a new, unfamiliar way.

The Social Photo-Matrix as a newly developed method for understanding organizations in depth has not least grown out of my experience with action research and group relations work over some decades. There are mainly three roots that had a particular major impact in imagining and conceptualizing this method: (1) an increasing awareness of the meaning of artefacts in organizational contexts, (2) the experience of working with drawings in the context of Organizational Role Analysis (for example Newton, Long, and Sievers 2006), and (3) Social Dreaming.

The actual design of the SPM sessions was quite similar to the one we used in a seminar on Social Dreaming: a one-hour SPM was followed by an hour of reflection and application of the thinking generated in the previous session to the university context and experience. The photos were projected on a screen. During both the SPM and the following reflection session, one of the students took minutes, which, together with copies of the photos from the last matrix, were sent to the participants before the next meeting in order to help us make links between sessions.

SOME ASSOCIATIONS FROM THE SOCIAL PHOTO-MATRIX

In retrospect, it seems that the six photos from the first SPM session and the very first picture in particular somehow set the tone for most of the following sessions. All photos of this session showed parts of buildings and were empty, sterile, mainly frightening spaces. The very first picture showed a view through a glass door with a sign asking to keep it closed in order to prevent, in case of a fire, smoke extending into further parts of the building, opening up the view into an empty part of a hall in front of an elevator. Like most of the subsequent photos, it raised associations of prison, clinical laboratory, and psychiatric hospital and fantasies of persecution and annihilation:

'This is a zone of high danger. The atmosphere is precarious.' 'Maybe the students are already evacuated.' 'The wire grid in the door adds to the feeling of being imprisoned.' 'The picture reminds me of the movie "One flew over the cuckoo's nest" '—'or "The Cube" in which people were trying to escape.' 'The photo is mirroring two decisive dynamics: you have to take care of either not going mad or not getting an infection.' 'Smoke and fire alarm are the only security and safety devices the university does provide.'

The second picture showed part of an iron fence in the parking lot, which was erected in front of an area that was under construction:

'It's like the view from a prison cell.' 'The grid is re-painted again and again in order to let it appear bearable.' 'To cover up the blood and the escape attempts.' 'Is this the place where the women have been ambushed?' 'Corpses in iron cages.' 'Cages of the Anabaptists hanging at a tower of a church in the city of Münster.' 'The cage in the fairy tail of Hansel and Gretel where the witch is keeping the boy in captivity and controls whether he has gained weight.' 'Maybe this is the place where it will be decided whether one will be admitted for examinations after one has put one's test through the grid.'

The two last associations, in particular, indicate how, as Stein (2004: 27) described, 'the teaching and learning situation is frequently fraught with various anxieties. Students may worry a great deal about whether they will get through their course; they may feel inadequate when they struggle to understand new ideas and recall new information; and they may have all kinds of worries about whether they are really accepted by their teacher and their fellow students' (cf. French 1997; Salzberger-Wittenberg, Henry, and Osborne 1983).

THOUGHTS, INSIGHTS, AND LEARNINGS FROM THE REFLECTION SESSIONS

The subsequent session provided space for reflection on the associations during the preceding first SPM. It raised the following thoughts:

'Taking photos is an unconscious process. There is a difference between what one wanted to catch and what actually has been caught.' 'It is interesting to notice that others have seen things differently to those I wanted to present.' 'The photos are almost always mirroring how ugly the building actually is.' 'They have simply chosen what was cheapest in the 1970s.'

'There are no spaces to linger.' 'It is like in a factory.' 'It well may be that the depression that is there is privatised. One does not have a choice. Why grumble? And thus it disappears.'— 'Towards the end of the session we no longer talked about the photos. But a lot about the university.' 'Yes, and would we have been able to do so without the photos?'

As the frame of this chapter does not provide the space to go through all of the sessions to the same extent, what follows is a summary of the main issues and thoughts we were able to address: the experience and anxiety of being imprisoned raised the question to what extent the totalitarianism ascribed to the university and the buildings in particular were actually a projection of one's own inner totalitarian tendencies that usually do not become conscious. Referring to the fact that Bergische Universität is not a campus university but one with a high number of students commuting on a daily basis, the university was referred to as a *drive-in university*. In other associations it was a bunker from the Second World War, a factory, a Fata Morgana, a laying battery, or a wrapped mausoleum. As one participant put it: *This university was built for science—not for people!*

The fact that both students and members of staff quite often disappeared without a word (in the case of the former either as dropouts, changing to another university, or finishing their studies; the latter either due to new appointments at other places, retirement, or death) nurtured the fear of sharing a similar fate—of just disappearing from the book of life.

The lack of containment fuelled many associations throughout the various sessions. Contrary to the traditional symbol of a (German) university as *alma mater*, the big mother, many photos showed the lack of anything that could be perceived as motherliness. This reconfirms what Höpfl (2003: p. xvii) states, i.e. that 'without an image of the mother...the textual matrix becomes a mechanism for male reproduction and regulation'. Though women as professors are highly underrepresented in German universities in general and extremely so in our department, female professors were perceived as tough men lacking any capacity for support, sponsoring, or warmth. This is paralleled by the experience that being a student in our department means to perceive oneself and co-students as sexually neutral.

With its primary emphasis on the teaching of knowledge for future (business) careers, the department does not acknowledge and therefore cannot provide containment for the inner 'incompleteness' and immaturity of the students. Personal development and growth of students are considered at best as a private matter— while apparent imperfection and deficiency is at the same time met by faculty's contempt. The department apparently does not 'provide an experience of living as well as an opportunity for learning' (Sloman 1964: 51). 'It is a factory run on Tayloristic principles of standardisation, measurement and control' (Höpfl 2005: 65).

That none of the pictures actually showed one of the professors also confirmed the above impression and reinforced the idea that *there is no relatedness between students and professors*. Members of staff are perceived as depreciating their teaching assignments. That they are not supposed to take students seriously and are contemptuous is paralleled by the fact that students often carry contempt both towards their professors and the content of study presented in their teaching.

Taking the role of a student more often than not may be a painful process. The extent to which students' ego ideal might be shattered was expressed by one participant: *When I first went to university, I felt free like a bird—but had to realize at the beginning day-in, day-out that I could not fly.* The first part of this contribution nicely catches in everyday language what for example Schwartz (1993: 194) describes as the function of the ego ideal in a more abstract way: 'The ego ideal pictures us as perfectly at home in the world, without anxiety, sure of ourselves, certain of the validity of our behaviour, without doubt or marginality.' While the predominance of the ego ideal, nurtured by (the fantasy of) love, is related to the mother, it is quite obvious that a university 'under the psychology of the ego ideal ... functions ... as a maternal imago' (ibid. 202). 'Within the psychology of the superego, the university is an arena of competition for respect based on achievement. Here the university functions as a father, who prepares students to achieve something in the world' (ibid.).

As students experience a high degree of anonymity, lack of identification with the university or a department, and loneliness, they are very much the singleton as described by Pierre Turquet (1975). As if they are saying: *All we have in common is to feel lonely!*—or: *the knowledge that the other one is equally just learning on his or her own. As everyone is a lone wolf amongst strangers all we have in common is this consciousness and experience*—which itself has to be privatized and turned into 'private misery'. And as others cannot be made out nor be related to, it is not too much of a surprise that the enormous threat students experience is but anonymous too.

This was further confirmed by the fact that there were extremely few photos showing people. This raised the question of what it might elucidate about us, the photographers. The fact that only one photo explicitly showed 'nature', i.e. a tree on top of a hill, led to the remark that the university apparently had a way of viewing (and thinking) in which living objects were either not well regarded or even useless. Students were timid about taking pictures of their co-students and felt ashamed to make 'real life' pictures of working and learning people.

As the work with photos in the SPM progressed from session to session, the photos gained another meaning: they were increasingly seen as means for new ways of thinking about the university: *We are just thinking the university through the pictures.—The photos actually are not what we are interested in, what really counts is disclosing our inner pictures.—There is no room in traditional science (and the humanities) for this kind of work and for free associations in particular.*

The Photo-Matrix allows speaking out what cannot be expressed officially. There is also an acknowledgement that the thinking initiated by the SPM creates awareness for those processes and connections that are not supposed to become known or obvious. This work is seen as giving access to the university's (and department's) shadow.

THE SOCIAL PHOTO-MATRIX AS A MEANS OF EXPERIENTIAL LEARNING AND MANAGEMENT EDUCATION

The use of photos and photography in experiential learning for management education or organizational analysis is, as such, obviously not new. Warren (2002, 2005, 2006), for example, describes how she uses photos in her work with organizations. Whereas most approaches resemble that of an ethnographer or anthropologist insofar as they are based on the perception of an outside observer, SPM is a method of action research that uses the very eyes (hearts and minds) of organizational role holders. They have the direct experience with the organization and are the genuine source for giving meaning to the photos through free associations, amplifications, and reflection. While the photos of an external observer, researcher, or consultant can be a means of telling the client what the photographer sees at the very moment they are taken and/or a way of encouraging the client to find its own meaning, the photos in the SPM, so to say, speak for themselves and to those who 'collectively' have made them.

What follows is my effort to put what we attempted to accomplish with the SPM into a broader context and to reflect on the experience of this first SPM in order to derive further learning from it—for the participants of this SPM, the reader of this chapter, and not least for myself.

Underneath the Surface of the University

The first part of this chapter's title 'Pictures from below the Surface of the University' is derived from the title of Wim Wenders's (2001, 2004: 299) recent photo exhibition *Pictures from the Surface of the Earth*. Many of his photos are not only very fascinating, but are also an expression of what he stated in a presentation relating to his work as film director some ten years earlier: 'My dreams and my nightmares are not only part of my life as "Artist", if you want so, they equally are part of my daily life as man, just like for everyone of you too' (Wenders 1992b: 94).

Even though dreams are not the immediate focus of this experiential method, there was sufficient evidence during this seminar that many of the photos had a dreamlike quality. Many appeared as nightmares that either had been ignored or had been too private to be addressed openly as a constituent part of what it means to hold a role in the university and the department in particular.

Instead of reviewing the 'theory of photography' for how various authors have conceptualized the 'function' and meaning of photography and its relatedness to the unconscious, I would like to confine myself, on this occasion, to some thoughts of Roland Barthes, Wilfred Wiegand, and Wim Wenders.

Though in our daily experience we tend to take what we see as an expression of reality—often a reality in the present even though we know all too well that every photo is a picture from the past—every photo actually is 'but' an image of what we are accustomed to perceiving as reality. Not only is what we 'see' in a photo seldom the same as what the photographer had intended to show when she or he took it, it also often differs from what others see. 'The PHOTO . . . cannot say what it shows' (Barthes 1980/1985: 111). In a sense, photos are like metaphors and dreams. They give access to a variety of social meaning. For Barthes (ibid. 17, cf. 22 f., 102 f., 108) photos—and portraits in particular—always have the uncanny hint of 'the return of the dead'—of a death that either has occurred in the past or will occur in the future. This may have a double meaning: It literally can refer to the object(s) of a photo as well as to the photographer who is either already dead or has changed significantly since the photo was taken. But 'the return of the dead' can also be related to the death of one's own remembrance, to the displacement of previous experience, thoughts, and emotions that once had been related to the object(s) shown on a photo.

Taking—or actually making—a photo may, from this perspective, mainly be seen as a defence against mortality, both on the side of the object and the photographer. Even though photographers (like their objects) disappear and ultimately die, through their photos they gain at least a temporary immortality insofar as they mostly survive the actual moment the photograph has been taken. Wiegand (1981, as quoted in Molderings 2005) observed: 'It is not fantasy which is the uppermost instance in the creative process of the photographer, but remembrance.' Remembrance since Freud 'is not only a supplier of raw materials of phantasy but its sister of equal rank, chained to the unconscious like the former' (ibid.). A photographic image, according to Wiegand, must represent beauty in order to serve as remembrance. To the extent that amateur photos more often than not are actually remembrances of other photos they are mere remembrances of remembrances (ibid.) and thus mainly lack the unconscious content and quality related to the original object.

Wiegand's emphasis on remembrance as the uppermost instance of the creative process is reminiscent of what Wenders (1992a: 24) stated about his film work: 'One cannot invent what has not been in oneself before.' Applying these thoughts to the photos of our SPM, it occurs to me that—despite the fact that they primarily show ugly, nasty, and uncanny parts of the university buildings—most of them were captivating in their beauty. In mirroring their own 'poetry of images' (Gombrich 1972: 94), they brought back participants' remembrances of their role as student, in particular, and most likely of earlier roles as well. The making of photos thus can be seen as taking place in a potential or transitional space (Winnicott 1967, 1971), a space between the 'inner' world of the photographer and the 'outer' one of the 'object' which mainly unconsciously catches not only 'a picture' but, above all, the remembrance of earlier experience.

As already mentioned in the above sketch of the SPM, the vast majority of photos did not show people as objects but artefacts. Though we usually tend to regard artefacts as part of the non-human world and environment, the work with these photos frequently gave convincing evidence that the normal differentiation between the human and non-human world was not valid.

The American psychoanalyst Searles (1960) was the first who questioned taking for granted this differentiation between the human and non-human environment and showed that the latter actually 'constitutes one of the most basically important ingredients of human psychological existence' (ibid. 6). Though Searles mainly focuses on the individual and does not explicitly refer to the non-human world of organizations, his thoughts on the meaning and function of the non-human environment for our culture are significant in the present context. As members of our culture, we 'tend to *project* the "nonhuman" part of the self and perceive it as a nonhuman thing which threatens the conscious self with destruction; it is too threatening to let oneself recognize the extent to which the nonhuman environment has, as it were, already invaded and become *part* of one's own personality' (ibid. 397).

The psychic and social implications of our relatedness to the non-human environment and 'things' or artefacts in particular have, since Searles's pioneering work, received increasing attention in the social sciences and in psychoanalysis, in particular (for example Habermas 1999; Heubach 1996; Guderian 2004; Jüngst 2002; Lütkehaus 2002; Selle 1997). Some of these authors explicitly emphasize its relevance and meaning for the context of organizations (for example Beumer 1998, 2005; Gagliardi 1990; Mersky 2005; Warren 2002, 2005, 2006). As Beumer (1998, 2005) indicates, artefacts always have a double function, an instrumental one referring to their potential use as 'tools' and an expressive one related to emotions, memories, former or present owners, etc. They have an important impact on the unconscious relatedness between people and organizations and provide at the same time unique possibilities and doorway for understanding their reciprocal exchange processes, awaken and stimulate pre- and unconsciousness, and at the same time represent or dispose of individually and socially unconscious material. The use and representation of artefacts in organizations are potential means both for providing containment, integration, and development for organizational members as well as for their colonization, exploitation, and subjugation (cf. Mersky 2005).

The SPM Offers New Awareness and Experience of the Social

In a similar way as the Social Dreaming Matrix questions the predominant assumption that dreams are the property of an individual and are to be interpreted respectively, the SPM is based on the assumption that a photo is not owned by the photographer. It became obvious that photographers in the context of the SPM are making different kinds of photos from those published in an official university brochure. What is characteristic for dreams, i.e. that they are always related to the *context* of the dreamer, is equally valid for photos. In the case of this SPM it was obvious that the photos were explicitly made to throw light on the participants' 'working place', i.e. the university and the department in particular. They were part of a collective venture to grasp at the hidden meaning of one's quotidian and long-standing experience with an organization of which one is a member.

While the university as the 'object of investigation' was the foreground, the particular photographer was in the background; it usually was not even asked who had taken a certain photo. The photographers somehow were all interchangeable. One student expressed this: *Even though I actually didn't, I myself easily could have made many of the pictures we have seen.* The SPM experience is suggestive of what Viola (2004: 275), the video artist, describes in relation to his own work. Once he had been able to give up what he had learned at the art academy, i.e. that pictures and ideas are the private property of an individual, his 'studio became a social space of work in common'. For the participants in this seminar, the experience of the photos as something 'social' and something they had in common apparently was quite a rare if not a totally new phenomenon in the context of the university; an experience of 'we-identity' as opposed to 'I-identity' as Norbert Elias (1987), the sociologist, puts it.

I invited participants to a Social Photo-*Matrix*—and not to a 'group'—based on my experience with Social Dreaming. Unlike a group, which is often preoccupied with the maintenance of its identity, rivalry about power and reputation, and, particularly with a work group in an organization, pursuing its task,

the matrix, on the other hand, is a collection of minds opening and being available for dwelling in possibility. It demands a different kind of leadership—one inspired by the recognition of the infinite, of not-knowing, of being in doubt and uncertainty, as opposed to knowing and repeating banal facts. (Lawrence 2005: 40)

A 'matrix is also to experience a democratic environment' not least because of the fact that 'free association means saying what comes to mind; it is not subject to rational control' (ibid. 38). While a group often tends to be dominated by tyrannical dynamics or individuals, in a matrix everyone can feel free to associate without a need for agreement or the obligation to reach a predominant opinion.

The SPM thus did not only give space for a variety of new thoughts and thinking about the university, it also provided an experience of learning quite different from the traditional rational and cognitive way of learning in a university. While the latter is mainly based on a 'transmission' of knowledge and theories accumulated by individual scientists (scholars or 'common sense') into the 'brains' of students as individuals, the SPM fosters a kind of action research learning that emphasizes thinking on the basis of not-knowing, of being in doubt and uncertainty, and thus of being available for new thoughts that have not been thought before—either by the participants themselves or by thinkers in general.

As with Elias's (1987) 'we-identity', these thoughts are the result of a kind of 'we-thinking' that is quite contrary for example to the Cartesian axiom '*I* think, therefore *I* am'. Often enough the thinking in the SPM revealed part of the 'unthought known' (Bollas 1987, 1989) of the university and its role holders, i.e. that which 'is known at some level but has never been thought or put into words, and so is not available for further thinking' (Lawrence 1999b: 6). In analogy to Bollas's unthought known, the SPM provides opportunities to make an organization's 'unseen visible' noticeable and available for further thinking.

The thinking in the SPM was, in addition to the unthought known, also to a major extent related to the uncanny and the organizational shadow. There were actually several explicit references to the uncanny in both the SPM and the reflection sessions. As one student stated, 'While it may be the "job" of dreams to get in contact with the tragic, the "job" of photos may be to get in contact with the uncanny.' Freud (1919) circumscribes the uncanny as 'that class of the frightening which leads back to what is known of old and long familiar'. The SPM made obvious that not only movies (for example Arnzen 1997) but photos in particular have a high affinity for the uncanny. It also demonstrated what Vidler (1994) describes in his book *The Architectural Uncanny: Essays in the Modern Unhomely*. If it is true that to the extent that the experience of dread can be allowed, 'the uncanny announces the destruction of the canny, the removal of the familiar' (Pfreundschuh 2003), this seminar may be said to have destroyed much of what had been taken for granted about the university in order to allow new ways of seeing and thinking.

Most of what we explored would, from a Jungian perspective, be part of the realm of the organizational shadow (Denhardt 1981; Bowles 1991; Sievers 1999a). The organizational shadow refers to those parts which organizations wish to deny about themselves, due to the threat posed to self-image and self-understanding and, more generally, the need to be viewed in a favourable light by others. The shadow is repressed, and, as unconscious content, projected onto others, often onto those who are incapable of resisting it. All organizations possess a shadow, and its intensity will be unknown until confronted. As long as the organization shadow is not confronted, it can be assumed that an organizational psyche is at war with itself. The experience with this SPM suggests that a prominent way this university deals with its shadow is to cast it on its students.

The SPM Allows Access to Some of the Anxieties (and Defences) that Are Part of the Organizational Psychodynamic

From a Kleinian and Bionic point of view it can be assumed that both the photos and the setting of the SPM provide some kind of container for the process of transformation of 'mental raw material' into thinking and thoughts (Bion 1970). As the threatening, paranoid, annihilating, persecuting, and despairing fantasies in the various SPM sessions can be seen as expressions of the psychotic part of the organization (cf. Bion 1957/1967; Sievers 1999b, 2006), these containers provide a means of experiencing, reflecting, and digesting the psychotic dynamic as something that is induced by the organization. While getting in touch with the psychotic parts of the organization or its 'normal madness' stimulates feelings and emotions such as inadequacy, shame, rage, abandonment, and despair, the attempt to learn from this experience would, in the present context, be futile in the frame of individual psychopathology. As these experiences predominantly belong to the realm of the organization, they require a social way of working with them.

The SPM as a New Way of Seeing the University and Department

Though some of the new thinking which we were able to reveal in the SPM certainly may be unique insofar as it is related to this particular university and department, some of these thoughts may be of a more general relevance for contemporary universities in general and for business schools in particular.

The thinking during the SPM often referred to changes in the university that have occurred since its founding in the early 1970s. The buildings of Bergische Universität were erected as prefabricated constructions in order to reduce costs— but also with the side effect of creating a certain uniformity. Lecture rooms and staff office equipment and furniture are at least 'minimalist'; almost no rooms were included for formal or informal meetings or gatherings.

Quite in line with the vast majority of German universities, which are (federal) state universities, some 800 new students are enrolled in our department every year. As opposed to the Anglo-American system, students are not in certain class cohorts, but choose their lectures and seminars freely in accordance with a broad syllabus. As the number of students in a classroom varies from some 60 to 450, no space or effort seems to have been provided to build sentient boundaries. The more recent reorganization of Bergische Universität, guided by the primary aim of increasing efficiency while reducing costs, has sadly made traditional values, ideas, and visions obsolete. The new organization appears to be mainly driven by the conviction that new wine requires new wineskins—or to reflect the present context, plastic containers (cf. Weiler 2004; Sievers 2005).

Many of the thoughts in the SPM and the subsequent reflection sessions reflected the disillusion felt by a majority of both students and faculty. They also indicated that studying in the same department of the same university is not really experienced as having something in common. Gaining new knowledge, new thoughts, and new insights is not seen as something that grows out of a common 'search and production process'—as in the matrix—but is predominantly seen to be transmitted and accumulated by books or computers. According to the underlying frame, knowledge thus has become a commodity—which sooner or later may turn universities into mere production centres or warehouses (cf. Chattopadhyay 2005; Long 2004: 11f.). Studying at the university with the intention of getting a degree is exclusively regarded as an individual matter. This mirrors 'a denial of the importance of the collective' (Long 2004: 103) and the broadly unconscious attitude described by Lawrence, Bain, and Gould (1996) as basic assumption 'me-ness'. The perception of oneself as self-made man (or woman) apparently seems to fit all too well into what broadly is assumed to be required for a successful management career.

The lack of a more substantial 'vision' can be understood as the lack of a primary task for both the university as a whole and its respective departments. Though learning from experience may not be part of the *primary* task of a university but rather a *secondary* one (Long 2004: 133), Habermas's (1971) warning three decades ago requires even more attention today. He pointed out 'the dangers of the university fulfilling only a part of its task—that is, the generation and transmission of technologically exploitable knowledge—and losing that part of the task that engaged students in genuine critical reflection' (Long 2004: 119). Not knowing that one actually does not know what the task of the university is, is not only a defence against experience—and thinking—but ultimately leads to the result that hatred of experience and thinking will be regarded as normal because this hatred is understood as an indispensable prerequisite both for scientific learning and research and both for making a management career.

Participants realized that, unlike what they experience in their roles as students at the university, the experience of the SPM made them a 'partner in participating in the task of the system' (Chattopadhyay 2005: 1). As long as faculty and students predominantly perceive a university, as a production line, the experience of being partners in the common attempt of creating new knowledge through new thinking may only survive in certain niches. A primary task for the university, as, for example, suggested by Chattopadhyay, would certainly foster further initiatives for experiential learning. As he articulates 'the primary task of an educational institution is engaging in activities that will create new knowledge, which in its turn can be transformed into wisdom by those engaged in the task. This would be a valid task for both students and teachers' (ibid.).

The experiential learning of the SPM is in major contrast to what Hoggett (1992) calls 'cultural autism' 'in which objects are emptied of their symbolic content and so lose their capacity to contain meaning' (Newton 1999: 161). The SPM is apparently a possible way to perceive a whole variety of symbolic content in our non-human environment and organizational artefacts and encourages through new thinking and thoughts the possibilities of finding existing meaning as well as finding new meaning.

It apparently has been of great advantage that a majority of participants in this first SPM already had experience with various other methods of experiential learning aimed at understanding organizations in depth. Despite all the difficulties we had in attempting to contain and digest the emotions, feelings, and fantasies during the process of this action research project, I hope we all developed a certain passion for this kind of work.

NOTE

For W. Gordon Lawrence who has introduced me to this kind of thinking. This chapter could not have been written without the work and thinking of those who took part in the Social Photo-Matrix during the winter term 2004/5. I am very grateful to them and also want to thank Arndt Ahlers-Niemann, Gilles Arnaud, Alastair Bain, Larry Gould, Larry Hirschhorn, Rose Mersky, Gerard van Reekum, Russ Vince, and Simon Western for their help in writing this chapter.

REFERENCES

Arnzen, M. (1997). 'The Return of the Uncanny', *Paradoxa*, 3: 3–4, http://paradoxa.com/excerpts/3–3intro.htm.

Barthes, R. (1980/1985). *Die helle Kammer. Bemerkungen zur Photographie*. Frankfurt: Suhrkamp.

Beumer, U. (1998). ' "Schläft ein Lied in allen Dingen…". Dingliche Objekte und räumliche Szenarien in der psychoanalytischen Organisationssupervision', *Freie Assoziation*, 1: 277–303.

—— (2005). 'Symbols and Artifacts in Organisational Life' Symbole und dingliche Objekte im Leben von Organisationen. Workshop presentation, Coesfeld, Germany, 15 Apr. 2005—MS.

Bion, W. R. (1957/1967). 'Differentiation of the Psychotic from the Non-psychotic Personalities', *International Journal of Psycho-analysis*, 38: 266–75 (repr. in W. R. Bion, *Second Thoughts: Selected Papers on Psycho-analysis*. London: Heinemann, 1967).

—— (1962/1967). 'A Theory of Thinking', *International Journal of Psycho-analysis*, 43: 306–10 (repr. in W. R. Bion, *Second Thoughts: Selected Papers on Psycho-analysis*. London: Heinemann, 1967).

—— (1970). *Attention and Interpretation*. London: Tavistock.

Bollas, C. (1987). *The Shadow of the Object: Psychoanalysis of the Unthought Known*. London: Free Associations Books.

—— (1989). *Forces of Destiny*. London: Free Associations Books.

Bowles, M. L. (1991). 'The Organization Shadow', *Organization Studies*, 12: 387–404.

Brock, B. (1986). *Ästhetik gegen erzwungene Unmittelbarkeit. Die Gottsucherbande. Schriften 1978–1986*. Cologne: DuMont.

—— (2004). ' "Quid Tum". Was folgt aus dem Iconic Turn?' in C. Maar and H. Burda (eds.), *Iconic Turn. Die neue Macht der Bilder*. Cologne: DuMont.

Chattopadhyay, G. P. (2005). 'Effectiveness as Manager Depending on Managing Self in Role'. MS, Institute of Management Development and Research (Pune) Convocation Address 15 Feb.

Denhardt, R. D. (1981). *In the Shadow of Organization*. Lawrence: Regents Press of Kansas.

Elias, N. (1987). 'Wandlungen der Wir–Ich-Balance', in *Die Gesellschaft der Individuen*. Frankfurt am Main: Suhrkamp.

Figlio, K. (1996). 'Thinking Psychoanalytically in the University', in M. Stanton and D. Reason (eds.), *Teaching Transference: On the Foundation of Psychoanalytic Studies*. London: Rebus Press.

French, R. (1997). 'The Teacher as Container of Anxiety: Psychoanalysis and the Role of the Teacher', *Journal of Management Education*, 21/4: 483–95.

Freud, S. (1919). *The Uncanny*, ed. James Strochey et al., Standard Edn. xvii. London: Hogarth Press.

Gagliardi, P. (ed.) (1990). *Symbols and Artefacts: Views of the Corporate Landscape*. Berlin: de Gruyter.

Gombrich, E. H. (1972). 'The Visual Image', *Scientific American*, 227/3: 82–96.

Guderian, C. (2004). *Die Couch in der Psychoanalyse. Geschichte und Gegenwart von Raum und Setting*. Stuttgart: Kohlhammer.

Habermas, J. (1971). *Toward a Rational Society*. London: Heinemann.

Habermas, T. (1999). *Geliebte Objekte. Symbole und Instrumente der Identitätsbildung*. Frankfurt: Suhrkamp.

Heubach, F. W. (1996). *Das bedingte Leben. Entwurf zu einer Theorie der psycho-logischen Gegenständlichkeit der Dinge. Ein Beitrag zur Psychologie des Alltags*. Munich: Fink.

Hoggett, P. (1992). 'A Place for Experience: A Psychoanalytic Perspective on Boundary, Identity, and Culture', *Environment and Planning D: Society and Space*, 10: 345–56.

Höpfl, H. (2003). 'Introduction', in H. Höpfl and M. Kostera (eds.), *Interpreting the Maternal Organisation*. London: Routledge.

—— (2005). 'Indifference', in C. Jones and D. O'Doherty (eds.), *Manifestos for the Business School of Tomorrow*. Åbo: Dvalin Books.

Jüngst, P. (2002). *Territorialität und Psychodynamik. Eine Einführung in die Psychogeographie*. Gießen: Psychosozial-Verlag.

Lawrence, W. G. (ed.) (1998). *Social Dreaming @ Work*. London: Karnac.

—— (1999a). 'The Contribution of Social Dreaming to Socio-analysis', *Socio-analysis*, 1/1: 18–33.

—— (1999b). 'Thinking Refracted in Organisations: The Finite and the Infinite/the Conscious and the Unconscious'. Presentation at the 1999 Symposium International Society for the Psychoanalytic Study of Organizations, Toronto (pub. as: 'Thinking Refracted', in W. G. Lawrence, *Tongued with Fire: Groups in Experience*. London: Karnac, 2000).

—— (ed.) (2003). *Experiences in Social Dreaming*. London: Karnac.

Lawrence, W. G. (ed.) (2005). *Introduction to Social Dreaming: Transforming Thinking*. London: Karnac.

—— Bain, A., and Gould, L. (1996). 'The Fifth Basic Assumption', *Free Associations*, 6, 1/37: 28–55.

Long, S. (2004). 'Building an Institution for Experiential Learning', in L. J. Gould, L. F. Stapley, and M. Stein, *Experiential Learning in Organizations: Applications of the Tavistock Group Relations Approach*. London: Karnac.

Lütkehaus, L. (2002). *Unterwegs zu einer Dingspsychologie. Für einen Paradigmenwechsel in der Psychologie*. Gießen: Psychosozial-Verlag.

Mersky, R. Redding (2005). 'Lost in Transition: A Psychoanalytic Exploration of Object Attachment in Today's Post-modern Organizations'. Paper presented at the 2005 Baltimore Symposium: 'New Psychoanalytic Responses in our Work with Organizations and Society', International Society for the Psychoanalytic Study of Organizations.

Molderings, H. (2005). 'Gefundene Schönheit des Augenblicks. Dem Klassischen auf der Spur: Wilfred Wiegand, Sammler, Kritiker und Interpret der Fotografie', *Frankfurter Allgemeine Zeitung*, Dec. 24/300: 40.

Newton, J. F. (1999). 'Clinging to the MBA "Syndicate": Shallowness and Second Skin Functioning in Management Education', *Socio-analysis*, 1: 152–75.

—— Long, S., and Sievers, B. (eds.) (2005). *Coaching in Depth: The Organizational Role Analysis Approach*. London: Karnac.

Pfreundschuh, W. (2003). 'Das Unheimliche', in W. Pfreundschuh (ed.), *Kulturkritisches Lexikon*, http://kulturkritik.net/Begriffe/u.html.

Salzberger-Wittenberg, I., Henry, G., and Osborne, E. (1983). *The Emotional Experience of Learning and Teaching*. London: Routledge.

Schwartz, H. (1993). 'Narcissistic Emotion and University Administration: An Analysis of "Political Correctness",' in S. Fineman (ed.), *Emotion in Organizations*. London: Sage.

Searles, H. F. (1960). *The Nonhuman Environment in Normal Development and in Schizophrenia*. Madison, Conn.: International Universities Press.

Selle, G. (1997). *Siebensachen. Ein Buch über die Dinge*. Frankfurt am Main: Campus.

Sievers, B. (1999a). 'The Organization Shadow'. Workshop MS.

—— (1999b). ' "Psychotic Organization" as a Metaphoric Frame for the Socio-analysis of Organizational and Interorganizational Dynamics', *Administration and Society*, 31/5, Nov.: 588–615.

—— (2005). ' "It is new, and it has to be done!" Socio-analytic Thoughts on Betrayal and Cynicism in Organizational Transformation'. Paper presented at the 2005 Baltimore Symposium: 'New Psychoanalytic Responses in our Work with Organizations and Society', International Society for the Psychoanalytic Study of Organizations; *Culture & Organization* (forthcoming 2007).

—— (2006). 'Psychotic Organization: A Socio-analytic Perspective', *ephemera*, 6/2: 104–20, http://www.ephemeraweb.org/journal/6-2/6-2sievers.pdf.

Sloman, A. E. (1964). *A University in the Making*. London: British Broadcasting Corporation.

Stein, M. (2004). 'Theories of Experiential Learning and the Unconscious', in L. J. Gould, L. F. Stapley, and M. Stein, *Experiential Learning in Organizations: Applications of the Tavistock Group Relations Approach*. London: Karnac.

Turquet, P. M. (1975). 'Threats to Identity in the Large Group', in L. Kreeger (ed.), *The Large Group: Therapy and Dynamics*. London: Constable.

Vidler, A. (1994). *The Architectural Uncanny: Essays in the Modern Unhomely*. Cambridge, Mass.: MIT Press.

Viola, W. (2004). 'Das Bild in mir: Videokunst offenbart die Welt des Verborgenen', in C. Maar and H. Burda (eds.), *Iconic Turn. Die neue Macht der Bilder*. Cologne: DuMont.

Warren, S. (2002). ' "Show me how it feels to work here": Using Photography to Research Organizational Aesthetics', *ephemera*, 2/3: 224–45, http://www.ephemeraweb.org.

—— (2005). 'Photography and Voice in Critical Qualitative Management Research', *Accounting, Auditing and Accountability Journal*, 18/6: 861–82.

—— (2006). 'Hot Nesting? A Visual Exploration of Personalised Workspaces in a "Hot-Desk" Office Environment', in P. Case, S. Lilley, and T. Owens (eds.), *The Speed of Organization*. Copenhagen: Copenhagen Business School Press (forthcoming).

Weiler, H. N. (2004). 'Neuer Wein braucht neue Schläuche. Organisationsformen und-reformen im deutschen Hochschulwesen'. Keynote anlässlich des Symposiums zum zehn-jährigen Bestehen des Centrums für Hochschulentwicklung (CHE) in Berlin, 29 Apr. 2004, http://www.stanford.edu/~weiler/Vortrag_CHE.pdf.

Wenders, W. (1992a). 'The Act of Seeing', in *The Act of Seeing. Texte und Gespräche*. Frankfurt am Main: Verlag der Autoren (Eng. trans. W. Wenders and M. Hofmann, *The Act of Seeing: Essays and Conversations*. London: Faber & Faber, 1997).

—— (1992b). 'High Definition', in *The Act of Seeing. Texte und Gespräche*. Frankfurt am Main: Verlag der Autoren.

—— (2001). *Bilder von der Oberfläche der Erde. Photographien von Wim Wenders*. Munich: Schirmer/Mosel.

—— (2004). 'Auf der Suche nach Bildern. Orte sind meine stärksten Bildgeber', in C. Maar and H. Burda (eds.), *Iconic Turn. Die neue Macht der Bilder*. Cologne: DuMont.

Wiegand, W. (1981). 'Was ist Photographie?', in *Die Wahrheit der Photographie. Klassische Bekenntnisse zu einer neuen Kunst*. Frankfurt am Main: S. Fischer.

Winnicott, D. W. (1967). 'The Location of Cultural Experience', *International Journal of Psychoanalysis*, 48: 368–72 (repr. in *Playing and Reality*. London: Tavistock/Routledge, 1971).

—— (1971). 'The Place Where We Live', in *Playing and Reality*. London: Tavistock/Routledge.

....

CHAPTER 15

BECOMING BETTER CONSULTANTS THROUGH VARIETIES OF EXPERIENTIAL LEARNING

....

JEAN E. NEUMANN

ORGANIZATIONAL consultants help their clients understand difficulties, address problems, and anticipate challenges by applying social science theory and methodology. Depending on their consultancy domain and requests brought by their typical clients practitioners evolve approaches that work sufficiently to enable continued practice (Neumann 2004). At some point in their careers, most consultants experience frustration and dissatisfaction with the state of their own consultancy. When this happens, they might turn to education for help.

Educational design for the professional development of organizational consultants needs both to reflect the nature of consultancy work in general and to exemplify the characteristics of an organizationally oriented consultancy in particular. Expressed concisely, consultants relate theory to practice in ways that make clients feel motivated and enabled. They help clients to connect suggested models and practical reasoning with experienced difficulties and challenges. Organizationally oriented consultants, by definition, do so with an implied concern for the complicated social, political, emotional, and relational issues that affect progress on enterprise goals.

Since 1993, the Tavistock Institute in London has offered professional development for practising consultants, entitled the Advanced Organizational Consultation (AOC) programme. Faculty have used experiential learning methodologies from the beginning, embedding different varieties throughout the educational design. Experiential learning brings 'real life' consultancy work into the classroom, and serves as a basic strategy for teaching and learning about the dynamics of organizational analysis and intervention. Combined with theoretical inputs and analytical tasks, the AOC provides consultants with opportunities to reflect on experience in order to integrate theory and practice in a way that works for them and their clients. In 2001, the Institute undertook a process of validation for the AOC, adding the option of studying for a master's degree via City University, London, to the retained outcome of the Institute's qualification. Thus, AOC became subject to the legal processes and related bureaucratic procedures intended to ensure compatibility across British and European higher education. In 2006, a postgraduate diploma was added to the AOC offerings.

Education for Scholarly Practitioners

The Tavistock Institute accepts candidates to its Advanced Organizational Consultation (AOC) programme whose roles require their continuous improvement in group development, organizational change, or technological innovation. Participants come from a wide range of occupational backgrounds and current positions (Czerniawska 1999), for example: senior HR and training and development specialists; freelance organizational development consultants; managerial consultants from niche firms; change managers in public and private agencies; individual coaches and group process specialists from service sectors; and systems development personnel in medium to large commercial firms.

Designed for participants who are mature learners, AOC candidates enter with substantial experience related to at least one of the three main theoretical orientations emphasized in the programme: organizational theory, consultancy competence, and systems psychodynamic perspectives. During the time period covered by this part-time course, participants undertake self-generated projects that can be understood as 'organizational consultancy', 'change management', or 'social systems development'. These consultancy requirements underpin the formal course structure, which is made up of a twenty-four-month educational process combining seven residential modules, five application days, self-directed learning, and written assignments.

Both the Tavistock Institute's history and current preoccupations demonstrate commitment to practical theory drawn from across the social sciences. The AOC exemplifies this commitment. Publicity documents state explicitly: an advanced organizational consultant enacts a high degree of consultancy competence, integrated with a lively understanding of organizational theory and psychodynamic perspectives. 'Advanced' refers to a practical necessity for organizational consultants to undertake self-directed learning in relation to their consultancy activities with clients. A consultant committed to such action-related learning (Argyris, Putnam, and Smith 1985) can be understood as developing a 'scholarly practice'—one that works towards an integration of theory and practice in support of a consultant's domain and typical clients' agenda (Marrow 1984).

Experiential learning stands as an integral component of AOC strategy in educating for scholarly practice (Argyris and Schön 1974). Five varieties of experiential learning operate within the educational design. Each will be described in terms of how they are used educationally, the theories and intentions that inform their use, the broad arena of social science theory each addresses, and some indication of participants' and faculty reactions. The varieties are:

- Curriculum and module design;
- Experiential activities and reflection;
- Consultancy experience and reflection;
- Vicarious learning;
- Institutional reflexivity.

These varieties of experiential learning are complemented and contained by theory and reflection—two other integral components of AOC considered necessary for educating practising consultants. For all seven modules, faculty selects theory for input and recommends reading based on their judgement of relevance to organizational analysis and consultancy practice. By the second module, participants begin to swap their own articles and suggest useful reading to each other. Reflection processes are woven throughout every aspect of the AOC course. The purpose of such reflection is twofold: to learn from experience, generalizing from a particular instance to others, and to make explicit connections between theory and practical experience.

VARIETY ONE: CURRICULUM AND MODULE DESIGN

The AOC curriculum overall, and each residential module, has been designed according to experiential learning approaches rooted historically in the Tavistock Institute (Miller 1990) and NTL Institute (Benne et al. 1975). From the 1940s to the

1970s, both organizations developed experiential learning as innovative laboratory research about social-psychological dynamics of groups and organizations. The enquiry methodology evolved rapidly into strategies for normative, re-educative change (Chin and Benne 1976). The original developers aspired to education that involved participants simultaneously in cognitive understanding about social systems, while providing direct emotional and relational experience in 'here and now' dynamics to connect understanding with behaviour.

Within AOC, the overall content flow of the curriculum mirrors a normative process for professionally planned organizational development (Neumann 1997). Theory and practice corresponding to different sizes and complexity of social system ground detailed work on organizational analysis and intervention. The initial approach to programme planning came directly from adult education theory (Knowles 1970). Thus, educational designers pay close attention to the interests and needs of practitioners and their organizational clients. Faculty feel equal concern that participants develop as self-directed learners in order to be able to combine their consultancy careers with lifelong learning.

Faculty match the content of a module to the anticipated stage of development for a particular cohort. Some matches are obvious: beginning with a client matched to beginning the AOC programme; ending with a client matched to ending classroom time with AOC colleagues. Faculty intend to maximize the likelihood that theoretical inputs can be studied both cognitively and in the light of predicted 'here and now' experiences at residential modules. Thus, the second module addresses early in the AOC life cycle the content issues of diagnosing and intervening in small social systems—the size which most closely approximates the size of the AOC learning community. Similarly, a module on 'consulting to messes and impossible tasks' appears towards the end of participants' time together when they are likely to be experiencing some recurring frustrations with themselves, their progress, and their learning institution.

Other aspects of the combined approaches from the two institutes are not readily apparent to the uninitiated. Faculty use their accumulated knowledge of applied social science and adult learning theory in order to develop trust and enhance willingness to learn. For example, the systems model applied to experiential learning requires that participants are prepared for input into each module, have the time and space necessary to become engaged in the more challenging learning during the middle of the module, and then are gradually prepared for exiting the module (Rice 1965). Combining that orientation with progressive group development (Gibb 1978) emphasizes the need for participants to be included with each other before being challenged with learning likely to stir up competition and power struggles. Anticipating and responding to emerging moments of affection (positive, negative, and neutral) are part and parcel of normative, re-educative learning strategies (Schultz 1969). While these elements of the design demonstrate good educational practice with adult learners, they also enact practical theories that can make or break an organizational intervention. The design models good practice supported by theoretical inputs and recommended reading.

Generally, both faculty and participants appreciate the flow of the overall curriculum and the designs for each module. Faculty find it possible to update and otherwise improve on the modules within the established patterns, as well as responding to the demands of university validation procedures. Participants regularly comment on the quality of the overall design. They speak about the degree of interconnection across the programme and how learning builds on preceding elements. This strength, however, makes changing the overall educational design difficult. Programme managers would like to open participation on modules to others outside of AOC; and, occasionally, AOC participants would like more flexibility about when they attend. The current curriculum and module design work against these options.

Variety Two: Experiential Activities and Reflection

Faculty choose a handful of topics around which they finalize module designs. Typically, learning opportunities include a theoretical input for each topic, with experiential or analytic activities, followed by structured reflection for all participants and faculty. Faculty ensure that each module incorporates all three AOC orientations—organizational theory, systems psychodynamics, and consultancy competence. Experiential exercises are used to keep the learning content and processes flowing between and within the three orientations. As teaching strategies, they are intended to stimulate different aspects of participants' intelligence (Gardner 1993).

Again, faculty use adult education methodology for selecting and incorporating specific experiential activities (Knowles, Holton, and Swanson 2005). Such exercises provide participants with a 'here and now' experience of the complexity inherent in a particular topic under consideration, However, these AOC experiential activities should not be confused with techniques that one might experience in basic human relations training (Pfeiffer and Jones 1986). While personal development of participants may result, the AOC focus is very much on professional competence. Therefore, the complexity under consideration refers to the social, political, emotional, and relational issues inherent in the practice of organizational consultancy.

Faculty have evolved the use of experiential exercises to illustrate critical management and organizational theories. As AOC faculty are required to practise as consultants themselves, they can select their own real life cases for simulations, role-plays, and case studies that enact pivotal moments. Multiple stakeholders, plurality of opinions, diverse identities, and conflicts of interests (for example while negotiating a contract, understanding resistance to particular developments, deciding who to involve in an evaluation meeting)—these are a few of the normal, practical challenges that AOC participants need to 'take in'. This sort of experiential exercise can run between two to five sessions on the same day or spread over two days. Despite their cognitive understanding, participants usually amaze themselves with the speed and intensity with which they recreate political and psychological dynamics.

Other experiential exercises tend to be 'here and now' use of particular interventions (for example process consulting, intergroup relationship clearing processes), or partial simulations of longer-term interventions or those for larger systems (for example STS design of repetitive jobs, future search conference). While more analytical in nature, some exercises focus on applying scientific methodology to consultancy tasks (for example writing a working note, developing meaningful codes for qualitative data during diagnosis, and feeding back data to clients).

Experiential exercises are only used alongside corresponding opportunities for reflection. Shorter experiential exercises have at least one session of reflection, called a 'plenary distillation'. Longer simulations will have been timed to incorporate reflections that start with a plenary distillation, and then revisit the experience as needed via other mechanisms spread over subsequent days (for example consultation groups and module reviews). Participants are taught an explicit model for reflecting on experience in order to learn, and plenary distillations are used to practise the model, roughly based on discovery learning (Bruner 1977).

Generally, participants find the experiential activities useful and compelling. Moving from debriefing experiences to reflecting on the experience, however, can be difficult. Experiential learning captures deep feelings and reactions, and the time needed to distance from those 'here and now' feelings in order to analyse the experience varies. The mental ability to identify aspects of the experience, analyse them, and generalize comes hard to most participants. The preferred pull tends to be in the direction of asking for 'real life' details, justifying one's own behaviour, and confronting one's colleagues. Participants typically strain to turn the plenary distillations into small study groups or t-groups. They put energy into avoiding the collective experience, and thus actively resist learning how to work with the complexity of collective dynamics.

Faculty hold the boundary on the primary task of reflecting on the experience, linking it to the selected theory (wherein the collective cannot be avoided), and considering implications for practice. Basic assumption behaviour tends to be very strong during these sessions. Participants often ask theoretical questions, complain about the design, or make evaluative comments about faculty. It is not unusual for some to feel overstimulated and shut down. That said, this form of experiential learning tends to stay with participants. The capability to learn from practice is crucial for the scholarly practitioner. All participants need to demonstrate 'good enough' proficiency by graduation. Faculty recognize that collective learning from experience, as a methodology for learning how to diagnose and intervene in collective dynamics, demands much from themselves and participants. Indeed, organizational consultancy makes the same demands on client and consultant.

VARIETY THREE: CONSULTANCY EXPERIENCE AND REFLECTION

Mechanisms are built into the AOC course structure—both during and between the modules—for reflecting on past and current consultancy practice. Faculty intend such reflection to assist participants in incorporating learning from modules, reading, and structured reflection into their practice with clients. During each module, a minimum of three consultation groups are set aside for individuals to work with colleagues and one member of faculty. Between modules, regional groups perform the same function but within a different timeframe. In the regional groups, participants often feel less prepared and messier in their practice: thus, the readiness to learn tends to be stronger, more immediate and the gap between meeting and application time shorter.

All participants must complete, during the time they are studying on AOC, one full cycle of planned development with an organizational client plus be well under way with a second project. Cases are plentiful for full-time internal and external consultants. Those working as change managers need to learn to conceptualize their practice in consultancy terms; those who are building up a new or different type of practice need to focus early on attracting suitable client systems.

Faculty assert that active engagement in the practice of organizational consultancy, from whatever occupational role the participant holds, develops and otherwise educates the consultant (Neumann 2004). Interacting with potential and actual organizational clients motivates the participant's felt need for self-directed learning. Consultancy processes teach the consultant as well as providing the client with assistance: attracting clients, negotiating entry into social systems, building relationships good enough for collaborating on an organizational issue, diagnosing and agreeing a plan of intervention for that issue, intervening with representatives of the client system, conducting a process of critique, reviewing with the client system and with one's professional colleagues.

Participants introduce for group reflection that which they 'want to work on' (for example a particular issue with an existing or potential case, the frustrations and joys of work development, expressions of a mismatch between self and client systems). The ability to articulate the nature of such concerns, proficiency in the frameworks and conventions of applied social science, develops over time. Colleagues and faculty work with whatever the participant brings, relating to the individual as 'client' to their consultancy. Results might include: selection of promising theoretical models, suggestions for suitable intervention approaches, insights about political and psychological dynamics, clarification of the consultant's role, confrontation about 'blind spots' and collusions, and study of 'parallel processes' that emerge in the room related to the topic under consideration.

Participants can choose to offer the same consultancy site repeatedly (common for those working as change managers or internal consultants of large and medium-sized enterprises). Or, they use cases that speak to the topic of the module or bring a case for immediate action or pressing concern. All participants must choose one case to present for a full session to the entire learning community, which is also written up in a final case analysis. Those who are working for the master's degree will have selected an actual consultancy challenge or change management case around which they will shape their thesis. Additional written assignments are tied to topics within each module, and often call on case reflection as well.

Thus, the more emergent and informal reflection of the module-based and between module groups complements structured verbal and written reflection. The written reflection explicitly requires participants to select theory relevant to their practice. Faculty intend these requirements to assist participants in the formation of consultancy identity, and in asserting their consultancy domain. Their ability to report generalizations emerging for their consideration of practice in light of theory (and vice versa) meets course requirements while improving their ability to offer such learning for use to client systems.

Participants benefit greatly from consultation and application groups, gaining enough confidence to work without faculty involvement during the times when such groups are not scheduled. At least one regional group from each cohort has continued to meet on its own after graduation. Faculty benefits from closer work with individuals and observing participants as they consult with each other. Such information often improves the quality of feedback for professional development that faculty can offer individuals; such feedback itself takes place in these groups. As both faculty and membership of these groups change a few times throughout the programme, repetitive patterns can be worked with in different ways in different groups.

Reactions to written reflection, in the form of assessed assignments, get bad press all around. Both participants and faculty complain about the workload. Since requirements for written reflection have been increased, however, participants' capability to generalize from experience in a way that links practice and theory has improved noticeably.

VARIETY FOUR: VICARIOUS LEARNING

During the small groups designed for reflection on consultancy cases, identity formation, and practice development, AOC participants learn vicariously from their peers' practical concerns. Their inner worlds are stirred by listening to their colleagues' emotionally intense stories. Usually without conscious intent, they imagine themselves in one or more positions within or otherwise in relation to their colleague's story. Through established psychological mechanisms like identification and projective identification (Horwitz 1985), they discover themselves taking up roles in relation to their colleague. As they react and interact with their 'client' colleague, they both help and hinder their colleague's progress in working through their concerns. The others within the group are doing the same. Multiple levels of learning become possible in this context.

These dynamics mimic what happens when working with 'real life' organizational clients. Participants discover their own and their colleagues' ideological biases and unresolved feelings about status and power (for example being aggressive towards executives, treating the needs of front-line staff as irrelevant, ignoring internal HRM personnel). They grow irritated with overuse or avoidance of particular frameworks or methods in relation to typical clients (for example complaining about tenders without crafting an entry approach consistent with one's values, continually offering workshops as a solution without diagnosis for fear of being rejected by clients, over-structuring interventions without involving appropriate representatives of the client system).

Sometimes, the dynamics of these consultancy groups can be studied directly as 'parallel processes' for insights and understanding related to the particular case. Different faculty work with such processes differently and at different times with the same or different groups. These are not t-groups or small study groups, although issues of group formation and defensiveness against the primary task may need to be addressed at some points. Faculty model feedback processes targeted at professional development, and mostly avoid that which might be understood as personal or interpersonal feedback. Equally, they are not solely problem-solving groups although solving immediate problems for the participants' practical concerns emerges during the work and often afterwards in the corridors and over meals. The experience of the group concentrating together on the organizational issue becomes the 'medium' through which 'the message' is communicated.

Observing someone else learn as a substitute for having to go through it oneself takes place during other times in the AOC programme. Notably, the times when the entire learning community gathers for reflecting on the course become points when individuals feel compelled to speak. The space tends to be constructed as 'public' because faculty and participants are together. All participants are struggling with the choice to speak or not, and how they use the opportunity for self-reflection, for study of 'here and now' dynamics, for disclosing excitement and confusion related to theory, for demonstrating learning and reading, for confronting norms with which they are dissatisfied. Despite explicit assistance from faculty, insights about how such struggles characterize client systems come slowly to some.

Participants often speak of the usefulness of learning from each other. They readily identify the consultation and application groups as places in which this happens. However, faculty would counter that projective identification, parallel processes, and the refusal to learn from each other rarely get mentioned. This does not mean that learning about enacted resistance does not take place; but that shame and envy militate against admitting it. Plenary distillations and collective review processes are fraught with the avoidance of being seen to learn openly from each other and faculty. Further, using others as substitutes for one's own learning has downsides that cannot be openly addressed. Even when faculty attempt to study how these dynamics might relate to organizational development and change, they often feel ignored or critiqued. Participants learn intimately that one cannot expect clients to embrace revelations about the downsides of their organizations, even if clients do learn and develop from such study.

VARIETY FIVE: INSTITUTIONAL REFLEXIVITY

Processes of mutual reflexivity for all members of AOC as a learning community require participants and faculty to reflect on the dynamics between them and in relation to the Tavistock Institute, City University, and other aspects of their work and lives. Within hours of entering the first module of the AOC programme, participants are put into experiential activity that begins institutional reflexivity. Participants enact many preconceived and idealized notions about the people and processes they expect to encounter within professional development, university education, consultancy services, and client relationships.

Faculty understand that their and participants' judgements of AOC—and each other—begin earlier than the first module, and continue throughout the time, space, and tasks that constitute the total programme. Faculty persistently work to expand participants' notions of what 'being in the programme' and 'reforming their consultancy identity' means. This usually involves consulting with participants about how to manage their boundaries in such a way that their consultancy practice, their reading, their assignments, their attendance at modules and application days can be balanced with other demands and desires in their lives.

While this has always been a part of the experiential learning within AOC, the introduction of the master's degree has changed dramatically the institutional context for the course. Many stakeholders can be understood as invested in the AOC programme: the Tavistock Institute, the participants' occupational context, the faculties' occupational context, organizational clients, publication outlets, personal and social relationships, competitors, the university, etc. Going from being solely informal professional development, wherein participants typically knew about and identified with the Tavistock Institute, to incorporating a formal educational credential seems to increase the 'victim' mentality of both faculty and participants.

Actively working through the political and psychological dynamics of the institutional context, as it is enacted and experienced and avoided within the programme, seems to be difficult. The study of authority dynamics, disclosure of social comparison, work with other social psychological mechanisms, and defences against learning—these and other aspects of institutional reflexivity are central to the experiential elements of the AOC programme. The perceived risk in engaging in this process, however, has always been difficult; with the MA element, it seems to feels impossible.

Thus, more formal mechanisms for institutional reflexivity have had to be introduced. Participants now design and conduct their own evaluation of the programme, sending their representative to the Institute's AOC Board of Studies. A record of the evaluation is then sent to the University's AOC Course Board. This formal process lays the groundwork for 'here and now' organizational change within the AOC programme itself. Reflecting on this experience of institutional reflexivity is still a new element of the programme. Intriguingly, some unreconstructed 'shoulds' about the people and processes within professional development, university education, consultancy services, and client relationships are resurfacing, having persisted unchallenged from the first module.

EXPERIENTIAL LEARNING ESSENTIAL TO BECOMING BETTER CONSULTANTS

These types of experiential learning make a crucial contribution to educating AOC participants in organizational change and development. They become better consultants to the extent that they take up the role of learner: within the modules, in relation to their self-study and individual assignments, with their colleagues on small group assignments, and in relation to their active practice with organizational change and development. Regardless of their particular consultancy domain, the institutional environments in which they work present numerous opportunities and challenges to think about the application of social science theory and methodology to systems change. How they practise organizational change and development, and their role within that practice, varies depending on where they are located in relation to their organizational client: internal consultant, external consultant from a firm, established within the sector, new to the sector, recognized as experienced, carving out a new patch, sole practitioner, etc. The variables that any one participant juggles to craft a better consultancy practice are numerous. It is possible, however, to identify patterns for how each type of experiential learning contributes to the education of consultants, their institutional contexts, and to organizational changes within the systems with which they work.

Curriculum and module design. Experiential learning underpins this approach for normative, re-educative change based on adult learning theory. Direct experience of 'here and now' dynamics, or reflection on 'there and then' experiences, help connect emotions and behaviours of self and others with cognitive understanding about social systems and how they change and develop. Within AOC, curriculum content mirrors prescriptive processes for planned organizational development and change. For example, entry and contracting is taught during the first module, ending with a client taught during the last. Modules match anticipated stages of individual and group development within the student body with specialized content. For example, diagnosis and intervention is introduced sequentially from small to larger to interorganizational systems, incorporating progressively more complex concepts and practices. These are timed as students' capability increases. Attention to trust, readiness to learn, and emotions pervade academic content.

In most institutions, rational-empirical and power-coercive approaches to change predominate. The need for normative, re-educative strategies might be neglected, mishandled, and discredited. Commercial pressures for rapid evidence of successful change and development can coexist with, and be contained alongside, a practical appreciation for the non-linear and less predictable reality of how people participate in their own processes of changing themselves and their organizations. AOC participants gain confidence in this contradictory social fact by having lived through it themselves, with their clients, and with their colleagues.

Experiential activities and reflection. The word 'experiential' defines this approach for relating theoretical inputs, experiential or analytic activities, and reflecting on both in order to generalize to other situations. The ability to reflect on experiences across many aspects of organizations requires concepts to articulate that reflection. Such an ability lays the groundwork for professionally applying social science theory and methodology to practice. Being able to work with others (for example one's clients and colleagues) as they reflect on experience to learn enhances an action research orientation to planned change. Within AOC, emphasis is placed on integrating organizational theory, systems psychodynamics, consultancy competence, and self-directed learning. Case simulations based on 'real life', practising interventions, using data analysis techniques, learning how to use disciplined reflection tools—all aid integration when combined with relevant theoretical inputs. Plenary distillations and module reviews provide additional opportunities to revisit that which confuses, catches one's attention, or otherwise niggles at the conscious mind. Differences between espoused theory and theory-in-action become apparent.

These issues are important to the institutional environments in which the students work. Norms about time, cost, and control tend to deny that organizational changes and developments present unique challenges and opportunities. Modern pressures embedded in social systems and institutional contexts need customized approaches flexibly evolving over time, space, and task. Understanding multiple levels within, across, and between social systems can be uncovered from the smallest to largest projects. An action research methodology begins with limits set early on by organizational leaders and evolves into something unique and customized as more organizational members become involved. Through this type of experiential learning, AOC participants grasp the idea that the best-laid plans go awry and that striving to know and take everything into account from the beginning is futile and not particularly desirable. The impact of multiple stakeholders, as well as new possibilities emerging as states of readiness develop, means that organizational change can—and perhaps should—be a movable feast.

Consultancy experience and reflection. Working with organizational clients provides the most compelling developmental experiences that consultants encounter. Reflecting on these experiences through the lens of theories, methodologies, and the eyes and ears of experienced colleagues and faculty brings insights and understanding that suggest different practical actions (and help work through feelings from the past). Within AOC, numerous opportunities for face-to-face reflection repeat throughout the programme: consultation groups, application groups, distillations, reviews, and case simulations. Written case analyses require the application of theory and methodologies to one's own experienced successes and failures.

Experiential learning of this type is of direct importance to the institutional environments in which the students work. Understandings from 'real life' examples— past, current, and potential—translate directly into changes in behaviour, actions, and recommendations to clients. Social systems and institutional contexts usually have a preferred approach to comprehensive change, including project management processes for incremental developments. Leaders enact such approaches regardless of repeated experiences with the downsides. Indeed, they often hire consultancy firms that cooperate with re-enacting their unsatisfactory approaches. Change agents, change managers, and consultants with exposure to a wide range of available theories and methodologies carry hope for something different to happen. The ability to combine and create interventions, working collaboratively with stakeholders through a planned cycle of change and development, has immediate impact. Short-term incremental projects as well as multiple, simultaneous initiatives benefit from consultants who reflect on their experiences and assist clients to do so.

Vicarious learning. Observing someone else learning as a substitute for having to go through it oneself provides opportunities to discover values and attitudes critical to consultancy practice. Participants sense biases and unresolved issues more easily in others than themselves, for example: that which might help or hinder a consultant's ability to include or work with groups with differential status and power; difficulties with cases due to gaps in understanding or methodological ignorance; neglecting to take in concepts readily taken up by others; and, patterns of conflict and frustration that repeat across cases. Vicarious learning takes place when participants are present while colleagues and faculty present cases, disclose issues in forming their occupational identities, report on successes and trials with commercial and business issues.

Comparisons happen naturally between the institutional environment in which the students work and the ones apparent in their colleagues' stories. Institutional routines and industrial or sector cultures carry within them often unexamined and otherwise taken for granted assumptions about how change should happen. The nature and methodology of that change, who gets included and excluded, and the roles necessary to make the change successful (and whose fault it is if it fails) pre-exist in the organization prior to the start of new initiatives. Working while keeping an eye and ear open for such routines and cultures becomes possible for a consultant who has clarified their own domain and their own preferred learning and development processes for re-engaging hope and creativity. The more influence a consultant feels over domain—with its sector or types of sectors—the more desire and patience he or she may have for understanding and working with biases, attitudes, and assumptions that may be preventing effective organizational change and development.

Institutional reflexivity. This experiential element of educational design structures time and space for when faculty and participants reflect together. Focus combines dynamics between and amongst them, and in relation to the sponsoring organizations, the university, other aspects of their work and life, and consultancy as an industry. Participants internalize models for structuring conversations for 'working through' thoughts and feelings during development and change. At AOC, participants study authority relations between themselves and faculty, considering how similarities between themselves and clients might operate. The role of judgement gets concentrated treatment during a mid-programme module on 'evaluating organizational change', when participants design and implement an evaluation of AOC. Their representatives present the results to university and institute governance boards.

An argument could be made that understanding political and psychological dynamics within and across organizations, and between organizations and their environments, constitutes 'institutional environment'. This level of cognitive development—both in systems psychodynamic and organizational theory terms—is a unique value added for any consultancy. Regressive dynamics that excite political and psychological anxieties and conflicts substantially delay or block many strategically important changes and developments in organizations. Competence in working effectively with such dynamics needs to be more broadly distributed within organizational systems to discover what progress is possible. Certainly AOC participants have been presented with experiential learning opportunities that confront their own and their colleagues' motivation and cooperation. Constructing and consulting to processes for 'working through', consultants help bring about unpredictable benefits.

CONCLUDING THOUGHTS

Both reflecting on experience in order to learn—and connecting that experience to social science theory and methodology—have moved from background to foreground as an essential ability over these fourteen years of the Tavistock Institute's Advanced Organizational Consultation programme. Experience for experience sake does not guarantee that a participant becomes a better consultant. Reflecting on experience without reading social science theory, and without using that reading as a basis for analysing consultancy cases, does not guarantee that a participant becomes a better consultant. The two need to be present and practised together in relation to consulting with organizational clients.

Jerome Bruner's EIAG model (short for experience, identify, analyse, and generalize) has been useful in teaching students a disciplined approach to reflection (1977). Combining that idea with Matthew Miles and Michael Huberman's levels of qualitative analysis (1994) shows students a way to move from identification and description of experience, through analysis of qualitative data, to making interpretations based on theory. Developing interpretations for process consultation (Bion 1959; Schein 1987) echoes similar concepts and mental abilities. Indeed, core faculty consider the possible need to be even more explicit in educating for this ability to reflect on experience in order to learn. Robert Kegan's (1994) research on mental organization of meaning and cognitive development may provide some assistance in taking this further. Educating for mental development 'across categories' and 'trans-categories' resonates with some of the challenges presented by the AOC aim of integrating organizational theory, systems psychodynamics, consultancy competence, and self-directed learning.

NOTE

This chapter has been written in association with a programme of work entitled 'Refreshing the Tavistock Institute's Traditions'.

REFERENCES

Argyris, C., Putnam, R., and Smith, D. M. (1985). *Action Science: Concepts, Methods and Skills for Research and Intervention*. San Francisco: Jossey-Bass.

Argyris, C. and Schön, D. A. (1974). *Theory in Action: Increasing Professional Effectiveness.* San Francisco: Jossey-Bass Publishers.

Benne, K. D., Bradford, L. P., Gibb, J. R., and Lippitt, R. O. (1975). *The Laboratory Method of Changing and Learning: Theory and Application.* Palo Alto, Calif.: Science and Behavior Books.

Bion, W. R. (1959). *Experiences in Groups.* New York: Ballantine Books.

Bruner, J. S. (1977). *The Process of Education.* Cambridge, Mass.: Harvard University Press.

Chin, R., and Benne, K. D. (1976). 'General Strategies for Effecting Changes in Human Systems', in W. G. Bennis, K. D. Benne, R. Chin, and K. E. Corey (eds.), *The Planning of Change*, 3rd edn. New York: Holt, Rinehart & Winston.

Czerniawska, F. (1999). *Management Consultancy in the 21st Century.* West Lafayette, Ind.: Ichor Business Books.

Gardner, H. (1993). *Multiple Intelligences: The Theory in Practice.* New York: Basic Books.

Gibb, J. R. (1978). *Trust: A New View of Personal and Organizational Development.* Los Angeles: The Guild of Tutors Press.

Horwitz, L. (1985). 'Projective Identification in Dyads and Groups', in A. D. Colman and M. H. Geller (eds.), *Group Relations Reader 2.* Washington: A. K. Rice Institute.

Kegan, R. (1994). *In over our Heads: The Mental Demands of Modern Life.* Cambridge, Mass.: Harvard University Press.

Knowles, M. S. (1970). *The Modern Practice of Adult Education: Andragogy Versus Pedagogy.* New York: Association Press.

—— Holton, E. F., and Swanson, R. A. (2005). *The Adult Learner: The Definitive Classic in Adult Education and Human Resource Management.* London: Elsevier, Inc.

Marrow, A. J. (1984). *The Practical Theorist: The Life and Work of Kurt Lewin.* Annapolis, Md.: BDR Learning Products, Inc.

Miles, M., and Huberman, M. (1994). *Qualitative Data Analysis*, 2nd edn. London: Sage.

Miller, E. J. (1990). 'Experiential Learning in Groups I: The Development of the Leicester Model', in E. Trist and H. Murray (eds.), *The Social Engagement of Social Science*, i: *The Socio-Psychological Perspective.* London: Free Association Books.

Neumann, J. E. (1997). 'Negotiating Entry and Contracting', in J. E. Neumann, K. Kellner, and A. Dawson-Shepherd (eds.), *Developing Organisational Consultancy.* London: Routledge.

—— (2004). 'Reforming Consultancy Identity in Relation to Discontinuities with Clients'. Paper presented at the meeting of the Academy of Management on Creating Actionable Knowledge, New Orleans, Aug.

Pfeiffer, J. W., and Jones, J. E. (1986). *Handbook of Structured Experiences in Human Relations Training*, vols. i–x. San Francisco: Pfeiffer Wiley.

Rice, A. K. (1965). *Learning for Leadership: Interpersonal and Intergroup Relations.* London: Tavistock Publications.

Schein, E. H. (1987). *Process Consultation: Lessons for Managers and Consultants*, 2nd edn. Reading, Mass.: Addison-Wesley.

Schultz, W. C. (1969). *Joy: Expanding Human Awareness.* New York: Grove Press.

CHAPTER 16

BALANCING THE ON-LINE TEACHING OF CRITICAL EXPERIENTIAL DESIGN

A CAUTIONARY TALE OF PARALLEL PROCESS

ELIZABETH CREESE

Lonely desperate and desolate
That's how it feels—words needing to be got from another—
To want help.

Children, students, people
Tug at my 'holding'
Well-practised disconnection
From my feelings
To bear uncomplainingly theirs.

I need your help
So that I can really listen and hear
Without rejecting or being overwhelmed
By others' feelings
While staying connected to mine.
> (Extract from one of Creese's first truly reflexive diary
> entries, Wed., 9 Nov. 2004)

THIS chapter tells a cautionary tale—the danger of 'not really knowing' what on-line experiential design we are teaching—until we have been able to be critically reflexive. Reynolds (2000) has similarly warned of problems such as adopting a critical curriculum approach when a more traditional pedagogical basis might belie this. The tale of my gap between theory and practice is based on my critical action research (Kemmis and McTaggart 1988). It is a story about a Tavistock School of Group Relations 'struggle' to learn from experience (French and Vince 1999) about my on-line teaching practice. To tell it I take a deliberate focus not upon the wider systemic issues, but my internal responses to them: hence the microscopic prism of self-scrutiny.

My Class as Virtual Learning Organization (CAVLO) adapted Tyson's (1999) Class as Learning Organization (CALO) model for the on-line environment. In this design I sought to encourage students to learn along critical experiential lines. It is with the benefit of five action research cycles that I have been subsequently able to recognize a gap between the theory I espoused in my design and on-line moderation and my actual practice of it (Argyris and Schön 1974, 1978).

Tyson based his design on Cohen's (1976) seminal work in America using the classroom experientially as a domain of organizational study. To this he added a teaching role informed by the Group Relations idea of anxiety containment (French 1997). In a previous study (Creese 2001) I had found that the dual role of on-line teacher as designer and moderator naturally aligned with such a notion. Extending Group Relations thinking to virtual group space I considered the psychological place, bounded by the teacher in which learning can occur, to be comparable. Within the virtual classroom containment of learning anxiety becomes possible through the complementary roles of on-line teacher: task boundaries can be potentially maintained both by the social 'here and now' presence, albeit virtual, and articulated in the design.

Technological breakthroughs have enabled the recording of the virtual interactions which occur in this bounded space via Computer Mediated Communication (CMC). CMC occurs both through synchronous networks in real time and asynchronous in delayed time. I use archives of CMC to tell the story of the parallel processes between the students' and my own resistance to reflexivity (Creese 2005).

For me reflexivity is critical self-reflection. This by definition is about self-in-relation and involves the collective theory–practice interplay integral to the Group

Relations notion of experiential learning. Such a process is capable of producing knowledge about internal group dynamics and relatedness that can be practised and by definition improved. Through the collective processing of the 'here and now', the emergent group dynamics, or ebbs and flows of emotional energy, can be processed, thereby containing anxiety about the task of learning. It is in becoming collectively aware of, reflecting on, and theorizing about the emotional and relational issues, both conscious and unconscious, that groups can adapt and transform their behaviours.

Framing the teacher role as one of containment of student anxiety assumes that theory and practice of this process are in tandem. My own experience shows, however, that espoused focus on reflexivity was not matched with theory supportive of it. In actuality the CAVLO design used a model of reflection that does not extend to the creation and practice of internal, often assumptional-level, emotional and relational knowledge encompassed by Group Relations theory. Instead it used Kolb's (1984) experiential learning model, with its emphasis on reflection upon past experience rather than the 'here and now'. In contrast to the Group Relations model Kolb's framework lends itself to theories that are external to the behavioural experience.

As my story will demonstrate, and with the benefit of hindsight, the disconnection between the espoused model of reflexivity and the practice of Kolb's was due to separation, albeit unconscious, within me between reason and emotion. It seems that when much of my emotional energy was expended in resisting reflexivity, there was little remaining for rational recognition of what I was actually doing. While Group Relations aims for a balance between reason and emotion its theoretical basis is able to encompass such emotion–reason imbalances. As Vince (1998) points out, unconscious emotional reactions are most likely to occur in the reflective observational part of Kolb's cycle.

It seems that I, despite my best intentions, unconsciously projected my own fear about reflexivity onto the students. I did this by increasingly focusing in my design and moderation the need for this type of reflection. A concurrent emphasis upon Kolb's model paradoxically ensured that the student group reflection, like my own, would be unable to capture the internal 'here and now' dynamics between myself in relation to them and them in relation to one another. Rather student group reflection would consequently be limited to reflection on past or asynchronous interaction, external to, and distanced from, the 'here and now' teacher–student group inter–relationship. It seems as if by operating largely from Kolb's asynchronous feedback on students' anxiety about reflection, I was then able to deny my own.

As I became more anxious this was reflected in my on-line design and moderation and it in turn impacted upon my students. Over time our collective resistance to reflexivity intensified as did our simultaneous inability to think. As I became more aware of the students' reactions to meaningful reflection, perhaps as a deflection, my denial and projection of both parts deepened. The students similarly followed suit. When the maintenance of our collective resistance became too emotionally exhausting, as it surely will, the defences eventually collapsed with neither party attempting any type of reflection or critical use of theory.

My story embodies the problem of splitting parts that are integral. The divide between reason and emotion can, as the case of my CAVLO design demonstrates, have the unfortunate tendency for idealization of one and a concomitant denigration of the other (Krantz and Gilmore 1990). Our behaviours then end up oscillating between defensiveness and non-defensiveness. It is those parts that we might not be able to bear or contain, that we may find it easier to deny or project onto others. Krantz and Gilmore (1990) have showed how these defences can operate at the organizational, societal, and even global level.

My story also highlights the enormity of the challenge relationally and emotionally of actually bringing theory and practice, in critical experiential design, even 'well-enough' together to use Winnicott's (1971) term. We might recognize intellectually the importance of such a balance, which is possibly the greatest challenge for managers and management educators today. Krantz and Gilmore (1990) call this a paradox of the New Order. We may in fact have underestimated the difficulties for us, and our students in partnership, of actually being reflexive. Such are the layers of anxiety involved in learning, in groups and group learning, and organizational life, let alone innovative experiential on-line design, that the containment of ours and our students' anxiety may be a charge that initially is too great for some if not most educators.

The story does however have a happier ending, with the moral being that in this case, critical experiential design can, after much 'struggle', produce the transformational organizational learning it promises. Eventually my increasing denial of anxiety and its projection onto students accelerated into what Maiteny (2000) calls 'creative regression to dependence'. No longer able to bear the increasingly unsettling feeling that something was severely amiss, I started to be receptive to the help and feedback offered by a peer. The sharing of reflexive space acted as sufficient anxiety container for me to reanalyse my research data. Hence I came to the recognition that the problem was not just the students' anxiety, as I had reported earlier (Creese 2003). Students' anxiety was not separate from mine as I suggested at the time. Rather the ability for students to be reflexive is in part related to me and my role as on-line teacher. I was forced to at last begin to acknowledge the emotional learning relationship or partnership with students that had hitherto remained hidden from my conscious awareness.

So it is with the help of another, and through the nature of the virtual teaching environment, that I am learning to take up my teacher role as anxiety container. It is through appreciating my students' behaviour—and in particular their emotional responses to such a process of collective scrutiny in the 'here and now'—that I eventually learnt about mine—in parallel.

The chapter ends with a description of some of the subsequent changes in the CAVLO design, and my facilitation within it, that have assisted transformational learning also in students. It seems once I was able to practise reflexivity so were students. In this way the theory–practice interplay is based on a connection, rather than a separation, between our collective reason and emotions. Such a separation is comparable to the positivist phenomenology divide that Kolb's (1984) traditional experiential model of learning seems to embrace (Vince 1998). Before illustrating the story of this assisted experiential journey I outline some background to the dynamics of the collective learning experience.

BACKGROUND TO MY SPLIT BETWEEN REASON AND EMOTION

Before teaching Organization Behaviour (OB), I worked in the performing arts where I was promoted from the practice of the art to its management. I was faced as a manager, within a context of ongoing and silent revolution against perceived rationalization and privatization of the public sector, with the challenge of no longer being required to be creative but to be rational. The split I identified in performing arts organizations (Creese 1998) is comparable with the emotion–reason divide that I explore here. My introduction to experiential management education, which enabled such discovery, was not within an MBA, but serendipitously, in a postgraduate management course in OB run along the lines of Group Relations. In contrast to the ivory towers in which I had originally studied 'pure' academic concepts, largely separated from the real and, by implication, dirty world, the course was in a working man's university of technology. Such are the paradoxical challenges it seems for managers of all organizations of the New Order including universities and management schools within them.

My resistance to the emotional and relational aspects of learning can be seen in my defensive flight (Bion 1961) from both this university and research area. I can only now acknowledge fully that my entrée into on-line education at my current university enabled my continued defence against the Group Relations theory that might implicate me emotionally and relationally.

I could now add to this defence by aligning with my new university's own emotional investment in flexible delivery. Whereas improvement in student learning was espoused as the real concern, in practice the university seemed to be preoccupied with its growing financial difficulties. These were in part due to the need to offset nearly 50 per cent reduction in government funding. At some level the university wanted to believe that having a Strategic Flagship, such as the on-line Bachelor of Commerce (B.Com.), of which OB was a first-year core subject, would somehow magically (Krantz and Gilmore 1990) solve all their problems. Both the organization and I can be seen to be similarly operating defensively rather than actually facing painful realities. For the university the belief seemed to be that not only would the quality of education be improved, but the programme could be flexibly delivered to multiple contexts. My ongoing process of cyclical design changes seemed to be based on an assumption that these in themselves would be able to address the fundamental issues.

The university's belief in on-line education has subsequently proved to be based, however, on insufficient consideration of what on-line learning actually entails. The reality is that, due to the resource intensity of on-line design, teaching hours necessarily must increase rather than decrease if Laurillard's (1993) conversational framework is to be realized.

It is in this context that I adapted Tyson's CALO design for on-line teaching. I simultaneously emphasized the process parts of the Group Relations approach while disregarding, or at least putting into shadow, its theoretical underpinnings. This *pre-existing separation between reason and emotion* is the first stage in the story of *increasing split between reason and emotion* before the foreshadowed *escalation of the split between reason and emotion* mirrored by the students.

To tell the story that now follows I use these stages of the intensification of our parallel defences against reflexivity. The final stage of *my regression to creative dependence and good-enough maintenance of the tension between reason and emotion* culminates in the student learning now possible within the CAVLO.

It should be noted that the CAVLOs were subdivided into groups of four or five. This is because of the communication difficulties of keeping track of multiple randomly typed synchronous entries. Asynchronous organizational-level announcements, comprising discussion boards and e-mails, however, were retained and managed accordingly. The virtual groups were allocated dedicated group spaces within the Classroom or organizational shell, which contain devices making up CMC, namely chatroom, discussion board, file exchange, and e-mail facilities. To distinguish between synchronous and asynchronous communication in the extracts from the group electronic communications, I have identified virtual chat with date, time, and message indented and threaded discussion with date and message only indented.

Pre-Existing Separation between Reason and Emotion

When team teaching the CALO with Tyson I had been unaware of a shared gap between our theory and practice. We espoused the CALO's primary task as that of a Group Relations focus on 'becoming aware of the here and now'. Our shared preoccupation with the surfacing of others' unconscious assumptions enabled us to remove ourselves from any connection we might have to the Group Relations theory. This was informed by an unconscious fear of what might be revealed about us. For example the theory used to justify the CALO model was not from Group Relations, but rather the fields of adult, self-directed learning. Integral to this more traditional theory was Kolb's model of experiential learning.

Again unknowingly, it was this pre-existing separation between reason and emotion that I extended to the CAVLO. The virtual nature of the setting enabled me first to put the mainstream OB lectures into the on-line ether conveniently removing me from them. I knew that such commercially available lectures, like their text bases, comprised the more traditional OB theories, none of which matched Group Relations theory. However it seemed that it was emotions rather than reason that were my driving force.

In the initial design the primary task of the CAVLO, as with the CALO, was reiterated as becoming aware of the 'here and now'. At this stage however there was no overt design requirement for the more objective kind of reflection possible within Kolb. Busying myself with the design of the group activities, I delegated to a colleague assisting the design team the composition of an introductory on-line lecture. Here the suggestion was that students keep a voluntary individual learning journal on their individual and group learning experiences. Kolb's model was presented as an example of how a student can have an experience, think about it afterwards, and find some theory 'out there' in the weekly topic-by-topic on-line lectures to explain it.

This defence of separating me from theory generally, and a theory of reflexivity in particular, meant that I could deny my own fear of reflexivity by passing it on to my students. Groups like Blue Angels understood clearly from my on-line moderation that my passion was for the reflexive processing of the 'here and now'. During a face-to-face interview Blue Angels, members described this as *having a group experience, looking at how this operates as it happens and using ourselves as means of study.* Milly, chair of the Blue Angels pragmatically articulates this task for the group's first meeting as:

23 July 09: 22: 08 . . . evaluate each team member and how they are perceived within the team, and respond as you see it in our meetings

This is sufficient to raise, albeit unconsciously, group member Stella's fears about reflexivity. The on-line dynamics of Blue Angels outlined now show how Stella is able to pass her fear on to the group, as I seem to have passed mine on to her.

Stella admits that she is

23 July 09: 04: 23 very wary of people who will make personal comments about me in a public forum especially when I think they are not correct. I do not feel safe, I feel vulnerable and I don't enjoy that.

Stella's fear is about the process of reflexivity I have espoused both in my moderation and design. It is her fear that leads to the unceremonious dumping of Chair Milly. It happens like this. At the meeting on 23 July Stella has made it clear that she does not want to reflect. Milly nevertheless at the next meeting echoes me and insists on process feedback. Stella now moves to deflect the group from any attempts the chair makes towards this. Stella does this by butting in and changing the subject continuously. When Milly becomes more adept at stopping Stella's constant interruptions Stella tries another tack and begins doodling on the virtual whiteboard. This is a blank group space above the chat facility. When no one notices her visual doodles Stella draws the words: *we need a new chairman*.

Milly tries initially to ignore this but eventually it becomes too much for her and she screams back at Stella in capitals:

9 Aug. 09: 06: 16 . . . one of the norms of the team was that the chairman would control it and ask questions, . . . BUT YOU DON'T GIVE ME A CHANCE.

Milly now seems to have had enough. She is becoming increasingly isolated in the group and is now clearly in need of the type of containment that, at this stage, I am not yet emotionally able to provide. While being possibly over-responsive to students by being timely and available, it seems that my facilitation has not yet been able to model the provision of the required psychosocial support. In addition the design has not provided theory that equates with Blue Angels' experience or a model of the type of reflection I have nevertheless emphasized. I can rationalize the problem, as I did in my yet-to-be-reflexive diary in 2000:

When involved in the action I get emotionally involved and react defensively and judgmentally. It would be great if I could develop the ability to observe [rationally] as I do [be emotionally, relationally].

The bracketed comments have been added, now that I am able to be reflexive. But at the time, it is as if I was powerless to bridge the gap between my emotions and reason. The morning after Milly is dumped I phone both Milly and Stella to talk for several hours about what I have read in the archive. However, this seems insufficient in the containment of Stella's fear about reflexivity now shared by the group. Milly is absent for the next meeting in which Stella denies that her challenge to Milly is a 'coup', as the other group members describe it. From then on Milly, lacking sufficient support, takes a low profile. By 16 August there is group agreement for

16 Aug.
08: 24: 02 . . . no personal comments . . .
08: 24: 07 . . . no judgements . . .
08: 24: 16 . . . no negative apologies.

It is in this way that student groups like the Blue Angels defend against any type of reflection. So you must ask, how did I respond at the time? It seems to me that the considerable logistics of on-line served sufficiently as 'objective stressors' (Ledford 1985) to cloud the real issue. I continued with the redesign process but the collective separation between reason and emotion, demonstrated by the Blue Angels dynamics, was now only to increase.

THE INCREASING SPLIT BETWEEN REASON AND EMOTION

My immediate concern in the next two designs was with a permanent repetitive strain injury developed while teaching the initial design. While seemingly unable to provide sufficient anxiety containment in our shared struggle with reflexivity, I had, as suggested above, attempted to support the students in my accustomed manner. This was by being over-responsive to students, as implied by the reflexive poem quoted at the beginning of the chapter. It is almost as if an 'unthought known' that something was amiss was propelling me into over-compensatory behaviour.

At the external level I attempted to redress the communication imbalance that resulted from being overly available via CMC twenty-four hours a day, seven days a week. I introduced more intra-student-group interaction and teacher-to-organization-level communication. However, beginning to surface from my unconscious was a realization that there was an issue about anxiety and reflection. Increasing awareness of this problem led to the growing split between reason and emotion as I moved to further remove myself from the possibility that I too might be anxious about reflexivity. I reasoned that I could continue to give students Group Relations type feedback including that about their reflection anxiety. The asynchronous typing of my responses to students, after reading their virtual 'here and now' electronic archives, meant, however, that I could remain separate.

My design reinforced this individual asynchronous feedback both with a requirement for reflection and also the prescription of both its type and content. The increasing emphasis on the Kolb cycle meant that reflection was restricted to external matters and theories that might explain these. The organizational experience was now limited to set group exercises and review questions as outlined by Gibbs's (1994) more traditional learning in teams. The design explicitly interwove each part of Kolb's model into the Gibbs group activities. For example the 'concrete experience' was linked to the exercises and the 'reflective observation' to review questions such as 'What difficulties did the group encounter?'

As an afterthought I added to Gibbs and Kolb what I knew was missing from the design. This was a Process Consultancy Sheet with Group Relations-type trigger questions. However the centrality of the Gibbs exercises and review-type questions, now so inextricably interwoven with Kolb, overshadowed the process sheet in the weekly CAVLO instructions. Groups struggling to complete the schedule of weekly group tasks had therefore little remaining energy for the type of processing that might reveal unconscious emotional and relational issues.

The design had the effect I unconsciously desired, which was denial of an in-creasing separation between my reason and emotion. The summary of the Yay team's dynamics illustrates this. Clarissa has had a long discussion with me about the need for reflexivity. She pushes for this, but on the Yay team's discussion board.

21 May I know I have been harping on about CONFLICT of late but find Liz's point that our team seems to avoid conflict quite interesting.

Clarissa analyses the reasons for their avoidance, a lack of trust and the limitations of on-line communication. She adds a final question:

21 May Can you think for any other possible reasons?

Two members respond but simply echo Clarissa's analysis. She brings up the issue again on 30 May. When no one responds, she suggests a solution with which the group feels comfortable. She suggests that each member post to the discussion board a Kolb reflection about one of the issues flagged in the formative feedback I have given. Clarissa's suggestion is eventually endorsed by Chairman Cliff, but at the last meeting, when it is too late for a group discussion. The group has eventually fulfilled my requirement for reflection and, like me, carefully managed to keep themselves removed from it.

So the Yay team did to one another as I did to them: asynchronous individual reflective feedback on others through typing. The fact of reflection of any kind may appear to be a progression from the first stage when no reflection of any kind occurred. At the time I liked to think so. But given its disembodied nature this type of reflection was more of a regression. The enforced reliance upon Kolb meant the Yay team was restricted to reflection on conscious and rational matters. Given that such feedback was individual it appeared separate from and unrelated to the sender. It was also delivered in a manner where any response was inevitably delayed, again providing distance for both sender and receiver. Students and I seemed now incapable of being emotionally or relationally involved with others. This regression seems now only to intensify.

ESCALATION OF THE SPLIT BETWEEN REASON AND EMOTION

Such impossible repression
With its emotional outbursts
Tired, worn out and down
I am literally eaten up
Simply unable
To re-erect the regime of control

This other extract from my Wednesday, 9 November 2004 journal highlights the eventual learning breakdown that can and did occur in the CAVLO. When so much emotional energy had been expended in our collective defence against reflexivity there was little remaining for learning. The inevitable emotional collapse highlights the importance of the internal support of anxiety containment for both teacher and students. This is especially in critical experiential learning that is also on-line.

As my split between theory and practice deepened, the direction of defensive emotions eventually became too much to bear. Rather I gave in to the student complaint that there seemed never to be enough time for reflection. In the fourth and fifth designs, I radically reduced the weekly group activities to four phases. These comprised team formation/reflection, team building/reflection, team production/reflection, and overall team reflection. Phase two consisted of only four of the Gibbs activities based around team roles, goals and norms, and definition of the team task. While I simultaneously intensified in my facilitation the need for reflection, I countered its possibility by reinforcing theory unrelated to it. Kolb's model was mandatory in specific reflection meetings now required at the end of phases two and four. As evidence of their occurrence electronic archives of these meetings were to be attached to the two reflection reports.

I further removed students and myself from any theory that might be connected to our collective emotional behaviour by also giving in to the student request for a task perceived to be more tangible than that of reflection. A Learning Resource could actually allow students to make a virtual presentation on conflict resolution based on the critique of external traditional OB theories entirely unrelated to their group experience of conflict or reflection about it.

Not only was I seemingly giving in internally but also externally. The requirement for reflection meeting archives was in contrast to the previous one for electronic archives of all interactions. Similarly my constant, possible over- communication with students was now slashed to the requirement of my participation at only one group meeting at the end of phase two. It is almost as if, in a process paralleling my flight from my previous university, I was again in flight from the CAVLO.

The collapse of my emotional energy seemed to coincide with the increase in the number of contexts to which the B.Com. was now being delivered and over which I had design responsibility. I had previously been accustomed to a genuinely collaborative relationship with instructional designers. However, by the fourth and fifth designs the spread of funds meant that there was only time for electronic communication about design changes.

Student groups like Virtual Co-alition now lacked not only my external over-support, but as well the internal anxiety containment mechanisms we both increasingly needed. The following summary of Virtual Co-alition's (VC) own regression to denial of both reflection and theory mirrors my own.

VC held obsessively and defensively onto the belief that attendance was the reason why they were unable to reflect. Lyn, chair of VC, tries in their first meeting on 25 March to get the three group members present to agree to at least

25 Mar. 02: 14: 53 give apologies for non-attendance.

With six members operating from different time zones in Australia it is difficult but not impossible to find a mutually convenient time. Lyn however delays reflection until Thursday as she does

1 Apr. 02: 44: 05 not know if reflection will be very useful with only three of us,

Some members arrive late for the required reflection meeting on 3 April and others leave early, one *for a work/client dinner* (3 Apr. 10:07:00), another to complete his *individual assignment* (3 Apr. 10:12:46). One member's father has *passed away* (3 Apr. 09:30:51). These seem to be legitimate stressors. It is also possible however that the technical logistics of on-line serve to cloud the real issue of a breakdown between emotion and reason.

There is some attempt to set a future norm of having

3 Apr. 09: 52: 03 people log in on time within the first five minutes or risk???

But the group seems reluctant to impose any 'penalties' for non-attendance

Only two male members log on for the meeting on 8 April. By May, the group is resorting to what they think needs to be done. The rest of the semester is spent in continuing to avoid the task of any type of reflection. Occasionally someone mentions that they have not yet reflected. When 90 per cent of the group actually logs on simultaneously Lyn types:

8 May 09: 35: 14 FIVE OF US AT A MEETING!!!! QUICK ALERT THE MEDIA

The use of capitals suggests both the level of desperation about getting people together and the possibility therefore of being able to reflect. Even now Lyn points out that

8 May 09: 19: 51 it is also difficult to reflect upon a meeting when we have never had a meeting where we are all present ... therefore we can only reflection upon certain interactions and relationships within the group.

At the 29 May meeting Lyn mentions that

29 May 09: 20: 09 we will need to do some reflection as well as this the end of both phases for the course ... we may need to schedule another meeting early next week so that we can get everything done.

But the next meeting never happens nor does the required group reflection meeting. Our shared emotional collapse seems now to be complete. So having given up, how did our collective regression lead to bridging the gap between our theory and practice? How is it that I can now contain my own and students' anxiety sufficiently so that together we can learn through collective reflexivity? Let us turn now to the final stage in the story.

My Regression to Creative Dependence and Good Enough Maintenance of the Tension between Reason and Emotion

As suggested above, I eventually began to emerge from working in isolation and to be receptive to the help offered by others. This was after having spent a further year seemingly unable yet to recognize my own anxiety and reiterating my thesis that students' defensiveness was unrelated to me (Creese 2004). Clearly, I had reached a stalemate. I was dismayed that the radical reduction in design to phases had not only produced less quantity but also less quality learning. I was also in disbelief that there seemed to be no sign even of the individual typed asynchronous reflection in the previous weekly design. But at this time I was still unable to offer further rational explanation. It is almost as if I had run out of excuses.

It was the sharing of reflexive space with a colleague, with a Group Relations background similar to mine, that finally enabled me to feel sufficiently emotionally supported to begin to re-examine my findings. Her feedback suggested that the reason that I seemed almost apologetic about my use of Group Relations theory for students might be perhaps that this theory could also apply to me. As I continue to reflect it emerged that disconnection from my own feelings was a defence against being in relation, as the extract from my journal quoted at the beginning of the chapter suggests. Once I was able to recognize 'me' (Klein 1959) emotionally in relation to my students, I could begin to take up my on-line teaching role more fully. This has entailed bringing into balance my theory and practice of reflexivity, a process of constantly maintaining the tension between my tendency to separate emotion from reason.

I trust that the story of my vivid 'struggle' over the years demonstrates the challenge critical experiential on-line design can be not only for some management educators but also for students. This is no matter how good our intentions and within management schools that seem to continue to reinforce individual organizing while espousing the need for collective reflexivity (Reynolds and Vince 2004). As a finale, I share some of the changes in design and on-line facilitation that have helped critical learning through meaningful reflection by students.

BALANCING THE ON-LINE TEACHING ROLE

I have kept the phased approach in keeping with trends in on-line design. Within the constraint of the on-line teaching model within my university, the first two phases give time for students to manage some of the stressors that might otherwise be managed more easily with the addition, for example, of face-to-face orientations. These include the vagaries of enrolment, access to the course site, and acquaintance with and practice of the various types of CMC. Much of the task preparation for example for a virtual meeting can be via asynchronous communication. This is so members can focus their attention on the processing of the 'here and now' within their virtual group meetings. Other issues that might impact on the motivation for, rather than anxiety about, collective reflexivity such as the feeling of isolation need to be identified and constantly managed. As technological breakdown remains a reality there is also ongoing need for contingency plans. This is so that technological problems do not become a convenient excuse.

I have removed the end of phase and overall reflection meetings as they encourage reflection after the event. The required virtual meeting with groups by the end of the first phase allows for facilitation of the processing of the 'here and now' generally in a discussion about definition of the team task. In containing student groups' resistance to reflexivity and modelling for them the processing of inter-and intragroup dynamics I can use the example of my own similar emotional struggle. This helps to highlight how such difficulties can in fact be turned around rather than defended against. Kolb's model has been replaced with Vince's (1998) revision. My modelling of reflexivity is reinforced explicitly in the articulation of the on-line instructions both for reading on screen and to be heard via audio. The learning resource has become a mapping of groups' learning. Demonstration of a group's ability to critically process the 'here and now' is possible also by cutting and pasting from their electronic archives. Examples of previous groups' learning resources can be posted on the web as the current ones are for peer assessment learning and feedback from other groups within the CAVLO.

With my increased emotional robustness it now feels right to expect more of my students. Previously my over-responsiveness, constant availability, and valency for in taking on, rather than containing, students' anxiety may have provided some false sense of security. In Group Relations terms my ability now to hold the task boundaries more strongly in both design and moderation assists on-line student groups to take up their collective authority.

However, not all student groups have deepened their learning as a result of such teacher improvements. Some like Group J continue to take defensive flight (Bion 1961) from the course, first fighting everything from learning, on-line, the course, to other courses and universities. Group J seemed to start with the best of intentions and with my facilitation could begin to process the 'here and now'. However, once I was unable to be present, their collective shared fear of failure after previous negative experiences of tertiary study seemed soon to take over. Group J's subsequent virtual chats regressed to discussion focusing on a shared love of sport. It seems that, constrained by a teaching model that fails to recognize even the equivalent of face-to-face teaching hours, there was little I could do to turn Group J's dynamics around.

In contrast, however are the Global Warriors. This group is made up of equally motivated and hard-working middle managers of considerable experience. Accustomed to balancing, in addition to family, full-time work and part-time study, group members also run their own extremely successful small businesses. They also pride themselves on being able, as at work, to take responsibility for supporting one another, in being reflexive, without the need for a facilitator. Having the requisite organization skills for the effective management of electronic communication assists this. Global Warriors were able immediately to see the benefit of reflexive practice, not only to their virtual group but their own work organizations. They valued the opportunity of a safe space to experiment and learn away from the pressures of work. Many Global Warriors members have reported on subsequent promotions.

Most virtual groups, however, continue to fall somewhere between Group J and Global Warriors. As a first-year course, and with the imposition by the university of an inadequate on-line teaching model, I am now satisfied that CAVLOs are at least introduced to a critical and collective way of operating. As I continue to critique my practice collectively with students, I am now more accepting that what students do with this knowledge is ultimately up to them.

NOTE

I would like to acknowledge friend and colleague Peliwe Mnguni as it is through sharing reflexive space with her that my learning and this chapter were made possible.

REFERENCES

Argyis, C., and Schön, D. A. (1974). *Theory in Practice: Increasing Professional Effectiveness.* San Francisco: Jossey-Bass.

————— (1978). *Organizational Learning: A Theory of Action Perspective.* Reading, Mass.: Addison-Wesley.

Bion, W. R. (1961). *Experiences in Groups.* London: Tavistock.

Cohen, A. R. (1976). 'Beyond Simulation: Treating the Classroom as Organisation', *Teaching of Organizational Behaviour*, 2/1: 13–19.

Creese, E. (1998). 'The Balance of Arts and Management Culture in Performing Arts Organizations'. Unpublished master's thesis, Australian Graduate School of Entrepreneurship.

—— (2001). 'From Dependency towards Self-Direction via Virtual Chat: The Case of One TAFE Class', in G. Kennedy, M. Keppel, C. McNaught, and T. Petrovic (eds.), *Meeting at the Crossroads.* Short Paper Proceedings of the 18th Conference of the Australian Society for Computers in Learning in Tertiary Education. Melbourne: Biomedical Multimedia Unit, the University of Melbourne.

—— (2003). 'Group Dynamics and Learning in an Organization Behaviour Virtual Learning Community: The Case of Six Virtual Peer Learning Teams', *Ultibase*, Nov., http://ultibase.rmit.edu.au/Journal/journal.htm.

—— (2004). 'The Impact of Group Dynamics in an Online Learning Community: A Class as Virtual Learning Organization', *Proceedings of International Conference on Computers in Education* (ICCE2004).

—— (2005). 'The Parallel Processes between Teacher and Students in Tacit Knowledge Production in a Class as Virtual Learning Organisation in Organization Behavior', *International Journal of Knowledge, Culture and Change Management*, 5.

French, R. B. (1997). 'The Teacher as Container of Anxiety: Psychoanalysis and the Role of the Teacher', *Journal of Management Education*, 21/4: 483–95.

—— and Vince, R. (1999). 'Learning, Managing and Organizing: The Continuing Contribution of Group Relations to Management and Organization', in R. French and R. Vince (eds.), *Group Relations, Management and Organisation.* Oxford: Oxford University Press.

Gibbs, G. (1994). *Learning in Teams: A Student Manual.* Oxford: Oxford Centre for Staff Development.

Kemmis, S., and McTaggart, R. (eds.) (1988). *The Action Research Planner.* Geelong, Victoria: Deakin University.

Klein, M. (1959). 'Our Adult World and its Roots in Infancy', *Human Relations*, 12: 291–301.

Kolb, D. A. (1984). *Experiential Learning.* Englewood Cliffs, NJ: Prentice-Hall.

Krantz, J. (1995). 'Anxiety and the New Order', in E. Klein, F. Gablenick, and P. Herr (eds.), *Dynamics of Leadership.* Madison: Psycho-social Press.

—— and Gilmore, T. N. (1990). 'The Splitting of Leadership and Management as a Social Defense', *Human Relations*, 43/2: 183–204.

Laurillard, D. (1993). *Rethinking University Teaching: A Framework for the Effective Use of Educational Technology.* London: Routledge.

Ledford, G. R. (1985). 'Transference and Countertransference in Action Research Relationships', *Consultation*, 4/1: 36–51.

Maiteny, P. (2000). 'The Psychodynamics of Meaning and Action for a Sustainable Future', *Futures*, 32: 339–60.

Reynolds, M. (2000). 'Bright Lights and the Pastoral Idyll: Ideas of Community Underlying Management Education Methodologies', *Management Learning*, 31/1: 67–81.

Reynolds, M., and Vince, R. (eds.) (2004). *Organizing Reflection*. Aldershot: Ashgate.

Tyson, T. (1999). *CALO—the Class as a Learning Organisation: The CAO model Revisited and Revitalised*. Human Resource Management/Organisation Behaviour, Working Paper Series, School of Business, Swinburne University of Technology, Melbourne.

Vince, R. (1998). 'Behind and Beyond Kolb's Learning Cycle', *Journal of Management Learning*, 22/3: 304–19.

Winnicott, D. W. (1971). *Playing and Reality*. London: Penguin.

CHAPTER 17

INTEGRATING EXPERIENTIAL LEARNING THROUGH 'LIVE' PROJECTS

A PSYCHODYNAMIC ACCOUNT

PAULA HYDE

INTRODUCTION

RECENT critiques of management education programmes have suggested that they are failing to develop appropriate technical and personal skills in their graduates, thus failing to prepare them for organizational life (Mintzberg 2004; Gabriel 2005; Whitley 1984). It has been suggested that radical changes are needed to programme content and modes of delivery to address these criticisms and to better prepare management graduates of the future. Whilst this view is not held universally, several writers have suggested means by which students may be better prepared. They have advocated reassessment of MBA curricula and the establishment of closer links with businesses (Mintzberg 2004). Such proposals require students to encounter and work with organizations as part of an experiential programme of study. Educators have also been challenged to encourage students to integrate theory and practice without succumbing to uncritical absorption of managerialist values (Burgoyne and Reynolds 1997).

In this chapter, one means of engaging students in experiential work with organizations is explored. 'Live' projects offer students the opportunity for involvement with organizations as an integral and experiential part of their management education. Some of the challenges of running this type of project are discussed. Live projects form part of a management programme involving a series of projects sponsored by, and taking place within, real organizations, and offering the opportunity to incorporate previous learning in future project experiences. Students take increasing responsibility for acquisition and organization of project groups and project management over the course of the programme. Rather than representing an innovation in management education this approach has been used over many years in an attempt to integrate experiential features into the programme as a whole (Rickards, Hyde, and Papamichail 2005).

The longevity of the programme (over forty years) offers the opportunity to illuminate the relationship between 'live' projects and experiential learning, whilst recognizing the continuing tensions and problems inherent in such pedagogic systems. In the past, collaboration across academic disciplines within the business school at Manchester has been an important component in the development of the approach. However, in recent years, the business school has adopted a more traditional subject-based approach both to organizing academics and to programme content. Organizational structures such as these are common to universities and their effect upon access to experience for students and tutors is considered here using psychodynamic ideas about containment of anxiety. Whilst this chapter will focus on the use of live projects in management education, it will conclude by exploring the challenges involved in attempting to integrate experiential approaches to management education in university settings in order that students might move between 'not knowing', 'knowing', and 'established knowledge' as part of their experience of learning.

EXPERIENTIAL LEARNING IN MANAGEMENT EDUCATION

The possibility of accounting for what is learnt during an 'experiential event' remains elusive. Moreover the simple reality of failing to learn from experience is a common personal phenomenon. Kolb perhaps came closest to simplifying the cyclical and iterative process of experiential learning for individuals, groups, and organizations (Kolb 1985). He described a process that begins with an experience occurring in a planned or accidental way. The capacity to observe and reflect upon the experience is required, followed by the ability to theorize including both the application of concepts to the phenomena and being able to construct theories that suggest how specific or generalizable the theories are. Finally, there is a further process of experimentation whereby the practical implications of such learning are explored. This makes experience and action critical components in learning from experience (Stein 2004).

Whilst Kolb's learning cycle is frequently presented to students as a means of learning and whilst universities ought to be able to offer a potential site for learning from experience, the process is not simple. Susan Long suggests that access to experience in universities is authorized and enacted or, indeed, made impossible through various structures and processes experienced by teachers and learners alike;

> the authorization of experience by the institution occurs predominantly through its organization—that is through the ways in which boundaries are created for work or, conversely, for non-work. The structure and dynamics of the institution give out strong messages to members, both at conscious and unconscious levels about what to think, feel and express. (Long 2004: 107)

University organization and structures commonly create boundaries around subject areas as well as around specialist courses units. Such conscious boundaries are created for task performance. These boundaries can lead to abuses of power, for example, where one subject claims a dominant position on a generalist course. The provision of boundaries, then, as containers for experience, may preclude or enable learning to take place, by enabling containment of anxiety to the extent that one may live in an experience and learn from it (Thomas 1982).

There are many accounts of diverse approaches to experiential learning in preparing management students for organizational life (see Wankel and DeFillipi 2005), many of which have some grounding in the group relations approach (see Gould, Stapley, and Stein 2004). Yiannis Gabriel (2005) described an innovative experiential leadership programme where participants were provided with the opportunity to experience leading their fellow group members. The programme was designed to enable the students to experience, reflect upon, theorize about, and experiment with their leadership experiences. Far from claiming this approach produced leaders, he illustrated the many ways participants manoeuvred themselves into acting as followers. He concluded that MBA programmes are fundamentally flawed as they continue to educate followers rather than leaders. In coming to this depressing, but convincing, conclusion he suggested that leadership students seek simple solutions, 'the vibrant vision, the motivating mission, the merger, the techno-fix, the new appointment and so on' (p. 159), whereas, in reality, problems may only be overcome by multifaceted, unpredictable, and highly varied solutions.

Furthermore, he acknowledged that some problems defy resolution through any device. It is at these moments that leaders are called upon to be able to contain their uncertainty and doubt through a capacity that has been termed, by the poet John Keats, 'negative capability': where a person is capable of experiencing 'uncertainties, mysteries, doubts, without any irritable reaching after fact and reason' (H. F. Bartlett in Gabriel 2005: 160).

It is this capacity for containment of anxiety in the face of uncertainty that is an important feature of experiential learning. Anxiety can arise from conflicts at an unconscious level as well as conflicts generated by the work task itself. Such anxiety can lead to a range of psychological defences aimed primarily at reducing anxiety and possibly at reducing uncertainty, the paradox of creativity being that the mind that can think about unbound experiences is also the mind that defends against them (Long 2004). Such defences have been described elsewhere and include rationalization, regression to more childlike behaviours, projection, and displacement (Klein et al. 1970). Mark Stein described his experiences of teaching a group of MBA students and illustrated how his own responses to anxiety influenced the experiences and reactions of the student group. As he sought to reflect upon and revisit events, he experimented with different interpretations and ideas about their meaning, offering him alternative means of dealing with them. He detailed the interdependencies of learners and facilitator as each projected their anxieties onto the other. His account illustrates how both learner and facilitator need to be actively engaged in thinking about their experiences to enable learning from experience. This interdependency between learner and facilitator is another important feature of experiential learning (Stein 2004).

Not only is experiential learning influenced by emotions, but it is also influenced by social phenomena. Stein also recognized how the content of the work itself may generate anxiety leading to particular group or organizational defences. Bion's work with groups explored task and fantasy as features of group life (Bion 1968). According to Bion, groups engage in what he called work group mode for only a minority of the time where they deal with work issues in realistic manner. He observed the tendency of groups to be driven by unrecognized emotionally powerful fantasies, which he referred to as basic assumptions. Specifically he identified three forms of basic assumption: dependency; fight-flight; and pairing. Each assumption relates to a fantasy state, which affects group function through the formation of unhelpful coalitions, member–member, or leader–group dynamics, which perpetuate the fantasy that some future resolution will overcome the unpleasantnesses of the present. Similar defensive processes have been described in organizations (Hyde and Thomas 2002; Menzies 1970). These individual defences, and basic assumptions in groups, enable participants to avoid experiencing the pain of uncertainty and to avoid thinking, thus to prevent learning. In learning from experience, both participants and learners move between task and fantasy. In fact, frenzied activity around a task may become a defence in itself that precludes the opportunity to think or reflect upon, and learn from, experience (Gabriel 2005).

Moreover, universities generate fantasies of their own. Freud named education as one of the impossible professions and this has been explained as follows;

> While seeming to be a place of learning where new knowledge could be generated and genuine questioning encouraged, [Freud] believed that the university was primarily a cover... for the master/slave discourse. The assumption in this discourse is that the master is all-powerful and makes demands of the slave who must carry them out. The master's pleasure is gained through the labour of the slave...
>
> ... In the university, the master (authority) is in a particular position of power. The position is what Lacan (1992) terms 'the subject supposed-to-know'. The fantasy behind this position contains the assumptions that (1) knowledge is a commodity, (2) there is a hierarchy of those who have increasing amounts of it, (3) the highest authority has ultimate knowledge, and, (4) the existence of such an authority is possible now or in the future. Such a fantasy will not only lead to grandiosity and the possibility of abuse of power or its counterpart, rebelliousness and the rebuke of authority, but it also makes the avowed task of the university indeed impossible. (Long 2004: 116)

The binding of knowledge into units or blocks makes dependent subjects of students. Packaging and marketing and premium pricing of MBA programmes may make students and teachers on these programmes more, rather than less, susceptible to the grandiose fantasy that conceives of knowledge as a commodity for consumption. The alternative, knowing, calls on intuition and is less easily packaged or commodified. Learning involves establishing knowledge through experiences of knowing and vice versa.

LIVE PROJECTS AS PART OF A MANAGEMENT PROGRAMME

The MBA programme at Manchester Business School originated over forty years ago with the ambitious intention of providing a radically different approach to management education. The intention was to sustain only loose divisions between subject areas with most project work, undertaken by students, crossing interdisciplinary boundaries. The design decision was to cluster learning experiences around multidisciplinary projects. Whilst the business school was unable to sustain such a loose structure, and academics grouped themselves under disciplinary banners, some elements of the approach remain. One such element is the inclusion of live projects in the MBA programme supported by tutors from a range of disciplinary backgrounds.

The programme incorporates subject-based lectures alongside group projects in organizational settings. Students are involved in a series of group projects. Each of these projects is sponsored by different organizations and requires the student groups to explore a particular area of interest or aspiration of the organization, within a prescribed time period. Each student group has access to a tutor from the business school but may draw on others as required. The term 'live' refers to the propensity of these areas of interest (projects) to be experienced as organic and changing, because they relate to current organizational situations, which are likely to evolve during the course of a project. Moreover, the sponsor and others in the organization have varying expectations of the project that alter over time. Groups of students work on a project and seek to understand and manage a range of competing expectations to produce a report and/or presentation that satisfies a range of interests, including their own. Uncertainty is inherent in these projects as outcomes are largely undefined and expectations vary between student, tutors, sponsors, and examiners.

Rather than a single 'one-off' event, students are involved in an iterative process of learning whereby they play an increasing part in negotiating their learning experiences as they progress through the course. They are supported initially with taught courses, which may be subject-specific. They move towards less taught courses and more live project group work, supported by in-house opportunities to review their learning. These in-house opportunities to review learning include both large group reviews and tutorial sessions where the focus of attention includes the opportunity to review project group processes as well as project content and development. The process of increasing autonomy for project teams is achieved by being given projects acquired by the business school, initially, and by their seeking out and bidding for specific projects later in the programme. The projects themselves come from a range of organizations, for example, IT, pharmaceutical, consulting, and public sector organizations. These one-off projects occasionally lead to future project work. One example of the regenerating effect of these types of projects took place at UNESCO (UK region). UNESCO operated across the world to find ways of transferring knowledge aimed at economic development from developed countries. Regional centres faced enormous challenges in translating local knowledge for global transfer. Three MBA project groups worked on this problem with different regions in 2003 for a 'business and environment' project. By 2004, the project was extended to a global challenge involving twenty groups of MBA students.

The 'live' nature of projects means that one project may lead directly to future projects and business developments. The development of the Business School Incubator in 2002 was a direct outcome of an internally generated 'live' project. A group of MBA students opted to find their own project and conduct it as a summer elective. They took responsibility for finding a sponsor (the head of school) whom they convinced of the benefits that would accrue from such an incubator. They also negotiated terms of reference for the project with their sponsor, conducted an investigation through direct interviews at existing incubators nationally and internationally, and reported their findings, which included evidence for the financial viability as well as the academic rationale for the incubator. As a direct result, an externally funded incubator was established, with the added objective of providing learning experiences within future MBA programmes. Moreover, members of the original project team act as operational executives. Financial support comes from several international financial and professional sponsors. New businesses are being created and supported, particularly through (yet more) 'live' project teams. Several incubator electives are now offered within the MBA, giving a focus for those interested in entrepreneurial careers, and new businesses supported by the incubator have been developed (Rickards, Hyde, and Papamichail 2005).

As the MBA programme progresses projects become less bounded and offer greater scope for individual and project team negotiation as seen in the incubator example above. Later in the programme students form their own groups, whereas these groups are given in the early projects. In later projects students are involved in a competitive process bidding for projects and negotiating the terms and scope of the project brief. Opportunities for reflexivity are high in the MBA programme as students take part in events aimed at allowing personal and reflective learning from the early stages. Experiential features of the programme are introduced from the beginning of the programme and students are encouraged to acknowledge high levels of knowledge uncertainty as live project work ensures frequent opportunities for unintended and personal learning. Uncertainty arises from the fact that projects are not designed with one answer in mind. Rather, they present project groups with problems to explore and to which they may suggest potential approaches. This approach generates high levels of creativity and anxiety (Rickards, Hyde, and Papamichail 2005).

These live projects reveal recurring themes, which challenge those involved. These include encountering issues around personal and team development, leadership, reflexivity, and the management of ambiguity. The content uniqueness of projects as 'living cases' has provided a context for these themes to be surfaced, explored, and addressed. This is not to suggest that recurrent tensions are removed, rather they resurface with familiar and timely regularity for re-inspection and serve to emphasize the emotional effort required to sustain a dynamic approach to student learning. Indeed, many, including those involved with this programme, would argue that this sort of approach cannot be sustained over many iterations of the programme without consideration, reflection, and learning from each experience for the facilitators themselves. It has been recognized that experiential learning of facilitators themselves is an important facet of experiential learning programmes. Except for a small number of examples such as those included at the start of the chapter, this appears to be an unrecognized feature in MBA programmes. Where tutors act as subject-supposed-to-know, they may be isolated within their own disciplinary boundaries and their own access to experiential learning may reduce. Opportunities for learning arise from each iteration of the project and offer familiarity that sometimes precludes learning from experience.

EXPERIENTIAL LEARNING
THROUGH LIVE PROJECTS

Each iteration of a live project brings with it new challenges for students and tutors alike. These new circumstances can generate a range of familiar themes including tensions within the project group, tensions between students and tutors, and confusion about the nature of a 'live' project. Students are encouraged to explore these tensions whilst recognizing the overall uncertainty of their project task. These tensions arise from conflicts with 'oneself, with the "other", with authority, with ideas, and with nature itself' (Lazar 2004: 139). These conflicts give rise to anxiety, defences, and basic assumptions.

Project Group Processes

The ability of tutors and participants to experience uncertainty, mystery, and doubt and contain their anxiety, their 'negative capability', is an important aspect of the live project. Participants look to tutors for solutions, for clues as to what they should do, or for the answers they suspect are being withheld from them. The lack of a clear answer, similar to one that may be attained from a case study approach, leaves the students with some level of uncertainty around what is expected of them. Additionally, they may be uncertain about what help they can expect from their tutors and their host business. The resultant anxieties occasionally spill over into group meetings with the tutors. Recently there have been increasing numbers of staff ambivalent or hostile to group projects. The staff group as a whole have grown increasingly fragmented along subject specialisms, which mitigate against the generalist role of project tutor. Moreover, experiential learning means different things to different people. Student anxieties have not always been contained or surfaced. Instead some members of faculty have absorbed the anxiety and colluded with the group in the search for the 'right' answer. This has sometimes led to frustrations with the approach itself and to a push for more 'concrete' student assignments. There is rarely a call to move away from the 'live' element of projects, i.e. working with businesses on current problems; rather, the call is for tighter definitions, specifications, or more written documentation about what is expected from whom. Notwithstanding these tensions, students who have completed the MBA programme often record the live projects as one of the most memorable and influential aspects of the programme (Rickards, Hyde, and Papamichail 2005).

Each project group seeks to find a way to work to complete their task, notwith-standing the likelihood of engaging in counterproductive behaviours relating to basic assumptions driven by the anxiety of the uncertainty of the task. To further complicate matters each project team is highly international, with students origi-nating from more than thirty-four countries in a cohort of around eighty students. These differences within the team can become the focus of attention and a source of destructive rather than creative activity. At this point, group members may seek the help of a tutor in confirming the view that the group is hampered by the language difficulties or characteristics of particular members. The interdependence of facilitator and learner is crucial here as such pleas can feed into the anxieties of the tutor who may start to doubt the ability of the group to succeed and seek to intervene. This in turn can confirm anxieties in the group that they may not be able to succeed. Similar attempts may be made to gain special consideration for extraordinary individual efforts or for punishment of a lazy individual. On the whole, tutors seek to explore with the group the nature of the problem they face without seeking to intervene on their behalf. The intention would be to enable individuals to think about their experiences in order that they may return to the task of the group. Constructive dynamics of international teams have been described as including involvement of all team members, developing bridges to support issues of language, cross-cultural curiosity, and developing a diversity of ideas. On the other hand destructive processes are characterized by a dependence on dominant groups or cultures, avoidance of anxiety, under- or overplaying language difficulty, task rather than learning focus, use and misuse of communications technology (Heimer and Vince 1998). These dynamics are played out with each iteration of a live project.

Heimer and Vince went on to argue that sustainable learning is only possible by working through such tensions. They argue that it is those very tensions and difficulties that are essential to effective experiential learning as the material that inspires learning and change. Learning becomes sustainable where students are able to question and challenge evolving norms and see and reflect on group processes as they emerge. Project groups learn to sustain uncertainty created through the interaction of different cultures and the task itself. This sustainable learning is the goal, but not always the outcome, of a live project.

The Task Itself: Consultancy or Experiential Learning

Live projects are easily mistaken for consultancy projects. Business schools have existed symbiotically with management consultancy firms, with a proportion of MBA participants undertaking the course as a direct route into consulting. Consultant business models pass in an interactive fashion from business schools to consulting firms and vice versa. Indeed, arguments have been made for the benefits of approaching business projects in order to develop consulting skills

(Clifford and Hillar Farran 2004). There are, however, tensions between projects regarded primarily as consultant-type experiences and those more concerned with broader aspects of personal development, particularly where students are encouraged not to accept uncritically managerialist approaches (Burgoyne and Reynolds 1997). The consultant–client relationship is often transactional and is generally exercised around pre-established and negotiated parameters. This is distinct from live projects wherein the relationship is between project team and project sponsor rather than a client. Here learning is openly accepted as a central part of the process: the sponsor learns through fresh insights into their interests; the project teams experience a range of knowledge, skills, and behavioural elements both directly and indirectly. The language used in marketing brochures for students and sponsors, as well as administrative arrangements for project acquisition and support, influence perceptions of projects as experiential or consultancy in nature.

Absorption in a consultancy project is one possible avenue for tutors and students alike. The distinction between consultancy and live projects is far from clear-cut and some projects are closer to traditional consulting arrangements: indeed, some staff are themselves more disposed to encourage the development of consulting skills. Experiences are mediated through relationships between the sponsor, the team, and the tutors. Arrangements are not made solely around a financial contract, but include the additional recognition of a learning contract. Sponsors contribute financially in recognition of obligations and costs incurred by participants whilst achieving the mutually agreed objectives of the project. Furthermore, the live project is influenced by the preferences of the faculty team, the language they use, and the manner in which a specific project develops over time.

Conflict between consultancy approaches and experiential learning reflects the tensions inherent within live projects and the wider business school and the manner in which diverse views jostle for a negotiated acceptance. Attempts to integrate live projects as part of a wider programme of management education offer one example of experiential learning in a university context.

EXPERIENTIAL LEARNING AS AN INTEGRAL FEATURE OF MANAGEMENT EDUCATION PROGRAMMES

Whilst MBA programmes have proliferated globally, three types of provision can be identified (Rickards, Hyde, and Papamichail 2005). These distinctions do not define MBA programmes as discrete entities, they may be better understood as points in a continuum that range from highly controlled taught programmes with low levels of uncertainty for students and teachers, through to loosely bounded programmes with high levels of uncertainty and opportunities for experiential learning for participants and facilitators alike. As such, these distinctions can be useful in thinking about learning opportunities provided to participants on management education programmes. Table 17.1 shows some differentiating features of MBA programmes.

The 'lecture-centred' MBA involves students in specialist courses which are taught and assessed by traditional means. Lectures provide a coherent knowledge base and levels of uncertainty are bounded. Scope for creativity lies in the presentational approach of the teacher, and opportunities for student reflection and personal learning have less emphasis. In contrast, 'project-added' MBA programmes build on established courses by providing projects that allow for some personal and experiential learning. These programmes increase the possibility for uncertainty, unintended outcomes, and creativity in the course of completing a project task. The final category could be called experiential programmes. These programmes take participants through a series of projects, whereby the level of external control and specification of projects can be reduced over time. Subject area boundaries are loosely defined in relation to project work and facilitators and participants are faced with uncertainty and novelty in each project experience and the anxieties these

Table 17.1 Comparative features of MBA programmes

Dimension	Lecture-centred MBAs	Project-added MBAs	Experiential MBAs
Delivery style	Controlled and bounded delivery of established knowledge categories (marketing, finance, operations management, etc.)	Controlled and bounded projects designed to supplement established course lecture categories, while permitting some personal and experiential learning	Level of external control and boundedness of projects moderated and increased over the course of the MBA. Subject area boundaries loosely defined in relation to project work
Mode of assessment	Well-established assessment procedures permitting external quality control and examination	Each project may present challenges and novelty to students and tutors. Assessment of project outputs possible with well-codified pedagogic interventions	Facilitators have to approach the novelties within each project as presenting challenges and opportunities to students and facilitators

(cont.)

Table 17.1 (continued)

Dimension	Lecture-centred MBAs	Project-added MBAs	Experiential MBAs
Reflexivity	Personal and reflective learning has less emphasis	Personal and reflective learning possible under controlled conditions	Personal and reflective learning possible, with greater scope for personal experiences, challenges, and setbacks
Experiential features	Psychologically safe learning zone within expectations of students and faculty	Experiential learning boundaries can be managed to permit some uncertainties, but avoid over-threatening challenges (Moderate scope for developmental 'stretching')	Challenges and setbacks require facilitated negotiation, so that they lead to qualitatively different experiential learning. The learning model permits reflective critique of group processes and anxieties
Degree of knowledge uncertainty	Lectures provide a coherent and convincing knowledge base	Projects provide realistic experiences equipping MBAs for industrial work as a unitary culture (shared goals etc.), and less frequently as a negotiable pluralism	Projects reveal the 'messiness' of pluralistic and fragmented group cultures, which sometimes are susceptible to negotiable outcomes
Organization of learning opportunities	Personal and unintended learning opportunities few	Personal and unintended learning opportunities possible	Personal and unintended learning opportunities frequent
Scope for creativity	Presentational approach of teacher	Presentational approach of teams; some scope for exceptional insights in content	As for other project-based approaches, plus additional opportunities for resilient and creative responses to unanticipated challenges
Knowledge management	Knowledge management structures mostly codified	Knowledge management structures partly codified (with scope for some integration of learning)	Knowledge management structures integral to the method ensuring recurrent developmental features

Source: Adapted from Rickards, Hyde, and Papamichail 2005.

experiences generate. There are increased opportunities for personal and reflective learning and for understanding and working with group processes. Such projects reveal the messiness of group work and allow for creative responses to unanticipated challenges.

Whilst the MBA programme at Manchester may have once claimed to be an experiential MBA (see Table 17.1), this was probably never fully realized. The programme structure and design have the features of a project added programme with live projects, at times, more closely resembling consultancy projects. These projects do however incorporate features of experiential learning in their provision of an experience which involves planned and unpredicted features, and students are encouraged to expect accidental opportunities to learn. The extent to which students are able to observe and reflect on their experiences varies between groups and between group members and tutors. There are a range of familiar behaviours exhibited by students and tutors during live projects, which can include classic group processes of fight-flight, dependency, or pairing. In reality, boundaries between subject area groups in the Business School are more clearly delineated than hitherto, resulting in perhaps a more conservative-looking department at some distance from its radical roots.

Whilst there are many examples of experiential events for management students, incorporation of such events into a programme of management education also requires tutors to learn from experience. Susan Long suggests that universities authorize the defence of 'isolation' (2004: 131) where learning from experience that is available to students is less available to tutors as staff are 'supposed-to-know'. Theoretical differences act as containers for anxieties and isolate the problem of competition between staff. The task of the university—to bind knowing into knowledge and commodify learning—means that knowledge is packaged into small parcels isolated from other units/courses/sessions and few courses integrate knowing across subjects. Whilst the tutors lack access to their own experience, students lose the ability to relate to the wider institution, its authority, and its boundaries. This leads to the development of specialist graduates. It is perhaps the generalists' ability to work across disciplinary boundaries that management graduates are lacking. It could also be that the aspiration towards an idealized future where graduates are capable and organizational life is simple, unproblematic, and easily managed is also a fantasy.

In order to enable experiential learning as a feature of the institutional life of the university, Long suggests three factors for consideration;

1. The creation of times and spaces for reflection where members may seriously look inward to their own inner experience, in connection to task and role. Some of these spaces should allow for the public sharing of reflections.
2. The search for ways to understand how current structures and practices make some experiences legitimate and not others. This can be done in everyday

practice through testing out taken for granted ideas, values, attitudes, and behaviours. It requires the courage of everyone to face the taken-for-granted views that come with power, position, and hierarchy, to question one's own assumptions about the ones-supposed-to-know, or the part of oneself supposed-to-know.

3. Understanding that this can only be achieved if it is legitimated within the institution not simply in rhetoric, but in practice. Without such authorization, learning from experience becomes isolated and unavailable to others—and often to the subject whose experience it is. (Long 2004: 134–5)

These suggestions apply to all staff and students, including administrators and others, and illustrate the enormity of the task, should one seek to incorporate experiential learning as a central feature of management education programmes.

Conclusions

This account of the use of live projects within a wider management education programme has shown that these projects offer opportunities for experiential learning that remain memorable to students over long time periods. Students are able to experience a range of project group processes (taking account of task and fantasy) that allow for the development of negative capability, including living with the experience of not knowing. They are able to work with 'not knowing', 'knowing', and 'establishing knowledge' and to move between these states. The tutors are as much a part of these processes and movements between knowledge states as the student group. Live projects run the risk of being transformed into consultancy projects as students and tutors seek to reduce uncertainties inherent in the projects.

One further critical issue is that the type of learning system described represents a moving target, ever striving to address possibilities for self-initiated change and development. There are necessary challenges in sustaining a dynamic approach to management education. Such approaches to learning generate tensions between faculty and staff and can conflate sponsor–client relationships. Furthermore, they require the continuous emotional engagement of participants to live with uncertainties and anxieties arising from the negotiated nature of live projects. Such tensions concern personal and team development, leadership, reflexivity, and the management of ambiguity. Live projects allow for the possibility of surfacing, exploring, and resolving conflicts. Rather than being removed, these conflicts recur, in novel forms, upon the advent of each new live project, re-emphasizing the emotional engagement required to sustain the approach.

Live projects cannot be separated from the programmes within which they occur, nor from wider university structures. The susceptibility of universities to the defence of isolation, built on assumptions of commodified knowledge consumption, acts against the possibility of experiential learning except as isolated pockets of student experience. Tutors find themselves in the position of those 'supposed-to-know', which limits their opportunities for learning from experience still further. Integrating experiential learning into management education programmes presents a challenging task that would require system-wide adaptation to achieve and sustain. By creating opportunities for experiential learning, management education programmes may be able to offer the student the opportunity to move between not knowing, knowing, and established knowledge and to learn from their experiences. Without the opportunity for experiential learning of some sort, management education programmes will continue to produce students unprepared for the realities of organizational life.

REFERENCES

Bion, W. R. (1968). *Experience in Groups*. London: Tavistock (repr. London: Routledge, 1989).

Burgoyne, J., and Reynolds, M. (1997). *Management Learning: Integrating Perspectives in Theory and Practice*. London: Sage.

Clifford, P., and Hillar Farran, J. (2004). *Wharton's Global Consulting Practicum*. New Orleans: Academy of Management Conference Procedings.

Gabriel, Y. (2005). 'MBA and the Education of Leaders: The New Playing Fields of Eton', *Leadership*, 1/2: 147–61.

Gould, L. J., Stapley, L. F., and Stein, M. (2004). *Experiential Learning in Organizations: Applications of the Tavistock Group Relations Approach*. London: H. Karnac Books Ltd.

Heimer, C., and Vince, R. (1998). 'Sustainable Learning and Change in International Teams: From Imperceptible Behaviour to Rigorous Practice', *Leadership and Organization Development Journal*, 19/2: 83–8.

Hyde, P., and Thomas, A. B. (2002). 'Organisational Defences Revisited: Systems and Contexts', *Journal of Managerial Psychology*, 17/5: 408–21.

Klein, M., Heimann, P., Isaacs, S., and Riviere, J. (1970). *Developments in Psychoanalysis*. London: Hogarth Press.

Kolb, D. A. (1985). *Experiential Learning: Experiences as the Source of Learning and Development*. Englewood Cliffs, NJ: Prentice Hall.

Lacan, J. (1992). *The Ethics of Psychoanalysis*. London: Routledge.

Lazar, R. (2004). 'Experiencing, Understanding, and Dealing with Intergroup and Institutional Conflict', in L. J. Gould, L. F. Stapley, and M. Stein (eds.), *Experiential Learning in Organizations: Applications of the Tavistock Group Relations Approach*. London: H. Karnac Books Ltd.

Long, S. (2004). 'Building an Institution for Experiential Learning', in L. J. Gould, L. F. Stapley, and M. Stein (eds.), *Experiential Learning in Organizations: Applications of the Tavistock Group Relations Approach*. London: H. Karnac Books Ltd.

Menzies, I. E. P. (1970). *The Functioning of Social Systems as a Defence against Anxiety*. London: Tavistock Institute.

Mintzberg, H. (2004). *Managers Not MBAs: A Hard Look at the Soft Practice of Managing and Management Practice*. San Fransisco: Berrett-Koehler Publishers.

Rickards, T., Hyde, P., and Papamichail, N. (2005). 'The Manchester Method: A Critical Review of a Learning Experiment', in C. Wankel and R. DeFillipi (eds.), *Educating Managers through Real World Projects*. Greenwich, Conn.: Information Age Publishers.

Stein, M. (2004). 'Theories of Experiential Learning and the Unconscious', in L. J. Gould, L. F. Stapley, and M. Stein (2004). *Experiential Learning in Organizations: Applications of the Tavistock Group Relations Approach*. London: H. Karnac Books Ltd.

Thomas, A. B. (1982). 'Inside Story: Managing Boundaries', *Organization Studies*, 3/2: 183–8.

Wankel, C., and DeFillipi, R. (2005). *Educating Managers through Real World Projects*. Greenwich, Conn.: Information Age Publishing.

Whitley, R., (1984). 'The Fragmented State of Management Studies: Reasons and Consequences', *Journal of Management Studies*, 21/3: 331–48.

PART V

DOCTORAL STUDENTS' EXPERIENCE OF LEARNING

CHAPTER 18

EXPERIENCING SCHOLARLY WRITING THROUGH A COLLABORATIVE COURSE PROJECT

ANDREA D. ELLINGER

WITH

RAYNIKA TRENT, YU-LIN WANG,
GRANT WOFFORD, YVONNE HOWARD,
INSIK CHO, MARA FREEMAN,
EUNJEE KIM, SOOYOUNG KIM,
PAT McGLAUGHLIN, SEOK YOUNG OH,
WAYNE SUTTON, BRAD WOOTEN

All life experiences hold the potential for learning. Some experiences result in learning, and some do not.

(Merriam and Caffarella 1999: 287)

INTRODUCTION

THIS chapter will describe a collaborative writing project that was designed to encourage doctoral students enrolled in a doctoral seminar at a midwestern university in the United States to become more immersed in the scholarly literatures on organizational learning and the learning organization concept. The chapter begins by situating experience and learning and briefly introducing experiential learning theory. Then, an overview of the purpose of the collaborative writing project in the broader context of experiential learning will be provided along with the processes followed by seminar participants to review and synthesize empirical work on the learning organization concept. Finally, doctoral seminar participants' reflections about key learnings as a result of participating in this experiential writing project will be discussed.

Several scholars have acknowledged the important role that experience plays in learning (Dewey 1938; Jarvis 1987; Knowles 1980; Kolb 1984; Merriam and Caffarella 1999). For example, Dewey (1938) asserted that 'all genuine education comes about through experience' (p. 25), but acknowledged that not all experiences educate and that some experiences may actually mis-educate.

For learning to occur through experience, Dewey (1938) articulated that the experience must exhibit the principles of continuity and interaction. The principle of continuity, or the experiential continuum, suggests that 'every experience both takes up something from those which have gone before and modifies in some way the quality of those which come after' (p. 35). In terms of the principle of interaction, 'an experience is always what it is because of the transaction taking place between an individual and what, at the time, constitutes his environment' (p. 43). For Dewey, these principles are interconnected and are the 'longitudinal and lateral aspects of experience' (p. 44). Dewey asserts that as learners encounter situations, what one has 'learned in the way of knowledge and skill in one situation becomes an instrument of understanding and dealing effectively with the situations that follow' (p. 44).

Drawing upon Dewey and others, Kolb (1984) conceptualized a theory of learning from experience, experiential learning theory (ELT), which suggests that learning is 'the process whereby knowledge is created through the transformation of experience' (Kolb 1984: 41). Kolb's experiential learning theory 'portrays two dialectically related modes of grasping experience—Concrete Experience (CE) and Abstract Conceptualization (AC)—and two dialectically related modes of transforming experience—Reflective Observation (RO) and Active Experimentation (AE)' (Kolb and Kolb 2005). According to Kolb, concrete experiences are the basis for observations and reflections which are then assimilated and distilled into abstract concepts. Implications can be drawn from these abstract concepts and action can be taken to test them which serves to create new experiences (in Kolb and Kolb

2005). Experiential learning is portrayed as a 'spiral where the learner "touches all the bases"—experiencing, reflecting, thinking, and acting—in a recursive process that is responsive to the learning situation and what is being learned' (p. 194). As Kayes (2002) has acknowledged, 'What distinguishes ELT is not its concern for any single aspect of learning, but rather its concern for the interaction between multiple aspects' (p. 139).

Design of the Course and Collaborative Writing Project in the Context of Experiential Learning Theory

Efforts to improve higher education have become increasingly focused on experiential learning as a core stream of research to improve learning processes (Kolb and Kolb 2005: 207–10). At the doctoral level within higher education institutions, this type of experiential approach is important. Although doctoral students have developed a foundational base of experience and knowledge throughout their undergraduate and graduate education upon which to build, further developing their core competencies as researchers and writers is fundamental to their successful completion of the dissertation and ultimately the awarding of their doctoral degree as well as their transition into academic career paths. As Boote and Beile (2005) have acknowledged,

We have all heard the joke before—as we move through graduate school, we learn more and more about less and less until we know everything about nothing. It is expected that someone earning a doctorate has a thorough and sophisticated understanding of an area of research and scholarship. Unfortunately, many doctoral dissertations in education belie the joke, their authors failing to master the literature that is supposed to be the foundation of their research. (p. 3)

While it is often assumed that doctoral candidates have well-developed writing skills, Boote and Beile have acknowledged that many doctoral students 'have not explicitly studied writing and rhetoric since their freshmen composition classes' (p. 12). Furthermore, it is also assumed that a dissertation literature review is indicative of the doctoral student's ability to identify, critically read, understand, and synthesize the scholarly literature. Yet, most doctoral students are novice researchers and Boote and Beile suggest that they are often insufficiently prepared. As they note, 'the dirty secret known by those who sit on dissertation committees is that most literature reviews are poorly conceptualized and written' (p. 4). They acknowledge that reviewing literature should be a central focus within doctoral programmes and integrated throughout the curriculum.

Since researching, synthesizing, and writing about the scholarly literature are critical core competencies required for doctoral study, it was thought that drawing upon these conceptions of experiential learning and Kolb and Kolb's (2005: 207–10) principles to enhance experiential learning:

- respect for learners and their experience
- beginning learning with the learner's experience of the subject matter
- creating and holding a hospitable space for learning
- making space for conversational learning
- making space for development of expertise
- making spaces for acting and reflecting
- making spaces for feeling and thinking
- making space for inside-out learning
- making space for learners to take charge of their own learning

would enable the course facilitator to help doctoral students to further develop these competencies. Therefore, the course facilitator at the University of Illinois at Urbana-Champaign attempted to design a doctoral seminar so that learners could engage in the experiential learning spiral in which the learner 'touches all the bases'—experiencing, reflecting, thinking, and acting' (Kolb and Kolb 2005: 194). The primary purpose of the course was to introduce learners to the multidisciplinary literature on the concepts of organizational learning and the learning organization through reading and in-depth discussion of these concepts so that learners would be able to meet the following objectives at the completion of the course:

- Describe different conceptualizations of the concepts of organizational learning and the learning organization;
- Discuss core philosophical and theoretical principles related to these concepts;
- Articulate the importance of these concepts and their application to the field of HRD;
- Examine and critique contemporary research literature on these topics;
- Gain knowledge and expertise in selected areas as a result of course projects and activities;
- Integrate knowledge and expertise through in-depth discussion and class facilitation;
- Experience group dynamics through collaborative learning projects and in-class activities; and
- Further develop research, writing, and critical thinking skills.

All twelve learners enrolled in the course were doctoral students. The composition of the course was diverse, with nearly 50 per cent of the course participants being from countries outside the United States. Approximately one-third of the course participants were first-semester doctoral students, another third were within their first year or two in their programme of study, and the final third were nearing the final stages of their degree programmes. During the sixteen-week progression of the course, the facilitator's intent was to expose learners to seminal readings on the concepts of organizational learning and the learning organization so that learners could build upon any of their pre-existing knowledge of these concepts, understand the historical evolution of these concepts, and how scholars have built upon each other's work to further advance these literature bases through conceptual writing and empirical research. It was also intended that learners would search for current literature on these concepts to develop further both individual and collective knowledge. It was also expected that learners would each assume responsibility for facilitating class discussions on assigned readings. Lastly, the course facilitator had proposed that the collective output of the course be a conference paper submission that would focus on the concept of the learning organization and current issues and research in this area. Through this collaborative writing project, it was intended that learners would experience reading, reflecting upon the readings, engaging in discussions and facilitation activities to deepen individual and collective knowledge, conducting focused reviews of the literature, and synthesizing and writing up mini-literature reviews conducted within smaller enquiry groups that would be integrated to form a collective conference paper submission.

Rationale for Focusing on the Learning Organization Concept for the Collaborative Writing Project

The course facilitator chose to focus the collaborative writing project on the concept of the learning organization because it has generated considerable attention in recent years given the importance of learning as a sustainable competitive advantage in the highly turbulent global marketplace (Boud and Garrick 1999; Colteryahn and Davis 2004; Garvin 2000; James 2003; Marquardt and Berger 2003; Marsick and Watkins 1999; Ruona, Lynham, and Chermack 2003; Senge 1990a, 1990b; Watkins and Marsick 1993, 1996). Despite the growing interest in learning organizations much of the existing literature base has been criticized for being overly prescriptive and descriptive as opposed to being empirically grounded. Several scholars have suggested that the literature base should be further explicated (Altman and Iles 1998; Iles 1994; Jacobs 1995; Johnson 1998; Kaiser and Holton 1998; Leitch et al. 1996; Slater and Narver 1995; Sun and Scott 2003; Tsang 1997; Ulrich, Von Glinow, and Jick 1993).

In particular, several areas have been critiqued as requiring more attention. Issues around management and leadership in building and sustaining learning organizations have been an area in need of additional research as it has been suggested that leaders lack guidance and an understanding of specific behaviours that impact learning (Prewitt 2003; Vera and Crossan 2004). Issues around power, gender, and emotions have also not been adequately addressed. Contrasting the philosophies of Senge, Coopey (1995) has indicated 'that the absence from the learning organization model of specific features to facilitate changes in the framework and institutions of governance, and in the political processes constrained by them, detracts considerably from the model's prescriptive value' (p. 197). Easterby-Smith, Snell, and Gherardi (1998) have also lamented the lack of literature identifying the relationships of power and politics to organizational learning and learning organizations. Furthermore, Long and Newton (1997) have expressed concern that while 'the ideas of the learning organization promote some excellent ideals, they never quite address those emotional processes whereby one moves from say, the destructive competitiveness inherent in fractured experiences of the world, to the more holistic co-operative experiences inherent in a broader sense of mutuality—a model perhaps of organizational maturation' (p. 288). While emotions 'are now being recognized as an inevitable feature of organizational life' (Gabriel and Griffiths 2002: 215), the domain of emotion in the study of organizational learning is underpresented (Turnbull 2004) and limited empirical research exists within the context of learning organizations.

Lastly, issues around assessment and measurement and how the learning organization concept may be linked to performance improvement have been an area demanding more scholarly attention (Moilanen 2001). Furthermore, while proponents of the learning organization contend that becoming a learning organization should result in improved performance, the linkage of the learning organization concept with organizational performance outcomes has been an area of enquiry demanding scholarly attention (Jacobs 1995; Kuchinke 1995; Smith and Tosey 1999).

Therefore, it was determined that the purpose of this collaborative writing project would be to conduct a focused review of the state of current empirical literature on the learning organization concept related to these thematic areas as well as to develop some directions for future research. While not exhaustive or comprehensive, it was assumed that the collective paper emerging from this collaborative writing process would provide some insights into these issues as well as present some implications for practice and future research. It was anticipated that this collective output would become a conference proposal submission for the Sixth International Conference on HRD Research and Practice across Europe. This venue was determined to be the most appropriate for the content of this submission and the submission timeframe corresponded to the completion of the course and project timetable.

Method for Conducting the Collective Literature Review and Writing the Paper

The collaborative process began with the course facilitator's preliminary identification of several broad themes: learning organization and leadership/management; learning organization and innovation; learning organization and culture/performance/assessment; learning organization and employee perceptions; learning organization and knowledge management/technology; learning organization and gender/power issues; learning organization and emotions; other topics. Course participants formed smaller enquiry groups and selected areas of interest so they could begin to conduct literature searches on their respective broad theme relative to the shortcomings in the literature. ABI-Inform and EBSCO were the primary databases that were searched using some of the following search terms: learning organization, employees, organizational behaviour, job satisfaction, commitment, workers, emotion, power, politics, political, assessment, gender, measurement, performance improvement, leadership, management, and a combination of these terms with the learning organization term.

Following a cursory review of the conceptual and empirical literature, several of these broad categories were collapsed and merged. Through this process, it was determined that the resulting collective review of literature would incorporate empirical research identified around the issues of leadership/management, power, gender, emotions, measurement/assessment, and performance improvement. These issues were determined to represent the acknowledged voids in the learning organization literature.

Doctoral students individually explored their thematic areas and then worked within their enquiry teams to collectively discuss and synthesize the empirical research they had gathered. They were encouraged to bring their laptop computers to the seminar so that the final two weeks of the semester could be used to integrate and assemble the work of the enquiry teams into a cohesive final product. During the final two weeks of the course, the facilitator also provided laptop computers and began to integrate the enquiry teams' files into one file that would serve as the initial draft of the collective paper. The facilitator and doctoral students reviewed the guidelines for the EHRD proposal submission process and discussed the general format of a conference paper submission and the type of content that each section within the paper should contain. A general outline of the content of the EHRD proposal submission was developed and sections were then cut and pasted into the respective sections. The facilitator used projection capabilities and highlighting features to display the initial and subsequently revised drafts to the students on a large projection screen. Once a reasonable near final draft was developed, a team of four students served as editors and the facilitator worked closely with them to finalize the paper to meet the conference submission deadline. The course concluded with the facilitator indicating that she would keep students apprised of the outcome of the submission.

Following receipt of the favourable outcome about the conference submission two months later, the facilitator contacted all of the students, who met to discuss the reviewers' feedback. The enquiry teams independently worked on enhancing their sections and pursuing recommended readings by reviewers to enhance the final draft of the paper. The final paper, 'Some Current Perspectives on the Learning Organization: A Review of the Literature', was submitted and the paper was presented jointly by the facilitator and one of the doctoral students who was able to travel to the conference on behalf of all of the seminar participants. This paper appears in the Proceedings of the Sixth International Conference on HRD Research and Practice across Europe, Leeds.

LEARNERS' REFLECTIONS ON THE COLLABORATIVE WRITING PROJECT EXPERIENCE

Following the completion of the course and presentation of the paper at the Sixth International Conference on HRD Research and Practice across Europe in May 2005, the course facilitator contacted all twelve learners and asked the learners to reflect on four questions:

1. As you reflect on your experiences, how did this writing project shape, challenge, and transform your individual understanding of organizational learning/learning organization? Do you and how do you come to understand organizational learning/learning organization concepts/literature differently?

2. As you reflect on your experiences, how did this writing project shape, challenge, and transform your group/collective understanding of organizational learning/learning organization? Did your group and how did your group come to understand organizational learning/learning organization concepts/literature differently?

3. As you reflect on your own experiential learning experiences, what if anything did you feel you learned from this project that has contributed to your scholarly writing?

4. Have you and how have you been transformed as an emerging and developing scholar in the doctoral programme?

The written reflections provided by all twelve learners were then examined by the course facilitator. While the facilitator had hoped that some of the learners indicating an interest in continuing work on this project would participate in the content analysis of the written responses, the four learners most committed to furthering this project had not yet taken qualitative data analysis courses. Therefore, the course facilitator asked these four learners to serve as critical reviewers of the content analysis as a form of member checking for this process. The following sections provide insights into the learners' reflections about their experiences in participating in this collaborative writing project.

REFLECTIONS ON INDIVIDUAL UNDERSTANDING

The learners' responses to the first question revealed an overarching theme related to the participation in the course and collaborative writing project as one that *broadened my scope of understanding*. Within this overarching theme, there was some variation as to how this occurred. Learners referred to the notions of being able to *distinguish between these concepts, deepen their knowledge about these concepts by understanding the vastness of the literature, its historical evolution and influential scholars, the dynamics that shape these concepts, and future research directions.*

The majority of course participants may have initially considered themselves to be organizational learning and learning organization neophytes. For example, learner 5 indicated, 'at the beginning of the class, I did not recognize the differences between organizational learning and the learning organization...however, throughout the semester, I came to realize the huge dissimilarity between [the] two terms.' Similarly, learner 3 mentioned, 'I just knew that organizational learning and the learning organization [were] the same thing...after reading tons of literature related to definitions, theories, and empirical research, I could...classify them in different points of view by scholars.' For learner 12, she indicated, 'honestly, the differences in concepts of organizational learning/learning organization was not clear to me until I read a few articles which changed my views of organizational learning/learning organization'.

In slight contrast to many of the other learners in the course, two learners had indicated that they had some knowledge of organizational learning and the learning organization concepts prior to enrolling in this course but gained new insights as a result. As learner 8 acknowledged,

I have a research project that focus[es] on one of organizational learning's constructs, information acquisition.... Based on my previous literature reviews on organizational learning, this writing assignment made me extend and review more organizational learning/learning organization concepts in depth.... I understand organizational learning and the learning organization in a time series [and] from various perspectives.... the historical literature review truly led me [to] understand the development [of these concepts].... hence, I merge these diverse concepts to transform my own understanding [of them].

Learner 10 stated,

Before the [writing] project began, my understanding of organizational learning was as learning as a process at an organizational level and that of the learning organization was as just and one type of organization that emphasize[s] learning, respectively. As the project went on, I got to understand that learning organization is a type of organization as an open system that the rapidly changing world demands to [ensure] its survival in competitive markets. The transition occurred from differentiating mere definition[s] to identifying several factors to facilitate or prevent organizations to become learning organizations: Learning organization is one type of organization that [is] good at organizational learning whose leaders play a major role in 'change'; power and politics come into play either in a positive or negative way; knowledge management is essential since knowledge and innovation are major players.

For learner 4, 'the writing project was a vehicle that guided me through the literature review process by providing an insight to organizational learning/learning organization and the distinction between the two. It challenged me to engage in how the various authors viewed [these concepts] and how their interpretations influenced and added to the body of knowledge.' As learner 2 acknowledged, 'This collaborative activity provided a foundation of where the learning organization concept had come from and where we are in the quest for understanding the learning organization, further, it facilitates future discussion identifying trends and illuminating missing or incomplete areas of our knowledge and understanding.'

Two learners specifically referred to their own research interests as being stimulated though their work on this project. As learner 1 noted, 'through my participation in this seminar and the organizational learning/learning organization literature, I began seeing that what I was interested in was how organizations were participating in the education and learning development of employees for them to contribute to the long term success of the organization.' Similarly, learner 3 suggested, 'As the [project] goes on, I began to find my own interest.' And for two other learners, how they approach their reading and work has been changed. For learner 6, 'as a result of participating in the assignment I now approach understanding [these concepts] differently than prior to my participation. I now seek to classify literature that I read regarding [these concepts] into broad categories, similar, but not limited to those developed during the collective class assignment. This mental classification allows me to organize my thinking by ensuring that I review literature with the appropriate "lens" if you will, as I conduct research.' For learner 11, 'the experience made me want to share some [of] the concepts that we explored during our project with colleagues in an effort to make a more positive impact on current situations in our "learning organization" '.

Overall, the individual reflections suggest that the writing project did enhance their individual understanding of these concepts. One learner commented that 'working together on this paper almost epitomize[d] what the learning organization/organizational learning [are]' (learner 9).

REFLECTIONS ON GROUP/COLLECTIVE UNDERSTANDING

Learners' responses to question 2 regarding their reflections about how the writing project shaped, challenged, and transformed group/collective understanding of organizational learning/learning organization concepts revealed an overarching theme associated with *stimulating conversations and exchange to refine, reshape, challenge, and sacrifice perspectives to develop niche knowledge and expertise.*

Learners' responses consistently described a similar approach among the smaller collaborative enquiry groups. Group members typically each conducted independent searches of the literature related to their respective thematic area and then met with their group members to share and potentially transform their insights with each other as well as work toward the development of a synthesized section of the literature review on their particular thematic area. Learner 2 captures the essence of the process that most groups used:

Within my particular sub-group were five students. Each of us commenced a search of the literature sources seeking material along the general line of our chosen topic of interest in organizational learning/learning organization. During our collaboration the diverse ideas and findings of this group became more refined and were narrowed down through individual reflection and feedback to express what we believed to be the salient issues expressed in the literature. This process elaborated some areas, such as the prevalence of power and gender issues recorded in the literature, but also reshaped our perceptions of other areas where we expected to find a substantial literature base but instead found little material. Through this process our perceptions [of these concepts] were modified and provided a sense that the literature base of organizational learning/learning organization was dynamic in nature and changing as it grows and faces new challenges and opportunities.

Sometimes during this process, though, 'we could not always explain our perspectives and relationship of topics to each other, some perspectives were sacrificed', according to learner 1. Furthermore, learner 1 felt that 'group members who had a stronger or more direct study that linked to the learning organization literature were able to contribute more and members who felt their research was repetitive or reinforcing of the other direct study contributed less...'. Learner 4 pointed out the challenges to the group because 'members had their own interpretation of [these concepts] and how they perceived power, gender, and emotions within an organization. . . . afterwards [obtaining our literature] [we] collaborated within the group to reach consensus of what power, gender and emotions represented in the [learning organization]. This interaction of reaching consensus transformed the group's understanding of [these concepts].'

Learner 6 said, 'I was free to focus my energy toward my particular niche and be as thorough as possible in its development . . . in addition, the particular subgroup in which I was a member had some very stimulating conversations which deepened our collective understanding and individual understanding. . . . I was the expert for my particular niche and took on the responsibility of teaching my section to other members [of my subgroup], linking with other's sections [in the subgroup], and editing as necessary to make sure there was a decent "fit" between our sections.' Similarly, learner 9 acknowledged, 'I think the best part was getting together and collaborating to put our thoughts and ideas together.' But, as learner 8 noted, 'my group members and I can exchange and articulate our ideas based on the same literatures on [leadership], on the other hand, I only read one to two articles on power and gender issues on the learning organization . . . and therefore, I cannot say I am the expert on gender and power on learning organization literature.' Learner 10 suggested that '[in her small subgroup initial topics overlapped] and we got to figure out how to organize our portion of the paper and to put [it] into one big paper'.

Overall, learners appeared to acknowledge learning about their thematic area from each other through their group processes, perhaps with some variation of group dynamics between groups. However, the focus on a specific thematic area enabled learners to become more immersed in the empirical research in that thematic area perhaps at the expense of total immersion in literature covering all areas. It was anticipated that learners would learn about all thematic areas once the final paper was produced.

REFLECTIONS ON WRITING/RESEARCH

In response to question 3 which sought to better understand how participation in the writing project contributed to scholarly writing, an overarching theme emerged: *benefits derived from working in these small groups* for which there were several manifestations.

For the majority of the learners, the *benefits derived from working in these small groups* on this project enabled them to gain a *personal perspective and niche engagement, learn from each other through the sharing of multiple viewpoints, more critically look at their own research and writing skills,* and *become intellectually stimulated to conduct research.* In terms of personal perspective and niche engagement, the majority of learners found the experience to be a positive one that immersed them in their small group. Learner 6 described developing a 'renewed understanding and respect for the collaborative process in researching [these concepts] and how it allows the individual collaborators to focus their energies in specific areas, become the "expert", and teach the other members of the group about his/her specific area'. In terms of learning from each other, learner 5 acknowledged, 'other students interpreted the same literature about organizational learning and the learning organization somewhat differently in comparison with me. That was also a valuable lesson from being involved in this writing project.' Similarly, learner 11 said, 'the experience reinforced my understanding of the need to be flexible and open to ideas that may differ from my own'.

A few learners did acknowledge some contrasting perspectives that illustrated the frustrations of not knowing it all. For learner 1, 'the significance of personal perspective and engagement most influenced my experience...as the project became more collaborative it included more perspectives and in some ways was less personal...as the project grew I felt less connected not having participated in either discussion and writing of the other sections.' Similarly, learner 7 did comment on the frustration associated with the inability to 'review all of the information that the other groups assessed and presented in their portion of the paper that was a source, albeit insane and impractical, of frustration'. Further, she acknowledged, 'pragmatic consideration does impart a genuine appreciation for how experiential group processes can provide such a multiplicity of knowledge in an efficient and productive manner'.

In terms of writing and research skills, learner 4 indicated, 'my experience with this project led to a closer examination of my research and writing skills and techniques while conducting keyword searches and reading articles pertaining to power, gender, and emotions within organizational learning/learning organization [literature]'. Similarly, learner 2 suggested, 'the group effort and group dynamics helped me to look more critically at my own writing and thought process and through feedback enabled me to improve my writing and amend my frame of reference for increased understanding of the organizational learning/learning organization literature'. Learner 9 also commented on the value of feedback when he said, 'in any type of scholarly writing, I feel it is important to have someone else reread and look at your work to get a second, third, etc. opinion'. For learner 8, 'learning how to synthesize related or different concepts, as a well-reasoned academic writing is what I learned most from the process'. And learner 10 acknowledged, 'this collaborative work was an opportunity to learn how to synthesize each member's ideas into one paper and to learn to write a paper together. Each of us could write a paper according to APA format.'

Lastly, several learners alluded to their intellectual desire to further research these topics. For example, learner 3 acknowledged, 'so this project impacts my study about learning organization [concept] in Korean [context]'. Learner 5 suggested that 'the writing project ... stimulate[d] my intellectual desire to research about organizational learning'. Lastly, one learner specifically acknowledged learning more about the need for more leadership/management research in the context of learning organizations (learner 12) as a result of her immersion in the smaller collaborative group exploring this thematic area.

In slight contrast to the overarching theme, two learners made additional observations that reflected on the challenges of group learning as a dynamic: 'As our learning was on the group level, I could see where the application of learning may fail in organizations because the members may not fully engage throughout the learning activities and therefore be less able to apply their learning to the organization's goals' (learner 1). Learner 1 seemed to consider that 'developing an understanding of the literature and desire to be understood and perceived as knowledgeable' may have impacted some learners' contributions to the group process. Learner 7 described the challenge of time to engage in the collaborative project as one that may have 'prevented the typical "growing pains" or developmental stages that are involved in any effective group process. ... It is thought that the time constraints did influence the lack of distractions re: power struggles, expressionistic differences, etc, as well as the fact that the dismal amount of empirical data on this sub-group's assigned categories left little to tussle about!'

REFLECTIONS AS AN EMERGING SCHOLAR

In their reflections about becoming an emerging scholar, two broad themes emerged across learners' responses: *Exposure and immersion in the scholarly exchange on these concepts* and *developing a broad base of knowledge of research, writing, and publication processes.*

Exposure, immersion, and participation in the scholarly exchange on these concepts reflected learners' perspectives about having read a volume of diverse literature on these concepts and having had an opportunity to interact with their peers to think more deeply and reflectively about them. Learner 5 noted that 'the collaborative writing project gave me an opportunity to experience various types of literature'. Learner 4 indicated that 'the experience of participating in a group writing project helped to generate scholarly exchange on information that is important in the research field'. Similarly, learner 1 acknowledged, 'I am now a scholar that looks at the relationship of [these concepts] with other concepts/constructs,' and learner 12 suggested that, 'I would say my viewpoint of [the] learning organization has been expanded through this class.' Learner 2 also shared,

I believe the saturation of the literature coupled with the interaction with my peers during the weekly class meetings led me to some deep reflective thinking regarding [these concepts]. This activity raised illuminating and intriguing questions that I hope to pursue through further study and research which I believe apart from this interaction I would not have [been] likely to have encountered.

In terms of *developing a broad base of knowledge of research, writing, and publication processes for doctoral study*, learner 7 acknowledged, 'it was a part of my initiation into the doctoral programme. The immersion in this process awarded the indispensable tools of research, literature reviews, writing in an intimate, scholarly setting and notably aided in the reduction of what formidably could have been a paralyzing culture shock.' For learner 3, he discovered 'how strict the conference paper was in form and process', and learner 8 felt that 'this writing process taught me to synthesize literatures and transform it into a logical and well-reasoned paper... [which are] critical to doctoral programme training'. Learner 6 acknowledged that he had a 'much better understanding and respect for what an exhaustive literature review could look like'. For learner 10, the project 'was another opportunity to write up an academic paper and to know some emerging topics about learning organizations. I am still in the process of [becoming] a scholar. I am sure that this collaborative group project showed me how to search topics and synthesize articles and ultimately expose myself to a possible and potential topic I will be interested in for the future.' Tangentially related to this, learner 11 suggested that she didn't know if she had been transformed, but she had 'been inspired to make some adjustments in my life/work so that I can redefine my doctoral plan, develop a completion timeline, and focus more of my energies in that direction'. And learner 9 felt that he had 'gained independence and I am able to look for things that interest me... while working with my advisor I am able to shape my thoughts and interests into research and then create the process of writing papers'. Three learners acknowledged their interests in conducting future research on these concepts.

Overall, while learners may not fully know if they have been transformed, it appears that they have derived value from this project and developed skills that will enable them to engage more fully in their doctoral studies.

Concluding Thoughts

At the doctoral level, Boote and Beile (2005) have acknowledged that 'acquiring the skills and knowledge required to be education scholars, able to analyze and synthesize the research in a field of specialization, should be the focal, integrative activity of predissertation doctoral education' (p. 3). However, they assert that the centrality of the literature review has largely been ignored by faculty which has weakened the quality of education research. Quality dissertations and research 'must be cumulative; it must build on and learn from prior research' (Boote and Beile 2005: 3). Similarly, experiential learning theory posits that learning should be cumulative and built upon prior experiences according to the principles of continuity and interaction.

The reflections provided by the doctoral students tend to suggest that the collaborative writing project was a positive experience that engaged the multiple facets of the experiential learning cycle. As can be seen from the reflections, initial immersion in the scholarly literature on the learning organization during the progression of the course helped to build a foundation upon which concepts could be clarified and internalized. For some learners, pre-existing knowledge of the learning organization concept and organizational learning was ill informed, whereas for others, the concepts were a part of the learners' experiential continuum. Through reading, facilitation activities, and in-depth discussion, learners could challenge their own understandings to form more abstract conceptualizations of the concepts. The learners also had to take action to locate relevant literature, to synthesize it, as well as discuss it in depth with their peers within their enquiry teams. Lastly, they had to engage in the writing process at a team level and then experience the process of transforming this team-level contribution into a collective product representative of all of the seminar participants and course facilitator.

By engaging doctoral students in this type of seminar where they were able to experience the dynamics of experiential learning, it is hoped that a more holistic and integrated approach to learning occurred that afforded them opportunities to develop themselves as emergent researchers and scholars. It is further hoped that their engagement enhanced the development of their research and writing skills. As Kayes (2002) asserts, 'Methods that increase vocabularies, introduce proximity of knowledge sharing, aid in making connections between personal and social knowledge, and organization experience in meaningful ways' (p. 147) lead to learning in academic and managerial contexts.

REFERENCES

Altman, Y., and Iles, P. (1998). 'Learning, Leadership, Teams: Corporate Learning and Organizational Change', *Journal of Management Development*, 17/1: 44–55.

Boote, D. N., and Beile, P. (2005). 'Scholars before Researchers: On the Centrality of the Dissertation Literature Review in Research Preparation', *Educational Researcher*, 34/2: 3–15.

Boud, D., and Garrick, J. (1999). 'Understandings of Workplace Learning', in D. Boud and J. Garrick (eds.), *Understanding Learning at Work*. London: Routledge.

Colteryahn, K., and Davis, P. (2004). '8 Trends You Need to Know Now', *T and D*, 58/1: 28–36.

Coopey, J. (1995). 'The Learning Organization, Power, Politics and Ideology', *Management Learning*, 26: 193–213.

Dewey, J. (1938). *Experience and Education.* New York: Simon & Schuster.

Easterby-Smith, M., Snell, R., and Gherardi, S. (1998). 'Organizational Learning: Diverging Communities of Practice?', *Management Learning*, 29/3: 259.

Gabriel, Y., and Griffiths, D. S. (2002). 'Emotion, Learning and Organizing', *Learning Organization*, 9/5: 214.

Garvin, D. (2000). *Learning in Action.* Boston: Harvard Business School Press.

Iles, P. (1994). 'Developing a Learning Environment: Challenges for Theory, Research and Practice', *Journal of European Industrial Training*, 18/3: 3–9.

Jacobs, R. L. (1995). 'Impressions about the Learning Organization: Looking to See What is behind the Curtain', *Human Resource Development Quarterly*, 6/2: 119–22.

James, C. R. (2003). 'Designing Learning Organizations', *Organizational Dynamics*, 32/1: 46–61.

Jarvis, P. (1987). *Adult Learning in the Social Context.* London: Croom Helm.

Johnson, J. R. (1998). 'Embracing Change: A Leadership Model for the Learning Organization', *International Journal of Training and Development*, 2/2: 141–50.

Kaiser, S. M., and Holton, E. F. (1998). 'The Learning Organization as a Performance Improvement Strategy', in R. Torraco (ed.), *Proceedings of the Academy of Human Resource Development Conference.* Oak Brook, Ill: Academy of Human Resource Development.

Kayes, D. C. (2002). 'Experiential Learning and its Critics: Preserving the Role of Experience in Management Learning and Education', *Academy of Management Learning and Education*, 1/2: 137–49.

Knowles, M. S. (1980). *The Modern Practice of Adult Education: From Pedagogy to Andragogy*, 2nd edn. New York: Cambridge Books.

Kolb, A. Y., and Kolb, D. A. (2005). 'Learning Styles and Learning Spaces: Enhancing Experiential Learning in Higher Education', *Academy of Management Learning and Education*, 4/2: 193–212.

Kolb, D. A. (1984). *Experiential Learning: Experience as the Source of Learning and Development.* Englewood Cliffs, NJ: Prentice Hall.

Kuchinke, K. P. (1995). 'Managing Learning for Performance', *Human Resource Development Quarterly*, 6/3: 307–16.

Leitch, C., Harrison, R., Burgoyne, J., and Blantern, C. (1996). 'Learning Organizations: The Measurement of Company Performance', *Journal of European Industrial Training*, 20/1: 31–44.

Long, S., and Newton, J. (1997). 'Educating the Gut: Socio-emotional Aspects of the Learning Organization', *Journal of Management Development*, 16/4: 284–98.

Marquardt, M., and Berger, N. O. (2003). 'The Future: Globalization and New Roles for HRD', *Advances in Developing Human Resources*, 5/3: 283–95.

Marsick, V. J., and Watkins, K. E. (1999). *Facilitating Learning Organizations: Making Learning Count.* Aldershot: Gower.

Merriam, S. B., and Caffarella, R. S. (1999). *Learning in Adulthood: A Comprehensive Guide*, 2nd edn. San Francisco: Jossey-Bass.

Moilanen, R. (2001). 'Diagnostic Tools for Learning Organizations', *Learning Organization*, 8/1: 6–20.

Prewitt, V. (2003). 'Leadership Development for Learning Organizations', *Leadership and Organization Development Journal*, 24/2: 58–61.

Ruona, W. E. A., Lynham, S. A., and Chermack, T. J. (2003). 'Insights on Emerging Trends and the Future of Human Resource Development', *Advances in Developing Human Resources*, 5/3: 272–82.

Senge, P. (1990*a*). *The Fifth Discipline: The Art and Practice of the Learning Organization*. New York: Doubleday.

——(1990*b*). 'The Leader's New Work: Building Learning Organizations', *Sloan Management Review*, 32/1: 7–23.

Slater, S. F., and Narver, J. C. (1995). 'Market Orientation and the Learning Organization', *Journal of Marketing*, 59: 63–74.

Smith, P. A. C., and Tosey, P. (1999). 'Assessing the Learning Organization: Part I— Theoretical Foundations', *Learning Organization*, 6/2: 70–5.

Sun, P. Y. T., and Scott, J. L. (2003). 'Exploring the Divide: Organizational Learning and the Learning Organization', *Learning Organization*, 10/4: 202–15.

Tsang, E. W. K. (1997). 'Organizational Learning and the Learning Organization: A Dichotomy between Descriptive and Prescriptive Research', *Human Relations*, 50/1: 73–89.

Turnbull, S. (2004). 'Emotion in Organizational Learning: Implications for HRD', in T. M. Egan and M. L. Morris (eds.), *Proceedings of the Academy of Human Resource Development Conference*. Austin, Tex.

Ulrich, D., Von Glinow, M. A., and Jick., T. (1993). 'High-Impact Learning: Building and Diffusing Learning Capability', *Organizational Dynamics*, 22/2: 52–66.

Vera, D., and Crossan, M. (2004). 'Strategic Leadership and Organizational Learning', *Academy of Management Review*, 29/2: 222–41.

Watkins, K. E., and Marsick, V. J. (1993). *Sculpting the Learning Organization: Lessons in the Art and Science of Systemic Change*. San Francisco: Jossey-Bass.

————(1996). *In Action: Creating the Learning Organization*. Alexandris, Va.: American Society for Training and Development.

CHAPTER 19

··

EXPERIENCING A COLLECTIVE[1] MODEL OF DOCTORAL RESEARCH SUPERVISION

··

SANDRA JONES (AND DOCTORAL STUDENTS)

INTRODUCTION

··

THE increasing number of candidates enrolled in doctorates (especially in the growing area of professional doctorates), in combination with industry demand for more relevant research into professional practice, is leading to growing recognition that university doctorates are 'occupying a more central role, both institutionally and nationally' (Neumann 2003: 4). This is resulting in wide-ranging discourse about the most effective form and structure of doctoral programmes to support candidates and lead to maximum output (completions). In the early 1990s in the USA Bowen and Rudenstine (1992) undertook research into completion rates, in the UK Becher, Henkel, and Kogan (1994) explored the educational experience, while

Clark (1993) and Burgess (1997) explored issues associated with postgraduate education and lifelong learning. In addition several authors have undertaken research to compare doctoral education in different countries (Clark 1993; Holdaway, Deblois, and Winchester 1995).

One of the important issues raised is the most appropriate supervisory relationship, especially in regard to the newly emerging professional doctorates. The professional doctorate differs from the more traditional Doctor of Philosophy (Ph.D.) in attracting part-time candidates with several years in the workforce in addition to their past academic success, rather than the full-time (recently graduated) candidates with a strong academic performance attracted to the Ph.D. The professional doctorate also differs from the Ph.D. in the expected contribution of advancement of professional practice rather than the advancement of knowledge within an academic discipline (Bourner, Bowden, and Laing 2001). Gibbons et al. (1994) describe this as the difference between Mode 1 (new) and Mode 2 (applied and integrated) knowledge. Lee, Green, and Brennan (2000) describe the professional doctorate as situated at the nexus of the profession, the workplace, and the university. While Green, Maxwell, and Shanahan (2001) state that the professional doctoral qualification represents

a significant challenge to the traditional orientation of universities, especially with regard to existing policies and practices of research and research training . . . it involves a fundamental reconsideration of matters such as knowledge, practice, supervision and methodology, as well as issues such as diversity and flexibility. (p. 2)

This is particularly the case in the management area where professional Doctorates of Business Administration (DBA) are attracting increasing numbers of candidates in the UK and Australia (Bourner, Bowden, and Laing 2001), with candidates seeing this as the next step beyond the Master of Business Administration (MBA).

Experiential learning has long been acknowledged as appropriate for management education. This has led to an increase in practice-based/action-based research, evidence-based, reflective practice, situated learning, and experiential learning. Practitioner-based research is often described as the 'pull' of research that differs from the traditional Ph.D. research 'push' approach through which academic researchers disseminate their results to practitioners (Bourner, Bowden, and Laing 2001). In response to business and industry criticism of the quality and skills of graduates from traditionally academic focused doctorates (Clarke 1996), this 'pull' approach is influencing both professional doctoral and Ph.D. research, especially in the 'soft' disciplines such as management.

Recognizing that this shift holds many challenges for organizations, universities, and candidates, the issue of interest for this chapter is: what should an appropriate student–supervision relationship for practice-based research include? In so doing it is acknowledged that any new experiential model of supervision for management doctorates should take account of the perceived limitations as well as advantages of experiential learning, particularly the need to focus beyond the individual to the collective (social), to link theory and practice, to expand reflection to the present, and to establish a process that reduces defensive responses (Vince 1998; Reynolds and Vince 2004).

This chapter proposes the addition of an experiential research Community of Practice (CoP) to provide peer-supported knowledge sharing and discovery for candidates whose doctoral research is in a similar domain. The chapter presents reflections of the supervisor (the author) and several doctoral candidates (DBA and Ph.D.) in an experiential research CoP established in 2003. The conclusion from this example is that a research CoP can provide a valuable experiential learning opportunity for doctoral candidates, especially those undertaking research into professional practice, particularly in addition to 'outsider' peer reflection on 'insider' first-person action reflections.

Student–Supervisory Relationship

Research has found that effective supervision is crucial to the successful completion of a Ph.D. (Hockey 1994). In so saying, several models of supervisory relationships, associated with different philosophies of doctoral education, have evolved. Under the more traditional research-based Ph.D., supervision tends to adhere closely to a master–apprentice tradition as identified by Frankland (1999), or a mentoring process as discussed by Hockey (1994). Neumann (2003: 38) found that students generally look for supervisors with similar research interests who are 'enthusiastic about their area of research, are experienced researchers, show an interest in students and respect them as people'. Supervisors in this traditional relationship are expected to have the expert academic knowledge to lead and support a candidate in their research. Examples of such supervisory modes include individual student–supervisor relationship (the major form of supervision in the 'soft fields'); small to medium-sized teams or groups under one or two supervisors with possibly a post-doctoral fellow (generally in laboratory-based hard pure disciplines); very large research groups of centres (soft pure fields); and finally, a supervisory panel (hard disciplines) (Neumann 2003). In all these models the emphasis is upon the individual relationship between the student (or groups of students) and the supervisor (sometimes supported by a post-doctoral student), with the supervisor providing the student with intellectual stimulation and excitement, academic rigour, and an appropriate framework within which to develop ideas without being too prescriptive.

New models of research supervision are needed for more practice-based professional doctorates and more mature-aged, work-experienced Ph.D. candidates.

These models need to be more cognizant of the candidates' greater practitioner knowledge, skills, and experience. Morley (2002) summarized the different supervisory relationship as:

in a PhD ... the emphasis is on academic knowledge and experience, supervisors are usually well ahead of their students in the vital knowledge areas at the commencement of the study ... DBA candidates can have much more relevant, practical knowledge than their senior (academic) supervisor. This means that the candidates' maturity, practical judgment and knowledge need to be respected in the supervisory relationship. (p. 8)

One way to respond to this challenge is to adopt a more experiential learning approach to the supervisory–candidate relationship.

EXPERIENTIAL LEARNING AND DOCTORAL SUPERVISION

Experiential learning covers a variety of techniques that seek to assist a continual process of learning through four circular 'stages' that include observation and reflection upon concrete experience leading to the development and testing of abstract concepts and generalizations through active experimentation (Kolb 1984).

Underpinning the 'Learning Cycle' that evolved into a theory of experiential learning are Kolb's theoretical principles that learning should be a holistic and continuous process grounded in experience rather than an outcome during which the learner resolves conflicts between dialectically opposed modes of adaptation to the world through transactions between people and between people and the environment. This Learning Cycle thus accommodates both deductive and inductive approaches enabling learning to occur as abstract concepts are tested in practice as well as reflection upon concrete experience.

There are many examples of experiential learning in management education with the most popularly discussed including: action-based learning, situated learning, experiential professional practice activities based on case studies and role-plays, reflective practice, and practice-based research (Schön 1983; Lave and Wenger 1991). Applied to doctoral supervision, examples of experiential learning as part of the supervisory relationship are more common in the emerging professional doctorate arena, although there is some discussion in relation to Ph.D. supervision (see for example McMorland et al. 2003 and their research into first- and second-person action research/peer partnership enquiry).

Action-based and practice-based research places the candidate-as-practitioner as the source of knowledge, with opportunities provided for practitioners to develop a research methodology that includes reflection upon both their practice and the practice of others from a deeper knowledge perspective (Schön 1983, 1987). It is the contention of this chapter that principles of experiential learning design can be of assistance in redesigning the doctoral supervisory–candidate model from the traditional master–apprentice, paternalistic approach (Sharp and Howard 1996).

In developing such a model, cognizance of the limitations of the experiential approach in a general education context is needed. Vince (1998), for example, criticized the learning cycle as being, first, limited by the individual experience that often does not recognize complexity and the unequal power relationships of social reality. This results in only certain 'voices' being heard and unequal power relations being hidden. Second, he identified the limitation of the focus of reflection on past events rather than on current experiences. Third, he pointed out that reflection can be limited by participant defensiveness about what may be exposed during the educative process. The solution he offered to address these limitations was more open dialogue to provide 'simultaneous access both to individual experience and to the translation of that experience through the social context' (Vince 1998: 313).

More recently Reynolds and Vince (2004) suggest that applying critical perspectives to management theory and practice, combined with an action-based learning approach, may address many of the limitations of the experiential learning approach. This is achieved by placing emphasis on the value of questioning and challenging existing power relations, enabling questioning of individual practice, while at the same time focusing on social and cultural processes rather than individual practice:

situating management learning in the workplace...complemented by formal education within management and business schools....[enables academics to]...work with managers in critically examining the challenges and problems with which they must work, drawing on our (academics) ideas and experiences in conjunction with theirs.

(Reynolds and Vince 2004: 445)

This chapter presents a model of an experiential collective peer-supported doctoral supervision process through the establishment of a Community of Practice (CoP).

CoPs and Doctoral Supervision

The term Communities of Practice was first coined in 1991 when Lave and Wenger (1991) refocused learning on the 'journeyman' or 'master–servant' apprenticeship models through their concept of 'practice-based learning in Situated Learning environment'. The resultant focus on 'communities of practitioners...[in which]...mastery of knowledge and skills requires newcomers to move toward full participation in the sociocultural practices of the community' (Lave and Wenger 1991: 29) led to a model of CoPs through which older members introduce newer members to their knowledge and skills through a process of *legitimate peripheral participation* (LPP) as the newer members move from the edge of the community to the centre. Building on this theory, Brown and Duguid (1991: 40) suggest that learning is a 'natural connection between working and innovating...the central issue in learning is about becoming a practitioner, not learning about practice.'

This has led to a surge in business interest in how organizations can use CoPs as a source of networking to encourage knowledge sharing. Literature on the theory and potential of CoPs by Snyder (1997), Wenger (1998), Lesser, Fontaine, and Slusher (2000), and Lesser and Prusak (2000), has been supplemented more recently by case studies of the practice of CoPs by Brown and Duguid (2000) and Hildreth and Kimble (2004). As Wenger, McDermott, and Snyder (2002: 6) state 'it is not that CoPs themselves are new, but the need for organizations to become more intentional and systematic about "managing" knowledge'. In this sense CoPs have been defined as:

groups of people who share a concern, a set of problems, or a passion about a topic, and who deepen their knowledge and expertise in this area by interacting on an ongoing basis.
(Wenger, McDermott, and Snyder 2002: 4)

CoPs are explained as fluid, not structurally rigid, voluntary groups of people who care about an issue (domain), share their practice, and often tacit knowledge, such that individual knowledge becomes social knowledge, and/or new knowledge is created. Organizations are encouraged to allow CoP to evolve and end organically, rather than have a particular 'task' or timescale (Wenger, McDermott, and Snyder 2002: 27 and 42).

CoPs are not a new concept in academia. Scholars naturally establish research collegiality around a common issue (*domain*), although such collegiality is often limited by competition for research grants and promotion (part of the 'publish or perish' performance criteria of academia). Thorne (2001) has also claimed that team or group research is a CoP. However, similarly to the recognized difference between teams and CoPs in organizations, the team research approach selects members rather than encouraging self-selection and has a specific task with clear boundaries that is held together by specific research goals and milestones. This is different from CoPs that aim to create, expand, and exchange knowledge around 'fuzzy' boundaries in which members are held together by passion, commitment, and identification with each other (Wenger, McDermott, and Snyder 2002).

A new model of research CoPs proposed in this chapter aims to bring candidates, supervisor, and other interested persons together to explore knowledge within a mutually defined domain that may be either directly or indirectly related to a candidate's specific research topic. This model assumes, first, that the role of the doctoral supervisor is to create the research environment, support candidates, and provide knowledge networking opportunities. Second, that continual peer review and feedback is useful for both research and improving practice through providing the means to explore new approaches to responding to ambiguity in a knowledge era. The model uses the concept of legitimate peripheral participation in a new way whereby the 'expert' and the peripheral 'newcomer' change according to the particular discourse. In this sense the research CoP becomes an experiential learning environment as members develop new knowledge by sharing experiences and reflecting on their own and other experiences.

The CoP model of doctoral supervision addresses many of the challenges identified above of practice-based doctoral research. First, by providing the opportunity for open discourse, analysis, and reflection on each individual candidate's experiences and research, it broadens the individual practitioner reflection to a more collective social reflection as other members of the CoP contribute an 'outsider' perspective on the 'insider' reflection. Second, it changes the power relationship between supervisor and candidate as the discourse recognizes the legitimacy of many 'voices' and the supervisor focuses more on providing an appropriate framework for the research rather than on providing expert knowledge. Third, members are enabled to reflect on their current experience within the CoP and then use reflection upon their experience as a contribution to their particular research topic. Finally, it links theory and practice as practitioners and academics share their knowledge. In their description of the eight months' lived experience of supervisors and supervisees in a community of practice (or what they termed 'relational learning community'), McMorland et al. (2003) state, 'it is only seeing supervision and research collaboration as a relationship as well as a project, that intellectual intimacy, reflexive practice and creative inquiry can be fostered and enhanced' (p. 6).

In order to 'test' this collective model of doctoral supervision the next section presents the 'lived' experience of the author and several doctoral candidates (Ph.D. and DBA) in a CoP established as a voluntary addition to the traditional one-on-one supervisory model. In so doing a first-person action research reflective research method is used to present the experience, with anecdotal comments of various members of the CoP used to demonstrate, in a narrative tradition, the contribution of membership of the CoP to the doctoral supervisory process.

Experiencing a Collective Model of Doctoral Supervision

Background

The Business Portfolio of the University of the Royal Melbourne Institute of Technology (RMIT) offers both a Ph.D. and a DBA. The Ph.D. generally attracts less work-experienced, more academically focused candidates, many of whom are international students. The DBA attracts practitioners with an appropriate post-graduate award and significant work experience. The DBA programme differs from the Ph.D. in the aim of contributing to professional practice rather than knowledge, and its structure, with a coursework component (33 per cent) that provides advanced specialist knowledge as well as academic analysis and writing skills. It also differs in the candidates it attracts—mature, high-achieving professionals, rather than the younger, more academically focused Ph.D. candidates. Finally, there is a difference in the ambitions of the candidates, with Ph.D. candidates focused more on an academic career, while DBA candidates wish to contribute to professional practice (Morley 1999).

The supervisory process offered by the university also differs. Ph.D. candidates are provided with a principal supervisor with whom they meet on a weekly basis, have twice-yearly formal reviews in which they present a summary of their progress to their supervisor and the research director, and a further public progress presentation to their peers. DBA candidates have a senior supervisor (academic) and a second supervisor (industry expert), plus a Supervised Professional Practice Review Session that provides opportunities for candidates to report on, and discuss, professional work relating to their thesis to colleagues and supervisors (RMIT 2003).

Experiential Learning: a CoP Model of and Doctoral Supervision

Establishment of the CoP

In 2003 the author (here after referred to as I) was the principal supervisor of four DBA and two Ph.D. research candidates in management (a third Ph.D. candidate was added in 2004). As a senior academic I was experienced in one-on-one research supervision of candidates in my area of research expertise, namely the challenges facing organizations in the ever-emergent knowledge era. Of the two Ph.D. candidates, one was an experienced practitioner. The DBA candidates were all practitioners with many years' experience operating in senior management positions from a cross-section of industry sectors (public service, manufacturing, academia, service), and disciplines (engineering, physics, design, human resource management). All candidates were at different stages of their research (one of the Ph.D. candidates was well advanced in his thesis write-up, the second Ph.D. candidate was involved in the first (quantitative) phase of her multi-method research. Two of the DBA candidates were new candidates undertaking the initial (coursework) part of their candidature, while the other two candidates had completed their coursework segments and were embarking upon their practice-led research. The research methodologies also varied from a more traditional external researcher using case study methodologies through questionnaires and interviews, to 'lived experience' through action-research methodologies such as participant observation, first-person reflection narrative of 'lived experience', and interpretativism (using an abductive epistemology).

Having supervised the two Ph.D. candidates for a year, and the four DBA candidates for six months through traditional one-on-one supervisory meetings, I had identified that although all were undertaking research in diverse topics, a domain common to all was management of change in a knowledge era. I was keen to establish an opportunity for candidates to meet and share their thoughts, ideas, and experiences in a more collective and collaborative environment. Given that my own research included identifying the potential for CoPs to assist the sharing of knowledge (particularly tacit knowledge), I invited each of the candidates to join with me in establishing a research CoP as an experiential learning opportunity. I identified the potential of a research CoP to contribute to their own research by providing a forum to network research (theory and practice) and to create, exchange, and expand knowledge around the theme of the contribution of CoPs to organizations' knowledge strategy. To initially assist identification of whether the candidates might find value in a CoP I suggested that all candidates read Wenger, McDermott, and Snyder (2002) on how to cultivate CoPs.

All DBA candidates and one of the Ph.D. candidates (henceforth called members) attended the first meeting. All candidates acknowledged that my suggested domain for the CoP of 'the contribution of CoPs to an organization's knowledge strategy' did, directly or indirectly, relate to their particular practice-based research. One candidate stated that the CoP could provide 'a space in which all participants can share their thoughts, ideas, experiences and findings'. In so doing it was thought that the CoP would add a different dimension to their DBA supervised professional practice review sessions that involved more formal presentations on a more eclectic range of issues in the issues. The Ph.D. candidate was less certain about the connection between her research focus (a more macro view of knowledge transfer between organizations in research alliances) and consequently attended the CoP meetings irregularly.

It was agreed that meetings would commence at monthly intervals at a mutually convenient time. One of the DBA students with skills and experience in establishing virtual discussion facilities suggested using the university Distributed Learning System (DLS) to provide the opportunity for a more continuous discourse. It was also agreed that the discourse in the CoP would emerge organically, with no set agenda and no formal notes, although I agreed to circulate any notes I took, especially interesting or 'breakthrough' ideas, to assist the opportunity for double-loop learning through reflection and feedback between meetings (Argyris 1990). A number of issues related to the domain emerged during discussion in the first meeting and these have continued to underpin discourse throughout the life of the CoP:

- relationship between CoPs and social capital
- organizational commitment to CoPs (resource commitment or verbal rhetoric)
- apparent dichotomy between knowledge sharing and organizational commitment to the individual
- relationship between trust and knowledge sharing
- potential role of CoPs in assisting the development of lateral thinking
- cultural influences on knowledge sharing
- role and measurement of resources people bring to organizations
- potential knowledge sharing/partnership between universities and organizations
- link between knowledge and organizational sustainability (triple bottom line)
- difference between CoPs and other employee participative practices.

The CoP in Practice

The CoP met monthly between August and December 2003, varying more in 2004, sometimes on a fortnightly basis, sometimes on a bi-monthly basis, depending on the work demands of the members. All DBA candidates and the supervisor attended regularly, the Ph.D. candidates attended less regularly, with a new Ph.D. candidate who commenced in March 2004 also becoming a regular attendee. One of the DBA members summarized attendance at meetings as follows:

the ongoing participation in these sessions, for those who have senior full-time roles testifies to their perceived value to all. It is rare to not have a quorum for fresh discussions and directions.

Membership grew in 2004 with a new Ph.D. candidate, an academic colleague undertaking a Ph.D. within the domain of knowledge management at another university, an honours student from the design area undertaking research into 'virtual' CoPs in local communities, and an external expert from a not-for-profit organization. The latter person was invited after members expressed a desire to ensure that the discourse extended from a 'business' perspective into more 'social' aspects. The external expert continued to attend meetings periodically because it provided an open, less pressured environment to discuss issues with senior representatives of the business community.

CoP meetings were held for an hour, once a month on a Friday morning starting at 8.30. This time limit was the only structural feature of CoP meetings and was maintained to make sure that members were able to fit the opportunity for open discourse into their heavy work schedules. Discussion was also unstructured and varied from continuation of a discourse begun at the previous meeting, to discussion on an article that a member might have circulated between meetings, or to ideas or reflection that a member may have had under consideration. Discourse was open, with everyone engaging in, and contributing to, the discourse.

Assessment of the CoP

In assessing the value of the CoPs I have used a combination of the advantages and limitations of experiential learning discussed earlier in this chapter including:

- value added to the individual doctoral researcher
- extension of doctoral research from an individual to a social experience
- combination of management theory and professional practice
- more equal supervisory–candidate relationship
- reflection in the 'here and now'
- opportunities for frank, open (non defensive) discourse and reflection.

In so doing, in keeping with the views of the CoP members emphasis has been placed on a qualitative rather than quantitative form of evaluation. Qualitative comments from members were collected in a variety of ways: collectively during one CoP meeting in which discussion focused on what may be the identified 'artefacts' emerging from CoP meetings, individually when a decision was taken to submit the CoP experience to the university as an example of an innovation. This evaluation revealed the following.

Value Added to the Individual Doctoral Researcher

The CoP was credited with assisting the individual doctoral candidates to develop their research skills, gain a broader understanding of their topic through the sharing of discussion on the various literature reviews undertaken, and develop a more holistic view of their research area. In their individual comments CoP members stated the following:

Deanne:

- I have fast-tracked my development as a researcher through the collaborative collegiate culture that is generated through CoP engagement
- The CoP facilitated
  - o my ability to articulate and discuss my research amongst a diverse community of researchers
  - o the maturing of my research process; greater clarity of focus and research method
  - o a deeper level of self-reflection and personal understanding of research intent
  - o an exchange of research paradigms, encouraging open debate and discussion

Owen: for me, our COP is a valued research paradigm that:

- broadens my academic and social networks and learning.
- adds to my research design and approach by my living the CoP experience.
- gives increased 'value adding' to my DBA time allocation and efforts.

Jackie: the value in the CoP environment is in the:

- free and proactive sharing of information amongst the participants who are participating voluntarily.
- removal of pressure of formal outcomes, and competitive influences.

- students participating in the CoPs are already highly skilled business people, but meeting for purely intellectual reasons is not a common opportunity.
- help in developing skills and rigour in theory development and defence.

Extension of Doctoral Research from an Individual to a Social Experience

During the collective feedback a number of statements about the CoP as a source of social learning experience were made including:

the CoP creates a sense of belonging … reduces the loneliness of the part-time post-graduate student: it builds a sense of community and not just a group of colleagues coming together for lectures which are driven by somebody else's agenda … it creates a tie that binds, bringing together candidates from various backgrounds, professions and experiences.

This led to recognition of similarities underpinning their different research topics that:

despite the divergence in backgrounds, knowledge, industry and thesis title, members recognised that discussion within the CoP led to an extraordinary commonality and convergence of topics that originally only Sandra had seen.

Owen summarized the CoP experience as:

providing a base for members to codify new models of social interaction, generate substantial bonding/linking social capital … manifested in the trust displayed and knowledge shared.

Jackie stated:

the group functions as a collection of intellectual equals who come to learn and to pass on knowledge wherever the opportunity arises in the free-flowing discussion … what the CoP does is provide the environment to capture the social energy of the collective.

From my perspective the CoP supplied the opportunity for candidates to provide peer support for each other. This was both intellectual (through sharing literature they came across as well as the exploration of different ideas) and social and emotional (through sharing the 'journey' through the academic process). The experience confirmed my initial belief that candidates could assist and support each other better by sharing their journey in this collective manner than through me as an intermediary.

Combination of Management Theory and Professional Practice

Members contributed both their professional practice and academic insights from their literature reviews. Jackie described the opportunity for true intellectual engagement provided by the CoP as providing 'a chance to work-out my brain that I don't get in my current work/life situation'. She went on to liken the environment created in the CoP to a university 'where academics can stop an expert in the corridor and discuss new research findings... a luxury not normally available in the world of the practitioner... it was quite a creative process'. She summarized the experience as:

there are frequent 'epiphanies' experienced by participants as the group exploration of theories from the wide variety of disciplines use experiments in language and narrative as sense-making methods, both supporting and challenging their fellow researchers. There is much cross-fertilisation of ideas, and sharing of readings and practice examples which would not happen in the competitive environment of course-based discussion groups.

Owen described the CoP as providing 'time and ambience for reflective thinking'. Indeed, the open interchange within the CoP reduced the concern often expressed about practitioner research that it may lack a critical external 'voice'.

Deanne commented:

the CoP broadened my original frame of reference to include a range of literature and views from other CoP participants that may not have been identified had I worked entirely on my own. It challenged my interpretations of literature, allowing deeper analysis and discussion from community members. It exposed [me] to new ideas, new ways of interpreting and greater appreciation for the input of others, and it provided greater openness to diverse views and inputs and the value to my own research endeavour.

Jackie commented:

Whilst the meetings are 'themed' the discussions are allowed to take any path which emerges and this unstructured approach leads often to innovative linking of concepts, introduction of new areas of interest, and breakthroughs in terms of removing boundaries and other scope limiters.

More Equal Supervisory–Candidate Relationship

Candidate members stated that the CoP did provide a more equal, mutually beneficial supervisory–candidate relationship. During the collective feedback session one comment was that the CoP provided 'a new way of engaging in teaching and research supervision' that assisted the development of 'common understanding'. The CoP was described as being built on a foundation of 'here is an opportunity to collaborate' rather than 'you will collaborate'. Another comment was that the CoP created a more equal environment by 'allowing candidates the freedom to make the connections and search for common threads as a gathering of equals, rather than being supervisor driven where candidates work to someone else's theme'.

Apart from a more equal supervisory relationship, Owen stated that the benefits of a more equal interchange within the CoP 'demonstrated the value of a non-hierarchal structure and minimalist (but essential) functional roles that distinguish CoPs from other social structures'. Deanne commented that she developed 'a greater understanding of the supervisor role as research agent within the CoPs context—opening up new levels of interaction and guidance'.

As the supervisor, I noted the expanded opportunities for the candidates to share information and knowledge rather than rely solely on the supervisor. The major challenge for me was to restrain myself from assuming responsibility for CoP meetings, the direction of the discourse, and circulating notes from the meetings. Candidate members assisted me in making this transition by sharing responsibility for reminders of meeting dates. Furthermore, whenever I suggested the cessation of meetings in busy work periods, candidate members resisted this, and other solutions, such as meeting at alternating times to suit work commitments, were instituted.

Reflection in the 'Here and Now'

Members stated that the discourse that occurred within the CoP assisted them to identify and reflect on their own tacit knowledge and the assumptions made by individuals. This was described as 'starting with one tiny thread and then expanding'. The CoP was described as providing members with the opportunity to influence their professional practice as part of a double-loop learning process by transferring knowledge developed during CoP meetings to their individual workplaces. Jackie stated that the CoP 'provided the opportunity for insider practice-based researchers to broaden their perspective and ensure that their reflection upon practice assists them in considering change required in a knowledge era'.

Opportunities for Frank, Open (Non-Defensive) Discourse and Reflection

Members remarked that the CoP, being voluntary and free of the structural rigidities and requirements of formal academic interchange, meant that the subject material remained interesting and members were honest and willing to offer their views. Jackie stated, 'it is in fact a luxury that we don't often get'.

The CoP was credited with providing members with emotional support, intellectual stimulation, and an opportunity to discuss emerging ideas in a 'safe' environment, through support given to each other. Trust being established between CoP members was identified as an important requirement to encourage the sharing of confidential information and to encourage members to contribute their views. One member stated, 'the supportive atmosphere created encouraged members to openly share their thoughts'. This was a surprising comment for me, as I had not considered the potential 'threat' of individuals 'revealing' their vulnerabilities in the more open environment of a CoP than in the one-on-one supervisory relationship. This could also have been influenced by the fairly senior role that most of the members had as practitioners. Indeed one member stated that the CoP provided a 'forum where contentious thinking can progress to free discussion without retribution or diminishment'.

The outcome was that members believed that their research had been improved, their knowledge expanded, and their own personality developed through their participation in the CoP. Jackie stated that the CoP provides the opportunity to 'challenge and be challenged, to try on the theories and beliefs of others and see how they felt—this cannot be achieved in a group smaller than three or four'.

In summary, as an experiential approach to doctoral supervision, the CoP served to provide opportunities for practitioners to share their individual practice-based knowledge in a collective research environment. Although the attendance of the Ph.D. candidates was limited, this can be seen as a result of the stage of their research when the CoP was established as well as their broader focus and less practical experience. This conclusion is borne out by the fact that the newer Ph.D. candidate became a regular and enthusiastic attendee at meetings.

It is, however, also important to record that, despite the positive evaluation of the CoP by candidate/members and myself as supervisor, as an innovative form of research supervision, the university was restricted in its ability to recognize its true value by a focus on government-established measures of supervisory excellence. The major current measure is 'number of research completions within time'. As any causal link between the CoP and 'timely' research completions could not be evidenced, the university was unable to recognize the CoP as a major experiential research supervision innovation. This has implications for the level of future university support that may be provided for innovations associated with experiential research supervisory arrangement such as a CoP.

CONCLUSION

The model of an experiential, collective (social) approach to doctoral research supervision through a CoP has been shown to demonstrate the advantage of enabling a number of doctoral candidates to share their practice-based knowledge, their reflection as 'outside' observers, and their academic research, to the mutual advantage of all members. In so doing the CoP provides the opportunity to expand each individual's research beyond the individual to the collective through which knowledge is extended from the individual to the social. This provides an expanded opportunity to link management practice and theory in a less hierarchical research environment in which the supervisor becomes a member of the CoP rather than a separate 'expert'. In so doing the supervisor still has the opportunity to contribute their 'expertise' as required, be that about the domain under discussion, or how the domain can be translated to reflect a theoretical approach, with the result being that the supervisory relationship becomes more mutually rewarding. It also adds a more contemporary aspect to the reflective process.

The advantage of a CoP over other research groups or teams is that attendance is voluntary, with members building relationships, learning together, and developing a sense of belonging, trust, and mutual commitment. As a model of research supervision, the CoP also provides the opportunity for ongoing membership at the conclusion of the doctoral candidature, an advantage for candidates who desire to continue the opportunity for open discourse, and universities that desire an ongoing relationship with their alumni.

However, the CoP model of 'collective' supervision is not without its challenges and limitations. First, the supervisor has to be prepared to become more a facilitator of knowledge sharing rather than the 'expert', and although there is some sharing of the administration of CoP meetings, this falls more to the supervisor than the doctoral candidate members. Second, the university needs to support and recognize the additional time contribution of the supervisor in establishing and supporting the CoP. Academic workload and 'performance appraisal' negotiations need to consider the supervisory process rather than just outcomes (number of successful completions) if this new supervisory process is to be adopted. Third, candidates can become so involved in the breadth of the discourse that they find it difficult to confine their research within the boundaries of their research topic. This can especially become a problem when there is pressure (from the university or the candidate sponsor) to finish the doctorate within a set period of time. Fourth, the research CoP can go through periods during which the combination of work, family, and thesis demands leads to a decrease in ability to attend meetings. Both the supervisor and candidate members need to accept that this is a natural characteristic of CoPs, and be comfortable with the need to reassess the value of any particular CoP at any time.

Notes

Written by Sandra Jones on behalf of doctoral candidates/CoP members: Deanne Koelmeyer; Owen Lockwood; Jackie McCann; Ahmad Mousa; Frank Tait.

1. Note: collective in this sense refers to a collective process rather than a co-creation of a dissertation.

References

Argyris, C. (1990). *Overcoming Organizational Differences: Facilitating Organizational Learning.* Boston: Allyn & Bacon.

Becher, T., Henkel, M., and Kogan, M. (1994). *Graduate Education in Britain.* London: Jessica Kingsley.

Bourner, T., Bowden, R., and Laing, S. (2001). 'The Adoption of Professional Doctorates in English Universities: Why Here? Why Now?', in B. Green, T. Maxwell, and P. Shanahan (eds.), *Doctoral Education and Professional Practice: The Next Generation.* Armidale: Kardoorair.

Bowen, W., and Rudenstine, N. (1992). *In Pursuit of the PhD.* Princeton: Princeton University.

Brown, J., and Duguid, D. (1991). 'Organizational Learning and Communities of Practice: Towards a Unified View of Working, Learning and Innovating', *Organizational Science*, 2/1: 40–57.

———— (2000). 'Organizational Learning and Communities of Practice: Towards a Unified View of Working, Learning and Innovation', in E. Lesser, M. Fontaine, and J. Slusher (eds.), *Knowledge and Communities.* Boston: Butterworth-Heinemann.

Burgess, R. (1997). *Beyond the First Degree: Graduate Education, Lifelong Learning and Careers.* Buckingham: SRHE and Open University.

Clark, B. (1993). 'The Research Foundations of Postgraduate Education', *Higher Education Quarterly*, 47/4: 301–15.

Clarke, H. (1996). 'Dumbing-Down in Australian Universities', *Quadrant*, Sept.: 55–9.

Frankland, M. (1999). 'The Master/Apprentice Model for the Supervision of Postgraduate Research and a New Policy for Research Education', *Australian Universities' Review*, 42/1: 8–11.

Gibbons, M., Limoges, C., Nowotny, H., Schwartzman, S., Scott, P., and Trow, M. (1994). *The New Production of Knowledge: The Dynamics of Science and Research in Contemporary Societies.* London: Sage.

Green, B., Maxwell, T., and Shanahan, P. (2001). *Doctoral Education and Professional Practice: The Next Generation.* Armidale: Kardoorair.

Hildreth, P., and Kimble, C. (eds.) (2004). *Knowledge Networks: Innovation through Communities of Practice.* Hershey, Pa.: Idea Group.

Hockey, J. (1994). 'New Territory: Problems of Adjusting to the First Year of a Social Science PhD', *Studies in Higher Education*, 19/2: 177–90.

Holdaway, E., Deblois, C., and Winchester, I. (1995). *Organization and Administration of Graduate Programs.* Edmonton: Department of Educational Policy Studies, University of Alberta.

Kolb, D. (1984). *Experiential Learning.* Englewood Cliffs, NJ: Prentice-Hall.

Lave, J., and Wenger, E. (1991). *Situated Learning Legitimate Peripheral Participation.* Cambridge: Cambridge University Press.

Lee, A., Green, B., and Brennan, M. (2000). 'Organizational Knowledge, Professional Practice and the Professional Doctorate at Work', in J. Garrick and C. Rhodes (eds.), *Research and Knowledge at Work: Perspectives, Case-Studies and Innovative Strategies.* New York: Routledge.

Lesser, E., Fontaine, M., and Slusher, J. (eds.) (2000). *Knowledge and Communities.* Boston: Butterworth-Heinemann.

—— and Prusak, L. (2000). 'Communities of Practice: Social Capital and Organizational Knowledge', in E. Lesser, M. Fontaine, and J. Slusher (eds.), *Knowledge and Communities.* Boston: Butterworth-Heinemann.

McMorland, J., Carroll, B., Copas, S., and Pringle, J. (2003). 'Enhancing the Practice of Phd Supervisory Relationships through First-and-Second-Person Action Research/Peer Relationship Inquiry', *Forum: Qualitative Social Research*, FQS. http://www.qualitative-research.net/fqs/.

Morley, C. (1999). 'A Professional Doctorate in Business: The New Height of Management Education', in S. Neelamegham, D. Midgley, and C. Sen (eds.), *Enterprise Management*. New Delhi: Tata McGraw-Hill Publishing Company.

Morley, C. (2002). 'Different Doctors: A Comparison of PhD and Professional Doctorate Supervision, *Proceedings Annual Conference ANZAM*. Beechworth, Australia.

Neumann, R. (2003). *The Doctoral Education Experience*. Canberra: Department of Education, Science and Technology, Australian Government Publishing Service.

Reynolds, M., and Vince, R. (2004). 'Critical Management Education and Action-Based Learning: Synergies and Contradictions', *Academy of Management Learning and Education*, 3/4: 442–56.

RMIT (2003). *DBA Brochure*. Melbourne.

Schön, D. (1983). *The Reflective Practitioner*. San Francisco: Jossey-Bass.

—— (1987). *Educating the Reflective Practitioner*. San Francisco: Jossey-Bass.

Sharp, J., and Howard, K. (1996). *The Management of the Student Research Projects*, 2nd edn. Aldershot: Gower.

Snyder, W. (1997). 'Communities of Practice: Combining Organizational Learning and Strategy Insights to Create a Bridge to the 21st Century'. Presented at the 1997 Academy of Management Conference.

Thorne, L. (2001). 'Doctoral-Level Learning: Customisation for Communities of Practice', in B. Green, T. Maxwell, and P. Shanahan (eds.), *Doctoral Education and Professional Practice: The Next Generation*. Armidale: Kardoorair.

Vince, R. (1998). 'Behind and Beyond Kolb's Learning Cycle', *Journal of Management Education*, June, 22/3: 304–19.

Wenger, E. (1998). *Communities of Practice: Learning, Meaning and Identity*. New York: Cambridge University Press.

—— McDermott, R., and Snyder, W. (2002). *Cultivating Communities of Practice*. Combridge, Mass.: Harvard Business School Press.

Action Research

Candidate Statements (D. Koelymer, O. Lockwood, J. McCann, and A. Mousa). RMIT Research Supervision Award Application, 2004.

CoP Notes from meetings: 6 August 2003; 22 August 2003; 10 October 2003; 14 November 2003; 28 November 2003; 18 June 2004; 24 September 2004.

Jones, S., Koelmeyer, D., Lockwood, O., McCann, J., and Mousa, A. (2004). 'A Community Approach to Research Supervision'. RMIT Research Colloquium. Internal mimeo.

CHAPTER 20

DRAWINGS AS A LINK TO EMOTIONAL DATA

A SLIPPERY TERRITORY

TUSSE SIDENIUS JENSEN

JANE ROHDE VOIGT

ENRICO MARIA PIRAS

BENTE RUGAARD THORSEN

INTRODUCTION

At the time of writing this chapter, we are Ph.D. students with an interest in learning about research from emotional and aesthetic perspectives. The specific context of this writing was a Ph.D. short course on 'Emotions and Aesthetics in Organizational Learning Research' arranged by the Doctoral School of Organizational Learning (DOCSOL) at the Danish University of Education, for European researchers and doctoral students. The task we were involved in was to take part in a drawing event and afterwards to work together to make a written contribution to knowledge in this field. Our interest in emotions and aesthetics was evoked because the course introduced methods to study complex social arenas in organizations that were new (to us) and that immediately seemed more promising than conventional methods.

One thing that we discovered on this course was that emotions and personal experiences are easily revealed by the use of drawings and that drawings can be used as a research method for capturing emotional and aesthetic aspects of experience. We have included four case stories from our experience of the course in order to reflect on the researchers' experiences as research participants as well as developing our knowledge about this method.

The drawing method is seen as a good way of gaining knowledge and generating interpretations from research participants. However, we also describe how certain skills are required in using this method in order to handle both the 'sensitive' information (information relating to senses and emotions) and the process itself. We do not specify the nature of the required skills, since we are still learning about these ourselves, but we do recommend some ideas for further research on this topic. Generally, it seems to us that the researcher's role changes when she or he is working with the drawing method, because the emotional data that emerges from the method easily becomes a slippery territory (meaning difficult to keep one's footing) if not handled with care.

We are aware that the classic research paradigms prescribed by positivist methodologies have been challenged by an increasing number of scholars. We are also aware that there is not necessarily agreement about the assumptions that underpin this approach to research. For example, there are different perspectives and positions within an 'aesthetic approach' to research in organizational and management theory. While some advocate a vision of the aesthetic as translatable in rational terms (Gagliardi 1996), others consider rational/clear-cut knowledge as intrinsically opposed to aesthetic/ambiguous knowledge (Strati 1992, 1999). We are learning that one of the most intriguing ways to rethink the path of research has been to put 'artful' expressions into it, generally as a complementary part of a qualitative approach. Barry (1996) considers artefacts intrinsically ambiguous and facilitative of a process of interpretation, where researcher(s) and interviewee(s) cooperate, and always leave room for open and contradictory explanations. Such reflections have opened a field of experimentation where artefacts like drawings, sculptures, pictures, and dramatization have gained a legitimate position as valid tools for analysis. We are part of an emerging understanding that non-rational forms of self expression can elicit the non-verbal, tacit, emotional knowledge that is often ignored or discarded by conventional techniques. A key question for researchers like us therefore is how to use artful expressions as a research device?

THE EXPERIENTIAL DRAWING EVENT

We took part in a research experiment during this short course that involved making drawings as a way of engaging with the emotional experience of being a researcher and of doing research. The experiment involved working with lived experiences and with reflections, as participants and as researchers, respectively. The four phases of the research method we experienced were the same as the approach outlined in a paper by Vince and Broussine (1996), which used drawings as a research method for investigating the emotions and politics mobilized by attempts to make change happen within organizations. The learning event was facilitated by our guest tutor Russ Vince and the process we undertook included one individual drawing session, a group process with individual and group reflections, a group discussion of emerging categories, and finally a plenary discussion of the method. At the plenary discussion we were invited to consider using the data collected during the learning event as the basis for writing a chapter for this book. This chapter focuses on our experience of this workshop, its content, and our reflections on the research method. We used drawings to generate data about the experience of being a doctoral student/researcher; including being both a research participant and a collector of data within complex qualitative processes.

In his introduction to the event, Russ Vince explained that drawings give rise to emotional data, and that they represent a method to sustain the connection between personal and political data. The drawing approach is a participative research process, which gives access to and has an influence on organizational members' emotional responses (see Vince forthcoming). This kind of research asks the researcher to pay attention to the interactive and developmental nature of research processes. As researchers and as participants in the process of learning about using drawings in research, this was what we were introduced to as well as inspired by.

To use drawings as a method within (for example) management education, the drawings have to be explicitly placed within a range of contextually specific dialogues (intra-interpersonal and intra-intergroup) and must be regarded as an expression of context (Vince and Broussine 1996). One way to strengthen these processes of disparate and consensual dialogues is to differentiate between them as either antagonistically destructive or constructive. This distinction generates knowledge of how to intensify group processes, and can be an agent for developing an atmosphere of openness, active listening, and retaining mutual goals; an atmosphere that is important when emotional and personal information is included because of the risks of humiliation, vulnerability, and other feelings of exposure (Darsø 2001, 2004). Darsø's research is particularly relevant to add to this experiential session, because her studies build on risky innovative processes and experiences of disclosure within teams in Danish organizations.

A Description of the Drawing Event

It was made clear from the beginning that all the steps of the event would give rise to research data collected as drawings and audio records. Something more than a lesson was at stake. An overview of the stages was provided in advance, but the experiences we had could never have been included in a workshop introduction. This workshop came to mean a lot for us—both as participants and researchers.

We were asked to draw a picture of our experience of being a Ph.D. student on large sheets of paper with markers in different colours. The only requirement was to include ourselves in the picture. Some protested and claimed to lack drawing abilities, but we were assured that the ability to draw was not required. After drawing in a tense and complete silence for twenty minutes—a phase we still easily recall— we were situated in two random groups with four and five members, respectively. The individual stage gave way to a group process; the awareness of the stages made the process systemic. An awareness, which was reinforced by the facilitators as they walked around observing our work progressing and took photos of the event and the drawings. Within the groups, each of us explained in detail what the image meant to us, and we shared our thoughts, feelings, and interpretations of each image, asking 'Is this a melody that is catching up on you?' or 'What was is like to do that? How did you feel?'

The processes of (a) telling others about one's drawing and (b) listening to others commenting on it made the non-verbal explicit and allowed a verbal form of communication. It was a process of continuous immersion, and detachment was only allowed by the physical presence of the drawings. The participants explained their drawing, its embedded meaning and emotions, by continuously pointing to or addressing specific parts ('in this part I represent . . . this figure stands for . . .'). Those who commented acted in much the same way. Thus, each individual drawing continuously provided a way of discussing the common topic and the drawings' potential for inspiring and for playing with the different interpretations which emerged in the group. The most significant moments of this phase happened when insight would suddenly hit the person who had made the drawing; showing that she or he had not realized fully what she or he had drawn. One participant realized during this phase that she had depicted herself naked!

We were encouraged to include emotional data in the process, which was easy enough because the subjects were highly relevant to us. Energy was intense, communication was unrestrained and intimate, and we shared little pieces about our lives with each other. When each member of the group had presented their image and received comments and reflections, the group's task changed; we now had to agree on some common categories or differences emerging from the discussions of the drawings. In this phase, there was more energy and conversation. The individual comments and reflections merged into the collective work of finding common categories from the session. Some categories emerged quickly from the material, for example the loneliness of being a Ph.D. student, others emerged from working with the subject, and this last part of the session closed down the event properly so that everyone had at least an opportunity for closure after the emotions that the experiment had raised.

DRAWINGS AND STORIES

The research material from this drawing session comprises images, audio recordings of the group discussions, and written descriptions of the experiences from the session. The descriptions vary somewhat in terms of focus and style because they are produced individually by each participant.

Case No. 1

I look at the white paper and think that this is a hard one to do. I find it difficult to structure my thoughts. My thoughts come sporadically. Especially my thoughts of what is difficult are hard to pin down. Then the picture is there and I begin to draw. I draw myself sitting in front of the computer. I sense frustration—frustration that I cannot capture the soft and not-verbal knowledge. The soft waving and melodious aspects of knowledge, which come into action, when describing playful learning and movements, are not easily categorized. Just to describe them verbally is difficult.

Case No. 20.1 Drawing

My hair is all wild; it is like energy that radiates from me—so much so that I look electric and rather weird.

I had thought it would be difficult to draw these experiences with problematic and chaotic writing processes, but it turned out fairly recognizable and, to me, captures the experience rather well. I presented my picture to the others and told them about it and I sense that once I have shared my story with the others, I am somehow closer to them.

The comments I get from the other participants are somehow difficult to take in—I kind of defend myself, until I am asked by the facilitator to try and listen to the comments instead of rejecting them. By listening I come to a better understanding of what they see in my picture, and the important thing is that I can suddenly look into areas that I haven't noticed or wanted to look into before. By contemplating, taking inspiration from it and perhaps implementing these insights into my own interpretation of my experiences, I can learn something from others, see different takes upon my experiences, and do a reinterpretation of my experiences.

Case No. 2

Normally I don't like to draw, but I felt that I was forced to do so as part of this course. Having been a Ph.D. student for two years now, I have come to realize that being forced into something new is a part of the Ph.D. learning process! The atmosphere in the course was supportive, and I felt fine. I immediately picked up an image of a tree in my mind. The image of a tree just came to me and I began to draw a picture. My drawing is quite simple and naive. What I found interesting was not the drawing itself, but the process of explaining the story about my Ph.D. that came after the drawing part, the group reflection, and the storytelling in relation to all the different drawings.

The group process was interesting because it was an intensive process. Emotions were on the agenda and the stories were intense. The group was inquisitive and reflective in relation to the drawings, and details gradually entered the discussions that followed. At the group level, we learned from each other's experiences, realizing the differences, for example culture, stages, the hard work, and similarities within the Ph.D. processes, for example being curious, knowing, being vulnerable, having to write academic articles. Aside from the group process, I found the individual reflective level following the event to be a very valuable part of the learning process. My self-reflection was mainly concerned with what I felt was missing in my own drawing in relation to my Ph.D. process, and I have reflected a lot on that. I think that to some extent this process made me more conscious about being a Ph.D. student.

Case No. 20.2 Drawing

Case No. 3

As a new Ph.D. student I feel I am entering a world with many aspects and many challenges, but also with new friendships and a lot of fun along the way. I am entering the new world with a smile on my face because I am full of positive expectations. In this new world, I have drawn the writing process in the middle and my senses like seeing, hearing, and talking just next to that. I find it a little strange that my body only is about to enter the world, when my senses are already inside. Yet I think the answer is that I already began this Ph.D. project in my mind when I graduated in 2003.

In my drawing, a man wearing glasses symbolizes my supervisor. I see him as a solid anchor for this ride I am about to begin. I also think there are a lot of rules and regulations one must be aware of, and that is why the paragraphs are in there. There

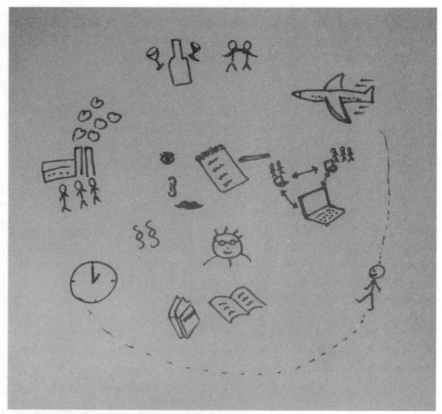

Case No. 20.3 Drawing

are three computers and they symbolize the importance of networking with others. Another social aspect is the wineglasses and the friendly persons, because I think this process is impossible without help from friends. The aeroplane symbolizes the amount of travelling to conferences and seminars in other countries, the factory symbolizes contact with the industry I am investigating, and the books represent the tremendous amount of literature I have to read. Finally, there is Time; a big, overwhelming, and dangerous part of the project. Dangerous, because you at first feel like you have all the time in the world to do your project, but suddenly you are in a hurry and have a hard time catching up. The group process made me see and say things to the group that I was not aware of about my own view of being a Ph.D. student.

Case No. 4

'It's not about drawing skill.' It's been repeated quite a few times before we all started to draw. Still it was embarrassing. I felt somehow forced to do something I didn't

Case No. 20.4 Drawing

like and was not skilled at. This feeling of inadequacy was reinforced by supervisors walking around the tables, looking at my work, and taking pictures. I felt observed. A few lines on the paper: I didn't like it and I started drawing on the other side.

I drew myself walking away from home, towards a place made of bicycles, book-butterflies, pentagrams, and pictures. These things are all related to my research, they surround me, but I felt like I haven't yet grasped them. In a while it became easier to draw and I kept adding details. 'We are supposed to explain it to others,' I kept repeating to myself, so I thought about drawing as a prelude to something I am keener at: speaking. When I presented my drawing to the group I knew exactly what every line meant. I explained the steadiness of my parents' house as counterpoint to the instability of my new situation. Pentagrams, pictures, and flying books were a clear symbol (to me) of the aesthetic perspective on organizations. It was something completely new for me, I explained. I was proud of my butterfly-book: a symbol that stands for beauty (of the topic), difficulty (to understand and use new concept), and the challenges of being a Ph.D. student. Then a supervisor passed by. He heard my explanation, looked at the drawing, and said: 'It looks like they are shitting on you.' I believe it's now I understand what the facilitator meant when he said you put things in the drawing you are not aware of. I'm fascinated. But, I don't know if I like it.

REFLECTIONS ON THE DRAWING EVENT

The task we had been assigned was simply to draw our experience as Ph.D. students with ourselves in the picture. The underlying assumption that justifies this is that artful activities, such as drawing, elicit the non-verbal and elusive dimensions of knowledge. They are a means to express something synoptically, rather than linearly; it facilitates the complex, chaotic, and unspeakable rather than the consequential, rational, and clear-cut. During the process, emotions inextricably emerged from our drawings, associated to our lived experiences, unintentionally and unconsciously. Just look at the artefacts in the pictures: what have trees, wineglasses, pentagrams, aeroplanes, and private houses to do with Ph.D. students? How come we all put these artefacts in the drawings? Are they part of our professional life or just something that belongs to our private life? We concluded that it was probably our emotions that connected these different aspects of our life.

The Experience of being a Participant in Research

One of our reflections addresses the distinction between our professional and private lives, a distinction that seems to lose some of its relevance when personal experiences and emotions are associated with it. Even if we were asked merely to depict ourselves as organizational actors, none of us restricted her or his representation to a classic organizational space, and we believe that this drawing method and experiential research session contributed to revealing things that we, as research participants, were only partly conscious of. This may also explain the difficulty we had as individuals in accepting and taking in comments from others, as well as realizing just how much others could construct, construe, misconstrue, and reflect on from a simple drawing. In the plenary session many agreed it had been a challenging experience, 'emotionally involving but not necessary pleasant', as one said.

Unlike conventional research methods we were quite able to understand that this method required an unusual trust in the others: 'It's a part of me I give to others, and others give something back to me.' This 'give and take' required openness and it included having to allow others to comment on our stories. Once we had put something in the drawing, even if we were unaware of it at the time, it became a matter of discussion and it was not easy to accept that a fellow Ph.D. student was allowed an opinion about our lives. This led us to reflect on the climate generated by the use of this technique, and on the high emotional investment that is expected of the research participants when cooperating in such research. We concluded that to be the analysed subjects for once was a highly valuable experience in order to understand what we are 'really' asking people to do within qualitative methods. By experiencing an intensive processes of data collection ourselves on a relevant topic, the lived emotion can be recalled and emphatically relived in order to understand the difficulties of respondents and research participants within our own research projects.

Another thing to keep in mind is how to protect oneself in sessions like this. Some of us believed that more explicit precautions were needed and emphasized the risks of this approach in the study of organizations. The plenary discussion touched on the risks by implicitly asking people to share their feelings from this session, to put the feelings down on paper, and to give others possibilities to discuss and reflect upon them. On the other hand, it was discussed whether it was possible to ask someone to repress their emotions in a research process, or make a sharp distinction between home and work or past, present, and future. Organizational theory has traditionally applied similar distinctions, often as dichotomies, which leads to a certain interpretation of organizational phenomena. In the drawing sessions, we found that it is impossible to separate emotions from professional life. It is interesting that this intense and, for some, scary process seemed to be able to break down well-established boundaries between organizational and personal life, but it also pinpoints that the researcher must possess certain competencies in facilitating group processes.

The experiment demonstrated the development of a research process from an individual to a group level. The drawing phase was a rather solitary one. As a result of this phase, there was a continuous change of focus from a material artefact, the drawing, to a verbal one; the discussions and the development of initial categories emerging from these discussions. The aim of this phase was, in fact, to come up with some shared preliminary conclusions on the commonalities that had emerged in the process so far. Because we were immersed in the process, this stage did not make immediate sense to all of us; thus, as part of research data it is important for the participants to understand the aim of this part of the event.

Emotions as a Slippery Territory

The two groups of Ph.D. students brought the following initial categorizations to the plenary session: ambivalence, loneliness, challenges (group A); peer networking, navigation in multiplicity, practice vs. academia, time, supervisor, theory, and approaching the field (group B). Loneliness and ambivalence were the only emotions that were mentioned. Other categories could easily be associated with emotions, for example 'challenges' could encompass fear or pride. It is difficult to determine which emotions we have identified just from looking at the categories. We were not asked to use emotions as categories and so the point here is not to judge the value of the categories, but it can easily be interpreted as the willingness of the participants to leave the slippery territory of emotions and step back to the comfortable realm of the rational.

We think that this research approach can be helpful for the development of knowledge about organizational group processes. In drawing sessions all the material is gathered and analysed in terms of the specific context and the theoretical implications. This implies that, at the event, emotions were regarded as an organizational dimension of a specific phenomenon rather than as characteristic of the event. At the same time, the choice of rational categories instead of emotions indicates the difficulties in handling emotions when we analyse an event like this. Thus, this method reveals our difficulties in expressing and being in emotional processes, but it also makes a difference to be a part of this slippery territory; the participants recall the event regardless of the individual evaluation of this experience.

When analysing the research data from the drawing session we found that the process we went through confirms that handling emotions is complicated and fraught with uneasiness (expressed for example in complaints about lack of drawing abilities and when receiving others' comments). In the plenary session, the unease reached a climax; the discussions can be characterized as rather emotional: an oppressive silence interrupted by bursts of collective noisy laughter, which felt as though it was a collective ritual to mitigate the tension. When we discussed the emotions that were expressed and hidden in the drawings, we noted that they were associated with events, situations, and conditions not generally considered to be part of 'being a Ph.D. student', which we found highly significant. We realized that this process gave us an opportunity to come to grips with the emotional aspects of being a Ph.D. student, aspects that are not generally included in the formal academic education, but are known to have an immense influence on learning processes. Thus, we realized that the drawing was a welcome event that gave us possibilities to share and discuss our common experiences of being a Ph.D. student.

REFLECTIONS ON HOW DRAWINGS CAN ELUCIDATE EXPERIENCES

In this section we move from a focus on the learning event to a short discussion of some theoretical references, which help in a description of knowledge about aesthetically informed learning processes.

Conceptualizing Experiential Learning Related to the Group Process

We are aware of the importance of the group processes and the collective reflections which support our experiences of an event. It is important to include reflections on individual and collective learning processes when one is facilitating research using drawings as a method. Some of the discussions, when we reflected on and evaluated the event in the group, concerned the benefits of sharing one's drawing with the others. According to our personal descriptions of the event, a lot of learning, considerations, and consolidation took place in the group processes; they were very important to the overall process of the research. At this stage, earlier experiences were taken into account, others' interpretations were taken into consideration, and a lively debate took place about common and disparate experiences. According to Boud (1994), such events can transform perceptions, and old patterns of learning can be challenged through critical reflection. Thus, the process of (for example) rethinking one's experiences through a drawing in a group can make a difference because taken for granted assumptions can be discovered in disparate and consensual dialogues (Cunliffe and Easterby-Smith 2004). The images are individuals' interpretation of experiences based upon the original signs of emotional and bodily states, and this interpretation can be changed by reducing the representation of bodily signs and by enhancing the rational aspect. Thus a different interpretation can emerge by rethinking or re-elaborating the interpretation (Damasio 1994). Through our listening to comments and reflecting upon them, these explicit dialogues facilitated our awareness of assumptions that we were not conscious of either as individuals or as part of research and other communities. It is, however, important that as members of the group we are willing to disclose our assumptions, thoughts, and feelings in an open and enquiring way (Cunliffe and Easterby-Smith 2004). These thoughts link to and support the structure of the experience/event, but they also strengthen the importance of a solid and elaborate environment for reflection on the experience/event. A lot of emotional data emerged from both the individual and the group processes, and we can see that emotional data must be expected when we use the drawing method.

Conceptualizing Emotions

Emotions are an inescapable feature in organizational life. Far from being emotional deserts, organizations are now reconfigured as arenas for the deployment, management, and resourcing of human emotions. As a consequence, Gabriel and Griffiths (2002) stress that organizational life and learning has to be aligned at three levels: the individual, group, and organizational level. A differentiation of emotions can facilitate an understanding of each level and across levels, and particularly important organizational changes seem to bring emotions into the social arena (Gabriel and Griffiths 2002). Organizational change concerns negotiation of power relations and how employers/employees deal with emotions that arise from change. The dynamic character of emotions and emotional experiences explains the difficulty of defining emotions theoretically (Poder 2004). The different theories through which emotions in organizations have been understood include psychoanalytic perspectives, social constructionist views (Gabriel and Griffiths 2002), and the embodied mind approach (Damasio 1994). It is not our aim within this chapter to go into the nature, advantages, and disadvantages of different approaches to understanding emotion in organizations. However, we can see that different ways of thinking about emotions will be found within organizational life and will influence how emotions are handled within an organization and how emotional phenomenon are 'constructed' when analysed, theorized, and presented as part of research into organizational life and experience. Even though the drawing event at our Ph.D. short course did not focus on the organizational context Ph.D. students are part of, we realize that this is an important issue for Ph.D. students to reflect upon.

Emotions are Connected to Political Processes in Organizations

When facilitating organizational change, people need to be engaged in the change process, and in this respect it is important to be aware of the power relations that are associated with the 'need' or desire for change. Any research method that is designed to reveal emotions and/or underlying assumptions is also likely to reveal at least some of the political context within which emotions are experienced. People within organizations are subjected to a significant amount of emotional processes beyond their conscious control. Since one emotion arises as a response to another, the interrelatedness of participants (whether in enquiry or organization) depends on this exchange, as well as on the extent to which others' emotions are internalized within and help to construct one's own feelings and emotional responses.

It seems to us to be important to notice when people act differently from what was expected. During our event, it was difficult within the group when others either disclosed too much or too little information. If people disclosed too much, a sense of over-involvement or embarrassment would result; when people disclosed too little, a sense of not meeting shared expectations or disappointment would spread. It is therefore important to work with expectations in events like this as well as with explicit agreements concerning confidentiality after the event. The researcher's ability to contain and react competently to all personal emotional data that comes out in the process must be unquestionable. Our general experience of the event was that drawing an image of one's experiences within a certain topic was a lot easier than expected. Much of our individual knowledge, including our memory of experiences, is recalled as visual and auditory images because of its basic topographical representation. This means that all thinking, even words and arbitrary signs, starts as a vague image before it becomes a thought (Damasio 1994). Thus, the human brain is familiar with images, though this does not explain how the vague image is transformed into the finished expression in the picture, or how memories are evoked as a multidimensional experience in contrast to speech. This corresponds to our experience of the event; the drawing kept us focused on what we included and did not. We are assuming that this would be different in a 'spoken' method like an interview, which would involve progression through a set of questions.

CONCLUSION

In this chapter, we have discussed drawing as an experimental research method from a researcher's point of view as well as the point of view of a research participant. We found it was a highly valuable experience to work with processes that include emotional and other personal experiences and it is important as a researcher to be able to understand the different dimensions of the collected data as well as the difficulties we create for respondents in addition to the difficulties they bring along for themselves. The assumption underlying the drawing session concept, that non-rational forms of self-expression can elicit the non-verbal, tacit, emotional knowledge that is ignored by conventional research methods, has indeed been confirmed in our drawing experience. We believe that artful expressions are an important approach to research because of the capacity of this method to yield knowledge that the informants are not even aware of themselves. At the same time, it is very important to note that such methods demand certain skills in handling sensitive and personal information from research participants as well as group processes.

The drawing method represents a powerful tool to reveal emotions and personal experiences, but this slippery territory must be handled with respect; this concerns learning processes as well as research in organizations due to the politics and power relations that are an integral part of social and organizational experience. We think that with such a method, risk becomes a key word. Risk can be associated with fear and discomfort, but can also be related to the pleasure and excitement of the discovery of the emotions as a powerful tool and not simply as a dimension to be explored in isolation from the others. 'A beautiful risk', as one of the participants said.

REFERENCES

Barry, D. (1996). 'Artful Inquiry: A Symbolic Constructivist Approach to Social Science Research', *Qualitative Inquiry*, 2/4: 411–38.
Boud, D. (1994). 'Conceptualizing Learning from Experience: Developing a Model for Facilitation', *Proceedings of the 35th Adult Education Research Conference*. Knoxville, Tenn.

Cunliffe, A. L., and Easterby-Smith, M. (2004). 'From Reflection to Practical and Organized Reflection', in M. Reynolds and R. Vince (eds.), *Organizing Reflection*. Aldershot: Ashgate.

Damasio, A. R. (1994). *Descartes' Error: Emotion, Reason and the Human Brain*. New York: G. P. Putnam's Sons.

Darsø, L. (2001). *Learning Lab: Vidensskabelse i nye forskningskonfigurationer*. Undervisningsministeriet, http://www.uvm.dk/cgi.

—— (2004). *Innovation in the Making*. Copenhagen: Samfundslitteratur, Narayana Press.

Gabriel,Y., and Griffiths, D. S. (2002). 'Emotion, Learning and Organizing', *Learning Organization*, 9/5: 214–21.

Gagliardi, P. (1996). 'Exploring the Aesthetic Side of Organizational Life', in S. R. Clegg, C. Hardy, and W. R. North, *Handbook of Organization Studies*. London: Sage.

Poder, P. (2004). 'Feelings of Power and the Power of Feeling: Handling Emotion in Organizational Change'. Ph.D. thesis, Faculty of Social Sciences, University of Copenhagen.

Strati, A. (1992). 'Aesthetic Understanding of Organizational Life', *Academy of Management Review*, 17: 568–81.

—— (1999). *Organization and Aesthetics*. London: Sage.

Vince, R. (forthcoming). 'Drawings and Images in Management Research', in R. Thorpe and R. Holt (eds.), *The Dictionary of Qualitative Management Research*. London: Sage.

—— and Broussine, M. (1996). 'Paradox, Defence and Attachment: Accessing and Working with Emotions and Relations Underlying Organizational Change', *Organization Studies*, 17/1: 1–21.

PART VI

··

CRITICALLY FOCUSED EXPERIENTIAL LEARNING

··

CHAPTER 21

POWER AND EXPERIENCE

EMANCIPATION THROUGH GUIDED LEADERSHIP NARRATIVES

ANNA B. KAYES

INTRODUCTION

ONE goal of management education is to help students organize experience in meaningful ways. Scholars have suggested that organizational storytelling (Klein 1998), the use of experiential-based simulations (Kayes et al. 2004; Kayes, Kayes, and Kolb 2005), reflective exercises, myth analysis (Gabriel 2000), and the use of metaphor (Morgan 1997; Kayes and Kayes 2003) all provide noteworthy methods that promote the use of experiential learning in the context of management education. But although these methods may encourage learning, they may not allow students to explore the complexities of organizational power that have an impact on learning. Also, they may not focus on how students can articulate and actively reconfigure their individual experiences of power. In this chapter I argue that when students of management engage in conversation, their experiences of power actually become transformed and, through a social process of conversation, take on new meaning.

This approach to experiential learning follows a process called *guided leadership narratives*, which draws on Kolb's (1984) experiential learning theory and conversational learning (Baker, Jensen, and Kolb 2002). Guided leadership narratives help participants increase awareness of power in organizations, understand limitations in individual experience, and gain the benefits of learning in a social setting. Students expand this awareness through conversational learning, drawing on multiple student viewpoints and articulating new insights and shared perspectives of power in organizations. My role in this process is that of facilitator, structuring the narrative assignment, providing guidelines for deconstruction, and creating space for conversation.

In this chapter I begin by describing conversational learning in relationship to experiential learning theory. I then show how conversational learning can be used as the basis for developing a guided leadership narrative. I explain how these narratives help participants to identify experiences of power dynamics in organizations related to roles, influencing behaviours, prejudice, and stereotypes, as well as through personal and positional power. Ultimately, students have expressed how writing these narratives and then engaging in the conversational process provide insights into themselves as leaders. The guided leadership narrative process provides meaningful learning in that students reconfigure their individual experiences into new meaning through conversation. Thus, students can see how individual experience is made meaningful through a social process.

EXPERIENTIAL LEARNING THEORY

Experiential learning theory (ELT) provides a holistic description of the learning process and is often represented in four stages. I rely mainly on Kolb's (1984) description of experiential learning: a four-phase process of (1) *concrete experience*, where an initial experience provides the basis for (2) *reflective observation*, where retrospective review of the experience leads to (3) *abstract conceptualization*, which puts the experience into an integrated framework, which in turn leads to (4) *active experimentation*, which tests the framework, thereby continuing the cycle with yet another concrete experience. More recently, Kolb and his colleagues (Baker, Jensen, and Kolb 2002) have taken a more conscious look at the social dimension of experiential learning in the form of conversational learning.

Conversational Learning

If we take as a starting point the idea that education mainly occurs as a social and interactive process, rather than a solitary process, conversational learning becomes especially relevant in understanding the role of experiential learning in management education. It is within conversation that people begin to understand and make sense of experience. Baker, Jensen, and Kolb (2002) described conversation as 'a process whereby learners construct meaning and transform experiences into knowledge through conversation' (p. 51). Years of observation and participation in experiential learning exercises, such as field exercises, internships, and role-plays, led Kolb and his colleagues to conclude that when learners combine these various experiences with deliberate conversations about the experiences, student learning becomes shared.

Conversational learning consists of five dialectic poles. These dialectic poles allow for learning because contradictions and opposites are explored simultaneously in conversation. The first of the five poles is *apprehension*, or 'concrete knowing', and *comprehension*, or 'abstract knowing'. Apprehension is feeling oriented and involves tacit knowledge, manifested by feelings and openness to new experiences. The other end of this dialectic pole, comprehension, is reason oriented and involves the interpretative process, manifested by analysing or theorizing. The second of the dialectic poles consists of *intension* and *extension*. Intension is the act of reflection and is manifested when people show contemplative behaviours such as listening and observing. Extension is action that can be deliberate or experimental, manifested by trying things out or the desire to accomplish goals. The third dialectic pole consists of *individuality* and *relationality*. Individuality emphasizes the individual, and relationality emphasizes the connection with others. The fourth dialectic pole consists of *status* and *solidarity*, where status emphasizes one's position in the group and solidarity emphasizes equality. The fifth dialectic pole includes a *discursive orientation* and a *recursive orientation*. Discursive orientation is guided by linear time, such as agendas and direction; and recursive orientation is guided by cyclical time and individual interests.

Learning occurs because of the contradictions and opposites that emerge during the conversation. Conversational learning is especially relevant for students to explore power in organizations, because the dialectics of conversational learning form a process that is inherently emotional and cognitive, social rather than solitary, and complex and not simple. Conversational learning serves to surface various dynamics of power. For example, students' experiences of prejudice, stereotyping, and powerlessness, often difficult topics and not simply abstract and theoretical concepts, can be explored in a safe place through the structure of guided narratives and group conversation. Conversation allows students to share these experiences and construct new knowledge and perspectives on these topics. Power dynamics in organizations are social dynamics and as such should be made sense of in a social setting. Conversational learning emancipates a participant from the personal knowledge of power, gained from personal experiences, into social knowledge of power, gained from class concepts and experiences of others shared through conversation. Power dynamics, discussed in the next section in more detail, consist of multiple topics and multiple variables and have been described by researchers in multiple terms. The method to provide management students with an understanding of the complexity of power dynamics in organizations should be a complex and holistic method. Simple memorization techniques or solo study would not serve the purpose of creating new and meaningful knowledge. It is through these *conversational spaces*, or places where different meaning is explored, reconciled, and adopted, that learning occurs.

The exercise described in this chapter addresses the criticism that experiential learning fails to adequately consider power inherent in social systems and that ELT disregards the context of power relations such as gender, social context, and cultural dominance and how these factors influence the learning process (see for example Reynolds 1998; Vince 1998). Specifically, the exercise reveals how the use of guided leadership narratives and conversational learning permits students to understand the power dynamics in their organizations and to make new meaning out of experience embedded in conversation with other students who are inherently different—different socio-economic status, race, gender, ethnicity, and positions in community and work organizations. It is these categorial differences that impact the facilitation of the dialectics and contradictions in the conversational learning process.

POWER DYNAMICS

Power and influence are not synonymous terms. Rather, both terms represent important ways of viewing human interactions in organizations. Power describes a type of resource that one would use to change the behaviour of another. Influence describes the actual process of change attempt. The terms *power* and *influence* are broad and include many variables. At the intersection lies the term *power dynamics*, which I use to describe the interaction of power (as a resource) with an attempt to change someone's behaviour (influence). Leadership research over the past twenty years has shifted from a focus solely on power, such as power bases (French and Raven 1959) in the abstract, to a wider focus that includes power and influence behaviours (Kipnis, Schmidt, and Wilkinson 1980; Yukl 2002). This shift in focus stemmed from the misalignment of actual behaviours that people exhibit with traditional power classification schemata. Power bases, or power resources, can rest on personal or positional capital, such as expertise, or the ability to use organizational sanctions and rewards. Influence behaviours, in contrast, could include more than 346 (Falbo 1977) different behaviours. In order to understand the full range of power and influence behaviours, and the impact these behaviours have on an organization, some causes and consequences are also worth mentioning.

Causes and Consequences of Power Dynamics

Power dynamics in organizations have been understood in different ways. For example, as structural and decision based (see, for example, Yukl, Kim, and Falbe 1996); stemming from powerlessness (for example Bies and Tripp 1998); and as part of organizational culture and the (hierarchical) organization of the firm, including levels of hierarchy (for example Mintzberg 1983). Decision-based factors include decision errors such as stereotyping and prior experience of influence attempts. Researchers have also examined consequences for the individual and the organization after influence attempts; these consequences include such variables as resistance to the influence attempt, accomplishment of individual goals at the expense of organizational goals, or loss of trust (for example, Zand 1997). Other consequences, described in more favourable terms, include salary increases, promotions, and visibility.

Power dynamics are an integral part of behaviour in organizations, and I would argue that a better understanding of these power dynamics is an important part of management education and learning about leadership. Power dynamics increasingly are used as a prescriptive means to increase leadership effectiveness. Research and practice continue to advocate the use of power dynamics as a means to become more effective and creative in leadership (Porter, Angle, and Allen 2003). Power dynamic effectiveness has been linked with successful performance evaluations (for example Kipnis and Schmidt 1998), the accomplishment of goals (for example Yukl, Guinan, and Sottolano 1995), the success of 'selling an idea', and even salary increases (for example Ferris et al. 1994).

THE GUIDED LEADERSHIP NARRATIVE

The leadership narrative is a guided exercise that can be used in different types of management education courses. In these written narratives, students are prompted to write, over a semester, a series of reflections on their leadership and followership experiences in their organizations, paying particular attention to themes of power dynamics. They might identify various bases of power, comment on what factors lead to influence effectiveness, and review how they have used influence to change other people's behaviour. Invariably, other connections to power dynamics are made, such as the decision process prior to influence usage. This decision process may include such decision-making errors as prejudice and stereotyping. Other connections are also made, like the consequences to the individual and to the organization after the influence attempts, such as resistance to the influence attempt, loss of trust, or powerlessness. They discuss these written leadership narratives over the duration of the semester in small groups guided by the instructor and revise their initial drafts after they have engaged in conversational learning. Some of the questions that students are asked to write about have included the following:

1. How would you describe your ability to influence others in your organization? From what bases of power do you interact with others?
2. Describe your organization's culture and the types of influence behaviour that are seen as acceptable and unacceptable. What is your leadership role in the organization?
3. Describe a situation where you addressed conflict with a subordinate or a manager. What did you do to change their behaviour? How did others respond? Did you use power appropriately in this situation?

These questions correspond to content that the students are learning. For instance, as they learn about theories of how leaders manage conflict in organizations, they also write about their personal experiences with conflict and how they might use power and influence to resolve conflict. As they learn about leadership strategy and structure, they write about their experiences exerting influence and managing up and managing down the organization's hierarchy. These initial narratives serve as a starting point for conversation. Once the first draft of the leadership narrative is written, students bring it to class and discuss it in small groups.

Changing the Narrative

One of the most important considerations is that the initial narrative is a starting point for the conversation in groups and that the narrative will be revised. Students are instructed to pay attention to the themes of power dynamics that emerge in writing and to note how these themes change over the semester. These themes are highlighted as being fluid, and students are encouraged to rewrite their narratives as they enter into the process of conversation in the small groups. Each week, the students focus on a different theme to converse about in order to continue the process of conversational learning. Because the process of conversational learning often seems abstract, I have adopted a series of concrete guidelines developed by Boje and Dennehy (1993) to facilitate conversational learning in the classroom. These guidelines provide an important framework for conversation. Without them, student teams would agree with each other's experiences and make little progress towards embracing differences and contradictions. As an instructor, I needed a detailed method for facilitating contradictions in team conversations—telling the students to have a conversation and to look for contradictions and multiple opinions was not concrete enough to stimulate conversation. Once these guidelines were adopted to stimulate this exploration of contradictions, however, conversation progressed.

The individual written narratives serve as the starting point for a team of students to utilize one or more of the themes listed below. These themes are subjected to a series of practical steps adapted from Boje and Dennehy (1993):

1. Duality search: The student team makes a list of any one-sided terms. An example is a narrative where only one gender is emphasized.

2. Reinterpreting the hierarchy: The team dissects the hierarchical relationships present in a narrative and reinterprets the hierarchy. An example is where a manager dominates the actions of a subordinate; this would be reinterpreted where a manager affects the actions of a boss.

3. Rebel voices: The team identifies the missing voices or opinions from a student's writing. What perspectives are not expressed in the writing? An example is where a student would rewrite an entry from the perspective of his or her manager.

4. Other side of the story: The student team finds the other sides of the story, as stories always have multiple sides. The student is prompted to reverse the story so that what is emphasized initially becomes marginal, what is vertical becomes horizontal, and so on.

5. Denying the plot: Students unearth the type of plot they have written and change it to another type of plot. An example is where students identify a narrative as a 'tragedy' and change it to a 'comedy'.

6. Finding the exception: Student stories have rules and scripts in which they can identify the exceptions and change them. An example is where a student has made a seemingly logical conclusion about an outcome, and the team reconsiders a seemingly absurd outcome as an alternative.

7. Tracing what is between the lines: Students are prompted to fill in the blanks and add more script to the backstage or the in-between. An example is where a student adds history or context to the story she has written.

8. Resituate: The final step is where the student has completely reconfigured the initial narrative that he or she wrote. The final story is completely different from the initial story and is the product of multiple perspectives. This final story is based on steps 1 to 7. This is where the individual articulates a new meaning based on shared experiences.

Student Narratives

This section uses examples of student writing to illustrate how the guided leadership narratives work. Students bring many differences into the classroom, including position and organization experience, gender, socio-economic background, race, ethnicity, sexual orientation. These differences impact on individual and collective experiences and are expressed in the conversational process. The first step is for an individual student to write a conversational starter, or a leadership narrative, based on a specific question such as 'How would you describe your ability to influence others in your organization? What bases of power do you interact with others from?' Next, the student brings the narrative to class, and the student team picks one or more guidelines for deconstruction from the eight steps listed above. These guidelines will help the students enter into the process of conversation and experience the five dialectical processes: (1) apprehension and comprehension, (2) intension versus extension, (3) individuality and relationality, (4) status and solidarity, and (5) discursive and recursive orientations. In the final step, the student rewrites the initial leadership narrative based on new meaning.

In the following example, a student wrote of how she highlighted her accomplishments and became 'visible' in her large organization. Note how she changed her initial journal entry after conversation with her team. Her team decided to follow Boje and Dennehy's (1993) step 6, 'finding the exception', to prompt their conversation.

Leadership Journal entry one:

Making a move to XXXX, a large conservative company with an extremely rigid hierarchical structure and culture, I have found the need to use 'friendliness' in order to better influence my manager and those around me. I am humble and do not point out my accomplishments to anyone above my manager in the hierarchy. I believe that I have to be overly friendly because as a large company, XXXX, doesn't look favorably on those that break out of the organizational structure it has created. (MBA student)

As the instructor, I guided this student and others in her group through the process of conversational learning, listening for overemphasis on one or more process dialectic and then encouraging the students to shift to emphasize the opposite dialectic. In the example above, the students in this group initially tended to overemphasize the *extension* or 'action' phase to start the rewriting process of the narrative. Rather, I encouraged them to spend adequate time creating a *conversational space* or place where differences are encouraged and individuals are receptive.

The narrative from this first student embedded gender assumptions in the role of an employee, specifically a female employee, in the hierarchy, and the importance of being liked through the use of 'friendliness' as opposed to other ways of relating, such as through negotiations or assertiveness. In order to encourage the student team to spend more time experiencing the dialectic process of *intension* and *extension*, I encouraged them to look at all sides of the themes before acting (intension). I had them discuss the role of gender and socialized assumptions in relation to managing, given gender and organizational hierarchy.

I also asked them to explore why they labelled behaviours as 'male' and 'female'. Only after they observed these differences were they to discuss these reflections and assign a framework that synthesized their various points of view (*extension*).

This student was encouraged by her classmates to highlight her accomplishments at work and to explore alternatives to her initial logic. One of her group members suggested that she should be more visible in her organization. Another student suggested that perhaps the organizational hierarchy was not as rigid as she assumed.

The next week, the student team selected another conversation starter, Boje and Dennehy's (1993) 'absurd outcome', for an alternative.

Leadership Journal entry two:

Making a move to XXXX, a large conservative company with an extremely rigid hierarchical structure and culture, I have found the need to use 'friendliness' in order to better influence my manager and those around me. I have made an active effort to form networks that involve key personnel outside my immediate department and include directors and managers outside of my immediate hierarchy. I point out my accomplishments at every opportunity I have. I believe that I do not have to be overly friendly but do have to make sure people see my accomplishment. As a large company, XXXX wants to be innovative and looks favorably on those that break out of the organizational structure it has created. (MBA student)

The student expressed in this entry that perhaps the constraints that she felt on sharing her accomplishments were more related to her fears and that she was limiting her visibility in her organization by not standing out from her peers. When she considered what she initially thought was 'absurd', or the team's perspective—different from her own experience—she allowed herself to become open to the possibility that it was not the hierarchical structure or culture of the organization that was holding her back from exerting influence, but rather it was her own self-imposed barriers. The students in her team had decided that, in their experience, pointing out accomplishments was a more 'male' behaviour than a 'female' behaviour. She considered this perspective on influence to be incongruous with how she traditionally viewed her role in her organization, acknowledging that she constrained herself from promoting her accomplishments at work. In their exploration of why they labelled influence behaviours as 'male' and 'female', the students even reconfigured the simplistic view of influence behaviours classified as an absolute category (for example, either male or female) to behaviours as a relative category (for example, effective or ineffective given the particular context).

Conversational Outcomes

After each class in which a leadership narrative entry is discussed and changed, the students share the insights or meaning that they have generated from this activity. The learning that this student team experienced included understanding

- The conversational learning processes and how to encourage contradiction and opposites in understanding power
- The importance of conversation with different others to expand personal experiences of power relations
- The inherently restrictive assumptions that bind individuals to rote patterns of influence behaviour
- The benefits of deconstructing narratives and considering multiple perspectives and outcomes

The next example is from a manager who changed her written narrative in response to step 7, 'tracing what is between the lines':

Leadership Journal entry one:

Today I addressed the project leader's poor performance as it related to a specific deliverable he provided to me. As the first conversation I've ever had with a superior regarding their lack of understanding of the task and unacceptable results, I would say I did a fine job. I think I could have approached the subject more delicately, but that would not be a true reflection of my personality to do so ... The project leader became defensive and physically agitated. He raised his voice and in response, I did the same. He doled out several subjective criticisms of my work product. (MBA student)

The learning group wanted to discuss the experience and to express the emotions connected with the experience (apprehension), without theorizing about what transpired (comprehension). They continued to discuss this experience without assembling a meaningful framework to make sense of their multiple perspectives. As an instructor, in order to help them organize their experiences, I asked them to draw a figure that would illustrate an effective performance feedback loop and that considered gender, trust (or distrust), and hierarchy. I selected these particular constructs for them to include in their model because these were the constructs with which they kept emotionally engaging. Once they drew their figure, their conversation continued to evolve and included elements of the other conversational dialectics. For instance, the team imposed time limits on their conversation (discursive), and two members wanted to continue the conversation after class on e-mail (recursive).

After this conversation with her student team, this manager admitted that she had addressed the project leader's poor performance in front of the rest of the project team and did so after she gained approval from a director higher in the organization's hierarchy. She also expressed her fear that the project leader would not take criticism from her because she was a female and less influential, whereas he was a male and had more power resources at his disposal. She rewrote her entry to reflect this additional context and, interestingly, reconfigured her analysis of the situation.

Leadership Journal entry two:

Today I addressed the project leader's poor performance as it related to a specific deliverable he provided to me. My supervisor's supervisor, the division director, proposed the idea of confronting the project leader's dismal performance. As the first conversation I've ever had with a superior regarding their lack of understanding of the task and unacceptable results, I would say I did not do such a fine job. I was afraid that if I did not confront the project leader publicly, in front of the rest of the team, the division director would think I was weak and not suitable for my job . . . The project leader became defensive and physically agitated. He raised his voice and in response, I did the same. He doled out several subjective criticisms of my work product. He didn't criticize me because I was a woman but because he was embarrassed in front of everyone. Upon further reflection, I understand how my actions could have been misconstrued. I pledge to continually observe and learn from the people around me. (MBA student)

Conversational Outcomes

The learning insights that students expressed after this experience included the following:

- There is an interaction between fear and influence behaviours in organizations (for example, fear of being seen as a 'weak female' led this student to give performance feedback in a publicly humiliating context).
- It is easy to see only one's own experience with power dynamics until these experiences are discussed in a group. Group members are all so different, and their experiences of power and influence differ vastly.
- There is much learning value in deconstructing and rewriting personal narratives and experiencing the change from initial perspective to perspective after team conversation.

Conclusions

Guided leadership narratives illustrate the process of experiential learning in conversation. This tool offers management educators a practical mechanism for helping management students to learn about power dynamics in organizations. Additionally, this pedagogical event responds to two criticisms of experiential learning: that it disregards power relations and focuses too narrowly on reflection at the expense of experience. Individual leadership narratives contain themes of power and influence that are transformed from individual knowledge into social knowledge through the process of conversational learning. That is, dominant themes of power in organizations are explored through this process of learning.

This process of learning does not privilege reflection over the 'here and now' of experience, but rather privileges the shared meaning making through conversation over the initial set of assumptions that the individual held prior to experiencing this pedagogical event. Learning about power dynamics as a collective event promises to unearth and reconfigure meaning as the students share in the process of meaning making.

Written leadership narratives combined with conversational learning together highlight the sometimes dialectically opposing views that managers hold of themselves and their role in organizations. This method seeks to emancipate managers from the limits of their initial interpretations of experience. Writing a guided leadership narrative, deconstructing the narrative through conversation, and rewriting the narrative allows managers to unearth their assumptions, to modify their perceptions, to make new shared meanings, and to understand the fluid nature of experience. This approach to learning emphasizes new knowledge and individual development. It acknowledges and explores contradictions that are inevitably part of working in social and political settings. As students move from their individual knowledge of power relations into more complex and social knowledge, this process of change leads to their individual growth and development.

REFERENCES

Baker, A., Jensen, P., and Kolb, D. A. (2002). *Conversational Learning: An Experiential Approach to Knowledge Creation*. Westport, Conn.: Quorum Books.

Bies, R. J., and Tripp, T. M. (1998). 'Two Faces of the Powerless: Coping with Tyranny in Organizations', in R. M. Kramer and M. A. Neale (eds.), *Power and Influence in Organizations*. Thousand Oaks, Calif.: Sage.

Boje, D. M., and Dennehy, R. F. (1993). *Managing in the Postmodern World: America's Revolution against Exploitation*. Dubuque, Ia.: Kendall-Hunt,

Falbo, T. (1977). 'Multidimensional Scaling of Power Strategies', *Journal of Personality and Social Psychology*, 35: 537–47.

Ferris, G. R., Judge, T. A., Rowland, K. M., and Fitzgibbons, D. E. (1994). 'Subordinate Influence and the Performance Evaluation Process: Test of a Model', *Organizational Behaviour and Human Decision Process*, 58: 101–35.

French, J. R., and Raven, B. (1959). 'The Bases of Social Power', in D. Cartwright (ed.), *Studies in Social Power*. Ann Arbor: University of Michigan Press.

Gabriel, Y. (2000). *Storytelling in Organizations: Facts, Fictions, and Fantasies*. London: Oxford University Press.

Kayes, A., Kayes, D. C., and Kolb, D. A. (2005), 'Developing Teams Using the Kolb Team Learning Experience', *Simulation and Gaming*, 36/3: 330–54.

———— Kolb, A. Y., and Kolb, D. A. (2004). *The Kolb Team Learning Experience: Improving Team Effectiveness through Structured Learning Experiences*. Boston: Hay Resources Direct.

Kayes, D. C., and Kayes, A. B. (2003). 'Through the Looking Glass: Management Education Gone Awry', *Journal of Management Education*, 27/6: 1–17.

Kipnis, D., and Schmidt, S. M. (1988). 'Upward Influence Styles: Relationship with Performance Evaluation', *Administrative Science Quarterly*, 33: 528–43.

——— and Wilkinson, I. (1980). 'Intraorganizational Influence Strategies: Explorations in Getting one's Way', *Journal of Applied Psychology*, 65/4: 440–52.

Klein, G. (1998). *Sources of Power: How People Make Decisions*. Cambridge Mass.: MIT Press.

Kolb, D. A. (1984). *Experiential Learning: Experience as the Source of Learning and Development*. Englewood Cliffs, NJ: Prentice-Hall.

Mintzberg, H. (1983). *Power in and around Organizations*. Englewood Cliffs, NJ: Prentice Hall.

Morgan, G. (1997). *Images of Organization*. Newbury Park, Conn.: Sage.

Porter, L. W., Angle, H. L., and Allen, R. W. (2003). *Organizational Influence Processes*. Armonk, NY: M. E. Sharpe, Inc.

Reynolds, M. (1998). 'Reflection and Critical Reflection in Management Learning', *Management Learning*, 29/2: 183–200.

Vince, R. (1998). 'Behind and beyond Kolb's Learning Cycle', *Journal of Management Education*, 22/3: 304–19.

Yukl, G. (2002). *Leadership in Organizations*. Upper Saddle River, NJ: Prentice Hall.

—— Guinan, P. J., and Sottolano, D. (1995). 'Influence Strategies Used for Different Objectives with Subordinates, Peers, and Superiors', *Group and Organization Management*, 20: 272–96.

——— Kim, H., and Falbe, C. M. (1996). 'Antecedents of Influence Outcomes', *Journal of Applied Psychology*, 81: 309–17.

Zand, D. E. (1997). *The Leadership Triad: Knowledge, Trust and Power*. New York: Oxford University Press.

CHAPTER 22

WORK ORIENTATIONS AND MANAGERIAL PRACTICES

AN EXPERIENTIAL AND THEORETICAL LEARNING EVENT

TONY WATSON

SETTING THE CONTEXT

THE set of events which are to be reported and reflected upon here were those experienced by undergraduate students taking a final-year module on work organization and management. The students attended a lecture and a seminar each week for twelve weeks. The seminars for two of the fifteen student groups were run by me and I gave the twelve lectures, these all being closely tied to the module textbook which I had developed and tested in modules with a variety of different types of student. In the department in which the module was located, the phrase 'the book of the module and module of the book' was used for this approach to simultaneously developing teaching modules and supporting textbooks—an approach which several other staff members also followed. What all of this suggests is that this top-level module was a highly integrated one. This was indeed the case. It was quite deliberate and seemed to be very much appreciated by the students, who responded to it with almost completely full attendance at both lectures and seminars (and produced very high-quality seminar performances and examination scripts in the view of the team of tutors who worked on the module as well as in the opinion of the external examiner).

Later, I shall focus on just one of the seminars that I took part in and this single event has been chosen for two reasons. First, it was the seminar at which I took notes as part of my preparation for writing a second edition of the textbook (Watson 2006). Second, the topic being covered by the module has a particular significance in terms of the whole spirit of the module. It deals with 'work orientations'—the meanings which work has for people as an element of their 'whole lives'—as well as the implicit contract which is at the heart of the exchange between organizations and their employees. So how does this relate to what I've called the 'spirit' of the module? Perhaps the best way to answer this is to refer to the informal 'contract' that was offered to the students at the beginning of the module. This was a contract which was very much influenced by the awareness shared by myself and the students that their lives generally and the meanings to them of work (both academic work and career work) were at a significant point of change. They were now in the final year of study and, I said to them in the first lecture,

This time next year, you will be coming to terms with the realities of life in organizations. You will deal with attempts by others to manage you and many of you will be reflecting on just how, later on, you might go about managing work situations yourselves.

And the offer made to them was expressed something like this:

If you all attend the whole module, read everything that is recommended to you and put real energy into the very participative seminars that we will be having, I promise that you will really see the cliché that good theory and good practice are closely related becoming a reality. I promise that you will be much better placed to cope with the highly political, ambiguous and emotionally challenging world of organizing and managing.

I added to this that the module would be challenging in that there will be 'some tough theoretical work to do'. 'Nevertheless', I went on, 'I hope that you will recognize, perhaps at the end of the module or perhaps when you are out there in the organizational jungle, that this was the most practical course you ever did.'

It was also explained in this introductory lecture that all the case study material with which they were going to be presented had come out of first-hand research done by their lecturer/text writer—much of this having been done in a participant observer way within managements. I explained that from the very beginning of my own industrial career I had been an ethnographic researcher at the same time as a practitioner and that, as a very young manager early on, and as a seconded senior manager in the 1990s (when I worked in GEC Plessey to 'update my management experience' and to prepare a book which became *In Search of Management*, Watson 2001), I was constantly 'using and testing organizational and management theories'. I wanted, I said, to pass on as much as I could of the benefits of all this to course members, as long as they put as much effort and commitment into the programme as I and my tutorial team wanted to do.

I would not claim that this initial 'presentation of the lecturer self' to students is fundamentally different from what many colleagues do. But this particular version of the standard 'trust me, I am a professor' speech needs to be explained here to contextualize all the subsequent events. To create a relationship with the students—however limited that would have to be for the majority of the 300 or so of them—I was telling them a lot about my own 'work orientation' and I was trying to establish a broad contract with them. I suggested to them that if they thought that I was attempting to 'be a manager' in my first talk to them, they were absolutely right. I was putting into practice my beliefs about theory and practice. And I told them that, 'later on, when we study the notion of "implicit contracts" you will get a good idea of some of the theory that is behind my practice today'.

Having set the context in this way, I shall now proceed to outline the theory behind the basic approach to experiential learning that I was applying in this work before returning to the specific theoretical notions of work orientation and implicit contract that were part of the course content. I shall then sketch out the case material that was used in the seminar that dealt with these ideas before going on to look at how the students related their personal experiences to the experiences of the figures in the two cases that they were required to reflect upon.

A NEGOTIATED NARRATIVE APPROACH TO EXPERIENTIAL LEARNING

The negotiated narrative approach to teaching and learning was first articulated in the process of reflecting upon my approach to postgraduate, post-experience group work (Watson 2001). In that work I was using ethnographic and participant observation material with managers and asking them, in effect, to throw their own managerial experience into a 'mix' of academic research materials, theories and concepts, and personal managerial experiences. The reflective manager notion (Schön 1983) and the philosophical pragmatist assumptions (Watson 1997) behind the model and the theoretical recognition of the power of 'narrative learning' (Tsoukas 1998) are discussed in the above (Watson 2001) reference. The model has also been applied to innovations in entrepreneurship learning (Fletcher and Watson 2007).

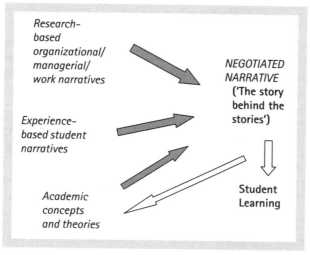

Fig. 22.1 A negotiated narrative approach to teaching and learning

The challenge of applying this approach to undergraduate students of business and management is inevitably much greater than that of applying it to experienced managers of the type attending the 'executive MBA' programme in which it was originally developed. However, a belief that has always informed my undergraduate teaching is that there is a lot more *managerially and organizationally relevant* experience among management undergraduates than at first sight we would expect to be the case. All have had experience of organizations, even if this only as the pupils of schools and the customers of retailing organizations. But few will have experience of observing managers at close hand, let alone trying to do a managerial job. This does not mean that we should not try to find areas of undergraduate experience where some 'negotiation of narratives' can occur based on potential links between material in the research literature and experiences in students' lives along the lines seen in Figure 22.1. Light should be thrown on just what is and what is not possible when we look at what occurred in the seminar event we will focus upon later.

The diagram shown here as Figure 22.1 was presented to students with the following explanation:

The diagram illustrates how we are going to use the ethnographic narratives or 'tales of the field' in the learning and teaching processes of the module. In preparation for seminars you will be asked to pre-read one or two of the book's cases and to bring along your reflections on the case together with accounts of your own experiences or observations in that aspect of working or organizational life. You might, for example, have read the case material on mischief at work. You and your colleagues would thus bring along an appreciation of this material together with accounts of events and activities which you have encountered yourselves—at school if not in a workplace. A valuable comparing of the research based and the personal would then occur, this comparison leading to the shaping of generalizations that might be derived from all this 'empirical' evidence. In effect a 'story behind the stories' (more formally, a 'negotiated narrative') is being worked upon by the seminar participants.

It is not the stories alone that are put into this mix, however. There are also the theoretical and research ideas which are presented in the textbook, further reading, and lectures. The 'negotiated narrative' experience, at its best, then becomes one in which students and tutor become involved in a process of 'research'-based theorizing about the particular topic under examination. This should result in significant student learning on your part. And it should also be possible (as the diagram suggests) for there to be learning on the part of the tutors. We all hope so! Tutors are thus enabled to feed back into their own learning, and indeed scholarly writing, insights and ideas emerging from the learning/teaching experience. We are going beyond the idea of the tutor acting as a 'learning resource' for the students. We see you, the students, becoming a learning resource and, indeed, a source of research ideas for the tutor!

Having now established the model upon which the learning events were based we can turn to a sample of the theory element of the module. This is an example of the 'academic concepts and theories' input to the mix represented in Figure 22.1.

LEARNING 'CONTENT': WORK ORIENTATIONS AND IMPLICIT CONTRACTS

In presenting the work orientations concept (originating with Goldthorpe et al. 1968) and the concept of implicit contract (originating with Levinson et al., 1966) to the students, it was argued that to understand any individual's or group's work behaviour it is necessary to examine

   (a) how they are predisposed to act in certain ways in the light of the meaning of work to them at that time and, within this,
   (b) their perception of the deal they are making with the employer.

Both of these things, it was explained in the text and the lecture, have to be looked at in the context of employees' lives before they enter an organization. This is especially the case with a person's work meaning or *orientation to work*. This was formally defined as *the meaning individuals attach to their work which predisposes them both to think and act in particular ways with regard to that work*. And it was pointed out that one can distinguish between an *initial orientation* at the point of entry to work and the *dynamic orientation* that follows later. Work orientations are always liable to change as circumstances and interests change within the continuing employment relationship. And various changes in people's broader lives (including job changes themselves) will mean that orientations shift, sometimes in a minor and sometimes in a major way. But each time that a new job is entered a broad 'deal' is made with the employer, large parts of which may never be formally stated, let alone written down. This deal is conceptualized as *the tacit agreement between an employing organization and the employed individual about what the employee will 'put in' to the job and the rewards and benefits for which this will be exchanged.* This focal element of the work orientation is similarly likely to change over time as both organizational and personal circumstances change.

This summary of a complex series of ideas emerging from decades of industrial sociology and organization theory (see Watson 2008) barely scratches the surface of the account given to students in the lecture and the text. In the lecture, especially, numerous examples were given of 'real life' cases of changes in people's work meanings and in the associated exchanges which they made in different ways at different times with employing organizations. An illustration which was given particular emphasis, in order to make links with students' own lives, was that of the lecturer himself and the approach he took to student vacation jobs (basically a work orientation which prioritized monetary reward whilst having a secondary concern with having experiences that might be helpful in a future career as an industrial sociologist). That early orientation was contrasted with the very different one that applied after graduation and marriage. The aim of this, fairly obviously, was to encourage students to think about the way in which their own work meanings were liable to be different in a year's time, when they were to enter full-time careers, from what might have been the case previously. They were being prompted to reflect on the very different sorts of implicit contract they might to make with graduate employers from the ones they had been making with employers of students over the past few years. And this theme was central to the first of the two case studies that they would be reading in preparation for the seminar on orientations and tacit employment contracts. This was the story of Ravi Barr.

ENTER RAVI

The first of the two case studies—these representing the research-based narratives in Figure 22.1—is that of Ravi, a young man who moves from school, through student work experiences, into a graduate and then a managerial career—his work orientation changing all the time. The material takes the form of an interview with Ravi who explains that in his first experience of employment, 'I worked enthusiastically in the family business [after school]. I simply fitted into the business, like my older brothers, and did whatever my father asked me, whether it was delivering orders or sorting out the invoices. I didn't think of myself as cheap family labour. I was their dutiful Indian boy.' Later, however, when he was at university, 'I started to see myself then as cheap family labour. I began to resent this and I got more and more awkward with my father and brothers—doing the minimum amount of work and refusing to take any kind of initiative at all. This all ended up in a big row and for the next few vacations I got work near the university.'

The employment Ravi undertook whilst at university (part-time in term, full-time in vacations) was sometimes labouring work, sometimes bar work, and, once, 'something horrible in a chicken factory'. He said that the work was 'a means to an end'. That 'end' was 'having a good time...the money I made enabled me to carry on partying in term time too. I was sort of shaking off all those years of being the quiet conscientious boy. And I was also refusing the plan my parents had for me, as the first one in our family to go to university and, hence, the one who would eventually run the business. I knew that this was something my older brothers really resented.' At the time of the interview, however, Ravi talks of how he has changed his orientation since then: 'I am very career oriented now. I am making sure that I am learning about every aspect of this business so that I can eventually be a chief executive of a large retailing outfit. My parents have now accepted that I do not want to work in the family business...and they are proud of what I am achieving. I think my marriage has been an important factor in my approach to career. Her family wanted to arrange a marriage for her and she had to fight them to marry me. So we have both had to make our way, and establish who we are "making careers away from the Asian community". '

ENTER SACHA

The second case deals with a group of workers in the corporate affairs department of an organization and looks at the way Sacha, the manager of the group, comes to terms with the varying work orientations of the individuals who make up her department. And this 'coming to terms' means active intervention in certain cases. She is seen to influence or 'manipulate' the workers' perceptions of their implicit contract with the company (something that was to be a key theoretical point later in the module when the notion of 'managerial manipulation of perceived implicit contracts' was to be put forward as an alternative frame of reference for managers to the standard 'motivation' one). Sacha talks about all of her seven staff. And this is what she says about three of them:

Biffy and Sniffy are amazing cases of people who have changed. When I came here I was told they were simply miserable types. It was also said that they both had 'chips on their shoulders' because they had lost their jobs when the second of the town's papers closed down. They felt they were demeaning themselves by working in public relations. Both were well on the way to becoming alcoholics and they ruined their marriages, largely because of the drink. However, about a year ago there was this amazing change. In part, it was down to my giving them the most almighty shouting at—'Shape up or ship out' is what

I basically said. But it was also to do with some kind of conversion experience they had, as our managing director put it. They had both joined Alcoholics Anonymous and, at the same time, they discovered the delights of line dancing. Somehow the smartening up that went on with getting off the booze and their meeting women at the dancing sessions translated into their work. It was amazing. Almost over night they changed from lazy and uninspired individuals who were in danger of letting the company down to smart and reliable characters who I can happily allow to speak for the company.

Smithy, on the other hand, is somebody I increasingly can't trust. In her case, the change seems to have come about after moving in with a new partner, as opposed to losing a partner. She is my languages person and used to be brilliant at dealing with almost any issue where we needed to deal with Europe. It seems that her bloke has been getting resentful about her travelling abroad for us and this has led to her taking it out on all of us in the office. She's managed not to go abroad for six months now and the other day she rushed out of the office screaming, 'Oh, sod the French'. One of my best people has become a complete liability for reasons which, it seems, have nothing to do with the company.

We have now seen excerpts of the material that the students carefully read, alongside the relevant academic reading and their lecture notes. I recognize, though, that some readers will find this claimed high participation level hard to believe. The explanation for it lies, in part anyway, in what a student once called a 'cunning managerial device' within the module design—a device designed to ensure full seminar and preparation! Thirty per cent of the assessment was for *leading and chairing* one of the seminars. And the main criterion for this assessment was that of gaining a high quality of participation by the group. The implication of this was that each individual was strongly discouraged from 'opting out' in any sense whatsoever. If you 'let down' the fellow students who were leading their allocated seminar, those students would get a bad mark. And the likely consequence of this was that these people would retaliate by failing to turn up to do the reading for the people who had failed to appear or contribute to their session!

SCENES FROM THE SEMINAR EVENT

It is in the seminar event that we see the 'experience-based student narratives' of Figure 22.1 coming into play. The seminar at which I took notes was led by Emma and Nihal. They did the job in an impressive way and, as was the case with most of the subsequent seminars, I only contributed, like the students themselves, when invited to by the chairpersons. This was in spite of the fact that everyone knew I would be filling in a pro-forma and, after the event, awarding a mark to the event leaders. They all, I think, assumed that my note taking was part of the assessment process.

Emma and Nihal had prepared their own thoughts on the academic material. They gave a ten-minute summary of the key theoretical ideas with which the seminar was concerned but they insisted to the group that they would reveal nothing of their own analyses of the two cases until 'everyone else in the room' has made a contribution. This was said in a friendly and unthreatening manner and was well received by the seminar group—who were functioning very well together, having at this stage experienced three previous seminar events. This was the first week of the module, however, in which the seminars were student led (the module design required the tutors to lead the first three seminars). The group were rather grateful to Emma and Nihal for volunteering to be the first ones to take over from the tutor 'in the chair', so to speak. To my surprise, the first student to speak was one of the three Asian students in the group. He had been very shy in the earlier events and I had struggled to get him to speak in front of the group. He told us about working as a boy in the family business and feeling, just like Ravi, that this was a simple matter of duty and 'how things are meant to be'. Again, like Ravi, his 'orientation towards my family and the work in the business changed when I came to Uni'. To everyone's amusement (they clearly knew him as a quiet and shy colleague) he said that he was 'not the partying type' and therefore did not look for student employment in order to 'pay for going out on the town'. His orientation was nevertheless, he said, 'money oriented'. But he wanted the money for savings and he said that, after several arguments with his parents, they had agreed to pay him whatever he would have got paid by other employers if he still worked in the family business in his vacations. He said he 'liked the orientations theory' and he felt sure that it would influence him when it came to 'sorting out a proper job when I leave here'.

The next student to speak, Tom, started with, 'I just want to pick up on something that Sandeep has just said'. This was the phrase 'partying type' and, to laughter from the group, he reminded the group that he really was a 'partying type' and went on to argue that 'this is really much more of who I am than just an orientation—as was probably the case with Ravi who, I reckon, was just going through a phase. So, yes: an orientation for Ravi, but something different for me.' Mandy tackled him hard on this, suggesting that when he faced the pressures of 'the real world' next year, he was bound to reorient himself. I wondered if she had a close personal relationship with Tom, especially given the tone of what she went on to say, 'And if you don't get a new orientation to work very soon, you will never get to the point of making an implicit contract with a company, because you won't have a degree.' Emma intervened, at this point, to say, 'we need to move on to other people', but the group appeared to want more on this matter. And Nihal suggested that this should be related to the theoretical point of whether there was 'something about people being types which clashed with the work orientation approach'. He reminded people that it had been argued in the lecture that it was more helpful, in work situations, to look at how people were orienting themselves at any given time rather than speculating on what 'sort of people' they were. Tom said that his father was a 'partying type' and that this had not stopped him being a very successful businessman. 'And you are just like your father?' Sandeep asked him. 'Without doubt,' Tom responded, 'my mother often says I have inherited his personality.'

The discussion then proceeded with people arguing about the issue of 'basic personality' versus 'emergent orientation'. This was skilfully chaired by Emma and Nihal, who made sure they brought most people into the debate. They became visibly uncomfortable, however, on several occasions when they had to cut short contributions 'because we have only got an hour'. But one of the skilful things they did was to ensure that the characters in Sacha's story were brought into the discussion. Because few of them felt they had ever got sufficiently close to anyone in a work situation to know them as well as it appeared Sacha knew 'her people', they tended to drift into arguing about such things as whether or not 'deep down Smithy always was someone you couldn't really trust' and that 'this had simply taken some time to come out' or whether or not, as one student put it, 'Sacha was mistaken to call Biffy and Sniffy miserable types: they were simply sick alcoholics who got cured'. The majority, however, thought that the Sacha story showed how valuable the orientations and implicit contract ideas were for managers trying to understand people in their departments. Emma and Nihal (who, incidentally, never got time to tell how his personal story compared with Ravi's) tried hard to get people to report experiences relating to managerial attempts to influence work orientations through manipulating people's perceived implicit contracts with their employer.

Only one student had anything to say on managerial interventions. And he had a lot to say. Perhaps not surprisingly, this was because, in his early twenties before coming to university, he had worked as a manager in a retail clothing business. Paul told how he had been 'totally up against it when I took over this bunch of unco-operative, stroppy bastards'. He continued, 'If I hadn't worked to turn these people around I could not have stayed in the job.' 'So how did you do it?', he was asked. He responded by talking in detail about how he'd tried to show them ways in which they could build into the work 'some good laughs'. Emma struggled to make sure this was related back to the theories under consideration and she put it to the group that what Paul was doing was 'inserting into the unwritten agreement between the shop and these workers the reward of fun at work and, I take it Paul, a better level of companionship with you and the rest of the team'. I presumed that they agreed with this because the group simply gave Emma a round of applause for her observation. And she and Nihal then moved to 'draw things together to see if we have a "story behind the story" as a result of our debates' (this being the 'negotiated narrative' element of Figure 22.1). The discussion, unfortunately, was severely curtailed by the clock. As the sound of other students gathering at the door of the seminar room built up, Nihal wrote up on the flip chart under the heading 'Our theory':

- people change their orientations to work as things in their lives and their jobs change;

- managers can make an input into implicit contracts to change behaviours;
- some types of people are easier to change than others.

The group then applauded Emma and Nihal. As the group started to file out of the room I approached the two 'leaders'. They looked worried and Nihal simply pointed at the flip chart and said, 'Sorry about that, Tony. I know you wouldn't want to sign up to this "types of people stuff".' I assured them that this was no problem because I had set up the event to be one where, between us as a group, we were to 'negotiate a narrative' and this was what we negotiated. I then assured the two of them that I would be awarding them a first-class mark for the outstanding way in which they had managed the group and gained a high level of participation in an event in which theory, research, and people's real life experiences were brought into play with each other. They both looked very pleased—and deservedly so.

In Conclusion

It is hoped that this fairly full account of a set of learning and teaching activities demonstrates the potential that exists for incorporating experiential learning relating to 'whole life' issues as opposed to 'work placement' experiences with undergraduate students. More importantly, though, it shows that quite a sophisticated level of achievement in relating 'theory and practice' is possible with such students if a suitable vehicle is created—one which carefully integrates, and makes mutually supportive, lectures, seminars, reading, and, very relevantly, assessment. In addition to this, there is the matter of the nature of the relationship established between teachers and students. This cannot be of the more personal type once possible when numbers were smaller. So what we saw here was an informal contract or *effort bargain* made between lecturer and student in which, in return for hard work and commitment, a promise was made of learning which would not be only relevant to students' own past and current experiences but which would help them manage their future experiences. This would relate not just to their initial experiences of entering the employment 'jungle' but to their later experiences when they might be confronting the challenges of *doing management* themselves.

References

Fletcher, D. E., and Watson, T. J. (2007). 'Entrepreneurship, Management Learning and Negotiated Narratives', *Management Learning*, 38/1: 9–26.

Goldthorpe, J. H., Lockwood, D., Bechhofer, F., and Platt, J. (1968). *The Affluent Worker: Attitudes and Behaviour*. Cambridge: Cambridge University Press.

Levinson, H., Price, C., Munden, K., and Solley, C. (1966). *Men, Management and Mental Health*. Cambridge, Mass.: Harvard University Press.

Schön, D. (1983). *The Reflective Practitioner*. New York: Basic Books.

Tsoukas, H. (1998). 'Forms of Knowledge and Forms of Life in Organised Contexts,' in R. Chia (ed.), *In the Realm of Organization: Essays for Robert Cooper*. London: Routledge.

Watson, T. J. (1997). 'Theorising Managerial Work: A Pragmatic Pluralist Approach to Interdisciplinary Research', *British Journal of Management*, 8: 3–8.

—— (2001). *In Search of Management*, rev. edn. London: Thomson Learning (1st pub. 1994).

—— (2006). *Organising and Managing Work*, 2nd edn. Harlow: FT Prentice-Hall.

—— (2008 forthcoming). *Sociology, Work and Industry*, 5th edn. London: Routledge.

CHAPTER 23

MAXIMUM DISORDER

WORKING EXPERIENTIALLY WITH HRM AND BUSINESS STUDIES UNDERGRADUATES

JANE THOMPSON

TRACY LAMPING

INTRODUCTION AND CONTEXT

IN this chapter we discuss an experiential seminar activity entitled 'Maximum Disorder'.[1] We demonstrate how we encourage our students to gain an understanding of the complexity of 'management', thus affording them the opportunity to gain insight and skills, as they negotiate the social, emotional, and political aspects of managing/managerial work. Debate with regard to critical pedagogy in management education is now well developed. Transferring this into practice at the level of curricula, or what we term 'critical pedagogy in action', is less so. In this chapter we illustrate how we have extrapolated from this debate and developed ideas/activities to establish a firmer foundation for the *practice* of a critical pedagogy.

To contextualize our practice, first we identity our pedagogic approach. We begin by introducing ourselves as senior lecturers at the University of Lincoln. We have worked in the Faculty of Business and Law for many years, designing and delivering a range of business studies courses. During this time our working environment has been turbulent (not unlike that of many of our colleagues in other universities), with increasing pressures from our own university to recruit students, in the midst of a large-scale voluntary severance programme.

Making meaningful subject areas such as HRM/Organizational Behaviour/Management to undergraduates (our seminars include a mix of business studies and HRM students) who have little work experience is challenging. While many students now, of course, undertake part-time work, or have been employed in at least one McJob, most of our full-time undergraduates have little experience of business environments and tend to hold a view of 'management' that is imbued with what Anthony (1986) describes as 'official theory'. Such a view is further reinforced by many traditional business studies/HRM/OB texts which have tended to present a prescriptive approach to the nature of managing (Grey and French 1996). In recent years, however, there has been a concern to get students to engage with 'real theory' which begins with the premiss that 'management' is a social and political activity; and 'power', in its various guises, requires recognition and deconstruction, thus equipping students for their future roles.

Texts such as Gareth Morgan's *Images of Organization* (1986), Tony Watson's *In Search of Management* (1994), Paul Thompson and David McHugh's *Work Organizations* (1990), Fiona Wilson's *Organizational Behaviour: A Critical Introduction* (2004), Norman Jackson and Pippa Carter's *Organizational Behaviour* (2004), and Chris Grey's *A Very Short, Fairly Interesting and Reasonably Cheap Book about Studying Organizations* (2005) do indeed acknowledge 'real theory' as described by Anthony. On the HRM front the work of Karen Legge (1995), Barbara Townley (1994), Richard Hyman (1975), and Tony Redman and Adrian Wilkinson (2001) is particularly helpful in that these authors adopt a more critical stance with regard to the employment relationship. 'Real theory' is reflected in their writings, encapsulating in their texts an acknowledgement of power relationships and the politicking that takes place in organizational life.

Many commentators, of course, have stated that 'teaching management' is problematic (see, for example, Grey and Mitev 1995) even at postgraduate level when there is often some experience of the business world on which to draw. It is our view, however, that with the adoption of an experiential critical pedagogy, based on 'real theory', students can be encouraged to consider aspects of managerial work which involve a critical understanding of power relations at the level of ownership, symbolic manifestion/personal interest, and the (in)equalities endemic of capitalist cultures. Such critical pedagogy can promote insight, skills, and a sense of 'morality' for (future) organizational roles, thus enabling a questioning of domi-nant managerial ideologies. We see this as extending Schön's model of the reflective practitioner (1987) to that of *reflexive* practitioner (see Thompson and McGivern 1996).

It is important to acknowledge that we have found the debates in *Management Learning* useful in stimulating our ideas. In particular we recognize some of the dilemmas raised by Michael Reynolds (1998), Christopher Grey and Robert French (1996), and Graeme Currie and David Knights (2003) in attempts to develop a critical pedagogy. Such theoretical debates do not, however, easily translate to the *practice* of a critical pedagogy, and by this we mean curricular development in terms of what actually takes place in the seminar room. This omission of debate about actual critical content is noted by Dehler, Welsh, and Lewis who, remarking on such absence, comment, 'Curricular content...but debate about what?' (2001: 500). However, it is important to point out that in recent years more attention has been given to critical curricular development, or as we term it 'critical peda-gogy in action', and indeed chapters within this text are concerned with this very issue.

So how do we help our students to understand the complexity of 'managing' and to become what we have referred to as reflexive practitioners? In year 1 of our Business Studies/HRM courses all undergraduates undertake the modules Per-spectives in Management and Management and Context in which we encourage them to think of themselves as possessing 'management skills' from the outset. We suggest 'management' is often reified, presented to us in a mystical manner, as deeds carried out by remote and unapproachable individuals in the name of 'the organization'. Mike Pedler's work provides an accessible framework through which students may identify their strengths and their development needs (Pedler, Burgoyne, and Boydell 1994). This approach also offers the possibility to students that they are *already* managers and may practise their skills in order to become adept at understanding organizations through 'reading situations' (Morgan 1986). Notions of management development as well as human resource management are introduced in this context. This approach acknowledges that there is no particu-lar point at which one 'becomes' a manager but rather it is an ongoing process (Watson 2001). The Perspectives in Management and Management in Context modules are built upon at level 3/4 (when many of our students have undertaken a placement year) with the introduction of a double semester module entitled Management Action in Practice (MAP); an activity from this unit is used to exemplify our approach in this chapter. Before we discuss this, and in order to provide further contextualization, we briefly add a little more information on our approach.

Given our interest in the development of an experiential critical pedagogy, over the years we have designed and developed activities which have enabled us to establish curricula-content which encourages students to experience in a 'here and now' situation the social, political and emotional behaviour that occurs in groups/organizations (McGivern and Thompson 2000). We have also tried to engender a critical reflexivity by encouraging students to consider debate that questions dominant ideologies around the way work is organized, the (in)equality of employment relationships, and the way in which particular interests are served and sustained. We would argue, therefore, that we engage with 'critical' aspects. Hence we emphasize that such an approach has the potential to develop what we have described as *reflexive* practitioners. The main purpose of this chapter therefore is to provide an example of an experiential event whereby we argue students are afforded the opportunity to recognize the complexity of managing, in the 'here and now' situation of the seminar, thus experiencing the power dynamics of group working, while also reflecting on wider critical reading.

THE MANAGEMENT ACTION IN PRACTICE MODULE (MAP)

The final-year MAP module consists of a structured lecture programme and alternate weekly two-hourly seminars/workshops where we use experiential activities. It is in this context, faced with 'management issues' such as struggles for power/leadership, collusion/exclusion, trust/mistrust, that students can learn to develop skills and qualities to negotiate the socio-political and emotional aspects of organizational life. Confronted by such dilemmas in these seminars, and through dialogic practice, new insights can occur. At this point it is worth mentioning that our own dialogue with our managers has been ongoing, particularly in the way we wish to organize our work. Our managers at Lincoln have been very supportive of the development of a critical pedagogy. Not only have they edited *Thinking about Management* (Golding and Currie 2000) which encapsulates much of our learning philosophy, but they have also been instrumental in curricular development and negotiating with the staff who organize timetabling. This has enabled us to be allocated a two-hour slot and, up until recently, a dual-tutor system for these experiential seminars has prevailed. We have found that one hour is insufficient as an activity and discussion cannot be sufficiently developed within such a timeframe. Having a co-worker has been invaluable as we have been able to engage in an explicit dialogic method in front of, and with, our students, thus reflecting on our dilemmas and uncertainties with regard to our own learning and the questioning of our own assumptions. It can, of course, be very challenging to move out of the 'traditional' tutor role (as generally perceived by students), but we consider it important to do this, not only so our students can actually take responsibility for what occurs, thus practising their managerial/organizational skills, but also it provides us with an opportunity to expose our own dilemmas, thus problematizing 'knowledge' and modelling 'a lack of closure' through dialogic practice (Cunliffe 2002).

In order to illustrate some of the above, we now describe the activity 'Maximum Disorder'.

THE ACTIVITY ... MAXIMUM DISORDER

Tuesday, 10.45 a.m., Room 304 (on this particular occasion this activity took place in week 8 of semester 1).

We arrive early to set out the room in preparation for the activity. We expect seventeen students in this final-level seminar group so begin by placing a small table in the centre of the room, surrounded by four chairs. This is then surrounded by an outer circle of thirteen chairs (see Figure 23.1). On the table we place a

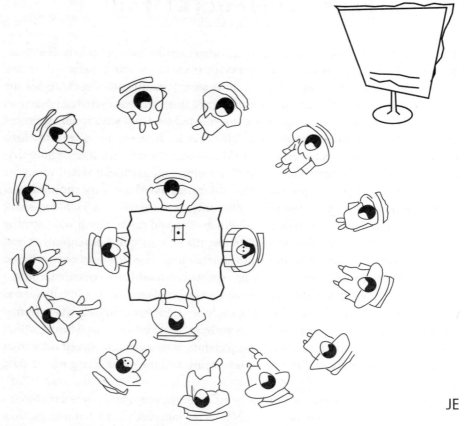

JE

Fig. 23.1 Maximum disorder

pack of playing cards. On the whiteboard we write 'Plan to sort the cards into maximum disorder. Only those sitting in the inner circle may speak. You have 40 minutes.'

We are ready and just before 11.00 a.m. we open the door to see how many students are waiting to enter. We count fifteen on this occasion so we swiftly remove two chairs from the outer circle. The students are invited in.

Today (as we have witnessed on previous occasions) the outer seats are taken first, and those last in take the chairs around the small table on which the cards have been placed. And as usual, one can observe a marked reluctance in the steps of the last four who take their seats in the inner circle, which can be interpreted as having a 'higher profile' and thus requiring a more active role.

Silence ensues . . . (this is not unusual and can last for quite a few minutes and we can experience a sense of unease as eyes are focused on us, awaiting further instructions—the instructions are actually written on the whiteboard but we do not draw attention to these, waiting instead for students to observe, and take the initiative). Meanwhile we take seats at the back of the room, and occupy ourselves with our own reading. In our learning environment we want students to take responsibility from the outset—a central prerequisite of managerial work—so we do not intervene at this point.

The silence continues today. Several members of the group look at the floor, avoiding eye contact, while others gaze towards the window. Sue,[2] Sally, Kevin, and Bill have the inner seats. Suddenly, Sue in a rather anxious voice says, 'What are we supposed to do now?' This question does not seem to be directed at anyone in particular. The silence continues but is interrupted by John who is sitting in the outer circle. He taps her on the shoulder, and points a finger in the direction of the whiteboard. 'Oh, right', says Sue, looking at the board. 'What is maximum disorder,' asks Sally, directing her attention to Sue. Ten minutes pass while the four round the table attempt to address the questions they raise such as: 'What is maximum disor-der?' 'It is impossible as it is a contradiction' . . . 'what is order?' . . . 'what is disorder'? The cards are removed from the pack by Bill and picked up by Kevin who shuffles them. There is talk as to the best way to achieve the task (as they have interpreted it) with voices becoming raised as they put forward their points. The conversation in the inner circle becomes quite muddled, seemingly no one is listening to another until Kevin confidently asserts, 'lets just throw them up in the air . . . that is max-imum disorder'. There is laughter. 'That can't be right', says Bill who has another go at passing cards to the three others in what he describes as a 'random pattern'. 'How can a pattern be random?' asks Sue and there is some good-humoured banter at this point; Kevin suggests a game of three-card brag, while Bill argues for strip poker.

Meanwhile, half an hour into the activity, those in the outer circle are looking bored and there are obvious signs of frustration, represented by a leaning low in seats, with heads bowed. 'We have got nowhere and look at the time', says Sue, commanding attention from the other three in what some might perceive as a quest for leadership. Sue turns round and looks at members of the outer circle and says, 'What do you think?' Kevin reminds her, 'they cannot speak'. (In debrief it is useful, for example, to pose questions such as 'Who makes the rules in here and "out there" in organizations, and why do we follow them?') At this point John from the outer circle gets up and his body language indicates that he wishes to swap places with Sally. Once in the circle John articulates his version of maximum disorder. This is very similar to Bill's idea and is soon rejected by Kevin. Meanwhile the sighs in the outer circle continue, and one or two exchange jottings on their notepads. Julia writes a note, folds it, and passes it into the inner circle. It is read by Sue but no comment is made.

By now it is 11.40. More notes are passed into the inner circle and Bill reads out the suggestions: 'Burn the cards,' and in very large writing 'Lets go to the pub.' A third jotting states, 'You've had your forty minutes, you're fired!' and another, 'Give a card to everyone in the room at random and see what happens.' Kevin picks up Julia's earlier note, reads it and says to the group, 'Ah, I get it, we don't have to actually sort the cards, we just have to PLAN [his emphasis] to sort them but we don't actually have to do it.' There is no acknowledgement of the group member who provided this suggestion. (Such an omission can be picked up in a debrief drawing attention as to why there was a lack of acknowl-edgement of what could be recognized as an important point of progression—to what extent do trust, liking structure, collusion, etc. impact on whose voice is heard and whose is ignored). Sue states, 'so, that is what we have actually been doing for the last 40 minutes,' trying to catch the eye of one of the tutors. 'What "planning?"' says Kevin, 'I don't call that *planning*' (his emphasis); a discussion ensues as to what constitutes a plan and so debate in the inner circle takes off once again.

More swap places so their voices can be heard; Demetrius suggests throwing the cards out of the window; Malcolm advocates cutting them up but others reject this idea, looking with amusement at the tutors who continue to appear preoc-cupied with their reading. Our role throughout the activity has been one of non-direction/non-interference thus enabling the group to take full responsibility for what occurs, encouraging them to be active in their learning; but we are listening, and at appropriate points (later), in what can be described as a 'debrief', we question various patterns of behaviour, as we observed, thus prompting the group to engage in further reflection/discussion.

By noon the circle has become one, all participants are now in one large circle, the instructions on the board are no longer acknowledged, and conversation is in full flow. However, at 12.15 on this occasion, the group appear to be in depen-dency mode, displaying the need for some form of leadership (Bion 1959), with students looking to the tutors to help them resolve their predicament. As stated above, we have made no explicit intervention for well over an hour. At this point

Demetrius says the task is complete, and all eyes focus on the tutors. 'What have you done?' is the tutor response. Sally says somewhat impatiently, 'we have completed the task by planning to sort the cards into maximum disorder...well, we didn't actually "plan" exactly but we did talk.' This prompts further discussion within the group on how events/actions are interpreted differently...when is a 'plan' a 'plan'...and the problematic nature of language. The difficulty of establishing 'meaning' is recognized by some, and reference is made to an earlier lecture on postmodernism, and the reading Demetrius and Sam had done from Jackson and Carter in preparation for today's activity. There appears to be a genuine attempt to deal with the difficulties they are encountering in terms of agreement/consensus and their discourse structures the next ten minutes with most participants making useful contributions, particularly with reference to the reading from the module core text, Jackson and Carter.

We ask, 'what has actually occurred in the last hour or so' and 'what implications might this have for managerial work, particularly if interpretation/meaning is so problematic with regard to instructions and achieving a task', as they have suggested. One student stated this would not happen in 'the real world' as instructions would be clear and 'therefore there wouldn't have been a problem'. At this point another describes an experience he had on his work placement and how no one understood 'what the boss was on about so we just did it how we thought'.

We then ask the group if they think there should be an 'answer' or 'solution' to the activity, thus prompting further discussion. This is not addressed at this point and instead there is talk of 'being set up' (by us), and, 'had the tutor been more clear and given more feedback at various points, there would not have been a problem'. 'What problem...who has a problem?' asks Kevin, at which point the tension is relieved by laughter.

'What is happening now?' we ask. Students look confused and then Angela states 'at least we are talking to each other... in many seminars we do not even do that, so that is a bonus'. (Given that we remind them, throughout this module, of the importance of 'talk' in managerial work, see Stewart 1982; Boden and Zimmerman 1991; and Boden 1994, this can be a useful prompt in debrief). We pose another question: 'how can we (you) progress when we (you) cannot agree as to what constitutes maximum disorder?' Someone mutters, 'THIS [their emphasis] is maximum disorder!' A reference is then made to the previous week's lecture which focused on intersubjectivity when Kevin states, 'but we are agreeing to agree, rather than agree whatever maximum disorder means so we can move on'. There follows a brief discussion about 'meaning' being negotiated through discourse to achieve some sort of closure. The role of power, leaders, and language is further discussed. This group have certainly done their reading and have been able to relate ideas to the activity. We might add that this is not always the case!

THE ONGOING DEBRIEF AND DEBATE

Indeed there is so much that can be drawn from the material that this group has generated in this one activity, and over the weeks, after such experiential activities, references are made to behaviours, dilemmas, and tensions that they highlight as being significant. In particular, points for discussion that are often raised during, or towards the end of, an experiential activity such as Maximum Disorder might include: the behaviour/feelings of those in the inner/outer circle; the making of 'good' contact when asking questions, the importance of developed listening skills and body language; rule making and the legitimization of such; gendering; lack of clarity and the ambiguity of language/meaning; the role of friendship, trust; inclusion, exclusion, and mistrust; the role of tutors; and reaction to silence. There are, of course, many other issues that can surface and may require skilful facilitation by both tutors and students (see further examples in McGivern and Thompson 2004). We do, however, encourage students to raise issues themselves—rather than for us to prompt particular issues—thus enabling them to take responsibility and ownership for the discussion, thereby practising for their future organizational roles. This particular session was lively: there has been lots of 'talk', laughter, jokes, and innuendo. Most have engaged with the activity (we are sensitive to the feelings of those who appear not to engage, and again, careful facilitation is required by both students and tutors), and participants have identified and reflected on behaviour patterns/postures/roles as well as relating their reading.

We referred earlier to the group being 'set up' (their words) by us and indeed, we did, of course, stage an activity that had the potential to create conflict and a range of emotions. We find this particular activity very appropriate as it departs from traditional role-plays which can be highly structured and solution based. Apart from the initial layout of materials and space, Maximum Disorder requires very little intervention from us and therefore students are put in a position whereby they have to reflect on the power dynamics in the 'here and now' and 'manage' for themselves. Being 'set up', as this group so describe, is necessary in order to expose the power relations within the seminar room, not only within the group but also within the tutor–student relationships. We have considered elsewhere the debate as to whether power can be decentred in the classroom (McGivern and Thompson 2004: 150), but maintain that by exposing power dynamics within the tutor–student relationship we are at least able to encourage students to gain a greater awareness of 'political' behaviour, thus enabling them to practise the skills they need in order to 'read' organizational situations.

One of the key features of working with our students is an explicit focus on their learning. Managing one's learning is central to the task of organizing and we believe that an understanding of one's own learning process and that of others is an essential prerequisite for future organizational roles. Reflecting on learning therefore is an integral part of our programme. Using a dialogic methodology (McGivern and Thompson 1995) we encourage our students to share their thoughts about their own learning. Such an approach is compatible with the reflective journal practices we establish in order to help them make explicit links between their own experience and conceptual material, thus leading to reflexive practitioners capable of significant learning through linking explicit knowledge and tacit knowledge. We suggest our critical pedagogy in action adds a further dimension to experiential approaches and, as Ann Cunliffe suggests, creating opportunities for reflexive dialogue 'in which we question and surface taken for granted aspects of our everyday experience' (2002: 46) is an essential prerequisite for a critical pedagogy. Through raising the problematic rooted in the assumptions underpinning managerial practice, we aim to reveal the socially constructed nature of the discipline, liberating students to deconstruct and reconstruct.

In this chapter we have explained how we work with our final-level HRM/Business Studies undergraduates with a view to encouraging them to become reflexive practitioners. We have described an experiential activity entitled Maximum Disorder and attempt to show how extrapolations can be made from this that have the potential to promote insight and skills. We are, of course, mindful of the debates as to whether critical content can actually initiate a process which extends beyond the 'traditional' (wherein the tutor retains control over the passive student via their 'expertise') and authoritative discourse reigns (as noted in Currie and Knights 2003: 32). However, by linking curricular (activities) such as described to a process where *we* and students problematize and develop 'knowledge' and understanding through dialogue and debate, a critical pedagogy in action can be engendered. As we have noted, the wider hierarchical/meritocratic cultures in which our discourse takes place are not ignored, but raised as issues for debate.

Notes

We are grateful to John Elliott for reproducing Figure 23.1.

Michael Reynolds and Russ Vince dedicated *Organizing Reflection* (2004, Ashgate) to Janet McGivern. Janet was our colleague and very dear friend and we have been inspired and encouraged by her experiential practice. Without her we could not have written this chapter, and it is to her that this is dedicated.

1. We have been using this activity for many years but the precise source cannot be located. The 'Instructions for Tutors' are these:
   - Create an inner circle with 4–5 chairs and place a table in the middle.
   - Create a larger outer circle with the required number of chairs (depending on number of participants).
   - Place a pack of playing cards on the table in the inner circle.

- Write on the board, 'Plan to sort the cards into maximum disorder. Only those in the inner circle may speak. You have 40 minutes.'
- Check the number of seats correspond with those waiting to enter and then invite participants into the room.

2. As we have asserted, our students are indeed aware of our research into our practice, and several have read (and, on occasion contributed to) our papers, but we consider it appropriate in this case to protect identity, hence names have been changed.

REFERENCES

Anthony, P. (1986). *The Foundation of Management*. London: Tavistock.

Bion, W. R. (1959). *Experiences in Groups*. New York: Basic Books.

Boden, D. (1994). *The Business of Talk*. Cambridge: Polity.

—— and Zimmerman, D. H. (1991). *Talk and Social Structure: Studies in Ethnomethodology and Conversation Analysis*. Oxford: Polity in Association with Blackwell.

Cunliffe, A. L. (2002). 'Reflexive Dialogue Practice in Management Learning', *Management Learning*, 33/1: 35–61.

Currie, G., and Knights, D. (2003). 'Reflecting on a Critical Pedagogy in MBA Education', *Management Learning*, 34/1: 27–49.

Dehler, G. E., Welsh, A. M., and Lewis, M. W. (2001). 'Critical Pedagogy in the "New Paradigm": Raising Complicated Understanding in Management Learning', *Management Learning*, 32/4: 493–511.

Golding, D., and Currie, D. (eds.) (2000). *Thinking about Management*. London: Routledge.

Grey, C. (2005). *A Very Short, Fairly Interesting and Reasonably Cheap Book about Studying Organizatins*. London: Sage.

—— and French, R. (1996). 'Rethinking Management Education', in R. French and C. Grey (eds.), *Rethinking Management Education*. London: Sage.

—— and Mitev, N. (1995). 'Management Education: A Polemic', *Management Learning*, 26/1: 73–90.

Hyman, R. (1975). *Industrial Relations: A Marxist Introduction*. London: Macmillan.

Jackson, N., and Carter, P. (2000). *Rethinking Organizational Behaviour*. Englewood Cliffs, NJ: Prentice Hall.

Legge, K. (1995). *Human Resource Management: Rhetorics and Realities*. London: Macmillan.

McGivern, J., and Thompson, J. (1995). 'Dialoguing for Development', in G. Gibbs (ed.), *Improving Student Learning*. Oxford: OCSD.

———— (2000). 'Teaching Management through Reflective Practice', in D. Golding and D. Currie (eds.), *Thinking about Management: A Reflective Practice Approach*. London: Routledge.

———— (2004). 'Dialoguing for Development: Lessons for Reflection', in M. Reynolds and R. Vince (eds.), *Organizing Reflection*. London: Ashgate.

Morgan, G. (1986). *Images of Organization*. London: Sage.

Pedler, M., Burgoyne, J., and Boydell, T. H. (1994). *A Managers Guide to Self Development*. London: McGraw Hill.

Redman, T., and Wilkinson, A. (2001). *Contemporary Human Resource Management*. Englewood Cliffs, NJ: Prentice Hall.

Reynolds, M. (1998). 'Reflection and Critical Reflection in Management Learning', *Management Learning*, 29/2: 183–200.

Schön, D. (1987). *Educating the Reflective Practitioner*. San Francisco: Jossey-Bass.

Stewart, R. (1982). *Choices for the Manager: A Guide to Managerial Work and Behaviour*. Maidenhead: McGraw Hill.

Thompson, J., and McGivern, J. (1996). 'Parody, Process and Practice: Perspectives for Management Education?', *Management Learning*, 27/1: 21–35.

Thompson, P., and McHugh, D. (1990). *Work Organizations*. London: Macmillan.

Townley, B. (1994). *Reframing Human Resource Management*. London: Sage.

Watson, T. (1994). *In Search of Management*. London: Routledge.

—— (2001). 'The Emergent Manager and Processes of Management Pre-learning', *Management Learning*, 32/2: 221–35.

Wilson, F. (2004). *Organizational Behaviour: A Critical Introduction*. Oxford: Oxford University Press.

CHAPTER 24

WORKING WITH EXPERIENTIAL LEARNING

A CRITICAL PERSPECTIVE IN PRACTICE

KIRAN TREHAN

CLARE RIGG

INTRODUCTION

THIS chapter reflects on experiences of running a management development programme where the pedagogical process is as significant as the content for participants' learning. The programme works through an approach to experiential
learning that incorporates insights from Critical Management Learning, integrating
action learning and critical reflection with a central focus on the notions of power,
empowerment, and openness that have been pivotal to the aspirations of experiential learning. This chapter does two main things. First, it elucidates the elements
and processes that make the programme experiential. But secondly, it identifies
some of the problematics that are frequently glossed over in the idealistic treatment
of much experiential learning literature. Threaded throughout are evaluations of

The week is actually quite structured, but because it does not conform to participants' expectations of themselves as passive learners and tutors as the expert givers of knowledge, many experience the initial uncertainty as chaos. It is their comments after the event that illustrate the importance of the week, exemplified by one woman who said, 'It was like a great jolt. It made me sit up and think what I want to do with my life. I'm drifting along in a job I don't enjoy and nobody else is going to sort it out.'

Throughout the programme many features aim to reinforce proactivity. The question of who owns the learning, diagnosis of issues or problems, and the solutions to these is central to the students' learning. Tutors take two basic, mutually supportive roles: those of Task Consultant—offering information, models, or reading related to the task, and Process Consultant—making the participants aware of group processes. Tutors take care in responding to participants' questions not to position them as dependent and passive. The courses are structured around individual and group tasks framed in terms of learning outcomes. However, there is room for interpretation, which provides considerable leeway for participants to influence the content of the curriculum. But this is also a situation of uncertainty, through which students have to direct their own paths, individually and collectively. One participant described this as:

The total refusal, well not so much refusal, more slippery than that, an avoidance of allowing the students to inscribe the tutors as knowledge bearers or themselves as empty vessels to be filled with knowledge.

Another said,

The loose style of the [programme] acts more rigidly upon the student...because I had to pace out and set my own boundaries upon my learning. (UCE 2001a)

Summary

So far we have explained four core elements of the UCE's Management Development Programme, action learning, praxis, process, and proactivity, which comprise an experiential pedagogy in which the learning *process* is considered as being as significant as the *content* in developing participants' learning about managing.

In the next section we explain how ideas from Critical Management Learning are integral to our approach to experiential learning, particularly through the use of Critical Reflection and Participative Assessment. We explore how a Critical perspective enhances our understanding of how course participants make connections between their learning and work experience as a basis for understanding and changing interpersonal and management practice.

A CRITICAL APPROACH IN PRACTICE

Critical management learning has emerged as a field that goes beyond ideas of traditional management education. Burgoyne and Reynolds (1997) see as central an emphasis on understanding the whole person as mediated through experience, thus paying attention to more connectedness to daily personal and professional life. Also, by avoiding the passivity associated with more conventional management education methods, critical approaches offer more opportunity for development than seemed possible in focusing exclusively on the acquisitions of knowledge and skills.

A key principle of the UCE Programme is what Reynolds (1997) describes as 'process radical' pedagogy. Through action learning sets, process facilitation, action research, and the idea of a learning community, not only do participants learn about organizational dynamics, they also learn about themselves in relation to others. Reflexivity is seen as integral to learning and self-development in several fields: adult learning (Jarvis 1995), work-based reflective practice (Argyris and Schön 1974), qualitative research (Blaxter, Hughes, and Tight 2001), and critical reflection (Trehan and Rigg 2005: Reynolds and Vince 2004). The most content-radical elements occur in the master's year, through a critical reflection paper and an action research dissertation. In the former, students are asked to reflect critically on their development as a manager, and are introduced to critical ideas, drawing on feminism, Foucault's ideas on power, and concepts of critical education based on Habermas and Giroux. This form of critical education is seen as embodying Kemmis's principles (1985) of critical reflection. As such it differs from the more instrumental, individualized, and introspection-based approaches to reflection promoted by some experiential learning methodologies. An action research methodology is deployed for the dissertation and students are encouraged to explore the epistemological basis of action research. Action research has a long history of use for radical community action and this leads many students to engage with the critical theory on which it is based.[1]

Self-Development through Critical Reflective Practice

Reflection and reflective practice have been gaining validity in recent years within higher education generally including the fields of management and organization development. Reflection is argued to improve the depth and relevance of individual learning (Moon 2000), to support emergence of self-insight and growth (Miller 2005), to develop the transferable ideal of the reflective practitioner, and to offer potential for organizational learning and change (Vince 2002a; Nicolini et al. 2004). However, the theory and practice of reflection has been subject to critique for being instrumental, individualized (Vince 2002a), for simply meaning introspection (Hoyrup 2004), or for serving narrowly defined purposes of individual growth. Lather, for example, criticized the fashion for exalting empowerment as 'individual self-assertion, upward mobility and the psychological experience of feeling powerful' (1991: 3).

Critical reflection, itself broadly interpreted, aims to go beyond these critiques. Mezirow (1991) defines critical reflection as reflection on assumptions and presuppositions. Brookfield (1988) highlights four elements as central to critical reflection: assumption analysis; contextual awareness; imaginative speculation; and reflective scepticism. Others advocate more explicit engagement from participants in a process of drawing from critical perspectives to make connections between their learning and work experiences, to understand and change personal, interpersonal, and organizational practices.

We differentiate critical reflection from critical thinking or engaging in critique in the following way. Critical thinking as critique is

the application of all the traditional scholarly criteria of rigour, challenge to taken-for-granted assumptions, debate, logical consistency and the setting of claims to valid generalisation and theories against the best evidence that can be mustered about what occurs in the world. (Watson 2000: 387)

Whilst there is no assumption of neutrality or pretence of objectivity here, it is the process of critical thinking that is emphasized, and implicitly there is a belief that the thinkers/researchers should attempt to be impartial as to the outcomes of their activity.

This contrasts with the use of the term 'critical reflection' by critical management writers, where it has a specific meaning, namely to achieve a society with social justice and free from oppression (howsoever defined). Critical reflection here is intertwined with the use of and generation of Critical Theory. For example, Guba and Lincoln suggest the aim of critical enquiry is 'the "critique and transformation" of the social, political, cultural, economic, ethnic and gender structures that constrain and exploit humankind' (1994: 113). Likewise, Carr and Kemmis exhibit a concern for the outcome of critical reflection, 'to articulate a view of theory that has the central task of emancipating people from the "positivist domination of thought"' (1986: 130).

On the UCE programme participants write reflective papers, both individually on their learning, and collectively about their learning from the group process within their ALS. On the master's stage they write a critical self-reflection paper, an autobiographical reflection on their development. In this participants are encouraged to identify their core assumptions, to understand some of their patterns, and the contextual influences on them. Depending on their particular focus, individuals may be introduced to critical concepts derived from such perspectives as feminism, post-colonial literature, Marxism, social constructionism, or critical pedagogy.

It has proved important to have individual knowledge of each student in order to judge what might be appropriate for them, and to help them make sense of their particular experiences. For example, some of the black students on the course attributed what they described as a sense of enlightenment to the literature to which they were introduced from anti-racist pedagogy (Mirza 1997).

This form of critical self-development is qualitatively different from the concept of reflection in experiential learning theory. While reflection focuses on the immediate, presenting details of a task or problem, critical reflection involves an analysis of power and control and an examination of the taken-for-granteds within which the issues are situated. The potential for critical reflection derives from the tensions, contradictions, emotions, and power dynamics that inevitably exist in managers' lives. Critical reflection as a pedagogical approach emerges on the programme because these dynamics are treated centrally as a site of learning about managing. McLaughlin and Thorpe (1993) argue:

At the level of their own expertise, managers undertaking critical reflection can come to know themselves and their organization much better. In particular, they can become aware of the primacy of politics, both macro and micro, and the influence of power on decision making and non-decision making, not to mention the 'mobilization of bias'. (p. 23)

Vince (1996) argues that the influential action learning and learning cycle models of Revans (1982) and Kolb (1984) both fall short of providing a way of integrating the emotional and political into experiential approaches to management education. Vince claims that these models lead, in some cases, to reflection on experience being constructed or interpreted as managers 'thinking about their experience', emphasizing the rational nature of the reflective process, and argues that if part of learning from experience is about working with the emotional and power dynamics generated in learning processes, then the reflective process also needs to involve the *rational*, the *emotional*, and the *political*.

Thus, on the UCE programme critical reflection is part of both formal and informal learning processes, and fits with Watson and Harris's (1999) concept of the individual as emergent, and of there being 'a clear continuity between the management of one's personal life and the formal managerial work done in the organisation' (1999: 237).

This integration of critical reflection with action learning is a significant aspect of the UCE programme as the following extract from a student's reflective paper highlights:

The action learning sets represented a move towards a critical approach to management, where the frustrations, power differentials, emotions, indifferences and conflicts which occur within groups can be focused upon and treated as topics for the exploration of management issues that are sensitive in our everyday experience. By focusing on our experiences as students in the action learning set context, a forum was provided for critical reflection on that experience, as a means of countering our conventional knowledge about the world.

ASSESSMENT

On this programme we define *participative* assessment as a process in which students and tutors share, to some degree, the responsibility for making evaluations and judgements about students' written work, gaining insight into how such judgements are made, and finding appropriate ways to communicate them. The criteria for assessment may be given, or there may be an opportunity for students to influence them. At most this can mean students on the course being involved with peer assessment, which takes the form of evaluation and commentary on written work and in reaching agreement with student colleagues as to its grading (Reynolds and Trehan 2000).

Peer assessment is intended to evaluate each student's understanding of their chosen topic area and how it relates to the practice of management. They are expected to record the comments and grades that result from group discussions. In this sense, students' dialogue and social support is fundamental to the assessment process. A member of staff is present to facilitate decision making, but not to pass judgement on the assignment.

This process provides a backdrop for students to engage reflexively with power relations in the classroom. The emphasis on students learning from each other in small groups, and the opportunity for their evaluation of each other's work to influence the assessment outcome, would seem to provide the foundations for 'diffusing authority along horizontal lines' (Giroux 1988: 39). Assessment on the programme is not simply another aspect of education method, as Reynolds and Trehan highlight: 'its function in providing the basis for granting or withholding qualifications makes it a primary location for power relations' (2000: 2). Individuals on the programme have different status and influence within the learning sets, informed by who they are in the wider society in relation to age, gender, religion, class, and ethnicity. Those differences will surface through assessment, as the following extract from a student illuminates:

> ...on the course, peer assessment invariably includes feedback from a wide range of intellect and knowledge within which the person assessed probably falls in at some point with the range...this implies that some assessment is made by individuals of a lower intellect/knowledge...how valid does that make this assessment?
>
> One consequence of this approach is that in my group people would make allowances for some of the women's experience and abilities, or rather, lack of it.

The above accounts demonstrate how the social processes taking place within participative assessment provide opportunities for students to learn experientially, developing their understanding of relationships and social dynamics as they unfold in the classroom. Operating such assessment methods is a challenging, complex process but is fundamental to the principles of a critically experiential pedagogy in practice.

CRITICALLY EXPERIENTIAL:
RICH *AND* COMPLEX

In this final section we draw insights from Critical Management Learning to illuminate how experiential learning can simultaneously be both a rich source of learning and problematically complex. We reconsider the theme of action learning through the discourse of learning communities, and draw on psychodynamic insights to highlight both the value and the challenge of feelings and emotions for experiential management development. The section also provides an exploration of experiential processes within classroom interaction that illuminate the complexity of managing and working with experiential learning.

Action Learning and Learning Communities

Generally considered fundamental to action learning approaches, the concept of the learning community has recently been examined from more critical perspectives. Fox (2001), for example, claims that learning community-based pedagogy aims to maximize student and/or pupil participation in the framing of the topic of learning and the skill of critique. He points out that without participation, and its consequence, the problematization and customization of content, the individual teacher and student confront bureaucratically standardized intellectual curricula and are alienated from the process of learning, just as the worker is alienated from the means of production.

Fox further claims that the learning community seeks to reverse the alienating effect of traditional authoritarian education, and quotes hooks (1994: 8) who tells us:

To begin, the professor must genuinely value everyone's presence. There must be an ongoing recognition that everyone influences the classroom dynamic, that everyone contributes. These contributions are resources. Used constructively they enhance the capacity of any class to create an open learning community.

The learning community concept involves increased levels of participation: each individual is recognized, their presence is valued, and their contributions produce resources which enhance the collective good. Further, the learning community concept involves 'some deconstruction of the traditional notion that only the professor is responsible for classroom dynamics' (hooks 1994). The professor cannot escape a higher level of responsibility for these dynamics, but ultimately 'excitement is generated by collective effort' (ibid.). The learning community approach requires sharing responsibility for choosing learning methods, the curricular content, and, ideally, in assessment. While these participative practices take time, they allow participants to customize their own pursuit of learning, helping to prevent the estrangement of the person from the knowledge they produce and own.

Furthermore, a challenge of working with a diverse community on an experiential learning programme is that issues emerge which might not be obvious for more homogeneous student groups or with less participative methods. Our observations reinforce criticisms from feminist and post-colonial pedagogy, that action learning is not a utopian, non-hierarchical environment and that the concept of learning 'community' has often been presented naively (for example Ellsworth 1992). Action learning groups tend to mirror the sociodynamics of wider society, so the influence of race, class, or gender on the habitus students enact at university often serves to recreate oppressive environments that silence and disempower some people (hooks 1994; McGill and Beaty 1995).

Core values of experiential learning, such as equality, openness, and honesty, are challenged by the imbalances of power, status, and social/cultural capital which exist within groups that are diverse in ethnicity, gender, religion, and class. For example, we have observed that for some participants on the programmes their experiences of action learning sets can at times be disempowering, so deep are the interconnected consequences of racism and sexism (Rigg and Trehan 1998). Issues of power and powerlessness, silence and openness challenge tutors, but cannot be avoided. They are also an important opportunity for learning. As students have said (UCE 2001a): 'exploring questions of power, as an action researcher and change agent, has provoked new insights into organisational politics more broadly.'

Engaging with Feelings: A Psychodynamic Insight

Learning from experience is also central to psychodynamic and systemic traditions with their focus on development, insight, and understanding. But what separates psychodynamic from other approaches is the idea of learning from unconscious phenomena. Psychodynamic perspectives illuminate approaches which differentiate between behaviours and activities geared towards rational task performance and those geared to emotional needs and anxieties. The application of this approach on the programme emphasizes the importance of understanding human relationships through the idea of connectedness and relatedness. In doing so the emphasis is placed on 'learning from the conscious and unconscious levels of connection that exist between and shape selves and others, people and systems' (French and Vince 1999: 7). In addition, growing awareness of the influence of emotions in shaping pedagogical agendas has provided interesting impetus for the issue of emotional learning on the programme.

It is very common as tutors to be on the receiving end of course participants' anger, as well as to observe, within the ALS, a range of emotional behaviour such as withdrawal, silence, aggression, or scapegoating. A psychodynamic perspective helps make sense of such behaviour and informs students' understanding of social processes and our facilitation of them. Tutors have to develop resilience in the face of participants' emotions, the insights to interpret them, and the skills to facilitate groups and individuals. Such learning is transferable to organizational development (Fineman 1999) and as Vince (2002b) has argued:

The importance of psychodynamic theory to the study of organizational learning is that it provides one way of thinking about the inseparability of emotion and politics, and acknowledges that this relationship is at the heart of what it means both to learn and to organise. (p. 73)

If we are to accept that engaging with emotions and associated feelings of fear and anxiety is an important element in the learning process, then questions of feelings, power, and authority need to be embedded in the curriculum. Risks are many and varied in learning groups, the expressions of powerful feelings such as anger, the risk of speaking or not speaking, the risk of leading, fear, and anxiety all have important implications for our programme, and students are actively encouraged to work with these issues as they surface. As Vince (1996) argues, any consideration of learning needs to take account of the emotions experienced by learners in the learning context. A Critically experiential course is likely, as a result of the level of social engagement it entails, to touch participants' emotions. Changes to learner—teacher power relations may have similar consequences, as Vince writes: 'Approaches to learning that break free of dependency on the teacher, and place emphasis on the responsibilities of the learner, always create anxiety' (1996: 121).

From our experience, active engagement in experiential learning can be painful and, contrary to its intention, can be disempowering. We should not expect it to be comfortable. Indeed, as has been observed more generally, learning cannot take place without anxiety or critical learning without personal struggle (hooks 1994). As the following extract from a student highlights;

I can recall incidents when my own uncertainty, that feeling of being on the edge of change, created the conditions for risk and it was in these situations that I think I learned most.

Vince (1996) states that it is the anxiety created from fear that gives rise to the uncertainty which can lead to learning and change, as is illustrated by the above extract. He also observes that learning environments are a powerful and contained arena for viewing negotiations on autonomy and dependence. Within the programme therefore, it is important that all the stakeholders acknowledge the inequalities of power which can be generated and which in any case can develop between students. Learning groups are permeated with relations of power, which contribute to the construction of individual and group identity.

CONCLUSION: EXPERIENTIAL LEARNING FOR THE TUTORS?

In this chapter we set out to explain the particular approach to experiential learning that characterizes the UCE Masters for Managers programme and that we have characterized as Critically Experiential. We have highlighted four key features of action learning, praxis, process, and proactivity that combine with insights from Critical Management Learning and psychodynamics to develop participants' management practice. A Critical perspective also enhances our understanding of both the potential and the pitfalls of experiential learning. It explains the opportunities for course participants to make connections between their action learning experiences and management practice. However, Critical insights also illuminate the complexity of managing and working with experiential learning.

We have identified some of the ways in which core facets of experiential learning, such as empowerment, openness, and trust, can simultaneously be challenged, whilst continuing to offer a wealth of unparalleled opportunity for learning to manage and practising organization development. So what does this demand of tutors? This is the question we turn to in this concluding section. We also need to explore the responsibilities of course tutors when initiating a process of experiential learning, when the consequences of such an approach are potentially disturbing and 'unmanageable'. We do not aim to offer a prescription, but some of the issues that we conclude are important include: the fundamental importance of facilitating the action learning set; tutors' reflexivity; and students' informed choice.

Learning is a social as well as an individual process (Jarvis 1987). Brookfield (1994) talks of the value to students of a supportive peer community, and we found the action learning sets had high importance as a site of learning, a place for dialogue, and a source of emotional support. Establishment and facilitation of the sets is therefore of great consequence, and demands skilled facilitators with good group work skills and insight into the social dynamics of diverse groups.

Our experience reminds us of the power that lecturers can have to influence students' lives, which clearly places a responsibility on us to question our own intentions, motives, and practices. Tutors have to be prepared for emotionality and conflict, and be aware of their own needs and impetuses. It is also incumbent upon us to be aware of, and be reflective about, the 'expert practitioner' label, which students often fix upon us, to query the roots of our own assumptions, and to be reflexive about our own awareness and practice concerning race and gender issues. The learning we gained from past action learning sets, for example, might not be adequate for the next year. As we have seen in Birmingham over the life of the programme, power dynamics between 'Us' and the 'Other' change: once women were few in number (less than 10 per cent), now they represent over 40 per cent. Where once white faces prevailed, black and minority managers now make up more than a third. However, in the very recent past, the 'other' has become students from refugee backgrounds, whilst the majority 'Us' is British, whether black, minority ethnic, or white. Notions of who has status, who has cultural capital, and how participants might ally across the learning community shift.

Our understanding as tutors has to keep up. Diversity in a staff group is therefore essential, to straddle the literature that can be offered, to be present as hetero-geneous individuals that different students can approach, and also to challenge and stretch each other. We need to be constantly developing ourselves, in a sense mirroring the risk taking we ask course participants to engage in. Just as we ask of our students, we also need to engage in reflexive practice.

NOTE

1. For distinctions between action learning and action research—both of which are ap-plied in the programme—see Pedler 1983 and Eden and Huxham 2001.

REFERENCES

Argyris, C., and Schön, D. (1974). *Theories in Practice*. San Francisco: Jossey-Bass.
Bateson, G. (1973). *Steps towards an Ecology of the Mind*. London: Paladin.
Belbin, M. R. (1981), *Management Teams: Why They Succeed or Fail* London: Heinemann.
Belenky, F. M., Clinchy, B. M., Golderger, N. R., and Tarube, J. M. (1986). *Women's Ways of Knowing: The Development of Self, Voice and Mind*. New York: Basic Books.
Blaxter, L., Hughes, C., and Tight, M. (2001). *How to Research*. Buckingham: Open University Press.
Brookfield, S. (1988). 'Developing Critically Reflective Practitioners: A Rationale for Train-ing Educators of Adults', in S. Brookfield (ed.), *Training Educators of Adults: The Theory and Practice of Graduate Adult Education*. New York: Routledge.
—— (1994). 'Tales from the Darker Side: A Phenomenology of Adult Critical Reflection', *International Journal of Lifelong Education*, 13/3: 203–16.
Burgoyne, J., and Reynolds, M. (eds.) (1997). *Management Learning: Integrating Perspectives in Theory and Practice*. London: Sage.
Carr, W., and Kemmis, S. (1986). *Becoming Critical: Knowing through Action Research*. Geelong: Deakin University.
Eden, C., and Huxham, C. (2001). 'Action Research for the Study of Organizations', in S. Clegg, C. Hardy, and W. Nord (eds.), *Studying Organization*. Beverly Hills, Calif.: Sage.
Ellsworth, E. (1992). 'Why Doesn't This Feel Empowering? Working through the Repressive Myths of Critical Pedagogy', in C. Luke and J. Gore (eds.), *Feminisms and Critical Peda-gogy*. New York: Routledge.

Fineman, S. (1999). 'Emotion and Organizing', in R. Stewart, S. Clegg, and C. Hardy (eds.), *Studying Organization*. London: Sage.

Fox, S. (2001). 'Studying Networked Learning: Same Implications from Socially Situated Learning Theory and Actor-Network Theory', in C. Steeples and C. Jones (eds.), Networked Learning: Perspectives and Issues. London: Springer.

French, R., and Vince, R. (1999). *Group Relations: Management and Organisation*. Oxford: Oxford University Press.

Giroux, H. (1988). *Teachers as Intellectuals*. New York: Bergin & Garvey.

Guba, E., and Lincoln, Y. (1994). 'Competing Paradigms', in N. K. Denzin and Y. S. Lincoln (eds.), *Handbook of Qualitative Research*. Thousand Oaks, Calif.: Sage.

Hooks, b. (1994). *Teaching to Transgress: Education as the Practice of Freedom*. New York: Routledge.

Hoyrup, S. (2004). 'Reflection as a Core Process in Organisational Learning', *Journal of Workplace Learning*, 16/8: 442–54.

Jarvis, P. (1987). *Adult Learning in the Social Context*. London: Croom Helm.

—— (1995). *Adult and Continuing Education: Theory and Practice*. London: Routledge.

Kemmis, S. (1985). 'Action Research and the Politics of Reflection', in D. Boud, R. Keogh, and D. Walker (eds.), *Reflection: Turning Experience into Learning*. London: Kogan Page.

Kolb, D. A. (1984). *Experiential Learning*. Englewood Cliffs, NJ: Prentice Hall.

Lather, P. (1991). *Getting Smart: Feminist Research and Pedagogy with/in the Postmodern*. New York: Routledge.

Lewin, K. (1947). 'Frontiers in Group Dynamics: Channel of Group Life: Social Planning and Action Research', *Human Relations*, 1: 143–53.

—— (1951). *Field Theory in Social Sciences*. New York: Harper & Row.

McGill, I., and Beaty, L. (1995). *Action Learning*. London: Kogan Page.

McLaughlin, H., and Thorpe, R. (1993). 'Action Learning: A Paradigm in Emergence: The Problems Facing a Challenge to Traditional Management Education and Development', *British Journal of Management*, 4/1: 19–27.

Mezirow, J. (1991). *Fostering Critical Reflection in Adulthood: A Guide to Transformative and Emancipatory Learning*. San Francisco: Jossey-Bass.

Miller, S. (1990). 'Experiential Learning in Groups: The Development of the Leicester Model', in E. L. Trist and H. Murray (eds.), *The Social Engagement of the Social Science: A Tavistock Anthropology*. London: Free Association Books.

—— (2005). 'What it's Like Being the "Holder of the Space": A Narrative on Working with Reflective Practice in Groups', *Reflective Practice*, 6/3: 367–77.

Mirza, H. (1997). *Black British Feminism: A Reader*. London: Routledge.

Moon, J. (2000). *Reflection in Learning and Professional Development: Theory and Practice*. London: Routledge.

Nicolini, D., Sher, M., Childerstone, S., and Gorli, M. (2004). 'In Search of the "Structure that Reflects": Promoting Organizational Reflection Practices in a UK Health Authority', in M. Reynolds and R. Vince (eds.) (2004), *Organizing Reflection*. Abingdon: Ashgate.

Pedler, M. (1983). *Action Learning in Practice*. Aldershot: Gower.

Revans, R. W. (ed.) (1982). *The Origins and Growth of Action Learning*. Bromley: Chartwell-Bratt.

Reynolds, M. (1997). 'Towards a Critical Pedagogy', in J. Burgoyne and M. Reynolds (eds.), *Management Learning: Integrating Perspectives in Theory and Practice*. London: Sage.

Reynolds, M. and Trehan, K. (2000). 'Assessment: A Critical Perspective', *Studies in Higher Education*, 25/3: 267–78.

—— —— (2001). 'Classroom as Real World: Propositions for a Pedagogy of Difference', *Gender and Education*, 13/4: 357–72.

—— and Vince, R. (eds.) (2004). *Organizing Reflection*. Abingdon: Ashgate.

Rice, A. K. (1999). *Learning for Leadership: Interpersonal and Intergroup Relations*. London: Tavistock.

Rigg, C., and Trehan, K. (1998). 'Not Critical Enough? Black Women Raise Challenges for Critical Management Learning', *Gender and Education*, 2/3: 265–80.

—— —— and Ram, M. (2002). 'Using Action Research to Explore the Development Needs of Second Generation Asian Small Businesses', in J. McGoldrick, J. Stewart, and S. Watson (eds.), *Researching HRD*. London: Routledge.

Schein, E. (1987). *Process Consultation: Lessons for Managers and Consultants*, vol.ii. Wokingham: Addison Wesley.

Schön, D. (1983). *The Reflective Practitioner: How Professionals Think in Action*. New York: Basic Books.

Trehan, K., and Rigg, C. (2005). 'Beware of the Unbottled Genie: Unspoken Aspects of Critical Self Reflection', in C. Elliott and S. Turnbull (eds.), *Critical Thinking in Human Resource Development*. London: Routledge.

UCE (2001a). *Postgraduate Management Development Programme Student Evaluation Questionnaire*. Birmingham: UCE.

—— (2001b). *Postgraduate Management Development Programme Student Handbook (Certificate in Management)*. Birmingham: UCE.

—— (2005). *Masters for Managers Brochure*. Birmingham: UCE.

Vince, R. (1996). 'Experiential Management Education as the Practice of Change', in R. French and C. Grey (eds.), *Rethinking Management Education*. London: Sage.

—— (2002a). 'Organizing Reflection', *Management Learning*, 33/1: 63–78.

—— (2002b). 'The Impact of Emotion on Organizational Learning', *Human Resource Development*, 15/1: 73–86.

Watson, T. (2000). 'Beyond Managism: Negotiated Narratives and Critical Management Education in Practice', *British Journal of Management*, 12/4: 385–96.

—— and Harris, P. (1999). *The Emergent Manager*. London: Sage.

CONCLUSION

INSTITUTIONAL BARRIERS TO EXPERIENTIAL LEARNING REVISITED

D. CHRISTOPHER KAYES

REARRANGING THE CHAIRS: AN OPPORTUNITY TO REVISIT EXPERIENTIAL LEARNING IN PRACTICE

AFTER I had been teaching in my first full-time faculty position for only a week, the Dean's office called and asked me to stop by. The Dean's assistant simply asked that I kindly place the chairs in the classroom back into rows after my classes were complete. This, she assured me, was only being considerate of the other faculty members who used the room. The request of the assistant wasn't earth shattering. I simply said 'okay' and left the encounter at that.

Confusion set in as I returned to my office. I may have engaged in what Chris Argyris calls defensive routines, or my counter-institutional orientation in general may have led to my confusion. I kept asking myself: Why was it inconsiderate for me not to put the chairs back into rows after my class, when other professors failed to put the chairs back into a circle after finance, accounting, or marketing? Why were rows the standard and circles or clusters or pairs or complete disarray considered deviant? In retrospect, this was my first encounter with the institutional barriers to experiential learning-based education. I don't think I can describe my experience any better than the student described in Kiran Trehan and Clare Rigg's chapter when she said of her experience, 'It was like a great jolt!'

The confusion I felt that first year of teaching continues to this day, although I have come to accept the situation, just as any teacher must do to keep from becoming weary from cynicism. The figure of 'maximum disorder' depicted by Jane Thompson and Tracy Lamping in this volume reminded me of this early career experience and put me on the path not only of reflecting upon my own experiences as a teacher, lecturer, and student of experiential learning, but of revisiting, more generally, the institutional barriers to using experiential learning in the contemporary classroom.

This chapter explores, from a different angle, a challenge put forth by Anne Herbert and Sari Stenfors in their chapter about experiential methods. The challenge they put forth, as I understand it, can be stated more generally as this: how do educators reconcile the use of experiential learning methods, which are clearly consistent with stated goals and strategies of most universities, with institutional practices that may not support, or in some cases run directly counter to, the use of experiential methods?

My answer to this question centres on the notion that, despite the growing acceptance of experiential approaches to education around the world, adopting experiential exercises remains a difficult, almost counter-institutional task. Despite the long, successful, and continued use of experiential events as a means to educate managers in and out of the classroom, institutional barriers to successful experiential learning still abound.

I begin by briefly explaining experiential learning in the context of institutional norms that emphasize the assessment of learning outcomes. I then rely on this framework to explore how experiential learning events described in this book challenge these norms. The purpose of this chapter is not to provide a comprehensive analysis of the barriers to adopting experiential learning methods in the classroom but to increase awareness of the potential barriers that might emerge as the reader seeks to apply the methods found throughout this book. I then use this volume as the basis to draw some broader conclusions about the state of experiential learning practice.

EXPERIENTIAL LEARNING IN CONTEXT

To better understand the nature of experiential learning, it can be viewed in relation to other forms of learning. In Figure 25.1, I present a framework

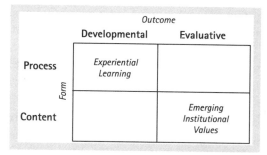

Fig. 25.1 Experiential learning in the context of management education

that considers learning in the context of formal education based on two dimensions.

The first dimension considers that learning outcomes generally relate to the development of individual participants or the evaluation of individual participants. Developmental outcomes focus more on creating individuals, building skills or abilities, or increasing knowledge in the form of critical thinking or similar knowledge management approaches. Developmental outcomes focus on individual growth, change, and reflexivity. In the context of learning theory, development involves a variety of potential changes, including growing (Kegan 1994), learning (Kolb 1984), failing and recovering (Weick, Sutcliffe, and Obstfeld 1999), creating new knowledge, questioning existing problems (Marquardt 1999), and viewing situations as dilemmas (Mezirow 1991). In contrast, evaluation outcomes focus more on how individual participants can better serve a greater end, through their improved performance or more effectual contributions to an organization's goals. Evaluation emphasizes topics such as measuring specific quantifiable outcomes, achieving goals, improving existing processes, solving existing problems, rewarding successes, and getting it right the first time.

The form of the educational experience can be considered either process driven or content driven. Processes consist of the course 'how', or the procedures, exercises, and/or method for teaching. Content, as I use the term here, refers to course and professional content, rather than the content of experience. Content focuses on the specific knowledge, language, or skills that students might gain from participation in the course.

This framework helps to distinguish between experiential learning and other, more pervasive forms of management education. Based on the matrix, I hypothesize that experiential learning is process oriented and developmental, while more prevalent forms of pedagogy, such as lectures and case studies, are content oriented and evaluative. At the end of the chapter, I will use the chapters in this book to test the hypothesis.

The framework, of course, contains a number of Parsonian functionalist assumptions that may be limiting to a full understanding of the phenomenon of experiential learning. The use of Parsonian logic here suggests an underlying belief that educational institutions perform the powerful function of social control and behavioural control.

To be sure, the framework's overly simplistic nature fails to serve as a theory of education. Yet, the framework has proven practical since it provides a basis to compare experiential learning and more institutionally centred practices. The chapters presented in this volume provide an important source of data for both the practice and conceptualization of experiential learning. Before moving more deliberately into the substance of these fascinating chapters, I want to briefly explore a few of the more potent institutional norms and values working against the further development of experiential learning.

INSTITUTIONAL NORMS AND VALUES AS A BARRIER TO EXPERIENTIAL LEARNING

Despite the vigour and enthusiasm for experiential learning presented in this book, in my experience teachers find it increasingly difficult to implement and justify the use of experiential learning events in management education. Evidence suggests that management education is moving from the process-driven/developmental quadrant to the content-driven/evaluative quadrant of the framework with alarming speed. While a number of reasons for this move exist, two trends in particular push institutional norms towards the content-driven/evaluative approach: outcome-based education and continued uncertainty about the professional identity of management educators.

Outcome-Based Education

One important factor limiting the application of experiential learning is the drive towards more outcome-based or evidence-based education. This drive can be seen in the recent revised accreditation standards issued by the Association to Advance Collegiate Schools of Business. Each school seeking accreditation must develop a short list of learning goals by which to 'demonstrate assurance of learning' and measure its success. The goals need to denote an outcome of individual students (as opposed, for example, to teams or cohorts) and must have a clear measurement. In and of themselves, such goals are not inherently anti-experiential learning, but the implementation often results in narrowly defined outcomes that are antithetical to experiential learning.

The problem with these goals is that they focus on the outcomes at the expense of process and focus on the individual and not the group. Since the problems with these kinds of goals have been addressed elsewhere (Kayes 2006), I will not go into further details. The barrier that these goals present to experiential learning might best be expressed as a question. How can the possibility of insight, engagement, or serendipity—just a few of the goals of experiential learning expressed in these chapters—be measured by such a narrowly defined outcome?

Jeff Gold, Robin Holt, and Richard Thorpe expose some of the folly of this kind of abstract goal setting. They show, although maybe unintentionally, what can happen when goal setting is treated as a lawlike predictive system rather than a context specific activity. They point to the social significance of goal setting and the implications of normative standards and traditions in determining what constitutes an 'appropriate goal'. If I am reading them correctly, oftentimes what constitutes a goal is actually an object of activity, not necessarily the intended outcome itself. We should seek to learn more from their use of activity theory to deconstruct the goal-setting process as it relates to the effective (or ineffective) use of goals in the context of learning. This might lead us to consider more fully the implications that goals are essentially 'informed by different people, and norms, and produce differing outcomes (in terms of expectations and results), in the context of management education'.

Professional Identity

Not only are the demands of outcome-based education pulling management education towards an unflattering narrowness, but the search by management education practitioners, i.e. professors, for a professional identity seems to pull us towards the content-driven/evaluative quadrant of our framework as well. Bennis and O'Toole (2005) have discussed at length the identity crisis faced by educators in schools of management, particularly in the United States, in relation to their more academic-minded counterparts in the arts and sciences, not to mention economics and finance. In order to become more academically credible, these educators have sought their validation through basic research.

The professionalization of management education had its benefits, as it assured a more secure or at least a recognized place for management scholars in the academy more generally. But this professionalization came at a cost. This drive for basic research may make us more academic in the eyes of our colleagues in arts and sciences, but it alienates us from the practice of management. Management scholars became increasingly dissociated from the world of practising managers. More interested in writing for and gaining accolades from other academic professionals, professors of management began to teach and think in academic jargon rather than management practice. This professionalization has had important consequences for experiential learning since professional disciplines, by nature, are more concerned with content than process, more interested in codification than application. The content of experience is particularly suspect because it is difficult to measure, codify, and evaluate.

Both the trend towards outcome-based education and the felt need to build a professional identity have moved schools of business in the direction of increased focus on accreditation standards and procedures, what Julian and Ofori-Dankwa (2006) term *accreditocracy*. Accreditocracy carries four systems. (1) *Formalized assessment processes* shift control of classroom activities from cultural control in the hands of specific disciplines to bureaucratic control in the hands of administrators. (2) *Documentation for external accountability* increases accounting procedures. (3) *Hard data-driven outcomes* require 'objective' learning outcomes that are easily measurable. (4) *A focus on continuous improvement* encourages safe, step-by-step changes rather than dynamic progressive change. I think Julian and Ofori-Dankwa's characteristics of accreditocracy provide a nice summary of the forces working against the use of experiential learning in management education, as well as the forces pulling institutions in the direction of evaluation/content.

THEMES FROM THIS BOOK

Using the previous chapters as the basis to test my beliefs that institutional norms pose a threat to experiential learning, I want to explore this theme of threat more deeply within the chapters of this book. Russ Vince and Michael Reynolds provide me with an exceptional opportunity to explore this idea. The rich selection of chapters in this book offers an opportunity to partake in a more nuanced comparison between process-driven/developmental experiential learning and emerging trends towards content-driven/evaluative practices. In addition, the book allows me to take stock of experiential learning and to make some general comments about the current state of, as well as future directions for, experiential learning theory and practice.

Outcomes and Forms of Management Education

Generally speaking, the experiential approaches described here appear to focus on process. The authors call for learning activities that generate the opportunity to reflect upon and take stock of experience. These experiential learning activities are designed to produce a wide variety of experiences in the form of engagement, serendipity, reflection, and surprise. The call for process seems to outweigh the need for outcome-based measures, although there is some call for better measures as well.

A little more might be said about content/process as well. The process of experiential learning seems to play a more important role in experiential learning than content-related issues. The evidence for this statement is that the content of the course seems to be secondary to the process by which it is taught. One might expect process to trump content in a book about experiential learning. I do think, however, that the lack of focus on specific course content represents a broader theme in experiential learning. On the one hand, the chapters here may point to an increasing reliance on experiential learning techniques (for example, the generation of events). On the other hand, at the same time there may be an increasing movement of experiential events into diverse content.

Many of the authors invite us to integrate experience with content. This book speaks to the diversity of fields in which experiential learning is beginning to have an impact. To gain a better understanding of the relationship between content and process, we can turn to Tony Watson's chapter. Watson shows the role of academic content as an important part of his experiential exercise of the negotiated narrative. He considers research-based narratives alongside experience-based narratives and not as something that exists independently. Watson talks of content as 'something you bring along with your reflections', again emphasizing that content does not stand alone from one's experience of it. This, of course, takes us back to Kolb's (1984) formulation of experience and content (for example, abstraction) as a dialectic relationship.

The chapters generate the opportunity to reflect upon experiences using a variety of techniques. Some of the new and exciting techniques include narratives, role-plays, drama, photography, deliberate reflection, and focused observation, just to name a few. The techniques generally cluster around taking stock of one's self and one's environment, especially in the context of others. To many, these techniques are not new. What is new and exciting, however, is to see these techniques being applied to pedagogy and to see them relative to experiential learning. The chapters provide many helpful hints on how to facilitate experiential learning events. Andrea Ellinger may provide the best advice in counselling teachers like me to get out of the way and let students learn.

In many cases, the techniques emerge from critical pedagogy and critical management studies. In the past (Kayes 2004), I have argued that critical management studies and experiential learning approaches have always had much to learn from each other. This volume marks an important step forward in seeing how the combination of critical and experiential-based pedagogy can lead to even richer experiences in the classroom.

Nowhere has the tension between experience and content been more prevalent than in the prolific work of Chris Argyris. Argyris's contribution to this book is that we need to take learning in organizations to a different level for it to make a difference. Dr Argyris's (1991) well-known *Harvard Business Review* article 'Teaching Smart People How to Learn' is the first reading I assign to each of my MBA classes. It doesn't take students long to realize that this chapter is talking about them, and that sets the tone for learning. Perhaps by reading Argyris's article, students make sense of why they are sitting in a circle of chairs rather than a row of chairs for the first time.

Argyris's arguments are important to our understanding of institutional barriers because they help us think a different way about the barriers to learning. With all my ranting about the institutional barriers, Argyris reminds me that many of the barriers to learning lie not in the order of my chairs, but in the order of my thinking. I am more likely to learn by releasing my mind than releasing myself from the organization.

The notion of being released by experiential learning may bring to mind prisons and other total institutions. Burkard Sievers finds a striking similarity between prisons and universities, a comparison that can be traced back at least as far as Foucault. Sievers points to the triteness of a 'chair' metaphor in light of the other, much stronger visual images of institutional structure. He proves that 'institutions of higher learning' are ultimately 'institutions' first and educational second. Through photography, Sievers's students provide us with an image of educational institutions through their very physical structure. We can learn from these photographs that those who enlist experiential learning activities must overcome substantial challenges simply because of bricks and mortar.

Barriers to Experiential Learning

Most, if not all, of the events described in this book shed some light on the problem of institutional pressures working counter to experiential learning.

The metaphor of institutions of higher education creeps into Paula Hyde's chapter just as it did in Sievers's chapter. Hyde returns to Freud to explain how educational institutions enlist relationships of domination. In particular, we see the master–slave relationship manifested in the teacher–student interaction. Whether the theme describes simply a metaphor or a re-enactment of the master–slave relationship itself, Hyde does not make clear. Either way, she surfaces a vivid and disturbing view of the barriers inherent in the relationship between student and teacher. Here, professionals enslave students by dangling knowledge. Not surprisingly, Hyde highlights Gabriel's idea that most of higher education in this form is about creating followers rather than about creating leaders.

Luckily, we are provided with at least two explicit examples of how to overcome the limitations posed by the bricks and mortar of our institutions. Peter Reason offers us an opportunity to move outdoors and away from institutional building blocks through wilderness experiences.

If some authors point out the physical and cultural limitations our institutions pose to realizing the potential of experiential learning, then others show us how to manage or even use these barriers to our advantage. Moving from prisons to the police, Ruth Colquhoun, Nelarine Cornelius, Meretta Elliott, Amar Mistry, and Stephen Smith explain the complexity of the constraints. They show how institutions can serve an important purpose. Institutions help us know what experiences are appropriate. Once we learn this 'institutional code' then we can endorse and display certain emotions that are institutionally appropriate. The chapter provides an example of how to explain and even codify the range of expressed emotions that emerge in a detention cell and the concurrent responses available to the facilitator to manage the particular expressed emotions that emerge.

John Coopey outlines some additional barriers to the effectiveness of experiential events. Coopey explores the rising interest in theatre techniques as a way to help managers manage and champion change. One of the most important limitations to realizing the benefits of experiential learning events is time. If what Coopey observes about dramatic techniques can be generalized, we are all conducting our experiences on borrowed time. Given that only a limited amount of time is devoted to experiential techniques, usually a day or less, it is surprising that these experiences can have much of an impact at all.

Some of the institutional constraints to experiential learning have become taken for granted. Reason, for example, recognizes that this use of wilderness experiences may be useful in 'a business programme in a prestigious business school'. This is a helpful counsel because I am not sure how many business schools include an introduction to Gaia theory as a regular part of their programme. But many business programmes would benefit from a goal that sought 'to open the possibility of a different way of addressing' one's experience in organizations. Imagine the possibility of using this as the sentence root for serial institutional goals. Imagine the possibility of a different way of seeing your career. Imagine the possibility of different ways of seeing your workplace, your coworkers, your financial statements, your education. It would be difficult to imagine how to evaluate such goals in the current outcome-based environment. It would also be difficult to imagine how accreditation standards would evaluate such a goal.

Antonio Strati's chapter brings up an important question about the nature of evaluation in light of experiential exercises. How do you respectfully evaluate someone's performance when you are asking them to 'invest something of themselves' in their coursework? The movement from abstraction to concrete experience is not a simple one, and measuring someone's 'infantile ability to engage in play' may not be an easy thing to get at, especially if it is up for evaluation. As Strati rightly notes, in institutions of higher learning, some teaching techniques like the riddle prove just too bizarre. The riddle, with its 'serious irony, playfulness, and non-sense', is likely to work only in the hands of the most skilled facilitator.

Defining Experience

In this section, I want to pick up a theme that underlies the chapter by Elaine Swan. One of the many issues her chapter surfaces is the problem of defining what we in fact mean by 'experience'. The project to define experience brings up issues related to the institutionalization of experiential learning itself. Interestingly, experiential learning, once a counter-cultural approach to management education, has now become a kind of institution itself. This institutionalization of experiential learning creates problems for defining experiential learning in consistent terms.

Yet, the institutionalization of this anti-institution has characteristics that keep it fresh and open in light of new approaches to learning. Experiential learning tends not to be defined by a clear-cut set of rules and shared assumptions. Rather, experiential learning tends to be defined by diversity rather than homogeneity, complexity rather than simplicity, and disagreement rather than consensus (see Kayes 2004). From the looks of the events described in this text, these tendencies have allowed experiential learning theory to thrive in practice as it incorporates newer understandings of the learning processes described as critical management learning (Reynolds and Vince 2004b), narrative, humanism, and psychoanalysis (Kayes 2002), just to name a few. From reading the texts in this volume, it appears that experiential learning has even experienced its own postmodern moment. One might conclude, after reading this volume, that those who practise experiential learning have adopted, for their own purposes, the postmodern belief that to name (or define) experience is to undermine its very definition.

The lack of a common (experience) referent is indeed anxiety provoking in the same way that circles of chairs provoke more anxiety than rows of chairs. Concerns that experiential learning has yet to develop a consensus definition of experience may have actually aided in the development of our understanding of what experience is and how people learn from it. This lack of a defining character of experience seems to have encouraged an interesting and wide-ranging set of individuals to partake in exploring how learning can emerge from something we call 'experience'.

Silvia Gherardi and Barbara Poggio provide a line of argument—rather, a line of illustration—that experiential learning theory, like leadership, is not an absolute. Rather, experience is best thought of as a contextualized event. The goal of identifying a common definition or set of words to describe experience may itself be problematic. The attempt to name experience simply seeks to further institutionalize it, making it more content driven/evaluative than process driven/developmental. Yet, I want to identify a few themes, no doubt to relieve my own anxiety, that might help at least put experiential learning within the current discussion of management learning.

Characteristics of Experiential Learning that Help Define It

One theme that emerged from my reading of these chapters is a strong connection between experience and narrative. A number of the chapters use narrative as a means to understand experience. These narratives take different forms, including negotiated (for example, Tony Watson), facilitated (for example, Anna Kayes), and gendered (for example, Silvia Gherardi and Barbara Poggio), to help configure experience. These chapters in particular help to highlight the narrative quality of experience. Although they might not agree on exactly what a narrative is, they offer a few insights in how to think about experience. Experience is encapsulated or at least expressed in words that take on a particular sequence.

Experiential learning seems to share something in common with critical theories. Both approaches to management pedagogy work on the fringes of mainstream thinking. In some ways, experiential learning and critical theory may have opposite problems. Jane Thompson and Tracy Lamping argue that, despite the extensive work done in critical pedagogy, few practices have emerged. Experiential learning may suffer the opposite problem. Despite substantial theoretical foundations that emerged in the 1970s and 1980s, few theoretical innovations have occurred since that time. In the meantime, as evidenced by the chapters in this volume, the practice of experiential learning has flourished. In fact, the efforts of Reynolds and Vince in compiling this volume highlight how experiential learning has flourished, despite the gathering storm of institutional controls over the form and outcome of management education. My reading is that, unlike other recent works produced by Reynolds and Vince, practice has taken centre stage to theory.

Taking these chapters as data, we can learn that experiential learning is moving more toward social and group dynamics. Group dynamics have always had an implicit role in experiential learning. After all, Kolb's (1984) initial formation was based, in large part, on action learning theory that emerged from t-group observation. More recently, the group or social dynamics characteristic of experience has become more explicit. For example, Baker, Jansen, and Kolb (2002) talked about experiential learning as a kind of conversation, and Kayes, Kayes, and Kolb (2005) provided a systematic way to think about how individual experiential learning works towards team learning. The trends toward the social dynamics of experiential learning emerged in Reynolds and Vince (2004a) and can be seen in a number of the chapters of this book, especially in Sandra Jones's use of communities of practice.

Ultimately, the social dynamics of practice help us to understand, in a more complex way, that experiences are constructed, not simply constructs, and Keijo Räsänen and Kirsi Korpiaho help us make this distinction. The distinction is not trivial. Constructs put experience into play while constructing plays with experience. Tusse Sidenius Jensen, Jane Rohde Voigt, Enrico Maria Piras, and Bente

Rugaard Thorsen remind us that such experiences occur in many symbolic forms, including drawings and art, not simply language.

As I have come to expect from their work, Ann Welsh, Gordon Dehler, and Dale Murray provide an interesting and thoughtful chapter on experiential learning that serves as a summary of what I have learned from this book. We might learn from their students who are trying to engineer better experiences or commercial products. What is brewing underneath the commercial application of the products these students are designing is an underlying structure to the experiential event of learning. If I may put their chapter into my own words, then I would suggest that an experiential learning event emerges from the following laundry list of considerations:

- *Emotionally intense.* Emotions work with cognition to create a concentrated experience.
- *Decentred.* The purpose of the exercise is determined by the participant (student) as much as the facilitator (teacher).
- *Multidisciplinary.* Traditional academic boundaries matter less than the usefulness of the knowledge.
- *Non-hierarchical.* Traditional power dynamics are named, imagined, and dealt with in explicit ways.
- *Action oriented.* The outcome of events is designed to be useful, even if usefulness is defined by the participants themselves.
- *Team based.* The interaction among participants and facilitator creates something that would not exist without such interaction.
- *Technologically enhanced.* Experiential events do not shy away from and even embrace new technology.

The students that Welsh, Dehler, and Dale describe focus on developing 'experiences' for customers: custom brewing experiences, custom in-flight experiences, etc. It is this very notion of 'experience', as intangible as it may be, that serves as the organizing principle for experiential learning practice and theory.

Although Welsh, Dehler, and Dale, like authors of other chapters, refrain from explicitly defining experience, hidden within the chapter is a kind of direction for understanding what is meant by experience. Experiential learning generates many emotional and cognitive events brought together and juxtaposed through language and arranged through conversation. Joseph Champoux builds on Welsh, Dehler, and Dale's definition of experience to describe experiential learning as a 'wide range of learning and teaching practices' that help learners focus on process, rather than strictly the outcomes of learning.

While surely this definition is not designed to encompass all definitions of experience, it provides me a starting point to limit anxiety about not having a definition, avoid the pitfall of the postmodern agenda that defiantly defies definition, and at the same time begin serious discussion of what experiential events actually are.

In short, I share the optimism described by Martin Hornyak, Steve Green, and Kurt Heppard about the promise of experiential learning to generate positive learning experiences. I am, however, less assured than they are that experiential learning will be used appropriately in the push for greater measurement and 'accountability' in management education. Not unlike the organization re-engineering craze, the growing accountability craze in education is more likely to assure measurement *per se*, than it is likely to assure learning itself. Luckily, these authors provide an example of how organizations can avoid the measurement pitfalls and focus on learning more directly.

Final Thoughts: Evaluating the Hypothesis about Experiential Learning

I have limited my reading of experiential learning to the chapters in this book. This method, of course, proves somewhat problematic. In addition to the biases inherent in the selection process utilized by editors Reynolds and Vince in this book, their reputations probably preceded them, and thus, they probably experienced some self-selection by authors interested in their particular viewpoint. The conclusions I draw here about the state of experiential learning must be made with some scepticism, since I am working with a representative sample of experiential learning efforts across the globe. I would suggest that, based on my knowledge of the editors' interests, there are probably more examples of functionalist, quantitative, and outcome-driven experiential exercises in the marketplace than are represented in this book. Nonetheless, the chapters selected by the editors of this book do provide some promising and interesting applications of experience into pedagogy.

My reading of the chapters implies that management education today is more about replication, socialization, imprinting, and conformity. Innovation and learning in management education may be secondary objectives. This book reaffirms my belief that the emergent institutional values and norms of management education reward pedagogy that is content driven and evaluative. Thus, the unscientific hypothesis that I proposed in the beginning of this chapter is supported. Experiential learning-based pedagogy tends to buck the forces of institutional priorities to provide an alternative to the growing reach of institutionalization.

Within this book we can see the mechanisms of experiential pedagogy at work in a variety of philosophical viewpoints, from functionalism to critical theory, from humanism to pragmatism. Experiential learning seems to have come into its own as an eclectic approach that accepts and integrates a variety of viewpoints, methods, and desired outcomes.

Despite my inclination to view my role as an educator to help individuals become more self-aware, I have become more accepting of the notion that most situations of learning in business schools are not going to be as insight producing as t-groups or even small study groups. Business schools today are targeted mainly toward professional development, not personal growth. I became more aware of my own assumptions about the value of personal development in management education by reading Jean E. Neumann's chapter on the work at the Tavistock Institute in London. There is no small irony here. The irony comes in two forms. First, I became more self-aware after reading about Tavistock, known, at least historically, for its work in making individuals more aware of personal blind spots. The deeper irony is that the Tavistock programme advocates as much for professional development as it does for personal development.

Despite the many barriers from within and without, I sense a general optimism about the breadth, depth, and diversity of experiential learning, which is being used in a variety of settings to teach a wide range of content. Experiential learning encompasses many different types of pedagogical strategies, including critical pedagogy, narrative-inspired self-reflections, simulations, and electronic technology. I continue to be optimistic about the future of experiential learning, Reading this volume, and reflecting on the experiences of Elizabeth Creese, I am more aware than ever that learning is a struggle, both between individual and institution, as well as within oneself.

REARRANGING THE CHAIRS: AN UPDATE

I appreciate the opportunity to revisit the troubling experience I encountered years ago when I was teaching in my first full-time position. I recall the situation of moving chairs into circles and then back into rows as challenging, more mentally than physically.

I was reminded of this situation once again as I walked into a new classroom, especially designed to include the latest teaching technology. Indeed, the classroom contained computers and internet hook-up, project-screen TVs, and other video recording devices. The wireless network permeated the room.

As I walked up the aisles of the multitiered classroom to move the chairs of the new lecture hall into a more experiential friendly arrangement, I noticed something both odd and expected. Here, in the brand new, technology-enhanced classroom, the chairs were bolted to the floor. No matter what configuration I wanted, I was trapped by institutional barriers from moving things out of order. And so I continued along with my exercises that semester, without so much as moving a chair. Working around institutional barriers may be the only way to survive.

REFERENCES

Argyris, C. (1991). 'Teaching Smart People How to Learn', *Harvard Business Review*, 69/3: 99–109.

Baker, A. C., Jansen, P. J., and Kolb, D. A. (2002). *Conversational Learning: An Experiential Approach to Knowledge Creation*. Westport, Conn.: Quorum Books.

Bennis, W. G., and O'Toole, J. (2005). 'How Business Schools Lost their Way', *Harvard Business Review*, 83/5: 96–104.

Julian, S. D., and Ofori-Dankwa, J. C. (2006). 'Is Accreditation Good for the Strategic Decision Making of Traditional Business Schools', *Academy of Management Learning and Education*, 5/2: 225–33.

Kayes, A. B. , Kayes, D. C., and Kolb, D. A. (2005). 'Experiential Learning in Teams', *Simulation and Gaming*, 36/3: 330–54.

Kayes, D. C. (2002). 'Experiential Learning and its Critics: Preserving the Role of Experience in Management Learning and Education', *Academy of Management Learning and Education*, 1/2: 137–49.

—— (2004). 'The Limits and Consequences of Experience-Absent Reflection: Implications for Learning and Organizing', in M. Reynolds and R. Vince (eds.), *Organizing Reflection*. London: Ashgate.

—— (2006). *Destructive Goal Pursuit: The Mount Everest Disaster*. London: Palgrave-Macmillan.

Kegan, R. (1994). *In over our Heads*. Cambridge, Mass.: Harvard University Press.

Kolb, D. A. (1984). *Experiential Learning: Experience as the Source of Learning and Development*. Englewood Cliffs, NJ: Prentice-Hall.

Marquardt, M. J. (1999). *Action Learning in Action*. Palo Alto, Calif.: Davies-Black.

Mezirow, J. (1991). *Transformative Dimensions of Adult Learning*. San Francisco: Jossey-Bass.

Reynolds, M., and Vince, R. (eds.) (2004a). *Organizing Reflection*. London: Ashgate.

—— —— (2004b). 'Critical Management Education and Action-Based Learning: Synergies and Contradictions', *Academy of Management Learning and Education*, 3/4: 442–58.

Weick, K. E., Sutcliffe, K. M., and Obstfeld, D. (1999). 'Organizing for High Reliability: Processes of Collective Mindfulness', *Research in Organizational Behavior*, 21: 81–123.

AUTHOR INDEX

Abma, T A 161
Abram, David 196
Ahmed, S 204, 209, 214–15, 217
Allen, E D 226, 227, 228
Allen, R W 367
Altman, Y 313
Alvesson, M 36, 112, 158, 159
Anderson, L 141
Angle, H L 367
Anthias, F 206, 208
Anthony, P 389
Argyris, C 32, 33, 260, 275, 335, 403, 406,
    423
Arkin, A 176, 178
Arnzen, M 251
Arora, Ranjit 203, 205, 206
Astin, A 149
Atherton, J S 92

Baier, A 172
Bailey, A 214
Bain, A 253
Baker, A 364, 365
Bakhurst, D 40
Bandura, A 125
Bannister, D 109
Barr, R 138, 140
Barry, D 73, 346
Barthes, R 248
Bartlett, F C 125
Bartlett, H F 294
Bateson, Gregory 190, 403
Beard, C 139
Beaty, L 226, 402, 411
Beccali, B 159
Becher, T 327
Bedny, G 39
Beech, N 162
Beile, P 311, 323–4
Belenky, F M 403
Bell, V 206–7
Benne, K D 260, 261
Bennis, W 36, 421

Ben-Tovim, G 208
Berger, N O 313
Berhman, J 138
Berlant, L 213, 214, 217
Berry, Thomas 198
Beumer, U 249
Bhavnani, Reena 203, 205
Billing, Y 159
Bion, W R 242, 252, 278, 288, 294, 394
Blaxter, L 406
Blixen, Karen 157, 161
Bloom, B S 124
Boal, A 112, 173–4, 181
Boden, D 395
Boje, D 165, 368, 369, 370, 371
Bollas, C 251
Bonnett, A 205, 206, 208
Boote, D N 311, 323–4
Born, D 150
Boud, D 125, 156, 313, 357
Bourdieu, Pierre 171
Bourner, T 328
Bouwen, R 173
Bowden, R 328
Bowen, W 327
Bowker, G C 101
Bowles, G 157
Bowles, M L 251
Boydell, T H 390
Bradbury, H 65, 66, 188
Brady, E M 158
Brah, A 125, 203, 204, 214
Brennan, M 328
Brock, B 243
Brockbank, A 162
Brookfield, S 204, 407, 413
Broussine, M 347
Brown, C 208
Brown, J 64, 92, 125, 199, 332
Brown, M Y 190
Brown, S 210
Bruner, J S 42, 65, 125, 163, 263, 272
Bruni, A 159

Subject Index

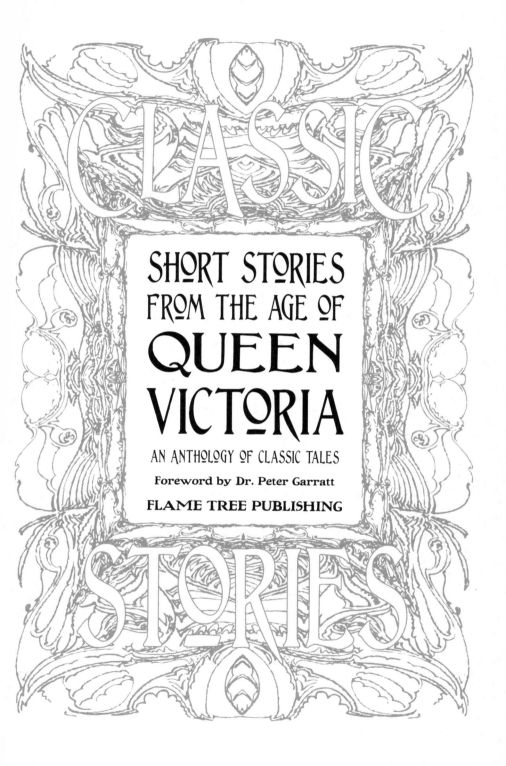

CLASSIC

SHORT STORIES FROM THE AGE OF QUEEN VICTORIA

AN ANTHOLOGY OF CLASSIC TALES

Foreword by Dr. Peter Garratt

FLAME TREE PUBLISHING

STORIES

This is a FLAME TREE Book

Publisher & Creative Director: Nick Wells
Project Editors: Polly Prior, Josie Mitchell
Editorial Assistant: Taylor Bentley
Editorial Board: Gillian Whitaker, Catherine Taylor

Publisher's Note: Due to the historical nature of the classic text, we're aware that there may be some language used which has the potential to cause offence to the modern reader. However, wishing overall to preserve the integrity of the text, rather than imposing contemporary sensibilities, we have left it unaltered.

FLAME TREE PUBLISHING
6 Melbray Mews, Fulham,
London SW6 3NS, United Kingdom
www.flametreepublishing.com

First published 2019

19 21 22 20 18
1 3 5 7 9 10 8 6 4 2

ISBN: 978-1-78755-286-9

The cover image is created by Flame Tree Studio
based on artwork by Slava Gerj and Gabor Ruszkai.

A copy of the CIP data for this book is available from the British Library.

Printed and bound in China

see our new fiction imprint
FLAME TREE PRESS | FICTION WITHOUT FRONTIERS
New and original writing in Horror, Crime, SF and Fantasy
flametreepress.com

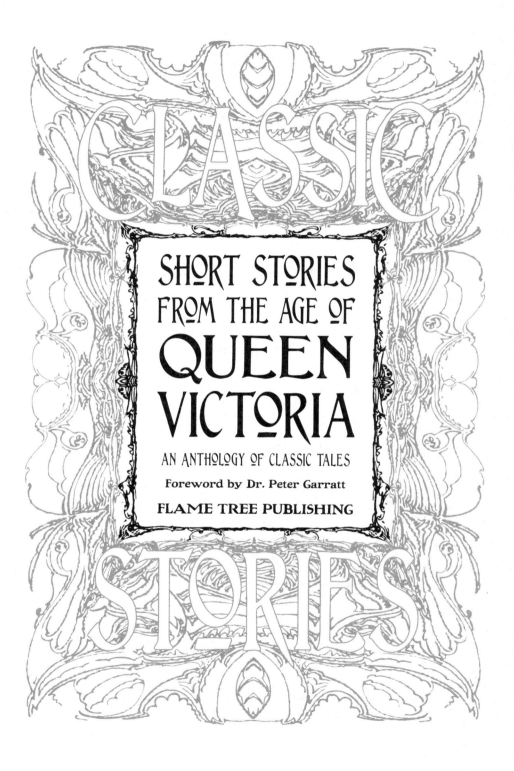

SHORT STORIES FROM THE AGE OF QUEEN VICTORIA

AN ANTHOLOGY OF CLASSIC TALES

Foreword by Dr. Peter Garratt

FLAME TREE PUBLISHING

Contents

Danger & Disorder

The Modern Marriage

Science & the Supernatural

Darkness & Light

Foreword

'FROM THE HUMBLEST of writers to one of the greatest', wrote Queen Victoria to Charles Dickens in 1870, inscribing these words in a copy of her own recently published *Leaves from the Journal of our Life in the Highlands*. That book was no great literary achievement, lacking any of the dazzling charm or imaginative energy of Dickens's own writing. All the same, as a gift to the 'The Inimitable' it seems to crystallize the acclaim and cultural centrality accorded to novelists and poets in the nineteenth century, not only by the monarch herself but by the age that bears her name. This was a period, in other words, when serious writers held a privileged vantage point upon society and its moral norms – and, in Dickens's case, a position of high celebrity – of a kind that would not outlast Victoria's reign. If Modernism's motifs of exile and alienation would help define the writer's role differently after 1901, the figure of the author was understood to be a vital arbiter of Victorian values.

The stories collected here suggestively evoke some of those Victorian values and the extent to which they were tested against changing social realities and radical ideas. They are narratives of darkness as well as light, of danger and disorder almost as often as refuge and affirmation. Elizabeth Gaskell's story 'Lizzie Leigh' (1850), which confronts the loss of a child, movingly examines the possibility of redemption and the necessity of suffering; in George Eliot's 'The Lifted Veil' (1859), the narrator is condemned to foresee the moment of his own death as a recurring living nightmare; while Anthony Trollope's portrait of an aspiring writer in 'The Spotted Dog' (1870) pitches its gentlemanly protagonist Mackenzie into a painful social descent ending in penury, literary failure, and an untimely abject death ('his throat cut from ear to ear'). Astonishingly varied though such examples are, the Victorian short story had certain common ingredients: usually a single unifying idea, seasoned with surprise, shock, or some cautionary revelation, artfully compressed exposition, climactic incident, and economic or even sparing narrative detail. Both in tone and storytelling technique, individual stories could be worlds apart, and certainly not always detained by grim or unsettling subjects. But, like the long novel form, short fiction became notably more artistically serious as the Victorian period progressed.

Romantic Victorians

DICKENS REMARKED, famously, that *Bleak House* dwelt on 'the romantic side of familiar things'. By 'romantic' he was allowing for the play of fantastical powers or agencies, including ghosts, in the course of ordinary life, while signalling a heightened style so widely enjoyed by his readers. Dickens's moral intuition, guided somewhat by Thomas Carlyle before him, was that the social ills caused by rapid industrialization (disease, hunger, rioting, corrosive inequalities) might be addressed using a vivid and visionary literary mode, something particularly true of his short fiction and Christmas ghost stories.

Like most writers of the early Victorian era, Dickens was also seeking ways of emerging as a writer from the Romantic age. Literary life in the 1830s still existed in the shadow of Sir Walter Scott and two generations of great Romantic poets: Lord Byron had died in 1824, and Wordsworth lived on (dying in 1850, having been made Poet Laureate in 1843). Romantic and Victorian shared a fuzzily defined boundary. Dickens's *Oliver Twist*, which began as monthly instalments in *Bentley's Miscellany* in

1837, is a novel that looks both forwards and backwards. Through the orphan Oliver, it explores a murky and murderous stratum of London society – workhouses, prostitutes, thieves, prison and the gallows – where Fagin's criminal gang acts as an alternative, if corrupting, family structure for displaced urban youths. Yet the plot does not simply reward Oliver for being immune to these degrading influences but implies, in a rather old-fashioned way, that his purity and resilience express an identity conferred innately at birth by station or rank (something apparent in Oliver's inexplicably middle-class manner of speaking). Dickens gave his readers excitement and even revulsion by absorbing elements of 'Newgate' fiction (a forerunner of today's 'true crime' genre) into a providential plot structure commonly found in eighteenth-century novels.

Crime and Sensation

A MENACING SENSE of being plotted against links aspects of *Oliver Twist* with later Victorian writing about criminal intrigue, including the 'sensation fiction' of Wilkie Collins in the 1860s and the *Suicide Club* stories of R.L. Stevenson. If Stevenson accelerated 'the revolt from Victorian respectability', as G.K. Chesterton remarked, then Collins's mode of popular fiction toyed in its own way with the boundaries of middle-class taste. Both liberally sprinkled plots with the thrills of secrecy and detection.

The *Suicide Club* stories (the third and final of which, 'The Adventures of a Hansom Cab', appears here) formed part of a group of stories styled by Stevenson in 1882 as the *New Arabian Nights*: in other words, modern romances connected by a common narrative frame. For one literary critic of the day, the authoritative George Saintsbury, the *Suicide Club* stories were a major achievement and a serious literary pleasure. Their effect, Saintsbury gushed, lay in a 'contrast of the fertility of extravagant incident, grim, amusing or simply bizarre, with the quiet play of the author's humour in the construction of character, the skill of his description, the thoroughly literary character of his apparently childish burlesque'. As in *The Strange Case of Dr. Jekyll and Mr. Hyde*, which appeared just a few years later, they also point at a darkness underpinning the outwardly civilised metropolis.

Progress and Reform

CRIME, PUNISHMENT, and reward had a grip on the Victorian reading public, for it was an age of social transformation. Towns and cities expanded rapidly in the wake of the industrial revolution, swelled by migrations from the countryside and population growth. The growing political and economic dominance of the wealthy middle class was recognised by the Reform Act of 1832 and subsequent constitutional reforms that widened the electoral franchise, symbolically marking the end of the *ancien régime*. Social critics such as John Ruskin came to associate urban forms of modernity with ruin and loss; in his unconventional autobiography *Praeterita* (1884), Ruskin evokes the world of his childhood as a vanished Eden. Thomas Hardy's Wessex stories, in a different way, register the passing of an old world and the threat of modern existence to human fulfilment and flourishing. In a different manner, the shape and possibilities of working class existence are the subject of Walter Besant's widely read 1882 novel *All Sorts and Conditions of Men*, set in east London and centring on the social and spiritual improvement of Victorian slum dwellers.

In common with writers of 'New Woman' fiction and drama, such as George Egerton (Mary Chavelita Dunne), Hardy's story 'An Imaginative Woman' (1894) explores the limiting effects of marriage on women, extending the critique of that social institution found elsewhere in his oeuvre. In the figure of its thwarted main character Ella, Hardy links failed artistic ambitions and marital disappointment. Hardy was not alone in exposing the unhappy interior of a marriage: Eliot's 'The Lifted Veil' and Trollope's 'The Spotted Dog' both dramatize monstrously selfish wives who tyrannize pitiful husbands. If reliant on unedifying images of femininity, these narratives are also sufficiently degraded to counter the Victorian ideal of bourgeois marriage.

Science and the Supernatural

GHOSTS, a staple of Victorian short stories, could also be used as a means of questioning the claim of progress. Dickens does this to chilling effect in 'The Signalman' (1866), one his most celebrated stories, which combines haunting voices and visions with the new technological environment of the Victorian railway. 'Main Line: The Boy at Mugby', featured here, belongs to the same group of eight stories (not all by Dickens himself). In a different voice, with a markedly different tone, 'The Boy at Mugby' similarly registers the strangeness of an accelerated modern world. Chapter VIII of *Great Expectations*, also included, in which Pip makes a first visit to Satis House, illustrates another kind of unnerving strangeness linked to the ghost-like presence of Miss Havisham, a shrunken skeletal figure recalling a 'ghastly waxwork at the Fair'. Her vision-like quality in the scene pushes Dickens's writing to the limits of realism, and perhaps beyond.

Visions and voices feature, too, in Eliot's 'The Lifted Veil', a dark 'jeu de mélancholie' as the author put it, in which a man, Latimer, suffers accurate 'previsions' of future events and unwillingly accesses the inner thoughts and feelings of those around him. The narrative ends with Latimer dying in his chair, exactly as its opening scene has predicted. Remarkably, these seemingly supernatural abilities are repeatedly captured in a language of scientific psychology and medical diagnosis ('superadded consciousness' and other terminology). Even if they reveal his wife's plans to kill him, Latimer's powers are not gifts but abnormalities. And yet through this strange story Eliot probes how Victorian science and materialism risked colonising the individual soul and spirit.

By the end of the century, after the impact of Darwin's ideas and the growth of Empire, a reading public enlarged by education reform was able to look back sceptically on the Victorian values that dominated the middle decades of the period – what Oscar Wilde would call its 'earnestness'. Aestheticism and decadence were two cultural labels associated with this fin de siècle mood. Short fiction thrived in periodicals such as *The Strand*, and the once dominant format of the three-volume novel – dubbed 'large, loose, baggy monsters' by Henry James – came to an end in the 1890s. New social and sexual identities emerged, such as the dandy and the flâneur, and writers such as Joseph Conrad began to search for new narrative forms adjusted to collapsing metaphysical certainties. His story 'Amy Foster' gestures, in fact, towards dawning literary Modernism, in its mood and method. A huge distance can consequently be marked between the early short fiction of Dickens, begun as descriptive urban scenes and character sketches, and the later stylistic complexity of Conrad. And yet what connects them, and connects all of the writing in this volume, is the incessant vitality of the Victorian creative imagination, always social, frequently sensational, and sometimes penetratingly critical.

Dr. Peter Garratt

Publisher's Note

Queen Victoria was on the throne from 1837 until her death in 1901; her 63-year reign was, until our present monarch's, unprecedented in its length. The Victorian era was a time of rapid change: economic, scientific, cultural, and a large part of the population lived in dire poverty while the lucky ones watched from their newly-built villas. Fiction bore witness to this; writers offered a commentary on all aspects of society: poverty, class, wealth, religion, gender, with many, such as Charles Dickens, hoping to achieve lasting reform as a result of their work.

We want this book to offer a selection of stories and extracts that will open a door into the darker side of Victorian society, and show the seamier side of this long-ago world. The popularity of the short story during the Victorian era meant that although we had an abundance of choice, narrowing down a final selection was extremely difficult. We have included stories by a variety of writers, some well known (Oscar Wilde, Thomas Hardy, Elizabeth Gaskell), others less so (Arthur Machen, Walter Besant, George Egerton) but who all in their own way, offer us in the twenty-first century a glimpse of what it was like to live and work during those transformative years. We hope you enjoy visiting *Short Stories from the Age of Queen Victoria*.

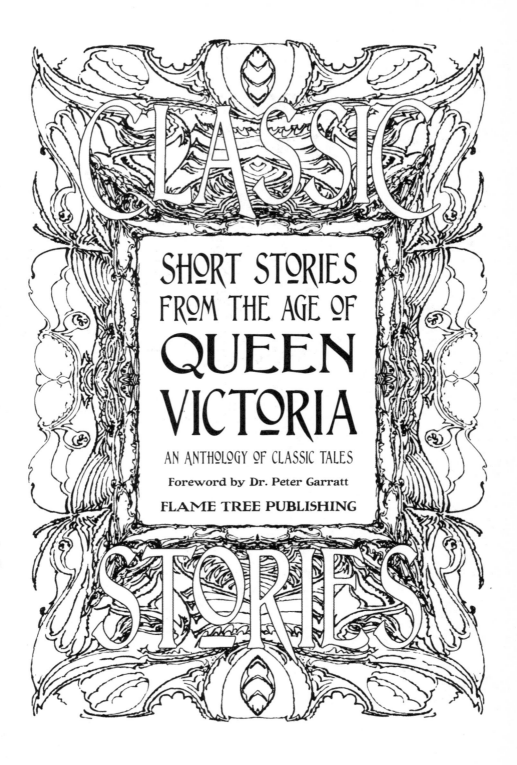

CLASSIC

SHORT STORIES FROM THE AGE OF
QUEEN VICTORIA

AN ANTHOLOGY OF CLASSIC TALES

Foreword by Dr. Peter Garratt

FLAME TREE PUBLISHING

STORIES

Danger & Disorder

Oliver Twist
Chapter VIII

Charles Dickens

OLIVER REACHED THE STYLE at which the bypath terminated, and once more gained the high-road. It was eight o'clock now; and, though he was nearly five miles away from the town, he ran, and hid behind the hedges by turns, till noon, fearing that he might be pursued and overtaken. Then he sat down to rest by the side of a milestone, and began to think for the first time where he had better go and try to live.

The stone by which he was seated bore in large characters an intimation that it was just seventy miles from that spot to London. The name awakened a new train of ideas in the boy's mind. London! – that great large place! – nobody – not even Mr. Bumble – could ever find him there. He had often heard the old men in the workhouse, too, say that no lad of spirit need want in London, and that there were ways of living in that vast city which those who had been bred up in country parts had no idea of. It was the very place for a homeless boy, who must die in the streets unless some one helped him. As these things passed through his thoughts, he jumped upon his feet, and again walked forward.

He had diminished the distance between himself and London by full four miles more, before he recollected how much he must undergo ere he could hope to reach his place of destination. As this consideration forced itself upon him, he slackened his pace a little, and meditated upon his means of getting there. He had a crust of bread, a coarse shirt, and two pairs of stockings in his bundle; and a penny – a gift of Sowerberry's after some funeral in which he had acquitted himself more than ordinarily well – in his pocket. "A clean shirt," thought Oliver, "is a very comfortable thing, – very; and so are two pairs of darned stockings, and so is a penny, but they are small helps to a sixty-five miles' walk in winter time." But Oliver's thoughts, like those of most other people, although they were extremely ready and active to point out his difficulties, were wholly at a loss to suggest any feasible mode of surmounting them; so, after a good deal of thinking to no particular purpose, he changed his little bundle over to the other shoulder, and trudged on.

Oliver walked twenty miles that day, and all that time tasted nothing but the crust of dry bread, and a few draughts of water which he begged at the cottage-doors by the road-side. When the night came, he turned into a meadow, and, creeping close under a hay-rick, determined to lie there till morning. He felt frightened at first, for the wind moaned dismally over the empty fields, and he was cold and hungry, and more alone than he had ever felt before. Being very tired with his walk, however, he soon fell asleep and forgot his troubles.

He felt cold and stiff when he got up next morning, and so hungry that he was obliged to exchange the penny for a small loaf in the very first village through which he passed. He had walked no more than twelve miles, when night closed in again; for his feet were sore, and his legs so weak that they trembled beneath him. Another night passed in the bleak damp air only made him worse; and, when he set forward on his journey next morning, he could hardly crawl along.

He waited at the bottom of a steep hill till a stage-coach came up, and then begged of the outside passengers; but there were very few who took any notice of him, and even those, told him to wait till they got to the top of the hill, and then let them see how far he could run for a halfpenny. Poor Oliver tried to keep up with the coach a little way, but was unable to do it, by reason of his fatigue and sore feet. When the outsides saw this, they put their halfpence back into their pockets again, declaring that he was an idle young dog, and didn't deserve anything; and the coach rattled away, and left only a cloud of dust behind.

In some villages large painted boards were fixed up warning all persons who begged within the district that they would be sent to jail, which frightened Oliver very much, and made him very glad to get out of them with all possible expedition. In others he would stand about the inn-yards, and look mournfully at every one who passed; a proceeding which generally terminated in the landlady's ordering one of the post-boys who were lounging about, to drive that strange boy out of the place, for she was sure he had come to steal something. If he begged at a farmer's house, ten to one but they threatened to set the dog on him; and when he showed his nose in a shop, they talked about the beadle, which brought Oliver's heart into his mouth, – very often the only thing he had there, for many hours together.

In fact, if it had not been for a good-hearted turnpike-man, and a benevolent old lady, Oliver's troubles would have been shortened by the very same process which put an end to his mother's; in other words, he would most assuredly have fallen dead upon the king's highway. But the turnpike-man gave him a meal of bread and cheese; and the old lady, who had a shipwrecked grandson wandering barefooted in some distant part of the earth, took pity upon the poor orphan, and gave him what little she could afford – and more – with such kind and gentle words, and such tears of sympathy and compassion, that they sank deeper into Oliver's soul than all the sufferings he had ever undergone.

Early on the seventh morning after he had left his native place, Oliver limped slowly into the little town of Barnet. The window-shutters were closed, the street was empty, not a soul had awakened to the business of the day. The sun was rising in all his splendid beauty, but the light only served to show the boy his own lonesomeness and desolation as he sat with bleeding feet and covered with dust upon a cold door-step.

By degrees the shutters were opened, the window-blinds were drawn up, and people began passing to and fro. Some few stopped to gaze at Oliver for a moment or two, or turned round to stare at him as they hurried by; but none relieved him, or troubled themselves to inquire how he came there. He had no heart to beg, and there he sat.

He had been crouching on the step for some time, wondering at the great number of public houses (every other house in Barnet is a tavern, large or small), gazing listlessly at the coaches as they passed through, and thinking how strange it seemed that they could do with ease in a few hours what it had taken him a whole week of courage and determination beyond his years to accomplish, when he was roused by observing that a boy who had passed him carelessly some minutes before, had returned, and was now surveying him most earnestly from the opposite side of the way. He took little heed of

this at first; but the boy remained in the same attitude of close observation so long, that
Oliver raised his head, and returned his steady look. Upon this, the boy crossed over,
and, walking close up to Oliver, said, "Hullo! my covey, what's the row?"

The boy who addressed this inquiry to the young wayfarer was about his own age,
but one of the queerest-looking boys that Oliver had ever seen. He was a snub-nosed,
flat-browed, common-faced boy enough, and as dirty a juvenile as one would wish to
see; but he had about him all the airs and manners of a man. He was short of his age,
with rather bow-legs, and little sharp ugly eyes. His hat was stuck on the top of his
head so slightly that it threatened to fall off every moment, and would have done so
very often if the wearer had not had a knack of every now and then giving his head
a sudden twitch, which brought it back to its old place again. He wore a man's coat,
which reached nearly to his heels. He had turned the cuffs back halfway up his arm to
get his hands out of the sleeves, apparently with the ultimate view of thrusting them
into the pockets of his corduroy trousers, for there he kept them. He was altogether as
roystering and swaggering a young gentleman as ever stood four feet six, or something
less, in his bluchers.

"Hullo, my covey, what's the row?" said this strange young gentleman to Oliver.

"I am very hungry and tired," replied Oliver, the tears standing in his eyes as he
spoke. "I have walked a long way – I have been walking these seven days."

"Walking for sivin days!" said the young gentleman. "Oh, I see. Beak's order, eh?
But," he added, noticing Oliver's look of surprise, "I suppose you don't know what a
beak is, my flash com-pan-i-on."

Oliver mildly replied, that he had always heard a bird's mouth described by the term
in question.

"My eyes, how green!" exclaimed the young gentleman. "Why, a beak's a madgst'rate;
and when you walk by a beak's order, it's not straight forerd, but always going up, and
nivir coming down agen. Was you never on the mill?"

"What mill?" inquired Oliver.

"What mill! – why, *the* mill – the mill as takes up so little room that'll work inside
a stone jug, and always goes better when the wind's low with people than when it's
high, acos then they can't get workmen. But come," said the young gentleman; "you
want grub, and you shall have it. I'm at low-water-mark – only one bob and a magpie;
but, *as* far *as* it goes, I'll fork out and stump. Up with you on your pins. There: now
then. Morrice."

Assisting Oliver to rise, the young gentleman took him to an adjacent chandler's
shop, where he purchased a sufficiency of ready-dressed ham and a half-quartern
loaf, or, as he himself expressed it, "a fourpenny bran;" the ham being kept clean and
preserved from dust by the ingenious expedient of making a hole in the loaf by pulling
out a portion of the crumb, and stuffing it therein. Taking the bread under his arm,
the young gentleman turned into a small public-house, and led the way to a tap-room
in the rear of the premises. Here, a pot of beer was brought in by the direction of the
mysterious youth; and Oliver, falling to, at his new friend's bidding, made a long and
hearty meal, during the progress of which the strange boy eyed him from time to time
with great attention.

"Going to London?" said the strange boy, when Oliver had at length concluded.

"Yes."

"Got any lodgings?"

"No."

"Money?"

"No."

The strange boy whistled, and put his arms into his pockets as far as the big-coat sleeves would let them go.

"Do you live in London?" inquired Oliver.

"Yes, I do, when I'm at home," replied the boy. "I suppose you want some place to sleep in to-night, don't you?"

"I do indeed," answered Oliver. "I have not slept under a roof since I left the country."

"Don't fret your eyelids on that score," said the young gentleman. "I've got to be in London to-night, and I know a 'spectable old genelman as lives there, wot'll give you lodgings for nothink, and never ask for the change; that is, if any genelman he knows interduces you. And don't he know me? – Oh, no – not in the least – by no means – certainly not."

The young gentleman smiled, as if to intimate that the latter fragments of discourse were playfully ironical, and finished the beer as he did so.

This unexpected offer of shelter was too tempting to be resisted, especially as it was immediately followed up by the assurance that the old gentleman already referred to, would doubtless provide Oliver with a comfortable place without loss of time. This led to a more friendly and confidential dialogue, from which Oliver discovered that his friend's name was Jack Dawkins, and that he was a peculiar pet and *protégé* of the elderly gentleman before mentioned.

Mr. Dawkins's appearance did not say a vast deal in favour of the comforts which his patron's interest obtained for those whom he took under his protection; but as he had a rather flighty and dissolute mode of conversing, and furthermore avowed that among his intimate friends he was better known by the *soubriquet* of "The artful Dodger," Oliver concluded that, being of a dissipated and careless turn, the moral precepts of his benefactor had hitherto been thrown away upon him. Under this impression, he secretly resolved to cultivate the good opinion of the old gentleman as quickly as possible; and, if he found the Dodger incorrigible, as he more than half suspected he should, to decline the honour of his farther acquaintance.

As John Dawkins objected to their entering London before nightfall, it was nearly eleven o'clock when they reached the turnpike at Islington. They crossed from the Angel into St. John's-road, struck down the small street which terminates at Sadler's Wells theatre, through Exmouth-street and Coppice-row, down the little court by the side of the workhouse, across the classic ground which once bore the name of Hockley-in-the-Hole, thence into Little Saffron-hill, and so into Saffron-hill the Great, along which the Dodger scudded at a rapid pace, directing Oliver to follow close at his heels.

Although Oliver had enough to occupy his attention in keeping sight of his leader, he could not help bestowing a few hasty glances on either side of the way as he passed along. A dirtier or more wretched place he had never seen. The street was very narrow and muddy, and the air was impregnated with filthy odours. There were a good many small shops; but the only stock in trade appeared to be heaps of children, who, even at that time of night, were crawling in and out at the doors, or screaming from the inside. The sole places that seemed to prosper amid the general blight of the place were the public-houses, and in them, the lowest orders of Irish (who are generally the lowest orders of anything) were wrangling with might and main. Covered ways and yards, which here and there diverged from the main street, disclosed little knots of houses where drunken men and women were positively wallowing in the filth; and from several of the door-ways, great ill-looking fellows were cautiously emerging, bound, to all appearance, upon no very well-disposed or harmless errands.

Oliver was just considering whether he hadn't better run away, when they reached the bottom of the hill: his conductor catching him by the arm, pushed open the door of a house near Field-lane, and, drawing him into the passage, closed it behind them.

"Now, then," cried a voice from below, in reply to a whistle from the Dodger.

"*Plummy and slam!*" was the reply.

This seemed to be some watchword or signal that all was right; for the light of a feeble candle gleamed on the wall at the farther end of the passage, and a man's face peeped out from where a balustrade of the old kitchen staircase had been broken away.

"There's two on you," said the man, thrusting the candle farther out, and shading his eyes with his hand. "Who's the t'other one?"

"A new pal," replied Jack Dawkins, pulling Oliver forward.

"Where did he come from?"

"Greenland. Is Fagin up stairs?"

"Yes, he's a sortin' the wipes. Up with you." The candle was drawn back, and the face disappeared.

Oliver, groping his way with one hand, and with the other firmly grasped by his companion, ascended with much difficulty the dark and broken stairs, which his conductor mounted with an ease and expedition that showed he was well acquainted with them. He threw open the door of a back-room, and drew Oliver in after him.

The walls and ceiling of the room were perfectly black with age and dirt. There was a deal table before the fire, upon which was a candle stuck in a ginger-beer bottle; two or three pewter pots, a loaf and butter, and a plate. In a frying-pan which was on the fire, and which was secured to the mantelshelf by a string, some sausages were cooking; and standing over them, with a toasting-fork in his hand, was a very old shrivelled Jew, whose villanous-looking and repulsive face was obscured by a quantity of matted red hair. He was dressed in a greasy flannel gown, with his throat bare, and seemed to be dividing his attention between the frying-pan and a clothes-horse, over which a great number of silk handkerchiefs were hanging. Several rough beds made of old sacks were huddled side by side on the floor; and seated round the table were four or five boys, none older than the Dodger, smoking long clay pipes and drinking spirits with the air of middle-aged men. These all crowded about their associate as he whispered a few words to the Jew, and then turned round and grinned at Oliver, as did the Jew himself: toasting-fork in hand.

"This is him, Fagin," said Jack Dawkins; "my friend, Oliver Twist."

The Jew grinned; and, making a low obeisance to Oliver, took him by the hand, and hoped he should have the honour of his intimate acquaintance. Upon this, the young gentlemen with the pipes came round him, and shook both his hands very hard – especially the one in which he held his little bundle. One young gentleman was very anxious to hang up his cap for him; and another was so obliging as to put his hands in his pockets, in order that, as he was very tired, he might not have the trouble of emptying them when he went to bed. These civilities would probably have been extended much further, but for a liberal exercise of the Jew's toasting-fork on the heads and shoulders of the affectionate youths who offered them.

"We are very glad to see you, Oliver – very," said the Jew. "Dodger, take off the sausages, and draw a tub near the fire for Oliver. Ah, you're a-staring at the pocket-handkerchiefs! eh, my dear? There are a good many of 'em, ain't there? We've just looked 'em out ready for the wash; that's all, Oliver; that's all. Ha! ha! ha!"

The latter part of this speech was hailed by a boisterous shout from all the hopeful pupils of the merry old gentleman, in the midst of which they went to supper.

Oliver ate his share; and the Jew then mixed him a glass of hot gin and water, telling him he must drink it off directly, because another gentleman wanted the tumbler. Oliver did as he was desired. Almost instantly afterwards, he felt himself gently lifted on to one of the sacks, and then he sunk into a deep sleep.

If you enjoyed this, you might also like...
Great Expectations, see page 371
Main Line: The Boy at Mugby, see page 379

Lizzie Leigh

Elizabeth Gaskell

Chapter I

WHEN DEATH is present in a household on a Christmas Day, the very contrast between the time as it now is, and the day as it has often been, gives a poignancy to sorrow – a more utter blankness to the desolation. James Leigh died just as the far-away bells of Rochdale Church were ringing for morning service on Christmas Day, 1836. A few minutes before his death, he opened his already glazing eyes, and made a sign to his wife, by the faint motion of his lips, that he had yet something to say. She stooped close down, and caught the broken whisper, "I forgive her, Annie! May God forgive me!"

"Oh, my love, my dear! only get well, and I will never cease showing my thanks for those words. May God in heaven bless thee for saying them. Thou'rt not so restless, my lad! may be—Oh, God!"

For even while she spoke he died.

They had been two-and-twenty years man and wife; for nineteen of those years their life had been as calm and happy as the most perfect uprightness on the one side, and the most complete confidence and loving submission on the other, could make it. Milton's famous line might have been framed and hung up as the rule of their married life, for he was truly the interpreter, who stood between God and her; she would have considered herself wicked if she had ever dared even to think him austere, though as certainly as he was an upright man, so surely was he hard, stern, and inflexible. But for three years the moan and the murmur had never been out of her heart; she had rebelled against her husband as against a tyrant, with a hidden, sullen rebellion, which tore up the old landmarks of wifely duty and affection, and poisoned the fountains whence gentlest love and reverence had once been for ever springing.

But those last blessed words replaced him on his throne in her heart, and called out penitent anguish for all the bitter estrangement of later years. It was this which made her refuse all the entreaties of her sons, that she would see the kind-hearted neighbours, who called on their way from church, to sympathize and condole. No! she would stay with the dead husband that had spoken tenderly at last, if for three years he had kept silence; who knew but what, if she had only been more gentle and less angrily reserved he might have relented earlier – and in time?

She sat rocking herself to and fro by the side of the bed, while the footsteps below went in and out; she had been in sorrow too long to have any violent burst of deep grief now; the furrows were well worn in her cheeks, and the tears flowed quietly, if incessantly, all the day long. But when the winter's night drew on, and the neighbours had gone away to their homes, she stole to the window, and gazed out, long and wistfully, over the dark grey moors. She did not hear her son's voice, as he spoke to her from the door, nor his footstep as he drew nearer. She started when he touched her.

"Mother! come down to us. There's no one but Will and me. Dearest mother, we do so want you." The poor lad's voice trembled, and he began to cry. It appeared to require an effort on Mrs. Leigh's part to tear herself away from the window, but with a sigh she complied with his request.

The two boys (for though Will was nearly twenty-one, she still thought of him as a lad) had done everything in their power to make the house-place comfortable for her. She herself, in the old days before her sorrow, had never made a brighter fire or a cleaner hearth, ready for her husband's return home, than now awaited her. The tea-things were all put out, and the kettle was boiling; and the boys had calmed their grief down into a kind of sober cheerfulness. They paid her every attention they could think of, but received little notice on her part; she did not resist, she rather submitted to all their arrangements; but they did not seem to touch her heart.

When tea was ended – it was merely the form of tea that had been gone through— Will moved the things away to the dresser. His mother leant back languidly in her chair.

"Mother, shall Tom read you a chapter? He's a better scholar than I."

"Ay, lad!" said she, almost eagerly. "That's it. Read me the Prodigal Son. Ay, ay, lad. Thank thee."

Tom found the chapter, and read it in the high-pitched voice which is customary in village schools. His mother bent forward, her lips parted, her eyes dilated; her whole body instinct with eager attention. Will sat with his head depressed and hung down. He knew why that chapter had been chosen; and to him it recalled the family's disgrace. When the reading was ended, he still hung down his head in gloomy silence. But her face was brighter than it had been before for the day. Her eyes looked dreamy, as if she saw a vision; and by-and-by she pulled the Bible towards her, and, putting her finger underneath each word, began to read them aloud in a low voice to herself; she read again the words of bitter sorrow and deep humiliation; but most of all, she paused and brightened over the father's tender reception of the repentant prodigal.

So passed the Christmas evening in the Upclose Farm.

The snow had fallen heavily over the dark waving moorland before the day of the funeral. The black storm-laden dome of heaven lay very still and close upon the white earth, as they carried the body forth out of the house which had known his presence so long as its ruling power. Two and two the mourners followed, making a black procession, in their winding march over the unbeaten snow, to Milne Row Church; now lost in some hollow of the bleak moors, now slowly climbing the heaving ascents. There was no long tarrying after the funeral, for many of the neighbours who accompanied the body to the grave had far to go, and the great white flakes which came slowly down were the boding forerunners of a heavy storm. One old friend alone accompanied the widow and her sons to their home.

The Upclose Farm had belonged for generations to the Leighs; and yet its possession hardly raised them above the rank of labourers. There was the house and out-buildings, all of an old-fashioned kind, and about seven acres of barren unproductive land, which they had never possessed capital enough to improve; indeed, they could hardly rely upon it for subsistence; and it had been customary to bring up the sons to some trade, such as a wheelwright's or blacksmith's.

James Leigh had left a will in the possession of the old man who accompanied them home. He read it aloud. James had bequeathed the farm to his faithful wife, Anne

Leigh, for her lifetime, and afterwards to his son William. The hundred and odd pounds in the savings bank was to accumulate for Thomas.

After the reading was ended, Anne Leigh sat silent for a time and then she asked to speak to Samuel Orme alone. The sons went into the back kitchen, and thence strolled out into the fields regardless of the driving snow. The brothers were dearly fond of each other, although they were very different in character. Will, the elder, was like his father, stern, reserved, and scrupulously upright. Tom (who was ten years younger) was gentle and delicate as a girl, both in appearance and character. He had always clung to his mother and dreaded his father. They did not speak as they walked, for they were only in the habit of talking about facts, and hardly knew the more sophisticated language applied to the description of feelings.

Meanwhile their mother had taken hold of Samuel Orme's arm with her trembling hand.

"Samuel, I must let the farm – I must."

"Let the farm! What's come o'er the woman?"

"Oh, Samuel!" said she, her eyes swimming in tears, "I'm just fain to go and live in Manchester. I mun let the farm."

Samuel looked, and pondered, but did not speak for some time. At last he said –

"If thou hast made up thy mind, there's no speaking again it; and thou must e'en go. Thou'lt be sadly pottered wi' Manchester ways; but that's not my look out. Why, thou'lt have to buy potatoes, a thing thou hast never done afore in all thy born life. Well! it's not my look out. It's rather for me than again me. Our Jenny is going to be married to Tom Higginbotham, and he was speaking of wanting a bit of land to begin upon. His father will be dying sometime, I reckon, and then he'll step into the Croft Farm. But meanwhile—"

"Then, thou'lt let the farm," said she, still as eagerly as ever.

"Ay, ay, he'll take it fast enough, I've a notion. But I'll not drive a bargain with thee just now; it would not be right; we'll wait a bit."

"No; I cannot wait; settle it out at once."

"Well, well; I'll speak to Will about it. I see him out yonder. I'll step to him and talk it over."

Accordingly he went and joined the two lads, and, without more ado, began the subject to them.

"Will, thy mother is fain to go live in Manchester, and covets to let the farm. Now, I'm willing to take it for Tom Higginbotham; but I like to drive a keen bargain, and there would be no fun chaffering with thy mother just now. Let thee and me buckle to, my lad! and try and cheat each other; it will warm us this cold day."

"Let the farm!" said both the lads at once, with infinite surprise. "Go live in Manchester!"

When Samuel Orme found that the plan had never before been named to either Will or Tom, he would have nothing to do with it, he said, until they had spoken to their mother. Likely she was "dazed" by her husband's death; he would wait a day or two, and not name it to anyone; not to Tom Higginbotham himself, or may be he would set his heart upon it. The lads had better go in and talk it over with their mother. He bade them good-day, and left them.

Will looked very gloomy, but he did not speak till they got near the house. Then he said –

"Tom, go to th' shippon, and supper the cows. I want to speak to mother alone."

When he entered the house-place, she was sitting before the fire, looking into its embers. She did not hear him come in: for some time she had lost her quick perception of outward things.

"Mother! what's this about going to Manchester?" asked he.

"Oh, lad!" said she, turning round, and speaking in a beseeching tone, "I must go and seek our Lizzie. I cannot rest here for thinking on her. Many's the time I've left thy father sleeping in bed, and stole to th' window, and looked and looked my heart out towards Manchester, till I thought I must just set out and tramp over moor and moss straight away till I got there, and then lift up every downcast face till I came to our Lizzie. And often, when the south wind was blowing soft among the hollows, I've fancied (it could but be fancy, thou knowest) I heard her crying upon me; and I've thought the voice came closer and closer, till at last it was sobbing out, 'Mother!' close to the door; and I've stolen down, and undone the latch before now, and looked out into the still, black night, thinking to see her – and turned sick and sorrowful when I heard no living sound but the sough of the wind dying away. Oh, speak not to me of stopping here, when she may be perishing for hunger, like the poor lad in the parable." And now she lifted up her voice, and wept aloud.

Will was deeply grieved. He had been old enough to be told the family shame when, more than two years before, his father had had his letter to his daughter returned by her mistress in Manchester, telling him that Lizzie had left her service some time – and why. He had sympathized with his father's stern anger; though he had thought him something hard, it is true, when he had forbidden his weeping, heart-broken wife to go and try to find her poor sinning child, and declared that henceforth they would have no daughter; that she should be as one dead, and her name never more be named at market or at meal time, in blessing or in prayer. He had held his peace, with compressed lips and contracted brow, when the neighbours had noticed to him how poor Lizzie's death had aged both his father and his mother; and how they thought the bereaved couple would never hold up their heads again. He himself had felt as if that one event had made him old before his time; and had envied Tom the tears he had shed over poor, pretty, innocent, dead Lizzie. He thought about her sometimes, till he ground his teeth together, and could have struck her down in her shame. His mother had never named her to him until now.

"Mother!" said he, at last. "She may be dead. Most likely she is."

"No, Will; she is not dead," said Mrs. Leigh. "God will not let her die till I've seen her once again. Thou dost not know how I've prayed and prayed just once again to see her sweet face, and tell her I've forgiven her, though she's broken my heart – she has, Will." She could not go on for a minute or two for the choking sobs. "Thou dost not know that, or thou wouldst not say she could be dead – for God is very merciful, Will; He is: He is much more pitiful than man. I could never ha' spoken to thy father as I did to Him – and yet thy father forgave her at last. The last words he said were that he forgave her. Thou'lt not be harder than thy father, Will? Do not try and hinder me going to seek her, for it's no use."

Will sat very still for a long time before he spoke. At last he said, "I'll not hinder you. I think she's dead, but that's no matter."

"She's not dead," said her mother, with low earnestness. Will took no notice of the interruption.

"We will all go to Manchester for a twelvemonth, and let the farm to Tom Higginbotham. I'll get blacksmith's work; and Tom can have good schooling for awhile, which he's always craving for. At the end of the year you'll come back, mother, and give over fretting for Lizzie, and think with me that she is dead – and, to my mind, that would be more comfort than to think of her living;" he dropped his voice as he spoke these last words. She shook her head but made no answer. He asked again – "Will you, mother, agree to this?"

"I'll agree to it a-this-ns," said she. "If I hear and see nought of her for a twelvemonth, me being in Manchester looking out, I'll just ha' broken my heart fairly before the year's ended, and then I shall know neither love nor sorrow for her any more, when I'm at rest in my grave. I'll agree to that, Will."

"Well, I suppose it must be so. I shall not tell Tom, mother, why we're flitting to Manchester. Best spare him."

"As thou wilt," said she, sadly, "so that we go, that's all."

Before the wild daffodils were in flower in the sheltered copses round Upclose Farm, the Leighs were settled in their Manchester home; if they could ever grow to consider that place as a home, where there was no garden or outbuilding, no fresh breezy outlet, no far-stretching view, over moor and hollow; no dumb animals to be tended, and, what more than all they missed, no old haunting memories, even though those remembrances told of sorrow, and the dead and gone.

Mrs. Leigh heeded the loss of all these things less than her sons. She had more spirit in her countenance than she had had for months, because now she had hope; of a sad enough kind, to be sure, but still it was hope. She performed all her household duties, strange and complicated as they were, and bewildered as she was with all the town necessities of her new manner of life; but when her house was "sided," and the boys come home from their work in the evening, she would put on her things and steal out, unnoticed, as she thought, but not without many a heavy sigh from Will, after she had closed the house-door and departed. It was often past midnight before she came back, pale and weary, with almost a guilty look upon her face; but that face so full of disappointment and hope deferred, that Will had never the heart to say what he thought of the folly and hopelessness of the search. Night after night it was renewed, till days grew to weeks, and weeks to months. All this time Will did his duty towards her as well as he could, without having sympathy with her. He stayed at home in the evenings for Tom's sake, and often wished he had Tom's pleasure in reading, for the time hung heavy on his hands as he sat up for his mother.

I need not tell you how the mother spent the weary hours. And yet I will tell you something. She used to wander out, at first as if without a purpose, till she rallied her thoughts, and brought all her energies to bear on the one point; then she went with earnest patience along the least-known ways to some new part of the town, looking wistfully with dumb entreaty into people's faces; sometimes catching a glimpse of a figure which had a kind of momentary likeness to her child's, and following that figure with never-wearying perseverance, till some light from shop or lamp showed the cold strange face which was not her daughter's. Once or twice a kind-hearted passer-by, struck by her look of yearning woe, turned back and offered help, or asked her what she wanted. When so spoken to, she answered only, "You don't know a poor girl they call Lizzie Leigh, do you?" and when they denied all knowledge, she shook her head, and went on again. I think they believed her to be crazy. But she never spoke first to anyone. She sometimes took a few minutes' rest on the door-steps, and sometimes (very seldom) covered her face and cried; but she could not afford to lose time and chances in this way; while her eyes were blinded with tears, the lost one might pass by unseen.

One evening, in the rich time of shortening autumn-days, Will saw an old man, who, without being absolutely drunk, could not guide himself rightly along the foot-path, and was mocked for his unsteadiness of gait by the idle boys of the neighbourhood. For his father's sake, Will regarded old age with tenderness, even when most degraded and removed from the stern virtues which dignified that father; so he took the old man home, and seemed to believe his often-repeated assertions, that he drank nothing but water. The stranger tried to stiffen himself up into steadiness as he drew nearer home, as if there someone there for whose respect he cared even in his half-intoxicated state, or whose feelings he feared to grieve. His home was exquisitely clean and neat, even in outside appearance; threshold, window, and windowsill were outward signs of some spirit of purity within. Will was rewarded for his attention by a bright glance of thanks, succeeded by a blush of shame, from a young woman of twenty or thereabouts. She did not speak or second her father's hospitable invitations to him to be seated. She seemed unwilling that a stranger should witness her father's attempts at stately sobriety, and Will could not bear to stay and see her distress. But when the old man, with many a flabby shake of the hand, kept asking him to come again some other evening, and see them, Will sought her downcast eyes, and, though he could not read their veiled meaning, he answered, timidly, "If it's agreeable to everybody, I'll come, and thank ye." But there was no answer from the girl, to whom this speech was in reality addressed; and Will left the house, liking her all the better for never speaking.

He thought about her a great deal for the next day or two; he scolded himself for being so foolish as to think of her, and then fell to with fresh vigour, and thought of her more than ever. He tried to depreciate her: he told himself she was not pretty, and then made indignant answer that he liked her looks much better than any beauty of them all. He wished he was not so country-looking, so red-faced, so broad-shouldered; while she was like a lady, with her smooth, colourless complexion, her bright dark hair, and her spotless dress. Pretty or not pretty she drew his footsteps towards her; he could not resist the impulse that made him wish to see her once more, and find out some fault which should unloose his heart from her unconscious keeping. But there she was, pure and maidenly as before. He sat and looked, answering her father at cross-purposes, while she drew more and more into the shadow of the chimney-corner out of sight. Then the spirit that possessed him (it was not he himself, sure, that did so impudent a thing!) made him get up and carry the candle to a different place, under the pretence of giving her more light at her sewing, but in reality to be able to see her better. She could not stand this much longer, but jumped up and said she must put her little niece to bed; and surely there never was, before or since, so troublesome a child of two years old, for though Will stayed an hour and a half longer, she never came down again. He won the father's heart, though, by his capacity as a listener; for some people are not at all particular, and, so that they themselves may talk on undisturbed, are not so unreasonable as to expect attention to what they say.

Will did gather this much, however, from the old man's talk. He had once been quite in a genteel line of business, but had failed for more money than any greengrocer he had heard of; at least, any who did not mix up fish and game with green-grocery proper. This grand failure seemed to have been the event of his life, and one on which he dwelt with a strange kind of pride. It appeared as if at present he rested from his past exertions (in the bankrupt line), and depended on his daughter, who kept a small school for very young children. But all these particulars Will only remembered and understood when he had left the house; at the time he heard them, he was thinking of Susan. After he had made good his footing at Mr. Palmer's, he was not long, you may be sure, without finding some reason for returning again and again. He listened to her father, he talked to the little niece, but he looked at Susan, both while he listened and while he talked. Her father kept on insisting upon his former gentility, the details of which would have appeared very questionable to Will's mind, if the sweet, delicate, modest Susan had not thrown an inexplicable air of refinement over all she came near. She never spoke much; she was generally diligently at work; but when she moved it was so noiselessly, and when she did speak, it was in so low and soft a voice, that silence, speech, motion, and stillness alike seemed to remove her high above Will's reach into some saintly and inaccessible air of glory – high above his reach, even as she knew him! And, if she were made acquainted with the dark secret behind of his sister's shame, which was kept ever present to his mind by his mother's nightly search among the outcast and forsaken, would not Susan shrink away from him with loathing, as if he were tainted by the involuntary relationship? This was his dread; and thereupon followed a resolution that he would withdraw from her sweet company before it was too late. So he resisted internal temptation, and stayed at home, and suffered and sighed. He became angry with his mother for her untiring patience in seeking for one who he could not help hoping was dead rather than alive. He spoke sharply to her, and received only such sad deprecatory answers as made him reproach himself, and still more lose sight of peace of mind. This struggle could not last long without affecting his health; and Tom, his sole companion through the long evenings, noticed his increasing languor, his restless irritability, with perplexed anxiety, and at last resolved to call his mother's attention to his brother's haggard, careworn looks. She listened with a startled recollection of Will's claims upon her love. She noticed his decreasing appetite and half-checked sighs.

"Will, lad! what's come o'er thee?" said she to him, as he sat listlessly gazing into the fire.

"There's nought the matter with me," said he, as if annoyed at her remark.

"Nay, lad, but there is." He did not speak again to contradict her; indeed, she did not know if he had heard her, so unmoved did he look.

"Wouldst like to go to Upclose Farm?" asked she, sorrowfully.

"It's just blackberrying time," said Tom.

Will shook his head. She looked at him awhile, as if trying to read that expression of despondency, and trace it back to its source.

"Will and Tom could go," said she; "I must stay here till I've found her, thou knowest," continued she, dropping her voice.

He turned quickly round, and with the authority he at all times exercised over Tom, bade him begone to bed.

When Tom had left the room, he prepared to speak.

Chapter II

"MOTHER," then said Will, "why will you keep on thinking she's alive? If she were but dead, we need never name her name again. We've never heard nought on her since father wrote her that letter; we never knew whether she got it or not. She'd left her place before then. Many a one dies in—"

"Oh, my lad! dunnot speak so to me, or my heart will break outright," said his mother, with a sort of cry. Then she calmed herself, for she yearned to persuade him to her own belief. "Thou never asked, and thou'rt too like thy father for me to tell without asking – but it were all to be near Lizzie's old place that I settled down on this side o' Manchester; and the very day at after we came, I went to her old missus, and asked to speak a word wi' her. I had a strong mind to cast it up to her, that she should ha' sent my poor lass away, without telling on it to us first; but she were in black, and looked so sad I could na' find in my heart to threep it up. But I did ask her a bit about our Lizzie. The master would have turned her away at a day's warning (he's gone to t'other place; I hope he'll meet wi' more mercy there than he showed our Lizzie – I do), and when the missus asked her should she write to us, she says Lizzie shook her head; and when she speered at her again, the poor lass went down on her knees, and begged her not, for she said it would break my heart (as it has done, Will – God knows it has)," said the poor mother, choking with her struggle to keep down her hard overmastering grief, "and her father would curse her – Oh, God, teach me to be patient." She could not speak for a few minutes – "and the lass threatened, and said she'd go drown herself in the canal, if the missus wrote home – and so –

"Well! I'd got a trace of my child – the missus thought she'd gone to th' workhouse to be nursed; and there I went – and there, sure enough, she had been – and they'd turned her out as she were strong, and told her she were young enough to work – but whatten kind o' work would be open to her, lad, and her baby to keep?"

Will listened to his mother's tale with deep sympathy, not unmixed with the old bitter shame. But the opening of her heart had unlocked his, and after awhile he spoke –

"Mother! I think I'd e'en better go home. Tom can stay wi' thee. I know I should stay too, but I cannot stay in peace so near – her – without craving to see her – Susan Palmer, I mean."

"Has the old Mr. Palmer thou told me on a daughter?" asked Mrs. Leigh.

"Ay, he has. And I love her above a bit. And it's because I love her I want to leave Manchester. That's all."

Mrs. Leigh tried to understand this speech for some time, but found it difficult of interpretation.

"Why shouldst thou not tell her thou lov'st her? Thou'rt a likely lad, and sure o' work. Thou'lt have Upclose at my death; and as for that, I could let thee have it now, and keep mysel' by doing a bit of charring. It seems to me a very backwards sort o' way of winning her to think of leaving Manchester."

"Oh, mother, she's so gentle and so good – she's downright holy. She's never known a touch of sin; and can I ask her to marry me, knowing what we do about Lizzie, and fearing worse? I doubt if one like her could ever care for me; but if she knew about my sister, it would put a gulf between us, and she'd shudder up at the thought of crossing it. You don't know how good she is, mother!"

"Will, Will! if she's so good as thou say'st, she'll have pity on such as my Lizzie. If she has no pity for such, she's a cruel Pharisee, and thou'rt best without her."

But he only shook his head, and sighed; and for the time the conversation dropped.

But a new idea sprang up in Mrs. Leigh's head. She thought that she would go and see Susan Palmer, and speak up for Will, and tell her the truth about Lizzie; and according to her pity for the poor sinner, would she be worthy or unworthy of him. She resolved to go the very next afternoon, but without telling anyone of her plan. Accordingly she looked out the Sunday clothes she had never before had the heart to unpack since she came to Manchester, but which she now desired to appear in, in order to do credit to Will. She put on her old-fashioned black mode bonnet, trimmed with real lace; her scarlet cloth cloak, which she had had ever since she was married; and, always spotlessly clean, she set forth on her unauthorised embassy. She knew the Palmers lived in Crown Street, though where she had heard it she could not tell; and modestly asking her way, she arrived in the street about a quarter to four o'clock. She stopped to enquire the exact number, and the woman whom she addressed told her that Susan Palmer's school would not be loosed till four, and asked her to step in and wait until then at her house.

"For," said she, smiling, "them that wants Susan Palmer wants a kind friend of ours; so we, in a manner, call cousins. Sit down, missus, sit down. I'll wipe the chair, so that it shanna dirty your cloak. My mother used to wear them bright cloaks, and they're right gradely things again a green field."

"Han ye known Susan Palmer long?" asked Mrs. Leigh, pleased with the admiration of her cloak.

"Ever since they comed to live in our street. Our Sally goes to her school."

"Whatten sort of a lass is she, for I ha' never seen her?"

"Well, as for looks, I cannot say. It's so long since I first knowed her, that I've clean forgotten what I thought of her then. My master says he never saw such a smile for gladdening the heart. But maybe it's not looks you're asking about. The best thing I can say of her looks is, that she's just one a stranger would stop in the street to ask help from if he needed it. All the little childer creeps as close as they can to her; she'll have as many as three or four hanging to her apron all at once."

"Is she cocket at all?"

"Cocket, bless you! you never saw a creature less set up in all your life. Her father's cocket enough. No! she's not cocket any way. You've not heard much of Susan Palmer, I reckon, if you think she's cocket. She's just one to come quietly in, and do the very thing most wanted; little things, maybe, that anyone could do, but that few would think on, for another. She'll bring her thimble wi' her, and mend up after the childer o' nights; and she writes all Betty Harker's letters to her grandchild out at service; and she's in nobody's way, and that's a great matter, I take it. Here's the childer running past! School is loosed. You'll find her now, missus, ready to hear and to help. But we none on us frab her by going near her in school-time."

Poor Mrs. Leigh's heart began to beat, and she could almost have turned round and gone home again. Her country breeding had made her shy of strangers, and this Susan Palmer appeared to her like a real born lady by all accounts. So she knocked with a timid feeling at the indicated door, and when it was opened, dropped a simple curtsey without speaking. Susan had her little niece in her arms, curled up with fond endearment against her breast, but she put her gently down to the ground, and instantly placed a chair in the best corner of the room for Mrs. Leigh, when she told her who she was. "It's not Will as has asked me to come," said the mother, apologetically; "I'd a wish just to speak to you myself!"

Susan coloured up to her temples, and stooped to pick up the little toddling girl. In a minute or two Mrs. Leigh began again.

"Will thinks you would na respect us if you knew all; but I think you could na help feeling for us in the sorrow God has put upon us; so I just put on my bonnet, and came off unknownst to the lads. Everyone says you're very good, and that the Lord has kept you from falling from His ways; but maybe you've never yet been tried and tempted as some is. I'm perhaps speaking too plain, but my heart's welly broken, and I can't be choice in my words as them who are happy can. Well now! I'll tell you the truth. Will dreads you to hear it, but I'll just tell it you. You mun know—" but here the poor woman's words failed her, and she could do nothing but sit rocking herself backwards and forwards, with sad eyes, straight-gazing into Susan's face, as if they tried to tell the tale of agony which the quivering lips refused to utter. Those wretched, stony eyes forced the tears down Susan's cheeks, and, as if this sympathy gave the mother strength, she went on in a low voice – "I had a daughter once, my heart's darling. Her father thought I made too much on her, and that she'd grow marred staying at home; so he said she mun go among strangers and learn to rough it. She were young, and liked the thought of seeing a bit of the world; and her father heard on a place in Manchester. Well! I'll not weary you. That poor girl were led astray; and first thing we heard on it, was when a letter of her father's was sent back by her missus, saying she'd left her place, or, to speak right, the master had turned her into the street soon as he had heard of her condition – and she not seventeen!"

She now cried aloud; and Susan wept too. The little child looked up into their faces, and, catching their sorrow, began to whimper and wail. Susan took it softly up, and hiding her face in its little neck, tried to restrain her tears, and think of comfort for the mother. At last she said –

"Where is she now?"

"Lass! I dunnot know," said Mrs. Leigh, checking her sobs to communicate this addition to her distress. "Mrs. Lomax told me she went—"

"Mrs. Lomax – what Mrs. Lomax?"

"Her as lives in Brabazon Street. She told me my poor wench went to the workhouse fra there. I'll not speak again the dead; but if her father would but ha' letten me – but he were one who had no notion – no, I'll not say that; best say nought. He forgave her on his death-bed. I daresay I did na go th' right way to work."

"Will you hold the child for me one instant?" said Susan.

"Ay, if it will come to me. Childer used to be fond on me till I got the sad look on my face that scares them, I think."

But the little girl clung to Susan; so she carried it upstairs with her. Mrs. Leigh sat by herself – how long she did not know.

Susan came down with a bundle of far-worn baby-clothes.

"You must listen to me a bit, and not think too much about what I'm going to tell you. Nanny is not my niece, nor any kin to me, that I know of. I used to go out working by the day. One night, as I came home, I thought some woman was following me; I turned to look. The woman, before I could see her face (for she turned it to one side), offered me something. I held out my arms by instinct; she dropped a bundle into them, with a bursting sob that went straight to my heart. It was a baby. I looked round again; but the woman was gone. She had run away as quick as lightning. There was a little packet of clothes – very few – and as if they were made out of its mother's gowns, for they were large patterns to buy for a baby. I was always fond of babies; and I had not my wits about me, father says; for it was very cold, and when I'd seen as well as I could (for it was past ten) that there was no one in the street, I brought it in and warmed it. Father was very angry when he came, and said he'd take it to the workhouse the next morning, and flyted me sadly about it. But when morning came I could not bear to part with it; it had slept in my arms all night; and I've heard what workhouse bringing-up is. So I told father I'd give up going out working and stay at home and keep school, if I might only keep the baby; and, after a while, he said if I earned enough for him to have his comforts, he'd let me; but he's never taken to her. Now, don't tremble so – I've but a little more to tell – and maybe I'm wrong in telling it; but I used to work next door to Mrs. Lomax's, in Brabazon Street, and the servants were all thick together; and I heard about Bessy (they called her) being sent away. I don't know that ever I saw her; but the time would be about fitting to this child's age, and I've sometimes fancied it was hers. And now, will you look at the little clothes that came with her – bless her!"

But Mrs. Leigh had fainted. The strange joy and shame, and gushing love for the little child, had overpowered her; it was some time before Susan could bring her round. There she was all trembling, sick with impatience to look at the little frocks. Among them was a slip of paper which Susan had forgotten to name, that had been pinned to the bundle. On it was scrawled in a round stiff hand –

"Call her Anne. She does not cry much, and takes a deal of notice. God bless you and forgive me."

The writing was no clue at all; the name "Anne," common though it was, seemed something to build upon. But Mrs. Leigh recognised one of the frocks instantly, as being made out of a part of a gown that she and her daughter had bought together in Rochdale.

She stood up, and stretched out her hands in the attitude of blessing over Susan's bent head.

"God bless you, and show you His mercy in your need, as you have shown it to this little child."

She took the little creature in her arms, and smoothed away her sad looks to a smile, and kissed it fondly, saying over and over again, "Nanny, Nanny, my little Nanny." At last the child was soothed, and looked in her face and smiled back again.

"It has her eyes," said she to Susan.

"I never saw her to the best of my knowledge. I think it must be hers by the frock. But where can she be?"

"God knows," said Mrs. Leigh; "I dare not think she's dead. I'm sure she isn't."

"No; she's not dead. Every now and then a little packet is thrust in under our door, with, may be, two half-crowns in it; once it was half-a-sovereign. Altogether I've got seven-and-thirty shillings wrapped up for Nanny. I never touch it, but I've often thought the poor mother feels near to God when she brings this money. Father wanted to set the policeman to watch, but I said No; for I was afraid if she was watched she might not come, and it seemed such a holy thing to be checking her in, I could not find in my heart to do it."

"Oh, if we could but find her! I'd take her in my arms, and we'd just lie down and die together."

"Nay, don't speak so!" said Susan, gently; "for all that's come and gone, she may turn right at last. Mary Magdalen did, you know."

"Eh! but I were nearer right about thee than Will. He thought you would never look on him again if you knew about Lizzie. But thou'rt not a Pharisee."

"I'm sorry he thought I could be so hard," said Susan in a low voice, and colouring up. Then Mrs. Leigh was alarmed, and, in her motherly anxiety, she began to fear lest she had injured Will in Susan's estimation.

"You see Will thinks so much of you – gold would not be good enough for you to walk on, in his eye. He said you'd never look at him as he was, let alone his being brother to my poor wench. He loves you so, it makes him think meanly on everything belonging to himself, as not fit to come near ye; but he's a good lad, and a good son. Thou'lt be a happy woman if thou'lt have him, so don't let my words go against him – don't!"

But Susan hung her head, and made no answer. She had not known until now that Will thought so earnestly and seriously about her; and even now she felt afraid that Mrs. Leigh's words promised her too much happiness, and that they could not be true. At any rate, the instinct of modesty made her shrink from saying anything which might seem like a confession of her own feelings to a third person. Accordingly she turned the conversation on the child.

"I am sure he could not help loving Nanny," said she. "There never was such a good little darling; don't you think she'd win his heart if he knew she was his niece, and perhaps bring him to think kindly on his sister?"

"I dunnot know," said Mrs. Leigh, shaking her head. "He has a turn in his eye like his father, that makes me – He's right down good though. But you see, I've never been a good one at managing folk; one severe look turns me sick, and then I say just the wrong thing, I'm so fluttered. Now I should like nothing better than to take Nancy home with me, but Tom knows nothing but that his sister is dead, and I've not the knack of speaking rightly to Will. I dare not do it, and that's the truth. But you mun not think badly of Will. He's so good hissel, that he can't understand how anyone can do wrong; and, above all, I'm sure he loves you dearly."

"I don't think I could part with Nancy," said Susan, anxious to stop this revelation of Will's attachment to herself. "He'll come round to her soon; he can't fail; and I'll keep a sharp look-out after the poor mother, and try and catch her the next time she comes with her little parcels of money."

"Ay, lass; we mun get hold of her; my Lizzie. I love thee dearly for thy kindness to her child: but, if thou canst catch her for me, I'll pray for thee when I'm too near my death to speak words; and, while I live, I'll serve thee next to her – she mun come first, thou know'st. God bless thee, lass. My heart is lighter by a deal than it was when I comed in. Them lads will be looking for me home, and I mun go, and leave this little sweet one" (kissing it). "If I can take courage, I'll tell Will all that has come and gone between us two. He may come and see thee, mayn't he?"

"Father will be very glad to see him, I'm sure," replied Susan. The way in which this was spoken satisfied Mrs. Leigh's anxious heart that she had done Will no harm by what she had said; and, with many a kiss to the little one, and one more fervent tearful blessing on Susan, she went homewards.

Chapter III

THAT NIGHT Mrs. Leigh stopped at home – that only night for many months. Even Tom, the scholar, looked up from his books in amazement; but then he remembered that Will had not been well, and that his mother's attention having been called to the circumstance, it was only natural she should stay to watch him. And no watching could be more tender, or more complete. Her loving eyes seemed never averted from his face – his grave, sad, careworn face. When Tom went to bed the mother left her seat, and going up to Will, where he sat looking at the fire, but not seeing it, she kissed his forehead, and said – "Will! lad, I've been to see Susan Palmer!"

She felt the start under her hand which was placed on his shoulder, but he was silent for a minute or two. Then he said, –

"What took you there, mother?"

"Why, my lad, it was likely I should wish to see one you cared for; I did not put myself forward. I put on my Sunday clothes, and tried to behave as yo'd ha' liked me. At least, I remember trying at first; but after, I forgot all."

She rather wished that he would question her as to what made her forget all. But he only said –

"How was she looking, mother?"

"Well, thou seest I never set eyes on her before; but she's a good, gentle-looking creature; and I love her dearly, as I've reason to."

Will looked up with momentary surprise, for his mother was too shy to be usually taken with strangers. But, after all, it was naturally in this case, for who could look at Susan without loving her? So still he did not ask any questions, and his poor mother had to take courage, and try again to introduce the subject near to her heart. But how?

"Will!" said she (jerking it out in sudden despair of her own powers to lead to what she wanted to say), "I told her all."

"Mother! you've ruined me," said he, standing up, and standing opposite to her with a stern white look of affright on his face.

"No! my own dear lad; dunnot look so scared; I have not ruined you!" she exclaimed, placing her two hands on his shoulders, and looking fondly into his face. "She's not one to harden her heart against a mother's sorrow. My own lad, she's too good for that. She's not one to judge and scorn the sinner. She's too deep read in her New Testament for that. Take courage, Will; and thou mayst, for I watched her well, though it is not for one woman to let out another's secret. Sit thee down, lad, for thou look'st very white."

He sat down. His mother drew a stool towards him, and sat at his feet.

"Did you tell her about Lizzie, then?" asked he, hoarse and low.

"I did; I told her all! and she fell a-crying over my deep sorrow, and the poor wench's sin. And then a light comed into her face, trembling and quivering with some new glad thought; and what dost thou think it was, Will, lad? Nay, I'll not misdoubt but that thy heart will give thanks as mine did, afore God and His angels, for her great goodness. That little Nanny is not her niece, she's our Lizzie's own child, my little grandchild." She could no longer restrain her tears; and they fell hot and fast, but still she looked into his face.

"Did she know it was Lizzie's child? I do not comprehend," said he, flushing red.

"She knows now: she did not at first, but took the little helpless creature in, out of her own pitiful, loving heart, guessing only that it was the child of shame; and she's worked for it, and kept it, and tended it ever sin' it were a mere baby, and loves it fondly. Will! won't you love it?" asked she, beseechingly.

He was silent for an instant; then he said, "Mother, I'll try. Give me time, for all these things startle me. To think of Susan having to do with such a child!"

"Ay, Will! and to think, as may be, yet of Susan having to do with the child's mother! For she is tender and pitiful, and speaks hopefully of my lost one, and will try and find her for me, when she comes, as she does sometimes, to thrust money under the door, for her baby. Think of that, Will. Here's Susan, good and pure as the angels in heaven, yet, like them, full of hope and mercy, and one who, like them, will rejoice over her as repents. Will, my lad, I'm not afeard of you now; and I must speak, and you must listen. I am your mother, and I dare to command you, because I know I am in the right, and that God is on my side. If He should lead the poor wandering lassie to Susan's door, and she comes back, crying and sorryful, led by that good angel to us once more, thou shalt never say a casting-up word to her about her sin, but be tender and helpful towards one 'who was lost and is found;' so may God's blessing rest on thee, and so mayst thou lead Susan home as thy wife."

She stood no longer as the meek, imploring, gentle mother, but firm and dignified, as if the interpreter of God's will. Her manner was so unusual and solemn, that it overcame all Will's pride and stubbornness. He rose softly while she was speaking, and bent his head, as if in reverence at her words, and the solemn injunction which they conveyed. When she had spoken, he said, in so subdued a voice that she was almost surprised at the sound, "Mother, I will."

"I may be dead and gone; but, all the same, thou wilt take home the wandering sinner, and heal up her sorrows, and lead her to her Father's house. My lad! I can speak no more; I'm turned very faint."

He placed her in a chair; he ran for water. She opened her eyes, and smiled.

"God bless you, Will. Oh! I am so happy. It seems as if she were found; my heart is so filled with gladness."

That night Mr. Palmer stayed out late and long. Susan was afraid that he was at his old haunts and habits – getting tipsy at some public-house; and this thought oppressed her, even though she had so much to make her happy in the consciousness that Will loved her. She sat up long, and then she went to bed, leaving all arranged as well as she could for her father's return. She looked at the little rosy, sleeping girl who was her bed-fellow, with redoubled tenderness, and with many a prayerful thought. The little arms entwined her neck as she lay down, for Nanny was a light sleeper, and was conscious that she, who was loved with all the power of that sweet, childish heart, was near her, and by her, although she was too sleepy to utter any of her half-formed words.

And, by-and-by, she heard her father come home, stumbling uncertain, trying first the windows, and next the door fastenings, with many a loud incoherent murmur. The little innocent twined around her seemed all the sweeter and more lovely, when she thought sadly of her erring father. And presently he called aloud for a light. She had left matches and all arranged as usual on the dresser; but, fearful of some accident from fire, in his unusually intoxicated state, she now got up softly, and putting on a cloak, went down to his assistance.

Alas! the little arms that were unclosed from her soft neck belonged to a light, easily awakened sleeper. Nanny missed her darling Susy; and terrified at being left alone, in the vast mysterious darkness, which had no bounds and seemed infinite, she slipped out of bed, and tottered, in her little nightgown, towards the door. There was a light below, and there was Susy and safety! So she went onwards two steps towards the steep, abrupt stairs; and then, dazzled by sleepiness, she stood, she wavered, she fell! Down on her head on the stone floor she fell! Susan flew to her, and spoke all soft, entreating, loving words; but her white lids covered up the blue violets of eyes, and there was no murmur came out of the pale lips. The warm tears that rained down did not awaken her;

she lay stiff, and weary with her short life, on Susan's knee. Susan went sick with terror. She carried her upstairs, and laid her tenderly in bed; she dressed herself most hastily, with her trembling fingers. Her father was asleep on the settle downstairs; and useless, and worse than useless, if awake. But Susan flew out of the door, and down the quiet resounding street, towards the nearest doctor's house. Quickly she went, but as quickly a shadow followed, as if impelled by some sudden terror. Susan rang wildly at the night-bell – the shadow crouched near. The doctor looked out from an upstairs window.

"A little child has fallen downstairs, at No. 9 Crown Street, and is very ill – dying, I'm afraid. Please, for God's sake, sir, come directly. No. 9 Crown Street."

"I'll be there directly," said he, and shut the window.

"For that God you have just spoken about – for His sake – tell me, are you Susan Palmer? Is it my child that lies a-dying?" said the shadow, springing forwards, and clutching poor Susan's arm.

"It is a little child of two years old. I do not know whose it is; I love it as my own. Come with me, whoever you are; come with me."

The two sped along the silent streets – as silent as the night were they. They entered the house; Susan snatched up the light, and carried it upstairs. The other followed.

She stood with wild, glaring eyes by the bedside, never looking at Susan, but hungrily gazing at the little, white, still child. She stooped down, and put her hand tight on her own heart, as if to still its beating, and bent her ear to the pale lips. Whatever the result was, she did not speak; but threw off the bed-clothes wherewith Susan had tenderly covered up the little creature, and felt its left side.

Then she threw up her arms, with a cry of wild despair.

"She is dead! she is dead!"

She looked so fierce, so mad, so haggard, that, for an instant, Susan was terrified; the next, the holy God had put courage into her heart, and her pure arms were round that guilty, wretched creature, and her tears were falling fast and warm upon her breast. But she was thrown off with violence.

"You killed her – you slighted her – you let her fall down those stairs! you killed her!"

Susan cleared off the thick mist before her, and, gazing at the mother with her clear, sweet angel eyes, said, mournfully – "I would have laid down my own life for her."

"Oh, the murder is on my soul!" exclaimed the wild, bereaved mother, with the fierce impetuosity of one who has none to love her, and to be beloved, regard to whom might teach self-restraint.

"Hush!" said Susan, her finger on her lips. "Here is the doctor. God may suffer her to live."

The poor mother turned sharp round. The doctor mounted the stair. Ah! that mother was right; the little child was really dead and gone.

And when he confirmed her judgment, the mother fell down in a fit. Susan, with her deep grief, had to forget herself, and forget her darling (her charge for years), and question the doctor what she must do with the poor wretch, who lay on the floor in such extreme of misery.

"She is the mother!" said she.

"Why did she not take better care of her child?" asked he, almost angrily.

But Susan only said, "The little child slept with me; and it was I that left her."

"I will go back and make up a composing draught; and while I am away you must get her to bed."

Susan took out some of her own clothes, and softly undressed the stiff, powerless form. There was no other bed in the house but the one in which her father slept. So she tenderly lifted the body of her darling; and was going to take it downstairs, but the mother opened her eyes, and seeing what she was about, she said – "I am not worthy to touch her, I am so wicked. I have spoken to you as I never should have spoken; but I think you are very good. May I have my own child to lie in my arms for a little while?"

Her voice was so strange a contrast to what it had been before she had gone into the fit, that Susan hardly recognised it: it was now so unspeakably soft, so irresistibly pleading; the features too had lost their fierce expression, and were almost as placid as death. Susan could not speak, but she carried the little child, and laid it in its mother's arms; then, as she looked at them, something overpowered her, and she knelt down, crying aloud – "Oh, my God, my God, have mercy on her, and forgive and comfort her."

But the mother kept smiling, and stroking the little face, murmuring soft, tender words, as if it were alive. She was going mad, Susan thought; but she prayed on, and on, and ever still she prayed with streaming eyes.

The doctor came with the draught. The mother took it, with docile unconsciousness of its nature as medicine. The doctor sat by her; and soon she fell asleep. Then he rose softly, and beckoning Susan to the door, he spoke to her there.

"You must take the corpse out of her arms. She will not awake. That draught will make her sleep for many hours. I will call before noon again. It is now daylight. Goodbye."

Susan shut him out; and then, gently extricating the dead child from its mother's arms, she could not resist making her own quiet moan over her darling. She tried to learn off its little placid face, dumb and pale before her.

> Not all the scalding tears of care
> Shall wash away that vision fair;
> Not all the thousand thoughts that rise,
> Not all the sights that dim her eyes,
> Shall e'er usurp the place
> Of that little angel-face.

And then she remembered what remained to be done. She saw that all was right in the house; her father was still dead asleep on the settle, in spite of all the noise of the night. She went out through the quiet streets, deserted still, although it was broad daylight, and to where the Leighs lived. Mrs. Leigh, who kept her country hours, was opening her window-shutters. Susan took her by the arm, and, without speaking, went into the house-place. There she knelt down before the astonished Mrs. Leigh, and cried as she had never done before; but the miserable night had overpowered her, and she who had gone through so much calmly, now that the pressure seemed removed could not find the power to speak.

"My poor dear! What has made thy heart so sore as to come and cry a-this-ons? Speak and tell me. Nay, cry on, poor wench, if thou canst not speak yet. It will ease the heart, and then thou canst tell me."

"Nanny is dead!" said Susan. "I left her to go to father, and she fell downstairs, and never breathed again. Oh, that's my sorrow! But I've more to tell. Her mother is come – is in our house! Come and see if it's your Lizzie."

Mrs. Leigh could not speak, but, trembling, put on her things and went with Susan in dizzy haste back to Crown Street.

Chapter IV

AS THEY ENTERED THE HOUSE in Crown Street, they perceived that the door would not open freely on its hinges, and Susan instinctively looked behind to see the cause of the obstruction. She immediately recognised the appearance of a little parcel, wrapped in a scrap of newspaper, and evidently containing money. She stooped and picked it up. "Look!" said she, sorrowfully, "the mother was bringing this for her child last night."

But Mrs. Leigh did not answer. So near to the ascertaining if it were her lost child or no, she could not be arrested, but pressed onwards with trembling steps and a beating, fluttering heart. She entered the bedroom, dark and still. She took no heed of the little corpse over which Susan paused, but she went straight to the bed, and, withdrawing the curtain, saw Lizzie; but not the former Lizzie, bright, gay, buoyant, and undimmed. This Lizzie was old before her time; her beauty was gone; deep lines of care, and, alas! of want (or thus the mother imagined) were printed on the cheek, so round, and fair, and smooth, when last she gladdened her mother's eyes. Even in her sleep she bore the look of woe and despair which was the prevalent expression of her face by day; even in her sleep she had forgotten how to smile. But all these marks of the sin and sorrow she had passed through only made her mother love her the more. She stood looking at her with greedy eyes, which seemed as though no gazing could satisfy their longing; and at last she stooped down and kissed the pale, worn hand that lay outside the bed-clothes. No touch disturbed the sleeper; the mother need not have laid the hand so gently down upon the counterpane. There was no sign of life, save only now and then a deep sob-like sigh. Mrs. Leigh sat down beside the bed, and still holding back the curtain, looked on and on, as if she could never be satisfied.

Susan would fain have stayed by her darling one; but she had many calls upon her time and thoughts, and her will had now, as ever, to be given up to that of others. All seemed to devolve the burden of their cares on her. Her father, ill-humoured from his last night's intemperance, did not scruple to reproach her with being the cause of little Nanny's death; and when, after bearing his upbraiding meekly for some time, she could no longer restrain herself, but began to cry, he wounded her even more by his injudicious attempts at comfort; for he said it was as well the child was dead; it was none of theirs, and why should they be troubled with it? Susan wrung her hands at this, and came and stood before her father, and implored him to forbear. Then she had to take all requisite steps for the coroner's inquest; she had to arrange for the dismissal of her school; she had to summons a little neighbour, and send his willing feet on a message to William Leigh, who, she felt, ought to be informed of his mother's whereabouts, and of the whole state of affairs. She asked her messenger to tell him to come and speak to her; that his mother was at her house. She was thankful that her father sauntered out to have a gossip at the nearest coach-stand, and to relate as many of the night's adventures as he knew; for as yet he was in ignorance of the watcher and the watched, who silently passed away the hours upstairs.

At dinner-time Will came. He looked red, glad, impatient, excited. Susan stood calm and white before him, her soft, loving eyes gazing straight into his.

"Will," said she, in a low, quiet voice, "your sister is upstairs."

"My sister!" said he, as if affrighted at the idea, and losing his glad look in one of gloom. Susan saw it, and her heart sank a little, but she went on as calm to all appearance as ever.

"She was little Nanny's mother, as perhaps you know. Poor little Nanny was killed last night by a fall downstairs." All the calmness was gone; all the suppressed feeling was displayed in spite of every effort. She sat down, and hid her face from him, and cried bitterly. He forgot everything but the wish, the longing to comfort her. He put his arm round her waist, and bent over her. But all he could say, was, "Oh, Susan, how can I comfort you? Don't take on so – pray don't!" He never changed the words, but the tone varied every time he spoke. At last she seemed to regain her power over herself; and she wiped her eyes, and once more looked upon him with her own quiet, earnest, unfearing gaze.

"Your sister was near the house. She came in on hearing my words to the doctor. She is asleep now, and your mother is watching her. I wanted to tell you all myself. Would you like to see your mother?"

"No!" said he. "I would rather see none but thee. Mother told me thou knew'st all." His eyes were downcast in their shame.

But the holy and pure did not lower or veil her eyes.

She said, "Yes, I know all – all but her sufferings. Think what they must have been!"

He made answer, low and stern, "She deserved them all; every jot."

"In the eye of God, perhaps she does. He is the Judge; we are not."

"Oh!" she said, with a sudden burst, "Will Leigh! I have thought so well of you; don't go and make me think you cruel and hard. Goodness is not goodness unless there is mercy and tenderness with it. There is your mother, who has been nearly heart-broken, now full of rejoicing over her child. Think of your mother."

"I do think of her," said he. "I remember the promise I gave her last night. Thou shouldst give me time. I would do right in time. I never think it o'er in quiet. But I will do what is right and fitting, never fear. Thou hast spoken out very plain to me, and misdoubted me, Susan; I love thee so, that thy words cut me. If I did hang back a bit from making sudden promises, it was because not even for love of thee, would I say what I was not feeling; and at first I could not feel all at once as thou wouldst have me. But I'm not cruel and hard; for if I had been, I should na' have grieved as I have done."

He made as if he were going away; and indeed he did feel he would rather think it over in quiet. But Susan, grieved at her incautious words, which had all the appearance of harshness, went a step or two nearer – paused – and then, all over blushes, said in a low, soft whisper –

"Oh, Will! I beg your pardon. I am very sorry. Won't you forgive me?"

She who had always drawn back, and been so reserved, said this in the very softest manner; with eyes now uplifted beseechingly, now dropped to the ground. Her sweet confusion told more than words could do; and Will turned back, all joyous in his certainty of being beloved, and took her in his arms, and kissed her.

"My own Susan!" he said.

Meanwhile the mother watched her child in the room above.

It was late in the afternoon before she awoke, for the sleeping draught had been very powerful. The instant she awoke, her eyes were fixed on her mother's face with a gaze as unflinching as if she were fascinated. Mrs. Leigh did not turn away, nor move; for it seemed as if motion would unlock the stony command over herself which, while so perfectly still, she was enabled to preserve. But by-and-by Lizzie cried out, in a piercing voice of agony –

"Mother, don't look at me! I have been so wicked!" and instantly she hid her face, and grovelled among the bed-clothes, and lay like one dead, so motionless was she.

Mrs. Leigh knelt down by the bed, and spoke in the most soothing tones.

"Lizzie, dear, don't speak so. I'm thy mother, darling; don't be afeard of me. I never left off loving thee, Lizzie. I was always a-thinking of thee. Thy father forgave thee afore he died." (There was a little start here, but no sound was heard.) "Lizzie, lass, I'll do aught for thee; I'll live for thee; only don't be afeard of me. Whate'er thou art or hast been, we'll ne'er speak on't. We'll leave th' oud times behind us, and go back to the Upclose Farm. I but left it to find thee, my lass; and God has led me to thee. Blessed be His name. And God is good, too, Lizzie. Thou hast not forgot thy Bible, I'll be bound, for thou wert always a scholar. I'm no reader, but I learnt off them texts to comfort me a bit, and I've said them many a time a day to myself. Lizzie, lass, don't hide thy head so; it's thy mother as is speaking to thee. Thy little child clung to me only yesterday; and if it's gone to be an angel, it will speak to God for thee. Nay, don't sob a that 'as; thou shalt have it again in heaven; I know thou'lt strive to get there, for thy little Nancy's sake – and listen! I'll tell thee God's promises to them that are penitent – only doan't be afeard."

Mrs. Leigh folded her hands, and strove to speak very clearly, while she repeated every tender and merciful text she could remember. She could tell from the breathing that her daughter was listening; but she was so dizzy and sick herself when she had ended, that she could not go on speaking. It was all she could do to keep from crying aloud.

At last she heard her daughter's voice.

"Where have they taken her to?" she asked.

"She is downstairs. So quiet, and peaceful, and happy she looks."

"Could she speak! Oh, if God – if I might but have heard her little voice! Mother, I used to dream of it. May I see her once again? Oh, mother, if I strive very hard and God is very merciful, and I go to heaven, I shall not know her – I shall not know my own again: she will shun me as a stranger, and chug to Susan Palmer and to you. Oh, woe! Oh, woe!" She shook with exceeding sorrow.

In her earnestness of speech she had uncovered her face, and tried to read Mrs. Leigh's thoughts through her looks. And when she saw those aged eyes brimming full of tears, and marked the quivering lips, she threw her arms round the faithful mother's neck, and wept there, as she had done in many a childish sorrow, but with a deeper, a more wretched grief.

Her mother hushed her on her breast; and lulled her as if she were a baby; and she grew still and quiet.

They sat thus for a long, long time. At last, Susan Palmer came up with some tea and bread and butter for Mrs. Leigh. She watched the mother feed her sick, unwilling child, with every fond inducement to eat which she could devise; they neither of them took notice of Susan's presence. That night they lay in each other's arms; but Susan slept on the ground beside them.

They took the little corpse (the little unconscious sacrifice, whose early calling-home had reclaimed her poor wandering mother) to the hills, which in her lifetime she had never seen. They dared not lay her by the stern grandfather in Milne Row churchyard, but they bore her to a lone moorland graveyard, where, long ago, the Quakers used to bury their dead. They laid her there on the sunny slope, where the earliest spring flowers blow.

Will and Susan live at the Upclose Farm. Mrs. Leigh and Lizzie dwell in a cottage so secluded that, until you drop into the very hollow where it is placed, you do not see it. Tom is a schoolmaster in Rochdale, and he and Will help to support their mother. I only know that, if the cottage be hidden in a green hollow of the hills, every sound of sorrow in the whole upland is heard there – every call of suffering or of sickness for help is listened to by a sad, gentle-looking woman, who rarely smiles (and when she does her smile is more sad than other people's tears), but who comes out of her seclusion whenever there is a shadow in any household. Many hearts bless Lizzie Leigh, but she – she prays always and ever for forgiveness – such forgiveness as may enable her to see her child once more. Mrs. Leigh is quiet and happy. Lizzie is, to her eyes, something precious – as the lost piece of silver – found once more. Susan is the bright one who brings sunshine to all. Children grow around her and call her blessed. One is called Nanny; her Lizzie often takes to the sunny graveyard in the uplands, and while the little creature gathers the daisies, and makes chains, Lizzie sits by a little grave and weeps bitterly.

If you enjoyed this, you might also like...
From the Dead, see page 249
Irremediable, see page 155

The Spotted Dog

Anthony Trollope

Part I
The Attempt

SOME few years since we received the following letter:

> *Dear Sir,*
>
> *I write to you for literary employment, and I implore you to provide me with it if it be within your power to do so. My capacity for such work is not small, and my acquirements are considerable. My need is very great, and my views in regard to remuneration are modest. I was educated at —, and was afterwards a scholar of — College, Cambridge. I left the university without a degree, in consequence of a quarrel with the college tutor. I was rusticated, and not allowed to return. After that I became for awhile a student for the Chancery Bar. I then lived for some years in Paris, and I understand and speak French as though it were my own language. For all purposes of literature I am equally conversant with German. I read Italian. I am, of course, familiar with Latin. In regard to Greek I will only say that I am less ignorant of it than nineteen-twentieths of our national scholars. I am well read in modern and ancient history. I have especially studied political economy. I have not neglected other matters necessary to the education of an enlightened man, – unless it be natural philosophy. I can write English, and can write it with rapidity. I am a poet; – at least, I so esteem myself. I am not a believer. My character will not bear investigation; – in saying which, I mean you to understand, not that I steal or cheat, but that I live in a dirty lodging, spend many of my hours in a public-house, and cannot pay tradesmen's bills where tradesmen have been found to trust me. I have a wife and four children, – which burden forbids me to free myself from all care by a bare bodkin. I am just past forty, and since I quarrelled with my family because I could not understand The Trinity, I have never been the owner of a ten-pound note. My wife was not a lady. I married her because I was determined to take refuge from the conventional thraldom of so-called 'gentlemen' amidst the liberty of the lower orders. My life, of course, has been a mistake. Indeed, to live at all, – is it not a folly?*
>
> *"I am at present employed on the staff of two or three of the 'Penny Dreadfuls.' Your august highness in literature has perhaps never heard of a 'Penny Dreadful.' I write for them matter, which we among ourselves call 'blood and nastiness,' – and which is copied from one to another. For this I am paid forty-five shillings a week. For thirty shillings a week I will do any work that you may impose upon me for the term of six months. I write this letter as a last effort to rescue myself from the filth of my present position, but I entertain no hope of*

any success. If you ask it I will come and see you; but do not send for me unless you mean to employ me, as I am ashamed of myself. I live at No. 3, Cucumber Court, Gray's Inn Lane; – but if you write, address to the care of Mr. Grimes, the Spotted Dog, Liquorpond Street. Now I have told you my whole life, and you may help me if you will. I do not expect an answer.

    Yours truly,
    Julius Mackenzie.

Indeed he had told us his whole life, and what a picture of a life he had drawn! There was something in the letter which compelled attention. It was impossible to throw it, half read, into the waste-paper basket, and to think of it not at all. We did read it, probably twice, and then put ourselves to work to consider how much of it might be true and how much false. Had the man been a boy at —, and then a scholar of his college? We concluded that, so far, the narrative was true. Had he abandoned his dependence on wealthy friends from conscientious scruples, as he pretended; or had other and less creditable reasons caused the severance? On that point we did not quite believe him. And then, as to those assertions made by himself in regard to his own capabilities, – how far did they gain credence with us? We think that we believed them all, making some small discount, – with the exception of that one in which he proclaimed himself to be a poet. A man may know whether he understands French, and be quite ignorant whether the rhymed lines which he produces are or are not poetry. When he told us that he was an infidel, and that his character would not bear investigation, we went with him altogether. His allusion to suicide we regarded as a foolish boast. We gave him credit for the four children, but were not certain about the wife. We quite believed the general assertion of his impecuniosity. That stuff about "conventional thraldom" we hope we took at its worth. When he told us that his life had been a mistake he spoke to us Gospel truth.

Of the "Penny Dreadfuls," and of "blood and nastiness," so called, we had never before heard, but we did not think it remarkable that a man so gifted as our correspondent should earn forty-five shillings a week by writing for the cheaper periodicals. It did not, however, appear to us probable that anyone so remunerated would be willing to leave that engagement for another which should give him only thirty shillings. When he spoke of the "filth of his present position," our heart began to bleed for him. We know what it is so well, and can fathom so accurately the degradation of the educated man who, having been ambitious in the career of literature, falls into that slough of despond by which the profession of literature is almost surrounded. There we were with him, as brothers together. When we came to Mr. Grimes and the Spotted Dog, in Liquorpond Street, we thought that we had better refrain from answering the letter, – by which decision on our part he would not, according to his own statement, be much disappointed. Mr. Julius Mackenzie! Perhaps at this very time rich uncles and aunts were buttoning up their pockets against the sinner because of his devotion to the Spotted Dog. There are well-to-do people among the Mackenzies. It might be the case that that heterodox want of comprehension in regard to The Trinity was the cause of it: but we have observed that in most families, grievous as are doubts upon such sacred subjects, they are not held to be cause of hostility so invincible as is a thorough-going devotion to a Spotted Dog. If the Spotted Dog had brought about these troubles, any interposition from ourselves would be useless.

For twenty-four hours we had given up all idea of answering the letter; but it then occurred to us that men who have become disreputable as drunkards do not put forth their own abominations when making appeals for aid. If this man were really given to drink he would hardly have told us of his association with the public-house. Probably he was much at the Spotted Dog, and hated himself for being there. The more we thought of it the more we fancied that the gist of his letter might be true. It seemed that the man had desired to tell the truth as he himself believed it.

It so happened that at that time we had been asked to provide an index to a certain learned manuscript in three volumes. The intended publisher of the work had already procured an index from a professional compiler of such matters; but the thing had been so badly done that it could not be used. Some knowledge of the classics was required, though it was not much more than a familiarity with the names of Latin and Greek authors, to which perhaps should be added some acquaintance, with the names also, of the better-known editors and commentators. The gentleman who had had the task in hand had failed conspicuously, and I had been told by my enterprising friend Mr. X—, the publisher, that £25 would be freely paid on the proper accomplishment of the undertaking. The work, apparently so trifling in its nature, demanded a scholar's acquirements, and could hardly be completed in less than two months. We had snubbed the offer, saying that we should be ashamed to ask an educated man to give his time and labour for so small a remuneration; – but to Mr. Julius Mackenzie £25 for two months' work would manifestly be a godsend. If Mr. Julius Mackenzie did in truth possess the knowledge for which he gave himself credit; if he was, as he said, "familiar with Latin," and was "less ignorant of Greek than nineteen-twentieths of our national scholars," he might perhaps be able to earn this £25. We certainly knew no one else who could and who would do the work properly for that money. We therefore wrote to Mr. Julius Mackenzie, and requested his presence. Our note was short, cautious, and also courteous. We regretted that a man so gifted should be driven by stress of circumstances to such need. We could undertake nothing, but if it would not put him to too much trouble to call upon us, we might perhaps be able to suggest something to him. Precisely at the hour named Mr. Julius Mackenzie came to us.

We well remember his appearance, which was one unutterably painful to behold. He was a tall man, very thin, – thin we might say as a whipping-post, were it not that one's idea of a whipping-post conveys erectness and rigidity, whereas this man, as he stood before us, was full of bends, and curves, and crookedness. His big head seemed to lean forward over his miserably narrow chest. His back was bowed, and his legs were crooked and tottering. He had told us that he was over forty, but we doubted, and doubt now, whether he had not added something to his years, in order partially to excuse the wan, worn weariness of his countenance. He carried an infinity of thick, ragged, wild, dirty hair, dark in colour, though not black, which age had not yet begun to grizzle. He wore a miserable attempt at a beard, stubbly, uneven, and half shorn, – as though it had been cut down within an inch of his chin with blunt scissors. He had two ugly projecting teeth, and his cheeks were hollow. His eyes were deep-set, but very bright, illuminating his whole face; so that it was impossible to look at him and to think him to be one wholly insignificant. His eyebrows were large and shaggy, but well formed, not meeting across the brow, with single, stiffly-projecting hairs, – a pair of eyebrows which added much strength to his countenance. His nose was long and well shaped, – but red as a huge carbuncle. The moment we saw him we connected that nose with the Spotted Dog. It was not a blotched nose, not a nose covered with many carbuncles, but a brightly red, smooth, well-formed nose, one glowing carbuncle in itself. He was dressed in a long brown great-coat, which was buttoned up round his throat, and which came nearly to his feet. The binding of the coat was frayed, the buttons were half uncovered, the button-holes were tattered, the velvet collar had become party-coloured with dirt and usage. It was in the month of December, and a great-coat was needed; but this great-coat looked as though it were worn because other garments were not at his command. Not an inch of linen or even of flannel shirt was visible. Below his coat we could only see his broken boots and the soiled legs of his trousers, which had reached that age which in trousers defies description. When we looked at him we could not but ask ourselves whether this man had been born a gentleman and was still a scholar. And yet there was that in his face which prompted us to believe the account he had given of himself. As we looked at him we felt sure that he possessed keen intellect, and that he was too much of a man to boast of acquirements which he did not believe himself to possess. We shook hands with him, asked him to sit down, and murmured something of our sorrow that he should be in distress.

"I am pretty well used to it," said he. There was nothing mean in his voice; – there was indeed a touch of humour in it, and in his manner there was nothing of the abjectness of supplication. We had his letter in our hands, and we read a portion of it again as he sat opposite to us. We then remarked that we did not understand how he, having a wife and family dependent on him, could offer to give up a third of his income with the mere object of changing the nature of his work. "You don't know what it is," said he, "to write for the 'Penny Dreadfuls.' I'm at it seven hours a day, and hate the very words that I write. I cursed myself afterwards for sending that letter. I know that to hope is to be an ass. But I did send it, and here I am."

We looked at his nose and felt that we must be careful before we suggested to our learned friend Dr. — to put his manuscript into the hands of Mr. Julius Mackenzie. If it had been a printed book the attempt might have been made without much hazard, but our friend's work, which was elaborate, and very learned, had not yet reached the honours of the printing-house. We had had our own doubts whether it might ever assume the form of a real book; but our friend, who was a wealthy as well as a learned man, was, as yet, very determined. He desired, at any rate, that the thing should be perfected, and his publisher had therefore come to us offering £25 for the codification and index. Were anything other than good to befall his manuscript, his lamentations would be loud, not on his own score, – but on behalf of learning in general. It behoved us therefore to be cautious. We pretended to read the letter again, in order that we might gain time for a decision, for we were greatly frightened by that gleaming nose.

Let the reader understand that the nose was by no means Bardolphian. If we have read Shakespeare aright Bardolph's nose was a thing of terror from its size as well as its hue. It was a mighty vat, into which had ascended all the divinest particles distilled from the cellars of the hostelrie in Eastcheap. Such at least is the idea which stage representations have left upon all our minds. But the nose now before us was a well-formed nose, would have been a commanding nose, – for the power of command shows itself much in the nasal organ, – had it not been for its colour. While we were thinking of this, and doubting much as to our friend's manuscript, Mr. Mackenzie interrupted us. "You think I am a drunkard," said he. The man's mother-wit had enabled him to read our inmost thoughts.

As we looked up the man had risen from his chair, and was standing over us. He loomed upon us very tall, although his legs were crooked, and his back bent. Those piercing eyes, and that nose which almost assumed an air of authority as he carried it, were a great way above us. There seemed to be an infinity of that old brown great-coat. He had divined our thoughts, and we did not dare to contradict him. We felt that a weak, vapid, unmanly smile was creeping over our face. We were smiling as a man smiles who intends to imply some contemptuous assent with the self-depreciating comment of his companion. Such a mode of expression is in our estimation most cowardly, and most odious. We had not intended it, but we knew that the smile had pervaded us. "Of course you do," said he. "I was a drunkard, but I am not one now. It doesn't matter; – only I wish you hadn't sent for me. I'll go away at once."

So saying, he was about to depart, but we stopped him. We assured him with much energy that we did not mean to offend him. He protested that there was no offence. He was too well used to that kind of thing to be made "more than wretched by it." Such was his heart-breaking phrase. "As for anger, I've lost all that long ago. Of course you take me for a drunkard, and I should still be a drunkard, only—"

"Only what?" I asked.

"It don't matter," said he. "I need not trouble you more than I have said already. You haven't got anything for me to do, I suppose?" Then I explained to him that I had something he might do, if I could venture to entrust him with the work. With some trouble I got him to sit down again, and to listen while I explained to him the circumstances. I had been grievously afflicted when he alluded to his former habit of drinking, – a former habit as he himself now stated, – but I entertained no hesitation in raising questions as to his erudition. I felt almost assured that his answers would be satisfactory, and that no discomfiture would arise from such questioning. We were quickly able to perceive that we at any rate could not examine him in classical literature. As soon as we mentioned the name and nature of the work he went off at score, and satisfied us amply that he was familiar at least with the title-pages of editions. We began, indeed, to fear whether he might not be too caustic a critic on our own friend's performance. "Dr. — is only an amateur himself," said we, deprecating in advance any such exercise of the red-nosed man's too severe erudition. "We never get much beyond dilettanteism here," said he, "as far as Greek and Latin are concerned." What a terrible man he would have been could he have got upon the staff of the Saturday Review, instead of going to the Spotted Dog!

We endeavoured to bring the interview to an end by telling him that we would consult the learned doctor from whom the manuscript had emanated; and we hinted that a reference would be of course acceptable. His impudence, – or perhaps we should rather call it his straightforward sincere audacity, – was unbounded. "Mr. Grimes of the Spotted Dog knows me better than anyone else," said he. We blew the breath out of our mouth with astonishment. "I'm not asking you to go to him to find out whether I know Latin and Greek," said Mr. Mackenzie. "You must find that out for yourself." We assured him that we thought we had found that out. "But he can tell you that I won't pawn your manuscript." The man was so grim and brave that he almost frightened us. We hinted, however, that literary reference should be given. The gentleman who paid him forty-five shillings a week, – the manager, in short, of the "Penny Dreadful," – might tell us something of him. Then he wrote for us a name on a scrap of paper, and added to it an address in the close vicinity of Fleet Street, at which we remembered to have seen the title of a periodical which we now knew to be a "Penny Dreadful."

Before he took his leave he made us a speech, again standing up over us, though we also were on our legs. It was that bend in his neck, combined with his natural height, which gave him such an air of superiority in conversation. He seemed to overshadow us, and to have his own way with us, because he was enabled to look down upon us. There was a footstool on our hearth-rug, and we remember to have attempted to stand upon that, in order that we might escape this supervision; but we stumbled and had to kick it from us, and something was added to our sense of inferiority by this little failure. "I don't expect much from this," he said. "I never do expect much. And I have misfortunes independent of my poverty which make it impossible that I should be other than a miserable wretch."

"Bad health?" we asked.

"No; – nothing absolutely personal; – but never mind. I must not trouble you with more of my history. But if you can do this thing for me, it may be the means of redeeming me from utter degradation." We then assured him that we would do our best, and he left us with a promise that he would call again on that day week.

The first step which we took on his behalf was one the very idea of which had at first almost moved us to ridicule. We made enquiry respecting Mr. Julius Mackenzie, of Mr. Grimes, the landlord of the Spotted Dog. Though Mr. Grimes did keep the Spotted Dog, he might be a man of sense and, possibly, of conscience. At any rate he would tell us something, or confirm our doubts by refusing to tell us anything. We found Mr. Grimes seated in a very neat little back parlour, and were peculiarly taken by the appearance of a lady in a little cap and black silk gown, whom we soon found to be Mrs. Grimes. Had we ventured to employ our intellect in personifying for ourselves an imaginary Mrs. Grimes as the landlady of a Spotted Dog public-house in Liquorpond Street, the figure we should have built up for ourselves would have been the very opposite of that which this lady presented to us. She was slim, and young, and pretty, and had pleasant little tricks of words, in spite of occasional slips in her grammar, which made us almost think that it might be our duty to come very often to the Spotted Dog to enquire about Mr. Julius Mackenzie. Mr. Grimes was a man about forty, – fully ten years the senior of his wife, – with a clear gray eye, and a mouth and chin from which we surmised that he would be competent to clear the Spotted Dog of unruly visitors after twelve o'clock, whenever it might be his wish to do so. We soon made known our request. Mr. Mackenzie had come to us for literary employment. Could they tell us anything about Mr. Mackenzie?

"He's as clever an author, in the way of writing and that kind of thing, as there is in all London," said Mrs. Grimes with energy. Perhaps her opinion ought not to have been taken for much, but it had its weight. We explained, however, that at the present moment we were specially anxious to know something of the gentleman's character and mode of life. Mr. Grimes, whose manner to us was quite courteous, sat silent, thinking how to answer us. His more impulsive and friendly wife was again ready with her assurance. "There ain't an honester gentleman breathing; – and I say he is a gentleman, though he's that poor he hasn't sometimes a shirt to his back."

"I don't think he's ever very well off for shirts," said Mr. Grimes.

"I wouldn't be slow to give him one of yours, John, only I know he wouldn't take it," said Mrs. Grimes. "Well now, look here, Sir; – we've that feeling for him that our young woman there would draw anything for him he'd ask – money or no money. She'd never venture to name money to him if he wanted a glass of anything, – hot or cold, beer or spirits. Isn't that so, John?"

"She's fool enough for anything as far as I know," said Mr. Grimes.

"She ain't no fool at all; and I'd do the same if I was there, and so'd you, John. There is nothing Mackenzie'd ask as he wouldn't give him," said Mrs. Grimes, pointing with her thumb over her shoulder to her husband, who was standing on the hearth-rug; – "that is, in the way of drawing liquor, and refreshments, and such like. But he never raised a glass to his lips in this house as he didn't pay for, nor yet took a biscuit out of that basket. He's a gentleman all over, is Mackenzie."

It was strong testimony; but still we had not quite got at the bottom of the matter. "Doesn't he raise a great many glasses to his lips?" we asked.

"No he don't," said Mrs. Grimes, – "only in reason."

"He's had misfortunes," said Mr. Grimes.

"Indeed he has," said the lady, – "what I call the very troublesomest of troubles. If you was troubled like him, John, where'd you be?"

"I know where you'd be," said John.

"He's got a bad wife, Sir; the worst as ever was," continued Mrs. Grimes. "Talk of drink; – there is nothing that woman wouldn't do for it. She'd pawn the very clothes off her children's back in mid-winter to get it. She'd rob the food out of her husband's mouth for a drop of gin. As for herself, – she ain't no woman's notions left of keeping herself any way. She'd as soon be picked out of the gutter as not; – and as for words out of her mouth or clothes on her back, she hasn't got, Sir, not an item of a female's feelings left about her."

Mrs. Grimes had been very eloquent, and had painted the "troublesomest of all troubles" with glowing words. This was what the wretched man had come to by marrying a woman who was not a lady in order that he might escape the "conventional thraldom" of gentility! But still the drunken wife was not all. There was the evidence of his own nose against himself, and the additional fact that he had acknowledged himself to have been formerly a drunkard. "I suppose he has drunk, himself?" we said.

"He has drunk, in course," said Mrs. Grimes.

"The world has been pretty rough with him, Sir," said Mr. Grimes.

"But he don't drink now," continued the lady. "At least if he do, we don't see it. As for her, she wouldn't show herself inside our door."

"It ain't often that man and wife draws their milk from the same cow," said Mr. Grimes.

"But Mackenzie is here every day of his life," said Mrs. Grimes. "When he's got a sixpence to pay for it, he'll come in here and have a glass of beer and a bit of something to eat. We does make him a little extra welcome, and that's the truth of it. We knows what he is, and we knows what he was. As for book learning, Sir; – it don't matter what language it is, it's all as one to him. He knows 'em all round just as I know my catechism."

"Can't you say fairer than that for him, Polly?" asked Mr. Grimes.

"Don't you talk of catechisms, John, nor yet of nothing else as a man ought to set his mind to; – unless it is keeping the Spotted Dog. But as for Mackenzie; – he knows off by heart whole books full of learning. There was some furreners here as come from, – I don't know where it was they come from, only it wasn't France, nor yet Germany, and he talked to them just as though he hadn't been born in England at all. I don't think there ever was such a man for knowing things. He'll go on with poetry out of his own head till you think it comes from him like web from a spider." We could not help thinking of the wonderful companionship which there must have been in that parlour while the reduced man was spinning his web and Mrs. Grimes, with her needlework lying idle in her lap, was sitting by, listening with rapt admiration. In passing by the Spotted Dog one would not imagine such a scene to have its existence within. But then so many things do have existence of which we imagine nothing!

Mr. Grimes ended the interview. "The fact is, Sir, if you can give him employment better than what he has now, you'll be helping a man who has seen better days, and who only wants help to see 'em again. He's got it all there," and Mr. Grimes put his finger up to his head.

"He's got it all here too," said Mrs. Grimes, laying her hand upon her heart. Hereupon we took our leave, suggesting to these excellent friends that if it should come to pass that we had further dealings with Mr. Mackenzie we might perhaps trouble them again. They assured us that we should always be welcome, and Mr. Grimes himself saw us to the door, having made profuse offers of such good cheer as the house afforded. We were upon the whole much taken with the Spotted Dog.

From thence we went to the office of the "Penny Dreadful," in the vicinity of Fleet Street. As we walked thither we could not but think of Mrs. Grimes's words. The troublesomest of troubles! We acknowledged to ourselves that they were true words. Can there be any trouble more troublesome than that of suffering from the shame inflicted by a degraded wife? We had just parted from Mr. Grimes, – not, indeed, having seen very much of him in the course of our interview; – but little as we had seen, we were sure that he was assisted in his position by a buoyant pride in that he called himself the master, and owner, and husband of Mrs. Grimes. In the very step with which he passed in and out of his own door you could see that there was nothing that he was ashamed of about his household. When abroad he could talk of his "missus" with a conviction that the picture which the word would convey to all who heard him would redound to his honour. But what must have been the reflections of Julius Mackenzie when his mind dwelt upon his wife? We remembered the words of his letter. "I have a wife and four children, which burden forbids me to free myself from all care with a bare bodkin." As we thought of them, and of the story which had been told to us at the Spotted Dog, they lost that tone of rhodomontade with which they had invested themselves when we first read them. A wife who is indifferent to being picked out of the gutter, and who will pawn her children's clothes for gin, must be a trouble than which none can be more troublesome.

We did not find that we ingratiated ourselves with the people at the office of the periodical for which Mr. Mackenzie worked; and yet we endeavoured to do so, assuming in our manner and tone something of the familiarity of a common pursuit. After much delay we came upon a gentleman sitting in a dark cupboard, who twisted round his stool to face us while he spoke to us. We believe that he was the editor of more than one "Penny Dreadful," and that as many as a dozen serial novels were being issued to the world at the same time under his supervision. "Oh!" said he, "so you're at that game, are you?" We assured him that we were at no game at all, but were simply influenced by a desire to assist a distressed scholar. "That be blowed," said our brother. "Mackenzie's doing as well here as he'll do anywhere. He's a drunken blackguard, when all's said and done. So you're going to buy him up, are you? You won't keep him long, – and then he'll have to starve." We assured the gentleman that we had no desire to buy up Mr. Mackenzie; we explained our ideas as to the freedom of the literary profession, in accordance with which Mr. Mackenzie could not be wrong in applying to us for work; and we especially deprecated any severity on our brother's part towards the man, more especially begging that nothing might be decided, as we were far from thinking it certain that we could provide Mr. Mackenzie with any literary employment. "That's all right," said our brother, twisting back his stool. "He can't work for both of us; – that's all. He has his bread here regular, week after week; and I don't suppose you'll do as much as that for him." Then we went away, shaking the dust off our feet, and wondering much at the great development of literature which latter years have produced. We had not even known of the existence of these papers; – and yet there they were, going forth into the hands of hundreds of thousands of readers, all of whom were being, more or less, instructed in their modes of life and manner of thinking by the stories which were thus brought before them.

But there might be truth in what our brother had said to us. Should Mr. Mackenzie abandon his present engagement for the sake of the job which we proposed to put in his hands, might he not thereby injure rather than improve his prospects? We were acquainted with only one learned doctor desirous of having his manuscripts codified and indexed at his own expense. As for writing for the periodical with which we were connected, we knew enough of the business to be aware that Mr. Mackenzie's gifts of erudition would very probably not so much assist him in attempting such work as would his late training act against him. A man might be able to read and even talk a dozen languages, – "just as though he hadn't been born in England at all," – and yet not write the language with which we dealt after the fashion which suited our readers. It might be that he would fly much above our heads, and do work infinitely too big for us. We did not regard our own heads as being very high. But, for such altitude as they held, a certain class of writing was adapted. The gentleman whom we had just left would require, no doubt, altogether another style. It was probable that Mr. Mackenzie had already fitted himself to his present audience. And, even were it not so, we could not promise him forty-five shillings a week, or even that thirty shillings for which he asked. There is nothing more dangerous than the attempt to befriend a man in middle life by transplanting him from one soil to another.

When Mr. Mackenzie came to us again we endeavoured to explain all this to him. We had in the meantime seen our friend the Doctor, whose beneficence of spirit in regard to the unfortunate man of letters was extreme. He was charmed with our account of the man, and saw with his mind's eye the work, for the performance of which he was pining, perfected in a manner that would be a blessing to the scholars of all future ages. He was at first anxious to ask Julius Mackenzie down to his rectory, and, even after we had explained to him that this would not at present be expedient, was full of a dream of future friendship with a man who would be able to discuss the digamma with him, who would have studied Greek metres, and have an opinion of his own as to Porson's canon. We were in possession of the manuscript, and had our friend's authority for handing it over to Mr. Mackenzie.

He came to us according to appointment, and his nose seemed to be redder than ever. We thought that we discovered a discouraging flavour of spirits in his breath. Mrs. Grimes had declared that he drank, – only in reason; but the ideas of the wife of a publican, – even though that wife were Mrs. Grimes, – might be very different from our own as to what was reasonable in that matter. And as we looked at him he seemed to be more rough, more ragged, almost more wretched than before. It might be that, in taking his part with my brother of the "Penny Dreadful," with the Doctor, and even with myself in thinking over his claims, I had endowed him with higher qualities than I had been justified in giving to him. As I considered him and his appearance I certainly could not assure myself that he looked like a man worthy to be trusted. A policeman, seeing him at a street corner, would have had an eye upon him in a moment. He rubbed himself together within his old coat, as men do when they come out of gin-shops. His eye was as bright as before, but we thought that his mouth was meaner, and his nose redder. We were almost disenchanted with him. We said nothing to him at first about the Spotted Dog, but suggested to him our fears that if he undertook work at our hands he would lose the much more permanent employment which he got from the gentleman whom we had seen in the cupboard. We then explained to him that we could promise to him no continuation of employment.

The violence with which he cursed the gentleman who had sat in the cupboard appalled us, and had, we think, some effect in bringing back to us that feeling of respect for him which we had almost lost. It may be difficult to explain why we respected him because he cursed and swore horribly. We do not like cursing and swearing, and were any of our younger contributors to indulge themselves after that fashion in our presence we should, at the very least, – frown upon them. We did not frown upon Julius Mackenzie, but stood up, gazing into his face above us, again feeling that the man was powerful. Perhaps we respected him because he was not in the least afraid of us. He went on to assert that he cared not, – not a straw, we will say, – for the gentleman in the cupboard. He knew the gentleman in the cupboard very well; and the gentleman in the cupboard knew him. As long as he took his work to the gentleman in the cupboard, the gentleman in the cupboard would be only too happy to purchase that work at the rate of sixpence for a page of manuscript containing two hundred and fifty words. That was his rate of payment for prose fiction, and at that rate he could earn forty-five shillings a week. He wasn't afraid of the gentleman in the cupboard. He had had some words with the gentleman in the cupboard before now, and they two understood each other very well. He hinted, moreover, that there were other gentlemen in other cupboards; but with none of them could he advance beyond forty-five shillings a week. For this he had to sit, with his pen in his hand, seven hours seven days a week, and the very paper, pens, and ink came to fifteenpence out of the money. He had struck for wages once, and for a halcyon month or two had carried his point of sevenpence halfpenny a page; but the gentlemen in the cupboards had told him that it could not be. They, too, must live. His matter was no doubt attractive; but any price above sixpence a page unfitted it for their market. All this Mr. Julius Mackenzie explained to us with much violence of expression. When I named Mrs. Grimes to him the tone of his voice was altered. "Yes," said he, "I thought they'd say a word for me. They're the best friends I've got now. I don't know that you ought quite to believe her, for I think she'd perhaps tell a lie to do me a service." We assured him that we did believe every word Mrs. Grimes had said to us.

After much pausing over the matter we told him that we were empowered to trust him with our friend's work, and the manuscript was produced upon the table. If he would undertake the work and perform it, he should be paid £8: 6s.: 8d. for each of the three volumes as they were completed. And we undertook, moreover, on our own responsibility, to advance him money in small amounts through the hands of Mrs.

Grimes, if he really settled himself to the task. At first he was in ecstasies, and as we explained to him the way in which the index should be brought out and the codification performed, he turned over the pages rapidly, and showed us that he understood at any rate the nature of the work to be done. But when we came to details he was less happy. In what workshop was this new work to be performed? There was a moment in which we almost thought of telling him to do the work in our own room; but we hesitated, luckily, remembering that his continual presence with us for two or three months would probably destroy us altogether. It appeared that his present work was done sometimes at the Spotted Dog, and sometimes at home in his lodgings. He said not a word to us about his wife, but we could understand that there would be periods in which to work at home would be impossible to him. He did not pretend to deny that there might be danger on that score, nor did he ask permission to take the entire manuscript at once away to his abode. We knew that if he took part he must take the whole, as the work could not be done in parts. Counter references would be needed. "My circumstances are bad; – very bad indeed," he said. We expressed the great trouble to which we should be subjected if any evil should happen to the manuscript. "I will give it up," he said, towering over us again, and shaking his head. "I cannot expect that I should be trusted." But we were determined that it should not be given up. Sooner than give the matter up we would make some arrangement by hiring a place in which he might work. Even though we were to pay ten shillings a week for a room for him out of the money, the bargain would be a good one for him. At last we determined that we would pay a second visit to the Spotted Dog, and consult Mrs. Grimes. We felt that we should have a pleasure in arranging together with Mrs. Grimes any scheme of benevolence on behalf of this unfortunate and remarkable man. So we told him that we would think over the matter, and send a letter to his address at the Spotted Dog, which he should receive on the following morning. He then gathered himself up, rubbed himself together again inside his coat, and took his departure.

As soon as he was gone we sat looking at the learned Doctor's manuscript, and thinking of what we had done. There lay the work of years, by which our dear and venerable old friend expected that he would take rank among the great commentators of modern times. We, in truth, did not anticipate for him all the glory to which he looked forward. We feared that there might be disappointment. Hot discussion on verbal accuracies or on rules of metre are perhaps not so much in vogue now as they were a hundred years ago. There might be disappointment and great sorrow; but we could not with equanimity anticipate the prevention of this sorrow by the possible loss or destruction of the manuscript which had been entrusted to us. The Doctor himself had seemed to anticipate no such danger. When we told him of Mackenzie's learning and misfortunes, he was eager at once that the thing should be done, merely stipulating that he should have an interview with Mr. Mackenzie before he returned to his rectory.

That same day we went to the Spotted Dog, and found Mrs. Grimes alone. Mackenzie had been there immediately after leaving our room, and had told her what had taken place. She was full of the subject and anxious to give every possible assistance. She confessed at once that the papers would not be safe in the rooms inhabited by Mackenzie and his wife. "He pays five shillings a week," she said, "for a wretched place round in Cucumber Court. They are all huddled together, any way; and how he manages to do a thing at all there, – in the way of author-work, – is a wonder to everybody. Sometimes he can't, and then he'll sit for hours together at the little table in our tap-room." We went into the tap-room and saw the little table. It was a wonder indeed that anyone should be able to compose and write tales of imagination in a place so dreary, dark, and ill-omened. The little table was hardly more than a long slab or plank, perhaps eighteen inches wide. When we visited the place there were two brewers' draymen seated there, and three draggled, wretched-looking women. The carters were eating enormous hunches of bread and bacon, which they cut and put into their mouths slowly, solemnly, and in silence. The three women were seated on a bench, and when I saw them had no signs of festivity before them. It must be presumed that they had paid for something, or they would hardly have been allowed to sit there. "It's empty now," said Mrs. Grimes, taking no immediate notice of the men or of the women; "but sometimes he'll sit writing in that corner, when there's such a jabber of voices as you wouldn't hear a cannon go off over at Reid's, and that thick with smoke you'd a'most cut it with a knife. Don't he, Peter?" The man whom she addressed endeavoured to prepare himself for answer by swallowing at the moment three square inches of bread and bacon, which he had just put into his mouth. He made an awful effort, but failed; and, failing, nodded his head three times. "They all know him here, Sir," continued Mrs. Grimes. "He'll go on writing, writing, writing, for hours together; and nobody'll say nothing to him. Will they, Peter?" Peter, who was now half-way through the work he had laid out for himself, muttered some inarticulate grunt of assent.

We then went back to the snug little room inside the bar. It was quite clear to me that the man could not manipulate the Doctor's manuscript, of which he would have to spread a dozen sheets before him at the same time, in the place I had just visited. Even could he have occupied the chamber alone, the accommodation would not have been sufficient for the purpose. It was equally clear that he could not be allowed to use Mrs. Grimes's snuggery. "How are we to get a place for him?" said I, appealing to the lady. "He shall have a place," she said, "I'll go bail; he sha'n't lose the job for want of a workshop." Then she sat down and began to think it over. I was just about to propose the hiring of some decent room in the neighbourhood, when she made a suggestion, which I acknowledge startled me. "I'll have a big table put into my own bed-room," said she, "and he shall do it there. There ain't another hole or corner about the place as'd suit; and he can lay the gentleman's papers all about on the bed, square and clean and orderly. Can't he now? And I can see after 'em, as he don't lose 'em. Can't I now?"

By this time there had sprung up an intimacy between ourselves and Mrs. Grimes which seemed to justify an expression of the doubt which I then threw on the propriety of such a disarrangement of her most private domestic affairs. "Mr. Grimes will hardly approve of that," we said.

"Oh, John won't mind. What'll it matter to John as long as Mackenzie is out in time for him to go to bed? We ain't early birds, morning or night, – that's true. In our line folks can't be early. But from ten to six there's the room, and he shall have it. Come up and see, Sir." So we followed Mrs. Grimes up the narrow staircase to the marital bower. "It ain't large, but there'll be room for the table, and for him to sit at it; – won't there now?"

It was a dark little room, with one small window looking out under the low roof, and facing the heavy high dead wall of the brewery opposite. But it was clean and sweet, and the furniture in it was all solid and good, old-fashioned, and made of mahogany. Two or three of Mrs. Grimes's gowns were laid upon the bed, and other portions of her dress were hung on pegs behind the doors. The only untidy article in the room was a pair of "John's" trousers, which he had failed to put out of sight. She was not a bit abashed, but took them up and folded them and patted them, and laid them in the capacious wardrobe. "We'll have all these things away," she said, "and then he can have all his papers out upon the bed just as he pleases."

We own that there was something in the proposed arrangement which dismayed us. We also were married, and what would our wife have said had we proposed that a contributor, – even a contributor not red-nosed and seething with gin, – that any best-disciplined contributor should be invited to write an article within the precincts of our sanctum? We could not bring ourselves to believe that Mr. Grimes would authorise the proposition. There is something holy about the bed-room of a married couple; and there would be a special desecration in the continued presence of Mr. Julius Mackenzie. We thought it better that we should explain something of all this to her. "Do you know," we said, "this seems to be hardly prudent?"

"Why not prudent?" she asked.

"Up in your bed-room, you know! Mr. Grimes will be sure to dislike it."

"What, – John! Not he. I know what you're a-thinking of, Mr. —," she said. "But we're different in our ways than what you are. Things to us are only just what they are. We haven't time, nor yet money, nor perhaps edication, for seemings and thinkings as you have. If you was travelling out amongst the wild Injeans, you'd ask anyone to have a bit in your bed-room as soon as look at 'em, if you'd got a bit for 'em to eat. We're travelling among wild Injeans all our lives, and a bed-room ain't no more to us than any other room. Mackenzie shall come up here, and I'll have the table fixed for him, just there by the window." I hadn't another word to say to her, and I could not keep myself from thinking for many an hour afterwards, whether it may not be a good thing for men, and for women also, to believe that they are always travelling among wild Indians.

When we went down Mr. Grimes himself was in the little parlour. He did not seem at all surprised at seeing his wife enter the room from above accompanied by a stranger. She at once began her story, and told the arrangement which she proposed, – which she did, as I observed, without any actual request for his sanction. Looking at Mr. Grimes's face, I thought that he did not quite like it; but he accepted it, almost without a word, scratching his head and raising his eyebrows. "You know, John, he could no more do it at home than he could fly," said Mrs. Grimes.

"Who said he could do it at home?"

"And he couldn't do it in the tap-room; – could he? If so, there ain't no other place, and so that's settled." John Grimes again scratched his head, and the matter was settled. Before we left the house Mackenzie himself came in, and was told in our presence of the accommodation which was to be prepared for him. "It's just like you, Mrs. Grimes," was all he said in the way of thanks. Then Mrs. Grimes made her bargain with him somewhat sternly. He should have the room for five hours a day, – ten till three, or twelve till five; but he must settle which, and then stick to his hours. "And I won't have nothing up there in the way of drink," said John Grimes.

"Who's asking to have drink there?" said Mackenzie.

"You're not asking now, but maybe you will. I won't have it, that's all."

"That shall be all right, John," said Mrs. Grimes, nodding her head.

"Women are that soft, – in the way of judgment, – that they'll go and do a'most anything, good or bad, when they've got their feelings up." Such was the only rebuke which in our hearing Mr. Grimes administered to his pretty wife. Mackenzie whispered something to the publican, but Grimes only shook his head. We understood it all thoroughly. He did not like the scheme, but he would not contradict his wife in an act of real kindness. We then made an appointment with the scholar for meeting our friend and his future patron at our rooms, and took our leave of the Spotted Dog. Before we went, however, Mrs. Grimes insisted on producing some cherry-bounce, as she called it, which, after sundry refusals on our part, was brought in on a small round shining tray, in a little bottle covered all over with gold sprigs, with four tiny glasses similarly ornamented. Mrs. Grimes poured out the liquor, using a very sparing hand when she came to the glass which was intended for herself. We find it, as a rule, easier to talk with the Grimeses of the world than to eat with them or to drink with them. When the glass was handed to us we did not know whether or not we were expected to say something. We waited, however, till Mr. Grimes and Mackenzie had been provided with their glasses. "Proud to see you at the Spotted Dog, Mr. —," said Grimes. "That we are," said Mrs. Grimes, smiling at us over her almost imperceptible drop of drink. Julius Mackenzie just bobbed his head, and swallowed the cordial at a gulp, – as a dog does a lump of meat, leaving the impression on his friends around him that he has not got from it half the enjoyment which it might have given him had he been a little more patient in the process. I could not but think that had Mackenzie allowed the cherry-bounce to trickle a little in his palate, as I did myself, it would have gratified him more than it did in being chucked down his throat with all the impetus which his elbow could give to the glass. "That's tidy tipple," said Mr. Grimes, winking his eye. We acknowledged that it was tidy. "My mother made it, as used to keep the Pig and Magpie, at Colchester," said Mrs. Grimes. In this way we learned a good deal of Mrs. Grimes's history. Her very earliest years had been passed among wild Indians.

Then came the interview between the Doctor and Mr. Mackenzie. We must confess that we greatly feared the impression which our younger friend might make on the elder. We had of course told the Doctor of the red nose, and he had accepted the information with a smile. But he was a man who would feel the contamination of contact with a drunkard, and who would shrink from an unpleasant association. There are vices of which we habitually take altogether different views in accordance with the manner in which they are brought under our notice. This vice of drunkenness is often a joke in the mouths of those to whom the thing itself is a horror. Even before our boys we talk of it as being rather funny, though to see one of them funny himself would almost break our hearts. The learned commentator had accepted our account of the red nose as though it were simply a part of the undeserved misery of the wretched man; but should he find the wretched man to be actually redolent of gin his feelings might be changed. The Doctor was with us first, and the volumes of the MS. were displayed upon the table. The compiler of them, as he lifted here a page and there a page, handled them with the gentleness of a lover. They had been exquisitely arranged, and were very fair. The pagings, and the margins, and the chapterings, and all the complementary paraphernalia of authorship, were perfect. "A lifetime, my friend; just a lifetime!" the Doctor had said to us, speaking of his own work while we were waiting for the man to whose hands was to be entrusted the result of so much labour and scholarship. We wished at that moment that we had never been called on to interfere in the matter.

Mackenzie came, and the introduction was made. The Doctor was a gentleman of the old school, very neat in his attire, – dressed in perfect black, with kneebreeches and black gaiters, with a closely-shorn chin, and an exquisitely white cravat. Though he was in truth simply the rector of his parish, his parish was one which entitled him to call himself a dean, and he wore a clerical rosette on his hat. He was a well-made, tall, portly gentleman, with whom to take the slightest liberty would have been impossible. His well-formed full face was singularly expressive of benevolence, but there was in it too an air of command which created an involuntary respect. He was a man whose means were ample, and who could afford to keep two curates, so that the appanages of a Church dignitary did in some sort belong to him. We doubt whether he really understood what work meant, – even when he spoke with so much pathos of the labour of his life; but he was a man not at all exacting in regard to the work of others, and who was anxious to make the world as smooth and rosy to those around him as it had been to himself. He came forward, paused a moment, and then shook hands with Mackenzie. Our work had been done, and we remained in the background during the interview. It was now for the Doctor to satisfy himself with the scholarship, – and, if he chose to take cognizance of the matter, with the morals of his proposed assistant.

Mackenzie himself was more subdued in his manner than he had been when talking with ourselves. The Doctor made a little speech, standing at the table with one hand on one volume and the other on another. He told of all his work, with a mixture of modesty as to the thing done, and self-assertion as to his interest in doing it, which was charming. He acknowledged that the sum proposed for the aid which he required was inconsiderable; – but it had been fixed by the proposed publisher. Should Mr. Mackenzie find that the labour was long he would willingly increase it. Then he commenced a conversation respecting the Greek dramatists, which had none of the air or tone of an examination, but which still served the purpose of enabling Mackenzie to show his scholarship. In that respect there was no doubt that the ragged, red-nosed, disreputable man, who stood there longing for his job, was the greater proficient of the two. We never discovered that he had had access to books in later years; but his memory of the old things seemed to be perfect. When it was suggested that references would be required, it seemed that he did know his way into the library of the British Museum. "When I wasn't quite so shabby," he said boldly, "I used to be there." The Doctor instantly produced a ten-pound note, and insisted that it should be taken in advance. Mackenzie hesitated, and we suggested that it was premature; but the Doctor was firm. "If an old scholar mayn't assist one younger than himself," he said, "I don't know when one man may aid another. And this is no alms. It is simply a pledge for work to be done." Mackenzie took the money, muttering something of an assurance that as far as his ability went, the work should be done well. "It should certainly," he said, "be done diligently."

When money had passed, of course the thing was settled; but in truth the bank-note had been given, not from judgment in settling the matter, but from the generous impulse of the moment. There was, however, no receding. The Doctor expressed by no hint a doubt as to the safety of his manuscript. He was by far too fine a gentleman to give the man whom he employed pain in that direction. If there were risk, he would now run the risk. And so the thing was settled.

We did not, however, give the manuscript on that occasion into Mackenzie's hands, but took it down afterwards, locked in an old despatch box of our own, to the Spotted

Dog, and left the box with the key of it in the hands of Mrs. Grimes. Again we went up into that lady's bed-room, and saw that the big table had been placed by the window for Mackenzie's accommodation. It so nearly filled the room, that as we observed, John Grimes could not get round at all to his side of the bed. It was arranged that Mackenzie was to begin on the morrow.

Part II
The Result

DURING the next month we saw a good deal of Mr. Julius Mackenzie, and made ourselves quite at home in Mrs. Grimes's bed-room. We went in and out of the Spotted Dog as if we had known that establishment all our lives, and spent many a quarter of an hour with the hostess in her little parlour, discussing the prospects of Mr. Mackenzie and his family. He had procured to himself decent, if not exactly new, garments out of the money so liberally provided by my learned friend the Doctor, and spent much of his time in the library of the British Museum. He certainly worked very hard, for he did not altogether abandon his old engagement. Before the end of the first month the index of the first volume, nearly completed had been sent down for the inspection of the Doctor, and had been returned with ample eulogium and some little criticism. The criticisms Mackenzie answered by letter, with true scholarly spirit, and the Doctor was delighted. Nothing could be more pleasant to him than a correspondence, prolonged almost indefinitely, as to the respective merits of a τό or a τον, or on the demand for a spondee or an iamb. When he found that the work was really in industrious hands, he ceased to be clamorous for early publication, and gave us to understand privately that Mr. Mackenzie was not to be limited to the sum named. The matter of remuneration was, indeed, left very much to ourselves, and Mackenzie had certainly found a most efficient friend in the author whose works had been confided to his hands.

All this was very pleasant, and Mackenzie throughout that month worked very hard. According to the statements made to me by Mrs. Grimes he took no more gin than what was necessary for a hard-working man. As to the exact quantity of that cordial which she imagined to be beneficial and needful, we made no close enquiry. He certainly kept himself in a condition for work, and so far all went on happily. Nevertheless, there was a terrible skeleton in the cupboard, – or rather out of the cupboard, for the skeleton could not be got to hide itself. A certain portion of his prosperity reached the hands of his wife, and she was behaving herself worse than ever. The four children had been covered with decent garments under Mrs. Grimes's care, and then Mrs. Mackenzie had appeared at the Spotted Dog, loudly demanding a new outfit for herself. She came not only once, but often, and Mr. Grimes was beginning to protest that he saw too much of the family. We had become very intimate with Mrs. Grimes, and she did not hesitate to confide to us her fears lest "John should cut up rough," before the thing was completed. "You see," she said, "it is against the house, no doubt, that woman coming nigh it." But still she was firm, and Mackenzie was not disturbed in the possession of the bed-room. At last Mrs. Mackenzie was provided with some articles of female attire; – and then, on the very next day, she and the four children were again stripped almost naked. The wretched creature must have steeped herself in gin to the shoulders, for in one day she made a sweep of everything. She then came in a state of furious intoxication to the Spotted Dog, and was removed by the police under the express order of the landlord.

We can hardly say which was the most surprising to us, the loyalty of Mrs. Grimes or the patience of John. During that night, as we were told two days afterwards by his wife, he stormed with passion. The papers she had locked up in order that he should not get at them and destroy them. He swore that everything should be cleared out on the following morning. But when the morning came he did not even say a word to Mackenzie, as the wretched, downcast, broken-hearted creature passed up stairs to his work. "You see I knows him, and how to deal with him," said Mrs. Grimes, speaking of her husband. "There ain't another like himself nowheres; – he's that good. A softer-hearteder man there ain't in the public line. He can speak dreadful when his dander is up, and can look—; oh, laws, he just can look at you! But he could no more put his hands upon a woman, in the way of hurting, – no more than be an archbishop." Where could be the man, thought we to ourselves as this was said to us, who could have put a hand, – in the way of hurting, – upon Mrs. Grimes?

On that occasion, to the best of our belief, the policeman contented himself with depositing Mrs. Mackenzie at her own lodgings. On the next day she was picked up drunk in the street, and carried away to the lock-up house. At the very moment in which the story was being told to us by Mrs. Grimes, Mackenzie had gone to the police office to pay the fine, and to bring his wife home. We asked with dismay and surprise why he should interfere to rescue her – why he did not leave her in custody as long as the police would keep her? "Who'd there be to look after the children?" asked Mrs. Grimes, as though she were offended at our suggestion. Then she went on to explain that in such a household as that of poor Mackenzie the wife is absolutely a necessity, even though she be an habitual drunkard. Intolerable as she was, her services were necessary to him. "A husband as drinks is bad," said Mrs. Grimes, – with something, we thought, of an apologetic tone for the vice upon which her own prosperity was partly built, – "but when a woman takes to it, it's the — devil." We thought that she was right, as we pictured to ourselves that man of letters satisfying the magistrate's demand for his wife's misconduct, and taking the degraded, half-naked creature once more home to his children.

We saw him about twelve o'clock on that day, and he had then, too evidently, been endeavouring to support his misery by the free use of alcohol. We did not speak of it down in the parlour; but even Mrs. Grimes, we think, would have admitted that he had taken more than was good for him. He was sitting up in the bed-room with his head hanging upon his hand, with a swarm of our learned friend's papers spread on the table before him. Mrs. Grimes, when he entered the house, had gone up stairs to give them out to him; but he had made no attempt to settle himself to his work. "This kind of thing must come to an end," he said to us with a thick, husky voice. We muttered something to him as to the need there was that he should exert a manly courage in his troubles. "Manly!" he said. "Well, yes; manly. A man should be a man, of course. There are some things which a man can't bear. I've borne more than enough, and I'll have an end of it."

We shall never forget that scene. After awhile he got up, and became almost violent. Talk of bearing! Who had borne half as much as he? There were things a man should not bear. As for manliness, he believed that the truly manly thing would be to put an end to the lives of his wife, his children, and himself at one swoop. Of course the judgment of a mealy-mouthed world would be against him, but what would that matter to him when he and they had vanished out of this miserable place into the infinite realms of nothingness? Was he fit to live, or were they? Was there any chance for his children but that of becoming thieves and prostitutes? And for that poor wretch of a woman, from out of whose bosom even her human instincts had been washed by gin, – would not death to her be, indeed, a charity? There was but one drawback to all this. When he should have destroyed them, how would it be with him if he should afterwards fail to make sure work with his own life? In such case it was not hanging that he would fear, but the self-reproach that would come upon him in that he had succeeded in sending others out of their misery, but had flinched when his own turn had come. Though he was drunk when he said these horrid things, or so nearly drunk that he could not perfect the articulation of his words, still there was a marvellous eloquence with him. When we attempted to answer, and told him of that canon which had been set against self-slaughter, he laughed us to scorn. There was something terrible to us in the audacity of the arguments which he used, when he asserted for himself the right to shuffle off from his shoulders a burden which they had not been made broad enough to bear. There was an intensity and a thorough hopelessness of suffering in his case, an openness of acknowledged degradation, which robbed us for the time of all that power which the respectable ones of the earth have over the disreputable. When we came upon him with our wise saws, our wisdom was shattered instantly, and flung back upon us in fragments. What promise could we dare to hold out to him that further patience would produce any result that could be beneficial? What further harm could any such doing on his part bring upon him? Did we think that were he brought out to stand at the gallows' foot with the knowledge that ten minutes would usher him into what folks called eternity, his sense of suffering would be as great as it had been when he conducted that woman out of court and along the streets to his home, amidst the jeering congratulations of his neighbours? "When you have fallen so low," said he, "that you can fall no lower, the ordinary trammels of the world cease to bind you." Though his words were knocked against each other with the dulled utterances of intoxication, his intellect was terribly clear, and his scorn for himself, and for the world that had so treated him, was irrepressible.

We must have been over an hour with him up there in the bed-room, and even then we did not leave him. As it was manifest that he could do no work on that day, we collected the papers together, and proposed that he should take a walk with us. He was patient as we shovelled together the Doctor's pages, and did not object to our suggestion. We found it necessary to call up Mrs. Grimes to assist us in putting away the "Opus magnum," and were astonished to find how much she had come to know about the work. Added to the Doctor's manuscript there were now the pages of Mackenzie's indexes, – and there were other pages of reference, for use in making future indexes, – as to all of which Mrs. Grimes seemed to be quite at home. We have no doubt that she was familiar with the names of Greek tragedians, and could have pointed out to us in print the performances of the chorus. "A little fresh air'll do you a deal of good, Mr. Mackenzie," she said to the unfortunate man, – "only take a biscuit in your pocket." We got him out to the street, but he angrily refused to take the biscuit which she endeavoured to force into his hands.

That was a memorable walk. Turning from the end of Liquorpond Street up Gray's Inn Lane towards Holborn, we at once came upon the entrance into a miserable court. "There," said he; "it is down there that I live. She is sleeping it off now, and the children are hanging about her, wondering whether mother has got money to have another go at it when she rises. I'd take you down to see it all, only it'd sicken you." We did not offer to go down the court, abstaining rather for his sake than for our own. The look of the place was as of a spot squalid, fever-stricken, and utterly degraded. And this man who was our companion had been born and bred a gentleman, – had been nourished with that soft and gentle care which comes of wealth and love combined, – had received the education which the country gives to her most favoured sons, and had taken such advantage of that education as is seldom taken by any of those favoured ones; – and Cucumber Court, with a drunken wife and four half-clothed, half-starved children, was the condition to which he had brought himself! The world knows nothing higher nor brighter than had been his outset in life, – nothing lower nor more debased than the result. And yet he was one whose time and intellect had been employed upon the pursuit of knowledge, – who even up to this day had high ideas of what should be a man's career, – who worked very hard and had always worked, – who as far as we knew had struck upon no rocks in the pursuit of mere pleasure. It had all come to him from that idea of his youth that it would be good for him "to take refuge from the conventional thraldom of so-called gentlemen amidst the liberty of the lower orders." His life, as he had himself owned, had indeed been a mistake.

We passed on from the court, and crossing the road went through the squares of Gray's Inn, down Chancery Lane, through the little iron gate into Lincoln's Inn, round through the old square, – than which we know no place in London more conducive to suicide; and the new square, – which has a gloom of its own, not so potent, and savouring only of madness, till at last we found ourselves in the Temple Gardens. I do not know why we had thus clung to the purlieus of the Law, except it was that he was telling us how in his early days, when he had been sent away from Cambridge, – as on this occasion he acknowledged to us, for an attempt to pull the tutor's nose, in revenge for a supposed insult, – he had intended to push his fortunes as a barrister. He pointed up to a certain window in a dark corner of that suicidal old court, and told us that for one year he had there sat at the feet of a great Gamaliel in Chancery, and had worked with all his energies. Of course we asked him why he had left a prospect so alluring. Though his answers to us were not quite explicit, we think that he did not attempt to conceal the truth. He learned to drink, and that Gamaliel took upon himself to rebuke the failing, and by the end of that year he had quarrelled irreconcilably with his family. There had been great wrath at home when he was sent from Cambridge, greater wrath when he expressed his opinion upon certain questions of religious faith, and wrath to the final severance of all family relations when he told the chosen Gamaliel that he should get drunk as often as he pleased. After that he had "taken refuge among the lower orders," and his life, such as it was, had come of it.

In Fleet Street, as we came out of the Temple, we turned into an eating-house and had some food. By this time the exercise and the air had carried off the fumes of the liquor which he had taken, and I knew that it would be well that he should eat. We had a mutton chop and a hot potato and a pint of beer each, and sat down to table for the first and last time as mutual friends. It was odd to see how in his converse with us on that day he seemed to possess a double identity. Though the hopeless misery of his condition was always present to him, was constantly on his tongue, yet he could talk about his own career and his own character as though they belonged to a third person. He could even laugh at the wretched mistake he had made in life, and speculate as to its consequences. For himself he was well aware that death was the only release that he could expect. We did not dare to tell him that if his wife should die, then things might be better with him. We could only suggest to him that work itself, if he would do honest work, would console him for many sufferings. "You don't know the filth of it," he said to us. Ah, dear! how well we remember the terrible word, and the gesture with which he pronounced it, and the gleam of his eyes as he said it! His manner to us on this occasion was completely changed, and we had a gratification in feeling that a sense had come back upon him of his old associations. "I remember this room so well," he said, – "when I used to have friends and money." And, indeed, the room was one which has been made memorable by Genius. "I did not think ever to have found myself here again." We observed, however, that he could not eat the food that was placed before him. A morsel or two of the meat he swallowed, and struggled to eat the crust of his bread, but he could not make a clean plate of it, as we did, – regretting that the nature of chops did not allow of ampler dimensions. His beer was quickly finished, and we suggested to him a second tankard. With a queer, half-abashed twinkle of the eye, he accepted our offer, and then the second pint disappeared also. We had our doubts on the subject, but at last decided against any further offer. Had he chosen to call for it he must have had a third; but he did not call for it. We left him at the door of the tavern, and he then promised that in spite of all that he had suffered and all that he had said he would make another effort to complete the Doctor's work. "Whether I go or stay," he said, "I'd like to earn the money that I've spent." There was something terrible in that idea of his going! Whither was he to go?

The Doctor heard nothing of the misfortune of these three or four inauspicious days; and the work was again going on prosperously when he came up again to London at the end of the second month. He told us something of his banker, and something of his lawyer, and murmured a word or two as to a new curate whom he needed; but we knew that he had come up to London because he could not bear a longer absence from the great object of his affections. He could not endure to be thus parted from his manuscript, and was again childishly anxious that a portion of it should be in the printer's hands. "At sixty-five, Sir," he said to us, "a man has no time to dally with his work." He had been dallying with his work all his life, and we sincerely believed that it would be well with him if he could be contented to dally with it to the end. If all that Mackenzie said of it was true, the Doctor's erudition was not equalled by his originality, or by his judgment. Of that question, however, we could take no cognizance. He was bent upon publishing, and as he was willing and able to pay for his whim and was his own master, nothing that we could do would keep him out of the printer's hands.

He was desirous of seeing Mackenzie, and was anxious even to see him once at his work. Of course he could meet his assistant in our editorial room, and all the papers could easily be brought backwards and forwards in the old despatch-box. But in the interest of all parties we hesitated as to taking our revered and reverend friend to the Spotted Dog. Though we had told him that his work was being done at a public-house, we thought that his mind had conceived the idea of some modest inn, and that he would be shocked at being introduced to a place which he would regard simply as a gin-shop. Mrs. Grimes, or if not Mrs. Grimes, then Mr. Grimes, might object to another visitor to their bed-room; and Mackenzie himself would be thrown out of gear by the appearance of those clerical gaiters upon the humble scene of his labours. We, therefore, gave him such reasons as were available for submitting, at any rate for the present, to having the papers brought up to him at our room. And we ourselves went down to the Spotted Dog to make an appointment with Mackenzie for the following day. We had last seen him about a week before, and then the task was progressing well. He had told us that another fortnight would finish it. We had enquired also of Mrs. Grimes about the man's wife. All she could tell us was that the woman had not again troubled them at the Spotted Dog. She expressed her belief, however, that the drunkard had been more than once in the hands of the police since the day on which Mackenzie had walked with us through the squares of the Inns of Court.

It was late when we reached the public-house on the occasion to which we now allude, and the evening was dark and rainy. It was then the end of January, and it might have been about six o'clock. We knew that we should not find Mackenzie at the public-house; but it was probable that Mrs. Grimes could send for him, or, at least, could make the appointment for us. We went into the little parlour, where she was seated with her husband, and we could immediately see, from the countenance of both of them, that something was amiss. We began by telling Mrs. Grimes that the Doctor had come to town. "Mackenzie ain't here, Sir," said Mrs. Grimes, and we almost thought that the very tone of her voice was altered. We explained that we had not expected to find him at that hour, and asked if she could send for him. She only shook her head. Grimes was standing with his back to the fire and his hands in his trousers pockets. Up to this moment he had not spoken a word. We asked if the man was drunk. She again shook her head. Could she bid him to come to us tomorrow, and bring the box and the papers with him? Again she shook her head.

"I've told her that I won't have no more of it," said Grimes; "nor yet I won't. He was drunk this morning, – as drunk as an owl."

"He was sober, John, as you are, when he came for the papers this afternoon at two o'clock." So the box and the papers had all been taken away!

"And she was here yesterday rampaging about the place, without as much clothes on as would cover her nakedness," said Mr. Grimes. "I won't have no more of it. I've done for that man what his own flesh and blood wouldn't do. I know that; and I won't have no more of it. Mary Anne, you'll have that table cleared out after breakfast tomorrow." When a man, to whom his wife is usually Polly, addresses her as Mary Anne, then it may be surmised that that man is in earnest. We knew that he was in earnest, and she knew it also.

"He wasn't drunk, John, – no, nor yet in liquor, when he come and took away that box this afternoon." We understood this reiterated assertion. It was in some sort excusing to us her own breach of trust in having allowed the manuscript to be withdrawn from her own charge, or was assuring us that, at the worst, she had not been guilty of the impropriety of allowing the man to take it away when he was unfit to have it in his charge. As for blaming her, who could have thought of it? Had Mackenzie at any time chosen to pass down stairs with the box in his hands, it was not to be expected that she should stop him violently. And now that he had done so we could not blame her; but we felt that a great weight had fallen upon our own hearts. If evil should come to the manuscript would not the Doctor's wrath fall upon us with a crushing weight? Something must be done at once. And we suggested that it would be well that somebody should go round to Cucumber Court. "I'd go as soon as look," said Mrs. Grimes, "but he won't let me."

"You don't stir a foot out of this tonight; – not that way," said Mr. Grimes.

"Who wants to stir?" said Mrs. Grimes.

We felt that there was something more to be told than we had yet heard, and a great fear fell upon us. The woman's manner to us was altered, and we were sure that this had come not from altered feelings on her part, but from circumstances which had frightened her. It was not her husband that she feared, but the truth of something that her husband had said to her. "If there is anything more to tell, for God's sake tell it," we said, addressing ourselves rather to the man than to the woman. Then Grimes did tell us his story. On the previous evening Mackenzie had received three or four sovereigns from Mrs. Grimes, being, of course, a portion of the Doctor's payments; and early on that morning all Liquorpond Street had been in a state of excitement with the drunken fury of Mackenzie's wife. She had found her way into the Spotted Dog, and was being actually extruded by the strength of Grimes himself, – of Grimes, who had been brought down, half dressed, from his bed-room by the row, – when Mackenzie himself, equally drunk, appeared upon the scene. "No, John; – not equally drunk," said Mrs. Grimes. "Bother!" exclaimed her husband, going on with his story. The man had struggled to take the woman by the arm, and the two had fallen and rolled in the street together. "I was looking out of the window, and it was awful to see," said Mrs. Grimes. We felt that it was "awful to hear." A man, – and such a man, rolling in the gutter with a drunken woman, – himself drunk, – and that woman his wife! "There ain't to be no more of it at the Spotted Dog; that's all," said John Grimes, as he finished his part of the story.

Then, at last, Mrs. Grimes became voluble. All this had occurred before nine in the morning. "The woman must have been at it all night," she said. "So must the man," said John. "Anyways he came back about dinner, and he was sober then. I asked him not to go up, and offered to make him a cup of tea. It was just as you'd gone out after dinner, John."

"He won't have no more tea here," said John.

"And he didn't have any then. He wouldn't, he said, have any tea, but went up stairs. What was I to do? I couldn't tell him as he shouldn't. Well; – during the row in the morning John had said something as to Mackenzie not coming about the premises any more."

"Of course I did," said Grimes.

"He was a little cut, then, no doubt," continued the lady; "and I didn't think as he would have noticed what John had said."

"I mean it to be noticed now."

"He had noticed it then, Sir, though he wasn't just as he should be at that hour of the morning. Well; – what does he do? He goes up stairs and packs up all the papers at once. Leastways, that's as I suppose. They ain't there now. You can go and look if you please, Sir. Well; when he came down, whether I was in the kitchen, – though it isn't often as my eyes is off the bar, or in the tap-room, or busy drawing, which I do do sometimes, Sir, when there are a many calling for liquor, I can't say; – but if I ain't never to stand upright again, I didn't see him pass out with the box. But Miss Wilcox did. You can ask her." Miss Wilcox was the young lady in the bar, whom we did not think ourselves called upon to examine, feeling no doubt whatever as to the fact of the box having been taken away by Mackenzie. In all this Mrs. Grimes seemed to defend herself, as though some serious charge was to be brought against her; whereas all that she had done had been done out of pure charity; and in exercising her charity towards Mackenzie she had shown an almost exaggerated kindness towards ourselves.

"If there's anything wrong, it isn't your fault," we said.

"Nor yet mine," said John Grimes.

"No, indeed," we replied.

"It ain't none of our faults," continued he; "only this; – you can't wash a blackamoor white, nor it ain't no use trying. He don't come here any more, that's all. A man in drink we don't mind. We has to put up with it. And they ain't that tarnation desperate as is a woman. As long as a man can keep his legs he'll try to steady hisself; but there is women who, when they've liquor, gets a fury for rampaging. There ain't a many as can beat this one, Sir. She's that strong, it took four of us to hold her; though she can't hardly do a stroke of work, she's that weak when she's sober."

We had now heard the whole story, and, while hearing it, had determined that it was our duty to go round into Cucumber Court and seek the manuscript and the box. We were unwilling to pry into the wretchedness of the man's home; but something was due to the Doctor; and we had to make that appointment for the morrow, if it were still possible that such an appointment should be kept. We asked for the number of the house, remembering well the entrance into the court. Then there was a whisper between John and his wife, and the husband offered to accompany us. "It's a roughish place," he said, "but they know me." "He'd better go along with you," said Mrs. Grimes. We, of course, were glad of such companionship, and glad also to find that the landlord, upon whom we had inflicted so much trouble, was still sufficiently our friend to take this trouble on our behalf.

"It's a dreary place enough," said Grimes, as he led us up the narrow archway. Indeed it was a dreary place. The court spread itself a little in breadth, but very little, when the passage was passed, and there were houses on each side of it. There was neither gutter nor, as far as we saw, drain, but the broken flags were slippery with moist mud, and here and there, strewed about between the houses, there were the remains of cabbages and turnip-tops. The place swarmed with children, over whom one ghastly gas-lamp at the end of the court threw a flickering and uncertain light. There was a clamour of scolding voices, to which it seemed that no heed was paid; and there was a smell of damp rotting nastiness, amidst which it seemed to us to be almost impossible that life should be continued. Grimes led the way without further speech, to the middle house on the left hand of the court, and asked a man who was sitting on the low threshold of the door whether Mackenzie was within. "So that be you, Muster Grimes; be it?" said the man, without stirring. "Yes; he's there I guess, but they've been and took her." Then we passed on into the house. "No matter about that," said the man, as we apologised for kicking him in our passage. He had not moved, and it had been impossible to enter without kicking him.

It seemed that Mackenzie held the two rooms on the ground floor, and we entered them at once. There was no light, but we could see the glimmer of a fire in the grate; and presently we became aware of the presence of children. Grimes asked after Mackenzie, and a girl's voice told us that he was in the inner room. The publican then demanded a light, and the girl with some hesitation, lit the end of a farthing candle, which was fixed in a small bottle. We endeavoured to look round the room by the glimmer which this afforded, but could see nothing but the presence of four children, three of whom seemed to be seated in apathy on the floor. Grimes, taking the candle in his hand, passed at once into the other room, and we followed him. Holding the bottle something over his head, he contrived to throw a gleam of light upon one of the two beds with which the room was fitted, and there we saw the body of Julius Mackenzie stretched in the torpor of dead intoxication. His head lay against the wall, his body was across the bed, and his feet dangled on to the floor. He still wore his dirty boots, and his clothes as he had worn them in the morning. No sight so piteous, so wretched, and at the same time so eloquent had we ever seen before. His eyes were closed, and the light of his face was therefore quenched. His mouth was open, and the slaver had fallen upon his beard. His dark, clotted hair had been pulled over his face by the unconscious movement of his hands. There came from him a stertorous sound of breathing, as though he were being choked by the attitude in which he lay; and even in his drunkenness there was an uneasy twitching as of pain about his face. And there sat, and had been sitting for hours past, the four children in the other room, knowing the condition of the parent whom they most respected, but not even endeavouring to do anything for his comfort. What could they do? They knew, by long training and thorough experience, that a fit of drunkenness had to be got out of by sleep. To them there was nothing shocking in it. It was but a periodical misfortune. "She'll have to own he's been and done it now," said Grimes, looking down upon the man, and alluding to his wife's good-natured obstinacy. He handed the candle to us, and, with a mixture of tenderness and roughness, of which the roughness was only in the manner and the tenderness was real, he raised Mackenzie's head and placed it on the bolster, and lifted the man's legs on to the bed. Then he took off the man's boots, and the old silk handkerchief from the neck, and pulled the trousers straight, and arranged the folds of the coat. It was almost as though he were laying out one that was dead. The eldest girl was now standing by us, and Grimes asked her how long her father had been in that condition. "Jack Hoggart brought him in just afore it was dark," said the girl. Then it was explained to us that Jack Hoggart was the man whom we had seen sitting on the door-step.

"And your mother?" asked Grimes.

"The perlice took her afore dinner."

"And you children; – what have you had to eat?" In answer to this the girl only shook her head. Grimes took no immediate notice of this, but called the drunken man by his name, and shook his shoulder, and looked round to a broken ewer which stood on the little table, for water to dash upon him; – but there was no water in the jug. He called again and repeated the shaking, and at last Mackenzie opened his eyes, and in a dull, half-conscious manner looked up at us. "Come, my man," said Grimes, "shake this off and have done with it."

"Hadn't you better try to get up?" we asked.

There was a faint attempt at rising, then a smile, – a smile which was terrible to witness, so sad was all which it said; then a look of utter, abject misery, coming, as we thought, from a momentary remembrance of his degradation; and after that he sank back in the dull, brutal, painless, death-like apathy of absolute unconsciousness.

"It'll be morning afore he'll move," said the girl.

"She's about right," said Grimes. "He's got it too heavy for us to do anything but just leave him. We'll take a look for the box and the papers."

And the man upon whom we were looking down had been born a gentleman, and was a finished scholar, – one so well educated, so ripe in literary acquirement, that we knew few whom we could call his equal. Judging of the matter by the light of our reason, we cannot say that the horror of the scene should have been enhanced to us by these recollections. Had the man been a shoemaker or a coalheaver there would have been enough of tragedy in it to make an angel weep, – that sight of the child standing by the bedside of her drunken father, while the other parent was away in custody, – and in no degree shocked at what she saw, because the thing was so common to her! But the thought of what the man had been, of what he was, of what he might have been, and the steps by which he had brought himself to the foul degradation which we witnessed, filled us with a dismay which we should hardly have felt had the gifts which he had polluted and the intellect which he had wasted been less capable of noble uses.

Our purpose in coming to the court was to rescue the Doctor's papers from danger, and we turned to accompany Grimes into the other room. As we did so the publican asked the girl if she knew anything of a black box which her father had taken away from the Spotted Dog. "The box is here," said the girl.

"And the papers?" asked Grimes. Thereupon the girl shook her head, and we both hurried into the outer room. I hardly know who first discovered the sight which we encountered, or whether it was shown to us by the child. The whole fire-place was strewn with half-burnt sheets of manuscript. There were scraps of pages of which almost the whole had been destroyed, others which were hardly more than scorched, and heaps of paper-ashes all lying tumbled together about the fender. We went down on our knees to examine them, thinking at the moment that the poor creature might in his despair have burned his own work and have spared that of the Doctor. But it was not so. We found scores of charred pages of the Doctor's elaborate handwriting. By this time Grimes had found the open box, and we perceived that the sheets remaining in it were tumbled and huddled together in absolute confusion. There were pages of the various volumes mixed with those which Mackenzie himself had written, and they were all crushed, and rolled, and twisted as though they had been thrust thither as waste-paper, – out of the way. "'Twas mother as done it," said the girl, "and we put 'em back again when the perlice took her."

There was nothing more to learn, – nothing more by the hearing which any useful clue could be obtained. What had been the exact course of the scenes which had been enacted there that morning it little booted us to enquire. It was enough and more than enough that we knew that the mischief had been done. We went down on our knees before the fire, and rescued from the ashes with our hands every fragment of manuscript that we could find. Then we put the mass altogether in the box, and gazed upon the wretched remnants almost in tears. "You had better go and get a bit of some'at to eat," said Grimes, handing a coin to the elder girl. "It's hard on them to starve 'cause their father's drunk, Sir." Then he took the closed box in his hand and we followed him out into the street. "I'll send or step up to look after him tomorrow," said Grimes, as he put us and the box into a cab. We little thought when we made to the drunkard that foolish request to arise, that we should never speak to him again.

As we returned to our office in the cab that we might deposit the box there ready for the following day, our mind was chiefly occupied in thinking over the undeserved grievances which had fallen upon ourselves. We had been moved by the charitable desire to do services to two different persons, – to the learned Doctor and to the red-nosed drunkard, and this had come of it! There had been nothing for us to gain by assisting either the one or the other. We had taken infinite trouble, attempting to bring together two men who wanted each other's services, – working hard in sheer benevolence; and what had been the result? We had spent half an hour on our knees in the undignified and almost disreputable work of raking among Mrs. Mackenzie's cinders, and now we had to face the anger, the dismay, the reproach, and, – worse than all, – the agony of the Doctor. As to Mackenzie, – we asserted to ourselves again and again that nothing further could be done for him. He had made his bed, and he must lie upon it; but, oh! why, – why had we attempted to meddle with a being so degraded? We got out of the cab at our office door, thinking of the Doctor's countenance as we should see it on the morrow. Our heart sank within us, and we asked ourselves, if it was so bad with us now, how it would be with us when we returned to the place on the following morning.

But on the following morning we did return. No doubt each individual reader to whom we address ourselves has at some period felt that indescribable load of personal, short-lived care, which causes the heart to sink down into the boots. It is not great grief that does it; – nor is it excessive fear; but the unpleasant operation comes from the mixture of the two. It is the anticipation of some imperfectly-understood evil that does it, – some evil out of which there might perhaps be an escape if we could only see the way. In this case we saw no way out of it. The Doctor was to be with us at one o'clock, and he would come with smiles, expecting to meet his learned colleague. How should we break it to the Doctor? We might indeed send to him, putting off the meeting, but the advantage coming from that would be slight, if any. We must see the injured Grecian sooner or later; and we had resolved, much as we feared, that the evil hour should not be postponed. We spent an hour that morning in arranging the fragments. Of the first volume about a third had been destroyed. Of the second nearly every page had been either burned or mutilated. Of the third but little had been injured. Mackenzie's own work had fared better than the Doctor's; but there was no comfort in that. After what had passed I thought it quite improbable that the Doctor would make any use of Mackenzie's work. So much of the manuscript as could still be placed in continuous pages we laid out upon the table, volume by volume, – that in the middle sinking down from its original goodly bulk almost to the dimensions of a poor sermon; – and the half-burned bits we left in the box. Then we sat ourselves down at our accustomed table, and pretended to try to work. Our ears were very sharp, and we heard the Doctor's step upon our stairs within a minute or two of the appointed time. Our heart went to the very toes of our boots. We shuffled in our chair, rose from it, and sat down again, – and were conscious that we were not equal to the occasion. Hitherto we had, after some mild literary form, patronised the Doctor, – as a man of letters in town will patronise his literary friend from the country; – but we now feared him as a truant school-boy fears his master. And yet it was so necessary that we should wear some air of self-assurance!

In a moment he was with us, wearing that bland smile which we knew so well, and which at the present moment almost overpowered us. We had been sure that he would wear that smile, and had especially feared it. "Ah," said he, grasping us by the hand, "I thought I should have been late. I see that our friend is not here yet."

"Doctor," we replied, "a great misfortune has happened."

"A great misfortune! Mr. Mackenzie is not dead?"

"No; – he is not dead. Perhaps it would have been better that he had died long since. He has destroyed your manuscript." The Doctor's face fell, and his hands at the same time, and he stood looking at us. "I need not tell you, Doctor, what my feelings are, and how great my remorse."

"Destroyed it!" Then we took him by the hand and led him to the table. He turned first upon the appetising and comparatively uninjured third volume, and seemed to think that we had hoaxed him. "This is not destroyed," he said, with a smile. But before I could explain anything, his hands were among the fragments in the box. "As I am a living man, they have burned it!" he exclaimed. "I—I—I—" Then he turned from us, and walked twice the length of the room, backwards and forwards, while we stood still, patiently waiting the explosion of his wrath. "My friend," he said, when his walk was over, "a great man underwent the same sorrow. Newton's manuscript was burned. I will take it home with me, and we will say no more about it." I never thought very much of the Doctor as a divine, but I hold him to have been as good a Christian as I ever met.

But that plan of his of saying no more about it could not quite be carried out. I was endeavouring to explain to him, as I thought it necessary to do, the circumstances of the case, and he was protesting his indifference to any such details, when there came a knock at the door, and the boy who waited on us below ushered Mrs. Grimes into the room. As the reader is aware, we had, during the last two months, become very intimate with the landlady of the Spotted Dog, but we had never hitherto had the pleasure of seeing her outside her own house. "Oh, Mr. ----" she began, and then she paused, seeing the Doctor.

We thought it expedient that there should be some introduction. "Mrs. Grimes," we said, "this is the gentleman whose invaluable manuscript has been destroyed by that unfortunate drunkard."

"Oh, then you're the Doctor, Sir?" The Doctor bowed and smiled. His heart must have been very heavy, but he bowed politely and smiled sweetly. "Oh, dear," she said, "I don't know how to tell you!"

"To tell us what?" asked the Doctor.

"What has happened since?" we demanded. The woman stood shaking before us, and then sank into a chair. Then arose to us at the moment some idea that the drunken woman, in her mad rage, had done some great damage to the Spotted Dog, – had set fire to the house, or injured Mr. Grimes personally, or perhaps run a muck amidst the jugs and pitchers, window glass, and gas lights. Something had been done which would give the Grimeses a pecuniary claim on me or on the Doctor, and the woman had been sent hither to make the first protest. Oh, – when should I see the last of the results of my imprudence in having attempted to befriend such a one as Julius Mackenzie! "If you have anything to tell, you had better tell it," we said, gravely.

"He's been, and—"

"Not destroyed himself?" asked the Doctor.

"Oh yes, Sir. He have indeed, – from ear to ear, – and is now a lying at the Spotted Dog!"

* * *

And so, after all, that was the end of Julius Mackenzie! We need hardly say that our feelings, which up to that moment had been very hostile to the man, underwent a sudden revulsion. Poor, overburdened, struggling, ill-used, abandoned creature! The world had been hard upon him, with a severity which almost induced one to make complaint against Omnipotence. The poor wretch had been willing to work, had been industrious in his calling, had had capacity for work; and he had also struggled gallantly against his evil fate, had recognised and endeavoured to perform his duty to his children and to the miserable woman who had brought him to his ruin!

And that sin of drunkenness had seemed to us to be in him rather the reflex of her vice than the result of his own vicious tendencies. Still it might be doubtful whether she had not learned the vice from him. They had both in truth been drunkards as long as they had been known in the neighbourhood of the Spotted Dog; but it was stated by all who had known them there that he was never seen to be drunk unless when she had disgraced him by the public exposure of her own abomination. Such as he was he had now come to his end! This was the upshot of his loud claims for liberty from his youth upwards; – liberty as against his father and family; liberty as against his college tutor; liberty as against all pastors, masters, and instructors; liberty as against the conventional thraldom of the world. He was now lying a wretched corpse at the Spotted Dog, with his throat cut from ear to ear, till the coroner's jury should have decided whether or not they would call him a suicide!

Mrs. Grimes had come to tell us that the coroner was to be at the Spotted Dog at four o'clock, and to say that her husband hoped that we would be present. We had seen Mackenzie so lately, and had so much to do with the employment of the last days of his life, that we could not refuse this request, though it came accompanied by no legal summons. Then Mrs. Grimes again became voluble and poured out to us her biography of Mackenzie as far as she knew it. He had been married to the woman ten years, and certainly had been a drunkard before he married her. "As for her, she'd been well-nigh suckled on gin," said Mrs. Grimes, "though he didn't know it, poor fellow." Whether this was true or not, she had certainly taken to drink soon after her marriage, and then his life had been passed in alternate fits of despondency and of desperate efforts to improve his own condition and that of his children. Mrs. Grimes declared to us that when the fit came on them, – when the woman had begun and the man had followed, – they would expend upon drink in two days what would have kept the family for a fortnight. "They say as how it was nothing for them to swallow forty shillings' worth of gin in forty-eight hours." The Doctor held up his hands in horror. "And it didn't, none of it, come our way," said Mrs. Grimes. "Indeed, John wouldn't let us serve it for 'em."

She sat there for half an hour, and during the whole time she was telling us of the man's life; but the reader will already have heard more than enough of it. By what immediate demon the woman had been instigated to burn the husband's work almost immediately on its production within her own home, we never heard. Doubtless there had been some terrible scene in which the man's sufferings must have been carried almost beyond endurance. "And he had feelings, Sir, he had," said Mrs. Grimes; "he knew as a woman should be decent, and a man's wife especial; I'm sure we pitied him so, John and I, that we could have cried over him. John would say a hard word to him at times, but he'd have walked round London to do him a good turn. John ain't to say edicated hisself, but he do respect learning."

When she had told us all, Mrs. Grimes went, and we were left alone with the Doctor. He at once consented to accompany us to the Spotted Dog, and we spent the hour that still remained to us in discussing the fate of the unfortunate man. We doubt whether an allusion was made during the time to the burned manuscript. If so, it was certainly not made by the Doctor himself. The tragedy which had occurred in connection with it had made him feel it to be unfitting even to mention his own loss. That such a one should have gone to his account in such a manner, without hope, without belief, and without fear, – as Burley said to Bothwell, and Bothwell boasted to Burley, – that was the theme of the Doctor's discourse. "The mercy of God is infinite," he said, bowing his head, with closed eyes and folded hands. To threaten while the life is in the man is human. To believe in the execution of those threats when the life has passed away is almost beyond the power of humanity.

At the hour fixed we were at the Spotted Dog, and found there a crowd assembled. The coroner was already seated in Mrs. Grimes's little parlour, and the body as we were told had been laid out in the tap-room. The inquest was soon over. The fact that he had destroyed himself in the low state of physical suffering and mental despondency which followed his intoxication was not doubted. At the very time that he was doing it, his wife was being taken from the lock-up house to the police office in the police van. He was not penniless, for he had sent the children out with money for their breakfasts, giving special caution as to the youngest, a little toddling thing of three years old; – and then he had done it. The eldest girl, returning to the house, had found him lying dead upon the floor. We were called upon for our evidence, and went into the tap-room accompanied by the Doctor. Alas! the very table which had been dragged up stairs into the landlady's bed-room with the charitable object of assisting Mackenzie in his work, – the table at which we had sat with him conning the Doctor's pages – had now been dragged down again and was used for another purpose. We had little to say as to the matter, except that we had known the man to be industrious and capable, and that we had, alas! seen him utterly prostrated by drink on the evening before his death.

The saddest sight of all on this occasion was the appearance of Mackenzie's wife, – whom we had never before seen. She had been brought there by a policeman, but whether she was still in custody we did not know. She had been dressed, either by the decency of the police or by the care of her neighbours, in an old black gown, which was a world too large and too long for her. And on her head there was a black bonnet which nearly enveloped her. She was a small woman, and, as far as we could judge from the glance we got of her face, pale, and worn, and wan. She had not such outward marks of a drunkard's career as those which poor Mackenzie always carried with him. She was taken up to the coroner, and what answers she gave to him were spoken in so low a voice that they did not reach us. The policeman, with whom we spoke, told us that she did not feel it much, – that she was callous now and beyond the power of mental suffering. "She's frightened just this minute, Sir; but it isn't more than that," said the policeman. We gave one glance along the table at the burden which it bore, but we saw nothing beyond the outward lines of that which had so lately been the figure of a man. We should have liked to see the countenance once more. The morbid curiosity to see such horrid sights is strong with most of us. But we did not wish to be thought to wish to see it, – especially by our friend the Doctor, – and we abstained from pushing our way to the head of the table. The Doctor himself remained quiescent in the corner of the room the farthest from the spectacle. When the matter was submitted to them, the jury lost not a moment in declaring their verdict. They said that the man had destroyed himself while suffering under temporary insanity produced by intoxication. And that was the end of Julius Mackenzie, the scholar.

On the following day the Doctor returned to the country, taking with him our black box, to the continued use of which, as a sarcophagus, he had been made very welcome. For our share in bringing upon him the great catastrophe of his life, he never uttered to us, either by spoken or written word, a single reproach. That idea of suffering as the great philosopher had suffered seemed to comfort him. "If Newton bore it, surely I can," he said to us with his bland smile, when we renewed the expression of our regret. Something passed between us, coming more from us than from him, as to the expediency of finding out some youthful scholar who could go down to the rectory, and reconstruct from its ruins the edifice of our friend's learning. The Doctor had given us some encouragement, and we had begun to make enquiry, when we received the following letter:

"— Rectory, — —, 18—.

"Dear Mr. —, —You were so kind as to say that you would endeavour to find for me an assistant in arranging and reconstructing the fragments of my work on The Metres of the Greek Dramatists. Your promise has been an additional kindness." Dear, courteous, kind old gentleman! For we knew well that no slightest sting of sarcasm was intended to be conveyed in these words. "Your promise has been an additional kindness; but looking upon the matter carefully, and giving to it the best consideration in my power, I have determined to relinquish the design. That which has been destroyed cannot be replaced; and it may well be that it was not worth replacing. I am old now, and never could do again that which perhaps I was never fitted to do with any fair prospect of success. I will never turn again to the ashes of my unborn child; but will console myself with the memory of my grievance, knowing well, as I do so, that consolation from the severity of harsh but just criticism might have been more difficult to find. When I think of the end of my efforts as a scholar, my mind reverts to the terrible and fatal catastrophe of one whose scholarship was infinitely more finished and more ripe than mine.

"Whenever it may suit you to come into this part of the country, pray remember that it will give very great pleasure to myself and to my daughter to welcome you at our parsonage.

"Believe me to be,
"My dear Mr. —,
"Yours very sincerely,
"— —."

We never have found the time to accept the Doctor's invitation, and our eyes have never again rested on the black box containing the ashes of the unborn child to which the Doctor will never turn again. We can picture him to ourselves standing, full of thought, with his hand upon the lid, but never venturing to turn the lock. Indeed, we do not doubt but that the key of the box is put away among other secret treasures, a lock of his wife's hair, perhaps, and the little shoe of the boy who did not live long enough to stand at his father's knee. For a tender, soft-hearted man was the Doctor, and one who fed much on the memories of the past.

We often called upon Mr. and Mrs. Grimes at the Spotted Dog, and would sit there talking of Mackenzie and his family. Mackenzie's widow soon vanished out of the neighbourhood, and no one there knew what was the fate of her or of her children. And then also Mr. Grimes went and took his wife with him. But they could not be said to vanish. Scratching his head one day, he told me with a dolorous voice that he had – made his fortune. "We've got as snug a little place as ever you see, just two mile out of Colchester," said Mrs. Grimes triumphantly, – "with thirty acres of land just to amuse John. And as for the Spotted Dog, I'm that sick of it, another year'd wear me to a dry bone." We looked at her, and saw no tendency that way. And we looked at John, and thought that he was not triumphant.

Who followed Mr. and Mrs. Grimes at the Spotted Dog we have never visited Liquorpond Street to see.

If you enjoyed this, you might also like...
A Cross Line, see page 143
Our New House, see page 423

Who Killed Zebedee?

Wilkie Collins

BEFORE THE DOCTOR left me one evening, I asked him how much longer I was likely to live. He answered: "It's not easy to say; you may die before I can get back to you in the morning, or you may live to the end of the month."

I was alive enough on the next morning to think of the needs of my soul, and (being a member of the Roman Catholic Church) to send for the priest.

The history of my sins, related in confession, included blameworthy neglect of a duty which I owed to the laws of my country. In the priest's opinion – and I agreed with him – I was bound to make public acknowledgment of my fault, as an act of penance becoming to a Catholic Englishman. We concluded, thereupon, to try a division of labor. I related the circumstances, while his reverence took the pen and put the matter into shape.

Here follows what came of it:

Chapter I

WHEN I WAS a young man of five-and-twenty, I became a member of the London police force. After nearly two years' ordinary experience of the responsible and ill-paid duties of that vocation, I found myself employed on my first serious and terrible case of official inquiry – relating to nothing less than the crime of Murder.

The circumstances were these:

I was then attached to a station in the northern district of London – which I beg permission not to mention more particularly. On a certain Monday in the week, I took my turn of night duty. Up to four in the morning, nothing occurred at the station-house out of the ordinary way. It was then springtime, and, between the gas and the fire, the room became rather hot. I went to the door to get a breath of fresh air – much to the surprise of our Inspector on duty, who was constitutionally a chilly man. There was a fine rain falling; and a nasty damp in the air sent me back to the fireside. I don't suppose I had sat down for more than a minute when the swinging-door was violently pushed open. A frantic woman ran in with a scream, and said: "Is this the station-house?"

Our Inspector (otherwise an excellent officer) had, by some perversity of nature, a hot temper in his chilly constitution. "Why, bless the woman, can't you see it is?" he says. "What's the matter now?"

"Murder's the matter!" she burst out. "For God's sake, come back with me. It's at Mrs. Crosscapel's lodging-house, number 14 Lehigh Street. A young woman has murdered her husband in the night! With a knife, sir. She says she thinks she did it in her sleep."

I confess I was startled by this; and the third man on duty (a sergeant) seemed to feel it too. She was a nice-looking young woman, even in her terrified condition, just out of bed, with her clothes huddled on anyhow. I was partial in those days to a tall figure – and she was, as they say, my style. I put a chair for her; and the sergeant poked the fire. As for the Inspector, nothing ever upset him. He questioned her as coolly as if it had been a case of petty larceny.

"Have you seen the murdered man?" he asked.

"No, sir."

"Or the wife?"

"No, sir. I didn't dare go into the room; I only heard about it!"

"Oh? And who are You? One of the lodgers?"

"No, sir. I'm the cook."

"Isn't there a master in the house?"

"Yes, sir. He's frightened out of his wits. And the housemaid's gone for the doctor. It all falls on the poor servants, of course. Oh, why did I ever set foot in that horrible house?"

The poor soul burst out crying, and shivered from head to foot. The Inspector made a note of her statement, and then asked her to read it, and sign it with her name. The object of this proceeding was to get her to come near enough to give him the opportunity of smelling her breath. "When people make extraordinary statements," he afterward said to me, "it sometimes saves trouble to satisfy yourself that they are not drunk. I've known them to be mad – but not often. You will generally find that in their eyes."

She roused herself and signed her name – "Priscilla Thurlby." The Inspector's own test proved her to be sober; and her eyes – a nice light blue color, mild and pleasant, no doubt, when they were not staring with fear, and red with crying – satisfied him (as I supposed) that she was not mad. He turned the case over to me, in the first instance. I saw that he didn't believe in it, even yet.

"Go back with her to the house," he says. "This may be a stupid hoax, or a quarrel exaggerated. See to it yourself, and hear what the doctor says. If it is serious, send word back here directly, and let nobody enter the place or leave it till we come. Stop! You know the form if any statement is volunteered?"

"Yes, sir. I am to caution the persons that whatever they say will be taken down, and may be used against them."

"Quite right. You'll be an Inspector yourself one of these days. Now, miss!" With that he dismissed her, under my care.

Lehigh Street was not very far off – about twenty minutes' walk from the station. I confess I thought the Inspector had been rather hard on Priscilla. She was herself naturally angry with him. "What does he mean," she says, "by talking of a hoax? I wish he was as frightened as I am. This is the first time I have been out at service, sir – and I did think I had found a respectable place."

I said very little to her – feeling, if the truth must be told, rather anxious about the duty committed to me. On reaching the house the door was opened from within, before I could knock. A gentleman stepped out, who proved to be the doctor. He stopped the moment he saw me.

"You must be careful, policeman," he says. "I found the man lying on his back, in bed, dead – with the knife that had killed him left sticking in the wound."

Hearing this, I felt the necessity of sending at once to the station. Where could I find a trustworthy messenger? I took the liberty of asking the doctor if he would repeat to the police what he had already said to me. The station was not much out of his way home. He kindly granted my request.

The landlady (Mrs. Crosscapel) joined us while we were talking. She was still a young woman; not easily frightened, as far as I could see, even by a murder in the house. Her husband was in the passage behind her. He looked old enough to be her father; and he so trembled with terror that some people might have taken him for the guilty person. I removed the key from the street door, after locking it; and I said to the landlady: "Nobody must leave the house, or enter the house, till the Inspector comes. I must examine the premises to see if any on e has broken in."

"There is the key of the area gate," she said, in answer to me. "It's always kept locked. Come downstairs and see for yourself." Priscilla went with us. Her mistress set her to work to light the kitchen fire. "Some of us," says Mrs. Crosscapel, "may be the better for a cup of tea." I remarked that she took things easy, under the circumstances. She answered that the landlady of a London lodging-house could not afford to lose her wits, no matter what might happen.

I found the gate locked, and the shutters of the kitchen window fastened. The back kitchen and back door were secured in the same way. No person was concealed anywhere. Returning upstairs, I examined the front parlor window. There, again, the barred shutters answered for the security of that room. A cracked voice spoke through the door of the back parlor. "The policeman can come in," it said, "if he will promise not to look at me." I turned to the landlady for information. "It's my parlor lodger, Miss Mybus," she said, "a most respectable lady." Going into the room, I saw something rolled up perpendicularly in the bed curtains. Miss Mybus had made herself modestly invisible in that way. Having now satisfied my mind about the security of the lower part of the house, and having the keys safe in my pocket, I was ready to go upstairs.

On our way to the upper regions I asked if there had been any visitors on the previous day. There had been only two visitors, friends of the lodgers – and Mrs. Crosscapel herself had let them both out. My next inquiry related to the lodgers themselves. On the ground floor there was Miss Mybus. On the first floor (occupying both rooms) Mr. Barfield, an old bachelor, employed in a merchant's office. On the second floor, in the front room, Mr. John Zebedee, the murdered man, and his wife. In the back room, Mr. Deluc; described as a cigar agent, and supposed to be a Creole gentleman from Martinique. In the front garret, Mr. and Mrs. Crosscapel. In the back garret, the cook and the housemaid. These were the inhabitants, regularly accounted for. I asked about the servants. "Both excellent characters," says the landlady, "or they would not be in my service."

We reached the second floor, and found the housemaid on the watch outside the door of the front room. Not as nice a woman, personally, as the cook, and sadly frightened of course. Her mistress had posted her, to give the alarm in the case of an outbreak on the part of Mrs. Zebedee, kept locked up in the room. My arrival relieved the housemaid of further responsibility. She ran downstairs to her fellow-servant in the kitchen.

I asked Mrs. Crosscapel how and when the alarm of the murder had been given.

"Soon after three this morning," says she, "I was woke by the screams of Mrs. Zebedee. I found her out here on the landing, and Mr. Deluc, in great alarm, trying to quiet her. Sleeping in the next room he had only to open his door, when her screams woke him. 'My dear John's murdered! I am the miserable wretch – I did it in my sleep!' She repeated these frantic words over and over again, until she dropped in a swoon. Mr. Deluc and I carried her back into the bedroom. We both thought the poor creature had been driven distracted by some dreadful dream. But when we got to the bedside – don't ask me what we saw; the doctor has told you about it already. I was once a nurse in a hospital, and accustomed, as such, to horrid sights. It turned me cold and giddy, notwithstanding. As for Mr. Deluc, I thought he would have had a fainting fit next."

Hearing this, I inquired if Mrs. Zebedee had said or done any strange things since she had been Mrs. Crosscapel's lodger.

"You think she's mad?" says the landlady. "And anybody would be of your mind, when a woman accuses herself of murdering her husband in her sleep. All I can say is that, up to this morning, a more quiet, sensible, well-behaved little person than Mrs. Zebedee I never met with. Only just married, mind, and as fond of her unfortunate husband as a woman could be. I should have called them a pattern couple, in their own line of life."

There was no more to be said on the landing. We unlocked the door and went into the room.

Chapter II

HE LAY IN BED on his back as the doctor had described him. On the left side of his nightgown, just over his heart, the blood on the linen told its terrible tale. As well as one could judge, looking unwillingly at a dead face, he must have been a handsome young man in his lifetime. It was a sight to sadden anybody – but I think the most painful sensation was when my eyes fell next on his miserable wife.

She was down on the floor, crouched up in a corner – a dark little woman, smartly dressed in gay colors. Her black hair and her big brown eyes made the horrid paleness of her face look even more deadly white than perhaps it really was. She stared straight at us without appearing to see us. We spoke to her, and she never answered a word. She might have been dead – like her husband – except that she perpetually picked at her fingers, and shuddered every now and then as if she was cold. I went to her and tried to lift her up. She shrank back with a cry that well-nigh frightened me – not because it was loud, but because it was more like the cry of some animal than of a human being. However quietly she might have behaved in the landlady's previous experience of her, she was beside herself now. I might have been moved by a natural pity for her, or I might have been completely upset in my mind – I only know this, I could not persuade myself that she was guilty. I even said to Mrs. Crosscapel, "I don't believe she did it."

While I spoke there was a knock at the door. I went downstairs at once, and admitted (to my great relief) the Inspector, accompanied by one of our men.

He waited downstairs to hear my report, and he approved of what I had done. "It looks as if the murder had been committed by somebody in the house." Saying this, he left the man below, and went up with me to the second floor.

Before he had been a minute in the room, he discovered an object which had escaped my observation.

It was the knife that had done the deed.

The doctor had found it left in the body – had withdrawn it to probe the wound – and had laid it on the bedside table. It was one of those useful knives which contain a saw, a corkscrew, and other like implements. The big blade fastened back, when open, with a spring. Except where the blood was on it, it was as bright as when it had been purchased. A small metal plate was fastened to the horn handle, containing an inscription, only partly engraved, which ran thus: "To John Zebedee, from —" There it stopped, strangely enough.

Who or what had interrupted the engraver's work? It was impossible even to guess. Nevertheless, the Inspector was encouraged.

"This ought to help us," he said – and then he gave an attentive ear (looking all the while at the poor creature in the corner) to what Mrs. Crosscapel had to tell him.

The landlady having done, he said he must now see the lodger who slept in the next bed-chamber.

Mr. Deluc made his appearance, standing at the door of the room, and turning away his head with horror from the sight inside.

He was wrapped in a splendid blue dressing-gown, with a golden girdle and trimmings. His scanty brownish hair curled (whether artificially or not, I am unable to say) in little ringlets. His complexion was yellow; his greenish-brown eyes were of the sort called "goggle" – they looked as if they might drop out of his face, if you held a spoon under them. His mustache and goat's beard were beautifully oiled; and, to complete his equipment, he had a long black cigar in his mouth.

"It isn't insensibility to this terrible tragedy," he explained. "My nerves have been shattered, Mr. Policeman, and I can only repair the mischief in this way. Be pleased to excuse and feel for me."

The Inspector questioned this witness sharply and closely. He was not a man to be misled by appearances; but I could see that he was far from liking, or even trusting, Mr. Deluc. Nothing came of the examination, except what Mrs. Crosscapel had in substance already mentioned to me. Mr. Deluc returned to his room.

"How long has he been lodging with you?" the Inspector asked, as soon as his back was turned.

"Nearly a year," the landlady answered.

"Did he give you a reference?"

"As good a reference as I could wish for." Thereupon, she mentioned the names of a well-known firm of cigar merchants in the city. The Inspector noted the information in his pocketbook.

I would rather not relate in detail what happened next: it is too distressing to be dwelt on. Let me only say that the poor demented woman was taken away in a cab to the station-house. The Inspector possessed himself of the knife, and of a book found on the floor, called "The World of Sleep." The portmanteau containing the luggage was locked – and then the door of the room was secured, the keys in both cases being left in my charge. My instructions were to remain in the house, and allow nobody to leave it, until I heard again shortly from the Inspector.

Chapter III

THE CORONER'S INQUEST was adjourned; and the examination before the magistrate ended in a remand – Mrs. Zebedee being in no condition to understand the proceedings in either case. The surgeon reported her to be completely prostrated by a terrible nervous shock. When he was asked if he considered her to have been a sane woman before the murder took place, he refused to answer positively at that time.

A week passed. The murdered man was buried; his old father attending the funeral. I occasionally saw Mrs. Crosscapel, and the two servants, for the purpose of getting such further information as was thought desirable. Both the cook and the housemaid had given their month's notice to quit; declining, in the interest of their characters, to remain in a house which had been the scene of a murder. Mr. Deluc's nerves led also to his removal; his rest was now disturbed by frightful dreams. He paid the necessary forfeit-money, and left without notice. The first-floor lodger, Mr. Barfield, kept his rooms, but obtained leave of absence from his employers, and took refuge with some friends in the country. Miss Mybus alone remained in the parlors. "When I am comfortable," the old lady said, "nothing moves me, at my age. A murder up two pairs of stairs is nearly the same thing as a murder in the next house. Distance, you see, makes all the difference."

It mattered little to the police what the lodgers did. We had men in plain clothes watching the house night and day. Everybody who went away was privately followed; and the police in the district to which they retired were warned to keep an eye on them, after that. As long as we failed to put Mrs. Zebedee's extraordinary statement to any sort of test – to say nothing of having proved unsuccessful, thus far, in tracing the knife to its purchaser – we were bound to let no person living under Mr. Crosscapel's roof, on the night of the murder, slip through our fingers.

Chapter IV

IN A FORTNIGHT more, Mrs. Zebedee had sufficiently recovered to make the necessary statement – after the preliminary caution addressed to persons in such cases. The surgeon had no hesitation, now, in reporting her to be a sane woman.

Her station in life had been domestic service. She had lived for four years in her last place as lady's-maid, with a family residing in Dorsetshire. The one objection to her had been the occasional infirmity of sleep-walking, which made it necessary that one of the other female servants should sleep in the same room, with the door locked and the key under her pillow. In all other respects the lady's-maid was described by her mistress as "a perfect treasure."

In the last six months of her service, a young man named John Zebedee entered the house (with a written character) as a footman. He soon fell in love with the nice little lady's-maid, and she heartily returned the feeling. They might have waited for years before they were in a pecuniary position to marry, but for the death of Zebedee's uncle, who left him a little fortune of two thousand pounds. They were now, for persons in their station, rich enough to please themselves; and they were married from the house in which they had served together, the little daughters of the family showing their affection for Mrs. Zebedee by acting as her bridesmaids.

The young husband was a careful man. He decided to employ his small capital to the best advantage, by sheep-farming in Australia. His wife made no objection; she was ready to go wherever John went.

Accordingly they spent their short honeymoon in London, so as to see for themselves the vessel in which their passage was to be taken. They went to Mrs. Crosscapel's lodging-house because Zebedee's uncle had always stayed there when in London. Ten days were to pass before the day of embarkation arrived. This gave the young couple a welcome holiday, and a prospect of amusing themselves to their heart's content among the sights and shows of the great city.

On their first evening in London they went to the theater. They were both accustomed to the fresh air of the country, and they felt half stifled by the heat and the gas. However, they were so pleased with an amusement which was new to them that they went to another theater on the next evening. On this second occasion, John Zebedee found the heat unendurable. They left the theater, and got back to their lodgings toward ten o'clock.

Let the rest be told in the words used by Mrs. Zebedee herself. She said:

"We sat talking for a little while in our room, and John's headache got worse and worse. I persuaded him to go to bed, and I put out the candle (the fire giving sufficient light to undress by), so that he might the sooner fall asleep. But he was too restless to sleep. He asked me to read him something. Books always made him drowsy at the best of times.

"I had not myself begun to undress. So I lit the candle again, and I opened the only book I had. John had noticed it at the railway bookstall by the name of 'The World of Sleep.' He used to joke with me about my being a sleepwalker; and he said, 'Here's something that's sure to interest you' – and he made me a present of the book.

"Before I had read to him for more than half an hour he was fast asleep. Not feeling that way inclined, I went on reading to myself.

"The book did indeed interest me. There was one terrible story which took a hold on my mind – the story of a man who stabbed his own wife in a sleep-walking dream. I thought of putting down my book after that, and then changed my mind again and went on. The next chapters were not so interesting; they were full of learned accounts of why we fall asleep, and what our brains do in that state, and such like. It ended in my falling asleep, too, in my armchair by the fireside.

"I don't know what o'clock it was when I went to sleep. I don't know how long I slept, or whether I dreamed or not. The candle and the fire had both burned out, and it was pitch dark when I woke. I can't even say why I woke – unless it was the coldness of the room.

"There was a spare candle on the chimney-piece. I found the matchbox, and got a light. Then for the first time, I turned round toward the bed; and I saw—"

She had seen the dead body of her husband, murdered while she was unconsciously at his side – and she fainted, poor creature, at the bare remembrance of it.

The proceedings were adjourned. She received every possible care and attention; the chaplain looking after her welfare as well as the surgeon.

I have said nothing of the evidence of the landlady and servants. It was taken as a mere formality. What little they knew proved nothing against Mrs. Zebedee. The police made no discoveries that supported her first frantic accusation of herself. Her master and mistress, where she had been last in service, spoke of her in the highest terms. We were at a complete deadlock.

It had been thought best not to surprise Mr. Deluc, as yet, by citing him as a witness. The action of the law was, however, hurried in this case by a private communication received from the chaplain.

After twice seeing, and speaking with, Mrs. Zebedee, the reverend gentleman was persuaded that she had no more to do than himself with the murder of her husband. He did not consider that he was justified in repeating a confidential communication

– he would only recommend that Mr. Deluc should be summoned to appear at the next examination. This advice was followed.

The police had no evidence against Mrs. Zebedee when the inquiry was resumed. To assist the ends of justice she was now put into the witness-box. The discovery of her murdered husband, when she woke in the small hours of the morning, was passed over as rapidly as possible. Only three questions of importance were put to her.

First, the knife was produced. Had she ever seen it in her husband's possession? Never. Did she know anything about it? Nothing whatever.

Secondly: Did she, or did her husband, lock the bedroom door when they returned from the theater? No. Did she afterward lock the door herself? No.

Thirdly: Had she any sort of reason to give for supposing that she had murdered her husband in a sleep-walking dream? No reason, except that she was beside herself at the time, and the book put the thought into her head.

After this the other witnesses were sent out of court The motive for the chaplain's communication now appeared. Mrs. Zebedee was asked if anything unpleasant had occurred between Mr. Deluc and herself.

Yes. He had caught her alone on the stairs at the lodging-house; had presumed to make love to her; and had carried the insult still farther by attempting to kiss her. She had slapped his face, and had declared that her husband should know of it, if his misconduct was repeated. He was in a furious rage at having his face slapped; and he said to her: "Madam, you may live to regret this."

After consultation, and at the request of our Inspector, it was decided to keep Mr. Deluc in ignorance of Mrs. Zebedee's statement for the present. When the witnesses were recalled, he gave the same evidence which he had already given to the Inspector – and he was then asked if he knew anything of the knife. He looked at it without any guilty signs in his face, and swore that he had never seen it until that moment. The resumed inquiry ended, and still nothing had been discovered.

But we kept an eye on Mr. Deluc. Our next effort was to try if we could associate him with the purchase of the knife.

Here again (there really did seem to be a sort of fatality in this case) we reached no useful result. It was easy enough to find out the wholesale cutlers, who had manufactured the knife at Sheffield, by the mark on the blade. But they made tens of thousands of such knives, and disposed of them to retail dealers all over Great Britain – to say nothing of foreign parts. As to finding out the person who had engraved the imperfect inscription (without knowing where, or by whom, the knife had been purchased) we might as well have looked for the proverbial needle in the bundle of hay. Our last resource was to have the knife photographed, with the inscribed side uppermost, and to send copies to every police-station in the kingdom.

At the same time we reckoned up Mr. Deluc – I mean that we made investigations into his past life – on the chance that he and the murdered man might have known each other, and might have had a quarrel, or a rivalry about a woman, on some former occasion. No such discovery rewarded us.

We found Deluc to have led a dissipated life, and to have mixed with very bad company. But he had kept out of reach of the law. A man may be a profligate vagabond; may insult a lady; may say threatening things to her, in the first stinging sensation of having his face slapped – but it doesn't follow from these blots on his character that he has murdered her husband in the dead of the night.

Once more, then, when we were called upon to report ourselves, we had no evidence to produce. The photographs failed to discover the owner of the knife, and to explain its interrupted inscription. Poor Mrs. Zebedee was allowed to go back to her friends, on entering into her own recognizance to appear again if called upon. Articles in the newspapers began to inquire how many more murderers would succeed in baffling the police. The authorities at the Treasury offered a reward of a hundred pounds for the necessary information. And the weeks passed and nobody claimed the reward.

Our Inspector was not a man to be easily beaten. More inquiries and examinations followed. It is needless to say anything about them. We were defeated – and there, so far as the police and the public were concerned, was an end of it.

The assassination of the poor young husband soon passed out of notice, like other undiscovered murders. One obscure person only was foolish enough, in his leisure hours, to persist in trying to solve the problem of Who Killed Zebedee? He felt that he might rise to the highest position in the police force if he succeeded where his elders and betters had failed – and he held to his own little ambition, though everybody laughed at him. In plain English, I was the man.

Chapter V

WITHOUT meaning it, I have told my story ungratefully.

There were two persons who saw nothing ridiculous in my resolution to continue the investigation, single-handed. One of them was Miss Mybus; and the other was the cook, Priscilla Thurlby.

Mentioning the lady first, Miss Mybus was indignant at the resigned manner in which the police accepted their defeat. She was a little bright-eyed wiry woman; and she spoke her mind freely.

"This comes home to me," she said. "Just look back for a year or two. I can call to mind two cases of persons found murdered in London – and the assassins have never been traced. I am a person, too; and I ask myself if my turn is not coming next. You're a nice-looking fellow and I like your pluck and perseverance. Come here as often as you think right; and say you are my visitor, if they make any difficulty about letting you in. One thing more! I have nothing particular to do, and I am no fool. Here, in the parlors, I see everybody who comes into the house or goes out of the house. Leave me your address – I may get some information for you yet."

With the best intentions, Miss Mybus found no opportunity of helping me. Of the two, Priscilla Thurlby seemed more likely to be of use.

In the first place, she was sharp and active, and (not having succeeded in getting another situation as yet) was mistress of her own movements.

In the second place, she was a woman I could trust. Before she left home to try domestic service in London, the parson of her native parish gave her a written testimonial, of which I append a copy. Thus it ran:

> *I gladly recommend Priscilla Thurlby for any respectable employment which she may be competent to undertake. Her father and mother are infirm old people, who have lately suffered a diminution of their income; and they have a younger daughter to maintain. Rather than be a burden on her parents, Priscilla goes to London to find domestic employment, and to devote her earnings to the assistance*

of her father and mother. This circumstance speaks for itself. I have known the family many years; and I only regret that I have no vacant place in my own household which I can offer to this good girl,
          (Signed) HENRY DEERINGTON, Rector of Roth.

After reading those words, I could safely ask Priscilla to help me in reopening the mysterious murder case to some good purpose.

My notion was that the proceedings of the persons in Mrs. Crosscapel's house had not been closely enough inquired into yet. By way of continuing the investigation, I asked Priscilla if she could tell me anything which associated the housemaid with Mr. Deluc. She was unwilling to answer. "I may be casting suspicion on an innocent person," she said. "Besides, I was for so short a time the housemaid's fellow servant—"

"You slept in the same room with her," I remarked; "and you had opportunities of observing her conduct toward the lodgers. If they had asked you, at the examination, what I now ask, you would have answered as an honest woman."

To this argument she yielded. I heard from her certain particulars, which threw a new light on Mr. Deluc, and on the case generally. On that information I acted. It was slow work, owing to the claims on me of my regular duties; but with Priscilla's help, I steadily advanced toward the end I had in view.

Besides this, I owed another obligation to Mrs. Crosscapel's nice-looking cook. The confession must be made sooner or later – and I may as well make it now. I first knew what love was, thanks to Priscilla. I had delicious kisses, thanks to Priscilla. And, when I asked if she would marry me, she didn't say No. She looked, I must own, a little sadly, and she said: "How can two such poor people as we are ever hope to marry?" To this I answered: "It won't be long before I lay my hand on the clew which my Inspector has failed to find. I shall be in a position to marry you, my dear, when that time comes."

At our next meeting we spoke of her parents. I was now her promised husband. Judging by what I had heard of the proceedings of other people in my position, it seemed to be only right that I should be made known to her father and mother. She entirely agreed with me; and she wrote home that day to tell them to expect us at the end of the week.

I took my turn of night-duty, and so gained my liberty for the greater part of the next day. I dressed myself in plain clothes, and we took our tickets on the railway for Yateland, being the nearest station to the village in which Priscilla's parents lived.

Chapter VI

THE TRAIN STOPPED, as usual, at the big town of Waterbank. Supporting herself by her needle, while she was still unprovided with a situation, Priscilla had been at work late in the night – she was tired and thirsty. I left the carriage to get her some soda-water. The stupid girl in the refreshment room failed to pull the cork out of the bottle, and refused to let me help her. She took a corkscrew, and used it crookedly. I lost all patience, and snatched the bottle out of her hand. Just as I drew the cork, the bell rang on the platform. I only waited to pour the soda-water into a glass – but the train was moving as I left the refreshment room. The porters stopped me when I tried to jump on to the step of the carriage. I was left behind.

As soon as I had recovered my temper, I looked at the time-table. We had reached Waterbank at five minutes past one. By good luck, the next train was due at forty-four minutes past one, and arrived at Yateland (the next station) ten minutes afterward. I could only hope that Priscilla would look at the time-table too, and wait for me. If I had attempted to walk the distance between the two places, I should have lost time instead of saving it. The interval before me was not very long; I occupied it in looking over the town.

Speaking with all due respect to the inhabitants, Waterbank (to other people) is a dull place. I went up one street and down another – and stopped to look at a shop which struck me; not from anything in itself, but because it was the only shop in the street with the shutters closed.

A bill was posted on the shutters, announcing that the place was to let. The outgoing tradesman's name and business, announced in the customary painted letters, ran thus:

James Wycomb, Cutler, etc.

For the first time, it occurred to me that we had forgotten an obstacle in our way, when we distributed our photographs of the knife. We had none of us remembered that a certain proportion of cutlers might be placed, by circumstances, out of our reach – either by retiring from business or by becoming bankrupt. I always carried a copy of the photograph about me; and I thought to myself, "Here is the ghost of a chance of tracing the knife to Mr. Deluc!"

The shop door was opened, after I had twice rung the bell, by an old man, very dirty and very deaf. He said "You had better go upstairs, and speak to Mr. Scorrier – top of the house."

I put my lips to the old fellow's ear-trumpet, and asked who Mr. Scorrier was.

"Brother-in-law to Mr. Wycomb. Mr. Wycomb's dead. If you want to buy the business apply to Mr. Scorrier."

Receiving that reply, I went upstairs, and found Mr. Scorrier engaged in engraving a brass door-plate. He was a middle-aged man, with a cadaverous face and dim eyes. After the necessary apologies, I produced my photograph.

"May I ask, sir, if you know anything of the inscription on that knife?" I said.

He took his magnifying glass to look at it.

"This is curious," he remarked quietly. "I remember the queer name – Zebedee. Yes, sir; I did the engraving, as far as it goes. I wonder what prevented me from finishing it?"

The name of Zebedee, and the unfinished inscription on the knife, had appeared in every English newspaper. He took the matter so coolly that I was doubtful how to interpret his answer. Was it possible that he had not seen the account of the murder? Or was he an accomplice with prodigious powers of self-control?

"Excuse me," I said, "do you read the newspapers?"

"Never! My eyesight is failing me. I abstain from reading, in the interests of my occupation."

"Have you not heard the name of Zebedee mentioned – particularly by people who do read the newspapers?"

"Very likely; but I didn't attend to it. When the day's work is done, I take my walk. Then I have my supper, my drop of grog, and my pipe. Then I go to bed. A dull existence you think, I daresay! I had a miserable life, sir, when I was young. A bare subsistence, and a little rest, before the last perfect rest in the grave – that is all I want. The world has gone by me long ago. So much the better."

The poor man spoke honestly. I was ashamed of having doubted him. I returned to the subject of the knife.

"Do you know where it was purchased, and by whom?" I asked.

"My memory is not so good as it was," he said; "but I have got something by me that helps it."

He took from a cupboard a dirty old scrapbook. Strips of paper, with writing on them, were pasted on the pages, as well as I could see. He turned to an index, or table of contents, and opened a page. Something like a flash of life showed itself on his dismal face.

"Ha! now I remember," he said. "The knife was bought of my late brother-in-law, in the shop downstairs. It all comes back to me, sir. A person in a state of frenzy burst into this very room, and snatched the knife away from me, when I was only half way through the inscription!"

I felt that I was now close on discovery. "May I see what it is that has assisted your memory?" I asked.

"Oh yes. You must know, sir, I live by engraving inscriptions and addresses, and I paste in this book the manuscript instructions which I receive, with marks of my own on the margin. For one thing, they serve as a reference to new customers. And for another thing, they do certainly help my memory."

He turned the book toward me, and pointed to a slip of paper which occupied the lower half of a page.

I read the complete inscription, intended for the knife that killed Zebedee, and written as follows:

"To John Zebedee. From Priscilla Thurlby."

Chapter VII

I DECLARE that it is impossible for me to describe what I felt when Priscilla's name confronted me like a written confession of guilt. How long it was before I recovered myself in some degree, I cannot say. The only thing I can clearly call to mind is, that I frightened the poor engraver.

My first desire was to get possession of the manuscript inscription. I told him I was a policeman, and summoned him to assist me in the discovery of a crime. I even offered him money. He drew back from my hand. "You shall have it for nothing," he said, "if you will only go away and never come here again." He tried to cut it out of the page – but his trembling hands were helpless. I cut it out myself, and attempted to thank him. He wouldn't hear me. "Go away!" he said, "I don't like the look of you."

It may be here objected that I ought not to have felt so sure as I did of the woman's guilt, until I had got more evidence against her. The knife might have been stolen from her, supposing she was the person who had snatched it out of the engraver's hands, and might have been afterward used by the thief to commit the murder. All very true. But I never had a moment's doubt in my own mind, from the time when I read the damnable line in the engraver's book.

I went back to the railway without any plan in my head. The train by which I had proposed to follow her had left Waterbank. The next train that arrived was for London. I took my place in it – still without any plan in my head.

At Charing Cross a friend met me. He said, "You're looking miserably ill. Come and have a drink."

I went with him. The liquor was what I really wanted; it strung me up, and cleared my head. He went his way, and I went mine. In a little while more, I determined what I would do.

In the first place, I decided to resign my situation in the police, from a motive which will presently appear. In the second place, I took a bed at a public-house. She would no doubt return to London, and she would go to my lodgings to find out why I had broken my appointment. To bring to justice the one woman whom I had dearly loved was too cruel a duty for a poor creature like me. I preferred leaving the police force. On the other hand, if she and I met before time had helped me to control myself, I had a horrid fear that I might turn murderer next, and kill her then and there. The wretch had not only all but misled me into marrying her, but also into charging the innocent housemaid with being concerned in the murder.

The same night I hit on a way of clearing up such doubts as still harassed my mind. I wrote to the rector of Roth, informing him that I was engaged to marry her, and asking if he would tell me (in consideration of my position) what her former relations might have been with the person named John Zebedee.

By return of post I got this reply:

"SIR – Under the circumstances, I think I am bound to tell you confidentially what the friends and well-wishers of Priscilla have kept secret, for her sake.

"Zebedee was in service in this neighborhood. I am sorry to say it, of a man who has come to such a miserable end – but his behavior to Priscilla proves him to have been a vicious and heartless wretch. They were engaged – and, I add with indignation, he tried to seduce her under a promise of marriage. Her virtue resisted him, and he pretended to be ashamed of himself. The banns were published in my church. On the next day Zebedee disappeared, and cruelly deserted her. He was a capable servant; and I believe he got another place. I leave you to imagine what the poor girl suffered under the outrage inflicted on her. Going to London, with my recommendation, she answered the first advertisement that she saw, and was unfortunate enough to begin her career in domestic service in the very lodging-house to which (as I gather from the newspaper report of the murder) the man Zebedee took the person whom he married, after deserting Priscilla. Be assured that you are about to unite yourself to an excellent girl, and accept my best wishes for your happiness."

It was plain from this that neither the rector nor the parents and friends knew anything of the purchase of the knife. The one miserable man who knew the truth was the man who had asked her to be his wife.

I owed it to myself – at least so it seemed to me – not to let it be supposed that I, too, had meanly deserted her. Dreadful as the prospect was, I felt that I must see her once more, and for the last time.

She was at work when I went into her room. As I opened the door she started to her feet. Her cheeks reddened, and her eyes flashed with anger. I stepped forward – and she saw my face. My face silenced her.

I spoke in the fewest words I could find.

"I have been to the cutler's shop at Waterbank," I said. "There is the unfinished inscription on the knife, complete in your handwriting. I could hang you by a word. God forgive me – I can't say the word."

Her bright complexion turned to a dreadful clay-color. Her eyes were fixed and staring, like the eyes of a person in a fit. She stood before me, still and silent. Without saying more, I dropped the inscription into the fire. Without saying more, I left her.

I never saw her again.

Chapter VIII

BUT I HEARD from her a few days later. The letter has long since been burned. I wish I could have forgotten it as well. It sticks to my memory. If I die with my senses about me, Priscilla's letter will be my last recollection on earth.

In substance it repeated what the rector had already told me. Further, it informed me that she had bought the knife as a keepsake for Zebedee, in place of a similar knife which he had lost. On the Saturday, she made the purchase, and left it to be engraved. On the Sunday, the banns were put up. On the Monday, she was deserted; and she snatched the knife from the table while the engraver was at work.

She only knew that Zebedee had added a new sting to the insult inflicted on her when he arrived at the lodgings with his wife. Her duties as cook kept her in the kitchen – and Zebedee never discovered that she was in the house. I still remember the last lines of her confession:

> *"The devil entered into me when I tried their door, on my way up to bed, and found it unlocked, and listened a while, and peeped in. I saw them by the dying light of the candle – one asleep on the bed, the other asleep by the fireside. I had the knife in my hand, and the thought came to me to do it, so that they might hang her for the murder. I couldn't take the knife out again, when I had done it. Mind this! I did really like you – I didn't say Yes, because you could hardly hang your own wife, if you found out who killed Zebedee."*

Since the past time I have never heard again of Priscilla Thurlby; I don't know whether she is living or dead. Many people may think I deserve to be hanged myself for not having given her up to the gallows. They may, perhaps, be disappointed when they see this confession, and hear that I have died decently in my bed. I don't blame them. I am a penitent sinner. I wish all merciful Christians goodbye forever.

If you enjoyed this, you might also like...
Brother Owen's Story of Anne Rodway, see page 345
The Day of Silence, see page 103

The Adventure of the Hansom Cabs

Robert Louis Stevenson

LIEUTENANT BRACKENBURY RICH had greatly distinguished himself in one of the lesser Indian hill wars. He it was who took the chieftain prisoner with his own hand; his gallantry was universally applauded; and when he came home, prostrated by an ugly sabre cut and a protracted jungle fever, society was prepared to welcome the Lieutenant as a celebrity of minor lustre. But his was a character remarkable for unaffected modesty; adventure was dear to his heart, but he cared little for adulation; and he waited at foreign watering-places and in Algiers until the fame of his exploits had run through its nine days' vitality and begun to be forgotten. He arrived in London at last, in the early season, with as little observation as he could desire; and as he was an orphan and had none but distant relatives who lived in the provinces, it was almost as a foreigner that he installed himself in the capital of the country for which he had shed his blood.

On the day following his arrival he dined alone at a military club. He shook hands with a few old comrades, and received their warm congratulations; but as one and all had some engagement for the evening, he found himself left entirely to his own resources. He was in dress, for he had entertained the notion of visiting a theatre. But the great city was new to him; he had gone from a provincial school to a military college, and thence direct to the Eastern Empire; and he promised himself a variety of delights in this world for exploration. Swinging his cane, he took his way westward. It was a mild evening, already dark, and now and then threatening rain. The succession of faces in the lamplight stirred the Lieutenant's imagination; and it seemed to him as if he could walk for ever in that stimulating city atmosphere and surrounded by the mystery of four million private lives. He glanced at the houses, and marvelled what was passing behind those warmly-lighted windows; he looked into face after face, and saw them each intent upon some unknown interest, criminal or kindly.

"They talk of war," he thought, "but this is the great battlefield of mankind."

And then he began to wonder that he should walk so long in this complicated scene, and not chance upon so much as the shadow of an adventure for himself.

"All in good time," he reflected. "I am still a stranger, and perhaps wear a strange air. But I must be drawn into the eddy before long."

The night was already well advanced when a plump of cold rain fell suddenly out of the darkness. Brackenbury paused under some trees, and as he did so he caught sight of a hansom cabman making him a sign that he was disengaged. The circumstance fell in so happily to the occasion that he at once raised his cane in answer, and had soon ensconced himself in the London gondola.

"Where to, sir?" asked the driver.

"Where you please," said Brackenbury.

And immediately, at a pace of surprising swiftness, the hansom drove off through the rain into a maze of villas. One villa was so like another, each with its front garden, and there was so little to distinguish the deserted lamp-lit streets and crescents through which the flying hansom took its way, that Brackenbury soon lost all idea of direction.

He would have been tempted to believe that the cabman was amusing himself by driving him round and round and in and out about a small quarter, but there was something business-like in the speed which convinced him of the contrary. The man had an object in view, he was hastening towards a definite end; and Brackenbury was at once astonished at the fellow's skill in picking a way through such a labyrinth, and a little concerned to imagine what was the occasion of his hurry. He had heard tales of strangers falling ill in London. Did the driver belong to some bloody and treacherous association? and was he himself being whirled to a murderous death?

The thought had scarcely presented itself, when the cab swung sharply round a corner and pulled up before the garden gate of a villa in a long and wide road. The house was brilliantly lighted up. Another hansom had just driven away, and Brackenbury could see a gentleman being admitted at the front door and received by several liveried servants. He was surprised that the cabman should have stopped so immediately in front of a house where a reception was being held; but he did not doubt it was the result of accident, and sat placidly smoking where he was, until he heard the trap thrown open over his head.

"Here we are, sir," said the driver.

"Here!" repeated Brackenbury. "Where?"

"You told me to take you where I pleased, sir," returned the man with a chuckle, "and here we are."

It struck Brackenbury that the voice was wonderfully smooth and courteous for a man in so inferior a position; he remembered the speed at which he had been driven; and now it occurred to him that the hansom was more luxuriously appointed than the common run of public conveyances.

"I must ask you to explain," said he. "Do you mean to turn me out into the rain? My good man, I suspect the choice is mine."

"The choice is certainly yours," replied the driver; "but when I tell you all, I believe I know how a gentleman of your figure will decide. There is a gentlemen's party in this house. I do not know whether the master be a stranger to London and without acquaintances of his own; or whether he is a man of odd notions. But certainly I was hired to kidnap single gentlemen in evening dress, as many as I pleased, but military officers by preference. You have simply to go in and say that Mr. Morris invited you."

"Are you Mr. Morris?" inquired the Lieutenant.

"Oh, no," replied the cabman. "Mr. Morris is the person of the house."

"It is not a common way of collecting guests," said Brackenbury: "but an eccentric man might very well indulge the whim without any intention to offend. And suppose that I refuse Mr. Morris's invitation," he went on, "what then?"

"My orders are to drive you back where I took you from," replied the man, "and set out to look for others up to midnight. Those who have no fancy for such an adventure, Mr. Morris said, were not the guests for him."

These words decided the Lieutenant on the spot.

"After all," he reflected, as he descended from the hansom, "I have not had long to wait for my adventure."

He had hardly found footing on the side-walk, and was still feeling in his pocket for the fare, when the cab swung about and drove off by the way it came at the former break-neck velocity. Brackenbury shouted after the man, who paid no heed, and continued to drive away; but the sound of his voice was overheard in the house, the door was again thrown open, emitting a flood of light upon the garden, and a servant ran down to meet him holding an umbrella.

"The cabman has been paid," observed the servant in a very civil tone; and he proceeded to escort Brackenbury along the path and up the steps. In the hall several other attendants relieved him of his hat, cane, and paletot, gave him a ticket with a number in return, and politely hurried him up a stair adorned with tropical flowers, to the door of an apartment on the first storey. Here a grave butler inquired his name, and announcing "Lieutenant Brackenbury Rich," ushered him into the drawing-room of the house.

A young man, slender and singularly handsome, came forward and greeted him with an air at once courtly and affectionate. Hundreds of candles, of the finest wax, lit up a room that was perfumed, like the staircase, with a profusion of rare and beautiful flowering shrubs. A side-table was loaded with tempting viands. Several servants went to and fro with fruits and goblets of champagne. The company was perhaps sixteen in number, all men, few beyond the prime of life, and with hardly an exception, of a dashing and capable exterior. They were divided into two groups, one about a roulette board, and the other surrounding a table at which one of their number held a bank of baccarat.

"I see," thought Brackenbury, "I am in a private gambling saloon, and the cabman was a tout."

His eye had embraced the details, and his mind formed the conclusion, while his host was still holding him by the hand; and to him his looks returned from this rapid survey. At a second view Mr. Morris surprised him still more than on the first. The easy elegance of his manners, the distinction, amiability, and courage that appeared upon his features, fitted very ill with the Lieutenant's preconceptions on the subject of the proprietor of a hell; and the tone of his conversation seemed to mark him out for a man of position and merit. Brackenbury found he had an instinctive liking for his entertainer; and though he chid himself for the weakness, he was unable to resist a sort of friendly attraction for Mr. Morris's person and character.

"I have heard of you, Lieutenant Rich," said Mr. Morris, lowering his tone; "and believe me I am gratified to make your acquaintance. Your looks accord with the reputation that has preceded you from India. And if you will forget for a while the irregularity of your presentation in my house, I shall feel it not only an honour, but a genuine pleasure besides. A man who makes a mouthful of barbarian cavaliers," he added with a laugh, "should not be appalled by a breach of etiquette, however serious."

And he led him towards the sideboard and pressed him to partake of some refreshment.

"Upon my word," the Lieutenant reflected, "this is one of the pleasantest fellows and, I do not doubt, one of the most agreeable societies in London."

He partook of some champagne, which he found excellent; and observing that many of the company were already smoking, he lit one of his own Manillas, and strolled up to the roulette board, where he sometimes made a stake and sometimes looked on smilingly on the fortune of others. It was while he was thus idling that he became aware of a sharp scrutiny to which the whole of the guests were subjected. Mr. Morris went here and there, ostensibly busied on hospitable concerns; but he had ever a shrewd glance at disposal; not a man of the party escaped his sudden, searching looks;

he took stock of the bearing of heavy losers, he valued the amount of the stakes, he paused behind couples who were deep in conversation; and, in a word, there was hardly a characteristic of anyone present but he seemed to catch and make a note of it. Brackenbury began to wonder if this were indeed a gambling hell: it had so much the air of a private inquisition. He followed Mr. Morris in all his movements; and although the man had a ready smile, he seemed to perceive, as it were under a mask, a haggard, careworn, and preoccupied spirit. The fellows around him laughed and made their game; but Brackenbury had lost interest in the guests.

"This Morris," thought he, "is no idler in the room. Some deep purpose inspires him; let it be mine to fathom it."

Now and then Mr. Morris would call one of his visitors aside; and after a brief colloquy in an ante-room, he would return alone, and the visitors in question reappeared no more. After a certain number of repetitions, this performance excited Brackenbury's curiosity to a high degree. He determined to be at the bottom of this minor mystery at once; and strolling into the ante-room, found a deep window recess concealed by curtains of the fashionable green. Here he hurriedly ensconced himself; nor had he to wait long before the sound of steps and voices drew near him from the principal apartment. Peering through the division, he saw Mr. Morris escorting a fat and ruddy personage, with somewhat the look of a commercial traveller, whom Brackenbury had already remarked for his coarse laugh and under-bred behaviour at the table. The pair halted immediately before the window, so that Brackenbury lost not a word of the following discourse: –

"I beg you a thousand pardons!" began Mr. Morris, with the most conciliatory manner; "and, if I appear rude, I am sure you will readily forgive me. In a place so great as London accidents must continually happen; and the best that we can hope is to remedy them with as small delay as possible. I will not deny that I fear you have made a mistake and honoured my poor house by inadvertence; for, to speak openly, I cannot at all remember your appearance. Let me put the question without unnecessary circumlocution – between gentlemen of honour a word will suffice – Under whose roof do you suppose yourself to be?"

"That of Mr. Morris," replied the other, with a prodigious display of confusion, which had been visibly growing upon him throughout the last few words.

"Mr. John or Mr. James Morris?" inquired the host.

"I really cannot tell you," returned the unfortunate guest. "I am not personally acquainted with the gentleman, any more than I am with yourself."

"I see," said Mr. Morris. "There is another person of the same name farther down the street; and I have no doubt the policeman will be able to supply you with his number. Believe me, I felicitate myself on the misunderstanding which has procured me the pleasure of your company for so long; and let me express a hope that we may meet again upon a more regular footing. Meantime, I would not for the world detain you longer from your friends. John," he added, raising his voice, "will you see that this gentleman finds his great-coat?"

And with the most agreeable air Mr. Morris escorted his visitor as far as the ante-room door, where he left him under conduct of the butler. As he passed the window, on his return to the drawing-room, Brackenbury could hear him utter a profound sigh, as though his mind was loaded with a great anxiety, and his nerves already fatigued with the task on which he was engaged.

For perhaps an hour the hansoms kept arriving with such frequency, that Mr. Morris had to receive a new guest for every old one that he sent away, and the company preserved its number undiminished. But towards the end of that time the arrivals grew few and far between, and at length ceased entirely, while the process of elimination was continued with unimpaired activity. The drawing-room began to look empty: the baccarat was discontinued for lack of a banker; more than one person said goodnight of his own accord, and was suffered to depart without expostulation; and in the meanwhile Mr. Morris redoubled in agreeable attentions to those who stayed behind. He went from group to group and from person to person with looks of the readiest sympathy and the most pertinent and pleasing talk; he was not so much like a host as like a hostess, and there was a feminine coquetry and condescension in his manner which charmed the hearts of all.

As the guests grew thinner, Lieutenant Rich strolled for a moment out of the drawing-room into the hall in quest of fresher air. But he had no sooner passed the threshold of the ante-chamber than he was brought to a dead halt by a discovery of the most surprising nature. The flowering shrubs had disappeared from the staircase; three large furniture waggons stood before the garden gate; the servants were busy dismantling the house upon all sides; and some of them had already donned their great-coats and were preparing to depart. It was like the end of a country ball, where everything has been supplied by contract. Brackenbury had indeed some matter for reflection. First, the guests, who were no real guests after all, had been dismissed; and now the servants, who could hardly be genuine servants, were actively dispersing.

"Was the whole establishment a sham?" he asked himself. "The mushroom of a single night which should disappear before morning?"

Watching a favourable opportunity, Brackenbury dashed upstairs to the highest regions of the house. It was as he had expected. He ran from room to room, and saw not a stick of furniture nor so much as a picture on the walls. Although the house had been painted and papered, it was not only uninhabited at present, but plainly had never been inhabited at all. The young officer remembered with astonishment its specious, settled, and hospitable air on his arrival. It was only at a prodigious cost that the imposture could have been carried out upon so great a scale.

Who, then, was Mr. Morris? What was his intention in thus playing the householder for a single night in the remote west of London? And why did he collect his visitors at hazard from the streets?

Brackenbury remembered that he had already delayed too long, and hastened to join the company. Many had left during his absence; and counting the Lieutenant and his host, there were not more than five persons in the drawing-room – recently so thronged. Mr. Morris greeted him, as he re-entered the apartment, with a smile, and immediately rose to his feet.

"It is now time, gentlemen," said he, "to explain my purpose in decoying you from your amusements. I trust you did not find the evening hang very dully on your hands; but my object, I will confess it, was not to entertain your leisure, but to help myself in an unfortunate necessity. You are all gentlemen," he continued, "your appearance does you that much justice, and I ask for no better security. Hence, I speak it without concealment, I ask you to render me a dangerous and delicate service; dangerous because you may run the hazard of your lives, and delicate because I must ask an absolute discretion upon all that you shall see or hear. From an utter stranger the request is almost comically extravagant; I am well aware of this; and I would add at once, if there be anyone present who has heard enough, if there be one among the party who recoils from a dangerous confidence and a piece of Quixotic devotion to he knows not whom – here is my hand ready, and I shall wish him goodnight and God-speed with all the sincerity in the world."

A very tall, black man, with a heavy stoop, immediately responded to this appeal.

"I commend your frankness, Sir," said he; "and, for my part, I go. I make no reflections; but I cannot deny that you fill me with suspicious thoughts. I go myself, as I say; and perhaps you will think I have no right to add words to my example."

"On the contrary," replied Mr. Morris, "I am obliged to you for all you say. It would be impossible to exaggerate the gravity of my proposal."

"Well, gentlemen, what do you say?" said the tall man, addressing the others. "We have had our evening's frolic; shall we all go homeward peaceably in a body? You will think well of my suggestion in the morning, when you see the sun again in innocence and safety."

The speaker pronounced the last words with an intonation which added to their force; and his face wore a singular expression, full of gravity and significance. Another of the company rose hastily, and, with some appearance of alarm, prepared to take his leave. There were only two who held their ground, Brackenbury and an old red-nosed cavalry Major; but these two preserved a nonchalant demeanour, and, beyond a look of intelligence which they rapidly exchanged, appeared entirely foreign to the discussion that had just been terminated.

Mr. Morris conducted the deserters as far as the door, which he closed upon their heels; then he turned round, disclosing a countenance of mingled relief and animation, and addressed the two officers as follows.

"I have chosen my men like Joshua in the Bible," said Mr. Morris, "and I now believe I have the pick of London. Your appearance pleased my hansom cabmen; then it delighted me; I have watched your behaviour in a strange company, and under the most unusual circumstances: I have studied how you played and how you bore your losses; lastly, I have put you to the test of a staggering announcement, and you received it like an invitation to dinner. It is not for nothing," he cried, "that I have been for years the companion and the pupil of the bravest and wisest potentate in Europe."

"At the affair of Bunderchang," observed the Major, "I asked for twelve volunteers, and every trooper in the ranks replied to my appeal. But a gaming party is not the same thing as a regiment under fire. You may be pleased, I suppose, to have found two, and two who will not fail you at a push. As for the pair who ran away, I count them among the most pitiful hounds I ever met with. Lieutenant Rich," he added, addressing Brackenbury, "I have heard much of you of late; and I cannot doubt but you have also heard of me. I am Major O'Rooke."

And the veteran tendered his hand, which was red and tremulous, to the young Lieutenant.

"Who has not?" answered Brackenbury.

"When this little matter is settled," said Mr. Morris, "you will think I have sufficiently rewarded you; for I could offer neither a more valuable service than to make him acquainted with the other."

"And now," said Major O'Rooke, "is it a duel?"

"A duel after a fashion," replied Mr. Morris, "a duel with unknown and dangerous enemies, and, as I gravely fear, a duel to the death. I must ask you," he continued, "to call me Morris no longer; call me, if you please, Hammersmith; my real name, as well as that of another person to whom I hope to present you before long, you will gratify me by not asking and not seeking to discover for yourselves. Three days ago the person of whom I speak disappeared suddenly from home; and, until this morning, I received no hint of his situation. You will fancy my alarm when I tell you that he is engaged upon a work of private justice. Bound by an unhappy oath, too lightly sworn, he finds it necessary, without the help of law, to rid the earth of an insidious and bloody villain. Already two of our friends, and one of them my own born brother, have perished in the enterprise. He himself, or I am much deceived, is taken in the same fatal toils. But at least he still lives and still hopes, as this billet sufficiently proves."

And the speaker, no other than Colonel Geraldine, proffered a letter, thus conceived:

Major Hammersmith, – On Wednesday, at 3 a.m., you will be admitted by the small door to the gardens of Rochester House, Regent's Park, by a man who is entirely in my interest. I must request you not to fail me by a second. Pray bring my case of swords, and, if you can find them, one or two gentlemen of conduct and discretion to whom my person is unknown. My name must not be used in this affair.
T. Godall.

"From his wisdom alone, if he had no other title," pursued Colonel Geraldine, when the others had each satisfied his curiosity, "my friend is a man whose directions should implicitly be followed. I need not tell you, therefore, that I have not so much as visited the neighbourhood of Rochester House; and that I am still as wholly in the dark as either of yourselves as to the nature of my friend's dilemma. I betook myself, as soon as I had received this order, to a furnishing contractor, and, in a few hours, the house in which we now are had assumed its late air of festival. My scheme was at least original; and I am far from regretting an action which has procured me the services of Major O'Rooke and Lieutenant Brackenbury Rich. But the servants in the street will have a strange awakening. The house which this evening was full of lights and visitors they will find uninhabited and for sale tomorrow morning. Thus even the most serious concerns," added the Colonel, "have a merry side."

"And let us add a merry ending," said Brackenbury.

The Colonel consulted his watch.

"It is now hard on two," he said. "We have an hour before us, and a swift cab is at the door. Tell me if I may count upon your help."

"During a long life," replied Major O'Rooke, "I never took back my hand from anything, nor so much as hedged a bet."

Brackenbury signified his readiness in the most becoming terms; and after they had drunk a glass or two of wine, the Colonel gave each of them a loaded revolver, and the three mounted into the cab and drove off for the address in question.

Rochester House was a magnificent residence on the banks of the canal. The large extent of the garden isolated it in an unusual degree from the annoyances of neighbourhood. It seemed the *parc aux cerfs* of some great nobleman or millionaire. As far as could be seen from the street, there was not a glimmer of light in any of the numerous windows of the mansion; and the place had a look of neglect, as though the master had been long from home.

The cab was discharged, and the three gentlemen were not long in discovering the small door, which was a sort of postern in a lane between two garden walls. It still wanted ten or fifteen minutes of the appointed time; the rain fell heavily, and the adventurers sheltered themselves below some pendant ivy, and spoke in low tones of the approaching trial.

Suddenly Geraldine raised his finger to command silence, and all three bent their hearing to the utmost. Through the continuous noise of the rain, the steps and voices of two men became audible from the other side of the wall; and, as they drew nearer, Brackenbury, whose sense of hearing was remarkably acute, could even distinguish some fragments of their talk.

"Is the grave dug?" asked one.

"It is," replied the other; "behind the laurel hedge. When the job is done, we can cover it with a pile of stakes."

The first speaker laughed, and the sound of his merriment was shocking to the listeners on the other side.

"In an hour from now," he said.

And by the sound of the steps it was obvious that the pair had separated, and were proceeding in contrary directions.

Almost immediately after the postern door was cautiously opened, a white face was protruded into the lane, and a hand was seen beckoning to the watchers. In dead silence the three passed the door, which was immediately locked behind them, and followed their guide through several garden alleys to the kitchen entrance of the house. A single candle burned in the great paved kitchen, which was destitute of the customary furniture; and as the party proceeded to ascend from thence by a flight of winding stairs, a prodigious noise of rats testified still more plainly to the dilapidation of the house.

Their conductor preceded them, carrying the candle. He was a lean man, much bent, but still agile; and he turned from time to time and admonished silence and caution by his gestures. Colonel Geraldine followed on his heels, the case of swords under one arm, and a pistol ready in the other. Brackenbury's heart beat thickly. He perceived that they were still in time; but he judged from the alacrity of the old man that the hour of action must be near at hand; and the circumstances of this adventure were so obscure and menacing, the place seemed so well chosen for the darkest acts, that an older man than Brackenbury might have been pardoned a measure of emotion as he closed the procession up the winding stair.

At the top the guide threw open a door and ushered the three officers before him into a small apartment, lighted by a smoky lamp and the glow of a modest fire. At the chimney corner sat a man in the early prime of life, and of a stout but courtly and commanding appearance. His attitude and expression were those of the most unmoved composure; he was smoking a cheroot with much enjoyment and deliberation, and on a table by his elbow stood a long glass of some effervescing beverage which diffused an agreeable odour through the room.

"Welcome," said he, extending his hand to Colonel Geraldine. "I knew I might count on your exactitude."

"On my devotion," replied the Colonel, with a bow.

"Present me to your friends," continued the first; and, when that ceremony had been performed, "I wish, gentlemen," he added, with the most exquisite affability, "that I could offer you a more cheerful programme; it is ungracious to inaugurate an acquaintance upon serious affairs; but the compulsion of events is stronger than the obligations of good-fellowship. I hope and believe you will be able to forgive me this unpleasant evening; and for men of your stamp it will be enough to know that you are conferring a considerable favour."

"Your Highness," said the Major, "must pardon my bluntness. I am unable to hide what I know. For some time back I have suspected Major Hammersmith, but Mr. Godall is unmistakable. To seek two men in London unacquainted with Prince Florizel of Bohemia was to ask too much at Fortune's hands."

"Prince Florizel!" cried Brackenbury in amazement.

And he gazed with the deepest interest on the features of the celebrated personage before him.

"I shall not lament the loss of my incognito," remarked the Prince, "for it enables me to thank you with the more authority. You would have done as much for Mr. Godall, I feel sure, as for the Prince of Bohemia; but the latter can perhaps do more for you. The gain is mine," he added, with a courteous gesture.

And the next moment he was conversing with the two officers about the Indian army and the native troops, a subject on which, as on all others, he had a remarkable fund of information and the soundest views.

There was something so striking in this man's attitude at a moment of deadly peril that Brackenbury was overcome with respectful admiration; nor was he less sensible to the charm of his conversation or the surprising amenity of his address. Every gesture, every intonation, was not only noble in itself, but seemed to ennoble the fortunate mortal for whom it was intended; and Brackenbury confessed to himself with enthusiasm that this was a sovereign for whom a brave man might thankfully lay down his life.

Many minutes had thus passed, when the person who had introduced them into the house, and who had sat ever since in a corner, and with his watch in his hand, arose and whispered a word into the Prince's ear.

"It is well, Dr. Noel," replied Florizel, aloud; and then addressing the others, "You will excuse me, gentlemen," he added, "if I have to leave you in the dark. The moment now approaches."

Dr. Noel extinguished the lamp. A faint, grey light, premonitory of the dawn, illuminated the window, but was not sufficient to illuminate the room; and when the Prince rose to his feet, it was impossible to distinguish his features or to make a guess at the nature of the emotion which obviously affected him as he spoke. He moved towards the door, and placed himself at one side of it in an attitude of the wariest attention.

"You will have the kindness," he said, "to maintain the strictest silence, and to conceal yourselves in the densest of the shadow."

The three officers and the physician hastened to obey, and for nearly ten minutes the only sound in Rochester House was occasioned by the excursions of the rats behind the woodwork. At the end of that period, a loud creak of a hinge broke in with surprising distinctness on the silence; and shortly after, the watchers could distinguish a slow and cautious tread approaching up the kitchen stair. At every second step the intruder seemed to pause and lend an ear, and during these intervals, which seemed of an incalculable duration, a profound disquiet possessed the spirit of the listeners. Dr. Noel, accustomed as he was to dangerous emotions, suffered an almost pitiful physical prostration; his breath whistled in his lungs, his teeth grated one upon another, and his joints cracked aloud as he nervously shifted his position.

At last a hand was laid upon the door, and the bolt shot back with a slight report. There followed another pause, during which Brackenbury could see the Prince draw himself together noiselessly as if for some unusual exertion. Then the door opened, letting in a little more of the light of the morning; and the figure of a man appeared upon the threshold and stood motionless. He was tall, and carried a knife in his hand. Even in the twilight they could see his upper teeth bare and glistening, for his mouth was open like that of a hound about to leap. The man had evidently been over the head in water but a minute or two before; and even while he stood there the drops kept falling from his wet clothes and pattered on the floor.

The next moment he crossed the threshold. There was a leap, a stifled cry, an instantaneous struggle; and before Colonel Geraldine could spring to his aid, the Prince held the man disarmed and helpless, by the shoulders.

"Dr. Noel," he said, "you will be so good as to re-light the lamp."

And relinquishing the charge of his prisoner to Geraldine and Brackenbury, he crossed the room and set his back against the chimney-piece. As soon as the lamp had kindled, the party beheld an unaccustomed sternness on the Prince's features. It was no longer Florizel, the careless gentleman; it was the Prince of Bohemia, justly incensed and full of deadly purpose, who now raised his head and addressed the captive President of the Suicide Club.

"President," he said, "you have laid your last snare, and your own feet are taken in it. The day is beginning; it is your last morning. You have just swum the Regent's Canal; it is your last bathe in this world. Your old accomplice, Dr. Noel, so far from betraying me, has delivered you into my hands for judgment. And the grave you had dug for me this afternoon shall serve, in God's almighty providence, to hide your own just doom from the curiosity of mankind. Kneel and pray, sir, if you have a mind that way; for your time is short, and God is weary of your iniquities."

The President made no answer either by word or sign; but continued to hang his head and gaze sullenly on the floor, as though he were conscious of the Prince's prolonged and unsparing regard.

"Gentlemen," continued Florizel, resuming the ordinary tone of his conversation, "this is a fellow who has long eluded me, but whom, thanks to Dr. Noel, I now have tightly by the heels. To tell the story of his misdeeds would occupy more time than we can now afford; but if the canal had contained nothing but the blood of his victims, I believe the wretch would have been no drier than you see him. Even in an affair of this sort I desire to preserve the forms of honour. But I make you the judges, gentlemen – this is more an execution than a duel and to give the rogue his choice of weapons would be to push too far a point of etiquette. I cannot afford to lose my life in such a business," he continued, unlocking the case of swords; "and as a pistol-bullet travels so often on the wings of chance, and skill and courage may fall by the most trembling marksman, I have decided, and I feel sure you will approve my determination, to put this question to the touch of swords."

When Brackenbury and Major O'Rooke, to whom these remarks were particularly addressed, had each intimated his approval, "Quick, sir," added Prince Florizel to the President, "choose a blade and do not keep me waiting; I have an impatience to be done with you for ever."

For the first time since he was captured and disarmed the President raised his head, and it was plain that he began instantly to pluck up courage.

"Is it to be stand up?" he asked eagerly, "and between you and me?"

"I mean so far to honour you," replied the Prince.

"Oh, come!" cried the President. "With a fair field, who knows how things may happen? I must add that I consider it handsome behaviour on your Highness's part; and if the worst comes to the worst I shall die by one of the most gallant gentlemen in Europe."

And the President, liberated by those who had detained him, stepped up to the table and began, with minute attention, to select a sword. He was highly elated, and seemed to feel no doubt that he should issue victorious from the contest. The spectators grew alarmed in the face of so entire a confidence, and adjured Prince Florizel to reconsider his intention.

"It is but a farce," he answered; "and I think I can promise you, gentlemen, that it will not be long a-playing."

"Your Highness will be careful not to over-reach," said Colonel Geraldine.

"Geraldine," returned the Prince, "did you ever know me fail in a debt of honour? I owe you this man's death, and you shall have it."

The President at last satisfied himself with one of the rapiers, and signified his readiness by a gesture that was not devoid of a rude nobility. The nearness of peril, and the sense of courage, even to this obnoxious villain, lent an air of manhood and a certain grace.

The Prince helped himself at random to a sword.

"Colonel Geraldine and Doctor Noel," he said, "will have the goodness to await me in this room. I wish no personal friend of mine to be involved in this transaction. Major O'Rooke, you are a man of some years and a settled reputation – let me recommend the President to your good graces. Lieutenant Rich will be so good as lend me his attentions: a young man cannot have too much experience in such affairs."

"Your Highness," replied Brackenbury, "it is an honour I shall prize extremely."

"It is well," returned Prince Florizel; "I shall hope to stand your friend in more important circumstances."

And so saying he led the way out of the apartment and down the kitchen stairs.

The two men who were thus left alone threw open the window and leaned out, straining every sense to catch an indication of the tragical events that were about to follow. The rain was now over; day had almost come, and the birds were piping in the shrubbery and on the forest trees of the garden. The Prince and his companions were visible for a moment as they followed an alley between two flowering thickets; but at the first corner a clump of foliage intervened, and they were again concealed from view. This was all that the Colonel and the Physician had an opportunity to see, and the garden was so vast, and the place of combat evidently so remote from the house, that not even the noise of sword-play reached their ears.

"He has taken him towards the grave," said Dr. Noel, with a shudder.

"God," cried the Colonel, "God defend the right!"

And they awaited the event in silence, the Doctor shaking with fear, the Colonel in an agony of sweat. Many minutes must have elapsed, the day was sensibly broader, and the birds were singing more heartily in the garden before a sound of returning footsteps recalled their glances towards the door. It was the Prince and the two Indian officers who entered. God had defended the right.

"I am ashamed of my emotion," said Prince Florizel; "I feel it is a weakness unworthy of my station, but the continued existence of that hound of hell had begun to prey upon me like a disease, and his death has more refreshed me than a night of slumber. Look, Geraldine," he continued, throwing his sword upon the floor, "there is the blood of the man who killed your brother. It should be a welcome sight. And yet," he added, "see how strangely we men are made! my revenge is not yet five minutes old, and already I am beginning to ask myself if even revenge be attainable on this precarious stage of life. The ill he did, who can undo it? The career in which he amassed a huge fortune (for the house itself in which we stand belonged to him) – that career is now a part of the destiny of mankind for ever; and I might weary myself making thrusts in carte until the crack of judgment, and Geraldine's brother would be none the less dead, and a thousand other innocent persons would be none the less dishonoured and debauched! The existence of a man is so small a thing to take, so mighty a thing to employ! Alas!" he cried, "is there anything in life so disenchanting as attainment?"

"God's justice has been done," replied the Doctor. "So much I behold. The lesson, your Highness, has been a cruel one for me; and I await my own turn with deadly apprehension."

"What was I saying?" cried the Prince. "I have punished, and here is the man beside us who can help me to undo. Ah, Dr. Noel! you and I have before us many a day of hard and honourable toil; and perhaps, before we have none, you may have more than redeemed your early errors."

"And in the meantime," said the Doctor, "let me go and bury my oldest friend."

If you enjoyed this, you might also like...
Markheim, see page 238
That Brute Simmons, see page 111

All Sorts and Conditions of Men
Chapter XII

Walter Besant

Sunday at the East End

SUNDAY MORNING in and about the Whitechapel and Mile End roads Angela discovered to be a time of peculiar interest. The closing of the shops adds to the dignity of the broad thoroughfares, because it hides so many disagreeable and even humiliating things. But it by no means puts a stop to traffic, which is conducted with an ostentatious disregard of the Fourth Commandment or Christian custom. At one end, the city end, is Houndsditch, crowded with men who come to buy and sell; and while the bells of St. Botolph call upon the faithful with a clanging and clashing which ring like a cry of despair, the footpath is filled with the busy loungers, who have long since ceased to regard the invitation as having anything at all to do with them.

Strange and wonderful result of the gathering of men in great cities! It is not a French, or an English, or a German, or an American result – it is universal. In every great city of the world, below a certain level, there is no religion – men have grown dead to their higher instincts; they no longer feel the possibilities of humanity; faith brings to them no more the evidence of things unseen. They are crowded together, so that they have ceased to feel their individuality. The crowd is eternal – they are part of that eternity; if one drops out, he is not missed; nobody considers that it will be his own turn some day so to drop out. Life is nothing for ever and ever, but work in the week with as much beer and tobacco as the money will run to, and loafing on Sundays with more beer and tobacco. This, my friends, is a truly astonishing thing, and a thing unknown until this century. Perhaps, however, in ancient Rome the people had ceased to believe in their gods; perhaps, in Babylon, the sacred bricks were kicked about by the unthinking mob; perhaps, in every great city, the same loss of individual manhood may be found.

It was on a Sunday morning in August that Angela took a little journey of exploration, accompanied by the young workman who was her companion in these excursions. He led her into Houndsditch and the Minories, where she had the pleasure of inspecting the great mercantile interest of old clothes, and of gazing upon such as buy and sell therein. Then she turned her face northward, and entered upon a journey which twenty years ago would have been full of peril, and is now, to one who loves his fellow-man, full of interest.

The great boulevard of the East was thronged with the class of men who keep the Sabbath in holy laziness with tobacco. Some of them lounge, some talk, some listen, all have pipes in their mouths. Here was a circle gathered round a man who was waving his arms and shouting. He was an Apostle of Temperance; behind him stood a few of his private friends to act as a claque. The listeners seemed amused but not convinced. "They will probably," said Harry, "enjoy their dinner beer quite as much as if they had not heard this sermon." Another circle was gathered round a man in a cart, who had a flaming red flag to support him. He belonged, the flag told the world, to the Tower Hamlets Magna Charta Association. What he said was listened to with the same languid curiosity and tepid amusement. Angela stopped a moment to hear what he had to say. He was detailing, with immense energy, the particulars of some awful act of injustice committed upon a friend unknown, who got six months. The law of England is always trampling upon some innocent victim, according to this sympathizer with virtue. The working-men have heard it all before, and they continue to smoke their pipes, their blood not quickened by a single beat. The ear of the people is accustomed to vehemence; the case must be put strongly before it will listen at all; and listening, as most brawlers discover, is not conviction.

Next to the Magna Charta brethren a cheap-jack had placed his cart. He drove a roaring trade in two-penn'orths, which, out of compliment to a day which should be devoted to good works, consisted each of a bottle of sarsaparilla, which he called "sassaple," and a box of pills. Next to him the costers stood beside their carts loaded with cheap ices, ginger-beer, and lemonade – to show that there was no deception, a great glass jar stood upon each cart with actual undeniable slices of lemon floating in water and a lump of ice upon the top; there were also piles of plums, plums without end, early August apples, and windfall pears; also sweet things in foot-long lumps sticky and gruesome to look upon; Brazil nuts, also a favorite article of commerce in certain circles, though not often met with at the tables of the luxurious; late oranges, more plums, many more plums, plums in enormous quantities; and periwinkles, which last all the year round, with whelks and vinegar, and the toothsome shrimp. Then there came another circle, and in the midst stood a young man with long fair hair and large blue eyes. He was preaching the Gospel, as he understood it; his face was the face of an enthusiast: a little solitude, a little meditation among the mountains, would have made this man a seer of visions and a dreamer of dreams. He was not ridiculous, though his grammar was defective and his pronunciation had the cockney twang and his aspirates were wanting: nothing is ridiculous that is in earnest. On the right of the street they had passed the headquarters of the Salvation Army; the brave warriors were now in full blast, and the fighting, "knee-drill," singing, and storming of the enemy's fort were at their highest and most enjoyable point; Angela looked in and found an immense hall crammed with people who came to fight, or look on, to scoff, or gaze. Higher up, on the left, stands a rival in red-hot religion, the Hall of the Jubilee Singers, where another vast crowd was worshipping, exhorting, and singing.

"There seems," said Angela, "to be too much exhorting; can they not sit down somewhere in quiet for praise and prayer?"

"We working-people," replied her companion, "like everything loud and strong. If we are persuaded to take a side, we want to be always fighting on that side."

Streams of people passed them, lounging or walking with a steady purpose. The former were the indifferent and the callous, the hardened and the stupid, men to whom preachers and orators appealed in vain; to whom Peter the Hermit might have bawled himself hoarse, and Bernard would have thrown all his eloquence away; they smoked short pipes, with their hands in their pockets, and looked good-tempered; with them were boys, also smoking short pipes, with their hands in their pockets. Those who walked were young men dressed in long frock-coats of a shiny and lustrous black, who carried Bibles and prayer-books with some ostentation. They were on their way to church; with them were their sisters, for the most part well-dressed, quiet girls, to whom the noise and the crowds were a part of life – a thing not to be avoided, hardly felt as a trouble.

"I am always getting a new sensation," said Angela.

"What is the last?"

"I have just realized that there are thousands and thousands of people who never, all their lives, get to a place where they can be quiet. Always noise, always crowds, always buying and selling."

"Here, at least," said Harry, "there is no noise."

They were at the wicket-gate of the Trinity Almshouse.

"What do you think, Miss Kennedy?"

"It is a haven of rest," she replied, thinking of a certain picture. "Let us, too, seek peace awhile."

It was just eleven o'clock, and the beadsmen were going to their chapel. They entered the square, and joined the old men in their weekly service. Angela discovered, to her disappointment, that the splendid flight of steps leading to the magnificent portal was a dummy, because the real entrance to the chapel was a lowly door beneath the stone steps, suited, Mr. Bunker would have said, to the humble condition of the moneyless.

It is a plain chapel, with a small organ in the corner, a tiny altar, and over the altar the ten commandments in a black wood frame – rules of life for those whose life is well-nigh done – and a pulpit, which serves for reading the service as well as delivering the sermon. The congregation consisted of about thirty of the almsmen, with about half as many old ladies; and Angela wondered why these old ladies were all dressed in black, and all wore crape. Perhaps they desired by the use of this material to symbolize mourning for the loss of opportunities for making money; or for the days of beauty and courtship, or for children dead and gone, or to mark the humility which becomes an inmate, or to do honor to the day which is still revered by many Englishwomen as a day of humiliation and rebuke, or in the belief that crape confers dignity. We know not, we know nothing; the love which women bear for crape is a mystery; man can but speculate idly on their ways. We are like the philosopher picking up pebbles by the seaside. Among the old people sat Nelly Sorensen, a flower of youth and loveliness, in her simple black dress, and her light hair breaking out beneath her bonnet. The Catholics believe that no church is complete without a bone of some dead saint or beatified person. Angela made up her mind, on the spot, that no act of public worship is complete without the assistance of youth as well as of age.

The men were all dressed alike in blue coats and brass buttons, the uniform of the place; they seemed all, with the exception of one who was battered by time, and was fain to sit while the rest stood, to be of the same age, and that might be anything between a hearty sixty-five and a vigorous eighty. After the manner of sailors, they were all exact in the performance of their share in public worship, following the prayers in the book and the lessons in the Bible. When the time came for listening they straightened themselves out, in an attitude comfortable for listening. The Scotch elder assumes, during the sermon, the air of a hostile critic; the face of the British rustic becomes vacant; the eyes of the ordinary listener in church show that his thoughts are far away; but the expression of a sailor's face, while he is performing the duty – part of the day's duty – of listening to the sermon, shows respectful attention, although he may have heard it all before.

Angela did not listen much to the sermon: she was thinking of the old men for whom that sermon was prepared. There was a fresh color upon their faces, as if it was not so very long since their cheeks had been fanned by the strong sea-breeze; their eyes were clear, they possessed the bearing which comes of the habit of command, and they carried themselves as if they were not ashamed of their poverty. Now Bunker, Angela reflected, would have been very much ashamed, and would have hung his head in shame. But then Bunker was one of the nimble-footed hunters after money, while these ignoble persons had contented themselves with the simple and slavish record of duty done.

The service over, they were joined by Captain Sorensen and his daughter, and for half an hour walked in the quiet court behind the church, in peaceful converse. Angela walked with the old man, and Nelly with the young man. It matters little what they talked about, but it was something good, because when the Captain went home to his dinner he kissed his daughter, and said it seemed to him that it was the best day's work he ever did when he let her go to Miss Kennedy.

In the evening Angela made another journey of exploration with the same escort. They passed down Stepney Green, and plunged among the labyrinth of streets lying between the Mile End Road and the Thames. It is as unlovely a collection of houses as may be found anywhere, always excepting Hoxton, which may fairly be considered the Queen of Unloveliness. The houses in this part are small, and they are almost all of one pattern. There is no green thing to be seen; no one plants trees, there seem to be no gardens; no flowers are in the windows; there is no brightness of paint or of clean windows; there is nothing of joy, nothing to gladden the eye.

"Think," said Harry, almost in a whisper, as if in homage to the Powers of Dirt and Dreariness, "think what this people could be made if we could only carry out your scheme of the Palace of Delight."

"We could make them discontented, at least," said Angela. "Discontent must come before reform."

"We should leave them to reform themselves," said Harry. "The mistake of philanthropists is to think that they can do for people what can only be done by the people. As you said this morning, there is too much exhorting."

Presently they struck out of a street rather more dreary than its neighbors, and found themselves in a broad road with a great church.

"This is Limehouse Church," said Harry. "All round you are sailors. There is East India Dock Road. Here is West India Dock Road. There is the Foreign Sailors' Home; and we will go no farther, if you please, because the streets are all full, you perceive, of the foreign sailors and the English sailors and the sailors' friends."

Angela had seen enough of the sailors. They turned back. Harry led her through another labyrinth into another broad street, also crowded with sailors.

"This is Shadwell," said her guide; "and if there is anything in Shadwell to interest you, I do not know what it is. Survey Shadwell!"

Angela looked up the street and down the street; there was nothing for the eye in search of the beautiful or the picturesque to rest upon. But a great bawling of rough voices came from a great tent stuck up, oddly, beside the road. A white canvas sheet with black letters proclaimed this as the place of worship of the "Happy Gypsies." They were holding their Sunday Function.

"More exhorting!" said Angela.

"Now, this," he said, as they walked along, "is a more interesting place. It used to be called Ratcliffe Highway, and had the reputation of being the wickedest place in London. I dare say it was all brag, and that really it was not much worse than its neighbors."

It is a distinctly squalid street, that now called St. George's-in-the-East. But it has its points; it is picturesque, like a good many dirty places; the people are good-tempered, though they do not wash their faces even on Sundays. They have quite left off knocking down, picking pockets, kicking, and robbing the harmless stranger; they are advancing slowly toward civilization.

"Come this way," said Harry.

He passed through a narrow passage, and led the way into a place at the sight of which Angela was fain to cry out in surprise.

In it was nothing less than a fair and gracious garden planted with flowers, and these in the soft August sunshine showed sweet and lovely. The beds were well kept; the walks were of asphalt; there were seats set about, and on them old women and old men sat basking in the evening sun. The young men and maidens walked along the paths – an Arcadian scene.

"This little strip of Eden," said Harry, "was cut out of the old church-yard."

The rest of the church-yard was divided from the garden by a railing, and round the wall were the tombstones of the departed obscure. From the church itself was heard the rolling of the organ and the soft singing of a hymn.

"This," said Angela, "is better than exhortation. A garden for meditation and the church for prayer. I like this place better than the Whitechapel Road."

"I will show you a more quiet place still," said her guide. They walked a little way farther down the main street; then he turned into a narrow street on the north, and Angela found herself in a square of clean houses round an inclosure of grass. Within the inclosure was a chapel, and tombs were dotted on the grass.

They went into the chapel, a plain edifice of the Georgian kind with round windows, and the evening sun shone through the window in the west. The high pews were occupied by a congregation of forty or fifty, all men. They all had light-brown hair, and as they turned round to look at the new-comers, Angela saw that they all had blue eyes. The preacher, who wore a black gown and bands, was similarly provided as to hair and eyes. He preached in a foreign tongue, and as it is difficult to be edified by a sermon not in one's native speech, they shortly went out again. They were followed by the verger, who seemed not indisposed to break the monotony of the service by a few minutes' walk.

He talked English imperfectly, but he told them that it was the church of the Swedes. Angela asked if they were all sailors. He said, with some seeming contempt for sailors, that only a few of them were sailors. She then said that she supposed they were people engaged in trade. He shook his head again, and informed her with a mysterious air that many of the Swedish nobility lived in that neighborhood. After this they came away, for fear of greater surprises.

They followed St. George's-in-the-East to the end of the street. Then they turned to the right, and passed through a straight and quite ignoble road leading north. It is a street greatly affected by Germans. German names are over every shop and on every brass plate. They come hither, these honest Germans, because to get good work in London is better than going after it to New York or Philadelphia, and nearer home. In the second generation their names will be Anglicized, and their children will have become rich London merchants, and very likely Cabinet ministers. They have their churches, too, the Reformed and the Lutheran, with nothing to choose between them on the score of ugliness.

"Let us get home," said Angela; "I have seen enough."

"It is the joylessness of the life," she explained, "the ignorant, contented joylessness, which weighs upon one. And there is so much of it. Surely there is no other city in the world which is so utterly without joy as this East London."

"No," said Harry, "there is not in the whole world a city so devoid of pleasant things. They do not know how to be happy. They are like your work-girls when you told them to dance."

"Look!" she cried, "what is that?"

There was a hoarse roar of many voices from a court leading out of the main road; the roar became louder; Harry drew the girl aside as a mob of men and boys and women rushed headlong out of the place. It was not a fight apparently, yet there was beating with sticks and kicking. For those who were beaten did not strike back in return. After a little the beaters and kickers desisted, and returned to their court as to a stronghold whose rights they had vindicated.

Those who had been beaten were a band of about a dozen, men and women. The women's shawls were hanging in tatters, and they had lost their bonnets. The men were without hats, and their coats were grievously torn. There was a thing among them which had been a banner, but the pole was broken and the flag was dragged in the dirt and smirched.

One of them who, seemed to be the leader – he wore a uniform coat something like a volunteer's coat – stepped to the front and called upon them all to form. Then with a loud voice he led off a hymn, in which all joined as they marched down the street.

He was hatless, and his cheek was bleeding from an open wound. Yet he looked undaunted, and his hymn was a song of triumph. A wild-set-up young fellow with thick black hair and black beard, but pale cheeks. His forehead was square and firm; his eyes were black and fierce.

"Good heavens!" cried Harry. "It is my cousin Tom, captain in the Salvation Army. And that, I suppose, is his regiment. Well, if standing still to be kicked means a victory, they have scored one to-night."

The pavement was even more crowded than in the morning. The political agitators bawled more fiercely than in the forenoon to their circle of apathetic listeners; the preachers exhorted the unwilling more fervently to embrace the faith. Cheap-jacks was dispensing more volubly his two penn'orths of "sassaple." The workmen lounged along, with their pipes in their mouths, more lazily than in the morning. The only difference was that the shop-boys were now added to the crowd, every lad with a "twopenny smoke" between his lips; and that the throng was increased by those who were going home from church.

"Let us, too, go home," said Angela; "there is too much humanity here; we shall lose ourselves among the crowd."

If you enjoyed this, you might also like...
The Watcher, see page 276
The Death of the Lion, see page 449

The Day of Silence

George Gissing

FOR A WEEK the mid-day thermometer had marked eighty or more in the shade. Golden weather for those who could lie and watch the lazy breakers on a rocky shore, or tread the turf of deep woodland, or drink from the cold stream on some mountain side. But the by-ways of Southwark languished for a cloud upon the sun, for a cooling shower, or a breath from its old enemy, the east. The cry of fretful children sounded ceaselessly. Every window was wide open; women who had nothing to do lounged in the dusk of doorways and in arched passages, their money all gone in visits to the public-house. Ice-cream men found business at a standstill; it was Friday, and the youngsters ha'pence had long ago come to an end. Labourers who depended upon casual employment chose to sleep through the thirsty hours rather than go in search of jobs; a crust of bread served them for a meal. They lay about in the shadowed spots, shirt and trousers their only costume, their shaggy heads in every conceivable attitude of repose.

Where the sun fell the pavement burned like an oven floor. An evil smell hung about the butchers' and the fish shops. A public-house poisoned a whole street with alcoholic fumes; from sewer-grates rose a miasma that caught the breath. People who bought butter from the little dealers had to carry it away in a saucer, covered with a piece of paper, which in a few moments turned oily dark. Rotting fruit, flung out by costermongers, offered a dire regale to little ragamuffins prowling like the cats and dogs. Babies' bottles were choked with thick-curdling milk, and sweets melted in grimy little hands.

Among the children playing in a court deep down by Southwark Bridge was one boy, of about seven years old, who looked healthier and sweeter than most of his companions. The shirt he wore had been washed a week ago, and rents in it had obeyed the needle. His mother-made braces supported a pair of trousers cut short between the knee and ankle, evidently shaped out of a man's garment. Stockings he dispensed with; but his boots were new and strong. Though he amused himself vigorously, he seemed to keep cool; his curly hair was not matted with perspiration, like that of the other youngsters; the open shirt – in this time of holiday coat and waistcoat were put away to be in a good condition when school began again – showed a body not ill-nourished, and his legs were of sturdy growth. A shouting, laughing, altogether noisy little chap. When his shrill voice rang out, it gave his playmates the word of command; he was ready, too, with his fists when occasion offered. You should have seen him standing with arms akimbo, legs apart, his round little head thrown back and the brown eyes glistening in merriment. Billy Burden, they called him. He had neither brother nor sister – a fortunate thing, as it enabled his parents to give him more of their love and their attention than would have been possible if other mouths had clamoured for sustenance. Mrs. Burden was very proud of him, and all the more decent women in the court regarded Billy with affectionate admiration. True, he had to be kept in order now and then, when he lost his temper and began to punch the heads of boys several years older than himself; but his frank, winsome face soon overcame the anger of grown-up people.

His father, Solomon Burden by name, worked pretty regularly at a wharf on the Middlesex side, and sometimes earned as much as a pound a week. Having no baby to look after, his mother got a turn of work as often as possible, chiefly at warehouse-cleaning and the like. She could trust little Billy to go to school and come home at the right time; but holidays, when he had to spend the whole day out-of-doors, caused her some anxiety, for the child liked to be off and away on long explorations of unknown country – into Lambeth, or across the river to the great London streets, no distance tiring him. Her one fear was lest he should be run over. Today he had promised to keep well within reach of home, and did so. At Mrs. Burden's return from a job in Waterloo Road he was found fast asleep on the landing. She bent over him, and muttered words of tenderness as she wiped his dirty face with her apron.

Of course, they had only one room – an attic just large enough to hold a bed, a table, and Billy's little mattress down on the floor in a corner. Their housekeeping was of the simplest: a shelf of crockery, two saucepans, and a frying-pan supplied Mrs. Burden with all she needed for the preparation of meals. Apparel was kept in a box under the bed, where also was the washing-basin. Up to a year ago they had had a chest of drawers; but the hard winter had obliged them to part with this.

When Mrs. Burden unlocked and opened the door, the air within was so oppressive that she stood for a moment and drew a deep breath. The sound of the key wakened Billy, who sprang up joyfully.

"Ain't it been 'ot again, mummy!" the boy exclaimed. "There was a 'bus-horse fell dead. Ben Wilkins seen it!"

"I a'most feel as if I could drop myself," she answered, sinking upon the bed. "There ain't no hair to breathe: I wish we wasn't under the roof."

She stood up again and felt the ceiling – it was some six inches above her head.

"My gracious alive! It's fair bakin'."

"Let me feel – let me feel!"

She lifted him in her arms, and Billy proved for himself that the plaster of the ceiling was decidedly warm. Nevertheless, sticks had to be lighted to boil the kettle. Father might come home any moment, and he liked his cup of tea.

As she worked about, the woman now and then pressed a hand to her left side, and seemed to breathe with difficulty. Sweat-drops hung thick upon her face, which was the colour of dough. On going downstairs to draw water for the kettle she took a quart jug, and after filling this she drank almost the whole of it in one long draught. It made her perspire still more freely; moisture streamed from her forehead as she returned to the upper story, and on arriving she was obliged to seat herself.

"Do you feel bad, mummy?" asked the child, who was accustomed to these failings of strength when his mother came home from a day's work.

"I do, Billy, hawful bad; but it'll go in a minute. Put the kittle on – there's a good boy."

She was a woman of active habits, in her way a good housewife, loving moderate cleanliness and a home in order. Naturally, her clothing was coarse and begrimed; she did the coarsest and grimiest of work. Her sandy hair had thinned of late; it began to show the scalp in places. There was always a look of pain on her features, and her eyes were either very glassy or very dull. For thirty years – that is, since she was ten years old – struggle with poverty had been the law of her life, and she remained victorious; there was always a loaf in the house, always an ounce of tea; her child had never asked in vain for the food demanded by his hearty appetite. She did not drink; she kept a guard upon her tongue in the matter of base language; esteemed comely by her equals, she had no irregularity of behaviour wherewith to reproach herself. Often enough at variance with her husband, she yet loved him; and Billy she loved more.

About seven o'clock the father came home; he clumped heavily up the stairs, bent his head to pass the doorway, and uttered a good-natured growl as he saw the table ready for him.

"Well, Bill, bwoy, can you keep warm?"

"Sh' think so," the child answered. "Mummy's bad again with the 'eat. There ain't no air in this bloomin' 'ouse."

"Kick a 'ole in the roof, old chap!"

"Wish I could!"

Solomon flung off his coat, and turned up the sleeves of his shirt. The basin, full of water, awaited him; he thrust his great head into it and made a slop over the floor. Thereat Mrs. Burden first looked, then spoke wrathfully. As his habit was, her husband retorted, and for a few minutes they wrangled. But it was without bitterness, without vile abuse. Domestic calm as understood by the people who have a whole house to themselves is impossible in a Southwark garret; Burden and his wife were regarded by the neighbours, and rightly, as an exemplary pair; they never came to blows, never to curses, and neither of them had ever been known to make a scene in public.

Burden had a loud, deep voice; whether he spoke angrily or gently, he could be heard all over the house and out in the court. Impossible for the family to discuss anything in private. But, like all their neighbours, they accepted such a state of things as a matter of course. Everybody knew all about everybody else; the wonder was when nothing disgraceful came to listening ears.

"Say, Bill," remarked the man, when he had at length sat quietly down to his tea, "how would you like to go in a boat tomorrow afternoon?"

"Shouldn't I just!"

"Old Four-arf is goin' to have a swim," Burden explained to his wife; "wants me to go with him; and I feel it 'ud do me good, weather like this. Bunker's promised him a boat at Blackfriars Bridge. Shall I take the kid?"

Mrs. Burden looked uneasy, and answered sharply.

"What's the good o' asking when you've spoke of it before the boy?"

"Well, why shouldn't I take him? You might come along, too: only we're a-goin' to strip up beyond Chelsea."

This was kindness, and it pacified the wife.

"I couldn't go before six," she said.

"What's the job?"

"Orfices near St. Bride's – Mrs. Robins wants 'elp; she sent her Sally over to me this mornin'. It'll be an all-day job; eighteen-pence for me."

"Bloomin' little, too. You ain't fit for it this weather."

"I'm all right!"

"No, you ain't. Billy just said as you'd been took bad, an' I can see it in yer eyes. Have a day at 'ome, mother."

"Don't you go fidgetin' about me. Take Billy, if you like; but just be careful. No puttin' of him into the water."

"Tain't likely."

"Cawn't I bathe, dad?" asked Billy.

"Course you cawn't. We're going to swim in the middle of the river, Jem Pollock an' me – where it's hawful deep, deep enough to drownd you fifty times over."

"The other boys go bathin'," Billy remonstrated.

"Dessay they do," cried his mother, "but you won't – so you know! If you want for to bathe, arst Mrs. Crowther to lend you her washin'-tub, and fill it with water. That won't do you no 'arm, and I don't mind if you make a bit of a splash, s'long as you don't wet the bed through."

After all it was a home, a nesting place of human affections – this attic in which the occupants had scarcely room to take half-a-dozen steps. Father, mother, and child, despite the severing tendency of circumstances, clung together about this poor hearth, the centre of their world. In the strength of ignorance, they were proof against envy; their imaginations had never played about the fact of social superiority, which, indeed, they but dimly understood. Burden and his wife would have been glad, now and then, of some addition to the weekly income; beyond that they never aspired. Billy, when he had passed the prescribed grades of school, would begin to earn money: it did not much matter how: only let the means be honest. To that the parents looked forward with anticipation of pride. Billy's first wages! It would warm their hearts to see the coins clutched in his solid little fist. For this was he born, to develop thews and earn wages.

It did not enter into their conception of domestic happiness to spend the evening at home, sitting and talking together. They had very little to say: their attachment was not vocal. Besides, the stifling heat of the garret made it impossible to rest here until the sun had long set. So, when tea was finished, Billy ran down again into the street to mingle with his shouting comrades; Mrs. Burden found a seat on the doorstep, where she dozed awhile, and then chatted with bare-armed women; and Solomon sauntered forth for his wonted stroll 'round the 'ouses.' At ten o'clock the mother took a jug to the neighbouring beerhouse and returned with a 'pot' – that is to say, a quart – of 'four ale', which she and Solomon drank for supper. The lad was lying sound asleep on his mattress, naked but for the thin shirt which he wore day and night; the weather made bedclothes a superfluity.

Saturday morning showed a change of sky. There were clouds about, and a wind blew as if for rain. At half-past six Solomon was ready to start for work. Billy still slept, and the parents subdued their voices lest they should wake him.

"If it's wet," said Mrs. Burden, "you won't go on the river – will you?"

"Not if it's thorough wet. Leave the key with Billy, and if we go you'll find it on the top of the door."

He set forth as usual: as he had done any day these eight years, since their marriage. Word of parting seemed unnecessary. He just glanced round the room, and with bent head passed on to the landing. His wife did not look after him; she was cutting bread and butter for Billy. Solomon thought only of the pleasant fact that his labour that day ended at one o'clock, and that in the afternoon he would perhaps have a swim. Mrs. Burden, who had suffered a broken night, looked forward with dreary doggedness to ten hours or more of scrubbing and cleaning, which would bring in eighteen-pence. And little Billy slept the sleep of healthy childhood.

By mid-day the clouds had passed, but the heat of the sun was tempered; broad light and soft western breeze made the perfection of English summer. This Saturday was one of the golden days of a year to be long remembered.

When he came home from work, Solomon found Billy awaiting him, all eagerness. They went up to the attic, and ate some dinner which Burden had brought in his pocket – two-pennyworth of fried fish and potatoes, followed by bread and cheese. A visit to the public-house, where Billy drank from his father's pewter, and they were ready to start for Blackfriars Bridge, where Solomon's friend, Jem Pollock – affectionately known by the name of his favourite liquor, 'Four-half' – had the use of a boat belonging to one Thomas Bunker, a lighterman. It was not one of the nimble skiffs in which persons of a higher class take their pleasure upon the Thames, but an ungainly old tub, propelled by heavy oars. Solomon and his friend, of course, knew that the tide would help them upwards; it wanted about an hour to flood. He was a jovial fellow, this Jem Pollock, unmarried, and less orderly in his ways of life than Sol Burden; his nickname did him no injustice, for whenever he had money he drank. A kindly temper saved him from the worst results of this bibulous habit; after a few quarts of ale he was at his best, and if he took more it merely sent him to sleep. When Solomon and Billy found him on the stairs at the south side of the bridge he had just taken his third pint since dinner, and his red, pimply face beamed with contentment.

"Come along there!" he roared from below. "Brought that bloomin' big son of yours for ballast, Sol?"

"He can steer, can Bill."

"He won't 'ave a chawnce. There ain't no bloomin' rudder on this old ship."

Billy stepped into the boat, and his father followed; but their friend was not yet ready to depart. The cause of his delay appeared when a lad came running down the stairs with a big jar and a tin mug.

"You don't s'ppose I'm a-goin' without a drop o' refreshment," Pollock remarked. "It's water, this is; the best supplied by the Lambeth Water Company. I've took the pledge."

This primitive facetiousness helped them merrily off. Billy sat in the stern; the men each took an oar; they were soon making good way towards Westminster.

Their progress was noisy: without noise they could not have enjoyed themselves. The men's shouts and Billy's shrill pipe were audible on either bank. Opposite the Houses of Parliament they exchanged abusive pleasantries with two fellows on a barge; bellowing was kept up until the whole distance between Lambeth Bridge and that of Westminster taxed their lungs. At Vauxhall Jem Pollock uncorked his jar and poured out a mugful of tawny ale, vastly to the boy's delight, for Billy had persisted in declining to believe that the vessel contained mere water. All drank. Solomon refused to let Billy have more than half a mug, to the scorn of Jem Pollock, who maintained that four-ale never did anything but good to man, woman, or babe.

At Chelsea the jar was again opened. This time Pollock drank an indefinite number of mugs, and Solomon all but quarrelled with him for continuing to tempt Billy. The child had swallowed at least a pint, and began to show the effect of it: he lay back in the stern, laughing to himself, his eyes fixed on the blue sky.

A sky such as London rarely knows: of exquisite purity – a limpid sapphire, streaked about the horizon with creamy cloudlets. All the smoke of the city was borne eastward; the zenith shone translucent as over woodland solitudes. The torrid beams of the past week were forgotten; a mild and soothing splendour summoned mortals to come forth into the ways of summer and be glad.

With the last impulse of the flowing tide they reached the broad water beyond Battersea Bridge, where Solomon began to prepare himself for a delicious plunge. The boat could not be left to Billy alone; Pollock was content to wait until Burden had had the first swim. Quickly stripped, the big-limbed fellow stood where his boy had been sitting, and of a sudden leapt headlong. Billy yelled with delight at the great splash, and yelled again triumphantly when his father's head rose to the surface. Solomon was a fair swimmer, but did not pretend to great achievements; he struck out in the upward direction and swam for about a quarter of a mile, the boat keeping along with him; then he was glad to catch hold of the stern. Pollock began to fling off his clothes.

"My turn, old pal!" he shouted. "Tumble in, an' let's have a feel of the coolness."

Solomon got into the boat, and sat naked at one of the oars, Billy managing the other. Five minutes saw Jem back again: he had wallowed rather alarmingly, a result of the gallon or two of ale which freighted him. Then Burden took another plunge. When he had swum to a little distance, Pollock whispered to the boy:

"Like to have a dip, Bill?"

"Shouldn't I just! But I can't swim."

"What's the odds? Go over the side, an' I'll 'old you by the 'ands. Orff with yer things sharp, afore yer fawther sees what we're up to."

Billy needed no second invitation. In a minute he had his clothes off. Pollock seized him by both arms and let him down over the side of the boat. Solomon swam ahead, and, as the tide had ceased to drift the boat onwards, he was presently at some distance. With firm grip, Pollock bobbed the child up and down, the breadth of the tub allowing him to lean cautiously without risk.

Then the father turned to look, and saw what was going on. He gave a terrific shout.

"Damn your eyes, Jem! Pull him in, or I'll—"

"Old yer jaw," roared the other, laughing. "He's all right. Let the kid enjoy hisself – cawn't yer?"

Solomon struck out for the boat.

"He's a-comin'!" said Pollock, all but helpless with half-drunken laughter.

"Pull me in!" said the child, fearful of his father's wrath. "Pull me up!"

And at the same moment he made an effort to jump upon the gunwale. But Jem Pollock also had bent forward, and the result of the two movements was that the man overbalanced himself. He fell plump into the water and sank, Billy with him. From Burden sounded a hoarse cry of agony. Already tired with swimming, the terrified man impeded himself instead of coming on more quickly; he splashed and struggled, and again his voice sounded in a wild shout for help.

There was a boat in sight, but far off. On the Battersea side a few people could be seen; but they had not yet become aware of what had happened. From the other bank no aid could be expected.

Pollock came to the surface and alone. He thought only of making for the boat, as the one way of saving Billy, for he had no skill in supporting another person whilst he himself swam. But the stress of the moment was too much for him: like Burden, he lost his head, and by clutching at the boat pulled it over, so that it began to fill. A cry, a heartrending scream, from the helpless child, who had just risen, utterly distracted him; as the boat swamped, he clung madly to it; it capsized, and he hung by the keel.

Billy was being wafted down the river. Once or twice his little head appeared above the water, and his arms were flung up. The desperate father came onwards, but slowly; fear seemed to have unstrung his sinews, and he struggled like one who is himself in need of assistance. Once more his voice made itself heard; but Pollock, who was drifting with the boat, did not answer. And from the drowning child there came no sound.

A steamer was just putting in at Battersea pier – too far off to be of use. But by this time someone on the bank of the old church had seen the boat bottom upwards. An alarm was given.

Too late, save for the rescue of Jem Pollock. Burden had passed the boat, and was not far from the place where his child had gone down for the last time; with ordinary command of his strength and skill he might easily have kept afloat until help neared him; but he sank. Only his lifeless body was recovered.

And Billy poor little chap – disappeared altogether. The seaward-rushing Thames bore him along in its muddy depths, hiding him until the third day; then his body was seen and picked up not far from the place whence he had started on his merry excursion.

This disaster happened about four of the clock. Two hours later, Mrs. Burden, having done her day's work and received her pay, moved homeward.

Since noon she had been suffering greatly; whilst on her knees, scrubbing floors and staircases, she had several times felt herself in danger of fainting; the stooping posture intensified a pain from which she was seldom quite free; and the heat in this small-windowed warehouse, crowded among larger buildings in an alley off Fleet Street, was insufferably oppressive; once or twice she lay flat upon the boards, panting for breath. It was over now: she had earned the Sunday's dinner, and could return with the feeling of one who had done her duty.

On Monday she would go to Guy's Hospital and get something for that pain. Six months had passed since her last visit to the doctor, whose warnings she had heeded but little. It won't do to think too much of one's ailments. But they must give her a good large bottle of medicine this time, and she would be careful to take it at the right hours.

She came out into St. Bride's Churchyard, and was passing on towards Fleet Street when again the anguishing spasm seized upon her. She turned and looked at the seats under the wall of the church, where two or three people were resting in the shadowed quiet. It would be better to sit here for a moment. Her weak and weary limbs bore her with difficulty to the nearest bench, and she sank upon it with a sigh.

The pain lasted only a minute or two, and in the relief that followed she was glad to breathe the air of this little open space, where she could look up at the blue sky and enjoy the sense of repose. The places of business round about were still and vacant, closed till Monday morning. Only a dull sound of traffic came from the great thoroughfare, near at hand as it was. And the wonderful sky made her think of little Billy who was enjoying himself up the river. She had felt a slight uneasiness about him, now and then, for Jem Pollock was a reckless fellow at all times, and in weather like this he was sure to have been drinking freely; but Solomon would look after the boy.

They would get back about eight o'clock, most likely. Billy would be hungry; he must have a bit of something for supper – fried liver, or perhaps some stewed steak. It was time for her to be moving on.

She stood up, but the movement brought on another attack. Her body sank together, her head fell forwards.

Presently the man who was sitting on the next bench began to look at her; he smiled – another victim of the thirsty weather!

And half-an-hour passed before it was discovered that the woman sitting there in the shadow of St. Bride's Church was dead.

That night Jem Pollock went to the house in Southwark where Solomon Burden and his wife and his child had lived. He could hear nothing of Mrs. Burden. The key of the attic lay on the ledge above the door; no one had been seen, said the neighbours, since father and son went away together early that afternoon.

In the little home there was silence.

If you enjoyed this, you might also like...
The Time Machine, see page 300
An Imaginative Woman, see page 171

That Brute Simmons

Arthur Morrison

SIMMONS'S infamous behavior toward his wife is still matter for profound wonderment among the neighbours. The other women had all along regarded him as a model husband, and certainly Mrs. Simmons was a most conscientious wife. She toiled and slaved for that man, as any woman in the whole street would have maintained, far more than any husband had a right to expect. And now this was what she got for it. Perhaps he had suddenly gone mad.

Before she married Simmons, Mrs. Simmons had been the widowed Mrs. Ford. Ford had got a berth as donkeyman on a tramp steamer, and that steamer had gone down with all hands off the Cape: a judgment, the widow woman feared, for long years of contumacy which had culminated in the wickedness of taking to the sea, and taking to it as a donkeyman – an immeasurable fall for a capable engine-fitter. Twelve years as Mrs. Ford had left her still childless, and childless she remained as Mrs. Simmons.

As for Simmons, he, it was held, was fortunate in that capable wife. He was a moderately good carpenter and joiner, but no man of the world, and he wanted one. Nobody could tell what might not have happened to Tommy Simmons if there had been no Mrs. Simmons to take care of him. He was a meek and quiet man, with a boyish face and sparse, limp whiskers. He had no vices (even his pipe departed him after his marriage), and Mrs. Simmons had engrafted on him divers exotic virtues. He went solemnly to chapel every Sunday, under a tall hat, and put a penny – one returned to him for the purpose out of his week's wages – in the plate. Then, Mrs. Simmons overseeing, he took off his best clothes and brushed them with solicitude and pains. On Saturday afternoons he cleaned the knives, the forks, the boots, the kettles, and the windows, patiently and conscientiously. On Tuesday evenings he took the clothes to the mangling. And on Saturday nights he attended Mrs. Simmons in her marketing, to carry the parcels.

Mrs. Simmons's own virtues were native and numerous. She was a wonderful manager. Every penny of Tommy's thirty-six or thirty-eight shillings a week was bestowed to the greatest advantage, and Tommy never ventured to guess how much of it she saved. Her cleanliness in housewifery was distracting to behold. She met Simmons at the front door whenever he came home, and then and there he changed his boots for slippers, balancing himself painfully on alternate feet on the cold flags. This was because she scrubbed the passage and doorstep turn about with the wife of the downstairs family, and because the stair-carpet was her own. She vigilantly supervised her husband all through the process of "cleaning himself" after work, so as to come between her walls and the possibility of random splashes; and if, in spite of her diligence, a spot remained to tell the tale, she was at pains to impress the fact on Simmons's memory, and to set forth at length all the circumstances of his ungrateful selfishness. In the beginning she had always escorted him to the ready-made clothes shop, and had selected and paid for his clothes: for the reason that men are such perfect fools, and shopkeepers do as they like with them. But she presently improved on that. She found a man selling cheap remnants at a street corner, and straightway she conceived the idea of making Simmons's clothes herself. Decision was one of her virtues, and a suit of uproarious check tweeds was begun that afternoon from the pattern furnished by an old one. More: it was finished by Sunday; when Simmons, overcome by astonishment at the feat, was indued in it, and pushed off to chapel ere he could recover his senses. The things were not altogether comfortable, he found: the trousers clung tight against his shins, but hung loose behind his heels; and when he sat, it was on a wilderness of hard folds and seams. Also his waistcoat collar tickled his nape, but his coat collar went straining across from shoulder to shoulder; while the main garment bagged generously below his waist. Use made a habit of his discomfort, but it never reconciled him to the chaff of his shopmates; for as Mrs. Simmons elaborated successive suits, each one modelled on the last, the primal accidents of her design developed into principles, and grew even bolder and more hideously pronounced. It was vain for Simmons to hint – as hint he did – that he shouldn't like her to overwork herself, tailoring being bad for the eyes, and there was a new tailor's in the Mile End Road, very cheap, where... "Ho yus," she retorted, "you're very consid'rit I dessay sittin' there actin' a livin' lie before your own wife Thomas Simmons as though I couldn't see through you like a book. A lot you care about overworkin' me as long as your turn's served throwin' away money like dirt in the street on a lot o' swindlin' tailors an' me workin' an' slavin' 'ere to save a 'apenny an' this is my return for it anyone 'ud think you could pick up money in the 'orseroad an' I b'lieve I'd be thought better of if I laid in bed all day like some would that I do." So that Thomas Simmons avoided the subject, nor even murmured when she resolved to cut his hair.

So his placid fortune endured for years. Then there came a golden summer evening when Mrs. Simmons betook herself with a basket to do some small shopping, and Simmons was left at home. He washed and put away the tea-things, and then he fell to meditating on a new pair of trousers, finished that day and hanging behind the parlor door. There they hung, in all their decent innocence of shape in the seat, and they were shorter of leg, longer of waist, and wilder of pattern than he had ever worn before. And as he looked on them the small devil of Original Sin awoke and clamored in his breast. He was ashamed of it, of course, for well he knew the gratitude he owed his wife for those same trousers, among other blessings. Still, there the small devil was, and the small devil was fertile in base suggestions, and could not be kept from hinting at the new crop of workshop gibes that would spring at Tommy's first public appearance in such things.

"Pitch 'em in the dustbin!" said the small devil at last; "it's all they're fit for."

Simmons turned away in sheer horror of his wicked self, and for a moment thought of washing the tea-things over again by way of discipline. Then he made for the back room, but saw from the landing that the front door was standing open, probably by the fault of the child downstairs. Now a front door standing open was a thing that Mrs. Simmons would not abide: it looked low. So Simmons went down, that she might not be wroth with him for the thing when she came back; and, as he shut the door, he looked forth into the street.

A man was loitering on the pavement, and prying curiously about the door. His face was tanned, his hands were deep in the pockets of his unbraced blue trousers, and well back on his head he wore the high-crowned peaked cap topped with a knob of wool, which is affected by Jack ashore about the docks. He lurched a step nearer to the door, and "Mrs. Ford ain't in, is she?" he said.

Simmons stared at him for a matter of five seconds, and then said, "Eh?"

"Mrs. Ford as was, then – Simmons now, ain't it?"

He said this with a furtive leer that Simmons neither liked nor understood.

"No," said Simmons, "she ain't in now."

"You ain't her 'usband, are ye?"

"Yus."

The man took his pipe from his mouth, and grinned silently and long. "Blimy," he said at length, "you look the sort o' bloke she'd like," – and with that he grinned again. Then, seeing that Simmons made ready to shut the door, he put a foot on the sill and a hand against the panel. "Don't be in a 'urry, matey," he said, "I come 'ere t'ave a little talk with you, man to man, d'ye see?" And he frowned fiercely.

Tommy Simmons felt uncomfortable, but the door would not shut, so he parleyed. "Wotjer want?" he asked. "I dunno you."

"Then, if you'll excuse the liberty, I'll interdooce meself, in a manner of speaking." He touched his cap with a bob of mock humility. "I'm Bob Ford," he said, "come back out o' kingdom-come, so to say. Me as went down with the *Mooltan* – safe dead five year gone. I come to see my wife."

During this speech Thomas Simmons's jaw was dropping lower and lower. At the end of it he poked his fingers up through his hair, looked down at the mat, then up at the fanlight, then out into the street, then hard at his visitor. But he found nothing to say.

"Come to see my wife," the man repeated. "So now we can talk it over – as man to man."

Simmons slowly shut his mouth, and led the way upstairs mechanically, his fingers still in his hair. A sense of the state of affairs sank gradually into his brain, and the small devil woke again. Suppose this man was Ford? Suppose he *did* claim his wife? Would it be a knock-down blow? Would it hit him out? – or not? He thought of the trousers, the tea-things, the mangling, the knives, the kettles, and the windows; and he thought of them in the way of a backslider.

On the landing Ford clutched at his arm, and asked in a hoarse whisper: "'Ow long 'fore she's back?"

"'Bout a hour, I expect," Simmons replied, having first of all repeated the question in his own mind. And then he opened the parlor door.

"Ah," said Ford, looking about him, "you've bin pretty comf'table. Them chairs an' things" – jerking his pipe toward them – "was hers – mine that is to say, speaking straight, and man to man." He sat down, puffing meditatively at his pipe, and presently: "Well," he continued, "'ere I am agin, ol' Bob Ford dead an' done for – gawn down in the *Mooltan*. On'y I ain't done for, see?" – and he pointed the stem of his pipe at Simmons's waistcoat, – "I *ain't* done for, 'cause why? Cons'kence o' bein' picked up by a ol' German sailin'-'utch an' took to 'Frisco 'fore the mast. I've 'ad a few years o' knockin' about since then, an' now" – looking hard at Simmons – "I've come back to see my wife."

"She—she don't like smoke in 'ere," said Simmons, as it were at random.

"No, I bet she don't," Ford answered, taking his pipe from his mouth, and holding it low in his hand. "I know 'Anner. 'Ow d'you find 'er? Do she make ye clean the winders?"

"Well," Simmons admitted uneasily, "I – I do 'elp 'er sometimes, o' course."

"Ah! An' the knives too, I bet, an' the bloomin' kittles. I know. Wy" – he rose and bent to look behind Simmons's head – "s'elp me, I b'lieve she cuts yer 'air! Well, I'm damned! Jes' wot she would do, too."

He inspected the blushing Simmons from divers points of vantage. Then he lifted a leg of the trousers hanging behind the door. "I'd bet a trifle," he said, "she made these 'ere trucks. Nobody else 'ud do 'em like that. Damme – they're wuss'n wot you're got on."

The small devil began to have the argument all its own way. If this man took his wife back perhaps he'd have to wear those trousers.

"Ah!" Ford pursued, "she ain't got no milder. An' my davy, wot a jore!"

Simmons began to feel that this was no longer his business. Plainly, 'Anner was this other man's wife, and he was bound in honor to acknowledge the fact. The small devil put it to him as a matter of duty.

"Well," said Ford suddenly, "time's short an' this ain't business. I won't be 'ard on you, matey. I ought prop'ly to stand on my rights, but seein' as you're a well-meanin' young man, so to speak, an' all settled an' a-livin' 'ere quiet an' matrimonual, I'll" – this with a burst of generosity – "damme, yus, I'll compound the felony, an' take me 'ook. Come, I'll name a figure, as man to man, fust an' last, no less an' no more. Five pound does it."

Simmons hadn't five pounds – he hadn't even five pence – and he said so. "An' I wouldn't think for to come between a man an' 'is wife," he added, "not on no account. It may be rough on me, but it's a dooty. *I'll* 'ook it."

"No," said Ford hastily, clutching Simmons by the arm, "don't do that. I'll make it a bit cheaper. Say three quid – come, that's reasonable, ain't it? Three quid ain't much compensation for me goin' away forever – where the stormy winds do blow, so to say – an' never as much as seein' me own wife agin for better nor wuss. Between man an' man now – three quid; an' I'll shunt. That's fair, ain't it?"

"Of course it's fair," Simmons replied effusively. "It's more'n fair: it's noble – downright noble, *I* call it. But I ain't goin' to take a mean advantage o' your good-'artedness, Mr. Ford. She's your wife, an' I oughtn't to 'a' come between you. I apologize. You stop an' 'ave yer proper rights. It's me as ought to shunt, an' I will." And he made a step toward the door.

"'Old on," quoth Ford, and got between Simmons and the door; "don't do things rash. Look wot a loss it'll be to you with no 'ome to go to, an' nobody to look after ye, an' all that. It'll be dreadful. Say a couple – there, we won't quarrel, jest a single quid, between man an' man, an' I'll stand a pot out o' the money. You can easy raise a quid – the clock 'ud pretty nigh do it. A quid does it; an' I'll—"

There was a loud double-knock at the front door. In the East End a double-knock is always for the upstairs lodgers.

"Oo's that?" asked Bob Ford apprehensively.

"I'll see," said Thomas Simmons in reply, and he made a rush for the staircase.

Bob Ford heard him open the front door. Then he went to the window, and, just below him, he saw the crown of a bonnet. It vanished, and borne to him from within the door there fell upon his ear the sound of a well-remembered female voice.

"Where ye goin' now with no 'at?" asked the voice sharply.

"Awright, 'Anner—there's—there's somebody upstairs to see you," Simmons answered. And, as Bob Ford could see, a man went scuttling down the street in the gathering dusk. And behold, it was Thomas Simmons.

Ford reached the landing in three strides. His wife was still at the front door, staring after Simmons. He flung into the back room, threw open the window, dropped from the wash-house roof into the back-yard, scrambled desperately over the fence, and disappeared into the gloom. He was seen by no living soul. And that is why Simmons's base desertion—under his wife's very eyes, too – is still an astonishment to the neighbours.

If you enjoyed this, you might also like...
The Adventure of the Copper Beeches, see page 433
The Chaperon, see page 117

The Modern Marriage

The Chaperon

Henry James

Chapter I

AN OLD LADY, in a high drawing-room, had had her chair moved close to the fire, where she sat knitting and warming her knees. She was dressed in deep mourning; her face had a faded nobleness, tempered, however, by the somewhat illiberal compression assumed by her lips in obedience to something that was passing in her mind. She was far from the lamp, but though her eyes were fixed upon her active needles she was not looking at them. What she really saw was quite another train of affairs. The room was spacious and dim; the thick London fog had oozed into it even through its superior defences. It was full of dusky, massive, valuable things. The old lady sat motionless save for the regularity of her clicking needles, which seemed as personal to her and as expressive as prolonged fingers. If she was thinking something out, she was thinking it thoroughly.

When she looked up, on the entrance of a girl of twenty, it might have been guessed that the appearance of this young lady was not an interruption of her meditation, but rather a contribution to it. The young lady, who was charming to behold, was also in deep mourning, which had a freshness, if mourning can be fresh, an air of having been lately put on. She went straight to the bell beside the chimney-piece and pulled it, while in her other hand she held a sealed and directed letter. Her companion glanced in silence at the letter; then she looked still harder at her work. The girl hovered near the fireplace, without speaking, and after a due, a dignified interval the butler appeared in response to the bell. The time had been sufficient to make the silence between the ladies seem long. The younger one asked the butler to see that her letter should be posted; and after he had gone out she moved vaguely about the room, as if to give her grandmother – for such was the elder personage – a chance to begin a colloquy of which she herself preferred not to strike the first note. As equally with herself her companion was on the face of it capable of holding out, the tension, though it was already late in the evening, might have lasted long. But the old lady after a little appeared to recognise, a trifle ungraciously, the girl's superior resources.

"Have you written to your mother?"

"Yes, but only a few lines, to tell her I shall come and see her in the morning."

"Is that all you've got to say?" asked the grandmother.

"I don't quite know what you want me to say."

"I want you to say that you've made up your mind."

"Yes, I've done that, granny."

"You intend to respect your father's wishes?"

"It depends upon what you mean by respecting them. I do justice to the feelings by which they were dictated."

"What do you mean by justice?" the old lady retorted.

The girl was silent a moment; then she said: "You'll see my idea of it."

"I see it already! You'll go and live with her."

"I shall talk the situation over with her tomorrow and tell her that I think that will be best."

"Best for her, no doubt!"

"What's best for her is best for me."

"And for your brother and sister?" As the girl made no reply to this her grandmother went on: "What's best for them is that you should acknowledge some responsibility in regard to them and, considering how young they are, try and do something for them."

"They must do as I've done – they must act for themselves. They have their means now, and they're free."

"Free? They're mere children."

"Let me remind you that Eric is older than I."

"He doesn't like his mother," said the old lady, as if that were an answer.

"I never said he did. And she adores him."

"Oh, your mother's adorations!"

"Don't abuse her now," the girl rejoined, after a pause.

The old lady forbore to abuse her, but she made up for it the next moment by saying: "It will be dreadful for Edith."

"What will be dreadful?"

"Your desertion of her."

"The desertion's on her side."

"Her consideration for her father does her honour."

"Of course I'm a brute, *n'en parlons plus*," said the girl. "We must go our respective ways," she added, in a tone of extreme wisdom and philosophy.

Her grandmother straightened out her knitting and began to roll it up. "Be so good as to ring for my maid," she said, after a minute. The young lady rang, and there was another wait and another conscious hush. Before the maid came her mistress remarked: "Of course then you'll not come to *me*, you know."

"What do you mean by 'coming' to you?"

"I can't receive you on that footing."

"She'll not come *with* me, if you mean that."

"I don't mean that," said the old lady, getting up as her maid came in. This attendant took her work from her, gave her an arm and helped her out of the room, while Rose Tramore, standing before the fire and looking into it, faced the idea that her grandmother's door would now under all circumstances be closed to her. She lost no time however in brooding over this anomaly: it only added energy to her determination to act. All she could do tonight was to go to bed, for she felt utterly weary. She had been living, in imagination, in a prospective struggle, and it had left her as exhausted as a real fight. Moreover this was the culmination of a crisis, of weeks of suspense, of a long, hard strain. Her father had been laid in his grave five days before, and that morning his will had been read. In the afternoon she had got Edith off to St. Leonard's with their aunt Julia, and then she had had a wretched talk with Eric. Lastly, she had made up her mind to act in opposition to the formidable will, to a clause which embodied if not exactly a provision, a recommendation singularly emphatic. She went to bed and slept the sleep of the just.

"Oh, my dear, how charming! I must take another house!" It was in these words that her mother responded to the announcement Rose had just formally made and with which she had vaguely expected to produce a certain dignity of effect. In the way of emotion there was apparently no effect at all, and the girl was wise enough to know that this was not simply on account of the general line of non-allusion taken by the extremely pretty woman before her, who looked like her elder sister. Mrs. Tramore had never manifested, to her daughter, the slightest consciousness that her position was peculiar; but the recollection of something more than that fine policy was required to explain such a failure, to appreciate Rose's sacrifice. It was simply a fresh reminder that she had never appreciated anything, that she was nothing but a tinted and stippled surface. Her situation was peculiar indeed. She had been the heroine of a scandal which had grown dim only because, in the eyes of the London world, it paled in the lurid light of the contemporaneous. That attention had been fixed on it for several days, fifteen years before; there had been a high relish of the vivid evidence as to his wife's misconduct with which, in the divorce-court, Charles Tramore had judged well to regale a cynical public. The case was pronounced awfully bad, and he obtained his decree. The folly of the wife had been inconceivable, in spite of other examples: she had quitted her children, she had followed the "other fellow" abroad. The other fellow hadn't married her, not having had time: he had lost his life in the Mediterranean by the capsizing of a boat, before the prohibitory term had expired.

Mrs. Tramore had striven to extract from this accident something of the austerity of widowhood; but her mourning only made her deviation more public, she was a widow whose husband was awkwardly alive. She had not prowled about the Continent on the classic lines; she had come back to London to take her chance. But London would give her no chance, would have nothing to say to her; as many persons had remarked, you could never tell how London would behave. It would not receive Mrs. Tramore again on any terms, and when she was spoken of, which now was not often, it was inveterately said of her that she went nowhere. Apparently she had not the qualities for which London compounds; though in the cases in which it does compound you may often wonder what these qualities are. She had not at any rate been successful: her lover was dead, her husband was liked and her children were pitied, for in payment for a topic London will parenthetically pity. It was thought interesting and magnanimous that Charles Tramore had not married again. The disadvantage to his children of the miserable story was thus left uncorrected, and this, rather oddly, was counted as *his* sacrifice. His mother, whose arrangements were elaborate, looked after them a great deal, and they enjoyed a mixture of laxity and discipline under the roof of their aunt, Miss Tramore, who was independent, having, for reasons that the two ladies had exhaustively discussed, determined to lead her own life. She had set up a home at St. Leonard's, and that contracted shore had played a considerable part in the upbringing of the little Tramores. They knew about their mother, as the phrase was, but they didn't know her; which was naturally deemed more pathetic for them than for her. She had a house in Chester Square and an income and a victoria – it served all purposes, as she never went out in the evening – and flowers on her window-sills, and a remarkable appearance of youth. The income was supposed to be in part the result of a bequest from the man for whose sake she had committed the error of her life, and in the appearance of youth there was a slightly impertinent implication that it was a sort of afterglow of the same connection.

Her children, as they grew older, fortunately showed signs of some individuality of disposition. Edith, the second girl, clung to her aunt Julia; Eric, the son, clung frantically to polo; while Rose, the elder daughter, appeared to cling mainly to herself. Collectively, of course, they clung to their father, whose attitude in the family group, however, was casual and intermittent. He was charming and vague; he was like a clever actor who often didn't come to rehearsal. Fortune, which but for that one stroke had been generous to him, had provided him with deputies and trouble-takers, as well as with whimsical opinions, and a reputation for excellent taste, and whist at his club, and perpetual cigars on morocco sofas, and a beautiful absence of purpose. Nature had thrown in a remarkably fine hand, which he sometimes passed over his children's heads when they were glossy from the nursery brush. On Rose's eighteenth birthday he said to her that she might go to see her mother, on condition that her visits should be limited to an hour each time and to four in the year. She was to go alone; the other children were not included in the arrangement. This was the result of a visit that he himself had paid his repudiated wife at her urgent request, their only encounter during the fifteen years. The girl knew as much as this from her aunt Julia, who was full of tell-tale secrecies. She availed herself eagerly of the license, and in course of the period that elapsed before her father's death she spent with Mrs. Tramore exactly eight hours by the watch. Her father, who was as inconsistent and disappointing as he was amiable, spoke to her of her mother only once afterwards. This occasion had been the sequel of her first visit, and he had made no use of it to ask what she thought of the personality in Chester Square or how she liked it. He had only said "Did she take you out?" and when Rose answered "Yes, she put me straight into a carriage and drove me up and down Bond Street," had rejoined sharply "See that that never occurs again." It never did, but once was enough, everyone they knew having happened to be in Bond Street at that particular hour.

After this the periodical interview took place in private, in Mrs. Tramore's beautiful little wasted drawing-room. Rose knew that, rare as these occasions were, her mother would not have kept her "all to herself" had there been anybody she could have shown her to. But in the poor lady's social void there was no one; she had after all her own correctness and she consistently preferred isolation to inferior contacts. So her daughter was subjected only to the maternal; it was not necessary to be definite in qualifying that. The girl had by this time a collection of ideas, gathered by impenetrable processes; she had tasted, in the ostracism of her ambiguous parent, of the acrid fruit of the tree of knowledge. She not only had an approximate vision of what everyone had done, but she had a private judgment for each case. She had a particular vision of her father, which did not interfere with his being dear to her, but which was directly concerned in her resolution, after his death, to do the special thing he had expressed the wish she should not do. In the general estimate her grandmother and her grandmother's money had their place, and the strong probability that any enjoyment of the latter commodity would now be withheld from her. It included Edith's marked inclination to receive the law, and doubtless eventually a more substantial memento, from Miss Tramore, and opened the question whether her own course might not contribute to make her sister's appear heartless. The answer to this question however would depend on the success that might attend her own, which would very possibly be small. Eric's attitude was eminently simple; he didn't care to know people who didn't know *his* people. If his mother should ever get back into society perhaps he would take her up. Rose Tramore had decided to do what she could to bring this consummation about; and strangely enough – so mixed were her superstitions and her heresies – a large part of her motive lay in the value she attached to such a consecration.

Of her mother intrinsically she thought very little now, and if her eyes were fixed on a special achievement it was much more for the sake of that achievement and to satisfy a latent energy that was in her than because her heart was wrung by this sufferer. Her heart had not been wrung at all, though she had quite held it out for the experience. Her purpose was a pious game, but it was still essentially a game. Among the ideas I have mentioned she had her idea of triumph. She had caught the inevitable note, the pitch, on her very first visit to Chester Square. She had arrived there in intense excitement, and her excitement was left on her hands in a manner that reminded her of a difficult air she had once heard sung at the opera when no one applauded the performer. That flatness had made her sick, and so did this, in another way. A part of her agitation proceeded from the fact that her aunt Julia had told her, in the manner of a burst of confidence, something she was not to repeat, that she was in appearance the very image of the lady in Chester Square. The motive that prompted this declaration was between aunt Julia and her conscience; but it was a great emotion to the girl to find her entertainer so beautiful. She was tall and exquisitely slim; she had hair more exactly to Rose Tramore's taste than any other she had ever seen, even to every detail in the way it was dressed, and a complexion and a figure of the kind that are always spoken of as "lovely." Her eyes were irresistible, and so were her clothes, though the clothes were perhaps a little more precisely the right thing than the eyes. Her appearance was marked to her daughter's sense by the highest distinction; though it may be mentioned that this had never been the opinion of all the world. It was a revelation to Rose that she herself might look a little like that. She knew however that aunt Julia had not seen her deposed sister-in-law for a long time, and she had a general impression that Mrs. Tramore was today a more complete production – for instance as regarded her air of youth – than she had ever been. There was no excitement on her side – that was all her visitor's; there was no emotion – that was excluded by the plan, to say nothing of conditions more primal. Rose had from the first a glimpse of her mother's plan. It was to mention nothing and imply nothing, neither to acknowledge, to explain nor to extenuate. She would leave everything to her child; with her child she was secure. She only wanted to get back into society; she would leave even that to her child, whom she treated not as a high-strung and heroic daughter, a creature of exaltation, of devotion, but as a new, charming, clever, useful friend, a little younger than herself. Already on that first day she had talked about dressmakers. Of course, poor thing, it was to be remembered that in her circumstances there were not many things she *could* talk about. "She wants to go out again; that's the only thing in the wide world she wants," Rose had promptly, compendiously said to herself. There had been a sequel to this observation, uttered, in intense engrossment, in her own room half an hour before she had, on the important evening, made known her decision to her grandmother: "Then I'll *take* her out!"

"She'll drag you down, she'll drag you down!" Julia Tramore permitted herself to remark to her niece, the next day, in a tone of feverish prophecy.

As the girl's own theory was that all the dragging there might be would be upward, and moreover administered by herself, she could look at her aunt with a cold and inscrutable eye.

"Very well, then, I shall be out of your sight, from the pinnacle you occupy, and I sha'n't trouble you."

"Do you reproach me for my disinterested exertions, for the way I've toiled over you, the way I've lived for you?" Miss Tramore demanded.

"Don't reproach *me* for being kind to my mother and I won't reproach you for anything."

"She'll keep you out of everything – she'll make you miss everything," Miss Tramore continued.

"Then she'll make me miss a great deal that's odious," said the girl.

"You're too young for such extravagances," her aunt declared.

"And yet Edith, who is younger than I, seems to be too old for them: how do you arrange that? My mother's society will make me older," Rose replied.

"Don't speak to me of your mother; you *have* no mother."

"Then if I'm an orphan I must settle things for myself."

"Do you justify her, do you approve of her?" cried Miss Tramore, who was inferior to her niece in capacity for retort and whose limitations made the girl appear pert.

Rose looked at her a moment in silence; then she said, turning away: "I think she's charming."

"And do you propose to become charming in the same manner?"

"Her manner is perfect; it would be an excellent model. But I can't discuss my mother with you."

"You'll have to discuss her with some other people!" Miss Tramore proclaimed, going out of the room.

Rose wondered whether this were a general or a particular vaticination. There was something her aunt might have meant by it, but her aunt rarely meant the best thing she might have meant. Miss Tramore had come up from St. Leonard's in response to a telegram from her own parent, for an occasion like the present brought with it, for a few hours, a certain relaxation of their dissent. "Do what you can to stop her," the old lady had said; but her daughter found that the most she could do was not much. They both had a baffled sense that Rose had thought the question out a good deal further than they; and this was particularly irritating to Mrs. Tramore, as consciously the cleverer of the two. A question thought out as far as *she* could think it had always appeared to her to have performed its human uses; she had never encountered a ghost emerging from that extinction. Their great contention was that Rose would cut herself off; and certainly if she wasn't afraid of that she wasn't afraid of anything. Julia Tramore could only tell her mother how little the girl was afraid. She was already prepared to leave the house, taking with her the possessions, or her share of them, that had accumulated there during her father's illness. There had been a going and coming of her maid, a thumping about of boxes, an ordering of four-wheelers; it appeared to old Mrs. Tramore that something of the objectionableness, the indecency, of her granddaughter's prospective connection had already gathered about the place. It was a violation of the decorum of bereavement which was still fresh there, and from the indignant gloom of the mistress of the house you might have inferred not so much that the daughter was about to depart as that the mother was about to arrive. There had been no conversation on the dreadful subject at luncheon; for at luncheon at Mrs. Tramore's (her son never came to it) there were always, even after funerals and other miseries, stray guests of both sexes whose policy it was to be cheerful and superficial. Rose had sat down as if nothing had happened – nothing worse, that is, than her father's death; but no one had spoken of anything that anyone else was thinking of.

Before she left the house a servant brought her a message from her grandmother – the old lady desired to see her in the drawing-room. She had on her bonnet, and she went down as if she were about to step into her cab. Mrs. Tramore sat there with her eternal knitting, from which she forebore even to raise her eyes as, after a silence that seemed to express the fulness of her reprobation, while Rose stood motionless, she began: "I wonder if you really understand what you're doing."

"I think so. I'm not so stupid."

"I never thought you were; but I don't know what to make of you now. You're giving up everything."

The girl was tempted to inquire whether her grandmother called herself "everything"; but she checked this question, answering instead that she knew she was giving up much.

"You're taking a step of which you will feel the effect to the end of your days," Mrs. Tramore went on.

"In a good conscience, I heartily hope," said Rose.

"Your father's conscience was good enough for his mother; it ought to be good enough for his daughter."

Rose sat down – she could afford to – as if she wished to be very attentive and were still accessible to argument. But this demonstration only ushered in, after a moment, the surprising words "I don't think papa had any conscience."

"What in the name of all that's unnatural do you mean?" Mrs. Tramore cried, over her glasses. "The dearest and best creature that ever lived!"

"He was kind, he had charming impulses, he was delightful. But he never reflected."

Mrs. Tramore stared, as if at a language she had never heard, a farrago, a *galimatias*. Her life was made up of items, but she had never had to deal, intellectually, with a fine shade. Then while her needles, which had paused an instant, began to fly again, she rejoined: "Do you know what you are, my dear? You're a dreadful little prig. Where do you pick up such talk?"

"Of course I don't mean to judge between them," Rose pursued. "I can only judge between my mother and myself. Papa couldn't judge for me." And with this she got up.

"One would think you were horrid. I never thought so before."

"Thank you for that."

"You're embarking on a struggle with society," continued Mrs. Tramore, indulging in an unusual flight of oratory. "Society will put you in your place."

"Hasn't it too many other things to do?" asked the girl.

This question had an ingenuity which led her grandmother to meet it with a merely provisional and somewhat sketchy answer. "Your ignorance would be melancholy if your behaviour were not so insane."

"Oh, no; I know perfectly what she'll do!" Rose replied, almost gaily. "She'll drag me down."

"She won't even do that," the old lady declared contradictiously. "She'll keep you forever in the same dull hole."

"I shall come and see *you*, granny, when I want something more lively."

"You may come if you like, but you'll come no further than the door. If you leave this house now you don't enter it again."

Rose hesitated a moment. "Do you really mean that?"

"You may judge whether I choose such a time to joke."

"Goodbye, then," said the girl.

"Goodbye."

Rose quitted the room successfully enough; but on the other side of the door, on the landing, she sank into a chair and buried her face in her hands. She had burst into tears, and she sobbed there for a moment, trying hard to recover herself, so as to go downstairs without showing any traces of emotion, passing before the servants and again perhaps before aunt Julia. Mrs. Tramore was too old to cry; she could only drop her knitting and, for a long time, sit with her head bowed and her eyes closed.

Rose had reckoned justly with her aunt Julia; there were no footmen, but this vigilant virgin was posted at the foot of the stairs. She offered no challenge however; she only said: "There's someone in the parlour who wants to see you." The girl demanded a name, but Miss Tramore only mouthed inaudibly and winked and waved. Rose instantly reflected that there was only one man in the world her aunt would look such deep things about. "Captain Jay?" her own eyes asked, while Miss Tramore's were those of a conspirator: they were, for a moment, the only embarrassed eyes Rose had encountered that day. They contributed to make aunt Julia's further response evasive, after her niece inquired if she had communicated in advance with this visitor. Miss Tramore merely said that he had been upstairs with her mother – hadn't she mentioned it? – and had been waiting for her. She thought herself acute in not putting the question of the girl's seeing him before her as a favour to him or to herself; she presented it as a duty, and wound up with the proposition: "It's not fair to him, it's not kind, not to let him speak to you before you go."

"What does he want to say?" Rose demanded.

"Go in and find out."

She really knew, for she had found out before; but after standing uncertain an instant she went in. "The parlour" was the name that had always been borne by a spacious sitting-room downstairs, an apartment occupied by her father during his frequent phases of residence in Hill Street – episodes increasingly frequent after his house in the country had, in consequence, as Rose perfectly knew, of his spending too much money, been disposed of at a sacrifice which he always characterised as horrid. He had been left with the place in Hertfordshire and his mother with the London house, on the general understanding that they would change about; but during the last years the community had grown more rigid, mainly at his mother's expense. The parlour was full of his memory and his habits and his things – his books and pictures and *bibelots*, objects that belonged now to Eric. Rose had sat in it for hours since his death; it was the place in which she could still be nearest to him. But she felt far from him as Captain Jay rose erect on her opening the door. This was a very different presence. He had not liked Captain Jay. She herself had, but not enough to make a great complication of her father's coldness. This afternoon however she foresaw complications. At the very outset for instance she was not pleased with his having arranged such a surprise for her with her grandmother and her aunt. It was probably aunt Julia who had sent for him; her grandmother wouldn't have done it. It placed him immediately on their side, and Rose was almost as disappointed at this as if she had not known it was quite where he would naturally be. He had never paid her a special visit, but if that was what he wished to do why shouldn't he have waited till she should be under her mother's roof? She knew the reason, but she had an angry prospect of enjoyment in making him express it. She liked him enough, after all, if it were measured by the idea of what she could make him do.

In Bertram Jay the elements were surprisingly mingled; you would have gone astray, in reading him, if you had counted on finding the complements of some of his qualities. He would not however have struck you in the least as incomplete, for in every case in which you didn't find the complement you would have found the contradiction. He was in the Royal Engineers, and was tall, lean and high-shouldered. He looked every inch a soldier, yet there were people who considered that he had missed his vocation in not becoming a parson. He took a public interest in the spiritual life of the army. Other persons still, on closer observation, would have felt that his most appropriate field was neither the army nor the church, but simply the world – the social, successful, worldly world. If he had a sword in one hand and a Bible in the other he had a Court Guide concealed somewhere about his person. His profile was hard and handsome, his eyes were both cold and kind, his dark straight hair was imperturbably smooth and prematurely streaked with grey. There was nothing in existence that he didn't take seriously. He had a first-rate power of work and an ambition as minutely organised as a German plan of invasion. His only real recreation was to go to church, but he went to parties when he had time. If he was in love with Rose Tramore this was distracting to him only in the same sense as his religion, and it was included in that department of his extremely sub-divided life. His religion indeed was of an encroaching, annexing sort. Seen from in front he looked diffident and blank, but he was capable of exposing himself in a way (to speak only of the paths of peace) wholly inconsistent with shyness. He had a passion for instance for open-air speaking, but was not thought on the whole to excel in it unless he could help himself out with a hymn. In conversation he kept his eyes on you with a kind of colourless candour, as if he had not understood what you were saying and, in a fashion that made many people turn red, waited before answering. This was only because he was considering their remarks in more relations than they had intended. He had in his face no expression whatever save the one just mentioned, and was, in his profession, already very distinguished.

He had seen Rose Tramore for the first time on a Sunday of the previous March, at a house in the country at which she was staying with her father, and five weeks later he had made her, by letter, an offer of marriage. She showed her father the letter of course, and he told her that it would give him great pleasure that she should send Captain Jay about his business. "My dear child," he said, "we must really have someone who will be better fun than that." Rose had declined the honour, very considerately and kindly, but not simply because her father wished it. She didn't herself wish to detach this flower from the stem, though when the young man wrote again, to express the hope that he *might* hope – so long was he willing to wait – and ask if he might not still sometimes see her, she answered even more indulgently than at first. She had shown her father her former letter, but she didn't show him this one; she only told him what it contained, submitting to him also that of her correspondent. Captain Jay moreover wrote to Mr. Tramore, who replied sociably, but so vaguely that he almost neglected the subject under discussion – a communication that made poor Bertram ponder long. He could never get to the bottom of the superficial, and all the proprieties and conventions of life were profound to him. Fortunately for him old Mrs. Tramore liked him, he was satisfactory to her long-sightedness; so that a relation was established under cover of which he still occasionally presented himself in Hill Street – presented himself nominally to the mistress of the house. He had had scruples about the veracity of his visits, but he had disposed of them; he had scruples about so many things that he had had to invent a general way, to dig a central drain. Julia Tramore happened to meet him when she came up to town, and she took a view of him more benevolent than her usual estimate of people encouraged by her mother. The fear of agreeing with that lady was a motive, but there was a stronger one, in this particular case, in the fear of agreeing with her niece, who had rejected him. His situation might be held to have improved when Mr. Tramore was taken so gravely ill that with regard to his recovery those about him left their eyes to speak for their lips; and in the light of the poor gentleman's recent death it was doubtless better than it had ever been.

He was only a quarter of an hour with the girl, but this gave him time to take the measure of it. After he had spoken to her about her bereavement, very much as an especially mild missionary might have spoken to a beautiful Polynesian, he let her know that he had learned from her companions the very strong step she was about to take. This led to their spending together ten minutes which, to her mind, threw more light on his character than anything that had ever passed between them. She had always felt with him as if she were standing on an edge, looking down into something decidedly deep. Today the impression of the perpendicular shaft was there, but it was rather an abyss of confusion and disorder than the large bright space in which she had figured everything as ranged and pigeon-holed, presenting the appearance of the labelled shelves and drawers at a chemist's. He discussed without an invitation to discuss, he appealed without a right to appeal. He was nothing but a suitor tolerated after dismissal, but he took strangely for granted a participation in her affairs. He assumed all sorts of things that made her draw back. He implied that there was everything now to assist them in arriving at an agreement, since she had never informed him that he was positively objectionable; but that this symmetry would be spoiled if she should not be willing to take a little longer to think of certain consequences. She was greatly disconcerted when she saw what consequences he meant and at his reminding her of them. What on earth was the use of a lover if he was to speak only like one's grandmother and one's aunt? He struck her as much in love with her and as particularly careful at the same time as to what he might say. He never mentioned her mother; he only alluded, indirectly but earnestly, to the "step." He disapproved of it altogether, took an unexpectedly prudent, politic view of it. He evidently also believed that she would be dragged down; in other words that she would not be asked out. It was his idea that her mother would contaminate her, so that he should find himself interested in a young person discredited and virtually unmarriageable. All this was more obvious to him than the consideration that a daughter should be merciful. Where was his religion if he understood mercy so little, and where were his talent and his courage if he were so miserably afraid of trumpery social penalties? Rose's heart sank when she reflected that a man supposed to be first-rate hadn't guessed that rather than not do what she could for her mother she would give up all the Engineers in the world. She became aware that she probably would have been moved to place her hand in his on the spot if he had come to her saying "Your idea is the right one; put it through at every cost." She couldn't discuss this with him, though he impressed her as having too much at stake for her to treat him with mere disdain. She sickened at the revelation that a gentleman could see so much in mere vulgarities of opinion, and though she uttered as few words as possible, conversing only in sad smiles and headshakes and in intercepted movements toward the door, she happened, in some unguarded lapse from her reticence, to use the expression that she was disappointed in him. He caught at it and, seeming to drop his field-glass, pressed upon her with nearer, tenderer eyes.

"Can I be so happy as to believe, then, that you had thought of me with some confidence, with some faith?"

"If you didn't suppose so, what is the sense of this visit?" Rose asked.

"One can be faithful without reciprocity," said the young man. "I regard you in a light which makes me want to protect you even if I have nothing to gain by it."

"Yet you speak as if you thought you might keep me for yourself."

"For *yourself*. I don't want you to suffer."

"Nor to suffer yourself by my doing so," said Rose, looking down.

"Ah, if you would only marry me next month!" he broke out inconsequently.

"And give up going to mamma?" Rose waited to see if he would say "What need that matter? Can't your mother come to us?" But he said nothing of the sort; he only answered –

"She surely would be sorry to interfere with the exercise of any other affection which I might have the bliss of believing that you are now free, in however small a degree, to entertain."

Rose knew that her mother wouldn't be sorry at all; but she contented herself with rejoining, her hand on the door: "Goodbye. I sha'n't suffer. I'm not afraid."

"You don't know how terrible, how cruel, the world can be."

"Yes, I do know. I know everything!"

The declaration sprang from her lips in a tone which made him look at her as he had never looked before, as if he saw something new in her face, as if he had never yet known her. He hadn't displeased her so much but that she would like to give him that impression, and since she felt that she was doing so she lingered an instant for the purpose. It enabled her to see, further, that he turned red; then to become aware that a carriage had stopped at the door. Captain Jay's eyes, from where he stood, fell upon this arrival, and the nature of their glance made Rose step forward to look. Her mother sat there, brilliant, conspicuous, in the eternal victoria, and the footman was already sounding the knocker. It had been no part of the arrangement that she should come to fetch her; it had been out of the question – a stroke in such bad taste as would have put Rose in the wrong. The girl had never dreamed of it, but somehow, suddenly, perversely, she was glad of it now; she even hoped that her grandmother and her aunt were looking out upstairs.

"My mother has come for me. Goodbye," she repeated; but this time her visitor had got between her and the door.

"Listen to me before you go. I will give you a life's devotion," the young man pleaded. He really barred the way.

She wondered whether her grandmother had told him that if her flight were not prevented she would forfeit money. Then, vividly, it came over her that this would be what he was occupied with. "I shall never think of you – let me go!" she cried, with passion.

Captain Jay opened the door, but Rose didn't see his face, and in a moment she was out of the house. Aunt Julia, who was sure to have been hovering, had taken flight before the profanity of the knock.

"Heavens, dear, where did you get your mourning?" the lady in the victoria asked of her daughter as they drove away.

Chapter II

LADY MARESFIELD had given her boy a push in his plump back and had said to him, "Go and speak to her now; it's your chance." She had for a long time wanted this scion to make himself audible to Rose Tramore, but the opportunity was not easy to come by. The case was complicated. Lady Maresfield had four daughters, of whom only one was married. It so happened moreover that this one, Mrs. Vaughan-Vesey, the only person in the world her mother was afraid of, was the most to be reckoned with. The Honourable Guy was in appearance all his mother's child, though he was really a simpler soul. He was large and pink; large, that is, as to everything but the eyes, which were diminishing points, and pink as to everything but the hair, which was comparable, faintly, to the hue of the richer rose. He had also, it must be conceded, very small neat teeth, which made his smile look like a young lady's. He had no wish to resemble any such person, but he was perpetually smiling, and he smiled more than ever as he approached Rose Tramore, who, looking altogether, to his mind, as a pretty girl should, and wearing a soft white opera-cloak over a softer black dress, leaned alone against the wall of the vestibule at Covent Garden while, a few paces off, an old gentleman engaged her mother in conversation. Madame Patti had been singing, and they were all waiting for their carriages. To their ears at present came a vociferation of names and a rattle of wheels. The air, through banging doors, entered in damp, warm gusts, heavy with the stale, slightly sweet taste of the London season when the London season is overripe and spoiling.

Guy Mangler had only three minutes to re-establish an interrupted acquaintance with our young lady. He reminded her that he had danced with her the year before, and he mentioned that he knew her brother. His mother had lately been to see old Mrs. Tramore, but this he did not mention, not being aware of it. That visit had produced, on Lady Maresfield's part, a private crisis, engendered ideas. One of them was that the grandmother in Hill Street had really forgiven the wilful girl much more than she admitted. Another was that there would still be some money for Rose when the others should come into theirs. Still another was that the others would come into theirs at no distant date; the old lady was so visibly going to pieces. There were several more besides, as for instance that Rose had already fifteen hundred a year from her father. The figure had been betrayed in Hill Street; it was part of the proof of Mrs. Tramore's decrepitude. Then there was an equal amount that her mother had to dispose of and on which the girl could absolutely count, though of course it might involve much waiting, as the mother, a person of gross insensibility, evidently wouldn't die of cold-shouldering. Equally definite, to do it justice, was the conception that Rose was in truth remarkably good looking, and that what she had undertaken to do showed, and would show even should it fail, cleverness of the right sort. Cleverness of the right sort was exactly the quality that Lady Maresfield prefigured as indispensable in a young lady to whom she should marry her second son, over whose own deficiencies she flung the veil of a maternal theory that *his* cleverness was of a sort that was wrong. Those who knew him less well were content to wish that he might not conceal it for such a scruple. This enumeration of his mother's views does not exhaust the list, and it was in obedience to one too profound to be uttered even by the historian that, after a very brief delay, she decided to move across the crowded lobby. Her daughter Bessie was the only one with her; Maggie was dining with the Vaughan-Veseys, and Fanny was not of an age. Mrs. Tramore the younger showed only an admirable back – her face was to her old gentleman – and Bessie had drifted to some other people; so that it was comparatively easy for Lady Maresfield to say to Rose, in a moment: "My dear child, are you never coming to see us?"

"We shall be delighted to come if you'll ask us," Rose smiled.

Lady Maresfield had been prepared for the plural number, and she was a woman whom it took many plurals to disconcert. "I'm sure Guy is longing for another dance with you," she rejoined, with the most unblinking irrelevance.

"I'm afraid we're not dancing again quite yet," said Rose, glancing at her mother's exposed shoulders, but speaking as if they were muffled in crape.

Lady Maresfield leaned her head on one side and seemed almost wistful. "Not even at my sister's ball? She's to have something next week. She'll write to you."

Rose Tramore, on the spot, looking bright but vague, turned three or four things over in her mind. She remembered that the sister of her interlocutress was the proverbially rich Mrs. Bray, a bankeress or a breweress or a builderess, who had so big a house that she couldn't fill it unless she opened her doors, or her mouth, very wide. Rose had learnt more about London society during these lonely months with her mother than she had ever picked up in Hill Street. The younger Mrs. Tramore was a mine of *commérages*, and she had no need to go out to bring home the latest intelligence. At any rate Mrs. Bray might serve as the end of a wedge. "Oh, I dare say we might think of that," Rose said. "It would be very kind of your sister."

"Guy'll think of it, won't you, Guy?" asked Lady Maresfield.

"Rather!" Guy responded, with an intonation as fine as if he had learnt it at a music hall; while at the same moment the name of his mother's carriage was bawled through the place. Mrs. Tramore had parted with her old gentleman; she turned again to her daughter. Nothing occurred but what always occurred, which was exactly this absence of everything – a universal lapse. She didn't exist, even for a second, to any recognising eye. The people who looked at her – of course there were plenty of those – were only the people who didn't exist for hers. Lady Maresfield surged away on her son's arm.

It was this noble matron herself who wrote, the next day, inclosing a card of invitation from Mrs. Bray and expressing the hope that Rose would come and dine and let her ladyship take her. She should have only one of her own girls; Gwendolen Vesey was to take the other. Rose handed both the note and the card in silence to her mother; the latter exhibited only the name of Miss Tramore. "You had much better go, dear," her mother said; in answer to which Miss Tramore slowly tore up the documents, looking with clear, meditative eyes out of the window. Her mother always said "You had better go" – there had been other incidents – and Rose had never even once taken account of the observation. She would make no first advances, only plenty of second ones, and, condoning no discrimination, would treat no omission as venial. She would keep all concessions till afterwards; then she would make them one by one. Fighting society was quite as hard as her grandmother had said it would be; but there was a tension in it which made the dreariness vibrate – the dreariness of such a winter as she had just passed. Her companion had cried at the end of it, and she had cried all through; only her tears had been private, while her mother's had fallen once for all, at luncheon on the bleak Easter Monday – produced by the way a silent survey of the deadly square brought home to her that every creature but themselves was out of town and having tremendous fun. Rose felt that it was useless to attempt to explain simply by her mourning this severity of solitude; for if people didn't go to parties (at least a few didn't) for six months after their father died, this was the very time other people took for coming to see them. It was not too much to say that during this first winter of Rose's period with her mother she had no communication whatever with the world. It had the effect of making her take to reading the new American books: she wanted to see how girls got on by themselves. She had never read so much before, and there was a legitimate indifference in it when topics failed with her mother. They often failed after the first days, and then, while she bent over instructive volumes, this lady, dressed as if for an impending function, sat on the sofa and watched her. Rose was not embarrassed by such an appearance, for she could reflect that, a little before, her companion had not even a girl who had taken refuge in queer researches to look at. She was moreover used to her mother's attitude by this time. She had her own description of it: it was the attitude of waiting for the carriage. If they didn't go out it was not that Mrs. Tramore was not ready in time, and Rose had even an alarmed prevision of their some day always arriving first. Mrs. Tramore's conversation at such moments was abrupt, inconsequent and personal. She sat on the edge of sofas and chairs and glanced occasionally at the fit of her gloves (she was perpetually gloved, and the fit was a thing it was melancholy to see wasted), as people do who are expecting guests to dinner. Rose used almost to fancy herself at times a perfunctory husband on the other side of the fire.

What she was not yet used to – there was still a charm in it – was her mother's extraordinary tact. During the years they lived together they never had a discussion; a circumstance all the more remarkable since if the girl had a reason for sparing her companion (that of being sorry for her) Mrs. Tramore had none for sparing her child. She only showed in doing so a happy instinct – the happiest thing about her. She took in perfection a course which represented everything and covered everything; she utterly abjured all authority. She testified to her abjuration in hourly ingenious, touching ways. In this manner nothing had to be talked over, which was a mercy all round. The tears on Easter Monday were merely a nervous gust, to help show she was not a Christmas doll from the Burlington Arcade; and there was no lifting up of the repentant Magdalen, no uttered remorse for the former abandonment of children. Of the way she could treat her children her demeanour to this one was an example; it was an uninterrupted appeal to her eldest daughter for direction. She took the law from Rose in every circumstance, and if you had noticed these ladies without knowing their history you would have wondered what tie was fine enough to make maturity so respectful to youth. No mother was ever so filial as Mrs. Tramore, and there had never been such a difference of position between sisters. Not that the elder one fawned, which would have been fearful; she only renounced – whatever she had to renounce. If the amount was not much she at any rate made no scene over it. Her hand was so light that Rose said of her secretly, in vague glances at the past, "No wonder people liked her!" She never characterised the old element of interference with her mother's respectability more definitely than as "people." They were people, it was true, for whom gentleness must have been everything and who didn't demand a variety of interests. The desire to "go out" was the one passion that even a closer acquaintance with her parent revealed to Rose Tramore. She marvelled at its strength, in the light of the poor lady's history: there was comedy enough in this unquenchable flame on the part of a woman who had known such misery. She had drunk deep of every dishonour, but the bitter cup had left her with a taste for lighted candles, for squeezing up staircases and hooking herself to the human elbow. Rose had a vision of the future years in which this taste would grow with restored exercise – of her mother, in a long-tailed dress, jogging on and on and on, jogging further and further from her sins, through a century of the "Morning Post" and down the fashionable avenue of time. She herself would then be very old – she herself would be dead. Mrs. Tramore would cover a span of life for which such an allowance of sin was small. The girl could laugh indeed now at that theory of her being dragged down. If one thing were more present to her than another it was the very desolation of their propriety. As she glanced at her companion, it sometimes seemed to her that if she had been a bad woman she would have been worse than that. There were compensations for being "cut" which Mrs. Tramore too much neglected.

The lonely old lady in Hill Street – Rose thought of her that way now – was the one person to whom she was ready to say that she would come to her on any terms. She wrote this to her three times over, and she knocked still oftener at her door. But the old lady answered no letters; if Rose had remained in Hill Street it would have been her own function to answer them; and at the door, the butler, whom the girl had known for ten years, considered her, when he told her his mistress was not at home, quite as he might have considered a young person who had come about a place and of whose eligibility he took a negative view. That was Rose's one pang, that she probably appeared rather heartless. Her aunt Julia had gone to Florence with Edith for the winter, on purpose to make her appear more so; for Miss Tramore was still the person most scandalised by her secession. Edith and she, doubtless, often talked over in Florence the destitution of the aged victim in Hill Street. Eric never came to see his sister, because, being full both of family and of personal feeling, he thought she really ought to have stayed with his grandmother. If she had had such an appurtenance all to herself she might have done what she liked with it; but he couldn't forgive such a want of consideration for anything of his. There were moments when Rose would have been ready to take her hand from the plough and insist upon reintegration, if only the fierce voice of the old house had allowed people to look her up. But she read, ever so clearly, that her grandmother had made this a question of loyalty to seventy years of virtue. Mrs. Tramore's forlornness didn't prevent her drawing-room from being a very public place, in which Rose could hear certain words reverberate: "Leave her alone; it's the only way to see how long she'll hold out." The old woman's visitors were people who didn't wish to quarrel, and the girl was conscious that if they had not let her alone – that is if they had come to her from her grandmother – she might perhaps not have held out. She had no friends quite of her own; she had not been brought up to have them, and it would not have been easy in a house which two such persons as her father and his mother divided between them. Her father disapproved of crude intimacies, and all the intimacies of youth were crude. He had married at five-and-twenty and could testify to such a truth. Rose felt that she shared even Captain Jay with her grandmother; she had seen what *he* was worth. Moreover, she had spoken to him at that last moment in Hill Street in a way which, taken with her former refusal, made it impossible that he should come near her again. She hoped he went to see his protectress: he could be a kind of substitute and administer comfort.

It so happened, however, that the day after she threw Lady Maresfield's invitation into the wastepaper basket she received a visit from a certain Mrs. Donovan, whom she had occasionally seen in Hill Street. She vaguely knew this lady for a busybody, but she was in a situation which even busybodies might alleviate. Mrs. Donovan was poor, but honest – so scrupulously honest that she was perpetually returning visits she had never received. She was always clad in weather-beaten sealskin, and had an odd air of being prepared for the worst, which was borne out by her denying that she was Irish. She was of the English Donovans.

"Dear child, won't you go out with me?" she asked.

Rose looked at her a moment and then rang the bell. She spoke of something else, without answering the question, and when the servant came she said: "Please tell Mrs. Tramore that Mrs. Donovan has come to see her."

"Oh, that'll be delightful; only you mustn't tell your grandmother!" the visitor exclaimed.

"Tell her what?"

"That I come to see your mamma."

"You don't," said Rose.

"Sure I hoped you'd introduce me!" cried Mrs. Donovan, compromising herself in her embarrassment.

"It's not necessary; you knew her once."

"Indeed and I've known everyone once," the visitor confessed.

Mrs. Tramore, when she came in, was charming and exactly right; she greeted Mrs. Donovan as if she had met her the week before last, giving her daughter such a new illustration of her tact that Rose again had the idea that it was no wonder "people" had liked her. The girl grudged Mrs. Donovan so fresh a morsel as a description of her mother at home, rejoicing that she would be inconvenienced by having to keep the story out of Hill Street. Her mother went away before Mrs. Donovan departed, and Rose was touched by guessing her reason – the thought that since even this circuitous personage had been moved to come, the two might, if left together, invent some remedy. Rose waited to see what Mrs. Donovan had in fact invented.

"You won't come out with me then?"

"Come out with you?"

"My daughters are married. You know I'm a lone woman. It would be an immense pleasure to me to have so charming a creature as yourself to present to the world."

"I go out with my mother," said Rose, after a moment.

"Yes, but sometimes when she's not inclined?"

"She goes everywhere she wants to go," Rose continued, uttering the biggest fib of her life and only regretting it should be wasted on Mrs. Donovan.

"Ah, but do you go everywhere *you* want?" the lady asked sociably.

"One goes even to places one hates. Everyone does that."

"Oh, what I go through!" this social martyr cried. Then she laid a persuasive hand on the girl's arm. "Let me show you at a few places first, and then we'll see. I'll bring them all here."

"I don't think I understand you," replied Rose, though in Mrs. Donovan's words she perfectly saw her own theory of the case reflected. For a quarter of a minute she asked herself whether she might not, after all, do so much evil that good might come. Mrs. Donovan would take her out the next day, and be thankful enough to annex such an attraction as a pretty girl. Various consequences would ensue and the long delay would be shortened; her mother's drawing-room would resound with the clatter of teacups.

"Mrs. Bray's having some big thing next week; come with me there and I'll show you what I mane," Mrs. Donovan pleaded.

"I see what you mane," Rose answered, brushing away her temptation and getting up. "I'm much obliged to you."

"You know you're wrong, my dear," said her interlocutress, with angry little eyes.

"I'm not going to Mrs. Bray's."

"I'll get you a kyard; it'll only cost me a penny stamp."

"I've got one," said the girl, smiling.

"Do you mean a penny stamp?" Mrs. Donovan, especially at departure, always observed all the forms of amity. "You can't do it alone, my darling," she declared.

"Shall they call you a cab?" Rose asked.

"I'll pick one up. I choose my horse. You know you require your start," her visitor went on.

"Excuse my mother," was Rose's only reply.

"Don't mention it. Come to me when you need me. You'll find me in the Red Book."

"It's awfully kind of you."

Mrs. Donovan lingered a moment on the threshold. "Who will you *have* now, my child?" she appealed.

"I won't have anyone!" Rose turned away, blushing for her. "She came on speculation," she said afterwards to Mrs. Tramore.

Her mother looked at her a moment in silence. "You can do it if you like, you know."

Rose made no direct answer to this observation; she remarked instead: "See what our quiet life allows us to escape."

"We don't escape it. She has been here an hour."

"Once in twenty years! We might meet her three times a day."

"Oh, I'd take her with the rest!" sighed Mrs. Tramore; while her daughter recognised that what her companion wanted to do was just what Mrs. Donovan was doing. Mrs. Donovan's life was her ideal.

On a Sunday, ten days later, Rose went to see one of her old governesses, of whom she had lost sight for some time and who had written to her that she was in London, unoccupied and ill. This was just the sort of relation into which she could throw herself now with inordinate zeal; the idea of it, however, not preventing a foretaste of the queer expression in the excellent lady's face when she should mention with whom she was living. While she smiled at this picture she threw in another joke, asking herself if Miss Hack could be held in any degree to constitute the nucleus of a circle. She would come to see her, in any event – come the more the further she was dragged down. Sunday was always a difficult day with the two ladies – the afternoons made it so apparent that they were not frequented. Her mother, it is true, was comprised in the habits of two or three old gentlemen – she had for a long time avoided male friends of less than seventy – who disliked each other enough to make the room, when they were there at once, crack with pressure. Rose sat for a long time with Miss Hack, doing conscientious justice to the conception that there could be troubles in the world worse than her own; and when she came back her mother was alone, but with a story to tell of a long visit from Mr. Guy Mangler, who had waited and waited for her return. "He's in love with you; he's coming again on Tuesday," Mrs. Tramore announced.

"Did he say so?"

"That he's coming back on Tuesday?"

"No, that he's in love with me."

"He didn't need, when he stayed two hours."

"With you? It's you he's in love with, mamma!"

"That will do as well," laughed Mrs. Tramore. "For all the use we shall make of him!" she added in a moment.

"We shall make great use of him. His mother sent him."

"Oh, she'll never come!"

"Then *he* sha'n't," said Rose. Yet he was admitted on the Tuesday, and after she had given him his tea Mrs. Tramore left the young people alone. Rose wished she hadn't – she herself had another view. At any rate she disliked her mother's view, which she had easily guessed. Mr. Mangler did nothing but say how charming he thought his hostess of the Sunday, and what a tremendously jolly visit he had had. He didn't remark in so many words "I had no idea your mother was such a good sort"; but this was the spirit of his simple discourse. Rose liked it at first – a little of it gratified her; then she thought there was too much of it for good taste. She had to reflect that one does what one can and that Mr. Mangler probably thought he was delicate. He wished to convey that he desired to make up to her for the injustice of society. Why shouldn't her mother receive gracefully, she asked (not audibly) and who had ever said she didn't? Mr. Mangler had a great deal to say about the disappointment of his own parent over Miss Tramore's not having come to dine with them the night of his aunt's ball.

"Lady Maresfield knows why I didn't come," Rose answered at last.

"Ah, now, but *I* don't, you know; can't you tell *me*?" asked the young man.

"It doesn't matter, if your mother's clear about it."

"Oh, but why make such an awful mystery of it, when I'm dying to know?"

He talked about this, he chaffed her about it for the rest of his visit: he had at last found a topic after his own heart. If her mother considered that he might be the emblem of their redemption he was an engine of the most primitive construction. He stayed and stayed; he struck Rose as on the point of bringing out something for which he had not quite, as he would have said, the cheek. Sometimes she thought he was going to begin: "By the way, my mother told me to propose to you." At other moments he seemed charged with the admission: "I say, of course I really know what you're trying to do for her," nodding at the door: "therefore hadn't we better speak of it frankly, so that I can help you with my mother, and more particularly with my sister Gwendolen, who's the difficult one? The fact is, you see, they won't do anything for nothing. If you'll accept me they'll call, but they won't call without something 'down.'" Mr. Mangler departed without their speaking frankly, and Rose Tramore had a hot hour during which she almost entertained, vindictively, the project of "accepting" the limpid youth until after she should have got her mother into circulation. The cream of the vision was that she might break with him later. She could read that this was what her mother would have liked, but the next time he came the door was closed to him, and the next and the next.

In August there was nothing to do but to go abroad, with the sense on Rose's part that the battle was still all to fight; for a round of country visits was not in prospect, and English watering-places constituted one of the few subjects on which the girl had heard her mother express herself with disgust. Continental autumns had been indeed for years, one of the various forms of Mrs. Tramore's atonement, but Rose could only infer that such fruit as they had borne was bitter. The stony stare of Belgravia could be practised at Homburg; and somehow it was inveterately only gentlemen who sat next to her at the *table d'hôte* at Cadenabbia. Gentlemen had never been of any use to Mrs. Tramore for getting back into society; they had only helped her effectually to get out of it. She once dropped, to her daughter, in a moralising mood, the remark that it was astonishing how many of them one could know without its doing one any good. Fifty of them – even very clever ones – represented a value inferior to that of one stupid woman. Rose wondered at the offhand way in which her mother could talk of fifty clever men; it seemed to her that the whole world couldn't contain such a number. She had a sombre sense that mankind must be dull and mean. These cogitations took place in a cold hotel, in an eternal Swiss rain, and they had a flat echo in the transalpine valleys, as the lonely ladies went vaguely down to the Italian lakes and cities. Rose guided their course, at moments, with a kind of aimless ferocity; she moved abruptly, feeling vulgar and hating their life, though destitute of any definite vision of another life that would have been open to her. She had set herself a task and she clung to it; but she appeared to herself despicably idle. She had succeeded in not going to Homburg waters, where London was trying to wash away some of its stains; that would be too staring an advertisement of their situation. The main difference in situations to her now was the difference of being more or less pitied, at the best an intolerable danger; so that the places she preferred were the unsuspicious ones. She wanted to triumph with contempt, not with submission.

One morning in September, coming with her mother out of the marble church at Milan, she perceived that a gentleman who had just passed her on his way into the cathedral and whose face she had not noticed, had quickly raised his hat, with a suppressed ejaculation. She involuntarily glanced back; the gentleman had paused, again uncovering, and Captain Jay stood saluting her in the Italian sunshine. "Oh, good-morning!" she said, and walked on, pursuing her course; her mother was a little in front. She overtook her in a moment, with an unreasonable sense, like a gust of cold air, that men were worse than ever, for Captain Jay had apparently moved into the church. Her mother turned as they met, and suddenly, as she looked back, an expression of peculiar sweetness came into this lady's eyes. It made Rose's take the same direction and rest a second time on Captain Jay, who was planted just where he had stood a minute before. He immediately came forward, asking Rose with great gravity if he might speak to her a moment, while Mrs. Tramore went her way again. He had the expression of a man who wished to say something very important; yet his next words were simple enough and consisted of the remark that he had not seen her for a year.

"Is it really so much as that?" asked Rose.

"Very nearly. I would have looked you up, but in the first place I have been very little in London, and in the second I believed it wouldn't have done any good."

"You should have put that first," said the girl. "It wouldn't have done any good."

He was silent over this a moment, in his customary deciphering way; but the view he took of it did not prevent him from inquiring, as she slowly followed her mother, if he mightn't walk with her now. She answered with a laugh that it wouldn't do any good but that he might do as he liked. He replied without the slightest manifestation of levity that it would do more good than if he didn't, and they strolled together, with

Mrs. Tramore well before them, across the big, amusing piazza, where the front of the cathedral makes a sort of builded light. He asked a question or two and he explained his own presence: having a month's holiday, the first clear time for several years, he had just popped over the Alps. He inquired if Rose had recent news of the old lady in Hill Street, and it was the only tortuous thing she had ever heard him say.

"I have had no communication of any kind from her since I parted with you under her roof. Hasn't she mentioned that?" said Rose.

"I haven't seen her."

"I thought you were such great friends."

Bertram Jay hesitated a moment. "Well, not so much now."

"What has she done to you?" Rose demanded.

He fidgeted a little, as if he were thinking of something that made him unconscious of her question; then, with mild violence, he brought out the inquiry: "Miss Tramore, are you happy?"

She was startled by the words, for she on her side had been reflecting – reflecting that he had broken with her grandmother and that this pointed to a reason. It suggested at least that he wouldn't now be so much like a mouthpiece for that cold ancestral tone. She turned off his question – said it never was a fair one, as you gave yourself away however you answered it. When he repeated "You give yourself away?" as if he didn't understand, she remembered that he had not read the funny American books. This brought them to a silence, for she had enlightened him only by another laugh, and he was evidently preparing another question, which he wished carefully to disconnect from the former. Presently, just as they were coming near Mrs. Tramore, it arrived in the words "Is this lady your mother?" On Rose's assenting, with the addition that she was travelling with her, he said: "Will you be so kind as to introduce me to her?" They were so close to Mrs. Tramore that she probably heard, but she floated away with a single stroke of her paddle and an inattentive poise of her head. It was a striking exhibition of the famous tact, for Rose delayed to answer, which was exactly what might have made her mother wish to turn; and indeed when at last the girl spoke she only said to her companion: "Why do you ask me that?"

"Because I desire the pleasure of making her acquaintance."

Rose had stopped, and in the middle of the square they stood looking at each other. "Do you remember what you said to me the last time I saw you?"

"Oh, don't speak of that!"

"It's better to speak of it now than to speak of it later."

Bertram Jay looked round him, as if to see whether anyone would hear; but the bright foreignness gave him a sense of safety, and he unexpectedly exclaimed: "Miss Tramore, I love you more than ever!"

"Then you ought to have come to see us," declared the girl, quickly walking on.

"You treated me the last time as if I were positively offensive to you."

"So I did, but you know my reason."

"Because I protested against the course you were taking? I did, I did!" the young man rang out, as if he still, a little, stuck to that.

His tone made Rose say gaily: "Perhaps you do so yet?"

"I can't tell till I've seen more of your circumstances," he replied with eminent honesty.

The girl stared; her light laugh filled the air. "And it's in order to see more of them and judge that you wish to make my mother's acquaintance?"

He coloured at this and he evaded; then he broke out with a confused "Miss Tramore, let me stay with you a little!" which made her stop again.

"Your company will do us great honour, but there must be a rigid condition attached to our acceptance of it."

"Kindly mention it," said Captain Jay, staring at the façade of the cathedral.

"You don't take us on trial."

"On trial?"

"You don't make an observation to me – not a single one, ever, ever! – on the matter that, in Hill Street, we had our last words about."

Captain Jay appeared to be counting the thousand pinnacles of the church. "I think you really must be right," he remarked at last.

"There you are!" cried Rose Tramore, and walked rapidly away.

He caught up with her, he laid his hand upon her arm to stay her. "If you're going to Venice, let me go to Venice with you!"

"You don't even understand my condition."

"I'm sure you're right, then: you must be right about everything."

"That's not in the least true, and I don't care a fig whether you're sure or not. Please let me go."

He had barred her way, he kept her longer. "I'll go and speak to your mother myself!"

Even in the midst of another emotion she was amused at the air of audacity accompanying this declaration. Poor Captain Jay might have been on the point of marching up to a battery. She looked at him a moment; then she said: "You'll be disappointed!"

"Disappointed?"

"She's much more proper than grandmamma, because she's much more amiable."

"Dear Miss Tramore – dear Miss Tramore!" the young man murmured helplessly.

"You'll see for yourself. Only there's another condition," Rose went on.

"Another?" he cried, with discouragement and alarm.

"You must understand thoroughly, before you throw in your lot with us even for a few days, what our position really is."

"Is it very bad?" asked Bertram Jay artlessly.

"No one has anything to do with us, no one speaks to us, no one looks at us."

"Really?" stared the young man.

"We've no social existence, we're utterly despised."

"Oh, Miss Tramore!" Captain Jay interposed. He added quickly, vaguely, and with a want of presence of mind of which he as quickly felt ashamed: "Do none of your family—?" The question collapsed; the brilliant girl was looking at him.

"We're extraordinarily happy," she threw out.

"Now that's all I wanted to know!" he exclaimed, with a kind of exaggerated cheery reproach, walking on with her briskly to overtake her mother.

He was not dining at their inn, but he insisted on coming that evening to their *table d'hôte*. He sat next Mrs. Tramore, and in the evening he accompanied them gallantly to the opera, at a third-rate theatre where they were almost the only ladies in the boxes. The next day they went together by rail to the Charterhouse of Pavia, and while he strolled with the girl, as they waited for the homeward train, he said to her candidly: "Your mother's remarkably pretty." She remembered the words and the feeling they gave her: they were the first note of new era. The feeling was somewhat that of an anxious, gratified matron who has "presented" her child and is thinking of the matrimonial market. Men might be of no use, as Mrs. Tramore said, yet it was from this moment Rose dated the rosy dawn of her confidence that her *protégée* would go off; and when later, in crowded assemblies, the phrase, or something like it behind a hat or a fan, fell repeatedly on her anxious ear, "Your mother *is* in beauty!" or "I've never seen her look better!" she had a faint vision of the yellow sunshine and the afternoon shadows on the dusty Italian platform.

Mrs. Tramore's behaviour at this period was a revelation of her native understanding of delicate situations. She needed no account of this one from her daughter – it was one of the things for which she had a scent; and there was a kind of loyalty to the rules of a game in the silent sweetness with which she smoothed the path of Bertram Jay. It was clear that she was in her element in fostering the exercise of the affections, and if she ever spoke without thinking twice it is probable that she would have exclaimed, with some gaiety, "Oh, I know all about *love*!" Rose could see that she thought their companion would be a help, in spite of his being no dispenser of patronage. The key to the gates of fashion had not been placed in his hand, and no one had ever heard of the ladies of his family, who lived in some vague hollow of the Yorkshire moors; but none the less he might administer a muscular push. Yes indeed, men in general were broken reeds, but Captain Jay was peculiarly representative. Respectability was the woman's maximum, as honour was the man's, but this distinguished young soldier inspired more than one kind of confidence. Rose had a great deal of attention for the use to which his respectability was put; and there mingled with this attention some amusement and much compassion. She saw that after a couple of days he decidedly liked her mother, and that he was yet not in the least aware of it. He took for granted that he believed in her but little; notwithstanding which he would have trusted her with anything except Rose herself. His trusting her with Rose would come very soon. He never spoke to her daughter about her qualities of character, but two or three of them (and indeed these were all the poor lady had, and they made the best show) were what he had in mind in praising her appearance. When he remarked: "What attention Mrs. Tramore seems to attract everywhere!" he meant: "What a beautifully simple nature it is!" and when he said: "There's something extraordinarily harmonious in the colours she wears," it signified: "Upon my word, I never saw such a sweet temper in my life!" She lost one of her boxes at Verona, and made the prettiest joke of it to Captain Jay. When Rose saw this she said to herself, "Next season we shall have only to choose." Rose knew what was in the box.

By the time they reached Venice (they had stopped at half a dozen little old romantic cities in the most frolicsome æsthetic way) she liked their companion better than she had ever liked him before. She did him the justice to recognise that if he was not quite honest with himself he was at least wholly honest with *her*. She reckoned up everything he had been since he joined them, and put upon it all an interpretation so favourable to his devotion that, catching herself in the act of glossing over one or two episodes that had not struck her at the time as disinterested she exclaimed, beneath her breath, "Look out – you're falling in love!" But if he liked correctness wasn't he quite right? Could anyone possibly like it more than *she* did? And if he had protested against her throwing in her lot with her mother, this was not because of the benefit conferred but because of the injury received. He exaggerated that injury, but this was the privilege of a lover perfectly willing to be selfish on behalf of his mistress. He might have wanted her grandmother's money for her, but if he had given her up on first discovering that she was throwing away her chance of it (oh, this was *her* doing too!) he had given up her grandmother as much: not keeping well with the old woman, as some men would have done; not waiting to see how the perverse experiment would turn out and appeasing her, if it should promise tolerably, with a view to future operations. He had had a simple-minded, evangelical, lurid view of what the girl he loved would find herself in for. She could see this now – she could see it from his present bewilderment and mystification, and she liked him and pitied him, with the kindest smile, for the original *naïveté* as well as for the actual meekness. No wonder he hadn't known what she was in for, since he now didn't even know what he was in for himself. Were there not moments when he thought his companions almost unnaturally good, almost suspiciously safe? He had lost all power to verify that sketch of their isolation and *déclassement* to which she had treated him on the great square at Milan. The last thing he noticed was that they were neglected, and he had never, for himself, had such an impression of society.

It could scarcely be enhanced even by the apparition of a large, fair, hot, red-haired young man, carrying a lady's fan in his hand, who suddenly stood before their little party as, on the third evening after their arrival in Venice, it partook of ices at one of the tables before the celebrated Café Florian. The lamplit Venetian dusk appeared to have revealed them to this gentleman as he sat with other friends at a neighbouring table, and he had sprung up, with unsophisticated glee, to shake hands with Mrs. Tramore and her daughter. Rose recalled him to her mother, who looked at first as though she didn't remember him but presently bestowed a sufficiently gracious smile on Mr. Guy Mangler. He gave with youthful candour the history of his movements and indicated the whereabouts of his family: he was with his mother and sisters; they had met the Bob Veseys, who had taken Lord Whiteroy's yacht and were going to Constantinople. His mother and the girls, poor things, were at the Grand Hotel, but he was on the yacht with the Veseys, where they had Lord Whiteroy's cook. Wasn't the food in Venice filthy, and wouldn't they come and look at the yacht? She wasn't very fast, but she was awfully jolly. His mother might have come if she would, but she wouldn't at first, and now, when she wanted to, there were other people, who naturally wouldn't turn out for her. Mr. Mangler sat down; he alluded with artless resentment to the way, in July, the door of his friends had been closed to him. He was going to Constantinople, but he didn't care – if *they* were going anywhere; meanwhile his mother hoped awfully they would look her up.

Lady Maresfield, if she had given her son any such message, which Rose disbelieved, entertained her hope in a manner compatible with her sitting for half an hour, surrounded by her little retinue, without glancing in the direction of Mrs. Tramore. The girl, however, was aware that this was not a good enough instance of their humiliation; inasmuch as it was rather she who, on the occasion of their last contact, had held off from Lady Maresfield. She was a little ashamed now of not having answered the note in which this affable personage ignored her mother. She couldn't help perceiving indeed a dim movement on the part of some of the other members of the group; she made out an attitude of observation in the high-plumed head of Mrs. Vaughan-Vesey. Mrs. Vesey, perhaps, might have been looking at Captain Jay, for as this gentleman walked back to the hotel with our young lady (they were at the "Britannia," and young Mangler, who clung to them, went in front with Mrs. Tramore) he revealed to Rose that he had some acquaintance with Lady Maresfield's eldest daughter, though he didn't know and didn't particularly want to know, her ladyship. He expressed himself with more acerbity than she had ever heard him use (Christian charity so generally governed his speech) about the young donkey who had been prattling to them. They separated at the door of the hotel. Mrs. Tramore had got rid of Mr. Mangler, and Bertram Jay was in other quarters.

"If you know Mrs. Vesey, why didn't you go and speak to her? I'm sure she saw you," Rose said.

Captain Jay replied even more circumspectly than usual. "Because I didn't want to leave you."

"Well, you can go now; you're free," Rose rejoined.

"Thank you. I shall never go again."

"That won't be civil," said Rose.

"I don't care to be civil. I don't like her."

"Why don't you like her?"

"You ask too many questions."

"I know I do," the girl acknowledged.

Captain Jay had already shaken hands with her, but at this he put out his hand again. "She's too worldly," he murmured, while he held Rose Tramore's a moment.

"Ah, you dear!" Rose exclaimed almost audibly as, with her mother, she turned away.

The next morning, upon the Grand Canal, the gondola of our three friends encountered a stately barge which, though it contained several persons, seemed pervaded mainly by one majestic presence. During the instant the gondolas were passing each other it was impossible either for Rose Tramore or for her companions not to become conscious that this distinguished identity had markedly inclined itself – a circumstance commemorated the next moment, almost within earshot of the other boat, by the most spontaneous cry that had issued for many a day from the lips of Mrs. Tramore. "Fancy, my dear, Lady Maresfield has bowed to us!"

"We ought to have returned it," Rose answered; but she looked at Bertram Jay, who was opposite to her. He blushed, and she blushed, and during this moment was born a deeper understanding than had yet existed between these associated spirits. It had something to do with their going together that afternoon, without her mother, to look at certain out-of-the-way pictures as to which Ruskin had inspired her with a desire to see sincerely. Mrs. Tramore expressed the wish to stay at home, and the motive of this wish – a finer shade than any that even Ruskin had ever found a phrase for – was not translated into misrepresenting words by either the mother or the daughter. At San Giovanni in Bragora the girl and her companion came upon Mrs. Vaughan-Vesey, who, with one of her sisters, was also endeavouring to do the earnest thing. She did it to Rose, she did it to Captain Jay, as well as to Gianbellini; she was a handsome, long-necked, aquiline person, of a different type from the rest of her family, and she did it remarkably well. She secured our friends – it was her own expression – for luncheon, on the morrow, on the yacht, and she made it public to Rose that she would come that afternoon to invite her mother. When the girl returned to the hotel, Mrs. Tramore mentioned, before Captain Jay, who had come up to their sitting-room, that Lady Maresfield had called. "She stayed a long time – at least it seemed long!" laughed Mrs. Tramore.

The poor lady could laugh freely now; yet there was some grimness in a colloquy that she had with her daughter after Bertram Jay had departed. Before this happened

Mrs. Vesey's card, scrawled over in pencil and referring to the morrow's luncheon, was brought up to Mrs. Tramore.

"They mean it all as a bribe," said the principal recipient of these civilities.

"As a bribe?" Rose repeated.

"She wants to marry you to that boy; they've seen Captain Jay and they're frightened."

"Well, dear mamma, I can't take Mr. Mangler for a husband."

"Of course not. But oughtn't we to go to the luncheon?"

"Certainly we'll go to the luncheon," Rose said; and when the affair took place, on the morrow, she could feel for the first time that she was taking her mother out. This appearance was somehow brought home to everyone else, and it was really the agent of her success. For it is of the essence of this simple history that, in the first place, that success dated from Mrs. Vesey's Venetian *déjeuner*, and in the second reposed, by a subtle social logic, on the very anomaly that had made it dubious. There is always a chance in things, and Rose Tramore's chance was in the fact that Gwendolen Vesey was, as someone had said, awfully modern, an immense improvement on the exploded science of her mother, and capable of seeing what a "draw" there would be in the comedy, if properly brought out, of the reversed positions of Mrs. Tramore and Mrs. Tramore's diplomatic daughter. With a first-rate managerial eye she perceived that people would flock into any room – and all the more into one of hers – to see Rose bring in her dreadful mother. She treated the cream of English society to this thrilling spectacle later in the autumn, when she once more "secured" both the performers for a week at Brimble. It made a hit on the spot, the very first evening – the girl was felt to play her part so well. The rumour of the performance spread; everyone wanted to see it. It was an entertainment of which, that winter in the country, and the next season in town, persons of taste desired to give their friends the freshness. The thing was to make the Tramores come late, after everyone had arrived. They were engaged for a fixed hour, like the American imitator and the Patagonian contralto. Mrs. Vesey had been the first to say the girl was awfully original, but that became the general view.

Gwendolen Vesey had with her mother one of the few quarrels in which Lady Maresfield had really stood up to such an antagonist (the elder woman had to recognise in general in whose veins it was that the blood of the Manglers flowed) on account of this very circumstance of her attaching more importance to Miss Tramore's originality ("Her originality be hanged!" her ladyship had gone so far as unintelligently to exclaim) than to the prospects of the unfortunate Guy. Mrs. Vesey actually lost sight of these pressing problems in her admiration of the way the mother and the daughter, or rather the daughter and the mother (it was slightly confusing) "drew." It was Lady Maresfield's version of the case that the brazen girl (she was shockingly coarse) had treated poor Guy abominably. At any rate it was made known, just after Easter, that Miss Tramore was to be married to Captain Jay. The marriage was not to take place till the summer; but Rose felt that before this the field would practically be won. There had been some bad moments, there had been several warm corners and a certain number of cold shoulders and closed doors and stony stares; but the breach was effectually made – the rest was only a question of time. Mrs. Tramore could be trusted to keep what she had gained, and it was the dowagers, the old dragons with prominent fangs and glittering scales, whom the trick had already mainly caught. By this time there were several houses into which the liberated lady had crept alone. Her daughter had been expected with her, but they couldn't turn her out because the girl had stayed behind, and she was fast acquiring a new identity, that of a parental connection with the heroine of such a romantic story. She was at least the next best thing to her daughter, and Rose foresaw the day when she would be valued principally as a memento of one of the prettiest episodes in the annals of London. At a big official party, in June, Rose had the joy of introducing Eric to his mother. She was a little sorry it was an official party – there were some other such queer people there; but Eric called, observing the shade, the next day but one.

No observer, probably, would have been acute enough to fix exactly the moment at which the girl ceased to take out her mother and began to be taken out by her. A later phase was more distinguishable – that at which Rose forbore to inflict on her companion a duality that might become oppressive. She began to economise her force, she went only when the particular effect was required. Her marriage was delayed by the period of mourning consequent upon the death of her grandmother, who, the younger Mrs. Tramore averred, was killed by the rumour of her own new birth. She was the only one of the dragons who had not been tamed. Julia Tramore knew the truth about this – she was determined such things should not kill *her*. She would live to do something – she hardly knew what. The provisions of her mother's will were published in the "Illustrated News"; from which it appeared that everything that was not to go to Eric and to Julia was to go to the fortunate Edith. Miss Tramore makes no secret of her own intentions as regards this favourite.

Edith is not pretty, but Lady Maresfield is waiting for her; she is determined Gwendolen Vesey shall not get hold of her. Mrs. Vesey however takes no interest in her at all. She is whimsical, as befits a woman of her fashion; but there are two persons she is still very fond of, the delightful Bertram Jays. The fondness of this pair, it must be added, is not wholly expended in return. They are extremely united, but their life is more domestic than might have been expected from the preliminary signs. It owes a portion of its concentration to the fact that Mrs. Tramore has now so many places to go to that she has almost no time to come to her daughter's. She is, under her son-in-law's roof, a brilliant but a rare apparition, and the other day he remarked upon the circumstance to his wife.

"If it hadn't been for you," she replied, smiling, "she might have had her regular place at our fireside."

"Good heavens, how did I prevent it?" cried Captain Jay, with all the consciousness of virtue.

"You ordered it otherwise, you goose!" And she says, in the same spirit, whenever her husband commends her (which he does, sometimes, extravagantly) for the way she launched her mother: "Nonsense, my dear – practically it was *you*!"

If you enjoyed this, you might also like...
The Day of Silence, see page 103
A Yellow Duster, see page 187

A Cross Line

George Egerton

THE RATHER FLAT notes of a man's voice float out into the clear air, singing the refrain of a popular music-hall ditty. There is something incongruous between the melody and the surroundings. It seems profane, indelicate, to bring this slangy, vulgar tune, and with it the mental picture of footlight flare and fantastic dance, into the lovely freshness of this perfect spring day.

A woman sitting on a felled tree turns her head to meet its coming, and an expression flits across her face in which disgust and humorous appreciation are subtly blended. Her mind is nothing if not picturesque; her busy brain, with all its capabilities choked by a thousand vagrant fancies, is always producing pictures and finding associations between the most unlikely objects. She has been reading a little sketch written in the daintiest language of a fountain scene in Tanagra, and her vivid imagination has made it real to her. The slim, graceful maids grouped around it filling their exquisitely-formed earthen jars, the dainty poise of their classic heads, and the flowing folds of their draperies have been actually present with her; and now, – why, it is like the entrance of a half-tipsy vagabond player bedizened in tawdry finery: the picture is blurred. She rests her head against the trunk of a pine-tree behind her, and awaits the singer. She is sitting on an incline in the midst of a wilderness of trees; some have blown down, some have been cut down, and the lopped branches lie about; moss and bracken and trailing bramble bushes, fir-cones, wild rose-bushes, and speckled red "fairy hats" fight for life in wild confusion. A disused quarry to the left is an ideal haunt of pike, and to the right a little river rushes along in haste to join a greater sister that is fighting a troubled way to the sea. A row of stepping-stones cross it, and if you were to stand on one you would see shoals of restless stone-loach "beardies" darting from side to side. The tails of several ducks can be seen above the water, and the paddle of their balancing feet and the gurgling suction of their bills as they search for larvae can be heard distinctly between the hum of insect, twitter of bird, and rustle of stream and leaf. The singer has changed his lay to a whistle, and presently he comes down the path a cool, neat, gray-clad figure, with a fishing creel slung across his back, and a trout rod held on his shoulder. The air ceases abruptly, and his cold, gray eyes scan the seated figure with its gypsy ease of attitude, a scarlet shawl that has fallen from her shoulders forming an accentuative background to the slim roundness of her waist.

Persistent study, coupled with a varied experience of the female animal, has given the owner of the said gray eyes some facility in classing her, although it has not supplied him with any definite data as to what any one of the species may do in a given circumstance. To put it in his own words, in answer to a friend who chaffed him on his untiring pursuit of women as an interesting problem, –

"If a fellow has had much experience of his fellow-man he may divide him into types, and given a certain number of men and a certain number of circumstances, he is pretty safe on hitting on the line of action each type will strike. 'T ain't so with woman. You may always look out for the unexpected; she generally upsets a fellow's calculations, and you are never safe in laying odds on her. Tell you what, old chappie, we may talk about superior intellect; but if a woman wasn't handicapped by her affection or need of it, the cleverest chap in Christendom would be just a bit of putty in her hands. I find them more fascinating as problems than anything going. Never let an opportunity slip to get new data – never!"

He did not now. He met the frank, unembarrassed gaze of eyes that would have looked with just the same bright inquiry at the advent of a hare or a toad, or any other object that might cross her path, and raised his hat with respectful courtesy, saying, in the drawling tone habitual with him, –

"I hope I am not trespassing?"

"I can't say; you may be; so may I, but no one has ever told me so!"

A pause. His quick glance has noted the thick wedding ring on her slim brown hand and the flash of a diamond in its keeper. A lady decidedly. Fast? – perhaps. Original? – undoubtedly. Worth knowing? – rather.

"I am looking for a trout stream, but the directions I got were rather vague; might I—"

"It's straight ahead; but you won't catch anything now, at least not here, – sun 's too glaring and water too low; a mile up you may in an hour's time."

"Oh, thanks awfully for the tip. You fish then?"

"Yes, sometimes."

"Trout run big here?" (What odd eyes the woman has! kind of magnetic.)

"No, seldom over a pound; but they are very game."

"Rare good sport, isn't it, whipping a stream? There is so much besides the mere catching of fish; the river and the trees and the quiet sets a fellow thinking; kind of sermon; makes a chap feel good, don't it?"

She smiles assentingly, and yet what the devil is she amused at, he queries mentally. An inspiration! he acts upon it, and says eagerly, –

"I wonder – I don't half like to ask, but fishing puts people on a common footing, don't it? You knowing the stream, you know, would you tell me what are the best flies to use?"

"I tie my own, but—"

"Do you? How clever of you! Wish I could;" and sitting down on the other end of the tree, he takes out his fly-book. "But I interrupted you, you were going to say –"

"Only," – stretching out her hand, of a perfect shape but decidedly brown, for the book, – "that you might give the local fly-tyer a trial; he 'tell you. Later on, end of next month, or perhaps later, you might try the oak-fly, – the natural fly, you know. A horn is the best thing to hold them in, they get out of anything else; and put two on at a time."

"By Jove, I must try that dodge!"

He watches her as she handles his book and examines the contents critically, turning aside some with a glance, fingering others almost tenderly, holding them daintily, and noting the cock of wings and the hint of tinsel, with her head on one side, – a trick of hers, he thinks.

"Which do you like most, wet or dry fly?" She is looking at some dry flies.

"Oh," with that rare smile, "at the time I swear by whichever happens to catch most fish, – perhaps really dry fly. I fancy most of these flies are better for Scotland or England. Up to this, March-brown has been the most killing thing. But you might try an 'orange-grouse,' – that's always good here, – with perhaps a 'hare's ear' for a change, and put on a 'coach-man' for the evenings. My husband [he steals a side look at her] brought home some beauties yesterday evening."

"Lucky fellow!"

She returns the book. There is a tone in his voice as he says this that jars on her, sensitive as she is to every inflection of a voice, with an intuition that is almost second sight. She gathers up her shawl, – she has a cream-colored woollen gown on, and her skin looks duskily foreign by contrast. She is on her feet before he can regain his, and says, with a cool little bend of her head: "Good afternoon, I wish you a full basket!"

Before he can raise his cap she is down the slope, gliding with easy steps that have a strange grace, and then springing lightly from stone to stone across the stream. He feels small; snubbed someway; and he sits down on the spot where she sat, and lighting his pipe says, "Check!"

* * *

She is walking slowly up the garden path; a man in his shirt-sleeves is stooping among the tender young peas; a bundle of stakes lies next him, and he whistles softly and all out of tune as he twines the little tendrils round each new support. She looks at his broad shoulders and narrow flanks; his back is too long for great strength she thinks. He hears her step, and smiles up at her from under the shadow of his broad-leafed hat.

"How do you feel now, old woman?"

"Beastly! I've got that horrid qualmish feeling again. I can't get rid of it."

He has spread his coat on the side of the path, and pats it for her to sit down.

"What is it?" anxiously. "If you were a mare I 'd know what to do for you. Have a nip of whiskey?"

He strides off without waiting for her reply, and comes back with it and a biscuit, kneels down and holds the glass to her lips. "Poor little woman, buck up! You'll see that'll fix you. Then you go, by-and-by, and have a shy at the fish."

She is about to say something, when a fresh qualm attacks her and she does not. He goes back to his tying.

"By Jove!" he says suddenly, "I forgot; got something to show you!"

After a few minutes he returns, carrying a basket covered with a piece of sacking; a dishevelled-looking hen, with spread wings trailing and her breast bare from sitting on her eggs, screeches after him. He puts it carefully down and uncovers it, disclosing seven little balls of yellow fluff splashed with olive-green; they look up sideways with bright round eyes, and their little spoon-bills look disproportionately large.

"Aren't they beauties?" enthusiastically. "This one is just out," taking up an egg; "mustn't let it get chilled; there is a chip out of it and a piece of hanging skin. Isn't it funny?" he asks, showing her how it is curled in the shell, with its paddles flattened and its bill breaking through the chip, and the slimy feathers sticking to its violet skin.

She suppresses an exclamation of disgust, and looks at his fresh-tinted skin instead. He is covering basket, hen, and all.

"How you love young things!" she says.

"Some! I had a filly once; she turned out a lovely mare! I cried when I had to sell her; I wouldn't have let anyone in God's world mount her."

"Yes, you would!"

"Who?" with a quick look of resentment.

"Me!"

"I wouldn't!"

"What! you wouldn't?"

"I wouldn't!"

"I think you would if I wanted to!" with a flash out of the tail of her eye.

"No, I wouldn't!"

"Then you would care more for her than for me. I would give you your choice," passionately, "her or me!"

"What nonsense!"

"Maybe," concentrated; but it's lucky she isn't here to make deadly sense of it." A humble-bee buzzes close to her ear, and she is roused to a sense of facts, and laughs to think how nearly they have quarrelled over a mare that was sold before she knew him.

Some evenings later she is stretched motionless in a chair; and yet she conveys an impression of restlessness, – a sensitively nervous person would feel it. She is gazing at her husband; her brows are drawn together, and make three little lines. He is reading, reading quietly, without moving his eyes quickly from side to side of the page as she does when she reads, and he pulls away at a big pipe with steady enjoyment. Her eyes turn from him to the window, and follow the course of two clouds; then they close for a few seconds, then open to watch him again. He looks up and smiles.

"Finished your book?"

There is a singular, soft monotony in his voice; the organ with which she replies is capable of more varied expression.

"Yes, it is a book makes one think. It would be a greater book if he were not an Englishman; he's afraid of shocking the big middle class. You wouldn't care about it."

"Finished your smoke?"

"No, it went out; too much fag to light up again! No," protestingly, "never you mind, old boy, why do you?"

He has drawn his long length out of his chair, and kneeling down beside her guards a lighted match from the incoming evening air. She draws in the smoke contentedly, and her eyes smile back with a general vague tenderness.

"Thank you, dear old man!"

"Going out again?" Negative head-shake.

"Back aching?" Affirmative nod, accompanied by a steadily aimed puff of smoke, that she has been carefully inhaling, into his eyes.

"Scamp! Have your booties off?"

"Oh, don't you bother! Lizzie will do it."

He has seized a foot from under the rocker, and sitting on his heels holds it on his knee, while he unlaces the boot; then he loosens the stocking under her toes, and strokes her foot gently. "Now the other!" Then he drops both boots outside the door, and fetching a little pair of slippers, past their first smartness, from the bedroom, puts one on. He examines the left foot: it is a little swollen round the ankle, and he presses his broad fingers gently round it as one sees a man do to a horse with windgalls. Then he pulls the rocker nearer to his chair, and rests the slipperless foot on his thigh. He relights his pipe, takes up his book, and rubs softly from ankle to toes as he reads.

She smokes, and watches him, diverting her- self by imagining him in the hats of different periods. His is a delicate skinned face, with regular features; the eyes are fine in color and shape, with the luminous clearness of a child's; his pointed beard is soft and curly. She looks at his hand, – a broad, strong hand with capable fingers; the hand of a craftsman, a contradiction to the face with its distinguished delicacy. She holds her own up, with a cigarette poised between the first and second fingers, idly pleased with its beauty of form and delicate, nervous slightness. One speculation chases the other in her quick brain: odd questions as to race arise; she dives into theories as to the why and wherefore of their distinctive natures, and holds a mental debate in which she takes both sides of the question impartially. He has finished his pipe, laid down his book, and is gazing dreamily into space, with his eyes darkened by their long lashes and a look of tender melancholy in their clear depths.

"What are you thinking of? "There is a look of expectation in her quivering nervous little face.

He turns to her, chafing her ankle again. "I was wondering if lob-worms would do for—"

He stops: a strange look of disappointment flits across her face and is lost in an hysterical peal of laughter.

"You are the best emotional check I ever knew," she gasps.

He stares at her in utter bewilderment, and then a slow smile creeps to his eyes and curves the thin lips under his mustache, – a smile at her. "You seem amused, Gypsy!"

She springs out of her chair, and takes book and pipe; he follows the latter anxiously with his eyes until he sees it laid safely on the table. Then she perches herself, resting her knees against one of his legs, while she hooks her feet back under the other.

"Now I am all up, don't I look small?"

He smiles his slow smile. "Yes, I believe you are made of gutta percha."

She is stroking out all the lines in his face with the tip of her finger; then she runs it through his hair. He twists his head half impatiently; she desists.

"I divide all the people in the world," she says, "into those who like their hair played with, and those who don't. Having my hair brushed gives me more pleasure than anything else; it's delicious. I'd *purr* if I knew how. I notice," meditatively, "I am never in sympathy with those who don't like it. I am with those who do; I always get on with them."

"You are a queer little devil!"

"Am I? I shouldn't have thought you would have found out I was the latter at all. I wish I were a man! I believe if I were a man, I 'd be a disgrace to my family."

"Why?"

"I'd go on a jolly old spree!"

He laughs: "Poor little woman! is it so dull?"

There is a gleam of deviltry in her eyes, and she whispers solemnly, –

"Begin with a D," and she traces imaginary letters across his forehead, and ending with a flick over his ear, says, "and that is the tail of the y!" After a short silence she queries: "Are you fond of me?" She is rubbing her chin up and down his face.

"Of course I am, don't you know it?"

"Yes, perhaps I do," impatiently: "but I want to be told it. A woman doesn't care a fig for a love as deep as the death-sea and as silent; she wants something that tells her it in little waves all the time. It isn't the *love*, you know, it's the *being loved*; it isn't really the *man*, it's his *loving*!"

"By Jove, you're a rum un!"

"I wish I wasn't, then. I wish I was as commonplace as – You don't tell me anything about myself," a fierce little kiss; "you might, even if it were lies. Other men who cared for me told me things about my eyes, my hands, anything. I don't believe you notice."

"Yes I *do*, little one, only I think it."

"Yes, but I don't care a bit for your thinking; if I can't see what's in your head, what good is it to me?"

"I wish I could understand you, dear!"

"I wish to God you could! Perhaps if you were badder and I were gooder we 'd meet half-way. *You* are an awfully good old chap; it's just men like you send women like me to the devil!"

"But you are good," kissing her, – "a real good chum! You understand a fellow's weak points; you don't blow him up if he gets on a bit. Why," enthusiastically, "being married to you is like chumming with a chap! Why," admiringly, "do you remember before we were married, when I let that card fall out of my pocket? Why, I couldn't have told another girl about her! she would n't have beheved that I was straight; she'd have thrown me over, and you sent her a quid because she was sick. You are a great little woman!"

"Don't see it!" she is biting his ear. Perhaps I was a man last time, and some hereditary memories are cropping up in this incarnation!"

He looks so utterly at sea that she must laugh again, and, kneeling up, shuts his eyes with kisses, and bites his chin and shakes it like a terrier in her strong little teeth.

"You imp! was there ever such a woman!"

Catching her wrists, he parts his knees and drops her on to the rug; then perhaps the subtle magnetism that is in her affects him, for he stoops and snatches her up and carries her up and down, and then over to the window, and lets the fading light with its glimmer of moonshine play on her odd face with its tantalizing changes, and his eyes dilate and his color deepens as he crushes her soft little body to him and carries her off to her room.

* * *

Summer is waning, and the harvest is ripe for ingathering, and the voice of the reaping machine is loud in the land. She is stretched on her back on the short, heather-mixed moss at the side of a bog stream. Rod and creel are flung aside, and the wanton breeze with the breath of coolness it has gathered in its passage over the murky dykes of black bog-water is playing with the tail-fly, tossing it to and fro with a half threat to fasten it to a prickly spine of golden gorse. Bunches of bog-wool nod their fluffy heads, and through the myriad indefinite sounds comes the regular scrape of a strickle on the scythe of a reaper in a neighboring meadow. Overhead a flotilla of clouds is steering from the south in a northeasterly direction. Her eyes follow them, – old-time galleons, she thinks, with their wealth of snowy sail spread, riding breast to breast up a wide, blue fjord after victory. The sails of the last are rose-flushed, with a silver edge. Someway she thinks of Cleopatra sailing down to meet Antony, and a great longing fills her soul to sail off some-where too, – away from the daily need of dinner-getting and the recurring Monday with its washing, life with its tame duties and virtuous monotony. She fancies herself in Arabia on the back of a swift steed; flashing eyes set in dark faces surround her, and she can see the clouds of sand swirl, and feel the swing under her of his rushing stride; and her thoughts shape themselves into a wild song, – a song to her steed of flowing mane and satin skin, an un- couth rhythmical jingle with a feverish beat; a song to the untamed spirit that dwells in her. Then she fancies she is on the stage of an ancient theatre, out in the open air, with hundreds of faces upturned toward her. She is gauze-clad in a cobweb garment of wondrous tissue; her arms are clasped by jewelled snakes, and one with quivering diamond fangs coils round her hips; her hair floats loosely, and her feet are sandal-clad, and the delicate breath of vines and the salt freshness of an incoming sea seem to fill her nostrils. She bounds forward and dances, bends her lissome waist, and curves her slender arms, and gives to the soul of each man what he craves, be it good or evil. And she can feel now, lying here in the shade of Irish hills, with her head resting on her scarlet shawl and her eyes closed, the grand, intoxicating power of swaying all these human souls to wonder and applause. She can see herself with parted lips and panting, rounded breasts, and a dancing devil in each glowing eye, sway voluptuously to the wild music that rises, now slow, now fast, now deliriously wild, seductive, intoxicating, with a human note of passion in its strain. She can feel the answering shiver of emotion that quivers up to her from the dense audience, spellbound by the motion of her glancing feet; and she flies swifter and swifter, and lighter and lighter, till the very serpents seem alive with jewelled scintillations. One quivering, gleaming, daring bound, and she stands with outstretched arms and passion- filled eyes, poised on one slender foot, asking a supreme note to finish her dream of motion; and the men rise to a man and answer her, and cheer, cheer till the echoes shout from the surrounding hills and tumble wildly down the crags.

The clouds have sailed away, leaving long feathery streaks in their wake. Her eyes have an inseeing look, and she is tremulous with excitement; she can hear yet that last grand shout, and the strain of that old-time music that she has never heard in this life of hers, save as an inner accompaniment to the memory of hidden things, born with her, not of this time.

And her thoughts go to other women she has known, women good and bad, school friends, casual acquaintances, women workers, – joyless machines for grinding daily corn, unwilling maids grown old in the endeavor to get settled, patient wives who bear little ones to indifferent husbands until they wear out, – a long array. She busies herself with questioning. Have they, too, this thirst for excitement, for change, this restless craving for sun and love and motion? Stray words, half confidences, glimpses through soul-chinks of suppressed fires, actual outbreaks, domestic catastrophes, – how the ghosts dance in the cells of her memory! And she laughs, laughs softly to herself, because the denseness of man, his chivalrous, conservative devotion to the female idea he has created, blinds him, perhaps happily, to the problems of her complex nature. "Ay," she mutters musingly, "the wisest of them can only say we are enigmas; each one of them sets about solving the riddle of the *ewigweibliche*, – and well it is that the workings of our hearts are closed to them, that we are cunning enough or great enough to seem to be what they would have us, rather than be what we are. But few of them have had the insight to find out the key to our seeming contradictions, – the why a refined, physically fragile woman will mate with a brute, a mere male animal with primitive passions, and love him; the why strength and beauty appeal more often than the more subtly fine qualities of mind or heart; the why women (and not the innocent ones) will condone sins that men find hard to forgive in their fellows. They have all overlooked the eternal wildness, the untamed primitive savage temperament that lurks in the mildest, best woman. Deep in through ages of convention this primeval trait burns, – an untamable quantity that may be concealed but is never eradicated by culture, the keynote of woman's witchcraft and woman's strength. But it is there, sure enough, and each woman is conscious of it in her truth-telling hours of quiet self-scrutiny; and each woman in God's wide world will deny it, and each woman will help another to conceal it, – for the woman who tells the truth and is not a liar about these things is untrue to her sex and abhorrent to man, for he has fashioned a model on imaginary lines, and he has said, 'So I would have you!' and every woman is an unconscious liar, for so man loves her. And when a Strindberg or a Nietzsche arises and peers into the recesses of her nature and dissects her ruthlessly, the men shriek out louder than the women, because the truth is at all times unpalatable, and the gods they have set up are dear to them—"

"Dreaming, or speering into futurity? You have the look of a seer. I believe you are half a witch!" And he drops his gray-clad figure on the turf; he has dropped his drawl long ago in midsummer.

"Is not every woman that? Let us hope I'm for my friends a white one."

"A-ah! Have you many friends?"

"That is a query! If you mean many correspondents, many persons who send me Christmas cards, or remember my birthday, or figure in my address book, – no."

"Well, grant I don't mean that!"

"Well, perhaps, yes. Scattered over the world, if my death were belled out, many women would give me a tear, and some a prayer; and many men would turn back a page in their memory and give me a kind thought, perhaps a regret, and go back to their work with a feeling of having lost something that they never possessed. I am a creature of moments. Women have told me that I came into their lives just when they needed me; men had no need to tell me, I felt it. People have needed me more than I them. I have given freely whatever they craved from me in the way of understanding or love; I have touched sore places they showed me, and healed them, – but they never got at me. I have been for myself, and helped myself, and borne the burden of my own mistakes. Some have chafed at my self-sufficiency, and have called me fickle, – not understanding that they gave me nothing, and that when I had served them their moment was ended, and I was to pass on. I read people easily, I am written in black letter to most—"

"To your husband?"

"He," quickly, – "we will not speak of him; it is not loyal."

"Do not I understand you a little?"

"You do not misunderstand me."

"That is something."

"It is much!"

"Is it?" searching her face. "It is not one grain of sand in the desert that stretches between you and me, and you are as impenetrable as a sphinx at the end of it. This," passionately, "is my moment, and what have you given me?"

"Perhaps less than other men I have known; but you want less. You are a little like me, – you can stand alone; and yet," her voice is shaking, "have I given you nothing?"

He laughs, and she winces; and they sit silent, and they both feel as if the earth between them is laid with infinitesimal electric threads vibrating with a common pain.

Her eyes are filled with tears that burn but don't fall; and she can see his some way through her closed lids, see their cool grayness troubled by sudden fire, and she rolls her handkerchief into a moist cambric ball between her cold palms.

"You have given me something, something to carry away with me, – an infernal want. You ought to be satisfied: I am infernally miserable. You," nearer, "have the most tantalizing mouth in the world when your lips tremble like that. I – What! can you cry? You?"

"Yes, even I can cry!"

"You dear woman!" pause; "and I can't help you?"

"You can't help me; no man can. Don't think it is because you are you I cry, but because you probe a little nearer into the real me that I feel so."

"Was it necessary to say that?" reproachfully; "do you think I don't know it? I can't for the life of me think how you, with that free gypsy nature of yours, could bind yourself to a monotonous country life, with no excitement, no change. I wish I could offer you my yacht; do you like the sea?"

"I love it; it answers one's moods."

"Well, let us play pretending, as the children say. Grant that I could, I would hang your cabin with your own colors, fill it with books (all those I have heard you say you care for), make it a nest as rare as the bird it would shelter. You would reign supreme. When your highness would deign to honor her servant, I would come and humor your every whim. If you were glad, you could clap your hands and order music, and we would dance on the white deck, and we would skim through the sunshine of Southern seas on a spice-scented breeze. You make me poetical. And if you were angry, you could vent your feelings on me, and I would give in and bow my head to your mood. And we would drop anchor, and stroll through strange cities, – go far inland and glean folk-lore out of the beaten track of everyday tourists; and at night, when the harbor slept, we would sail out through the moonlight over silver seas. You are smiling, – you look so different when you smile; do you like my picture?"

"Some of it!"

"What not?"

"You!"

"Thank you."

"You asked me. Can't you understand where the spell lies? It is the freedom, the freshness, the vague danger, the unknown that has a witchery for me, – ay, for every woman!"

"Are you incapable of affection, then?"

"Of course not. I share," bitterly, "that crowning disability of my sex; but not willingly, – I chafe under it. My God! if it were not for that, we women would master the world! I tell you, men would be no match for us! At heart we care nothing for laws, nothing for systems; all your elaborately reasoned codes for controlling morals or man do not weigh a jot with us against an impulse, an instinct. We learn those things from you, – you tamed, amenable animals; they are not natural to us. It is a wise disposition of Providence that this untamableness of ours is corrected by our affections. We forge our own chains in a moment of softness, and then," bitterly, "we may as well wear them with a good grace. Perhaps many of our seeming contradictions are only the outward evidences of inward chafing. Bah! the qualities that go to make a Napoleon

– superstition, want of honor, disregard of opinion, and the eternal I – are oftener to be found in a woman than a man. Lucky for the world, perhaps, that all these attributes weigh as nothing in the balance with the need to love, if she be a good woman; to be loved, if she is of a coarser fibre."

"I never met anyone like you; you are a strange woman!"

"No, I am merely a truthful one. Women talk to me – why? I can't say; but always they come, strip their hearts and souls naked, and let me see the hidden folds of their natures. The greatest tragedies I have ever read are child's play to those I have seen acted in the inner life of outwardly commonplace women. A woman must beware of speaking the truth to a man; he loves her the less for it. It is the elusive spirit in her, that he divines but cannot seize, that fascinates and keeps him."

There is a long silence; the sun is waning and the scythes are silent, and overhead the crows are circling, – a croaking, irregular army, homeward bound from a long day's pillage.

She has made no sign, yet so subtilely is the air charged with her that he feels but a few moments remain to him. He goes over and kneels beside her, and fixes his eyes on her odd, dark face. They both tremble, yet neither speaks. His breath is coming quickly, and the bistre stains about her eyes seem to have deepened, perhaps by contrast, as she has paled.

"Look at me!"

She turns her head right round and gazes straight into his face; a few drops of sweat glisten on his forehead.

"You witch woman! What am I to do with myself? Is my moment ended?"

"I think so."

"Lord, what a mouth!"

"Don't! Oh, don't!"

"No, I won't. But do you mean it? Am I, who understand your every mood, your restless spirit, to vanish out of your life? You can't mean it! Listen! – are you listening to me? I can't see your face; take down your hands. Go back over every chance meeting you and I have had together since I met you first by the river, and judge them fairly. Today is Monday: Wednesday afternoon I shall pass your gate, and if – if my moment is ended, and you mean to send me away, to let me go with this weary aching—"

"A-ah!" she stretches out one brown hand appealingly, but he does not touch it.

Hang something white on the lilac bush!

She gathers up creel and rod, and he takes her shawl, and wrapping it round her holds her a moment in it, and looks searchingly into her eyes, then stands back and raises his hat, and she glides away through the reedy grass.

* * *

Wednesday morning she lies watching the clouds sail by. A late rose-spray nods into the open window, and the petals fall every time. A big bee buzzes in and fills the room with his bass note, and then dances out again. She can hear his footstep on the gravel. Presently he looks in over the half window, –

"Get up and come out, – 'twill do you good; have a brisk walk!"

She shakes her head languidly, and he throws a great soft, dewy rose with sure aim on her breast.

"Shall I go in and lift you out and put you, 'nighty' and all, into your tub?"

"No!" impatiently. "I'll get up just now."

The head disappears, and she rises wearily and gets through her dressing slowly, stopped every moment by a feeling of faintness. He finds her presently rocking slowly to and fro with closed eyes, and drops a leaf with three plums in it on to her lap.

"I have been watching four for the last week, but a bird, greedy beggar, got one this morning early: try them. Don't you mind, old girl, I'll pour out my own tea!"

She bites into one and tries to finish it, but cannot. You are a good old man!" she says, and the tears come unbidden to her eyes, and trickle down her cheeks, dropping on to the plums, streaking their delicate bloom.

He looks uneasily at her, but doesn't know what to do; and when he has finished his breakfast he stoops over her chair and strokes her hair, saying, as he leaves a kiss on the top of her head, "Come out into the air, little woman; do you a world of good!"

And presently she hears the sharp thrust of his spade above the bee's hum, leaf rustle, and the myriad late summer sounds that thrill through the air. It irritates her almost to screaming point; there is a practical non-sympathy about it; she can distinguish the regular one, two, three, the thrust, interval, then pat, pat, on the upturned sod. Today she wants someone, and her thoughts wander to, and she wonders what, the gray-eyed man who never misunderstands her, would say to her. Oh, she wants someone so badly to soothe her; and she yearns for the little mother who is twenty years under the daisies, – the little mother who is a faint memory strengthened by a daguerreotype in which she sits with silk-mittened hands primly crossed on the lap of her moiré gown. a diamond brooch fastening the black-velvet ribbon crossed so stiffly over her lace collar, the shining tender eyes looking steadily out, and her hair in the fashion of fifty-six. How that spade dominates over every sound! and what a sickening pain she has, an odd pain; she never felt It before. Supposing she were to die, she tries to fancy how she would look; they would be sure to plaster her curls down. He might be digging her grave – no, it is the patch where the early peas grew, the peas that were eaten with the twelve weeks' ducklings: she remembers them, little fluffy golden balls with waxen bills, and such dainty paddles, – remembers holding an egg to her ear and listening to it cheep inside before even there was a chip in the shell. Strange how things come to life! What! she sits bolt upright and holds tightly to the chair, and a questioning, awesome look comes over her face; and then the quick blood creeps up through her olive skin right up to her temples, and she buries her face in her hands and sits so a long time.

The maid comes in and watches her curiously, and moves softly about. The look in her eyes is the look of a faithful dog, and she loves her with the same rare fidelity. She hesitates, then goes into the bedroom and stands thoughtfully, with her hands clasped over her breast. She is a tall, thin, flat-waisted woman, with misty blue eyes and a receding chin. Her hair is pretty. She turns as her mistress comes in, with an expectant look on her face. She has taken up a nightgown, but holds it idly.

"Lizzie, had you ever a child?"

The girl's long left hand is ringless; yet she asks it with a quiet insistence, as if she knew what the answer would be, and her odd eyes read her face with an almost cruel steadiness. The girl flushes painfully, and then whitens; her very eyes seem to pale, and her under lip twitches as she jerks out huskily, –

"Yes!"

"What happened to it?"

"It died, Ma'am."

"Poor thing! Poor old Liz!"

She pats the girl's hand softly, and the latter stands dumbly and looks down at both hands, as if fearful to break the wonder of a caress. She whispers hesitatingly, –

"Have you – have you any little things left?" And she laughs such a soft, cooing little laugh, like the chirring of a ring-dove, and nods shyly back in reply to the tall maid's questioning look. The latter goes out, and comes back with a flat, red-painted deal box, and unlocks it. It does not hold very much, and the tiny garments are not of costly material; but the two women pore over them as a gem collector over a rare stone. She has a glimpse of thick-crested paper as the girl unties a packet of letters, and looks away until she says tenderly, –

"Look, Ma'am!"

A little bit of hair inside a paper heart. It is almost white, so silky and so fine that it is more like a thread of bog-wool than a baby's hair; and the mistress, who is a wife, puts her arms round the tall maid, who has never had more than a moral claim to the name, and kisses her in her quick way.

The afternoon is drawing on; she is kneeling before an open trunk, with flushed cheeks and sparkling eyes. A heap of unused, dainty lace-trimmed ribbon-decked cambric garments are scattered around her. She holds the soft, scented web to her cheek and smiles musingly; and then she rouses herself and sets to work, sorting out the finest, with the narrowest lace and tiniest ribbon, and puckers her swarthy brows, and measures lengths along her middle finger, and then gets slowly up, as if careful of herself as a precious thing, and half afraid.

"Lizzie!"

"Yes, Ma'am!"

"Wasn't it lucky they were too fine for every day? They will be so pretty. Look at this one with the tiny Valenciennes edging. Why, one nightgown will make a dozen little shirts, – such elfin-shirts as they are too; and Lizzie!"

"Yes, M'am!"

"Just hang it out on the lilac-bush, – mind, the lilac-bush!"

"Yes, M'am!"

"Or, Lizzie, wait: I'll do it myself!"

If you enjoyed this, you might also like...

The Cone, see page 322

A Yellow Duster, see page 187

Irremediable

Ella D'Arcy

A YOUNG MAN strolled along a country road one August evening after a long delicious day – a day of that blessed idleness the man of leisure never knows: one must be a bank clerk forty-nine weeks out of the fifty-two before one can really appreciate the exquisite enjoyment of doing nothing for twelve hours at a stretch. Willoughby had spent the morning lounging about a sunny rickyard; then, when the heat grew unbearable, he had retreated to an orchard, where, lying on his back in the long cool grass, he had traced the pattern of the apple-leaves diapered above him upon the summer sky; now that the heat of the day was over he had come to roam whither sweet fancy led him, to lean over gates, view the prospect and meditate upon the pleasures of a well-spent day. Five such days had already passed over his head, fifteen more remained to him. Then farewell to freedom and clean country air! Back again to London and another year's toil.

He came to a gate on the right of the road. Behind it a foot path meandered up over a glassy slope. The sheep nibbling on its summit cast long shadows down the hill almost to his feet. Road and field-path were equally new to him, but the latter offered greener attractions; he vaulted lightly over the gate and had so little idea he was taking thus the first step towards ruin that he began to whistle "White Wings" from pure joy of life.

The sheep stopped feeding and raised their heads to stare at him from pale-lashed eyes; first one and then another broke into a startled run, until there was a sudden woolly stampede of the entire flock. When Willoughby gained the ridge from which they had just scattered he came in sight of a woman sitting on a stile at the further end of the field. As he advanced towards her he saw that she was young and that she was not what is called "a lady" – of which he was glad: an earlier episode in his career having indissolubly associated in his mind ideas of feminine refinement with those of feminine treachery.

He thought it probable this girl would be willing to dispense with the formalities of an introduction and that he might venture with her on some pleasant foolish chat.

As she made no movement to let him pass he stood still, and, looking at her, began to smile.

She returned his gaze from unabashed dark eyes and then laughed, showing teeth white, sound, and smooth as split hazel-nuts.

"Do you wanter get over?" she remarked familiarly.

"I'm afraid I can't without disturbing you."

"Dontcher think you're much better where you are?" said the girl, on which Willoughby hazarded:

"You mean to say looking at you? Well, perhaps I am!"

The girl at this laughed again, but nevertheless dropped herself down into the further field; then, leaning her arms upon the cross bar, she informed the young man: "No, I don't wanter spoil your walk. You were goin' p'raps ter Beacon Point? It's very pretty that wye."

"I was going nowhere in particular," he replied: "just exploring, so to speak. I'm a stranger in these parts."

"How funny! Imer stranger here too. I only come down larse Friday to stye with a Naunter mine in Horton. Are you stying in Horton?"

Willoughby told her he was not in Orton, but at Povey Cross Farm out in the other direction.

"Oh, Mrs. Payne's, ain't it? I've heard aunt speak ovver. She takes summer boarders, don't chee? I egspec you come from London, heh?"

"And I expect you come from London too?" said Willoughby, recognising the familiar accent.

"You're as sharp as a needle," cried the girl with her unrestrained laugh;" so I do. I'm here for a hollerday 'cos I was so done up with the work and the hot weather. I don't look as though I'd bin ill, do I? But I was, though: for it was just stifflin' hot up in our workrooms all larse month, an' tailorin's awful hard work at the bester times."

Willoughby felt a sudden accession of interest in her. Like many intelligent young men, he had dabbled a little in Socialism and at one time had wandered among the dispossessed; but since then, had caught up and held loosely the new doctrine – It is a good and fitting thing that woman also should earn her bread by the sweat of her brow. Always in reference to the woman who, fifteen months before, had treated him ill, he had said to himself that even the breaking of stones in the road should be considered a more feminine employment than the breaking of hearts.

He gave way therefore to a movement of friendliness for this working daughter of the people, and joined her on the other side of the stile in token of his approval. She, twisting round to face him, leaned now with her back against the bar, and the sunset fires lent a fleeting glory to her face. Perhaps she guessed how becoming the light was, for she took off her hat and let it touch to gold the ends and fringes of her rough abundant hair. Thus and at this moment she made an agreeable picture, to which stood as background all the beautiful wooded Southshire view.

"You don't really mean to say you are a tailoress?" said Willoughby with a sort of eager compassion.

"I do, though! An I've bin one ever since I was fourteen. Look at my fingers if you don't b'lieve me."

She put out her right hand, and he took hold of it, as he was expected to do. The finger-ends were frayed and blackened by needle-pricks, but the hand itself was plump, moist, and not unshapely. She meanwhile examined Willoughby's fingers enclosing hers.

"It's easy ter see you've never done no work!" she said, half admiring, half envious. "I s'pose you re a tip-top swell, ain't you?"

"Oh, yes! I'm a tremendous swell indeed!" said Willoughby ironically. He thought of his hundred and thirty pounds salary; and he mentioned his position in the British and Colonial Banking house, without shedding much illumination on her mind; for she insisted:

"Well, anyhow, you're a gentleman. I've often wished I was a lady. It must be so nice ter wear fine clo'es an never have ter do any work all day long."

Willoughby thought it innocent of the girl to say this; it reminded him of his own notion as a child – that kings and queens put on their crowns the first thing on rising in the morning. His cordiality rose another degree.

"If being a gentleman means having nothing to do," said he, smiling, "I can certainly lay no claim to the title. Life isn't all beer and skittles with me, any more than it is with you. Which is the better reason for enjoying the present moment, don't you think? Suppose, now, like a kind little girl, you were to show me the way to Beacon Point, which you say is so pretty?"

She required no further persuasion. As he walked beside her through the upland fields where the dusk was beginning to fall, and the white evening moths to emerge from their daytime hiding-places, she asked him many personal questions, most of which he thought fit to parry. Taking no offence thereat, she told him, instead, much concerning herself and her family. Thus he learned her name was Esther Stables, that she and her people lived Whitechapel way; that her father was seldom sober, and her mother always ill; and that the aunt with whom she was staying kept the post-office and general shop in Orton village. He learned, too, that Esther was discontented with life in general; that, though she hated being at home, she found the country dreadfully dull; and that, consequently, she was extremely glad to have made his acquaintance. But what he chiefly realised when they parted was that he had spent a couple of pleasant hours talking nonsense with a girl who was natural, simple-minded, and entirely free from that repellently protective atmosphere with which a woman of the "classes" so carefully surrounds herself. He and Esther had "made friends" with the ease and rapidity of children before they have learned the dread meaning of "etiquette," and they said goodnight, not without some talk of meeting each other again.

Obliged to breakfast at a quarter to eight in town, Willoughby was always luxuriously late when in the country, where he took his meals also in leisurely fashion, often reading from a book propped up on the table before him. But the morning after his meeting with Esther Stables found him less disposed to read than usual. Her image obtruded itself upon the printed page, and at length grew so importunate he came to the conclusion the only way to lay it was to confront it with the girl herself.

Wanting some tobacco, he saw a good reason for going into Orton. Esther had told him he could get tobacco and everything else at her aunt's. He found the post-office to be one of the first houses in the widely spaced village-street. In front of the cottage was a small garden ablaze with old-fashioned flowers; and in a larger garden at one side were apple-trees, raspberry and currant bushes, and six thatched beehives on a bench. The bowed windows of the little shop were partly screened by sunblinds; nevertheless the lower panes still displayed a heterogeneous collection of goods – lemons, hanks of yarn, white linen buttons upon blue cards, sugar cones, warden pipes, and tobacco jars. A letter-box opened its narrow mouth low down in one wall, and over the door swung the sign, "Stamps and money-order office," in black letters on white enamelled iron.

The interior of the shop was cool and dark. A second glass-door at the back permitted Willoughby to see into a small sitting-room, and out again through a low and square-paned window to the sunny landscape beyond. Silhouetted against the light were the heads of two women: the rough young head of yesterday's Esther, the lean outline and bugled cap of Esther's aunt.

It was the latter who at the jingling of the door-bell rose from her work and came forward to serve the customer; but the girl, with much mute meaning in her eyes and a finger laid upon her smiling mouth, followed behind. Her aunt heard her footfall. "What do you want here, Esther?" she said with thin disapproval; "get back to your sewing."

Esther gave the young man a signal seen only by him and slipped out into the side-garden, where he found her when his purchases were made. She leaned over the privet-hedge to intercept him as he passed.

"Aunt's an awful ole maid," she remarked apologetically; "I b'lieve she'd never let me say a word to enny one if she could help it."

"So you got home all right last night?" Willoughby inquired; "what did your aunt say to you?"

"Oh, she arst me where I'd been, and I tolder a lotter lies!" Then, with woman's intuition, perceiving that this speech jarred, Esther made haste to add, "She's so dreadful hard on me! I dursn't tell her I'd been with a gentleman or she'd never have let me out alone again."

"And at present I suppose you'll be found somewhere about that same stile every evening?" said Willoughby foolishly, for he really did not much care whether he met her again or not. Now he was actually in her company he was surprised at himself for having given her a whole morning's thought; yet the eagerness of her answer flattered him, too.

"Tonight I can't come, worse luck! It's Thursday, and the shops here close of a Thursday at five. I'll havter keep aunt company. But to-morrer? – I can be there to-morrer. You'll come, say?"

"Esther!" cried a vexed voice, and the precise, right-minded aunt emerged through the row of raspberry-bushes; "whatever are you thinking about, delayin the gentleman in this fashion?" She was full of rustic and official civility for "the gentleman," but indignant with her niece. "I don't want none of your London manners down here," Willoughby heard her say as she marched the girl off.

He himself was not sorry to be released from Esther's too friendly eyes, and he spent an agreeable evening over a book, and this time managed to forget her completely.

Though he remembered her first thing next morning, it was to smile wisely and determine he would not meet her again. Yet by dinner-time the day seemed long; why, after all, should he not meet her? By tea-time prudence triumphed anew – no, he would not go. Then he drank his tea hastily and set off for the stile.

Esther was waiting for him. Expectation had given an additional colour to her cheeks, and her red-brown hair showed here and there a beautiful glint of gold. He could not help admiring the vigorous way in which it waved and twisted, or the little curls which grew at the nape of her neck, tight and close as those of a young lamb's fleece. Her neck here was admirable, too, in its smooth creaminess; and when her eyes lighted up with such evident pleasure at his coming, how avoid the conviction she was a good and nice girl after all?

He proposed they should go down into the little copse on the right, where they would be less disturbed by the occasional passer by. Here, seated on a felled tree-trunk, Willoughby began that bantering silly meaningless form of conversation known among the "classes" as flirting. He had but the wish to make himself agreeable, and to while away the time. Esther, however, misunderstood him.

Willoughby's hand lay palm downwards on his knee, and she noticing a ring which he wore on his little finger, took hold of it.

"What a funny ring!" she said; "let's look?"

To disembarrass himself of her touch he pulled the ring off and gave it her to examine.

"What's that ugly dark green stone?" she asked.

"It's called a sardonyx."

"What's it for?" she said, turning it about.

"It's a signet ring, to seal letters with."

"An' there's a sorter king's head scratched on it, an' some writin' too, only I carn't make it out?"

"It isn't the head of a king, although it wears a crown," Willoughby explained, "but the head and bust of a Saracen against whom my ancestor of many hundred years ago went to fight in the Holy Land. And the words cut round it are the motto of our house, Vertue vaunceth, which means virtue prevails."

Willoughby may have displayed some slight accession of dignity in giving this bit of family history, for Esther fell into uncontrolled laughter, at which he was much displeased. And when the girl made as though she would put the ring on her own finger, asking, "Shall I keep it?" he coloured up with sudden annoyance.

"It was only my fun!" said Esther hastily, and gave him the ring back, but his cordiality was gone. He felt no inclination to renew the idle-word pastime, said it was time to go back, and, swinging his cane vexedly, struck off the heads of the flowers and the weeds as he went. Esther walked by his side in complete silence, a phenomenon of which he presently became conscious. He felt rather ashamed of having shown temper.

"Well, here's your way home," said he with an effort at friendliness. "Goodbye, we've had a nice evening anyhow. It was pleasant down there in the woods, eh?"

He was astonished to see her eyes soften with tears, and to hear the real emotion in her voice as she answered, "It was just heaven down there with you until you turned so funny-like. What had I done to make you cross? Say you forgive me, do!"

"Silly child!" said Willoughby, completely mollified, "I'm not the least angry. There! goodbye!" and like a fool he kissed her.

He anathematised his folly in the white light of next morning, and, remembering the kiss he had given her, repented it very sincerely. He had an uncomfortable suspicion she had not received it in the same spirit in which it had been bestowed, but, attaching more serious meaning to it, would build expectations thereon which must be left unfulfilled. It were best indeed not to meet her again; for he acknowledged to himself that, though he only half liked, and even slightly feared, her, there was a certain attraction about her – was it in her dark unflinching eyes or in her very red lips? – which might lead him into greater follies still.

Thus it came about that for two successive evenings Esther waited for him in vain, and on the third evening he said to himself with a grudging relief that by this time she had probably transferred her affections to someone else.

It was Saturday, the second Saturday since he left town. He spent the day about the farm, contemplated the pigs, inspected the feeding of the stock, and assisted at the afternoon milking. Then at evening, with a refilled pipe, he went for a long lean over the west gate, while he traced fantastic pictures and wove romances in the glories of the sunset clouds.

He watched the colours glow from gold to scarlet, change to crimson, sink at last to sad purple reefs and isles, when the sudden consciousness of someone being near him made him turn round. There stood Esther, and her eyes were full of eagerness and anger.

"Why have you never been to the stile again?" she asked him. "You promised to come faithful, and you never came. Why have you not kep your promise? Why? – why?" she persisted, stamping her foot because Willoughby remained silent.

What could he say! Tell her she had no business to follow him like this; or own, what was, unfortunately, the truth, he was just a little glad to see her?

"P'raps you don't care to see me?" she said. " Well, why did you kiss me, then?"

Why, indeed! thought Willoughby, marvelling at his own idiotcy, and yet – such is the inconsistency of man – not wholly without the desire to kiss her again. And while he looked at her she suddenly flung herself down on the hedge-bank at his feet and burst into tears. She did not cover up her face, but simply pressed one cheek down upon the grass while the water poured from her eyes with astonishing abundance. Willoughby saw the dry earth turn dark and moist as it drank the tears in. This, his first experience of Esther's powers of weeping, distressed him horribly; never in his life before had he seen anyone weep like that; he should not have believed such a thing possible, and he was alarmed, too, lest she should be noticed from the house. He opened the gate; "Esther!" he begged, "don't cry. Come out here, like a dear girl, and let us talk sensibly."

Because she stumbled, unable to see her way through wet eyes, he gave her his hand, and they found themselves in a field of corn, walking along the narrow grass-path that skirted it, in the shadow of the hedgerow.

"What is there to cry about because you have not seen me for two days?" he began; "why, Esther, we are only strangers, after all. When we have been at home a week or two we shall scarcely remember each other's names."

Esther sobbed at intervals, but her tears had ceased. "It's fine for you to talk of home," she said to this. "You've got some thing that is a home, I s'pose? But me! my home's like hell, with nothing but quarrellin' and cursin', and father who beats us whether sober or drunk. Yes!" she repeated shrewdly, seeing the lively disgust on Willoughby's face, "he beat me, all ill as I was, jus' before I come away. I could show you the bruises on my arms still. And now to go back there after knowin' you! It'll be worse than ever. I can't endure it and I won't! I'll put an end to it or myself somehow, I swear!"

"But, my poor Esther, how can I help it, what can I do?" said Willoughby. He was greatly moved, full of wrath with her father, with all the world which makes women suffer. He had suffered himself at the hands of a woman, and severely, but this, instead of hardening his heart, had only rendered it the more supple. And yet he had a vivid perception of the peril in which he stood. An interior voice urged him to break away, to seek safety in flight even at the cost of appearing cruel or ridiculous; so, coming to a point in the field where an elm-bole jutted out across the path, he saw with relief he could now withdraw his hand from the girl's, since they must walk singly to skirt round it.

Esther took a step in advance, stopped and suddenly turned to face him; she held out her two hands and her face was very near his own.

"Don't you care for me one little bit?" she said wistfully, and surely sudden madness fell upon him. For he kissed her again, he kissed her many times, and pushed all thoughts of the consequences far from him.

But some of these consequences already called loudly to him as he and Esther reached the last gate on the road to Orton.

"You know I have only £130 a year?" he told her: "it's no very brilliant prospect for you to marry me on that."

For he had actually offered her marriage, although such conduct to the mediocre man must appear incredible or at least uncalled for. But to Willoughby it seemed the only course possible. How else justify his kisses, rescue her from her father's brutality, or bring back the smiles to her face?

As for Esther, sudden exultation had leaped in her heart; then 'ere fifty seconds were gone by, she was certain she would never have consented to anything less.

"O! I'me used to managin'," she told him confidently, and mentally resolved to buy herself, so soon as she was married, a black feather boa, such as she had coveted last winter.

Willoughby spent the remaining days of his holiday in thinking out and planning with Esther the details of his return to London and her own, the secrecy to be observed, the necessary legal steps to be taken, and the quiet suburb in which they would set up housekeeping. And, so successfully did he carry out his arrangements, that within five weeks from the day on which he had first met Esther Stables he and she came out one morning from a Lucy Rimmerton in Highbury husband and wife. It was a mellow September day, the streets were filled with sunshine, and Willoughby, in reckless high spirits, imagined he saw a reflection of his own gaiety on the indifferent faces of the passers-by. There being no one else to perform the office he congratulated himself very warmly, and Esther's frequent laughter filled in the pauses of the day.

Three months later Willoughby was dining with a friend, and the hour-hand of the clock nearing ten the host no longer resisted the guest's growing anxiety to be gone. He arose and exchanged with him good wishes and goodbyes.

"Marriage is evidently a most successful institution," said he, half jesting, half sincere; "you almost make me inclined to go and get married myself. Confess now your thoughts have been at home the whole evening?"

Willoughby thus addressed turned red to the roots of his hair, but did not deny the soft impeachment.

The other laughed. "And very commendable they should be," he continued, "since you are scarcely, so to speak, out of your honeymoon."

With a social smile on his lips Willoughby calculated a moment before replying, "I have been married exactly three months and three days;" then, after a few words respecting their next meeting, the two shook hands and parted, the young host to finish the evening with books and pipe, the young husband to set out on a twenty minutes walk to his home.

It was a cold clear December night following a day of rain. A touch of frost in the air had dried the pavements, and Willoughby's footfall ringing upon the stones re-echoed down the empty suburban street. Above his head was a dark remote sky thickly powdered with stars, and as he turned westward Alpherat hung for a moment "comme le point sur un i," over the slender spire of St. John's. But he was insensible to the worlds about him; he was absorbed in his own thoughts, and these, as his friend had surmised, were entirely with his wife. For Esther's face was always before his eyes, her voice was always in his ears, she filled the universe for him; yet only four months ago he had never seen her, had never heard her name. This was the curious part of it – here in December he found himself the husband of a girl who was completely dependent upon him not only for food, clothes, and lodging, but for her present happiness, her whole future life; and last July he had been scarcely more than a boy himself, with no greater care on his mind than the pleasant difficulty of deciding where he should spend his annual three weeks holiday.

But it is events, not months or years, which age. Willoughby, who was only twenty-six, remembered his youth as a sometime companion irrevocably lost to him; its vague, delightful hopes were now crystallised into definite ties, and its happy irresponsibility displaced by a sense of care inseparable perhaps from the most fortunate of marriages.

As he reached the street in which he lodged his pace involuntarily slackened. While still some distance off his eye sought out and distinguished the windows of the room in which Esther awaited him. Through the broken slats of the Venetian blinds he could see the yellow gaslight within. The parlour beneath was in darkness; his landlady had evidently gone to bed, there being no light over the hall door either. In some apprehension he consulted his watch under the last street-lamp he passed, to find comfort in assuring himself it was only ten minutes after ten. He let himself in with his latch-key, hung up his hat and overcoat by the sense of touch, and, groping his way upstairs, opened the door of the first floor sitting-room.

At the table in the centre of the room sat his wife, leaning upon her elbows, her two hands thrust up into her ruffled hair; spread out before her was a crumpled yesterday's newspaper, and so interested was she to all appearance in its contents that she neither spoke nor looked up as Willoughby entered. Around her were the still uncleared tokens of her last meal: tea-slops, bread-crumbs, and an eggshell crushed to fragments upon a plate, which was one of those trifles that set Willoughby's teeth on edge – whenever his wife ate an egg she persisted in turning the egg-cup upside down upon the tablecloth, and pounding the shell to pieces in her plate with her spoon.

The room was repulsive in its disorder. The one lighted burner of the gaselier, turned too high, hissed up into a long tongue of flame. The fire smoked feebly under a newly administered shovelful of "slack," and a heap of ashes and cinders littered the grate. A pair of walking boots, caked in dry mud, lay on the hearthrug just where they had been thrown off. On the mantelpiece, amidst a dozen other articles which had no business there, was a bedroom-candlestick; and every single article of furniture stood crookedly out of its place.

Willoughby took in the whole intolerable picture, and yet spoke with kindliness. "Well, Esther! I'm not so late, after all. I hope you did not feel the time dull by yourself?" Then he explained the reason of his absence. He had met a friend he had not seen for a couple of years, who had insisted on taking him home to dine.

His wife gave no sign of having heard him; she kept he eyes rivetted on the paper before her.

"You received my wire, of course," Willoughby went on, "and did not wait?"

Now she crushed the newspaper up with a passionate movement, and threw it from her. She raised her head, showing cheeks blazing with anger, and dark, sullen, unflinching eyes.

"I did wyte then!" she cried. "I wyted till near eight before I got your old telegraph! I s'pose that's what you call the manners of a gentleman, to keep your wife mewed up here, while you go gallivantin' off with your fine friends?"

Whenever Esther was angry, which was often, she taunted Willoughby with being "a gentleman," although this was the precise point about him which at other times found most favour in her eyes. But tonight she was envenomed by the idea he had been enjoying himself without her, stung by fear lest he should have been in company with some other woman.

Willoughby, hearing the taunt, resigned himself to the inevitable. Nothing that he could do might now avert the breaking storm, all his words would only be twisted into fresh griefs. But sad experience had taught him that to take refuge in silence was more fatal still. When Esther was in such a mood as this it was best to supply the fire with fuel, that, through the very violence of the conflagration, it might the sooner burn itself out.

So he said what soothing things he could, and Esther caught them up, disfigured them, and flung them back at him with scorn. She reproached him with no longer caring for her; she vituperated the conduct of his family in never taking the smallest notice of her marriage; and she detailed the insolence of the landlady, who had told her that morning she pitied "poor Mr. Willoughby," and had refused to go out and buy herrings for Esther's early dinner.

Every affront or grievance, real or imaginary, since the day she and Willoughby had first met, she poured forth with a fluency due to frequent repetition, for, with the exception of today's added injuries, Willoughby had heard the whole litany many times before.

While she raged and he looked at her, he remembered he had once thought her pretty. He had seen beauty in her rough brown hair, her strong colouring, her full red mouth. He fell into musing... a woman may lack beauty, he told himself, and yet be loved...

Meantime Esther reached white heats of passion, and the strain could no longer be sustained. She broke into sobs and began to shed tears with the facility peculiar to her. In a moment her face was all wet with the big drops which rolled down her cheeks faster and faster and fell with audible splashes on to the table, on to her lap, on to the floor. To this tearful abundance, formerly a surprising spectacle, Willoughby was now acclimatised; but the remnant of chivalrous feeling not yet extinguished in his bosom forbade him to sit stolidly by while a woman wept, without seeking to console her. As on previous occasions, his peace-overtures were eventually accepted. Esther's tears gradually ceased to flow, she began to exhibit a sort of compunction, she wished to be forgiven, and, with the kiss of reconciliation, passed into a phase of demonstrative affection perhaps more trying to Willoughby's patience than all that had preceded it. "You don't love me?" she questioned, "I'm sure you don't love me?" she reiterated; and he asseverated that he loved her until he loathed himself. Then at last, only half satisfied, but wearied out with vexation – possibly, too, with a movement of pity at the sight of his haggard face – she consented to leave him; only what was he going to do? she asked suspiciously: write those rubbishing stories of his? Well, he must promise not to stay up more than half an hour at the latest only until he had smoked one pipe!

Willoughby promised, as he would have promised anything on earth to secure to himself a half-hour's peace and solitude. Esther groped for her slippers, which were kicked off under the table; scratched four or five matches along the box and threw them away before she succeeded in lighting her candle; set it down again to contemplate her tear-swollen reflection in the chimney-glass, and burst out laughing.

"What a fright I do look, to be sure!" she remarked complacently, and again thrust her two hands up through her disordered curls. Then, holding the candle at such an angle that the grease ran over on to the carpet, she gave Willoughby another vehement kiss and trailed out of the room with an ineffectual attempt to close the door behind her.

Willoughby got up to shut it himself, and wondered why it was that Esther never did any one mortal thing efficiently or well. Good God! how irritable he felt! It was impossible to write. He must find an outlet for his impatience, rend or mend something. He began to straighten the room, but a wave or disgust came over him before the task was fairly commenced. What was the use? Tomorrow all would be bad as ever. What was the use of doing anything? He sat down by the table and leaned his head upon his hands.

The past came back to him in pictures: his boyhood's past first of all. He saw again the old home, every inch of which was familiar to him as his own name; he reconstructed in his thought all the old well-known furniture, and replaced it precisely as it had stood long ago. He passed again a childish finger over the rough surface of the faded Utrecht velvet chairs, and smelled again the strong fragrance of the white lilac-tree, blowing in through the open parlour-window. He savoured anew the pleasant mental atmosphere produced by the dainty neatness of cultured women, the companionship of a few good pictures, of a few good books. Yet this home had been broken up years ago, the dear familiar things had been scattered far and wide, never to find themselves under the same roof again; and from those near relatives who still remained to him he lived now hopelessly estranged.

Then came the past of his first love-dream, when he worshipped at the feet of Nora Beresford, and, with the wholeheartedness of the true fanatic, clothed his idol with every imaginable attribute of virtue and tenderness. To this day there remained a secret shrine in his heart wherein the Lady of his young ideal was still enthroned, although it was long since he had come to perceive she had nothing whatever in common with the Nora of reality. For the real Nora he had no longer any sentiment: she had passed altogether out of his life and thoughts; and yet, so permanent is all influence, whether good or evil, that the effect she wrought upon his character remained. He recognised tonight that her treatment of him in the past did not count for nothing among the various factors which had determined his fate.

Now the past of only last year returned, and, strangely enough, this seemed farther removed from him than all the rest. He had been particularly strong, well and happy this time last year. Nora was dismissed from his mind, and he had thrown all his energies into his work. His tastes were sane and simple, and his dingy, furnished rooms had become through habit very pleasant to him. In being his own they were invested with a greater charm than another man's castle. Here he had smoked and studied, here he had made many a glorious voyage into the land of books. Many a home-coming, too, rose up before him out of the dark ungenial streets to a clean blazing fire, a neatly laid cloth, an evening of ideal enjoyment; many a summer twilight when he mused at the open window, plunging his gaze deep into the recesses of his neighbour's lime-tree, where the unseen sparrows chattered with such unflagging gaiety.

He had always been given to much day-dreaming, and it was in the silence of his rooms of an evening that he turned his phantas-mal adventures into stories for the magazines; here had come to him many an editorial refusal, but, here, too, he had received the news of his first unexpected success. All his happiest memories were embalmed in those shabby, badly furnished rooms.

Now all was changed. Now might there be no longer any soft indulgence of the hour's mood. His rooms and everything he owned belonged now to Esther, too. She had objected to most of his photographs, and had removed them. She hated books, and were he ever so ill-advised as to open one in her presence, she immediately began to talk, no matter how silent or how sullen her previous mood had been. If he read aloud to her she either yawned despairingly, or was tickled into laughter where there was no reasonable cause. At first, Willoughby had tried to educate her and had gone hopefully to the task. It is so natural to think you may make what you will of the woman who loves you. But Esther had no wish to improve. She evinced all the self-satisfaction of an illiterate mind. To her husband's gentle admonitions she replied with brevity that she thought her way quite as good as his; or, if he didn't approve of her pronunciation, he might do the other thing, she was too old to go to school again. He gave up the attempt, and, with humiliation at his previous fatuity, perceived that it was folly to expect a few weeks of his companionship could alter or pull up the impressions of years, or rather of generations.

Yet here he paused to admit a curious thing: it was not only Esther's bad habits which vexed him, but habits quite unblame-worthy in themselves, and which he never would have noticed in another, irritated him in her. He disliked her manner of standing, of walking, of sitting in a chair, of folding her hands. Like a lover he was conscious of her proximity without seeing her. Like a lover, too, his eyes followed her every movement, his ear noted every change in her voice. But, then, instead of being charmed by everything as the lover is, everything jarred upon him.

What was the meaning of this? Tonight the anomaly pressed upon him: he reviewed his position. Here was he quite a young man, just twenty-six years of age, married to Esther, and bound to live with her so long as life should last twenty, forty, perhaps fifty years more. Every day of those years to be spent in her society; he and she face to face, soul to soul; they two alone amid all the whirling, busy, indifferent world. So near together in semblance, in truth so far apart as regards all that makes life dear.

Willoughby groaned. From the woman he did not love, whom he had never loved, he might not again go free; so much he recognised. The feeling he had once entertained for Esther, strange compound of mistaken chivalry and flattered vanity, was long since extinct; but what, then, was the sentiment with which she inspired him? For he was not indifferent to her – no, never for one instant could he persuade himself he was indifferent, never for one instant could he banish her from his thoughts. His mind's eye followed her during his hours of absence as pertinaciously as his bodily eye dwelt upon her actual presence. She was the principal object of the universe to him, the centre around which his wheel of life revolved with an appalling fidelity.

What did it mean? What could it mean? he asked himself with anguish.

And the sweat broke out upon his forehead and his hands grew cold, for on a sudden the truth lay there like a written word upon the tablecloth before him. This woman, whom he had taken to himself for better for worse, inspired him with a passion intense indeed, all-masterful, soul-subduing as Love itself –... But when he understood the terror of his Hatred, he laid his head upon his arms and wept, not facile tears like Esther's, but tears wrung out from his agonising, unavailing regret.

If you enjoyed this, you might also like...
The Houseboat, see page 330
From the Dead, see page 249

A Lost Masterpiece
A City Mood, Aug. '93

George Egerton

I REGRET it, but what am I to do? It was not my fault – I can only regret it. It was thus it happened to me.

I had come to town straight from a hillside cottage in a lonely ploughland, with the smell of the turf in my nostrils, and the swish of the scythes in my ears; the scythes that flashed in the meadows where the upland hay, drought-parched, stretched thirstily up to the clouds that mustered upon the mountain-tops, and marched mockingly away, and held no rain.

The desire to mix with the crowd, to lay my ear once more to the heart of the world and listen to its life-throbs, had grown too strong for me; and so I had come back – but the sights and sounds of my late life clung to me – it is singular how the most opposite things often fill one with associative memory.

That *gamin* of the bird-tribe, the Cockney sparrow, recalled the swallows that built in the tumble-down shed; and I could almost see the gleam of their white bellies, as they circled in ever narrowing sweeps and clove the air with forked wings, uttering a shrill note, with a querulous grace-note in front of it.

The freshness of the country still lurked in me, unconsciously influencing my attitude towards the city.

One forenoon business drove me citywards, and following an inclination that always impels me to water-ways rather than roadways, I elected to go by river steamer.

I left home in a glad mood, disposed to view the whole world with kindly eyes. I was filled with a happy-go-lucky *insouciance* that made walking the pavements a loafing in Elysian fields. The coarser touches of street-life, the oddities of accent, the idiosyncrasies of that most eccentric of city-dwellers, the Londoner, did not jar as at other times – rather added a zest to enjoyment; impressions crowded in too quickly to admit of analysis, I was simply an interested spectator of a varied panorama.

I was conscious, too, of a peculiar dual action of brain and senses, for, though keenly alive to every unimportant detail of the life about me, I was yet able to follow a process by which delicate inner threads were being spun into a fanciful web that had nothing to do with my outer self.

At Chelsea I boarded a river steamer bound for London Bridge. The river was wrapped in a delicate grey haze with a golden subtone, like a beautiful bright thought struggling for utterance through a mist of obscure words. It glowed through the turbid waters under the arches, so that I feared to see a face or a hand wave through its dull amber – for I always think of drowned creatures washing wearily in its murky depths – it lit up the great warehouses, and warmed the brickwork of the monster chimneys in the background. No detail escaped my outer eyes – not the hideous green of the velveteen in the sleeves of the woman on my left, nor the supercilious giggle of the young ladies on my right, who made audible remarks about my personal appearance.

But what cared I? Was I not happy, absurdly happy? – because all the while my inner eyes saw undercurrents of beauty and pathos, quaint contrasts, whimsical details that tickled my sense of humour deliciously. The elf that lurks in some inner cell was very busy, now throwing out tender mimosa-like threads of creative fancy, now recording fleeting impressions with delicate sure brushwork for future use; touching a hundred vagrant things with the magic of imagination, making a running comment on the scenes we passed.

The warehouses told a tale of an up-to-date Soll und Haben, one of my very own, one that would thrust old Freytag out of the book-mart. The tall chimneys ceased to be giraffic throats belching soot and smoke over the blackening city. They were obelisks rearing granite heads heavenwards! Joints in the bricks, weather-stains? You are mistaken; they were hieroglyphics, setting down for posterity a tragic epic of man the conqueror, and fire his slave; and how they strangled beauty in the grip of gain. A theme for a Whitman!

And so it talks and I listen with my inner ear – and yet nothing outward escapes me – the slackening of the boat – the stepping on and off of folk – the lowering of the funnel – the name "Stanley" on the little tug, with its self-sufficient puff-puff, fussing by with a line of grimy barges in tow; freight-laden, for the water washes over them – and on the last a woman sits suckling her baby, and a terrier with badly cropped ears yaps at us as we pass...

And as this English river scene flashes by, lines of association form angles in my brain; and the point of each is a dot of light that expands into a background for forgotten canal scenes, with green-grey water, and leaning balconies, and strange crafts – Canaletti and Guardi seen long ago in picture galleries...

A delicate featured youth with gold-laced cap, scrapes a prelude on a thin-toned violin, and his companion thrums an accompaniment on a harp.

I don't know what they play, some tuneful thing with an undernote of sadness and sentiment running through its commonplace – likely a music-hall ditty; for a lad with a cheap silk hat, and the hateful expression of knowingness that makes him a type of his kind, grins appreciatively and hums the words.

I turn from him to the harp. It is the wreck of a handsome instrument, its gold is tarnished, its white is smirched, its stucco rose-wreaths sadly battered. It has the air of an antique beauty in dirty ball finery; and is it fancy, or does not a shamed wail lurk in the tone of its strings?

The whimsical idea occurs to me that it has once belonged to a lady with drooping ringlets and an embroidered spencer; and that she touched its chords to the words of a song by Thomas Haynes Baily, and that Miss La Creevy transferred them both to ivory.

The youth played mechanically, without a trace of emotion; whilst the harpist, whose nose is a study in purples and whose bloodshot eyes have the glassy brightness of drink, felt every touch of beauty in the poor little tune, and drew it tenderly forth.

They added the musical note to my joyous mood; the poetry of the city dovetailed harmoniously with country scenes too recent to be treated as memories – and I stepped off the boat with the melody vibrating through the city sounds.

I swung from place to place in happy, lightsome mood, glad as a fairy prince in quest of adventures. The air of the city was exhilarating ether – and all mankind my brethren – in fact I felt effusively affectionate.

I smiled at a pretty anaemic city girl, and only remembered that she was a stranger when she flashed back an indignant look of affected affront.

But what cared I? Not a jot! I could afford to say pityingly: Go thy way, little city maid, get thee to thy typing.

And all the while that these outward insignificant things occupied me, I knew that a precious little pearl of a thought was evolving slowly out of the inner chaos.

It was such an unique little gem, with the lustre of a tear, and the light of moonlight and streamlight and love smiles reflected in its pure sheen – and, best of all, it was all my own – a priceless possession, not to be bartered for the Jagersfontein diamond – a city childling with the prepotency of the country working in it – and I revelled in its fresh charm and dainty strength; it seemed original, it was so frankly natural.

And as I dodged through the great waggons laden with wares from outer continents, I listened and watched it forming inside, until my soul became filled with the light of its brightness; and a wild elation possessed me at the thought of this darling brain-child, this offspring of my fancy, this rare little creation, perhaps embryo of genius that was my very own.

I smiled benevolently at the passers-by, with their harassed business faces, and shiny black bags bulging with the weight of common every-day documents, as I thought of the treat I would give them later on; the delicate feast I held in store for them, when I would transfer this dainty elusive birthling of my brain to paper for their benefit.

It would make them dream of moonlit lanes and sweethearting; reveal to them the golden threads in the sober city woof; creep in close and whisper good cheer, and smooth out tired creases in heart and brain; a draught from the fountain of Jouvence could work no greater miracle than the tale I had to unfold.

Aye, they might pass me by now, not even give me the inside of the pavement, I would not blame them for it! – but later on, later on, they would flock to thank me. They just didn't realise, poor money-grubbers! How could they? But later on... I grew perfectly radiant at the thought of what I would do for poor humanity, and absurdly self-satisfied as the conviction grew upon me that this would prove a work of genius – no mere glimmer of the spiritual afflatus – but a solid chunk of genius.

Meanwhile I took a bus and paid my penny. I leant back and chuckled to myself as each fresh thought-atom added to the precious quality of my pearl. Pearl? Not one any longer – a whole quarrelet of pearls, Oriental pearls of the greatest price! Ah, how happy I was as I fondled my conceit!

It was near Chancery Lane that a foreign element cropped up and disturbed the rich flow of my fancy.

I happened to glance at the side-walk. A woman, a little woman, was hurrying along in a most remarkable way. It annoyed me, for I could not help wondering why she was in such a desperate hurry. Bother the jade! what business had she to thrust herself on my observation like that, and tangle the threads of a web of genius, undoubted genius?

I closed my eyes to avoid seeing her; I could see her through the lids. She had square shoulders and a high bust, and a white gauze tie, like a snowy feather in the breast of a pouter pigeon.

We stop – I look again – aye, there she is! Her black eyes stare boldly through her kohol-tinted lids, her face has a violet tint. She grips her gloves in one hand, her white-handled umbrella in the other, handle up, like a knobkerrie.

She has great feet, too, in pointed shoes, and the heels are under her insteps; and as we outdistance her I fancy I can hear their decisive tap-tap above the thousand sounds of the street.

I breathe a sigh of relief as I return to my pearl – my pearl that is to bring *me* kudos and make countless thousands rejoice. It is dimmed a little, I must nurse it tenderly.

Jerk, jerk, jangle – stop. – Bother the bell! We pull up to drop some passengers, the idiots! and, as I live, she overtakes us! How the men and women cede her the middle of the pavement! How her figure dominates it, and her great feet emphasise her ridiculous haste! Why should she disturb me? My nerves are quivering pitifully; the sweet inner light is waning, I am in mortal dread of losing my little masterpiece. Thank heaven, we are off again...

Charing Cross, Army and Navy, V'toria! – Stop!

Of course, naturally! Here she comes, elbows out, umbrella waving! How the steel in her bonnet glistens! She recalls something, what is it? – what is it? A-ah! I have it! – a strident voice, on the deck of a steamer in the glorious bay of Rio, singing:

"Je suis le vr-r-rai pompier, Le seul pompier..."

and *la mióla* snaps her fingers gaily and trills her *r's*; and the Corcovado is outlined clearly on the purple background as if bending to listen; and the palms and the mosque-like buildings, and the fair islets bathed in the witchery of moonlight, and the star-gems twinned in the lap of the bay, intoxicate as a dream of the East.

"Je suis le vr-r-rai pompier, Le seul pompier..."

What in the world is a *pompier*? What connection has the word with this creature who is murdering, deliberately murdering, a delicate creation of my brain, begotten by the fusion of country and town?

"Je suis le vr-r-rai pompier,

I am convinced *pompier* expresses her in some subtle way – absurd word! I look back at her, I criticise her, I anathematise her, I *hate* her!

What is she hurrying for? We can't escape her – always we stop and let her overtake us with her elbowing gait, and tight skirt shortened to show her great splay feet – ugh!

My brain is void, all is dark within; the flowers are faded, the music stilled; the lovely illusive little being has flown, and yet she pounds along untiringly.

Is she a feminine presentment of the wandering Jew, a living embodiment of the ghoul-like spirit that haunts the city and murders fancy?

What business had she, I ask, to come and thrust her white-handled umbrella into the delicate network of my nerves and untune their harmony?

Does she realise what she has done? She has trampled a rare little mind-being unto death, destroyed a precious literary gem. Aye, one that, for aught I know, might have worked a revolution in modern thought; added a new human document to the archives of man; been the keystone to psychic investigations; solved problems that lurk in the depths of our natures and tantalise us with elusive gleams of truth; heralded in, perchance, the new era; when such simple problems as Home Rule, Bimetallism, or the Woman Question will be mere themes for schoolboard compositions – who can tell?

Well, it was not my fault. – No one regrets it more, no one – but what could I do? Blame her, woman of the great feet and dominating gait, and waving umbrella-handle! – blame her! I can only regret it – regret it!

If you enjoyed this, you might also like...
A Cross Line, see page 143
The Chaperon, see page 117

An Imaginative Woman

Thomas Hardy

WHEN WILLIAM MARCHMILL had finished his inquiries for lodgings at the well-known watering-place of Solentsea in Upper Wessex, he returned to the hotel to find his wife. She, with the children, had rambled along the shore, and Marchmill followed in the direction indicated by the military-looking hall-porter.

"By Jove, how far you've gone! I am quite out of breath," Marchmill said, rather impatiently, when he came up with his wife, who was reading as she walked, the three children being considerably further ahead with the nurse.

Mrs. Marchmill started out of the reverie into which the book had thrown her. "Yes," she said, "you've been such a long time. I was tired of staying in that dreary hotel. But I am sorry if you have wanted me, Will?"

"Well I have had trouble to suit myself. When you see the airy and comfortable rooms heard of, you find they are stuffy and uncomfortable. Will you come and see if what I've fixed on will do? There is not much room, I am afraid; but I can light on nothing better. The town is rather full."

The pair left the children and nurse to continue their ramble, and went back together.

In age well-balanced, in personal appearance fairly matched, and in domestic requirements conformable, in temper this couple differed, though even here they did not often clash, he being equable, if not lymphatic, and she decidedly nervous and sanguine. It was to their tastes and fancies, those smallest, greatest particulars, that no common denominator could be applied. Marchmill considered his wife's likes and inclinations somewhat silly; she considered his sordid and material. The husband's business was that of a gunmaker in a thriving city northwards, and his soul was in that business always; the lady was best characterized by that superannuated phrase of elegance "a votary of the muse." An impressionable, palpitating creature was Ella, shrinking humanely from detailed knowledge of her husband's trade whenever she reflected that everything he manufactured had for its purpose the destruction of life. She could only recover her equanimity by assuring herself that some, at least, of his weapons were sooner or later used for the extermination of horrid vermin and animals almost as cruel to their inferiors in species as human beings were to theirs.

She had never antecedently regarded this occupation of his as any objection to having him for a husband. Indeed, the necessity of getting life-leased at all cost, a cardinal virtue which all good mothers teach, kept her from thinking of it at all till she had closed with William, had passed the honeymoon, and reached the reflecting stage. Then, like a person who has stumbled upon some object in the dark, she wondered what she had got; mentally walked round it, estimated it; whether it were rare or common; contained gold, silver, or lead; were a clog or a pedestal, everything to her or nothing.

She came to some vague conclusions, and since then had kept her heart alive by pitying her proprietor's obtuseness and want of refinement, pitying herself, and letting off her delicate and ethereal emotions in imaginative occupations, daydreams, and night-sighs, which perhaps would not much have disturbed William if he had known of them.

Her figure was small, elegant, and slight in build, tripping, or rather bounding, in movement. She was dark-eyed, and had that marvelously bright and liquid sparkle in each pupil which characterizes persons of Ella's cast of soul, and is too often a cause of heartache to the possessor's male friends, ultimately sometimes to herself. Her husband was a tall, long-featured man, with a brown beard; he had a pondering regard; and was, it must be added, usually kind and tolerant to her. He spoke in squarely shaped sentences, and was supremely satisfied with a condition of sublunary things which made weapons a necessity.

Husband and wife walked till they had reached the house they were in search of, which stood in a terrace facing the sea, and was fronted by a small garden of windproof and salt-proof evergreens, stone steps leading up to the porch. It had its number in the row, but, being rather larger than the rest, was in addition sedulously distinguished as Coburg House by its landlady, though everybody else called it "Thirteen, New Parade." The spot was bright and lively now; but in winter it became necessary to place sandbags against the door, and to stuff up the keyhole against the wind and rain, which had worn the paint so thin that the priming and knotting showed through.

The householder, who had been watching for the gentleman's return, met them in the passage, and showed the rooms. She informed them that she was a professional man's widow, left in needy circumstances by the rather sudden death of her husband, and she spoke anxiously of the conveniences of the establishment.

Mrs. Marchmill said that she liked the situation and the house; but, it being small, there would not be accommodation enough, unless she could have all the rooms.

The landlady mused with an air of disappointment. She wanted the visitors to be her tenants very badly, she said, with obvious honesty. But unfortunately two of the rooms were occupied permanently by a bachelor gentleman. He did not pay season prices, it was true; but as he kept on his apartments all the year round, and was all extremely nice and interesting young man, who gave no trouble, she did not like to turn him out for a month's "let," even at a high figure. "Perhaps, however," she added, "he might offer to go for a time."

They would not hear of this, and went back to the hotel, intending to proceed to the agent's to inquire further. Hardly had they sat down to tea when the landlady called. Her gentleman, she said, had been so obliging as to offer to give up his rooms three or four weeks rather than drive the newcomers away.

"It is very kind, but we won't inconvenience him in that way," said the Marchmills.

O, it won't inconvenience him, I assure you!" said the landlady eloquently. "You see, he's a different sort of young man from most – dreamy, solitary, rather melancholy – and he cares more to be here when the south-westerly gales are beating against the door, and the sea washes over the Parade, and there's not a soul in the place, than he does now in the season. He'd just as soon be where, in fact, he's going temporarily to a little cottage on the Island opposite, for a change." She hoped therefore that they would come.

The Marchmill family accordingly took possession of the house next day, and it seemed to suit them very well. After luncheon Mr. Marchmill strolled out toward the pier, and Mrs. Marchmill, having despatched the children to their outdoor amusements on the sands, settled herself in more completely, examining this and that article, and testing the reflecting powers of the mirror in the wardrobe door.

In the small back sitting room, which had been the young bachelor's, she found furniture of a more personal nature than in the rest. Shabby books, of correct rather than rare editions, were piled up in a queerly reserved manner in corners, as if the previous occupant had not conceived the possibility that any incoming person of the season's bringing could care to look inside them. The landlady hovered on the threshold to rectify anything that Mrs. Marchmill might not find to her satisfaction.

"I'll make this my own little room," said the latter, "because the books are here. By the way, the person who has left seems to have a good many. He won't mind my reading some of them, Mrs. Hooper, I hope?"

"O, dear no, ma'am. Yes, he has a good many. You see, he is in the literary line himself somewhat. He is a poet – yes, really a poet – and he has a little income of his own, which is enough to write verses on, but not enough for cutting a figure, even if he cared to."

"A Poet! O, I did not know that."

Mrs. Marchmill opened one of the books, and saw the owner's name written on the title-page. "Dear me!" she continued; "I know his name very well – Robert Trewe – of course I do; and his writings! And it is his rooms we have taken, and him we have turned out of his home?"

Ella Marchmill, sitting down alone a few minutes later, thought with interested surprise of Robert Trewe. Her own latter history will best explain that interest. Herself the only daughter of a struggling man of letters, she had during the last year or two taken to writing poems, in an endeavor to find a congenial channel in which let flow her painfully embayed emotions, whose former limpidity and sparkle seemed departing in the stagnation caused by the routine of a practical household and the gloom of bearing children to a commonplace father. These poems, subscribed with masculine pseudonym, had appeared in various obscure magazines, and in two cases in rather prominent ones. In the second of the latter the page which bore her effusion at the bottom, in smallish print, bore at the top, in large print, a few verses on the same subject by this very man, Robert Trewe. Both of them, had, in fact, been struck by a tragic incident reported in the daily papers, and had used it simultaneously as an inspiration, the editor remarking in a note upon the coincidence, and that the excellence of both poems prompted him to give them together.

After that event Ella, otherwise "John Ivy," had watched with much attention the appearance anywhere in print of verse bearing the signature of Robert Trewe, who, with a man's unsusceptibility on the question of sex, had never once thought of passing himself off as a woman. To be sure, Mrs. Marchmill had satisfied herself with a sort of reason for doing the contrary in her case; since nobody might believe in her inspiration if they found that the sentiments came from a pushing tradesman's wife, from the mother of three children by a matter-of-fact small-arms manufacturer.

Trewe's verse contrasted with that of the rank and file of recent minor poets in being impassioned rather than ingenious, luxuriant rather than finished. Neither *symboliste* nor *decadent*, he was a pessimist in so far as that character applies to a man who looks at the worst contingencies as well as the best in the human condition. Being little attracted by excellences of form and rhythm apart from content, he sometimes, when feeling outran his artistic speed, perpetrated sonnets in the loosely rhymed Elizabethan fashion, which every right-minded reviewer said he ought not to have done.

With sad and hopeless envy Ella Marchmill had often and often scanned the rival poet's work, so much stronger as it always was than her own feeble lines. She had imitated him, and her inability to touch his level would send her into fits of despondency. Months passed away thus, till she observed from the publishers' list that Trewe had collected his fugitive pieces into a volume, which was duly issued, and was much or little praised according to chance, and had a sale quite sufficient to pay for the printing.

This step onward had suggested to John Ivy the idea of collecting her pieces also, or at any rate of making up a book of her rhymes by adding many in manuscript to the few that had seen the light, for she had been able to get no great number into print. A ruinous charge was made for costs of publication; a few reviews noticed her poor little volume; but nobody talked of it, nobody bought it, and it fell dead in a fortnight – if it had ever been alive.

The author's thoughts were diverted to another groove just then by the discovery that she was going to have a third child, and the collapse of her poetical venture had perhaps less effect upon her mind than it might have done if she had been domestically unoccupied. Her husband had paid the publisher's bill with the doctor's, and there it all had ended for the time. But, though less than a poet of her century, Ella was more than a mere multiplier of her kind, and latterly she had begun to feel the old afflatus once more. And now by an odd conjunction she found herself in the rooms of Robert Trewe.

She thoughtfully rose from her chair and searched the apartment with the interest of a fellow-tradesman. Yes, the volume of his own verse was among the rest. Though quite familiar with its contents, she read it here as if it spoke aloud to her, then called up Mrs. Hooper, the landlady, for some trivial service, and inquired again about the young man.

"Well, I'm sure you'd be interested in him, ma'am, if you could see him, only he's so shy that I don't suppose you will." Mrs. Hooper seemed nothing loth to minister to her tenant's curiosity about her predecessor. "Lived here long? Yes, nearly two years. He keeps on his rooms even when he's not here: the soft air of this place suits his chest, and he likes to be able to come back at any time. He is mostly writing or reading, and doesn't see many people, though, for the matter of that, he is such a good, kind young fellow that folks would only be too glad to be friendly with him if they knew him. You don't meet kind-hearted people everyday."

"Ah, he's kind-hearted... and good."

"Yes; he'll oblige me in anything if I ask him. 'Mr. Trewe,' I say to him sometimes, you are rather out of spirits.' 'Well, I am, Mrs. Hooper,' he'll say, 'though I don't know how you should find it out.' 'Why not take a little change?' I ask. Then in a day or two he'll say that he will take a trip to Paris, or Norway, or somewhere; and I assure you he comes back all the better for it."

"Ah, indeed! His is a sensitive nature, no doubt."

"Yes. Still he's odd in some things. Once when he had finished a poem of his composition late at night he walked up and down the room rehearsing it; and the floors being so thin – jerry-built houses, you know, though I say it myself – he kept me awake up above him till I wished him further... But we get on very well."

This was but the beginning of a series of conversations about the rising poet as the days went on. On one of these occasions Mrs. Hooper drew Ella's attention to what she had not noticed before: minute scribblings in pencil on the wallpaper behind the curtains at the head of the bed.

"O! let me look," said Mrs. Marchmill, unable to conceal a rush of tender curiosity as she bent her pretty face close to the wall.

"These," said Mrs. Hooper, with the manner of a woman who knew things, "are the very beginnings and first thoughts of his verses. He has tried to rub most of them out, but you can read them still. My belief is that he wakes up in the night, you know, with some rhyme in his head, and jots it down there on the wall lest he should forget it by the morning. Some of these very lines you see here I have seen afterwards in print in the magazines. Some are newer; indeed, I have not seen that one before. It must have been done only a few days ago."

"O, yes!..." Ella Marchmill flushed without knowing why, and suddenly wished her companion would go away, now that the information was imparted. An indescribable consciousness of personal interest rather than literary made her anxious to read the inscription alone; and she accordingly waited till she could do so, with a sense that a great store of emotion would be enjoyed in the act.

Perhaps because the sea was choppy outside the Island, Ella's husband found it much pleasanter to go sailing and steaming about without his wife, who was a bad sailor, than with her. He did not disdain to go thus alone on board the steamboats of the cheap-trippers, where there was dancing by moonlight, and where the couples would come suddenly down with a lurch into each other's arms; for, as he blandly told her, the company was too mixed for him to take her amid such scenes. Thus, while this thriving manufacturer got a great deal of change and sea-air out of his sojourn here, the life, external at least, of Ella was monotonous enough, and mainly consisted in passing a certain number of hours each day in bathing and walking up and down a stretch of shore. But the poetic impulse having again waxed strong, she was possessed by an inner flame which left her hardly conscious of what was proceeding around her.

She had read till she knew by heart Trewe's last little volume of verses, and spent a great deal of time in vainly attempting to rival some of them, till, in her failure, she burst into tears. The personal element in the magnetic attraction exercised by this circumambient, unapproachable master of hers was so much stronger than the intellectual and abstract that she could not understand it. To be sure, she was surrounded noon and night by his customary environment, which literally whispered of him to her at every moment; but he was a man she had never seen, and that all that moved her was the instinct to specialize a waiting emotion on the first fit thing that came to hand did not, of course, suggest itself to Ella.

In the natural way of passion under the too practical conditions which civilization has devised for its fruition, her husband's love for her had not survived, except in the form of fitful friendship, anymore than, or even so much as, her own for him; and, being a woman of very living ardors, that required sustenance of some sort, they were beginning to feed on this chancing material, which was, indeed, of a quality far better than chance usually offers.

One day the children had been playing hide-and-seek in a closet, whence, in their excitement they pulled out some clothing. Mrs. Hooper explained that it belonged to Mr. Trewe, and hung it up in the closet again. Possessed of her fantasy, Ella went later in the afternoon, when nobody was in that part of the house, opened the closet, unhitched one of the articles, a mackintosh, and put it on, with the waterproof cap belonging to it.

"The mantle of Elijah!" she said. "Would it might inspire me to rival him, glorious genius that he is!"

Her eyes always grew wet when she thought like that, and she turned to look at herself in the glass. His heart had beat inside that coat, and his brain had worked under that hat at levels of thought she would never reach. The consciousness of her weakness beside him made her feel quite sick. Before she had got the things off her the door opened, and her husband entered the room.

"What the devil—"

She blushed, and removed them. "I found them in the closet here," she said, "and put them on in a freak. What have I else to do? You are always away!"

"Always away? Well..."

That evening she had a further talk with the landlady, who might herself have nourished a half-tender regard for the poet, so ready was she to discourse ardently about him. "You are interested in Mr. Trewe, I know, ma'am," she said; "and he has just sent to say that he is going to call tomorrow afternoon to look up some books of his that he wants, if I'll be in, and he may select them from your room?"

"O, yes!"

"You could very well meet Mr. Trewe then, if you'd like to be in the way!"

She promised with secret delight, and went to bed musing of him.

Next morning her husband observed: "I've been thinking of what you said, Ell: that I have gone about a good deal and left you without much to amuse you. Perhaps it's true. Today, as there's not much sea, I'll take you with me on board the yacht."

For the first time in her experience of such an offer Ella was not glad. But she accepted it for the moment. The time for setting out drew near, and she went to get ready. She stood reflecting. The longing to see the poet she was now distinctly in love with overpowered all other considerations.

"I don't want to go," she said to herself. "I can't bear to be away! And I won't go."

She told her husband that she had changed her mind about wishing to sail. He was indifferent, and went his way. For the rest of the day the house was quiet, the children having gone out upon the sands. The blinds waved in the sunshine to the soft, steady stroke of the sea beyond the wall; and the notes of the Green Silesian band, a troop of foreign gentlemen hired for the season, had drawn almost all the residents and promenaders away from the vicinity of Coburg House. A knock was audible at the door.

Mrs. Marchmill did not hear any servant go to answer it, and she became impatient. The books were in the room where she sat; but nobody came up. She rang the bell. "There is some person waiting at the door," she said.

"O, no, ma'am' he's gone long ago. I answered it," the servant replied, and Mrs. Hooper came in herself.

"So dissappointing!" she said. "Mr. Trewe not coming after all!"

"But I heard him knock, I fancy!"

"No; that was somebody inquiring for lodgings who came to the wrong house. I tell you that Mr. Trewe sent a note just before lunch to say I needn't get any tea for him, as he should not require the books, and wouldn't come to select them."

Ella was miserable, and for a long time could not even reread his mournful ballad on "Severed Lives," so aching was her erratic little heart, and so tearful her eyes. When the children came in with wet stockings, and ran up to her to tell her of their adventures, she could not feel that she cared about them half as much as usual.

"Mrs. Hooper, have you a photograph of – the gentleman who lived here?" She was getting to be curiously shy in mentioning his name.

"Why, yes. It's in the ornamental frame on the mantelpiece in your own bedroom, ma'am."

"No; the Royal Duke and Duchess are in that."

"Yes, so they are; but he's behind them. He belongs rightly to that frame, which I bought on purpose; but as he went away he said: 'Cover me up from those strangers that are coming, for God's sake. I don't want them staring at me, and I am sure they won't want me staring at them.' So I slipped in the Duke and Duchess temporarily in front of him, as they had no frame, and Royalties are more suitable for letting furnished than a private young man. If you take 'em out you'll see him under. Lord, ma'am, he wouldn't mind if he knew it! He didn't think the next tenant would be such an attractive lady as you, or he wouldn't have thought of hiding himself, perhaps."

"Is he handsome?" she asked timidly.

"I call him so. Some, perhaps, wouldn't."

"Should I?" she asked, with eagerness.

"I think you would, though some would say he's more striking than handsome; a large-eyed thoughtful fellow, you know, with a very electric flash in his eye when he looks round quickly, such as you'd expect a poet to be who doesn't get his living by it."

"How old is he?"

"Several years older than yourself, ma'am; about thirty-one or two, I think."

Ella was a matter of fact, a few months over thirty herself; but she did not look nearly so much. Though so immature in nature, she was entering on that tract of life in which emotional women begin to suspect that last love may be stronger than first love; and she would soon, alas, enter on the still more melancholy tract when at least the vainer ones of her sex shrink from receiving a male visitor otherwise than with their backs to the window or the blinds half down. She reflected on Mrs. Hooper's remark, and said no more about age.

Just then a telegram was brought up. It came from her husband, who had gone down the Channel as far as Budmouth with his friends in the yacht, and would not be able to get back till next day.

After her light dinner Ella idled about the shore with the children till dusk, thinking of the yet uncovered photograph in her room, with a serene sense of in which this something ecstatic to come. For, with the subtle luxuriousness of fancy in which this young woman was an adept, on learning that her husband was to be absent that night she had refrained from incontinently rushing upstairs and, opening the picture-frame, preferring to reserve the inspection till she could be alone, and a more romantic tinge be imparted to the occasion by silence, candles, solemn sea and stars outside, than was afforded by the garish afternoon sunlight.

The children had been sent to bed, and Ella soon followed, though it was not yet ten o'clock. To gratify her passionate curiosity she now made her preparations, first getting rid of superfluous garments and putting on her dressing-gown, then arranging a chair in front of the table and reading several pages of Trewe's tenderest utterances. Next she fetched the portrait-frame to the light, opened the back, took out the likeness, and set it up before her.

It was a striking countenance to look upon. The poet wore a luxuriant black moustache and imperial, and a slouched hat which shaded the forehead. The large dark eyes described by the landlady showed an unlimited capacity for misery, they looked out from beneath well-shaped brows as if they were reading the universe in the microcosm of the confronter's face, and were not altogether overjoyed at what the spectacle portended.

Ella murmured in her lowest, richest, tenderest tone: "And it's *you* who've so cruelly eclipsed me these many times!"

As she gazed long at the portrait she fell into thought, till her eyes filled with tears, and she touched the cardboard with her lips. Then she laughed with a nervous lightness, and wiped her eyes.

She thought how wicked she was, a woman having a husband and three children, to let her mind stray to a stranger in this unconscionable manner. No, he was not a stranger! She knew his thoughts and feelings as well as she knew her own; they were, in fact, the self-same thoughts and feelings as hers, which her husband distinctly lacked; perhaps luckily for himself, considering that he had to provide for family expenses.

"He's nearer my real self, he's more intimate with the real me than Will is, after all, even though I've never seen him," she said.

She laid his book and picture on the table at the bedside, and when she was reclining on the pillow she re-read those of Robert Trewe's verses which she had marked from time to time as most touching and true. Putting these aside she set up the photograph on its edge upon the coverlet, and contemplated it as she lay. Then she scanned again by the light of the candle the half-obliterated pencillings on the wallpaper beside her head. There they were – phrases, couplets, *bouts-rimes*, beginnings and middles of lines, ideas in the rough, like Shelley's scraps, and the least of them so intense, so sweet, so palpitating, that it seemed as if his very breath, warm and loving, fanned her cheeks from those walls, walls that had surrounded his head times and times as they surrounded her own now. He must often have put up his hand so – with the pencil in it. Yes, the writing was sideways, as it would be if executed by one who extended his arm thus.

These inscribed shapes of the poet's world,

"Forms more real than living man,
Nurslings of immortality,"

were, no doubt, the thoughts and spirit-strivings which had come to him in the dead of night, when he could let himself go and have no fear of the frost of criticism. No doubt they had often been written up hastily by the light of the moon, the rays of the lamp, in the blue-gray dawn, in full daylight perhaps never. And now her hair was dragging where his arm had lain when he secured the fugitive fancies; she was sleeping on a poet's lips, immersed in the very essence of him, permeated by his spirit as by an ether.

While she was dreaming the minutes away thus, a footstep came upon the stairs, and in a moment she heard her husband's heavy step on the landing immediately without.

"Ell, where are you?"

What possessed her she could not have described, but, with an instinctive objection to let her husband know what she had been doing, she slipped the photograph under the pillow just as he flung open the door with the air of a man who had dined not badly.

"O, I beg pardon," said William Marchmill. "Have you a headache? I am afraid I have disturbed you."

"No, I've not got a headache," said she. "How is it you've come?"

"Well, we found we could get back in very good time after all, and I didn't want to make another day of it, because of going somewhere else tomorrow."

"Shall I come down again?"

"O, no. I'm as tired as a dog. I've had a good feed, and I shall turn in straight off. I want to get out at six o'clock tomorrow if I can... I shan't disturb you by my getting up; it will be long before you are awake." And he came forward into the room.

While her eyes followed his movements, Ella softly pushed the photograph further out of sight.

"Sure you're not ill?" he asked, bending over her.

"No, only wicked!"

"Never mind that." And he stooped and kissed her. "I wanted to be with you tonight."

Next morning Marchmill was called at six o'clock; and in waking and yawning he heard him muttering to himself. "What the deuce is this that's been crackling under me so?" Imagining her asleep he searched round him and withdrew something. Through her half-opened eyes she perceived it to be Mr. Trewe.

"Well, I'm damned!" her husband exclaimed.

"What, dear?" said she.

"O, you are awake? Ha! ha!"

"What *do* you mean?"

"Some bloke's photograph – a friend of our landlady's, I suppose. I wonder how it came here; whisked off the mantelpiece by accident perhaps when they were making the bed."

"I was looking at it yesterday, and it must have dropped in then."

"O, he's a friend of yours? Bless his picturesque heart!"

Ella's loyalty to the object of her admiration could not endure to hear him ridiculed. "He's a clever man!" she said, with a tremor in her gentle voice which she herself felt to be absurdly uncalled for. "He is a rising poet – the gentleman who occupied two of these rooms before we came, though I've never seen him."

"How do you know, if you've never seen him?"

"Mrs. Hooper told me when she showed me the photograph."

"O, well, I must up and be off. I shall be home rather early. Sorry I can't take you today dear. Mind the children don't go getting drowned."

That day Mrs. Marchmill inquired if Mr. Trewe were likely to call at any other time.

"Yes," said Mrs. Hooper. "He's coming this day week to stay with a friend near here till you leave. He'll be sure to call."

Marchmill did return quite early in the afternoon; and, opening some letters which had arrived in his absence, declared suddenly that he and his family would have to leave a week earlier than they had expected to do – in short, in three days.

"Surely we can stay a week longer?" she pleaded. "I like it here."

"I don't. It is getting rather slow."

"Then you might leave me and the children!"

"How perverse you are, Ell! What's the use? And have to come to fetch you! No: we'll all return together; and we'll make out our time in North Wales or Brighton a little later on. Besides, you've three days longer yet."

It seemed to be her doom not to meet the man for whose rival talent she had a despairing admiration, and to whose person she was now absolutely attached. Yet she determined to make a last effort; and having gathered from her landlady that Trewe was living in a lonely spot not far from the fashionable town on the Island opposite, she crossed over in the packet from the neighboring pier the following afternoon.

What a useless journey it was! Ella knew but vaguely where the house stood, and when she fancied she had found it, and ventured to inquire of a pedestrian if he lived there, the answer returned by the man was that he did not know. And if he did live there, how could she call upon him? Some women might have the assurance to do it, but she had not. How crazy he would think her. She might have asked him to call upon her, perhaps; but she had not the courage for that, either. She lingered mournfully about the picturesque seaside eminence till it was time to return to the town and enter the steamer for recrossing, reaching home for dinner without having been greatly missed.

At the last moment, unexpectedly enough, her husband said that he should have no objection to letting her and the children stay on till the end of the week, since she wished to do so, if she felt herself able to get home without him. She concealed the pleasure this extension of time gave her; and Marchmill went off the next morning alone.

But the week passed, and Trewe did not call.

On Saturday morning the remaining members of the Marchmill family departed from the place which had been productive of so much fervor in her. The dreary, dreary train; the sun shining in moted beams upon the hot cushions; the dusty permanent way; the mean rows of wire – these things were her accompaniment: while out of the window the deep blue sea-levels disappeared from her gaze, and with them her poet's home. Heavy-hearted, she tried to read, and wept instead.

Mr. Marchmill was in a thriving way of business, and he and his family lived in a large new house, which stood in rather extensive grounds a few miles outside the midland city wherein he carried on his trade. Ella's life was lonely here, as the suburban life is apt to be, particularly at certain seasons; and she had ample time to indulge her taste for lyric and elegiac composition. She had hardly got back when she encountered a piece by Robert Trewe in the new number of her favorite magazine, which must have been written almost immediately before her visit to Solentsea, for it contained the very couplet she had seen penciled on the wallpaper by the bed, and Mrs. Hooper had declared to be recent. Ella could resist no longer, but seizing a pen impulsively, wrote to him as a brother-poet, using the name of John Ivy, congratulating him in her letter on his triumphant executions in meter and rhythm of thoughts that moved his soul, as compared with her own brow-beaten efforts in the same pathetic trade.

To this address there came a response in a few days, little as she had dared to hope for it – a civil and brief note, in which the young poet stated that, though he was not well acquainted with Mr. Ivy's verse, he recalled the name as being one he had seen attached to some very promising pieces; that he was glad to gain Mr. Ivy's acquaintance by letter, and should certainly look with much interest for his productions in the future.

There must have been something juvenile or timid in her own epistle, as one ostensibly coming from a man, she declared to herself; for Trewe quite adopted the tone of an elder and superior in this reply. But what did it matter? He had replied; he had written to her with his own hand from that very room she knew so well, for he was now back again in his quarters.

The correspondence thus begun was continued for two months or more, Ella Marchmill sending him from time to time some that she considered to be the best her pieces, which he very kindly accepted, though he did not say he sedulously read them, nor did he send her any of his own in return. Ella would have been more hurt at this than she was if she had not known that Trewe labored under the impression that she was one of his own sex.

Yet the situation was unsatisfactory. A flattering little voice told her that, were he only to see her, matters would be otherwise. No doubt she would have helped on this by making a frank confession of womanhood, to begin with, if something had not appeared, to her delight, to render it unnecessary. A friend of her husband's, the editor of the most important newspaper in their city and county, who was dining with them one day, observed during their conversation about the poet that his (the editor's) brother the landscape-painter was a friend of Mr. Trewe's, and that the two men were at that very moment in Wales together.

Ella was slightly acquainted with the editor's brother. The next morning down she sat and wrote, inviting him to stay at her house for a short time on his way back, and to bring with him, if practicable, his companion Mr. Trewe, whose acquaintance she was anxious to make. The answer arrived after some few days. Her correspondent and his friend Trewe would have much satisfaction in accepting her invitation on their way southward, which would be on such and such a day in the following week.

Ella was blithe and buoyant. Her scheme had succeeded; her beloved though as yet unseen was coming. "Behold, he standeth behind our wall; he looked forth at the windows, showing himself through the lattice," she thought ecstatically. "And, lo, the winter is past, the rain is over and gone, the flowers appear on the earth, the time of the singing of birds is come, and the voice of the turtle is heard in our land."

But it was necessary to consider the details of lodging and feeding him. This she did most solicitously, and awaited the pregnant day and hour.

It was about five in the afternoon when she heard a ring at the door and the editor's brother's voice in the hall. Poetess as she was, or as she thought herself, she had not been too sublime that day to dress with infinite trouble in a fashionable robe of rich material, having a faint resemblance to the chiton of the Greeks, a style just then in vogue among ladies of an artistic and romantic turn, which had been obtained by Ella of her Bond Street dressmaker when she was last in London. Her visitor entered the drawing room. She looked toward his rear; nobody else came through the door. Where, in the name of the God of Love, was Robert Trewe?

"O, I'm sorry," said the painter, after their introductory words had been spoken. "Trewe is a curious fellow, you know, Mrs. Marchmill. He said he'd come; then he said he couldn't. He's rather dusty. We've been doing a few miles with knapsacks, you know; and he wanted to get on home."

"He—he's not coming?"

"He's not; and he asked me to make his apologies."

"When did you p-p-part from him?" she asked, her nether lip starting off quivering so much that it was like a tremolo-stop opened in her speech. She longed to run away from this dreadful bore and cry her eyes out.

"Just now, in the turnpike road yonder there."

"What! he has actually gone past my gates?"

"Yes. When we got to them – handsome gates they are, too, the finest bit of modern wrought-iron work I have seen – when we came to them we stopped, talking there a little while, and then he wished me goodbye and went on. The truth is, he's a little bit depressed just now, and doesn't want to see anybody. He's a very good fellow, and a warm friend, but a little uncertain and gloomy sometimes; he thinks too much of things. His poetry is rather too erotic and passionate, you know, for some tastes; and he has just come in for a terrible slating from the — *Review* that was published yesterday; he saw a copy of it at the station by accident. Perhaps you've read it?"

"No."

"So much the better. O, it is not worth thinking of; just one of those articles written to order, to please the narrow-minded set of subscribers upon whom the circulation depends. But he's upset by it. He says it is the misrepresentation that hurts him so; that, though he can stand a fair attack, he can't stand lies that he's powerless to refute and stop from spreading. That's just Trewe's weak point. He lives so much by himself that these things affect him much more than they would if he were in the bustle of fashionable or commercial life. So he wouldn't come here, making the excuse that it all looked so new and monied – if you'll pardon—"

"But – he must have known – there was sympathy here! Has he never said anything about getting letters from this address?"

"Yes, yes, he has, from John Ivy – perhaps a relative of yours, he thought, visiting here at the time?"

"Did he—like Ivy, did he say?"

"Well, I don't know that he took any great interest in Ivy."

"Or in his poems?"

"Or in his poems – so far as I know, that is."

Robert Trewe took no interest in her house, in her poems, or in their writer. As soon as she could get away she went into the nursery and tried to let off her emotion by unnecessarily kissing the children, till she had a sudden sense of disgust at being reminded how plain-looking they were, like their father.

The obtuse and single-minded landscape-painter never once perceived from her conversation that it was only Trewe she wanted, and not himself. He made the best of his visit, seeming to enjoy the society of Ella's husband, who also took a great fancy to him, and showed him everywhere about the neighborhood, neither of them noticing Ella's mood.

The painter had been gone only a day or two when, while sitting upstairs alone one morning, she glanced over the London paper just arrived, and read the following paragraph:

> *"SUICIDE OF A POET" Mr. Robert Trewe, who has been favorably known for some years as one of our rising lyrists, committed suicide at his lodgings at Solentsea on Saturday evening last by shooting himself in the right temple with a revolver. Readers hardly need to be reminded that Mr. Trewe recently attracted the attention of a much wider public than had hitherto known him, by his new volume of verse, mostly of an impassioned kind, entitled 'Lyrics to a Woman Unknown,' which has been already favorably noticed in these pages for the extraordinary gamut of feeling it traverses, and which has been made the subject of a severe, if not ferocious, criticism in the — Review. It is supposed, though not certainly known, that the article may have partially conduced to the sad act, as a copy of the review in question was found on his writing-table; and he has been observed to be in a somewhat depressed state of mind since the critique appeared.*

Then came the report of the inquest, at which the following letter was read, it having been addressed to a friend at a distance:

> *Dear —, Before these lines reach your hands I shall be delivered from the inconveniences of seeing, hearing, and knowing more of the things around me. I will not trouble you by giving my reasons for the step I have taken, though I can assure you they were sound and logical. Perhaps had I been blessed with a mother, or a sister, or a female friend of another sort tenderly devoted to me, I might have thought it worth while to continue my present existence. I have long dreamt of such an unattainable creature, as you know; and she, this undiscoverable, elusive one, inspired my last volume; the imaginary woman alone, for, in spite of what has been said in some quarters, there is no real woman behind the title. She has continued to the last unrevealed, unmet, unwon. I think it desirable to mention this in order that no blame may attach to any real woman as having been the cause of my decease by cruel or cavalier treatment of me. Tell my landlady that I am sorry to have caused her this unpleasantness; but my occupancy of the rooms will soon be forgotten. There are ample funds in my name at the bank to pay all expenses. R. TREWE.*

Ella sat for a while as if stunned, then rushed into the adjoining chamber and flung herself upon her face on the bed.

Her grief and distraction shook her to pieces; and she lay in this frenzy of sorrow for more than an hour. Broken words came every now and then from her quivering lips: "O, if he had only known of me – known of me – me!... O, if I had only once met him – only once; and put my hand upon his hot forehead – kissed him – let him know how I loved him – that I would have suffered shame and scorn, would have lived and died, for him! Perhaps it would have saved his dear life!... But no – it was not allowed! God is a jealous God; and that happiness was not for him and me!"

All possibilities were over; the meeting was stultified. Yet it was almost visible to her in her fantasy even now, though it could never be substantiated –

> *The hour which might have been, yet might not be,*
> *Which man's and woman's heart conceived and bore,*
> *Yet whereof life was barren.*

She wrote to the landlady at Solentsea in the third person, in as subdued a style as she could command, enclosing a postal order for a sovereign, and informing Mrs. Hooper that Mrs. Marchmill had seen in the papers the sad account of the poet's death, and having been, as Mrs. Hooper was aware, much interested in Mr. Trewe during her stay at Coburg House, she would be obliged if Mrs. Hooper could obtain a small portion of his hair before his coffin was closed down, and send it her as a memorial of him, as also the photograph that was in the frame.

By the return-post a letter arrived containing what had been requested. Ella wept over the portrait and secured it in her private drawer; the lock of hair she tied with white ribbon and put in her bosom, whence she drew it and kissed it every now and then in some unobserved nook.

"What's the matter?" said her husband, looking up from his newspaper on one of these occasions. "Crying over something? A lock of hair? Whose is it?"

"He's dead!" she murmured.

"Who?"

"I don't want to tell you, Will, just now, unless you insist!" she said, a sob hanging heavy in her voice.

"O, all right."

"Do you mind my refusing? I will tell you someday."

"It doesn't matter in the least, of course."

He walked away whistling a few bars of no tune in particular; and when he had got down to his factory in the city the subject came into Marchmill's head again.

He, too, was aware that a suicide had taken place recently at the house they had occupied at Solentsea. Having seen the volume of poems in his wife's hand of late, and heard fragments of the landlady's conversation about Trewe when they were her tenants, he all at once said to himself, "Why of course it's he! How the devil did she get to know him? What sly animals women are!"

Then he placidly dismissed the matter, and went on with his daily affairs. By this time Ella at home had come to a determination. Mrs. Hooper, in sending the hair and photograph, had informed her of the day of the funeral; and as the morning and noon wore on an overpowering wish to know where they were laying him took possession of the sympathetic woman. Caring very little now what her husband or anyone else might think of her eccentricities, she wrote Marchmill a brief note, stating that she was called away for the afternoon and evening, but would return on the following morning. This she left on his desk, and having given the same information to the servants, went out of the house on foot.

When Mr. Marchmill reached home early in the afternoon the servants looked anxious. The nurse took him privately aside, and hinted that her mistress's sadness during the past few days had been such that she feared she had gone out to drown herself. Marchmill reflected. Upon the whole he thought that she had not done that. Without saying whither he was bound he also started off, telling them not to sit up for him. He drove to the railway-station, and took a ticket for Solentsea.

It was dark when he reached the place, though he had come by a fast train, and he knew that if his wife had preceded him thither it could only have been by a slower train, arriving not a great while before his own. The season at Solentsea was now past: the parade was gloomy, and the flys were few and cheap. He asked the way to the Cemetery, and soon reached it. The gate was locked, but the keeper let him in, declaring, however, that there was nobody within the precincts. Although it was not late, the autumnal darkness had now become intense; and he found some difficulty in keeping to the serpentine path which led to the quarter where, as the man had told him, the one or two interments for the day had taken place. He stepped upon the grass, and, stumbling over some pegs, stooped now and then to discern if possible a figure against the sky. He could see none; but lighting on a spot where the soil was trodden, beheld a crouching object beside a newly made grave. She heard him, and sprang up.

"Ell, how silly this is!" he said indignantly. "Running away from home – I never heard such a thing! Of course I am not jealous of this unfortunate man; but it is too ridiculous that you, a married woman with three children and a fourth coming, should go losing your head like this over a dead lover!... Do you know you were locked in? You might not have been able to get out all night."

She did not answer.

"I hope it didn't go far between you and him, for your own sake."

"Don't insult me, Will."

"Mind, I won't have anymore of this sort of thing; do you hear?"

"Very well," she said.

He drew her arm within his own, and conducted her out of the Cemetery. It was impossible to get back that night; and not wishing to be recognized in their present sorry condition he took her to a miserable little coffee-house close to the station, whence they departed early in the morning, traveling almost without speaking, under the sense that it was one of those dreary situations occurring in married life which words could not mend, and reaching their own door at noon.

The months passed, and neither of the twain ever ventured to start a conversation upon this episode. Ella seemed to be only too frequently in a sad and listless mood, which might almost have been called pining. The time was approaching when she would have to undergo the stress of childbirth for a fourth time, and that apparently not tend to raise her spirits.

"I don't think I shall get over it this time!" she said one day. "Pooh! what childish foreboding! Why shouldn't it be as well now as ever?"

She shook her head. "I feel almost sure I am going to die; and I should be glad, if it were not for Nelly, and Frank, and Tiny."

"And me!"

"You'll soon find somebody to fill my place," she murmured, with a sad smile. "And you'll have a perfect right to; I assure you of that."

"Ell, you are not thinking still about that—poetical friend of yours?"

She neither admitted nor denied the charge. "I am not going to get over my illness this time," she reiterated. "Something tells me I shan't."

This view of things was rather a bad beginning, as it usually is; and, in fact, six weeks later, in the month of May, she was lying in her room, pulseless and bloodless, with hardly strength enough left to follow up one feeble breath with another, the infant for whose unnecessary life she was slowly parting with her own being fat and well. Just before her death she spoke to Marchmill softly: –

"Will, I want to confess to you the entire circumstances of that – about you know what – that time we visited Solentsea. I can't tell what possessed me – how I could forget you so, my husband! But I had got into a morbid state: I thought you had been unkind; that you had neglected me; that you weren't up to my intellectual level, while he was, and far above it. I wanted a fuller appreciator, perhaps, rather than another lover –"

She could get no further then for very exhaustion; and she went off in sudden collapse a few hours later, without having said anything more to her husband on the subject of her love for the poet. William Marchmill, in truth, like most husbands of several years' standing, was little disturbed by retrospective jealousies, and had not shown the least anxiety to press her for confessions concerning a man dead and gone beyond any power of inconveniencing him more.

But when she had been buried a couple of years it chanced one day that, in turning over some forgotten papers that he wished to destroy before his second wife entered the house, he lighted on a lock of hair in an envelope, with the photograph of the deceased poet, a date being written on the back in his late wife's hand. It was that of the time they spent at Solentsea.

Marchmill looked long and musingly at the hair and portrait, for something struck him. Fetching the little boy who had been the death of his mother, now a noisy toddler, he took him on his knee, held the lock of hair against the child's head, and set up the photograph on the table behind, so that he could closely compare the features each countenance presented. By a known but inexplicable trick of Nature there were undoubtedly strong traces of resemblance to the man Ella had never seen; the dreamy and peculiar expression of the poet's face sat, as the transmitted idea,, upon the child's, and the hair was of the same hue.

"I'm damned if I didn't think so!" murmured Marchmill. "Then *she* did play me false with that fellow at the lodgings! Let me see: the dates – the second week in August... the third week in May... Yes... yes... Get away, you poor little brat! You are nothing to me!"

If you enjoyed this, you might also like...
The Distracted Preacher, see page 386
The Model Millionnaire, see page 429

A Yellow Duster

Bram Stoker

WHEN MY old friend Stanhope came unexpectedly, late in life, into a huge fortune he went traveling round the world for a whole year with his wife before settling down. We had been friends in college days, but I had seen little of him during his busy professional life. Now, however, in our declining years, chance threw us together again, and our old intimacy became renewed. I often stayed with him, both at Stanhope Towers and in his beautiful house in St. James's square; and I noticed that wherever he was, certain of his curios went with him. He had always been a collector in a small way, and I have no doubt that in his hard-working time, though he had not the means to gratify his exquisite taste, the little he could do served as a relief to the worry and tedium of daily toil. His great-uncle, from whom he inherited, had a wonderful collection of interesting things; and Stanhope kept them much in the same way as he had found them – not grouped or classified in any way, but placed in juxtaposition as taste or pleasure prompted. There was one glass-covered table which stood always in the small drawing room, or rather sitting room, which Mr. and Mrs. Stanhope held as their own particular sanctum. In it was a small but very wonderful collection of precious and beautiful things; an enormous gold scarib with graven pictures on its natural panels, such a scarib as is not to be found even amongst the wonderful collection at Leyden; a carved star ruby from Persia, a New Zealand chieftain's head wrought in greenstone, a jade amulet from Central India, an enamelled watch with an exquisitely-painted miniature of Madame du Barri, a perfect Queen Anne farthing laid in a contemporary pounce-box of gold and enamel, a Borgia ring, a coiled serpent with emerald eyes, a miniature of Peg Woffington by Gainsborough, in a quaint frame of aqua marines, a tiny Elzivir Bible in cover of lapis lazuli mounted in red gold, a chain of wrought iron as delicate as hair, and many other such things, which were not only rare and costly as well as beautiful, but each of which seemed to have some personal association.

And yet in the very middle of the case was placed a common cotton duster, carefully folded. It was not only coarse and common in its texture, but it was of such crude and vulgar colours that it looked startlingly out of place in such a congeries of beautiful treasures. It was so manifestly a personal relic that for a long time I felt some diffidence in alluding to it; though I always looked at that particular table, for as Mrs. Stanhope was good enough to share her husband's liking for me, I was always treated as one of themselves and admitted to their special sitting-room.

One day when Stanhope and I were bending over the case, I remarked:

"I see one treasure there which must be supreme, for it has not the same intrinsic claim as the others!" He smiled as he said:

"Oh, that! You are right; that is one of the best treasures I have got. Only for it all the rest might be of no avail!"

This piqued my curiosity, so I said:

"May an old friend hear the story? Of course, it is evident by its being there that it is not a subject to be shunned."

"Right again!" he answered, and opening the case he took out the duster and held it in his hand lovingly. I could see that it was not even clean; it was one that had manifestly done service.

"You ask the missis," he said: "and if she doesn't mind I'll tell you with pleasure."

At tea that afternoon, when we were alone, I asked Mrs. Stanhope if I might hear the story. Her reply was quick and hearty:

"Indeed you may! Moreover, I hope I may hear it, too!"

"Do you mean to tell me," I said, "that you don't know why it is there?" She smiled as she replied:

"I have often wondered; but Frank never told me, and I never asked. It is a long, long time since he kept it. It used to be in the safe of his study till he came into Stanhope Towers; and then he put it where it is now. He keeps the key of the table himself, and no one touches the things in it but him. You noticed, I suppose, that every thing in it is fastened down for traveling?"

When I told Stanhope that his wife permitted him to tell me the story, I added her own hope that she, too, might hear it. He said:

"Very well! Tonight after dinner – we are alone this evening – we will come in here and I shall tell you."

When we were alone in the room and the coffee cups had been removed he began:

"Of all the possessions I have, which come under the designation of real or personal estate, that old, dirty, flaring, common duster is the most precious. It is, and has been, a secret pleasure to me for all these years to surround it with the most pretty and costly of my treasures; for so it has a symbolical effect to me. I was once near a grave misunderstanding with my wife – indeed it had begun. This was not long into the second year of our marriage, when the bloom of young wedlock had worn off, and we had begun to settle down to the grim realities of working life. You know my wife is a good many years younger than I am, and when we married I had just about come to that time of life when a man begins to distrust himself as important in the eyes of a beautiful young woman. Lily was always so sweet to me, however, that out of her very sweetness I began to distrust her somewhat. It seemed almost unreasonable that she should be always willing to yield her wishes to mine. At first this distrust was on a very shadowy and unreal basis; but as we grew into the realities of life on small means, it was not always possible for her to forego her wishes in the same way. I had my work to do; and she had her own life to lead, and her own plans to make. I daresay I was pretty unreasonable at times. A man gets worried about his work, and if he tries to keep the worry to himself he sometimes overlooks the fact that his wife, not knowing the facts, cannot understand the almost vital importance of small arrangements which he has to make. So she unconsciously thwarts him."

Here Mrs. Stanhope came over and sat on a stool beside him, and put her hand in his. He stroked it gently and went on:

"I was especially anxious not to worry her about this time, for there was a hope that our wishes for a child were to be realised, and in my very anxiety to save her from trouble I created the very thing I dreaded. Some little question arose between us; a matter in itself of so small importance that I have quite forgotten it, though the issues then bearing on it were big enough to be remembered. For the purpose of my work things had to be settled in my way, but I could not explain to her without letting her share the worry, and, in addition, I feared that as we were at two, my having held back anything from her might be construed into a want of confidence. Thus it was that her opposition to me became far graver than the occasion itself warranted; and in my blind helplessness, with no one to confide in, I began to fancy that the reason of her opposition was that she did not love me. Let me tell you, old friend – you cannot know, since you were never married – that when once you raise this spirit it is hard to exorcise it. It grows, and grows, and grows, like the genius in the 'Arabian Nights,' until it fills the universe. With this fatal suspicion in my mind every little act of petulance or self-will, everything done or undone, said or unsaid, became 'proof as strong as Holy Writ' that she did not love me; until I grew morbid on the subject. Like the people of old, I wanted a sign.

"One day the strain of silence became too great for me to bear. I broke my resolution of reticence, and taxed her that she did not love me. At first he laughed; for she felt, as she told me afterwards, that the idea was ridiculous. Anyhow, I did not wait to understand, or to weigh her feeling. Her laughter maddened me, and I spoke out some bitter things. 'Oh, yes, my dear, I did!' [This in response to a pressure from the hand that held his, and a warning finger of the other raised.] She tried to bear with me bravely for a while; but at length her feelings mastered her, and the tears rose in her eyes and trickled down her cheeks. But even then I was obdurate. The suspicion of weeks, and all the bitterness of it which had kept me awake so many nights, could not be allayed in a moment. I began to doubt even her very tears. They might, I thought, have come from annoyance at having to explain, from chagrin, from vexation, from anything except the real cause, true womanly and wifely feeling. Again I wanted a sign. And I got it."

His wife's hand closed harder on his; I could see the answering pressure of his hand as he went on:

"She had been dusting the little knick-knacks in the drawing-room, using for the purpose a duster of a peculiarly aggressive pattern. It was one of a set put aside for this special purpose, and therefore chosen of a colour not to be confused with the rest of the domestic appliances. She still held this in her hand; and whilst I stood looking at her with something like rage in my heart, and with my brain a seething mass of doubt as to her half- hysterical sobbing, she raised the duster unconsciously to her face and began to wipe her tears away with it.

"That settled me! Here was a sign that not even a jealous idiot could mistake! Had the thing been less gaudily hideous, had it even been clean, I might still have wallowed in my doubt; but now the conviction of the genuineness of her grief swept me like a great burst of sunshine through fog, and cleared it away for ever. I took her in my arms and tried to comfort her; and from that hour to this there has never been – I thank God for it with all my heart – a doubt between us. Nothing but love and trust and affection! I noticed where she placed the duster, and in the night I came and took it and put it safely away. Do you wonder now, old friend, why I value that rag; why it has a sacred value in my eyes?"

By this time Mrs. Stanhope was shading her face, and I could see the tears roll down her cheeks. "Frank, dear," she said, "let me have your key a moment?" He handed the bunch to her without a word. She selected the key, opened the table top, and took out the duster, which she kissed. Then turning to her husband, as she dried her eyes, she said, "Frank, dear, this is the second time you have made me cry in my long, happy life; but, ho, how different!" Stanhope spoke: "Lily, dear, the first time you used that duster I noticed the glaring contrast of its colour to your black hair, and now it holds its own against the coming grey," and he took her in his arms and kissed her. She turned to me and said: "I think the story was worth the telling – and the hearing – don't you? I have allowed this poor, dear old rag to remain in its place of honour all these years because my husband wished it so; but now it shall hold its place in my heart as well as his. God does not always speak in thunder; there are softer notes in the expression of His love and tenderness. Oh, Frank!"

What more she said I know not; for by this time I had stolen quietly away, leaving them alone together.

If you enjoyed this, you might also like...
Amy Foster, see opposite
The Cone, see page 322

Amy Foster

Joseph Conrad

KENNEDY is a country doctor, and lives in Colebrook, on the shores of Eastbay. The high ground rising abruptly behind the red roofs of the little town crowds the quaint High Street against the wall which defends it from the sea. Beyond the sea-wall there curves for miles in a vast and regular sweep the barren beach of shingle, with the village of Brenzett standing out darkly across the water, a spire in a clump of trees; and still further out the perpendicular column of a lighthouse, looking in the distance no bigger than a lead pencil, marks the vanishing-point of the land. The country at the back of Brenzett is low and flat, but the bay is fairly well sheltered from the seas, and occasionally a big ship, windbound or through stress of weather, makes use of the anchoring ground a mile and a half due north from you as you stand at the back door of the "Ship Inn" in Brenzett. A dilapidated windmill near by lifting its shattered arms from a mound no loftier than a rubbish heap, and a Martello tower squatting at the water's edge half a mile to the south of the Coastguard cottages, are familiar to the skippers of small craft. These are the official seamarks for the patch of trustworthy bottom represented on the Admiralty charts by an irregular oval of dots enclosing several figures six, with a tiny anchor engraved among them, and the legend "mud and shells" over all.

The brow of the upland overtops the square tower of the Colebrook Church. The slope is green and looped by a white road. Ascending along this road, you open a valley broad and shallow, a wide green trough of pastures and hedges merging inland into a vista of purple tints and flowing lines closing the view.

In this valley down to Brenzett and Colebrook and up to Darnford, the market town fourteen miles away, lies the practice of my friend Kennedy. He had begun life as surgeon in the Navy, and afterwards had been the companion of a famous traveller, in the days when there were continents with unexplored interiors. His papers on the fauna and flora made him known to scientific societies. And now he had come to a country practice – from choice. The penetrating power of his mind, acting like a corrosive fluid, had destroyed his ambition, I fancy. His intelligence is of a scientific order, of an investigating habit, and of that unappeasable curiosity which believes that there is a particle of a general truth in every mystery.

A good many years ago now, on my return from abroad, he invited me to stay with him. I came readily enough, and as he could not neglect his patients to keep me company, he took me on his rounds – thirty miles or so of an afternoon, sometimes. I waited for him on the roads; the horse reached after the leafy twigs, and, sitting in the dogcart, I could hear Kennedy's laugh through the half-open door left open of some cottage. He had a big, hearty laugh that would have fitted a man twice his size, a brisk manner, a bronzed face, and a pair of grey, profoundly attentive eyes. He had the talent of making people talk to him freely, and an inexhaustible patience in listening to their tales.

One day, as we trotted out of a large village into a shady bit of road, I saw on our left hand a low, black cottage, with diamond panes in the windows, a creeper on the end wall, a roof of shingle, and some roses climbing on the rickety trellis-work of the tiny porch. Kennedy pulled up to a walk. A woman, in full sunlight, was throwing a dripping blanket over a line stretched between two old apple-trees. And as the bobtailed, long-necked chestnut, trying to get his head, jerked the left hand, covered by a thick dog-skin glove, the doctor raised his voice over the hedge: "How's your child, Amy?"

I had the time to see her dull face, red, not with a mantling blush, but as if her flat cheeks had been vigorously slapped, and to take in the squat figure, the scanty, dusty brown hair drawn into a tight knot at the back of the head. She looked quite young. With a distinct catch in her breath, her voice sounded low and timid.

"He's well, thank you."

We trotted again. "A young patient of yours," I said; and the doctor, flicking the chestnut absently, muttered, "Her husband used to be."

"She seems a dull creature," I remarked listlessly.

"Precisely," said Kennedy. "She is very passive. It's enough to look at the red hands hanging at the end of those short arms, at those slow, prominent brown eyes, to know the inertness of her mind – an inertness that one would think made it everlastingly safe from all the surprises of imagination. And yet which of us is safe? At any rate, such as you see her, she had enough imagination to fall in love. She's the daughter of one Isaac Foster, who from a small farmer has sunk into a shepherd; the beginning of his misfortunes dating from his runaway marriage with the cook of his widowed father – a well-to-do, apoplectic grazier, who passionately struck his name off his will, and had been heard to utter threats against his life. But this old affair, scandalous enough to serve as a motive for a Greek tragedy, arose from the similarity of their characters. There are other tragedies, less scandalous and of a subtler poignancy, arising from irreconcilable differences and from that fear of the Incomprehensible that hangs over all our heads – over all our heads..."

The tired chestnut dropped into a walk; and the rim of the sun, all red in a speckless sky, touched familiarly the smooth top of a ploughed rise near the road as I had seen it times innumerable touch the distant horizon of the sea. The uniform brownness of the harrowed field glowed with a rosy tinge, as though the powdered clods had sweated out in minute pearls of blood the toil of uncounted ploughmen. From the edge of a copse a waggon with two horses was rolling gently along the ridge. Raised above our heads upon the sky-line, it loomed up against the red sun, triumphantly big, enormous, like a chariot of giants drawn by two slow-stepping steeds of legendary proportions. And the clumsy figure of the man plodding at the head of the leading horse projected itself on the background of the Infinite with a heroic uncouthness. The end of his carter's whip quivered high up in the blue. Kennedy discoursed.

"She's the eldest of a large family. At the age of fifteen they put her out to service at the New Barns Farm. I attended Mrs. Smith, the tenant's wife, and saw that girl there for the first time. Mrs. Smith, a genteel person with a sharp nose, made her put on a black dress every afternoon. I don't know what induced me to notice her at all. There are faces that call your attention by a curious want of definiteness in their whole aspect, as, walking in a mist, you peer attentively at a vague shape which, after all, may be nothing more curious or strange than a signpost. The only peculiarity I perceived in her was a slight hesitation in her utterance, a sort of preliminary stammer which passes away with the first word. When sharply spoken to, she was apt to lose her head at once; but her heart was of the kindest. She had never been heard to express a dislike for a single human being, and she was tender to every living creature. She was devoted to Mrs. Smith, to Mr. Smith, to their dogs, cats, canaries; and as to Mrs. Smith's grey parrot, its peculiarities exercised upon her a positive fascination. Nevertheless, when that outlandish bird, attacked by the cat, shrieked for help in human accents, she ran out into the yard stopping her ears, and did not prevent the crime. For Mrs. Smith this was another evidence of her stupidity; on the other hand, her want of charm, in view of Smith's well-known frivolousness, was a great recommendation. Her short-sighted eyes would swim with pity for a poor mouse in a trap, and she had been seen once by some boys on her knees in the wet grass helping a toad in difficulties. If it's true, as some German fellow has said, that without phosphorus there is no thought, it is still more true that there is no kindness of heart without a certain amount of imagination. She had some. She had even more than is necessary to understand suffering and to be moved by pity. She fell in love under circumstances that leave no room for doubt in the matter; for you need imagination to form a notion of beauty at all, and still more to discover your ideal in an unfamiliar shape.

"How this aptitude came to her, what it did feed upon, is an inscrutable mystery. She was born in the village, and had never been further away from it than Colebrook or perhaps Darnford. She lived for four years with the Smiths. New Barns is an isolated farmhouse a mile away from the road, and she was content to look day after day at the same fields, hollows, rises; at the trees and the hedgerows; at the faces of the four men about the farm, always the same – day after day, month after month, year after year. She never showed a desire for conversation, and, as it seemed to me, she did not know how to smile. Sometimes of a fine Sunday afternoon she would put on her best dress, a pair of stout boots, a large grey hat trimmed with a black feather (I've seen her in that finery), seize an absurdly slender parasol, climb over two stiles, tramp over three fields and along two hundred yards of road – never further. There stood Foster's cottage. She would help her mother to give their tea to the younger children, wash up the crockery, kiss the little ones, and go back to the farm. That was all. All the rest, all the change, all the relaxation. She never seemed to wish for anything more. And then she fell in love. She fell in love silently, obstinately – perhaps helplessly. It came slowly, but when it came it worked like a powerful spell; it was love as the Ancients understood it: an irresistible and fateful impulse – a possession! Yes, it was in her to become haunted and possessed by a face, by a presence, fatally, as though she had been a pagan worshipper of form under a joyous sky – and to be awakened at last from that mysterious forgetfulness of self, from that enchantment, from that transport, by a fear resembling the unaccountable terror of a brute..."

With the sun hanging low on its western limit, the expanse of the grass-lands framed in the counter-scarps of the rising ground took on a gorgeous and sombre aspect. A sense of penetrating sadness, like that inspired by a grave strain of music, disengaged itself from the silence of the fields. The men we met walked past slow, unsmiling, with downcast eyes, as if the melancholy of an over-burdened earth had weighted their feet, bowed their shoulders, borne down their glances.

"Yes," said the doctor to my remark, "one would think the earth is under a curse, since of all her children these that cling to her the closest are uncouth in body and as leaden of gait as if their very hearts were loaded with chains. But here on this same road you might have seen amongst these heavy men a being lithe, supple, and long-limbed, straight like a pine with something striving upwards in his appearance as though the heart within him had been buoyant. Perhaps it was only the force of the contrast, but when he was passing one of these villagers here, the soles of his feet did not seem to me to touch the dust of the road. He vaulted over the stiles, paced these slopes with a long elastic stride that made him noticeable at a great distance, and had lustrous black eyes. He was so different from the mankind around that, with his freedom of movement, his soft – a little startled, glance, his olive complexion and graceful bearing, his humanity suggested to me the nature of a woodland creature. He came from there."

The doctor pointed with his whip, and from the summit of the descent seen over the rolling tops of the trees in a park by the side of the road, appeared the level sea far below us, like the floor of an immense edifice inlaid with bands of dark ripple, with still trails of glitter, ending in a belt of glassy water at the foot of the sky. The light blur of smoke, from an invisible steamer, faded on the great clearness of the horizon like the mist of a breath on a mirror; and, inshore, the white sails of a coaster, with the appearance of disentangling themselves slowly from under the branches, floated clear of the foliage of the trees.

"Shipwrecked in the bay?" I said.

"Yes; he was a castaway. A poor emigrant from Central Europe bound to America and washed ashore here in a storm. And for him, who knew nothing of the earth, England was an undiscovered country. It was some time before he learned its name; and for all I know he might have expected to find wild beasts or wild men here, when, crawling in the dark over the sea-wall, he rolled down the other side into a dyke, where it was another miracle he didn't get drowned. But he struggled instinctively like an animal under a net, and this blind struggle threw him out into a field. He must have been, indeed, of a tougher fibre than he looked to withstand without expiring such buffetings, the violence of his exertions, and so much fear. Later on, in his broken English that resembled curiously the speech of a young child, he told me himself that he put his trust in God, believing he was no longer in this world. And truly – he would add – how was he to know? He fought his way against the rain and the gale on all fours, and crawled at last among some sheep huddled close under the lee of a hedge. They ran off in all directions, bleating in the darkness, and he welcomed the first familiar sound he heard on these shores. It must have been two in the morning then. And this is all we know of the manner of his landing, though he did not arrive unattended by any means. Only his grisly company did not begin to come ashore till much later in the day…"

The doctor gathered the reins, clicked his tongue; we trotted down the hill. Then turning, almost directly, a sharp corner into the High Street, we rattled over the stones and were home.

Late in the evening Kennedy, breaking a spell of moodiness that had come over him, returned to the story. Smoking his pipe, he paced the long room from end to end. A reading-lamp concentrated all its light upon the papers on his desk; and, sitting by the open window, I saw, after the windless, scorching day, the frigid splendour of a hazy sea lying motionless under the moon. Not a whisper, not a splash, not a stir of the shingle, not a footstep, not a sigh came up from the earth below – never a sign of life but the scent of climbing jasmine; and Kennedy's voice, speaking behind me, passed through the wide casement, to vanish outside in a chill and sumptuous stillness.

"...The relations of shipwrecks in the olden time tell us of much suffering. Often the castaways were only saved from drowning to die miserably from starvation on a barren coast; others suffered violent death or else slavery, passing through years of precarious existence with people to whom their strangeness was an object of suspicion, dislike or fear. We read about these things, and they are very pitiful. It is indeed hard upon a man to find himself a lost stranger, helpless, incomprehensible, and of a mysterious origin, in some obscure corner of the earth. Yet amongst all the adventurers shipwrecked in all the wild parts of the world there is not one, it seems to me, that ever had to suffer a fate so simply tragic as the man I am speaking of, the most innocent of adventurers cast out by the sea in the bight of this bay, almost within sight from this very window.

"He did not know the name of his ship. Indeed, in the course of time we discovered he did not even know that ships had names – 'like Christian people'; and when, one day, from the top of the Talfourd Hill, he beheld the sea lying open to his view, his eyes roamed afar, lost in an air of wild surprise, as though he had never seen such a sight before. And probably he had not. As far as I could make out, he had been hustled together with many others on board an emigrant-ship lying at the mouth of the Elbe, too bewildered to take note of his surroundings, too weary to see anything, too anxious to care. They were driven below into the 'tweendeck and battened down from the very start. It was a low timber dwelling – he would say – with wooden beams overhead, like the houses in his country, but you went into it down a ladder. It was very large, very cold, damp and sombre, with places in the manner of wooden boxes where people had to sleep, one above another, and it kept on rocking all ways at once all the time. He crept into one of these boxes and laid down there in the clothes in which he had left his home many days before, keeping his bundle and his stick by his side. People groaned, children cried, water dripped, the lights went out, the walls of the place creaked, and everything was being shaken so that in one's little box one dared not lift one's head. He had lost touch with his only companion (a young man from the same valley, he said), and all the time a great noise of wind went on outside and heavy blows fell – boom! boom! An awful sickness overcame him, even to the point of making him neglect his prayers. Besides, one could not tell whether it was morning or evening. It seemed always to be night in that place.

"Before that he had been travelling a long, long time on the iron track. He looked out of the window, which had a wonderfully clear glass in it, and the trees, the houses, the fields, and the long roads seemed to fly round and round about him till his head swam. He gave me to understand that he had on his passage beheld uncounted multitudes of people – whole nations – all dressed in such clothes as the rich wear. Once he was made to get out of the carriage, and slept through a night on a bench in a house of bricks with his bundle under his head; and once for many hours he had to sit on a floor of flat stones dozing, with his knees up and with his bundle between his feet. There was a roof over him, which seemed made of glass, and was so high that the tallest mountain-pine he had ever seen would have had room to grow under it. Steam-machines rolled in at one end and out at the other. People swarmed more than you can see on a feast-day round the miraculous Holy Image in the yard of the Carmelite Convent down in the plains where, before he left his home, he drove his mother in a wooden cart – a pious old woman who wanted to offer prayers and make a vow for his safety. He could not give me an idea of how large and lofty and full of noise and smoke and gloom, and clang of iron, the place was, but someone had told him it was called Berlin. Then they rang a bell, and another steam-machine came in, and again he was taken on and on through a land that wearied his eyes by its flatness without a single bit of a hill to be seen anywhere. One more night he spent shut up in a building like a good stable with a litter of straw on the floor, guarding his bundle amongst a lot of men, of whom not one could understand a single word he said. In the morning they were all led down to the stony shores of an extremely broad muddy river, flowing not between hills but between houses that seemed immense. There was a steam-machine that went on the water, and they all stood upon it packed tight, only now there were with them many women and children who made much noise. A cold rain fell, the wind blew in his face; he was wet through, and his teeth chattered. He and the young man from the same valley took each other by the hand.

"They thought they were being taken to America straight away, but suddenly the steam-machine bumped against the side of a thing like a house on the water. The walls were smooth and black, and there uprose, growing from the roof as it were, bare trees in the shape of crosses, extremely high. That's how it appeared to him then, for he had never seen a ship before. This was the ship that was going to swim all the way to America. Voices shouted, everything swayed; there was a ladder dipping up and down. He went up on his hands and knees in mortal fear of falling into the water below, which made a great splashing. He got separated from his companion, and when he descended into the bottom of that ship his heart seemed to melt suddenly within him.

"It was then also, as he told me, that he lost contact for good and all with one of those three men who the summer before had been going about through all the little towns in the foothills of his country. They would arrive on market days driving in a peasant's cart, and would set up an office in an inn or some other Jew's house. There were three of them, of whom one with a long beard looked venerable; and they had red cloth collars round their necks and gold lace on their sleeves like Government officials. They sat proudly behind a long table; and in the next room, so that the common people shouldn't hear, they kept a cunning telegraph machine, through which they could talk to the Emperor of America. The fathers hung about the door, but the young men of the mountains would crowd up to the table asking many questions, for there was work to be got all the year round at three dollars a day in America, and no military service to do.

"But the American Kaiser would not take everybody. Oh, no! He himself had a great difficulty in getting accepted, and the venerable man in uniform had to go out of the room several times to work the telegraph on his behalf. The American Kaiser engaged him at last at three dollars, he being young and strong. However, many able young men backed out, afraid of the great distance; besides, those only who had some money could be taken. There were some who sold their huts and their land because it cost a lot of money to get to America; but then, once there, you had three dollars a day, and if you were clever you could find places where true gold could be picked up on the ground. His father's house was getting over full. Two of his brothers were married and had children. He promised to send money home from America by post twice a year. His father sold an old cow, a pair of piebald mountain ponies of his own raising, and a cleared plot of fair pasture land on the sunny slope of a pine-clad pass to a Jew inn-keeper in order to pay the people of the ship that took men to America to get rich in a short time.

"He must have been a real adventurer at heart, for how many of the greatest enterprises in the conquest of the earth had for their beginning just such a bargaining away of the paternal cow for the mirage or true gold far away! I have been telling you more or less in my own words what I learned fragmentarily in the course of two or three years, during which I seldom missed an opportunity of a friendly chat with him. He told me this story of his adventure with many flashes of white teeth and lively glances of black eyes, at first in a sort of anxious baby-talk, then, as he acquired the language, with great fluency, but always with that singing, soft, and at the same time vibrating intonation that instilled a strangely penetrating power into the sound of the most familiar English words, as if they had been the words of an unearthly language. And he always would come to an end, with many emphatic shakes of his head, upon that awful sensation of his heart melting within him directly he set foot on board that ship. Afterwards there seemed to come for him a period of blank ignorance, at any rate as to facts. No doubt he must have been abominably sea-sick and abominably unhappy – this soft and passionate adventurer, taken thus out of his knowledge, and feeling bitterly as he lay in his emigrant bunk his utter loneliness; for his was a highly sensitive nature. The next thing we know of him for certain is that he had been hiding in Hammond's pig-pound by the side of the road to Norton six miles, as the crow flies, from the sea. Of these experiences he was unwilling to speak: they seemed to have seared into his soul a sombre sort of wonder and indignation. Through the rumours of the country-side, which lasted for a good many days after his arrival, we know that the fishermen of West Colebrook had been disturbed and startled by heavy knocks against the walls of weatherboard cottages, and by a voice crying piercingly strange words in the night. Several of them turned out even, but, no doubt, he had fled in sudden alarm at their rough angry tones hailing each other in the darkness. A sort of frenzy must have helped him up the steep Norton hill. It was he, no doubt, who early the following morning had been seen lying (in a swoon, I should say) on the roadside grass by the Brenzett carrier, who actually got down to have a nearer look, but drew back, intimidated by the perfect immobility, and by something queer in the aspect of that tramp, sleeping so still under the showers. As the day advanced, some children came dashing into school at Norton in such a fright that the schoolmistress went out and spoke indignantly to a 'horrid-looking man' on the road. He edged away, hanging his head, for a few steps, and then suddenly ran off with extraordinary fleetness. The driver of Mr. Bradley's milk-cart made no secret of it that he had lashed with his whip at a hairy sort of gipsy fellow who, jumping up at a turn of the road by the Vents, made a snatch at the pony's bridle. And he caught him a good one too, right over the face, he said, that made him drop down in the mud a jolly sight quicker than he had jumped up; but it was a good half-a-mile before he could stop the pony. Maybe that in his desperate endeavours to get help, and in his need to get in touch with someone, the poor devil had tried to stop the cart. Also three boys confessed afterwards to throwing stones at a funny tramp, knocking about all wet and muddy, and, it seemed, very drunk, in the narrow deep lane by the limekilns. All this was the talk of three villages for days; but we have Mrs. Finn's (the wife of Smith's waggoner) unimpeachable testimony that she saw him get over the low wall of Hammond's pig-pound and lurch straight at her, babbling aloud in a voice that was enough to make one die of fright. Having the baby with her in a perambulator, Mrs. Finn called out to him to go away, and as he persisted in coming nearer, she hit him courageously with her umbrella over the head and, without once looking back, ran like the wind with the perambulator as far as the first house in the village. She stopped then, out of breath, and spoke to old Lewis, hammering there at a heap of stones; and the old chap, taking off his immense black wire goggles, got up on his shaky legs to look where she pointed. Together they followed with their eyes the figure of the man running over a field; they saw him fall down, pick himself up, and run on again, staggering and waving his long arms above his head, in the direction of the New Barns Farm. From that moment he is plainly in the toils of his obscure and touching destiny. There is no doubt after this of what happened to him. All is certain now: Mrs. Smith's intense terror; Amy Foster's stolid conviction held against the other's nervous attack, that the man 'meant no harm'; Smith's exasperation (on his return from Darnford Market) at finding the dog barking himself into a fit, the back-door locked, his wife in hysterics; and all for an unfortunate dirty tramp, supposed to be even then lurking in his stackyard. Was he? He would teach him to frighten women.

"Smith is notoriously hot-tempered, but the sight of some nondescript and miry creature sitting cross-legged amongst a lot of loose straw, and swinging itself to and fro like a bear in a cage, made him pause. Then this tramp stood up silently before him, one mass of mud and filth from head to foot. Smith, alone amongst his stacks with this apparition, in the stormy twilight ringing with the infuriated barking of the dog, felt the dread of an inexplicable strangeness. But when that being, parting with his black hands the long matted locks that hung before his face, as you part the two halves of a curtain, looked out at him with glistening, wild, black-and-white eyes, the weirdness of this silent encounter fairly staggered him. He had admitted since (for the story has been a legitimate subject of conversation about here for years) that he made more than one step backwards. Then a sudden burst of rapid, senseless speech persuaded him at once that he had to do with an escaped lunatic. In fact, that impression never wore off completely. Smith has not in his heart given up his secret conviction of the man's essential insanity to this very day.

"As the creature approached him, jabbering in a most discomposing manner, Smith (unaware that he was being addressed as 'gracious lord,' and adjured in God's name to afford food and shelter) kept on speaking firmly but gently to it, and retreating all the time into the other yard. At last, watching his chance, by a sudden charge he bundled him headlong into the wood-lodge, and instantly shot the bolt. Thereupon he wiped his brow, though the day was cold. He had done his duty to the community by shutting up a wandering and probably dangerous maniac. Smith isn't a hard man at all, but he had room in his brain only for that one idea of lunacy. He was not imaginative enough to ask himself whether the man might not be perishing with cold and hunger. Meantime, at first, the maniac made a great deal of noise in the lodge. Mrs. Smith was screaming upstairs, where she had locked herself in her bedroom; but Amy Foster sobbed piteously at the kitchen door, wringing her hands and muttering,

'Don't! don't!' I daresay Smith had a rough time of it that evening with one noise and another, and this insane, disturbing voice crying obstinately through the door only added to his irritation. He couldn't possibly have connected this troublesome lunatic with the sinking of a ship in Eastbay, of which there had been a rumour in the Darnford marketplace. And I daresay the man inside had been very near to insanity on that night. Before his excitement collapsed and he became unconscious he was throwing himself violently about in the dark, rolling on some dirty sacks, and biting his fists with rage, cold, hunger, amazement, and despair.

"He was a mountaineer of the eastern range of the Carpathians, and the vessel sunk the night before in Eastbay was the Hamburg emigrant-ship Herzogin Sophia-Dorothea, of appalling memory.

"A few months later we could read in the papers the accounts of the bogus 'Emigration Agencies' among the Sclavonian peasantry in the more remote provinces of Austria. The object of these scoundrels was to get hold of the poor ignorant people's homesteads, and they were in league with the local usurers. They exported their victims through Hamburg mostly. As to the ship, I had watched her out of this very window, reaching close-hauled under short canvas into the bay on a dark, threatening afternoon. She came to an anchor, correctly by the chart, off the Brenzett Coastguard station. I remember before the night fell looking out again at the outlines of her spars and rigging that stood out dark and pointed on a background of ragged, slaty clouds like another and a slighter spire to the left of the Brenzett church-tower. In the evening the wind rose. At midnight I could hear in my bed the terrific gusts and the sounds of a driving deluge.

"About that time the Coastguardmen thought they saw the lights of a steamer over the anchoring-ground. In a moment they vanished; but it is clear that another vessel of some sort had tried for shelter in the bay on that awful, blind night, had rammed the German ship amidships (a breach – as one of the divers told me afterwards – 'that you could sail a Thames barge through'), and then had gone out either scathless or damaged, who shall say; but had gone out, unknown, unseen, and fatal, to perish mysteriously at sea. Of her nothing ever came to light, and yet the hue and cry that was raised all over the world would have found her out if she had been in existence anywhere on the face of the waters.

"A completeness without a clue, and a stealthy silence as of a neatly executed crime, characterise this murderous disaster, which, as you may remember, had its gruesome celebrity. The wind would have prevented the loudest outcries from reaching the shore; there had been evidently no time for signals of distress. It was death without any sort of fuss. The Hamburg ship, filling all at once, capsized as she sank, and at daylight there was not even the end of a spar to be seen above water. She was missed, of course, and at first the Coastguardmen surmised that she had either dragged her anchor or parted her cable some time during the night, and had been blown out to sea. Then, after the tide turned, the wreck must have shifted a little and released some of the bodies, because a child – a little fair-haired child in a red frock – came ashore abreast of the Martello tower. By the afternoon you could see along three miles of beach dark figures with bare legs dashing in and out of the tumbling foam, and rough-looking men, women with hard faces, children, mostly fair-haired, were being carried, stiff and dripping, on stretchers, on wattles, on ladders, in a long procession past the door of the 'Ship Inn,' to be laid out in a row under the north wall of the Brenzett Church.

"Officially, the body of the little girl in the red frock is the first thing that came ashore from that ship. But I have patients amongst the seafaring population of West Colebrook, and, unofficially, I am informed that very early that morning two brothers, who went down to look after their cobble hauled up on the beach, found, a good way from Brenzett, an ordinary ship's hencoop lying high and dry on the shore, with eleven drowned ducks inside. Their families ate the birds, and the hencoop was split into firewood with a hatchet. It is possible that a man (supposing he happened to be on deck at the time of the accident) might have floated ashore on that hencoop. He might. I admit it is improbable, but there was the man – and for days, nay, for weeks – it didn't enter our heads that we had amongst us the only living soul that had escaped from that disaster. The man himself, even when he learned to speak intelligibly, could tell us very little. He remembered he had felt better (after the ship had anchored, I suppose), and that the darkness, the wind, and the rain took his breath away. This looks as if he had been on deck some time during that night. But we mustn't forget he had been taken out of his knowledge, that he had been sea-sick and battened down below for four days, that he had no general notion of a ship or of the sea, and therefore could have no definite idea of what was happening to him. The rain, the wind, the darkness he knew; he understood the bleating of the sheep, and he remembered the pain of his wretchedness and misery, his heartbroken astonishment that it was neither seen nor understood, his dismay at finding all the men angry and all the women fierce. He had approached them as a beggar, it is true, he said; but in his country, even if they gave nothing, they spoke gently to beggars. The children in his country were not taught to throw stones at those who asked for compassion. Smith's strategy overcame him completely. The wood-lodge presented the horrible aspect of a dungeon. What would be done to him next?... No wonder that Amy Foster appeared to his eyes with the aureole of an angel of light. The girl had not been able to sleep for thinking of the poor man, and in the morning, before the Smiths were up, she slipped out across the back yard. Holding the door of the wood-lodge ajar, she looked in and extended to him half a loaf of white bread – 'such bread as the rich eat in my country,' he used to say.

"At this he got up slowly from amongst all sorts of rubbish, stiff, hungry, trembling, miserable, and doubtful. 'Can you eat this?' she asked in her soft and timid voice. He must have taken her for a 'gracious lady.' He devoured ferociously, and tears were falling on the crust. Suddenly he dropped the bread, seized her wrist, and imprinted a kiss on her hand. She was not frightened. Through his forlorn condition she had observed that he was good-looking. She shut the door and walked back slowly to the kitchen. Much later on, she told Mrs. Smith, who shuddered at the bare idea of being touched by that creature.

"Through this act of impulsive pity he was brought back again within the pale of human relations with his new surroundings. He never forgot it – never.

"That very same morning old Mr. Swaffer (Smith's nearest neighbour) came over to give his advice, and ended by carrying him off. He stood, unsteady on his legs, meek, and caked over in half-dried mud, while the two men talked around him in an incomprehensible tongue. Mrs. Smith had refused to come downstairs till the madman was off the premises; Amy Foster, far from within the dark kitchen, watched through the open back door; and he obeyed the signs that were made to him to the best of his ability. But Smith was full of mistrust. 'Mind, sir! It may be all his cunning,' he cried repeatedly in a tone of warning. When Mr. Swaffer started the mare, the deplorable being sitting humbly by his side, through weakness, nearly fell out over the back of the high two-wheeled cart. Swaffer took him straight home. And it is then that I come upon the scene.

"I was called in by the simple process of the old man beckoning to me with his forefinger over the gate of his house as I happened to be driving past. I got down, of course.

"'I've got something here,' he mumbled, leading the way to an outhouse at a little distance from his other farm-buildings.

"It was there that I saw him first, in a long low room taken upon the space of that sort of coach-house. It was bare and whitewashed, with a small square aperture glazed with one cracked, dusty pane at its further end. He was lying on his back upon a straw pallet; they had given him a couple of horse-blankets, and he seemed to have spent the remainder of his strength in the exertion of cleaning himself. He was almost speechless; his quick breathing under the blankets pulled up to his chin, his glittering, restless black eyes reminded me of a wild bird caught in a snare. While I was examining him, old Swaffer stood silently by the door, passing the tips of his fingers along his shaven upper lip. I gave some directions, promised to send a bottle of medicine, and naturally made some inquiries.

"'Smith caught him in the stackyard at New Barns,' said the old chap in his deliberate, unmoved manner, and as if the other had been indeed a sort of wild animal. 'That's how I came by him. Quite a curiosity, isn't he? Now tell me, doctor – you've been all over the world – don't you think that's a bit of a Hindoo we've got hold of here.'

"I was greatly surprised. His long black hair scattered over the straw bolster contrasted with the olive pallor of his face. It occurred to me he might be a Basque. It didn't necessarily follow that he should understand Spanish; but I tried him with the few words I know, and also with some French. The whispered sounds I caught by bending my ear to his lips puzzled me utterly. That afternoon the young ladies from the Rectory (one of them read Goethe with a dictionary, and the other had struggled with Dante for years), coming to see Miss Swaffer, tried their German and Italian on him from the doorway. They retreated, just the least bit scared by the flood of passionate speech which, turning on his pallet, he let out at them. They admitted that the sound was pleasant, soft, musical – but, in conjunction with his looks perhaps, it was startling – so excitable, so utterly unlike anything one had ever heard. The village boys climbed up the bank to have a peep through the little square aperture. Everybody was wondering what Mr. Swaffer would do with him.

"He simply kept him.

"Swaffer would be called eccentric were he not so much respected. They will tell you that Mr. Swaffer sits up as late as ten o'clock at night to read books, and they will tell you also that he can write a cheque for two hundred pounds without thinking twice about it. He himself would tell you that the Swaffers had owned land between this and Darnford for these three hundred years. He must be eighty-five today, but he does not look a bit older than when I first came here. He is a great breeder of sheep, and deals extensively in cattle. He attends market days for miles around in every sort of weather, and drives sitting bowed low over the reins, his lank grey hair curling over the collar of his warm coat, and with a green plaid rug round his legs. The calmness of advanced age gives a solemnity to his manner. He is clean-shaved; his lips are thin and sensitive;

something rigid and monarchal in the set of his features lends a certain elevation to the character of his face. He has been known to drive miles in the rain to see a new kind of rose in somebody's garden, or a monstrous cabbage grown by a cottager. He loves to hear tell of or to be shown something that he calls 'outlandish.' Perhaps it was just that outlandishness of the man which influenced old Swaffer. Perhaps it was only an inexplicable caprice. All I know is that at the end of three weeks I caught sight of Smith's lunatic digging in Swaffer's kitchen garden. They had found out he could use a spade. He dug barefooted.

"His black hair flowed over his shoulders. I suppose it was Swaffer who had given him the striped old cotton shirt; but he wore still the national brown cloth trousers (in which he had been washed ashore) fitting to the leg almost like tights; was belted with a broad leathern belt studded with little brass discs; and had never yet ventured into the village. The land he looked upon seemed to him kept neatly, like the grounds round a landowner's house; the size of the cart-horses struck him with astonishment; the roads resembled garden walks, and the aspect of the people, especially on Sundays, spoke of opulence. He wondered what made them so hardhearted and their children so bold. He got his food at the back door, carried it in both hands carefully to his outhouse, and, sitting alone on his pallet, would make the sign of the cross before he began. Beside the same pallet, kneeling in the early darkness of the short days, he recited aloud the Lord's Prayer before he slept. Whenever he saw old Swaffer he would bow with veneration from the waist, and stand erect while the old man, with his fingers over his upper lip, surveyed him silently. He bowed also to Miss Swaffer, who kept house frugally for her father – a broad-shouldered, big-boned woman of forty-five, with the pocket of her dress full of keys, and a grey, steady eye. She was Church – as people said (while her father was one of the trustees of the Baptist Chapel) – and wore a little steel cross at her waist. She dressed severely in black, in memory of one of the innumerable Bradleys of the neighbourhood, to whom she had been engaged some twenty-five years ago – a young farmer who broke his neck out hunting on the eve of the wedding day. She had the unmoved countenance of the deaf, spoke very seldom, and her lips, thin like her father's, astonished one sometimes by a mysteriously ironic curl.

"These were the people to whom he owed allegiance, and an overwhelming loneliness seemed to fall from the leaden sky of that winter without sunshine. All the faces were sad. He could talk to no one, and had no hope of ever understanding anybody. It was as if these had been the faces of people from the other world – dead people – he used to tell me years afterwards. Upon my word, I wonder he did not go mad. He didn't know where he was. Somewhere very far from his mountains – somewhere over the water. Was this America, he wondered?

"If it hadn't been for the steel cross at Miss Swaffer's belt he would not, he confessed, have known whether he was in a Christian country at all. He used to cast stealthy glances at it, and feel comforted. There was nothing here the same as in his country! The earth and the water were different; there were no images of the Redeemer by the roadside. The very grass was different, and the trees. All the trees but the three old Norway pines on the bit of lawn before Swaffer's house, and these reminded him of his country. He had been detected once, after dusk, with his forehead against the trunk of one of them, sobbing, and talking to himself. They had been like brothers to him at that time, he affirmed. Everything else was strange. Conceive you the kind of an existence overshadowed, oppressed, by the everyday material appearances, as if by the visions of a nightmare. At night, when he could not sleep, he kept on thinking of the girl who gave him the first piece of bread he had eaten in this foreign land. She had been neither fierce nor angry, nor frightened. Her face he remembered as the only comprehensible face amongst all these faces that were as closed, as mysterious, and as mute as the faces of the dead who are possessed of a knowledge beyond the comprehension of the living. I wonder whether the memory of her compassion prevented him from cutting his throat. But there! I suppose I am an old sentimentalist, and forget the instinctive love of life which it takes all the strength of an uncommon despair to overcome.

"He did the work which was given him with an intelligence which surprised old Swaffer. By-and-by it was discovered that he could help at the ploughing, could milk the cows, feed the bullocks in the cattle-yard, and was of some use with the sheep. He began to pick up words, too, very fast; and suddenly, one fine morning in spring, he rescued from an untimely death a grand-child of old Swaffer.

"Swaffer's younger daughter is married to Willcox, a solicitor and the Town Clerk of Colebrook. Regularly twice a year they come to stay with the old man for a few days. Their only child, a little girl not three years old at the time, ran out of the house alone in her little white pinafore, and, toddling across the grass of a terraced garden, pitched herself over a low wall head first into the horse-pond in the yard below.

"Our man was out with the waggoner and the plough in the field nearest to the house, and as he was leading the team round to begin a fresh furrow, he saw, through the gap of the gate, what for anybody else would have been a mere flutter of something white. But he had straight-glancing, quick, far-reaching eyes, that only seemed to flinch and lose their amazing power before the immensity of the sea. He was barefooted, and looking as outlandish as the heart of Swaffer could desire. Leaving the horses on the turn, to the inexpressible disgust of the waggoner he bounded off, going over the ploughed ground in long leaps, and suddenly appeared before the mother, thrust the child into her arms, and strode away.

"The pond was not very deep; but still, if he had not had such good eyes, the child would have perished – miserably suffocated in the foot or so of sticky mud at the bottom. Old Swaffer walked out slowly into the field, waited till the plough came over to his side, had a good look at him, and without saying a word went back to the house. But from that time they laid out his meals on the kitchen table; and at first, Miss Swaffer, all in black and with an inscrutable face, would come and stand in the doorway of the living-room to see him make a big sign of the cross before he fell to. I believe that from that day, too, Swaffer began to pay him regular wages.

"I can't follow step by step his development. He cut his hair short, was seen in the village and along the road going to and fro to his work like any other man. Children ceased to shout after him. He became aware of social differences, but remained for a long time surprised at the bare poverty of the churches among so much wealth. He couldn't understand either why they were kept shut up on week days. There was nothing to steal in them. Was it to keep people from praying too often? The rectory took much notice of him about that time, and I believe the young ladies attempted to prepare the ground for his conversion. They could not, however, break him of his habit of crossing himself, but he went so far as to take off the string with a couple of brass medals the size of a sixpence, a tiny metal cross, and a square sort of scapulary which he wore round his neck. He hung them on the wall by the side of his bed, and he was still to be heard every evening reciting the Lord's Prayer, in incomprehensible words and in a slow, fervent tone, as he had heard his old father do at the head of all the kneeling family, big and little, on every evening of his life. And though he wore corduroys at work, and a slop-made pepper-and-salt suit on Sundays, strangers would turn round to look after him on the road. His foreignness had a peculiar and indelible stamp. At last people became used to see him. But they never became used to him. His rapid, skimming walk; his swarthy complexion; his hat cocked on the left ear; his habit, on warm evenings, of wearing his coat over one shoulder, like a hussar's dolman; his manner of leaping over the stiles, not as a feat of agility, but in the ordinary course of progression – all these peculiarities were, as one may say, so many causes of scorn and offence to the inhabitants of the village. They wouldn't in their dinner hour lie flat on their backs on the grass to stare at the sky. Neither did they go about the fields screaming dismal tunes. Many times have I heard his high-pitched voice from behind the ridge of some sloping sheep-walk, a voice light and soaring, like a lark's, but with a melancholy human note, over our fields that hear only the song of birds. And I should be startled myself. Ah! He was different: innocent of heart, and full of good will, which nobody wanted, this castaway, that, like a man transplanted into another planet, was separated by an immense space from his past and by an immense ignorance from his future. His quick, fervent utterance positively shocked everybody. 'An excitable devil,' they called him. One evening, in the tap-room of the Coach and Horses (having drunk some whisky), he upset them all by singing a love song of his country. They hooted him down, and he was pained; but Preble, the lame wheelwright, and Vincent, the fat blacksmith, and the other notables too, wanted to drink their evening beer in peace. On another occasion he tried to show them how to dance. The dust rose in clouds from the sanded floor; he leaped straight up amongst the deal tables, struck his heels together, squatted on one heel in front of old Preble, shooting out the other leg, uttered wild and exulting cries, jumped up to whirl on one foot, snapping his fingers above his head – and a strange carter who was having a drink in there began to swear, and cleared out with his half-pint in his hand into the bar. But when suddenly he sprang upon a table and continued to dance among the glasses, the landlord interfered. He didn't want any 'acrobat tricks in the taproom.' They laid their hands on him. Having had a glass or two, Mr. Swaffer's foreigner tried to expostulate: was ejected forcibly: got a black eye.

"I believe he felt the hostility of his human surroundings. But he was tough – tough in spirit, too, as well as in body. Only the memory of the sea frightened him, with that vague terror that is left by a bad dream. His home was far away; and he did not want now to go to America. I had often explained to him that there is no place on earth where true gold can be found lying ready and to be got for the trouble of the picking up. How then, he asked, could he ever return home with empty hands when there had been sold a cow, two ponies, and a bit of land to pay for his going? His eyes would fill with tears, and, averting them from the immense shimmer of the sea, he would throw himself face down on the grass. But sometimes, cocking his hat with a little conquering air, he would defy my wisdom. He had found his bit of true gold. That was Amy Foster's heart; which was 'a golden heart, and soft to people's misery,' he would say in the accents of overwhelming conviction.

"He was called Yanko. He had explained that this meant little John; but as he would also repeat very often that he was a mountaineer (some word sounding in the dialect of his country like Goorall) he got it for his surname. And this is the only trace of him that the succeeding ages may find in the marriage register of the parish. There it stands – Yanko Goorall – in the rector's handwriting. The crooked cross made by the castaway, a cross whose tracing no doubt seemed to him the most solemn part of the whole ceremony, is all that remains now to perpetuate the memory of his name.

"His courtship had lasted some time – ever since he got his precarious footing in the community. It began by his buying for Amy Foster a green satin ribbon in Darnford. This was what you did in his country. You bought a ribbon at a Jew's stall on a fair-day. I don't suppose the girl knew what to do with it, but he seemed to think that his honourable intentions could not be mistaken.

"It was only when he declared his purpose to get married that I fully understood how, for a hundred futile and inappreciable reasons, how – shall I say odious? – he was to all the countryside. Every old woman in the village was up in arms. Smith, coming upon him near the farm, promised to break his head for him if he found him about again. But he twisted his little black moustache with such a bellicose air and rolled such big, black fierce eyes at Smith that this promise came to nothing. Smith, however, told the girl that she must be mad to take up with a man who was surely wrong in his head. All the same, when she heard him in the gloaming whistle from beyond the orchard a couple of bars of a weird and mournful tune, she would drop whatever she had in her hand – she would leave Mrs. Smith in the middle of a sentence – and she would run out to his call. Mrs. Smith called her a shameless hussy. She answered nothing. She said nothing at all to anybody, and went on her way as if she had been deaf. She and I alone all in the land, I fancy, could see his very real beauty. He was very good-looking, and most graceful in his bearing, with that something wild as of a woodland creature in his aspect. Her mother moaned over her dismally whenever the girl came to see her on her day out. The father was surly, but pretended not to know; and Mrs. Finn once told her plainly that 'this man, my dear, will do you some harm some day yet.' And so it went on. They could be seen on the roads, she tramping stolidly in her finery – grey dress, black feather, stout boots, prominent white cotton gloves that caught your eye a hundred yards away; and he, his coat slung picturesquely over one shoulder, pacing by her side, gallant of bearing and casting tender glances upon the girl with the golden heart. I wonder whether he saw how plain she was. Perhaps among types so different from what he had ever seen, he had not the power to judge; or perhaps he was seduced by the divine quality of her pity.

"Yanko was in great trouble meantime. In his country you get an old man for an ambassador in marriage affairs. He did not know how to proceed. However, one day in the midst of sheep in a field (he was now Swaffer's under-shepherd with Foster) he took off his hat to the father and declared himself humbly. 'I daresay she's fool enough to marry you,' was all Foster said. 'And then,' he used to relate, 'he puts his hat on his head, looks black at me as if he wanted to cut my throat, whistles the dog, and off he goes, leaving me to do the work.' The Fosters, of course, didn't like to lose the wages the girl earned: Amy used to give all her money to her mother. But there was in Foster a very genuine aversion to that match. He contended that the fellow was very good with sheep, but was not fit for any girl to marry. For one thing, he used to go along the hedges muttering to himself like a dam' fool; and then, these foreigners behave very queerly to women sometimes. And perhaps he would want to carry her off somewhere – or run off himself. It was not safe. He preached it to his daughter that the fellow might ill-use her in some way. She made no answer. It was, they said in the village, as if the man had done something to her. People discussed the matter. It was quite an excitement, and the two went on 'walking out' together in the face of opposition. Then something unexpected happened.

"I don't know whether old Swaffer ever understood how much he was regarded in the light of a father by his foreign retainer. Anyway the relation was curiously feudal. So when Yanko asked formally for an interview – 'and the Miss too' (he called the severe, deaf Miss Swaffer simply Miss) – it was to obtain their permission to marry. Swaffer heard him unmoved, dismissed him by a nod, and then shouted the intelligence into Miss Swaffer's best ear. She showed no surprise, and only remarked grimly, in a veiled blank voice, 'He certainly won't get any other girl to marry him.'

"It is Miss Swaffer who has all the credit of the munificence: but in a very few days it came out that Mr. Swaffer had presented Yanko with a cottage (the cottage you've seen this morning) and something like an acre of ground – had made it over to him in absolute property. Willcox expedited the deed, and I remember him telling me he had a great pleasure in making it ready. It recited: 'In consideration of saving the life of my beloved grandchild, Bertha Willcox.'

"Of course, after that no power on earth could prevent them from getting married.

"Her infatuation endured. People saw her going out to meet him in the evening. She stared with unblinking, fascinated eyes up the road where he was expected to appear, walking freely, with a swing from the hip, and humming one of the love-tunes of his country. When the boy was born, he got elevated at the 'Coach and Horses,' essayed again a song and a dance, and was again ejected. People expressed their commiseration for a woman married to that Jack-in-the-box. He didn't care. There was a man now (he told me boastfully) to whom he could sing and talk in the language of his country, and show how to dance by-and-by.

"But I don't know. To me he appeared to have grown less springy of step, heavier in body, less keen of eye. Imagination, no doubt; but it seems to me now as if the net of fate had been drawn closer round him already.

"One day I met him on the footpath over the Talfourd Hill. He told me that 'women were funny.' I had heard already of domestic differences. People were saying that Amy Foster was beginning to find out what sort of man she had married. He looked upon the sea with indifferent, unseeing eyes. His wife had snatched the child out of his arms one day as he sat on the doorstep crooning to it a song such as the mothers sing to babies in his mountains. She seemed to think he was doing it some harm. Women are funny. And she had objected to him praying aloud in the evening. Why? He expected the boy to repeat the prayer aloud after him by-and-by, as he used to do after his old father when he was a child – in his own country. And I discovered he longed for their boy to grow up so that he could have a man to talk with in that language that to our ears sounded so disturbing, so passionate, and so bizarre. Why his wife should dislike the idea he couldn't tell. But that would pass, he said. And tilting his head knowingly, he tapped his breastbone to indicate that she had a good heart: not hard, not fierce, open to compassion, charitable to the poor!

"I walked away thoughtfully; I wondered whether his difference, his strangeness, were not penetrating with repulsion that dull nature they had begun by irresistibly attracting. I wondered..."

The Doctor came to the window and looked out at the frigid splendour of the sea, immense in the haze, as if enclosing all the earth with all the hearts lost among the passions of love and fear.

"Physiologically, now," he said, turning away abruptly, "it was possible. It was possible."

He remained silent. Then went on – "At all events, the next time I saw him he was ill – lung trouble. He was tough, but I daresay he was not acclimatised as well as I had supposed. It was a bad winter; and, of course, these mountaineers do get fits of home sickness; and a state of depression would make him vulnerable. He was lying half dressed on a couch downstairs.

"A table covered with a dark oilcloth took up all the middle of the little room. There was a wicker cradle on the floor, a kettle spouting steam on the hob, and some child's linen lay drying on the fender. The room was warm, but the door opens right into the garden, as you noticed perhaps.

"He was very feverish, and kept on muttering to himself. She sat on a chair and looked at him fixedly across the table with her brown, blurred eyes. 'Why don't you have him upstairs?' I asked. With a start and a confused stammer she said, 'Oh! ah! I couldn't sit with him upstairs, Sir.'

"I gave her certain directions; and going outside, I said again that he ought to be in bed upstairs. She wrung her hands. 'I couldn't. I couldn't. He keeps on saying something – I don't know what.' With the memory of all the talk against the man that had been dinned into her ears, I looked at her narrowly. I looked into her shortsighted eyes, at her dumb eyes that once in her life had seen an enticing shape, but seemed, staring at me, to see nothing at all now. But I saw she was uneasy.

"'What's the matter with him?' she asked in a sort of vacant trepidation. 'He doesn't look very ill. I never did see anybody look like this before...'

"'Do you think,' I asked indignantly, 'he is shamming?'

"'I can't help it, sir,' she said stolidly. And suddenly she clapped her hands and looked right and left. 'And there's the baby. I am so frightened. He wanted me just now to give him the baby. I can't understand what he says to it.'

"'Can't you ask a neighbour to come in tonight?' I asked.

"'Please, sir, nobody seems to care to come,' she muttered, dully resigned all at once.

"I impressed upon her the necessity of the greatest care, and then had to go. There was a good deal of sickness that winter. 'Oh, I hope he won't talk!' she exclaimed softly just as I was going away.

"I don't know how it is I did not see – but I didn't. And yet, turning in my trap, I saw her lingering before the door, very still, and as if meditating a flight up the miry road.

"Towards the night his fever increased.

"He tossed, moaned, and now and then muttered a complaint. And she sat with the table between her and the couch, watching every movement and every sound, with the terror, the unreasonable terror, of that man she could not understand creeping over her. She had drawn the wicker cradle close to her feet. There was nothing in her now but the maternal instinct and that unaccountable fear.

"Suddenly coming to himself, parched, he demanded a drink of water. She did not move. She had not understood, though he may have thought he was speaking in English. He waited, looking at her, burning with fever, amazed at her silence and immobility, and then he shouted impatiently, 'Water! Give me water!'

"She jumped to her feet, snatched up the child, and stood still. He spoke to her, and his passionate remonstrances only increased her fear of that strange man. I believe he spoke to her for a long time, entreating, wondering, pleading, ordering, I suppose. She says she bore it as long as she could. And then a gust of rage came over him.

"He sat up and called out terribly one word – some word. Then he got up as though he hadn't been ill at all, she says. And as in fevered dismay, indignation, and wonder he tried to get to her round the table, she simply opened the door and ran out with the child in her arms. She heard him call twice after her down the road in a terrible voice – and fled... Ah! but you should have seen stirring behind the dull, blurred glance of these eyes the spectre of the fear which had hunted her on that night three miles and a half to the door of Foster's cottage! I did the next day.

"And it was I who found him lying face down and his body in a puddle, just outside the little wicket-gate.

"I had been called out that night to an urgent case in the village, and on my way home at daybreak passed by the cottage. The door stood open. My man helped me to carry him in. We laid him on the couch. The lamp smoked, the fire was out, the chill of the stormy night oozed from the cheerless yellow paper on the wall. 'Amy!' I called aloud, and my voice seemed to lose itself in the emptiness of this tiny house as if I had cried in a desert. He opened his eyes. 'Gone!' he said distinctly. 'I had only asked for water – only for a little water...'

"He was muddy. I covered him up and stood waiting in silence, catching a painfully gasped word now and then. They were no longer in his own language. The fever had left him, taking with it the heat of life. And with his panting breast and lustrous eyes he reminded me again of a wild creature under the net; of a bird caught in a snare. She had left him. She had left him – sick – helpless – thirsty. The spear of the hunter had entered his very soul. 'Why?' he cried in the penetrating and indignant voice of a man calling to a responsible Maker. A gust of wind and a swish of rain answered.

"And as I turned away to shut the door he pronounced the word 'Merciful!' and expired.

"Eventually I certified heart-failure as the immediate cause of death. His heart must have indeed failed him, or else he might have stood this night of storm and exposure, too. I closed his eyes and drove away. Not very far from the cottage I met Foster walking sturdily between the dripping hedges with his collie at his heels.

"'Do you know where your daughter is?' I asked.

"'Don't I!' he cried. 'I am going to talk to him a bit. Frightening a poor woman like this.'

"'He won't frighten her any more,' I said. 'He is dead.'

"He struck with his stick at the mud.

"'And there's the child.'

"Then, after thinking deeply for a while – "'I don't know that it isn't for the best.'

"That's what he said. And she says nothing at all now. Not a word of him. Never. Is his image as utterly gone from her mind as his lithe and striding figure, his carolling voice are gone from our fields? He is no longer before her eyes to excite her imagination into a passion of love or fear; and his memory seems to have vanished from her dull brain as a shadow passes away upon a white screen. She lives in the cottage and works for Miss

Swaffer. She is Amy Foster for everybody, and the child is 'Amy Foster's boy.' She calls him Johnny – which means Little John.

"It is impossible to say whether this name recalls anything to her. Does she ever think of the past? I have seen her hanging over the boy's cot in a very passion of maternal tenderness. The little fellow was lying on his back, a little frightened at me, but very still, with his big black eyes, with his fluttered air of a bird in a snare. And looking at him I seemed to see again the other one – the father, cast out mysteriously by the sea to perish in the supreme disaster of loneliness and despair."

If you enjoyed this, you might also like...
The Watcher, see page 276
A Lost Masterpiece, see page 166

Science & the Supernatural

The Lifted Veil

George Eliot

Give me no light, great Heaven, but such as turns
To energy of human fellowship;
No powers beyond the growing heritage
That makes completer manhood.

Chapter I

THE TIME of my end approaches. I have lately been subject to attacks of angina pectoris; and in the ordinary course of things, my physician tells me, I may fairly hope that my life will not be protracted many months. Unless, then, I am cursed with an exceptional physical constitution, as I am cursed with an exceptional mental character, I shall not much longer groan under the wearisome burthen of this earthly existence. If it were to be otherwise – if I were to live on to the age most men desire and provide for – I should for once have known whether the miseries of delusive expectation can outweigh the miseries of true provision. For I foresee when I shall die, and everything that will happen in my last moments.

Just a month from this day, on September 20, 1850, I shall be sitting in this chair, in this study, at ten o'clock at night, longing to die, weary of incessant insight and foresight, without delusions and without hope. Just as I am watching a tongue of blue flame rising in the fire, and my lamp is burning low, the horrible contraction will begin at my chest. I shall only have time to reach the bell, and pull it violently, before the sense of suffocation will come. No one will answer my bell. I know why. My two servants are lovers, and will have quarrelled. My housekeeper will have rushed out of the house in a fury, two hours before, hoping that Perry will believe she has gone to drown herself. Perry is alarmed at last, and is gone out after her. The little scullery-maid is asleep on a bench: she never answers the bell; it does not wake her. The sense of suffocation increases: my lamp goes out with a horrible stench: I make a great effort, and snatch at the bell again. I long for life, and there is no help. I thirsted for the unknown: the thirst is gone. O God, let me stay with the known, and be weary of it: I am content. Agony of pain and suffocation – and all the while the earth, the fields, the pebbly brook at the bottom of the rookery, the fresh scent after the rain, the light of the morning through my chamber-window, the warmth of the hearth after the frosty air – will darkness close over them for ever?

Darkness – darkness – no pain – nothing but darkness: but I am passing on and on through the darkness: my thought stays in the darkness, but always with a sense of moving onward...

Before that time comes, I wish to use my last hours of ease and strength in telling the strange story of my experience. I have never fully unbosomed myself to any human being; I have never been encouraged to trust much in the sympathy of my fellow-men. But we have all a chance of meeting with some pity, some tenderness, some charity, when we are dead: it is the living only who cannot be forgiven – the living only from whom men's indulgence and reverence are held off, like the rain by the hard east wind. While the heart beats, bruise it – it is your only opportunity; while the eye can still turn towards you with moist, timid entreaty, freeze it with an icy unanswering gaze; while the ear, that delicate messenger to the inmost sanctuary of the soul, can still take in the tones of kindness, put it off with hard civility, or sneering compliment, or envious affectation of indifference; while the creative brain can still throb with the sense of injustice, with the yearning for brotherly recognition – make haste – oppress it with your ill-considered judgements, your trivial comparisons, your careless misrepresentations. The heart will by and by be still – "ubi saeva indignatio ulterius cor lacerare nequit"; the eye will cease to entreat; the ear will be deaf; the brain will have ceased from all wants as well as from all work. Then your charitable speeches may find vent; then you may remember and pity the toil and the struggle and the failure; then you may give due honour to the work achieved; then you may find extenuation for errors, and may consent to bury them.

That is a trivial schoolboy text; why do I dwell on it? It has little reference to me, for I shall leave no works behind me for men to honour. I have no near relatives who will make up, by weeping over my grave, for the wounds they inflicted on me when I was among them. It is only the story of my life that will perhaps win a little more sympathy from strangers when I am dead, than I ever believed it would obtain from my friends while I was living.

My childhood perhaps seems happier to me than it really was, by contrast with all the after-years. For then the curtain of the future was as impenetrable to me as to other children: I had all their delight in the present hour, their sweet indefinite hopes for the morrow; and I had a tender mother: even now, after the dreary lapse of long years, a slight trace of sensation accompanies the remembrance of her caress as she held me on her knee – her arms round my little body, her cheek pressed on mine. I had a complaint of the eyes that made me blind for a little while, and she kept me on her knee from morning till night. That unequalled love soon vanished out of my life, and even to my childish consciousness it was as if that life had become more chill I rode my little white pony with the groom by my side as before, but there were no loving eyes looking at me as I mounted, no glad arms opened to me when I came back. Perhaps I missed my mother's love more than most children of seven or eight would have done, to whom the other pleasures of life remained as before; for I was certainly a very sensitive child. I remember still the mingled trepidation and delicious excitement with which I was affected by the tramping of the horses on the pavement in the echoing stables, by the loud resonance of the groom's voices, by the booming bark of the dogs as my father's carriage thundered under the archway of the courtyard, by the din of the gong as it gave notice of luncheon and dinner. The measured tramp of soldiery which I sometimes heard – for my father's house lay near a county town where there were large barracks – made me sob and tremble; and yet when they were gone past, I longed for them to come back again.

I fancy my father thought me an odd child, and had little fondness for me; though he was very careful in fulfilling what he regarded as a parent's duties. But he was already past the middle of life, and I was not his only son. My mother had been his second wife, and he was five-and-forty when he married her. He was a firm, unbending, intensely orderly man, in root and stem a banker, but with a flourishing graft of the active landholder, aspiring to county influence: one of those people who are always like themselves from day to day, who are uninfluenced by the weather, and neither know melancholy nor high spirits. I held him in great awe, and appeared more timid and sensitive in his presence than at other times; a circumstance which, perhaps, helped to confirm him in the intention to educate me on a different plan from the prescriptive one with which he had complied in the case of my elder brother, already a tall youth at Eton. My brother was to be his representative and successor; he must go to Eton and Oxford, for the sake of making connexions, of course: my father was not a man to underrate the bearing of Latin satirists or Greek dramatists on the attainment of an aristocratic position. But, intrinsically, he had slight esteem for "those dead but sceptred spirits"; having qualified himself for forming an independent opinion by reading Potter's Æschylus, and dipping into Francis's Horace. To this negative view he added a positive one, derived from a recent connexion with mining speculations; namely, that a scientific education was the really useful training for a younger son. Moreover, it was clear that a shy, sensitive boy like me was not fit to encounter the rough experience of a public school. Mr. Letherall had said so very decidedly. Mr. Letherall was a large man in spectacles, who one day took my small head between his large hands, and pressed it here and there in an exploratory, auspicious manner – then placed each of his great thumbs on my temples, and pushed me a little way from him, and stared at me with glittering spectacles. The contemplation appeared to displease him, for he frowned sternly, and said to my father, drawing his thumbs across my eyebrows –

"The deficiency is there, sir – there; and here," he added, touching the upper sides of my head, "here is the excess. That must be brought out, sir, and this must be laid to sleep."

I was in a state of tremor, partly at the vague idea that I was the object of reprobation, partly in the agitation of my first hatred – hatred of this big, spectacled man, who pulled my head about as if he wanted to buy and cheapen it.

I am not aware how much Mr. Letherall had to do with the system afterwards adopted towards me, but it was presently clear that private tutors, natural history, science, and the modern languages, were the appliances by which the defects of my organization were to be remedied. I was very stupid about machines, so I was to be greatly occupied with them; I had no memory for classification, so it was particularly necessary that I should study systematic zoology and botany; I was hungry for human deeds and humane motions, so I was to be plentifully crammed with the mechanical powers, the elementary bodies, and the phenomena of electricity and magnetism. A better-constituted boy would certainly have profited under my intelligent tutors, with their scientific apparatus; and would, doubtless, have found the phenomena of electricity and magnetism as fascinating as I was, every Thursday, assured they were. As it was, I could have paired off, for ignorance of whatever was taught me, with the worst Latin scholar that was ever turned out of a classical academy. I read Plutarch, and Shakespeare, and Don Quixote by the sly, and supplied myself in that way with wandering thoughts, while my tutor was assuring me that "an improved man, as distinguished from an ignorant one, was a man who knew the reason why water ran downhill." I had no desire to be this improved man; I was glad of the running water; I could watch it and listen to it gurgling among the pebbles, and bathing the bright green water-plants, by the hour together. I did not want to know why it ran; I had perfect confidence that there were good reasons for what was so very beautiful.

There is no need to dwell on this part of my life. I have said enough to indicate that my nature was of the sensitive, unpractical order, and that it grew up in an uncongenial medium, which could never foster it into happy, healthy development. When I was sixteen I was sent to Geneva to complete my course of education; and the change was a very happy one to me, for the first sight of the Alps, with the setting sun on them, as we descended the Jura, seemed to me like an entrance into heaven; and the three years of my life there were spent in a perpetual sense of exaltation, as if from a draught of delicious wine, at the presence of Nature in all her awful loveliness. You will think, perhaps, that I must have been a poet, from this early sensibility to Nature. But my lot was not so happy as that. A poet pours forth his song and believes in the listening ear and answering soul, to which his song will be floated sooner or later. But the poet's sensibility without his voice – the poet's sensibility that finds no vent but in silent tears on the sunny bank, when the noonday light sparkles on the water, or in an inward shudder at the sound of harsh human tones, the sight of a cold human eye – this dumb passion brings with it a fatal solitude of soul in the society of one's fellow-men. My least solitary moments were those in which I pushed off in my boat, at evening, towards the centre of the lake; it seemed to me that the sky, and the glowing mountain-tops, and the wide blue water, surrounded me with a cherishing love such as no human face had shed on me since my mother's love had vanished out of my life. I used to do as Jean Jacques did – lie down in my boat and let it glide where it would, while I looked up at the departing glow leaving one mountain-top after the other, as if the prophet's chariot of fire were passing over them on its way to the home of light. Then, when the white summits were all sad and corpse-like, I had to push homeward, for I was under careful surveillance, and was allowed no late wanderings. This disposition of mine was not favourable to the formation of intimate friendships among the numerous youths of my own age who are always to be found studying at Geneva. Yet I made one such friendship; and, singularly enough, it was with a youth whose intellectual tendencies were the very reverse of my own. I shall call him Charles Meunier; his real surname – an English one, for he was of English extraction – having since become celebrated. He was an orphan, who lived on a miserable pittance while he pursued the medical studies for which he had a special genius. Strange! that with my vague mind, susceptible and unobservant, hating inquiry and given up to contemplation, I should have been drawn towards a youth whose strongest passion was science. But the bond was not an intellectual one; it came from a source that can happily blend the stupid with the brilliant, the dreamy with the practical: it came from community of feeling. Charles was poor and ugly, derided by Genevese gamins, and not acceptable in drawing-rooms. I saw that he was isolated, as I was, though from a different cause, and, stimulated by a sympathetic resentment, I made timid advances towards him. It is enough to say that there sprang up as much comradeship between us as our different habits would allow; and in Charles's rare holidays we went up the Salève together, or took the boat to Vevay, while I listened dreamily to the monologues in which he unfolded his bold conceptions of future experiment and discovery. I mingled them confusedly in my thought with glimpses of blue water and delicate floating cloud, with the notes of birds and the distant glitter of the glacier. He knew quite well that my mind was half absent, yet he liked to talk to me in this way; for don't we talk of our hopes and our projects even to dogs and birds, when they love us? I have mentioned this one friendship because of its connexion with a strange and terrible scene which I shall have to narrate in my subsequent life.

This happier life at Geneva was put an end to by a severe illness, which is partly a blank to me, partly a time of dimly-remembered suffering, with the presence of my father by my bed from time to time. Then came the languid monotony of convalescence, the days gradually breaking into variety and distinctness as my strength enabled me to take longer and longer drives. On one of these more vividly remembered days, my father said to me, as he sat beside my sofa—

"When you are quite well enough to travel, Latimer, I shall take you home with me. The journey will amuse you and do you good, for I shall go through the Tyrol and Austria, and you will see many new places. Our neighbours, the Filmores, are come; Alfred will join us at Basle, and we shall all go together to Vienna, and back by Prague" ...

My father was called away before he had finished his sentence, and he left my mind resting on the word Prague, with a strange sense that a new and wondrous scene was breaking upon me: a city under the broad sunshine, that seemed to me as if it were the summer sunshine of a long-past century arrested in its course – unrefreshed for ages by dews of night, or the rushing rain-cloud; scorching the dusty, weary, time-eaten grandeur of a people doomed to live on in the stale repetition of memories, like deposed and superannuated kings in their regal gold-inwoven tatters. The city looked so thirsty that the broad river seemed to me a sheet of metal; and the blackened statues, as I passed under their blank gaze, along the unending bridge, with their ancient garments and their saintly crowns, seemed to me the real inhabitants and owners of this place, while the busy, trivial men and women, hurrying to and fro, were a swarm of ephemeral visitants infesting it for a day. It is such grim, stony beings as these, I thought, who are the fathers of ancient faded children, in those tanned time-fretted dwellings that crowd the steep before me; who pay their court in the worn and crumbling pomp of the palace which stretches its monotonous length on the height; who worship wearily in the stifling air of the churches, urged by no fear or hope, but compelled by their doom to be ever old and undying, to live on in the rigidity of habit, as they live on in perpetual midday, without the repose of night or the new birth of morning.

A stunning clang of metal suddenly thrilled through me, and I became conscious of the objects in my room again: one of the fire-irons had fallen as Pierre opened the door to bring me my draught. My heart was palpitating violently, and I begged Pierre to leave my draught beside me; I would take it presently.

As soon as I was alone again, I began to ask myself whether I had been sleeping. Was this a dream – this wonderfully distinct vision – minute in its distinctness down to a patch of rainbow light on the pavement, transmitted through a coloured lamp in the shape of a star – of a strange city, quite unfamiliar to my imagination? I had seen no picture of Prague: it lay in my mind as a mere name, with vaguely-remembered historical associations – ill-defined memories of imperial grandeur and religious wars.

Nothing of this sort had ever occurred in my dreaming experience before, for I had often been humiliated because my dreams were only saved from being utterly disjointed and commonplace by the frequent terrors of nightmare. But I could not believe that

I had been asleep, for I remembered distinctly the gradual breaking-in of the vision upon me, like the new images in a dissolving view, or the growing distinctness of the landscape as the sun lifts up the veil of the morning mist. And while I was conscious of this incipient vision, I was also conscious that Pierre came to tell my father Mr. Filmore was waiting for him, and that my father hurried out of the room. No, it was not a dream; was it – the thought was full of tremulous exultation – was it the poet's nature in me, hitherto only a troubled yearning sensibility, now manifesting itself suddenly as spontaneous creation? Surely it was in this way that Homer saw the plain of Troy, that Dante saw the abodes of the departed, that Milton saw the earthward flight of the Tempter. Was it that my illness had wrought some happy change in my organization – given a firmer tension to my nerves – carried off some dull obstruction? I had often read of such effects – in works of fiction at least. Nay; in genuine biographies I had read of the subtilizing or exalting influence of some diseases on the mental powers. Did not Novalis feel his inspiration intensified under the progress of consumption?

When my mind had dwelt for some time on this blissful idea, it seemed to me that I might perhaps test it by an exertion of my will. The vision had begun when my father was speaking of our going to Prague. I did not for a moment believe it was really a representation of that city; I believed – I hoped it was a picture that my newly liberated genius had painted in fiery haste, with the colours snatched from lazy memory. Suppose I were to fix my mind on some other place – Venice, for example, which was far more familiar to my imagination than Prague: perhaps the same sort of result would follow. I concentrated my thoughts on Venice; I stimulated my imagination with poetic memories, and strove to feel myself present in Venice, as I had felt myself present in Prague. But in vain. I was only colouring the Canaletto engravings that hung in my old bedroom at home; the picture was a shifting one, my mind wandering uncertainly in search of more vivid images; I could see no accident of form or shadow without conscious labour after the necessary conditions. It was all prosaic effort, not rapt passivity, such as I had experienced half an hour before. I was discouraged; but I remembered that inspiration was fitful.

For several days I was in a state of excited expectation, watching for a recurrence of my new gift. I sent my thoughts ranging over my world of knowledge, in the hope that they would find some object which would send a reawakening vibration through my slumbering genius. But no; my world remained as dim as ever, and that flash of strange light refused to come again, though I watched for it with palpitating eagerness.

My father accompanied me every day in a drive, and a gradually lengthening walk as my powers of walking increased; and one evening he had agreed to come and fetch me at twelve the next day, that we might go together to select a musical box, and other purchases rigorously demanded of a rich Englishman visiting Geneva. He was one of the most punctual of men and bankers, and I was always nervously anxious to be quite ready for him at the appointed time. But, to my surprise, at a quarter past twelve he had not appeared. I felt all the impatience of a convalescent who has nothing particular to do, and who has just taken a tonic in the prospect of immediate exercise that would carry off the stimulus.

Unable to sit still and reserve my strength, I walked up and down the room, looking out on the current of the Rhone, just where it leaves the dark-blue lake; but thinking all the while of the possible causes that could detain my father.

Suddenly I was conscious that my father was in the room, but not alone: there were two persons with him. Strange! I had heard no footstep, I had not seen the door open; but I saw my father, and at his right hand our neighbour Mrs. Filmore, whom I remembered very well, though I had not seen her for five years. She was a commonplace middle-aged woman, in silk and cashmere; but the lady on the left of my father was not more than twenty, a tall, slim, willowy figure, with luxuriant blond hair, arranged in cunning braids and folds that looked almost too massive for the slight figure and the small-featured, thin-lipped face they crowned. But the face had not a girlish expression: the features were sharp, the pale grey eyes at once acute, restless, and sarcastic. They were fixed on me in half-smiling curiosity, and I felt a painful sensation as if a sharp wind were cutting me. The pale-green dress, and the green leaves that seemed to form a border about her pale blond hair, made me think of a Water-Nixie – for my mind was full of German lyrics, and this pale, fatal-eyed woman, with the green weeds, looked like a birth from some cold sedgy stream, the daughter of an aged river.

"Well, Latimer, you thought me long," my father said...

But while the last word was in my ears, the whole group vanished, and there was nothing between me and the Chinese printed folding-screen that stood before the door. I was cold and trembling; I could only totter forward and throw myself on the sofa. This strange new power had manifested itself again... But was it a power? Might it not rather be a disease – a sort of intermittent delirium, concentrating my energy of brain into moments of unhealthy activity, and leaving my saner hours all the more barren? I felt a dizzy sense of unreality in what my eye rested on; I grasped the bell convulsively, like one trying to free himself from nightmare, and rang it twice. Pierre came with a look of alarm in his face.

"Monsieur ne se trouve pas bien?" he said anxiously.

"I'm tired of waiting, Pierre," I said, as distinctly and emphatically as I could, like a man determined to be sober in spite of wine; "I'm afraid something has happened to my father – he's usually so punctual. Run to the Hôtel des Bergues and see if he is there."

Pierre left the room at once, with a soothing "Bien, Monsieur"; and I felt the better for this scene of simple, waking prose. Seeking to calm myself still further, I went into my bedroom, adjoining the salon, and opened a case of eau-de-Cologne; took out a bottle; went through the process of taking out the cork very neatly, and then rubbed the reviving spirit over my hands and forehead, and under my nostrils, drawing a new delight from the scent because I had procured it by slow details of labour, and by no strange sudden madness. Already I had begun to taste something of the horror that belongs to the lot of a human being whose nature is not adjusted to simple human conditions.

Still enjoying the scent, I returned to the salon, but it was not unoccupied, as it had been before I left it. In front of the Chinese folding-screen there was my father, with Mrs. Filmore on his right hand, and on his left – the slim, blond-haired girl, with the keen face and the keen eyes fixed on me in half-smiling curiosity.

"Well, Latimer, you thought me long," my father said...

I heard no more, felt no more, till I became conscious that I was lying with my head low on the sofa, Pierre, and my father by my side. As soon as I was thoroughly revived, my father left the room, and presently returned, saying –

"I've been to tell the ladies how you are, Latimer. They were waiting in the next room. We shall put off our shopping expedition today."

Presently he said, "That young lady is Bertha Grant, Mrs. Filmore's orphan niece. Filmore has adopted her, and she lives with them, so you will have her for a neighbour when we go home – perhaps for a near relation; for there is a tenderness between her and Alfred, I suspect, and I should be gratified by the match, since Filmore means to provide for her in every way as if she were his daughter. It had not occurred to me that you knew nothing about her living with the Filmores."

He made no further allusion to the fact of my having fainted at the moment of seeing her, and I would not for the world have told him the reason: I shrank from the idea of disclosing to anyone what might be regarded as a pitiable peculiarity, most of all from betraying it to my father, who would have suspected my sanity ever after.

I do not mean to dwell with particularity on the details of my experience. I have described these two cases at length, because they had definite, clearly traceable results in my after-lot.

Shortly after this last occurrence – I think the very next day – I began to be aware of a phase in my abnormal sensibility, to which, from the languid and slight nature of my intercourse with others since my illness, I had not been alive before. This was the obtrusion on my mind of the mental process going forward in first one person, and then another, with whom I happened to be in contact: the vagrant, frivolous ideas and emotions of some uninteresting acquaintance – Mrs. Filmore, for example – would force themselves on my consciousness like an importunate, ill-played musical instrument, or the loud activity of an imprisoned insect. But this unpleasant sensibility was fitful, and left me moments of rest, when the souls of my companions were once more shut out from me, and I felt a relief such as silence brings to wearied nerves. I might have believed this importunate insight to be merely a diseased activity of the imagination, but that my prevision of incalculable words and actions proved it to have a fixed relation to the mental process in other minds. But this superadded consciousness, wearying and annoying enough when it urged on me the trivial experience of indifferent people, became an intense pain and grief when it seemed to be opening to me the souls of those who were in a close relation to me – when the rational talk, the graceful attentions, the wittily-turned phrases, and the kindly deeds, which used to make the web of their characters, were seen as if thrust asunder by a microscopic vision, that showed all the intermediate frivolities, all the suppressed egoism, all the struggling chaos of puerilities, meanness, vague capricious memories, and indolent make-shift thoughts, from which human words and deeds emerge like leaflets covering a fermenting heap.

At Basle we were joined by my brother Alfred, now a handsome, self-confident man of six-and-twenty – a thorough contrast to my fragile, nervous, ineffectual self. I believe I was held to have a sort of half-womanish, half-ghostly beauty; for the portrait-painters, who are thick as weeds at Geneva, had often asked me to sit to them, and I had been the model of a dying minstrel in a fancy picture. But I thoroughly disliked my own physique and nothing but the belief that it was a condition of poetic genius would have reconciled me to it. That brief hope was quite fled, and I saw in my face now nothing but the stamp of a morbid organization, framed for passive suffering – too feeble for the sublime resistance of poetic production. Alfred, from whom I had been almost constantly separated, and who, in his present stage of character and appearance, came before me as a perfect stranger, was bent on being extremely friendly and brother-like to me. He had the superficial kindness of a good-humoured, self-satisfied nature, that fears no rivalry, and has encountered no contrarieties. I am not sure that my disposition was good enough for me to have been quite free from envy towards him, even if our desires had not clashed, and if I had been in the healthy human condition which admits of generous confidence and charitable construction. There must always have been an antipathy between our natures. As it was, he became in a few weeks an object of intense hatred to me; and when he entered the room, still more when he spoke, it was as if a sensation of grating metal had set my teeth on edge. My diseased consciousness was more intensely and continually occupied with his thoughts and emotions, than with those of any other person who came in my way. I was perpetually exasperated with the petty promptings of his conceit and his love of patronage, with his self-complacent belief in Bertha Grant's passion for him, with his half-pitying contempt for me – seen not in the ordinary indications of intonation and phrase and slight action, which an acute and suspicious mind is on the watch for, but in all their naked skinless complication.

For we were rivals, and our desires clashed, though he was not aware of it. I have said nothing yet of the effect Bertha Grant produced in me on a nearer acquaintance. That effect was chiefly determined by the fact that she made the only exception, among all the human beings about me, to my unhappy gift of insight. About Bertha I was always in a state of uncertainty: I could watch the expression of her face, and speculate on its meaning; I could ask for her opinion with the real interest of ignorance; I could listen for her words and watch for her smile with hope and fear: she had for me the fascination of an unravelled destiny. I say it was this fact that chiefly determined the strong effect she produced on me: for, in the abstract, no womanly character could seem to have less affinity for that of a shrinking, romantic, passionate youth than Bertha's. She was keen, sarcastic, unimaginative, prematurely cynical, remaining critical and unmoved in the most impressive scenes, inclined to dissect all my favourite poems, and especially contemptous towards the German lyrics which were my pet literature at that time. To this moment I am unable to define my feeling towards her: it was not ordinary boyish admiration, for she was the very opposite, even to the colour of her hair, of the ideal woman who still remained to me the type of loveliness; and she was without that enthusiasm for the great and good, which, even at the moment of her strongest dominion over me, I should have declared to be the highest element of character. But there is no tyranny more complete than that which a self-centred negative nature exercises over a morbidly sensitive nature perpetually craving sympathy and support. The most independent people feel the effect of a man's silence in heightening their value for his opinion – feel an additional triumph in conquering the reverence of a critic habitually captious and satirical: no wonder, then, that an enthusiastic self-distrusting youth should watch and wait before the closed secret of a sarcastic woman's face, as if it were the shrine of the doubtfully benignant deity who ruled his destiny. For a young enthusiast is unable to imagine the total negation in another mind of the emotions which are stirring his own: they may be feeble, latent, inactive, he thinks, but they are there – they may be called forth; sometimes, in moments of happy hallucination, he believes they may be there in all the greater strength because he sees no outward sign of them. And this effect, as I have intimated, was heightened to its utmost intensity in me, because Bertha was the only being who remained for me in the mysterious seclusion of soul that renders such youthful delusion possible. Doubtless there was another sort of fascination at work – that subtle physical attraction which delights in cheating our psychological predictions, and in compelling the men who paint sylphs, to fall in love with some bonne et brave femme, heavy-heeled and freckled.

Bertha's behaviour towards me was such as to encourage all my illusions, to heighten my boyish passion, and make me more and more dependent on her smiles. Looking back with my present wretched knowledge, I conclude that her vanity and love of power were intensely gratified by the belief that I had fainted on first seeing her purely from the strong impression her person had produced on me. The most prosaic woman likes to believe herself the object of a violent, a poetic passion; and without a grain of romance in her, Bertha had that spirit of intrigue which gave piquancy to the idea that the brother of the man she meant to marry was dying with love and jealousy for her sake. That she meant to marry my brother, was what at that time I did not believe; for though he was assiduous in his attentions to her, and I knew well enough that both he and my father had made up their minds to this result, there was not yet an understood engagement – there had been no explicit declaration; and Bertha habitually, while she flirted with my brother, and accepted his homage in a way that implied to him a thorough recognition of its intention, made me believe, by the subtlest looks and phrases – feminine nothings which could never be quoted against her – that he was really the object of her secret ridicule; that she thought him, as I did, a coxcomb, whom she would have pleasure in disappointing. Me she openly petted in my brother's presence, as if I were too young and sickly ever to be thought of as a lover; and that was the view he took of me. But I believe she must inwardly have delighted in the tremors into which she threw me by the coaxing way in which she patted my curls, while she laughed at my quotations. Such caresses were always given in the presence of our friends; for when we were alone together, she affected a much greater distance towards me, and now and then took the opportunity, by words or slight actions, to stimulate my foolish timid hope that she really preferred me. And why should she not follow her inclination? I was not in so advantageous a position as my brother, but I had fortune, I was not a year younger than she was, and she was an heiress, who would soon be of age to decide for herself.

The fluctuations of hope and fear, confined to this one channel, made each day in her presence a delicious torment. There was one deliberate act of hers which especially helped to intoxicate me. When we were at Vienna her twentieth birthday occurred, and as she was very fond of ornaments, we all took the opportunity of the splendid jewellers' shops in that Teutonic Paris to purchase her a birthday present of jewellery. Mine, naturally, was the least expensive; it was an opal ring – the opal was my favourite stone, because it seems to blush and turn pale as if it had a soul. I told Bertha so when I gave it her, and said that it was an emblem of the poetic nature, changing with the changing light of heaven and of woman's eyes. In the evening she appeared elegantly dressed, and wearing conspicuously all the birthday presents except mine. I looked eagerly at her fingers, but saw no opal. I had no opportunity of noticing this to her during the evening; but the next day, when I found her seated near the window alone, after breakfast, I said, "You scorn to wear my poor opal. I should have remembered that you despised poetic natures, and should have given you coral, or turquoise, or some other opaque unresponsive stone." "Do I despise it?" she answered, taking hold of a delicate gold chain which she always wore round her neck and drawing out the end from her bosom with my ring hanging to it; "it hurts me a little, I can tell you," she said, with her usual dubious smile, "to wear it in that secret place; and since your poetical nature is so stupid as to prefer a more public position, I shall not endure the pain any longer."

She took off the ring from the chain and put it on her finger, smiling still, while the blood rushed to my cheeks, and I could not trust myself to say a word of entreaty that she would keep the ring where it was before.

I was completely fooled by this, and for two days shut myself up in my own room whenever Bertha was absent, that I might intoxicate myself afresh with the thought of this scene and all it implied.

I should mention that during these two months – which seemed a long life to me from the novelty and intensity of the pleasures and pains I underwent – my diseased anticipation in other people's consciousness continued to torment me; now it was my father, and now my brother, now Mrs. Filmore or her husband, and now our German courier, whose stream of thought rushed upon me like a ringing in the ears not to be got rid of, though it allowed my own impulses and ideas to continue their uninterrupted course. It was like a preternaturally heightened sense of hearing, making audible to one a roar of sound where others find perfect stillness. The weariness and disgust of this involuntary intrusion into other souls was counteracted only by my ignorance of Bertha, and my growing passion for her; a passion enormously stimulated, if not produced, by that ignorance. She was my oasis of mystery in the dreary desert of knowledge. I had never allowed my diseased condition to betray itself, or to drive me into any unusual speech or action, except once, when, in a moment of peculiar bitterness against my brother, I had forestalled some words which I knew he was going to utter – a clever observation, which he had prepared beforehand. He had occasionally a slightly affected hesitation in his speech, and when he paused an instant after the second word, my impatience and jealousy impelled me to continue the speech for him, as if it were something we had both learned by rote. He coloured and looked astonished, as well as annoyed; and the words had no sooner escaped my lips than I felt a shock of alarm lest such an anticipation of words – very far from being words of course, easy to divine – should have betrayed me as an exceptional being, a sort of quiet energumen, whom everyone, Bertha above all, would shudder at and avoid. But I magnified, as usual, the impression any word or deed of mine could produce on others; for no one gave any sign of having noticed my interruption as more than a rudeness, to be forgiven me on the score of my feeble nervous condition.

While this superadded consciousness of the actual was almost constant with me, I had never had a recurrence of that distinct prevision which I have described in relation to my first interview with Bertha; and I was waiting with eager curiosity to know whether or not my vision of Prague would prove to have been an instance of the same kind. A few days after the incident of the opal ring, we were paying one of our frequent visits to the Lichtenberg Palace. I could never look at many pictures in succession; for pictures, when they are at all powerful, affect me so strongly that one or two exhaust all my capability of contemplation. This morning I had been looking at Giorgione's picture of the cruel-eyed woman, said to be a likeness of Lucrezia Borgia. I had stood long alone before it, fascinated by the terrible reality of that cunning, relentless face, till I felt a strange poisoned sensation, as if I had long been inhaling a fatal odour, and was just beginning to be conscious of its effects. Perhaps even then I should not have moved away, if the rest of the party had not returned to this room, and announced that they were going to the Belvedere Gallery to settle a bet which had arisen between my brother and Mr. Filmore about a portrait. I followed them dreamily, and was hardly alive to what occurred till they had all gone up to the gallery, leaving me below; for I refused to come within sight of another picture that day. I made my way to the Grand Terrace, since it was agreed that we should saunter in the gardens when the dispute had been decided. I had been sitting here a short space, vaguely conscious of trim gardens, with a city and green hills in the distance, when, wishing to avoid the proximity of the sentinel, I rose and walked down the broad stone steps, intending to seat myself farther on in the gardens. Just as I reached the gravel-walk, I felt an arm slipped within mine, and a light hand gently pressing my wrist. In the same instant a strange intoxicating numbness passed over me, like the continuance or climax of the sensation I was still feeling from the gaze of Lucrezia Borgia. The gardens, the summer sky, the consciousness of Bertha's arm being within mine, all vanished, and I seemed to be suddenly in darkness, out of which there gradually broke a dim firelight, and I felt myself sitting in my father's leather chair in the library at home. I knew the fireplace – the dogs for the wood-fire – the black marble chimney-piece with the white marble medallion of the dying Cleopatra in the centre. Intense and hopeless misery was pressing on my soul; the light became stronger, for Bertha was entering with a candle in her hand – Bertha, my wife – with cruel eyes, with green jewels and green leaves on her white ball-dress; every hateful thought within her present to me... "Madman, idiot! why don't you kill yourself, then?" It was a moment of hell. I saw into her pitiless soul – saw its barren worldliness, its scorching hate – and felt it clothe me round like an air I was obliged to breathe. She came with her candle and stood over me with a bitter smile of contempt; I saw the great emerald brooch on her bosom, a studded serpent with diamond eyes. I shuddered – I despised this woman with the barren soul and mean thoughts; but I felt helpless before her, as if she clutched my bleeding heart, and would clutch it till the last drop of life-blood ebbed away. She was my wife, and we hated each other. Gradually the hearth, the dim library, the candle-light disappeared – seemed to melt away into a background of light, the green serpent with the diamond eyes remaining a dark image on the retina. Then I had a sense of my eyelids quivering, and the living daylight broke in upon me; I saw gardens, and heard voices; I was seated on the steps of the Belvedere Terrace, and my friends were round me.

The tumult of mind into which I was thrown by this hideous vision made me ill for several days, and prolonged our stay at Vienna. I shuddered with horror as the scene recurred to me; and it recurred constantly, with all its minutiæ, as if they had been burnt into my memory; and yet, such is the madness of the human heart under the influence of its immediate desires, I felt a wild hell-braving joy that Bertha was to be mine; for the fulfilment of my former prevision concerning her first appearance before me, left me little hope that this last hideous glimpse of the future was the mere diseased play of my own mind, and had no relation to external realities. One thing alone I looked towards as a possible means of casting doubt on my terrible conviction – the discovery that my vision of Prague had been false – and Prague was the next city on our route.

Meanwhile, I was no sooner in Bertha's society again than I was as completely under her sway as before. What if I saw into the heart of Bertha, the matured woman – Bertha, my wife? Bertha, the girl, was a fascinating secret to me still: I trembled under her touch; I felt the witchery of her presence; I yearned to be assured of her love. The fear of poison is feeble against the sense of thirst. Nay, I was just as jealous of my brother as before – just as much irritated by his small patronizing ways; for my pride, my diseased sensibility, were there as they had always been, and winced as inevitably under every offence as my eye winced from an intruding mote. The future, even when brought within the compass of feeling by a vision that made me shudder, had still no more than the force of an idea, compared with the force of present emotion – of my love for Bertha, of my dislike and jealousy towards my brother.

It is an old story, that men sell themselves to the tempter, and sign a bond with their blood, because it is only to take effect at a distant day; then rush on to snatch the cup their souls thirst after with an impulse not the less savage because there is a dark shadow beside them for evermore. There is no short cut, no patent tram-road, to wisdom: after all the centuries of invention, the soul's path lies through the thorny wilderness which must be still trodden in solitude, with bleeding feet, with sobs for help, as it was trodden by them of old time.

My mind speculated eagerly on the means by which I should become my brother's successful rival, for I was still too timid, in my ignorance of Bertha's actual feeling, to venture on any step that would urge from her an avowal of it. I thought I should gain confidence even for this, if my vision of Prague proved to have been veracious; and yet, the horror of that certitude! Behind the slim girl Bertha, whose words and looks I watched for, whose touch was bliss, there stood continually that Bertha with the fuller form, the harder eyes, the more rigid mouth – with the barren, selfish soul laid bare; no longer a fascinating secret, but a measured fact, urging itself perpetually on my unwilling sight. Are you unable to give me your sympathy – you who react this? Are you unable to imagine this double consciousness at work within me, flowing on like two parallel streams which never mingle their waters and blend into a common hue? Yet you must have known something of the presentiments that spring from an insight at war with passion; and my visions were only like presentiments intensified to horror. You have known the powerlessness of ideas before the might of impulse; and my visions, when once they had passed into memory, were mere ideas – pale shadows that beckoned in vain, while my hand was grasped by the living and the loved.

In after-days I thought with bitter regret that if I had foreseen something more or something different – if instead of that hideous vision which poisoned the passion it could not destroy, or if even along with it I could have had a foreshadowing of that moment when I looked on my brother's face for the last time, some softening influence would have been shed over my feeling towards him: pride and hatred would surely have been subdued into pity, and the record of those hidden sins would have been shortened. But this is one of the vain thoughts with which we men flatter ourselves. We try to believe that the egoism within us would have easily been melted, and that it was only the narrowness of our knowledge which hemmed in our generosity, our awe, our human piety, and hindered them from submerging our hard indifference to the sensations and emotions of our fellows. Our tenderness and self-renunciation seem strong when our egoism has had its day – when, after our mean striving for a triumph that is to be another's loss, the triumph comes suddenly, and we shudder at it, because it is held out by the chill hand of death.

Our arrival in Prague happened at night, and I was glad of this, for it seemed like a deferring of a terribly decisive moment, to be in the city for hours without seeing it. As we were not to remain long in Prague, but to go on speedily to Dresden, it was proposed that we should drive out the next morning and take a general view of the place, as well as visit some of its specially interesting spots, before the heat became oppressive – for we were in August, and the season was hot and dry. But it happened that the ladies were rather late at their morning toilet, and to my father's politely-repressed but perceptible annoyance, we were not in the carriage till the morning was far advanced. I thought with a sense of relief, as we entered the Jews' quarter, where we were to visit the old synagogue, that we should be kept in this flat, shut-up part of the city, until we should all be too tired and too warm to go farther, and so we should return without seeing more than the streets through which we had already passed. That would give me another day's suspense – suspense, the only form in which a fearful spirit knows the solace of hope. But, as I stood under the blackened, groined arches of that old synagogue, made dimly visible by the seven thin candles in the sacred lamp, while our Jewish cicerone reached down the Book of the Law, and read to us in its ancient tongue – I felt a shuddering impression that this strange building, with its shrunken lights, this surviving withered remnant of medieval Judaism, was of a piece with my vision. Those darkened dusty Christian saints, with their loftier arches and their larger candles, needed the consolatory scorn with which they might point to a more shrivelled death-in-life than their own.

As I expected, when we left the Jews' quarter the elders of our party wished to return to the hotel. But now, instead of rejoicing in this, as I had done beforehand, I felt a sudden overpowering impulse to go on at once to the bridge, and put an end to the suspense I had been wishing to protract. I declared, with unusual decision, that I would get out of the carriage and walk on alone; they might return without me. My father, thinking this merely a sample of my usual "poetic nonsense," objected that I should only do myself harm by walking in the heat; but when I persisted, he said angrily that I might follow my own absurd devices, but that Schmidt (our courier) must go with me. I assented to this, and set off with Schmidt towards the bridge. I had no sooner passed from under the archway of the grand old gate leading an to the bridge, than a trembling seized me, and I turned cold under the midday sun; yet I went on; I was in search of something – a small detail which I remembered with special intensity as part of my vision. There it was – the patch of rainbow light on the pavement transmitted through a lamp in the shape of a star.

Chapter II

BEFORE THE AUTUMN was at an end, and while the brown leaves still stood thick on the beeches in our park, my brother and Bertha were engaged to each other, and it was understood that their marriage was to take place early in the next spring. In spite of the certainty I had felt from that moment on the bridge at Prague, that Bertha would one day be my wife, my constitutional timidity and distrust had continued to benumb me, and the words in which I had sometimes premeditated a confession of my love, had died away unuttered. The same conflict had gone on within me as before – the longing for an assurance of love from Bertha's lips, the dread lest a word of contempt and denial should fall upon me like a corrosive acid. What was the conviction of a distant necessity to me? I trembled under a present glance, I hungered after a present joy, I was clogged and chilled by a present fear. And so the days passed on: I witnessed Bertha's engagement and heard her marriage discussed as if I were under a conscious nightmare – knowing it was a dream that would vanish, but feeling stifled under the grasp of hard-clutching fingers.

When I was not in Bertha's presence – and I was with her very often, for she continued to treat me with a playful patronage that wakened no jealousy in my brother – I spent my time chiefly in wandering, in strolling, or taking long rides while the daylight lasted, and then shutting myself up with my unread books; for books had lost the power of chaining my attention. My self-consciousness was heightened to that pitch of intensity in which our own emotions take the form of a drama which urges itself imperatively on our contemplation, and we begin to weep, less under the sense of our suffering than at the thought of it. I felt a sort of pitying anguish over the pathos of my own lot: the lot of a being finely organized for pain, but with hardly any fibres that responded to pleasure – to whom the idea of future evil robbed the present of its joy, and for whom the idea of future good did not still the uneasiness of a present yearning or a present dread. I went dumbly through that stage of the poet's suffering, in which he feels the delicious pang of utterance, and makes an image of his sorrows.

I was left entirely without remonstrance concerning this dreamy wayward life: I knew my father's thought about me: "That lad will never be good for anything in life: he may waste his years in an insignificant way on the income that falls to him: I shall not trouble myself about a career for him."

One mild morning in the beginning of November, it happened that I was standing outside the portico patting lazy old Cæsar, a Newfoundland almost blind with age, the only dog that ever took any notice of me – for the very dogs shunned me, and fawned on the happier people about me – when the groom brought up my brother's horse which was to carry him to the hunt, and my brother himself appeared at the door, florid, broad-chested, and self-complacent, feeling what a good-natured fellow he was not to behave insolently to us all on the strength of his great advantages.

"Latimer, old boy," he said to me in a tone of compassionate cordiality, "what a pity it is you don't have a run with the hounds now and then! The finest thing in the world for low spirits!"

"Low spirits!" I thought bitterly, as he rode away; "that is the sort of phrase with which coarse, narrow natures like yours think to describe experience of which you can know no more than your horse knows. It is to such as you that the good of this world falls: ready dulness, healthy selfishness, good-tempered conceit – these are the keys to happiness."

The quick thought came, that my selfishness was even stronger than his – it was only a suffering selfishness instead of an enjoying one. But then, again, my exasperating insight into Alfred's self-complacent soul, his freedom from all the doubts and fears, the unsatisfied yearnings, the exquisite tortures of sensitiveness, that had made the web of my life, seemed to absolve me from all bonds towards him. This man needed no pity, no love; those fine influences would have been as little felt by him as the delicate white mist is felt by the rock it caresses. There was no evil in store for him: if he was not to marry Bertha, it would be because he had found a lot pleasanter to himself.

Mr. Filmore's house lay not more than half a mile beyond our own gates, and whenever I knew my brother was gone in another direction, I went there for the chance of finding Bertha at home. Later on in the day I walked thither. By a rare accident she was alone, and we walked out in the grounds together, for she seldom went on foot beyond the trimly-swept gravel-walks. I remember what a beautiful sylph she looked to me as the low November sun shone on her blond hair, and she tripped along teasing me with her usual light banter, to which I listened half fondly, half moodily; it was all the sign Bertha's mysterious inner self ever made to me. Today perhaps, the moodiness predominated, for I had not yet shaken off the access of jealous hate which my brother had raised in me by his parting patronage. Suddenly I interrupted and startled her by saying, almost fiercely, "Bertha, how can you love Alfred?"

She looked at me with surprise for a moment, but soon her light smile came again, and she answered sarcastically, "Why do you suppose I love him?"

"How can you ask that, Bertha?"

"What! your wisdom thinks I must love the man I'm going to marry? The most unpleasant thing in the world. I should quarrel with him; I should be jealous of him; our ménage would be conducted in a very ill-bred manner. A little quiet contempt contributes greatly to the elegance of life."

"Bertha, that is not your real feeling. Why do you delight in trying to deceive me by inventing such cynical speeches?"

"I need never take the trouble of invention in order to deceive you, my small Tasso" – (that was the mocking name she usually gave me). "The easiest way to deceive a poet is to tell him the truth."

She was testing the validity of her epigram in a daring way, and for a moment the shadow of my vision – the Bertha whose soul was no secret to me – passed between me and the radiant girl, the playful sylph whose feelings were a fascinating mystery. I suppose I must have shuddered, or betrayed in some other way my momentary chill of horror.

"Tasso!" she said, seizing my wrist, and peeping round into my face, "are you really beginning to discern what a heartless girl I am? Why, you are not half the poet I thought you were; you are actually capable of believing the truth about me."

The shadow passed from between us, and was no longer the object nearest to me. The girl whose light fingers grasped me, whose elfish charming face looked into mine – who, I thought, was betraying an interest in my feelings that she would not have directly avowed, – this warm breathing presence again possessed my senses and imagination like a returning siren melody which had been overpowered for an instant by the roar of threatening waves. It was a moment as delicious to me as the waking up to a consciousness of youth after a dream of middle age. I forgot everything but my passion, and said with swimming eyes—

"Bertha, shall you love me when we are first married? I wouldn't mind if you really loved me only for a little while."

Her look of astonishment, as she loosed my hand and started away from me, recalled me to a sense of my strange, my criminal indiscretion.

"Forgive me," I said, hurriedly, as soon as I could speak again; "I did not know what I was saying."

"Ah, Tasso's mad fit has come on, I see," she answered quietly, for she had recovered herself sooner than I had. "Let him go home and keep his head cool. I must go in, for the sun is setting."

I left her – full of indignation against myself. I had let slip words which, if she reflected on them, might rouse in her a suspicion of my abnormal mental condition – a suspicion which of all things I dreaded. And besides that, I was ashamed of the apparent baseness I had committed in uttering them to my brother's betrothed wife. I wandered home slowly, entering our park through a private gate instead of by the lodges. As I approached the house, I saw a man dashing off at full speed from the stable-yard across the park. Had any accident happened at home? No; perhaps it was only one of my father's peremptory business errands that required this headlong haste.

Nevertheless I quickened my pace without any distinct motive, and was soon at the house. I will not dwell on the scene I found there. My brother was dead – had been pitched from his horse, and killed on the spot by a concussion of the brain.

I went up to the room where he lay, and where my father was seated beside him with a look of rigid despair. I had shunned my father more than anyone since our return home, for the radical antipathy between our natures made my insight into his inner self a constant affliction to me. But now, as I went up to him, and stood beside him in sad silence, I felt the presence of a new element that blended us as we had never been blent before. My father had been one of the most successful men in the money-getting world: he had had no sentimental sufferings, no illness. The heaviest trouble that had befallen him was the death of his first wife. But he married my mother soon after; and I remember he seemed exactly the same, to my keen childish observation, the week after her death as before. But now, at last, a sorrow had come – the sorrow of old age, which suffers the more from the crushing of its pride and its hopes, in proportion as the pride and hope are narrow and prosaic. His son was to have been married soon – would probably have stood for the borough at the next election. That son's existence was the best motive that could be alleged for making new purchases of land every year to round off the estate. It is a dreary thing onto live on doing the same things year after year, without knowing why we do them. Perhaps the tragedy of disappointed youth and passion is less piteous than the tragedy of disappointed age and worldliness.

As I saw into the desolation of my father's heart, I felt a movement of deep pity towards him, which was the beginning of a new affection – an affection that grew and strengthened in spite of the strange bitterness with which he regarded me in the first month or two after my brother's death. If it had not been for the softening influence of my compassion for him – the first deep compassion I had ever felt – I should have been stung by the perception that my father transferred the inheritance of an eldest son to me with a mortified sense that fate had compelled him to the unwelcome course of caring for me as an important being. It was only in spite of himself that he began to think of me with anxious regard. There is hardly any neglected child for whom death has made vacant a more favoured place, who will not understand what I mean.

Gradually, however, my new deference to his wishes, the effect of that patience which was born of my pity for him, won upon his affection, and he began to please himself with the endeavour to make me fill any brother's place as fully as my feebler personality would admit. I saw that the prospect which by and by presented itself of my becoming Bertha's husband was welcome to him, and he even contemplated in my case what he had not intended in my brother's – that his son and daughter-in-law should make one household with him. My softened feelings towards my father made this the happiest time I had known since childhood; – these last months in which I retained the delicious illusion of loving Bertha, of longing and doubting and hoping that she might love me. She behaved with a certain new consciousness and distance towards me after my brother's death; and I too was under a double constraint – that of delicacy towards my brother's memory and of anxiety as to the impression my abrupt words had left on her mind. But the additional screen this mutual reserve erected between us only brought me more completely under her power: no matter how empty the adytum, so that the veil be thick enough. So absolute is our soul's need of something hidden and uncertain for the maintenance of that doubt and hope and effort which are the breath of its life, that if the whole future were laid bare to us beyond today, the interest of all mankind would be bent on the hours that lie between; we should pant after the uncertainties of our one morning and our one afternoon; we should rush fiercely to the Exchange for our last possibility of speculation, of success, of disappointment: we should have a glut of political prophets foretelling a crisis or a no-crisis within the only twenty-four hours left open to prophecy. Conceive the condition of the human mind if all propositions whatsoever were self-evident except one, which was to become self-evident at the close of a summer's day, but in the meantime might be the subject of question, of hypothesis, of debate. Art and philosophy, literature and science, would fasten like bees on that one proposition which had the honey of probability in it, and be the more eager because their enjoyment would end with sunset. Our impulses, our spiritual activities, no more adjust themselves to the idea of their future nullity, than the beating of our heart, or the irritability of our muscles.

Bertha, the slim, fair-haired girl, whose present thoughts and emotions were an enigma to me amidst the fatiguing obviousness of the other minds around me, was as absorbing to me as a single unknown today – as a single hypothetic proposition to remain problematic till sunset; and all the cramped, hemmed-in belief and disbelief, trust and distrust, of my nature, welled out in this one narrow channel.

And she made me believe that she loved me. Without ever quitting her tone of badinage and playful superiority, she intoxicated me with the sense that I was necessary to her, that she was never at ease, unless I was near her, submitting to her playful tyranny. It costs a woman so little effort to beset us in this way! A half-repressed word, a moment's unexpected silence, even an easy fit of petulance on our account, will serve us as hashish for a long while. Out of the subtlest web of scarcely perceptible signs, she set me weaving the fancy that she had always unconsciously loved me better than Alfred, but that, with the ignorant fluttered sensibility of a young girl, she had been imposed on by the charm that lay for her in the distinction of being admired and chosen by a man who made so brilliant a figure in the world as my brother. She satirized herself in a very graceful way for her vanity and ambition. What was it to me that I had the light of my wretched provision on the fact that now it was I who possessed at least all but the personal part of my brother's advantages? Our sweet illusions are half of them conscious illusions, like effects of colour that we know to be made up of tinsel, broken glass, and rags.

We were married eighteen months after Alfred's death, one cold, clear morning in April, when there came hail and sunshine both together; and Bertha, in her white silk and pale-green leaves, and the pale hues of her hair and face, looked like the spirit of the morning. My father was happier than he had thought of being again: my marriage, he felt sure, would complete the desirable modification of my character, and make me practical and worldly enough to take my place in society among sane men. For he delighted in Bertha's tact and acuteness, and felt sure she would be mistress of me, and make me what she chose: I was only twenty-one, and madly in love with her. Poor father! He kept that hope a little while after our first year of marriage, and it was not quite extinct when paralysis came and saved him from utter disappointment.

I shall hurry through the rest of my story, not dwelling so much as I have hitherto done on my inward experience. When people are well known to each other, they talk rather of what befalls them externally, leaving their feelings and sentiments to be inferred.

We lived in a round of visits for some time after our return home, giving splendid dinner-parties, and making a sensation in our neighbourhood by the new lustre of our equipage, for my father had reserved this display of his increased wealth for the period of his son's marriage; and we gave our acquaintances liberal opportunity for remarking that it was a pity I made so poor a figure as an heir and a bridegroom. The nervous fatigue of this existence, the insincerities and platitudes which I had to live through twice over – through my inner and outward sense – would have been maddening to me, if I had not had that sort of intoxicated callousness which came from the delights of a first passion. A bride and bridegroom, surrounded by all the appliances of wealth, hurried through the day by the whirl of society, filling their solitary moments with hastily-snatched caresses, are prepared for their future life together as the novice is prepared for the cloister – by experiencing its utmost contrast.

Through all these crowded excited months, Bertha's inward self remained shrouded from me, and I still read her thoughts only through the language of her lips and demeanour: I had still the human interest of wondering whether what I did and said pleased her, of longing to hear a word of affection, of giving a delicious exaggeration of meaning to her smile. But I was conscious of a growing difference in her manner towards me; sometimes strong enough to be called haughty coldness, cutting and chilling me as the hail had done that came across the sunshine on our marriage morning; sometimes only perceptible in the dexterous avoidance of a tête-à-tête walk or dinner to which I had been looking forward. I had been deeply pained by this – had even felt a sort of crushing of the heart, from the sense that my brief day of happiness was near its setting; but still I remained dependent on Bertha, eager for the last rays of a bliss that would soon be gone for ever, hoping and watching for some after-glow more beautiful from the impending night.

I remember – how should I not remember? – the time when that dependence and hope utterly left me, when the sadness I had felt in Bertha's growing estrangement became a joy that I looked back upon with longing as a man might look back on the last pains in a paralysed limb. It was just after the close of my father's last illness, which had necessarily withdrawn us from society and thrown us more on each other. It was the evening of father's death. On that evening the veil which had shrouded Bertha's soul from me – had made me find in her alone among my fellow-beings the blessed possibility of mystery, and doubt, and expectation – was first withdrawn. Perhaps it was the first day since the beginning of my passion for her, in which that passion was completely neutralized by the presence of an absorbing feeling of another kind. I had been watching by my father's deathbed: I had been witnessing the last fitful yearning glance his soul had cast back on the spent inheritance of life – the last faint consciousness of love he had gathered from the pressure of my hand. What are all our personal loves when we have been sharing in that supreme agony? In the first moments when we come away from the presence of death, every other relation to the living is merged, to our feeling, in the great relation of a common nature and a common destiny.

In that state of mind I joined Bertha in her private sitting-room. She was seated in a leaning posture on a settee, with her back towards the door; the great rich coils of her pale blond hair surmounting her small neck, visible above the back of the settee. I remember, as I closed the door behind me, a cold tremulousness seizing me, and a vague sense of being hated and lonely – vague and strong, like a presentiment. I know how I looked at that moment, for I saw myself in Bertha's thought as she lifted her cutting grey eyes, and looked at me: a miserable ghost-seer, surrounded by phantoms in the noonday, trembling under a breeze when the leaves were still, without appetite for the common objects of human desires, but pining after the moon-beams. We were front to front with each other, and judged each other. The terrible moment of complete illumination had come to me, and I saw that the darkness had hidden no landscape from me, but only a blank prosaic wall: from that evening forth, through the sickening years which followed, I saw all round the narrow room of this woman's soul – saw petty artifice and mere negation where I had delighted to believe in coy sensibilities and in wit at war with latent feeling – saw the light floating vanities of the girl defining themselves into the systematic coquetry, the scheming selfishness, of the woman – saw repulsion and antipathy harden into cruel hatred, giving pain only for the sake of wreaking itself.

For Bertha too, after her kind, felt the bitterness of disillusion. She had believed that my wild poet's passion for her would make me her slave; and that, being her slave, I should execute her will in all things. With the essential shallowness of a negative, unimaginative nature, she was unable to conceive the fact that sensibilities were anything else than weaknesses. She had thought my weaknesses would put me in her power, and she found them unmanageable forces. Our positions were reversed. Before marriage she had completely mastered my imagination, for she was a secret to me; and I created the unknown thought before which I trembled as if it were hers. But now that her soul was laid open to me, now that I was compelled to share the privacy of her motives, to follow all the petty devices that preceded her words and acts, she found herself powerless with me, except to produce in me the chill shudder of repulsion – powerless, because I could be acted on by no lever within her reach. I was dead to worldly ambitions, to social vanities, to all the incentives within the compass of her narrow imagination, and I lived under influences utterly invisible to her.

She was really pitiable to have such a husband, and so all the world thought. A graceful, brilliant woman, like Bertha, who smiled on morning callers, made a figure in ball-rooms, and was capable of that light repartee which, from such a woman, is accepted as wit, was secure of carrying off all sympathy from a husband who was sickly, abstracted, and, as some suspected, crack-brained. Even the servants in our house gave her the balance of their regard and pity. For there were no audible quarrels between us; our alienation, our repulsion from each other, lay within the silence of our own hearts; and if the mistress went out a great deal, and seemed to dislike the master's society, was it not natural, poor thing? The master was odd. I was kind and just to my dependants, but I excited in them a shrinking, half-contemptuous pity; for this class of men and women are but slightly determined in their estimate of others by general considerations, or even experience, of character. They judge of persons as they judge of coins, and value those who pass current at a high rate.

After a time I interfered so little with Bertha's habits that it might seem wonderful how her hatred towards me could grow so intense and active as it did. But she had begun to suspect, by some involuntary betrayal of mine, that there was an abnormal power of penetration in me – that fitfully, at least, I was strangely cognizant of her thoughts and intentions, and she began to be haunted by a terror of me, which alternated every now and then with defiance. She meditated continually how the incubus could be shaken off her life – how she could be freed from this hateful bond to a being whom she at once despised as an imbecile, and dreaded as an inquisitor. For a long while she lived in the hope that my evident wretchedness would drive me to the commission of suicide; but suicide was not in my nature. I was too completely swayed by the sense that I was in the grasp of unknown forces, to believe in my power of self-release. Towards my own destiny I had become entirely passive; for my one ardent desire had spent itself, and impulse no longer predominated over knowledge. For this reason I never thought of taking any steps towards a complete separation, which would have made our alienation evident to the world. Why should I rush for help to a new course, when I was only suffering from the consequences of a deed which had been the act of my intensest will? That would have been the logic of one who had desires to gratify, and I had no desires. But Bertha and I lived more and more aloof from each other. The rich find it easy to live married and apart.

That course of our life which I have indicated in a few sentences filled the space of years. So much misery – so slow and hideous a growth of hatred and sin, may be compressed into a sentence! And men judge of each other's lives through this summary medium. They epitomize the experience of their fellow-mortal, and pronounce judgment on him in neat syntax, and feel themselves wise and virtuous – conquerors over the temptations they define in well-selected predicates. Seven years of wretchedness glide glibly over the lips of the man who has never counted them out in moments of chill disappointment, of head and heart throbbings, of dread and vain wrestling, of remorse and despair. We learn words by rote, but not their meaning; that must be paid for with our life-blood, and printed in the subtle fibres of our nerves.

But I will hasten to finish my story. Brevity is justified at once to those who readily understand, and to those who will never understand.

Some years after my father's death, I was sitting by the dim firelight in my library one January evening – sitting in the leather chair that used to be my father's – when Bertha appeared at the door, with a candle in her hand, and advanced towards me. I knew the ball-dress she had on – the white ball-dress, with the green jewels, shone upon by the light of the wax candle which lit up the medallion of the dying Cleopatra on the mantelpiece. Why did she come to me before going out? I had not seen her in the library, which was my habitual place for months. Why did she stand before me with the candle in her hand, with her cruel contemptuous eyes fixed on me, and the glittering serpent, like a familiar demon, on her breast? For a moment I thought this fulfilment of my vision at Vienna marked some dreadful crisis in my fate, but I saw nothing in Bertha's mind, as she stood before me, except scorn for the look of overwhelming misery with which I sat before her... "Fool, idiot, why don't you kill yourself, then?" – that was her thought. But at length her thoughts reverted to her errand, and she spoke aloud. The apparently indifferent nature of the errand seemed to make a ridiculous anticlimax to my prevision and my agitation.

"I have had to hire a new maid. Fletcher is going to be married, and she wants me to ask you to let her husband have the public-house and farm at Molton. I wish him to have it. You must give the promise now, because Fletcher is going tomorrow morning – and quickly, because I'm in a hurry."

"Very well; you may promise her," I said, indifferently, and Bertha swept out of the library again.

I always shrank from the sight of a new person, and all the more when it was a person whose mental life was likely to weary my reluctant insight with worldly ignorant trivialities. But I shrank especially from the sight of this new maid, because her advent had been announced to me at a moment to which I could not cease to attach some fatality: I had a vague dread that I should find her mixed up with the dreary drama of my life – that some new sickening vision would reveal her to me as an evil genius. When at last I did unavoidably meet her, the vague dread was changed into definite disgust. She was a tall, wiry, dark-eyed woman, this Mrs. Archer, with a face handsome enough to give her coarse hard nature the odious finish of bold, self-confident coquetry. That was enough to make me avoid her, quite apart from the contemptuous feeling with which she contemplated me. I seldom saw her; but I perceived that she rapidly became a favourite with her mistress, and, after the lapse of eight or nine months, I began to be aware that there had arisen in Bertha's mind towards this woman a mingled feeling of fear and dependence, and that this feeling was associated with ill-defined images of candle-light scenes in her dressing-room, and the locking-up of something in Bertha's cabinet. My interviews with my wife had become so brief and so rarely solitary, that I had no opportunity of perceiving these images in her mind with more definiteness. The recollections of the past become contracted in the rapidity of thought till they sometimes bear hardly a more distinct resemblance to the external reality than the forms of an oriental alphabet to the objects that suggested them.

Besides, for the last year or more a modification had been going forward in my mental condition, and was growing more and more marked. My insight into the minds of those around me was becoming dimmer and more fitful, and the ideas that crowded my double consciousness became less and less dependent on any personal contact. All that was personal in me seemed to be suffering a gradual death, so that I was losing the organ through which the personal agitations and projects of others could affect me. But along with this relief from wearisome insight, there was a new development of what I concluded – as I have since found rightly – to be a provision of external scenes. It was as if the relation between me and my fellow-men was more and more deadened, and my relation to what we call the inanimate was quickened into new life. The more I lived apart from society, and in proportion as my wretchedness subsided from the violent throb of agonized passion into the dulness of habitual pain, the more frequent and vivid became such visions as that I had had of Prague – of strange cities, of sandy plains, of gigantic ruins, of midnight skies with strange bright constellations, of mountain-passes, of grassy nooks flecked with the afternoon sunshine through the boughs: I was in the midst of such scenes, and in all of them one presence seemed to weigh on me in all these mighty shapes – the presence of something unknown and pitiless. For continual suffering had annihilated religious faith within me: to the utterly miserable – the unloving and the unloved – there is no religion possible, no worship but a worship of devils. And beyond all these, and continually recurring, was the vision of my death – the pangs, the suffocation, the last struggle, when life would be grasped at in vain.

Things were in this state near the end of the seventh year. I had become entirely free from insight, from my abnormal cognizance of any other consciousness than my own, and instead of intruding involuntarily into the world of other minds, was living continually in my own solitary future. Bertha was aware that I was greatly changed. To my surprise she had of late seemed to seek opportunities of remaining in my society, and had cultivated that kind of distant yet familiar talk which is customary between a husband and wife who live in polite and irrevocable alienation. I bore this with languid submission, and without feeling enough interest in her motives to be roused into keen observation; yet I could not help perceiving something triumphant and excited in her carriage and the expression of her face – something too subtle to express itself in words or tones, but giving one the idea that she lived in a state of expectation or hopeful suspense. My chief feeling was satisfaction that her inner self was once more shut out from me; and I almost revelled for the moment in the absent melancholy that made me answer her at cross purposes, and betray utter ignorance of what she had been saying. I remember well the look and the smile with which she one day said, after a mistake of this kind on my part: "I used to think you were a clairvoyant, and that was the reason why you were so bitter against other clairvoyants, wanting to keep your monopoly; but I see now you have become rather duller than the rest of the world."

I said nothing in reply. It occurred to me that her recent obtrusion of herself upon me might have been prompted by the wish to test my power of detecting some of her secrets; but I let the thought drop again at once: her motives and her deeds had no interest for me, and whatever pleasures she might be seeking, I had no wish to baulk her. There was still pity in my soul for every living thing, and Bertha was living – was surrounded with possibilities of misery.

Just at this time there occurred an event which roused me somewhat from my inertia, and gave me an interest in the passing moment that I had thought impossible for me. It was a visit from Charles Meunier, who had written me word that he was coming to England for relaxation from too strenuous labour, and would like too see me. Meunier had now a European reputation; but his letter to me expressed that keen remembrance of an early regard, an early debt of sympathy, which is inseparable from nobility of character: and I too felt as if his presence would be to me like a transient resurrection into a happier pre-existence.

He came, and as far as possible, I renewed our old pleasure of making tête-à-tête excursions, though, instead of mountains and glacers and the wide blue lake, we had to content ourselves with mere slopes and ponds and artificial plantations. The years had changed us both, but with what different result! Meunier was now a brilliant figure in society, to whom elegant women pretended to listen, and whose acquaintance was boasted of by noblemen ambitious of brains. He repressed with the utmost delicacy all betrayal of the shock which I am sure he must have received from our meeting, or of a desire to penetrate into my condition and circumstances, and sought by the utmost exertion of his charming social powers to make our reunion agreeable. Bertha was much struck by the unexpected fascinations of a visitor whom she had expected to find presentable only on the score of his celebrity, and put forth all her coquetries and accomplishments. Apparently she succeeded in attracting his admiration, for his manner towards her was attentive and flattering. The effect of his presence on me was so benignant, especially in those renewals of our old tête-à-tête wanderings, when he poured forth to me wonderful narratives of his professional experience, that more than once, when his talk turned on the psychological relations of disease, the thought crossed my mind that, if his stay with me were long enough, I might possibly bring myself to tell this man the secrets of my lot. Might there not lie some remedy for me, too, in his science? Might there not at least lie some comprehension and sympathy ready for me in his large and susceptible mind? But the thought only flickered feebly now and then, and died out before it could become a wish. The horror I had of again breaking in on the privacy of another soul, made me, by an irrational instinct, draw the shroud of concealment more closely around my own, as we automatically perform the gesture we feel to be wanting in another.

When Meunier's visit was approaching its conclusion, there happened an event which caused some excitement in our household, owing to the surprisingly strong effect it appeared to produce on Bertha – on Bertha, the self-possessed, who usually seemed inaccessible to feminine agitations, and did even her hate in a self-restrained hygienic manner. This event was the sudden severe illness of her maid, Mrs. Archer. I have reserved to this moment the mention of a circumstance which had forced itself on my notice shortly before Meunier's arrival, namely, that there had been some quarrel between Bertha and this maid, apparently during a visit to a distant family, in which she had accompanied her mistress. I had overheard Archer speaking in a tone of bitter insolence, which I should have thought an adequate reason for immediate dismissal. No dismissal followed; on the contrary, Bertha seemed to be silently putting up with personal inconveniences from the exhibitions of this woman's temper. I was the more astonished to observe that her illness seemed a cause of strong solicitude to Bertha; that she was at the bedside night and day, and would allow no one else to officiate as head-nurse. It happened that our family doctor was out on a holiday, an accident which made Meunier's presence in the house doubly welcome, and he apparently entered into the case with an interest which seemed so much stronger than the ordinary professional feeling, that one day when he had fallen into a long fit of silence after visiting her, I said to him –

"Is this a very peculiar case of disease, Meunier?"

"No," he answered, "it is an attack of peritonitis, which will be fatal, but which does not differ physically from many other cases that have come under my observation. But I'll tell you what I have on my mind. I want to make an experiment on this woman, if you will give me permission. It can do her no harm – will give her no pain – for I shall not make it until life is extinct to all purposes of sensation. I want to try the effect of transfusing blood into her arteries after the heart has ceased to beat for some minutes. I have tried the experiment again and again with animals that have died of this disease, with astounding results, and I want to try it on a human subject. I have the small tubes necessary, in a case I have with me, and the rest of the apparatus could be prepared readily. I should use my own blood – take it from my own arm. This woman won't live through the night, I'm convinced, and I want you to promise me your assistance in making the experiment. I can't do without another hand, but it would perhaps not be well to call in a medical assistant from among your provincial doctors. A disagreeable foolish version of the thing might get abroad."

"Have you spoken to my wife on the subject?" I said, "because she appears to be peculiarly sensitive about this woman: she has been a favourite maid."

"To tell you the truth," said Meunier, "I don't want her to know about it. There are always insuperable difficulties with women in these matters, and the effect on the supposed dead body may be startling. You and I will sit up together, and be in readiness. When certain symptoms appear I shall take you in, and at the right moment we must manage to get everyone else out of the room."

I need not give our farther conversation on the subject. He entered very fully into the details, and overcame my repulsion from them, by exciting in me a mingled awe and curiosity concerning the possible results of his experiment.

We prepared everything, and he instructed me in my part as assistant. He had not told Bertha of his absolute conviction that Archer would not survive through the night, and endeavoured to persuade her to leave the patient and take a night's rest. But she was obstinate, suspecting the fact that death was at hand, and supposing that he wished merely to save her nerves. She refused to leave the sick-room. Meunier and I sat up together in the library, he making frequent visits to the sick-room, and returning with the information that the case was taking precisely the course he expected. Once he said to me, "Can you imagine any cause of ill-feeling this woman has against her mistress, who is so devoted to her?"

"I think there was some misunderstanding between them before her illness. Why do you ask?"

"Because I have observed for the last five or six hours – since, I fancy, she has lost all hope of recovery – there seems a strange prompting in her to say something which pain and failing strength forbid her to utter; and there is a look of hideous meaning in her eyes, which she turns continually towards her mistress. In this disease the mind often remains singularly clear to the last."

"I am not surprised at an indication of malevolent feeling in her," I said. "She is a woman who has always inspired me with distrust and dislike, but she managed to insinuate herself into her mistress's favour." He was silent after this, looking at the fire with an air of absorption, till he went upstairs again. He stayed away longer than usual, and on returning, said to me quietly, "Come now."

I followed him to the chamber where death was hovering. The dark hangings of the large bed made a background that gave a strong relief to Bertha's pale face as I entered. She started forward as she saw me enter, and then looked at Meunier with an expression of angry inquiry; but he lifted up his hand as it to impose silence, while he fixed his glance on the dying woman and felt her pulse. The face was pinched and ghastly, a cold perspiration was on the forehead, and the eyelids were lowered so as to conceal the large dark eyes. After a minute or two, Meunier walked round to the other side of the bed where Bertha stood, and with his usual air of gentle politeness towards her begged her to leave the patient under our care – everything should be done for her – she was no longer in a state to be conscious of an affectionate presence. Bertha was hesitating, apparently almost willing to believe his assurance and to comply. She looked round at the ghastly dying face, as if to read the confirmation of that assurance, when for a moment the lowered eyelids were raised again, and it seemed as if the eyes were looking towards Bertha, but blankly. A shudder passed through Bertha's frame, and she returned to her station near the pillow, tacitly implying that she would not leave the room.

The eyelids were lifted no more. Once I looked at Bertha as she watched the face of the dying one. She wore a rich peignoir, and her blond hair was half covered by a lace cap: in her attire she was, as always, an elegant woman, fit to figure in a picture of modern aristocratic life: but I asked myself how that face of hers could ever have seemed to me the face of a woman born of woman, with memories of childhood, capable of pain, needing to be fondled? The features at that moment seemed so preternaturally sharp, the eyes were so hard and eager – she looked like a cruel immortal, finding her spiritual feast in the agonies of a dying race. For across those hard features there came something like a flash when the last hour had been breathed out, and we all felt that the dark veil had completely fallen. What secret was there between Bertha and this woman? I turned my eyes from her with a horrible dread lest my insight should return, and I should be obliged to see what had been breeding about two unloving women's hearts. I felt that Bertha had been watching for the moment of death as the sealing of her secret: I thanked Heaven it could remain sealed for me.

Meunier said quietly, "She is gone." He then gave his arm to Bertha, and she submitted to be led out of the room.

I suppose it was at her order that two female attendants came into the room, and dismissed the younger one who had been present before. When they entered, Meunier had already opened the artery in the long thin neck that lay rigid on the pillow, and I dismissed them, ordering them to remain at a distance till we rang: the doctor, I said, had an operation to perform – he was not sure about the death. For the next twenty minutes I forgot everything but Meunier and the experiment in which he was so absorbed, that I think his senses would have been closed against all sounds or sights which had no relation to it. It was my task at first to keep up the artificial respiration in the body after the transfusion had been effected, but presently Meunier relieved me, and I could see the wondrous slow return of life; the breast began to heave, the inspirations became stronger, the eyelids quivered, and the soul seemed to have returned beneath them. The artificial respiration was withdrawn: still the breathing continued, and there was a movement of the lips.

Just then I heard the handle of the door moving: I suppose Bertha had heard from the women that they had been dismissed: probably a vague fear had arisen in her mind, for she entered with a look of alarm. She came to the foot of the bed and gave a stifled cry.

The dead woman's eyes were wide open, and met hers in full recognition – the recognition of hate. With a sudden strong effort, the hand that Bertha had thought for ever still was pointed towards her, and the haggard face moved. The gasping eager voice said –

"You mean to poison your husband... the poison is in the black cabinet... I got it for you... you laughed at me, and told lies about me behind my back, to make me disgusting... because you were jealous... are you sorry... now?"

The lips continued to murmur, but the sounds were no longer distinct. Soon there was no sound – only a slight movement: the flame had leaped out, and was being extinguished the faster. The wretched woman's heart-strings had been set to hatred and vengeance; the spirit of life had swept the chords for an instant, and was gone again for ever. Great God! Is this what it is to live again... to wake up with our unstilled thirst upon us, with our unuttered curses rising to our lips, with our muscles ready to act out their half-committed sins?

Bertha stood pale at the foot of the bed, quivering and helpless, despairing of devices, like a cunning animal whose hiding-places are surrounded by swift-advancing flame. Even Meunier looked paralysed; life for that moment ceased to be a scientific problem to him. As for me, this scene seemed of one texture with the rest of my existence: horror was my familiar, and this new revelation was only like an old pain recurring with new circumstances.

* * *

Since then Bertha and I have lived apart – she in her own neighbourhood, the mistress of half our wealth, I as a wanderer in foreign countries, until I came to this Devonshire nest to die. Bertha lives pitied and admired; for what had I against that charming woman, whom everyone but myself could have been happy with? There had been no witness of the scene in the dying room except Meunier, and while Meunier lived his lips were sealed by a promise to me.

Once or twice, weary of wandering, I rested in a favourite spot, and my heart went out towards the men and women and children whose faces were becoming familiar to me; but I was driven away again in terror at the approach of my old insight – driven away to live continually with the one Unknown Presence revealed and yet hidden by the moving curtain of the earth and sky. Till at last disease took hold of me and forced me to rest here – forced me to live in dependence on my servants. And then the curse of insight – of my double consciousness, came again, and has never left me. I know all their narrow thoughts, their feeble regard, their half-wearied pity.

* * *

It is the 20th of September, 1850. I know these figures I have just written, as if they were a long familiar inscription. I have seen them on this pace in my desk unnumbered times, when the scene of my dying struggle has opened upon me...

If you enjoyed this, you might also like...
From the Dead, see page 249
An Imaginative Woman, see page 171

Markheim

Robert Louis Stevenson

"YES," SAID THE DEALER, "our windfalls are of various kinds. Some customers are ignorant, and then I touch a dividend on my superior knowledge. Some are dishonest," and here he held up the candle, so that the light fell strongly on his visitor, "and in that case," he continued, "I profit by my virtue."

Markheim had but just entered from the daylight streets, and his eyes had not yet grown familiar with the mingled shine and darkness in the shop. At these pointed words, and before the near presence of the flame, he blinked painfully and looked aside.

The dealer chuckled. "You come to me on Christmas Day," he resumed, "when you know that I am alone in my house, put up my shutters, and make a point of refusing business. Well, you will have to pay for that; you will have to pay for my loss of time, when I should be balancing my books; you will have to pay, besides, for a kind of manner that I remark in you today very strongly. I am the essence of discretion, and ask no awkward questions; but when a customer cannot look me in the eye, he has to pay for it." The dealer once more chuckled; and then, changing to his usual business voice, though still with a note of irony, "You can give, as usual, a clear account of how you came into the possession of the object?" he continued. "Still your uncle's cabinet? A remarkable collector, sir!"

And the little pale, round-shouldered dealer stood almost on tip-toe, looking over the top of his gold spectacles, and nodding his head with every mark of disbelief. Markheim returned his gaze with one of infinite pity, and a touch of horror.

"This time," said he, "you are in error. I have not come to sell, but to buy. I have no curios to dispose of; my uncle's cabinet is bare to the wainscot; even were it still intact, I have done well on the Stock Exchange, and should more likely add to it than otherwise, and my errand today is simplicity itself. I seek a Christmas present for a lady," he continued, waxing more fluent as he struck into the speech he had prepared; "and certainly I owe you every excuse for thus disturbing you upon so small a matter. But the thing was neglected yesterday; I must produce my little compliment at dinner; and, as you very well know, a rich marriage is not a thing to be neglected."

There followed a pause, during which the dealer seemed to weigh this statement incredulously. The ticking of many clocks among the curious lumber of the shop, and the faint rushing of the cabs in a near thoroughfare, filled up the interval of silence.

"Well, sir," said the dealer, "be it so. You are an old customer after all; and if, as you say, you have the chance of a good marriage, far be it from me to be an obstacle. Here is a nice thing for a lady now," he went on, "this hand glass – fifteenth century, warranted; comes from a good collection, too; but I reserve the name, in the interests of my customer, who was just like yourself, my dear sir, the nephew and sole heir of a remarkable collector."

The dealer, while he thus ran on in his dry and biting voice, had stooped to take the object from its place; and, as he had done so, a shock had passed through Markheim, a start both of hand and foot, a sudden leap of many tumultuous passions to the face. It passed as swiftly as it came, and left no trace beyond a certain trembling of the hand that now received the glass.

"A glass," he said hoarsely, and then paused, and repeated it more clearly. "A glass? For Christmas? Surely not?"

"And why not?" cried the dealer. "Why not a glass?"

Markheim was looking upon him with an indefinable expression. "You ask me why not?" he said. "Why, look here – look in it – look at yourself! Do you like to see it? No! nor I – nor any man."

The little man had jumped back when Markheim had so suddenly confronted him with the mirror; but now, perceiving there was nothing worse on hand, he chuckled. "Your future lady, sir, must be pretty hard favoured," said he.

"I ask you," said Markheim, "for a Christmas present, and you give me this – this damned reminder of years, and sins and follies – this hand-conscience! Did you mean it? Had you a thought in your mind? Tell me. It will be better for you if you do. Come, tell me about yourself. I hazard a guess now, that you are in secret a very charitable man?"

The dealer looked closely at his companion. It was very odd, Markheim did not appear to be laughing; there was something in his face like an eager sparkle of hope, but nothing of mirth.

"What are you driving at?" the dealer asked.

"Not charitable?" returned the other, gloomily. "Not charitable; not pious; not scrupulous; unloving, unbeloved; a hand to get money, a safe to keep it. Is that all? Dear God, man, is that all?"

"I will tell you what it is," began the dealer, with some sharpness, and then broke off again into a chuckle. "But I see this is a love match of yours, and you have been drinking the lady's health."

"Ah!" cried Markheim, with a strange curiosity. "Ah, have you been in love? Tell me about that."

"I," cried the dealer. "I in love! I never had the time, nor have I the time today for all this nonsense. Will you take the glass?"

"Where is the hurry?" returned Markheim. "It is very pleasant to stand here talking; and life is so short and insecure that I would not hurry away from any pleasure – no, not even from so mild a one as this. We should rather cling, cling to what little we can get, like a man at a cliff's edge. Every second is a cliff, if you think upon it – a cliff a mile high – high enough, if we fall, to dash us out of every feature of humanity. Hence it is best to talk pleasantly. Let us talk of each other: why should we wear this mask? Let us be confidential. Who knows, we might become friends?"

"I have just one word to say to you," said the dealer. "Either make your purchase, or walk out of my shop!"

"True true," said Markheim. "Enough, fooling. To business. Show me something else."

The dealer stooped once more, this time to replace the glass upon the shelf, his thin blond hair falling over his eyes as he did so. Markheim moved a little nearer, with one hand in the pocket of his greatcoat; he drew himself up and filled his lungs; at the same time many different emotions were depicted together on his face – terror, horror, and resolve, fascination and a physical repulsion; and through a haggard lift of his upper lip, his teeth looked out.

"This, perhaps, may suit," observed the dealer: and then, as he began to re-arise, Markheim bounded from behind upon his victim. The long, skewerlike dagger flashed and fell. The dealer struggled like a hen, striking his temple on the shelf, and then tumbled on the floor in a heap.

Time had some score of small voices in that shop, some stately and slow as was becoming to their great age; others garrulous and hurried. All these told out the seconds in an intricate, chorus of tickings. Then the passage of a lad's feet, heavily running on the pavement, broke in upon these smaller voices and startled Markheim into the consciousness of his surroundings. He looked about him awfully. The candle stood on the counter, its flame solemnly wagging in a draught; and by that inconsiderable movement, the whole room was filled with noiseless bustle and kept heaving like a sea: the tall shadows nodding, the gross blots of darkness swelling and dwindling as with respiration, the faces of the portraits and the china gods changing and wavering like images in water. The inner door stood ajar, and peered into that leaguer of shadows with a long slit of daylight like a pointing finger.

From these fear-stricken rovings, Markheim's eyes returned to the body of his victim, where it lay both humped and sprawling, incredibly small and strangely meaner than in life. In these poor, miserly clothes, in that ungainly attitude, the dealer lay like so much sawdust. Markheim had feared to see it, and, lo! it was nothing. And yet, as he gazed, this bundle of old clothes and pool of blood began to find eloquent voices. There it must lie; there was none to work the cunning hinges or direct the miracle of locomotion – there it must lie till it was found. Found! ay, and then? Then would this dead flesh lift up a cry that would ring over England, and fill the world with the echoes of pursuit. Ay, dead or not, this was still the enemy. "Time was that when the brains were out," he thought; and the first word struck into his mind. Time, now that the deed was accomplished – time, which had closed for the victim, had become instant and momentous for the slayer.

The thought was yet in his mind, when, first one and then another, with every variety of pace and voice – one deep as the bell from a cathedral turret, another ringing on its treble notes the prelude of a waltz-the clocks began to strike the hour of three in the afternoon.

The sudden outbreak of so many tongues in that dumb chamber staggered him. He began to bestir himself, going to and fro with the candle, beleaguered by moving shadows, and startled to the soul by chance reflections. In many rich mirrors, some of home design, some from Venice or Amsterdam, he saw his face repeated and repeated, as it were an army of spies; his own eyes met and detected him; and the sound of his own steps, lightly as they fell, vexed the surrounding quiet. And still, as he continued to fill his pockets, his mind accused him with a sickening iteration, of the thousand faults of his design. He should have chosen a more quiet hour; he should have prepared an alibi; he should not have used a knife; he should have been more cautious, and only bound and gagged the dealer, and not killed him; he should have been more bold, and killed the servant also; he should have done all things otherwise: poignant regrets, weary, incessant toiling of the mind to change what was unchangeable, to plan what was now useless, to be the architect of the irrevocable past. Meanwhile, and behind all this activity, brute terrors, like the scurrying of rats in a deserted attic, filled the more remote chambers of his brain with riot; the hand of the constable would fall heavy on his shoulder, and his nerves would jerk like a hooked fish; or he beheld, in galloping defile, the dock, the prison, the gallows, and the black coffin.

Terror of the people in the street sat down before his mind like a besieging army. It was impossible, he thought, but that some rumour of the struggle must have reached their ears and set on edge their curiosity; and now, in all the neighbouring houses, he divined them sitting motionless and with uplifted ear – solitary people, condemned to spend Christmas dwelling alone on memories of the past, and now startingly recalled from that tender exercise; happy family parties struck into silence round the table, the mother still with raised finger: every degree and age and humour, but all, by their own hearths, prying and hearkening and weaving the rope that was to hang him. Sometimes it seemed to him he could not move too softly; the clink of the tall Bohemian goblets rang out loudly like a bell; and alarmed by the bigness of the ticking, he was tempted to stop the clocks. And then, again, with a swift transition of his terrors, the very silence of the place appeared a source of peril, and a thing to strike and freeze the passer-by; and he would step more boldly, and bustle aloud among the contents of the shop, and imitate, with elaborate bravado, the movements of a busy man at ease in his own house.

But he was now so pulled about by different alarms that, while one portion of his mind was still alert and cunning, another trembled on the brink of lunacy. One hallucination in particular took a strong hold on his credulity. The neighbour hearkening with white face beside his window, the passer-by arrested by a horrible surmise on the pavement – these could at worst suspect, they could not know; through the brick walls and shuttered windows only sounds could penetrate. But here, within the house, was he alone? He knew he was; he had watched the servant set forth sweet-hearting, in her poor best, 'out for the day' written in every ribbon and smile. Yes, he was alone, of course; and yet, in the bulk of empty house above him, he could surely hear a stir of delicate footing – he was surely conscious, inexplicably conscious of some presence. Ay, surely; to every room and corner of the house his imagination followed it; and now it was a faceless thing, and yet had eyes to see with; and again it was a shadow of himself; and yet again behold the image of the dead dealer, reinspired with cunning and hatred.

At times, with a strong effort, he would glance at the open door which still seemed to repel his eyes. The house was tall, the skylight small and dirty, the day blind with fog; and the light that filtered down to the ground story was exceedingly faint, and showed dimly on the threshold of the shop. And yet, in that strip of doubtful brightness, did there not hang wavering a shadow?

Suddenly, from the street outside, a very jovial gentleman began to beat with a staff on the shop-door, accompanying his blows with shouts and railleries in which the dealer was continually called upon by name. Markheim, smitten into ice, glanced at the dead man. But no! he lay quite still; he was fled away far beyond earshot of these blows and shoutings; he was sunk beneath seas of silence; and his name, which would once have caught his notice above the howling of a storm, had become an empty sound. And presently the jovial gentleman desisted from his knocking, and departed.

Here was a broad hint to hurry what remained to be done, to get forth from this accusing neighbourhood, to plunge into a bath of London multitudes, and to reach, on the other side of day, that haven of safety and apparent innocence – his bed. One visitor had come: at any moment another might follow and be more obstinate. To have done the deed, and yet not to reap the profit, would be too abhorrent a failure. The money, that was now Markheim's concern; and as a means to that, the keys.

He glanced over his shoulder at the open door, where the shadow was still lingering and shivering; and with no conscious repugnance of the mind, yet with a tremor of the belly, he drew near the body of his victim. The human character had quite departed. Like a suit half-stuffed with bran, the limbs lay scattered, the trunk doubled, on the floor; and yet the thing repelled him. Although so dingy and inconsiderable to the eye, he feared it might have more significance to the touch. He took the body by the shoulders, and turned it on its back. It was strangely light and supple, and the limbs, as if they had been broken, fell into the oddest postures. The face was robbed of all expression; but it was as pale as wax, and shockingly smeared with blood about one temple. That was, for Markheim, the one displeasing circumstance. It carried him back, upon the instant, to a certain fair-day in a fishers' village: a gray day, a piping wind, a crowd upon the street, the blare of brasses, the booming of drums, the nasal voice of a ballad singer; and a boy going to and fro, buried over head in the crowd and divided between interest and fear, until, coming out upon the chief place of concourse, he beheld a booth and a great screen with pictures, dismally designed, garishly coloured: Brown-rigg with her apprentice; the Mannings with their murdered guest; Weare in the death-grip of Thurtell; and a score besides of famous crimes. The thing was as clear as an illusion; he was once again that little boy; he was looking once again, and with the same sense of physical revolt, at these vile pictures; he was still stunned by the thumping of the drums. A bar of that day's music returned upon his memory; and at that, for the first time, a qualm came over him, a breath of nausea, a sudden weakness of the joints, which he must instantly resist and conquer.

He judged it more prudent to confront than to flee from these considerations; looking the more hardily in the dead face, bending his mind to realise the nature and greatness of his crime. So little a while ago that face had moved with every change of sentiment, that pale mouth had spoken, that body had been all on fire with governable energies; and now, and by his act, that piece of life had been arrested, as the horologist, with interjected finger, arrests the beating of the clock. So he reasoned in vain; he could rise to no more remorseful consciousness; the same heart which had shuddered before the painted effigies of crime, looked on its reality unmoved. At best, he felt a gleam of pity for one who had been endowed in vain with all those faculties that can make the world a garden of enchantment, one who had never lived and who was now dead. But of penitence, no, not a tremor.

With that, shaking himself clear of these considerations, he found the keys and advanced towards the open door of the shop. Outside, it had begun to rain smartly; and the sound of the shower upon the roof had banished silence. Like some dripping cavern, the chambers of the house were haunted by an incessant echoing, which filled the ear and mingled with the ticking of the clocks. And, as Markheim approached the door, he seemed to hear, in answer to his own cautious tread, the steps of another foot withdrawing up the stair. The shadow still palpitated loosely on the threshold. He threw a ton's weight of resolve upon his muscles, and drew back the door.

The faint, foggy daylight glimmered dimly on the bare floor and stairs; on the bright suit of armour posted, halbert in hand, upon the landing; and on the dark wood-carvings, and framed pictures that hung against the yellow panels of the wainscot.

So loud was the beating of the rain through all the house that, in Markheim's ears, it began to be distinguished into many different sounds. Footsteps and sighs, the tread of regiments marching in the distance, the chink of money in the counting, and the creaking of doors held stealthily ajar, appeared to mingle with the patter of the drops upon the cupola and the gushing of the water in the pipes. The sense that he was not alone grew upon him to the verge of madness. On every side he was haunted and begirt by presences. He heard them moving in the upper chambers; from the shop, he heard the dead man getting to his legs; and as he began with a great effort to mount the stairs, feet fled quietly before him and followed stealthily behind. If he were but deaf, he thought, how tranquilly he would possess his soul! And then again, and hearkening with ever fresh attention, he blessed himself for that unresting sense which held the outposts and stood a trusty sentinel upon his life. His head turned continually on his neck; his eyes, which seemed starting from their orbits, scouted on every side, and on every side were half-rewarded as with the tail of something nameless vanishing. The four-and-twenty steps to the first floor were four-and-twenty agonies.

On that first storey, the doors stood ajar, three of them like three ambushes, shaking his nerves like the throats of cannon. He could never again, he felt, be sufficiently immured and fortified from men's observing eyes, he longed to be home, girt in by walls, buried among bedclothes, and invisible to all but God. And at that thought he wondered a little, recollecting tales of other murderers and the fear they were said to entertain of heavenly avengers. It was not so, at least, with him. He feared the laws of nature, lest, in their callous and immutable procedure, they should preserve some damning evidence of his crime. He feared tenfold more, with a slavish, superstitions terror, some scission in the continuity of man's experience, some wilful illegality of nature. He played a game of skill, depending on the rules, calculating consequence from cause; and what if nature, as the defeated tyrant overthrew the chess-board, should break the mould of their succession? The like had befallen Napoleon (so writers said) when the winter changed the time of its appearance. The like might befall Markheim: the solid walls might become transparent and reveal his doings like those of bees in a glass hive; the stout planks might yield under his foot like quicksands and detain him in their clutch; ay, and there were soberer accidents that might destroy him: if, for instance, the house should fall and imprison him beside the body of his victim; or the house next door should fly on fire, and the firemen invade him from all sides. These things he feared; and, in a sense, these things might be called the hands of God reached forth against sin. But about God himself he was at ease; his act was doubtless exceptional, but so were his excuses, which God knew; it was there, and not among men, that he felt sure of justice.

When he had got safe into the drawing-room, and shut the door behind him, he was aware of a respite from alarms. The room was quite dismantled, uncarpeted besides, and strewn with packing cases and incongruous furniture; several great pier-glasses, in which he beheld himself at various angles, like an actor on a stage; many pictures, framed and unframed, standing, with their faces to the wall; a fine Sheraton sideboard, a cabinet of marquetry, and a great old bed, with tapestry hangings. The windows opened to the floor; but by great good fortune the lower part of the shutters had been closed, and this concealed him from the neighbours. Here, then, Markheim drew in a packing case before the cabinet, and began to search among the keys. It was a long business, for there were many; and it was irksome, besides; for, after all, there might be nothing in the cabinet, and time was on the wing. But the closeness of the occupation sobered him. With the tail of his eye he saw the door – even glanced at it from time to time directly, like a besieged commander pleased to verify the good estate of his defences. But in truth he was at peace. The rain falling in the street sounded natural and pleasant. Presently, on the other side, the notes of a piano were wakened to the music of a hymn, and the voices of many children took up the air and words. How stately, how comfortable was the melody! How fresh the youthful voices! Markheim gave ear to it smilingly, as he sorted out the keys; and his mind was thronged with answerable ideas and images; church-going children and the pealing of the high organ; children afield, bathers by the brookside, ramblers on the brambly common, kite-flyers in the windy and cloud-navigated sky; and then, at another cadence of the hymn, back again to church, and the somnolence of summer Sundays, and the high genteel voice of the parson (which he smiled a little to recall) and the painted Jacobean tombs, and the dim lettering of the Ten Commandments in the chancel.

And as he sat thus, at once busy and absent, he was startled to his feet. A flash of ice, a flash of fire, a bursting gush of blood, went over him, and then he stood transfixed and thrilling. A step mounted the stair slowly and steadily, and presently a hand was laid upon the knob, and the lock clicked, and the door opened.

Fear held Markheim in a vice. What to expect he knew not, whether the dead man walking, or the official ministers of human justice, or some chance witness blindly stumbling in to consign him to the gallows. But when a face was thrust into the aperture, glanced round the room, looked at him, nodded and smiled as if in friendly recognition, and then withdrew again, and the door closed behind it, his fear broke loose from his control in a hoarse cry. At the sound of this the visitant returned.

"Did you call me?" he asked, pleasantly, and with that he entered the room and closed the door behind him.

Markheim stood and gazed at him with all his eyes. Perhaps there was a film upon his sight, but the outlines of the new comer seemed to change and waver like those of the idols in the wavering candle-light of the shop; and at times he thought he knew him; and at times he thought he bore a likeness to himself; and always, like a lump of living terror, there lay in his bosom the conviction that this thing was not of the earth and not of God.

And yet the creature had a strange air of the commonplace, as he stood looking on Markheim with a smile; and when he added: "You are looking for the money, I believe?" it was in the tones of everyday politeness.

Markheim made no answer.

"I should warn you," resumed the other, "that the maid has left her sweetheart earlier than usual and will soon be here. If Mr. Markheim be found in this house, I need not describe to him the consequences."

"You know me?" cried the murderer.

The visitor smiled. "You have long been a favourite of mine," he said; "and I have long observed and often sought to help you."

"What are you?" cried Markheim: "the devil?"

"What I may be," returned the other, "cannot affect the service I propose to render you."

"It can," cried Markheim; "it does! Be helped by you? No, never; not by you! You do not know me yet; thank God, you do not know me!"

"I know you," replied the visitant, with a sort of kind severity or rather firmness. "I know you to the soul."

"Know me!" cried Markheim. "Who can do so? My life is but a travesty and slander on myself. I have lived to belie my nature. All men do; all men are better than this disguise that grows about and stifles them. You see each dragged away by life, like one whom bravos have seized and muffled in a cloak. If they had their own control – if you could see their faces, they would be altogether different, they would shine out for heroes and saints! I am worse than most; myself is more overlaid; my excuse is known to me and God. But, had I the time, I could disclose myself."

"To me?" inquired the visitant.

"To you before all," returned the murderer. "I supposed you were intelligent. I thought – since you exist – you would prove a reader of the heart. And yet you would propose to judge me by my acts! Think of it; my acts! I was born and I have lived in a land of giants; giants have dragged me by the wrists since I was born out of my mother – the giants of circumstance. And you would judge me by my acts! But can you not look within? Can you not understand that evil is hateful to me? Can you not see within me the clear writing of conscience, never blurred by any wilful sophistry, although too often disregarded? Can you not read me for a thing that surely must be common as humanity – the unwilling sinner?"

"All this is very feelingly expressed," was the reply, "but it regards me not. These points of consistency are beyond my province, and I care not in the least by what compulsion you may have been dragged away, so as you are but carried in the right direction. But time flies; the servant delays, looking in the faces of the crowd and at the pictures on the hoardings, but still she keeps moving nearer; and remember, it is as if the gallows itself was striding towards you through the Christmas streets! Shall I help you; I, who know all? Shall I tell you where to find the money?"

"For what price?" asked Markheim.

"I offer you the service for a Christmas gift," returned the other.

Markheim could not refrain from smiling with a kind of bitter triumph. "No," said he, "I will take nothing at your hands; if I were dying of thirst, and it was your hand that put the pitcher to my lips, I should find the courage to refuse. It may be credulous, but I will do nothing to commit myself to evil."

"I have no objection to a death-bed repentance," observed the visitant.

"Because you disbelieve their efficacy!" Markheim cried.

"I do not say so," returned the other; "but I look on these things from a different side, and when the life is done my interest falls. The man has lived to serve me, to spread black looks under colour of religion, or to sow tares in the wheat-field, as you do, in a course of weak compliance with desire. Now that he draws so near to his deliverance, he can add but one act of service – to repent, to die smiling, and thus to build up in confidence and hope the more timorous of my surviving followers. I am not so hard a master. Try me. Accept my help. Please yourself in life as you have done hitherto; please yourself more amply, spread your elbows at the board; and when the night begins to fall and the curtains to be drawn, I tell you, for your greater comfort, that you will find it even easy to compound your quarrel with your conscience, and to make a truckling peace with God. I came but now from such a deathbed, and the room was full of sincere mourners, listening to the man's last words: and when I looked into that face, which had been set as a flint against mercy, I found it smiling with hope."

"And do you, then, suppose me such a creature?" asked Markheim. "Do you think I have no more generous aspirations than to sin, and sin, and sin, and, at the last, sneak into heaven? My heart rises at the thought. Is this, then, your experience of mankind? or is it because you find me with red hands that you presume such baseness? and is this crime of murder indeed so impious as to dry up the very springs of good?"

"Murder is to me no special category," replied the other. "All sins are murder, even as all life is war. I behold your race, like starving mariners on a raft, plucking crusts out of the hands of famine and feeding on each other's lives. I follow sins beyond the moment of their acting; I find in all that the last consequence is death; and to my eyes, the pretty maid who thwarts her mother with such taking graces on a question of a ball, drips no less visibly with human gore than such a murderer as yourself. Do I say that I follow sins? I follow virtues also; they differ not by the thickness of a nail, they are both scythes for the reaping angel of Death. Evil, for which I live, consists not in action but in character. The bad man is dear to me; not the bad act, whose fruits, if we could follow them far enough down the hurtling cataract of the ages, might yet be found more blessed than those of the rarest virtues. And it is not because you have killed a dealer, but because you are Markheim, that I offer to forward your escape."

"I will lay my heart open to you," answered Markheim. "This crime on which you find me is my last. On my way to it I have learned many lessons; itself is a lesson, a momentous lesson. Hitherto I have been driven with revolt to what I would not; I was a bond-slave to poverty, driven and scourged. There are robust virtues that can stand in these temptations; mine was not so: I had a thirst of pleasure. But today, and out of this deed, I pluck both warning and riches – both the power and a fresh resolve to be myself. I become in all things a free actor in the world; I begin to see myself all changed, these hands the agents of good, this heart at peace. Something comes over me out of the past; something of what I have dreamed on Sabbath evenings to the sound of the church organ, of what I forecast when I shed tears over noble books, or talked, an innocent child, with my mother. There lies my life; I have wandered a few years, but now I see once more my city of destination."

"You are to use this money on the Stock Exchange, I think?" remarked the visitor; "and there, if I mistake not, you have already lost some thousands?"

"Ah," said Markheim, "but this time I have a sure thing."

"This time, again, you will lose," replied the visitor quietly.

"Ah, but I keep back the half!" cried Markheim.

"That also you will lose," said the other.

The sweat started upon Markheim's brow. "Well, then, what matter?" he exclaimed. "Say it be lost, say I am plunged again in poverty, shall one part of me, and that the worse, continue until the end to override the better? Evil and good run strong in me, haling me both ways. I do not love the one thing, I love all. I can conceive great deeds, renunciations, martyrdoms; and though I be fallen to such a crime as murder, pity is no stranger to my thoughts. I pity the poor; who knows their trials better than myself? I pity and help them; I prize love, I love honest laughter; there is no good thing nor true thing on earth but I love it from my heart. And are my vices only to direct my life, and my virtues to lie without effect, like some passive lumber of the mind? Not so; good, also, is a spring of acts."

But the visitant raised his finger. "For six-and-thirty years that you have been in this world," said be, "through many changes of fortune and varieties of humour, I have watched you steadily fall. Fifteen years ago you would have started at a theft. Three years back you would have blenched at the name of murder. Is there any crime, is there any cruelty or meanness, from which you still recoil? – five years from now I shall detect you in the fact! Downward, downward, lies your way; nor can anything but death avail to stop you."

"It is true," Markheim said huskily, "I have in some degree complied with evil. But it is so with all: the very saints, in the mere exercise of living, grow less dainty, and take on the tone of their surroundings."

"I will propound to you one simple question," said the other; "and as you answer, I shall read to you your moral horoscope. You have grown in many things more lax; possibly you do right to be so – and at any account, it is the same with all men. But granting that, are you in any one particular, however trifling, more difficult to please with your own conduct, or do you go in all things with a looser rein?"

"In any one?" repeated Markheim, with an anguish of consideration. "No," he added, with despair, "in none! I have gone down in all."

"Then," said the visitor, "content yourself with what you are, for you will never change; and the words of your part on this stage are irrevocably written down."

Markheim stood for a long while silent, and indeed it was the visitor who first broke the silence. "That being so," he said, "shall I show you the money?"

"And grace?" cried Markheim.

"Have you not tried it?" returned the other. "Two or three years ago, did I not see you on the platform of revival meetings, and was not your voice the loudest in the hymn?"

"It is true," said Markheim; "and I see clearly what remains for me by way of duty. I thank you for these lessons from my soul; my eyes are opened, and I behold myself at last for what I am."

At this moment, the sharp note of the door-bell rang through the house; and the visitant, as though this were some concerted signal for which he had been waiting, changed at once in his demeanour.

"The maid!" he cried. "She has returned, as I forewarned you, and there is now before you one more difficult passage. Her master, you must say, is ill; you must let her in, with an assured but rather serious countenance – no smiles, no overacting, and I promise you success! Once the girl within, and the door closed, the same dexterity that has already rid you of the dealer will relieve you of this last danger in your path. Thenceforward you have the whole evening – the whole night, if needful – to ransack the treasures of the house and to make good your safety. This is help that comes to you with the mask of danger. Up!" he cried; "up, friend; your life hangs trembling in the scales: up, and act!"

Markheim steadily regarded his counsellor. "If I be condemned to evil acts," he said, "there is still one door of freedom open – I can cease from action. If my life be an ill thing, I can lay it down. Though I be, as you say truly, at the beck of every small temptation, I can yet, by one decisive gesture, place myself beyond the reach of all. My love of good is damned to barrenness; it may, and let it be! But I have still my hatred of evil; and from that, to your galling disappointment, you shall see that I can draw both energy and courage."

The features of the visitor began to undergo a wonderful and lovely change: they brightened and softened with a tender triumph, and, even as they brightened, faded and dislimned. But Markheim did not pause to watch or understand the transformation. He opened the door and went downstairs very slowly, thinking to himself. His past went soberly before him; he beheld it as it was, ugly and strenuous like a dream, random as chance-medley – a scene of defeat. Life, as he thus reviewed it, tempted him no longer; but on the further side he perceived a quiet haven for his bark. He paused in the passage, and looked into the shop, where the candle still burned by the dead body. It was strangely silent. Thoughts of the dealer swarmed into his mind, as he stood gazing. And then the bell once more broke out into impatient clamour.

He confronted the maid upon the threshold with something like a smile.

"You had better go for the police," said he: "I have killed your master."

If you enjoyed this, you might also like...
The Adventure of the Hansom Cabs, see page 85
A Lost Masterpiece, see page 166

From the Dead

Edith Nesbit

Chapter I

"BUT TRUE OR NOT true, your brother is a scoundrel. No man – no decent man – tells such things."

"He did not tell me. How dare you suppose it? I found the letter in his desk; and she being my friend and you being her lover, I never thought there could be any harm in my reading her letter to my brother. Give me back the letter. I was a fool to tell you."

Ida Helmont held out her hand for the letter.

"Not yet," I said, and I went to the window. The dull red of a London sunset burned on the paper, as I read in the quaint, dainty handwriting I knew so well and had kissed so often –

> Dear, I do – I do love you; but it's impossible. I must marry Arthur. My honour is engaged. If he would only set me free – but he never will. He loves me so foolishly. But as for me, it is you I love – body, soul, and spirit. There is no one in my heart but you. I think of you all day, and dream of you all night. And we must part. And that is the way of the world. Goodbye! – Yours, yours, yours,
> Elvire.

I had seen the handwriting, indeed, often enough. But the passion written there was new to me. That I had not seen.

I turned from the window wearily. My sitting-room looked strange to me. There were my books, my reading-lamp, my untasted dinner still on the table, as I had left it when I rose to dissemble my surprise at Ida Helmont's visit – Ida Helmont, who now sat in my easy-chair looking at me quietly.

"Well – do you give me no thanks?"

"You put a knife in my heart, and then ask for thanks?"

"Pardon me," she said, throwing up her chin. "I have done nothing but show you the truth. For that one should expect no gratitude – may I ask, out of mere curiosity, what you intend to do?"

"Your brother will tell you—"

She rose suddenly, pale to the lips.

"You will not tell my brother?" she began.

"That you have read his private letters? Certainly not!"

She came towards me – her gold hair flaming in the sunset light.

"Why are you so angry with me?" she said. "Be reasonable. What else could I do?"

"I don't know."

"Would it have been right not to tell you?"

"I don't know. I only know that you've put the sun out, and I haven't got used to the dark yet."

"Believe me," she said, coming still nearer to me, and laying her hands in the lightest light touch on my shoulders, "believe me, she never loved you."

There was a softness in her tone that irritated and stimulated me. I moved gently back, and her hands fell by her sides.

"I beg your pardon," I said. "I have behaved very badly. You were quite right to come, and I am not ungrateful. Will you post a letter for me?"

I sat down and wrote –

> *I give you back your freedom. The only gift of mine that can please you now. Arthur.*

I held the sheet out to Miss Helmont, and, when she had glanced at it, I sealed, stamped, and addressed it.

"Goodbye," I said then, and gave her the letter. As the door closed behind her I sank into my chair, and I am not ashamed to say that I cried like a child or a fool over my lost plaything – the little dark-haired woman who loved some one else with "body, soul, and spirit."

I did not hear the door open or any foot on the floor, and therefore I started when a voice behind me said –

"Are you so very unhappy? Oh, Arthur, don't think I am not sorry for you!"

"I don't want any one to be sorry for me, Miss Helmont," I said.

She was silent a moment. Then, with a quick, sudden, gentle movement she leaned down and kissed my forehead – and I heard the door softly close. Then I knew that the beautiful Miss Helmont loved me.

At first that thought only fleeted by – a light cloud against a grey sky – but the next day reason woke, and said –

"Was Miss Helmont speaking the truth? Was it possible that…?"

I determined to see Elvire, to know from her own lips whether by happy fortune this blow came, not from her, but from a woman in whom love might have killed honesty.

I walked from Hampstead to Gower Street. As I trod its long length, I saw a figure in pink come out of one of the houses. It was Elvire. She walked in front of me to the corner of Store Street. There she met Oscar Helmont. They turned and met me face to face, and I saw all I needed to see. They loved each other. Ida Helmont had spoken the truth. I bowed and passed on. Before six months were gone they were married, and before a year was over I had married Ida Helmont.

What did it I don't know. Whether it was remorse for having, even for half a day, dreamed that she could be so base as to forge a lie to gain a lover, or whether it was her beauty, or the sweet flattery of the preference of a woman who had half her acquaintances at her feet, I don't know; anyhow, my thoughts turned to her as to their natural home. My heart, too, took that road, and before very long I loved her as I had never loved Elvire. Let no one doubt that I loved her – as I shall never love again, please God!

There never was any one like her. She was brave and beautiful, witty and wise, and beyond all measure adorable. She was the only woman in the world. There was a frankness – a largeness of heart – about her that made all other women seem small and contemptible. She loved me and I worshipped her. I married her, I stayed with her for three golden weeks, and then I left her. Why?

Because she told me the truth. It was one night – late – we had sat all the evening in the verandah of our seaside lodging watching the moonlight on the water and listening to the soft sound of the sea on the sand. I have never been so happy; I never shall be happy any more, I hope.

"Heart's heart," she said, leaning her gold head against my shoulder, "how much do you love me?"

"How much?"

"Yes – how much? I want to know what place it is I hold in your heart. Am I more to you than any one else?"

"My love!"

"More than yourself?"

"More than my life!"

"I believe you," she said. Then she drew a long breath, and took my hands in hers. "It can make no difference. Nothing in heaven or earth can come between us now."

"Nothing," I said. "But, sweet, my wife, what is it?"

For she was deathly pale.

"I must tell you," she said; "I cannot hide anything now from you, because I am yours – body, soul, and spirit."

The phrase was an echo that stung me.

The moonlight shone on her gold hair, her warm, soft, gold hair, and on her pale face.

"Arthur," she said, "you remember my coming to you at Hampstead with that letter?"

"Yes, my sweet, and I remember how you—"

"Arthur!" – she spoke fast and low – "Arthur, that letter was a forgery. She never wrote it. I—"

She stopped, for I had risen and flung her hands from me, and stood looking at her. God help me! I thought it was anger at the lie I felt. I know now it was only wounded vanity that smarted in me. That I should have been tricked, that I should have been deceived, that I should have been led on to make a fool of myself! That I should have married the woman who had befooled me! At that moment she was no longer the wife I adored – she was only a woman who had forged a letter and tricked me into marrying her.

I spoke; I denounced her; I said I would never speak to her again. I felt it was rather creditable in me to be so angry. I said I would have no more to do with a liar and forger.

I don't know whether I expected her to creep to my knees and implore forgiveness. I think I had some vague idea that I could by-and-by consent with dignity to forgive and forget. I did not mean what I said. No, no; I did not mean a word of it. While I was saying it I was longing for her to weep and fall at my feet, that I might raise her and hold her in my arms again.

But she did not fall at my feet; she stood quietly looking at me.

"Arthur," she said, as I paused for breath, "let me explain – she – I—"

"There is nothing to explain," I said hotly, still with that foolish sense of there being something rather noble in my indignation, as one feels when one calls one's self a miserable sinner. "You are a liar and forger, and that is enough for me. I will never speak to you again. You have wrecked my life—"

"Do you mean that?" she said, interrupting me, and leaning forward to look at me. Tears lay on her cheeks, but she was not crying now.

I hesitated. I longed to take her in my arms and say – "Lay your head here, my darling, and cry here, and know how I love you."

But instead I kept silence.

"Do you mean it?" she persisted.

Then she put her hand on my arm. I longed to clasp it and draw her to me.

Instead, I shook it off, and said –

"Mean it? Yes – of course I mean it. Don't touch me, please! You have ruined my life." She turned away without a word, went into our room, and shut the door.

I longed to follow her, to tell her that if there was anything to forgive I forgave it.

Instead, I went out on the beach, and walked away under the cliffs.

The moonlight and the solitude, however, presently brought me to a better mind. Whatever she had done had been done for love of me – I knew that. I would go home and tell her so – tell her that whatever she had done she was my dearest life, my heart's one treasure. True, my ideal of her was shattered, but, even as she was, what was the whole world of women compared to her? I hurried back, but in my resentment and evil temper I had walked far, and the way back was very long. I had been parted from her for three hours by the time I opened the door of the little house where we lodged. The house was dark and very still. I slipped off my shoes and crept up the narrow stairs, and opened the door of our room quite softly. Perhaps she would have cried herself to sleep, and I would lean over her and waken her with my kisses and beg her to forgive me. Yes, it had come to that now.

I went into the room – I went towards the bed. She was not there. She was not in the room, as one glance showed me. She was not in the house, as I knew in two minutes. When I had wasted a priceless hour in searching the town for her, I found a note on the dressing-table –

"Goodbye! Make the best of what is left of your life. I will spoil it no more."

She was gone, utterly gone. I rushed to town by the earliest morning train, only to find that her people knew nothing of her. Advertisement failed. Only a tramp said he had met a white lady on the cliff, and a fisherman brought me a handkerchief marked with her name that he had found on the beach.

I searched the country far and wide, but I had to go back to London at last, and the months went by. I won't say much about those months, because even the memory of that suffering turns me faint and sick at heart. The police and detectives and the Press failed me utterly. Her friends could not help me, and were, moreover, wildly indignant with me, especially her brother, now living very happily with my first love.

I don't know how I got through those long weeks and months. I tried to write; I tried to read; I tried to live the life of a reasonable human being. But it was impossible. I could not endure the companionship of my kind. Day and night I almost saw her face – almost heard her voice. I took long walks in the country, and her figure was always just round the next turn of the road – in the next glade of the wood. But I never quite saw her – never quite heard her. I believe I was not altogether sane at that time. At last, one morning as I was setting out for one of those long walks that had no goal but weariness, I met a telegraph boy, and took the red envelope from his hand.

On the pink paper inside was written –

Come to me at once. I am dying. You must come. – Ida. – Apinshaw Farm, Mellor, Derbyshire.

There was a train at twelve to Marple, the nearest station. I took it. I tell you there are some things that cannot be written about. My life for those long months was one of them, that journey was another. What had her life been for those months? That question troubled me, as one is troubled in every nerve at the sight of a surgical operation or a wound inflicted on a being dear to one. But the overmastering sensation was joy – intense, unspeakable joy. She was alive! I should see her again. I took out the telegram and looked at it: "I am dying." I simply did not believe it. She could not die till she had seen me. And if she had lived all those months without me, she could live now, when I was with her again, when she knew of the hell I had endured apart from her, and the heaven of our meeting. She must live. I would not let her die.

There was a long drive over bleak hills. Dark, jolting, infinitely wearisome. At last we stopped before a long, low building, where one or two lights gleamed faintly. I sprang out.

The door opened. A blaze of light made me blink and draw back. A woman was standing in the doorway.

"Art thee Arthur Marsh?" she said.

"Yes."

"Then, th'art ower late. She's dead."

Chapter II

I WENT into the house, walked to the fire, and held out my hands to it mechanically, for, though the night was May, I was cold to the bone. There were some folks standing round the fire and lights flickering. Then an old woman came forward with the northern instinct of hospitality.

"Thou'rt tired," she said, "and mazed-like. Have a sup o' tea."

I burst out laughing. It was too funny. I had travelled two hundred miles to see her; and she was dead, and they offered me tea. They drew back from me as if I had been a wild beast, but I could not stop laughing. Then a hand was laid on my shoulder, and some one led me into a dark room, lighted a lamp, set me in a chair, and sat down opposite me. It was a bare parlour, coldly furnished with rush chairs and much-polished tables and presses. I caught my breath, and grew suddenly grave, and looked at the woman who sat opposite me.

"I was Miss Ida's nurse," said she; "and she told me to send for you. Who are you?"

"Her husband—"

The woman looked at me with hard eyes, where intense surprise struggled with resentment. "Then, may God forgive you!" she said. "What you've done I don't know; but it'll be 'ard work forgivin' you – even for Him!"

"Tell me," I said, "my wife—"

"Tell you?" The bitter contempt in the woman's tone did not hurt me; what was it to the self-contempt that had gnawed my heart all these months? "Tell you? Yes, I'll tell you. Your wife was that ashamed of you, she never so much as told me she was married. She let me think anything I pleased sooner than that. She just come 'ere an' she said,

'Nurse, take care of me, for I am in mortal trouble. And don't let them know where I am,' says she. An' me bein' well married to an honest man, and well-to-do here, I was able to do it, by the blessing."

"Why didn't you send for me before?" It was a cry of anguish wrung from me.

"I'd never 'a sent for you – it was her doin'. Oh, to think as God A'mighty's made men able to measure out such-like pecks o' trouble for us womenfolk! Young man, I dunno what you did to 'er to make 'er leave you; but it muster bin something cruel, for she loved the ground you walked on. She useter sit day after day, a-lookin' at your picture an' talkin' to it an' kissin' of it, when she thought I wasn't takin' no notice, and cryin' till she made me cry too. She useter cry all night 'most. An' one day, when I tells 'er to pray to God to 'elp 'er through 'er trouble, she outs with your putty face on a card, she doez, an', says she, with her poor little smile, 'That's my god, Nursey,' she says."

"Don't!" I said feebly, putting out my hands to keep off the torture; "not any more, not now."

"Don't?" she repeated. She had risen and was walking up and down the room with clasped hands – "don't, indeed! No, I won't; but I shan't forget you! I tell you I've had you in my prayers time and again, when I thought you'd made a light-o'-love o' my darling. I shan't drop you outer them now I know she was your own wedded wife as you chucked away when you'd tired of her, and left 'er to eat 'er 'art out with longin' for you. Oh! I pray to God above us to pay you scot and lot for all you done to 'er! You killed my pretty. The price will be required of you, young man, even to the uttermost farthing! O God in heaven, make him suffer! Make him feel it!"

She stamped her foot as she passed me. I stood quite still; I bit my lip till I tasted the blood hot and salt on my tongue.

"She was nothing to you!" cried the woman, walking faster up and down between the rush chairs and the table; "any fool can see that with half an eye. You didn't love her, so you don't feel nothin' now; but some day you'll care for some one, and then you shall know what she felt – if there's any justice in heaven!"

I, too, rose, walked across the room, and leaned against the wall. I heard her words without understanding them.

"Can't you feel nothin'? Are you mader stone? Come an' look at 'er lyin' there so quiet. She don't fret arter the likes o' you no more now. She won't sit no more a-lookin' outer winder an' sayin' nothin' – only droppin' 'er tears one by one, slow, slow on her lap. Come an' see 'er; come an' see what you done to my pretty – an' then ye can go. Nobody wants you 'ere. She don't want you now. But p'r'aps you'd like to see 'er safe underground fust? I'll be bound you'll put a big slab on 'er – to make sure she don't rise again."

I turned on her. Her thin face was white with grief and impotent rage. Her claw-like hands were clenched.

"Woman," I said, "have mercy!"

She paused, and looked at me.

"Eh?" she said.

"Have mercy!" I said again.

"Mercy? You should 'a thought o' that before. You 'adn't no mercy on 'er. She loved you – she died lovin' you. An' if I wasn't a Christian woman, I'd kill you for it – like the rat you are! That I would, though I 'ad to swing for it arterwards."

I caught the woman's hands and held them fast, in spite of her resistance.

"Don't you understand?" I said savagely. "We loved each other. She died loving me. I have to live loving her. And it's her you pity. I tell you it was all a mistake – a stupid, stupid mistake. Take me to her, and for pity's sake let me be left alone with her."

She hesitated; then said in a voice only a shade less hard –

"Well, come along, then."

We moved towards the door. As she opened it a faint, weak cry fell on my ear. My heart stood still.

"What's that?" I asked, stopping on the threshold.

"Your child," she said shortly.

That, too! Oh, my love! oh, my poor love! All these long months!

"She allus said she'd send for you when she'd got over her trouble," the woman said as we climbed the stairs. "'I'd like him to see his little baby, nurse,' she says; 'our little baby. It'll be all right when the baby's born,' she says. 'I know he'll come to me then. You'll see.' And I never said nothin' – not thinkin' you'd come if she was your leavins, and not dreamin' as you could be 'er husband an' could stay away from 'er a hour – her bein' as she was. Hush!"

She drew a key from her pocket and fitted it to the lock. She opened the door and I followed her in. It was a large, dark room, full of old-fashioned furniture. There were wax candles in brass candlesticks and a smell of lavender.

The big four-post bed was covered with white.

"My lamb – my poor pretty lamb!" said the woman, beginning to cry for the first time as she drew back the sheet. "Don't she look beautiful?"

I stood by the bedside. I looked down on my wife's face. Just so I had seen it lie on the pillow beside me in the early morning when the wind and the dawn came up from beyond the sea. She did not look like one dead. Her lips were still red, and it seemed to me that a tinge of colour lay on her cheek. It seemed to me, too, that if I kissed her she would wake, and put her slight hand on my neck, and lay her cheek against mine – and that we should tell each other everything, and weep together, and understand and be comforted.

So I stooped and laid my lips to hers as the old nurse stole from the room.

But the red lips were like marble, and she did not wake. She will not wake now ever any more.

I tell you again there are some things that cannot be written.

Chapter III

I LAY THAT NIGHT in a big room filled with heavy, dark furniture, in a great four-poster hung with heavy, dark curtains – a bed the counterpart of that other bed from whose side they had dragged me at last.

They fed me, I believe, and the old nurse was kind to me. I think she saw now that it is not the dead who are to be pitied most.

I lay at last in the big, roomy bed, and heard the household noises grow fewer and die out, the little wail of my child sounding latest. They had brought the child to me, and I had held it in my arms, and bowed my head over its tiny face and frail fingers. I did not love it then. I told myself it had cost me her life. But my heart told me that it was I who had done that. The tall clock at the stairhead sounded the hours – eleven, twelve, one, and still I could not sleep. The room was dark and very still.

I had not been able to look at my life quietly. I had been full of the intoxication of grief – a real drunkenness, more merciful than the calm that comes after.

Now I lay still as the dead woman in the next room, and looked at what was left of my life. I lay still, and thought, and thought, and thought. And in those hours I tasted the bitterness of death. It must have been about two that I first became aware of a slight sound that was not the ticking of the clock. I say I first became aware, and yet I knew perfectly that I had heard that sound more than once before, and had yet determined not to hear it, because it came from the next room – the room where the corpse lay.

And I did not wish to hear that sound, because I knew it meant that I was nervous – miserably nervous – a coward and a brute. It meant that I, having killed my wife as surely as though I had put a knife in her breast, had now sunk so low as to be afraid of her dead body – the dead body that lay in the room next to mine. The heads of the beds were placed against the same wall; and from that wall I had fancied I heard slight, slight, almost inaudible sounds. So when I say that I became aware of them I mean that I at last heard a sound so distinct as to leave no room for doubt or question. It brought me to a sitting position in the bed, and the drops of sweat gathered heavily on my forehead and fell on my cold hands as I held my breath and listened.

I don't know how long I sat there – there was no further sound – and at last my tense muscles relaxed, and I fell back on the pillow.

"You fool!" I said to myself; "dead or alive, is she not your darling, your heart's heart? Would you not go near to die of joy if she came to you? Pray God to let her spirit come back and tell you she forgives you!"

"I wish she would come," myself answered in words, while every fibre of my body and mind shrank and quivered in denial.

I struck a match, lighted a candle, and breathed more freely as I looked at the polished furniture – the commonplace details of an ordinary room. Then I thought of her, lying alone, so near me, so quiet under the white sheet. She was dead; she would not wake or move. But suppose she did move? Suppose she turned back the sheet and got up, and walked across the floor and turned the door-handle?

As I thought it, I heard – plainly, unmistakably heard – the door of the chamber of death open slowly – I heard slow steps in the passage, slow, heavy steps – I heard the touch of hands on my door outside, uncertain hands, that felt for the latch.

Sick with terror, I lay clenching the sheet in my hands.

I knew well enough what would come in when that door opened – that door on which my eyes were fixed. I dreaded to look, yet I dared not turn away my eyes. The door opened slowly, slowly, slowly, and the figure of my dead wife came in. It came straight towards the bed, and stood at the bed-foot in its white grave-clothes, with the white bandage under its chin. There was a scent of lavender. Its eyes were wide open and looked at me with love unspeakable.

I could have shrieked aloud.

My wife spoke. It was the same dear voice that I had loved so to hear, but it was very weak and faint now; and now I trembled as I listened.

"You aren't afraid of me, darling, are you, though I am dead? I heard all you said to me when you came, but I couldn't answer. But now I've come back from the dead to tell you. I wasn't really so bad as you thought me. Elvire had told me she loved Oscar. I only wrote the letter to make it easier for you. I was too proud to tell you when you were so angry, but I am not proud any more now. You'll love me again now, won't you, now I'm dead? One always forgives dead people."

The poor ghost's voice was hollow and faint. Abject terror paralyzed me. I could answer nothing.

"Say you forgive me," the thin, monotonous voice went on; "say you love me again."

I had to speak. Coward as I was, I did manage to stammer –

"Yes; I love you. I have always loved you, God help me!"

The sound of my own voice reassured me, and I ended more firmly than I began. The figure by the bed swayed a little unsteadily.

"I suppose," she said wearily, "you would be afraid, now I am dead, if I came round to you and kissed you?"

She made a movement as though she would have come to me.

Then I did shriek aloud, again and again, and covered my face with the sheet, and wound it round my head and body, and held it with all my force.

There was a moment's silence. Then I heard my door close, and then a sound of feet and of voices, and I heard something heavy fall. I disentangled my head from the sheet. My room was empty. Then reason came back to me. I leaped from the bed.

"Ida, my darling, come back! I am not afraid! I love you! Come back! Come back!"

I sprang to my door and flung it open. Some one was bringing a light along the passage. On the floor, outside the door of the death-chamber, was a huddled heap – the corpse, in its grave-clothes. Dead, dead, dead.

She is buried in Mellor churchyard, and there is no stone over her.

Now, whether it was catalepsy – as the doctors said – or whether my love came back even from the dead to me who loved her, I shall never know; but this I know – that, if I had held out my arms to her as she stood at my bed-foot – if I had said, "Yes, even from the grave, my darling – from hell itself, come back, come back to me!" – if I had had room in my coward's heart for anything but the unreasoning terror that killed love in that hour, I should not now be here alone. I shrank from her – I feared her – I would not take her to my heart. And now she will not come to me any more.

Why do I go on living?

You see, there is the child. It is four years old now, and it has never spoken and never smiled.

If you enjoyed this, you might also like...
From the Dead, see page 249
A Cross Line, see page 143

The Inmost Light

Arthur Machen

Chapter I

ONE EVENING in autumn, when the deformities of London were veiled in faint blue mist, and its vistas and far-reaching streets seemed splendid, Mr. Charles Salisbury was slowly pacing down Rupert Street, drawing nearer to his favourite restaurant by slow degrees. His eyes were downcast in study of the pavement, and thus it was that as he passed in at the narrow door a man who had come up from the lower end of the street jostled against him.

"I beg your pardon – wasn't looking where I was going. Why, it's Dyson!"

"Yes, quite so. How are you, Salisbury?"

"Quite well. But where have you been, Dyson? I don't think I can have seen you for the last five years?"

"No; I dare say not. You remember I was getting rather hard up when you came to my place at Charlotte Street?"

"Perfectly. I think I remember your telling me that you owed five weeks' rent, and that you had parted with your watch for a comparatively small sum."

"My dear Salisbury, your memory is admirable. Yes, I was hard up. But the curious thing is that soon after you saw me I became harder up. My financial state was described by a friend as 'stone broke.' I don't approve of slang, mind you, but such was my condition. But suppose we go in; there might be other people who would like to dine – it's a human weakness, Salisbury."

"Certainly; come along. I was wondering as I walked down whether the corner table were taken. It has a velvet back, you know."

"I know the spot; it's vacant. Yes, as I was saying, I became even harder up."

"What did you do then?" asked Salisbury, disposing of his hat, and settling down in the corner of the seat, with a glance of fond anticipation at the menu.

"What did I do? Why, I sat down and reflected. I had a good classical education, and a positive distaste for business of any kind: that was the capital with which I faced the world. Do you know, I have heard people describe olives as nasty! What lamentable Philistinism! I have often thought, Salisbury, that I could write genuine poetry under the influence of olives and red wine. Let us have Chianti; it may not be very good, but the flasks are simply charming."

"It is pretty good here. We may as well have a big flask."

"Very good. I reflected, then, on my want of prospects, and I determined to embark in literature."

"Really; that was strange. You seem in pretty comfortable circumstances, though."

"Though! What a satire upon a noble profession. I am afraid, Salisbury, you haven't a proper idea of the dignity of an artist. You see me sitting at my desk – or at least you can see me if you care to call – with pen and ink, and simple nothingness before me, and if you come again in a few hours you will (in all probability) find a creation!"

"Yes, quite so. I had an idea that literature was not remunerative."

"You are mistaken; its rewards are great. I may mention, by the way, that shortly after you saw me I succeeded to a small income. An uncle died, and proved unexpectedly generous."

"Ah, I see. That must have been convenient."

"It was pleasant – undeniably pleasant. I have always considered it in the light of an endowment of my researches. I told you I was a man of letters; it would, perhaps, be more correct to describe myself as a man of science."

"Dear me, Dyson, you have really changed very much in the last few years. I had a notion, don't you know, that you were a sort of idler about town, the kind of man one might meet on the north side of Piccadilly every day from May to July."

"Exactly. I was even then forming myself, though all unconsciously. You know my poor father could not afford to send me to the University. I used to grumble in my ignorance at not having completed my education. That was the folly of youth, Salisbury; my University was Piccadilly. There I began to study the great science which still occupies me."

"What science do you mean?"

"The science of the great city; the physiology of London; literally and metaphysically the greatest subject that the mind of man can conceive. What an admirable salmi this is; undoubtedly the final end of the pheasant. Yet I feel sometimes positively overwhelmed with the thought of the vastness and complexity of London. Paris a man may get to understand thoroughly with a reasonable amount of study; but London is always a mystery. In Paris you may say: 'Here live the actresses, here the Bohemians, and the Ratés'; but it is different in London. You may point out a street, correctly enough, as the abode of washerwomen; but, in that second floor, a man may be studying Chaldee roots, and in the garret over the way a forgotten artist is dying by inches."

"I see you are Dyson, unchanged and unchangeable," said Salisbury, slowly sipping his Chianti. "I think you are misled by a too fervid imagination; the mystery of London exists only in your fancy. It seems to me a dull place enough. We seldom hear of a really artistic crime in London, whereas I believe Paris abounds in that sort of thing."

"Give me some more wine. Thanks. You are mistaken, my dear fellow, you are really mistaken. London has nothing to be ashamed of in the way of crime. Where we fail is for want of Homers, not Agamemnons. Carent quia vate sacro, you know."

"I recall the quotation. But I don't think I quite follow you."

"Well, in plain language, we have no good writers in London who make a speciality of that kind of thing. Our common reporter is a dull dog; every story that he has to tell is spoilt in the telling. His idea of horror and of what excites horror is so lamentably deficient. Nothing will content the fellow but blood, vulgar red blood, and when he can get it he lays it on thick, and considers that he has produced a telling article. It's a poor notion. And, by some curious fatality, it is the most commonplace and brutal murders which always attract the most attention and get written up the most. For instance, I dare say that you never heard of the Harlesden case?"

"No; no, I don't remember anything about it."

"Of course not. And yet the story is a curious one. I will tell it you over our coffee. Harlesden, you know, or I expect you don't know, is quite on the out-quarters of

London; something curiously different from your fine old crusted suburb like Norwood or Hampstead, different as each of these is from the other. Hampstead, I mean, is where you look for the head of your great China house with his three acres of land and pine-houses, though of late there is the artistic substratum; while Norwood is the home of the prosperous middle-class family who took the house 'because it was near the Palace,' and sickened of the Palace six months afterwards; but Harlesden is a place of no character. It's too new to have any character as yet. There are the rows of red houses and the rows of white houses and the bright green Venetians, and the blistering doorways, and the little backyards they call gardens, and a few feeble shops, and then, just as you think you're going to grasp the physiognomy of the settlement, it all melts away."

"How the dickens is that? the houses don't tumble down before one's eyes, I suppose!"

"Well, no, not exactly that. But Harlesden as an entity disappears. Your street turns into a quiet lane, and your staring houses into elm trees, and the back-gardens into green meadows. You pass instantly from town to country; there is no transition as in a small country town, no soft gradations of wider lawns and orchards, with houses gradually becoming less dense, but a dead stop. I believe the people who live there mostly go into the City. I have seen once or twice a laden 'bus bound thitherwards. But however that may be, I can't conceive a greater loneliness in a desert at midnight than there is there at midday. It is like a city of the dead; the streets are glaring and desolate, and as you pass it suddenly strikes you that this too is part of London. Well, a year or two ago there was a doctor living there; he had set up his brass plate and his red lamp at the very end of one of those shining streets, and from the back of the house, the fields stretched away to the north. I don't know what his reason was in settling down in such an out-of-the-way place, perhaps Dr. Black, as we will call him, was a far-seeing man and looked ahead. His relations, so it appeared afterwards, had lost sight of him for many years and didn't even know he was a doctor, much less where he lived. However, there he was settled in Harlesden, with some fragments of a practice, and an uncommonly pretty wife. People used to see them walking out together in the summer evenings soon after they came to Harlesden, and, so far as could be observed, they seemed a very affectionate couple. These walks went on through the autumn, and then ceased; but, of course, as the days grew dark and the weather cold, the lanes near Harlesden might be expected to lose many of their attractions. All through the winter nobody saw anything of Mrs. Black; the doctor used to reply to his patients' inquiries that she was a 'little out of sorts, would be better, no doubt, in the spring.' But the spring came, and the summer, and no Mrs. Black appeared, and at last people began to rumour and talk amongst themselves, and all sorts of queer things were said at 'high teas,' which you may possibly have heard are the only form of entertainment known in such suburbs. Dr. Black began to surprise some very odd looks cast in his direction, and the practice, such as it was, fell off before his eyes. In short, when the neighbours whispered about the matter, they whispered that Mrs. Black was dead, and that the doctor had made away with her. But this wasn't the case; Mrs. Black was seen alive in June. It was a Sunday afternoon, one of those few exquisite days that an English climate offers, and half London had strayed out into the fields, north, south, east, and west to smell the scent of the white May, and to see if the wild roses were yet in blossom in the hedges. I had gone out myself early in the morning, and had had a long ramble, and somehow or other as I was steering homeward I found myself in this very Harlesden we have been talking about. To be exact, I had a glass of beer in the

'General Gordon,' the most flourishing house in the neighbourhood, and as I was wandering rather aimlessly about, I saw an uncommonly tempting gap in a hedgerow, and resolved to explore the meadow beyond. Soft grass is very grateful to the feet after the infernal grit strewn on suburban sidewalks, and after walking about for some time I thought I should like to sit down on a bank and have a smoke. While I was getting out my pouch, I looked up in the direction of the houses, and as I looked I felt my breath caught back, and my teeth began to chatter, and the stick I had in one hand snapped in two with the grip I gave it. It was as if I had had an electric current down my spine, and yet for some moment of time which seemed long, but which must have been very short, I caught myself wondering what on earth was the matter. Then I knew what had made my very heart shudder and my bones grind together in an agony. As I glanced up I had looked straight towards the last house in the row before me, and in an upper window of that house I had seen for some short fraction of a second a face. It was the face of a woman, and yet it was not human. You and I, Salisbury, have heard in our time, as we sat in our seats in church in sober English fashion, of a lust that cannot be satiated and of a fire that is unquenchable, but few of us have any notion what these words mean. I hope you never may, for as I saw that face at the window, with the blue sky above me and the warm air playing in gusts about me, I knew I had looked into another world – looked through the window of a commonplace, brand-new house, and seen hell open before me. When the first shock was over, I thought once or twice that I should have fainted; my face streamed with a cold sweat, and my breath came and went in sobs, as if I had been half drowned. I managed to get up at last, and walked round to the street, and there I saw the name 'Dr. Black' on the post by the front gate. As fate or my luck would have it, the door opened and a man came down the steps as I passed by. I had no doubt it was the doctor himself. He was of a type rather common in London; long and thin, with a pasty face and a dull black moustache. He gave me a look as we passed each other on the pavement, and though it was merely the casual glance which one foot-passenger bestows on another, I felt convinced in my mind that here was an ugly customer to deal with. As you may imagine, I went my way a good deal puzzled and horrified too by what I had seen; for I had paid another visit to the 'General Gordon,' and had got together a good deal of the common gossip of the place about the Blacks. I didn't mention the fact that I had seen a woman's face in the window; but I heard that Mrs. Black had been much admired for her beautiful golden hair, and round what had struck me with such a nameless terror, there was a mist of flowing yellow hair, as it were an aureole of glory round the visage of a satyr. The whole thing bothered me in an indescribable manner; and when I got home I tried my best to think of the impression I had received as an illusion, but it was no use. I knew very well I had seen what I have tried to describe to you, and I was morally certain that I had seen Mrs. Black. And then there was the gossip of the place, the suspicion of foul play, which I knew to be false, and my own conviction that there was some deadly mischief or other going on in that bright red house at the corner of Devon Road: how to construct a theory of a reasonable kind out of these two elements. In short, I found myself in a world of mystery; I puzzled my head over it and filled up my leisure moments by gathering together odd threads of speculation, but I never moved a step towards any real solution, and as the summer days went on the matter seemed to grow misty and indistinct, shadowing some vague terror, like a nightmare of last month. I suppose it would before long have faded into the background of my brain – I should not have forgotten it, for such a thing could never be forgotten – but one morning as I was looking over the paper my eye was caught by a heading over some two dozen lines of small type. The words I had seen were simply, 'The Harlesden Case,' and I knew what I was going to read. Mrs. Black was dead. Black had called in another medical man to certify as to cause of death, and something or other had aroused the strange doctor's suspicions and there had been an inquest and post-mortem. And the result? That, I will confess, did astonish me considerably; it was the triumph of the unexpected. The two doctors who made the autopsy were obliged to confess that they could not discover the faintest trace of any kind of foul play; their most exquisite tests and reagents failed to detect the presence of poison in the most infinitesimal quantity. Death, they found, had been caused by a somewhat obscure and scientifically interesting form of brain disease. The tissue of the brain and the molecules of the grey matter had undergone a most extraordinary series of changes; and the younger of the two doctors, who has some reputation, I believe, as a specialist in brain trouble, made some remarks in giving his evidence which struck me deeply at the time, though I did not then grasp their full significance. He said: 'At the commencement of the examination I was astonished to find appearances of a character entirely new to me, notwithstanding my somewhat large experience. I need not specify these appearances at present, it will be sufficient for me to state that as I proceeded in my task I could scarcely believe that the brain before me was that of a human being at all.' There was some surprise at this statement, as you may imagine, and the coroner asked the doctor if he meant to say that the brain resembled that of an animal. 'No,' he replied, 'I should not put it in that way. Some of the appearances I noticed seemed to point in that direction, but others, and these were the more surprising, indicated a nervous organization of a wholly different character from that either of man or the lower animals.' It was a curious thing to say, but of course the jury brought in a verdict of death from natural causes, and, so far as the public was concerned, the case came to an end. But after I had read what the doctor said I made up my mind that I should like to know a good deal more, and I set to work on what seemed likely to prove an interesting investigation. I had really a good deal of trouble, but I was successful in a measure. Though why – my dear fellow, I had no notion at the time. Are you aware that we have been here nearly four hours? The waiters are staring at us. Let's have the bill and be gone."

The two men went out in silence, and stood a moment in the cool air, watching the hurrying traffic of Coventry Street pass before them to the accompaniment of the ringing bells of hansoms and the cries of the newsboys; the deep far murmur of London surging up ever and again from beneath these louder noises.

"It is a strange case, isn't it?" said Dyson at length. "What do you think of it?"

"My dear fellow, I haven't heard the end, so I will reserve my opinion. When will you give me the sequel?"

"Come to my rooms some evening; say next Thursday. Here's the address. Goodnight; I want to get down to the Strand." Dyson hailed a passing hansom, and Salisbury turned northward to walk home to his lodgings.

Chapter II

MR. SALISBURY, as may have been gathered from the few remarks which he had found it possible to introduce in the course of the evening, was a young gentleman of a peculiarly solid form of intellect, coy and retiring before the mysterious and the uncommon, with a constitutional dislike of paradox. During the restaurant dinner he had been forced to listen in almost absolute silence to a strange tissue of improbabilities strung together with the ingenuity of a born meddler in plots and mysteries, and it was with a feeling of weariness that he crossed Shaftesbury Avenue, and dived into the recesses of Soho, for his lodgings were in a modest neighbourhood to the north of Oxford Street. As he walked he speculated on the probable fate of Dyson, relying on literature, unbefriended by a thoughtful relative, and could not help concluding that so much subtlety united to a too vivid imagination would in all likelihood have been rewarded with a pair of sandwich-boards or a super's banner. Absorbed in this train of thought, and admiring the perverse dexterity which could transmute the face of a sickly woman and a case of brain disease into the crude elements of romance, Salisbury strayed on through the dimly-lighted streets, not noticing the gusty wind which drove sharply round corners and whirled the stray rubbish of the pavement into the air in eddies, while black clouds gathered over the sickly yellow moon. Even a stray drop or two of rain blown into his face did not rouse him from his meditations, and it was only when with a sudden rush the storm tore down upon the street that he began to consider the expediency of finding some shelter. The rain, driven by the wind, pelted down with the violence of a thunderstorm, dashing up from the stones and hissing through the air, and soon a perfect torrent of water coursed along the kennels and accumulated in pools over the choked-up drains. The few stray passengers who had been loafing rather than walking about the street had scuttered away, like frightened rabbits, to some invisible places of refuge, and though Salisbury whistled loud and long for a hansom, no hansom appeared. He looked about him, as if to discover how far he might be from the haven of Oxford Street, but strolling carelessly along, he had turned out of his way, and found himself in an unknown region, and one to all appearance devoid even of a public-house where shelter could be bought for the modest sum of twopence. The street lamps were few and at long intervals, and burned behind grimy glasses with the sickly light of oil, and by this wavering glimmer Salisbury could make out the shadowy and vast old houses of which the street was composed. As he passed along, hurrying, and shrinking from the full sweep of the rain, he noticed the innumerable bell-handles, with names that seemed about to vanish of old age graven on brass plates beneath them, and here and there a richly carved penthouse overhung the door, blackening with the grime of fifty years. The storm seemed to grow more and more furious; he was wet through, and a new hat had become a ruin, and still Oxford Street seemed as far off as ever; it was with deep relief that the dripping man caught sight of a dark archway which seemed to promise shelter from the rain if not from the wind. Salisbury took up his position in the driest corner and looked about him; he was standing in a kind of passage contrived under part of a house, and behind him stretched a narrow footway leading between blank walls to regions unknown. He had stood there for some time, vainly endeavouring to rid himself of some of his superfluous moisture, and listening for the passing wheel of a hansom, when his attention was aroused by a loud noise coming from the direction of the passage behind, and growing louder as it drew nearer. In a couple of minutes he could make out the shrill, raucous voice of a woman, threatening and renouncing, and making the very stones echo with her accents, while now and then a man grumbled and expostulated. Though to all appearance devoid of romance, Salisbury had some relish for street rows, and was, indeed, somewhat of an amateur in the more amusing phases of drunkenness; he therefore composed himself to listen and observe with something of the air of a subscriber to grand opera. To his annoyance, however, the tempest seemed suddenly to be composed, and he could hear nothing but the impatient steps of the woman and the slow lurch of the man as they came towards him. Keeping back in the shadow of the wall, he could see the two drawing nearer; the man was evidently drunk, and had much ado to avoid frequent collision with the wall as he tacked across from one side to the other, like some bark beating up against a wind. The woman was looking straight in front of her, with tears streaming from her eyes, but suddenly as they went by the flame blazed up again, and she burst forth into a torrent of abuse, facing round upon her companion.

"You low rascal, you mean, contemptible cur," she went on, after an incoherent storm of curses, "you think I'm to work and slave for you always, I suppose, while you're after that Green Street girl and drinking every penny you've got? But you're mistaken, Sam – indeed, I'll bear it no longer. Damn you, you dirty thief, I've done with you and your master too, so you can go your own errands, and I only hope they'll get you into trouble."

The woman tore at the bosom of her dress, and taking something out that looked like paper, crumpled it up and flung it away. It fell at Salisbury's feet. She ran out and disappeared in the darkness, while the man lurched slowly into the street, grumbling indistinctly to himself in a perplexed tone of voice. Salisbury looked out after him and saw him maundering along the pavement, halting now and then and swaying indecisively, and then starting off at some fresh tangent. The sky had cleared, and white fleecy clouds were fleeting across the moon, high in the heaven. The light came and went by turns, as the clouds passed by, and, turning round as the clear, white rays shone into the passage, Salisbury saw the little ball of crumpled paper which the woman had cast down. Oddly curious to know what it might contain, he picked it up and put it in his pocket, and set out afresh on his journey.

Chapter III

SALISBURY was a man of habit. When he got home, drenched to the skin, his clothes hanging lank about him, and a ghastly dew besmearing his hat, his only thought was of his health, of which he took studious care. So, after changing his clothes and encasing himself in a warm dressing-gown, he proceeded to prepare a sudorific in the shape of a hot gin and water, warming the latter over one of those spirit-lamps which mitigate the austerities of the modern hermit's life. By the time this preparation had been exhibited, and Salisbury's disturbed feelings had been soothed by a pipe of tobacco, he was able to get into bed in a happy state of vacancy, without a thought of his adventure in the dark archway, or of the weird fancies with which Dyson had seasoned his dinner. It was the same at breakfast the next morning, for Salisbury made a point of not thinking of any thing until that meal was over; but when the cup and saucer were cleared away, and the morning pipe was lit, he remembered the little ball of paper, and began fumbling in the pockets of his wet coat. He did not remember into which pocket he had put it, and as he dived now into one and now into another, he experienced a strange feeling of apprehension lest it should not be there at all, though he could not for the life of him have explained the importance he attached to what was in all probability mere rubbish. But he sighed with relief when his fingers touched the crumpled surface in an inside pocket, and he drew it out gently and laid it on the little desk by his easy-chair with as much care as if it had been some rare jewel. Salisbury sat smoking and staring at his find for a few minutes, an odd temptation to throw the thing in the fire and have done with it struggling with as odd a speculation as to its possible contents, and as to the reason why the infuriated woman should have flung a bit of paper from her with such vehemence. As might be expected, it was the latter feeling that conquered in the end, and yet it was with something like repugnance that he at last took the paper and unrolled it, and laid it out before him. It was a piece of common dirty paper, to all appearance torn out of a cheap exercise-book, and in the middle were a few lines written in a queer cramped hand. Salisbury bent his head and stared eagerly at it for a moment, drawing a long breath, and then fell back in his chair gazing blankly before him, till at last with a sudden revulsion he burst into a peal of laughter, so long and loud and uproarious that the landlady's baby on the floor below awoke from sleep and echoed his mirth with hideous yells. But he laughed again and again, and took the paper up to read a second time what seemed such meaningless nonsense.

"Q. has had to go and see his friends in Paris," it began. "Traverse Handle S. 'Once around the grass, and twice around the lass, and thrice around the maple tree.'"

Salisbury took up the paper and crumpled it as the angry woman had done, and aimed it at the fire. He did not throw it there, however, but tossed it carelessly into the well of the desk, and laughed again. The sheer folly of the thing offended him, and he was ashamed of his own eager speculation, as one who pores over the high-sounding announcements in the agony column of the daily paper, and finds nothing but advertisement and triviality. He walked to the window, and stared out at the languid morning life of his quarter; the maids in slatternly print dresses washing door-steps, the fish-monger and the butcher on their rounds, and the tradesmen standing at the doors of their small shops, drooping for lack of trade and excitement. In the distance a blue haze gave some grandeur to the prospect, but the view as a whole was depressing, and would only have interested a student of the life of London, who finds something rare and choice in its very aspect. Salisbury turned away in disgust, and settled himself in the easy-chair, upholstered in a bright shade of green, and decked with yellow gimp, which was the pride and attraction of the apartments. Here he composed himself to his morning's occupation – the perusal of a novel that dealt with sport and love in a manner that suggested the collaboration of a stud-groom and a ladies' college. In an ordinary way, however, Salisbury would have been carried on by the interest of the story up to lunch-time, but this morning he fidgeted in and out of his chair, took the book up and laid it down again, and swore at last to himself and at himself in mere irritation. In point of fact the jingle of the paper found in the archway had 'got into his head,' and do what he would he could not help muttering over and over, "Once around the grass, and twice around the lass, and thrice around the maple tree." It became a positive pain, like the foolish burden of a music-hall song, everlastingly quoted, and sung at all hours of the day and night, and treasured by the street-boys as an unfailing resource for six months together. He went out into the streets, and tried to forget his enemy in the jostling of the crowds and the roar and clatter of the traffic, but presently he would find himself stealing quietly aside, and pacing some deserted byway, vainly puzzling his brains, and trying to fix some meaning to phrases that were meaningless. It was a positive relief when Thursday came, and he remembered that he had made an appointment to go and see Dyson; the flimsy reveries of the self-styled man of letters appeared entertaining when compared with this ceaseless iteration, this maze of thought from which there seemed no possibility of escape. Dyson's abode was in one of the quietest of the quiet streets that led down from the Strand to the river, and when Salisbury passed from the narrow stairway into his friend's room, he saw that the uncle had been beneficent indeed. The floor glowed and flamed with all the colours of the East; it was, as Dyson pompously remarked, "a sunset in a dream," and the lamplight, the twilight of London streets, was shut out with strangely worked curtains, glittering here and there with threads of gold. In the shelves of an oak armoire stood jars and plates of old French china, and the black and white of etchings not to be found in the Haymarket or in Bond Street, stood out against the splendour of a Japanese paper. Salisbury sat down on the settle by the hearth, and sniffed the mingled fumes of incense and tobacco, wondering and dumb before all this splendour after the green rep and the oleographs, the gilt-framed mirror, and the lustres of his own apartment.

"I am glad you have come," said Dyson. "Comfortable little room, isn't it? But you don't look very well, Salisbury. Nothing disagreed with you, has it?"

"No; but I have been a good deal bothered for the last few days. The fact is I had an odd kind of – of – adventure, I suppose I may call it, that night I saw you, and it has worried me a good deal. And the provoking part of it is that it's the merest nonsense – but, however, I will tell you all about it, by and by. You were going to let me have the rest of that odd story you began at the restaurant."

"Yes. But I am afraid, Salisbury, you are incorrigible. You are a slave to what you call matter of fact. You know perfectly well that in your heart you think the oddness in that case is of my making, and that it is all really as plain as the police reports. However, as I have begun, I will go on. But first we will have something to drink, and you may as well light your pipe."

Dyson went up to the oak cupboard, and drew from its depths a rotund bottle and two little glasses, quaintly gilded.

"It's Benedictine," he said. "You'll have some, won't you?"

Salisbury assented, and the two men sat sipping and smoking reflectively for some minutes before Dyson began.

"Let me see," he said at last, "we were at the inquest, weren't we? No, we had done with that. Ah, I remember. I was telling you that on the whole I had been successful in my inquiries, investigation, or whatever you like to call it, into the matter. Wasn't that where I left off?"

"Yes, that was it. To be precise, I think 'though' was the last word you said on the matter."

"Exactly. I have been thinking it all over since the other night, and I have come to the conclusion that that 'though' is a very big 'though' indeed. Not to put too fine a point on it, I have had to confess that what I found out, or thought I found out, amounts in reality to nothing. I am as far away from the heart of the case as ever. However, I may as well tell you what I do know. You may remember my saying that I was impressed a good deal by some remarks of one of the doctors who gave evidence at the inquest. Well, I determined that my first step must be to try if I could get something more definite and intelligible out of that doctor. Somehow or other I managed to get an introduction to the man, and he gave me an appointment to come and see him. He turned out to be a pleasant, genial fellow; rather young and not in the least like the typical medical man, and he began the conference by offering me whisky and cigars. I didn't think it worth while to beat about the bush, so I began by saying that part of his evidence at the Harlesden Inquest struck me as very peculiar, and I gave him the printed report, with the sentences in question underlined. He just glanced at the slip, and gave me a queer look. 'It struck you as peculiar, did it?' said he. 'Well, you must remember that the Harlesden case was very peculiar. In fact, I think I may safely say that in some features it was unique – quite unique.' 'Quite so,' I replied, 'and that's exactly why it interests me, and why I want to know more about it. And I thought that if anybody could give me any information it would be you. What is your opinion of the matter?'

"It was a pretty downright sort of question, and my doctor looked rather taken aback.

"'Well,' he said, 'as I fancy your motive in inquiring into the question must be mere curiosity, I think I may tell you my opinion with tolerable freedom. So, Mr., Mr. Dyson? if you want to know my theory, it is this: I believe that Dr. Black killed his wife.'

"'But the verdict,' I answered, 'the verdict was given from your own evidence.'

"'Quite so; the verdict was given in accordance with the evidence of my colleague and myself, and, under the circumstances, I think the jury acted very sensibly. In fact, I don't see what else they could have done. But I stick to my opinion, mind you, and I say this also. I don't wonder at Black's doing what I firmly believe he did. I think he was justified.'

"'Justified! How could that be?' I asked. I was astonished, as you may imagine, at the answer I had got. The doctor wheeled round his chair and looked steadily at me for a moment before he answered.

"'I suppose you are not a man of science yourself? No; then it would be of no use my going into detail. I have always been firmly opposed myself to any partnership between physiology and psychology. I believe that both are bound to suffer. No one recognizes more decidedly than I do the impassable gulf, the fathomless abyss that separates the world of consciousness from the sphere of matter. We know that every change of consciousness is accompanied by a rearrangement of the molecules in the grey matter; and that is all. What the link between them is, or why they occur together, we do not know, and most authorities believe that we never can know. Yet, I will tell you that as I did my work, the knife in my hand, I felt convinced, in spite of all theories, that what lay before me was not the brain of a dead woman – not the brain of a human being at all. Of course I saw the face; but it was quite placid, devoid of all expression. It must have been a beautiful face, no doubt, but I can honestly say that I would not have looked in that face when there was life behind it for a thousand guineas, no, nor for twice that sum.'

"'My dear sir,' I said, 'you surprise me extremely. You say that it was not the brain of a human being. What was it then?'

"'The brain of a devil.' He spoke quite coolly, and never moved a muscle. 'The brain of a devil,' he repeated, 'and I have no doubt that Black found some way of putting an end to it. I don't blame him if he did. Whatever Mrs. Black was, she was not fit to stay in this world. Will you have anything more? No? Goodnight, goodnight.'

"It was a queer sort of opinion to get from a man of science, wasn't it? When he was saying that he would not have looked on that face when alive for a thousand guineas, or two thousand guineas, I was thinking of the face I had seen, but I said nothing. I went again to Harlesden, and passed from one shop to another, making small purchases, and trying to find out whether there was anything about the Blacks which was not already common property, but there was very little to hear. One of the tradesmen to whom I spoke said he had known the dead woman well; she used to buy of him such quantities of grocery as were required for their small household, for they never kept a servant, but had a charwoman in occasionally, and she had not seen Mrs. Black for months before she died. According to this man Mrs. Black was 'a nice lady,' always kind and considerate, and so fond of her husband and he of her, as every one thought. And yet, to put the doctor's opinion on one side, I knew what I had seen. And then after thinking it all over, and putting one thing with another, it seemed to me that the only person likely to give me much assistance would be Black himself, and I made up my mind to find him. Of course he wasn't to be found in Harlesden; he had left, I was told, directly after the funeral. Everything in the house had been sold, and one fine day Black got into the train with a small portmanteau, and went, nobody knew where. It was a chance if he were ever heard of again, and it was by a mere chance that I came across him at last. I was walking one day along Gray's Inn Road, not bound for anywhere in particular, but looking about me, as usual, and holding on to my hat, for it was a gusty day in early March, and the wind was making the treetops in the Inn rock and quiver. I had come up from the Holborn end, and I had almost got to Theobald's Road when I noticed a man walking in front of me, leaning on a stick, and to all appearance very feeble. There was something about his look that made me curious, I don't know why, and I began to walk briskly with the idea of overtaking him, when of a sudden his hat blew off and came bounding along the pavement to my feet. Of course I rescued the hat, and gave it a glance as I went towards its owner. It was a biography in itself; a Piccadilly maker's name in the inside, but I don't think a beggar would have picked it out of the gutter. Then I looked up and saw Dr. Black of Harlesden waiting for me. A queer thing, wasn't it? But, Salisbury, what a change! When I saw Dr. Black come down the steps of his house at Harlesden he was an upright man, walking firmly with well-built limbs; a man, I should say, in the prime of his life. And now before me there crouched this wretched creature, bent and feeble, with shrunken cheeks, and hair that was whitening fast, and limbs that trembled and shook together, and misery in his eyes. He thanked me for bringing him his hat, saying, 'I don't think I should ever have got it, I can't run much now. A gusty day, sir, isn't it?' and with this he was turning away, but by little and little I contrived to draw him into the current of conversation, and we walked together eastward. I think the man would have been glad to get rid of me; but I didn't intend to let him go, and he stopped at last in front of a miserable house in a miserable street. It was, I verily believe, one of the most wretched quarters I have ever seen: houses that must have been sordid and hideous enough when new, that had gathered foulness with every year, and now seemed to lean and totter to their fall. 'I live up there,' said Black, pointing to the tiles, 'not in the front – in the back. I am very quiet there. I won't ask you to come in now, but perhaps some other day—' I caught him up at that, and told him I should be only too glad to come and see him. He gave me an odd sort of glance, as if he were wondering what on earth I or anybody else could care about him, and I left him fumbling with his latch-key. I think you will say I did pretty well when I tell you that within a few weeks I had made myself an intimate friend of Black's. I shall never forget the first time I went to his room; I hope I shall never see such abject, squalid misery again. The foul paper, from which all pattern or trace of a pattern had long vanished, subdued and penetrated with the grime of the evil street, was hanging in mouldering pennons from the wall. Only at the end of the room was it possible to stand upright, and the sight of the wretched bed and the odour of corruption that pervaded the place made me turn faint and sick. Here I found him munching a piece of bread; he seemed surprised to find that I had kept my promise, but he gave me his chair and sat on the bed while we talked. I used to go to see him often, and we had long conversations together, but he never mentioned Harlesden or his wife. I fancy that he supposed me ignorant of the matter, or thought that if I had heard of it, I should never connect the respectable Dr. Black of Harlesden with a poor garreteer in the backwoods of London. He was a strange man, and as we sat together smoking, I often wondered whether he were mad or sane, for I think the wildest dreams of Paracelsus and the Rosicrucians would appear plain and sober fact compared with the theories I have heard him earnestly advance in that grimy den of his. I once ventured to hint something of the sort to him. I suggested that something he had said was in flat contradiction to all science and all experience. 'No,' he answered, 'not all experience, for mine counts for something. I am no dealer in unproved theories; what I say I have proved for myself, and at a terrible cost. There is a region of knowledge which you will never know, which wise men seeing from afar off shun like the plague, as well they may, but into that region I have gone. If you knew, if you could even dream of what may be done, of what one or two men have done in this quiet world of ours, your very soul would shudder and faint within you. What you have heard from me has been but the merest husk and outer covering of true science – that science which means death, and that which is more awful than death, to those who gain it. No, when men say that there are strange things in the world, they little know the awe and the terror that dwell always with them and about them.' There was a sort of fascination about the man that drew me to him, and I was quite sorry to have to leave London for a month or two; I missed his odd talk. A few days after I came back to town I thought I would look him up, but when I gave the two rings at the bell that used to summon him, there was no answer. I rang and rang again, and was just turning to go away, when the door opened and a dirty woman asked me what I wanted. From her look I fancy she took me for a plain-clothes officer after one of her lodgers, but when I inquired if Mr. Black were in, she gave me a stare of another kind. 'There's no Mr. Black lives here,' she said. 'He's gone. He's dead this six weeks. I always thought he was a bit queer in his head, or else had been and got into some trouble or other. He used to go out every morning from ten till one, and one Monday morning we heard him come in, and go into his room and shut the door, and a few minutes after, just as we was a-sitting down to our dinner, there was such a scream that I thought I should have gone right off. And then we heard a stamping, and down he came, raging and cursing most dreadful, swearing he had been robbed of something that was worth millions. And then he just dropped down in the passage, and we thought he was dead. We got him up to his room, and put him on his bed, and I just sat there and waited, while my 'usband he went for the doctor. And there was the winder wide open, and a little tin box he had lying on the floor open and empty, but of course nobody could possible have got in at the winder, and as for him having anything that was worth anything, it's nonsense, for he was often weeks and weeks behind with his rent, and my 'usband he threatened often and often to turn him into the street, for, as he said, we've got a living to myke like other people – and, of course, that's true; but, somehow, I didn't like to do it, though he was an odd kind of a man, and I fancy had been better off. And then the doctor came and looked at him, and said as he couldn't do nothing, and that night he died as I was a-sitting by his bed; and I can tell you that, with one thing and another, we lost money by him, for the few bits of clothes as he had were worth next to nothing when they came to be sold.' I gave the woman half a sovereign for her trouble, and went home thinking of Dr. Black and the epitaph she had made him, and wondering at his strange fancy that he had been robbed. I take it that he had very little to fear on that score, poor fellow; but I suppose that he was really mad, and died in a sudden access of his mania. His landlady said that once or twice when she had had occasion to go into his room (to dun the poor wretch for his rent, most likely), he would keep her at the door for about a minute, and that when she came in she would find him putting away his tin box in the corner by the window; I suppose he had become possessed with the idea of some great treasure, and fancied himself a wealthy man in the midst of all his misery. Explicit, my tale is ended, and you see that though I knew Black, I know nothing of his wife or of the history of her death. – That's the Harlesden case, Salisbury, and I think it interests me all the more deeply because there does not seem the shadow of a possibility that I or any one else will ever know more about it. What do you think of it?"

"Well, Dyson, I must say that I think you have contrived to surround the whole thing with a mystery of your own making. I go for the doctor's solution: Black murdered his wife, being himself in all probability an undeveloped lunatic."

"What? Do you believe, then, that this woman was something too awful, too terrible to be allowed to remain on the earth? You will remember that the doctor said it was the brain of a devil?"

"Yes, yes, but he was speaking, of course, metaphorically. It's really quite a simple matter if you only look at it like that."

"Ah, well, you may be right; but yet I am sure you are not. Well, well, it's no good discussing it any more. A little more Benedictine? That's right; try some of this tobacco. Didn't you say that you had been bothered by something – something which happened that night we dined together?"

"Yes, I have been worried, Dyson, worried a great deal. I— But it's such a trivial matter – indeed, such an absurdity – that I feel ashamed to trouble you with it."

"Never mind, let's have it, absurd or not."

With many hesitations, and with much inward resentment of the folly of the thing, Salisbury told his tale, and repeated reluctantly the absurd intelligence and the absurder doggerel of the scrap of paper, expecting to hear Dyson burst out into a roar of laughter.

"Isn't it too bad that I should let myself be bothered by such stuff as that?" he asked, when he had stuttered out the jingle of once, and twice, and thrice.

Dyson listened to it all gravely, even to the end, and meditated for a few minutes in silence.

"Yes," he said at length, "it was a curious chance, your taking shelter in that archway just as those two went by. But I don't know that I should call what was written on the paper nonsense; it is bizarre certainly, but I expect it has a meaning for somebody. Just repeat it again, will you, and I will write it down. Perhaps we might find a cipher of some sort, though I hardly think we shall."

Again had the reluctant lips of Salisbury slowly to stammer out the rubbish that he abhorred, while Dyson jotted it down on a slip of paper.

"Look over it, will you?" he said, when it was done; "it may be important that I should have every word in its place. Is that all right?"

"Yes; that is an accurate copy. But I don't think you will get much out of it. Depend upon it, it is mere nonsense, a wanton scribble. I must be going now, Dyson. No, no more; that stuff of yours is pretty strong. Goodnight."

"I suppose you would like to hear from me, if I did find out anything?"

"No, not I; I don't want to hear about the thing again. You may regard the discovery, if it is one, as your own."

"Very well. Goodnight."

Chapter IV

A GOOD MANY HOURS after Salisbury had returned to the company of the green rep chairs, Dyson still sat at his desk, itself a Japanese romance, smoking many pipes, and meditating over his friend's story. The bizarre quality of the inscription which had annoyed Salisbury was to him an attraction, and now and again he took it up and scanned thoughtfully what he had written, especially the quaint jingle at the end. It was a token, a symbol, he decided, and not a cipher, and the woman who had flung it away was in all probability entirely ignorant of its meaning; she was but the agent of the 'Sam' she had abused and discarded, and he too was again the agent of some one unknown, possibly of the individual styled Q, who had been forced to visit his French friends. But what to make of 'Traverse Handle S.' Here was the root and source of the enigma, and not all the tobacco of Virginia seemed likely to suggest any clue here. It seemed almost hopeless, but Dyson regarded himself as the Wellington of mysteries, and went to bed feeling assured that sooner or later he would hit upon the right track. For the next few days he was deeply engaged in his literary labours, labours which were a profound mystery even to the most intimate of his friends, who searched the railway bookstalls in vain for the result of so many hours spent at the Japanese bureau in company with strong tobacco and black tea. On this occasion Dyson confined himself to his room for four days, and it was with genuine relief that he laid down his pen and went out into the streets in quest of relaxation and fresh air. The gas-lamps were being lighted, and the fifth edition of the evening papers was being howled through the streets, and Dyson, feeling that he wanted quiet, turned away from the clamorous Strand, and began to trend away to the north-west. Soon he found himself in streets that echoed to his footsteps, and crossing a broad new thoroughfare, and verging still to the west, Dyson discovered that he had penetrated to the depths of Soho. Here again was life; rare vintages of France and Italy, at prices which seemed contemptibly small, allured the passer-by; here were cheeses, vast and rich, here olive oil, and here a grove of Rabelaisian sausages; while in a neighbouring shop the whole Press of Paris appeared to be on sale. In the middle of the roadway a strange miscellany of nations sauntered to and fro, for there cab and hansom rarely ventured; and from window over window the inhabitants looked forth in pleased contemplation of the scene. Dyson made his way slowly along, mingling with the crowd on the cobble-stones, listening to the queer babel of French and German, and Italian and English, glancing now and again at the shop-windows with their levelled batteries of bottles, and had almost gained the end of the street, when his attention was arrested by a small shop at the corner, a vivid contrast to its neighbours. It was the typical shop of the poor quarter; a shop entirely English. Here were vended tobacco and sweets, cheap pipes of clay and cherry-wood; penny exercise-books and penholders jostled for precedence with comic songs, and story papers with appalling cuts showed that romance claimed its place beside the actualities of the evening paper, the bills of which fluttered at the doorway. Dyson glanced up at the name above the door, and stood by the kennel trembling, for a sharp pang, the pang of one who has made a discovery, had for a moment left him incapable of motion. The name over the shop was Travers. Dyson looked up again, this time at the corner of the wall above the lamp-post, and read in white letters on a blue ground the words 'Handel Street, W.C.,' and the legend was repeated in fainter letters just below. He gave a little sigh of satisfaction, and without more ado walked boldly into the shop, and stared full in the face the fat man who was sitting behind the counter. The fellow rose to his feet, and returned the stare a little curiously, and then began in stereotyped phrase—

"What can I do for you, sir?"

Dyson enjoyed the situation and a dawning perplexity on the man's face. He propped his stick carefully against the counter and leaning over it, said slowly and impressively—

"Once around the grass, and twice around the lass, and thrice around the maple-tree."

Dyson had calculated on his words producing an effect, and he was not disappointed. The vendor of miscellanies gasped, open-mouthed like a fish, and steadied himself against the counter. When he spoke, after a short interval, it was in a hoarse mutter, tremulous and unsteady.

"Would you mind saying that again, sir? I didn't quite catch it."

"My good man, I shall most certainly do nothing of the kind. You heard what I said perfectly well. You have got a clock in your shop, I see; an admirable timekeeper, I have no doubt. Well, I give you a minute by your own clock."

The man looked about him in a perplexed indecision, and Dyson felt that it was time to be bold.

"Look here, Travers, the time is nearly up. You have heard of Q, I think. Remember, I hold your life in my hands. Now!"

Dyson was shocked at the result of his own audacity. The man shrank and shrivelled in terror, the sweat poured down a face of ashy white, and he held up his hands before him.

"Mr. Davies, Mr. Davies, don't say that – don't for Heaven's sake. I didn't know you at first, I didn't indeed. Good God! Mr. Davies, you wouldn't ruin me? I'll get it in a moment."

"You had better not lose any more time."

The man slunk piteously out of his own shop, and went into a back parlour. Dyson heard his trembling fingers fumbling with a bunch of keys, and the creak of an opening box. He came back presently with a small package neatly tied up in brown paper in his hands, and, still full of terror, handed it to Dyson.

"I'm glad to be rid of it," he said. "I'll take no more jobs of this sort."

Dyson took the parcel and his stick, and walked out of the shop with a nod, turning round as he passed the door. Travers had sunk into his seat, his face still white with terror, with one hand over his eyes, and Dyson speculated a good deal as he walked rapidly away as to what queer chords those could be on which he had played so roughly. He hailed the first hansom he could see and drove home, and when he had lit his hanging lamp, and laid his parcel on the table, he paused for a moment, wondering on what strange thing the lamplight would soon shine. He locked his door, and cut the strings, and unfolded the paper layer after layer, and came at last to a small wooden box, simply but solidly made. There was no lock, and Dyson had simply to raise the lid, and as he did so he drew a long breath and started back. The lamp seemed to glimmer feebly like a single candle, but the whole room blazed with light – and not with light alone, but with a thousand colours, with all the glories of some painted window; and upon the walls of his room and on the familiar furniture, the glow flamed back and seemed to flow again to its source, the little wooden box. For there upon a bed of soft wool lay the most splendid jewel, a jewel such as Dyson had never dreamed of, and within it shone the blue of far skies, and the green of the sea by the shore, and the red of the ruby, and deep violet rays, and in the middle of all it seemed aflame as if a fountain of fire rose up, and fell, and rose again with sparks like stars for drops. Dyson gave a long deep sigh, and dropped into his chair, and put his hands over his eyes to think. The jewel was like an opal, but from a long experience of the shop-windows he knew there was no such thing as an opal one-quarter or one-eighth of its size. He looked at the stone again, with a feeling that was almost awe, and placed it gently on the table under the lamp, and watched the wonderful flame that shone and sparkled in its centre, and then turned to the box, curious to know whether it might contain other marvels. He lifted the bed of wool on which the opal had reclined, and saw beneath, no more jewels, but a little old pocket-book, worn and shabby with use. Dyson opened it at the first leaf, and dropped the book again appalled. He had read the name of the owner, neatly written in blue ink:

Steven Black, m. d.,
Oranmore,
Devon Road,
Harlesden.

It was several minutes before Dyson could bring himself to open the book a second time; he remembered the wretched exile in his garret; and his strange talk, and the memory too of the face he had seen at the window, and of what the specialist had said, surged up in his mind, and as he held his finger on the cover, he shivered, dreading what might be written within. When at last he held it in his hand, and turned the pages, he found that the first two leaves were blank, but the third was covered with clear, minute writing, and Dyson began to read with the light of the opal flaming in his eyes.

Chapter V

"EVER SINCE I was a young man" – the record began – "I devoted all my leisure and a good deal of time that ought to have been given to other studies to the investigation of curious and obscure branches of knowledge. What are commonly called the pleasures of life had never any attractions for me, and I lived alone in London, avoiding my fellow-students, and in my turn avoided by them as a man self-absorbed and unsympathetic. So long as I could gratify my desire of knowledge of a peculiar kind, knowledge of which the very existence is a profound secret to most men, I was intensely happy, and I have often spent whole nights sitting in the darkness of my room, and thinking of the strange world on the brink of which I trod. My professional studies, however, and the necessity of obtaining a degree, for some time forced my more obscure employment into the background, and soon after I had qualified I met Agnes, who became my wife. We took a new house in this remote suburb, and I began the regular routine of a sober practice, and for some months lived happily enough, sharing in the life about me, and only thinking at odd intervals of that occult science which had once fascinated my whole being. I had learnt enough of the paths I had begun to tread to know that they were beyond all expression difficult and dangerous, that to persevere meant in all probability the wreck of a life, and that they led to regions so terrible, that the mind of man shrinks appalled at the very thought. Moreover, the quiet and the peace I had enjoyed since my marriage had wiled me away to a great extent from places where I knew no peace could dwell. But suddenly – I think indeed it was the work of a single night, as I lay awake on my bed gazing into the darkness – suddenly, I say, the old desire, the former longing, returned, and returned with a force that had been intensified ten times by its absence; and when the day dawned and I looked out of the window, and saw with haggard eyes the sunrise in the east, I knew that my doom had been pronounced; that as I had gone far, so now I must go farther with unfaltering steps. I turned to the bed where my wife was sleeping peacefully, and lay down again, weeping bitter tears, for the sun had set on our happy life and had risen with a dawn of terror to us both. I will not set down here in minute detail what followed; outwardly I went about the day's labour as before, saying nothing to my wife. But she soon saw that I had changed; I spent my spare time in a room which I had fitted up as a laboratory, and often I crept upstairs in the grey dawn of the morning, when the light of many lamps still glowed over London; and each night I had stolen a step nearer to that great abyss which I was to bridge over, the gulf between the world of consciousness and the world of matter. My experiments were many and complicated in their nature, and it was some months before I realized whither they all pointed, and when this was borne in upon me in a moment's time, I felt my face whiten and my heart still within me. But the power to draw back, the power to stand before the doors that now opened wide before me and not to enter in, had long ago been absent; the way was closed, and I could only pass onward. My position was as utterly hopeless as that of the prisoner in an utter dungeon, whose only light is that of the dungeon above him; the doors were shut and escape was impossible. Experiment after experiment gave the same result, and I knew, and shrank even as the thought passed through my mind, that in the work I had to do there must be elements which no laboratory could furnish, which no scales could ever measure. In that work, from which even I doubted to escape with life, life itself must enter; from some human being there must be drawn that essence which men call the soul, and in its place (for in the scheme of the world there is no vacant chamber) – in its place would enter in what the lips can hardly utter, what the mind cannot conceive without a horror more awful than the horror of death itself. And when I knew this, I knew also on whom this fate would fall; I looked into my wife's eyes. Even at that hour, if I had gone out and taken a rope and hanged myself, I might have escaped, and she also, but in no other way. At last I told her all. She shuddered, and wept, and called on her dead mother for help, and asked me if I had no mercy, and I could only sigh. I concealed nothing from her; I told her what she would become, and what would enter in where her life had been; I told her of all the shame and of all the horror. You who will read this when I am dead – if indeed I allow this record to survive, – you who have opened the box and have seen what lies there, if you could understand what lies hidden in that opal! For one night my wife consented to what I asked of her, consented with the tears running down her beautiful face, and hot shame flushing red over her neck and breast, consented to undergo this for me. I threw open the window, and we looked together at the sky and the dark earth for the last time; it was a fine star-light night, and there was a pleasant breeze blowing, and I kissed her on her lips, and her tears ran down upon my face. That night she came down to my laboratory, and there, with shutters bolted and barred down, with curtains drawn thick and close, so that the very stars might be shut out from the sight of that room, while the crucible hissed and boiled over the lamp, I did what had to be done, and led out what was no longer a woman. But on the table the opal flamed and sparkled with such light as no eyes of man have ever gazed on, and the rays of the flame that was within it flashed and glittered, and shone even to my heart. My wife had only asked one thing of me; that when there came at last what I had told her, I would kill her. I have kept that promise."

There was nothing more. Dyson let the little pocket-book fall, and turned and looked again at the opal with its flaming inmost light, and then with unutterable irresistible horror surging up in his heart, grasped the jewel, and flung it on the ground, and trampled it beneath his heel. His face was white with terror as he turned away, and for a moment stood sick and trembling, and then with a start he leapt across the room and steadied himself against the door. There was an angry hiss, as of steam escaping under great pressure, and as he gazed, motionless, a volume of heavy yellow smoke was slowly issuing from the very centre of the jewel, and wreathing itself in snake-like coils above it. And then a thin white flame burst forth from the smoke, and shot up into the air and vanished; and on the ground there lay a thing like a cinder, black and crumbling to the touch.

If you enjoyed this, you might also like...
The Cone, see page 322
The Time Machine, see page 300

The Watcher

J. Sheridan Le Fanu

IT IS NOW more than fifty years since the occurrences which I am about to relate caused a strange sensation in the gay society of Dublin. The fashionable world, however, is no recorder of traditions; the memory of selfishness seldom reaches far; and the events which occasionally disturb the polite monotony of its pleasant and heartless progress, however stamped with the characters of misery and horror, scarcely outlive the gossip of a season, and (except, perhaps, in the remembrance of a few more directly interested in the consequences of the catastrophe) are in a little time lost to the recollection of all. The appetite for scandal, or for horror, has been sated; the incident can yield no more of interest or novelty; curiosity, frustrated by impenetrable mystery, gives over the pursuit in despair; the tale has ceased to be new, grows stale and flat; and so, in a few years, inquiry subsides into indifference.

Somewhere about the year 1794, the younger brother of a certain baronet, whom I shall call Sir James Barton, returned to Dublin. He had served in the navy with some distinction, having commanded one of his Majesty's frigates during the greater part of the American war. Captain Barton was now apparently some two or three-and-forty years of age. He was an intelligent and agreeable companion, when he chose it, though generally reserved, and occasionally even moody. In society, however, he deported himself as a man of the world and a gentleman. He had not contracted any of the noisy brusqueness sometimes acquired at sea; on the contrary, his manners were remarkably easy, quiet, and even polished. He was in person about the middle size, and somewhat strongly formed; his countenance was marked with the lines of thought, and on the whole wore an expression of gravity and even of melancholy. Being, however, as we have said, a man of perfect breeding, as well as of affluent circumstances and good family, he had, of course, ready access to the best society of the metropolis, without the necessity of any other credentials. In his personal habits Captain Barton was economical. He occupied lodgings in one of the then fashionable streets in the south side of the town, kept but one horse and one servant, and though a reputed free-thinker, he lived an orderly and moral life, indulging neither in gaming, drinking, nor any other vicious pursuit, living very much to himself, without forming any intimacies, or choosing any companions, and appearing to mix in gay society rather for the sake of its bustle and distraction, than for any opportunities which it offered of interchanging either thoughts or feelings with its votaries. Barton was therefore pronounced a saving, prudent, unsocial sort of a fellow, who bid fair to maintain his celibacy alike against stratagem and assault, and was likely to live to a good old age, die rich and leave his money to a hospital.

It was soon apparent, however, that the nature of Captain Barton's plans had been totally misconceived. A young lady, whom we shall call Miss Montague, was at this time introduced into the fashionable world of Dublin by her aunt, the Dowager Lady

Rochdale. Miss Montague was decidedly pretty and accomplished, and having some natural cleverness, and a great deal of gaiety, became for a while the reigning toast. Her popularity, however, gained her, for a time, nothing more than that unsubstantial admiration which, however pleasant as an incense to vanity, is by no means necessarily antecedent to matrimony, for, unhappily for the young lady in question, it was an understood thing, that, beyond her personal attractions, she had no kind of earthly provision. Such being the state of affairs, it will readily be believed that no little surprise was consequent upon the appearance of Captain Barton as the avowed lover of the penniless Miss Montague.

His suit prospered, as might have been expected, and in a short time it was confidentially communicated by old Lady Rochdale to each of her hundred and fifty particular friends in succession, that Captain Barton had actually tendered proposals of marriage, with her approbation, to her niece, Miss Montague, who had, moreover, accepted the offer of his hand, conditionally upon the consent of her father, who was then upon his homeward voyage from India, and expected in two or three months at furthest. About his consent there could be no doubt. The delay, therefore, was one merely of form; they were looked upon as absolutely engaged, and Lady Rochdale, with a vigour of old-fashioned decorum with which her niece would, no doubt, gladly have dispensed, withdrew her thenceforward from all further participation in the gaieties of the town. Captain Barton was a constant visitor as well as a frequent guest at the house, and was permitted all the privileges and intimacy which a betrothed suitor is usually accorded. Such was the relation of parties, when the mysterious circumstances which darken this narrative with inexplicable melancholy first began to unfold themselves.

Lady Rochdale resided in a handsome mansion at the north side of Dublin, and Captain Barton's lodgings, as we have already said, were situated at the south. The distance intervening was considerable, and it was Captain Barton's habit generally to walk home without an attendant, as often as he passed the evening with the old lady and her fair charge. His shortest way in such nocturnal walks lay, for a considerable space, through a line of streets which had as yet been merely laid out, and little more than the foundations of the houses constructed. One night, shortly after his engagement with Miss Montague had commenced, he happened to remain unusually late, in company only with her and Lady Rochdale. The conversation had turned upon the evidences of revelation, which he had disputed with the callous scepticism of a confirmed infidel. What were called "French principles" had, in those days, found their way a good deal into fashionable society, especially that portion of it which professed allegiance to Whiggism, and neither the old lady nor her charge was so perfectly free from the taint as to look upon Captain Barton's views as any serious objection to the proposed union. The discussion had degenerated into one upon the supernatural and the marvellous, in which he had pursued precisely the same line of argument and ridicule. In all this, it is but true to state, Captain Barton was guilty of no affectation; the doctrines upon which he insisted were, in reality, but too truly the basis of his own fixed belief, if so it might be called; and perhaps not the least strange of the many strange circumstances connected with this narrative, was the fact that the subject of the fearful influences we are about to describe was himself, from the deliberate conviction of years, an utter disbeliever in what are usually termed preternatural agencies.

It was considerably past midnight when Mr. Barton took his leave, and set out upon his solitary walk homeward. He rapidly reached the lonely road, with its unfinished dwarf walls tracing the foundations of the projected rows of houses on either side. The moon was shining mistily, and its imperfect light made the road he trod but additionally dreary; that utter silence, which has in it something indefinably exciting, reigned there, and made the sound of his steps, which alone broke it, unnaturally loud and distinct. He had proceeded thus some way, when on a sudden he heard other footsteps, pattering at a measured pace, and, as it seemed, about two score steps behind him. The suspicion of being dogged is at all times unpleasant; it is, however, especially so in a spot so desolate and lonely: and this suspicion became so strong in the mind of Captain Barton, that he abruptly turned about to confront his pursuers, but, though there was quite sufficient moonlight to disclose any object upon the road he had traversed, no form of any kind was visible.

The steps he had heard could not have been the reverberation of his own, for he stamped his foot upon the ground, and walked briskly up and down, in the vain attempt to wake an echo. Though by no means a fanciful person, he was at last compelled to charge the sounds upon his imagination, and treat them as an illusion. Thus satisfying himself, he resumed his walk, and before he had proceeded a dozen paces, the mysterious footfalls were again audible from behind, and this time, as if with the special design of showing that the sounds were not the responses of an echo, the steps sometimes slackened nearly to a halt, and sometimes hurried for six or eight strides to a run, and again abated to a walk.

Captain Barton, as before, turned suddenly round, and with the same result; no object was visible above the deserted level of the road. He walked back over the same ground, determined that, whatever might have been the cause of the sounds which had so disconcerted him, it should not escape his search; the endeavour, however, was unrewarded. In spite of all his scepticism, he felt something like a superstitious fear stealing fast upon him, and, with these unwonted and uncomfortable sensations, he once more turned and pursued his way. There was no repetition of these haunting sounds, until he had reached the point where he had last stopped to retrace his steps. Here they were resumed, and with sudden starts of running, which threatened to bring the unseen pursuer close up to the alarmed pedestrian. Captain Barton arrested his course as formerly; the unaccountable nature of the occurrence filled him with vague and almost horrible sensations, and, yielding to the excitement he felt gaining upon him, he shouted, sternly, "Who goes there?"

The sound of one's own voice, thus exerted, in utter solitude, and followed by total silence, has in it something unpleasantly exciting, and he felt a degree of nervousness which, perhaps, from no cause had he ever known before. To the very end of this solitary street the steps pursued him, and it required a strong effort of stubborn pride on his part to resist the impulse that prompted him every moment to run for safety at the top of his speed. It was not until he had reached his lodging, and sat by his own fireside, that he felt sufficiently reassured to arrange and reconsider in his own mind the occurrences which had so discomposed him: so little a matter, after all, is sufficient to upset the pride of scepticism, and vindicate the old simple laws of nature within us.

Mr. Barton was next morning sitting at a late breakfast, reflecting upon the incidents of the previous night, with more of inquisitiveness than awe – so speedily do gloomy impressions upon the fancy disappear under the cheerful influences of day – when a letter just delivered by the postman was placed upon the table before him. There was nothing remarkable in the address of this missive, except that it was written in a hand which he did not know – perhaps it was disguised – for the tall narrow characters were sloped backward; and with the self-inflicted suspense which we so often see practised in such cases, he puzzled over the inscription for a full minute before he broke the seal. When he did so, he read the following words, written in the same hand:

> *"Mr. Barton, late Captain of the Dolphin, is warned of danger. He will do wisely to avoid — Street – (here the locality of his last night's adventure was named) – if he walks there as usual, he will meet with something bad. Let him take warning, once for all, for he has good reason to dread The Watcher."*

Captain Barton read and re-read this strange effusion; in every light and in every direction he turned it over and over. He examined the paper on which it was written, and closely scrutinized the handwriting. Defeated here, he turned to the seal; it was nothing but a patch of wax, upon which the accidental impression of a coarse thumb was imperfectly visible. There was not the slightest mark, no clue or indication of any kind, to lead him to even a guess as to its possible origin. The writer's object seemed a friendly one, and yet he subscribed himself as one whom he had "good reason to dread." Altogether, the letter, its author, and its real purpose, were to him an inexplicable puzzle, and one, moreover, unpleasantly suggestive, in his mind, of associations connected with the last night's adventure.

In obedience to some feeling – perhaps of pride – Mr. Barton did not communicate, even to his intended bride, the occurrences which we have just detailed. Trifling as they might appear, they had in reality most disagreeably affected his imagination, and he cared not to disclose, even to the young lady in question, what she might possibly look upon as evidences of weakness. The letter might very well be but a hoax, and the mysterious footfall but a delusion of his fancy. But although he affected to treat the whole affair as unworthy of a thought, it yet haunted him pertinaciously, tormenting him with perplexing doubts, and depressing him with undefined apprehensions. Certain it is, that for a considerable time afterwards he carefully avoided the street indicated in the letter as the scene of danger.

It was not until about a week after the receipt of the letter which I have transcribed, that anything further occurred to remind Captain Barton of its contents, or to counteract the gradual disappearance from his mind of the disagreeable impressions which he had then received. He was returning one night, after the interval I have stated, from the theatre, which was then situated in Crow Street, and having there handed Miss Montague and Lady Rochdale into their carriage, he loitered for some time with two or three acquaintances. With these, however, he parted close to the College, and pursued his way alone. It was now about one o'clock, and the streets were quite deserted. During the whole of his walk with the companions from whom he had just parted, he had been at times painfully aware of the sound of steps, as it seemed, dogging them on their way. Once or twice he had looked back, in the uneasy anticipation that he was again about to experience the same mysterious annoyances which had so much disconcerted him a week before, and earnestly hoping that he might see some form from whom the sounds might naturally proceed. But the street was deserted; no form was visible. Proceeding now quite alone upon his homeward way, he grew really nervous and uncomfortable, as he became sensible, with increased distinctness, of the well-known and now absolutely dreaded sounds.

By the side of the dead wall which bounded the College Park, the sounds followed, recommencing almost simultaneously with his own steps. The same unequal pace, sometimes slow, sometimes, for a score yards or so, quickened to a run, was audible from behind him. Again and again he turned, quickly and stealthily he glanced over his shoulder almost at every half-dozen steps; but no one was visible. The horrors of this intangible and unseen persecution became gradually all but intolerable; and when at last he reached his home his nerves were strung to such a pitch of excitement that he could not rest, and did not attempt even to lie down until after the daylight had broken.

He was awakened by a knock at his chamber-door, and his servant entering, handed him several letters which had just been received by the early post. One among them instantly arrested his attention; a single glance at the direction aroused him thoroughly. He at once recognized its character, and read as follows:

> "You may as well think, Captain Barton, to escape from your own shadow as from me; do what you may, I will see you as often as I please, and you shall see me, for I do not want to hide myself, as you fancy. Do not let it trouble your rest, Captain Barton; for, with a good conscience, what need you fear from the eye of The Watcher?"

It is scarcely necessary to dwell upon the feelings elicited by a perusal of this strange communication. Captain Barton was observed to be unusually absent and out of spirits for several days afterwards; but no one divined the cause. Whatever he might think as to the phantom steps which followed him, there could be no possible illusion about the letters he had received; and, to say the least of it, their immediate sequence upon the mysterious sounds which had haunted him was an odd coincidence. The whole circumstance, in his own mind, was vaguely and instinctively connected with certain passages in his past life, which, of all others, he hated to remember.

It so happened that just about this time, in addition to his approaching nuptials, Captain Barton had fortunately, perhaps, for himself, some business of an engrossing kind connected with the adjustment of a large and long-litigated claim upon certain properties. The hurry and excitement of business had its natural effect in gradually dispelling the marked gloom which had for a time occasionally oppressed him, and in a little while his spirits had entirely resumed their accustomed tone.

During all this period, however, he was occasionally dismayed by indistinct and half-heard repetitions of the same annoyance, and that in lonely places, in the day time as well as after nightfall. These renewals of the strange impressions from which he had suffered so much were, however, desultory and faint, insomuch that often he really could not, to his own satisfaction, distinguish between them and the mere suggestions of an excited imagination. One evening he walked down to the House of Commons with a Mr. Norcott, a Member. As they walked down together he was observed to become absent and silent, and to a degree so marked as scarcely to consist with good breeding; and this, in one who was obviously in all his habits so perfectly a gentleman, seemed to argue the pressure of some urgent and absorbing anxiety. It was afterwards known that, during the whole of that walk, he had heard the well-known footsteps dogging him as he proceeded. This, however, was the last time he suffered from this phase of the persecution of which he was already the anxious victim. A new and a very different one was about to be presented.

Of the new series of impressions which were afterwards gradually to work out his destiny, that evening disclosed the first; and but for its relation to the train of events which followed, the incident would scarcely have been remembered by any one. As they were walking in at the passage, a man (of whom his friend could afterwards remember only that he was short in stature, looked like a foreigner, and wore a kind of travelling-cap) walked very rapidly, and, as if under some fierce excitement, directly towards them, muttering to himself fast and vehemently the while. This odd-looking person proceeded straight toward Barton, who was foremost, and halted, regarding him for a moment or two with a look of menace and fury almost maniacal; and then turning about as abruptly, he walked before them at the same agitated pace, and disappeared by a side passage. Norcott distinctly remembered being a good deal shocked at the countenance and bearing of this man, which indeed irresistibly impressed him with an undefined sense of danger, such as he never felt before or since from the presence of anything human; but these sensations were far from amounting to anything so disconcerting as to flurry or excite him – he had seen only a singularly evil countenance, agitated, as it seemed, with the excitement of madness. He was absolutely astonished, however, at the effect of this apparition upon Captain Barton. He knew him to be a man of proved courage and coolness in real danger, a circumstance which made his conduct upon this occasion the more conspicuously odd. He recoiled a step or two as the stranger advanced, and clutched his companion's arm in silence, with a spasm of agony or terror; and then, as the figure disappeared, shoving him roughly back, he followed it for a few paces, stopped in great disorder, and sat down upon a form. A countenance more ghastly and haggard it was impossible to fancy.

"For God's sake, Barton, what is the matter?" said Norcott, really alarmed at his friend's appearance. "You're not hurt, are you? nor unwell? What is it?"

"What did he say? I did not hear it. What was it?" asked Barton, wholly disregarding the question.

"Tut, tut, nonsense!" said Norcott, greatly surprised; "who cares what the fellow said? You are unwell, Barton, decidedly unwell; let me call a coach."

"Unwell! Yes, no, not exactly unwell," he said, evidently making an effort to recover his self-possession; "but, to say the truth, I am fatigued, a little overworked, and perhaps over anxious. You know I have been in Chancery, and the winding up of a suit is always a nervous affair. I have felt uncomfortable all this evening; but I am better now. Come, come, shall we go on?"

"No, no. Take my advice, Barton, and go home; you really do need rest; you are looking absolutely ill. I really do insist on your allowing me to see you home," replied his companion.

It was obvious that Barton was not himself disinclined to be persuaded. He accordingly took his leave, politely declining his friend's offered escort. Notwithstanding the few commonplace regrets which Norcott had expressed, it was plain that he was just as little deceived as Barton himself by the extempore plea of illness with which he had accounted for the strange exhibition, and that he even then suspected some lurking mystery in the matter.

Norcott called next day at Barton's lodgings, to inquire for him, and learned from the servant that he had not left his room since his return the night before; but that he was not seriously indisposed, and hoped to be out again in a few days. That evening he sent for Doctor Richards, then in large and fashionable practice in Dublin, and their interview was, it is said, an odd one.

He entered into a detail of his own symptoms in an abstracted and desultory kind of way, which seemed to argue a strange want of interest in his own cure, and, at all events, made it manifest that there was some topic engaging his mind of more engrossing importance than his present ailment. He complained of occasional palpitations, and headache. Doctor Richards asked him, among other questions, whether there was any irritating circumstance or anxiety to account for it. This he denied quickly and peevishly; and the physician thereupon declared his opinion, that there was nothing amiss except some slight derangement of the digestion, for which he accordingly wrote a prescription, and was about to withdraw, when Mr. Barton, with the air of a man who suddenly recollects a topic which had nearly escaped him, recalled him.

"I beg your pardon, doctor, but I had really almost forgot; will you permit me to ask you two or three medical questions? – rather odd ones, perhaps, but as a wager depends upon their solution, you will, I hope, excuse my unreasonableness."

The physician readily undertook to satisfy the inquirer.

Barton seemed to have some difficulty about opening the proposed interrogatories, for he was silent for a minute, then walked to his book-case and returned as he had gone; at last he sat down, and said,—

"You'll think them very childish questions, but I can't recover my wager without a decision; so I must put them. I want to know first about lock-jaw. If a man actually has had that complaint, and appears to have died of it – so that in fact a physician of average skill pronounces him actually dead – may he, after all, recover?"

Doctor Richards smiled, and shook his head.

"But – but a blunder may be made," resumed Barton. "Suppose an ignorant pretender to medical skill; may he be so deceived by any stage of the complaint, as to mistake what is only a part of the progress of the disease, for death itself?"

"No one who had ever seen death," answered he, "could mistake it in the case of lock-jaw."

Barton mused for a few minutes. "I am going to ask you a question, perhaps still more childish; but first tell me, are not the regulations of foreign hospitals, such as those of, let us say, Lisbon, very lax and bungling? May not all kinds of blunders and slips occur in their entries of names, and so forth?"

Doctor Richards professed his inability to answer that query.

"Well, then, doctor, here is the last of my questions. You will probably laugh at it; but it must out nevertheless. Is there any disease, in all the range of human maladies, which would have the effect of perceptibly contracting the stature, and the whole frame – causing the man to shrink in all his proportions, and yet to preserve his exact resemblance to himself in every particular – with the one exception, his height and bulk; any disease, mark, no matter how rare, how little believed in, generally, which could possibly result in producing such an effect?"

The physician replied with a smile, and a very decided negative.

"Tell me, then," said Barton, abruptly, "if a man be in reasonable fear of assault from a lunatic who is at large, can he not procure a warrant for his arrest and detention?"

"Really, that is more a lawyer's question than one in my way," replied Doctor Richards; "but I believe, on applying to a magistrate, such a course would be directed."

The physician then took his leave; but, just as he reached the hall-door, remembered that he had left his cane upstairs, and returned. His reappearance was awkward, for a piece of paper, which he recognized as his own prescription, was slowly burning upon the fire, and Barton sitting close by with an expression of settled gloom and dismay. Doctor Richards had too much tact to appear to observe what presented itself; but he had seen quite enough to assure him that the mind, and not the body, of Captain Barton was in reality the seat of his sufferings.

A few days afterwards, the following advertisement appeared in the Dublin newspapers:

"If Sylvester Yelland, formerly a foremast man on board his Majesty's frigate Dolphin, or his nearest of kin, will apply to Mr. Robery Smith, solicitor, at his office, Dame Street, he or they may hear of something greatly to his or their advantage. Admission may be had at any hour up to twelve o'clock at night for the next fortnight, should parties desire to avoid observation; and the strictest secrecy, as to all communications intended to be confidential, shall be honourably observed."

The Dolphin, as we have mentioned, was the vessel which Captain Barton had commanded; and this circumstance, connected with the extraordinary exertions made by the circulation of hand-bills, etc., as well as by repeated advertisements, to secure for this strange notice the utmost possible publicity, suggested to Doctor Richards the idea that Captain Barton's extreme uneasiness was somehow connected with the individual to whom the advertisement was addressed, and he himself the author of it. This, however, it is needless to add, was no more than a conjecture. No information whatsoever, as to the real purpose of the advertisement itself, was divulged by the agent, nor yet any hint as to who his employer might be.

Mr. Barton, although he had latterly begun to earn for himself the character of a hypochondriac, was yet very far from deserving it. Though by no means lively, he had yet, naturally, what are termed "even spirits," and was not subject to continual depressions. He soon, therefore, began to return to his former habits; and one of the earliest symptoms of this healthier tone of spirits was his appearing at a grand dinner of the Freemasons, of which worthy fraternity he was himself a brother. Barton, who had been at first gloomy and abstracted, drank much more freely than was his wont – possibly with the purpose of dispelling his own secret anxieties – and under the influence of good wine, and pleasant company, became gradually (unlike his usual self) talkative, and even noisy. It was under this unwonted excitement that he left his company at about half-past ten o'clock; and as conviviality is a strong incentive to gallantry, it occurred to him to proceed forthwith to Lady Rochdale's, and pass the remainder of the evening with her and his destined bride.

Accordingly, he was soon at — Street, and chatting gaily with the ladies. It is not to be supposed that Captain Barton had exceeded the limits which propriety prescribes to good fellowship; he had merely taken enough of wine to raise his spirits, without, however, in the least degree unsteadying his mind, or affecting his manners. With this undue elevation of spirits had supervened an entire oblivion or contempt of those undefined apprehensions which had for so long weighed upon his mind, and to a certain extent estranged him from society; but as the night wore away, and his artificial gaiety began to flag, these painful feelings gradually intruded themselves again, and he grew abstracted and anxious as heretofore. He took his leave at length, with an unpleasant foreboding of some coming mischief, and with a mind haunted with a thousand mysterious apprehensions, such as, even while he acutely felt their pressure, he, nevertheless, inwardly strove, or affected to contemn.

It was his proud defiance of what he considered to be his own weakness which prompted him upon this occasion to the course which brought about the adventure which we are now about to relate. Mr. Barton might have easily called a coach, but he was conscious that his strong inclination to do so proceeded from no cause other than what he desperately persisted in representing to himself to be his own superstitious tremors. He might also have returned home by a route different from that against which he had been warned by his mysterious correspondent; but for the same reason he dismissed this idea also, and with a dogged and half desperate resolution to force matters to a crisis of some kind, to see if there were any reality in the causes of his former suffering, and if not, satisfactorily to bring their delusiveness to the proof, he determined to follow precisely the course which he had trodden upon the night so painfully memorable in his own mind as that on which his strange persecution had commenced. Though, sooth to say, the pilot who for the first time steers his vessel under the muzzles of a hostile battery never felt his resolution more severely tasked than did Captain Barton, as he breathlessly pursued this solitary path; a path which, spite of every effort of scepticism and reason, he felt to be, as respected him, infested by a malignant influence.

He pursued his way steadily and rapidly, scarcely breathing from intensity of suspense; he, however, was troubled by no renewal of the dreaded footsteps, and was beginning to feel a return of confidence, as, more than three-fourths of the way being accomplished with impunity, he approached the long line of twinkling oil lamps which indicated the frequented streets. This feeling of self-congratulation was, however, but momentary. The report of a musket at some two hundred yards behind him, and the whistle of a bullet close to his head, disagreeably and startlingly dispelled it. His first impulse was to retrace his steps in pursuit of the assassin; but the road on either side was, as we have said, embarrassed by the foundations of a street, beyond which extended waste fields, full of rubbish and neglected lime and brick kilns, and all now as utterly silent as though no sound had ever disturbed their dark and unsightly solitude. The futility of attempting, single-handed, under such circumstances, a search for the murderer, was apparent, especially as no further sound whatever was audible to direct his pursuit.

With the tumultuous sensations of one whose life had just been exposed to a murderous attempt, and whose escape has been the narrowest possible, Captain Barton turned, and without, however, quickening his pace actually to a run, hurriedly pursued his way. He had turned, as we have said, after a pause of a few seconds, and had just commenced his rapid retreat, when on a sudden he met the well-remembered little man in the fur cap. The encounter was but momentary. The figure was walking at the same exaggerated pace, and with the same strange air of menace as before; and as it passed him, he thought he heard it say, in a furious whisper, "Still alive, still alive!"

The state of Mr. Barton's spirits began now to work a corresponding alteration in his health and looks, and to such a degree that it was impossible that the change should escape general remark. For some reasons, known but to himself, he took no step whatsoever to bring the attempt upon his life, which he had so narrowly escaped, under the notice of the authorities; on the contrary, he kept it jealously to himself; and it was not for many weeks after the occurrence that he mentioned it, and then in strict confidence to a gentleman, the torments of his mind at last compelled him to consult a friend.

Spite of his blue devils, however, poor Barton, having no satisfactory reason to render to the public for any undue remissness in the attentions which his relation to Miss Montague required, was obliged to exert himself, and present to the world a confident and cheerful bearing. The true source of his sufferings, and every circumstance connected with them, he guarded with a reserve so jealous, that it seemed dictated by at least a suspicion that the origin of his strange persecution was known to himself, and that it was of a nature which, upon his own account, he could not or dare not disclose.

The mind thus turned in upon itself, and constantly occupied with a haunting anxiety which it dared not reveal, or confide to any human breast, became daily more excited; and, of course, more vividly impressible, by a system of attack which operated through the nervous system; and in this state he was destined to sustain, with increasing frequency, the stealthy visitations of that apparition, which from the first had seemed to possess so unearthly and terrible a hold upon his imagination.

* * *

It was about this time that Captain Barton called upon the then celebrated preacher, Doctor Macklin, with whom he had a slight acquaintance; and an extraordinary conversation ensued. The divine was seated in his chambers in college, surrounded with works upon his favourite pursuit and deep in theology, when Barton was announced. There was something at once embarrassed and excited in his manner, which, along with his wan and haggard countenance, impressed the student with the unpleasant consciousness that his visitor must have recently suffered terribly indeed to account for an alteration so striking, so shocking.

After the usual interchange of polite greeting, and a few commonplace remarks, Captain Barton, who obviously perceived the surprise which his visit had excited, and which Doctor Macklin was unable wholly to conceal, interrupted a brief pause by remarking,—

"This is a strange call, Doctor Macklin, perhaps scarcely warranted by an acquaintance so slight as mine with you. I should not, under ordinary circumstances, have ventured to disturb you, but my visit is neither an idle nor impertinent intrusion. I am sure you will not so account it, when—"

Doctor Macklin interrupted him with assurances, such as good breeding suggested, and Barton resumed,—

"I am come to task your patience by asking your advice. When I say your patience, I might, indeed, say more; I might have said your humanity, your compassion; for I have been, and am a great sufferer."

"My dear sir," replied the churchman, "it will, indeed, afford me infinite gratification if I can give you comfort in any distress of mind, but – but—"

"I know what you would say," resumed Barton, quickly. "I am an unbeliever, and, therefore, incapable of deriving help from religion, but don't take that for granted. At least you must not assume that, however unsettled my convictions may be, I do not feel a deep, a very deep, interest in the subject. Circumstances have lately forced it upon my attention in such a way as to compel me to review the whole question in a more candid and teachable spirit, I believe, than I ever studied it in before."

"Your difficulties, I take it for granted, refer to the evidences of revelation," suggested the clergyman.

"Why – no – yes; in fact I am ashamed to say I have not considered even my objections sufficiently to state them connectedly; but – but there is one subject on which I feel a peculiar interest."

He paused again, and Doctor Macklin pressed him to proceed.

"The fact is," said Barton, "whatever may be my uncertainty as to the authenticity of what we are taught to call revelation, of one fact I am deeply and horribly convinced: that there does exist beyond this a spiritual world – a system whose workings are generally in mercy hidden from us – a system which may be, and which is sometimes, partially and terribly revealed. I am sure, I know," continued Barton, with increasing excitement, "there is a God – a dreadful God – and that retribution follows guilt. In ways, the most mysterious and stupendous; by agencies, the most inexplicable and terrific; there is a spiritual system – great Heavens, how frightfully I have been convinced! – a system malignant, and inexorable, and omnipotent, under whose persecutions I am, and have been, suffering the torments of the damned! – yes, sir – yes – the fires and frenzy of hell!"

As Barton continued, his agitation became so vehement that the divine was shocked and even alarmed. The wild and excited rapidity with which he spoke, and, above all, the indefinable horror which stamped his features, afforded a contrast to his ordinary cool and unimpassioned self-possession, striking and painful in the last degree.

"My dear sir," said Doctor Macklin, after a brief pause, "I fear you have been suffering much, indeed; but I venture to predict that the depression under which you labour will be found to originate in purely physical causes, and that with a change of air and the aid of a few tonics, your spirits will return, and the tone of your mind be once more cheerful and tranquil as heretofore. There was, after all, more truth than we are quite willing to admit in the classic theories which assigned the undue predominance of any one affection of the mind to the undue action or torpidity of one or other of our bodily organs. Believe me, that a little attention to diet, exercise, and the other essentials of health, under competent direction, will make you as much yourself as you can wish."

"Doctor Macklin," said Barton, with something like a shudder, "I cannot delude myself with such a hope. I have no hope to cling to but one, and that is, that by some other spiritual agency more potent than that which tortures me, it may be combated, and I delivered. If this may not be, I am lost – now and for ever lost."

"But, Mr. Barton, you must remember," urged his companion, "that others have suffered as you have done, and—"

"No, no, no," interrupted he with irritability; "no, sir, I am not a credulous – far from a superstitious man. I have been, perhaps, too much the reverse – too sceptical, too slow of belief; but unless I were one whom no amount of evidence could convince, unless I were to contemn the repeated, the perpetual evidence of my own senses, I am now – now at last constrained to believe I have no escape from the conviction, the overwhelming certainty, that I am haunted and dogged, go where I may, by – by a Demon."

There was an almost preternatural energy of horror in Barton's face, as, with its damp and death-like lineaments turned towards his companion, he thus delivered himself.

"God help you, my poor friend!" said Doctor Macklin, much shocked. "God help you; for, indeed, you are a sufferer, however your sufferings may have been caused."

"Ay, ay, God help me," echoed Barton sternly; "but will He help me? will He help me?"

"Pray to Him; pray in an humble and trusting spirit," said he.

"Pray, pray," echoed he again; "I can't pray; I could as easily move a mountain by an effort of my will. I have not belief enough to pray; there is something within me that will not pray. You prescribe impossibilities – literal impossibilities."

"You will not find it so, if you will but try," said Doctor Macklin.

"Try! I have tried, and the attempt only fills me with confusion and terror. I have tried in vain, and more than in vain. The awful, unutterable idea of eternity and infinity oppresses and maddens my brain, whenever my mind approaches the contemplation of the Creator; I recoil from the effort, scared, confounded, terrified. I tell you, Doctor Macklin, if I am to be saved, it must be by other means. The idea of the Creator is to me intolerable; my mind cannot support it."

"Say, then, my dear sir," urged he, "say how you would have me serve you. What you would learn of me. What can I do or say to relieve you?"

"Listen to me first," replied Captain Barton, with a subdued air, and an evident effort to suppress his excitement; "listen to me while I detail the circumstances of the terrible persecution under which my life has become all but intolerable – a persecution which has made me fear death and the world beyond the grave as much as I have grown to hate existence."

Barton then proceeded to relate the circumstances which we have already detailed, and then continued,—

"This has now become habitual – an accustomed thing. I do not mean the actual seeing him in the flesh; thank God, that at least is not permitted daily. Thank God, from the unutterable horrors of that visitation I have been mercifully allowed intervals of repose, though none of security; but from the consciousness that a malignant spirit is following and watching me wherever I go, I have never, for a single instant, a temporary respite: I am pursued with blasphemies, cries of despair, and appalling hatred; I hear those dreadful sounds called after me as I turn the corners of streets; they come in the night-time while I sit in my chamber alone; they haunt me everywhere, charging me with hideous crimes, and – great God! – threatening me with coming vengeance and eternal misery! Hush! do you hear that?" he cried, with a horrible smile of triumph. "There – there, will that convince you?"

The clergyman felt the chillness of horror irresistibly steal over him, while, during the wail of a sudden gust of wind, he heard, or fancied he heard, the half articulate sounds of rage and derision mingling in their sough.

"Well, what do you think of that?" at length Barton cried, drawing a long breath through his teeth.

"I heard the wind," said Doctor Macklin; "what should I think of it? What is there remarkable about it?"

"The prince of the powers of the air," muttered Barton, with a shudder.

"Tut, tut! my dear sir!" said the student, with an effort to reassure himself; for though it was broad daylight, there was nevertheless something disagreeably contagious in the nervous excitement under which his visitor so obviously suffered. "You must not give way to those wild fancies: you must resist those impulses of the imagination."

"Ay, ay; 'resist the devil, and he will flee from thee,'" said Barton, in the same tone; "but how resist him? Ay, there it is: there is the rub. What – what am I to do? What can I do?"

"My dear sir, this is fancy," said the man of folios; "you are your own tormentor."

"No, no, sir; fancy has no part in it," answered Barton, somewhat sternly. "Fancy, forsooth! Was it that made you, as well as me, hear, but this moment, those appalling accents of hell? Fancy, indeed! No, no."

"But you have seen this person frequently," said the ecclesiastic; "why have you not accosted or secured him? Is it not somewhat precipitate, to say no more, to assume, as you have done, the existence of preternatural agency, when, after all, everything may be easily accountable, if only proper means were taken to sift the matter."

"There are circumstances connected with this – this appearance," said Barton, "which it were needless to disclose, but which to me are proofs of its horrible and unearthly nature. I know that the being who haunts me is not man. I say I know this; I could prove it to your own conviction." He paused for a minute, and then added, "And as to accosting it, I dare not – I could not! When I see it I am powerless; I stand in the gaze of death, in the triumphant presence of preterhuman power and malignity; my strength, and faculties, and memory all forsake me. Oh, God! I fear, sir, you know not what you speak of. Mercy, mercy! heaven have pity on me!"

He leaned his elbow on the table, and passed his hand across his eyes, as if to exclude some image of horror, muttering the last words of the sentence he had just concluded, again and again.

"Dr. Macklin," he said, abruptly raising himself, and looking full upon the clergyman with an imploring eye, "I know you will do for me whatever may be done. You know now fully the circumstances and the nature of the mysterious agency of which I am the victim. I tell you I cannot help myself; I cannot hope to escape; I am utterly passive. I conjure you, then, to weigh my case well, and if anything may be done for me by vicarious supplication, by the intercession of the good, or by any aid or influence whatsoever, I implore of you, I adjure you in the name of the Most High, give me the benefit of that influence, deliver me from the body of this death! Strive for me; pity me! I know you will; you cannot refuse this; it is the purpose and object of my visit. Send me away with some hope, however little – some faint hope of ultimate deliverance, and I will nerve myself to endure, from hour to hour, the hideous dream into which my existence is transformed."

Doctor Macklin assured him that all he could do was to pray earnestly for him, and that so much he would not fail to do. They parted with a hurried and melancholy valediction. Barton hastened to the carriage which awaited him at the door, drew the blinds, and drove away, while Dr. Macklin returned to his chamber, to ruminate at leisure upon the strange interview which had just interrupted his studies.

It was not to be expected that Captain Barton's changed and eccentric habits should long escape remark and discussion. Various were the theories suggested to account for it. Some attributed the alteration to the pressure of secret pecuniary embarrassments; others to a repugnance to fulfil an engagement into which he was presumed to have too precipitately entered; and others, again, to the supposed incipiency of mental disease, which latter, indeed, was the most plausible, as well as the most generally received, of the hypotheses circulated in the gossip of the day.

From the very commencement of this change, at first so gradual in its advances, Miss Montague had, of course, been aware of it. The intimacy involved in their peculiar relation, as well as the near interest which it inspired, afforded, in her case, alike opportunity and motive for the successful exercise of that keen and penetrating observation peculiar to the sex. His visits became, at length, so interrupted, and his manner, while they lasted, so abstracted, strange, and agitated, that Lady Rochdale, after hinting her anxiety and her suspicions more than once, at length distinctly stated her anxiety, and pressed for an explanation. The explanation was given, and although its nature at first relieved the worst solicitudes of the old lady and her niece, yet the circumstances which attended it, and the really dreadful consequences which it obviously threatened as regarded the spirits, and, indeed, the reason, of the now wretched man who made the strange declaration, were enough, upon a little reflection, to fill their minds with perturbation and alarm.

General Montague, the young lady's father, at length arrived. He had himself slightly known Barton, some ten or twelve years previously, and being aware of his fortune and connections, was disposed to regard him as an unexceptionable and indeed a most desirable match for his daughter. He laughed at the story of Barton's supernatural visitations, and lost not a moment in calling upon his intended son-in-law.

"My dear Barton," he continued gaily, after a little conversation, "my sister tells me that you are a victim to blue devils in quite a new and original shape."

Barton changed countenance, and sighed profoundly.

"Come, come; I protest this will never do," continued the General; "you are more like a man on his way to the gallows than to the altar. These devils have made quite a saint of you."

Barton made an effort to change the conversation.

"No, no, it won't do," said his visitor, laughing; "I am resolved to say out what I have to say about this magnificent mock mystery of yours. Come, you must not be angry; but, really, it is too bad to see you, at your time of life, absolutely frightened into good behaviour, like a naughty child, by a bugaboo, and, as far as I can learn, a very particularly contemptible one. Seriously, though, my dear Barton, I have been a good deal annoyed at what they tell me; but, at the same time, thoroughly convinced that there is nothing in the matter that may not be cleared up, with just a little attention and management, within a week at furthest."

"Ah, General, you do not know—" he began.

"Yes, but I do know quite enough to warrant my confidence," interrupted the soldier. "I know that all your annoyance proceeds from the occasional appearance of a certain little man in a cap and great-coat, with a red vest and bad countenance, who follows you about, and pops upon you at the corners of lanes, and throws you into ague fits. Now, my dear fellow, I'll make it my business to catch this mischievous little mountebank, and either beat him into a jelly with my own hands, or have him whipped through the town at the cart's tail."

"If you knew what I know," said Barton, with gloomy agitation, "you would speak very differently. Don't imagine that I am so weak and foolish as to assume, without proof the most overwhelming, the conclusion to which I have been forced. The proofs are here, locked up here." As he spoke, he tapped upon his breast, and with an anxious sigh continued to walk up and down the room.

"Well, well, Barton," said his visitor, "I'll wager a rump and a dozen I collar the ghost, and convince yourself before many days are over."

He was running on in the same strain when he was suddenly arrested, and not a little shocked, by observing Barton, who had approached the window, stagger slowly back, like one who had received a stunning blow – his arm feebly extended towards the street, his face and his very lips white as ashes – while he uttered, "There – there – there!"

General Montague started mechanically to his feet, and, from the window of the drawing-room, saw a figure corresponding, as well as his hurry would permit him to discern, with the description of the person whose appearance so constantly and dreadfully disturbed the repose of his friend. The figure was just turning from the rails of the area upon which it had been leaning, and without waiting to see more, the old gentleman snatched his cane and hat, and rushed down the stairs and into the street, in the furious hope of securing the person, and punishing the audacity of the mysterious stranger. He looked around him, but in vain, for any trace of the form he had himself distinctly beheld. He ran breathlessly to the nearest corner, expecting to see from thence the retreating figure, but no such form was visible. Back and forward, from crossing to crossing, he ran at fault, and it was not until the curious gaze and laughing countenances of the passers-by reminded him of the absurdity of his pursuit, that he checked his hurried pace, lowered his walking-cane from the menacing altitude which he had mechanically given it, adjusted his hat, and walked composedly back again, inwardly vexed and flurried. He found Barton pale and trembling in every joint; they both remained silent, though under emotions very different. At last Barton whispered, "You saw it?"

"It!—him—someone—you mean—to be sure I did," replied Montague, testily. "But where is the good or the harm of seeing him? The fellow runs like a lamplighter. I wanted to catch him, but he had stolen away before I could reach the hall door. However, it is no great matter; next time, I dare say, I'll do better; and, egad, if I once come within reach of him, I'll introduce his shoulders to the weight of my cane, in a way to make him cry peccavi."

Notwithstanding General Montague's undertakings and exhortations, however, Barton continued to suffer from the self-same unexplained cause. Go how, when, or where he would, he was still constantly dogged or confronted by the hateful being who had established over him so dreadful and mysterious an influence; nowhere, and at no time, was he secure against the odious appearance which haunted him with such diabolical perseverance. His depression, misery, and excitement became more settled and alarming every day, and the mental agonies that ceaselessly preyed upon him began at last so sensibly to affect his general health, that Lady Rochdale and General Montague succeeded (without, indeed, much difficulty) in persuading him to try a short tour on the Continent, in the hope that an entire change of scene would, at all events, have the effect of breaking through the influences of local association, which the more sceptical of his friends assumed to be by no means inoperative in suggesting and perpetuating what they conceived to be a mere form of nervous illusion. General Montague, moreover, was persuaded that the figure which haunted his intended son-in-law was by no means the creation of his own imagination, but, on the contrary, a substantial form of flesh and blood, animated by a spiteful and obstinate resolution, perhaps with some murderous object in perspective, to watch and follow the unfortunate gentleman. Even this hypothesis was not a very pleasant one; yet it was plain that if Barton could once be convinced that there was nothing preternatural in the phenomenon, which he had hitherto regarded in that light, the affair would lose all its terrors in his eyes, and wholly cease to exercise upon his health and spirits the baneful influence which it had hitherto done. He therefore reasoned, that if the annoyance were actually escaped from by mere change of scene, it obviously could not have originated in any supernatural agency.

Yielding to their persuasions, Barton left Dublin for England, accompanied by General Montague. They posted rapidly to London, and thence to Dover, whence they took the packet with a fair wind for Calais. The General's confidence in the result of the expedition on Barton's spirits had risen day by day since their departure from the shores of Ireland; for, to the inexpressible relief and delight of the latter, he had not, since then, so much as even once fancied a repetition of those impressions which had, when at home, drawn him gradually down to the very abyss of horror and despair. This exemption from what he had begun to regard as the inevitable condition of his existence, and the sense of security which began to pervade his mind, were inexpressibly delightful; and in the exultation of what he considered his deliverance, he indulged in a thousand happy anticipations for a future into which so lately he had hardly dared to look. In short, both he and his companion secretly congratulated themselves upon the termination of that persecution which had been to its immediate victim a source of such unspeakable agony.

It was a beautiful day, and a crowd of idlers stood upon the jetty to receive the packet, and enjoy the bustle of the new arrivals. Montague walked a few paces in advance of his friend, and as he made his way through the crowd, a little man touched his arm, and said to him, in a broad provincial patois,—

"Monsieur is walking too fast; he will lose his sick comrade in the throng, for, by my faith, the poor gentleman seems to be fainting."

Montague turned quickly, and observed that Barton did indeed look deadly pale. He hastened to his side.

"My poor fellow, are you ill?" he asked anxiously.

The question was unheeded, and twice repeated, ere Barton stammered,—

"I saw him—by —, I saw him!"

"Him! – who? – where? – when did you see him? – where is he?" cried Montague, looking around him.

"I saw him – but he is gone," repeated Barton, faintly.

"But where – where? For God's sake, speak," urged Montague, vehemently.

"It is but this moment – here," said he.

"But what did he look like? – what had he on? – what did he wear? – quick, quick," urged his excited companion, ready to dart among the crowd, and collar the delinquent on the spot.

"He touched your arm – he spoke to you – he pointed to me. God be merciful to me, there is no escape!" said Barton, in the low, subdued tones of intense despair.

Montague had already bustled away in all the flurry of mingled hope and indignation; but though the singular personnel of the stranger who had accosted him was vividly and perfectly impressed upon his recollection, he failed to discover among the crowd even the slightest resemblance to him. After a fruitless search, in which he enlisted the services of several of the bystanders, who aided all the more zealously as they believed he had been robbed, he at length, out of breath and baffled, gave over the attempt.

"Ah, my friend, it won't do," said Barton, with the faint voice and bewildered, ghastly look of one who has been stunned by some mortal shock; "there is no use in contending with it; whatever it is, the dreadful association between me and it is now established; I shall never escape – never, never!"

"Nonsense, nonsense, my dear fellow; don't talk so," said Montague, with something at once of irritation and dismay; "you must not; never mind, I say – never mind, we'll jockey the scoundrel yet."

It was, however, but lost labour to endeavour henceforward to inspire Barton with one ray of hope; he became utterly desponding. This intangible and, as it seemed, utterly inadequate influence was fast destroying his energies of intellect, character, and health. His first object was now to return to Ireland, there, as he believed, and now almost hoped, speedily to die.

To Ireland, accordingly, he came, and one of the first faces he saw upon the shore was again that of his implacable and dreaded persecutor. Barton seemed at last to have lost not only all enjoyment and every hope in existence, but all independence of will besides. He now submitted himself passively to the management of the friends most nearly interested in his welfare. With the apathy of entire despair, he implicitly assented to whatever measures they suggested and advised; and, as a last resource, it was determined to remove him to a house of Lady Rochdale's in the neighbourhood of Clontarf, where, with the advice of his medical attendant (who persisted in his opinion that the whole train of impressions resulted merely from some nervous derangement) it was resolved that he was to confine himself strictly to the house, and to make use only of those apartments which commanded a view of an enclosed yard, the gates of which were to be kept jealously locked. These precautions would at least secure him against the casual appearance of any living form which his excited imagination might possibly confound with the spectre which, as it was contended, his fancy recognized in every figure that bore even a distant or general resemblance to the traits with which he had at first invested it. A month or six weeks' absolute seclusion under these conditions, it was hoped, might, by interrupting the series of these terrible impressions, gradually dispel the predisposing apprehension, and effectually break up the associations which had confirmed the supposed disease, and rendered recovery hopeless. Cheerful society and that of his friends was to be constantly supplied, and on the whole, very sanguine expectations were indulged in, that under this treatment the obstinate hypochondria of the patient might at length give way.

Accompanied, therefore, by Lady Rochdale, General Montague, and his daughter – his own affianced bride – poor Barton, himself never daring to cherish a hope of his ultimate emancipation from the strange horrors under which his life was literally wasting away, took possession of the apartments whose situation protected him against the dreadful intrusions from which he shrank with such unutterable terror.

After a little time, a steady persistence in this system began to manifest its results in a very marked though gradual improvement alike in the health and spirits of the invalid. Not, indeed, that anything at all approaching to complete recovery was yet discernible. On the contrary, to those who had not seen him since the commencement of his strange sufferings, such an alteration would have been apparent as might well have shocked them. The improvement, however, such as it was, was welcomed with gratitude and delight, especially by the poor young lady, whom her attachment to him, as well as her now singularly painful position, consequent on his mysterious and protracted illness, rendered an object of pity scarcely one degree less to be commiserated than himself.

A week passed – a fortnight – a month – and yet no recurrence of the hated visitation had agitated and terrified him as before. The treatment had, so far, been followed by complete success. The chain of association had been broken. The constant pressure upon the overtasked spirits had been removed, and, under these comparatively favourable circumstances, the sense of social community with the world about him, and something of human interest, if not of enjoyment, began to reanimate his mind.

It was about this time that Lady Rochdale, who, like most old ladies of the day, was deep in family receipts, and a great pretender to medical science, being engaged in the concoction of certain unpalatable mixtures of marvellous virtue, despatched her own maid to the kitchen garden with a list of herbs which were there to be carefully culled and brought back to her for the purpose stated. The hand-maiden, however, returned with her task scarce half-completed, and a good deal flurried and alarmed. Her mode of accounting for her precipitate retreat and evident agitation was odd, and to the old lady unpleasantly startling.

It appeared that she had repaired to the kitchen garden, pursuant to her mistress's directions, and had there begun to make the specified selection among the rank and neglected herbs which crowded one corner of the enclosure, and while engaged in this pleasant labour she carelessly sang a fragment of an old song, as she said, "to keep herself company." She was, however, interrupted by a sort of mocking echo of the air she was singing; and looking up, she saw through the old thorn hedge, which surrounded the garden, a singularly ill-looking, little man, whose countenance wore the stamp of menace and malignity, standing close to her at the other side of the hawthorn screen. She described herself as utterly unable to move or speak, while he charged her with a message for Captain Barton, the substance of which she distinctly remembered to have been to the effect that he, Captain Barton, must come abroad as usual, and show himself to his friends out of doors, or else prepare for a visit in his own chamber. On concluding this brief message, the stranger had, with a threatening air, got down into the outer ditch, and seizing the hawthorn stems in his hands, seemed on the point of climbing through the fence, a feat which might have been accomplished without much difficulty. Without, of course, awaiting this result, the girl, throwing down her treasures of thyme and rosemary, had turned and run, with the swiftness of terror, to the house. Lady Rochdale commanded her, on pain of instant dismissal, to observe an absolute silence respecting all that portion of the incident which related to Captain Barton; and, at the same time, directed instant search to be made by her men in the garden and fields adjacent. This measure, however, was attended with the usual unsuccess, and filled with fearful and indefinable misgivings, Lady Rochdale communicated the incident to her brother. The story, however, until long afterwards, went no further, and of course it was jealously guarded from Barton, who continued to mend, though slowly and imperfectly.

Barton now began to walk occasionally in the courtyard which we have mentioned, and which, being surrounded by a high wall, commanded no view beyond its own extent. Here he, therefore, considered himself perfectly secure; and, but for a careless violation of orders by one of the grooms, he might have enjoyed, at least for some time longer, his much-prized immunity. Opening upon the public road, this yard was entered by a wooden gate, with a wicket in it, which was further defended by an iron gate upon the outside. Strict orders had been given to keep them carefully locked; but, in spite of these, it had happened that one day, as Barton was slowly pacing this narrow enclosure, in his accustomed walk, and reaching the further extremity, was turning to retrace his steps, he saw the boarded wicket ajar, and the face of his tormentor immovably looking at him through the iron bars. For a few seconds he stood riveted to the earth, breathless and bloodless, in the fascination of that dreaded gaze, and then fell helplessly upon the pavement.

There was he found a few minutes afterwards, and conveyed to his room, the apartment which he was never afterwards to leave alive. Henceforward, a marked and unaccountable change was observable in the tone of his mind. Captain Barton was now no longer the excited and despairing man he had been before; a strange alteration had passed upon him, an unearthly tranquillity reigned in his mind; it was the anticipated stillness of the grave.

"Montague, my friend, this struggle is nearly ended now," he said, tranquilly, but with a look of fixed and fearful awe. "I have, at last, some comfort from that world of spirits, from which my punishment has come. I know now that my sufferings will be soon over."

Montague pressed him to speak on.

"Yes," said he, in a softened voice, "my punishment is nearly ended. From sorrow perhaps I shall never, in time or eternity, escape; but my agony is almost over. Comfort has been revealed to me, and what remains of my allotted struggle I will bear with submission, even with hope."

"I am glad to hear you speak so tranquilly, my dear fellow," said Montague; "peace and cheerfulness of mind are all you need to make you what you were."

"No, no, I never can be that," said he, mournfully. "I am no longer fit for life. I am soon to die: I do not shrink from death as I did. I am to see him but once again, and then all is ended."

"He said so, then?" suggested Montague.

"He? No, no; good tidings could scarcely come through him; and these were good and welcome; and they came so solemnly and sweetly, with unutterable love and melancholy, such as I could not, without saying more than is needful or fitting, of other long-past scenes and persons, fully explain to you." As Barton said this he shed tears.

"Come, come," said Montague, mistaking the source of his emotions, "you must not give way. What is it, after all, but a pack of dreams and nonsense; or, at worst, the practices of a scheming rascal that enjoys his power of playing upon your nerves, and loves to exert it; a sneaking vagabond that owes you a grudge, and pays it off this way, not daring to try a more manly one."

"A grudge, indeed, he owes me; you say rightly," said Barton, with a sullen shudder; "a grudge as you call it. Oh, God! when the justice of heaven permits the Evil One to carry out a scheme of vengeance, when its execution is committed to the lost and frightful victim of sin, who owes his own ruin to the man, the very man, whom he is commissioned to pursue; then, indeed, the torments and terrors of hell are anticipated on earth. But heaven has dealt mercifully with me: hope has opened to me at last; and if death could come without the dreadful sight I am doomed to see, I would gladly close my eyes this moment upon the world. But though death is welcome, I shrink with an agony you cannot understand; a maddening agony, an actual frenzy of terror, from the last encounter with that – that DEMON, who has drawn me thus to the verge of the chasm, and who is himself to plunge me down. I am to see him again, once more, but under circumstances unutterably more terrific than ever."

As Barton thus spoke, he trembled so violently that Montague was really alarmed at the extremity of his sudden agitation, and hastened to lead him back to the topic which had before seemed to exert so tranquillizing an effect upon his mind.

"It was not a dream," he said, after a time; "I was in a different state, I felt differently and strangely; and yet it was all as real, as clear and vivid, as what I now see and hear; it was a reality."

"And what did you see and hear?" urged his companion.

"When I awakened from the swoon I fell into on seeing him," said Barton, continuing, as if he had not heard the question, "it was slowly, very slowly; I was reclining by the margin of a broad lake, surrounded by misty hills, and a soft, melancholy, rose-coloured light illuminated it all. It was indescribably sad and lonely, and yet more beautiful than any earthly scene. My head was leaning on the lap of a girl, and she was singing a strange and wondrous song, that told, I know not how, whether by words or harmony, of all my life, all that is past, and all that is still to come. And with the song the old feelings that I thought had perished within me came back, and tears flowed from my eyes, partly for the song and its mysterious beauty, and partly for the unearthly sweetness of her voice; yet I know the voice, oh! how well; and I was spell-bound as I listened and looked at the strange and solitary scene, without stirring, almost without breathing, and, alas! alas! without turning my eyes toward the face that I knew was near me, so sweetly powerful was the enchantment that held me. And so, slowly and softly, the song and scene grew fainter, and ever fainter, to my senses, till all was dark and still again. And then I wakened to this world, as you saw, comforted, for I knew that I was forgiven much." Barton wept again long and bitterly.

From this time, as we have said, the prevailing tone of his mind was one of profound and tranquil melancholy. This, however, was not without its interruptions. He was thoroughly impressed with the conviction that he was to experience another and a final visitation, illimitably transcending in horror all he had before experienced. From this anticipated and unknown agony he often shrunk in such paroxysms of abject terror and distraction, as filled the whole household with dismay and superstitious panic. Even those among them who affected to discredit the supposition of preternatural agency in the matter, were often in their secret souls visited during the darkness and solitude of night with qualms and apprehensions which they would not have readily confessed; and none of them attempted to dissuade Barton from the resolution on which he now systematically acted, of shutting himself up in his own apartment. The window-blinds of this room were kept jealously down; and his own man was seldom out of his presence, day or night, his bed being placed in the same chamber.

This man was an attached and respectable servant; and his duties, in addition to those ordinarily imposed upon valets, but which Barton's independent habits generally dispensed with, were to attend carefully to the simple precautions by means of which his master hoped to exclude the dreaded intrusion of the "Watcher," as the strange letter he had at first received had designated his persecutor. And, in addition to attending to these arrangements, which consisted merely in anticipating the possibility of his master's being, through any unscreened window or opened door, exposed to the dreaded influence, the valet was never to suffer him to be for one moment alone: total solitude, even for a minute, had become to him now almost as intolerable as the idea of going abroad into the public ways; it was an instinctive anticipation of what was coming.

It is needless to say, that, under these mysterious and horrible circumstances, no steps were taken toward the fulfilment of that engagement into which he had entered. There was quite disparity enough in point of years, and indeed of habits, between the young lady and Captain Barton, to have precluded anything like very vehement or romantic attachment on her part. Though grieved and anxious, therefore, she was very far from being heart-broken; a circumstance which, for the sentimental purposes of our tale, is much to be deplored. But truth must be told, especially in a narrative whose chief, if not only, pretensions to interest consist in a rigid adherence to facts, or what are so reported to have been.

Miss Montague, nevertheless, devoted much of her time to a patient but fruitless attempt to cheer the unhappy invalid. She read for him, and conversed with him; but it was apparent that whatever exertions he made, the endeavour to escape from the one constant and ever-present fear that preyed upon him was utterly and miserably unavailing.

Young ladies, as all the world knows, are much given to the cultivation of pets; and among those who shared the favour of Miss Montague was a fine old owl, which the gardener, who caught him napping among the ivy of a ruined stable, had dutifully presented to that young lady.

The caprice which regulates such preferences was manifested in the extravagant favour with which this grim and ill-favoured bird was at once distinguished by his mistress; and, trifling as this whimsical circumstance may seem, I am forced to mention it, inasmuch as it is connected, oddly enough, with the concluding scene of the story. Barton, so far from sharing in this liking for the new favourite, regarded it from the first with an antipathy as violent as it was utterly unaccountable. Its very vicinity was insupportable to him. He seemed to hate and dread it with a vehemence absolutely laughable, and to those who have never witnessed the exhibition of antipathies of this kind, his dread would seem all but incredible.

With these few words of preliminary explanation, I shall proceed to state the particulars of the last scene in this strange series of incidents. It was almost two o'clock one winter's night, and Barton was, as usual at that hour, in his bed; the servant we have mentioned occupied a smaller bed in the same room, and a candle was burning. The man was on a sudden aroused by his master, who said,—

"I can't get it out of my head that that accursed bird has escaped somehow, and is lurking in some corner of the room. I have been dreaming of him. Get up, Smith, and look about; search for him. Such hateful dreams!"

The servant rose, and examined the chamber, and while engaged in so doing, he heard the well-known sound, more like a long-drawn gasp than a hiss, with which these birds from their secret haunts affright the quiet of the night. This ghostly indication of its proximity, for the sound proceeded from the passage upon which Barton's chamber-door opened, determined the search of the servant, who, opening the door, proceeded a step or two forward for the purpose of driving the bird away. He had, however, hardly entered the lobby, when the door behind him slowly swung to under the impulse, as it seemed, of some gentle current of air; but as immediately over the door there was a kind of window, intended in the daytime to aid in lighting the passage, and through which the rays of the candle were then issuing, the valet could see quite enough for his purpose. As he advanced he heard his master (who, lying in a well-curtained bed had not, as it seemed, perceived his exit from the room) call him by name, and direct him to place the candle on the table by his bed. The servant, who was now some way in the long passage, did not like to raise his voice for the purpose of replying, lest he should startle the sleeping inmates of the house, began to walk hurriedly and softly back again, when, to his amazement, he heard a voice in the interior of the chamber answering calmly, and the man actually saw, through the window which over-topped the door, that the light was slowly shifting, as if carried across the chamber in answer to his master's call. Palsied by a feeling akin to terror, yet not unmingled with a horrible curiosity, he stood breathless and listening at the threshold, unable to summon resolution to push open the door and enter. Then came a rustling of the curtains, and a sound like that of one who in a low voice hushes a child to rest, in the midst of which he heard Barton say, in a tone of stifled horror – "Oh, God – oh, my God!" and repeat the same exclamation several times. Then ensued a silence, which again was broken by the same strange soothing sound; and at last there burst forth, in one swelling peal, a yell of agony so appalling and hideous, that, under some impulse of ungovernable horror, the man rushed to the door, and with his whole strength strove to force it open. Whether it was that, in his agitation, he had himself but imperfectly turned the handle, or that the door was really secured upon the inside, he failed to effect an entrance; and as he tugged and pushed, yell after yell rang louder and wilder through the chamber, accompanied all the while by the same hushing sounds. Actually freezing with terror, and scarce knowing what he did, the man turned and ran down the passage, wringing his hands in the extremity of horror and irresolution. At the stair-head he was encountered by General Montague, scared and eager, and just as they met the fearful sounds had ceased.

"What is it? – who – where is your master?" said Montague, with the incoherence of extreme agitation. "Has anything – for God's sake, is anything wrong?"

"Lord have mercy on us, it's all over," said the man, staring wildly towards his master's chamber. "He's dead, sir; I'm sure he's dead."

Without waiting for inquiry or explanation, Montague, closely followed by the servant, hurried to the chamber-door, turned the handle, and pushed it open. As the door yielded to his pressure, the ill-omened bird of which the servant had been in search, uttering its spectral warning, started suddenly from the far side of the bed, and flying through the doorway close over their heads, and extinguishing, in its passage, the candle which Montague carried, crashed through the skylight that overlooked the lobby, and sailed away into the darkness of the outer space.

"There it is, God bless us!" whispered the man, after a breathless pause.

"Curse that bird!" muttered the general, startled by the suddenness of the apparition, and unable to conceal his discomposure.

"The candle was moved," said the man, after another breathless pause; "see, they put it by the bed!"

"Draw the curtains, fellow, and don't stand gaping there," whispered Montague, sternly. The man hesitated.

"Hold this, then," said Montague, impatiently, thrusting the candlestick into the servant's hand; and himself advancing to the bedside, he drew the curtains apart. The light of the candle, which was still burning at the bedside, fell upon a figure huddled together, and half upright, at the head of the bed. It seemed as though it had shrunk back as far as the solid panelling would allow, and the hands were still clutched in the bed-clothes.

"Barton, Barton, Barton!" cried the general, with a strange mixture of awe and vehemence.

He took the candle, and held it so that it shone full upon his face. The features were fixed, stern and white; the jaw was fallen, and the sightless eyes, still open, gazed vacantly forward toward the front of the bed.

"God Almighty, he's dead!" muttered the general, as he looked upon this fearful spectacle. They both continued to gaze upon it in silence for a minute or more. "And cold, too," said Montague, withdrawing his hand from that of the dead man.

"And see, see; may I never have life, sir," added the man, after another pause, with a shudder, "but there was something else on the bed with him! Look there – look there; see that, sir!"

As the man thus spoke, he pointed to a deep indenture, as if caused by a heavy pressure, near the foot of the bed.

Montague was silent.

"Come, sir, come away, for God's sake!" whispered the man, drawing close up to him, and holding fast by his arm, while he glanced fearfully round; "what good can be done here now? – come away, for God's sake!"

At this moment they heard the steps of more than one approaching, and Montague, hastily desiring the servant to arrest their progress, endeavoured to loose the rigid grip with which the fingers of the dead man were clutched in the bed-clothes, and drew, as well as he was able, the awful figure into a reclining posture. Then closing the curtains carefully upon it, he hastened himself to meet those who were approaching.

* * *

It is needless to follow the personages so slightly connected with this narrative into the events of their after lives; it is enough for us to remark that no clue to the solution of these mysterious occurrences was ever afterwards discovered; and so long an interval having now passed, it is scarcely to be expected that time can throw any new light upon their inexplicable obscurity. Until the secrets of the earth shall be no longer hidden these transactions must remain shrouded in mystery.

The only occurrence in Captain Barton's former life to which reference was ever made, as having any possible connection with the sufferings with which his existence closed, and which he himself seemed to regard as working out a retribution for some grievous sin of his past life, was a circumstance which not for several years after his death was brought to light. The nature of this disclosure was painful to his relatives and discreditable to his memory.

It appeared, then, that some eight years before Captain Barton's final return to Dublin, he had formed, in the town of Plymouth, a guilty attachment, the object of which was the daughter of one of the ship's crew under his command. The father had visited the frailty of his unhappy child with extreme harshness, and even brutality, and it was said that she had died heart-broken. Presuming upon Barton's implication in her guilt, this man had conducted himself towards him with marked insolence, and Barton resented this – and what he resented with still more exasperated bitterness, his treatment of the unfortunate girl – by a systematic exercise of those terrible and arbitrary severities with which the regulations of the navy arm those who are responsible for its discipline. The man had at length made his escape, while the vessel was in port at Lisbon, but died, as it was said, in an hospital in that town, of the wounds inflicted in one of his recent and sanguinary punishments.

Whether these circumstances in reality bear or not upon the occurrences of Barton's after-life, it is of course impossible to say. It seems, however, more than probable that they were, at least in his own mind, closely associated with them. But however the truth may be as to the origin and motives of this mysterious persecution, there can be no doubt that, with respect to the agencies by which it was accomplished, absolute and impenetrable mystery is like to prevail until the day of doom.

If you enjoyed this, you might also like...
All Sorts and Conditions of Men, see page 97
Amy Foster, see page 191

The Time Machine
Chapters VI–IX
H.G. Wells

Chapter VI

"**IT MAY** seem odd to you, but it was two days before I could follow up the new-found clue in what was manifestly the proper way. I felt a peculiar shrinking from those pallid bodies. They were just the half-bleached colour of the worms and things one sees preserved in spirit in a zoological museum. And they were filthily cold to the touch. Probably my shrinking was largely due to the sympathetic influence of the Eloi, whose disgust of the Morlocks I now began to appreciate.

"The next night I did not sleep well. Probably my health was a little disordered. I was oppressed with perplexity and doubt. Once or twice I had a feeling of intense fear for which I could perceive no definite reason. I remember creeping noiselessly into the great hall where the little people were sleeping in the moonlight – that night Weena was among them – and feeling reassured by their presence. It occurred to me even then, that in the course of a few days the moon must pass through its last quarter, and the nights grow dark, when the appearances of these unpleasant creatures from below, these whitened Lemurs, this new vermin that had replaced the old, might be more abundant. And on both these days I had the restless feeling of one who shirks an inevitable duty. I felt assured that the Time Machine was only to be recovered by boldly penetrating these underground mysteries. Yet I could not face the mystery. If only I had had a companion it would have been different. But I was so horribly alone, and even to clamber down into the darkness of the well appalled me. I don't know if you will understand my feeling, but I never felt quite safe at my back.

"It was this restlessness, this insecurity, perhaps, that drove me further and further afield in my exploring expeditions. Going to the south-westward towards the rising country that is now called Combe Wood, I observed far off, in the direction of nineteenth-century Banstead, a vast green structure, different in character from any I had hitherto seen. It was larger than the largest of the palaces or ruins I knew, and the facade had an Oriental look: the face of it having the lustre, as well as the pale-green tint, a kind of bluish-green, of a certain type of Chinese porcelain. This difference in aspect suggested a difference in use, and I was minded to push on and explore. But the day was growing late, and I had come upon the sight of the place after a long and tiring circuit; so I resolved to hold over the adventure for the following day, and I returned to the welcome and the caresses of little Weena. But next morning I perceived clearly enough that my curiosity regarding the Palace of Green Porcelain was a piece of self-deception, to enable me to shirk, by another day, an experience I dreaded. I resolved I would make the descent without further waste of time, and started out in the early morning towards a well near the ruins of granite and aluminium.

"Little Weena ran with me. She danced beside me to the well, but when she saw me lean over the mouth and look downward, she seemed strangely disconcerted. 'Goodbye, little Weena,' I said, kissing her; and then putting her down, I began to feel over the parapet for the climbing hooks. Rather hastily, I may as well confess, for I feared my courage might leak away! At first she watched me in amazement. Then she gave a most piteous cry, and running to me, she began to pull at me with her little hands. I think her opposition nerved me rather to proceed. I shook her off, perhaps a little roughly, and in another moment I was in the throat of the well. I saw her agonized face over the parapet, and smiled to reassure her. Then I had to look down at the unstable hooks to which I clung.

"I had to clamber down a shaft of perhaps two hundred yards. The descent was effected by means of metallic bars projecting from the sides of the well, and these being adapted to the needs of a creature much smaller and lighter than myself, I was speedily cramped and fatigued by the descent. And not simply fatigued! One of the bars bent suddenly under my weight, and almost swung me off into the blackness beneath. For a moment I hung by one hand, and after that experience I did not dare to rest again. Though my arms and back were presently acutely painful, I went on clambering down the sheer descent with as quick a motion as possible. Glancing upward, I saw the aperture, a small blue disk, in which a star was visible, while little Weena's head showed as a round black projection. The thudding sound of a machine below grew louder and more oppressive. Everything save that little disk above was profoundly dark, and when I looked up again Weena had disappeared.

"I was in an agony of discomfort. I had some thought of trying to go up the shaft again, and leave the Under-world alone. But even while I turned this over in my mind I continued to descend. At last, with intense relief, I saw dimly coming up, a foot to the right of me, a slender loophole in the wall. Swinging myself in, I found it was the aperture of a narrow horizontal tunnel in which I could lie down and rest. It was not too soon. My arms ached, my back was cramped, and I was trembling with the prolonged terror of a fall. Besides this, the unbroken darkness had had a distressing effect upon my eyes. The air was full of the throb and hum of machinery pumping air down the shaft.

"I do not know how long I lay. I was roused by a soft hand touching my face. Starting up in the darkness I snatched at my matches and, hastily striking one, I saw three stooping white creatures similar to the one I had seen above ground in the ruin, hastily retreating before the light. Living, as they did, in what appeared to me impenetrable darkness, their eyes were abnormally large and sensitive, just as are the pupils of the abysmal fishes, and they reflected the light in the same way. I have no doubt they could see me in that rayless obscurity, and they did not seem to have any fear of me apart from the light. But, so soon as I struck a match in order to see them, they fled incontinently, vanishing into dark gutters and tunnels, from which their eyes glared at me in the strangest fashion.

"I tried to call to them, but the language they had was apparently different from that of the Over-world people; so that I was needs left to my own unaided efforts, and the thought of flight before exploration was even then in my mind. But I said to myself, 'You are in for it now,' and, feeling my way along the tunnel, I found the noise of machinery grow louder. Presently the walls fell away from me, and I came to a large open space, and striking another match, saw that I had entered a vast arched cavern, which stretched into utter darkness beyond the range of my light. The view I had of it was as much as one could see in the burning of a match.

"Necessarily my memory is vague. Great shapes like big machines rose out of the dimness, and cast grotesque black shadows, in which dim spectral Morlocks sheltered from the glare. The place, by the by, was very stuffy and oppressive, and the faint halitus of freshly shed blood was in the air. Some way down the central vista was a little table of white metal, laid with what seemed a meal. The Morlocks at any rate were carnivorous! Even at the time, I remember wondering what large animal could have survived to furnish the red joint I saw. It was all very indistinct: the heavy smell, the big unmeaning shapes, the obscene figures lurking in the shadows, and only waiting for the darkness to come at me again! Then the match burned down, and stung my fingers, and fell, a wriggling red spot in the blackness.

"I have thought since how particularly ill-equipped I was for such an experience. When I had started with the Time Machine, I had started with the absurd assumption that the men of the Future would certainly be infinitely ahead of ourselves in all their appliances. I had come without arms, without medicine, without anything to smoke – at times I missed tobacco frightfully – even without enough matches. If only I had thought of a Kodak! I could have flashed that glimpse of the Underworld in a second, and examined it at leisure. But, as it was, I stood there with only the weapons and the powers that Nature had endowed me with – hands, feet, and teeth; these, and four safety-matches that still remained to me.

"I was afraid to push my way in among all this machinery in the dark, and it was only with my last glimpse of light I discovered that my store of matches had run low. It had never occurred to me until that moment that there was any need to economize them, and I had wasted almost half the box in astonishing the Upper-worlders, to whom fire was a novelty. Now, as I say, I had four left, and while I stood in the dark, a hand touched mine, lank fingers came feeling over my face, and I was sensible of a peculiar unpleasant odour. I fancied I heard the breathing of a crowd of those dreadful little beings about me. I felt the box of matches in my hand being gently disengaged, and other hands behind me plucking at my clothing. The sense of these unseen creatures examining me was indescribably unpleasant. The sudden realization of my ignorance of their ways of thinking and doing came home to me very vividly in the darkness. I shouted at them as loudly as I could. They started away, and then I could feel them approaching me again. They clutched at me more boldly, whispering odd sounds to each other. I shivered violently, and shouted again – rather discordantly. This time they were not so seriously alarmed, and they made a queer laughing noise as they came back at me. I will confess I was horribly frightened. I determined to strike another match and escape under the protection of its glare. I did so, and eking out the flicker with a scrap of paper from my pocket, I made good my retreat to the narrow tunnel. But I had scarce entered this when my light was blown out and in the blackness I could hear the Morlocks rustling like wind among leaves, and pattering like the rain, as they hurried after me.

"In a moment I was clutched by several hands, and there was no mistaking that they were trying to haul me back. I struck another light, and waved it in their dazzled faces. You can scarce imagine how nauseatingly inhuman they looked – those pale, chinless faces and great, lidless, pinkish-grey eyes! – as they stared in their blindness and bewilderment. But I did not stay to look, I promise you: I retreated again, and when my second match had ended, I struck my third. It had almost burned through when I reached the opening into the shaft. I lay down on the edge, for the throb of the great pump below made me giddy. Then I felt sideways for the projecting hooks, and, as I did so, my feet were grasped from behind, and I was violently tugged backward. I lit my last match ...and it incontinently went out. But I had my hand on the climbing bars now, and, kicking violently, I disengaged myself from the clutches of the Morlocks and was speedily clambering up the shaft, while they stayed peering and blinking up at me: all but one little wretch who followed me for some way, and well-nigh secured my boot as a trophy.

"That climb seemed interminable to me. With the last twenty or thirty feet of it a deadly nausea came upon me. I had the greatest difficulty in keeping my hold. The last few yards was a frightful struggle against this faintness. Several times my head swam, and I felt all the sensations of falling. At last, however, I got over the well-mouth somehow, and staggered out of the ruin into the blinding sunlight. I fell upon my face. Even the soil smelt sweet and clean. Then I remember Weena kissing my hands and ears, and the voices of others among the Eloi. Then, for a time, I was insensible.

Chapter VII

"**NOW, INDEED**, I seemed in a worse case than before. Hitherto, except during my night's anguish at the loss of the Time Machine, I had felt a sustaining hope of ultimate escape, but that hope was staggered by these new discoveries. Hitherto I had merely thought myself impeded by the childish simplicity of the little people, and by some unknown forces which I had only to understand to overcome; but there was an altogether new element in the sickening quality of the Morlocks – a something inhuman and malign. Instinctively I loathed them. Before, I had felt as a man might feel who had fallen into a pit: my concern was with the pit and how to get out of it. Now I felt like a beast in a trap, whose enemy would come upon him soon.

"The enemy I dreaded may surprise you. It was the darkness of the new moon. Weena had put this into my head by some at first incomprehensible remarks about the Dark Nights. It was not now such a very difficult problem to guess what the coming Dark Nights might mean. The moon was on the wane: each night there was a longer interval of darkness. And I now understood to some slight degree at least the reason of the fear of the little Upper-world people for the dark. I wondered vaguely what foul villainy it might be that the Morlocks did under the new moon. I felt pretty sure now that my second hypothesis was all wrong. The Upper-world people might once have been the favoured aristocracy, and the Morlocks their mechanical servants: but that had long since passed away. The two species that had resulted from the evolution of man were sliding down towards, or had already arrived at, an altogether new relationship. The Eloi, like the Carolingian kings, had decayed to a mere beautiful futility. They still possessed the earth on sufferance: since the Morlocks, subterranean for innumerable generations, had come at last to find the daylit surface intolerable. And the Morlocks made their garments, I inferred, and maintained them in their habitual needs, perhaps through the survival of an old habit of service. They did it as a standing horse paws with his foot, or as a man enjoys killing animals in sport: because ancient and departed necessities had impressed it on the organism. But, clearly, the old order was already in part reversed. The Nemesis of the delicate ones was creeping on apace. Ages ago, thousands of generations ago, man had thrust his brother man out of the ease and the sunshine. And now that brother was coming back changed! Already the Eloi had begun to learn one old lesson anew. They were becoming reacquainted with Fear. And suddenly there came into my head the memory of the meat I had seen in the Underworld. It seemed odd how it floated into my mind: not stirred up as it were by the current of my meditations, but coming in almost like a question from outside. I tried to recall the form of it. I had a vague sense of something familiar, but I could not tell what it was at the time.

"Still, however helpless the little people in the presence of their mysterious Fear, I was differently constituted. I came out of this age of ours, this ripe prime of the human race, when Fear does not paralyse and mystery has lost its terrors. I at least would defend myself. Without further delay I determined to make myself arms and a fastness where I might sleep. With that refuge as a base, I could face this strange world with some of that confidence I had lost in realizing to what creatures night by night I lay exposed. I felt I could never sleep again until my bed was secure from them. I shuddered with horror to think how they must already have examined me.

"I wandered during the afternoon along the valley of the Thames, but found nothing that commended itself to my mind as inaccessible. All the buildings and trees seemed easily practicable to such dexterous climbers as the Morlocks, to judge by their wells, must be. Then the tall pinnacles of the Palace of Green Porcelain and the polished gleam of its walls came back to my memory; and in the evening, taking Weena like a child upon my shoulder, I went up the hills towards the south-west. The distance, I had reckoned, was seven or eight miles, but it must have been nearer eighteen. I had first seen the place on a moist afternoon when distances are deceptively diminished. In addition, the heel of one of my shoes was loose, and a nail was working through the sole – they were comfortable old shoes I wore about indoors – so that I was lame. And it was already long past sunset when I came in sight of the palace, silhouetted black against the pale yellow of the sky.

"Weena had been hugely delighted when I began to carry her, but after a while she desired me to let her down, and ran along by the side of me, occasionally darting off on either hand to pick flowers to stick in my pockets. My pockets had always puzzled Weena, but at the last she had concluded that they were an eccentric kind of vase for floral decoration. At least she utilized them for that purpose. And that reminds me! In changing my jacket I found..."

The Time Traveller paused, put his hand into his pocket, and silently placed two withered flowers, not unlike very large white mallows, upon the little table. Then he resumed his narrative.

"As the hush of evening crept over the world and we proceeded over the hill crest towards Wimbledon, Weena grew tired and wanted to return to the house of grey stone. But I pointed out the distant pinnacles of the Palace of Green Porcelain to her, and contrived to make her understand that we were seeking a refuge there from her Fear. You know that great pause that comes upon things before the dusk? Even the breeze stops in the trees. To me there is always an air of expectation about that evening stillness. The sky was clear, remote, and empty save for a few horizontal bars far down in the sunset. Well, that night the expectation took the colour of my fears. In that darkling calm my senses seemed preternaturally sharpened. I fancied I could even feel the hollowness of the ground beneath my feet: could, indeed, almost see through it the Morlocks on their ant-hill going hither and thither and waiting for the dark. In my excitement I fancied that they would receive my invasion of their burrows as a declaration of war. And why had they taken my Time Machine?

"So we went on in the quiet, and the twilight deepened into night. The clear blue of the distance faded, and one star after another came out. The ground grew dim and the trees black. Weena's fears and her fatigue grew upon her. I took her in my arms and talked to her and caressed her. Then, as the darkness grew deeper, she put her arms round my neck, and, closing her eyes, tightly pressed her face against my shoulder. So we went down a long slope into a valley, and there in the dimness I almost walked into a little river. This I waded, and went up the opposite side of the valley, past a number of sleeping houses, and by a statue – a Faun, or some such figure, minus the head. Here too were acacias. So far I had seen nothing of the Morlocks, but it was yet early in the night, and the darker hours before the old moon rose were still to come.

"From the brow of the next hill I saw a thick wood spreading wide and black before me. I hesitated at this. I could see no end to it, either to the right or the left. Feeling tired – my feet, in particular, were very sore – I carefully lowered Weena from my shoulder as I halted, and sat down upon the turf. I could no longer see the Palace of Green Porcelain, and I was in doubt of my direction. I looked into the thickness of the wood and thought of what it might hide. Under that dense tangle of branches one would be out of sight of the stars. Even were there no other lurking danger – a danger I did not care to let my imagination loose upon – there would still be all the roots to stumble over and the tree-boles to strike against.

"I was very tired, too, after the excitements of the day; so I decided that I would not face it, but would pass the night upon the open hill.

"Weena, I was glad to find, was fast asleep. I carefully wrapped her in my jacket, and sat down beside her to wait for the moonrise. The hill-side was quiet and deserted, but from the black of the wood there came now and then a stir of living things. Above me shone the stars, for the night was very clear. I felt a certain sense of friendly comfort in their twinkling. All the old constellations had gone from the sky, however: that slow movement which is imperceptible in a hundred human lifetimes, had long since rearranged them in unfamiliar groupings. But the Milky Way, it seemed to me, was still the same tattered streamer of star-dust as of yore. Southward (as I judged it) was a very bright red star that was new to me; it was even more splendid than our own green Sirius. And amid all these scintillating points of light one bright planet shone kindly and steadily like the face of an old friend.

"Looking at these stars suddenly dwarfed my own troubles and all the gravities of terrestrial life. I thought of their unfathomable distance, and the slow inevitable drift of their movements out of the unknown past into the unknown future. I thought of the great precessional cycle that the pole of the earth describes. Only forty times had that silent revolution occurred during all the years that I had traversed. And during these few revolutions all the activity, all the traditions, the complex organizations, the nations, languages, literatures, aspirations, even the mere memory of Man as I knew him, had been swept out of existence. Instead were these frail creatures who had forgotten their high ancestry, and the white Things of which I went in terror. Then I thought of the Great Fear that was between the two species, and for the first time, with a sudden shiver, came the clear knowledge of what the meat I had seen might be. Yet it was too horrible! I looked at little Weena sleeping beside me, her face white and starlike under the stars, and forthwith dismissed the thought.

"Through that long night I held my mind off the Morlocks as well as I could, and whiled away the time by trying to fancy I could find signs of the old constellations in the new confusion. The sky kept very clear, except for a hazy cloud or so. No doubt I dozed at times. Then, as my vigil wore on, came a faintness in the eastward sky, like the reflection of some colourless fire, and the old moon rose, thin and peaked and white. And close behind, and overtaking it, and overflowing it, the dawn came, pale at first, and then growing pink and warm. No Morlocks had approached us. Indeed, I had seen none upon the hill that night. And in the confidence of renewed day it almost seemed to me that my fear had been unreasonable. I stood up and found my foot with the loose heel swollen at the ankle and painful under the heel; so I sat down again, took off my shoes, and flung them away.

"I awakened Weena, and we went down into the wood, now green and pleasant instead of black and forbidding. We found some fruit wherewith to break our fast. We soon met others of the dainty ones, laughing and dancing in the sunlight as though there was no such thing in nature as the night. And then I thought once more of the meat that I had seen. I felt assured now of what it was, and from the bottom of my heart I pitied this last feeble rill from the great flood of humanity. Clearly, at some time in the Long-Ago of human decay the Morlocks' food had run short. Possibly they had lived on rats and such-like vermin. Even now man is far less discriminating and exclusive in his food than he was – far less than any monkey. His prejudice against human flesh is no deep-seated instinct. And so these inhuman sons of men –! I tried to look at the thing in a scientific spirit. After all, they were less human and more remote than our cannibal ancestors of three or four thousand years ago. And the intelligence that would have made this state of things a torment had gone. Why should I trouble myself? These Eloi were mere fatted cattle, which the ant-like Morlocks preserved and preyed upon – probably saw to the breeding of. And there was Weena dancing at my side!

"Then I tried to preserve myself from the horror that was coming upon me, by regarding it as a rigorous punishment of human selfishness. Man had been content to live in ease and delight upon the labours of his fellow-man, had taken Necessity as his watchword and excuse, and in the fullness of time Necessity had come home to him. I even tried a Carlyle-like scorn of this wretched aristocracy in decay. But this attitude of mind was impossible. However great their intellectual degradation, the Eloi had kept too much of the human form not to claim my sympathy, and to make me perforce a sharer in their degradation and their Fear.

"I had at that time very vague ideas as to the course I should pursue. My first was to secure some safe place of refuge, and to make myself such arms of metal or stone as I could contrive. That necessity was immediate. In the next place, I hoped to procure some means of fire, so that I should have the weapon of a torch at hand, for nothing, I knew, would be more efficient against these Morlocks. Then I wanted to arrange some contrivance to break open the doors of bronze under the White Sphinx. I had in mind a battering ram. I had a persuasion that if I could enter those doors and carry a blaze of light before me I should discover the Time Machine and escape. I could not imagine the Morlocks were strong enough to move it far away. Weena I had resolved to bring with me to our own time. And turning such schemes over in my mind I pursued our way towards the building which my fancy had chosen as our dwelling.

Chapter VIII

"**I FOUND** the Palace of Green Porcelain, when we approached it about noon, deserted and falling into ruin. Only ragged vestiges of glass remained in its windows, and great sheets of the green facing had fallen away from the corroded metallic framework. It lay very high upon a turfy down, and looking north-eastward before I entered it, I was surprised to see a large estuary, or even creek, where I judged Wandsworth and Battersea must once have been. I thought then – though I never followed up the thought – of what might have happened, or might be happening, to the living things in the sea.

"The material of the Palace proved on examination to be indeed porcelain, and along the face of it I saw an inscription in some unknown character. I thought, rather foolishly, that Weena might help me to interpret this, but I only learned that the bare idea of writing had never entered her head. She always seemed to me, I fancy, more human than she was, perhaps because her affection was so human.

"Within the big valves of the door – which were open and broken – we found, instead of the customary hall, a long gallery lit by many side windows. At the first glance I was reminded of a museum. The tiled floor was thick with dust, and a remarkable array of miscellaneous objects was shrouded in the same grey covering. Then I perceived, standing strange and gaunt in the centre of the hall, what was clearly the lower part of a huge skeleton. I recognized by the oblique feet that it was some extinct creature after the fashion of the Megatherium. The skull and the upper bones lay beside it in the thick dust, and in one place, where rain-water had dropped through a leak in the roof, the thing itself had been worn away. Further in the gallery was the huge skeleton barrel of a Brontosaurus. My museum hypothesis was confirmed. Going towards the side I found what appeared to be sloping shelves, and clearing away the thick dust, I found the old familiar glass cases of our own time. But they must have been air-tight to judge from the fair preservation of some of their contents.

"Clearly we stood among the ruins of some latter-day South Kensington! Here, apparently, was the Palaeontological Section, and a very splendid array of fossils it must have been, though the inevitable process of decay that had been staved off for a time, and had, through the extinction of bacteria and fungi, lost ninety-nine hundredths of its force, was nevertheless, with extreme sureness if with extreme slowness at work again upon all its treasures. Here and there I found traces of the little people in the shape of rare fossils broken to pieces or threaded in strings upon reeds. And the cases had in some instances been bodily removed – by the Morlocks as I judged. The place was very silent. The thick dust deadened our footsteps. Weena, who had been rolling a sea urchin down the sloping glass of a case, presently came, as I stared about me, and very quietly took my hand and stood beside me.

"And at first I was so much surprised by this ancient monument of an intellectual age, that I gave no thought to the possibilities it presented. Even my preoccupation about the Time Machine receded a little from my mind.

"To judge from the size of the place, this Palace of Green Porcelain had a great deal more in it than a Gallery of Palaeontology; possibly historical galleries; it might be, even a library! To me, at least in my present circumstances, these would be vastly more interesting than this spectacle of oldtime geology in decay. Exploring, I found another short gallery running transversely to the first. This appeared to be devoted to minerals, and the sight of a block of sulphur set my mind running on gunpowder. But I could find no saltpeter; indeed, no nitrates of any kind. Doubtless they had deliquesced ages ago. Yet the sulphur hung in my mind, and set up a train of thinking. As for the rest of the contents of that gallery, though on the whole they were the best preserved of all I saw, I had little interest. I am no specialist in mineralogy, and I went on down a very ruinous aisle running parallel to the first hall I had entered. Apparently this section had been devoted to natural history, but everything had long since passed out of recognition. A few shrivelled and blackened vestiges of what had once been stuffed animals, desiccated mummies in jars that had once held spirit, a brown dust of departed plants: that was all! I was sorry for that, because I should have been glad to trace the patent readjustments by which the conquest of animated nature had been attained. Then we came to a gallery of simply colossal proportions, but singularly ill-lit, the floor of it running downward at a slight angle from the end at which I entered. At intervals white globes hung from the ceiling – many of them cracked and smashed – which suggested that originally the place had been artificially lit. Here I was more in my element, for rising on either side of me were the huge bulks of big machines, all greatly corroded and many broken down, but some still fairly complete. You know I have a certain weakness for mechanism, and I was inclined to linger among these; the more so as for the most part they had the interest of puzzles, and I could make only the vaguest guesses at what they were for. I fancied that if I could solve their puzzles I should find myself in possession of powers that might be of use against the Morlocks.

"Suddenly Weena came very close to my side. So suddenly that she startled me. Had it not been for her I do not think I should have noticed that the floor of the gallery sloped at all.. The end I had come in at was quite above ground, and was lit by rare slit-like windows. As you went down the length, the ground came up against these windows, until at last there was a pit like the 'area' of a London house before each, and only a narrow line of daylight at the top. I went slowly along, puzzling about the machines, and had been too intent upon them to notice the gradual diminution of the light, until Weena's increasing apprehensions drew my attention. Then I saw that the gallery ran down at last into a thick darkness. I hesitated, and then, as I looked round me, I saw that the dust was less abundant and its surface less even. Further away towards the dimness, it appeared to be broken by a number of small narrow footprints. My sense of the immediate presence of the Morlocks revived at that. I felt that I was wasting my time in the academic examination of machinery. I called to mind that it was already far advanced in the afternoon, and that I had still no weapon, no refuge, and no means of making a fire. And then down in the remote blackness of the gallery I heard a peculiar pattering, and the same odd noises I had heard down the well.

"I took Weena's hand. Then, struck with a sudden idea, I left her and turned to a machine from which projected a lever not unlike those in a signal-box. Clambering upon the stand, and grasping this lever in my hands, I put all my weight upon it sideways. Suddenly Weena, deserted in the central aisle, began to whimper. I had judged the strength of the lever pretty correctly, for it snapped after a minute's strain, and I rejoined her with a mace in my hand more than sufficient, I judged, for any Morlock skull I might encounter. And I longed very much to kill a Morlock or so. Very inhuman, you may think, to want to go killing one's own descendants! But it was impossible, somehow, to feel any humanity in the things. Only my disinclination to leave Weena, and a persuasion that if I began to slake my thirst for murder my Time

Machine might suffer, restrained me from going straight down the gallery and killing the brutes I heard.

"Well, mace in one hand and Weena in the other, I went out of that gallery and into another and still larger one, which at the first glance reminded me of a military chapel hung with tattered flags. The brown and charred rags that hung from the sides of it, I presently recognized as the decaying vestiges of books. They had long since dropped to pieces, and every semblance of print had left them. But here and there were warped boards and cracked metallic clasps that told the tale well enough. Had I been a literary man I might, perhaps, have moralized upon the futility of all ambition. But as it was, the thing that struck me with keenest force was the enormous waste of labour to which this sombre wilderness of rotting paper testified. At the time I will confess that I thought chiefly of the *Philosophical Transactions* and my own seventeen papers upon physical optics.

"Then, going up a broad staircase, we came to what may once have been a gallery of technical chemistry. And here I had not a little hope of useful discoveries. Except at one end where the roof had collapsed, this gallery was well preserved. I went eagerly to every unbroken case. And at last, in one of the really air-tight cases, I found a box of matches. Very eagerly I tried them. They were perfectly good. They were not even damp. I turned to Weena. 'Dance,' I cried to her in her own tongue. For now I had a weapon indeed against the horrible creatures we feared. And so, in that derelict museum, upon the thick soft carpeting of dust, to Weena's huge delight, I solemnly performed a kind of composite dance, whistling The Land of the Leal as cheerfully as I could. In part it was a modest cancan, in part a step dance, in part a skirt-dance (so far as my tail-coat permitted), and in part original. For I am naturally inventive, as you know.

"Now, I still think that for this box of matches to have escaped the wear of time for immemorial years was a most strange, as for me it was a most fortunate thing. Yet, oddly enough, I found a far unlikelier substance, and that was camphor. I found it in a sealed jar, that by chance, I suppose, had been really hermetically sealed. I fancied at first that it was paraffin wax, and smashed the glass accordingly. But the odour of camphor was unmistakable. In the universal decay this volatile substance had chanced to survive, perhaps through many thousands of centuries. It reminded me of a sepia painting I had once seen done from the ink of a fossil Belemnite that must have perished and become fossilized millions of years ago. I was about to throw it away, but I remembered that it was inflammable and burned with a good bright flame – was, in fact, an excellent candle – and I put it in my pocket. I found no explosives, however, nor any means of breaking down the bronze doors. As yet my iron crowbar was the most helpful thing I had chanced upon. Nevertheless I left that gallery greatly elated.

"I cannot tell you all the story of that long afternoon. It would require a great effort of memory to recall my explorations in at all the proper order. I remember a long gallery of rusting stands of arms, and how I hesitated between my crowbar and a hatchet or a sword. I could not carry both, however, and my bar of iron promised best against the bronze gates. There were numbers of guns, pistols, and rifles. The most were masses of rust, but many were of some new metal, and still fairly sound. But any cartridges or powder there may once have been had rotted into dust. One corner I saw was charred and shattered; perhaps, I thought, by an explosion among the specimens. In another place was a vast array of idols – Polynesian, Mexican, Grecian, Phoenician, every country on earth I should think. And here, yielding to an irresistible impulse, I wrote my name upon the nose of a steatite monster from South America that particularly took my fancy.

"As the evening drew on, my interest waned. I went through gallery after gallery, dusty, silent, often ruinous, the exhibits sometimes mere heaps of rust and lignite, sometimes fresher. In one place I suddenly found myself near the model of a tin-mine, and then by the merest accident I discovered, in an air-tight case, two dynamite cartridges! I shouted 'Eureka!' and smashed the case with joy. Then came a doubt. I hesitated. Then, selecting a little side gallery, I made my essay. I never felt such a disappointment as I did in waiting five, ten, fifteen minutes for an explosion that never came. Of course the things were dummies, as I might have guessed from their presence. I really believe that had they not been so, I should have rushed off incontinently and blown Sphinx, bronze doors, and (as it proved) my chances of finding the Time Machine, all together into non-existence.

"It was after that, I think, that we came to a little open court within the palace. It was turfed, and had three fruit-trees. So we rested and refreshed ourselves. Towards sunset I began to consider our position. Night was creeping upon us, and my inaccessible hiding-place had still to be found. But that troubled me very little now. I had in my possession a thing that was, perhaps, the best of all defences against the Morlocks – I had matches! I had the camphor in my pocket, too, if a blaze were needed. It seemed to me that the best thing we could do would be to pass the night in the open, protected by a fire. In the morning there was the getting of the Time Machine. Towards that, as yet, I had only my iron mace. But now, with my growing knowledge, I felt very differently towards those bronze doors. Up to this, I had refrained from forcing them, largely because of the mystery on the other side. They had never impressed me as being very strong, and I hoped to find my bar of iron not altogether inadequate for the work.

Chapter IX

"**WE EMERGED** from the palace while the sun was still in part above the horizon. I was determined to reach the White Sphinx early the next morning, and ere the dusk I purposed pushing through the woods that had stopped me on the previous journey. My plan was to go as far as possible that night, and then, building a fire, to sleep in the protection of its glare. Accordingly, as we went along I gathered any sticks or dried grass I saw, and presently had my arms full of such litter. Thus loaded, our progress was slower than I had anticipated, and besides Weena was tired. And I began to suffer from sleepiness too; so that it was full night before we reached the wood. Upon the shrubby hill of its edge Weena would have stopped, fearing the darkness before us; but a singular sense of impending calamity, that should indeed have served me as a warning, drove me onward. I had been without sleep for a night and two days, and I was feverish and irritable. I felt sleep coming upon me, and the Morlocks with it.

"While we hesitated, among the black bushes behind us, and dim against their blackness, I saw three crouching figures. There was scrub and long grass all about us, and I did not feel safe from their insidious approach. The forest, I calculated, was rather less than a mile across. If we could get through it to the bare hill-side, there, as it seemed to me, was an altogether safer resting-place; I thought that with my matches and my camphor I could contrive to keep my path illuminated through the woods. Yet it was evident that if I was to flourish matches with my hands I should have to abandon my firewood; so, rather reluctantly, I put it down. And then it came into my head that I would amaze our friends behind by lighting it. I was to discover the atrocious folly of this proceeding, but it came to my mind as an ingenious move for covering our retreat.

"I don't know if you have ever thought what a rare thing flame must be in the absence of man and in a temperate climate. The sun's heat is rarely strong enough to burn, even when it is focused by dewdrops, as is sometimes the case in more tropical districts. Lightning may blast and blacken, but it rarely gives rise to widespread fire. Decaying vegetation may occasionally smoulder with the heat of its fermentation, but this rarely results in flame. In this decadence, too, the art of fire-making had been forgotten on the earth. The red tongues that went licking up my heap of wood were an altogether new and strange thing to Weena.

"She wanted to run to it and play with it. I believe she would have cast herself into it had I not restrained her. But I caught her up, and in spite of her struggles, plunged boldly before me into the wood. For a little way the glare of my fire lit the path. Looking back presently, I could see, through the crowded stems, that from my heap of sticks the blaze had spread to some bushes adjacent, and a curved line of fire was creeping up the grass of the hill. I laughed at that, and turned again to the dark trees before me. It was very black, and Weena clung to me convulsively, but there was still, as my eyes grew accustomed to the darkness, sufficient light for me to avoid the stems. Overhead it was simply black, except where a gap of remote blue sky shone down upon us here and there. I struck none of my matches because I had no hand free. Upon my left arm I carried my little one, in my right hand I had my iron bar.

"For some way I heard nothing but the crackling twigs under my feet, the faint rustle of the breeze above, and my own breathing and the throb of the blood-vessels in my ears. Then I seemed to know of a pattering about me. I pushed on grimly. The pattering grew more distinct, and then I caught the same queer sound and voices I had heard in the Under-world. There were evidently several of the Morlocks, and they were closing in upon me. Indeed, in another minute I felt a tug at my coat, then something at my arm. And Weena shivered violently, and became quite still.

"It was time for a match. But to get one I must put her down. I did so, and, as I fumbled with my pocket, a struggle began in the darkness about my knees, perfectly silent on her part and with the same peculiar cooing sounds from the Morlocks. Soft little hands, too, were creeping over my coat and back, touching even my neck. Then the match scratched and fizzed. I held it flaring, and saw the white backs of the Morlocks in flight amid the trees. I hastily took a lump of camphor from my pocket, and prepared to light it as soon as the match should wane. Then I looked at Weena. She was lying clutching my feet and quite motionless, with her face to the ground. With a sudden fright I stooped to her. She seemed scarcely to breathe. I lit the block of camphor and flung it to the ground, and as it split and flared up and drove back the Morlocks and the shadows, I knelt down and lifted her. The wood behind seemed full of the stir and murmur of a great company!

"She seemed to have fainted. I put her carefully upon my shoulder and rose to push on, and then there came a horrible realization. In manoeuvring with my matches and Weena, I had turned myself about several times, and now I had not the faintest idea in what direction lay my path. For all I knew, I might be facing back towards the Palace of Green Porcelain. I found myself in a cold sweat. I had to think rapidly what to do. I determined to build a fire and encamp where we were. I put Weena, still motionless, down upon a turfy bole, and very hastily, as my first lump of camphor waned, I began collecting sticks and leaves. Here and there out of the darkness round me the Morlocks' eyes shone like carbuncles.

"The camphor flickered and went out. I lit a match, and as I did so, two white forms that had been approaching Weena dashed hastily away. One was so blinded by the light that he came straight for me, and I felt his bones grind under the blow of my fist. He gave a whoop of dismay, staggered a little way, and fell down. I lit another piece of camphor, and went on gathering my bonfire. Presently I noticed how dry was some of the foliage above me, for since my arrival on the Time Machine, a matter of a week, no rain had fallen. So, instead of casting about among the trees for fallen twigs, I began leaping up and dragging down branches. Very soon I had a choking smoky fire of green wood and dry sticks, and could economize my camphor. Then I turned to where Weena lay beside my iron mace. I tried what I could to revive her, but she lay like one dead. I could not even satisfy myself whether or not she breathed.

"Now, the smoke of the fire beat over towards me, and it must have made me heavy of a sudden. Moreover, the vapour of camphor was in the air. My fire would not need replenishing for an hour or so. I felt very weary after my exertion, and sat down. The wood, too, was full of a slumbrous murmur that I did not understand. I seemed just to nod and open my eyes. But all was dark, and the Morlocks had their hands upon me. Flinging off their clinging fingers I hastily felt in my pocket for the match-box, and – it had gone! Then they gripped and closed with me again. In a moment I knew what had happened. I had slept, and my fire had gone out, and the bitterness of death came over my soul. The forest seemed full of the smell of burning wood. I was caught by the neck, by the hair, by the arms, and pulled down. It was indescribably horrible in the darkness to feel all these soft creatures heaped upon me. I felt as if I was in a monstrous spider's web. I was overpowered, and went down. I felt little teeth nipping at my neck. I rolled over, and as I did so my hand came against my iron lever. It gave me strength. I struggled up, shaking the human rats from me, and, holding the bar short, I thrust where I judged their faces might be. I could feel the succulent giving of flesh and bone under my blows, and for a moment I was free.

"The strange exultation that so often seems to accompany hard fighting came upon me. I knew that both I and Weena were lost, but I determined to make the Morlocks pay for their meat. I stood with my back to a tree, swinging the iron bar before me. The whole wood was full of the stir and cries of them. A minute passed. Their voices seemed to rise to a higher pitch of excitement, and their movements grew faster. Yet none came within reach. I stood glaring at the blackness. Then suddenly came hope. What if the Morlocks were afraid? And close on the heels of that came a strange thing. The darkness seemed to grow luminous. Very dimly I began to see the Morlocks about me – three battered at my feet – and then I recognized, with incredulous surprise, that the others were running, in an incessant stream, as it seemed, from behind me, and away through the wood in front. And their backs seemed no longer white, but reddish. As I stood agape, I saw a little red spark go drifting across a gap of starlight between the branches, and vanish. And at that I understood the smell of burning wood, the slumbrous murmur that was growing now into a gusty roar, the red glow, and the Morlocks' flight.

"Stepping out from behind my tree and looking back, I saw, through the black pillars of the nearer trees, the flames of the burning forest. It was my first fire coming after me. With that I looked for Weena, but she was gone. The hissing and crackling behind me, the explosive thud as each fresh tree burst into flame, left little time for reflection. My iron bar still gripped, I followed in the Morlocks' path. It was a close race. Once the flames crept forward so swiftly on my right as I ran that I was outflanked and had to strike off to the left. But at last I emerged upon a small open space, and as I did so, a Morlock came blundering towards me, and past me, and went on straight into the fire!

"And now I was to see the most weird and horrible thing, I think, of all that I beheld in that future age. This whole space was as bright as day with the reflection of the fire. In the centre was a hillock or tumulus, surmounted by a scorched hawthorn. Beyond this was another arm of the burning forest, with yellow tongues already writhing from it, completely encircling the space with a fence of fire. Upon the hill-side were some thirty or forty Morlocks, dazzled by the light and heat, and blundering hither and thither against each other in their bewilderment. At first I did not realize their blindness, and struck furiously at them with my bar, in a frenzy of fear, as they approached me, killing one and crippling several more. But when I had watched the gestures of one of them groping under the hawthorn against the red sky, and heard their moans, I was assured of their absolute helplessness and misery in the glare, and I struck no more of them.

"Yet every now and then one would come straight towards me, setting loose a quivering horror that made me quick to elude him. At one time the flames died down somewhat, and I feared the foul creatures would presently be able to see me. I was thinking of beginning the fight by killing some of them before this should happen; but the fire burst out again brightly, and I stayed my hand. I walked about the hill among them and avoided them, looking for some trace of Weena. But Weena was gone.

"At last I sat down on the summit of the hillock, and watched this strange incredible company of blind things groping to and fro, and making uncanny noises to each other, as the glare of the fire beat on them. The coiling uprush of smoke streamed across the sky, and through the rare tatters of that red canopy, remote as though they belonged to another universe, shone the little stars. Two or three Morlocks came blundering into me, and I drove them off with blows of my fists, trembling as I did so.

"For the most part of that night I was persuaded it was a nightmare. I bit myself and screamed in a passionate desire to awake. I beat the ground with my hands, and got up and sat down again, and wandered here and there, and again sat down. Then I would fall to rubbing my eyes and calling upon God to let me awake. Thrice I saw Morlocks put their heads down in a kind of agony and rush into the flames. But, at last, above the subsiding red of the fire, above the streaming masses of black smoke and the whitening and blackening tree stumps, and the diminishing numbers of these dim creatures, came the white light of the day.

"I searched again for traces of Weena, but there were none. It was plain that they had left her poor little body in the forest. I cannot describe how it relieved me to think that it had escaped the awful fate to which it seemed destined. As I thought of that, I was almost moved to begin a massacre of the helpless abominations about me, but I contained myself. The hillock, as I have said, was a kind of island in the forest. From its summit I could now make out through a haze of smoke the Palace of Green Porcelain, and from that I could get my bearings for the White Sphinx. And so, leaving the remnant of these damned souls still going hither and thither and moaning, as the day grew clearer, I tied some grass about my feet and limped on across smoking ashes and among black stems, that still pulsated internally with fire, towards the hiding-place of the Time Machine. I walked slowly, for I was almost exhausted, as well as lame, and I felt the intensest wretchedness for the horrible death of little Weena. It seemed an overwhelming calamity. Now, in this old familiar room, it is more like the sorrow of a dream than an actual loss. But that morning it left me absolutely lonely again – terribly alone. I began to think of this house of mine, of this fireside, of some of you, and with such thoughts came a longing that was pain.

"But as I walked over the smoking ashes under the bright morning sky, I made a discovery. In my trouser pocket were still some loose matches. The box must have leaked before it was lost.

If you enjoyed this, you might also like...
The Lifted Veil, see page 211
The Inmost Light, see page 258

Lost Hearts

M.R. James

IT WAS, as far as I can ascertain, in September of the year 1811 that a post-chaise drew up before the door of Aswarby Hall, in the heart of Lincolnshire. The little boy who was the only passenger in the chaise, and who jumped out as soon as it had stopped, looked about him with the keenest curiosity during the short interval that elapsed between the ringing of the bell and the opening of the hall door. He saw a tall, square, red-brick house, built in the reign of Anne; a stone-pillared porch had been added in the purer classical style of 1790; the windows of the house were many, tall and narrow, with small panes and thick white woodwork. A pediment, pierced with a round window, crowned the front. There were wings to right and left, connected by curious glazed galleries, supported by colonnades, with the central block. These wings plainly contained the stables and offices of the house. Each was surmounted by an ornamental cupola with a gilded vane.

An evening light shone on the building, making the window-panes glow like so many fires. Away from the Hall in front stretched a flat park studded with oaks and fringed with firs, which stood out against the sky. The clock in the church-tower, buried in trees on the edge of the park, only its golden weather-cock catching the light, was striking six, and the sound came gently beating down the wind. It was altogether a pleasant impression, though tinged with the sort of melancholy appropriate to an evening in early autumn, that was conveyed to the mind of the boy who was standing in the porch waiting for the door to open to him.

The post-chaise had brought him from Warwickshire, where, some six months before, he had been left an orphan. Now, owing to the generous offer of his elderly cousin, Mr. Abney, he had come to live at Aswarby. The offer was unexpected, because all who knew anything of Mr. Abney looked upon him as a somewhat austere recluse, into whose steady-going household the advent of a small boy would import a new and, it seemed, incongruous element. The truth is that very little was known of Mr. Abney's pursuits or temper. The Professor of Greek at Cambridge had been heard to say that no one knew more of the religious beliefs of the later pagans than did the owner of Aswarby. Certainly his library contained all the then available books bearing on the Mysteries, the Orphic poems, the worship of Mithras, and the Neo-Platonists. In the marble-paved hall stood a fine group of Mithras slaying a bull, which had been imported from the Levant at great expense by the owner. He had contributed a description of it to the Gentleman's Magazine, and he had written a remarkable series of articles in the Critical Museum on the superstitions of the Romans of the Lower Empire. He was looked upon, in fine, as a man wrapped up in his books, and it was a matter of great surprise among his neighbours that he should ever have heard of his orphan cousin, Stephen Elliott, much more that he should have volunteered to make him an inmate of Aswarby Hall.

Whatever may have been expected by his neighbours, it is certain that Mr. Abney – the tall, the thin, the austere – seemed inclined to give his young cousin a kindly reception. The moment the front-door was opened he darted out of his study, rubbing his hands with delight.

"How are you, my boy? – how are you? How old are you?" said he – "that is, you are not too much tired, I hope, by your journey to eat your supper?"

"No, thank you, sir," said Master Elliott; "I am pretty well."

"That's a good lad," said Mr. Abney. "And how old are you, my boy?"

It seemed a little odd that he should have asked the question twice in the first two minutes of their acquaintance.

"I'm twelve years old next birthday, sir," said Stephen.

"And when is your birthday, my dear boy? Eleventh of September, eh? That's well – that's very well. Nearly a year hence, isn't it? I like – ha, ha! – I like to get these things down in my book. Sure it's twelve? Certain?"

"Yes, quite sure, sir."

"Well, well! Take him to Mrs. Bunch's room, Parkes, and let him have his tea – supper – whatever it is."

"Yes, sir," answered the staid Mr. Parkes; and conducted Stephen to the lower regions.

Mrs. Bunch was the most comfortable and human person whom Stephen had as yet met at Aswarby. She made him completely at home; they were great friends in a quarter of an hour: and great friends they remained. Mrs. Bunch had been born in the neighbourhood some fifty-five years before the date of Stephen's arrival, and her residence at the Hall was of twenty years' standing. Consequently, if anyone knew the ins and outs of the house and the district, Mrs. Bunch knew them; and she was by no means disinclined to communicate her information.

Certainly there were plenty of things about the Hall and the Hall gardens which Stephen, who was of an adventurous and inquiring turn, was anxious to have explained to him. "Who built the temple at the end of the laurel walk? Who was the old man whose picture hung on the staircase, sitting at a table, with a skull under his hand?" These and many similar points were cleared up by the resources of Mrs. Bunch's powerful intellect. There were others, however, of which the explanations furnished were less satisfactory.

One November evening Stephen was sitting by the fire in the housekeeper's room reflecting on his surroundings.

"Is Mr. Abney a good man, and will he go to heaven?" he suddenly asked, with the peculiar confidence which children possess in the ability of their elders to settle these questions, the decision of which is believed to be reserved for other tribunals.

"Good? – bless the child!" said Mrs. Bunch. "Master's as kind a soul as ever I see! Didn't I never tell you of the little boy as he took in out of the street, as you may say, this seven years back? and the little girl, two years after I first come here?"

"No. Do tell me all about them, Mrs. Bunch – now, this minute!"

"Well," said Mrs. Bunch, "the little girl I don't seem to recollect so much about. I know master brought her back with him from his walk one day, and give orders to Mrs. Ellis, as was housekeeper then, as she should be took every care with. And the pore child hadn't no one belonging to her – she told me so her own self – and here she lived with us a matter of three weeks it might be; and then, whether she were somethink of a gipsy in her blood or what not, but one morning she out of her bed afore any of us had opened a eye, and neither track nor yet trace of her have I set eyes on since. Master was wonderful put about, and had all the ponds dragged; but it's my belief she was had away by them gipsies, for there was singing round the house for as much as an hour the night she went, and Parkes, he declare as he heard them a-calling in the woods all that afternoon. Dear, dear! a hodd child she was, so silent in her ways and all, but I was wonderful taken up with her, so domesticated she was – surprising."

"And what about the little boy?" said Stephen.

"Ah, that pore boy!" sighed Mrs. Bunch. "He were a foreigner – Jevanny he called hisself – and he come a-tweaking his 'urdy-gurdy round and about the drive one winter day, and master 'ad him in that minute, and ast all about where he came from, and how old he was, and how he made his way, and where was his relatives, and all as kind as heart could wish. But it went the same way with him. They're a hunruly lot, them foreign nations, I do suppose, and he was off one fine morning just the same as the girl. Why he went and what he done was our question for as much as a year after; for he never took his 'urdy-gurdy, and there it lays on the shelf."

The remainder of the evening was spent by Stephen in miscellaneous cross-examination of Mrs. Bunch and in efforts to extract a tune from the hurdy-gurdy.

That night he had a curious dream. At the end of the passage at the top of the house, in which his bedroom was situated, there was an old disused bathroom. It was kept locked, but the upper half of the door was glazed, and, since the muslin curtains which used to hang there had long been gone, you could look in and see the lead-lined bath affixed to the wall on the right hand, with its head towards the window.

On the night of which I am speaking, Stephen Elliott found himself, as he thought, looking through the glazed door. The moon was shining through the window, and he was gazing at a figure which lay in the bath.

His description of what he saw reminds me of what I once beheld myself in the famous vaults of St Michan's Church in Dublin, which possesses the horrid property of preserving corpses from decay for centuries. A figure inexpressibly thin and pathetic, of a dusty leaden colour, enveloped in a shroud-like garment, the thin lips crooked into a faint and dreadful smile, the hands pressed tightly over the region of the heart.

As he looked upon it, a distant, almost inaudible moan seemed to issue from its lips, and the arms began to stir. The terror of the sight forced Stephen backwards and he awoke to the fact that he was indeed standing on the cold boarded floor of the passage in the full light of the moon. With a courage which I do not think can be common among boys of his age, he went to the door of the bathroom to ascertain if the figure of his dreams were really there. It was not, and he went back to bed.

Mrs. Bunch was much impressed next morning by his story, and went so far as to replace the muslin curtain over the glazed door of the bathroom. Mr. Abney, moreover, to whom he confided his experiences at breakfast, was greatly interested and made notes of the matter in what he called 'his book'.

The spring equinox was approaching, as Mr. Abney frequently reminded his cousin, adding that this had been always considered by the ancients to be a critical time for the young: that Stephen would do well to take care of himself, and to shut his bedroom window at night; and that Censorinus had some valuable remarks on the subject. Two incidents that occurred about this time made an impression upon Stephen's mind.

The first was after an unusually uneasy and oppressed night that he had passed – though he could not recall any particular dream that he had had.

The following evening Mrs. Bunch was occupying herself in mending his nightgown.

"Gracious me, Master Stephen!" she broke forth rather irritably, "how do you manage to tear your nightdress all to flinders this way? Look here, sir, what trouble you do give to poor servants that have to darn and mend after you!"

There was indeed a most destructive and apparently wanton series of slits or scorings in the garment, which would undoubtedly require a skilful needle to make good. They were confined to the left side of the chest – long, parallel slits about six inches in length, some of them not quite piercing the texture of the linen. Stephen could only express his entire ignorance of their origin: he was sure they were not there the night before.

"But," he said, "Mrs. Bunch, they are just the same as the scratches on the outside of my bedroom door: and I'm sure I never had anything to do with making them."

Mrs. Bunch gazed at him open-mouthed, then snatched up a candle, departed hastily from the room, and was heard making her way upstairs. In a few minutes she came down.

"Well," she said, "Master Stephen, it's a funny thing to me how them marks and scratches can 'a' come there – too high up for any cat or dog to 'ave made 'em, much less a rat: for all the world like a Chinaman's finger-nails, as my uncle in the tea-trade used to tell us of when we was girls together. I wouldn't say nothing to master, not if I was you, Master Stephen, my dear; and just turn the key of the door when you go to your bed."

"I always do, Mrs. Bunch, as soon as I've said my prayers."

"Ah, that's a good child: always say your prayers, and then no one can't hurt you."

Herewith Mrs. Bunch addressed herself to mending the injured nightgown, with intervals of meditation, until bed-time. This was on a Friday night in March, 1812.

On the following evening the usual duet of Stephen and Mrs. Bunch was augmented by the sudden arrival of Mr. Parkes, the butler, who as a rule kept himself rather to himself in his own pantry. He did not see that Stephen was there: he was, moreover, flustered and less slow of speech than was his wont.

"Master may get up his own wine, if he likes, of an evening," was his first remark. "Either I do it in the daytime or not at all, Mrs. Bunch. I don't know what it may be: very like it's the rats, or the wind got into the cellars; but I'm not so young as I was, and I can't go through with it as I have done."

"Well, Mr. Parkes, you know it is a surprising place for the rats, is the Hall."

"I'm not denying that, Mrs. Bunch; and, to be sure, many a time I've heard the tale from the men in the shipyards about the rat that could speak. I never laid no confidence in that before; but tonight, if I'd demeaned myself to lay my ear to the door of the further bin, I could pretty much have heard what they was saying."

"Oh, there, Mr. Parkes, I've no patience with your fancies! Rats talking in the wine-cellar indeed!"

"Well, Mrs. Bunch, I've no wish to argue with you: all I say is, if you choose to go to the far bin, and lay your ear to the door, you may prove my words this minute."

"What nonsense you do talk, Mr. Parkes – not fit for children to listen to! Why, you'll be frightening Master Stephen there out of his wits."

"What! Master Stephen?" said Parkes, awaking to the consciousness of the boy's presence. "Master Stephen knows well enough when I'm a-playing a joke with you, Mrs. Bunch."

In fact, Master Stephen knew much too well to suppose that Mr. Parkes had in the first instance intended a joke. He was interested, not altogether pleasantly, in the situation; but all his questions were unsuccessful in inducing the butler to give any more detailed account of his experiences in the wine-cellar.

* * *

We have now arrived at March 24, 1812. It was a day of curious experiences for Stephen: a windy, noisy day, which filled the house and the gardens with a restless impression. As Stephen stood by the fence of the grounds, and looked out into the park, he felt as if an endless procession of unseen people were sweeping past him on the wind, borne on resistlessly and aimlessly, vainly striving to stop themselves, to catch at something that might arrest their flight and bring them once again into contact with the living world of which they had formed a part. After luncheon that day Mr. Abney said:

"Stephen, my boy, do you think you could manage to come to me tonight as late as eleven o'clock in my study? I shall be busy until that time, and I wish to show you something connected with your future life which it is most important that you should know. You are not to mention this matter to Mrs. Bunch nor to anyone else in the house; and you had better go to your room at the usual time."

Here was a new excitement added to life: Stephen eagerly grasped at the opportunity of sitting up till eleven o'clock. He looked in at the library door on his way upstairs that evening, and saw a brazier, which he had often noticed in the corner of the room, moved out before the fire; an old silver-gilt cup stood on the table, filled with red wine, and some written sheets of paper lay near it. Mr. Abney was sprinkling some incense on the brazier from a round silver box as Stephen passed, but did not seem to notice his step.

The wind had fallen, and there was a still night and a full moon. At about ten o'clock Stephen was standing at the open window of his bedroom, looking out over the country. Still as the night was, the mysterious population of the distant moon-lit woods was not yet lulled to rest. From time to time strange cries as of lost and despairing wanderers sounded from across the mere. They might be the notes of owls or water-birds, yet they did not quite resemble either sound. Were not they coming nearer? Now they sounded from the nearer side of the water, and in a few moments they seemed to be floating about among the shrubberies. Then they ceased; but just as Stephen was thinking of shutting the window and resuming his reading of Robinson Crusoe, he caught sight of two figures standing on the gravelled terrace that ran along the garden side of the Hall – the figures of a boy and girl, as it seemed; they stood side by side, looking up at the windows. Something in the form of the girl recalled irresistibly his dream of the figure in the bath. The boy inspired him with more acute fear.

Whilst the girl stood still, half smiling, with her hands clasped over her heart, the boy, a thin shape, with black hair and ragged clothing, raised his arms in the air with an appearance of menace and of unappeasable hunger and longing. The moon shone upon his almost transparent hands, and Stephen saw that the nails were fearfully long and that the light shone through them. As he stood with his arms thus raised, he disclosed a terrifying spectacle. On the left side of his chest there opened a black and gaping rent; and there fell upon Stephen's brain, rather than upon his ear, the impression of one of those hungry and desolate cries that he had heard resounding over the woods of

Aswarby all that evening. In another moment this dreadful pair had moved swiftly and noiselessly over the dry gravel, and he saw them no more.

Inexpressibly frightened as he was, he determined to take his candle and go down to Mr. Abney's study, for the hour appointed for their meeting was near at hand. The study or library opened out of the front-hall on one side, and Stephen, urged on by his terrors, did not take long in getting there. To effect an entrance was not so easy. It was not locked, he felt sure, for the key was on the outside of the door as usual. His repeated knocks produced no answer. Mr. Abney was engaged: he was speaking. What! why did he try to cry out? and why was the cry choked in his throat? Had he, too, seen the mysterious children? But now everything was quiet, and the door yielded to Stephen's terrified and frantic pushing.

* * *

On the table in Mr. Abney's study certain papers were found which explained the situation to Stephen Elliott when he was of an age to understand them. The most important sentences were as follows:

"It was a belief very strongly and generally held by the ancients – of whose wisdom in these matters I have had such experience as induces me to place confidence in their assertions – that by enacting certain processes, which to us moderns have something of a barbaric complexion, a very remarkable enlightenment of the spiritual faculties in man may be attained: that, for example, by absorbing the personalities of a certain number of his fellow-creatures, an individual may gain a complete ascendancy over those orders of spiritual beings which control the elemental forces of our universe.

"It is recorded of Simon Magus that he was able to fly in the air, to become invisible, or to assume any form he pleased, by the agency of the soul of a boy whom, to use the libellous phrase employed by the author of the Clementine Recognitions, he had 'murdered'. I find it set down, moreover, with considerable detail in the writings of Hermes Trismegistus, that similar happy results may be produced by the absorption of the hearts of not less than three human beings below the age of twenty-one years. To the testing of the truth of this receipt I have devoted the greater part of the last twenty years, selecting as the corpora vilia of my experiment such persons as could conveniently be removed without occasioning a sensible gap in society. The first step I effected by the removal of one Phoebe Stanley, a girl of gipsy extraction, on March 24, 1792. The second, by the removal of a wandering Italian lad, named Giovanni Paoli, on the night of March 23, 1805. The final 'victim' – to employ a word repugnant in the highest degree to my feelings – must be my cousin, Stephen Elliott. His day must be this March 24, 1812.

"The best means of effecting the required absorption is to remove the heart from the living subject, to reduce it to ashes, and to mingle them with about a pint of some red wine, preferably port. The remains of the first two subjects, at least, it will be well to conceal: a disused bathroom or wine-cellar will be found convenient for such a purpose. Some annoyance may be experienced from the psychic portion of the subjects, which popular language dignifies with the name of ghosts. But the man of philosophic temperament – to whom alone the experiment is appropriate – will be little prone to attach importance to the feeble efforts of these beings to wreak their vengeance on him. I contemplate with the liveliest satisfaction the enlarged and emancipated existence which the experiment, if successful, will confer on me; not only placing me beyond the reach of human justice (so-called), but eliminating to a great extent the prospect of death itself."

* * *

Mr. Abney was found in his chair, his head thrown back, his face stamped with an expression of rage, fright, and mortal pain. In his left side was a terrible lacerated wound, exposing the heart. There was no blood on his hands, and a long knife that lay on the table was perfectly clean. A savage wild-cat might have inflicted the injuries. The window of the study was open, and it was the opinion of the coroner that Mr. Abney had met his death by the agency of some wild creature. But Stephen Elliott's study of the papers I have quoted led him to a very different conclusion.

If you enjoyed this, you might also like...
Markheim, see page 238
Irremediable, see page 155

The Cone

H.G. Wells

THE NIGHT was hot and overcast, the sky red-rimmed with the lingering sunset of midsummer. They sat at the open window, trying to fancy the air was fresher there. The trees and shrubs of the garden stood stiff and dark; beyond in the roadway a gas-lamp burnt, bright orange against the hazy blue of the evening. Farther were the three lights of the railway signal against the lowering sky. The man and woman spoke to one another in low tones.

"He does not suspect?" said the man, a little nervously.

"Not he," she said peevishly, as though that too irritated her. "He thinks of nothing but the works and the prices of fuel. He has no imagination, no poetry."

"None of these men of iron have," he said sententiously. "They have no hearts."

"*He* has not," she said. She turned her discontented face towards the window. The distant sound of a roaring and rushing drew nearer and grew in volume; the house quivered; one heard the metallic rattle of the tender. As the train passed, there was a glare of light above the cutting and a driving tumult of smoke; one, two, three, four, five, six, seven, eight black oblongs – eight trucks – passed across the dim grey of the embankment, and were suddenly extinguished one by one in the throat of the tunnel, which, with the last, seemed to swallow down train, smoke, and sound in one abrupt gulp.

"This country was all fresh and beautiful once," he said; "and now – it is Gehenna. Down that way – nothing but pot-banks and chimneys belching fire and dust into the face of heaven...But what does it matter? An end comes, an end to all this cruelty...*Tomorrow.*" He spoke the last word in a whisper.

"*Tomorrow,*" she said, speaking in a whisper too, and still staring out of the window.

"Dear!" he said, putting his hand on hers.

She turned with a start, and their eyes searched one another's. Hers softened to his gaze. "My dear one!" she said, and then: "It seems so strange – that you should have come into my life like this – to open—" She paused.

"To open?" he said.

"All this wonderful world" – she hesitated, and spoke still more softly – "this world of *love* to me."

Then suddenly the door clicked and closed. They turned their heads, and he started violently back. In the shadow of the room stood a great shadowy figure-silent. They saw the face dimly in the half-light, with unexpressive dark patches under the pent-house brows. Every muscle in Raut's body suddenly became tense. When could the door have opened? What had he heard? Had he heard all? What had he seen? A tumult of questions.

The new-comer's voice came at last, after a pause that seemed interminable. "Well?" he said.

"I was afraid I had missed you, Horrocks," said the man at the window, gripping the window-ledge with his hand. His voice was unsteady.

The clumsy figure of Horrocks came forward out of the shadow. He made no answer to Raut's remark. For a moment he stood above them.

The woman's heart was cold within her. "I told Mr. Raut it was just possible you might come back," she said in a voice that never quivered.

Horrocks, still silent, sat down abruptly in the chair by her little work-table. His big hands were clenched; one saw now the fire of his eyes under the shadow of his brows. He was trying to get his breath. His eyes went from the woman he had trusted to the friend he had trusted, and then back to the woman.

By this time and for the moment all three half understood one another. Yet none dared say a word to ease the pent-up things that choked them.

It was the husband's voice that broke the silence at last.

"You wanted to see me?" he said to Raut.

Raut started as he spoke. "I came to see you," he said, resolved to lie to the last.

"Yes," said Horrocks.

"You promised," said Raut, "to show me some fine effects of moonlight and smoke."

"I promised to show you some fine effects of moonlight and smoke," repeated Horrocks in a colourless voice.

"And I thought I might catch you tonight before you went down to the works," proceeded Raut, "and come with you."

There was another pause. Did the man mean to take the thing coolly? Did he, after all, know? How long had he been in the room? Yet even at the moment when they heard the door, their attitudes...Horrocks glanced at the profile of the woman, shadowy pallid in the half-light. Then he glanced at Raut, and seemed to recover himself suddenly. "Of course," he said, "I promised to show you the works under their proper dramatic conditions. It's odd how I could have forgotten."

"If I am troubling you—" began Raut.

Horrocks started again. A new light had suddenly come into the sultry gloom of his eyes. "Not in the least." he said.

"Have you been telling Mr. Raut of all these contrasts of flame and shadow you think so splendid?" said the woman, turning now to her husband for the first time, her confidence creeping back again, her voice just one half-note too high – "that dreadful theory of yours that machinery is beautiful, and everything else in the world ugly. I thought he would not spare you, Mr. Raut. It's his great theory, his one discovery in art."

"I am slow to make discoveries," said Horrocks grimly, damping her suddenly. "But what I discover...." He stopped.

"Well?" she said.

"Nothing;" and suddenly he rose to his feet.

"I promised to show you the works," he said to Raut, and put his big, clumsy hand on his friend's shoulder. "And you are ready to go?"

"Quite," said Raut, and stood up also.

There was another pause. Each of them peered through the indistinctness of the dusk at the other two.

Horrocks's hand still rested on Raut's shoulder. Raut half fancied still that the incident was trivial after all. But Mrs. Horrocks knew her husband better, knew that grim quiet in his voice, and the confusion in her mind took a vague shape of physical evil. "Very well," said Horrocks, and, dropping his hand, turned towards the door.

"My hat?" Raut looked round in the half-light.

"That's my work-basket," said Mrs. Horrocks with a gust of hysterical laughter. Their hands came together on the back of the chair. "Here it is!" he said. She had an impulse to warn him in an undertone, but she could not frame a word. "Don't go!" and "Beware of him!" struggled in her mind, and the swift moment passed.

"Got it?" said Horrocks, standing with the door half open.

Raut stepped towards him. "Better say goodbye to Mrs. Horrocks," said the ironmaster, even more grimly quiet in his tone than before.

Raut started and turned. "Good-evening, Mrs. Horrocks," he said, and their hands touched.

Horrocks held the door open with a ceremonial politeness unusual in him towards men. Raut went out, and then, after a wordless look at her, her husband followed. She stood motionless while Raut's light footfall and her husband's heavy tread, like bass and treble, passed down the passage together. The front door slammed heavily. She went to the window, moving slowly, and stood watching, leaning forward. The two men appeared for a moment at the gateway in the road, passed under the street lamp, and were hidden by the black masses of the shrubbery. The lamplight fell for a moment on their faces, showing only unmeaning pale patches, telling nothing of what she still feared, and doubted, and craved vainly to know. Then she sank down into a crouching attitude in the big arm-chair, her eyes-wide open and staring out at the red lights from the furnaces that flickered in the sky. An hour after she was still there, her attitude scarcely changed.

The oppressive stillness of the evening weighed heavily upon Raut. They went side by side down the road in silence, and in silence turned into the cinder-made byway that presently opened out the prospect of the valley.

A blue haze, half dust, half mist, touched the long valley with mystery. Beyond were Hanley and Etruria, grey and dark masses, outlined thinly by the rare golden dots of the street lamps, and here and there a gas-lit window, or the yellow glare of some late-working factory or crowded public-house. Out of the masses, clear and slender against the evening sky, rose a multitude of tall chimneys, many of them reeking, a few smokeless during a season of 'play.' Here and there a pallid patch and ghostly stunted beehive shapes showed the position of a pot-bank or a wheel, black and sharp against the hot lower sky, marked some colliery where they raise the iridescent coal of the place. Nearer at hand was the broad stretch of railway, and half-invisible trains shunted – a steady puffing and rumbling, with every run a ringing concussion and a rhymthic series of impacts, and a passage of intermittent puffs of white steam across the further view. And to the left, between the railway and the dark mass of the low hill beyond, dominating the whole view, colossal, inky-black, and crowned with smoke and fitful flames, stood the great cylinders of the Jeddah Company Blast Furnaces, the central edifices of the big ironworks of which Horrocks was the manager. They stood heavy and threatening, full of an incessant turmoil of flames and seething molten iron, and about the feet of them rattled the rolling-mills, and the steam-hammer beat heavily and splashed the white iron sparks hither and thither. Even as they looked, a truckful of fuel was shot into one of the giants, and the red flames gleamed out, and a confusion of smoke and black dust came boiling upwards towards the sky.

"Certainly you get some colour with your furnaces," said Raut, breaking a silence that had become apprehensive.

Horrocks grunted. He stood with his hands in his pockets, frowning down at the dim steaming railway and the busy ironworks beyond, frowning as if he were thinking out some knotty problem.

Raut glanced at him and away again. "At present your moonlight effect is hardly ripe," he continued, looking upward; "the moon is still smothered by the vestiges of daylight."

Horrocks stared at him with the expression of a man who has suddenly awakened. "Vestiges of daylight?...Of course, of course." He too looked up at the moon, pale still in the midsummer sky. "Come along," he said suddenly, and gripping Raut's arm in his hand, made a move towards the path that dropped from them to the railway.

Raut hung back. Their eyes met and saw a thousand things in a moment that their lips came near to say. Horrocks's hand tightened and then relaxed. He let go, and before Raut was aware of it, they were arm in arm, and walking, one unwillingly enough, down the path.

"You see the fine effect of the railway signals towards Burslem," said Horrocks, suddenly breaking into loquacity, striding fast and tightening the grip of his elbow the while – "little green lights and red and white lights, all against the haze. You have an eye for effect, Raut. It's fine. And look at those furnaces of mine, how they rise upon us as we come down the hill. That to the right is my pet – seventy feet of him. I packed him myself, and he's boiled away cheerfully with iron in his guts for five long years. I've a particular fancy for *him*. That line of red there – a lovely bit of warm orange you'd call it, Raut – that's the puddlers' furnaces, and there, in the hot light, three black figures – did you see the white splash of the steam-hammer then? – that's the rolling mills. Come along! Clang, clatter, how it goes rattling across the floor! Sheet tin, Raut, – amazing stuff. Glass mirrors are not in it when that stuff comes from the mill. And, squelch! There goes the hammer again. Come along!"

He had to stop talking to catch at his breath. His arm twisted into Raut's with benumbing tightness. He had come striding down the black path towards the railway as though he was possessed. Raut had not spoken a word, had simply hung back against Horrocks's pull with all his strength.

"I say," he said now, laughing nervously, but with an undertone of snarl in his voice, "why on earth are you nipping my arm off, Horrocks, and dragging me along like this?"

At length Horrocks released him. His manner changed again. "Nipping your arm off?" he said. "Sorry. But it's you taught me the trick of walking in that friendly way."

"You haven't learnt the refinements of it yet then," said Raut, laughing artificially again. "By Jove! I'm black and blue." Horrocks offered no apology. They stood now near the bottom of the hill, close to the fence that bordered the railway. The ironworks had grown larger and spread out with their approach. They looked up to the blast furnaces now instead of down; the further view of Etruria and Hanley had dropped out of sight with their descent. Before them, by the stile, rose a notice-board, bearing, still dimly visible, the words, *'Beware of the Trains,'* half hidden by splashes of coaly mud.

"Fine effects," said Horrocks, waving his arm. "Here comes a train. The puffs of smoke, the orange glare, the round eye of light in front of it, the melodious rattle. Fine effects! But these furnaces of mine used to be finer, before we shoved cones in their throats, and saved the gas."

"How?" said Raut. "Cones?"

"Cones, my man, cones. I'll show you one nearer. The flames used to flare out of the open throats, great – what is it? – pillars of cloud by day, red and black smoke, and pillars of fire by night. Now we run it off – in pipes, and burn it to heat the blast, and the top is shut by a cone. You'll be interested in that cone."

"But every now and then," said Raut, "you get a burst of fire and smoke up there."

"The cone's not fixed, it's hung by a chain from a lever, and balanced by an equipoise. You shall see it nearer. Else, of course, there'd be no way of getting fuel into the thing. Every now and then the cone dips, and out comes the flare."

"I see," said Raut. He looked over his shoulder. "The moon gets brighter," he said.

"Come along," said Horrocks abruptly, gripping his shoulder again, and moving him suddenly towards the railway crossing. And then came one of those swift incidents, vivid, but so rapid that they leave one doubtful and reeling. Half-way across, Horrocks's hand suddenly clenched upon him like a vice, and swung him backward and through a half-turn, so that he looked up the line. And there a chain of lamp-lit carriage windows telescoped swiftly as it came towards them, and the red and yellow lights of an engine grew larger and larger, rushing down upon them. As he grasped what this meant, he turned his face to Horrocks, and pushed with all his strength against the arm that held him back between the rails. The struggle did not last a moment. Just as certain as it was that Horrocks held him there, so certain was it that he had been violently lugged out of danger.

"Out of the way," said Horrocks with a gasp, as the train came rattling by, and they stood panting by the gate into the ironworks.

"I did not see it coming," said Raut, still, even in spite of his own apprehensions, trying to keep up an appearance of ordinary intercourse.

Horrocks answered with a grunt. "The cone," he said, and then, as one who recovers himself, "I thought you did not hear."

"I didn't," said Raut.

"I wouldn't have had you run over then for the world," said Horrocks.

"For a moment I lost my nerve," said Raut.

Horrocks stood for half a minute, then turned abruptly towards the ironworks again. "See how fine these great mounds of mine, these clinker-heaps, look in the night! That truck yonder, up above there! Up it goes, and out-tilts the slag. See the palpitating red stuff go sliding down the slope. As we get nearer, the heap rises up and cuts the blast furnaces. See the quiver up above the big one. Not that way! This way, between the heaps. That goes to the puddling furnaces, but I want to show you the canal first." He came and took Raut by the elbow, and so they went along side by side. Raut answered Horrocks vaguely. What, he asked himself, had really happened on the line? Was he deluding himself with his own fancies, or had Horrocks actually held him back in the way of the train? Had he just been within an ace of being murdered?

Suppose this slouching, scowling monster *did* know anything? For a minute or two then Raut was really afraid for his life, but the mood passed as he reasoned with himself. After all, Horrocks might have heard nothing. At any rate, he had pulled him out of the way in time. His odd manner might be due to the mere vague jealousy he had shown once before. He was talking now of the ash-heaps and the canal. "Eigh?" said Horrocks.

"What?" said Raut. "Rather! The haze in the moonlight. Fine!"

"Our canal," said Horrocks, stopping suddenly. "Our canal by moonlight and firelight is immense. You've never seen it? Fancy that! You've spent too many of your evenings philandering up in Newcastle there. I tell you, for real florid quality – But you shall see. Boiling water...."

As they came out of the labyrinth of clinker-heaps and mounds of coal and ore, the noises of the rolling-mill sprang upon them suddenly, loud, near, and distinct. Three shadowy workmen went by and touched their caps to Horrocks. Their faces were vague in the darkness. Raut felt a futile impulse to address them, and before he could frame his words they passed into the shadows. Horrocks pointed to the canal close before them now: a weird-looking place it seemed, in the blood-red reflections of the furnaces. The hot water that cooled the tuyères came into it, some fifty yards up – a tumultuous, almost boiling affluent, and the steam rose up from the water in silent white wisps and streaks, wrapping damply about them, an incessant succession of ghosts coming up from the black and red eddies, a white uprising that made the head swim. The shining black tower of the larger blast-furnace rose overhead out of the mist, and its tumultuous riot filled their ears. Raut kept away from the edge of the water, and watched Horrocks.

"Here it is red," said Horrocks, "blood-red vapour as red and hot as sin; but yonder there, where the moonlight falls on it, and it drives across the clinker-heaps, it is as white as death."

Raut turned his head for a moment, and then came back hastily to his watch on Horrocks. "Come along to the rolling-mills," said Horrocks. The threatening hold was not so evident that time, and Raut felt a little reassured. But all the same, what on earth did Horrocks mean about 'white as death' and 'red as sin'? Coincidence, perhaps?

They went and stood behind the puddlers for a little while, and then through the rolling-mills, where amidst an incessant din the deliberate steam-hammer beat the juice out of the succulent iron, and black, half-naked Titans rushed the plastic bars, like hot sealing-wax, between the wheels, "Come on," said Horrocks in Raut's ear; and they went and peeped through the little glass hole behind the tuyères, and saw the tumbled fire writhing in the pit of the blast-furnace. It left one eye blinded for a while. Then, with green and blue patches dancing across the dark, they went to the lift by which the trucks of ore and fuel and lime were raised to the top of the big cylinder.

And out upon the narrow rail that overhung the furnace Raut's doubts came upon him again. Was it wise to be here? If Horrocks did know – everything! Do what he would, he could not resist a violent trembling. Right under foot was a sheer depth of seventy feet. It was a dangerous place. They pushed by a truck of fuel to get to the railing that crowned the thing. The reek of the furnace, a sulphurous vapour streaked with pungent bitterness, seemed to make the distant hillside of Hanley quiver. The moon was riding out now from among a drift of clouds, half-way up the sky above the undulating wooded outlines of Newcastle. The steaming canal ran away from below them under an indistinct bridge, and vanished into the dim haze of the flat fields towards Burslem.

"That's the cone I've been telling you of," shouted Horrocks; "and, below that, sixty feet of fire and molten metal, with the air of the blast frothing through it like gas in soda-water."

Raut gripped the hand-rail tightly, and stared down at the cone. The heat was intense. The boiling of the iron and the tumult of the blast made a thunderous accompaniment to Horrocks's voice. But the thing had to be gone through now. Perhaps, after all...

"In the middle," bawled Horrocks, "temperature near a thousand degrees. If *you* were dropped into it ...flash into flame like a pinch of gunpowder in a candle. Put your hand out and feel the heat of his breath. Why, even up here I've seen the rain-water boiling off the trucks. And that cone there. It's a damned sight too hot for roasting cakes. The top side of it's three hundred degrees."

"Three hundred degrees!" said Raut.

"Three hundred centigrade, mind!" said Horrocks. "It will boil the blood out of you in no time."

"Eigh?" said Raut, and turned.

"Boil the blood out of you in ...No, you don't!"

"Let me go!" screamed Raut. "Let go my arm!"

With one hand he clutched at the hand-rail, then with both. For a moment the two men stood swaying. Then suddenly, with a violent jerk, Horrocks had twisted him from his hold. He clutched at Horrocks and missed, his foot went back into empty air; in mid-air he twisted himself, and then cheek and shoulder and knee struck the hot cone together.

He clutched the chain by which the cone hung, and the thing sank an infinitesimal amount as he struck it. A circle of glowing red appeared about him, and a tongue of flame, released from the chaos within, flickered up towards him. An intense pain assailed him at the knees, and he could smell the singeing of his hands. He raised himself to his feet, and tried to climb up the chain, and then something struck his head. Black and shining with the moonlight, the throat of the furnace rose about him.

Horrocks, he saw, stood above him by one of the trucks of fuel on the rail. The gesticulating figure was bright and white in the moonlight, and shouting, "Fizzle, you fool! Fizzle, you hunter of women! You hot-blooded hound! Boil! Boil! Boil!"

Suddenly he caught up a handful of coal out of the truck, and flung it deliberately, lump after lump, at Raut.

"Horrocks!" cried Raut. "Horrocks!"

He clung, crying, to the chain, pulling himself up from the burning of the cone. Each missile Horrocks flung hit him. His clothes charred and glowed, and as he struggled the cone dropped, and a rush of hot, suffocating gas whooped out and burned round him in a swift breath of flame.

His human likeness departed from him. When the momentary red had passed, Horrocks saw a charred, blackened figure, its head streaked with blood, still clutching and fumbling with the chain, and writhing in agony – a cindery animal, an inhuman, monstrous creature that began a sobbing, intermittent shriek.

Abruptly at the sight the ironmaster's anger passed. A deadly sickness came upon him. The heavy odour of burning flesh came drifting up to his nostrils. His sanity returned to him.

"God have mercy upon me!" he cried. "O God! What have I done?"

He knew the thing below him, save that it still moved and felt, was already a dead man – that the blood of the poor wretch must be boiling in his veins. An intense realisation of that agony came to his mind, and overcame every other feeling. For a moment he stood irresolute, and then, turning to the truck, he hastily tilted its contents upon the struggling thing that had once been a man. The mass fell with a thud, and went radiating over the cone. With the thud the shriek ended, and a boiling confusion of smoke, dust, and flame came rushing up towards him. As it passed, he saw the cone clear again.

Then he staggered back, and stood trembling, clinging to the rail with both hands. His lips moved, but no words came to them.

Down below was the sound of voices and running steps. The clangour of rolling in the shed ceased abruptly.

If you enjoyed this, you might also like...
From the Dead, see page 249
Our New House, see page 423

The Houseboat

Richard Marsh

Chapter I

"I AM SURE of it!"

Inglis laid down his knife and fork. He stared round and round the small apartment in a manner which was distinctly strange. My wife caught him up. She laid down her knife and fork.

"You're sure of what?"

Inglis seemed disturbed. He appeared unwilling to give a direct answer. "Perhaps, after all, it's only a coincidence."

But Violet insisted "What is a coincidence?"

Inglis addressed himself to me.

"The fact is, Millen, directly I came on board I tought I had seen this boat before."

"But I thought you said that you had never heard of the Water Lily."

"Nor have I. The truth is that when I knew it, it wasn't the Water Lily."

"I don't understand."

"They must have changed the name. Unless I am very much mistaken this – this used to be the Sylph."

"The Sylph?"

"You don't mean to say that you have never heard of the Sylph?" Inglis asked this question in a tone of voice which was peculiar.

"My dear fellow, I'm not a riverain authority. I am not acquainted with every houseboat between Richmond and Oxford. It was only at your special recommendation that I took the Water Lily!"

"Excuse me, Millen, I advised a houseboat. I didn't specify the Water Lily!"

"But," asked my wife, "what was the matter with the Sylph that she should so mysteriously have become the Water Lily?"

Inglis fenced with this question in a manner which seemed to suggest a state of mental confusion.

"Of course, Millen, I know that that sort of thing would not have the slightest influence on you. It is only people of a very different sort who would allow it to have any effect on them. Then, after all, I may be wrong. And, in any case, I don't see that it matters."

"Mr. Inglis, are you suggesting that the Sylph was haunted?"

"Haunted!" Inglis started "I never dropped a hint about its being haunted. So far as I remember I never heard a word of anything of the kind."

Violet placed her knife and fork together on her plate. She folded her hands upon her lap.

"Mr. Inglis, there is a mystery. Will you this mystery unfold?" "Didn't you really ever hear about the Sylph – two years ago?" "Two years ago we were out of England."

"So you were. Perhaps that explains it. You understand, this mayn't be the Sylph. I may be wrong – though I don't think I am." Inglis glanced uncomfortably at the chair on which he was sitting. "Why, I believe this is the very chair on which I sat! I remember noticing what a queer shape it was."

It was rather an odd-shaped chair. For that matter, all the things on board were odd.

"Then have you been on board this boat before?"

"Yes." Inglis positively shuddered. "I was, once; if it is the Sylph, that is." He thrust his hands into his trouser pockets. He leaned back in his chair. A curious look came into his face. "It is the Sylph, I'll swear to it. It all comes back to me. What an extraordinary coincidence! One might almost think there was something supernatural in the thing."

His manner fairly roused me.

"I wish you would stop speaking in riddles, and tell us what you are driving at."

He became prematurally solemn.

"Millen, I'm afraid I have made rather an ass of myself; I ought to have held my tongue. But the coincidence is such a strange one that it took me unawares, and since I have said so much I suppose I may as well say more. After dinner I will tell you all there is to tell. I don't think it's a story which Mrs. Millen would like to listen to."

Violet's face was a study.

"I don't understand you, Mr. Inglis, because you are quite well aware it is a principle of mine that what is good for a husband to hear is good for a wife. Come, don't be silly. Let us hear what the fuss is about. I daresay it's about nothing after all."

"You think so? Well, Mrs. Millen, you shall hear." He carefully wiped his moustache. He began: "Two years ago there was a houseboat on the river called the Sylph. It belonged to a man named Hambro. He lent it to a lady and a gentleman. She was rather a pretty woman, with a lot of fluffy, golden hair. He was a quiet unassuming-looking man, who looked as though he had something to do with horses. I made their acquaintance on the river. One evening he asked me on board to dine. I sat, as I believe, on this very chair, at this very table. Three days afterwards they disappeared."

"Well? " I asked. Inglis had paused.

"So far as I know, he has never been seen or heard of since."

"And the lady?"

"Some of us were getting up a picnic. We wanted them to come with us. We couldn't quite make out their sudden disappearance. So, two days after we had missed them, I and another man tried to rout them out I looked through the window. I saw something lying on the floor. 'Jarvis,' I whispered, 'I believe that Mrs. Bush is lying on the floor dead drunk.' 'She can't have been drunk two days,' he said. He came to my side. 'Why, she's in her nightdress. This is very queer. Inglis, I wonder if the door is locked.' It wasn't. We opened it and went inside."

Inglis emptied his glass of wine.

"The woman we had known as Mrs. Bush lay in her nightdress, dead upon the floor. She had been stabbed to the heart She was lying just about where Mrs. Millen is sitting now."

"Mr. Inglis!" Violet rose suddenly.

"There is reason to believe that, from one point of view, the woman was no better than she ought to have been. That is the story."

"But" – I confess it was not at all the story I had expected it was going to be; I did not altogether like it – "who killed her?"

"That is the question. There was no direct evidence to show. No weapon was discovered The man we had known as Bush had vanished, as it seemed, off the face of the earth. He had not left so much as a pocket-handkerchief behind him. Everything both of his and hers had gone. It turned out that nobody knew anything at all about him. They had no servant. What meals they had on board were sent in from the hotel. Hambro had advertised the Sylph. Bush had replied to the advertisement He had paid the rent in advance, and Hambro had asked no questions."

"And what became of the Sylph?"

"She also vanished. She had become a little too notorious. One doesn't fancy living on board a houseboat on which a murder has been committed; one is at too close quarters. I suppose Hambro sold her for what he could get, and the purchaser painted her, and rechristened her the Water Lily!"

"But are you sure this is the Sylph?"

"As sure as that I am sitting here. It is impossible that I could be mistaken. I still seem to see that woman lying dead just about where Mrs. Millen is standing now."

"Mr. Inglis!"

Violet was standing up. She moved away – towards me. Inglis left soon afterwards. He did not seem to care to stop. He had scarcely eaten any dinner. In fact, that was the case with all of us. Mason had exerted herself to prepare a decent meal in her cramped little kitchen, and we had been so ungrateful as not even to reach the end of her bill of fare. When Inglis had gone she appeared in her bonnet and cloak. We supposed that, very naturally, she had taken umbrage.

"If you please, ma'am, I'm going."

"Mason ! What do you mean?"

"I couldn't think of stopping in no place in which murder was committed, least of all a houseboat. Not to mention that last night I heard ghosts, if ever anyone heard them yet."

"Mason! Don't be absurd. I thought you had more sense."

"All I can say is, ma'am, that last night as I lay awake, listening to the splashing of the water, all at once I heard in here the sound of quarrelling. I couldn't make it out. I thought that you and the master was having words. Yet it didn't sound like your voices. Besides, you went on awful. Still, I didn't like to say nothing, because it might have been, and it wasn't my place to say that I had heard. But now I know that it was ghosts."

She went. She was not to be persuaded to stay any more than Inglis. She did not even stay to clear the table. I have seldom seen a woman in a greater hurry. As for wages, there was not a hint of them. Staid, elderly, self-possessed female though she was, she seemed to be in a perfect panic of fear. Nothing would satisfy her but that she should, with the greatest possible expedition, shake from her feet the dust of the Water Lily, When we were quit of her I looked at Violet and Violet looked at me. I laughed. I will not go so far as to say that I laughed genially; still, I laughed.

"We seem to be in for a pleasant river holiday."

"Eric, let us get outside."

We went on deck. The sun had already set. There was no moon, but there was a cloudless sky. The air was languorous and heavy. Boats were stealing over the waters. Someone in the distance was playing a banjo accompaniment while a clear girlish voice was singing "The Garden of Sleep." The other houseboats were radiant with Chinese lanterns. The Water Lily alone was still in shadow. We drew our deck-chairs close together. Violet's hand stole into mine.

"Eric, do you know that last night I, too, heard voices?"

"You!" I laughed again. "Violet!"

"I couldn't make it out at all. I was just going to wake you when they were still."

"You were dreaming, child. Inglis's story – confound him and his story! – has recalled your dream to mind. I hope you don't wish to follow Mason's example, and make a bolt of it. I have paid pretty stiffly for the honour of being the Water Lily tenant for a month, not to mention the fact of disarranging all our plans."

Violet paused before she answered.

"No; I don't think I want, as you say, to make a bolt of it. Indeed," she nestled closer to my side, "it is rather the other way. I should like to see it through. I have sometimes thought that I should like to be with someone I can trust in a situation such as this. Perhaps we may be able to fathom the mystery – who knows?"

This tickled me. "I thought you had done with romance."

"With one sort of romance I hope I shall never have done." She pressed my hand. She looked up archly into my face. I knew it, although we were in shadow. " With another sort of romance I may be only just beginning. I have never yet had dealings with a ghost."

Chapter II

AT FIRST I could not make out what it was that had roused me. Then I felt Violet's hand steal into mine. Her voice whispered in my ear, "Eric!" I turned over towards her on the pillow. "Be still. They're here." I did as she bade me. I was still. I heard no sound but the lazy rippling of the river.

"Who's here?" I asked, when, as I deemed, I had been silent long enough.

"S-sh!" I felt her finger pressed against my lips. I was still again. The silence was broken in rather a peculiar manner.

"I don't think you quite understand me."

The words were spoken in a man's voice, as it seemed to me, close behind my back. I was so startled by the unexpected presence of a third person that I made as if to spring up in bed. My wife caught me by the arm. Before I could remonstrate or shake off her grasp a woman's laughter rang through the little cabin. It was too metallic to be agreeable. And a woman's voice replied –

"I understand you well enough, don't you make any error!" There was a momentary pause.

"You don't understand me, fool!"

The first four words were spoken with a deliberation which meant volumes, while the final epithet came with a sudden malignant ferocity which took me aback. The speaker, whoever he might be, meant mischief. I sprang up and out of bed.

"What are you doing here?" I cried.

I addressed the inquiry apparently to the vacant air. The moonlight flooded the little cabin. It showed clearly enough that it was empty. My wife sat up in bed.

"Now," she observed, "you've done it."

"Done what? Who was that speaking?"

"The voices."

"The voices! What voices? I'll voice them! Where the dickens have they gone?"

I moved towards the cabin door, with the intention of pursuing my inquiries further. Violet's voice arrested me.

"It is no use your going to look for them. They will not be found by searching. The speakers were Mr. and Mrs. Bush."

"Mr. and Mrs. Bush?"

Violet's voice dropped to an awful whisper. "The murderer and his victim."

I stared at her in the moonlight. Inglis's pleasant little story had momentarily escaped my memory. Suddenly roused from a dreamless slumber, I had not yet had time to recall such trivialities. Now it all came back in a flash.

"Violet," I exclaimed, "have you gone mad?"

"They are the voices which I heard last night.They are the voices which Mason heard. Now you have heard them. If you had kept still the mystery might have been unravelled. The crime might have been re-acted before our eyes, or at least within sound of our ears."

I sat down upon the ingenious piece of furniture which did duty as a bed. I seemed to have struck upon a novel phase in my wife's character. It was not altogether a pleasing novelty. She spoke with a degree of judicial calmness which, under all the circumstances, I did not altogether relish.

"Violet, I wish you wouldn't talk like that. It makes my blood run cold."

"Why should it? My dear Eric, I have heard you yourself say that in the presence of the seemingly mysterious our attitude should be one of passionless criticism. A mysterious crime has been committed in this very chamber." I shivered. "Surely it is our duty to avail ourselves of any opportunities which may offer, and which may enable us to probe it to the bottom."

I made no answer. I examined the doors. They were locked and bolted. There was no sign that anyone had tampered with the fastenings. I returned to bed. As I was arranging myself between the sheets Violet whispered in my ear. "Perhaps if we are perfectly quiet they may come back again."

I am not a man given to adjectives; but I felt adjectival then. I was about to explain, in language which would not have been wanting in force, that I had no desire that they should come back again, when –

"You had better give it to me."

The words were spoken in a woman's voice, as it seemed, within twelve inches of my back. The voice was not that of a lady. I should have said without hesitation, had I heard the voice under any other circumstances, that the speaker had been bom within the sound of Bow Bells.

"Had I?"

It was a man's voice which put the question. There was something about the tone in which the speaker put it which reminded one of the line in the people's ballad, "It ain't exactly what 'e sez, it's the nasty way 'e sez it." The question was put in a very "nasty way" indeed.

"Yes, my boy, you had."

"Indeed?"

"Yes, you may say 'indeed,' but if you don't I tell you what I'll do – I'll spoil you."

"And what, my dear Gertie, am I to understand by the mystic threat of spoiling me?"

"I'll go straight to your wife, and I'll tell her everything."

"Oh, you will, will you?"

There was a movement of a chair. The male speaker was getting up. "Yes, I will"

There was a slight pause. One could fancy that the speakers were facing each other. One could picture the look of impudent defiance upon the woman's countenance, the suggestion of coming storm upon that of the man. It was the man's voice which broke the silence.

"It is odd, Gertrude, that you should have chosen this evening to threaten me, because I myself had chosen this evening, I won't say to threaten, but to make a communication to you."

"Give me a match." The request came from the woman.

"With pleasure. I will give you anything, my dear Gertrude, within reason." There was another pause...In the silence I seemed to hear my wife holding her breath – as I certainly was holding mine. All at once there came a sound of scratching, a flash of light. It came so unexpectedly, and such was the extreme tension of my nerves, that, with a stifled exclamation, I half rose in bed. My wife pressed her hand against my lips. She held me down. She spoke in so attenuated a whisper that it was only because all my senses were so keenly on the alert that I heard her.

"You goose ! He's only striking a match."

He might have been, but who? She took things for granted. I wanted to know. The light continued flickering to and fro, as a match does flicker. I would have given much to know who held it, or even what was its position in the room. As luck had it, my face was turned the other way. My wife seemed to understand what was passing in my mind.

"There's no one there," she whispered.

No one, I presumed, but the match. I took it for granted that was there. Though I did not venture to inquire, I felt that I might not have such perfect control over my voice as my wife appeared to have.

While the light continued to flicker there came stealing into my nostrils – I sniffed, the thing was unmistakable! – the odour of tobacco. The woman was lighting a cigarette. I knew it was the woman because presently there came this request from the man, "After you with the light, my dear."

I presume that the match was passed. Immediately the smell of tobacco redoubled. The man had lit a cigarette as well. I confess that I resented – silently, but still strongly – the idea of two strangers, whether ghosts or anybody else, smoking, uninvited, in my cabin.

The match went out The cigarettes were lit. The man continued speaking.

"The communication, my dear Gertrude, which I intended to make to you was this. The time has come for us to part."

He paused, possibly for an answer. None came.

"I need not enlarge on the reasons which necessitate our parting. They exist."

Pause again. Then the woman.

"What are you going to give me?"

"One of the reasons which necessitate our parting – a very strong reason, as you, I am sure, will be the first to admit – is that I have nothing left to give you."

"So you say."

"Precisely. So I say and so I mean."

"Do you mean that you are going to give me nothing?"

"I mean, my dear Gertrude, that I have nothing to give you. You have left me nothing."

"Bah!"

The sound which issued from the lady's lips was expressive of the most complete contempt. "Look here, my boy, you give me a hundred sovereigns or I'll spoil you."

Pause again. Probably the gentleman was thinking over the lady's observation.

"What benefit do you think you will do yourself by what you call 'spoiling' me?"

"Never mind about that: I'll do it You think I don't know all about you, but I do. Perhaps I'm not so soft as you think. Your wife's got some money if you haven't. Suppose you go back and ask her for some. You've treated me badly enough. I don't see why you shouldn't go and treat her the same. She wouldn't make things warm for you if she knew a few things I could tell her – not at all! You give me a hundred sovereigns or, I tell you straight, I'll go right to your house and I'll tell her all."

"Oh, no, you won't."

"Won't I? I say l will!"

"Oh, no, you won't."

"I say I will! I've warned you, that's all I'm not going to stop here, talking stuff to you. I'm going to bed. You can go and hang yourself for all I care."

There was a sound, an indubitable sound – the sound of a pair of shoes being thrown upon the floor. There were other sounds, equally capable of explanation: sounds which suggested – I wish the printer would put it in small type – that the lady was undressing. Undressing, too, with scant regard to ceremony. Garments were thrown off and tossed higgledy-piggledy here and there. They appeared to be thrown, with sublime indifference, upon table, chairs, and floor. I even felt something alight upon the bed. Some feminine garment, perhaps, which, although it fell by no means heavily, made me conscious, as it fell, of the most curious sensation I had in all my life – till then – experienced. It seemed that the lady, while she unrobed, continued smoking.

From her next words it appeared that the gentleman, also smoking, stood and stared at her.

"Don't stand staring at me like a gawk. I'm going to turn in."

"And I'm going to turn out. Not, as you suggested, to hang myself, but to finish this cigarette upon the roof. Perhaps, when I return, you will be in a more equable frame of mind."

"Don't you flatter yourself. What I say I mean. A hundred sovereigns, or I tell your wife."

He laughed very softly, as though he was determined not to be annoyed. Then we heard his footsteps as he crossed the floor. The door opened, then closed. We heard him ascend the steps. Then, with curious distinctness, his measured tramp, tramp, as he moved to and fro upon the roof. In the cabin for a moment there was silence. Then the woman said, with a curious faltering in her voice –

"I'll do it. I don't care what he says." There was a choking in her throat. "He don't care for me a bit."

Suddenly she flung herself upon her knees beside the bed. She pillowed her head and arms upon the coverlet. I lay near the outer edge of the bed, which was a small one, by the way. As I lay I felt the pressure of her limbs. My sensations, as I did, I am unable to describe. After a momentary interval there came the sound of sobbing. I could feel the woman quivering with the strength of her emotion. Violet and I were speechless. I do not think that, for the instant, we could have spoken even had we tried. The woman's presence was so evident, her grief so real. As she wept disjointed words came from her.

"I've given everything for him! If he only cared for me! If he only did."

All at once, with a rapid movement, she sprang up. The removal of the pressure was altogether unmistakable. I was conscious of her resting her hands upon the coverlet to assist her to her feet. I felt the little jerk; then the withdrawal of the hands. She choked back her sobs when she had gained her feet Her tone was changed.

"What a fool I am to make a fuss. He don't care for me – not that." We heard her snap her fingers in the air. "He never did. Us women are always fools – we're all the same. I'll go to bed."

Violet clutched my arm. She whispered, in that attenuated fashion she seemed to have caught the trick of—

"She's getting into bed. We must get out."

It certainly was a fact, someone was getting into bed. The bed-clothes were moved; not our bedclothes, but some phantom coverings. We heard them rustle, we were conscious of a current of air across our faces as someone caught them open. And then! – then someone stepped upon the bed.

"Let's get out!" gasped Violet.

Chapter III

SHE MOVED away from me. She squeezed herself against the side of the cabin. She withdrew her limbs from between the sheets. As for me, the person who had stepped upon the bed had actually stepped upon me, and that without seeming at all conscious of my presence. Someone sat down plump upon the sheet beside me. That was enough. I took advantage of my lying on the edge of the bed to slip out upon the floor. I might possess an unsuspected capacity for undergoing strange experiences, but I drew the line at sleeping with a ghost.

The moonlight streamed across the room. As I stood, in something very like a state of nature on the floor, I could clearly see Violet cowering on the further side of the bed. I could distinguish all her features. But when I looked upon the bed itself – there was nothing there. The moon's rays fell upon the pillow. They revealed its snowy whiteness. There seemed nothing else it could reveal. It was untenanted. And yet, if one looked closely at it, it seemed to be indented, just as it might have been indented had a human head been lying there. But about one thing there could be no mistake whatever – my ears did not play me false, I heard it too distinctly – the sound made by a person who settles himself between the sheets, and then the measured respiration of one who composes himself to slumber.

I remained there silent. On her hands and knees Violet crept towards the foot of the bed. When she had gained the floor she stole on tiptoe to my side.

"I did not dare to step across her." I felt her, as she nestled to me, give me a little shiver. " I could not do it. Can you see her?"

"What a fool I am!" As Violet asked her question there came this observation from the person in the bed – whom, by the way, I could not see. There was a long- drawn sigh. "What fools all we women are! What fools!"

There was a sincerity of bitterness about the tone, which, coming as it did from an unseen speaker – one so near and yet so far – had on one a most uncomfortable effect. Violet pressed closer to my side. The woman in the bed turned over. Overhead there still continued the measured tramp, tramping of the man. We were conscious, in some subtle way, that the woman lay listening to the footsteps. They spoke more audibly to her ears even than to ours.

"Ollie! Ollie!" she repeated the name softly to herself, with a degree of tenderness which was in startling contrast to her previous bitterness.

"I wish you would come to bed."

She was silent There was only the sound of her gentle breathing. Her bitter mood had been but transient. She was falling asleep with words of tenderness upon her lips. Above, the footsteps ceased. All was still. There was not even the murmur of the waters. The wife and I, side by side, stood looking down upon what seemed an empty bed.

"She is asleep," said Violet.

It seemed to me she was: although I could not see her, it seemed to me she was. I could hear her breathing as softly as a child. Violet continued whispering –

"How strange! Eric, what can it mean?"

I muttered a reply –

"A problem for the Psychical Research Society."

"It seems just like a dream."

"I wish it were a dream."

"S-sh! There is someone coming down the stairs."

There was – at least, if we could trust our ears, there was. Apparently the man above had had enough of solitude. We heard him move across the roof, then pause just by the steps, then descend them one by one. It seemed to us that in this step there was something stealthy, that he was endeavouring not to arouse attention, to make as little noise as possible. Half-way down he paused; at the foot he paused again.

"He's listening outside the door." It almost seemed that he was. We stood and listened too.

"Let's get away from the bed."

My wife drew me with her. At the opposite end of the cabin was a sort of little alcove, which was screened by a curtain, and behind which were hung one or two of our garments which we were not actually using. Violet drew me within the shadow of this alcove. I say drew me because, offering no resistance, I allowed myself to be completely passive in her hands. The alcove was not large enough to hold us. Still the curtain acted as a partial screen.

The silence endured for some moments. Then we heard without a hand softly turning the handle of the door. While I was wondering whether, after all, I was not the victim of an attack of indigestion, or whether I was about to witness an attempt at effecting a burglarious entry into a houseboat, a strange thing happened, the strangest thing that had happened yet.

As I have already mentioned, the moon's rays flooded the cabin. This was owing to the fact that a long narrow casement, which ran round the walls near the roof of the cabin, had been left open for the sake of admitting air and ventilation; but save for the moonbeams, the cabin was unlighted. When, however, we heard the handle being softly turned, a singular change occurred. It was like the transformation scene in a theatre. The whole place, all at once, was brilliantly illuminated. The moonbeams disappeared. Instead, a large swinging lamp was hanging from the centre of the cabin. So strong was the light which it shed around that our eyes were dazzled. It was not our lamp; we used small hand-lamps, which stood upon the table. By its glare we saw that the whole cabin was changed. For an instant we failed to clearly realise in what the change consisted. Then we understood it was a question of decoration. The contents of the cabin, for the most part, were the same, though they looked newer, and the positions of the various articles were altered; but the panels of the cabin of the Water Lily were painted blue and white. The panels of this cabin were coloured chocolate and gold.

"Eric, it's the Sylph!"

The suggestion conveyed by my wife's whispered words, even as she spoke, occurred to me. I under-stood where, for Inglis, had lain the difficulty of recognition. The two cabins were the same, and yet were not. It was just as though someone had endeavoured, without spending much cash, to render one as much as possible unlike the other.

In this cabin there were many things which were not ours. In fact, so far as I can see, there was nothing which was ours. Strange articles of costume were scattered about; the table was covered with a curious litter; and on the ingenious article of furniture which did duty as a bed, and which stood where our bed stood, and which, indeed, seemed to be our bed, there was someone sleeping.

As my startled eyes travelled round this amazing transformation scene, at last they reached the door. There they stayed. Mechanically I shrank back nearer to the wall. I felt my wife tighten her grasp upon my hand.

The door was open some few inches. Through the aperture thus formed there peered a man. He seemed to be listening. It was so still that one could hear the gentle breathing of the woman sleeping in the bed. Apparently satisfied, he opened the door sufficiently wide to admit of his entering the cabin. My impression was that he could not fail to perceive us, yet to all appearances he remained entirely unconscious of our neighbourhood. He was a man certainly under five feet six in height. He was slight in build, very dark, with face clean shaven; his face was long and narrow. In dress and bearing he seemed a gentleman, yet there was that about him which immediately reminded me of what Inglis had said of the man Bush – "he looked as though he had something to do with horses."

He stood for some seconds in an attitude of listening, so close to me that I had only to stretch out my hand to take him by the throat. I did not do it. I don't know what restrained me; I think, more than anything, it was the feeling that these things which were passing before me must be passing in a dream. His face was turned away. He looked intently towards the sleeping woman.

After he had had enough of listening he moved towards the bed. His step was soft and cat-like; it was absolutely noiseless. Glancing down, I perceived that he was without boots or shoes. He was in his stockinged feet. I had distinctly heard the tramp, tramping of a pair of shoes upon the cabin roof. I had heard them descend the steps. Possibly he had paused outside the door to take them off.

When he reached the bed he stood looking down upon the sleeper. He stooped over her, as if the better to catch her breathing. He whispered softly –

"Gerty!"

He paused for a moment, as if for an answer. None came. Standing up, he put his hand, as it seemed to me, into the bosom of his flannel shirt. He took out a leather sheath. From the sheath he drew a knife. It was a long, slender, glittering blade. Quite twelve inches in length, at no part was it broader than my little finger. With the empty sheath in his left hand, the knife behind his back in his right, he again leaned over the sleeper. Again he softly whispered, "Gerty!"

Again there was no answer. Again he stood upright, turning his back towards the bed, so that he looked towards us. His face was not an ugly one, though the expression was somewhat saturnine. On it, at the instant, there was a peculiar look, such a look as I could fancy upon the face of a jockey who, toward the close of a great race, settles himself in the saddle with the determination to "finish" well. The naked blade he placed upon the table, the empty sheath beside it Then he moved towards us. My first thought was that now, at last, we were discovered ; but something in the expression of his features told me that this was not so. He approached us with an indifference which was amazing. He passed so close to us that we were conscious of the slight disturbance of the air caused by his passage. There was a Gladstone bag on a chair within two feet of us. Picking it up, he bore it to the table. Opening it out, he commenced to pack it. All manner of things he placed within it, both masculine and feminine belongings, even the garments which the sleeper had taken off, and which lay scattered on the chair and on the floor, even her shoes and stockings! When the bag was filled he took a long brown ulster, which was thrown over the back of a chair. He stuffed the pockets with odds and ends. When he had completed his operations the cabin was stripped of everything except the actual furniture. He satisfied himself that this was so overhauling every nook and corner, in the process passing and repassing Violet and me with a perfect unconcern which was more and more amazing. Being apparently at last clear in his mind upon that point, he put on the ulster and a dark cloth cap, and began to fasten the Gladstone bag.

While he was doing so, his back being turned to the bed, without the slighest warning, the woman in the bed sat up. The man's movements had been noiseless. He had made no sound which could have roused her. Possibly some sudden intuition had come to her in her sleep. However that might be, she all at once was wide awake. She stared round the apartment with wondering eyes. Her glance fell on the man, dressed as for a journey.

"Where are you going?"

The words fell from her lips as unawares. Then some sudden conception of his purpose seemed to have flown to her brain. She sprang out of bed with a bound.

"You shan't go," she screamed.

She rushed to him. He put his hand on the table. He turned to her. Sometiiing flashed in the lamplight. It was the knife. As she came he plunged it into her side right to the hilt. For an instant he held her spitted on the blade. He put his hand to her throat. He thrust her from him. With the other hand he extricated the blade. He let her fall upon the floor. She had uttered a sort of sigh as the weapon was being driven home. Beyond that she had not made a sound.

All was still. He remained for some seconds looking down at her as she lay. Then he turned away. We saw his face. It was, if possible, paler than before. A smile distorted his lips. He stood for a moment as if listening. Then he glanced round the cabin, as if to make sure that he was unobserved.

His black eyes travelled over our startled features, in evident unconsciousness that we were there. Then he glanced at the blade in his hand. As he did so he perceptibly shuddered. The glittering steel was obscured with blood. As he perceived that this was so he gasped. He seemed to realise for the first time what it was that he had done. Taking an envelope from an inner pocket of his ulster he began to wipe the blood from off the blade. While doing so his wandering glance fell upon the woman lying on the floor. Some new aspect of the recumbent figure seemed to strike him with a sudden horror. He staggered backwards. I thought he would have fallen. He caught at the wall to help him stand – caught at the wall with the hand which held the blade. At that part of the cabin the wall was doubly panelled half-way to the roof. Between the outer and the inner panel there was evidently a cavity, because, when in his sudden alarm he clutched at the wall, the blade slipped from his relaxing grasp and fell between the panels. Such was his state of panic that he did not appear to perceive what had happened. And at that moment a cry rang out upon the river – possibly it was someone hailing the keeper of the lock – "Ahoy!"

The sound seemed to fill him with unreasoning terror. He rushed to the table. He closed the Gladstone with a hurried snap ; he caught it up ; he turned to flee. As he did so I stepped out of the alcove. I advanced right in front of him. I cannot say whether he saw me, or whether he didn't. But he seemed to see me. He started back. A look of the most awful terror came on his countenance. And at that same instant the whole scene vanished. I was standing in the cabin of the Water Lily. The moon was stealing through the little narrow casement Violet was creeping to my side. She stole into my arms. I held her to me.

"Eric," she moaned.

For myself, I am not ashamed to own that, temporarily, I had lost the use of my tongue. When, in a measure, the faculty of speech returned to me –

"Was it a dream?" I whispered. "It was a vision."

"A vision?" I shuddered. "Look!"

As I spoke she turned to look. There, in the moonbeams, we saw a woman in her nightdress, lying on the cabin floor. We saw that she had golden hair. It seemed to us that she was dead. We saw her but a moment – she was gone! It must have been imagination; we know that these things are not, but it belonged to that order of imagination which is stranger than reality.

My wife looked up at me.

"Eric, it is a vision which has been sent to us in order that we may expose in the light of day a crime which was hidden in the night."

I said nothing. I felt for a box of matches on the table. I lit a lamp. I looked round and round the cabin, holding the lamp above my head the better to assist my search. It was with a feeling of the most absurd relief that I perceived that everything was unchanged, that, so far as I could see, there was no one there but my wife and I.

"I think, Violet, if you don't mind, I'll have some whisky."

She offered no objection. She stood and watched me as I poured the stuff into a glass. I am bound to admit that the spirit did me good.

"And what," I asked, "do you make of the performance we have just now witnessed?" She was still. I took another drink. There can be no doubt that, under certain circumstances, whisky is a fluid which is not to be despised. "Have we both suddenly become insane, or do you attribute it to the cucumber we ate at lunch ? "

"How strange that Mr. Inglis should have told us the story only this afternoon."

"I wish Mr. Inglis had kept the story to himself entirely."

"They were the voices which I heard last night They were the voices Mason heard. It was all predestined. I understand it now."

"I wish that I could say the same."

"I see it all!"

She pressed her hands against her brow. Her eyes flashed fire.

"I see why it was sent to us, what it is we have to do. Eric, we have to find the knife."

I began to fear, from her frenzied manner, that her brain must in reality be softening.

"What knife?"

"The knife which he dropped between the panels. The boat has only been repainted. We know that in all essentials the Sylph and the Water Lily are one and the same. Mr. Inglis said that the weapon which did the deed was never found. No adequate search was ever made. It is waiting for us where he dropped it."

"My dear Violet, don't you think you had better have a little whisky? It will calm you."

"Have you a hamimer and a chisel?"

"What do you want them for?"

"It was here that he was standing; it was here that he dropped the knife." She had taken up her position against the wall at the foot of the bed. Frankly, I did not like her manner at all. It was certainly where, in the latter portion of that nightmare, the fellow had been standing. "I will wrench this panel away." She rapped against a particular panel with her knuckles. "Behind it we shall find the knife."

"My dear Violet, this houseboat isn't mine. We cannot destroy another man's property in that wanton fashion. He will hardly accept as an adequate excuse the fact that at the time we were suffering from a severe attack of indigestion."

"This will do."

She took a large carving-knife out of the knife-basket which was on the shelf close by her. She thrust the blade between the panel and the woodwork. It could scarcely have been securely fastened. In a surprisingly short space of time she had forced it loose. Then, grasping it with both her hands, she hauled the panel bodily away.

"Eric, it is there!"

Something was there, resting on a little ledge which had checked its fall on to the floor beneath – something which was covered with paint, and dust, and cobwebs, and Violet all at once grew timid.

"You take it; I dare not touch the thing."

"It is very curious; something is there, and, by George, it is a knife!"

It was a knife – the knife which we had seen in the vision, the dream, the nightmare, call it what you will – the something which had seemed so real. There was no mistaking it, tarnished though it was – the long, slender blade which we had seen the man draw from the leather sheath. Stuck to it by what was afterwards shown to be coagulated blood was an envelope – the envelope which we had seen the fellow take from his pocket to wipe off the crimson stain. It had adhered to the blade. When the knife fell the envelope fell too.

If you enjoyed this, you might also like...
A Yellow Duster, see page 187
That Brute Simmons, see page 111

Darkness
& Light

Brother Owen's Story of Anne Rodway

Wilkie Collins

March 3rd, 1840

A LONG LETTER today from Robert, which surprised and vexed me so that I have been sadly behindhand with my work ever since. He writes in worse spirits than last time, and absolutely declares that he is poorer even than when he went to America, and that he has made up his mind to come home to London.

How happy I should be at this news, if he only returned to me a prosperous man! As it is, though I love him dearly, I cannot look forward to the meeting him again, disappointed and broken down, and poorer than ever, without a feeling almost of dread for both of us. I was twenty-six last birthday and he was thirty-three, and there seems less chance now than ever of our being married. It is all I can do to keep myself by my needle; and his prospects, since he failed in the small stationery business three years ago, are worse, if possible, than mine.

Not that I mind so much for myself; women, in all ways of life, and especially in my dressmaking way, learn, I think, to be more patient than men. What I dread is Robert's despondency, and the hard struggle he will have in this cruel city to get his bread, let alone making money enough to marry me. So little as poor people want to set up in housekeeping and be happy together, it seems hard that they can't get it when they are honest and hearty, and willing to work. The clergyman said in his sermon last Sunday evening that all things were ordered for the best, and we are all put into the stations in life that are properest for us. I suppose he was right, being a very clever gentleman who fills the church to crowding; but I think I should have understood him better if I had not been very hungry at the time, in consequence of my own station in life being nothing but plain needlewoman.

March 4th

Mary Mallinson came down to my room to take a cup of tea with me. I read her bits of Robert's letter, to show her that, if she has her troubles, I have mine too; but I could not succeed in cheering her. She says she is born to misfortune, and that, as long back as she can remember, she has never had the least morsel of luck to be thankful for. I told her to go and look in my glass, and to say if she had nothing to be thankful for then; for Mary is a very pretty girl, and would look still prettier if she could be more cheerful and dress neater. However, my compliment did no good. She rattled her spoon impatiently in her tea-cup, and said, "If I was only as good a hand at needle-work as you are, Anne, I would change faces with the ugliest girl in London." "Not you!" says I, laughing. She looked at me for a moment, and shook her head, and was out of the room before I could get up and stop her. She always runs off in that way when she is going to cry, having a kind of pride about letting other people see her in tears.

345

March 5th

A fright about Mary. I had not seen her all day, as she does not work at the same place where I do; and in the evening she never came down to have tea with me, or sent me word to go to her; so, just before I went to bed, I ran upstairs to say goodnight.

She did not answer when I knocked; and when I stepped softly in the room I saw her in bed, asleep, with her work not half done, lying about the room in the untidiest way. There was nothing remarkable in that, and I was just going away on tiptoe, when a tiny bottle and wine-glass on the chair by her bedside caught my eye. I thought she was ill and had been taking physic, and looked at the bottle. It was marked in large letters, "Laudanum – Poison."

My heart gave a jump as if it was going to fly out of me. I laid hold of her with both hands, and shook her with all my might. She was sleeping heavily, and woke slowly, as it seemed to me – but still she did wake. I tried to pull her out of bed, having heard that people ought to be always walked up and down when they have taken laudanum but she resisted, and pushed me away violently.

"Anne!" says she, in a fright. "For gracious sake, what's come to you! Are you out of your senses?"

"Oh, Mary! Mary!" says I, holding up the bottle before her, "if I hadn't come in when I did—" And I laid hold of her to shake her again.

She looked puzzled at me for a moment – then smiled (the first time I had seen her do so for many a long day) – then put her arms round my neck.

"Don't be frightened about me, Anne," she says; "I am not worth it, and there is no need."

"No need!" says I, out of breath – "no need, when the bottle has got Poison marked on it!"

"Poison, dear, if you take it all," says Mary, looking at me very tenderly, "and a night's rest if you only take a little."

I watched her for a moment, doubtful whether I ought to believe what she said or to alarm the house. But there was no sleepiness now in her eyes, and nothing drowsy in her voice; and she sat up in bed quite easily, without anything to support her.

"You have given me a dreadful fright, Mary," says I, sitting down by her in the chair, and beginning by this time to feel rather faint after being startled so.

She jumped out of bed to get me a drop of water, and kissed me, and said how sorry she was, and how undeserving of so much interest being taken in her. At the same time, she tried to possess herself of the laudanum bottle which I still kept cuddled up tight in my own hands.

"No," says I. "You have got into a low-spirited, despairing way. I won't trust you with it."

"I am afraid I can't do without it," says Mary, in her usual quiet, hopeless voice. "What with work that I can't get through as I ought, and troubles that I can't help thinking of, sleep won't come to me unless I take a few drops out of that bottle. Don't keep it away from me, Anne; it's the only thing in the world that makes me forget myself."

"Forget yourself!" says I. "You have no right to talk in that way, at your age. There's something horrible in the notion of a girl of eighteen sleeping with a bottle of laudanum by her bedside every night. We all of us have our troubles. Haven't I got mine?"

"You can do twice the work I can, twice as well as me," says Mary. "You are never scolded and rated at for awkwardness with your needle, and I always am. You can pay for your room every week, and I am three weeks in debt for mine."

"A little more practice," says I, "and a little more courage, and you will soon do better. You have got all your life before you—"

"I wish I was at the end of it," says she, breaking in. "I am alone in the world, and my life's no good to me."

"You ought to be ashamed of yourself for saying so," says I. "Haven't you got me for a friend? Didn't I take a fancy to you when first you left your step-mother and came to lodge in this house? And haven't I been sisters with you ever since? Suppose you are alone in the world, am I much better off? I'm an orphan like you. I've almost as many things in pawn as you; and, if your pockets are empty, mine have only got ninepence in them, to last me for all the rest of the week."

"Your father and mother were honest people," says Mary, obstinately. "My mother ran away from home, and died in a hospital. My father was always drunk, and always beating me. My step-mother is as good as dead, for all she cares about me. My only brother is thousands of miles away in fore ign parts, and never writes to me, and never helps me with a farthing. My sweetheart—"

She stopped, and the red flew into her face. I knew, if she went on that way, she would only get to the saddest part of her sad story, and give both herself and me unnecessary pain.

"*My* sweetheart is too poor to marry me, Mary," I said, "so I'm not so much to be envied even there. But let's give over disputing which is worst off. Lie down in bed, and let me tuck you up. I'll put a stitch or two into that work of yours while you go to sleep."

Instead of doing what I told her, she burst out crying (being very like a child in some of her ways), and hugged me so tight round the neck that she quite hurt me. I let her go on till she had worn herself out, and was obliged to lie down. Even then, her last few words before she dropped off to sleep were such as I was half sorry, half frightened to hear.

"I won't plague you long, Anne," she said. "I haven't courage to go out of the world as you seem to fear I shall; but I began my life wretchedly, and wretchedly I am sentenced to end it."

It was of no use lecturing her again, for she closed her eyes.

I tucked her up as neatly as I could, and put her petticoat over her, for the bedclothes were scanty, and her hands felt cold. She looked so pretty and delicate as she fell asleep that it quite made my heart ache to see her, after such talk as we had held together. I just waited long enough to be quite sure that she was in the land of dreams, then emptied the horrible laudanum bottle into the grate, took up her half-done work, and, going out softly, left her for that night.

March 6th. Sent off a long letter to Robert, begging and entreating him not to be so down-hearted, and not to leave America without making another effort. I told him I could bear any trial except the wretchedness of seeing him come back a helpless, broken-down man, trying uselessly to begin life again when too old for a change.

It was not till after I had posted my own letter, and read over part of Robert's again, that the suspicion suddenly floated across me, for the first time, that he might have sailed for England immediately after writing to me. There were expressions in the letter which seemed to indicate that he had some such headlong project in his mind. And yet, surely, if it were so, I ought to have noticed them at the first reading. I can only hope I am wrong in my present interpretation of much of what he has written to me – hope it earnestly for both our sakes.

This has been a doleful day for me. I have been uneasy about Robert and uneasy about Mary. My mind is haunted by those last words of hers: "I began my life wretchedly, and wretchedly I am sentenced to end it." Her usual melancholy way of talking never produced the same impression on me that I feel now. Perhaps the discovery of the laudanum-bottle is the cause of this. I would give many a hard day's work to know what to do for Mary's good. My heart warmed to her when we first met in the same lodging-house two years ago, and, although I am not one of the over-affectionate sort myself, I feel as if I could go to the world's end to serve that girl. Yet, strange to say, if I was asked why I was so fond of her, I don't think I should know how to answer the question.

March 7th

I am almost ashamed to write it down, even in this journal, which no eyes but mine ever look on; yet I must honestly confess to myself that here I am, at nearly one in the morning, sitting up in a state of serious uneasiness because Mary has not yet come home.

I walked with her this morning to the place where she works, and tried to lead her into talking of the relations she has got who are still alive. My motive in doing this was to see if she dropped anything in the course of conversation which might suggest a way of helping her interests with those who are bound to give her all reasonable assistance. But the little I could get her to say to me led to nothing. Instead of answering my questions about her step-mother and her brother, she persisted at first, in the strangest way, in talking of her father, who was dead and gone, and of one Noah Truscott, who had been the worst of all the bad friends he had, and had taught him to drink and game. When I did get her to speak of her brother, she only knew that he had gone out to a place called Assam, where they grew tea. How he was doing, or whether he was there still, she did not seem to know, never having heard a word from him for years and years past.

As for her step-mother, Mary not unnaturally flew into a passion the moment I spoke of her. She keeps an eating-house at Hammersmith, and could have given Mary good employment in it; but she seems always to have hated her, and to have made her life so wretched with abuse and ill usage that she had no refuge left but to go away from home, and do her best to make a living for herself. Her husband (Mary's father) appears to have behaved badly to her, and, after his death, she took the wicked course of revenging herself on her step-daughter. I felt, after this, that it was impossible Mary could go back, and that it was the hard necessity of her position, as it is of mine, that she should struggle on to make a decent livelihood without assistance from any of her relations. I confessed as much as this to her; but I added that I would try to get her employment with the persons for whom I work, who pay higher wages, and show a little more indulgence to those under them than the people to whom she is now obliged to look for support.

I spoke much more confidently than I felt about being able to do this, and left her, as I thought, in better spirits than usual. She promised to be back tonight to tea at nine o'clock, and now it is nearly one in the morning, and she is not home yet. If it was any other girl I should not feel uneasy, for I should make up my mind that there was extra work to be done in a hurry, and that they were keeping her late, and I should go to bed. But Mary is so unfortunate in everything that happens to her, and her own melancholy talk about herself keeps hanging on my mind so, that I have fears on her account which would not distress me about anyone else. It seems inexcusably silly to think such a thing, much more to write it down; but I have a kind of nervous dread upon me that some accident—

What does that loud knocking at the street door mean? And those voices and heavy footsteps outside? Some lodger who has lost his key, I suppose. And yet, my heart – What a coward I have become all of a sudden!

More knocking and louder voices. I must run to the door and see what it is. Oh, Mary! Mary! I hope I am not going to have another fright about you, but I feel sadly like it.

March 8th–11th

Oh me! all the troubles I have ever had in my life are as nothing to the trouble I am in now. For three days I have not been able to write a single line in this journal, which I have kept so regularly ever since I was a girl. For three days I have not once thought of Robert – I, who am always thinking of him at other times.

My poor, dear, unhappy Mary! the worst I feared for you on that night when I sat up alone was far below the dreadful calamity that has really happened. How can I write about it, with my eyes full of tears and my hand all of a tremble? I don't even know why I am sitting down at my desk now, unless it is habit that keeps me to my old every-day task, in spite of all the grief and fear which seem to unfit me entirely for performing it.

The people of the house were asleep and lazy on that dreadful night, and I was the first to open the door. Never, never could I describe in writing, or even say in plain talk, though it is so much easier, what I felt when I saw two policemen come in, carrying between them what seemed to me to be a dead girl, and that girl Mary! I caught hold of her, and gave a scream that must have alarmed the whole house; for frightened people came crowding downstairs in their night-dresses. There was a dreadful confusion and noise of loud talking, but I heard nothing and saw nothing till I had got her into my room and laid on my bed. I stooped down, frantic-like, to kiss her, and saw an awful mark of a blow on the left temple, and felt, at the same time, a feeble flutter of her breath on my cheek. The discovery that she was not dead seemed to give me back my senses again. I told one of the policemen where the nearest doctor was to be found, and sat down by the bedside while he was gone, and bathed her poor head with cold water. She never opened her eyes, or moved, or spoke; but she breathed, and that was enough for me, because it was enough for life.

The policeman left in the room was a big, thick-voiced, pompous man, with a horrible unfeeling pleasure in hearing himself talk before an assembly of frightened, silent people. He told us how he had found her, as if he had been telling a story in a tap-room, and began with saying: "I don't think the young woman was drunk."

Drunk! My Mary, who might have been a born lady for all the spirits she ever touched – drunk! I could have struck the man for uttering the word, with her lying – poor suffering angel – so white, and still, and helpless before him. As it was, I gave him a look, but he was too stupid to understand it, and went droning on, saying the same thing over and over again in the same words. And yet the story of how they found her was, like all the sad stories I have ever heard told in real life, so very, very short. They had just seen her lying along on the curbstone a few streets off, and had taken her to the station-house. There she had been searched, and one of my cards, that I gave to ladies who promise me employment, had been found in her pocket, and so they had brought her to our house. This was all the man really had to tell. There was nobody near her when she was found, and no evidence to show how the blow on her temple had been inflicted.

What a time it was before the doctor came, and how dreadful to hear him say, after he had looked at her, that he was afraid all the medical men in the world could be of no use here! He could not get her to swallow anything; and the more he tried to bring her back to her senses the less chance there seemed of his succeeding. He examined the blow on her temple, and said he thought she must have fallen down in a fit of some sort, and struck her head against the pavement, and so have given her brain what he was afraid was a fatal shake. I asked what was to be done if she showed any return to sense in the night. He said: "Send for me directly"; and stopped for a little while afterward stroking her head gently with his hand, and whispering to himself: "Poor girl, so young and so pretty!" I had felt, some minutes before, as if I could have struck the policeman, and I felt now as if I could have thrown my arms round the doctor's neck and kissed him. I did put out my hand when he took up his hat, and he shook it in the friendliest way. "Don't hope, my dear," he said, and went out.

The rest of the lodgers followed him, all silent and shocked, except the inhuman wretch who owns the house and lives in idleness on the high rents he wrings from poor people like us.

"She's three weeks in my debt," says he, with a frown and an oath. "Where the devil is my money to come from now?" Brute! brute!

I had a long cry alone with her that seemed to ease my heart a little. She was not the least changed for the better when I had wiped away the tears and could see her clearly again. I took up her right hand, which lay nearest to me. It was tight clinched. I tried to unclasp the fingers, and succeeded after a little time. Something dark fell out of the palm of her hand as I straightened it.

I picked the thing up, and smoothed it out, and saw that it was an end of a man's cravat.

A very old, rotten, dingy strip of black silk, with thin lilac lines, all blurred and deadened with dirt, running across and across the stuff in a sort of trellis-work pattern. The small end of the cravat was hemmed in the usual way, but the other end was all jagged, as if the morsel then in my hands had been torn off violently from the rest of the stuff. A chill ran all over me as I looked at it; for that poor, stained, crumpled end of a cravat seemed to be saying to me, as though it had been in plain words: "If she dies, she has come to her death by foul means, and I am the witness of it."

I had been frightened enough before, lest she should die suddenly and quietly without my knowing it, while we were alone together; but I got into a perfect agony now, for fear this last worst affliction should take me by surprise. I don't suppose five minutes passed all that woful night through without my getting up and putting my cheek close to her mouth, to feel if the faint breaths still fluttered out of it. They came and went just the same as at first, though the fright I was in often made me fancy they were stilled forever.

Just as the church clocks were striking four I was startled by seeing the room door open. It was only Dusty Sal (as they call her in the house), the maid-of-all-work. She was wrapped up in the blanket off her bed; her hair was all tumbled over her face, and her eyes were heavy with sleep as she came up to the bedside where I was sitting.

"I've two hours good before I begin to work," says she, in her hoarse, drowsy voice, "and I've come to sit up and take my turn at watching her. You lay down and get some sleep on the rug. Here's my blanket for you. I don't mind the cold – it will keep me awake."

"You are very kind – very, very kind and thoughtful, Sally," says I, "but I am too wretched in my mind to want sleep, or rest, or to do anything but wait where I am, and try and hope for the best."

"Then I'll wait, too," says Sally. "I must do something; if there's nothing to do but waiting, I'll wait."

And she sat down opposite me at the foot of the bed, and drew the blanket close round her with a shiver.

"After working so hard as you do, I'm sure you must want all the little rest you can get," says I.

"Excepting only you," says Sally, putting her heavy arm very clumsily, but very gently at the same time, round Mary's feet, and looking hard at the pale, still face on the pillow. "Excepting you, she's the only soul in this house as never swore at me, or give me a hard word that I can remember. When you made puddings on Sundays, and give her half, she always give me a bit. The rest of 'em calls me Dusty Sal. Excepting only you, again, she always called me Sally, as if she knowed me in a friendly way. I ain't no good here, but I ain't no harm, neither; and I shall take my turn at the sitting up – that's what I shall do!"

She nestled her head down close at Mary's feet as she spoke those words, and said no more. I once or twice thought she had fallen asleep, but whenever I looked at her her heavy eyes were always wide open. She never changed her position an inch till the church clocks struck six; then she gave one little squeeze to Mary's feet with her arm, and shuffled out of the room without a word. A minute or two after, I heard her down below, lighting the kitchen fire just as usual.

A little later the doctor stepped over before his breakfast-time to see if there had been any change in the night. He only shook his head when he looked at her as if there was no hope. Having nobody else to consult that I could put trust in, I showed him the end of the cravat, and told him of the dreadful suspicion that had arisen in my mind when I found it in her hand.

"You must keep it carefully, and produce it at the inquest," he said. "I don't know, though, that it is likely to lead to anything. The bit of stuff may have been lying on the pavement near her, and her hand may have unconsciously clutched it when she fell. Was she subject to fainting-fits?"

"Not more so, sir, than other young girls who are hard-worked and anxious, and weakly from poor living," I answered.

"I can't say that she may not have got that blow from a fall," the doctor went on, looking at her temple again. "I can't say that it presents any positive appearance of having been inflicted by another person. It will be important, however, to ascertain what state of health she was in last night. Have you any idea where she was yesterday evening?"

I told him where she was employed at work, and said I imagined she must have been kept there later than usual.

"I shall pass the place this morning" said the doctor, "in going my rounds among my patients, and I'll just step in and make some inquiries."

I thanked him, and we parted. Just as he was closing the door he looked in again.

"Was she your sister?" he asked.

"No, sir, only my dear friend."

He said nothing more, but I heard him sigh as he shut the door softly. Perhaps he once had a sister of his own, and lost her? Perhaps she was like Mary in the face?

The doctor was hours gone away. I began to feel unspeakably forlorn and helpless, so much so as even to wish selfishly that Robert might really have sailed from America, and might get to London in time to assist and console me.

No living creature came into the room but Sally. The first time she brought me some tea; the second and third times she only looked in to see if there was any change, and glanced her eye toward the bed. I had never known her so silent before; it seemed almost as if this dreadful accident had struck her dumb. I ought to have spoken to her, perhaps, but there was something in her face that daunted me; and, besides, the fever of anxiety I was in began to dry up my lips, as if they would never be able to shape any words again. I was still tormented by that frightful apprehension of the past night, that she would die without my knowing it – die without saying one word to clear up the awful mystery of this blow, and set the suspicions at rest forever which I still felt whenever my eyes fell on the end of the old cravat.

At last the doctor came back.

"I think you may safely clear your mind of any doubts to which that bit of stuff may have given rise," he said. "She was, as you supposed, detained late by her employers, and she fainted in the work-room. They most unwisely and unkindly let her go home alone, without giving her any stimulant, as soon as she came to her senses again. Nothing is more probable, under these circumstances, than that she should faint a second time on her way here. A fall on the pavement, without any friendly arm to break it, might have produced even a worse injury than the injury we see. I believe that the only ill usage to which the poor girl was exposed was the neglect she met with in the work-room."

"You speak very reasonably, I own, sir," said I, not yet quite convinced. "Still, perhaps she may—"

"My poor girl, I told you not to hope," said the doctor, interrupting me. He went to Mary, and lifted up her eyelids, and looked at her eyes while he spoke; then added, "If you still doubt how she came by that blow, do not encourage the idea that any words of hers will ever enlighten you. She will never speak again."

"Not dead! Oh, sir, don't say she's dead!"

"She is dead to pain and sorrow – dead to speech and recognition. There is more animation in the life of the feeblest insect that flies than in the life that is left in her. When you look at her now, try to think that she is in heaven. That is the best comfort I can give you, after telling the hard truth."

I did not believe him. I could not believe him. So long as she breathed at all, so long I was resolved to hope. Soon after the doctor was gone, Sally came in again, and found me listening (if I may call it so) at Mary's lips. She went to where my little hand-glass hangs against the wall, took it down, and gave it to me.

"See if the breath marks it," she said.

Yes; her breath did mark it, but very faintly. Sally cleaned the glass with her apron, and gave it back to me. As she did so, she half stretched out her hand to Mary's face, but drew it in again suddenly, as if she was afraid of soiling Mary's delicate skin with her hard, horny fingers. Going out, she stopped at the foot of the bed, and scraped away a little patch of mud that was on one of Mary's shoes.

"I always used to clean 'em for her," said Sally, "to save her hands from getting blacked. May I take 'em off now, and clean 'em again?"

I nodded my head, for my heart was too heavy to speak. Sally took the shoes off with a slow, awkward tenderness, and went out.

An hour or more must have passed, when, putting the glass over her lips again, I saw no mark on it. I held it closer and closer. I dulled it accidentally with my own breath, and cleaned it. I held it over her again. Oh, Mary, Mary, the doctor was right! I ought to have only thought of you in heaven!

Dead, without a word, without a sign – without even a look to tell the true story of the blow that killed her! I could not call to anybody, I could not cry, I could not so much as put the glass down and give her a kiss for the last time. I don't know how long I had sat there with my eyes burning, and my hands deadly cold, when Sally came in with the shoes cleaned, and carried carefully in her apron for fear of a soil touching them. At the sight of that—

I can write no more. My tears drop so fast on the paper that I can see nothing.

March 12th

She died on the afternoon of the eighth. On the morning of the ninth, I wrote, as in duty bound, to her stepmother at Hammersmith. There was no answer. I wrote again; my letter was returned to me this morning unopened. For all that woman cares, Mary might be buried with a pauper's funeral; but this shall never be, if I pawn everything about me, down to the very gown that is on my back. The bare thought of Mary being buried by the workhouse gave me the spirit to dry my eyes, and go to the undertaker's, and tell him how I was placed. I said if he would get me an estimate of all that would have to be paid, from first to last, for the cheapest decent funeral that could be had, I would undertake to raise the money. He gave me the estimate, written in this way, like a common bill:

A walking funeral complete	Pounds 1 13 8
Vestry	0 4 4
Rector	0 4 4
Clerk	0 1 0
Sexton	0 1 0
Beadle	0 1 0
Bell	0 1 0
Six feet of ground	0 2 0
Total	**Pounds 2 8 4**

If I had the heart to give any thought to it, I should be inclined to wish that the Church could afford to do without so many small charges for burying poor people, to whose friends even shillings are of consequence. But it is useless to complain; the money must be raised at once. The charitable doctor – a poor man himself, or he would not be living in our neighborhood – has subscribed ten shillings toward the expenses; and the coroner, when the inquest was over, added five more. Perhaps others may assist me. If not, I have fortunately clothes and furniture of my own to pawn. And I must set about parting with them without delay, for the funeral is to be tomorrow, the thirteenth.

The funeral – Mary's funeral! It is well that the straits and difficulties I am in keep my mind on the stretch. If I had leisure to grieve, where should I find the courage to face tomorrow?

Thank God they did not want me at the inquest. The verdict given, with the doctor, the policeman, and two persons from the place where she worked, for witnesses, was Accidental Death. The end of the cravat was produced, and the coroner said that it was certainly enough to suggest suspicion; but the jury, in the absence of any positive evidence, held to the doctor's notion that she had fainted and fallen down, and so got the blow on her temple. They reproved the people where Mary worked for letting her go home alone, without so much as a drop of brandy to support her, after she had fallen into a swoon from exhaustion before their eyes. The coroner added, on his own account, that he thought the reproof was thoroughly deserved. After that, the cravat-end was given back to me by my own desire, the police saying that they could make no investigations with such a slight clew to guide them. They may think so, and the coroner, and doctor, and jury may think so; but, in spite of all that has passed, I am now more firmly persuaded than ever that there is some dreadful mystery in connection with that blow on my poor lost Mary's temple which has yet to be revealed, and which may come to be discovered through this very fragment of a cravat that I found in her hand. I cannot give any good reason for why I think so, but I know that if I had been one of the jury at the inquest, nothing should have induced me to consent to such a verdict as Accidental Death.

After I had pawned my things, and had begged a small advance of wages at the place where I work to make up what was still wanting to pay for Mary's funeral, I thought I might have had a little quiet time to prepare myself as I best could for tomorrow. But this was not to be. When I got home the landlord met me in the passage. He was in liquor, and more brutal and pitiless in his way of looking and speaking than ever I saw him before.

"So you're going to be fool enough to pay for her funeral, are you?" were his first words to me.

I was too weary and heart-sick to answer; I only tried to get by him to my own door.

"If you can pay for burying her," he went on, putting himself in front of me, "you can pay her lawful debts. She owes me three weeks' rent. Suppose you raise the money for that next, and hand it over to me? I'm not joking, I can promise you. I mean to have my rent; and, if somebody don't pay it, I'll have her body seized and sent to the workhouse!"

Between terror and disgust, I thought I should have dropped to the floor at his feet. But I determined not to let him see how he had horrified me, if I could possibly control myself. So I mustered resolution enough to answer that I did not believe the law gave him any such wicked power over the dead.

"I'll teach you what the law is!" he broke in; "you'll raise money to bury her like a born lady, when she's died in my debt, will you? And you think I'll let my rights be trampled upon like that, do you? See if I do! I'll give you till tonight to think about it. If I don't have the three weeks she owes before tomorrow, dead or alive, she shall go to the workhouse!"

This time I managed to push by him, and get to my own room, and lock the door in his face. As soon as I was alone I fell into a breathless, suffocating fit of crying that seemed to be shaking me to pieces. But there was no good and no help in tears; I did my best to calm myself after a little while, and tried to think who I should run to for help and protection.

The doctor was the first friend I thought of; but I knew he was always out seeing his patients of an afternoon. The beadle was the next person who came into my head. He had the look of being a very dignified, unapproachable kind of man when he came about the inquest; but he talked to me a little then, and said I was a good girl, and seemed, I really thought, to pity me. So to him I determined to apply in my great danger and distress.

Most fortunately, I found him at home. When I told him of the landlord's infamous threats, and of the misery I was suffering in consequence of them, he rose up with a stamp of his foot, and sent for his gold-laced cocked hat that he wears on Sundays, and his long cane with the ivory top to it.

"I'll give it to him," said the beadle. "Come along with me, my dear. I think I told you you were a good girl at the inquest – if I didn't, I tell you so now. I'll give it to him! Come along with me."

And he went out, striding on with his cocked hat and his great cane, and I followed him.

"Landlord!" he cries, the moment he gets into the passage, with a thump of his cane on the floor, "landlord!" with a look all round him as if he was King of England calling to a beast, "come out!"

The moment the landlord came out and saw who it was, his eye fixed on the cocked hat, and he turned as pale as ashes.

"How dare you frighten this poor girl?" says the beadle. "How dare you bully her at this sorrowful time with threatening to do what you know you can't do? How dare you be a cowardly, bullying, braggadocio of an unmanly landlord? Don't talk to me: I won't hear you. I'll pull you up, sir. If you say another word to the young woman, I'll pull you up before the authorities of this metropolitan parish. I've had my eye on you, and the authorities have had their eye on you, and the rector has had his eye on you. We don't like the look of your small shop round the corner; we don't like the look of some of the customers who deal at it; we don't like disorderly characters; and we don't by any manner of means like you. Go away. Leave the young woman alone. Hold your tongue, or I'll pull you up. If he says another word, or interferes with you again, my dear, come and tell me; and, as sure as he's a bullying, unmanly, braggadocio of a landlord, I'll pull him up."

With those words the beadle gave a loud cough to clear his throat, and another thump of his cane on the floor, and so went striding out again before I could open my lips to thank him. The landlord slunk back into his room without a word. I was left alone and unmolested at last, to strengthen myself for the hard trial of my poor love's funeral tomorrow.

March 13th

It is all over. A week ago her head rested on my bosom. It is laid in the churchyard now; the fresh earth lies heavy over her grave. I and my dearest friend, the sister of my love, are parted in this world forever.

I followed her funeral alone through the cruel, hustling streets. Sally, I thought, might have offered to go with me, but she never so much as came into my room. I did not like to think badly of her for this, and I am glad I restrained myself; for, when we got into the churchyard, among the two or three people who were standing by the open grave I saw Sally, in her ragged gray shawl and her patched black bonnet. She did not seem to notice me till the last words of the service had been read and the clergyman had gone away; then she came up and spoke to me.

"I couldn't follow along with you," she said, looking at her ragged shawl, "for I haven't a decent suit of clothes to walk in. I wish I could get vent in crying for her like you, but I can't; all the crying's been drudged and starved out of me long ago. Don't you think about lighting your fire when you get home. I'll do that, and get you a drop of tea to comfort you."

She seemed on the point of saying a kind word or two more, when, seeing the beadle coming toward me, she drew back, as if she was afraid of him, and left the churchyard.

"Here's my subscription toward the funeral," said the beadle, giving me back his shilling fee. "Don't say anything about it, for it mightn't be approved of in a business point of view, if it came to some people's ears. Has the landlord said anything more to you? no, I thought not. He's too polite a man to give me the trouble of pulling him up. Don't stop crying here, my dear. Take the advice of a man familiar with funerals, and go home."

I tried to take his advice, but it seemed like deserting Mary to go away when all the rest forsook her.

I waited about till the earth was thrown in and the man had left the place, then I returned to the grave. Oh, how bare and cruel it was, without so much as a bit of green turf to soften it! Oh, how much harder it seemed to live than to die, when I stood alone looking at the heavy piled-up lumps of clay, and thinking of what was hidden beneath them!

I was driven home by my own despairing thoughts. The sight of Sally lighting the fire in my room eased my heart a little. When she was gone, I took up Robert's letter again to keep my mind employed on the only subject in the world that has any interest for it now.

This fresh reading increased the doubts I had already felt relative to his having remained in America after writing to me. My grief and forlornness have made a strange alteration in my former feelings about his coming back. I seem to have lost all my prudence and self-denial, and to care so little about his poverty, and so much about himself, that the prospect of his return is really the only comforting thought I have now to support me. I know this is weak in me, and that his coming back can l ead to no good result for either of us; but he is the only living being left me to love; and – I can't explain it – but I want to put my arms round his neck and tell him about Mary.

March 14th

I locked up the end of the cravat in my writing-desk. No change in the dreadful suspicions that the bare sight of it rouses in me. I tremble if I so much as touch it.

March 15th–17th

Work, work, work. If I don't knock up, I shall be able to pay back the advance in another week; and then, with a little more pinching in my daily expenses, I may succeed in saving a shilling or two to get some turf to put over Mary's grave, and perhaps even a few flowers besides to grow round it.

March 18th

Thinking of Robert all day long. Does this mean that he is really coming back? If it does, reckoning the distance he is at from New York, and the time ships take to get to England, I might see him by the end of April or the beginning of May.

March 19th

I don't remember my mind running once on the end of the cravat yesterday, and I am certain I never looked at it; yet I had the strangest dream concerning it at night. I thought it was lengthened into a long clew, like the silken thread that led to Rosamond's Bower. I thought I took hold of it, and followed it a little way, and then got frightened and tried to go back, but found that I was obliged, in spite of myself, to go on. It led me through a place like the Valley of the Shadow of Death, in an old print I remember in my mother's copy of the Pilgrim's Progress. I seemed to be months and months following it without any respite, till at last it brought me, on a sudden, face to face with an angel whose eyes were like Mary's. He said to me, "Go on, still; the truth is at the end, waiting for you to find it." I burst out crying, for the angel had Mary's voice as well as Mary's eyes, and woke with my heart throbbing and my cheeks all wet. What is the meaning of this? Is it always superstitious, I wonder, to believe that dreams may come true?

April 30th

I have found it! God knows to what results it may lead; but it is as certain as that I am sitting here before my journal that I have found the cravat from which the end in Mary's hand was torn. I discovered it last night; but the flutter I was in, and the nervousness and uncertainty I felt, prevented me from noting down this most extraordinary and unexpected event at the time when it happened. Let me try if I can preserve the memory of it in writing now.

I was going home rather late from where I work, when I suddenly remembered that I had forgotten to buy myself any candles the evening before, and that I should be left in the dark if I did not manage to rectify this mistake in some way. The shop close to me, at which I usually deal, would be shut up, I knew, before I could get to it; so I determined to go into the first place I passed where candles were sold. This turned out to be a small shop with two counters, which did business on one side in the general grocery way, and on the other in the rag and bottle and old iron line.

There were several customers on the grocery side when I went in, so I waited on the empty rag side till I could be served. Glancing about me here at the worthless-looking things by which I was surrounded, my eye was caught by a bundle of rags lying on the counter, as if they had just been brought in and left there. From mere idle curiosity, I looked close at the rags, and saw among them something like an old cravat. I took it up directly and held it under a gaslight. The pattern was blurred lilac lines running across and across the dingy black ground in a trellis-work form. I looked at the ends: one of them was torn off.

How I managed to hide the breathless surprise into which this discovery threw me I cannot say, but I certainly contrived to steady my voice somehow, and to ask for my candles calmly when the man and woman serving in the shop, having disposed of their other customers, inquired of me what I wanted.

As the man took down the candles, my brain was all in a whirl with trying to think how I could get possession of the old cravat without exciting any suspicion. Chance, and a little quickness on my part in taking advantage of it, put the object within my reach in a moment. The man, having counted out the candles, asked the woman for some paper to wrap them in. She produced a piece much too small and flimsy for the purpose, and declared, when he called for something better, that the day's supply of stout paper was all exhausted. He flew into a rage with her for managing so badly. Just as they were beginning to quarrel violently, I stepped back to the rag-counter, took the old cravat carelessly out of the bundle, and said, in as light a tone as I could possibly assume:

"Come, come, don't let my candles be the cause of hard words between you. Tie this ragged old thing round them with a bit of string, and I shall carry them home quite comfortably."

The man seemed disposed to insist on the stout paper being produced; but the woman, as if she was glad of an opportunity of spiting him, snatched the candles away, and tied them up in a moment in the torn old cravat. I was afraid he would have struck her before my face, he seemed in such a fury; but, fortunately, another customer came in, and obliged him to put his hands to peaceable and proper use.

"Quite a bundle of all-sorts on the opposite counter there," I said to the woman, as I paid her for the candles.

"Yes, and all hoarded up for sale by a poor creature with a lazy brute of a husband, who lets his wife do all the work while he spends all the money," answered the woman, with a malicious look at the man by her side.

"He can't surely have much money to spend, if his wife has no better work to do than picking up rags," said I.

"It isn't her fault if she hasn't got no better," says the woman, rather angrily. "She's ready to turn her hand to anything. Charing, washing, laying-out, keeping empty houses – nothing comes amiss to her. She's my half-sister, and I think I ought to know."

"Did you say she went out charing?" I asked, making believe as if I knew of somebody who might employ her.

"Yes, of course I did," answered the woman; "and if you can put a job into her hands, you'll be doing a good turn to a poor hard-working creature as wants it. She lives down the Mews here to the right – name of Horlick, and as honest a woman as ever stood in shoe-leather. Now, then, ma'am, what for you?"

Another customer came in just then, and occupied her attention. I left the shop, passed the turning that led down to the Mews, looked up at the name of the street, so as to know how to find it again, and then ran home as fast as I could. Perhaps it was the remembrance of my strange dream striking me on a sudden, or perhaps it was the shock of the discovery I had just made, but I began to feel frightened without knowing why, and anxious to be under shelter in my own room.

It Robert should come back! Oh, what a relief and help it would be now if Robert should come back!

May 1st

On getting indoors last night, the first thing I did, after striking a light, was to take the ragged cravat off the candles, and smooth it out on the table. I then took the end that had been in poor Mary's hand out of my writing-desk, and smoothed that out too. It matched the torn side of the cravat exactly. I put them together, and satisfied myself that there was not a doubt of it.

Not once did I close my eyes that night. A kind of fever got possession of me – a vehement yearning to go on from this first discovery and find out more, no matter what the risk might be. The cravat now really became, to my mind, the clew that I thought I saw in my dream – the clew that I was resolved to follow. I determined to go to Mrs. Horlick this evening on my return from work.

I found the Mews easily. A crook-backed dwarf of a man was lounging at the corner of it smoking his pipe. Not liking his looks, I did not inquire of him where Mrs. Horlick lived, but went down the Mews till I met with a woman, and asked her. She directed me to the right number. I knocked at the door, and Mrs. Horlick herself – a lean, ill-tempered, miserable-looking woman – answered it. I told her at once that I had come to ask what her terms were for charing. She stared at me for a moment, then answered my question civilly enough.

"You look surprised at a stranger like me finding you out," I said. "I first came to hear of you last night, from a relation of yours, in rather an odd way."

And I told her all that had happened in the chandler's shop, bringing in the bundle of rags, and the circumstance of my carrying home the candles in the old torn cravat, as often as possible.

"It's the first time I've heard of anything belonging to him turning out any use," said Mrs. Horlick, bitterly.

"What! the spoiled old neck-handkerchief belonged to your husband, did it?" said I, at a venture.

"Yes; I pitched his rotten rag of a neck-'andkercher into the bundle along with the rest, and I wish I could have pitched him in after it," said Mrs. Horlick. "I'd sell him cheap at any ragshop. There he stands, smoking his pipe at the end of the Mews, out of work for weeks past, the idlest humpbacked pig in all London!"

She pointed to the man whom I had passed on entering the Mews. My cheeks began to burn and my knees to tremble, for I knew that in tracing the cravat to its owner I was advancing a step toward a fresh discovery. I wished Mrs. Horlick good evening, and said I would write and mention the day on which I wanted her.

What I had just been told put a thought into my mind that I was afraid to follow out. I have heard people talk of being light-headed, and I felt as I have heard them say they felt when I retraced my steps up the Mews. My head got giddy, and my eyes seemed able to see nothing but the figure of the little crook-backed man, still smoking his pipe in his former place. I could see nothing but that; I could think of nothing but the mark of the blow on my poor lost Mary's temple. I know that I must have been light-headed, for as I came close to the crook-backed man I stopped without meaning it. The minute before, there had been no idea in me of speaking to him. I did not know how to speak, or in what way it would be safest to begin; and yet, the moment I came face to face with him, something out of myself seemed to stop me, and to make me speak without considering beforehand, without thinking of consequences, without knowing, I may almost say, what words I was uttering till the instant when they rose to my lips.

"When your old neck-tie was torn, did you know that one end of it went to the rag-shop, and the other fell into my hands?"

I said these bold words to him suddenly, and, as it seemed, without my own will taking any part in them.

He started, stared, changed color. He was too much amazed by my sudden speaking to find an answer for me. When he did open his lips, it was to say rather to himself than me:

"You're not the girl."

"No," I said, with a strange choking at my heart, "I'm her friend."

By this time he had recovered his surprise, and he seemed to be aware that he had let out more than he ought.

"You may be anybody's friend you like," he said, brutally, "so long as you don't come jabbering nonsense here. I don't know you, and I don't understand your jokes."

He turned quickly away from me when he had said the last words. He had never once looked fairly at me since I first spoke to him.

Was it his hand that had struck the blow? I had only sixpence in my pocket, but I took it out and followed him. If it had been a five-pound note I should have done the same in the state I was in then.

"Would a pot of beer help you to understand me?" I said, and offered him the sixpence.

"A pot ain't no great things," he answered, taking the sixpence doubtfully.

"It may lead to something better," I said. His eyes began to twinkle, and he came close to me. Oh, how my legs trembled – how my head swam!

"This is all in a friendly way, is it?" he asked, in a whisper.

I nodded my head. At that moment I could not have spoken for worlds.

"Friendly, of course," he went on to himself, "or there would have been a policeman in it. She told you, I suppose, that I wasn't the man?"

I nodded my head again. It was all I could do to keep myself standing upright.

"I suppose it's a case of threatening to have him up, and make him settle it quietly for a pound or two? How much for me if you lay hold of him?"

"Half."

I began to be afraid that he would suspect something if I was still silent. The wretch's eyes twinkled again and he came yet closer.

"I drove him to the Red Lion, corner of Dodd Street and Rudgely Street. The house was shut up, but he was let in at the jug and bottle door, like a man who was known to the landlord. That's as much as I can tell you, and I'm certain I'm right. He was the last fare I took up at night. The next morning master gave me the sack – said I cribbed his corn and his fares. I wish I had."

I gathered from this that the crook-backed man had been a cab-driver.

"Why don't you speak?" he asked, suspiciously. "Has she been telling you a pack of lies about me? What did she say when she came home?"

"What ought she to have said?"

"She ought to have said my fare was drunk, and she came in the way as he was going to get into the cab. That's what she ought to have said to begin with."

"But after?"

"Well, after, my fare, by way of larking with her, puts out his leg for to trip her up, and she stumbles and catches at me for to save herself, and tears off one of the limp ends of my rotten old tie. 'What do you mean by that, you brute?' says she, turning round as soon as she was steady on her legs, to my fare. Says my fare to her: 'I means to teach you to keep a civil tongue in your head.' And he ups with his fist, and – what's come to you, now? What are you looking at me like that for? How do you think a man of my size was to take her part against a man big enough to have eaten me up? Look as much as you like, in my place you would have done what I done – drew off when he shook his fist at you, and swore he'd be the death of you if you didn't start your horse in no time."

I saw he was working himself up into a rage; but I could not, if my life had depended on it, have stood near him or looked at him any longer. I just managed to stammer out that I had been walking a long way, and that, not being used to much exercise, I felt faint and giddy with fatigue. He only changed from angry to sulky when I made that excuse. I got a little further away from him, and then added that if he would be at the Mews entrance the next evening I should have something more to say and something more to give him. He grumbled a few suspicious words in answer about doubting whether he should trust me to come back. Fortunately, at that moment, a policeman passed on the opposite side of the way. He slunk down the Mews immediately, and I was free to make my escape.

How I got home I can't say, except that I think I ran the greater part of the way. Sally opened the door, and asked if anything was the matter the moment she saw my face. I answered: "Nothing – nothing." She stopped me as I was going into my room, and said:

"Smooth your hair a bit, and put your collar straight. There's a gentleman in there waiting for you."

My heart gave one great bound: I knew who it was in an instant, and rushed into the room like a mad woman.

"Oh, Robert, Robert!"

All my heart went out to him in those two little words.

"Good God, Anne, has anything happened? Are you ill?"

"Mary! my poor, lost, murdered, dear, dear Mary!"

That was all I could say before I fell on his breast.

May 2nd

Misfortunes and disappointments have saddened him a little, but toward me he is unaltered. He is as good, as kind, as gently and truly affectionate as ever. I believe no other man in the world could have listened to the story of Mary's death with such tenderness and pity as he. Instead of cutting me short anywhere, he drew me on to tell more than I had intended; and his first generous words when I had done were to assure me that he would see himself to the grass being laid and the flowers planted on Mary's grave. I could almost have gone on my knees and worshiped him when he made me that promise.

Surely this best, and kindest, and noblest of men cannot always be unfortunate! My cheeks burn when I think that he has come back with only a few pounds in his pocket, after all his hard and honest struggles to do well in America. They must be bad people there when such a man as Robert cannot get on among them. He now talks calmly and resignedly of trying for any one of the lowest employments by which a man can earn his bread honestly in this great city – he who knows French, who can write so beautifully! Oh, if the people who have places to give away only knew Robert as well as I do, what a salary he would have, what a post he would be chosen to occupy!

I am writing these lines alone while he has gone to the Mews to treat with the dastardly, heartless wretch with whom I spoke yesterday.

Robert says the creature – I won't call him a man – must be humored and kept deceived about poor Mary's end, in order that we may discover and bring to justice the monster whose drunken blow was the death of her. I shall know no ease of mind till her murderer is secured, and till I am certain that he will be made to suffer for his crimes. I wanted to go with Robert to the Mews, but he said it was best that he should carry out the rest of the investigation alone, for my strength and resolution had been too hardly taxed already. He said more words in praise of me for what I have been able to do up to this time, which I am almost ashamed to write down with my own pen. Besides, there is no need; praise from his lips is one of the things that I can trust my memory to preserve to the latest day of my life.

May 3rd

Robert was very long last night before he came back to tell me what he had done. He easily recognized the hunchback at the corner of the Mews by my description of him; but he found it a hard matter, even with the help of money, to overcome the cowardly wretch's distrust of him as a stranger and a man. However, when this had been accomplished, the main difficulty was conquered. The hunchback, excited by the promise of more money, went at once to the Red Lion to inquire about the person whom he had driven there in his cab. Robert followed him, and waited at the corner of the street. The tidings brought by the cabman were of the most unexpected kind. The murderer – I can write of him by no other name – had fallen ill on the very night when he was driven to the Red Lion, had taken to his bed there and then, and was still confined to it at that very moment. His disease was of a kind that is brought on by excessive drinking, and that affects the mind as well as the body. The people at the public house call it the Horrors.

Hearing these things, Robert determined to see if he could not find out something more for himself by going and inquiring at the public house, in the character of one of the friends of the sick man in bed upstairs. He made two important discoveries. First, he found out the name and address of the doctor in attendance. Secondly, he entrapped the barman into mentioning the murderous wretch by his name. This last discovery adds an unspeakably fearful interest to the dreadful misfortune of Mary's death. Noah Truscott, as she told me herself in the last conversation I ever had with her, was the name of the man whose drunken example ruined her father, and Noah Truscott is also the name of the man whose drunken fury killed her. There is something that makes one shudder, something supernatural in this awful fact. Robert agrees with me that the hand of Providence must have guided my steps to that shop from which all the discoveries since made took their rise. He says he believes we are the instruments of effecting a righteous retribution; and, if he spends his last farthing, he will have the investigation brought to its full end in a court of justice.

May 4th

Robert went today to consult a lawyer whom he knew in former times The lawyer was much interested, though not so seriously impressed as he ought to have been by the story of Mary's death and of the events that have followed it. He gave Robert a confidential letter to take to the doctor in attendance on the double-dyed villain at the Red Lion. Robert left the letter, and called again and saw the doctor, who said his patient was getting better, and would most likely be up again in ten days or a fortnight. This statement Robert communicated to the lawyer, and the lawyer has undertaken to have the public house properly watched, and the hunchback (who is the most important witness) sharply looked after for the next fortnight, or longer if necessary. Here, then, the progress of this dreadful business stops for a while.

May 5th

Robert has got a little temporary employment in copying for his friend the lawyer. I am working harder than ever at my needle, to make up for the time that has been lost lately.

May 6th

Today was Sunday, and Robert proposed that we should go and look at Mary's grave. He, who forgets nothing where a kindness is to be done, has found time to perform the promise he made to me on the night when we first met. The grave is already, by his orders, covered with turf, and planted round with shrubs. Some flowers, and a low headstone, are to be added, to make the place look worthier of my poor lost darling who is beneath it. Oh, I hope I shall live long after I am married to Robert! I want so much time to show him all my gratitude!

May 20th

A hard trial to my courage today. I have given evidence at the police-office, and have seen the monster who murdered her.

I could only look at him once. I could just see that he was a giant in size, and that he kept his dull, lowering, bestial face turned toward the witness-box, and his bloodshot, vacant eyes staring on me. For an instant I tried to confront that look; for an instant I kept my attention fixed on him – on his blotched face – on the short, grizzled hair above it – on his knotty, murderous right hand, hanging loose over the bar in front of him, like the paw of a wild beast over the edge of its den. Then the horror of him – the double horror of confronting him, in the first place, and afterward of seeing that he was an old man – overcame me, and I turned away, faint, sick, and shuddering. I never faced him again; and, at the end of my evidence, Robert considerately took me out.

When we met once more at the end of the examination, Robert told me that the prisoner never spoke and never changed his position. He was either fortified by the cruel composure of a savage, or his faculties had not yet thoroughly recovered from the disease that had so lately shaken them. The magistrate seemed to doubt if he was in his right mind; but the evidence of the medical man relieved this uncertainty, and the prisoner was committed for trial on a charge of manslaughter.

Why not on a charge of murder? Robert explained the law to me when I asked that question. I accepted the explanation, but it did not satisfy me. Mary Mallinson was killed by a blow from the hand of Noah Truscott. That is murder in the sight of God. Why not murder in the sight of the law also?

June 18th

Tomorrow is the day appointed for the trial at the Old Bailey.

Before sunset this evening I went to look at Mary's grave. The turf has grown so green since I saw it last, and the flowers are springing up so prettily. A bird was perched dressing his feathers on the low white headstone that bears the inscription of her name and age. I did not go near enough to disturb the little creature. He looked innocent and pretty on the grave, as Mary herself was in her lifetime. When he flew away I went and sat for a little by the headstone, and read the mournful lines on it. Oh, my love! my love! what harm or wrong had you ever done in this world, that you should die at eighteen by a blow from a drunkard's hand?

June 19th

The trial. My experience of what happened at it is limited, like my experience of the examination at the police-office, to the time occupied in giving my own evidence. They made me say much more than I said before the magistrate. Between examination and cross-examination, I had to go into almost all the particulars about poor Mary and her funeral that I have written i n this journal; the jury listening to every word I spoke with the most anxious attention. At the end, the judge said a few words to me approving of my conduct, and then there was a clapping of hands among the people in court. I was so agitated and excited that I trembled all over when they let me go out into the air again.

I looked at the prisoner both when I entered the witness-box and when I left it. The lowering brutality of his face was unchanged, but his faculties seemed to be more alive and observant than they were at the police-office. A frightful blue change passed over his face, and he drew his breath so heavily that the gasps were distinctly audible while I mentioned Mary by name and described the mark or the blow on her temple. When they asked me if I knew anything of the prisoner, and I answered that I only knew what Mary herself had told me about his having been her father's ruin, he gave a kind of groan, and struck both his hands heavily on the dock. And when I passed beneath him on my way out of court, he leaned over suddenly, whether to speak to me or to strike me I can't say, for he was immediately made to stand upright again by the turnkeys on either side of him. While the evidence proceeded (as Robert described it to me), the signs that he was suffering under superstitious terror became more and more apparent; until, at last, just as the lawyer appointed to defend him was rising to speak, he suddenly cried out, in a voice that startled everyone, up to the very judge on the bench: "Stop!"

There was a pause, and all eyes looked at him. The perspiration was pouring over his face like water, and he made strange, uncouth signs with his hands to the judge opposite. "Stop all this!" he cried again; "I've been the ruin of the father and the death of the child. Hang me before I do more harm! Hang me, for God's sake, out of the way!" As soon as the shock produced by this extraordinary interruption had subsided, he was removed, and there followed a long discussion about whether he was of sound mind or not. The matter was left to the jury to decide by their verdict. They found him guilty of the charge of manslaughter, without the excuse of insanity. He was brought up again, and condemned to transportation for life. All he did, on hearing the dreadful sentence, was to reiterate his desperate words: "Hang me before I do more harm! Hang me, for God's sake, out of the way!"

June 20th

I made yesterday's entry in sadness of heart, and I have not been better in my spirits today. It is something to have brought the murderer to the punishment that he deserves. But the knowledge that this most righteous act of retribution is accomplished brings no consolation with it. The law does indeed punish Noah Truscott for his crime, but can it raise up Mary Mallinson from her last resting-place in the churchyard?

While writing of the law, I ought to record that the heartless wretch who allowed Mary to be struck down in his presence without making an attempt to defend her is not likely to escape with perfect impunity. The policeman who looked after him to insure his attendance at the trial discovered that he had committed past offenses, for which the law can make him answer. A summons was executed upon him, and he was taken before the magistrate the moment he left the court after giving his evidence.

I had just written these few lines, and was closing my journal, when there came a knock at the door. I answered it, thinking that Robert had called on his way home to say goodnight, and found myself face to face with a strange gentleman, who immediately asked for Anne Rodway. On hearing that I was the person inquired for, he requested five minutes' conversation with me. I showed him into the little empty room at the back of the house, and waited, rather surprised and fluttered, to hear what he had to say.

He was a dark man, with a serious manner, and a short, stern way of speaking I was certain that he was a stranger, and yet there seemed something in his face not unfamiliar to me. He began by taking a newspaper from his pocket, and asking me if I was the person who had given evidence at the trial of Noah Truscott on a charge of manslaughter. I answered immediately that I was.

"I have been for nearly two years in London seeking Mary Mallinson, and always seeking her in vain," he said. "The first and only news I have had of her I found in the newspaper report of the trial yesterday."

He still spoke calmly, but there was something in the look of his eyes which showed me that he was suffering in spirit. A sudden nervousness overcame me, and I was obliged to sit down.

"You knew Mary Mallinson, sir?" I asked, as quietly as I could.

"I am her brother."

I clasped my hands and hid my face in despair. Oh, the bitterness of heart with which I heard him say those simple words!

"You were very kind to her," said the calm, tearless man. "In her name and for her sake, I thank you."

"Oh, sir," I said, "why did you never write to her when you were in foreign parts?"

"I wrote often," he answered; "but each of my letters contained a remittance of money. Did Mary tell you she had a stepmother? If she did, you may guess why none of my letters were allowed to reach her. I now know that this woman robbed my sister. Has she lied in telling me that she was never informed of Mary's place of abode?"

I remembered that Mary had never communicated with her stepmother after the separation, and could therefore assure him that the woman had spoken the truth.

He paused for a moment after that, and sighed. Then he took out a pocket-book, and said:

"I have already arranged for the payment of any legal expenses that may have been incurred by the trial, but I have still to reimburse you for the funeral charges which you so generously defrayed. Excuse my speaking bluntly on this subject; I am accustomed to look on all matters where money is concerned purely as matters of business."

I saw that he was taking several bank-notes out of the pocket-book, and stopped him.

"I will gratefully receive back the little money I actually paid, sir, because I am not well off, and it would be an ungracious act of pride in me to refuse it from you," I said; "but I see you handling bank-notes, any one of which is far beyond the amount you have to repay me. Pray put them back, sir. What I did for your poor lost sister I did from my love and fondness for her. You have thanked me for that, and your thanks are all I can receive."

He had hitherto concealed his feelings, but I saw them now begin to get the better of him. His eyes softened, and he took my hand and squeezed it hard.

"I beg your pardon," he said; "I beg your pardon, with all my heart."

There was silence between us, for I was crying, and I believe, at heart, he was crying too. At last he dropped my hand, and seemed to change back, by an effort, to his former calmness.

"Is there no one belonging to you to whom I can be of service?" he asked. "I see among the witnesses on the trial the name of a young man who appears to have assisted you in the inquiries which led to the prisoner's conviction. Is he a relation?"

"No, sir – at least, not now – but I hope—"

"What?"

"I hope that he may, one day, be the nearest and dearest relation to me that a woman can have." I said those words boldly, because I was afraid of his otherwise taking some wrong view of the connection between Robert and me

"One day?" he repeated. "One day may be a long time hence."

"We are neither of us well off, sir," I said. "One day means the day when we are a little richer than we are now."

"Is the young man educated? Can he produce testimonials to his character? Oblige me by writing his name and address down on the back of that card."

When I had obeyed, in a handwriting which I am afraid did me no credit, he took out another card and gave it to me.

"I shall leave England tomorrow," he said. "There is nothing now to keep me in my own country. If you are ever in any difficulty or distress (which I pray God you may never be), apply to my London agent, whose address you have there."

He stopped, and looked at me attentively, then took my hand again.

"Where is she buried?" he said, suddenly, in a quick whisper, turning his head away.

I told him, and added that we had made the grave as beautiful as we could with grass and flowers. I saw his lips whiten and tremble.

"God bless and reward you!" he said, and drew me toward him quickly and kissed my forehead. I was quite overcome, and sank down and hid my face on the table. When I looked up again he was gone.

June 25th, 1841

I write these lines on my wedding morning, when little more than a year has passed since Robert returned to England.

His salary was increased yesterday to one hundred and fifty pounds a year. If I only knew where Mr. Mallinson was, I would write and tell him of our present happiness. But for the situation which his kindness procured for Robert, we might still have been waiting vainly for the day that has now come.

I am to work at home for the future, and Sally is to help us in our new abode. If Mary could have lived to see this day! I am not ungrateful for my blessings; but oh, how I miss that sweet face on this morning of all others!

I got up today early enough to go alone to the grave, and to gather the nosegay that now lies before me from the flowers that grow round it. I shall put it in my bosom when

Robert comes to fetch me to the church. Mary would have been my bridesmaid if she had lived; and I can't forget Mary, even on my wedding-day...

The Night

The last words of the last story fell low and trembling from Owen's lips. He waited for a moment while Jessie dried the tears which Anne Rodway's simple diary had drawn from her warm young heart, then closed the manuscript, and taking her hand patted it in his gentle, fatherly way.

"You will be glad to hear, my love," he said, "that I can speak from personal experience of Anne Rodway's happiness. She came to live in my parish soon after the trial at which she appeared as chief witness, and I was the clergyman who married her. Months before that I knew her story, and had read those portions of her diary which you have just heard. When I made her my little present on her wedding day, and when she gratefully entreated me to tell her what she could do for me in return, I asked for a copy of her diary to keep among the papers that I treasured most. 'The reading of it now and then,' I said, 'will encourage that faith in the brighter and better part of human nature which I hope, by God's help, to preserve pure to my dying day.' In that way I became possessed of the manuscript: it was Anne's husband who made the copy for me. You have noticed a few withered leaves scattered here and there between the pages. They were put there, years since, by the bride's own hand: they are all that now remain of the flowers that Anne Rodway gathered on her marriage morning from Mary Mallinson's grave."

Jessie tried to answer, but the words failed on her lips. Between the effect of the story, and the anticipation of the parting now so near at hand, the good, impulsive, affectionate creature was fairly overcome. She laid her head on Owen's shoulder, and kept tight hold of his hand, and let her heart speak simply for itself, without attempting to help it by a single word.

The silence that followed was broken harshly by the tower clock. The heavy hammer slowly rang out ten strokes through the gloomy night-time and the dying storm.

I waited till the last humming echo of the clock fainted into dead stillness. I listened once more attentively, and again listened in vain. Then I rose, and proposed to my brothers that we should leave our guest to compose herself for the night.

When Owen and Morgan were ready to quit the room, I took her by the hand, and drew her a little aside.

"You leave us early, my dear," I said; "but, before you go tomorrow morning—"

I stopped to listen for the last time, before the words were spoken which committed me to the desperate experiment of pleading George's cause in defiance of his own request. Nothing caught my ear but the sweep of the weary weakened wind and the melancholy surging of the shaken trees.

"But, before you go tomorrow morning," I resumed, "I want to speak to you in private. We shall breakfast at eight o'clock. Is it asking too much to beg you to come and see me alone in my study at half past seven?"

Just as her lips opened to answer me I saw a change pass over her face. I had kept her hand in mine while I was speaking, and I must have pressed it unconsciously so hard as almost to hurt her. She may even have uttered a few words of remonstrance; but they never reached me: my whole hearing sense was seized, absorbed, petrified.

At the very instant when I had ceased speaking, I, and I alone, heard a faint sound – a sound that was new to me – fly past the Glen Tower on the wings of the wind.

"Open the window, for God's sake!" I cried.

My hand mechanically held hers tighter and tighter. She struggled to free it, looking hard at me with pale cheeks and frightened eyes. Owen hastened up and released her, and put his arms round me.

"Griffith, Griffith!" he whispered, "control yourself, for George's sake."

Morgan hurried to the window and threw it wide open.

The wind and rain rushed in fiercely. Welcome, welcome wind! They all heard it now. "Oh, Father in heaven, so merciful to fathers on earth – my son, my son!"

It came in, louder and louder with every gust of wind – the joyous, rapid gathering roll of wheels. My eyes fastened on her as if they could see to her heart, while she stood there with her sweet face turned on me all pale and startled. I tried to speak to her; I tried to break away from Owen's arms, to throw my own arms round her, to keep her on my bosom, till *he* came to take her from me. But all my strength had gone in the long waiting and the long suspense. My head sank on Owen's breast – but I still heard the wheels. Morgan loosened my cravat, and sprinkled water over my face – I still heard the wheels. The poor terrified girl ran into her room, and came back with her smelling-salts – I heard the carriage stop at the house. The room whirled round and round with me; but I heard the eager hurry of footsteps in the hall, and the opening of the door. In another moment my son's voice rose clear and cheerful from below, greeting the old servants who loved him. The dear, familiar tones just poured into my ear, and then, the moment they filled it, hushed me suddenly to rest.

When I came to myself again my eyes opened upon George. I was lying on the sofa, still in the same room; the lights we had read by in the evening were burning on the table; my son was kneeling at my pillow, and we two were alone.

The Morning

The wind is fainter, but there is still no calm. The rain is ceasing, but there is still no sunshine. The view from my window shows me the mist heavy on the earth, and a dim gray veil drawn darkly over the sky. Less than twelve hours since, such a prospect would have saddened me for the day. I look out at it this morning, through the bright medium of my own happiness, and not the shadow of a shade falls across the steady inner sunshine that is poring over my heart.

The pen lingers fondly in my hand, and yet it is little, very little, that I have left to say. The Purple Volume lies open by my side, with the stories ranged together in it in the order in which they were read. My son has learned to prize them already as the faithful friends who served him at his utmost need. I have only to wind off the little thread of narrative on which they are all strung together before the volume is closed and our anxious literary experiment fairly ended.

My son and I had a quiet hour together on that happy night before we retired to rest. The little love-plot invented in George's interests now required one last stroke of diplomacy to complete it before we all threw off our masks and assumed our true characters for the future. When my son and I parted for the night, we had planned the necessary stratagem for taking our lovely guest by surprise as soon as she was out of her bed in the morning.

Shortly after seven o'clock I sent a message to Jessie by her maid, informing her that a good night's rest had done wonders for me, and that I expected to see her in my study at half past seven, as we had arranged the evening before. As soon as her answer, promising to be punctual to the appointment, had reached me, I took George into my study – left him in my place to plead his own cause – and stole away, five minutes before the half hour, to join my brothers in the breakfast-room.

Although the sense of my own happiness disposed me to take the brightest view of my son's chances, I must nevertheless acknowledge that some nervous anxieties still fluttered about my heart while the slow minutes of suspense were counting themselves out in the breakfast-room. I had as little attention to spare for Owen's quiet prognostications of success as for Morgan's pitiless sarcasms on love, courtship, and matrimony. A quarter of an hour elapsed – then twenty minutes. The hand moved on, and the clock pointed to five minutes to eight, before I heard the study door open, and before the sound of rapidly-advancing footsteps warned me that George was coming into the room.

His beaming face told the good news before a word could be spoken on either side. The excess of his happiness literally and truly deprived him of speech. He stood eagerly looking at us all three, with outstretched hands and glistening eyes.

"Have I folded up my surplice forever," asked Owen, "or am I to wear it once again, George, in your service?"

"Answer this question first," interposed Morgan, with a look of grim anxiety. "Have you actually taken your young woman off my hands, or have you not?"

No direct answer followed either question. George's feelings had been too deeply stirred to allow him to return jest for jest at a moment's notice.

"Oh, father, how can I thank you!" he said. "And you! and you!" he added, looking at Owen and Morgan gratefully.

"You must thank Chance as well as thank us," I replied, speaking as lightly as my heart would let me, to encourage him. "The advantage of numbers in our little love-plot was all on our side. Remember, George, we were three to one."

While I was speaking the breakfast-room door opened noiselessly, and showed us Jessie standing on the threshold, uncertain whether to join us or to run back to her own room. Her bright complexion heightened to a deep glow; the tears just rising in her eyes, and not yet falling from them; her delicate lips trembling a little, as if they were still shyly conscious of other lips that had pressed them but a few minutes since; her attitude irresolutely graceful; her hair just disturbed enough over her forehead and her cheeks to add to the charm of them – she stood before us, the loveliest living picture of youth, and tenderness, and virgin love that eyes ever looked on. George and I both advanced together to meet her at the door. But the good, grateful girl had heard from my son the true story of all that I had done, and hoped, and suffered for the last ten days, and showed charmingly how she felt it by turning at once to *me*.

"May I stop at the Glen Tower a little longer?" she asked, simply.

"If you think you can get through your evenings, my love," I answered. "'But surely you forget that the Purple Volume is closed, and that the stories have all come to an end?"

She clasped her arms round my neck, and laid her cheek fondly against mine.

"How you must have suffered yesterday!" she whispered, softly.

"And how happy I am today!"

The tears gathered in her eyes and dropped over her cheeks as she raised her head to look at me affectionately when I said those words. I gently unclasped her arms and led her to George.

"So you really did love him, then, after all," I whispered, "though you were too sly to let me discover it?"

A smile broke out among the tears as her eyes wandered away from mine and stole a look at my son. The clock struck the hour, and the servant came in with breakfast. A little domestic interruption of this kind was all that was wanted to put us at our ease. We drew round the table cheerfully, and set the Queen of Hearts at the head of it, in the character of mistress of the house already.

If you enjoyed this, you might also like...
Great Expectations, see opposite
The Death of the Lion, see page 449

Great Expectations
Chapter VIII

Charles Dickens

PUMBLECHOOK'S premises in the High Street of the market town, were of a peppercorny and farinaceous character, as the premises of a cornchandler and seedsman should be. It appeared to me that he must be a very happy man indeed, to have so many little drawers in his shop; and I wondered when I peeped into one or two on the lower tiers, and saw the tied-up brown paper packets inside, whether the flower-seeds and bulbs ever wanted of a fine day to break out of those jails, and bloom.

It was in the early morning after my arrival that I entertained this speculation. On the previous night, I had been sent straight to bed in an attic with a sloping roof, which was so low in the corner where the bedstead was, that I calculated the tiles as being within a foot of my eyebrows. In the same early morning, I discovered a singular affinity between seeds and corduroys. Mr. Pumblechook wore corduroys, and so did his shopman; and somehow, there was a general air and flavor about the corduroys, so much in the nature of seeds, and a general air and flavor about the seeds, so much in the nature of corduroys, that I hardly knew which was which. The same opportunity served me for noticing that Mr. Pumblechook appeared to conduct his business by looking across the street at the saddler, who appeared to transact his business by keeping his eye on the coachmaker, who appeared to get on in life by putting his hands in his pockets and contemplating the baker, who in his turn folded his arms and stared at the grocer, who stood at his door and yawned at the chemist. The watchmaker, always poring over a little desk with a magnifying-glass at his eye, and always inspected by a group of smock-frocks poring over him through the glass of his shop-window, seemed to be about the only person in the High Street whose trade engaged his attention.

Mr. Pumblechook and I breakfasted at eight o'clock in the parlor behind the shop, while the shopman took his mug of tea and hunch of bread and butter on a sack of peas in the front premises. I considered Mr. Pumblechook wretched company. Besides being possessed by my sister's idea that a mortifying and penitential character ought to be imparted to my diet, – besides giving me as much crumb as possible in combination with as little butter, and putting such a quantity of warm water into my milk that it would have been more candid to have left the milk out altogether, – his conversation consisted of nothing but arithmetic. On my politely bidding him Good morning, he said, pompously, "Seven times nine, boy?" And how should I be able to answer, dodged in that way, in a strange place, on an empty stomach! I was hungry, but before I had swallowed a morsel, he began a running sum that lasted all through the breakfast. "Seven?" "And four?" "And eight?" "And six?" "And two?" "And ten?" And so on. And after each figure was disposed of, it was as much as I could do to get a bite or a sup, before the next came; while he sat at his ease guessing nothing, and eating bacon and hot roll, in (if I may be allowed the expression) a gorging and gormandizing manner.

For such reasons, I was very glad when ten o'clock came and we started for Miss Havisham's; though I was not at all at my ease regarding the manner in which I should acquit myself under that lady's roof. Within a quarter of an hour we came to Miss Havisham's house, which was of old brick, and dismal, and had a great many iron bars to it. Some of the windows had been walled up; of those that remained, all the lower were rustily barred. There was a courtyard in front, and that was barred; so we had to wait, after ringing the bell, until some one should come to open it. While we waited at the gate, I peeped in (even then Mr. Pumblechook said, "And fourteen?" but I pretended not to hear him), and saw that at the side of the house there was a large brewery. No brewing was going on in it, and none seemed to have gone on for a long long time.

A window was raised, and a clear voice demanded "What name?" To which my conductor replied, "Pumblechook." The voice returned, "Quite right," and the window was shut again, and a young lady came across the court-yard, with keys in her hand.

"This," said Mr. Pumblechook, "is Pip."

"This is Pip, is it?" returned the young lady, who was very pretty and seemed very proud; "come in, Pip."

Mr. Pumblechook was coming in also, when she stopped him with the gate.

"Oh!" she said. "Did you wish to see Miss Havisham?"

"If Miss Havisham wished to see me," returned Mr. Pumblechook, discomfited.

"Ah!" said the girl; "but you see she don't."

She said it so finally, and in such an undiscussible way, that Mr. Pumblechook, though in a condition of ruffled dignity, could not protest. But he eyed me severely, – as if I had done anything to him! – and departed with the words reproachfully delivered: "Boy! Let your behavior here be a credit unto them which brought you up by hand!" I was not free from apprehension that he would come back to propound through the gate, "And sixteen?" But he didn't.

My young conductress locked the gate, and we went across the courtyard. It was paved and clean, but grass was growing in every crevice. The brewery buildings had a little lane of communication with it, and the wooden gates of that lane stood open, and all the brewery beyond stood open, away to the high enclosing wall; and all was empty and disused. The cold wind seemed to blow colder there than outside the gate; and it made a shrill noise in howling in and out at the open sides of the brewery, like the noise of wind in the rigging of a ship at sea.

She saw me looking at it, and she said, "You could drink without hurt all the strong beer that's brewed there now, boy."

"I should think I could, miss," said I, in a shy way.

"Better not try to brew beer there now, or it would turn out sour, boy; don't you think so?"

"It looks like it, miss."

"Not that anybody means to try," she added, "for that's all done with, and the place will stand as idle as it is till it falls. As to strong beer, there's enough of it in the cellars already, to drown the Manor House."

"Is that the name of this house, miss?"

"One of its names, boy."

"It has more than one, then, miss?"

"One more. Its other name was Satis; which is Greek, or Latin, or Hebrew, or all three – or all one to me – for enough."

"Enough House," said I; "that's a curious name, miss."

"Yes," she replied; "but it meant more than it said. It meant, when it was given, that whoever had this house could want nothing else. They must have been easily satisfied in those days, I should think. But don't loiter, boy."

Though she called me "boy" so often, and with a carelessness that was far from complimentary, she was of about my own age. She seemed much older than I, of course, being a girl, and beautiful and self-possessed; and she was as scornful of me as if she had been one-and-twenty, and a queen.

We went into the house by a side door, the great front entrance had two chains across it outside, – and the first thing I noticed was, that the passages were all dark, and that she had left a candle burning there. She took it up, and we went through more passages and up a staircase, and still it was all dark, and only the candle lighted us.

At last we came to the door of a room, and she said, "Go in."

I answered, more in shyness than politeness, "After you, miss."

To this she returned: "Don't be ridiculous, boy; I am not going in." And scornfully walked away, and – what was worse – took the candle with her.

This was very uncomfortable, and I was half afraid. However, the only thing to be done being to knock at the door, I knocked, and was told from within to enter. I entered, therefore, and found myself in a pretty large room, well lighted with wax candles. No glimpse of daylight was to be seen in it. It was a dressing-room, as I supposed from the furniture, though much of it was of forms and uses then quite unknown to me. But prominent in it was a draped table with a gilded looking-glass, and that I made out at first sight to be a fine lady's dressing-table.

Whether I should have made out this object so soon if there had been no fine lady sitting at it, I cannot say. In an arm-chair, with an elbow resting on the table and her head leaning on that hand, sat the strangest lady I have ever seen, or shall ever see.

She was dressed in rich materials, – satins, and lace, and silks, – all of white. Her shoes were white. And she had a long white veil dependent from her hair, and she had bridal flowers in her hair, but her hair was white. Some bright jewels sparkled on her neck and on her hands, and some other jewels lay sparkling on the table. Dresses, less splendid than the dress she wore, and half-packed trunks, were scattered about. She had not quite finished dressing, for she had but one shoe on, – the other was on the table near her hand, – her veil was but half arranged, her watch and chain were not put on, and some lace for her bosom lay with those trinkets, and with her handkerchief, and gloves, and some flowers, and a Prayer-Book all confusedly heaped about the looking-glass.

It was not in the first few moments that I saw all these things, though I saw more of them in the first moments than might be supposed. But I saw that everything within my view which ought to be white, had been white long ago, and had lost its lustre and was faded and yellow. I saw that the bride within the bridal dress had withered like the dress, and like the flowers, and had no brightness left but the brightness of her sunken eyes. I saw that the dress had been put upon the rounded figure of a young woman, and that the figure upon which it now hung loose had shrunk to skin and bone. Once, I had been taken to see some ghastly waxwork at the Fair, representing I know not what impossible personage lying in state. Once, I had been taken to one of our old marsh churches to see a skeleton in the ashes of a rich dress that had been dug out of a vault under the church pavement. Now, waxwork and skeleton seemed to have dark eyes that moved and looked at me. I should have cried out, if I could.

"Who is it?" said the lady at the table.

"Pip, ma'am."

"Pip?"

"Mr. Pumblechook's boy, ma'am. Come – to play."

"Come nearer; let me look at you. Come close."

It was when I stood before her, avoiding her eyes, that I took note of the surrounding objects in detail, and saw that her watch had stopped at twenty minutes to nine, and that a clock in the room had stopped at twenty minutes to nine.

"Look at me," said Miss Havisham. "You are not afraid of a woman who has never seen the sun since you were born?"

I regret to state that I was not afraid of telling the enormous lie comprehended in the answer "No."

"Do you know what I touch here?" she said, laying her hands, one upon the other, on her left side.

"Yes, ma'am." (It made me think of the young man.)

"What do I touch?"

"Your heart."

"Broken!"

She uttered the word with an eager look, and with strong emphasis, and with a weird smile that had a kind of boast in it. Afterwards she kept her hands there for a little while, and slowly took them away as if they were heavy.

"I am tired," said Miss Havisham. "I want diversion, and I have done with men and women. Play."

I think it will be conceded by my most disputatious reader, that she could hardly have directed an unfortunate boy to do anything in the wide world more difficult to be done under the circumstances.

"I sometimes have sick fancies," she went on, "and I have a sick fancy that I want to see some play. There, there!" with an impatient movement of the fingers of her right hand; "play, play, play!"

For a moment, with the fear of my sister's working me before my eyes, I had a desperate idea of starting round the room in the assumed character of Mr. Pumblechook's chaise-cart. But I felt myself so unequal to the performance that I gave it up, and stood looking at Miss Havisham in what I suppose she took for a dogged manner, inasmuch as she said, when we had taken a good look at each other, –

"Are you sullen and obstinate?"

"No, ma'am, I am very sorry for you, and very sorry I can't play just now. If you complain of me I shall get into trouble with my sister, so I would do it if I could; but it's so new here, and so strange, and so fine, – and melancholy—" I stopped, fearing I might say too much, or had already said it, and we took another look at each other.

Before she spoke again, she turned her eyes from me, and looked at the dress she wore, and at the dressing-table, and finally at herself in the looking-glass.

"So new to him," she muttered, "so old to me; so strange to him, so familiar to me; so melancholy to both of us! Call Estella."

As she was still looking at the reflection of herself, I thought she was still talking to herself, and kept quiet.

"Call Estella," she repeated, flashing a look at me. "You can do that. Call Estella. At the door."

To stand in the dark in a mysterious passage of an unknown house, bawling Estella to a scornful young lady neither visible nor responsive, and feeling it a dreadful liberty so to roar out her name, was almost as bad as playing to order. But she answered at last, and her light came along the dark passage like a star.

Miss Havisham beckoned her to come close, and took up a jewel from the table, and tried its effect upon her fair young bosom and against her pretty brown hair. "Your own, one day, my dear, and you will use it well. Let me see you play cards with this boy."

"With this boy? Why, he is a common laboring boy!"

I thought I overheard Miss Havisham answer, – only it seemed so unlikely, – "Well? You can break his heart."

"What do you play, boy?" asked Estella of myself, with the greatest disdain.

"Nothing but beggar my neighbor, miss."

"Beggar him," said Miss Havisham to Estella. So we sat down to cards.

It was then I began to understand that everything in the room had stopped, like the watch and the clock, a long time ago. I noticed that Miss Havisham put down the jewel exactly on the spot from which she had taken it up. As Estella dealt the cards, I glanced at the dressing-table again, and saw that the shoe upon it, once white, now yellow, had never been worn. I glanced down at the foot from which the shoe was absent, and saw that the silk stocking on it, once white, now yellow, had been trodden ragged. Without this arrest of everything, this standing still of all the pale decayed objects, not even the withered bridal dress on the collapsed form could have looked so like grave-clothes, or the long veil so like a shroud.

So she sat, corpse-like, as we played at cards; the frillings and trimmings on her bridal dress, looking like earthy paper. I knew nothing then of the discoveries that are occasionally made of bodies buried in ancient times, which fall to powder in the moment of being distinctly seen; but, I have often thought since, that she must have looked as if the admission of the natural light of day would have struck her to dust.

"He calls the knaves Jacks, this boy!" said Estella with disdain, before our first game was out. "And what coarse hands he has! And what thick boots!"

I had never thought of being ashamed of my hands before; but I began to consider them a very indifferent pair. Her contempt for me was so strong, that it became infectious, and I caught it.

She won the game, and I dealt. I misdealt, as was only natural, when I knew she was lying in wait for me to do wrong; and she denounced me for a stupid, clumsy laboring-boy.

"You say nothing of her," remarked Miss Havisham to me, as she looked on. "She says many hard things of you, but you say nothing of her. What do you think of her?"

"I don't like to say," I stammered.

"Tell me in my ear," said Miss Havisham, bending down.

"I think she is very proud," I replied, in a whisper.

"Anything else?"

"I think she is very pretty."

"Anything else?"

"I think she is very insulting." (She was looking at me then with a look of supreme aversion.)

"Anything else?"

"I think I should like to go home."

"And never see her again, though she is so pretty?"

"I am not sure that I shouldn't like to see her again, but I should like to go home now."

"You shall go soon," said Miss Havisham, aloud. "Play the game out."

Saving for the one weird smile at first, I should have felt almost sure that Miss Havisham's face could not smile. It had dropped into a watchful and brooding expression, – most likely when all the things about her had become transfixed, – and it looked as if nothing could ever lift it up again. Her chest had dropped, so that she stooped; and her voice had dropped, so that she spoke low, and with a dead lull upon her; altogether, she had the appearance of having dropped body and soul, within and without, under the weight of a crushing blow.

I played the game to an end with Estella, and she beggared me. She threw the cards down on the table when she had won them all, as if she despised them for having been won of me.

"When shall I have you here again?" said Miss Havisham. "Let me think."

I was beginning to remind her that today was Wednesday, when she checked me with her former impatient movement of the fingers of her right hand.

"There, there! I know nothing of days of the week; I know nothing of weeks of the year. Come again after six days. You hear?"

"Yes, ma'am."

"Estella, take him down. Let him have something to eat, and let him roam and look about him while he eats. Go, Pip."

I followed the candle down, as I had followed the candle up, and she stood it in the place where we had found it. Until she opened the side entrance, I had fancied, without thinking about it, that it must necessarily be night-time. The rush of the daylight quite confounded me, and made me feel as if I had been in the candlelight of the strange room many hours.

"You are to wait here, you boy," said Estella; and disappeared and closed the door.

I took the opportunity of being alone in the courtyard to look at my coarse hands and my common boots. My opinion of those accessories was not favorable. They had never troubled me before, but they troubled me now, as vulgar appendages. I determined to ask Joe why he had ever taught me to call those picture-cards Jacks, which ought to be called knaves. I wished Joe had been rather more genteelly brought up, and then I should have been so too.

She came back, with some bread and meat and a little mug of beer. She put the mug down on the stones of the yard, and gave me the bread and meat without looking at me, as insolently as if I were a dog in disgrace. I was so humiliated, hurt, spurned, offended, angry, sorry, – I cannot hit upon the right name for the smart – God knows what its name was, – that tears started to my eyes. The moment they sprang there, the girl looked at me with a quick delight in having been the cause of them. This gave me power to keep them back and to look at her: so, she gave a contemptuous toss – but with a sense, I thought, of having made too sure that I was so wounded – and left me.

But when she was gone, I looked about me for a place to hide my face in, and got behind one of the gates in the brewery-lane, and leaned my sleeve against the wall there, and leaned my forehead on it and cried. As I cried, I kicked the wall, and took a hard twist at my hair; so bitter were my feelings, and so sharp was the smart without a name, that needed counteraction.

My sister's bringing up had made me sensitive. In the little world in which children have their existence whosoever brings them up, there is nothing so finely perceived and so finely felt as injustice. It may be only small injustice that the child can be exposed to; but the child is small, and its world is small, and its rocking-horse stands as many hands high, according to scale, as a big-boned Irish hunter. Within myself, I had sustained, from my babyhood, a perpetual conflict with injustice. I had known, from the time when I could speak, that my sister, in her capricious and violent coercion, was unjust to me. I had cherished a profound conviction that her bringing me up by hand gave her no right to bring me up by jerks. Through all my punishments, disgraces, fasts, and vigils, and other penitential performances, I had nursed this assurance; and to my communing so much with it, in a solitary and unprotected way, I in great part refer the fact that I was morally timid and very sensitive.

I got rid of my injured feelings for the time by kicking them into the brewery wall, and twisting them out of my hair, and then I smoothed my face with my sleeve, and came from behind the gate. The bread and meat were acceptable, and the beer was warming and tingling, and I was soon in spirits to look about me.

To be sure, it was a deserted place, down to the pigeon-house in the brewery-yard, which had been blown crooked on its pole by some high wind, and would have made the pigeons think themselves at sea, if there had been any pigeons there to be rocked by it. But there were no pigeons in the dove-cot, no horses in the stable, no pigs in the sty, no malt in the storehouse, no smells of grains and beer in the copper or the vat. All the uses and scents of the brewery might have evaporated with its last reek of smoke. In a by-yard, there was a wilderness of empty casks, which had a certain sour remembrance of better days lingering about them; but it was too sour to be accepted as a sample of the beer that was gone, – and in this respect I remember those recluses as being like most others.

Behind the furthest end of the brewery, was a rank garden with an old wall; not so high but that I could struggle up and hold on long enough to look over it, and see that the rank garden was the garden of the house, and that it was overgrown with tangled weeds, but that there was a track upon the green and yellow paths, as if some one sometimes walked there, and that Estella was walking away from me even then. But she seemed to be everywhere. For when I yielded to the temptation presented by the casks, and began to walk on them, I saw her walking on them at the end of the yard of casks. She had her back towards me, and held her pretty brown hair spread out in her two hands, and never looked round, and passed out of my view directly. So, in the brewery itself, – by which I mean the large paved lofty place in which they used to make the beer, and where the brewing utensils still were. When I first went into it, and, rather oppressed by its gloom, stood near the door looking about me, I saw her pass among the extinguished fires, and ascend some light iron stairs, and go out by a gallery high overhead, as if she were going out into the sky.

It was in this place, and at this moment, that a strange thing happened to my fancy. I thought it a strange thing then, and I thought it a stranger thing long afterwards. I turned my eyes – a little dimmed by looking up at the frosty light – towards a great wooden beam in a low nook of the building near me on my right hand, and I saw a figure hanging there by the neck. A figure all in yellow white, with but one shoe to the feet; and it hung so, that I could see that the faded trimmings of the dress were like earthy paper, and that the face was Miss Havisham's, with a movement going over the whole countenance as if she were trying to call to me. In the terror of seeing the figure, and in the terror of being certain that it had not been there a moment before, I at first ran from it, and then ran towards it. And my terror was greatest of all when I found no figure there.

Nothing less than the frosty light of the cheerful sky, the sight of people passing beyond the bars of the court-yard gate, and the reviving influence of the rest of the bread and meat and beer, would have brought me round. Even with those aids, I might not have come to myself as soon as I did, but that I saw Estella approaching with the keys, to let me out. She would have some fair reason for looking down upon me, I thought, if she saw me frightened; and she would have no fair reason.

She gave me a triumphant glance in passing me, as if she rejoiced that my hands were so coarse and my boots were so thick, and she opened the gate, and stood holding it. I was passing out without looking at her, when she touched me with a taunting hand.

"Why don't you cry?"

"Because I don't want to."

"You do," said she. "You have been crying till you are half blind, and you are near crying again now."

She laughed contemptuously, pushed me out, and locked the gate upon me. I went straight to Mr. Pumblechook's, and was immensely relieved to find him not at home. So, leaving word with the shopman on what day I was wanted at Miss Havisham's again, I set off on the four-mile walk to our forge; pondering, as I went along, on all I had seen, and deeply revolving that I was a common laboring-boy; that my hands were coarse; that my boots were thick; that I had fallen into a despicable habit of calling knaves Jacks; that I was much more ignorant than I had considered myself last night, and generally that I was in a low-lived bad way.

If you enjoyed this, you might also like...
Lost Hearts, see page 315
Markheim, see page 238

Main Line: The Boy at Mugby

Charles Dickens

I AM the boy at Mugby. That's about what I am.

You don't know what I mean? What a pity! But I think you do. I think you must. Look here. I am the boy at what is called The Refreshment Room at Mugby Junction, and what's proudest boast is, that it never yet refreshed a mortal being.

Up in a corner of the Down Refreshment Room at Mugby Junction, in the height of twenty-seven cross draughts (I've often counted 'em while they brush the First-Class hair twenty-seven ways), behind the bottles, among the glasses, bounded on the nor'west by the beer, stood pretty far to the right of a metallic object that's at times the tea-urn and at times the soup-tureen, according to the nature of the last twang imparted to its contents which are the same groundwork, fended off from the traveller by a barrier of stale sponge-cakes erected atop of the counter, and lastly exposed sideways to the glare of Our Missis's eye – you ask a Boy so sitiwated, next time you stop in a hurry at Mugby, for anything to drink; you take particular notice that he'll try to seem not to hear you, that he'll appear in a absent manner to survey the Line through a transparent medium composed of your head and body, and that he won't serve you as long as you can possibly bear it. That's me.

What a lark it is! We are the Model Establishment, we are, at Mugby. Other Refreshment Rooms send their imperfect young ladies up to be finished off by our Missis. For some of the young ladies, when they're new to the business, come into it mild! Ah! Our Missis, she soon takes that out of 'em. Why, I originally come into the business meek myself. But Our Missis, she soon took that out of ME.

What a delightful lark it is! I look upon us Refreshmenters as ockipying the only proudly independent footing on the Line. There's Papers, for instance – my honourable friend, if he will allow me to call him so – him as belongs to Smith's bookstall. Why, he no more dares to be up to our Refreshmenting games than he dares to jump a top of a locomotive with her steam at full pressure, and cut away upon her alone, driving himself, at limited-mail speed. Papers, he'd get his head punched at every compartment, first, second, and third, the whole length of a train, if he was to ventur to imitate my demeanour. It's the same with the porters, the same with the guards, the same with the ticket clerks, the same the whole way up to the secretary, traffic-manager, or very chairman. There ain't a one among 'em on the nobly independent footing we are. Did you ever catch one of them, when you wanted anything of him, making a system of surveying the Line through a transparent medium composed of your head and body? I should hope not.

You should see our Bandolining Room at Mugby Junction. It's led to by the door behind the counter, which you'll notice usually stands ajar, and it's the room where Our Missis and our young ladies Bandolines their hair. You should see 'em at it, betwixt trains, Bandolining away, as if they was anointing themselves for the combat. When you're telegraphed, you should see their noses all a- going up with scorn, as if it was a part of the working of the same Cooke and Wheatstone electrical machinery. You should hear Our Missis give the word, "Here comes the Beast to be Fed!" and then you should see 'em indignantly skipping across the Line, from the Up to the Down, or Wicer Warsaw, and begin to pitch the stale pastry into the plates, and chuck the sawdust sangwiches under the glass covers, and get out the – ha, ha, ha! – the sherry – O my eye, my eye! – for your Refreshment.

It's only in the Isle of the Brave and Land of the Free (by which, of course, I mean to say Britannia) that Refreshmenting is so effective, so 'olesome, so constitutional a check upon the public. There was a Foreigner, which having politely, with his hat off, beseeched our young ladies and Our Missis for "a leetel gloss host prarndee," and having had the Line surveyed through him by all and no other acknowledgment, was a-proceeding at last to help himself, as seems to be the custom in his own country, when Our Missis, with her hair almost a-coming un-Bandolined with rage, and her eyes omitting sparks, flew at him, cotched the decanter out of his hand, and said, "Put it down! I won't allow that!" The foreigner turned pale, stepped back with his arms stretched out in front of him, his hands clasped, and his shoulders riz, and exclaimed: "Ah! Is it possible, this! That these disdaineous females and this ferocious old woman are placed here by the administration, not only to empoison the voyagers, but to affront them! Great Heaven! How arrives it? The English people. Or is he then a slave? Or idiot?" Another time, a merry, wideawake American gent had tried the sawdust and spit it out, and had tried the Sherry and spit that out, and had tried in vain to sustain exhausted natur upon Butter-Scotch, and had been rather extra Bandolined and Line-surveyed through, when, as the bell was ringing and he paid Our Missis, he says, very loud and good-tempered: "I tell Yew what 'tis, ma'arm. I la'af. Theer! I la'af. I Dew. I oughter ha' seen most things, for I hail from the Onlimited side of the Atlantic Ocean, and I haive travelled right slick over the Limited, head on through Jeerusalemm and the East, and likeways France and Italy, Europe Old World, and am now upon the track to the Chief Europian Village; but such an Institution as Yew, and Yewer young ladies, and Yewer fixin's solid and liquid, afore the glorious Tarnal I never did see yet! And if I hain't found the eighth wonder of monarchical Creation, in finding Yew and Yewer young ladies, and Yewer fixin's solid and liquid, all as aforesaid, established in a country where the people air not absolute Loo- naticks, I am Extra Double Darned with a Nip and Frizzle to the innermostest grit! Wheerfur – Theer! – I la'af! I Dew, ma'arm. I la'af!" And so he went, stamping and shaking his sides, along the platform all the way to his own compartment.

I think it was her standing up agin the Foreigner as giv' Our Missis the idea of going over to France, and droring a comparison betwixt Refreshmenting as followed among the frog-eaters, and Refreshmenting as triumphant in the Isle of the Brave and Land of the Free (by which, of course, I mean to say agin, Britannia). Our young ladies, Miss Whiff, Miss Piff, and Mrs. Sniff, was unanimous opposed to her going; for, as they says to Our Missis one and all, it is well beknown to the hends of the herth as no other nation except Britain has a idea of anythink, but above all of business. Why then should you tire yourself to prove what is already proved? Our Missis, however (being a teazer at all pints) stood out grim obstinate, and got a return pass by Southeastern Tidal, to go right through, if such should be her dispositions, to Marseilles.

Sniff is husband to Mrs. Sniff, and is a regular insignificant cove. He looks arter the sawdust department in a back room, and is sometimes, when we are very hard put to it, let behind the counter with a corkscrew; but never when it can be helped, his demeanour towards the public being disgusting servile. How Mrs. Sniff ever come so far to lower herself as to marry him, I don't know; but I suppose he does, and I should think he wished he didn't, for he leads a awful life. Mrs. Sniff couldn't be much harder with him if he was public. Similarly, Miss Whiff and Miss Piff, taking the tone of Mrs. Sniff, they shoulder Sniff about when he IS let in with a corkscrew, and they whisk things out of his hands when in his servility he is a-going to let the public have 'em, and they snap him up when in the crawling baseness of his spirit he is a-going to answer a public question, and they drore more tears into his eyes than ever the mustard does which he all day long lays on to the sawdust. (But it ain't strong.) Once, when Sniff had the repulsiveness to reach across to get the milk-pot to hand over for a baby, I see Our Missis in her rage catch him by both his shoulders, and spin him out into the Bandolining Room.

But Mrs. Sniff – how different! She's the one! She's the one as you'll notice to be always looking another way from you, when you look at her. She's the one with the small waist buckled in tight in front, and with the lace cuffs at her wrists, which she puts on the edge of the counter before her, and stands a smoothing while the public foams. This smoothing the cuffs and looking another way while the public foams is the last accomplishment taught to the young ladies as come to Mugby to be finished by Our Missis; and it's always taught by Mrs. Sniff.

When Our Missis went away upon her journey, Mrs. Sniff was left in charge. She did hold the public in check most beautiful! In all my time, I never see half so many cups of tea given without milk to people as wanted it with, nor half so many cups of tea with milk given to people as wanted it without. When foaming ensued, Mrs. Sniff would say: "Then you'd better settle it among yourselves, and change with one another." It was a most highly delicious lark. I enjoyed the Refreshmenting business more than ever, and was so glad I had took to it when young.

Our Missis returned. It got circulated among the young ladies, and it as it might be penetrated to me through the crevices of the Bandolining Room, that she had Orrors to reveal, if revelations so contemptible could be dignified with the name. Agitation become awakened. Excitement was up in the stirrups. Expectation stood a- tiptoe. At length it was put forth that on our slacked evening in the week, and at our slackest time of that evening betwixt trains, Our Missis would give her views of foreign Refreshmenting, in the Bandolining Room.

It was arranged tasteful for the purpose. The Bandolining table and glass was hid in a corner, a arm-chair was elevated on a packing- case for Our Missis's ockypation, a table and a tumbler of water (no sherry in it, thankee) was placed beside it. Two of the pupils, the season being autumn, and hollyhocks and dahlias being in, ornamented the wall with three devices in those flowers. On one might be read, "MAY ALBION NEVER LEARN;" on another "KEEP THE PUBLIC DOWN;" on another, "OUR REFRESHMENTING CHARTER." The whole had a beautiful appearance, with which the beauty of the sentiments corresponded.

On Our Missis's brow was wrote Severity, as she ascended the fatal platform. (Not that that was anythink new.) Miss Whiff and Miss Piff sat at her feet. Three chairs from the Waiting Room might have been perceived by a average eye, in front of her, on which the pupils was accommodated. Behind them a very close observer might have discerned a Boy. Myself.

"Where," said Our Missis, glancing gloomily around, "is Sniff?"

"I thought it better," answered Mrs. Sniff, "that he should not be let to come in. He is such an Ass."

"No doubt," assented Our Missis. "But for that reason is it not desirable to improve his mind?"

"Oh, nothing will ever improve HIM," said Mrs. Sniff.

"However," pursued Our Missis, "call him in, Ezekiel."

I called him in. The appearance of the low-minded cove was hailed with disapprobation from all sides, on account of his having brought his corkscrew with him. He pleaded "the force of habit."

"The force!" said Mrs. Sniff. "Don't let us have you talking about force, for Gracious' sake. There! Do stand still where you are, with your back against the wall."

He is a smiling piece of vacancy, and he smiled in the mean way in which he will even smile at the public if he gets a chance (language can say no meaner of him), and he stood upright near the door with the back of his head agin the wall, as if he was a waiting for somebody to come and measure his heighth for the Army.

"I should not enter, ladies," says Our Missis, "on the revolting disclosures I am about to make, if it was not in the hope that they will cause you to be yet more implacable in the exercise of the power you wield in a constitutional country, and yet more devoted to the constitutional motto which I see before me," – it was behind her, but the words sounded better so – "'May Albion never learn!'"

Here the pupils as had made the motto admired it, and cried, "Hear! Hear! Hear!" Sniff, showing an inclination to join in chorus, got himself frowned down by every brow.

"The baseness of the French," pursued Our Missis, "as displayed in the fawning nature of their Refreshmenting, equals, if not surpasses, anythink as was ever heard of the baseness of the celebrated Bonaparte."

Miss Whiff, Miss Piff, and me, we drored a heavy breath, equal to saying, "We thought as much!" Miss Whiff and Miss Piff seeming to object to my droring mine along with theirs, I drored another to aggravate 'em.

"Shall I be believed," says Our Missis, with flashing eyes, "when I tell you that no sooner had I set my foot upon that treacherous shore—"

Here Sniff, either bursting out mad, or thinking aloud, says, in a low voice: "Feet. Plural, you know."

The cowering that come upon him when he was spurned by all eyes, added to his being beneath contempt, was sufficient punishment for a cove so grovelling. In the midst of a silence rendered more impressive by the turned-up female noses with which it was pervaded, Our Missis went on:

"Shall I be believed when I tell you, that no sooner had I landed," this word with a killing look at Sniff, "on that treacherous shore, than I was ushered into a Refreshment Room where there were – I do not exaggerate – actually eatable things to eat?"

A groan burst from the ladies. I not only did myself the honour of jining, but also of lengthening it out.

"Where there were," Our Missis added, "not only eatable things to eat, but also drinkable things to drink?"

A murmur, swelling almost into a scream, ariz. Miss Piff, trembling with indignation, called out, "Name?"

"I WILL name," said Our Missis. "There was roast fowls, hot and cold; there was smoking roast veal surrounded with browned potatoes; there was hot soup with (again I ask shall I be credited?) nothing bitter in it, and no flour to choke off the consumer; there was a variety of cold dishes set off with jelly; there was salad; there was – mark me! FRESH pastry, and that of a light construction; there was a luscious show of fruit; there was bottles and decanters of sound small wine, of every size, and adapted to every pocket; the same odious statement will apply to brandy; and these were set out upon the counter so that all could help themselves."

Our Missis's lips so quivered, that Mrs. Sniff, though scarcely less convulsed than she were, got up and held the tumbler to them.

"This," proceeds Our Missis, "was my first unconstitutional experience. Well would it have been if it had been my last and worst. But no. As I proceeded farther into that enslaved and ignorant land, its aspect became more hideous. I need not explain to this assembly the ingredients and formation of the British Refreshment sangwich?"

Universal laughter – except from Sniff, who, as sangwich-cutter, shook his head in a state of the utmost dejection as he stood with it agin the wall.

"Well!" said Our Missis, with dilated nostrils. "Take a fresh, crisp, long, crusty penny loaf made of the whitest and best flour. Cut it longwise through the middle. Insert a fair and nicely fitting slice of ham. Tie a smart piece of ribbon round the middle of the whole to bind it together. Add at one end a neat wrapper of clean white paper by which to hold it. And the universal French Refreshment sangwich busts on your disgusted vision."

A cry of "Shame!" from all – except Sniff, which rubbed his stomach with a soothing hand.

"I need not," said Our Missis, "explain to this assembly the usual formation and fitting of the British Refreshment Room?"

No, no, and laughter. Sniff agin shaking his head in low spirits agin the wall.

"Well," said Our Missis, "what would you say to a general decoration of everythink, to hangings (sometimes elegant), to easy velvet furniture, to abundance of little tables, to abundance of little seats, to brisk bright waiters, to great convenience, to a pervading cleanliness and tastefulness positively addressing the public, and making the Beast thinking itself worth the pains?"

Contemptuous fury on the part of all the ladies. Mrs. Sniff looking as if she wanted somebody to hold her, and everbody else looking as if they'd rayther not.

"Three times," said Our Missis, working herself into a truly terrimenjious state – "three times did I see these shameful things, only between the coast and Paris, and not counting either: at Hazebroucke, at Arras, at Amiens. But worse remains. Tell me, what would you call a person who should propose in England that there should be kept, say at our own model Mugby Junction, pretty baskets, each holding an assorted cold lunch and dessert for one, each at a certain fixed price, and each within a passenger's power to take away, to empty in the carriage at perfect leisure, and to return at another station fifty or a hundred miles farther on?"

There was disagreement what such a person should be called. Whether revolutionise, atheist, Bright (I said him), or Un-English. Miss Piff screeched her shrill opinion last, in the words: "A malignant maniac!"

"I adopt," says Our Missis, "the brand set upon such a person by the righteous indignation of my friend Miss Piff. A malignant maniac. Know, then, that that malignant maniac has sprung from the congenial soil of France, and that his malignant madness was in unchecked action on this same part of my journey."

I noticed that Sniff was a-rubbing his hands, and that Mrs. Sniff had got her eye upon him. But I did not take more particular notice, owing to the excited state in which the young ladies was, and to feeling myself called upon to keep it up with a howl.

"On my experience south of Paris," said Our Missis, in a deep tone, "I will not expatiate. Too loathsome were the task! But fancy this. Fancy a guard coming round, with the train at full speed, to inquire how many for dinner. Fancy his telegraphing forward the number of dinners. Fancy everyone expected, and the table elegantly laid for the complete party. Fancy a charming dinner, in a charming room, and the head-cook, concerned for the honour of every dish, superintending in his clean white jacket and cap. Fancy the Beast travelling six hundred miles on end, very fast, and with great punctuality, yet being taught to expect all this to be done for it!"

A spirited chorus of "The Beast!"

I noticed that Sniff was agin a-rubbing his stomach with a soothing hand, and that he had drored up one leg. But agin I didn't take particular notice, looking on myself as called upon to stimulate public feeling. It being a lark besides.

"Putting everything together," said Our Missis, "French Refreshmenting comes to this, and oh, it comes to a nice total! First: eatable things to eat, and drinkable things to drink."

A groan from the young ladies, kep' up by me.

"Second: convenience, and even elegance."

Another groan from the young ladies, kep' up by me.

"Third: moderate charges."

This time a groan from me, kep' up by the young ladies.

"Fourth: – and here," says Our Missis, "I claim your angriest sympathy – attention, common civility, nay, even politeness!"

Me and the young ladies regularly raging mad all together.

"And I cannot in conclusion," says Our Missis, with her spitefullest sneer, "give you a completer pictur of that despicable nation (after what I have related), than assuring you that they wouldn't bear our constitutional ways and noble independence at Mugby Junction, for a single month, and that they would turn us to the right-about and put another system in our places, as soon as look at us; perhaps sooner, for I do not believe they have the good taste to care to look at us twice."

The swelling tumult was arrested in its rise. Sniff, bore away by his servile disposition, had drored up his leg with a higher and a higher relish, and was now discovered to be waving his corkscrew over his head. It was at this moment that Mrs. Sniff, who had kep' her eye upon him like the fabled obelisk, descended on her victim. Our Missis followed them both out, and cries was heard in the sawdust department.

You come into the Down Refreshment Room, at the Junction, making believe you don't know me, and I'll pint you out with my right thumb over my shoulder which is Our Missis, and which is Miss Whiff, and which is Miss Piff, and which is Mrs. Sniff. But you won't get a chance to see Sniff, because he disappeared that night. Whether he perished, tore to pieces, I cannot say; but his corkscrew alone remains, to bear witness to the servility of his disposition.

If you enjoyed this, you might also like...
Our New House, see page 423
Great Expectations, see page 371

The Distracted Preacher

Thomas Hardy

Chapter I
How His Cold Was Cured

SOMETHING DELAYED the arrival of the Wesleyan minister, and a young man came temporarily in his stead. It was the thirteenth of January, 18—, that Mr. Stockdale, the young man in question, made his humble entry into the village, unknown, and almost unseen. But when those of the inhabitants who styled themselves of his connection became acquainted with him, they were rather pleased with the substitute than otherwise, though he had scarcely as yet acquired ballast of character sufficient to steady the consciences of the hundred and forty Methodists of pure blood who, at this time, lived in Nether-Mynton, and to give in addition supplementary support to the mixed race which went to church in the morning and chapel in the evening, or when there was a tea – as many as a hundred and ten people more, all told, and including the parish-clerk in the winters time, when it was too dark for the vicar to observe who passed up the street at seven 'o clock – which, to be just to him, he was never anxious to do.

It was owing to his overlapping of creeds that the celebrated population-puzzle arose among the denser gentry of the district around Nether-Mynton; how could it be that a parish containing fifteen score of strong, full-grown Episcopalians, and nearly thirteen score of well-matured Dissenters, numbered barely two-and-twenty score adults in all?

The young man being personally interesting those with whom he came in contact were content to waive for a while the graver question of his sufficiency. It is said that at this time of his life his eyes were affectionate, though without a ray of levity; that his hair was curly, and his figure tall; that he was, in short, a very lovable youth, who won upon his female hearers as soon as they saw and heard him, and caused them to say, "Why didn't we know of this before he came, that we might have gied him a warmer welcome!"

The fact was that, knowing him to be only provisionally selected, and expecting nothing remarkable in his person or doctrine, they and the rest of his flock in Nether-Mynton had felt almost as indifferent about his advent as if they had been the soundest church-going parishioners in the country, and he their true and appointed parson. Thus when Stockdale set foot in the place nobody had secured a lodging for him, and though his journey had given him a bad cold in the head, he was forced to attend to that business himself. On inquiry he found that the only possible accommodation in the village would be found at the house of one Mrs. Lizzy Newberry, at the upper end of the street.

It was a youth who gave this information, and Stockdale asked him who Mrs. Newberry might be.

The boy said that she was a widow-woman, who had got no husband, because he was dead. Mr. Newberry, he added, had been a well-to-do man enough, as the saying was, and a farmer; but be had gone off in a decline. As regarded Mrs. Newberry's serious side, Stockdale gathered that she was one of the trimmers who went to church and chapel both.

"I'll go there," said Stockdale, feeling that, in the absence of purely sectarian lodgings, he could do no better.

"She's a little particular, and won't hae gover'ment folks, or curates, or the pa'son's friends, or such like," said the lad, dubiously.

"Ah, that may be a promising sign. I'll call. Or no; just you go up and ask first if she can find room for me. I have to see one or two persons on another matter. You will find me down to the carrier's."

In a quarter of an hour the lad came back, and said that Mrs. Newberry would have no objection to accommodate him, whereupon Stockdale called at the house. It stood within a garden hedge, and seemed to be roomy and comfortable. He saw an elderly woman, with whom he made arrangements to come the same night, since there was no inn in the place, and he wished to house himself as soon as possible; the village being a local center from which he was to radiate at once to the different small chapels in the neighborhood. He forthwith sent his luggage to Mrs. Newberry's from the carrier's, where he had taken shelter, and in the evening walked up to his temporary home.

As he now lived there, Stockdale felt it unnecessary to knock at the door; and entering quietly, he had the pleasure of hearing footsteps scudding away like mice into the back quarters. He advanced to the parlor, as the front room was called, though its stone floor was scarcely disguised by the carpet, which overlaid only the trodden areas, leaving sandy deserts under the furniture. But the room looked snug and cheerful. The firelight shone out brightly, trembling on the bulging moldings of the table-legs, playing with brass knobs and handles, and lurking in great strength on the under surface of the chimney-piece. A deep arm-chair, covered with horse-hair, and studded with a countless throng of brass nails, was pulled up on one side of the fireplace. The tea-things were on the table, the teapot cover was open, and a little hand-bell had been laid at that precise point toward which a person seated in the great chair might be expected instinctively to stretch his hand.

Stockdale sat down, not objecting to his experience of the room thus far, and began his residence by tinkling the bell. A little girl crept in at the summons, and made tea for him. Her name, she said, was Marther Sarer, and she lived out there, nodding toward the road and village generally. Before Stockdale had got far with his meal a tap sounded on the door behind him, and on his telling the inquirer to come in, a rustle of garments caused him to turn his head. He saw before him a fine and extremely well-made young woman, with dark hair, a wide, sensible, beautiful forehead, eyes that warmed him before he knew it, and a mouth that was in itself a picture to all appreciative souls.

"Can I get you anything else for tea?" she said, coming forward a step or two, an expression of liveliness on her features, and her hand waving the door by its edge.

"Nothing, thank you," said Stockdale, thinking less of what he replied than of what might be her relation to the household.

"You are quite sure?" said the young woman, apparently aware that he had not considered his answer.

He conscientiously examined the tea-things, and found them all there. "Quite sure, Miss Newberry," he said.

"It is Mrs. Newberry," said she. "Lizzy Newberry. I used to be Lizzy Simpkins."

"Oh, I beg your pardon, Mrs. Newberry." And before he had occasion to say more she left the room.

Stockdale remained in some doubt till Martha Sarah came to clear the table. "Whose house is this, my little woman?" said he.

"Mrs. Lizzy Newberry's, sir."

"Then Mrs. Newberry is not the old lady I saw this afternoon?"

"No. That's Mrs. Newberry's mother. It was Mrs. Newberry who comed in to you just by now, because she wanted to see if you was good-looking."

Later in the evening, when Stockdale was about to begin supper, she came again. "I have come myself, Mr. Stockdale," she said. The minister stood up in acknowledgment of the honor. "I am afraid little Marther might not make you understand. What will you have for supper? There's cold rabbit, and there's a ham uncut."

Stockdale said he could get on nicely with those viands, and supper was laid. He had no more than cut a slice when tap-tap came to the door again. The minister had already learned that this particular rhythm in taps denoted the fingers of his enkindling landlady, and the doomed young fellow buried his first mouthful under a look of receptive blandness.

"We have a chicken in the house, Mr. Stockdale; I quite forgot to mention it just now. Perhaps you would like Marther Sarer to bring it up?"

Stockdale had advanced far enough in the art of being a young man to say that he did not want the chicken, unless she brought it up herself but when it was uttered he blushed at the daring gallantry of the speech, perhaps a shade too strong for a serious man and a minister. In three minutes the chicken appeared, but, to his great surprise, only in the hands of Martha Sarah. Stockdale was disappointed, which perhaps it was intended that he should be.

He had finished supper, and was not in the least anticipating Mrs. Newberry again that night, when she tapped and entered as before.

Stockdale's gratified look told that she had lost nothing by not appearing when expected. It happened that the cold in the head from which the young man suffered had increased with the approach of night, and before she had spoken he was seized with a violent fit of sneezing, which he could not anyhow repress.

Mrs. Newberry looked full of pity. "Your cold is very bad tonight, Mr. Stockdale."

Stockdale replied that it was rather troublesome.

"And I've a good mind—" she added, archly, looking at the cheerless glass of water on the table, which the abstemious young minister was going to drink.

"Yes, Mrs. Newberry?"

"I've a good mind that you should have something more likely to cure it than that cold stuff."

"Well," said Stockdale, looking down at the glass, "as there is no inn here, and nothing better to be got in the village, of course it will do."

To this she replied, "There is something better, not far off, though not in the house. I really think you must try it, or you may be ill. Yes, Mr. Stockdale, you shall." She held up her finger, seeing that he was about to speak. "Don't ask what it is; wait, and you shall see."

Lizzy went away, and Stockdale waited in a pleasant mood. Presently she returned with her bonnet and cloak on, saying, "I am so sorry, but you must help me to get it. Mother has gone to bed. Will you wrap yourself up, and come this way, and please bring that cup with you?"

Stockdale, a lonely young fellow; who had for weeks felt a great craving for somebody on whom to throw away superfluous interest, and even tenderness, was not sorry to join her, and followed his guide through the back door, across the garden to the bottom, where the boundary was a wall. This wall was low, and beyond it Stockdale discerned in the night-shades several gray headstones, and the outlines of the church roof or tower.

"It is easy to get up this way," she said, stepping upon a bank which abutted on the wall; then putting her foot on the top of the stone-work, and descending by a spring inside, where the ground was much higher, as is the manner of grave-yards to be. Stockdale did the same, and followed her in the dusk across the irregular ground till they came to the tower door, which, when they had entered, she softly closed behind them.

"You can keep a secret?" she said, in a musical voice.

"Like an iron chest!" said he, fervently.

Then from under her cloak she produced a small lighted lantern, which the minister had not noticed that she carried at all. The light showed them to be close to the singing-gallery stairs, under which lay a heap of lumber of all sorts, but consisting mostly of decayed framework, pews, panels, and pieces of flooring, that from time to time had been removed from their original fixings in the body of the edifice and replaced by new.

"Perhaps you will drag some of those boards aside?" she said, holding the lantern over her head to light him better. "Or will you take the lantern while I move them?"

"I can manage it," said the young man; and acting as she ordered, he uncovered, to his surprise, a row of little barrels bound with wood hoops, each barrel being about as large as the nave of a common wagon-wheel. When they were laid open Lizzy fixed her eyes on him, as if she wondered what he would say.

"You know what they are?" she asked, finding that he did not speak.

"Yes, barrels," said Stockdale, simply. He was an inland man, the son of highly respectable parents, and brought up with a single eye to the ministry, and the sight suggested nothing beyond the fact that such articles were there.

"You are quite right; they are barrels," she said, in an emphatic tone of candor that was not without a touch of irony.

Stockdale looked at her with an eye of sudden misgiving. "Not smugglers' liquor?" he said.

"Yes," said she. "They are tubs of spirits that have accidentally come over in the dark from France."

In Nether-Mynton and its vicinity at this date people always smiled at the sort of sin called in the outside world illicit trading, and these little tubs of gin and brandy were as well known to the inhabitants as turnips. So that Stockdale's innocent ignorance, and his look of alarm when he guessed the sinister mystery, seemed to strike Lizzy first as ludicrous, and then as very awkward for the good impression that she wished to produce upon him.

"Smuggling is carried out here by some of the people," she said, in a gentle, apologetic voice. "It has been their practice for generations, and they think it no harm. Now, will you roll out one of the tubs?"

"What to do with it?" said the minister.

"To draw a little from it to cure your cold," she answered. "It is so burning strong that it drives away that sort of thing in a jiffy. Oh, it is all right about our taking it. I may have what I like; the owner of the tubs says so. I ought to have had some in the house, and then I shouldn't ha' been put to this trouble; but I drink none myself, and so I often forget to keep it indoors."

"You are allowed to help yourself, I suppose, that you may not inform where their hiding-place is?"

"Well, no, not that particularly, but I may take some if I want it. So help yourself."

"I will, to oblige you, since you have a right to it," murmured the minister; and though he was not quite satisfied with his part in the performance, he rolled one of the tubs out from the corner into the middle of the tower floor. "How do you wish me to get it out – with a gimlet, I suppose?"

"No; I'll show you," said his interesting companion. And she held up with her other hand a shoemaker's awl and a hammer. "You must never do these things with a gimlet, because the wood-dust gets in; and when the buyers pour out the brandy, that would tell them that the tub had been broached. An awl makes no dust, and the hole nearly closes up again. Now tap one of the hoops forward."

Stockdale took the hammer and did so.

"Now make the hole in the part that was covered by the hoop."

He made the hole as directed. "It won't run out," he said.

"Oh yes, it will," said she. "Take the tub between your knees and squeeze the heads, and I'll hold the cup."

Stockdale obeyed; and the pressure taking effect upon the tub, which seemed to be thin, the spirits spurted out in a stream. When the cup was full he ceased pressing, and the flow immediately stopped. "Now we must fill up keg with water," said Lizzy, "or it will look like forty hens when it is handled, and show that 'tis not full."

"But they tell you you may take it?"

"Yes, the *smugglers*; but the *buyers* must not know that the smugglers have been kind to me at their expense."

"I see," said Stockdale, doubtfully. "I much question the honesty of this proceeding."

By her direction be held the tub with the hole upward, and while he went through the process of alternately pressing and ceasing to press she produced a bottle of water, from which she took mouthfuls, then putting her pretty lips to the hole, where it was sucked in at each recovery of the cask from pressure. When it was again full be plugged the hole, knocked the hoop down to its place, and buried the tub in the lumber as before.

"Aren't the smugglers afraid that you will tell?" he asked, as they recrossed the churchyard.

"Oh no; they are not afraid of that. I couldn't do such a thing."

"They have put you into a very awkward corner," said Stockdale, emphatically. "You must, of course, as an honest person, sometimes feel that it is your duty to inform – really, you must."

"Well, I have never particularly felt it as a duty; and, besides, my first husband—" She stopped, and there was some confusion in her voice. Stockdale was so honest and unsophisticated that he did not at once discern why she paused; but at last he did perceive that the words were a slip, and that no women would have uttered "first husband" by accident unless she had thought pretty frequently of a second. He felt for her confusion, and allowed her time to recover and proceed. "My husband," she said, in a self-corrected tone, "used to know of their doings, and so did my father, and kept the secret. I cannot inform, in fact, against anybody."

"I see the hardness of it," he continued, like a man who looked far into the moral of things. "And it is very cruel that you should be tossed and tantalized between your memories and your conscience. I do hope, Mrs. Newberry, that you will soon see your way out of this unpleasant position."

"Well, I don't just now," she murmured.

By this time they had passed over the wall and entered the house, where she brought him a glass and hot water, and left him to his own reflections. He looked after her vanishing form, asking himself whether he, as a respectable man, and a minister, and a shining light, even though as yet only of the halfpenny-candle sort, were quite justified in doing this thing. A sneeze settled the question; and he found that when the fiery liquor was lowered by the addition of twice or thrice the quantity of water, it was one of the prettiest cures for a cold in the head that he had ever known, particularly at this chilly time of the year.

Stockdale sat in the deep chair about twenty minutes sipping and meditating, till he at length took warmer views of things, and longed for the morrow, when he would see Mrs. Newberry again. He then felt that, though chronologically at a short distance, it would, in an emotional sense, be very long before tomorrow came, and walked restlessly round the room. His eye was attracted by a framed and glazed sampler in which a running ornament of fir-trees and peacocks surrounded the following pretty bit of sentiment:

> *Rose leaves smell when roses thrive,*
> *Here's my work while I'm alive;*
> *Rose leaves smell when shrunk and shed,*
> *Here's my work when I am dead.*
> *Lizzie Simpkins. Fear God. Honor the King.*
> *Aged 11 years.*

"'Tis hers," he said to himself. "Heavens, how I like that name!"

Before he had done thinking that no other name from Abigail to Zenobia would have suited his young landlady so well, tap-tap came again upon the door; and the minister started as her face appeared yet another time, looking so disinterested that the most ingenious would refrained from asserting that she had come to affect his feelings by her seductive eyes.

"Would you like a fire in your room, Mr. Stockdale, on account of your cold?"

The minister, being still a little pricked in the conscience for countenancing her in watering the spirits, saw here a way to self-chastisement.

"No, I thank you," he said, firmly; "it is not necessary. I have never been used to one in my life, and it would be giving way to luxury too far."

"Then I won't insist," she said, and disconcerted him by vanishing instantly. Wondering if she was vexed by his refusal, he wished that he had chosen to have a fire, even though it should have scorched him out of bed and endangered his self-discipline for a dozen days. However, he consoled himself with what was in truth a rare consolation for a budding lover, that he was under the same roof with Lizzy – her guest, in fact, to take a poetical view of the term lodger; and that he would certainly see her on the morrow.

The morrow came, and Stockdale rose early, his cold quite gone. He had never in his life so longed for the breakfast-hour as he did that day, and punctually at eight o'clock, after a short walk, to reconnoiter the premises, he re-entered the door of his dwelling. Breakfast passed, and Martha Sarah attended, but nobody came voluntarily as on the night before to inquire if there were other wants which he had not mentioned, and which she would attempt to gratify. He was disappointed, and went out, hoping to see her at dinner. Dinner-time came; he sat down to the meal, finished it, lingered on for a whole hour, although two new teachers were at that moment waiting at the chapel door to speak to him by appointment. It was useless to wait longer, and he slowly went his way down the lane, cheered by the thought that, after all, he would see her in the evening, and perhaps engage again in the delightful tub-broaching in the neighboring church tower, which proceeding he resolved to render more moral by steadfastly insisting that no water should be introduced to fill up, though the tub should cluck like all the hens in Christendom. But nothing could disguise the fact that it was a queer business; and his countenance fell when he thought how much more his mind was interested in that matter than in his serious duties.

However, compunction vanished with the decline of day. Night came, and his tea and supper; but no Lizzy Newberry, and no sweet temptations. At last the minister could bear it no longer, and said to his quaint little attendant, "Where is Mrs. Newberry today?" judiciously handing a penny as he spoke.

"She's busy," said Martha.

"Anything serious happened?" he asked, handing another penny, and revealing yet additional pennies in the background.

"Oh no, nothing at all!" said she, with breathless confidence. "Nothing ever happens to her. She's only biding upstairs in bed, because 'tis her way sometimes."

Being a young man of some honor, he would not question further, and assuming that Lizzy must have a bad headache, or other slight ailment, in spite of what the girl had said, he went to bed dissatisfied, not even setting eyes on old Mrs. Simpkins. "I said last night that I should see her tomorrow," he reflected; "but that was not to be."

Next day he had better fortune, or worse, meeting her at the foot of the stairs in the morning, and being favored by a visit or two from her during the day – once for the purpose of making kindly inquiries about his comfort, as on the first evening, and at another time to place a bunch of winter-violets on his table, with a promise to renew them when they drooped. On these occasions there was something in her smile which showed how conscious she was of the effect she produced, though it must be said that it was rather a humorous than a designing consciousness, and savored more of pride than of vanity.

As for Stockdale, he clearly perceived that he possessed unlimited capacity for backsliding, and wished that tutelary saints were not denied to Dissenters. He set a watch upon his tongue and eyes for the space of one hour and a half, after which he found it was useless to struggle further, and gave himself up to the situation. "The other minister will be here in a month," he said to himself when sitting over the fire. "Then I shall be off, and she will distract my mind no more!... And then, shall I go on living by myself forever? No; when my two years of probation are finished, I shall have a furnished house to live in, with a varnished door and a brass knocker; and I'll march straight back to her, and ask her flat, as soon as the last plate is on the dresser!"

Thus a titillative fortnight was passed by young Stockdale, during which time things proceeded much as such matters have done ever since the beginning of history. He saw the object of attachment several times one day, did not see her at all the next, met her when he least expected to do so, missed her when hints and signs as to where she should be at a given hour almost amounted to an appointment. This mild coquetry was perhaps fair enough under the circumstances of their being so closely lodged, and Stockdale put up with it as philosophically as he was able. Being in her own house, she could, after vexing or disappointing him of her presence, easily win him back by suddenly surrounding him with those little attentions which her position as his landlady put it in her power to bestow. When he had waited indoors half the day to see her, and on finding that she would not be seen, had gone off in a huff to the dreariest and dampest walk he could discover, she would restore equilibrium in the evening with "Mr. Stockdale, I have fancied you must feel draught o' nights from your bedroom window, and so I have been putting up thicker curtains this afternoon while you were out." or "I noticed that you sneezed twice again this morning, Mr. Stockdale. Depend upon it, that cold is hanging about you yet; I am sure it is – I have thought of it continually; and you must let me make a posset for you."

Sometimes in coming home he found his sitting-room rearranged, chairs placed where the table had stood, and the table ornamented with the few fresh flowers and leaves that could be obtained at this season, so as to add a novelty to the room. At times she would be standing in a chair outside the house, trying to nail up a branch of the monthly rose which the winter wind had blown down; and of course he stepped forward to assist her, when their hands got mixed in passing the shreds and nails. Thus they became friends again after a disagreement. She would utter on these occasions some pretty and deprecatory remark on the necessity of her troubling him anew; and he would straightway say that he would do a hundred times as much for her if she should so require.

Chapter II
How He Saw Two Other Men

MATTERS BEING in this advanced state, Stockdale was rather surprised one cloudy evening, while sitting in his room, at hearing her speak in low tones of expostulation to someone at the door. It was nearly dark, but the shutters were not yet closed, nor the candles lighted; and Stockdale was tempted to stretch his head toward the window. He saw outside the door a young man in clothes of a whitish color, and upon reflection judged their wearer to be the well-built and rather handsome miller who lived below. The miller's voice was alternately low and firm, and sometimes it reached the level of positive entreaty; but what the words were Stockdale could in no way hear.

Before the colloquy had ended, the minister's attention was attracted by a second incident. Opposite Lizzy's home grew a clump of laurels, forming a thick and permanent shade. One of the laurel boughs now quivered against the light background of sky, and in a moment the head of a man peered out, and remained still. He seemed to be also much interested in the conversation at the door, and was plainly lingering there to watch and listen. Had Stockdale stood in any other relation to Lizzy than that of a lover, he might have gone out and examined I into the meaning of this; but being as yet but an unprivileged ally, he did nothing more than stand up and show himself in the lighted room, whereupon the listener disappeared, and Lizzy and the miller spoke in lower tones.

Stockdale was made so uneasy by the circumstance that as soon as the miller was gone, he said, "Mrs. Newberry, are you aware that you were watched just now, and your conversation heard?"

"When?" she said

'When you were talking to that miller. A man was looking from the laurel-tree as jealously as if he could have eaten you"

She showed more concern than the trifling event seemed to demand, and he added, "Perhaps you were talking of things you did not wish to be overheard?"

"I was talking only on business," she said.

"Lizzy, be frank!" said the young man. "If it was only on business, why should anybody wish to listen to you?"

She looked curiously at him. "What else do you think it could be, then?"

"Well, the only talk between a young woman and man that is likely to amuse an eavesdropper."

"Ah, yes," she said, smiling in spite of her preoccupation. "Well, Cousin Owlett has spoken to me about matrimony, every now and then, that's true; but he was not speaking of it then. I wish he had been speaking of it, with all my heart. It would have been much less serious for me."

"Oh, Mrs. Newberry!"

"It would. Not that I should ha' chimed in with him, of course. I wish it for other reasons. I am glad, Mr. Stockdale, that you have told me of that listener. It is a timely warning, and I must see my cousin again."

"But don't go away till I have spoken," said the minister. "I'll out with it at once, and make no more ado. Let it be Yes or No between us. Lizzy, please do!" And he held out his hand, in which she freely allowed her own to rest, but without speaking.

"You mean Yes by that?" he asked, after waiting a while.

"You may be my sweetheart, if you will."

"Why not say at once you will wait for me until I have a house and can come back to marry you?"

"Because I am thinking – thinking of something else," she said, with embarrassment. "It all comes upon me at once, and I must settle one thing at a time."

"At any rate, dear Lizzy, you can assure me that the miller shall not be allowed to speak to you except on business? You have never directly encouraged him?"

She parried the question by saying, "You see, he and his party have been in the habit of leaving things on my premises sometimes, and as I have not denied him, it makes him rather forward."

"Things – what things?"

"Tubs – they are called things here."

"But why don't you deny him, my dear Lizzy?"

"I cannot well."

"You are too timid. It is unfair of him to impose so upon you, and get your good name into danger by his smuggling tricks. Promise me that the next time he wants to leave his tubs here you will let me roll them into the street?"

She shook her head. "I would not venture to offend the neighbors so much as that," said she, "or do anything that would be so likely to put poor Owlett into the hands of the exciseman."

Stockdale sighed, and said that he thought hers a mistaken generosity when it extended to assisting those who cheated the king of his dues.

"At any rate, you will let me make him keep his distance as your lover, and tell him flatly that you are not for him?"

"Please not, at present," she said. "I don't wish to offend my old neighbors. It is not only Owlett who is concerned."

"This is too bad," said Stockdale, impatiently.

"On my honor, I won't encourage him as my lover," Lizzy answered, earnestly. "A reasonable man will be satisfied with that."

"Well, so I am," said Stockdale, his countenance clearing.

Chapter III
The Mysterious Great-Coat

STOCKDALE NOW began to notice more particularly a feature in the life of his fair landlady which he had casually observed, but scarcely ever thought of before. It was that she was markedly irregularly in her hours of rising. For a week or two she would be tolerably punctual, reaching the ground-floor within a few minutes of halfpast seven; then suddenly she would not be visible till twelve at noon, perhaps for three or four days in succession; and twice he had certain proof that she did not leave her room till halfpast three in the afternoon. The second time that this extreme lateness came under his notice was on a day when he had particularly wished to consult with her about his future movements; and he concluded, as he always had done, that she had a cold, headache, or other ailment unless she had kept herself invisible to avoid meeting and talking to him, which he could hardly believe. The former supposition was disproved, however, by her innocently saying, some days later; when they were speaking on a question of health, that she had never had a moment's heaviness, headache, or illness of any kind since the previous January twelvemonth.

"I am glad to hear it," said he. "I thought quite otherwise."

"What, do I look sickly?" she asked, turning up her face to show the impossibility of his gazing on it and holding such a belief for a moment.

"Not at all; I merely thought so from your being sometimes obliged to keep your room through the best part of the day."

"Oh, as for that, it means nothing," she murmured, with a look which some might have called cold, and which was the look that he worst liked to see upon her. "It is pure sleepiness, Mr. Stockdale."

"Never!"

"It is, I tell you. When I stay in my room till half-past three in the afternoon you may always be sure that I slept soundly till three, or I shouldn't have stayed there."

"It is dreadful," said Stockdale, thinking of the disastrous effects of such indulgence upon the household of a minister, should it become a habit of every-day occurrence.

"But then," she said, divining his good and prescient thoughts, "it happens only when I stay awake all night. I don't go to sleep till five or six in the morning sometimes."

"Ah, that's another matter," said Stockdale.

"Sleeplessness to such an alarming extent is real illness. Have you spoken to a doctor?"

"Oh no, there is no need for doing that; it is all natural to me." And she went away without further remark.

Stockdale might have waited a long time to know the real cause of her sleeplessness had it not happened that one dark night he was sitting in his bedroom jotting down notes for a sermon, which unintentionally occupied him for a considerable time after the other members of the household had retired. He did not get to bed till one o'clock. Before he had fallen asleep he heard a knocking at the door, first rather timidly performed, and then louder. Nobody answered it, and the person knocked again. As the house still remained undisturbed, Stockdale got out of bed, went to his window, which overlooked the door, and opening it, asked who was there.

A young woman's voice replied that Susan Wallis was there, and that she had come to ask if Mrs. Newberry could give her some mustard to make a plaster with, as her father was taken very ill on the chest.

The minister, having neither bell nor servant, was compelled to act in person. "I will call Mrs. Newberry," he said. Partly dressing himself, he went along the passage and tapped at Lizzy's door. She did not answer, and, thinking of her erratic habits in the matter of sleep, he thumped the door persistently, when he discovered, by its moving ajar under his knocking, that it had only been gently pushed to. As there was now a sufficient entry for the voice, he knocked no longer, but said, in firm tones: "Mrs. Newberry, you are wanted."

The room was quite silent; not a breathing, not a rustle, came from any part of it. Stock-dale now sent a positive shout through the open space of the door: "Mrs. Newberry!" still no answer, or movement of any kind within. Then he heard sounds from the opposite room, that of Lizzy's mother, as if she had been aroused by his uproar though Lizzy had not, and was dressing herself hastily. Stockdale softly closed the younger woman's door and went on to the other, which was opened by Mrs. Simpkins before he could reach it. She was in her ordinary clothes, and had a light in her hand.

"What's the person calling about?" she said, in alarm.

Stockdale told the girl's errand, adding, seriously: "I cannot wake Mrs. Newberry."

"It is no matter," said her mother. "I can let the girl have what she wants as well as my daughter." And she came out of the room and went downstairs.

Stockdale retired toward his own apartment, saying, however, to Mrs. Simpkins from the landing, as if on second thoughts: "I suppose there is nothing the matter with Mrs. Newberry, that I could not wake her?"

"Oh no," said the old lady, hastily. "Nothing at all."

Still the minister was not satisfied. "Will you go in and see?" he said. "I should be much more at ease."

Mrs. Simpkins returned up the staircase, went to her daughter's room, and came out again almost instantly. "There is nothing at all the matter with Lizzy," she said, and descended again to attend to the applicant, who, having seen the light, had remained quiet during this interval.

Stockdale went into his room and lay down as before. He heard Lizzy's mother open the front door, admit the girl, and then the murmured discourse of both as they went to the store-cupboard for the medicament required. The girl departed, the door was fastened, Mrs. Simpkins came upstairs, and the house was again in silence. Still the minister did not fall asleep. He could not get rid of a singular suspicion, which was all the more harassing, in beings if true, the most unaccountable thing within his experience. That Lizzy Newberry was in her bedroom when he made such a clamor at her door he could not possibly convince himself, notwithstanding that he had heard her come upstairs at the usual time, go into her chamber and shut herself up in the usual way. Yet all reason was so much against her being elsewhere that he was constrained to go back again to the unlikely theory of a heavy sleep, though he had heard neither breath nor movement during a shouting and knocking loud enough to rouse the Seven Sleepers.

Before coming to any positive conclusion he fell asleep himself, and did not awake till day. He saw nothing of Mrs. Newberry in the morning, before he went out to meet the rising sun, as he liked to do when the weather was fine; but as this was by no means unusual, he took no notice of it. At breakfast-time he knew that she was not far off by hearing her in the kitchen, and though he saw nothing of her person, that back apartment being rigorously closed against his eyes, she seemed to be talking, ordering, and bustling about among the pots and skimmers in so ordinary a manner that there was no reason for his wasting more time in fruitless surmise.

The minister suffered from these distractions, and his extemporized sermons were not improved thereby. Already he often said Romans for Corinthians in the pulpit, and gave out hymns in strange cramped meters that hitherto had always been skipped because the congregation could not raise a tune to fit them. He fully resolved that as soon as his few weeks of stay approached their end he would cut the matter short, and commit himself by proposing a definite engagement, repenting at leisure if necessary.

With this end in view, he suggested to her on the evening after her mysterious sleep that they should take a walk together just before dark, the latter part of the proposition being introduced that they might return home unseen. She consented to go; and away they went over a stile, to a shrouded foot-path suited for the occasion. But, in spite of attempts on both sides, they were unable to infuse much spirit into the ramble.

She looked rather paler than usual, and. sometimes turned her head away.

"Lizzy," said Stockdale, reproachfully, when they had walked in silence a long distance.

"Yes," said she.

"You yawned – much my company is to you!" He put it in that way, but he was really wondering whether her yawn could possibly have more to do with physical weariness from the night before than mental weariness of that present moment. Lizzy apologized, and owned that she was rather tired, which gave him an opening for a direct question on the point; but his modesty would not allow him to put it to her, and he uncomfortably resolved to wait.

The month of February passed with alternations of mud and frost, rain and sleet, east winds and northwesterly gales. The hollow places in the plowed fields showed themselves as pools of water, which had settled there from the higher levels, and had not yet found time to soak away. The birds began to get lively, and a single thrush came just before sunset each evening, and sang hopefully on the large elm tree which stood nearest to Mrs. Newberry's house. Cold blasts and brittle earth had given place to an oozing dampness more unpleasant in itself than frost; but it suggested coming spring, and its unpleasantness was of a bearable kind.

Stockdale had been going to bring about a practical understanding with Lizzy at least half a dozen times; but what with the mystery of her apparent absence on the night of the neighbor's call, and her curious way of lying in bed at unaccountable times, he felt a check within him whenever he wanted to speak out. Thus they still lived on as indefinitely affianced lovers, each of whom hardly acknowledged the other's claim to the name of chosen one. Stockdale persuaded himself that his hesitation was owing to the postponement of the ordained minister's arrival, and the consequent delay in his own departure, which did away with all necessity for haste in his courtship; but perhaps it was only that his discretion was re-asserting itself, and telling him that he had better get clearer ideas of Lizzy before arranging for the grand contract of his life with her. She, on her part, always seemed ready to be urged further on that question than he had hitherto attempted to go; but she was none the less independent, and to a degree which would have kept from flagging the passion of a far more mutable man.

On the evening of the first of March he went casually into his bedroom about dusk, and noticed lying on a chair a great-coat, hat and breeches. Having no recollection of leaving any clothes of his own in that spot, he went and examined them as well as he could in the twilight, and found that they did not belong to him. He paused for a moment to consider how they might have got there. He was the only man living in the house; and yet these were not his garments, unless he had made a mistake. No, they were not his. He called up Martha Sarah.

"How did these things come in my room?" he said, flinging the objectionable articles to the floor.

Martha said that Mrs. Newberry had given them to her to brush, and that she had brought them up there, thinking they must be Mr. Stockdale's, as there was no other gentleman a-lodging there.

"Of course you did," said Stockdale. "Now take them down to your mis'ess, and say they are some clothes I have found here and know nothing about."

As the door was left open he heard the conversation downstairs. "How stupid!" said Mrs. Newberry, in a tone of confusion. "Why, Marther Sarer, I did not tell you to take 'em to Mr. Stockdale's room!"

"I thought they must be his as they was so muddy," said Martha humbly.

"You should have left 'em on the clothes' horse," said the young mistress, severely; and she came upstairs with the garments on her arm quickly passed Stockdale's room, and threw them forcibly into a closet at the end of a passage. With this the incident ended, and the house was silent again.

There would have been nothing remarkable in finding such clothes in a widow's house had they been clean, or moth-eaten, or creased, or mouldy from long lying by; but that they should be splashed with recent mud bothered Stockdale a good deal. When a young pastor is in the aspen stage of attachment, and open to agitation at the merest trifles, a really substantial incongruity of this complexion is a disturbing thing. However, nothing further occurred at that time; but he became watchful and given to conjecture, and was unable to forget the circumstance.

One morning, on looking from his window, he saw Mrs. Newberry herself brushing the tails of a long drab great-coat, which, if he mistook not, was the very same garment as the one that had adorned the chair of his room. It was densely splashed up to the hollow of the back with neighboring Nether-Mynton mud, to judge by its color, the spots being distinctly visible to him in the sunlight. The previous day or two having been wet, the inference was irresistible that the wearer had quite recently been walking some considerable distance about the lanes and fields. Stockdale opened the window and looked out, and Mrs. Newberry turned her head. Her face became slowly red; she never had looked prettier or more incomprehensible. He waved his hand affectionately, and said good-morning; she answered with embarrassment, having ceased her occupation on the instant that she saw him, and rolled up the coat half-cleaned.

Stockdale shut the window. Some simple explanation of her proceeding was doubtless within the bounds of possibility; but he himself could not think of one; and he wished that she had placed the matter beyond conjecture by voluntarily saying something about it there and then.

But, though Lizzy had not offered an explanation at the moment, the subject was brought forward by her at the next time of their meeting. She was chatting to him concerning some other event, and remarked that it happened about the time when she was dusting some old clothes that had belonged to her poor husband.

"You keep them clean out of respect to his memory?" said Stockdale, tentatively.

"I air and dust them sometimes," she said, with the most charming innocence in the world.

"Do dead men come out of their graves and walk in mud?" murmured the minister, in a cold sweat at the deception that she was practicing.

"What did you say?" asked Lizzy

"Nothing, nothing," said he, mournfully.

"Mere words – a phrase that will do for my sermon next Sunday." It was too plain that Lizzy was unaware that he had seen actual pedestrian splashes upon the skirts of the tell-tale overcoat, and that she imagined him to believe it had come direct from some chest or drawer.

The aspect of the case was now considerably darker. Stockdale was so much depressed by it that he did not challenge her explanation, or threaten to go off as a missionary to benighted islanders, or reproach her in any way whatever. He simply parted from her when she had done talking, and lived on in perplexity, till by degrees his natural manner became sad and constrained.

Chapter IV
At the Time of the New Moon

THE FOLLOWING Thursday was changeable, damp, and gloomy, and the night threatened to be windy and unpleasant. Stockdale had gone away to Knollsea in the morning, to be present at some commemoration service there, and on his return he was met by the attractive Lizzy in the passage. Whether influenced by the tide of cheerfulness which had attended him that day, or by the drive through the open air, or whether from a natural disposition to let bygones alone, be allowed himself to be fascinated into forgetfulness of the great-coat incident, and, upon the whole, passed a pleasant evening; not so much in her society as within sound of her voice, as she sat talking in the back parlor to her mother, till the latter went to bed. Shortly after this Mrs. Newberry retired, and then Stockdale prepared to go upstairs himself. But before he left the room he remained standing by the dying embers a while, thinking long of one thing and another, and was only aroused by the flickering of his candle in the socket as it suddenly declined. and went out. Knowing that there were a tinder-box, matches, and another candle in his bedroom, he felt his way upstairs without a light. On reaching his chamber he laid his hand on every possible ledge and corner for the tinderbox, but for a long time in vain. Discovering it at length, Stockdale produced a spark and was kindling the brimstone when he fancied that he heard a movement in the passage. He blew harder at the lint, the match flared up, and looking by aid of the blue light through the door, which had been standing open all this time, he was surprised to see a male figure vanishing round the top of the staircase with the evident intention of escaping unobserved. The personage wore the clothes which Lizzy had been brushing, and something in the outline and gait suggested to the minister that the wearer was Lizzy herself.

But he was not sure of this; and, greatly excited, Stockdale determined to investigate the mystery, and to adopt his own way for doing it. He blew out the match without lighting the candle, went into the passage, and proceeded on tiptoe toward Lizzy's room. A faint gray square of light in the direction of the chamber window as he approached told him that the door was open, and at once suggested that the occupant was gone. He turned and brought down his fist upon the hand-rail of the staircase: "It was she, in her late husband's coat and hat!"

Somewhat relieved to find that there was no intruder in the case, yet none the less surprised, the minister crept down the stairs, softly put on his boots, overcoat, and hat, and tried the front door. It was fastened as usual; he went to the back door, found this unlocked, and emerged into the garden. The night was mild and moonless, and rain had lately been falling, though for the present it had ceased. There was a sudden dropping from the trees and bushes every now and then, as each passing wind shook their boughs. Among these sounds Stockdale heard the faint fall of feet upon the road outside, and he guessed from the step that it was Lizzy's. He followed the sound, and, helped by the circumstance of the wind blowing from the direction in which the pedestrian moved, he got nearly close to her, and kept there, without risk of being overheard. While he thus followed her up the street or lane, as it might indifferently be called, there being more hedge than houses on either side, a figure came forward to her from one of the cottage doors. Lizzy stopped; the minister stepped upon the grass and stopped also.

"Is that Mrs. Newberry?" said the man who had come out, whose voice Stockdale recognized as that of one of the most devout members of his congregation.

"It is," said Lizzy.

"I be quite ready – I've been here this quarter-hour."

"Ah, John," said she, "I have bad news; there is danger tonight for our venture."

"And d'ye tell o't! I dreamed there might be."

"Yes," she said, hurriedly; "and you must go at once round to where the chaps are waiting, and tell them they will not be wanted till tomorrow night at the same time. I go to burn the lugger off."

"I will," he said, and instantly went off through a gate, Lizzy continuing her way.

On she tripped at a quickening pace till the lane turned into the turnpike-road, which she crossed, and got into the track for Ringsworth. Here he ascended the hill without the least hesitation, passed the lonely hamlet of Holworth, and went down the vale on the other side. Stockdale had never taken any extensive walks in this direction, but he was aware that if she persisted in her course much longer she would draw near to the coast, which was here between two and three miles distant from Nether-Mynton; and as it had been about a quarter-past eleven o'clock when they set out, her intention seemed to be to reach the shore about midnight.

Lizzy soon ascended a small mound, which Stockdale at the same time adroitly-skirted on the left; and a dull monotonous roar burst upon his ear. The hillock was about fifty yards from the top of the cliffs, and by day it apparently commanded a full view of the bay. There was light enough in the sky to show her disguised figure against it when she reached the top, where she paused, and afterward sat down. Stockdale, not wishing on any account to alarm her at this moment, yet desirous of being near her, sank upon his hands and knees, crept a little higher up, and there stayed still.

The wind was chilly, the ground damp, and his position one in which he did not care to remain long. However, before he had decided to leave it, the young man heard voices behind him. What they signified he did not know; but, fearing that Lizzy was in danger, he was about to run forward and warn her that she might be seen, when she crept to the shelter of a little bush which maintained a precarious existence in that exposed spot; and her form was absorbed in its dark and stunted outline as she had become part of it. She had evidently heard the men as well as he. They passed near him, talking in loud and careless tones, which could be heard above the uninterrupted washings of the sea, and which suggested that they were not engaged in any business at their own risk. This proved to be the fact; some of their words floated across to him, and caused him to forget at once the coldness of his situation.

"What's the vessel?"

"A lugger, about fifty tons."

"From Cherbourg, I suppose?"

"Yes, a b'lieve".

"But it don't all belong to Owlett?"

"Oh no. He's only got a share. There's another or two in it – a farmer and such-like, but the names I don't know."

The voices died away, and the heads and shoulders of the men diminished toward the cliff, and dropped out of sight.

"My darling has been tempted to buy a share by that unbeliever Owlett," groaned the minister, his honest affection for Lizzy having quickened to its intensest point during these moments of risk to her person and name. "That's why she's here," he said to himself. "Oh, it will be the ruin of her."

His perturbation was interrupted by the sudden bursting out of a bright and increasing light from the spot where Lizzy was in hiding. A few seconds later, and before it had reached the height of a blaze, he heard her rush past him down the hollow like a stone from a sling, in the direction of home. The light now flared high and wide, and showed its position clearly. She had kindled a bough of furze and stuck it into the bush under which she had been crouching; the wind fanned the flame, which crackled fiercely, and threatened to consume the bush as well as the bough. Stockdale paused just long enough to notice thus much, and then followed rapidly the route taken by the young woman. His intention was to overtake her, and reveal himself as a friend; but run as he would he could see nothing of her. Thus he flew across the open country about Holworth, twisting his legs and ankles in unexpected fissures and descents, till, on coming to the gate between the downs and the road, he was forced to pause to get breath. There was no audible movement either in front or behind him, and he now concluded that she had not outrun him, but that, hearing him at her heels, and believing him one of the excise party, she had hidden herself somewhere on the way, and let him pass by.

He went on at a more leisurely pace toward the village. On reaching the house he found his surmise to be correct, for the gate was on the latch, and the door unfastened, just as he had left them. Stockdale closed the door behind him, and waited silently in the passage. In about-ten minutes he heard the same light footstep that he had heard in going out; it paused at the gate, which opened and shut softly, and then the door-latch was lifted and Lizzy came in.

Stockdale went forward and said at once, "Lizzy, don't be frightened. I have been waiting up for you."

She started, though she had recognized the voice. "It is Mr. Stockdale, isn't it?" she said.

"Yes," he answered, becoming angry now that she was safe indoors, and not alarmed. "And a nice game I've found you out in tonight. You are in man's clothes, and I am ashamed of you!"

Lizzy could hardly find a voice to answer this unexpected reproach.

"I am only partly in man's clothes," she faltered, shrinking back to the wall. "It is only his great-coat and hat and breeches that I've got on, which is no harm, as he was my own husband; and I do it only because a cloak blows about so, and you can't use your arms. I have got my own dress under just the same – it is only tucked in. Will you go away upstairs and let me pass? I didn't want you to see me at such a time as this."

"But I have a right to see you. How do you think there can be anything between us now?" Lizzy was silent.

"You are a smuggler," he continued sadly.

"I have only a share in the run," she said.

"That makes no difference. Whatever did you engage in such a trade as that for, and keep it such a secret from me all this time?"

"I don't do it always. I do it only in wintertime when 'tis new moon."

"Well, I suppose that's because it can't be done anywhen else. You have regularly upset me, Lizzy."

"I am sorry for that," Lizzy meekly replied.

"Well now," said he, more tenderly, "no harm is done as yet. Won't you, for the sake of me, give up this blamable and dangerous practice altogether?"

"I must do my best to save this run," said she, getting rather husky in the throat. "I don't want to give you up – you know that; but I don't want to lose my venture. I don't know what to do now! Why I have kept it so secret from you is that I was afraid you would be angry if you knew."

"I should think so. I suppose if I had married you without finding this out you'd have gone on with it just the same?"

"I don't know. I did not think so far ahead. I only went tonight to burn the folks off, because we found that the excisemen knew where the tubs were to be landed."

"It is a pretty mess to be in altogether, is this," said the distracted young minister. "Well, what will you do now?"

Lizzy slowly murmured the particulars of their plan, the chief of which were that they meant to try their luck at some other point of the shore the next night; that three landing-places were always agreed upon before the run was attempted, with the understanding that, if the vessel was burned off from the first point, which was Ringsworth, as it had been by her tonight the crew should attempt to make the second, which was Lullstead, on the second night; and if there, too, danger threatened, they should on the third night try the third place, which was behind a headland further west.

"Suppose the officers hinder them landing there too?" he said, his attention to this interesting programme displacing for a moment his concern at her share in it.

"Then we shan't try anywhere else all this dark – that's what we call the time between moon and moon – and perhaps they'll string the tubs to a stray-line, and sink 'em a little ways from shore, and take the bearings; and then when they have a chance they'll go to creep for 'em."

"What's that?"

"Oh, they'll go out in a boat and drag a creeper – that's a grapnel – along the bottom till it catch hold of the stray-line."

The minister stood thinking; and there was no sound within doors but the tick of the clock on the stairs, and the quick breathing of Lizzy, partly from her walk and partly from agitation, as she stood close to the wall, not in such complete darkness but that he could discern against its whitewashed surface the great-coat and broad hat which covered her.

"Lizzy, all this is very wrong," he said. "Don't you remember the lesson of the tribute-money – 'Render unto Caesar the things that are Caesar's?' Surely you have heard that read times enough in your growing up?"

"He's dead," she pouted.

"But the spirit of the text is in force just the same."

"My father did it, and so did my grandfather, and almost everybody in Nether-Mynton lives by it; and life would be so dull if it wasn't for that, that I should not care to live at all."

"I am nothing to live for, of course," he replied, bitterly. "You would not think it worth while to give up this wild business and live for me alone?"

"I have never looked at it like that."

"And you won't promise, and wait till I am ready?"

"I cannot give you my word tonight." And, looking thoughtfully down, she gradually moved and moved away, going into the adjoining room and closing the door between them. She remained there in the dark till he was tired of waiting, and had gone up to his own chamber.

Poor Stockdale was dreadfully depressed all the next day by the discoveries of the night before. Lizzy was unmistakably a fascinating young woman, but as a minister's wife she was hardly to be contemplated. "If I had only stuck to father's little grocery business, instead of going in for the ministry, she would have suited me beautifully!" he said, sadly, until he remembered that in that case he would never have come from his distant home to Nether-Mynton, and never have known her.

The estrangement between them was not complete, but it was sufficient to keep them out of each other's company. Once during the day he met her in the garden path, and said, turning a reproachful eye upon her, "Do you promise, Lizzy?" But she did not reply. The evening drew on, and he knew well enough that Lizzy would repeat her excursion at night – her half-offended manner had shown that she had not the slightest intention of altering her plans at present. He did not wish to repeat his own share of the adventure; but, act as he would, his uneasiness on her account increased with the decline of day. Supposing that an accident should befall her, he would never forgive himself for not being there to help, much as he disliked the idea of seeming to countenance such unlawful escapades.

Chapter V
How They Went to Lullstead and Back

AS HE HAD expected, she left the house at the same hour at night, this time passing his door without stealth, as if she knew very well that he would be watching, and were resolved to brave his displeasure. He was quite ready, opened the door quickly, and reached the back door almost as soon as she.

"Then you will go, Lizzy?" he said, as he stood on the step beside her, who now again appeared as a little man with a face altogether unsuited to his clothes.

"I must," she said, repressed by his stern manner.

"Then I shall go too," said he.

"And I am sure you will enjoy it!" she exclaimed, in more buoyant tones. "Everybody does who tries it."

"God forbid that I should," he said. "But I must look after you."

They opened the wicket and went up the road abreast of each other, but at some distance apart, scarcely a word passing between them. The evening was rather less favorable to smuggling enterprise than the last had been, the wind being lower, and the sky somewhat clear toward the north.

"It is rather lighter," said Stockdale.

"'Tis, unfortunately," said she. "But it is only from those few stars over there. The moon was new today at four o'clock, and I expected clouds. I hope we shall be able to do it this dark, for when we have to sink 'em for long it makes the stuff taste bleachy, and folks don't like it so well."

Her course was different from that of the preceding night, branching off to the left over Lord's Barrow as soon as they had got out of the lane and crossed the highway. By the time they reached Chaldon Down, Stockdale, who had been in perplexed thought as to what he should say to her, decided that he would not attempt expostulation now, while she was excited by the adventure, but wait till it was over, and endeavor to keep her from such practices in future. It occurred to him once or twice, as they rambled on, that should they be surprised by the excisemen, his situation would be more awkward than hers, for it would be difficult to prove his true motive in coming to the spot; but the risk was a slight consideration beside his wish to be with her.

They now arrived at a ravine which lay on the outskirts of Chaldon, a village two miles on their way toward the point of the shore they sought.

Lizzy broke the silence this time: "I have to wait here to meet the carriers. I don't know if they have come yet. As I told. you, we go to Lullstead tonight, and it is two miles further than Ringsworth."

It turned out that the men had already come; for while she spoke two or three dozen heads broke the line of the slope, and a company of men at once descended from the bushes where they had been lying in wait. These carriers were men whom Lizzy and other proprietors regularly employed to bring the tubs from the boat to a hiding-place inland. They were young fellows of Nether-Mynton, Chaldon, and the neighborhood, quiet and inoffensive persons, who simply engaged to carry the cargo for Lizzy and her cousin Owlett, as they would have engaged in any other labor for which they were fairly well paid.

At a word from her, they closed in together. "You had better take it now," she said to them, and handed to each a packet. It contained six shillings, their remuneration for the night's undertaking, which was paid beforehand without reference to success or failure; but, besides this, they had the privilege of selling as agents when the run was successfully made. As soon as it was done, she said to them, "The place is the old one at Lullstead;" the men till that moment not having been told whither they were bound, for obvious reasons. "Owlett will meet you there," added Lizzy. "I shall, follow behind, to see that we are not watched."

The carriers went on, and Stockdale and Mrs. Newberry followed at the distance of a stone's throw, "What do these men do by day?" he said.

"Twelve or fourteen of them are laboring men. Some are brickmakers, some carpenters, some masons, some thatchers. They are all known to me very well. Nine of 'em are of your own congregation."

"I can't help that," said Stockdale.

"Oh, I know you can't. I only told you. The others are more church-inclined, because they supply the pa'son with all the spirits he requires, and they don't wish to show unfriendliness to a customer."

"How do you choose them?" said Stockdale.

"We choose 'em for their closeness, and because they are strong and sure-footed, and able to carry a heavy load a long way without being tired."

Stockdale sighed as she enumerated each particular, for it proved how far involved in the business a woman must be who was so well acquainted with its conditions and needs. And yet he felt more tenderly toward her at this moment than he had felt all the foregoing day. Perhaps it was that her experienced manner and bold indifference stirred his admiration in spite of himself.

"Take my arm, Lizzy," he murmured.

"I don't want it," she said.

"Besides, we may never be to each other again what we once have been."

"That depends upon you," said he, and they went on again as before.

The hired carriers paced along over Chaldon Down with as little hesitation as if it had been day, avoiding the cart-way, and leaving the village of East Chaldon on the left, so as to reach the crest of the hill at a lonely, trackless place not far from the ancient earthwork called Round Pound. An hour's brisk walking brought them within sound of the sea, not many hundred yards from Lullstead Cove. Here they paused, and Lizzy and Stockdale came up with them, when they went on together to the verge of the cliff. One of the men now produced an iron bar, which he drove firmly into the soil a yard from the edge, and attached to it a rope that he had uncoiled from his body. They all began to descend, partly stepping, partly sliding down the incline, as the rope slipped through their hands.

"You will not go to the bottom, Lizzy?" said Stockdale, anxiously.

"No; I stay here to watch," she said. "Owlett is down there."

The men remained quite silent when they reached the shore; and the next thing audible to the two at the top was the dip of heavy oars, and the dashing of waves against a boat's bow. In a moment the keel gently touched the shingle, and Stockdale heard the footsteps of the thirty-six carriers running forward over the pebbles toward the point of landing.

There was a sousing in the water as of a brood of ducks plunging in, showing that the men had not been particular about keeping their legs, or even their waists, dry from the brine; but it was impossible to see what they were doing, and in a few minutes the shingle was trampled again. The iron bar sustaining the rope, on which Stockdale's hand rested, began to swerve a little, and the carriers one by one appeared climbing up the sloping cliff, dripping audibly as they came, and sustaining themselves by the guide-rope. Each man on reaching the top was seen to be carrying a pair of tubs, one on his back and one on his chest, the two being slung together by cords passing round the chine hoops, and resting on the carrier's shoulders. Some of the stronger men carried three by putting an extra one on the top behind, but the customary load was a pair, these being quite weighty enough to give their bearer the sensation of having chest and backbone in contact after a walk of four or five miles.

"Where is Owlett?" said Lizzy to one of them.

"He will not come up this way," said the carrier. "He's to bide on shore till we be safe off." Then, without waiting for the rest, the foremost men plunged across the down; and when the last had ascended, Lizzy pulled up the rope; wound it round her arm, wriggled the bar from the sod, and turned to follow the carriers.

"You are very anxious about Owlett's safety," said the minister.

"Was there ever such a man!" said Lizzy. "Why, isn't he my cousin?"

"Yes. Well, it is a bad night's work," said Stockdale, heavily. "But I'll carry the bar and rope for you."

"Thank God, the tubs have got so far all right," said she.

Stockdale shook his head, and taking the bar, walked by her side toward the down, and the moan of the sea was heard no more.

"Is this what you meant the other day when you spoke of having business with Owlett?" the young man asked.

"This is it," she replied. "I never see him on any other matter."

"A partnership of that kind with a young man is very odd"

"It was begun by my father and his, who were brother-laws."

Her companion could not blind himself to the fact that where tastes and pursuits were so akin as Lizzy's and Owlett's, and where risks were shared, as with them, in every undertaking, there would be a peculiar appropriateness in her answering Owlett's standing question on matrimony in the affirmative. This did not soothe Stockdale, its tendency being rather to stimulate in him an effort to make the pair as inappropriate as possible, and win her away from this nocturnal crew to correctness of conduct and a minister's parlor in some far-removed inland county.

They had been walking near enough to the file of carriers for Stockdale to perceive that, when they got into the road to the village, they split up into two companies of unequal size, each of which made off in a direction of its own. One company, the smaller of the two, went toward the church, and by the time that Lizzy and Stockdale reached their own house these men had scaled the churchyard wall and were proceeding noiselessly over the grass within.

"I see that Owlett has arranged for one batch to be put in the church again," observed Lizzy. "Do you remember my taking you there the first night you came?"

"Yes, of course," said Stockdale. "No wonder you had permission to broach the tubs – they were his, I suppose?"

"No, they were not – they were mine; I had permission from myself. The day after that they went several miles inland in a wagon-load of manure, and sold very well."

At this moment the group of men who had made off to the left some time before began leaping one by one from the hedge opposite Lizzy's house, and the first man, who had no tubs upon his shoulders, came forward.

"Mrs. Newberry, isn't it?" he said, hastily.

"Yes, Jim," said she. "What's the matter?"

"I find that we can't put any in Badger's Clump tonight, Lizzy," said Owlett. "The place is watched. We must sling the apple-tree in the orchard if there's time. We can't put any more under the church lumber than I have sent on there, and my mixen hev already more in en than is safe."

"Very well," she said. "Be quick about it – that's all. What can I do?"

"Nothing at all, please. Ah! it is the minister! – you two that can't do anything had better get indoors and not be seed."

While Owlett thus conversed, a tone so full of contraband anxiety and so free from lover's jealousy, the men who followed him had been descending one by one from the hedge; and it unfortunately happened that when the hindmost took his leap, the cord which sustained his tubs slipped; the result was that both the kegs fell into the road, one of them being stove in by the blow.

"'Od drown it all!" said Owlett, rushing back.

"It is worth a good deal, I suppose?" said Stockdale.

"Oh, no – about two guineas and a half to us now," said Lizzy, excitedly. "It isn't that – it is the smell! It is so blazing strong before it had been lowered by water that it smells dreadfully when spilled in the road like that! I do hope Latimer won't pass by till it is gone off. "

Owlett and one or two others picked up the burst tub and began to scrape and trample over the spot, to disperse the liquor as much as possible; and then they all entered the gate of Owlett's orchard, which adjoined Lizzy's garden on the right. Stockdale did not care to follow them, for several on recognizing him had looked wonderingly at his presence, though they said nothing. Lizzy left his side and went to the bottom of the garden, looking over the hedge into the orchard, where the men could be dimly seen bustling about, and apparently hiding the tubs. All was done noiselessly, and without a light; and when it was over they dispersed in different directions, those who had taken their cargoes to the church having already gone off to their homes.

Lizzy returned to the garden gate, over which Stockdale was still abstractedly leaning. "It is all finished; I am going indoors now," she said, gently. "I will leave the door ajar for you."

"Oh no, you needn't," said Stockdale; "I am coming, too."

But before either of them had moved, the faint clatter of horses' hoofs broke upon the ear, and it seemed to come from the point where the track across the down joined the hard road.

"They are just too late!" cried Lizzy, exultingly.

"Who?" said Stockdale.

"Latimer, the riding-officer, and some assistant of his. We had better go indoors."

They entered the house, and Lizzy bolted the door. "Please don't get a light, Mr. Stockdale," she said.

"Of course I will not," said he.

"I thought you might be on the side of the Ring," said, Lizzy, with faintest sarcasm.

"I am," said Stockdale. "But, Lizzy Newberry, I love you, and you know it perfectly well; and you ought to know, if you do not, what I have suffered in my conscience on your account these last few days!"

"I guess very well," she said, hurriedly. "Yet I don't see why. Ah, you are better than I!"

The trotting of the horses seemed to have again died away, and the pair of listeners touched each other's fingers in the cold "goodnight" of those whom something seriously divided. They were on the landing, but before they had taken three steps apart the tramp of the horsemen suddenly revived, almost close to the house. Lizzy turned to the staircase window, opened the casement about an inch, and put her face close to the aperture. "Yes one of 'em is Latimer," she whispered. "He always rides a white horse. One would think it was the last color for a man in that line."

Stockdale looked, and saw the white shape of the animal as it passed by; but before the riders had gone another ten yards Latimer reined in his horse, and said something to his companion which neither Stockdale nor Lizzy could hear. Its drift was, however, soon made evident, for the other man stopped also; and sharply turning the horses' heads they cautiously retraced their steps. When they were again opposite Mrs. Newberry's garden, Latimer dismounted, the man on the dark horse did the same. Lizzy and Stockdale, intently listening and observing the proceedings, naturally put their heads as close as possible to the slit formed by the slightly opened casement; and thus it occurred that at last their cheeks came positively into contact. They went on lIstening, as if they did not know of the singular circumstance which had happened to their faces, and the pressure of each to each rather increased than lessened with the lapse of time.

They could hear the excisemen sniffing the air like hounds as they paced slowly along. When they reached the spot where the tub had burst, both stopped on the instant.

"Ay, ay, 'tis quite strong here," said the second officer. "Shall we knock at the door?"

"Well, no," said Latimer. "Maybe this is only a trick to put us off the scent. They wouldn't kick up this stink anywhere near their hiding place. I have known such things before."

"Anyhow, the things, or some of 'em, must have been brought this way," said the other.

"Yes," said Latimer, musingly. "Unless 'tis all done to tole us the wrong way. I have a mind that we go home for tonight without saying a word, and come the first thing in the morning with more hands. I know they have storages about here, but we can do nothing by this owl's light. We will look round the parish and see if everybody is in bed, John; and if all is quiet, we will do as I say."

They went on, and the two inside the window could hear them passing leisurely through the whole village, the street of which curved round at the bottom and entered the turnpike-road at another junction. This way the excisemen followed, and the amble of their horses died quite away.

"What will you do?" said Stockdale, withdrawing from his position.

She knew that he alluded to the coming search by the officers, to divert her attention from their own tender incident by the casement, which he wished to be passed over as a thing rather dreamed of than done. "Oh, nothing," she replied, with as much coolness as she could command under her disappointment at his manner. "We often have such storms as this. You would not be frightened if you knew what fools they are. Fancy riding o' horseback through the place; of course they will hear and see nobody while they make that noise; but they are always afraid to get off, in case some of our fellows should burst out upon 'em, and tie them up to the gatepost, as they have done before now. Goodnight, Mr. Stockdale."

She closed the window and went to her room, where a tear fell from her eyes; and that not because of the alertness of the riding-officers.

Chapter VI
The Great Search at Nether-Mynton

STOCKDALE was so excited by the events of the evening, and the dilemma that he was placed in between conscience and love, that he did not sleep, or seven doze, but remained as broadly awake as at noonday. As soon as the gray light began to touch ever so faintly the whiter objects in his bedroom, he arose, dressed himself, and went downstairs into the road.

The village was already astir. Several of the carriers had heard the well-known tramp of Latimer's horse while they were undressing in the dark that night, and had already communicated with one another and Owlett on the subject. The only doubt seemed to be about the safely of those tubs which had been left under the church gallery stairs, and after a short discussion at the corner of the mill, it was agreed that these should be removed before it got lighter, and hidden in the middle of a double hedge bordering the adjoining field. However, before anything could be carried into effect, the footsteps of many men were heard coming down the lane from the highway.

"D— it, here they be," said Owlett, who, having already drawn the hatch and started his mill for the day, stood stolidly at the mill door covered with flour, as if the interest of his whole soul was bound up in the shaking walls around him.

The two or three with whom he had been talking dispersed to their usual work, and when the excise officers and the formidable body of men they had hired reached the village cross, between the mill and Mrs. Newberry's house, the village wore the natural aspect of a place beginning its morning labors.

"Now," said Latimer to his associates, who numbered thirteen men in all, "what I know is that the things are somewhere in this here place. We have got the day before us, and 'tis hard if we can't light upon 'em and get 'em to Budmouth Custom-house before night. First we will try the fuel-houses, and then we'll work our way into the chimmers, and then to the ricks and stables, and so creep round. You have nothing but your noses to guide ye, mind, so use 'em today if you never did in your lives before."

Then the search began. Owlett, during the early part, watched from his mill window, Lizzy from the door of her house, with the greatest self-possession. A farmer down below, who also had a share in the run, rode about with one eye on his fields and the other on Latimer and his myrmidons, prepared to put them off the scent if he should be asked a question. Stockdale, who was no smuggler at all, felt more anxiety than the worst of them, and went about his studies with a heavy heart, coming frequently to the door to ask Lizzy some question or other on the consequences to her of the tubs being found.

"The consequences," she said, quietly, "are simply that I shall lose 'em. As I have none in the house or garden, they can't touch me personally."

"But you have some in the orchard?"

"Owlett rents that of me, and he lends it to others. So it will be hard to say who had any tubs there if they should be found."

There was never such a tremendous sniffing known as that which took place in Nether-Mynton parish and its vicinity this day. All was done methodically, and mostly on hands and knees. At different hours of the day they had different plans. From daybreak to breakfast time the officers used their sense of smell in a direct and straightforward manner only, pausing nowhere but at such places as the tubs might be supposed to be secreted in at that very moment, pending their removal on the following night. Among the places tested and examined were:

Hollow trees.
Potato-graves.
Fuel-houses.
Bedrooms.
Apple-lofts.
Cupboards.
Clock-cases.
Chimney-flues.
Rain-water butts.
Pigsties.
Culverts.
Hedgerows.
Fagot-ricks.
Haystacks.
Coppers and ovens.

After breakfast they recommenced with renewed vigor, taking a new line; that is to say, directing their attention to clothes that might be supposed to have come in contact with the tubs in their removal from the shore, such garments being usually tainted with the spirits, owing to its oozing between the staves. They now sniffed at

Smock-frocks.
Old shirts and waistcoats.
Coats and hats.
Breeches and leggings.
Women's shawls and gowns.
Smiths' and shoemakers' aprons.
Knee-naps and hedging-gloves.
Tarpaulins.
Market-cloaks.
Scarecrows.

And, as soon as the mid-day meal was over, they pushed their search into places where the spirits might have been thrown away in alarm:

Horse-ponds.
Stable-drains.
Cinder-heaps.
Mixens.
Wet ditches.
Cesspools.
Sinks in yards.
Road-scrapings.
Back-door gutters.

But still these indefatigable excisemen discovered nothing more than the original telltale smell in the road opposite Lizzy's house, which even yet had not passed off.

"I'll tell ye what it is, men," said Latimer, about three o'clock in the afternoon, "we must begin over again. Find them tubs I will."

The men, who had been hired for the day, looked at their hands and knees, muddy with creeping on all fours so frequently, and rubbed their noses, as if they had had almost enough of it; for the quantity of bad air which had passed into each one's 'nostril had rendered it nearly as insensible as a flue. However, after a moment's hesitation, they prepared to start anew, except three, whose power of smell had quite succumbed under the excessive wear and tear of the day.

By this time not a male villager was to be seen in the parish. Owlett was not at his mill, the farmers were not in their fields, the parson was not in his garden, the smith had left his forge, and the wheelwright's shop was silent.

"Where the devil are the folk gone?" said Latimer, waking up to the fact of their absence, and looking round.

"I'll have 'em up for this! Why don't they come and help us? There's not a man about the place but the Methodist parson, and he's an old woman. I demand assistance in the king's name!"

"We must find the jineral public afore we can demand that," said his lieutenant.

"Well, well, we shall do better without 'em," said Latimer, who changed his moods at a moment's notice. "But there's great cause of suspicion in this silence and this keeping out of sight, and I'll bear it in mind. Now we will go across to Owlett's orchard, and see what we can find there."

Stockdale, who heard this discussion from the garden gate, over which he had been leaning, was rather alarmed, and thought it a mistake of the villagers to keep so completely out of the way. He himself, like the excisemen, had been wondering for the last half-hour what could have become of them. Some laborers were of necessity engaged in distant fields, but the master-workmen should have been at home; though one and all, after just showing themselves at their shops, had apparently gone off for the day. He went in to Lizzy, who sat at a back window sewing, and said, "Lizzy, where are the men?"

Lizzy laughed. "Where they mostly are when they are run so hard as this." She cast her eyes to heaven. "Up there," she said.

Stockdale looked up. "What – on the top of the church tower?" he asked, seeing the direction of her glance.

"Yes."

"Well, I expect they will soon have to come down," said he, gravely. "I have been listening to the officers and they are going to search the orchard over again and then every nook in the church."

Lizzy looked alarmed for the first time. "Will you go and tell our folk?" she said. "They ought to be let know." Seeing his conscience struggling within him like a boiling pot she added, "No, never mind, I'll go myself."

She went out, descended the garden, and climbed over the churchyard wall at the same time that the preventivemen were ascending the road to the orchard. Stockdale could do no less than follow her. By the time that she reached the tower entrance he was at her side, and they entered together.

Nether-Mynton church tower was, as in many villages, without a turret, and the only way to the top was by going up to the singers' gallery, and thence ascending by a ladder to a square trap-door in the floor of the bell-loft, above which a permanent ladder was fixed, passing through the bells to a hole in the roof. When Lizzy and Stockdale reached the gallery and looked up, nothing but the trap-door and the five holes for the bell-ropes appeared, The ladder was gone.

"There's no getting up," said Stockdale.

"Oh yes, there is," said she. "There's an eye looking at us at this moment through a knot-hole in that trap-door."

And as she spoke the trap opened, and the dark line of the ladder was seen descending against the whitewashed wall. When it touched the bottom Lizzy dragged it to its place, and said, "If you'll go up, I'll follow."

The young man ascended, and presently found himself among consecrated bells for the first time in his life, nonconformity having been in the Stockdale blood for some generations. He eyed them uneasily, and looked round for Lizzy. Owlett stood here, holding the top of the ladder "What, be you really one of us?" said the miller.

"It seems so," said Stockdale, sadly.

"He's not," said Lizzy, who overheard. "He's neither for nor against us. He'll do us no harm."

She stepped up beside them, and then they went on to the next stage, which, when they had clambered over the dusty bell-carriages, was of easy ascent, leading toward the hole through which the pale sky appeared, and into the open air. Owlett remained behind for a moment to pull up the lower ladder.

"Keep down your heads," said a voice, as soon as they set foot on the flat.

Stockdale here beheld all the missing parishioners, lying on their stomachs on the tower roof, except a few who, elevated on their hands and knees, were peeping through the embrasure of the parapet. Stockdale did the same, and saw the village lying like a map below him, over which moved the figures of the excisemen, each foreshortened to a crab-like object, the crown of his hat forming a circular disk in the center of him. Some of the men had turned their heads when the young preacher's figure arose among them.

"What, Mr. Stockdale?" said Matt Grey, in a tone of surprise.

"I'd' as lief that it hadn't been," said Jim Clarke. "If the pa'son should see him a trespassing here in his tower, 'twould be none the better for we, seeing how 'a do hate chapel members. He'd never buy a tub of us again, and he's as good a customer as we have got this side o' Warm'll,"

"Where is the pa'son?" said Lizzy.

"In his house, to be sure, that he may see nothing of what's going on – where all good folks ought to be, and this young man likewise."

"Well, he has brought some news," said Lizzy. "They are going to search the orchet and church; can we do anything if they should find?"

"Yes," said her cousin Owlett. "That's what we've been talking o', and we have settled our line. Well, be dazed!"

The exclamation was caused by his perceiving that some of the searchers, having got into the orchard, and begun stooping and creeping hither and thither, were pausing in the middle, where a tree smaller than the rest was growing. They drew closer, and bent lower than ever upon the ground.

"Oh, my tubs!" said Lizzy, faintly, as she peered through the parapet at them.

"They have got 'em, 'a b'lieve," said Owlett.

The interest in the movements of the officers was so keen that not a single eye was looking in any other direction; but at that moment a shout from the church beneath them attracted the attention of the smugglers, as it did also of the party in the orchard, who sprang to their feet and went toward the church-yard wall. At the same time those of the Government men who had entered the church unperceived by the smugglers cried aloud, "Here be some of 'em at last."

The smugglers remained in a blank silence, uncertain whether "some of 'em" meant tubs or men; but again peeping cautiously over the edge of the tower they learned that tube were the things described; and soon these fated articles were brought one by one into the middle of the church-yard from their hiding-place under the gallery stairs.

"They are going to put 'em on Hinton's vault till they find the rest," said Lizzy, hopelessly. The excisemen had, in fact, begun to pile up the tubs on a large stone slab which was fixed there; and when all were brought out from the tower, two or three of the men were left standing by them, the rest of the party again proceeding to the orchard.

The interest of the smugglers in the next maneuvers of their enemies became painfully intense. Only about thirty tubs had been secreted in the lumber of the tower, but seventy were hidden in the orchard, making up all that they had brought ashore as yet, the remainder of the cargo. having been tied to a sinker and dropped overboard for another night's operations. The excisemen, having re-entered the orchard, acted as if they were positive that here lay hidden the rest of the tubs, which they were determined to find before nightfall. They spread themselves out round the field, and advancing on all fours as before, went anew round every apple-tree in the inclosure. The young tree in the middle again led them to pause, and at length the whole company gathered there in a way which signified that a second chain of reasoning had led to the same results as the first.

When they had examined the sod hereabouts for some minutes, one of the men rose, ran to a disused porch of the church where tools were kept, and returned with the sexton's pickax and shovel, with which they set to work.

"Are they really buried there?" said the minister, for the grass was so green and uninjured that it was difficult to believe it had been disturbed. The smugglers were too interested to reply, and presently they saw, to their chagrin, the officers stand two on each side of the tree; and, stooping and applying their hands to the soil, they bodily lifted the tree and the turf around it. The apple-tree now showed itself to be growing in a shallow box, with handles for lifting at each of the four sides. Under the site of the tree a square hole was revealed, and an exciseman went and looked down.

"It is all up now," said Owlett, quietly. "And now all of ye get down before they notice we are here; and be ready for our next move. I had better bide here till dark, or they may take me on suspicion, as 'tis on my ground. I'll be with ye as soon as daylight begins to pink in."

"And I?" said Lizzy.

"You please look to the linchpins and screws; then go indoors and know nothing at all. The chaps will do the rest."

The ladder was replaced, and all but Owlett descended, the men passing off one by one at the back of the church, and vanishing on their respective errands.

Lizzy walked boldly along the street, followed closely by the minister.

"You are going indoors, Mrs. Newberry?" he said.

She knew from the words "Mrs. Newberry" that the division between them had widened yet another degree.

"I am not going home," she said. "I have a little thing to do before I go in. Martha Sarah will got your tea."

"Oh, I don't mean on that account," said Stockdale. "What can you have to do further in this unhallowed affair?"

"Only a little," she said.

"What is that? I'll go with you."

"No, I shall go by myself. Will you please go indoors? I shall be there in less than an hour."

"You are not going to run any danger, Lizzy?" said the young man, his tenderness reasserting itself.

"None whatever – worth mentioning," answered she, and went down toward the cross.

Stockdale entered the garden gate, and stood behind it looking on. The excisemen were still busy in the orchard, and at last he was tempted to enter, and watch their proceedings. When he came closer he found that the secret cellar, of whose existence he had been totally unaware, was formed by timbers placed across from side to side about a foot under the ground, and grassed over.

The excisemen looked up at Stockdale's fair and downy countenance, and evidently thinking him above suspicion, went on with their work again. As soon as all the tubs were taken out, they began tearing up the turf, pulling out the timbers, and breaking in the sides, till the cellar was wholly dismantled and shapeless, the apple tree lying with its roots high to the air. But the hole which had in its time held so much contraband merchandise was never completely filled up, either then or afterward, a depression in the greensward marking the spot to this day.

Chapter VII
The Walk to Warm'Ell Cross; and Afterward

AS THE GOODS had all to be carried to Budmouth that night, the excisemen's next object was to find horses and carts for the journey, and they went about the village for that purpose. Latimer strode hither and thither with a lump of chalk in his hand, marking broad arrows so vigorously on every vehicle and set of harness that he came across that it seemed as if he would chalk broad arrows on the very hedges and roads. The owner of every conveyance so marked was bound to give it up for Government purposes. Stockdale, who had had enough of the scene, turned indoors, thoughtful and depressed. Lizzy was already there, having come in at the back, though she had not yet taken off her bonnet. She looked tired, and her mood was not much brighter than his own. They had but little to say to each other; and the minister went away and attempted to read; but at this he could not succeed, and he shook the little bell for tea.

Lizzy herself brought in the tray, the girl having run off into the village during the afternoon, too full of excitement at the proceedings to remember her state of life. However, almost before the sad lovers had said anything to each other, Martha came in in a steaming state.

"Oh, there's such a stoor, Mrs. Newberry and Mr. Stockdale! The king's excisemen can't get the carts ready nohow at all! They pulled Thomas Ballam's, and William Roger's, and Stephen Sprake's carts into the road, and off came the wheels, and down fell the carts; and they found there was no linchpins in the arms; and then they tried Samuel Shane's wagon, and found that the screws were gone from he, and at last they looked at the dairyman's cart, and he's got none neither! They have gone now to the blacksmith's to get some made, but he's nowhere to be found!"

Stockdale looked at Lizzy, who blushed very slightly, and went out of the room, followed by Martha Sarah; but before they had got through the passage there was a rap at the front door, and Stockdale recognized Latimer's voice addressing Mrs. Newberry, who had turned back.

"For God's sake, Mrs. Newberry, have you seen Hardman the blacksmith up this way? If we could get hold of him, we'd e'en a'most drag him by the hair of his head to his anvil, where he ought to be."

"He's an idle man, Mr. Latimer," replied Lizzy, archly. "What do you want him for?"

"Why, there isn't a horse in the place that has got more than three shoes on, and some have only two. The wagon-wheels be without strakes, and there's no linchpins to the carts. What with that, and the bother about every set of harness being out of order, we shan't be off before night-fall – upon my soul we shan't. 'Tis a rough lot, Mrs. Newberry, that you've got about you here; but they'll play at this game once too often, mark my words they will! There's not a man in the parish that don't deserve to be whipped."

It happened that Hardman was at that moment a little further up the lane, smoking his pipe behind a holly-bush. When Latimer had done speaking he went on in this direction, and Hardman, hearing the exciseman's steps, found curiosity too strong for prudence. He peeped out from the bush at the very moment that Latimer's glance was on it. There was nothing left for him to do but to come forward with unconcern.

"I've been looking for you for the last hour!" said Latimer, with a glare in his eye.

"Sorry to hear that," said Hardman. "I've been out for a stroll, to look for more hid tubs, to deliver 'em up to Gover'ment."

"Oh yes, Hardman, we know it," said Latimer, with withering sarcasm. "We know that you'll deliver 'em up to Gover'ment. We know that all the parish is helping us, and have been all day! Now, you please walk along with me down to your shop, and kindly let me hire ye in the king's name."

They went down the lane together, and presently there, resounded from the smithy the ring of a hammer not very briskly swung. However, the carts and horses were got into some sort of traveling condition, but it was not until after the clock had struck six, when the muddy roads were glistening under the horizontal light of the fading day. The smuggled tubs were soon packed into the vehicles, and Latimer, with three of his assistants, drove slowly out of the village in the direction of the port of Budmouth, some considerable number of miles distant, the other excisemen being left to watch for, the remainder of the cargo, which they knew to have been sunk somewhere between Ringsworth and Lullstead Cove, and to unearth Owlett, the only person clearly implicated by the discovery of the cave.

Women and children stood at the doors as the carts, each chalked with the Government pitchfork, passed in the increasing twilight; and as they stood they looked at the confiscated property with a melancholy expression that told only too plainly the relation which they bore to the trade.

"Well, Lizzy," said Stockdale, when the crackle of the wheels had nearly died away, "this is a fit finish to your adventure. I am truly thankful that you have got off without suspicion, and the loss only of the liquor. Will you sit down and let me talk to you?"

"By-and-by," she said. "But I must go out now."

"Not to that horrid shore again?" he said, blankly.

"No, not there. I am only going to see the end of this day's business."

He did not answer to this, and she moved toward the door slowly, as if waiting for him to say something more.

"You don't offer to come with me," she added, at last. "I suppose that's because you hate me after all this?"

"Can you say it, Lizzy, when you know I only want to save you from such practices? Come with you? Of course I will, if it is only to take care of you. But why will you go out again?"

"Because I cannot rest indoors. Something is happening, and I must know what. Now come!" And they went into the dusk together. When they reached the turnpike road she turned to the right, and he soon perceived that they were following the direction of the excisemen and their loads. He had given her his arm, and every now and then she suddenly pulled it back, to signify that he was to halt a moment and listen. They had walked rather quickly along the first quarter of a mile, and on the second or third time of standing still she said, "I hear them ahead – don't you?"

"Yes," he said; "I hear the wheels. But what of that?"

"I only want to know if they get clear away from the neighborhood."

"Ah," said he, a light breaking upon him. "Something desperate is to be attempted – and now I remember, there was not a man about the village when we left."

"Hark!" she murmured. The noise of the cart-wheels had stopped, and given place to another sort of sound.

"'Tis a scuffle," said Stockdale. "There'll be murder! Lizzy, let go my arm; I am going on. On my conscience, I must not stay here and do nothing!"

"There'll he no murder, and not even a broken head," she said. "Our men are thirty to four of them; no harm will be done at all."

"Then there is an attack!" exclaimed Stockdale; "and you knew it was to be. Why should you side with men who break the laws like this?"

"Why should you side with men who take from country traders what they have honestly bought wi' their own money in France?" said' she, firmly.

"They are not honestly bought," said he.

"They are," she contradicted. "I and Owlett and the others paid thirty shillings for every one of the tubs before they were put on board at Cherbourg, and if a king who is nothing to us sends his people to steal our property, we have a right to steal it back again."

Stockdale did not stop to argue the matter, but went quickly in the direction of the noise, Lizzy keeping at his side. "Don't you interfere, will you, dear Richard?" she said, anxiously, as they drew near. "Don't let us go any closer; 'tis at Warm'ell Cross where they are seizing 'em. You can do no good, and you may meet with a hard blow!"

"Let us see first what is going on," he said. But before they had got much further the noise of the cart-wheels began again, and Stockdale soon found that they were coming toward him. In another minute the three carts came up, and Stockdale and Lizzy stood in the ditch to let them pass.

Instead of being conducted by four men, as had happened when they went out of the village, the horses and carts were now accompanied by a body of from twenty to thirty, all of whom, as Stockdale perceived to his astonishment, had blackened faces. Among them walked six or eight huge female figures, whom, from their wide strides, Stockdale guessed to be men in disguise. As soon as the party discerned Lizzy and her companion four or five fell back, and when the carts had passed came close to the pair.

"There is no walking up this way for the present," said one of the gaunt women, who wore curls a foot long, dangling down the sides of her face, in the fashion of the time. Stockdale recognized this lady's voice as Owlett's.

"Why not?" said Stockdale. "This is the public highway."

"Now, look here, youngster," said Owlett – "oh, 'tis the Methodist parson! – what, and Mrs. Newberry! Well, you'd better not go up that way, Lizzy. They've all run off, and folks have got their own again."

The miller then hastened on and joined his comrades. Stockdale and Lizzy also turned back. "I wish all this hadn't been forced upon us," she said, regretfully. "But if those excisemen had got off with the tubs, half the people in the parish would have been in want for the next month or two."

Stockdale was not paying much attention to her words, and he said, "I don't think I can go back like this. Those four poor excisemen may be murdered, for all I know."

"Murdered!" said, Lizzy, impatiently. "We don't do murder here."

"Well, I shall go as far as Warm'ell Cross to see," said Stockdale, decisively; and without wishing her safe home or anything else, the minister turned back. Lizzy stood, looking at him till his form was absorbed in the shades; and then, with sadness, she went in the direction of Nether-Mynton.

The road was lonely, and after nightfall at this time of the year there was often not a passer for hours. Stockdale pursued his way without hearing a sound beyond that of his own footsteps, and in due time he passed beneath the trees of the plantation which surrounded the Warm'ell Crossroad. Before he had reached the point of intersection he heard voices from the thicket.

"Hoi-hoi-hoi! Help! help!"

The voices were not at all feeble, or despairing, but they were unmistakably anxious. Stockdale had no weapon, and before plunging into the pitchy darkness of the plantation he pulled a stake from the hedge to use in case of need.

When he got among the trees he shouted, "What's the matter – where are you?"

"Here!" answered the voices; and pushing through the brambles in that direction, he came near the objects of his search.

"Why don't you come forward?" said Stockdale.

"We be tied to the trees."

"Who are you?"

"Poor Will Latimer the exciseman!" said one, plaintively. "Just come and cut these cords, there's a good man! We were afraid nobody would pass by tonight."

Stockdale soon loosened them, upon which they stretched their limbs and stood at their ease.

"The rascals!" said Latimer, getting now into a rage, though: he had seemed quite meek when Stockdale first came up. "'Tis the same sort of fellows. I know they were Mynton chaps to a man."

"But we can't swear to 'em," said another.

"Not one of 'em spoke."

"What are you going to do?" said Stockdale. "I'd fain go back to Mynton, and have at 'em again," said Latimer.

"So would we!" said his comrades.

"Fight till we die!" said Latimer.

"We will, we will!" said his men.

"But," said Latimer, more frigidly, as they came out of the plantation, "we don't know that these chaps with black faces were Mynton men. And proof is a hard thing."

"So it is," said the rest.

"And therefore we won't do nothing at all," said Latimer with complete dispassionateness. "For my part, I'd sooner be them than we. The clitches of my arms are burning like fire from the cords those two strapping women, tied round 'em. My opinion, is, now I have had time to think o't, that you may serve your gover'ment at too high a price. For these two nights and days, I have not had an hour's rest; and, please God, here's for home-along."

The other officers agreed heartily to this course,' and thanking Stockdale for his timely assistance, they parted from him at the cross, taking themselves the western road and Stockdale going back to Nether-Mynton.

During that walk the minister was lost in reverie of the most painful kind. As soon as he got into the house, and before entering his own rooms, he advanced to the door of the little back parlor in which Lizzy usually sat with her mother. He found her there alone. Stockdale went forward, and, like a man in a dream, looked down upon the table that stood between him and the young woman, who had her bonnet and cloak still on. As he did not speak, she looked up from her chair at him, with misgiving in her eye.

"Where are they gone?" he then said, listlessly.

"Who? – I don't know. I have seen nothing of them since. I came straight in here."

"If your men can manage to get off with those tubs it will be a great profit to you, I suppose?"

"A share will be mine, a share my cousin Owlett's, a share to each of the two farmers, and a share divided among the men who helped us."

"And you still think," he went on very slowly, "that you will not give this business up?"

Lizzy rose, and put her hand upon his shoulder.

"Don't ask that," she whispered. "You don't know what you are asking. I must tell you, though I meant not to do it. What I make by that trade is all I have to keep my mother and myself with."

He was astonished. "I did not dream of such a thing," he said. "I would rather have swept the streets, had I been you. What is money compared with a clear conscience?"

"My conscience is clear. I know my mother but the king I have never seen. His dues are nothing to me. But it is a great deal to me that my mother and I should live."

"Marry me, and promise to give it up. I will keep your mother."

"It is good of you," she said, trembling a little. "Let me think of it by myself. I would rather not answer now."

She reserved her answer till the next day, and came into his room with a solemn face. "I cannot do what you wished" she said, passionately.

"It is too much to ask. My whole life ha' been passed in this way." Her words and manner showed that before entering she had been struggling with herself in private, and that the contention had been strong.

Stockdale turned pale, but he spoke quietly.

"Then, Lizzy, we must part. I cannot go against my principles in this matter, and I cannot make my profession a mockery. You know how I love you, and what I would do for you; but this one thing I cannot do."

"But why should you belong to that profession?" she burst out. "I have got this large house; why can't you marry me and live here with us, and not be a Methodist preacher any more? I assure you, Richard, it is no harm, and I wish you could only see it as I do! We only carry it on in winter; in summer it is never done at all. It stirs up one's dull life at this time o' the year, and gives excitement, which I have got so used to now that I should hardly know how to do 'ithout it. At nights, when the wind blows, instead of being dull and stupid, and not noticing whether it do blow or not, your mind is afield, even if you are not afield yourself; and you are wondering how the chaps are getting on; and you walk up and down the room, and look out o' window, and then you go off yourself and know your way about as well by night as by day, and have hair-breadth escapes from old Latimer and his fellows, who are too stupid ever to really frighten us, and only make us a bit nimble."

"He frightened you a little last night, anyhow; and I would advise you to drop it before it is worse."

She shook her head. "No, I must go on as I have begun. I was born to it. It is in my blood, and I can't be cured. Oh, Richard, you cannot think what a hard thing you have asked, and how sharp you try me when you put me between this and my love for 'ee!"

Stockdale was leaning with his elbow on the mantel-piece, his hands over his eyes. "We ought never to have met, Lizzy," he said. "It was an ill day for us. I little thought there was anything so hopeless and impossible in our engagement as this. Well, it is too late now to regret consequences in this way. I have had the happiness of seeing you and knowing you at least."

"You dissent from Church and I dissent from State," she said, "and I don't see why we are not well-matched."

He smiled sadly, while Lizzy remained looking down, her eyes beginning to overflow.

That was an unhappy evening for both of them, and the days that followed were unhappy days. Both she and he went mechanically about their employments, and his depression was marked in the village by more than one of his denomination with whom he came in contact. But Lizzy, who passed her days indoors, was unsuspected of being the cause; for it was generally understood that a quiet engagement to marry existed between her and her cousin Owlett, and had existed for some time.

Thus uncertainly the week passed on, till one morning Stockdale said to her: "I have had a letter, Lizzy. I must call you that till I am gone."

"Gone?" said she, blankly.

"Yes," he said. "I am going from this place. I felt it would be better for us both that I should not stay after what has happened. In fact, I couldn't stay here, and look on you from day to day, without becoming weak and faltering in my course. I have just heard of an arrangement by which the other minister can arrive here in about a week and let me go elsewhere."

That he had all this time continued so firmly fixed in his resolution came upon her as a grievous surprise. "You never loved me!" she said, bitterly.

"I might say the same," he returned, "but I will not. Grant me one favor. Come and hear my last sermon on the day before I go."

Lizzy, who was a church-goer on Sunday mornings, frequently attended Stockdale's chapel in the evening with the rest of the double-minded, and she promised.

It became known that Stockdale was going to leave, and a good many people outside his own sect were sorry to hear it. The intervening days flew rapidly away, and on the evening of the Sunday which preceded the morning of his departure Lizzy sat in the chapel to hear him for the last time. The little building was full to overflowing, and he took up the subject which all had expected, that of the contraband trade so extensively practiced among them. His hearers, in laying his words to their own hearts, did not perceive that they were most particularly directed against Lizzy, till the sermon waxed warm and Stockdale nearly broke down with emotion. In truth, his own earnestness, and her sad eyes looking up at him, were too much for the young man's equanimity. He hardly knew how he ended. He saw Lizzy, as through a mist, turn and go away with the rest of the congregation, and shortly afterward followed her home.

She invited him to supper, and they sat down alone, her mother having, as was usual with her on Sunday nights, gone to bed early.

"We will part friends, won't we?" said Lizzy, forced gayety, and never alluding to the sermon – a reticence which rather disappointed him.

"We will," he said, with a forced smile on his part; and they sat down.

It was the first meal that they had ever shared together in their lives, and probably the last that they would so share. When it was over, and the indifferent conversation could no longer be continued, he arose and took her hand.

"Lizzy," he said, "do you say we must part – do you?"

"You do," she said, solemnly "I can say no more."

"Nor I," said he. "If that is your answer, goodbye!"

Stockdale bent over her and kissed her, and she involuntarily returned his kiss. "I shall go early," he said; hurriedly. "I shall not see you again."

And he did leave early. He fancied, when stepping into the gray morning light, to which was to carry him away, that he saw between the parted curtains of Lizzy's window; but the light was faint, and the panes glistened with wet; so he could not be sure. Stockdale mounted the vehicle, and was gone; and on the following Sunday the new minister preached in the chapel of the Mynton Wesleyans.

One day, two years after the parting, Stockdale, now settled in a midland town, came into Nether-Mynton by carrier in the original way. Jogging along in the van that afternoon, he had put questions to the driver, and the answers that he received interested, the minister deeply. The result of them was that he went without the least hesitation to the door of his former lodging. It was about six o'clock in the evening, and the same time of year as when he had left; now, too, the ground was damp and glistening, the west was bright, and Lizzy's snowdrops were raising their heads in the border under the wall.

Lizzy must have caught sight of him from the window, for by the time that he reached the door she was there holding it open; and then, as if she had not sufficiently considered her act of coming out, she drew herself back, saying, with some constraint: "Mr. Stockdale!"

"You knew it was," said Stockdale, taking her hand. "I wrote to say I should call."

"Yes, but you did not say when," she answered.

"I did not. I was not quite sure when my business would lead me to these parts." "You only came because business brought you near?"

"Well, that is the fact; but I have often thought I should like to come on purpose to see you. But what's all this that has happened? I told you how it would be, Lizzy, and you would not listen to me."

"I would not," she said, sadly. "But I had been brought up to that life, and it was second nature to me. However, it is all over now. The officers have blood-money for taking a man dead or alive, and the trade is going to nothing. We were hunted down like rats."

"Owlett is quite gone, I hear?"

"Yes, he is in America. We had a dreadful struggle that last time, when they tried to take him. It is a perfect miracle that he lived through and it is a wonder that I was not killed. I was shot in the hand. It was not by aim; the shot was really meant for my cousin; but I was behind, looking on as usual, and the bullet came to me. It bled terribly, but I got home without fainting, and it healed after a time. You know how he suffered?"

"No," said Stockdale. "I only heard that he just escaped with his life."

"He was shot in the back, but a rib turned the ball. He was badly hurt. We would not let him be took. The men carried him all night across the meads to Bere, and hid him in a barn, dressing his wound as well as they could, till he was so far recovered as to be able to get about. He had gied up his mill for some time, and at last he got to Bristol, and took a passage to America, and he's settled in Wisconsin."

"What do you think of smuggling now?" said the minister, gravely.

"I own that we were wrong," said she. "But I have suffered for it. I am very poor now, and my mother has been dead these twelve months. But won't you come in, Mr. Stockdale?"

Stockdale went in; and it is to be presumed that they came to an understanding, for a fortnight later there was a sale of Lizzy's furniture, and after that a wedding at a chapel in a neighboring town.

He took her away from her old haunts to the home that he had made for himself in his native county, where she studied her duties as a minister's wife with praiseworthy assiduity. It is said that in after-years she wrote an excellent tract called "Render unto Caesar; or, The Repentant Villagers," in which her own experience was anonymously used as the introductory story. Stockdale got it printed, after making some corrections, and putting in a few powerful sentences of his own; and many hundreds of copies were distributed by the couple in the course of their married life.

If you enjoyed this, you might also like...
The Lifted Veil, see page 211
Our New House, see opposite

Our New House

Bram Stoker

WE SPOKE of it as our New House simply because we thought of it as such and not from any claim to the title, for it was just about as old and as ricketty as a house supposed to be habitable could well be. It was only new to us. Indeed with the exception of the house there was nothing new about us. Neither my wife nor myself was, in any sense of the word, old, and we were still, comparatively speaking, new to each other.

It had been my habit, for the few years I had been in Somerset House, to take my holidays at Littlehampton, partly because I liked the place, and partly – and chiefly, because it was cheap. I used to have lodgings in the house of a widow, Mrs. Compton, in a quiet street off the sea frontage. I had this year, on my summer holiday, met there my fate in the person of Mrs. Compton's daughter Mary, just home from school. I returned to London engaged. There was no reason why we should wait, for I had few friends and no near relatives living, and Mary had the consent of her mother. I was told that her father, who was a merchant captain, had gone to sea shortly after her birth, but had never been heard of since, and had consequently been long ago reckoned as "with the majority." I never met any of my new relatives; indeed, there was not the family opportunity afforded by marriage under conventional social conditions. We were married in the early morning at the church at Littlehampton, and, without any formal wedding breakfast, came straight away in the train. As I had to attend to my duties at Somerset House, the preliminaries were all arranged by Mrs. Compton at Littlehampton, and Mary gave the required notice of residency. We were all in a hurry to be off, as we feared missing the train; indeed, whilst Mary was signing the registry I was settling the fees and tipping the verger.

When we began to look about for a house, we settled on one which was vacant in a small street near Sloane Square. There was absolutely nothing to recommend the place except the smallness of the rent – but this was everything to us. The landlord, Mr. Gradder, was the very hardest man I ever came across. He did not even go through the form of civility in his dealing.

"There is the house," he said, "and you can either take it or leave it. I have painted the outside, and you must paint the inside. Or, if you like it as it is, you can have it so; only you must paint and paper it before you give i t up to me again – be it in one year or more."

I was pretty much of a handy man, and felt equal to doing the work myself; so, having looked over the place carefully, we determined to take it. It was, however, in such a terribly neglected condition that I could not help asking my ironclad lessor as to who had been the former tenant, and what kind of person he had been to have been content with such a dwelling.

His answer was vague. "Who he was I don't know. I never knew more than his name. He was a regular oddity. Had this house and another of mine near here, and used to live in them both, and all by himself. Think he was afraid of being murdered or robbed. Never knew which he was in. Dead lately. Had to bury him – worse luck. Expenses swallowed up value of all he'd got."

We signed an agreement to take out a lease, and when, in a few days, I had put in order two rooms and a kitchen, my wife and I moved in. I worked hard every morning before I went to my office, and every evening after I got home, so I got the place in a couple of weeks in a state of comparative order. We had, in fact, arrived so far on our way to perfection that we had seriously begun to consider dispensing with the services of our charwoman and getting a regular servant.

One evening my landlord called on me. It was about nine o'clock, and, as our temporary servant had gone home, I opened the door myself. I was somewhat astonished at recognising my visitor, and not a little alarmed, for he was so brutally simple in dealing with me that I rather dreaded any kind of interview. To my astonishment he began to speak in what he evidently meant for a hearty manner.

"Well, how are you getting on with your touching up?"

"Pretty well," I answered, "but 'touching up' is rather a queer name for it. Why, the place was like an old ash heap. The very walls seemed pulled about."

"Indeed!" he said quickly.

I went on, "It is getting into something like order, however. There is only one more room to do, and then we shall be all right."

"Do you know," he said, "that I have been thinking it is hardly fair that you should have to do all this yourself."

I must say that I was astonished as well as pleased, and found myself forming a resolution not to condemn ever again anyone for hardness until I had come to know something about his real nature. I felt somewhat guilty as I answered, "You are very kind, Mr. Gradder. I shall let you know what it all costs me, and then you can repay me a part as you think fair."

"Oh, I don't mean that at all." This was said very quickly.

"Then what do you mean," I asked.

"That I should do some of it in my own way, at my own cost."

I did not feel at all inclined to have either Mr. Gradder or strange workmen in the house. Moreover, my pride rebelled at the thought that I should be seen by real workmen doing labourers' work – I suppose there is something of the spirit of snobbery in all of us. So I told him I could not think of such a thing; that all was going on very well; and more to the same effect. He seemed more irritated than the occasion warranted. Indeed, it struck me as odd that a man should be annoyed at his generous impulse being thwarted. He tried, with a struggle for calmness, to persuade me, but I did not like the controversy, and stood to my refusal of assistance. He went away in a positive fury of suppressed rage.

The next evening he called in to see me. Mary had, after he had gone, asked me not to allow him to assist, as she did not like him; so when he came in I refused again with what urbanity I could. Mary kept nudging me to be firm, and he could not help noticing it. He said: "Of course, if your wife objects" – and stopped. He spoke the words very rudely, and Mary spoke out:

"She does object, Mr. Gradder. We are all right, thank you, and do not want help from anyone."

For reply Mr. Gradder put on his hat, knocked it down on his head firmly and viciously, and walked out, banging the door behind him.

"There is a nice specimen of a philanthropist," said Mary, and we both laughed.

The next day, while I was in my office, Mr. Gradder called to see me. He was in a very amiable mood, and commenced by apologising for what he called "his unruly exit." "I am afraid you must have thought me rude," he said.

As the nearest approach to mendacity I could allow myself, was the suppressio veri, I was silent.

"You see," he went on, "your wife dislikes me, and that annoys me; so I just called to see you alone, and try if we could arrange this matter – we men alone."

"What matter?" I asked.

"You know – about the doing up those rooms."

I began to get annoyed myself, for there was evidently some underlying motive of advantage to himself in his persistence. Any shadowy belief I had ever entertained as to a benevolent idea had long ago vanished and left not a wrack behind. I told him promptly and briefly that I would not do as he desired, and that I did not care to enter any further upon the matter. He again made an "unruly exit." This time he nearly swept away in his violence a young man who was entering through the swing door, to get some papers stamped. The youth remonstrated with that satirical force which is characteristic of the lawyer's clerk. Mr. Gradder was too enraged to stop to listen, and the young man entered the room grumbling and looking back at him.

"Old brute!" he said. "I know him. Next time I see him I'll advise him to buy some manners with his new fortune."

"His new fortune?" I asked, naturally interested about him. "How do you mean, Wigley?"

"Lucky old brute! I wish I had a share of it. I heard all about it at Doctors Commons yesterday."

"Why, is it anything strange?"

"Strange! Why, it's no name for it. What do you think of an old flint like that having a miser for a tenant who goes and dies and leaves him all he's got – £40,000 or £50,000 – in a will, providing a child of his own doesn't turn up to claim it.

"He died recently, then?"

"About three or four weeks ago. Old Gradder only found the will a few days since. He had been finding pots of gold and bundles of notes all over the house, and it was like drawing a tooth from him to make an inventory, as he had to do under a clause of the will. The old thief would have pocketed all the coin without a word, only for the will, and he was afraid he'd risk everything if he did not do it legally.

"You know all about it," I remarked, wishing to hear more.

"I should think I did. I asked Cripps, of Bogg and Snagleys, about it this morning. They're working for him, and Cripps says that if they had not threatened him with the Public Prosecutor, he would not have given even a list of the money he found."

I began now to understand the motive of Mr. Gradder's anxiety to aid in working at my house. I said to Wigley:

"This is very interesting. Do you know that he is my landlord?"

"Your landlord! Well, I wish you joy of him. I must be off now. I have to go down to Doctors Commons before one o'clock. Would you mind getting these stamped for me, and keeping them till I come back?"

"With pleasure," I said, "and look here! Would you mind looking out that will of Gradder's, and make a mem. of it for me, if it isn't too long? I'll go a shilling on it." And I handed him the coin.

Later in the day he came hack and handed me a paper.

"It isn't long," he said. "We might put up the shutters if men made wills like that. That is an exact copy. It is duly witnessed, and all regular."

I took the paper and put it in my pocket, for I was very busy at the time.

After supper that evening I got a note from Gradder, saying that he had got an offer from another person who had been in treaty with him before I had taken the, house, wanting to have it, and offering to pay a premium. "He is an old friend," wrote Gradder, "and I would like to oblige him; so if you choose I will take back the lease and hand you over what he offers to pay." This was £25, altered from £20.

I then told Mary of his having called on me at the office, and of the subsequent revelation of the will. She was much impressed. "Oh, Bob," she said, "it is a real romance."

With a woman's quickness of perception, she guessed at once our landlord's reason for wishing to help us.

"Why, he thinks the old miser has hidden money here, and wants to look for it. Bob," this excitedly, "this house may be full of money; the walls round us may hold a fortune. Let us begin to look at once!"

I was as much excited as she was, but I felt that someone must keep cool, so I said:

"Mary, dear, there may be nothing; but even if there is, it does not belong to us."

"Why not?" she asked.

"Because it is all arranged in the will," I answered; "and, by the bye, I have a mem. of it here," and I took from my pocket the paper which Wigley had given me.

With intense interest we read it together, Mary holding me tightly by the arm. It certainly was short. It ran as follows:

"*7, Little Butler Street, S.W., London. – I hereby leave to my child or children, if I have any living, all I own, and in default of such everything is to go to John Gradder, my landlord, who is to make an inventory of all he can find in the two houses occupied by me, this house and 2, Lampeter Street, S.W. London, and to lodge all money and securities in Coutts's Bank. If my children or any of them do not claim in writing by an application before a Justice of the Peace within one calendar month from my decease, they are to forfeit all rights. Ignorance of my death or their relationship to be no reason for noncompliance. Lest there be any doubt of my intentions, I hereby declare that I wish in such default of my natural heirs John Gradder aforesaid to have my property, because he is the hardesthearted man I ever knew, and will not fool it away in charities or otherwise, but keep it together. If any fooling is to be done, it will be by my own.*

(Signed) GILES ARMER, Master Mariner,
Formerly of Whitby."

When I came near the end, Mary, who had been looking down the paper in advance of my reading, cried out; "Giles Armer! Why, that was my father!"

"Good God!" I cried out, as I jumped to my feet.

"Yes," she said, excitedly; "didn't you see me sign Mary Armer at the registry? We never spoke of the name because he had a quarrel with mother and deserted her, and after seven years she married my step-father, and I was always called by his name."

"And was he from Whitby?" I asked. I was nearly wild with excitement.

"Yes," said Mary. "Mother was married there, and I was born there."

I was reading over the will again. My hands were trembling so that I could hardly read. An awful thought struck me. What day did he die? Perhaps it was too late – it was now the thirtieth of October. However, we were determined to be on the safe side, and then and there Mary and I put on our hats and wraps and went to the nearest police-station.

There we learned the address of a magistrate, after we had explained to the inspector the urgency of the case.

We went to the address given, and after some delay were admitted to an interview.

The Magistrate was at first somewhat crusty at being disturbed at such an hour, for by this time it was pretty late in the evening. However, when we had explained matters to him he was greatly interested, and we went through the necessary formalities. When it was done he ordered in cake and wine, and wished us both luck. "But remember," he said to Mary, "that as yet your possible fortune is a long way off. There may be more Giles Armers than one, and moreover there may be some difficulty in proving legally that the dead man was the same person as your father. Then you will also have to prove, in a formal way, your mother's marriage and your own birth. This will probably involve heavy expenses, for lawyers fight hard when they are well paid. However, I do not wish to discourage you, but only to prevent false hopes; at any rate, you have done well in making your Declaration at once. So far you are on the high road to success." So he sent us away filled with hopes as well as fears.

When we got home we set to work to look for hidden treasures in the unfinished room. I knew too well that there was nothing hidden in the rooms which were finished, for I had done the work myself, and had even stripped the walls and uncovered the floors.

It took us a couple of hours to make an accurate search, but there was absolutely no result. The late Master Mariner had made his treasury in the other house.

Next morning I went to find out from the parish registry the date of the death of Giles Armer, and to my intense relief and joy learned that it had occurred on the 30th of September, so that by our prompt action in going at once to the magistrate's, we had, if not secured a fortune, at least, not forfeited our rights or allowed them to lapse.

The incident was a sort of good omen, and cheered us up; and we needed a little cheering, for, despite the possible good fortune, we feared we might have to contest a lawsuit, a luxury which we could not afford.

We determined to keep our own counsel for a little, and did not mention the matter to a soul.

That evening Mr. Gradder called again, and renewed his offer of taking the house off my hands. I still refused, for I did not wish him to see any difference in my demeanour. He evidently came determined to effect a surrender of the lease, and kept bidding higher and higher, till at last I thought it best to let him have his way; and so we agreed for no less a sum than a hundred pounds that I should give him immediate possession and cancel the agreement. I told him we would clear out within one hour after the money was handed to me.

Next morning at half-past nine o'clock he came with the money. I had all our effects – they were not many – packed up and taken to a new lodging, and before ten o'clock Mr. Gradder was in possession of the premises.

Whilst he was tearing down my new wall papers, and pulling out the grates, and sticking his head up the chimneys and down the water tanks in the search for more treasures, Mary and I were consulting the eminent solicitor, Mr. George, as to our method of procedure. He said he would not lose an hour, but go by the first train to Littlehampton himself to examine Mrs. Compton as to dates and places.

Mary and I went with him. In the course of the next twenty-four hours he had, by various documents and the recollections of my mother-in-law, made out a clear case, the details of which only wanted formal verification.

We all came back to London jubilant, and were engaged on a high tea when there came a loud knocking at the door. There was a noise and scuffle in the passage, and into the room rushed Mr. Gradder, covered with soot and lime dust, with hair dishevelled and eyes wild with anger, and haggard with want of sleep. He burst out at me in a torrent of invective.

"Give me back my money, you thief! You ransacked the house yourself, and have taken it all away! My money, do you hear? my money!" He grew positively speechless with rage, and almost foamed at the mouth.

I took Mary by the hand and led her up to him.

"Mr. Gradder," I said, "let us both thank you. Only for your hurry and persistency we might have let the time lapse, and have omitted the declaration which, on the evening before last, we, or rather, she, made.

He started as though struck.

"What declaration? What do you mean?"

"The declaration made by my wife, only daughter of Giles Armer, Master Mariner, late of Whitby."

If you enjoyed this, you might also like...
The Watcher, see page 276
The Cone, see page 322

The Model Millionaire
A Note of Admiration
Oscar Wilde

UNLESS ONE IS wealthy there is no use in being a charming fellow. Romance is the privilege of the rich, not the profession of the unemployed. The poor should be practical and prosaic. It is better to have a permanent income than to be fascinating. These are the great truths of modern life which Hughie Erskine never realised. Poor Hughie! Intellectually, we must admit, he was not of much importance. He never said a brilliant or even an ill-natured thing in his life. But then he was wonderfully good-looking, with his crisp brown hair, his clear-cut profile, and his grey eyes. He was as popular with men as he was with women and he had every accomplishment except that of making money. His father had bequeathed him his cavalry sword and a *History of the Peninsular War* in fifteen volumes. Hughie hung the first over his looking-glass, put the second on a shelf between *Ruff's Guide* and *Bailey's Magazine*, and lived on two hundred a year that an old aunt allowed him. He had tried everything. He had gone on the Stock Exchange for six months; but what was a butterfly to do among bulls and bears? He had been a tea-merchant for a little longer, but had soon tired of pekoe and souchong. Then he had tried selling dry sherry. That did not answer; the sherry was a little too dry. Ultimately he became nothing, a delightful, ineffectual young man with a perfect profile and no profession.

To make matters worse, he was in love. The girl he loved was Laura Merton, the daughter of a retired Colonel who had lost his temper and his digestion in India, and had never found either of them again. Laura adored him, and he was ready to kiss her shoe-strings. They were the handsomest couple in London, and had not a penny-piece between them. The Colonel was very fond of Hughie, but would not hear of any engagement.

"Come to me, my boy, when you have got ten thousand pounds of your own, and we will see about it," he used to say; and Hughie looked very glum in those days, and had to go to Laura for consolation.

One morning, as he was on his way to Holland Park, where the Mertons lived, he dropped in to see a great friend of his, Alan Trevor. Trevor was a painter. Indeed, few people escape that nowadays. But he was also an artist, and artists are rather rare. Personally he was a strange rough fellow, with a freckled face and a red ragged beard. However, when he took up the brush he was a real master, and his pictures were eagerly sought after. He had been very much attracted by Hughie at first, it must be acknowledged, entirely on account of his personal charm. "The only people a painter should know," he used to say, "are people who are *bête* and beautiful, people who are an artistic pleasure to look at and an intellectual repose to talk to. Men who are dandies and women who are darlings rule the world, at least they should do so." However, after he got to know Hughie better, he liked him quite as much for his bright, buoyant spirits and his generous, reckless nature, and had given him the permanent *entrée* to his studio.

When Hughie came in he found Trevor putting the finishing touches to a wonderful life-size picture of a beggar-man. The beggar himself was standing on a raised platform in a corner of the studio. He was a wizened old man, with a face like wrinkled parchment, and a most piteous expression. Over his shoulders was flung a coarse brown cloak, all tears and tatters; his thick boots were patched and cobbled, and with one hand he leant on a rough stick, while with the other he held out his battered hat for alms.

"What an amazing model!" whispered Hughie, as he shook hands with his friend.

"An amazing model?" shouted Trevor at the top of his voice; "I should think so! Such beggars as he are not to be met with every day. A *trouvaille, mon cher*; a living Velasquez! My stars! what an etching Rembrandt would have made of him!"

"Poor old chap!" said Hughie, "how miserable he looks! But I suppose, to you painters, his face is his fortune?"

"Certainly," replied Trevor, "you don't want a beggar to look happy, do you?"

"How much does a model get for sitting?" asked Hughie, as he found himself a comfortable seat on a divan.

"A shilling an hour."

"And how much do you get for your picture, Alan?"

"Oh, for this I get two thousand!"

"Pounds?"

"Guineas. Painters, poets, and physicians always get guineas."

"Well, I think the model should have a percentage," cried Hughie, laughing; "they work quite as hard as you do."

"Nonsense, nonsense! Why, look at the trouble of laying on the paint alone, and standing all day long at one's easel! It's all very well, Hughie, for you to talk, but I assure you that there are moments when Art almost attains to the dignity of manual labour. But you mustn't chatter; I'm very busy. Smoke a cigarette, and keep quiet."

After some time the servant came in, and told Trevor that the framemaker wanted to speak to him.

"Don't run away, Hughie," he said, as he went out, "I will be back in a moment."

The old beggar-man took advantage of Trevor's absence to rest for a moment on a wooden bench that was behind him. He looked so forlorn and wretched that Hughie could not help pitying him, and felt in his pockets to see what money he had. All he could find was a sovereign and some coppers. "Poor old fellow," he thought to himself, "he wants it more than I do, but it means no hansoms for a fortnight"; and he walked across the studio and slipped the sovereign into the beggar's hand.

The old man started, and a faint smile flitted across his withered lips. "Thank you, sir," he said, "thank you."

Then Trevor arrived, and Hughie took his leave, blushing a little at what he had done. He spent the day with Laura, got a charming scolding for his extravagance, and had to walk home.

That night he strolled into the Palette Club about eleven o'clock, and found Trevor sitting by himself in the smoking-room drinking hock and seltzer.

"Well, Alan, did you get the picture finished all right?" he said, as he lit his cigarette.

"Finished and framed, my boy!" answered Trevor; "and, by the bye, you have made a conquest. That old model you saw is quite devoted to you. I had to tell him all about you – who you are, where you live, what your income is, what prospects you have –"

"My dear Alan," cried Hughie, "I shall probably find him waiting for me when I go home. But of course you are only joking. Poor old wretch! I wish I could do something for him. I think it is dreadful that anyone should be so miserable. I have got heaps of old clothes at home – do you think he would care for any of them? Why, his rags were falling to bits."

"But he looks splendid in them," said Trevor. "I wouldn't paint him in a frock coat for anything. What you call rags I call romance. What seems poverty to you is picturesqueness to me. However, I'll tell him of your offer."

"Alan," said Hughie seriously, "you painters are a heartless lot."

"An artist's heart is his head," replied Trevor; "and besides, our business is to realise the world as we see it, not to reform it as we know it. À chacun son métier. And now tell me how Laura is. The old model was quite interested in her."

"You don't mean to say you talked to him about her?" said Hughie.

"Certainly I did. He knows all about the relentless colonel, the lovely Laura, and the £10,000."

"You told that old beggar all my private affairs?" cried Hughie, looking very red and angry.

"My dear boy," said Trevor, smiling, "that old beggar, as you call him, is one of the richest men in Europe. He could buy all London tomorrow without overdrawing his account. He has a house in every capital, dines off gold plate, and can prevent Russia going to war when he chooses."

"What on earth do you mean?" exclaimed Hughie.

"What I say," said Trevor. "The old man you saw today in the studio was Baron Hausberg. He is a great friend of mine, buys all my pictures and that sort of thing, and gave me a commission a month ago to paint him as a beggar. Que voulez-vous? La fantaisie d'un millionnaire! And I must say he made a magnificent figure in his rags, or perhaps I should say in my rags; they are an old suit I got in Spain."

"Baron Hausberg!" cried Hughie. "Good heavens! I gave him a sovereign!" and he sank into an armchair the picture of dismay.

"Gave him a sovereign!" shouted Trevor, and he burst into a roar of laughter. "My dear boy, you'll never see it again. Son affaire c'est l'argent des autres."

"I think you might have told me, Alan," said Hughie sulkily, "and not have let me make such a fool of myself."

"Well, to begin with, Hughie," said Trevor, "it never entered my mind that you went about distributing alms in that reckless way. I can understand your kissing a pretty model, but your giving a sovereign to an ugly one – by Jove, no! Besides, the fact is that I really was not at home today to anyone; and when you came in I didn't know whether Hausberg would like his name mentioned. You know he wasn't in full dress."

"What a duffer he must think me!" said Hughie.

"Not at all. He was in the highest spirits after you left; kept chuckling to himself and rubbing his old wrinkled hands together. I couldn't make out why he was so interested to know all about you; but I see it all now. He'll invest your sovereign for you, Hughie, pay you the interest every six months, and have a capital story to tell after dinner."

"I am an unlucky devil," growled Hughie. "The best thing I can do is to go to bed; and, my dear Alan, you mustn't tell anyone. I shouldn't dare show my face in the Row."

"Nonsense! It reflects the highest credit on your philanthropic spirit, Hughie. And don't run away. Have another cigarette, and you can talk about Laura as much as you like."

However, Hughie wouldn't stop, but walked home, feeling very unhappy, and leaving Alan Trevor in fits of laughter.

The next morning, as he was at breakfast, the servant brought him up a card on which was written, "Monsieur Gustave Naudin, *de la part de* M. le Baron Hausberg." "I suppose he has come for an apology," said Hughie to himself; and he told the servant to show the visitor up.

An old gentleman with gold spectacles and grey hair came into the room, and said, in a slight French accent, "Have I the honour of addressing Monsieur Erskine?"

Hughie bowed.

"I have come from Baron Hausberg," he continued. "The Baron—"

"I beg, sir, that you will offer him my sincerest apologies," stammered Hughie.

"The Baron," said the old gentleman with a smile, "has commissioned me to bring you this letter"; and he extended a sealed envelope.

On the outside was written, "A wedding present to Hugh Erskine and Laura Merton, from an old beggar," and inside was a cheque for £10,000.

When they were married Alan Trevor was the best man, and the Baron made a speech at the wedding breakfast.

"Millionaire models," remarked Alan, "are rare enough; but, by Jove, model millionaires are rarer still!"

If you enjoyed this, you might also like...
Our New House, see page 423
The Death of the Lion, see page 449

The Adventure of the Copper Beeches

Arthur Conan Doyle

"TO THE MAN who loves art for its own sake," remarked Sherlock Holmes, tossing aside the advertisement sheet of the *Daily Telegraph*, "it is frequently in its least important and lowliest manifestations that the keenest pleasure is to be derived. It is pleasant to me to observe, Watson, that you have so far grasped this truth that in these little records of our cases which you have been good enough to draw up, and, I am bound to say, occasionally to embellish, you have given prominence not so much to the many causes célèbres and sensational trials in which I have figured but rather to those incidents which may have been trivial in themselves, but which have given room for those faculties of deduction and of logical synthesis which I have made my special province."

"And yet," said I, smiling, "I cannot quite hold myself absolved from the charge of sensationalism which has been urged against my records."

"You have erred, perhaps," he observed, taking up a glowing cinder with the tongs and lighting with it the long cherry-wood pipe which was wont to replace his clay when he was in a disputatious rather than a meditative mood – "you have erred perhaps in attempting to put colour and life into each of your statements instead of confining yourself to the task of placing upon record that severe reasoning from cause to effect which is really the only notable feature about the thing."

"It seems to me that I have done you full justice in the matter," I remarked with some coldness, for I was repelled by the egotism which I had more than once observed to be a strong factor in my friend's singular character.

"No, it is not selfishness or conceit," said he, answering, as was his wont, my thoughts rather than my words. "If I claim full justice for my art, it is because it is an impersonal thing – a thing beyond myself. Crime is common. Logic is rare. Therefore it is upon the logic rather than upon the crime that you should dwell. You have degraded what should have been a course of lectures into a series of tales."

It was a cold morning of the early spring, and we sat after breakfast on either side of a cheery fire in the old room at Baker Street. A thick fog rolled down between the lines of dun-coloured houses, and the opposing windows loomed like dark, shapeless blurs through the heavy yellow wreaths. Our gas was lit and shone on the white cloth and glimmer of china and metal, for the table had not been cleared yet. Sherlock Holmes had been silent all the morning, dipping continuously into the advertisement columns of a succession of papers until at last, having apparently given up his search, he had emerged in no very sweet temper to lecture me upon my literary shortcomings.

"At the same time," he remarked after a pause, during which he had sat puffing at his long pipe and gazing down into the fire, "you can hardly be open to a charge of sensationalism, for out of these cases which you have been so kind as to interest yourself in, a fair proportion do not treat of crime, in its legal sense, at all. The small matter in which I endeavoured to help the King of Bohemia, the singular experience of Miss Mary Sutherland, the problem connected with the man with the twisted lip, and the incident of the noble bachelor, were all matters which are outside the pale of the law. But in avoiding the sensational, I fear that you may have bordered on the trivial."

"The end may have been so," I answered, "but the methods I hold to have been novel and of interest."

"Pshaw, my dear fellow, what do the public, the great unobservant public, who could hardly tell a weaver by his tooth or a compositor by his left thumb, care about the finer shades of analysis and deduction! But, indeed, if you are trivial, I cannot blame you, for the days of the great cases are past. Man, or at least criminal man, has lost all enterprise and originality. As to my own little practice, it seems to be degenerating into an agency for recovering lost lead pencils and giving advice to young ladies from boarding-schools. I think that I have touched bottom at last, however. This note I had this morning marks my zero-point, I fancy. Read it!" He tossed a crumpled letter across to me.

It was dated from Montague Place upon the preceding evening, and ran thus:

> *Dear Mr. Holmes:*
> *I am very anxious to consult you as to whether I should or should not accept a situation which has been offered to me as governess. I shall call at half-past ten tomorrow if I do not inconvenience you.*
> *Yours faithfully,*
> *Violet Hunter.*

"Do you know the young lady?" I asked.

"Not I."

"It is half-past ten now."

"Yes, and I have no doubt that is her ring."

"It may turn out to be of more interest than you think. You remember that the affair of the blue carbuncle, which appeared to be a mere whim at first, developed into a serious investigation. It may be so in this case, also."

"Well, let us hope so. But our doubts will very soon be solved, for here, unless I am much mistaken, is the person in question."

As he spoke the door opened and a young lady entered the room. She was plainly but neatly dressed, with a bright, quick face, freckled like a plover's egg, and with the brisk manner of a woman who has had her own way to make in the world.

"You will excuse my troubling you, I am sure," said she, as my companion rose to greet her, "but I have had a very strange experience, and as I have no parents or relations of any sort from whom I could ask advice, I thought that perhaps you would be kind enough to tell me what I should do."

"Pray take a seat, Miss Hunter. I shall be happy to do anything that I can to serve you."

I could see that Holmes was favourably impressed by the manner and speech of his new client. He looked her over in his searching fashion, and then composed himself, with his lids drooping and his fingertips together, to listen to her story.

"I have been a governess for five years," said she, "in the family of Colonel Spence Munro, but two months ago the colonel received an appointment at Halifax, in Nova Scotia, and took his children over to America with him, so that I found myself without a situation. I advertised, and I answered advertisements, but without success. At last the little money which I had saved began to run short, and I was at my wit's end as to what I should do.

"There is a well-known agency for governesses in the West End called Westaway's, and there I used to call about once a week in order to see whether anything had turned up which might suit me. Westaway was the name of the founder of the business, but it is really managed by Miss Stoper. She sits in her own little office, and the ladies who are seeking employment wait in an anteroom, and are then shown in one by one, when she consults her ledgers and sees whether she has anything which would suit them.

"Well, when I called last week I was shown into the little office as usual, but I found that Miss Stoper was not alone. A prodigiously stout man with a very smiling face and a great heavy chin which rolled down in fold upon fold over his throat sat at her elbow with a pair of glasses on his nose, looking very earnestly at the ladies who entered. As I came in he gave quite a jump in his chair and turned quickly to Miss Stoper.

"'That will do,' said he; 'I could not ask for anything better. Capital! Capital!' He seemed quite enthusiastic and rubbed his hands together in the most genial fashion. He was such a comfortable-looking man that it was quite a pleasure to look at him.

"'You are looking for a situation, miss?' he asked.

"'Yes, sir.'

"'As governess?'

"'Yes, sir.'

"'And what salary do you ask?'

"'I had 4 pounds a month in my last place with Colonel Spence Munro.'

"'Oh, tut, tut! Sweating – rank sweating!' he cried, throwing his fat hands out into the air like a man who is in a boiling passion. 'How could anyone offer so pitiful a sum to a lady with such attractions and accomplishments?'

"'My accomplishments, sir, may be less than you imagine,' said I. 'A little French, a little German, music, and drawing –'

"'Tut, tut!' he cried. 'This is all quite beside the question. The point is, have you or have you not the bearing and deportment of a lady? There it is in a nutshell. If you have not, you are not fitted for the rearing of a child who may some day play a considerable part in the history of the country. But if you have why, then, how could any gentleman ask you to condescend to accept anything under the three figures? Your salary with me, madam, would commence at 100 pounds a year.'

"You may imagine, Mr. Holmes, that to me, destitute as I was, such an offer seemed almost too good to be true. The gentleman, however, seeing perhaps the look of incredulity upon my face, opened a pocket-book and took out a note.

"'It is also my custom,' said he, smiling in the most pleasant fashion until his eyes were just two little shining slits amid the white creases of his face, 'to advance to my young ladies half their salary beforehand, so that they may meet any little expenses of their journey and their wardrobe.'

"It seemed to me that I had never met so fascinating and so thoughtful a man. As I was already in debt to my tradesmen, the advance was a great convenience, and yet there was something unnatural about the whole transaction which made me wish to know a little more before I quite committed myself.

"'May I ask where you live, sir?' said I.

"'Hampshire. Charming rural place. The Copper Beeches, five miles on the far side of Winchester. It is the most lovely country, my dear young lady, and the dearest old country-house.'

"'And my duties, sir? I should be glad to know what they would be.'

"'One child – one dear little romper just six years old. Oh, if you could see him killing cockroaches with a slipper! Smack! smack! smack! Three gone before you could wink!' He leaned back in his chair and laughed his eyes into his head again.

"I was a little startled at the nature of the child's amusement, but the father's laughter made me think that perhaps he was joking.

"'My sole duties, then,' I asked, 'are to take charge of a single child?'

"'No, no, not the sole, not the sole, my dear young lady,' he cried. 'Your duty would be, as I am sure your good sense would suggest, to obey any little commands my wife might give, provided always that they were such commands as a lady might with propriety obey. You see no difficulty, heh?'

"'I should be happy to make myself useful.'

"'Quite so. In dress now, for example. We are faddy people, you know – faddy but kind-hearted. If you were asked to wear any dress which we might give you, you would not object to our little whim. Heh?'

"'No,' said I, considerably astonished at his words.

"'Or to sit here, or sit there, that would not be offensive to you?'

"'Oh, no.'

"'Or to cut your hair quite short before you come to us?'

"I could hardly believe my ears. As you may observe, Mr. Holmes, my hair is somewhat luxuriant, and of a rather peculiar tint of chestnut. It has been considered artistic. I could not dream of sacrificing it in this offhand fashion.

"'I am afraid that that is quite impossible,' said I. He had been watching me eagerly out of his small eyes, and I could see a shadow pass over his face as I spoke.

"'I am afraid that it is quite essential,' said he. 'It is a little fancy of my wife's, and ladies' fancies, you know, madam, ladies' fancies must be consulted. And so you won't cut your hair?'

"'No, sir, I really could not,' I answered firmly.

"'Ah, very well; then that quite settles the matter. It is a pity, because in other respects you would really have done very nicely. In that case, Miss Stoper, I had best inspect a few more of your young ladies.'

"The manageress had sat all this while busy with her papers without a word to either of us, but she glanced at me now with so much annoyance upon her face that I could not help suspecting that she had lost a handsome commission through my refusal.

"'Do you desire your name to be kept upon the books?' she asked.

"'If you please, Miss Stoper.'

"'Well, really, it seems rather useless, since you refuse the most excellent offers in this fashion,' said she sharply. 'You can hardly expect us to exert ourselves to find another such opening for you. Good-day to you, Miss Hunter.' She struck a gong upon the table, and I was shown out by the page.

"Well, Mr. Holmes, when I got back to my lodgings and found little enough in the cupboard, and two or three bills upon the table. I began to ask myself whether I had not done a very foolish thing. After all, if these people had strange fads and expected obedience on the most extraordinary matters, they were at least ready to pay for their eccentricity. Very few governesses in England are getting 100 pounds a year. Besides, what use was my hair to me? Many people are improved by wearing it short and perhaps I should be among the number. Next day I was inclined to think that I had made a mistake, and by the day after I was sure of it. I had almost overcome my pride so far as to go back to the agency and inquire whether the place was still open when I received this letter from the gentleman himself. I have it here and I will read it to you:

The Copper Beeches, near Winchester.

Dear Miss Hunter:

Miss Stoper has very kindly given me your address, and I write from here to ask you whether you have reconsidered your decision. My wife is very anxious that you should come, for she has been much attracted by my description of you. We are willing to give 30 pounds a quarter, or 120 pounds a year, so as to recompense you for any little inconvenience which our fads may cause you. They are not very exacting, after all. My wife is fond of a particular shade of electric blue and would like you to wear such a dress indoors in the morning. You need not, however, go to the expense of purchasing one, as we have one belonging to my dear daughter Alice (now in Philadelphia), which would, I should think, fit you very well. Then, as to sitting here or there, or amusing yourself in any manner indicated, that need cause you no inconvenience. As regards your hair, it is no doubt a pity, especially as I could not help remarking its beauty during our short interview, but I am afraid that I must remain firm upon this point, and I only hope that the increased salary may recompense you for the loss. Your duties, as far as the child is concerned, are very light. Now do try to come, and I shall meet you with the dog-cart at Winchester. Let me know your train.

Yours faithfully,
Jephro Rucastle.

"That is the letter which I have just received, Mr. Holmes, and my mind is made up that I will accept it. I thought, however, that before taking the final step I should like to submit the whole matter to your consideration."

"Well, Miss Hunter, if your mind is made up, that settles the question," said Holmes, smiling.

"But you would not advise me to refuse?"

"I confess that it is not the situation which I should like to see a sister of mine apply for."

"What is the meaning of it all, Mr. Holmes?"

"Ah, I have no data. I cannot tell. Perhaps you have yourself formed some opinion?"

"Well, there seems to me to be only one possible solution. Mr. Rucastle seemed to be a very kind, good-natured man. Is it not possible that his wife is a lunatic, that he desires to keep the matter quiet for fear she should be taken to an asylum, and that he humours her fancies in every way in order to prevent an outbreak?"

"That is a possible solution – in fact, as matters stand, it is the most probable one. But in any case it does not seem to be a nice household for a young lady."

"But the money, Mr. Holmes the money!"

"Well, yes, of course the pay is good – too good. That is what makes me uneasy. Why should they give you 120 pounds a year, when they could have their pick for 40 pounds? There must be some strong reason behind."

"I thought that if I told you the circumstances you would understand afterwards if I wanted your help. I should feel so much stronger if I felt that you were at the back of me."

"Oh, you may carry that feeling away with you. I assure you that your little problem promises to be the most interesting which has come my way for some months. There is something distinctly novel about some of the features. If you should find yourself in doubt or in danger—"

"Danger! What danger do you foresee?"

Holmes shook his head gravely. "It would cease to be a danger if we could define it," said he. "But at any time, day or night, a telegram would bring me down to your help."

"That is enough." She rose briskly from her chair with the anxiety all swept from her face. "I shall go down to Hampshire quite easy in my mind now. I shall write to Mr. Rucastle at once, sacrifice my poor hair tonight, and start for Winchester tomorrow." With a few grateful words to Holmes she bade us both goodnight and bustled off upon her way.

"At least," said I as we heard her quick, firm steps descending the stairs, "she seems to be a young lady who is very well able to take care of herself."

"And she would need to be," said Holmes gravely. "I am much mistaken if we do not hear from her before many days are past."

It was not very long before my friend's prediction was fulfilled. A fortnight went by, during which I frequently found my thoughts turning in her direction and wondering what strange side-alley of human experience this lonely woman had strayed into. The unusual salary, the curious conditions, the light duties, all pointed to something abnormal, though whether a fad or a plot, or whether the man were a philanthropist or a villain, it was quite beyond my powers to determine. As to Holmes, I observed that he sat frequently for half an hour on end, with knitted brows and an abstracted air, but he swept the matter away with a wave of his hand when I mentioned it. "Data! Data! Data!" he cried impatiently. "I can't make bricks without clay." And yet he would always wind up by muttering that no sister of his should ever have accepted such a situation.

The telegram which we eventually received came late one night just as I was thinking of turning in and Holmes was settling down to one of those all-night chemical researches which he frequently indulged in, when I would leave him stooping over a retort and a test-tube at night and find him in the same position when I came down to breakfast in the morning. He opened the yellow envelope, and then, glancing at the message, threw it across to me.

"Just look up the trains in Bradshaw," said he, and turned back to his chemical studies. The summons was a brief and urgent one.

> *Please be at the Black Swan Hotel at Winchester at midday tomorrow* [it said].
> *Do come! I am at my wit's end.*
> *Hunter.*

"Will you come with me?" asked Holmes, glancing up.

"I should wish to."

"Just look it up, then."

"There is a train at half-past nine," said I, glancing over my Bradshaw. "It is due at Winchester at 11:30."

"That will do very nicely. Then perhaps I had better postpone my analysis of the acetones, as we may need to be at our best in the morning."

* * *

By eleven o'clock the next day we were well upon our way to the old English capital. Holmes had been buried in the morning papers all the way down, but after we had passed the Hampshire border he threw them down and began to admire the scenery. It was an ideal spring day, a light blue sky, flecked with little fleecy white clouds drifting across from west to east. The sun was shining very brightly, and yet there was an exhilarating nip in the air, which set an edge to a man's energy. All over the countryside, away to the rolling hills around Aldershot, the little red and grey roofs of the farm-steadings peeped out from amid the light green of the new foliage.

"Are they not fresh and beautiful?" I cried with all the enthusiasm of a man fresh from the fogs of Baker Street.

But Holmes shook his head gravely.

"Do you know, Watson," said he, "that it is one of the curses of a mind with a turn like mine that I must look at everything with reference to my own special subject. You look at these scattered houses, and you are impressed by their beauty. I look at them, and the only thought which comes to me is a feeling of their isolation and of the impunity with which crime may be committed there."

"Good heavens!" I cried. "Who would associate crime with these dear old homesteads?"

"They always fill me with a certain horror. It is my belief, Watson, founded upon my experience, that the lowest and vilest alleys in London do not present a more dreadful record of sin than does the smiling and beautiful countryside."

"You horrify me!"

"But the reason is very obvious. The pressure of public opinion can do in the town what the law cannot accomplish. There is no lane so vile that the scream of a tortured child, or the thud of a drunkard's blow, does not beget sympathy and indignation among the neighbours, and then the whole machinery of justice is ever so close that a word of complaint can set it going, and there is but a step between the crime and the dock. But look at these lonely houses, each in its own fields, filled for the most part with poor ignorant folk who know little of the law. Think of the deeds of hellish cruelty, the hidden wickedness which may go on, year in, year out, in such places, and none the wiser. Had this lady who appeals to us for help gone to live in Winchester, I should never have had a fear for her. It is the five miles of country which makes the danger. Still, it is clear that she is not personally threatened."

"No. If she can come to Winchester to meet us she can get away."

"Quite so. She has her freedom."

"What can be the matter, then? Can you suggest no explanation?"

"I have devised seven separate explanations, each of which would cover the facts as far as we know them. But which of these is correct can only be determined by the fresh information which we shall no doubt find waiting for us. Well, there is the tower of the cathedral, and we shall soon learn all that Miss Hunter has to tell."

The Black Swan is an inn of repute in the High Street, at no distance from the station, and there we found the young lady waiting for us. She had engaged a sitting-room, and our lunch awaited us upon the table.

"I am so delighted that you have come," she said earnestly. "It is so very kind of you both; but indeed I do not know what I should do. Your advice will be altogether invaluable to me."

"Pray tell us what has happened to you."

"I will do so, and I must be quick, for I have promised Mr. Rucastle to be back before three. I got his leave to come into town this morning, though he little knew for what purpose."

"Let us have everything in its due order." Holmes thrust his long thin legs out towards the fire and composed himself to listen.

"In the first place, I may say that I have met, on the whole, with no actual ill-treatment from Mr. and Mrs. Rucastle. It is only fair to them to say that. But I cannot understand them, and I am not easy in my mind about them."

"What can you not understand?"

"Their reasons for their conduct. But you shall have it all just as it occurred. When I came down, Mr. Rucastle met me here and drove me in his dog-cart to the Copper Beeches. It is, as he said, beautifully situated, but it is not beautiful in itself, for it is a large square block of a house, whitewashed, but all stained and streaked with damp and bad weather. There are grounds round it, woods on three sides, and on the fourth a field which slopes down to the Southampton highroad, which curves past about a hundred yards from the front door. This ground in front belongs to the house, but the woods all round are part of Lord Southerton's preserves. A clump of copper beeches immediately in front of the hall door has given its name to the place.

"I was driven over by my employer, who was as amiable as ever, and was introduced by him that evening to his wife and the child. There was no truth, Mr. Holmes, in the conjecture which seemed to us to be probable in your rooms at Baker Street. Mrs. Rucastle is not mad. I found her to be a silent, pale-faced woman, much younger than her husband, not more than thirty, I should think, while he can hardly be less than forty-five. From their conversation I have gathered that they have been married about seven years, that he was a widower, and that his only child by the first wife was the daughter who has gone to Philadelphia. Mr. Rucastle told me in private that the reason why she had left them was that she had an unreasoning aversion to her stepmother. As the daughter could not have been less than twenty, I can quite imagine that her position must have been uncomfortable with her father's young wife.

"Mrs. Rucastle seemed to me to be colourless in mind as well as in feature. She impressed me neither favourably nor the reverse. She was a nonentity. It was easy to see that she was passionately devoted both to her husband and to her little son. Her light grey eyes wandered continually from one to the other, noting every little want and forestalling it if possible. He was kind to her also in his bluff, boisterous fashion, and on the whole they seemed to be a happy couple. And yet she had some secret sorrow, this woman. She would often be lost in deep thought, with the saddest look upon her face. More than once I have surprised her in tears. I have thought sometimes that it was the disposition of her child which weighed upon her mind, for I have never met so utterly spoiled and so ill-natured a little creature. He is small for his age, with a head which is quite disproportionately large. His whole life appears to be spent in an alternation between savage fits of passion and gloomy intervals of sulking. Giving pain to any creature weaker than himself seems to be his one idea of amusement, and he shows quite remarkable talent in planning the capture of mice, little birds, and insects. But I would rather not talk about the creature, Mr. Holmes, and, indeed, he has little to do with my story."

"I am glad of all details," remarked my friend, "whether they seem to you to be relevant or not."

"I shall try not to miss anything of importance. The one unpleasant thing about the house, which struck me at once, was the appearance and conduct of the servants. There are only two, a man and his wife. Toller, for that is his name, is a rough, uncouth man, with grizzled hair and whiskers, and a perpetual smell of drink. Twice since I have been with them he has been quite drunk, and yet Mr. Rucastle seemed to take no notice of it. His wife is a very tall and strong woman with a sour face, as silent as Mrs. Rucastle and much less amiable. They are a most unpleasant couple, but fortunately I spend most of my time in the nursery and my own room, which are next to each other in one corner of the building.

"For two days after my arrival at the Copper Beeches my life was very quiet; on the third, Mrs. Rucastle came down just after breakfast and whispered something to her husband.

"'Oh, yes,' said he, turning to me, 'we are very much obliged to you, Miss Hunter, for falling in with our whims so far as to cut your hair. I assure you that it has not detracted in the tiniest iota from your appearance. We shall now see how the electric-blue dress will become you. You will find it laid out upon the bed in your room, and if you would be so good as to put it on we should both be extremely obliged.'

"The dress which I found waiting for me was of a peculiar shade of blue. It was of excellent material, a sort of beige, but it bore unmistakable signs of having been worn before. It could not have been a better fit if I had been measured for it. Both Mr. and Mrs. Rucastle expressed a delight at the look of it, which seemed quite exaggerated in its vehemence. They were waiting for me in the drawing-room, which is a very large room, stretching along the entire front of the house, with three long windows reaching down to the floor. A chair had been placed close to the central window, with its back turned towards it. In this I was asked to sit, and then Mr. Rucastle, walking up and down on the other side of the room, began to tell me a series of the funniest stories that I have ever listened to. You cannot imagine how comical he was, and I laughed until I was quite weary. Mrs. Rucastle, however, who has evidently no sense of humour, never so much as smiled, but sat with her hands in her lap, and a sad, anxious look upon her face. After an hour or so, Mr. Rucastle suddenly remarked that it was time to commence the duties of the day, and that I might change my dress and go to little Edward in the nursery.

"Two days later this same performance was gone through under exactly similar circumstances. Again I changed my dress, again I sat in the window, and again I laughed very heartily at the funny stories of which my employer had an immense repertoire, and which he told inimitably. Then he handed me a yellowbacked novel, and moving my chair a little sideways, that my own shadow might not fall upon the page, he begged me to read aloud to him. I read for about ten minutes, beginning in the heart of a chapter, and then suddenly, in the middle of a sentence, he ordered me to cease and to change my dress.

"You can easily imagine, Mr. Holmes, how curious I became as to what the meaning of this extraordinary performance could possibly be. They were always very careful, I observed, to turn my face away from the window, so that I became consumed with the desire to see what was going on behind my back. At first it seemed to be impossible, but I soon devised a means. My hand-mirror had been broken, so a happy thought seized me, and I concealed a piece of the glass in my handkerchief. On the next occasion, in the midst of my laughter, I put my handkerchief up to my eyes, and was able with a little management to see all that there was behind me. I confess that I was disappointed. There was nothing. At least that was my first impression. At the second glance, however, I perceived that there was a man standing in the Southampton Road, a small bearded man in a grey suit, who seemed to be looking in my direction. The road is an important highway, and there are usually people there. This man, however, was leaning against the railings which bordered our field and was looking earnestly up. I lowered my handkerchief and glanced at Mrs. Rucastle to find her eyes fixed upon me with a most searching gaze. She said nothing, but I am convinced that she had divined that I had a mirror in my hand and had seen what was behind me. She rose at once.

"'Jephro,' said she, 'there is an impertinent fellow upon the road there who stares up at Miss Hunter.'

"'No friend of yours, Miss Hunter?' he asked.

"'No, I know no one in these parts.'

"'Dear me! How very impertinent! Kindly turn round and motion to him to go away.'

"'Surely it would be better to take no notice.'

"'No, no, we should have him loitering here always. Kindly turn round and wave him away like that.'

"I did as I was told, and at the same instant Mrs. Rucastle drew down the blind. That was a week ago, and from that time I have not sat again in the window, nor have I worn the blue dress, nor seen the man in the road."

"Pray continue," said Holmes. "Your narrative promises to be a most interesting one."

"You will find it rather disconnected, I fear, and there may prove to be little relation between the different incidents of which I speak. On the very first day that I was at the Copper Beeches, Mr. Rucastle took me to a small outhouse which stands near the kitchen door. As we approached it I heard the sharp rattling of a chain, and the sound as of a large animal moving about.

"'Look in here!' said Mr. Rucastle, showing me a slit between two planks. 'Is he not a beauty?'

"I looked through and was conscious of two glowing eyes, and of a vague figure huddled up in the darkness.

"'Don't be frightened,' said my employer, laughing at the start which I had given. 'It's only Carlo, my mastiff. I call him mine, but really old Toller, my groom, is the only man who can do anything with him. We feed him once a day, and not too much then, so that he is always as keen as mustard. Toller lets him loose every night, and God help the trespasser whom he lays his fangs upon. For goodness' sake don't you ever on any pretext set your foot over the threshold at night, for it's as much as your life is worth.'

"The warning was no idle one, for two nights later I happened to look out of my bedroom window about two o'clock in the morning. It was a beautiful moonlight night, and the lawn in front of the house was silvered over and almost as bright as day. I was standing, rapt in the peaceful beauty of the scene, when I was aware that something was moving under the shadow of the copper beeches. As it emerged into the moonshine I saw what it was. It was a giant dog, as large as a calf, tawny tinted, with hanging jowl, black muzzle, and huge projecting bones. It walked slowly across the lawn and vanished into the shadow upon the other side. That dreadful sentinel sent a chill to my heart which I do not think that any burglar could have done.

"And now I have a very strange experience to tell you. I had, as you know, cut off my hair in London, and I had placed it in a great coil at the bottom of my trunk. One evening, after the child was in bed, I began to amuse myself by examining the furniture of my room and by rearranging my own little things. There was an old chest of drawers in the room, the two upper ones empty and open, the lower one locked. I had filled the first two with my linen, and as I had still much to pack away I was naturally annoyed at not having the use of the third drawer. It struck me that it might have been fastened by a mere oversight, so I took out my bunch of keys and tried to open it. The very first key fitted to perfection, and I drew the drawer open. There was only one thing in it, but I am sure that you would never guess what it was. It was my coil of hair.

"I took it up and examined it. It was of the same peculiar tint, and the same thickness. But then the impossibility of the thing obtruded itself upon me. How could my hair have been locked in the drawer? With trembling hands I undid my trunk, turned out the contents, and drew from the bottom my own hair. I laid the two tresses together, and I assure you that they were identical. Was it not extraordinary? Puzzle as I would, I could make nothing at all of what it meant. I returned the strange hair to the drawer, and I said nothing of the matter to the Rucastles as I felt that I had put myself in the wrong by opening a drawer which they had locked.

"I am naturally observant, as you may have remarked, Mr. Holmes, and I soon had a pretty good plan of the whole house in my head. There was one wing, however, which appeared not to be inhabited at all. A door which faced that which led into the quarters of the Tollers opened into this suite, but it was invariably locked. One day, however, as I ascended the stair, I met Mr. Rucastle coming out through this door, his keys in his hand, and a look on his face which made him a very different person to the round, jovial man to whom I was accustomed. His cheeks were red, his brow was all crinkled with anger, and the veins stood out at his temples with passion. He locked the door and hurried past me without a word or a look.

"This aroused my curiosity, so when I went out for a walk in the grounds with my charge, I strolled round to the side from which I could see the windows of this part of the house. There were four of them in a row, three of which were simply dirty, while the fourth was shuttered up. They were evidently all deserted. As I strolled up and down, glancing at them occasionally, Mr. Rucastle came out to me, looking as merry and jovial as ever.

"'Ah!' said he, 'you must not think me rude if I passed you without a word, my dear young lady. I was preoccupied with business matters.'

"I assured him that I was not offended. 'By the way,' said I, 'you seem to have quite a suite of spare rooms up there, and one of them has the shutters up.'

"He looked surprised and, as it seemed to me, a little startled at my remark.

"'Photography is one of my hobbies,' said he. 'I have made my dark room up there. But, dear me! What an observant young lady we have come upon. Who would have believed it? Who would have ever believed it?' He spoke in a jesting tone, but there was no jest in his eyes as he looked at me. I read suspicion there and annoyance, but no jest.

"Well, Mr. Holmes, from the moment that I understood that there was something about that suite of rooms which I was not to know, I was all on fire to go over them. It was not mere curiosity, though I have my share of that. It was more a feeling of duty – a feeling that some good might come from my penetrating to this place. They talk of woman's instinct; perhaps it was woman's instinct which gave me that feeling. At any rate, it was there, and I was keenly on the lookout for any chance to pass the forbidden door.

"It was only yesterday that the chance came. I may tell you that, besides Mr. Rucastle, both Toller and his wife find something to do in these deserted rooms, and I once saw him carrying a large black linen bag with him through the door. Recently he has been drinking hard, and yesterday evening he was very drunk; and when I came upstairs there was the key in the door. I have no doubt at all that he had left it there. Mr. and Mrs. Rucastle were both downstairs, and the child was with them, so that I had an admirable opportunity. I turned the key gently in the lock, opened the door, and slipped through.

"There was a little passage in front of me, unpapered and uncarpeted, which turned at a right angle at the farther end. Round this corner were three doors in a line, the first and third of which were open. They each led into an empty room, dusty and cheerless, with two windows in the one and one in the other, so thick with dirt that the evening light glimmered dimly through them. The centre door was closed, and across the outside of it had been fastened one of the broad bars of an iron bed, padlocked at one end to a ring in the wall, and fastened at the other with stout cord. The door itself was locked as well, and the key was not there. This barricaded door corresponded clearly with the shuttered window outside, and yet I could see by the glimmer from beneath it that the room was not in darkness. Evidently there was a skylight which let in light from above. As I stood in the passage gazing at the sinister door and wondering what secret it might veil, I suddenly heard the sound of steps within the room and saw a shadow pass backward and forward against the little slit of dim light which shone out from under the door. A mad, unreasoning terror rose up in me at the sight, Mr. Holmes. My overstrung nerves failed me suddenly, and I turned and ran – ran as though some dreadful hand were behind me clutching at the skirt of my dress. I rushed down the passage, through the door, and straight into the arms of Mr. Rucastle, who was waiting outside.

"'So,' said he, smiling, 'it was you, then. I thought that it must be when I saw the door open.'

"'Oh, I am so frightened!' I panted.

"'My dear young lady! My dear young lady!' – You cannot think how caressing and soothing his manner was – 'and what has frightened you, my dear young lady?'

"But his voice was just a little too coaxing. He overdid it. I was keenly on my guard against him.

"'I was foolish enough to go into the empty wing,' I answered. 'But it is so lonely and eerie in this dim light that I was frightened and ran out again. Oh, it is so dreadfully still in there!'

"'Only that?' said he, looking at me keenly.

"'Why, what did you think?' I asked.

"'Why do you think that I lock this door?'

"'I am sure that I do not know.'

"'It is to keep people out who have no business there. Do you see?' He was still smiling in the most amiable manner.

"'I am sure if I had known

"'Well, then, you know now. And if you ever put your foot over that threshold again' – here in an instant the smile hardened into a grin of rage, and he glared down at me with the face of a demon – 'I'll throw you to the mastiff.'

"I was so terrified that I do not know what I did. I suppose that I must have rushed past him into my room. I remember nothing until I found myself lying on my bed trembling all over. Then I thought of you, Mr. Holmes. I could not live there longer without some advice. I was frightened of the house, of the man of the woman, of the servants, even of the child. They were all horrible to me. If I could only bring you down all would be well. Of course I might have fled from the house, but my curiosity was almost as strong as my fears. My mind was soon made up. I would send you a wire. I put on my hat and cloak, went down to the office, which is about half a mile from the house, and then returned, feeling very much easier. A horrible doubt came into my mind as I approached the door lest the dog might be loose, but I remembered that Toller had drunk himself into a state of insensibility that evening, and I knew that he was the only one in the household who had any influence with the savage creature, or who would venture to set him free. I slipped in in safety and lay awake half the night in my joy at the thought of seeing you. I had no difficulty in getting leave to come into Winchester this morning, but I must be back before three o'clock, for Mr. and Mrs. Rucastle are going on a visit, and will be away all the evening, so that I must look after the child. Now I have told you all my adventures, Mr. Holmes, and I should be very glad if you could tell me what it all means, and, above all, what I should do."

Holmes and I had listened spellbound to this extraordinary story. My friend rose now and paced up and down the room, his hands in his pockets, and an expression of the most profound gravity upon his face.

"Is Toller still drunk?" he asked.

"Yes. I heard his wife tell Mrs. Rucastle that she could do nothing with him."

"That is well. And the Rucastles go out tonight?"

"Yes."

"Is there a cellar with a good strong lock?"

"Yes, the wine-cellar."

"You seem to me to have acted all through this matter like a very brave and sensible girl, Miss Hunter. Do you think that you could perform one more feat? I should not ask it of you if I did not think you a quite exceptional woman."

"I will try. What is it?"

"We shall be at the Copper Beeches by seven o'clock, my friend and I. The Rucastles will be gone by that time, and Toller will, we hope, be incapable. There only remains Mrs. Toller, who might give the alarm. If you could send her into the cellar on some errand, and then turn the key upon her, you would facilitate matters immensely."

"I will do it."

"Excellent! We shall then look thoroughly into the affair. Of course there is only one feasible explanation. You have been brought there to personate someone, and the real person is imprisoned in this chamber. That is obvious. As to who this prisoner is, I have no doubt that it is the daughter, Miss Alice Rucastle, if I remember right, who was said to have gone to America. You were chosen, doubtless, as resembling her in height, figure, and the colour of your hair. Hers had been cut off, very possibly in some illness through which she has passed, and so, of course, yours had to be sacrificed also. By a curious chance you came upon her tresses. The man in the road was undoubtedly some friend of hers – possibly her fiance – and no doubt, as you wore the girl's dress and were so like her, he was convinced from your laughter, whenever he saw you, and afterwards from your gesture, that Miss Rucastle was perfectly happy, and that she no longer desired his attentions. The dog is let loose at night to prevent him from endeavouring to communicate with her. So much is fairly clear. The most serious point in the case is the disposition of the child."

"What on earth has that to do with it?" I ejaculated.

"My dear Watson, you as a medical man are continually gaining light as to the tendencies of a child by the study of the parents. Don't you see that the converse is equally valid. I have frequently gained my first real insight into the character of parents by studying their children. This child's disposition is abnormally cruel, merely for cruelty's sake, and whether he derives this from his smiling father, as I should suspect, or from his mother, it bodes evil for the poor girl who is in their power."

"I am sure that you are right, Mr. Holmes," cried our client. "A thousand things come back to me which make me certain that you have hit it. Oh, let us lose not an instant in bringing help to this poor creature."

"We must be circumspect, for we are dealing with a very cunning man. We can do nothing until seven o'clock. At that hour we shall be with you, and it will not be long before we solve the mystery."

We were as good as our word, for it was just seven when we reached the Copper Beeches, having put up our trap at a wayside public-house. The group of trees, with their dark leaves shining like burnished metal in the light of the setting sun, were sufficient to mark the house even had Miss Hunter not been standing smiling on the door-step.

"Have you managed it?" asked Holmes.

A loud thudding noise came from somewhere downstairs. "That is Mrs. Toller in the cellar," said she. "Her husband lies snoring on the kitchen rug. Here are his keys, which are the duplicates of Mr. Rucastle's."

"You have done well indeed!" cried Holmes with enthusiasm. "Now lead the way, and we shall soon see the end of this black business."

We passed up the stair, unlocked the door, followed on down a passage, and found ourselves in front of the barricade which Miss Hunter had described. Holmes cut the cord and removed the transverse bar. Then he tried the various keys in the lock, but without success. No sound came from within, and at the silence Holmes's face clouded over.

"I trust that we are not too late," said he. "I think, Miss Hunter, that we had better go in without you. Now, Watson, put your shoulder to it, and we shall see whether we cannot make our way in."

It was an old rickety door and gave at once before our united strength. Together we rushed into the room. It was empty. There was no furniture save a little pallet bed, a small table, and a basketful of linen. The skylight above was open, and the prisoner gone.

"There has been some villainy here," said Holmes; "this beauty has guessed Miss Hunter's intentions and has carried his victim off."

"But how?"

"Through the skylight. We shall soon see how he managed it." He swung himself up onto the roof. "Ah, yes," he cried, "here's the end of a long light ladder against the eaves. That is how he did it."

"But it is impossible," said Miss Hunter; "the ladder was not there when the Rucastles went away."

"He has come back and done it. I tell you that he is a clever and dangerous man. I should not be very much surprised if this were he whose step I hear now upon the stair. I think, Watson, that it would be as well for you to have your pistol ready."

The words were hardly out of his mouth before a man appeared at the door of the room, a very fat and burly man, with a heavy stick in his hand. Miss Hunter screamed and shrunk against the wall at the sight of him, but Sherlock Holmes sprang forward and confronted him.

"You villain!" said he, "where's your daughter?"

The fat man cast his eyes round, and then up at the open skylight.

"It is for me to ask you that," he shrieked, "you thieves! Spies and thieves! I have caught you, have I? You are in my power. I'll serve you!" He turned and clattered down the stairs as hard as he could go.

"He's gone for the dog!" cried Miss Hunter.

"I have my revolver," said I.

"Better close the front door," cried Holmes, and we all rushed down the stairs together. We had hardly reached the hall when we heard the baying of a hound, and then a scream of agony, with a horrible worrying sound which it was dreadful to listen to. An elderly man with a red face and shaking limbs came staggering out at a side door.

"My God!" he cried. "Someone has loosed the dog. It's not been fed for two days. Quick, quick, or it'll be too late!"

Holmes and I rushed out and round the angle of the house, with Toller hurrying behind us. There was the huge famished brute, its black muzzle buried in Rucastle's throat, while he writhed and screamed upon the ground. Running up, I blew its brains out, and it fell over with its keen white teeth still meeting in the great creases of his neck. With much labour we separated them and carried him, living but horribly mangled, into the house. We laid him upon the drawing-room sofa, and having dispatched the sobered Toller to bear the news to his wife, I did what I could to relieve his pain. We were all assembled round him when the door opened, and a tall, gaunt woman entered the room.

"Mrs. Toller!" cried Miss Hunter.

"Yes, miss. Mr. Rucastle let me out when he came back before he went up to you. Ah, miss, it is a pity you didn't let me know what you were planning, for I would have told you that your pains were wasted."

"Ha!" said Holmes, looking keenly at her. "It is clear that Mrs. Toller knows more about this matter than anyone else."

"Yes, sir, I do, and I am ready enough to tell what I know."

"Then, pray, sit down, and let us hear it for there are several points on which I must confess that I am still in the dark."

"I will soon make it clear to you," said she; "and I'd have done so before now if I could ha' got out from the cellar. If there's police-court business over this, you'll remember that I was the one that stood your friend, and that I was Miss Alice's friend too.

"She was never happy at home, Miss Alice wasn't, from the time that her father married again. She was slighted like and had no say in anything, but it never really became bad for her until after she met Mr. Fowler at a friend's house. As well as I could learn, Miss Alice had rights of her own by will, but she was so quiet and patient, she was, that she never said a word about them but just left everything in Mr. Rucastle's hands. He knew he was safe with her; but when there was a chance of a husband coming forward, who would ask for all that the law would give him, then her father thought it time to put a stop on it. He wanted her to sign a paper, so that whether she married or not, he could use her money. When she wouldn't do it, he kept on worrying her until she got brain-fever, and for six weeks was at death's door. Then she got better at last, all worn to a shadow, and with her beautiful hair cut off; but that didn't make no change in her young man, and he stuck to her as true as man could be."

"Ah," said Holmes, "I think that what you have been good enough to tell us makes the matter fairly clear, and that I can deduce all that remains. Mr. Rucastle then, I presume, took to this system of imprisonment?"

"Yes, sir."

"And brought Miss Hunter down from London in order to get rid of the disagreeable persistence of Mr. Fowler."

"That was it, sir."

"But Mr. Fowler being a persevering man, as a good seaman should be, blockaded the house, and having met you succeeded by certain arguments, metallic or otherwise, in convincing you that your interests were the same as his."

"Mr. Fowler was a very kind-spoken, free-handed gentleman," said Mrs. Toller serenely.

"And in this way he managed that your good man should have no want of drink, and that a ladder should be ready at the moment when your master had gone out."

"You have it, sir, just as it happened."

"I am sure we owe you an apology, Mrs. Toller," said Holmes, "for you have certainly cleared up everything which puzzled us. And here comes the country surgeon and Mrs. Rucastle, so I think. Watson, that we had best escort Miss Hunter back to Winchester, as it seems to me that our *locus standi* now is rather a questionable one."

And thus was solved the mystery of the sinister house with the copper beeches in front of the door. Mr. Rucastle survived, but was always a broken man, kept alive solely through the care of his devoted wife. They still live with their old servants, who probably know so much of Rucastle's past life that he finds it difficult to part from them. Mr. Fowler and Miss Rucastle were married, by special license, in Southampton the day after their flight, and he is now the holder of a government appointment in the island of Mauritius. As to Miss Violet Hunter, my friend Holmes, rather to my disappointment, manifested no further interest in her when once she had ceased to be the centre of one of his problems, and she is now the head of a private school at Walsall, where I believe that she has met with considerable success.

If you enjoyed this, you might also like...
Who Killed Zebedee?, see page 71
Brother Owen's Story of Anne Rodway, see page 345

The Death of the Lion

Henry James

Chapter I

I HAD SIMPLY, I suppose, a change of heart, and it must have begun when I received my manuscript back from Mr. Pinhorn. Mr. Pinhorn was my "chief," as he was called in the office: he had the high mission of bringing the paper up. This was a weekly periodical, which had been supposed to be almost past redemption when he took hold of it. It was Mr. Deedy who had let the thing down so dreadfully: he was never mentioned in the office now save in connexion with that misdemeanour. Young as I was I had been in a manner taken over from Mr. Deedy, who had been owner as well as editor; forming part of a promiscuous lot, mainly plant and office-furniture, which poor Mrs. Deedy, in her bereavement and depression, parted with at a rough valuation. I could account for my continuity but on the supposition that I had been cheap. I rather resented the practice of fathering all flatness on my late protector, who was in his unhonoured grave; but as I had my way to make I found matter enough for complacency in being on a "staff." At the same time I was aware of my exposure to suspicion as a product of the old lowering system. This made me feel I was doubly bound to have ideas, and had doubtless been at the bottom of my proposing to Mr. Pinhorn that I should lay my lean hands on Neil Paraday. I remember how he looked at me – quite, to begin with, as if he had never heard of this celebrity, who indeed at that moment was by no means in the centre of the heavens; and even when I had knowingly explained he expressed but little confidence in the demand for any such stuff. When I had reminded him that the great principle on which we were supposed to work was just to create the demand we required, he considered a moment and then returned: "I see – you want to write him up."

"Call it that if you like."

"And what's your inducement?"

"Bless my soul – my admiration!"

Mr. Pinhorn pursed up his mouth. "Is there much to be done with him?"

"Whatever there is we should have it all to ourselves, for he hasn't been touched."

This argument was effective and Mr. Pinhorn responded. "Very well, touch him." Then he added: "But where can you do it?"

"Under the fifth rib!"

Mr. Pinhorn stared. "Where's that?"

"You want me to go down and see him?" I asked when I had enjoyed his visible search for the obscure suburb I seemed to have named.

"I don't 'want' anything – the proposal's your own. But you must remember that that's the way we do things *now*," said Mr. Pinhorn with another dig Mr. Deedy.

Unregenerate as I was I could read the queer implications of this speech. The present owner's superior virtue as well as his deeper craft spoke in his reference to the late editor as one of that baser sort who deal in false representations. Mr. Deedy would as soon have sent me to call on Neil Paraday as he would have published a "holiday-number"; but such scruples presented themselves as mere ignoble thrift to his successor, whose own sincerity took the form of ringing door-bells and whose definition of genius was the art of finding people at home. It was as if Mr. Deedy had published reports without his young men's having, as Pinhorn would have said, really been there. I was unregenerate, as I have hinted, and couldn't be concerned to straighten out the journalistic morals of my chief, feeling them indeed to be an abyss over the edge of which it was better not to peer. Really to be there this time moreover was a vision that made the idea of writing something subtle about Neil Paraday only the more inspiring. I would be as considerate as even Mr. Deedy could have wished, and yet I should be as present as only Mr. Pinhorn could conceive. My allusion to the sequestered manner in which Mr. Paraday lived – it had formed part of my explanation, though I knew of it only by hearsay – was, I could divine, very much what had made Mr. Pinhorn nibble. It struck him as inconsistent with the success of his paper that any one should be so sequestered as that. And then wasn't an immediate exposure of everything just what the public wanted? Mr. Pinhorn effectually called me to order by reminding me of the promptness with which I had met Miss Braby at Liverpool on her return from her fiasco in the States. Hadn't we published, while its freshness and flavour were unimpaired, Miss Braby's own version of that great international episode? I felt somewhat uneasy at this lumping of the actress and the author, and I confess that after having enlisted Mr. Pinhorn's sympathies I procrastinated a little. I had succeeded better than I wished, and I had, as it happened, work nearer at hand. A few days later I called on Lord Crouchley and carried off in triumph the most unintelligible statement that had yet appeared of his lordship's reasons for his change of front. I thus set in motion in the daily papers columns of virtuous verbiage. The following week I ran down to Brighton for a chat, as Mr. Pinhorn called it, with Mrs. Bounder, who gave me, on the subject of her divorce, many curious particulars that had not been articulated in court. If ever an article flowed from the primal fount it was that article on Mrs. Bounder. By this time, however, I became aware that Neil Paraday's new book was on the point of appearing and that its approach had been the ground of my original appeal to Mr. Pinhorn, who was now annoyed with me for having lost so many days. He bundled me off – we would at least not lose another. I've always thought his sudden alertness a remarkable example of the journalistic instinct. Nothing had occurred, since I first spoke to him, to create a visible urgency, and no enlightenment could possibly have reached him. It was a pure case of profession flair – he had smelt the coming glory as an animal smells its distant prey.

Chapter II

I MAY AS WELL say at once that this little record pretends in no degree to be a picture either of my introduction to Mr. Paraday or of certain proximate steps and stages. The scheme of my narrative allows no space for these things, and in any case a prohibitory sentiment would hang about my recollection of so rare an hour. These meagre notes are essentially private, so that if they see the light the insidious forces that, as my story itself shows, make at present for publicity will simply have overmastered my precautions. The curtain fell lately enough on the lamentable drama. My memory of the day I alighted at Mr. Paraday's door is a fresh memory of kindness, hospitality, compassion, and of the wonderful illuminating talk in which the welcome was conveyed. Some voice of the air had taught me the right moment, the moment of his life at which an act of unexpected young allegiance might most come home to him. He had recently recovered from a long, grave illness. I had gone to the neighbouring inn for the night, but I spent the evening in his company, and he insisted the next day on my sleeping under his roof. I hadn't an indefinite leave: Mr. Pinhorn supposed us to put our victims through on the gallop. It was later, in the office, that the rude motions of the jig were set to music. I fortified myself, however, as my training had taught me to do, by the conviction that nothing could be more advantageous for my article than to be written in the very atmosphere. I said nothing to Mr. Paraday about it, but in the morning, after my remove from the inn, while he was occupied in his study, as he had notified me he should need to be, I committed to paper the main heads of my impression. Then thinking to commend myself to Mr. Pinhorn by my celerity, I walked out and posted my little packet before luncheon. Once my paper was written I was free to stay on, and if it was calculated to divert attention from my levity in so doing I could reflect with satisfaction that I had never been so clever. I don't mean to deny of course that I was aware it was much too good for Mr. Pinhorn; but I was equally conscious that Mr. Pinhorn had the supreme shrewdness of recognising from time to time the cases in which an article was not too bad only because it was too good. There was nothing he loved so much as to print on the right occasion a thing he hated. I had begun my visit to the great man on a Monday, and on the Wednesday his book came out. A copy of it arrived by the first post, and he let me go out into the garden with it immediately after breakfast, I read it from beginning to end that day, and in the evening he asked me to remain with him the rest of the week and over the Sunday.

That night my manuscript came back from Mr. Pinhorn, accompanied with a letter the gist of which was the desire to know what I meant by trying to fob off on him such stuff. That was the meaning of the question, if not exactly its form, and it made my mistake immense to me. Such as this mistake was I could now only look it in the face and accept it. I knew where I had failed, but it was exactly where I couldn't have succeeded. I had been sent down to be personal and then in point of fact hadn't been personal at all: what I had dispatched to London was just a little finicking feverish study of my author's talent. Anything less relevant to Mr. Pinhorn's purpose couldn't well be imagined, and he was visibly angry at my having (at his expense, with a second-class ticket) approached the subject of our enterprise only to stand off so helplessly. For myself, I knew but too well what had happened, and how a miracle – as pretty as some old miracle of legend – had been wrought on the spot to save me. There had been a big brush of wings, the flash of an opaline robe, and then, with a great cool stir of the air, the sense of an angel's having swooped down and caught me to his bosom. He held me only till the danger was over, and it all took place in a minute. With my manuscript back on my hands I understood the phenomenon better, and the reflexions I made on it are what I meant, at the beginning of this anecdote, by my change of heart. Mr. Pinhorn's note was not only a rebuke decidedly stern, but an invitation immediately to send him – it was the case to say so – the genuine article, the revealing and reverberating sketch to the promise of which, and of which alone, I owed my squandered privilege. A week or two later I recast my peccant paper and, giving it a particular application to Mr. Paraday's new book, obtained for it the hospitality of another journal, where, I must admit, Mr. Pinhorn was so far vindicated as that it attracted not the least attention.

Chapter III

I WAS FRANKLY, at the end of three days, a very prejudiced critic, so that one morning when, in the garden, my great man had offered to read me something I quite held my breath as I listened. It was the written scheme of another book – something put aside long ago, before his illness, but that he had lately taken out again to reconsider. He had been turning it round when I came down on him, and it had grown magnificently under this second hand. Loose liberal confident, it might have passed for a great gossiping eloquent letter – the overflow into talk of an artist's amorous plan. The theme I thought singularly rich, quite the strongest he had yet treated; and this familiar statement of it, full too of fine maturities, was really, in summarised splendour, a mine of gold, a precious independent work. I remember rather profanely wondering whether the ultimate production could possibly keep at the pitch. His reading of the fond epistle, at any rate, made me feel as if I were, for the advantage of posterity, in close correspondence with him – were the distinguished person to whom it had been affectionately addressed. It was a high distinction simply to be told such things. The idea he now communicated had all the freshness, the flushed fairness, of the conception untouched and untried: it was Venus rising from the sea and before the airs had blown upon her. I had never been so throbbingly present at such an unveiling. But when he had tossed the last bright word after the others, as I had seen cashiers in banks, weighing mounds of coin, drop a final sovereign into the tray, I knew a sudden prudent alarm.

"My dear master, how, after all, are you going to do it? It's infinitely noble, but what time it will take, what patience and independence, what assured, what perfect conditions! Oh for a lone isle in a tepid sea!"

"Isn't this practically a lone isle, and aren't you, as an encircling medium, tepid enough?" he asked, alluding with a laugh to the wonder of my young admiration and the narrow limits of his little provincial home. "Time isn't what I've lacked hitherto: the question hasn't been to find it, but to use it. Of course my illness made, while it lasted, a great hole – but I dare say there would have been a hole at any rate. The earth we tread has more pockets than a billiard-table. The great thing is now to keep on my feet."

"That's exactly what I mean."

Neil Paraday looked at me with eyes – such pleasant eyes as he had – in which, as I now recall their expression, I seem to have seen a dim imagination of his fate. He was fifty years old, and his illness had been cruel, his convalescence slow. "It isn't as if I weren't all right."

"Oh if you weren't all right I wouldn't look at you!" I tenderly said.

We had both got up, quickened as by this clearer air, and he had lighted a cigarette. I had taken a fresh one, which with an intenser smile, by way of answer to my exclamation, he applied to the flame of his match. "If I weren't better I shouldn't have thought of *that*!" He flourished his script in his hand.

"I don't want to be discouraging, but that's not true," I returned. "I'm sure that during the months you lay here in pain you had visitations sublime. You thought of a thousand things. You think of more and more all the while. That's what makes you, if you'll pardon my familiarity, so respectable. At a time when so many people are spent you come into your second wind. But, thank God, all the same, you're better! Thank God, too, you're not, as you were telling me yesterday, 'successful.' If *you* weren't a failure what would be the use of trying? That's my one reserve on the subject of your recovery

– that it makes you 'score,' as the newspapers say. It looks well in the newspapers, and almost anything that does that's horrible. 'We are happy to announce that Mr. Paraday, the celebrated author, is again in the enjoyment of excellent health.' Somehow I shouldn't like to see it."

"You won't see it; I'm not in the least celebrated – my obscurity protects me. But couldn't you bear even to see I was dying or dead?" my host enquired.

"Dead – passe encore; there's nothing so safe. One never knows what a living artist may do – one has mourned so many. However, one must make the worst of it. You must be as dead as you can."

"Don't I meet that condition in having just published a book?"

"Adequately, let us hope; for the book's verily a masterpiece."

At this moment the parlour-maid appeared in the door that opened from the garden: Paraday lived at no great cost, and the frisk of petticoats, with a timorous "Sherry, sir?" was about his modest mahogany. He allowed half his income to his wife, from whom he had succeeded in separating without redundancy of legend. I had a general faith in his having behaved well, and I had once, in London, taken Mrs. Paraday down to dinner. He now turned to speak to the maid, who offered him, on a tray, some card or note, while, agitated, excited, I wandered to the end of the precinct. The idea of his security became supremely dear to me, and I asked myself if I were the same young man who had come down a few days before to scatter him to the four winds. When I retraced my steps he had gone into the house, and the woman – the second London post had come in – had placed my letters and a newspaper on a bench. I sat down there to the letters, which were a brief business, and then, without heeding the address, took the paper from its envelope. It was the journal of highest renown, *The Empire* of that morning. It regularly came to Paraday, but I remembered that neither of us had yet looked at the copy already delivered. This one had a great mark on the "editorial" page, and, uncrumpling the wrapper, I saw it to be directed to my host and stamped with the name of his publishers. I instantly divined that *The Empire* had spoken of him, and I've not forgotten the odd little shock of the circumstance. It checked all eagerness and made me drop the paper a moment. As I sat there conscious of a palpitation I think I had a vision of what was to be. I had also a vision of the letter I would presently address to Mr. Pinhorn, breaking, as it were, with Mr. Pinhorn. Of course, however, the next minute the voice of *The Empire* was in my ears.

The article wasn't, I thanked heaven, a review; it was a "leader," the last of three, presenting Neil Paraday to the human race. His new book, the fifth from his hand, had been but a day or two out, and *The Empire*, already aware of it, fired, as if on the birth of a prince, a salute of a whole column. The guns had been booming these three hours in the house without our suspecting them. The big blundering newspaper had discovered him, and now he was proclaimed and anointed and crowned. His place was assigned him as publicly as if a fat usher with a wand had pointed to the topmost chair; he was to pass up and still up, higher and higher, between the watching faces and the envious sounds – away up to the dais and the throne. The article was "epoch-making," a landmark in his life; he had taken rank at a bound, waked up a national glory. A national glory was needed, and it was an immense convenience he was there. What all this meant rolled over me, and I fear I grew a little faint – it meant so much more than I could say "yea" to on the spot. In a flash, somehow, all was different; the tremendous wave I speak of had swept something away. It had knocked down, I suppose, my little customary altar, my twinkling tapers and my flowers, and had reared itself into the likeness of a temple vast and bare. When Neil Paraday should come out of the house he would come out a contemporary. That was what had happened: the poor man was to be squeezed into his horrible age. I felt as if he had been overtaken on the crest of the hill and brought back to the city. A little more and he would have dipped down the short cut to posterity and escaped.

Chapter IV

WHEN HE CAME OUT it was exactly as if he had been in custody, for beside him walked a stout man with a big black beard, who, save that he wore spectacles, might have been a policeman, and in whom at a second glance I recognised the highest contemporary enterprise.

"This is Mr. Morrow," said Paraday, looking, I thought, rather white: "he wants to publish heaven knows what about me."

I winced as I remembered that this was exactly what I myself had wanted. "Already?" I cried with a sort of sense that my friend had fled to me for protection.

Mr. Morrow glared, agreeably, through his glasses: they suggested the electric headlights of some monstrous modern ship, and I felt as if Paraday and I were tossing terrified under his bows. I saw his momentum was irresistible. "I was confident that I should be the first in the field. A great interest is naturally felt in Mr. Paraday's surroundings," he heavily observed.

"I hadn't the least idea of it," said Paraday, as if he had been told he had been snoring.

"I find he hasn't read the article in *The Empire*," Mr. Morrow remarked to me. "That's so very interesting – it's something to start with," he smiled. He had begun to pull off his gloves, which were violently new, and to look encouragingly round the little garden. As a "surrounding" I felt how I myself had already been taken in; I was a little fish in the stomach of a bigger one. "I represent," our visitor continued, "a syndicate of influential journals, no less than thirty-seven, whose public – whose publics, I may say – are in peculiar sympathy with Mr. Paraday's line of thought. They would greatly appreciate any expression of his views on the subject of the art he so nobly exemplifies. In addition to my connexion with the syndicate just mentioned I hold a particular commission from *The Tatler*, whose most prominent department, 'Smatter and Chatter' – I dare say you've often enjoyed it – attracts such attention. I was honoured only last week, as a representative of *The Tatler*, with the confidence of Guy Walsingham, the brilliant author of 'Obsessions.' She pronounced herself thoroughly pleased with my sketch of her method; she went so far as to say that I had made her genius more comprehensible even to herself."

Neil Paraday had dropped on the garden-bench and sat there at once detached and confounded; he looked hard at a bare spot in the lawn, as if with an anxiety that had suddenly made him grave. His movement had been interpreted by his visitor as an invitation to sink sympathetically into a wicker chair that stood hard by, and while Mr. Morrow so settled himself I felt he had taken official possession and that there was no undoing it. One had heard of unfortunate people's having "a man in the house," and this was just what we had. There was a silence of a moment, during which we seemed to acknowledge in the only way that was possible the presence of universal fate; the sunny stillness took no pity, and my thought, as I was sure Paraday's was doing, performed within the minute a great distant revolution. I saw just how emphatic I should make my rejoinder to Mr. Pinhorn, and that having come, like Mr. Morrow, to betray, I must remain as long as possible to save. Not because I had brought my mind back, but because our visitors last words were in my ear, I presently enquired with gloomy irrelevance if Guy Walsingham were a woman.

"Oh yes, a mere pseudonym – rather pretty, isn't it? – and convenient, you know, for a lady who goes in for the larger latitude. 'Obsessions, by Miss So-and-so,' would look a little odd, but men are more naturally indelicate. Have you peeped into 'Obsessions'?" Mr. Morrow continued sociably to our companion.

Paraday, still absent, remote, made no answer, as if he hadn't heard the question: a form of intercourse that appeared to suit the cheerful Mr. Morrow as well as any other. Imperturbably bland, he was a man of resources – he only needed to be on the spot. He had pocketed the whole poor place while Paraday and I were wool-gathering, and I could imagine that he had already got his "heads." His system, at any rate, was justified by the inevitability with which I replied, to save my friend the trouble: "Dear no – he hasn't read it. He doesn't read such things!" I unwarily added.

"Things that are *too* far over the fence, eh?" I was indeed a godsend to Mr. Morrow. It was the psychological moment; it determined the appearance of his note-book, which, however, he at first kept slightly behind him, even as the dentist approaching his victim keeps the horrible forceps. "Mr. Paraday holds with the good old proprieties – I see!" And thinking of the thirty-seven influential journals, I found myself, as I found poor Paraday, helplessly assisting at the promulgation of this ineptitude. "There's no point on which distinguished views are so acceptable as on this question – raised perhaps more strikingly than ever by Guy Walsingham – of the permissibility of the larger latitude. I've an appointment, precisely in connexion with it, next week, with Dora Forbes, author of 'The Other Way Round,' which everybody's talking about. Has Mr. Paraday glanced at 'The Other Way Round'?" Mr. Morrow now frankly appealed to me. I took on myself to repudiate the supposition, while our companion, still silent, got up nervously and walked away. His visitor paid no heed to his withdrawal; but opened out the note-book with a more fatherly pat. "Dora Forbes, I gather, takes the ground, the same as Guy Walsingham's, that the larger latitude has simply got to come. He holds that it has got to be squarely faced. Of course his sex makes him a less prejudiced witness. But an authoritative word from Mr. Paraday – from the point of view of *his* sex, you know – would go right round the globe. He takes the line that we *haven't* got to face it?"

I was bewildered: it sounded somehow as if there were three sexes. My interlocutor's pencil was poised, my private responsibility great. I simply sat staring, none the less, and only found presence of mind to say: "Is this Miss Forbes a gentleman?"

Mr. Morrow had a subtle smile. "It wouldn't be 'Miss' – there's a wife!"

"I mean is she a man?"

"The wife?" – Mr. Morrow was for a moment as confused as myself. But when I explained that I alluded to Dora Forbes in person he informed me, with visible amusement at my being so out of it, that this was the "pen-name" of an indubitable male – he had a big red moustache. "He goes in for the slight mystification because the ladies are such popular favourites. A great deal of interest is felt in his acting on that idea – which *is* clever, isn't it? – and there's every prospect of its being widely imitated." Our host at this moment joined us again, and Mr. Morrow remarked invitingly that he should be happy to make a note of any observation the movement in question, the bid for success under a lady's name, might suggest to Mr. Paraday. But the poor man, without catching the allusion, excused himself, pleading that, though greatly honoured by his visitor's interest, he suddenly felt unwell and should have to take leave of him – have to go and lie down and keep quiet. His young friend might be trusted to answer for him, but he hoped Mr. Morrow didn't expect great things even of his young friend. His young friend, at this moment, looked at Neil Paraday with an anxious eye, greatly wondering if he were doomed to be ill again; but Paraday's own kind face met his question reassuringly, seemed to say in a glance intelligible enough: "Oh I'm not ill, but I'm scared: get him out of the house as quietly as possible." Getting newspaper-men out of the house was odd business for an emissary of Mr. Pinhorn, and I was so exhilarated by the idea of it that I called after him as he left us: "Read the article in *The Empire* and you'll soon be all right!"

Chapter V

"**DELICIOUS MY HAVING** come down to tell him of it!" Mr. Morrow ejaculated. "My cab was at the door twenty minutes after *The Empire* had been laid on my breakfast-table. Now what have you got for me?" he continued, dropping again into his chair, from which, however, he the next moment eagerly rose. "I was shown into the drawing-room, but there must be more to see – his study, his literary sanctum, the little things he has about, or other domestic objects and features. He wouldn't be lying down on his study-table? There's a great interest always felt in the scene of an author's labours. Sometimes we're favoured with very delightful peeps. Dora Forbes showed me all his table-drawers, and almost jammed my hand into one into which I made a dash! I don't ask that of you, but if we could talk things over right there where he sits I feel as if I should get the keynote."

I had no wish whatever to be rude to Mr. Morrow, I was much too initiated not to tend to more diplomacy; but I had a quick inspiration, and I entertained an insurmountable, an almost superstitious objection to his crossing the threshold of my friend's little lonely shabby consecrated workshop. "No, no – we shan't get at his life that way," I said. "The way to get at his life is to – But wait a moment!" I broke off and went quickly into the house, whence I in three minutes reappeared before Mr. Morrow with the two volumes of Paraday's new book. "His life's here," I went on, "and I'm so full of this admirable thing that I can't talk of anything else. The artist's life's his work, and this is the place to observe him. What he has to tell us he tells us with *this* perfection. My dear sir, the best interviewer is the best reader."

Mr. Morrow good-humouredly protested. "Do you mean to say that no other source of information should be open to us?"

"None other till this particular one – by far the most copious – has been quite exhausted. Have you exhausted it, my dear sir? Had you exhausted it when you came down here? It seems to me in our time almost wholly neglected, and something should surely be done to restore its ruined credit. It's the course to which the artist himself at every step, and with such pathetic confidence, refers us. This last book of Mr. Paraday's is full of revelations."

"Revelations?" panted Mr. Morrow, whom I had forced again into his chair.

"The only kind that count. It tells you with a perfection that seems to me quite final all the author thinks, for instance, about the advent of the 'larger latitude.'"

"Where does it do that?" asked Mr. Morrow, who had picked up the second volume and was insincerely thumbing it.

"Everywhere – in the whole treatment of his case. Extract the opinion, disengage the answer – those are the real acts of homage."

Mr. Morrow, after a minute, tossed the book away. "Ah but you mustn't take me for a reviewer."

"Heaven forbid I should take you for anything so dreadful! You came down to perform a little act of sympathy, and so, I may confide to you, did I. Let us perform our little act together. These pages overflow with the testimony we want: let us read them and taste them and interpret them. You'll of course have perceived for yourself that one scarcely does read Neil Paraday till one reads him aloud; he gives out to the ear an extraordinary full tone, and it's only when you expose it confidently to that test that you really get near his style. Take up your book again and let me listen, while you pay it out, to that wonderful fifteenth chapter. If you feel you can't do it justice, compose yourself to attention while I produce for you – I think I can! – this scarcely less admirable ninth."

Mr. Morrow gave me a straight look which was as hard as a blow between the eyes; he had turned rather red, and a question had formed itself in his mind which reached my sense as distinctly as if he had uttered it: "What sort of a damned fool are *you*?" Then he got up, gathering together his hat and gloves, buttoning his coat, projecting hungrily all over the place the big transparency of his mask. It seemed to flare over Fleet Street and somehow made the actual spot distressingly humble: there was so little for it to feed on unless he counted the blisters of our stucco or saw his way to do something with the roses. Even the poor roses were common kinds. Presently his eyes fell on the manuscript from which Paraday had been reading to me and which still lay on the bench. As my own followed them I saw it looked promising, looked pregnant, as if it gently throbbed with the life the reader had given it. Mr. Morrow indulged in a nod at it and a vague thrust of his umbrella. "What's that?"

"Oh, it's a plan – a secret."

"A secret!" There was an instant's silence, and then Mr. Morrow made another movement. I may have been mistaken, but it affected me as the translated impulse of the desire to lay hands on the manuscript, and this led me to indulge in a quick anticipatory grab which may very well have seemed ungraceful, or even impertinent, and which at any rate left Mr. Paraday's two admirers very erect, glaring at each other while one of them held a bundle of papers well behind him. An instant later Mr. Morrow quitted me abruptly, as if he had really carried something off with him. To reassure myself, watching his broad back recede, I only grasped my manuscript the tighter. He went to the back door of the house, the one he had come out from, but on trying the handle he appeared to find it fastened. So he passed round into the front garden, and by listening intently enough I could presently hear the outer gate close behind him with a bang. I thought again of the thirty-seven influential journals and wondered what would be his revenge. I hasten to add that he was magnanimous: which was just the most dreadful thing he could have been. *The Tatler* published a charming chatty familiar account of Mr. Paraday's "Home-life," and on the wings of the thirty-seven influential journals it went, to use Mr. Morrow's own expression, right round the globe.

Chapter VI

A WEEK LATER, early in May, my glorified friend came up to town, where, it may be veraciously recorded he was the king of the beasts of the year. No advancement was ever more rapid, no exaltation more complete, no bewilderment more teachable. His book sold but moderately, though the article in *The Empire* had done unwonted wonders for it; but he circulated in person to a measure that the libraries might well have envied. His formula had been found – he was a "revelation." His momentary terror had been real, just as mine had been – the overclouding of his passionate desire to be left to finish his work. He was far from unsociable, but he had the finest conception of being let alone that I've ever met. For the time, none the less, he took his profit where it seemed most to crowd on him, having in his pocket the portable sophistries about the nature of the artist's task. Observation too was a kind of work and experience a kind of success; London dinners were all material and London ladies were fruitful toil. "No one has the faintest conception of what I'm trying for," he said to me, "and not many have read three pages that I've written; but I must dine with them first – they'll find out why when they've time." It was rather rude justice perhaps; but the fatigue had the merit of being a new sort, while the phantasmagoric town was probably after all less of a battlefield than the haunted study. He once told me that he had had no personal life to speak of since his fortieth year, but had had more than was good for him before. London closed the parenthesis and exhibited him in relations; one of the most inevitable of these being that in which he found himself to Mrs. Weeks Wimbush, wife of the boundless brewer and proprietress of the universal menagerie. In this establishment, as everybody knows, on occasions when the crush is great, the animals rub shoulders freely with the spectators and the lions sit down for whole evenings with the lambs.

It had been ominously clear to me from the first that in Neil Paraday this lady, who, as all the world agreed, was tremendous fun, considered that she had secured a prime attraction, a creature of almost heraldic oddity. Nothing could exceed her enthusiasm over her capture, and nothing could exceed the confused apprehensions it excited in me. I had an instinctive fear of her which I tried without effect to conceal from her victim, but which I let her notice with perfect impunity. Paraday heeded it, but she never did, for her conscience was that of a romping child. She was a blind violent force to which I could attach no more idea of responsibility than to the creaking of a sign in the wind. It was difficult to say what she conduced to but circulation. She was constructed of steel and leather, and all I asked of her for our tractable friend was not to do him to death. He had consented for a time to be of india-rubber, but my thoughts were fixed on the day he should resume his shape or at least get back into his box. It was evidently all right, but I should be glad when it was well over. I had a special fear – the impression was ineffaceable of the hour when, after Mr. Morrow's departure, I had found him on the sofa in his study. That pretext of indisposition had not in the least been meant as a snub to the envoy of *The Tatler* – he had gone to lie down in very truth. He had felt a pang of his old pain, the result of the agitation wrought in him by this forcing open of a new period. His old programme, his old ideal even had to be changed. Say what one would, success was a complication and recognition had to be reciprocal. The monastic life, the pious illumination of the missal in the convent cell were things of the gathered past. It didn't engender despair, but at least it required adjustment. Before

I left him on that occasion we had passed a bargain, my part of which was that I should make it my business to take care of him. Let whoever would represent the interest in his presence (I must have had a mystical prevision of Mrs. Weeks Wimbush) I should represent the interest in his work – or otherwise expressed in his absence. These two interests were in their essence opposed; and I doubt, as youth is fleeting, if I shall ever again know the intensity of joy with which I felt that in so good a cause I was willing to make myself odious.

One day in Sloane Street I found myself questioning Paraday's landlord, who had come to the door in answer to my knock. Two vehicles, a barouche and a smart hansom, were drawn up before the house.

"In the drawing-room, sir? Mrs. Weeks Wimbush."

"And in the dining-room?"

"A young lady, sir – waiting: I think a foreigner."

It was three o'clock, and on days when Paraday didn't lunch out he attached a value to these appropriated hours. On which days, however, didn't the dear man lunch out? Mrs. Wimbush, at such a crisis, would have rushed round immediately after her own repast. I went into the dining-room first, postponing the pleasure of seeing how, upstairs, the lady of the barouche would, on my arrival, point the moral of my sweet solicitude. No one took such an interest as herself in his doing only what was good for him, and she was always on the spot to see that he did it. She made appointments with him to discuss the best means of economising his time and protecting his privacy. She further made his health her special business, and had so much sympathy with my own zeal for it that she was the author of pleasing fictions on the subject of what my devotion had led me to give up. I gave up nothing (I don't count Mr. Pinhorn) because I had nothing, and all I had as yet achieved was to find myself also in the menagerie. I had dashed in to save my friend, but I had only got domesticated and wedged; so that I could do little more for him than exchange with him over people's heads looks of intense but futile intelligence.

Chapter VII

THE YOUNG LADY in the dining-room had a brave face, black hair, blue eyes, and in her lap a big volume. "I've come for his autograph," she said when I had explained to her that I was under bonds to see people for him when he was occupied. "I've been waiting half an hour, but I'm prepared to wait all day." I don't know whether it was this that told me she was American, for the propensity to wait all day is not in general characteristic of her race. I was enlightened probably not so much by the spirit of the utterance as by some quality of its sound. At any rate I saw she had an individual patience and a lovely frock, together with an expression that played among her pretty features like a breeze among flowers. Putting her book on the table she showed me a massive album, showily bound and full of autographs of price. The collection of faded notes, of still more faded "thoughts," of quotations, platitudes, signatures, represented a formidable purpose.

I could only disclose my dread of it. "Most people apply to Mr. Paraday by letter, you know."

"Yes, but he doesn't answer. I've written three times."

"Very true," I reflected; "the sort of letter you mean goes straight into the fire."

"How do you know the sort I mean?" My interlocutress had blushed and smiled, and in a moment she added: "I don't believe he gets many like them!"

"I'm sure they're beautiful, but he burns without reading." I didn't add that I had convinced him he ought to.

"Isn't he then in danger of burning things of importance?"

"He would perhaps be so if distinguished men hadn't an infallible nose for nonsense."

She looked at me a moment – her face was sweet and gay. "Do *you* burn without reading too?" – in answer to which I assured her that if she'd trust me with her repository I'd see that Mr. Paraday should write his name in it.

She considered a little. "That's very well, but it wouldn't make me see him."

"Do you want very much to see him?" It seemed ungracious to catechise so charming a creature, but somehow I had never yet taken my duty to the great author so seriously.

"Enough to have come from America for the purpose."

I stared. "All alone?"

"I don't see that that's exactly your business, but if it will make me more seductive I'll confess that I'm quite by myself. I had to come alone or not come at all."

She was interesting; I could imagine she had lost parents, natural protectors – could conceive even she had inherited money. I was at a pass of my own fortunes when keeping hansoms at doors seemed to me pure swagger. As a trick of this bold and sensitive girl, however, it became romantic – a part of the general romance of her freedom, her errand, her innocence. The confidence of young Americans was notorious, and I speedily arrived at a conviction that no impulse could have been more generous than the impulse that had operated here. I foresaw at that moment that it would make her my peculiar charge, just as circumstances had made Neil Paraday. She would be another person to look after, so that one's honour would be concerned in guiding her straight. These things became clearer to me later on; at the instant I had scepticism enough to observe to her, as I turned the pages of her volume, that her net had all the same caught many a big fish. She appeared to have had fruitful access to the great ones of the earth; there were people moreover whose signatures she had presumably secured without a personal interview. She couldn't have worried George Washington and Friedrich Schiller and Hannah More. She met this argument, to my surprise, by throwing up the album without a pang. It wasn't even her own; she was responsible for none of its treasures. It belonged to a girl-friend in America, a young lady in a western city. This young lady had insisted on her bringing it, to pick up more autographs: she thought they might like to see, in Europe, in what company they would be. The "girl-friend," the western city, the immortal names, the curious errand, the idyllic faith, all made a story as strange to me, and as beguiling, as some tale in the Arabian Nights. Thus it was that my informant had encumbered herself with the ponderous tome; but she hastened to assure me that this was the first time she had brought it out. For her visit to Mr. Paraday it had simply been a pretext. She didn't really care a straw that he should write his name; what she did want was to look straight into his face.

I demurred a little. "And why do you require to do that?"

"Because I just love him!" Before I could recover from the agitating effect of this crystal ring my companion had continued: "Hasn't there ever been any face that you've wanted to look into?"

How could I tell her so soon how much I appreciated the opportunity of looking into hers? I could only assent in general to the proposition that there were certainly for every one such yearnings, and even such faces; and I felt the crisis demand all my lucidity, all my wisdom. "Oh yes, I'm a student of physiognomy. Do you mean," I pursued, "that you've a passion for Mr. Paraday's books?"

"They've been everything to me and a little more beside – I know them by heart. They've completely taken hold of me. There's no author about whom I'm in such a state as I'm in about Neil Paraday."

"Permit me to remark then," I presently returned, "that you're one of the right sort."

"One of the enthusiasts? Of course I am!"

"Oh there are enthusiasts who are quite of the wrong. I mean you're one of those to whom an appeal can be made."

"An appeal?" Her face lighted as if with the chance of some great sacrifice.

If she was ready for one it was only waiting for her, and in a moment I mentioned it. "Give up this crude purpose of seeing him! Go away without it. That will be far better."

She looked mystified, then turned visibly pale. "Why, hasn't he any personal charm?" The girl was terrible and laughable in her bright directness.

"Ah that dreadful word 'personally'!" I wailed; "we're dying of it, for you women bring it out with murderous effect. When you meet with a genius as fine as this idol of ours let him off the dreary duty of being a personality as well. Know him only by what's best in him and spare him for the same sweet sake."

My young lady continued to look at me in confusion and mistrust, and the result of her reflexion on what I had just said was to make her suddenly break out: "Look here, sir – what's the matter with him?"

"The matter with him is that if he doesn't look out people will eat a great hole in his life."

She turned it over. "He hasn't any disfigurement?"

"Nothing to speak of!"

"Do you mean that social engagements interfere with his occupations?"

"That but feebly expresses it."

"So that he can't give himself up to his beautiful imagination?"

"He's beset, badgered, bothered – he's pulled to pieces on the pretext of being applauded. People expect him to give them his time, his golden time, who wouldn't themselves give five shillings for one of his books."

"Five? I'd give five thousand!"

"Give your sympathy – give your forbearance. Two-thirds of those who approach him only do it to advertise themselves."

"Why it's too bad!" the girl exclaimed with the face of an angel. "It's the first time I was ever called crude!" she laughed.

I followed up my advantage. "There's a lady with him now who's a terrible complication, and who yet hasn't read, I'm sure, ten pages he ever wrote."

My visitor's wide eyes grew tenderer. "Then how does she talk – ?"

"Without ceasing. I only mention her as a single case. Do you want to know how to show a superlative consideration? Simply avoid him."

"Avoid him?" she despairingly breathed.

"Don't force him to have to take account of you; admire him in silence, cultivate him at a distance and secretly appropriate his message. Do you want to know," I continued, warming to my idea, "how to perform an act of homage really sublime?" Then as she hung on my words: "Succeed in never seeing him at all!"

"Never at all?" – she suppressed a shriek for it.

"The more you get into his writings the less you'll want to, and you'll be immensely sustained by the thought of the good you're doing him."

She looked at me without resentment or spite, and at the truth I had put before her with candour, credulity, pity. I was afterwards happy to remember that she must have gathered from my face the liveliness of my interest in herself. "I think I see what you mean."

"Oh I express it badly, but I should be delighted if you'd let me come to see you – to explain it better."

She made no response to this, and her thoughtful eyes fell on the big album, on which she presently laid her hands as if to take it away. "I did use to say out West that they might write a little less for autographs – to all the great poets, you know – and study the thoughts and style a little more."

"What do they care for the thoughts and style? They didn't even understand you. I'm not sure," I added, "that I do myself, and I dare say that you by no means make me out."

She had got up to go, and though I wanted her to succeed in not seeing Neil Paraday I wanted her also, inconsequently, to remain in the house. I was at any rate far from desiring to hustle her off. As Mrs. Weeks Wimbush, upstairs, was still saving our friend in her own way, I asked my young lady to let me briefly relate, in illustration of my point, the little incident of my having gone down into the country for a profane purpose and been converted on the spot to holiness. Sinking again into her chair to listen she showed a deep interest in the anecdote. Then thinking it over gravely she returned with her odd intonation: "Yes, but you do see him!" I had to admit that this was the case; and I wasn't so prepared with an effective attenuation as I could have wished. She eased the situation off, however, by the charming quaintness with which she finally said: "Well, I wouldn't want him to be lonely!" This time she rose in earnest, but I persuaded her to let me keep the album to show Mr. Paraday. I assured her I'd bring it back to her myself. "Well, you'll find my address somewhere in it on a paper!" she sighed all resignedly at the door.

Chapter VIII

I BLUSH TO CONFESS IT, but I invited Mr. Paraday that very day to transcribe into the album one of his most characteristic passages. I told him how I had got rid of the strange girl who had brought it – her ominous name was Miss Hurter and she lived at an hotel; quite agreeing with him moreover as to the wisdom of getting rid with equal promptitude of the book itself. This was why I carried it to Albemarle Street no later than on the morrow. I failed to find her at home, but she wrote to me and I went again; she wanted so much to hear more about Neil Paraday. I returned repeatedly, I may briefly declare, to supply her with this information. She had been immensely taken, the more she thought of it, with that idea of mine about the act of homage: it had ended by filling her with a generous rapture. She positively desired to do something sublime for him, though indeed I could see that, as this particular flight was difficult, she appreciated the fact that my visits kept her up. I had it on my conscience to keep her up: I neglected nothing that would contribute to it, and her conception of our cherished author's independence became at last as fine as his very own. "Read him, read him – *that* will be an education in decency," I constantly repeated; while, seeking him in his works even as God in nature, she represented herself as convinced that, according to my assurance, this was the system that had, as she expressed it, weaned her. We read him together when I could find time, and the generous creature's sacrifice was fed by our communion. There were twenty selfish women about whom I told her and who stirred her to a beautiful rage. Immediately after my first visit her sister, Mrs. Milsom, came over from Paris, and the two ladies began to present, as they called it, their letters. I thanked our stars that none had been presented to Mr. Paraday. They received invitations and dined out, and some of these occasions enabled Fanny Hurter to perform, for consistency's sake, touching feats of submission. Nothing indeed would now have induced her even to look at the object of her admiration. Once, hearing his name announced at a party, she instantly left the room by another door and then straightway quitted the house. At another time when I was at the opera with them – Mrs. Milsom had invited me to their box – I attempted to point Mr. Paraday out to her in the stalls. On this she asked her sister to change places with her and, while that lady devoured the great man through a powerful glass, presented, all the rest of the evening, her inspired back to the house. To torment her tenderly I pressed the glass upon her, telling her how wonderfully near it brought our friend's handsome head. By way of answer she simply looked at me in charged silence, letting me see that tears had gathered in her eyes. These tears, I may remark, produced an effect on me of which the end is not yet. There was a moment when I felt it my duty to mention them to Neil Paraday, but I was deterred by the reflexion that there were questions more relevant to his happiness.

These question indeed, by the end of the season, were reduced to a single one – the question of reconstituting so far as might be possible the conditions under which he had produced his best work. Such conditions could never all come back, for there was a new one that took up too much place; but some perhaps were not beyond recall. I wanted above all things to see him sit down to the subject he had, on my making his acquaintance, read me that admirable sketch of. Something told me there was no security but in his doing so before the new factor, as we used to say at Mr. Pinhorn's, should render the problem incalculable. It only half-reassured me that the sketch itself was so copious and so eloquent that even at the worst there would be the making of a small but complete book, a tiny volume which, for the faithful, might well become an object of adoration. There would even not be wanting critics to declare, I foresaw, that the plan was a thing to be more thankful for than the structure to have been reared on it. My impatience for the structure, none the less, grew and grew with the interruptions. He had on coming up to town begun to sit for his portrait to a young painter, Mr. Rumble, whose little game, as we also used to say at Mr. Pinhorn's, was to be the first to perch on the shoulders of renown. Mr. Rumble's studio was a circus in which the man of the hour, and still more the woman, leaped through the hoops of his showy frames almost as electrically as they burst into telegrams and "specials." He pranced into the exhibitions on their back; he was the reporter on canvas, the Vandyke up to date, and there was one roaring year in which Mrs. Bounder and Miss Braby, Guy Walsingham and Dora Forbes proclaimed in chorus from the same pictured walls that no one had yet got ahead of him.

Paraday had been promptly caught and saddled, accepting with characteristic good-humour his confidential hint that to figure in his show was not so much a consequence as a cause of immortality. From Mrs. Wimbush to the last "representative" who called to ascertain his twelve favourite dishes, it was the same ingenuous assumption that he would rejoice in the repercussion. There were moments when I fancied I might have had more patience with them if they hadn't been so fatally benevolent. I hated at all events Mr. Rumble's picture, and had my bottled resentment ready when, later on, I found my distracted friend had been stuffed by Mrs. Wimbush into the mouth of another cannon. A young artist in whom she was intensely interested, and who had no connexion with Mr. Rumble, was to show how far he could make him go. Poor Paraday, in return, was naturally to write something somewhere about the young artist. She played her victims against each other with admirable ingenuity, and her establishment was a huge machine in which the tiniest and the biggest wheels went round to the same treadle. I had a scene with her in which I tried to express that the function of such a man was to exercise his genius – not to serve as a hoarding for pictorial posters. The people I was perhaps angriest with were the editors of magazines who had introduced what they called new features, so aware were they that the newest feature of all would be to make him grind their axes by contributing his views on vital topics and taking part in the periodical prattle about the future of fiction. I made sure that before I should have done with him there would scarcely be a current form of words left me to be sick of; but meanwhile I could make surer still of my animosity to bustling ladies for whom he drew the water that irrigated their social flower-beds.

I had a battle with Mrs. Wimbush over the artist she protected, and another over the question of a certain week, at the end of July, that Mr. Paraday appeared to have contracted to spend with her in the country. I protested against this visit; I intimated that he was too unwell for hospitality without a nuance, for caresses without imagination; I begged he might rather take the time in some restorative way. A sultry air of promises, of ponderous parties, hung over his August, and he would greatly profit by the interval of rest. He hadn't told me he was ill again that he had had a warning; but I hadn't needed this, for I found his reticence his worst symptom. The only thing he said to me was that he believed a comfortable attack of something or other would set him up: it would put out of the question everything but the exemptions he prized. I'm afraid I shall have presented him as a martyr in a very small cause if I fail to explain that he surrendered himself much more liberally than I surrendered him. He filled his lungs, for the most part; with the comedy of his queer fate: the tragedy was in the spectacles through which I chose to look. He was conscious of inconvenience, and above all of a great renunciation; but how could he have heard a mere dirge in the bells of his accession? The sagacity and the jealousy were mine, and his the impressions and the harvest. Of course, as regards Mrs. Wimbush, I was worsted in my encounters, for wasn't the state of his health the very reason for his coming to her at Prestidge? Wasn't it precisely at Prestidge that he was to be coddled, and wasn't the dear Princess coming to help her to coddle him? The dear Princess, now on a visit to England, was of a famous foreign house, and, in her gilded cage, with her retinue of keepers and feeders, was the most expensive specimen in the good lady's collection. I don't think her august presence had had to do with Paraday's consenting to go, but it's not impossible he had operated as a bait to the illustrious stranger. The party had been made up for him, Mrs. Wimbush averred, and every one was counting on it, the dear Princess most of all. If he was well enough he was to read them something absolutely fresh, and it was on that particular prospect the Princess had set her heart. She was so fond of genius in *any* walk of life, and was so used to it and understood it so well: she was the greatest of Mr.

Paraday's admirers, she devoured everything he wrote. And then he read like an angel. Mrs. Wimbush reminded me that he had again and again given her, Mrs. Wimbush, the privilege of listening to him.

I looked at her a moment. "What has he read to you?" I crudely enquired.

For a moment too she met my eyes, and for the fraction of a moment she hesitated and coloured. "Oh all sorts of things!"

I wondered if this were an imperfect recollection or only a perfect fib, and she quite understood my unuttered comment on her measure of such things. But if she could forget Neil Paraday's beauties she could of course forget my rudeness, and three days later she invited me, by telegraph, to join the party at Prestidge. This time she might indeed have had a story about what I had given up to be near the master. I addressed from that fine residence several communications to a young lady in London, a young lady whom, I confess, I quitted with reluctance and whom the reminder of what she herself could give up was required to make me quit at all. It adds to the gratitude I owe her on other grounds that she kindly allows me to transcribe from my letters a few of the passages in which that hateful sojourn is candidly commemorated.

Chapter IX

"I SUPPOSE I ought to enjoy the joke of what's going on here," I wrote, "but somehow it doesn't amuse me. Pessimism on the contrary possesses me and cynicism deeply engages. I positively feel my own flesh sore from the brass nails in Neil Paraday's social harness. The house is full of people who like him, as they mention, awfully, and with whom his talent for talking nonsense has prodigious success. I delight in his nonsense myself; why is it therefore that I grudge these happy folk their artless satisfaction? Mystery of the human heart – abyss of the critical spirit! Mrs. Wimbush thinks she can answer that question, and as my want of gaiety has at last worn out her patience she has given me a glimpse of her shrewd guess. I'm made restless by the selfishness of the insincere friend – I want to monopolise Paraday in order that he may push me on. To be intimate with him is a feather in my cap; it gives me an importance that I couldn't naturally pretend to, and I seek to deprive him of social refreshment because I fear that meeting more disinterested people may enlighten him as to my real motive. All the disinterested people here are his particular admirers and have been carefully selected as such. There's supposed to be a copy of his last book in the house, and in the hall I come upon ladies, in attitudes, bending gracefully over the first volume. I discreetly avert my eyes, and when I next look round the precarious joy has been superseded by the book of life. There's a sociable circle or a confidential couple, and the relinquished volume lies open on its face and as dropped under extreme coercion. Somebody else presently finds it and transfers it, with its air of momentary desolation, to another piece of furniture. Every one's asking every one about it all day, and every one's telling every one where they put it last. I'm sure it's rather smudgy about the twentieth page. I've a strong impression, too, that the second volume is lost – has been packed in the bag of some departing guest; and yet everybody has the impression that somebody else has read to the end. You see therefore that the beautiful book plays a great part in our existence. Why should I take the occasion of such distinguished honours to say that I begin to see deeper into Gustave Flaubert's doleful refrain about the hatred of literature? I refer you again to the perverse constitution of man.

"The Princess is a massive lady with the organisation of an athlete and the confusion of tongues of a valet de place. She contrives to commit herself extraordinarily little in a great many languages, and is entertained and conversed with in detachments and relays, like an institution which goes on from generation to generation or a big building contracted for under a forfeit. She can't have a personal taste any more than, when her husband succeeds, she can have a personal crown, and her opinion on any matter is rusty and heavy and plain – made, in the night of ages, to last and be transmitted. I feel as if I ought to 'tip' some custode for my glimpse of it. She has been told everything in the world and has never perceived anything, and the echoes of her education respond awfully to the rash footfall – I mean the casual remark – in the cold Valhalla of her memory. Mrs. Wimbush delights in her wit and says there's nothing so charming as to hear Mr. Paraday draw it out. He's perpetually detailed for this job, and he tells me it has a peculiarly exhausting effect. Every one's beginning – at the end of two days – to sidle obsequiously away from her, and Mrs. Wimbush pushes him again and again into the breach. None of the uses I have yet seen him put to infuriate me quite so much. He looks very fagged and has at last confessed to me that his condition makes him uneasy – has even promised me he'll go straight home instead of returning to his final engagements in town. Last night I had some talk with him about going today, cutting his visit short; so sure am I that he'll be better as soon as he's shut up in his lighthouse. He told me that this is what he would like to do; reminding me, however, that the first lesson of his greatness has been precisely that he can't do what he likes. Mrs. Wimbush would never forgive him if he should leave her before the Princess has received the last hand. When I hint that a violent rupture with our hostess would be the best thing in the world for him he gives me to understand that if his reason assents to the proposition his courage hangs woefully back. He makes no secret of being mortally afraid of her, and when I ask what harm she can do him that she hasn't already done he simply repeats: 'I'm afraid, I'm afraid! Don't enquire too closely,' he said last night; 'only believe that I feel a sort of terror. It's strange, when she's so kind! At any rate, I'd as soon overturn that piece of priceless Sèvres as tell her I must go before my date.' It sounds dreadfully weak, but he has some reason, and he pays for his imagination, which puts him (I should hate it) in the place of others and makes him feel, even against himself, their feelings, their appetites, their motives. It's indeed inveterately against himself that he makes his imagination act. What a pity he has such a lot of it! He's too beastly intelligent. Besides, the famous reading's still to come off, and it has been postponed a day to allow Guy Walsingham to arrive. It appears this eminent lady's staying at a house a few miles off, which means of course that Mrs. Wimbush has forcibly annexed her. She's to come over in a day or two – Mrs. Wimbush wants her to hear Mr. Paraday.

"Today's wet and cold, and several of the company, at the invitation of the Duke, have driven over to luncheon at Bigwood. I saw poor Paraday wedge himself, by command, into the little supplementary seat of a brougham in which the Princess and our hostess were already ensconced. If the front glass isn't open on his dear old back perhaps he'll survive. Bigwood, I believe, is very grand and frigid, all marble and precedence, and I wish him well out of the adventure. I can't tell you how much more and more your attitude to him, in the midst of all this, shines out by contrast. I never willingly talk to these people about him, but see what a comfort I find it to scribble to you! I appreciate it – it keeps me warm; there are no fires in the house. Mrs. Wimbush goes by the calendar, the temperature goes by the weather, the weather goes by God knows what, and the Princess is easily heated. I've nothing but my acrimony to warm me, and have been out under an umbrella to restore my circulation. Coming in an hour ago I found Lady Augusta Minch rummaging about the hall. When I asked her what she was looking for she said she had mislaid something that Mr. Paraday had lent her. I ascertained in a moment that the article in question is a manuscript, and I've a foreboding that it's the noble morsel he read me six weeks ago. When I expressed my surprise that he should have bandied about anything so precious (I happen to know it's his only copy – in the most beautiful hand in all the world) Lady Augusta confessed to me that she hadn't had it from himself, but from Mrs. Wimbush, who had wished to give her a glimpse of it as a salve for her not being able to stay and hear it read.

"'Is that the piece he's to read,' I asked, 'when Guy Walsingham arrives?'

"'It's not for Guy Walsingham they're waiting now, it's for Dora Forbes,' Lady Augusta said. 'She's coming, I believe, early to-morrow. Meanwhile Mrs. Wimbush has found out about him, and is actively wiring to him. She says he also must hear him.'

"'You bewilder me a little,' I replied; 'in the age we live in one gets lost among the genders and the pronouns. The clear thing is that Mrs. Wimbush doesn't guard such a treasure so jealously as she might.'

"'Poor dear, she has the Princess to guard! Mr. Paraday lent her the manuscript to look over.'

"'She spoke, you mean, as if it were the morning paper?'

"Lady Augusta stared – my irony was lost on her. 'She didn't have time, so she gave me a chance first; because unfortunately I go to-morrow to Bigwood.'

"'And your chance has only proved a chance to lose it?'

"'I haven't lost it. I remember now – it was very stupid of me to have forgotten. I told my maid to give it to Lord Dorimont – or at least to his man.'

"'And Lord Dorimont went away directly after luncheon.'

"'Of course he gave it back to my maid – or else his man did,' said Lady Augusta. 'I dare say it's all right.'

"The conscience of these people is like a summer sea. They haven't time to look over a priceless composition; they've only time to kick it about the house. I suggested that the 'man,' fired with a noble emulation, had perhaps kept the work for his own perusal; and her ladyship wanted to know whether, if the thing shouldn't reappear for the grand occasion appointed by our hostess, the author wouldn't have something else to read that would do just as well. Their questions are too delightful! I declared to Lady Augusta briefly that nothing in the world can ever do so well as the thing that does best; and at this she looked a little disconcerted. But I added that if the manuscript had gone astray our little circle would have the less of an effort of attention to make. The piece in question was very long – it would keep them three hours.

"'Three hours! Oh the Princess will get up!' said Lady Augusta.

"'I thought she was Mr. Paraday's greatest admirer.'

"'I dare say she is – she's so awfully clever. But what's the use of being a Princess—'

"'If you can't dissemble your love?' I asked as Lady Augusta was vague. She said at any rate she'd question her maid; and I'm hoping that when I go down to dinner I shall find the manuscript has been recovered."

Chapter X

"IT HAS NOT been recovered," I wrote early the next day, "and I'm moreover much troubled about our friend. He came back from Bigwood with a chill and, being allowed to have a fire in his room, lay down a while before dinner. I tried to send him to bed and indeed thought I had put him in the way of it; but after I had gone to dress Mrs. Wimbush came up to see him, with the inevitable result that when I returned I found him under arms and flushed and feverish, though decorated with the rare flower she had brought him for his button-hole. He came down to dinner, but Lady Augusta Minch was very shy of him. Today he's in great pain, and the advent of ces dames – I mean of Guy Walsingham and Dora Forbes – doesn't at all console me. It does Mrs. Wimbush, however, for she has consented to his remaining in bed so that he may be all right to-morrow for the listening circle. Guy Walsingham's already on the scene, and the Doctor for Paraday also arrived early. I haven't yet seen the author of 'Obsessions,' but of course I've had a moment by myself with the Doctor. I tried to get him to say that our invalid must go straight home – I mean to-morrow or next day; but he quite refuses to talk about the future. Absolute quiet and warmth and the regular administration of an important remedy are the points he mainly insists on. He returns this afternoon, and I'm to go back to see the patient at one o'clock, when he next takes his medicine. It consoles me a little that he certainly won't be able to read – an exertion he was already more than unfit for. Lady Augusta went off after breakfast, assuring me her first care would be to follow up the lost manuscript. I can see she thinks me a shocking busybody and doesn't understand my alarm, but she'll do what she can, for she's a good-natured woman. 'So are they all honourable men.' That was precisely what made her give the thing to Lord Dorimont and made Lord Dorimont bag it. What use *he* has for it God only knows. I've the worst forebodings, but somehow I'm strangely without passion – desperately calm. As I consider the unconscious, the well-meaning ravages of our appreciative circle I bow my head in submission to some great natural, some universal accident; I'm rendered almost indifferent, in fact quite gay (ha-ha!) by the sense of immitigable fate. Lady Augusta promises me to trace the precious object and let me have it through the post by the time Paraday's well enough to play his part with it. The last evidence is that her maid did give it to his lordship's valet. One would suppose it some thrilling number of *The Family Budget*. Mrs. Wimbush, who's aware of the accident, is much less agitated by it than she would doubtless be were she not for the hour inevitably engrossed with Guy Walsingham."

Later in the day I informed my correspondent, for whom indeed I kept a loose diary of the situation, that I had made the acquaintance of this celebrity and that she was a pretty little girl who wore her hair in what used to be called a crop. She looked so juvenile and so innocent that if, as Mr. Morrow had announced, she was resigned to the larger latitude, her superiority to prejudice must have come to her early. I spent most of the day hovering about Neil Paraday's room, but it was communicated to me from below that Guy Walsingham, at Prestidge, was a success. Toward evening I became conscious somehow that her superiority was contagious, and by the time the company separated for the night I was sure the larger latitude had been generally accepted. I thought of Dora Forbes and felt that he had no time to lose. Before dinner I received a telegram from Lady Augusta

Minch. "Lord Dorimont thinks he must have left bundle in train – enquire." How could I enquire – if I was to take the word as a command? I was too worried and now too alarmed about Neil Paraday. The Doctor came back, and it was an immense satisfaction to me to be sure he was wise and interested. He was proud of being called to so distinguished a patient, but he admitted to me that night that my friend was gravely ill. It was really a relapse, a recrudescence of his old malady. There could be no question of moving him: we must at any rate see first, on the spot, what turn his condition would take. Meanwhile, on the morrow, he was to have a nurse. On the morrow the dear man was easier, and my spirits rose to such cheerfulness that I could almost laugh over Lady Augusta's second telegram: "Lord Dorimont's servant been to station – nothing found. Push enquiries." I did laugh, I'm sure, as I remembered this to be the mystic scroll I had scarcely allowed poor Mr. Morrow to point his umbrella at. Fool that I had been: the thirty-seven influential journals wouldn't have destroyed it, they'd only have printed it. Of course I said nothing to Paraday.

When the nurse arrived she turned me out of the room, on which I went downstairs. I should premise that at breakfast the news that our brilliant friend was doing well excited universal complacency, and the Princess graciously remarked that he was only to be commiserated for missing the society of Miss Collop. Mrs. Wimbush, whose social gift never shone brighter than in the dry decorum with which she accepted this fizzle in her fireworks, mentioned to me that Guy Walsingham had made a very favourable impression on her Imperial Highness. Indeed I think every one did so, and that, like the money-market or the national honour, her Imperial Highness was constitutionally sensitive. There was a certain gladness, a perceptible bustle in the air, however, which I thought slightly anomalous in a house where a great author lay critically ill. "Le roy est mort – vive le roy": I was reminded that another great author had already stepped into his shoes. When I came down again after the nurse had taken possession I found a strange gentleman hanging about the hall and pacing to and fro by the closed door of the drawing-room. This personage was florid and bald; he had a big red moustache and wore showy knickerbockers – characteristics all that fitted to my conception of the identity of Dora Forbes. In a moment I saw what had happened: the author of "The Other Way Round" had just alighted at the portals of Prestidge, but had suffered a scruple to restrain him from penetrating further. I recognised his scruple when, pausing to listen at his gesture of caution, I heard a shrill voice lifted in a sort of rhythmic uncanny chant. The famous reading had begun, only it was the author of "Obsessions" who now furnished the sacrifice. The new visitor whispered to me that he judged something was going on he oughtn't to interrupt.

"Miss Collop arrived last night," I smiled, "and the Princess has a thirst for the inédit."

Dora Forbes lifted his bushy brows. "Miss Collop?"

"Guy Walsingham, your distinguished confrère – or shall I say your formidable rival?"

"Oh!" growled Dora Forbes. Then he added: "Shall I spoil it if I go in?"

"I should think nothing could spoil it!" I ambiguously laughed.

Dora Forbes evidently felt the dilemma; he gave an irritated crook to his moustache. "*Shall* I go in?" he presently asked.

We looked at each other hard a moment; then I expressed something bitter that was in me, expressed it in an infernal "Do!" After this I got out into the air, but not so fast as not to hear, when the door of the drawing-room opened, the disconcerted drop of Miss Collop's public manner: she must have been in the midst of the larger latitude. Producing with extreme rapidity, Guy Walsingham has just published a work in which amiable people who are not initiated have been pained to see the genius of a sister-novelist held up to unmistakeable ridicule; so fresh an exhibition does it seem to them of the dreadful way men have always treated women. Dora Forbes, it's true, at the present hour, is immensely pushed by Mrs. Wimbush and has sat for his portrait to the young artists she protects, sat for it not only in oils but in monumental alabaster.

What happened at Prestidge later in the day is of course contemporary history. If the interruption I had whimsically sanctioned was almost a scandal, what is to be said of that general scatter of the company which, under the Doctor's rule, began to take place in the evening? His rule was soothing to behold, small comfort as I was to have at the end. He decreed in the interest of his patient an absolutely soundless house and a consequent break-up of the party. Little country practitioner as he was, he literally packed off the Princess. She departed as promptly as if a revolution had broken out, and Guy Walsingham emigrated with her. I was kindly permitted to remain, and this was not denied even to Mrs. Wimbush. The privilege was withheld indeed from Dora Forbes; so Mrs. Wimbush kept her latest capture temporarily concealed. This was so little, however, her usual way of dealing with her eminent friends that a couple of days of it exhausted her patience, and she went up to town with him in great publicity. The sudden turn for the worse her afflicted guest had, after a brief improvement, taken on the third night raised an obstacle to her seeing him before her retreat; a fortunate circumstance doubtless, for she was fundamentally disappointed in him. This was not the kind of performance for which she had invited him to Prestidge, let alone invited the Princess. I must add that none of the generous acts marking her patronage of intellectual and other merit have done so much for her reputation as her lending Neil Paraday the most beautiful of her numerous homes to die in. He took advantage to the utmost of the singular favour. Day by day I saw him sink, and I roamed alone about the empty terraces and gardens. His wife never came near him, but I scarcely noticed it: as I paced there with rage in my heart I was too full of another wrong. In the event of his death it would fall to me perhaps to bring out in some charming form, with notes, with the tenderest editorial care, that precious heritage of his written project. But where was that precious heritage and were both the author and the book to have been snatched from us? Lady Augusta wrote me that she had done all she could and that poor Lord Dorimont, who had really been worried to death, was extremely sorry. I couldn't have the matter out with Mrs. Wimbush, for I didn't want to be taunted by her with desiring to aggrandise myself by a public connexion with Mr. Paraday's sweepings. She had signified her willingness to meet the expense of all advertising, as indeed she was always ready to do. The last night of the horrible series, the night before he died, I put my ear closer to his pillow.

"That thing I read you that morning, you know."

"In your garden that dreadful day? Yes!"

"Won't it do as it is?"

"It would have been a glorious book."

"It *is* a glorious book," Neil Paraday murmured. "Print it as it stands – beautifully."

"Beautifully!" I passionately promised.

It may be imagined whether, now that he's gone, the promise seems to me less sacred. I'm convinced that if such pages had appeared in his lifetime the Abbey would hold him today. I've kept the advertising in my own hands, but the manuscript has not been recovered. It's impossible, and at any rate intolerable, to suppose it can have been wantonly destroyed. Perhaps some hazard of a blind hand, some brutal fatal ignorance has lighted kitchen-fires with it. Every stupid and hideous accident haunts my meditations. My undiscourageable search for the lost treasure would make a long chapter. Fortunately I've a devoted associate in the person of a young lady who has every day a fresh indignation and a fresh idea, and who maintains with intensity that the prize will still turn up. Sometimes I believe her, but I've quite ceased to believe myself. The only thing for us at all events is to go on seeking and hoping together; and we should be closely united by this firm tie even were we not at present by another.

If you enjoyed this, you might also like...
The Lifted Veil, see page 211
The Cone, see page 322

Biographies & Sources

Walter Besant
All Sorts and Conditions of Men
(Originally published by Chatto & Windus, 1882)
A novelist and hostorian, Walter Besant (1836–1901) was born in Portsmouth, Hampshire. He wrote throughout his life and worked as a professor of mathematics for many years. His most well-known novels include *All in a Garden Fair, Dorothy Forster* and *Children of Gibeon*.

Wilkie Collins
Brother Owen's Story of Anne Rodway
(Originally published in *Household Words*, 1856)
Who Killed Zebedee?
(Originally published in *The Seaside Library,* 1881)
William Wilkie Collins (1824–89) was born in London's Marylebone and he lived there almost consistently for 65 years. Writing over 30 major books, 100 articles, short stories and essays and a dozen or more plays, he is best known for *The Moonstone* and *The Woman in White*. He was good friends with novelist Charles Dickens with whom he collaborated as well as took inspiration from to help write novels like *The Lighthouse* and *The Frozen Deep*. Finally becoming internationally reputable in the 1860s, Collins truly showed himself as the master of his craft as he wrote many profitable novels in less than a decade and earned himself the title of a successful English novelist, playwright and author of short stories.

Joseph Conrad
Amy Foster
(Originally published in *Illustrated London News*, 1901)
Joseph Conrad (1857–1924) was a Polish-British author born in Ukraine who was greatly influenced by his years at sea. Travelling first on French ships and spending 16 years as a British merchant marine enabled him to gain experiences in various countries including Australia, Africa and Singapore. His writings show clear roots from his seafaring career and display themes of imperialism and colonialism. One of his most famous novels, *Lord Jim*, follows the story of a sailor dealing with his past. His works have influenced a number of authors such as F. Scott Fitzgerald, George Orwell and Salman Rushdie.

Ella D'Arcy
Irremediable
(Originally published in *The Yellow Book*, Volume I, 1894)
Though Constance Eleanor Mary Byrne D'Arcy (1857–1937) was born to an Irish family in Pimlico, London, she spent much of her youth on the Channel Islands, and was also variously educated in London, Germany, and France. While she aspired to be an artist, she gave it up in favour of a literary career, supposedly due to her failing eyesight. She is perhaps best known for her association with *The Yellow Book*, to which she was a frequent contributor – second only to its literary editor, Henry Harland. Moreover, as the periodical's sub-editor, D'Arcy played a significant part in shaping one of the most influential publications of the nineteenth century. D'Arcy's fiction, which was published in numerous magazines and

short story collections, was distinguished by its unsentimental psychological realism and exploration of modern relations between the sexes.

Charles Dickens
Oliver Twist (chapter VIII); Originally published in *Bentley's Miscellany*, 1837–39
Great Expectations (chapter VIII); Originally published in *All the Year Round*, 1861
Main Line: The Boy at Mugby; Originally published in *All the Year Round*, 1866
The iconic and much-loved Charles Dickens (1812–70) was born in Portsmouth, England, though he spent much of his life in Kent and London. At the age of 12 Charles was forced into working in a factory for a couple of months to support his family. He never forgot his harrowing experience there, and his novels always reflected the plight of the working class. A prolific writer, Dickens kept up a career in journalism as well as writing short stories and novels, with much of his work being serialized before being published as books. He gave a view of contemporary England with a strong sense of realism, yet incorporated the occasional ghost and horror elements. He continued to work hard until his death in 1870, leaving *The Mystery of Edwin Drood* unfinished.

Arthur Conan Doyle
The Adventure of the Copper Beeches
(Originally published in *The Strand Magazine*, 1892)
Arthur Conan Doyle (1859–1930) was born in Edinburgh, Scotland. As a medical student Doyle was so impressed by his professor's powers of deduction that he was inspired to create the illustrious and much-loved figure Sherlock Holmes. However, he became increasingly interested in spiritualism and the supernatural, leaving him keen to explore fantastical elements in his stories. Doyle's vibrant and remarkable characters have breathed life into all of his stories, engaging readers throughout the decades.

George Egerton
A Cross Line
(Originally published in *Keynotes*, 1893)
A Lost Masterpiece
(Originally published in *The Yellow Book*, Volume I, 1894)
Mary Chavelita Dunne (1859–1945), better known by the pen name George Egerton, is one of the earliest modernist writers in the English language. Born in Melbourne, Australia, she led a well-travelled life, spending years in New Zealand, Chile, Germany, New York and Norway, she identified as 'intensely Irish', having spent a significant portion of her youth near Dublin. One of the most outspoken female voices of her time, particularly in her advocacy for female sexual freedom, she quickly gained fame and acclaim with the publication of *Keynotes*, her first collection of short stories. Although Egerton's later literary efforts never matched the success of Keynotes, she remained a prolific, innovative writer throughout her life.

George Eliot
The Lifted Veil
(Originally published in *Blackwood's Magazine*, 1859)
Often lauded as one of the greatest English novelists, Mary Anne Evans (1819–1880) grew up in rural Warwickshire, where she witnessed the rise of Industrialisation firsthand. She eventually settled in London where she worked as a critic and editor for *The Westminster*

Review, and later decided to try her hand at fiction. Her pseudonym, George Eliot, was a means of avoiding the reductive stereotypes works by female authors were usually subjected to. Her first novel, *Adam Bede*, was an immediate sensation, though it is perhaps *Middlemarch*, her most celebrated work, that cemented her status in the English literary canon.

J. Sheridan Le Fanu
The Watcher
(Originally published in *The Watcher and Other Weird Stories*, 1894)
The remarkable father of Victorian ghost stories Joseph Thomas Sheridan Le Fanu (1814–73) was born in Dublin, Ireland. His gothic tales and mystery novels led to him become a leading ghost story writer of the nineteenth century. Three oft-cited works of his are *Uncle Silas*, *Carmilla* and *The House by the Churchyard*, which all are assumed to have influenced Bram Stoker's *Dracula*. Le Fanu wrote his most successful and productive works after his wife's tragic death and he remained a strong writer up until his own death.

Dr. Peter Garratt
(Foreword Writer of *Short Stories from the Age of Queen Victoria*)
Peter Garratt is Associate Professor in the Department of English Studies at Durham University. He teaches and researches nineteenth-century literature and culture, and is the author of *Victorian Empiricism* (2010) and essays and journal articles on writers such as Charles Dickens, John Ruskin and George Eliot.

Elizabeth Gaskell
Lizzie Leigh
(Originally published in *Household Words*, 1850)
Elizabeth Gaskell (1810–65) was born in Chelsea, London, and is widely known for her biography of her friend Charlotte Brontë. In a family of eight children, only Elizabeth and her brother John survived past childhood. Her mother's early death caused her to be raised by her aunt in Knutsford, a place that inspired her to write her most famous work, *Cranford*. Tragedy struck again when Gaskell's son died, and she began to write. All the misfortune in her life led her to write many gothic and horror tales, including *Lois the Witch*.

George Gissing
The Day of Silence
(Originally published in *The National Review*, 1893)
In his lifetime, Yorkshire-born author George Gissing's (1857–1903) talent as a writer and academic was displayed in his work. He published 23 novels over the course of as many years. Gissing's work received little attention until the 1890s, and his stories are recognized today for their sharply cynical, even sensational, depiction of life amongst the lower middle classes.

Thomas Hardy
The Distracted Preacher
(Originally published in *New Quarterly Magazine*, 1879)
An Imaginative Woman
(Originally published in *Pall Mall Magazine*, 1894)
Thomas Hardy (1840–1928), one of the most renowned poets and novelists in English literary history, was born in Stinsford, in Dorset, England. Influenced by Romanticism

and Charles Dickens, he wrote critically about the Victorian society. He quickly gained fame for his dedication to Naturalism, made evident through his novels *Far from the Madding Crowd*, *Jude the Obscure* and *The Mayor of Casterbridge*. Most of his stories contain tragic characters, which developed into the characters that feature in his horror novels, in for example *A Tragedy of Two Ambitions*.

Henry James

The Chaperon
(Originally published in *The Atlantic Monthly*, 1891)
The Death of the Lion
(Originally published in *The Yellow Book*, Volume I, 1894)
Henry James (1843–1916) was born in New York City, though spent a lot of time in England, with the dynamic between Europe and America playing a key role in his novels. Writing a massive amount of literary works throughout his lifetime, he published over 112 tales, 20 novels, 16 plays and various other autobiographies and literary criticisms. Each work is filled with characters of great social complexity as most of his works reflect his own complicated perspectives and satirical personality. James's works include *Daisy Miller*, *The Turn of the Screw*, *The Ambassadors*, *The Golden Bowl* and *The Portrait of a Lady*. James strongly believed novels had to be a recognizable representation of the realistic truth as well as filled with imaginative action.

M.R. James

Lost Hearts
(Originally published in *Pall Mall Magazine*, 1895)
Montague Rhodes ('M.R.') James (1862–1936), whose works are regarded as being at the forefront of the ghost story genre, was born in Kent, England. James dispensed with the traditional, predictable techniques of ghost story construction, instead using realistic contemporary settings for his works. He was also a British medieval scholar, so his stories often incorporated antiquarian elements. James wrote authoritatively in his essays about the best techniques for the genre, and his first collection of stories, *Ghost Stories of an Antiquary*, bred several sequels and remains popular today. His stories often reflect his childhood in Suffolk and talented acting career, which both seem to have assisted in the build-up of tension and horror in his works.

Arthur Machen

The Inmost Light
(Originally published by John Lane, 1894)
Welsh author Arthur Machen (1863–1941) played a key role in the Victorian revival of gothic fiction, and was also associated with the decadent movement of the 1890s. His most famous work, *The Great God Pan*, now considered a classic example of gothic horror, was initially considered depraved for its subversive content, hurting Machen's burgeoning career. He would go on to enjoy fits and starts of literary success throughout his life, supplementing his income by working variously as an actor, translator, cataloguer and journalist. Machen's fiction gained renewed attention in the 1920s, particularly in America, and would go on to influence the work of writers such as H.P. Lovecraft and Stephen King. 'The Inmost Light' was published in 1894, shortly after *The Great God Pan*, and was only the beginning of his writing career, with later stories such as 'The Bowmen' elevating his reputation.

Richard Marsh

The Houseboat

(Originally published in *The Seen and Unseen*, Methuen, 1900)

Known by the pseudonym Richard Marsh, London-born author Richard Bernard Heldman (1857–1915) was one of the most popular authors of his time. His extraordinary literary output – almost 80 volumes of fiction and many short stories – spanned numerous genres, from horror to romance. *The Beetle*, his most recognized work, is a thrilling piece of sensation fiction that simultaneously engaged with many of the issues of the Victorian era, including scientific development, urban impoverishment, the British empire, and the burgeoning Women's Movement.

Arthur Morrison

That Brute Simmons

(Originally published in *Tales of Mean Streets*, 1894)

Arthur Morrison (1863–1945) was born in the East End of London. He later became a writer for *The Globe* newspaper and showed a keen interest in relating the real and bleak plight of those living in London slums. When Arthur Conan Doyle killed off Sherlock Holmes in 1893, a vacuum opened up for detective heroes. In the wake Morrison created Martin Hewitt, publishing stories about him in *The Strand Magazine*, which had also first published Sherlock Holmes. Though a man with genius deductive skill, Morrison's Hewitt character was the polar opposite to Holmes: genial and helpful to the police. He was perhaps the most popular and successful of these new investigator fiction heroes.

Edith Nesbit

From the Dead

(Originally published in *Grim Tales*, 1893)

Edith Nesbit (1858–1924) was born in Kennington, England. Nesbit established herself as a successful author and poet, writing a variety of books ranging from children's books to adult horror stories. She was co-founded the Fabian Society and was also a strong political activist. Marrying young and frequently moving home, Edith Nesbit made many friendships including those with H.G. Wells and George Bernard Shaw. Although she gained most of her success from her children's books, including the ever-popular *The Railway Children*, she was also a well-known horror writer, with such collections as *Something Wrong* and *Grim Tales*. Her works are very well regarded and have often been cited by later authors as greatly influential.

Robert Louis Stevenson

The Adventure of the Hansom Cabs; Originally published as part of *The Suicide Club* collection in *The London Magazine*, 1878

Markheim; Originally published in *The Pall Mall Gazette*, 1884

Robert Louis Stevenson (1850–1894) was born in Edinburgh, Scotland. He became a well-known novelist, poet and travel writer, publishing the famous works *Treasure Island, Kidnapped* and *The Strange Case of Dr. Jekyll and Mr. Hyde*. All of his works were highly admired by many other artists, as he was a literary celebrity during his lifetime. Stevenson ended up writing a lot of his journeys into his works, writing primarily horror stories, as well as stories for children.

Bram Stoker

Our New House

(Originally published in *The Theatre Annual*, 1886)

A Yellow Duster

(Originally published in *Lloyd's Weekly Newspaper*, 1899)

Abraham 'Bram' Stoker (1847–1912) was born in Dublin, Ireland. Often ill during his childhood, he spent a lot of time in bed listening to his mother's grim stories, sparking his imagination. Striking up a friendship as an adult with the actor Henry Irving, Stoker eventually came to work and live in London, meeting notable authors such as Arthur Conan Doyle and Oscar Wilde. Stoker wrote several stories based on supernatural horror, such as the gothic masterpiece *Dracula* which has left an enduring and powerful impact on the genre, as well as chilling mysteries like *The Lair of the White Worm*.

Anthony Trollope

The Spotted Dog

(Originally published in *Saint Paul's Magazine*, 1870)

Born in Oxford, Anthony Trollope (1815–1882) was one of the most industrious and business-minded authors of the Victorian era, causing consternation amongst critics who had more romantic ideas of what a writer should be. A prolific writer throughout his career, his best-known works remain the *Chronicles of Barsetshire,* a set of novels which explore day-to-day life in the fictional county of Barsetshire. His work has remained enormously popular through the years, and has been championed by the likes of Nathaniel Hawthorne, David Mamet, Sue Grafton, and Alec Guinness.

H.G. Wells

The Time Machine (chapters VI–IX)

(Originally published in *The New Review*, 1895)

The Cone

(Originally published in *Unicorn*, 1895)

Herbert George Wells (1866–1946) was born in Kent, England. Novelist, journalist, social reformer and historian, Wells is one of the greatest ever science fiction writers and, along with Jules Verne, is sometimes referred to as a 'founding father' of the genre. With Aldous Huxley and, later, George Orwell, he defined the adventurous, social concern of early speculative fiction where the human condition was played out on a greater stage. Wells created over 50 novels, including his famous works *The Time Machine, The Invisible Man, The Island of Dr. Moreau* and *The War of the Worlds*, as well as a fantastic array of gothic short stories.

Oscar Wilde

The Model Millionaire

(Originally published in *The World*, 1887)

Oscar Wilde (1854–1900) was born in Dublin, Ireland, and was a successful author, poet, philosopher and playwright with an impressive gift for language. With several acclaimed works including his novel *The Picture of Dorian Gray* and the play *The Importance of Being Earnest*, Wilde was known for his biting wit and flamboyant personality in the Victorian era. He was famously imprisoned on homosexual charges, an imprisonment that proved disastrous to his health, but he continued to write.

Reading List

A selection of literature that helped shape and reflect *The Age of Queen Victoria*:

Samuel Butler, *Erewhon*

Anne Brontë, *The Tenant of Wildfell Hall*

Charlotte Brontë, *Jane Eyre*

Emily Brontë, *Wuthering Heights*

Robert Browning, *Men and Women*

Thomas Carlyle, *A History and On Heroes, Hero-Worship, and The Heroic in History*

Lewis Carroll, *Alice's Adventures in Wonderland*

Lewis Carroll, *Through the Looking Glass and What Alice Found There*

Joseph Conrad, *Heart of Darkness*

Charles Darwin, *On the Origin of Species*

Charles Dickens, *Hard Times*

Charles Dickens, *A Christmas Carol*

Charles Dickens, *Oliver Twist*

Benjamin Disraeli, *Sybil, or The Two Nations*

Arthur Conan Doyle, *The Adventures of Sherlock Holmes*

Friedrich Engels, *The Condition of the Working Class in England*

George Eliot (Mary Ann Evans) *The Mill on the Floss*

George Eliot (Mary Ann Evans), *Middlemarch*

Elizabeth Gaskell, *Mary Barton*

Elizabeth Gaskell, *North and South*

H. Rider Haggard, *She: A History of Adventure*

Thomas Hardy, *Far from the Madding Crowd*

Thomas Hardy, *Jude the Obscure*

Thomas Hardy, *Tess of the d'Urbervilles*

Thomas Hughes, *Tom Brown's School Days*

Andrew Lang, *The Blue Fairy Book*

Arthur Machen, *The Great God Pan*

William Morris, *News from Nowhere*

William Morris, *The Wood Beyond the Worlds*

Christina Rossetti, *Goblin Market and Other Poems*

John Ruskin, *Modern Painters*

Mary Shelley, *Frankenstein*

Robert Louis Stevenson, *The Strange Case of Dr. Jekyll and Mr. Hyde*

Robert Louis Stevenson, *Treasure Island*

Bram Stoker, *Dracula*

Alfred Lord Tennyson, 'The Charge of the Light Brigade'

William Thackeray, *Vanity Fair*

H.G. Wells, *The Time Machine*

H.G. Wells, *The War of the Worlds*

Oscar Wilde, *The Picture of Dorian Gray*

FLAME TREE PUBLISHING
Short Story Series
New & Classic Writing

Flame Tree's Gothic Fantasy books offer a carefully curated series of new titles, each with combinations of original and classic writing:

*Chilling Horror • Chilling Ghost • Science Fiction
Murder Mayhem • Crime & Mystery • Swords & Steam
Dystopia Utopia • Supernatural Horror • Lost Worlds • Time Travel
Heroic Fantasy • Pirates & Ghosts • Agents & Spies
Endless Apocalypse • Alien Invasion • Robots & AI
Lost Souls • Haunted House • Cosy Crime • American Gothic • Urban Crime*

**Also, new companion titles offer rich collections of
classic fiction, myths and tales in the gothic fantasy tradition:**

*H.G. Wells • Lovecraft • Sherlock Holmes
Edgar Allan Poe • Bram Stoker • Mary Shelley
Celtic Myths & Tales • Chinese Myths & Tales
Norse Myths & Tales • Greek Myths & Tales • African Myths & Tales
King Arthur & The Knights of the Round Table • Irish Fairy Tales
Alice's Adventures in Wonderland • The Divine Comedy
Brothers Grimm Fairy Tales • The Wonderful Wizard of Oz*

Available from all good bookstores, worldwide, and online at
flametreepublishing.com

See our new fiction imprint
FLAME TREE PRESS | FICTION WITHOUT FRONTIERS
New and original writing in Horror, Crime, SF and Fantasy

And join our monthly newsletter with offers and more stories:
FLAME TREE FICTION NEWSLETTER
flametreepress.com

GOTHIC FANTASY

For our books, calendars, blog
and latest special offers please see:
flametreepublishing.com